# BATTLE WEAPONS
## of the American Revolution

*The Historian's Complete Reference*
*By George C. Neumann*

**MOWBRAY PUBLISHERS**
54 E. SCHOOL STREET • WOONSOCKET, RI 02895 • www.gunandswordcollector.com

in cooperation with
SCURLOCK PUBLISHING CO., 1293 MYRTLE SPRINGS ROAD, TEXARKANA, TX 75503 • www.muzzleloadermagazine.com

# Battle Weapons of the American Revolution

*The Historian's Complete Reference*

*By George C. Neumann*

Copyright © 2011 George C. Neumann and Mowbray Publishers, Inc.

To order more copies of this book or to request a free catalog, contact Mowbray Publishers at 800-999-4697.

Publisher — Mowbray Publishers, Inc.
Editor — William H. Scurlock
Line Art Illustrator — George C. Woodbridge
Layout & Design — William H. Scurlock
Layout Assistants — Cherry Lloyd and Jason Dempsey
Copyright © 1998 Scurlock Publishing Co., Inc.

All rights reserved. No part of this book may be used or reproduced wthout the written permission of the publisher, except in the case of brief quotations embodied in critial essays and reviews.

**About the Cover:** *The Battle of Cowpens* by Don Troiani, Southbury, Connecticut. On January 17, 1781, General Daniel Morgan's mixed-American force of state militiamen, Continentals and dragoons met Banastre Tarleton's British Regulars and Loyalists at a South Carolina crossroads known as the Cowpens. The fighting was fierce and British victory seemed within reach until the withdrawing American troops unexpectedly wheeled around and delivered a devastating volley into the British ranks. The Continentals followed up with a bayonet assault of their own and were joined by the militiamen as the battle became a hand-to-hand contest. By noon, a much-needed victory had been added to the American cause, helping to pave the way for success at Yorktown, Virginia, nine months later. Acclaimed artist Don Troiani brings to life in this painting the climactic moment of this great American battle.

ISBN 1-931464-49-9

Printed in United States of America.

# Contents

| | |
|---|---|
| Introduction | 5 |
| **Chapter 1** *The Flintlock Evolves* | 6 |
| **Chapter 2** *Weapons Determine the Tactics* | 11 |
| **Chapter 3** *Smoothbore Shoulder Arms: Up Close by Volley* | 16 |
| **Chapter 4** *Rifles: The Precision Weapon* | 211 |
| **Chapter 5** *Pistols: One Shot, Man-to-Man* | 230 |
| **Chapter 6** *Bayonets: The Moment of Truth* | 277 |
| **Chapter 7** *Swords: Of Honor & Daring* | 302 |
| **Chapter 8** *Polearms: Traditions of Rank & Combat* | 366 |
| Glossary of Terms | 382 |
| Nomenclature Summary | 384 |
| Bibliography | 385 |
| Index | 390 |

*To Diana, the light of my life . . .
whose patience and encouragement made
this work possible.*

# Introduction

Our histories of America's War for Independence traditionally focus on the generals, statesmen, strategies and battles. We routinely omit one of the most critical factors in understanding how Washington achieved his incredible victory—the nature of the weapons with which he had to fight.

It was the capability of these arms that determined the tactics, and the tactics in turn that determined the type of army he desperately needed to create while simultaneously conducting the war. Because—and make no mistake about it—once the Revolution began, it was the continuance of America's army in the field that held together the tenuous association of thirteen autonomous states through eight years of pain.

Until recently the importance of flint ignition, black powder fouling, undersized bullets, volley fire, linear discipline and ultimate reliance on the bayonet had little relevance to the academic historian. Primarily through the growth of responsible reenactors, who re-create the armies of both sides and follow orders and procedures from the original manuals with authentic arms in the field, have we grasped the magnitude of the challenges and accomplishments of our Colonial military leaders.

This book is intended to provide a pictorial reference for identifying the typical hand weapons used from 1690 to 1783. Relatively few of them are accessible in public institutions but reside mostly in private collections. Thus, it is important that they be made known as part of our history. They reflect the manufacturing capabilities of that era, the enormous variety of patterns and sources used by the struggling rebels, plus the personal hand-to-hand courage and discipline demanded in linear tactics.

Although this work is similar to my first book of thirty years ago (*The History of Weapons of the American Revolution*), it includes many newly identified arms, which are illustrated in larger format and more defining photographs. Moreover, the coverage is expanded to include greater exposure of the relevant privately produced commercial and trade arms of that period. Because the great variety of weapons that saw service here came from so many sources—England, France, the German states, Spain, the Low Countries, American Colonies and the accumulated cast-offs of international arms dealers—I have chosen to include most of the established northern European patterns of that period. The identifications are based upon the best information available to me from written records, archaeological artifacts, the actual surviving weapons and my use of them in the field as a reenactor. For any of those incorrectly presented, I offer my apologies in advance. Where no specific dates are listed, it is assumed the item is representative of the period. Hopefully, the number of arms shown will enable the reader to progress beyond memorized details of specific models in order to evaluate individual pieces by their configuration.

It is impossible to list all of those who so generously contributed their time and assistance to help assemble this information. Many are listed with appreciation under illustrations from their collections, but special acknowledgment is also extended to these individuals:

To Robert Nittolo who generously provided the resources of his extensive collection; to Kit Ravenshear for sharing so much of his pioneering research and practical experience; to Herman O. Benninghoff who made available his personal collection and the material in the Valley Forge Historical Society; and to James D. Forman and Richard J. Ulbrich for access to their significant Colonial militaria.

To Dona M. McDermott and Scott P. Houting at the Valley Forge National Historical Park (plus the Sun Company whose gift made possible the location of my original collection at that site); Robert W. Fisch at the West Point Military Academy Museum; Nicholas Westbrook, Bruce M. Moseley, and Christopher D. Fox at Fort Ticonderoga; John Bosh; Jess Melot; Bruce S. Bazelon plus Eric Castle of the Pennsylvania Historical & Museum Commission; Donna-Belle Garvin and Douglas Copeley in the New Hampshire Historical Society; Joseph Serbaroli; Stacey A. Swigart of the Valley Forge Historical Society; Richard Patterson at the Old Barracks Museum (Trenton, N.J.); Anthony DeSantis, Michael Comeau, plus James Capobianco in the Massachusetts Archives; Sandy Balcom and Jim Campbell at Fortress Louisbourg NHS; S. James Gooding; René Chartrand; and Russel Bouchard.

Special appreciation is also extended to George C. Woodbridge, whose accurate, interpretative artwork has added immeasurably to all of my books; and to Richard McCaffrey for his skills and patience with the endless photographic prints.

*George C. Neumann*
*North Attleboro, Massachusetts*

# Chapter 1

# The Flintlock Evolves

Gunpowder first appeared in Europe early in the 13th century. The basic formula of saltpeter, charcoal and sulfur came from a mixture developed for pyrotechnics by the Chinese that found its way through Arab writings to the Europeans.

Initially this new substance was used in primitive "hand cannon," which were little more than an iron barrel with a handle and a touch-hole through which the powder was ignited by a live coal, burning cord or hot wire held in the other hand. By the beginning of the 14th century, however, a stocked shoulder arm had evolved and steadily replaced the traditional bows, crossbows, polearms and swords until the firearm became the basic infantry weapon at the end of the 1600s.

During America's colonial development in the 17th century, a successive series of firearm ignition systems became available. All of them were employed here and are briefly described as: the matchlock, circa 1410–1700; the wheel-lock, circa 1500–1700; and the flintlock, circa 1550–1840.

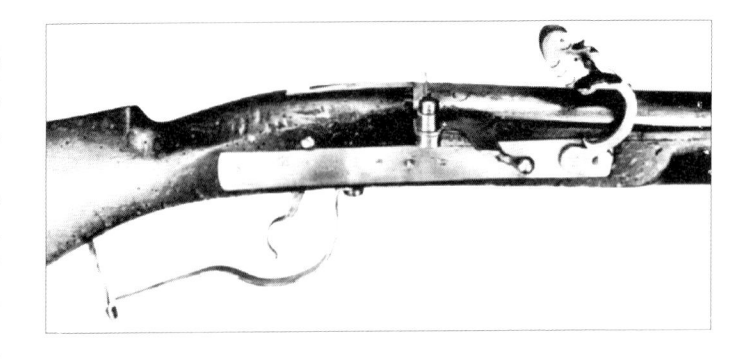

## THE MATCHLOCK

The matchlock provided a mechanical means of igniting the gunpowder in the barrel. A curved lever ("serpentine") was attached by a pin to a flat lock plate at the side of the breech. At its end were jaws that were normally tightened by a thumbscrew to secure the end of a slow burning "match rope." This rope was typically of

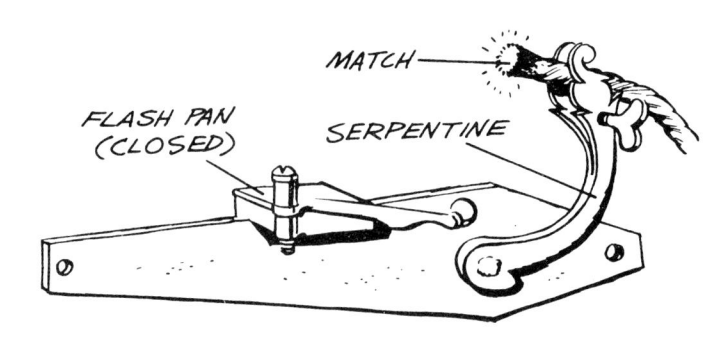

**EARLY MATCHLOCK ACTION** – Squeezing the trigger bar upward rotates lever arm on pivot (controlled by pressure from lever arm spring). The lever arm then rotates the linkage, attached by a horizontal axle to the outside serpentine. This rotation slowly lowers the serpentine and its lighted match into the pan (filled with priming powder) attached to the barrel outside the touch-hole, sending a flash into the barrel's main charge.

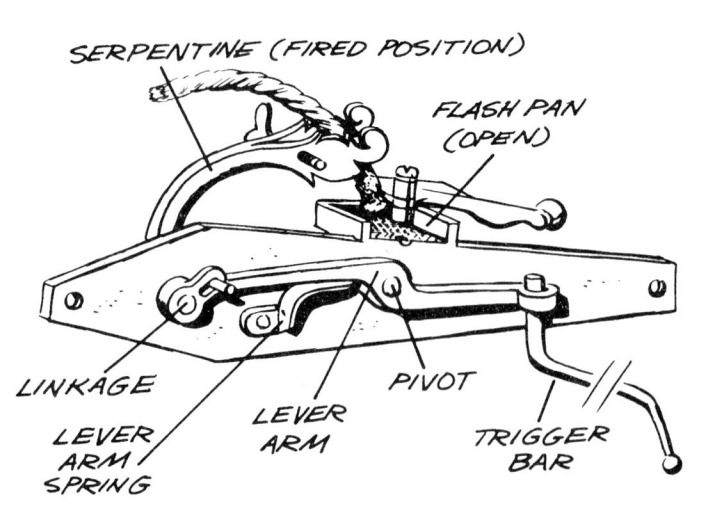

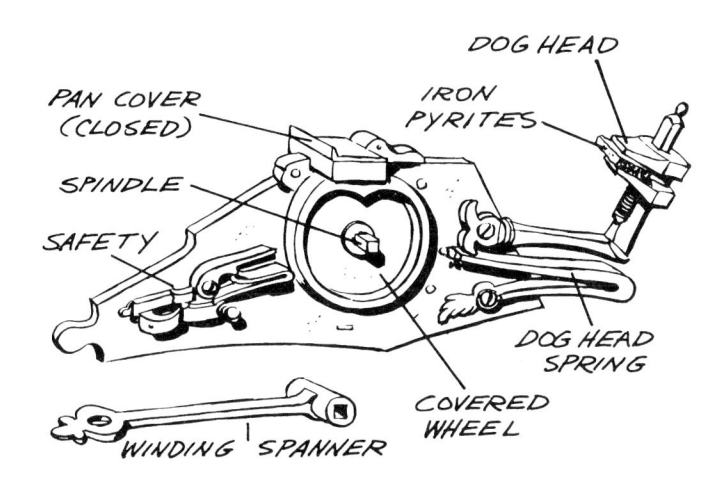

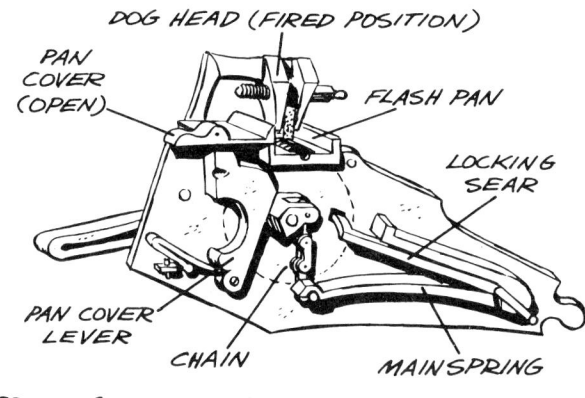

**WHEEL-LOCK ACTION** – A spanner wrench is fitted over the spindle and turned to wind up the wheel. This turning wraps the chain around the spindle, pulling up on the main spring. The sear also moves sideways through the lock plate into a hole in the wheel, locking it under tension. The dog head (holding an iron pyrites in its jaws) is then lowered against the top of the sliding pan cover, which covers the pan. Pulling the trigger retracts the sear, allowing the wheel to spin—automatically sliding back the pan cover. The dog head's pyrites is now forced down through a slit in the pan and against the rough edges of the spinning wheel. This sends a shower of sparks into the priming powder of the flashpan, igniting the main charge through the touch-hole in the barrel.

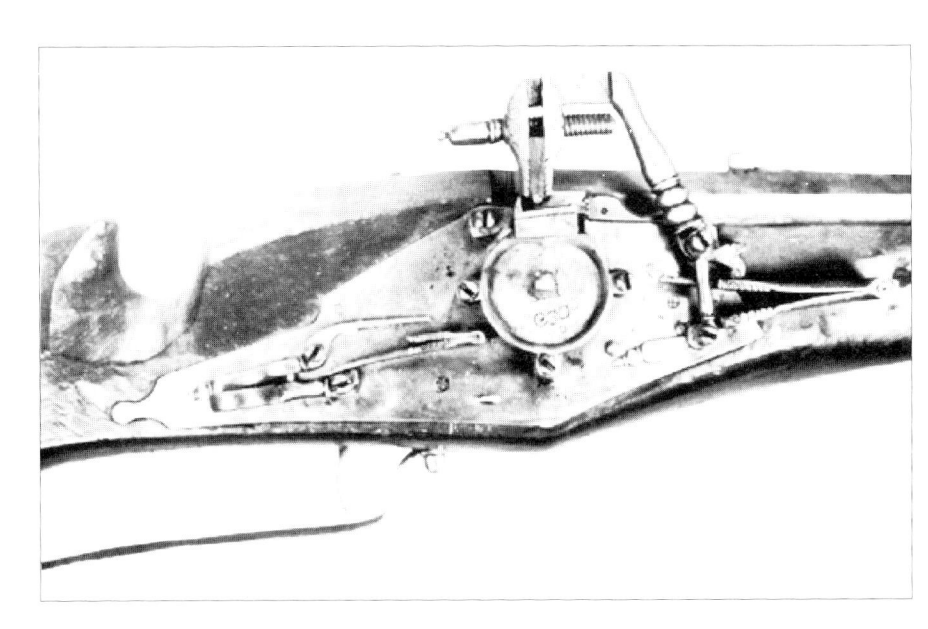

flax or hemp tow soaked in saltpeter and lighted at both ends to ensure a glowing spark when needed.

The barrel's touch-hole was at the side and adjacent to an open balcony-like flashpan that held a small portion of gunpowder. Depressing or pulling the trigger pivoted the serpentine down until the glowing "match" touched the pan of priming powder, which ignited and sent flame through the touch-hole to set off the main charge.

This form was modified following its circa 1410 introduction, so that by the time of America's colonization in the early 1600s, it had acquired a hand-operated pivoting cover over the flashpan (allowing safe portability while primed) and a modern vertical trigger to replace the earlier sloping bar. Yet the matchlock remained vulnerable, with a slow rate of fire, bulky size, unreliability in bad weather, visibility at night, plus a sound and smell from the match rope too easily detected by Indians in the forest.

## THE WHEEL-LOCK

The wheel-lock was more complicated to manufacture and repair. Its ignition came from a round serrated wheel that was wound like a clock. An external pivoting arm held a piece of iron pyrites in its jaws, which was lowered against the wheel. Pulling the trigger released the wheel to spin rapidly, generating a shower of sparks onto the priming powder in the pan and causing ignition through the touch-hole.

Although this system was easier to carry when loaded and made possible firing from horseback, its cost to produce and maintain in the field restricted acceptance largely to special units and sporting arms of the well-to-do.

## THE FLINTLOCK

In the middle of the 1500s, another ignition method appeared that functioned by using the sparks from flint striking steel. The flint was held in screw-tightened jaws of a pivoting "cock" (or "hammer") that snapped forward when the trigger was pulled to hit a piece of hardened steel ("battery," "steel" or "frizzen"). The resulting sparks dropped onto the priming powder in the flashpan, which sent flame through the touch-hole to reach the main charge. It would develop and emerge at the beginning of the 1700s as the ultimate firearm system for the 18th century. There were four primary versions of this method: the snaphaunce, the miquelet, the English lock, and the French lock.

*Chapter 1: The Flintlock Evolves*

## The Snaphaunce

This initial flint and steel arrangement probably appeared in Holland during the second half of the 1500s (others developed in Scotland, Italy and Scandinavia). Its basic mechanical action is described below. The primary difference in this case was that the battery was not attached to the flashpan cover; it pivoted back after impact. A separate flat cover slid clear of the pan before firing — in the early form by hand and later mechanically by a pushrod mounted on the inner surface of the lock plate. (Note: During the 17th century, *snaphaunce* commonly referred to any flintlock system.)

This action was less complex and cheaper than the wheel-lock, more reliable and faster to load than the matchlock and could be carried when loaded and primed. Drawbacks included the absence of a safety position for the battery while loading, plus a relatively complicated action. It became the primary ignition used by the Americans during the first half of the 1600s.

## The Miquelet

The miquelet was unique to Spain, Italy and the shores of the Mediterranean. Developed about 1620 by the Spanish, it combined the frizzen and pan cover in one piece like the evolving English lock. The primary difference was positioning the mainspring on the outside, although it required two sears that moved laterally through the lock plate. The larger exterior mainspring was thus able to utilize the poorer quality flint in those countries without weakening the stock by excessive hollowing of the wood. The miquelet continued in use up to about 1825 in Europe and far longer as a Mediterranean trade lock.

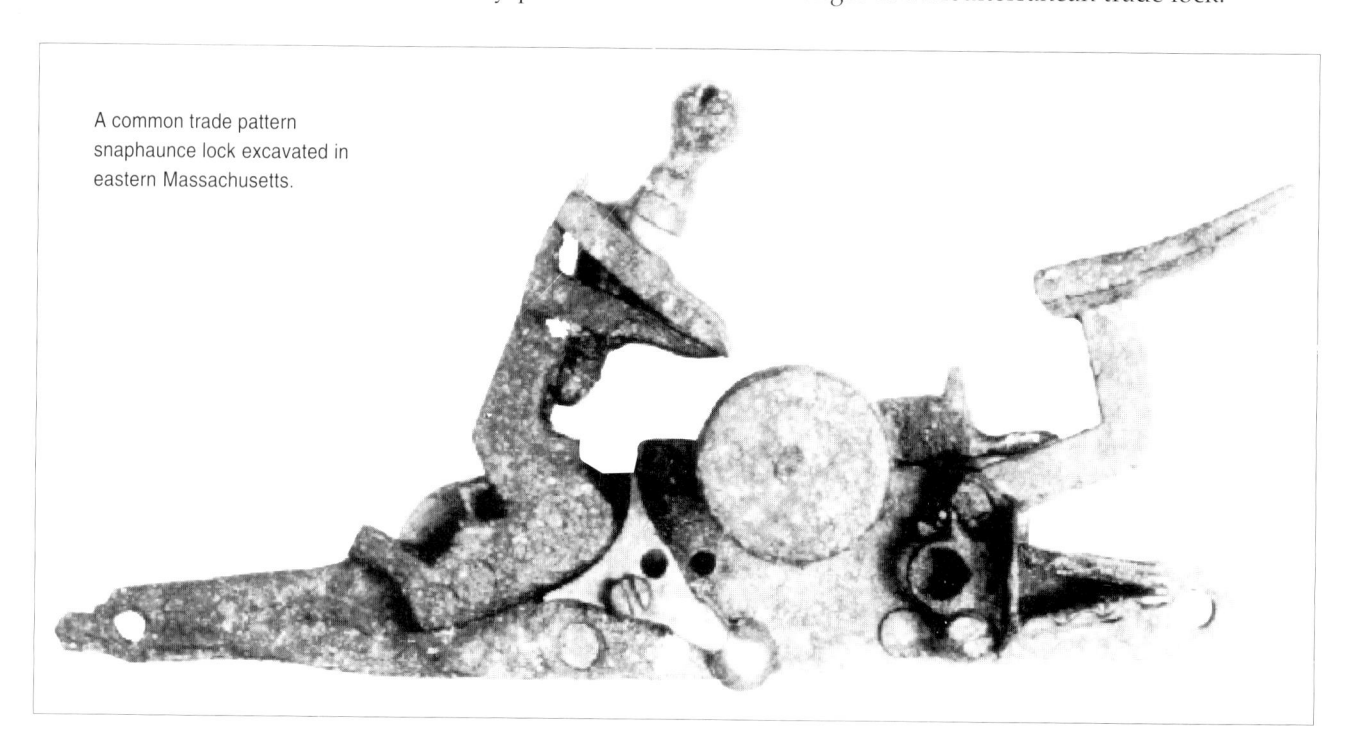

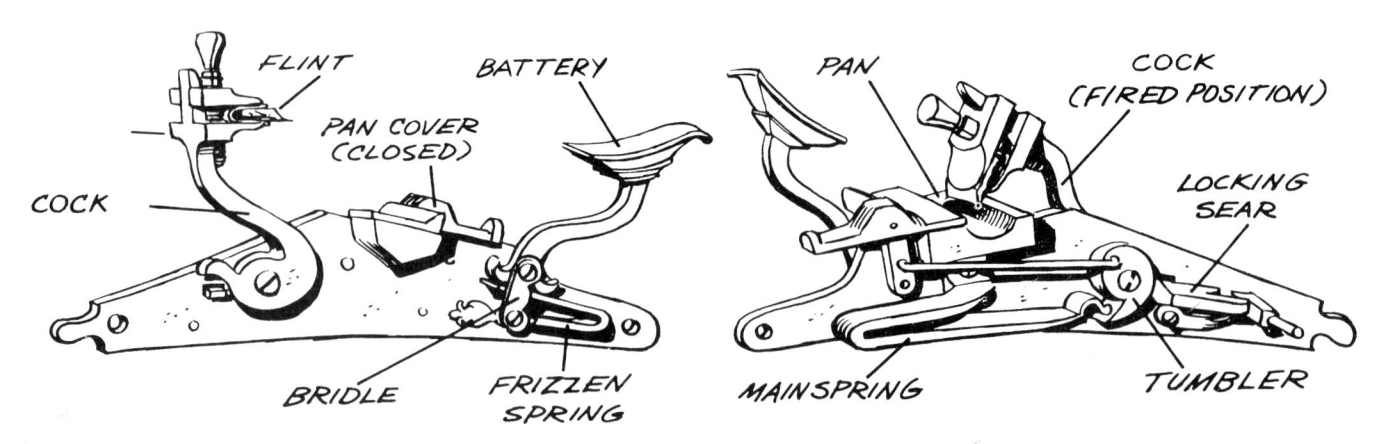

A common trade pattern snaphaunce lock excavated in eastern Massachusetts.

**SNAPHAUNCE LOCK ACTION** – Pulling back the cock rotates its pivot (through the lock plate) and the attached tumbler inside. This compresses the main spring and closes the pan cover over the pan. When the cock is pulled back into a cocked position, the locking sear moves sideways to catch in a hole on the cock's underside. The battery is then lowered into position over the pan. Pulling the trigger retracts the locking sear, allowing the cock to snap forward (automatically sliding back the pan cover) to hit the battery with its flint. The resulting sparks spray into the priming powder of the pan, firing the main charge through the barrel's touch-hole.

*Chapter 1: The Flintlock Evolves*

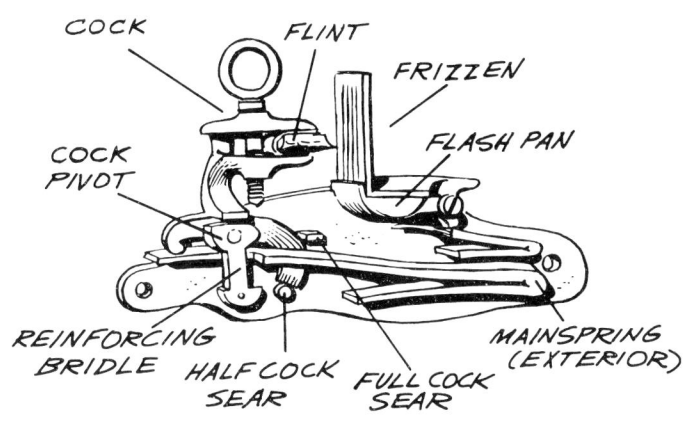

**MIQUELET LOCK ACTION** – When the cock is pulled back, it rotates on the pivot and compresses the main spring (on outside of lock). This cocking action causes two sears to move sideways through the lock plate to the outside. The lower half-cock sear comes out under the cock's lower arm, locking it in a "safe" or "half-cock" position. When rotated farther for firing, the cock's lower arm catches on the higher full-cock sear. As the trigger is pulled, both sears retract, and the cock snaps forward—hitting the frizzen. The blow springs the frizzen upward, as the sparks drop into the priming powder of the pan below. The resulting flash reaches the main barrel charge through the touch-hole.

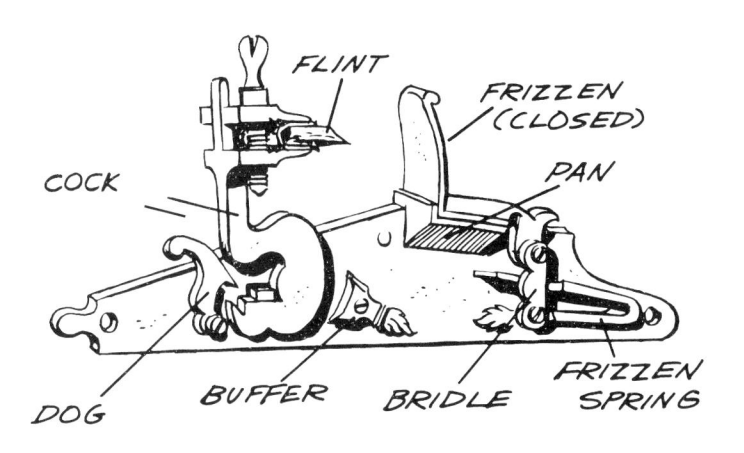

**ENGLISH DOG-LOCK ACTION** – The cock is pulled back, rotating its pivot and the attached inside tumbler. This compresses the mainspring and allows the locking sear to move sideways through the lock plate and engage the end of the cock. The outside dog is also latched onto the tail of the cock. To fire, this outside dog is disengaged by hand. Pulling the trigger retracts the locking sear letting the cock spring forward, striking and lifting the frizzen, and sending sparks down onto the priming powder in the pan below.

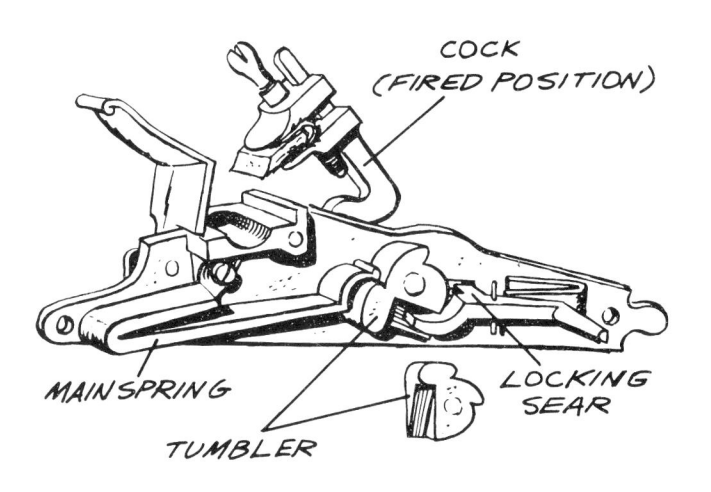

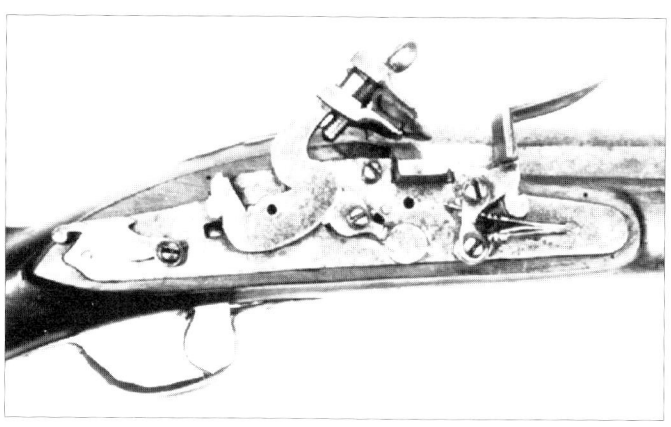

## The English Lock

The prelude to the final flintlock form was the English lock. First appearing during the 1600s, it incorporated two major innovations: (1) the ability to hold the cock in a locked position before firing by using a sear moving laterally through a hole in the lock plate and/or by using an exterior pivoting "dog" catch, which latched onto a notch in the rear of the cock; and (2) the separated pan cover and frizzen of the snaphaunce were now joined as a single L-shaped piece on a pivot screw. The sear feature disappeared about 1650, but the doglock persisted in British military arms until at least 1715 and well beyond that date in traditional trade patterns. It was apparently the most frequent system employed by the American Colonists during the second half of the 1600s.

*Chapter 1: The Flintlock Evolves* 9

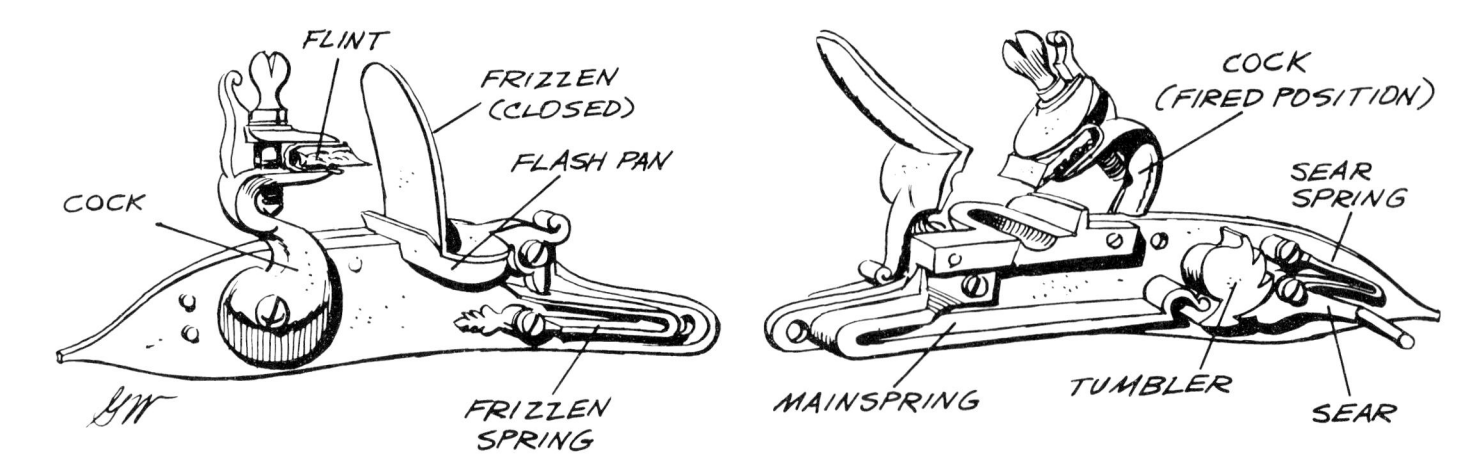

**TRUE (FRENCH) FLINTLOCK** – Pulling back the cock rotates its pivot and the attached tumbler. This compresses the mainspring, and when reaching the half cock position, the sharp edge of the sear slides into the first notch of the tumbler (the safe loading position). For firing the cock is pulled back farther until the sear catches in the second notch of the tumbler. Squeezing the trigger raises the horizontal arm of the sear and disengages its edge from the tumbler notch. The cock then snaps forward, hitting the frizzen with its flint and dropping sparks into the priming powder of the pan. Its flash ignites the main charge through the touch-hole in the barrel.

## The French Lock

This was the ultimate design that firmly established flintlocks as the dominant ignition system for the 18th century. Developed in France about 1610–1620, it simplified prior actions in two ways: (1) the horizontal safety sear of the English lock was replaced by a new internal sear that engaged notches in a rotating inside tumbler (attached to the external cock); and (2) a second notch on the tumbler created a half-cock safe position for use while loading or carrying a primed weapon.

Not burdened with large inventories of obsolete arms and having to cope with heavily wooded terrain instead of the open fields of Europe, the American Colonists embraced these new ignitions more quickly than the Europeans as they became available.

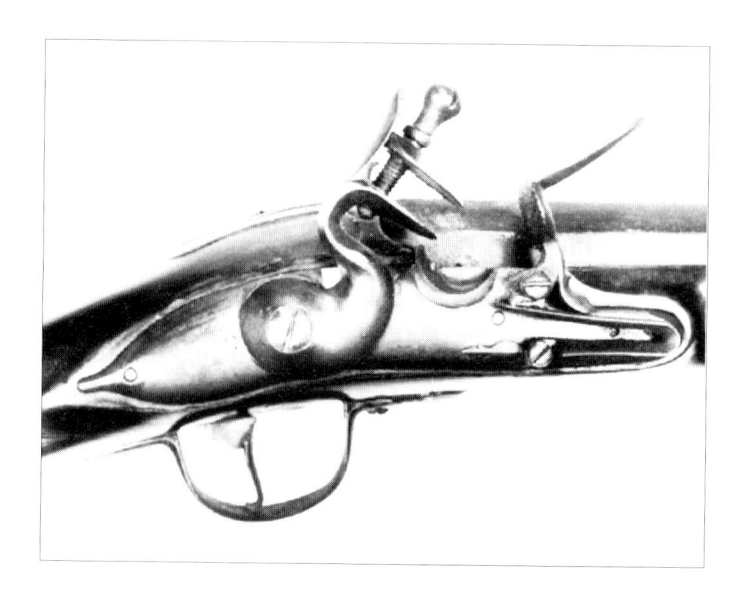

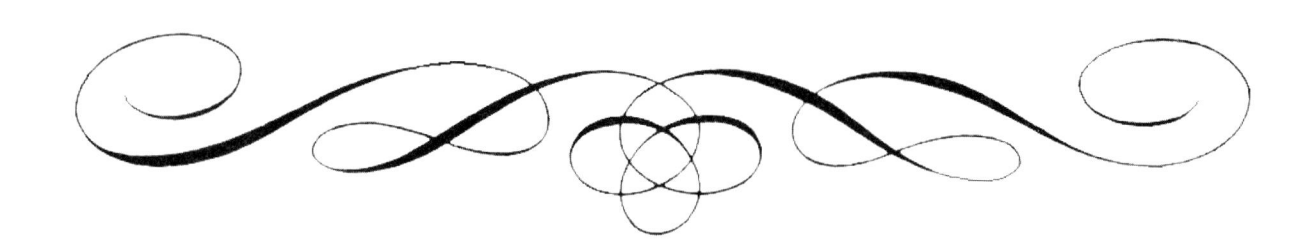

# Chapter 2

# *Weapons Determined the Tactics*

The evolution of firearm ignition systems during the 1600s described in the preceding chapter illustrates the many shortcomings and lack of reliability of the flintlock. Its performance depended upon the quality and striking edge of the flint, strength of both the main and frizzen springs, hardness of the steel frizzen, maintenance of an open touch-hole and favorable weather. The most vexing difficulty of these weapons, however, was the black powder.

To understand how the American Revolution was won, it is essential to appreciate the severe limitations that the firearms created because their capabilities determined the battlefield tactics. The tactics in turn determined the recruitment, training, equipment and leadership demands that Washington had to solve while simultaneously conducting a war against the finest troops in the world.

Black powder is a very "hot" explosive. When fired it creates a flash of flame close to two feet long from a smoothbore's muzzle and another ten-inch burst at the lock's flashpan. After only four or five rounds the barrel can become too hot to touch. The formula is also hygroscopic, which varies its shooting performance depending on the weather's humidity and temperature. The primary problem, however, is its residue.

An ideal gunpowder changes completely into a gas upon ignition to push the projectile out of the barrel with maximum force. The black powder in use until the late 1800s transformed less than half of itself into a gas. Close to 55 percent remained in the weapon after firing as a clinging black fouling. Successive layers from each round steadily reduced the effective diameter of the bore, as well as clogged the barrel's touch-hole and coated the striking surfaces of the flint and frizzen. The soldier carried a small pick and brush, usually suspended from one of his crossbelts, in an effort to keep the lock, pan and touch-hole clear. But the accumulation of fouling inside the bore meant that, following less than half a dozen firings of a tight-fitting

**DEFENSE OF BREED'S HILL, June 1775**
When the British regulars finally swarmed into the redoubt with leveled bayonets, they were surprised by the fierce response from its defenders—most of whom lacked bayonets but continued to resist with clubbed muskets and fowlers. As England's General Gage reported, they were "not the despicable rabble too many have supposed them to be."

**THE NEW YORK CITY CAMPAIGN, 1776**
British grenadiers of the 23rd Royal Welch Fusiliers present a solid line of charging bayonets against semi-trained Americans who were not yet prepared to oppose them in the open. It forced Washington to survive by surprise attack, rapid elusive movements, field entrenchments and the use of natural cover until a disciplined army could be created.

round lead bullet, the ball would become clogged after being rammed part-way down the barrel (with the danger of rupturing the breech if fired in that position). It thus created a steadily less reliable weapon during a battle as the fouling built up.

Their solution for this fundamental problem was the use of an undersized bullet (usually .04 to .06 caliber smaller than the bore). This made loading easier, but when fired much of the force of the ignition was lost around the loose projectile as it progressed up the barrel bouncing and skidding against opposite walls. The final trajectory was determined by which side it hit last at the muzzle. Such inherent inaccuracy demanded that these smoothbores be fired at close quarters to be effective and that the soldier be armed with a second bladed weapon that always "worked," such as a sword, belt ax or bayonet.

The rifle favored on the frontier—with its spiraled grooves that spun the ball for greater accuracy—usually employed a bullet wrapped in cloth or leather to help clear the fouling and better grip the rifling.

## TACTICS IN THE FIELD

Based upon these firearm limitations, the European nations developed "linear tactics." Since the arms lost accuracy beyond 50 to 60 yards, the smoothbore musket was used as a giant shotgun within that range, and the soldiers were trained for speed firing in place of accuracy. They would simply point their arms to the front or to either oblique and fire together in controlled volleys (successively by rank) to achieve maximum shock impact on the enemy. Their military musket, in fact, did not have a rear sight.

The typical 18th century battle began with each army entering the field in column and rapidly deploying into a long "line of battle" (usually including the artillery) perhaps 200 to 300 yards from their foes. Massed regimental snare drums immediately to the rear relayed all of the orders to the troops through specific beatings. The soldiers stood shoulder to shoulder (for maximum firepower) in two or three ranks, with additional "file closers" behind to move forward and plug gaps as casualties occurred. Since the line with its volley fire provided the most effective use of these weapons, the objective of the battle was to break

*12    Chapter 2: Weapons Determined the Tactics*

the enemy's line usually by assaulting the front or maneuvering around the flanks. Once the troops were scattered, the cavalry charged forward to ride among them with swinging sabers.

The formal combat began when one force advanced across the field with colors displayed, music playing and the noncoms continually dressing the lines. Enemy artillery, which had a range exceeding the shoulder arms, would begin firing solid iron balls and change to multiple-shot loads of grape and cannister at closer range against the solidly packed attackers. An advancing line normally halted about 50 to 60 yards from the enemy, at which time both forces began firing rapid volleys by successive ranks (four to five rounds per minute was claimed, but powder fouling steadily slowed the rate). Meanwhile, white powder smoke quickly enveloped the field. Finally, at an advantageous moment, one line would charge with the ultimate battlefield weapon—the bayonet.

This advance was methodical in dressed ranks that moved forward as a relentless wall. The American soldier early in the war lacked the disciplined training to cope with it—and in most cases did not even own a bayonet. When these closely packed enemy lines appeared through the powder smoke with leveled muskets mounting seventeen-inch bayonet blades, there was little he could do but break and run. Thus victory required more than the stubborn defiance of firing from behind stone walls, trees or entrenchments as at Lexington and Concord and at Bunker Hill.

Not until 1777 and 1778, when large numbers of French arms with bayonets began arriving and von Steuben indoctrinated the Americans in this highly controlled warfare, had Washington any hope of facing the King's troops successfully in the open. Until that time he survived by surprise attack, rapid elusive movements, field entrenchments and the use of natural cover.

## TWO AMERICAS AT WAR

The Americans who challenged the British forces in 1775 comprised two distinct societies that existed in dissimilar situations and employed different weapons. Along the East Coast, towns were established and much of the land had been cleared. These Colonists adopted the European tactics described above with smoothbore arms and the bayonet exercised in the disciplines of formal linear warfare. West of the Alleghenies on the frontier, however, the families were usually isolated, which forced many to use the slower loading but more accurate rifle from natural cover, with the belt knife and tomahawk as secondary weapons.

Two types of troops served the patriot cause: the militia and short term state units ("levies"), which were mustered for limited periods when needed; and the more permanent regular Continental line regiments.

The militia were local semi-military groups maintained in the English tradition. Each state had its own regulations, which normally required participation by men from sixteen to sixty years of age with few exceptions. Although lacking

**CONTINENTAL LINE SURCHARGES**
In 1777 a resolution of the Continental Congress ordered all government-owned arms and accoutrements to be branded "US," "UNITED STATES," or "U:STATES." Not all were marked and, because it was mostly done locally by each regiment, the final forms varied (as shown). Similar identification continued at armories after the war ended.
**Source: Author**

*Chapter 2: Weapons Determined the Tactics*

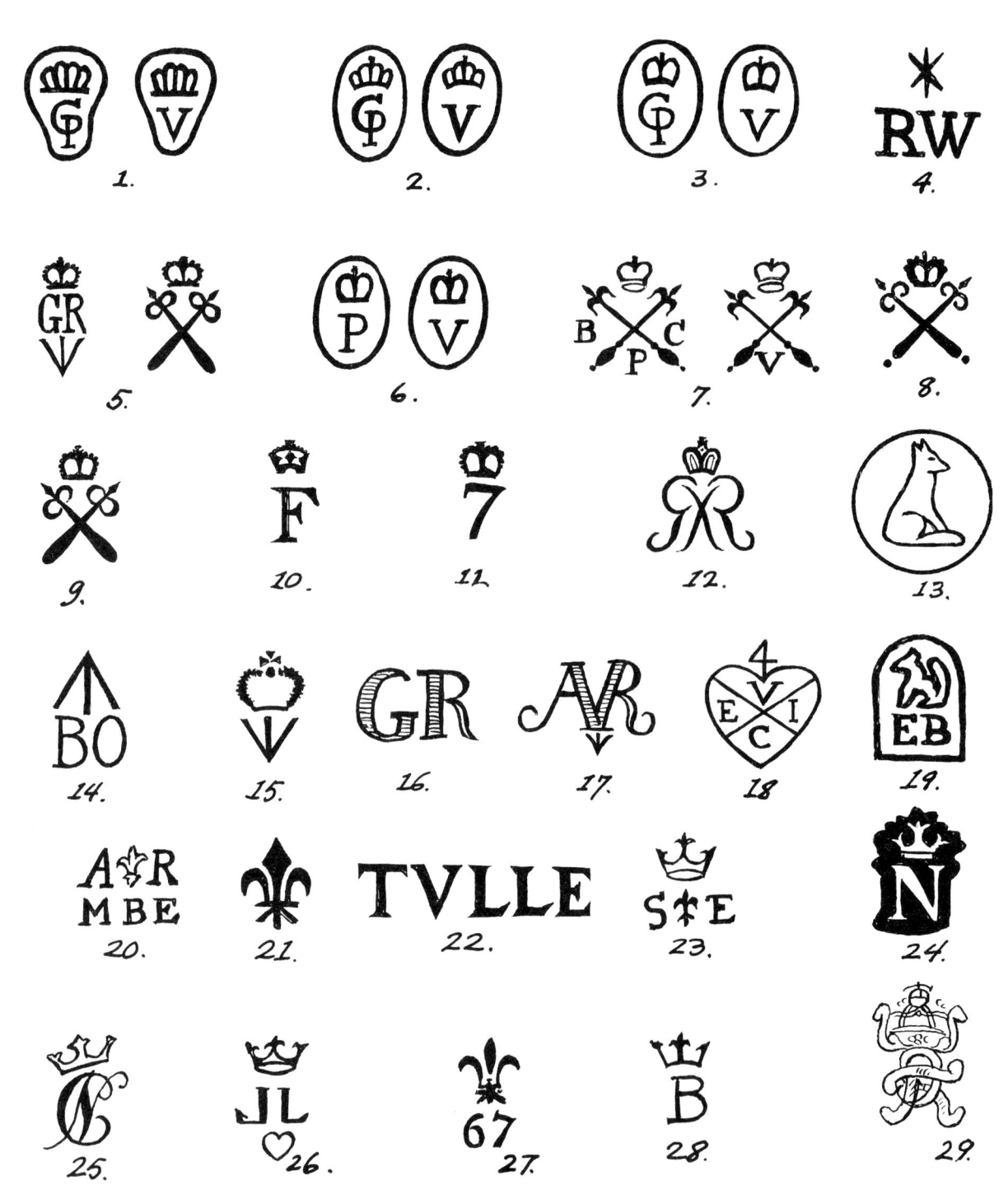

**TYPICAL WEAPON MARKINGS**

**ENGLISH:** **(1)** London Gunmakers Company of London 1637 proofs (private contractors), usually on the barrel breech, one above the other. **(2)** London Gunmakers 1672 proofs. **(3)** London Gunmakers 1702 proofs ("V" stamp—the first rough proof or "viewing;" "GP"—the final proof). **(4)** Typical London Gunmakers individual member's mark (usually struck between the two vertical proofs shown in 1–3); this was for Richard Wilson. **(5)** Gun barrel proofs of the English Royal Armory (on the breech); the initial scepters' "viewers" mark below the later and final "King's Proof" ("GR" with the broad arrow of ownership). **(6)** Birmingham proofs (private contractors) prior to 1813. **(7)** Proofs adopted in 1813 for new Birmingham Gunmakers proof house. **(8)** Birmingham private proof used by Ketland, circa 1780. **(9)** Board of Ordnance "private" proof for nongovernmental makers by the Tower Armory for a fee (struck twice, one above the other). **(10)** "Foreigners" mark; proof by London Gunmakers for non-members; post 1741. **(11)** Viewers (inspector's) stamp for government arms (the number identified each inspector). **(12)** Ordnance storekeeper's stamp; usually on side of the butt; used after 1770 (but retroactively applied to many earlier weapons). **(13)** Fox-in-circle view mark on trade guns by Northwest Company of Montreal circa 1790–1815 and on later presentation pieces (usually on lock plate and breech). **(14)** Board of Ordnance ownership mark (mostly on the stock); replaced by "WD" (War Department) in 1855. **(15)** Crown/broad arrow; government ownership stamp (struck sideways under pan on lock plate). **(16)** Royal cipher for "Georgius Rex" (Kings George I–III); appeared under a crown on lock plates and sword blades. **(17)** Royal cipher during Queen Anne's reign (1702–1714). **(18)** British East India Company mark. **(19)** "Tombstone Fox" lock stamp used mostly on Hudson Bay Company trade guns; "EB" mark was Hudson Bay "viewer" Edward Bond (1771–1776), continued by his family until 1879. **FRENCH:** **(20)** "AR" for Inspector Desjardins (1718–1755); "MBE" identified the Royal manufactory at Maubeuge. **(21)** Fleur-de-lis mark for the Charleville manufactory. **(22)** Stamp for Tulle private gunmaker; chief source of Naval Ministry arms for marine troops in Canada; the spelling (using the V) is pre-1745. **(23)** St. Etienne manufactory mark. **(24)** French date letter hallmark (this one 1776). **(25)** Cipher of Nicholas Carteron,

*14    Chapter 2: Weapons Determined the Tactics*

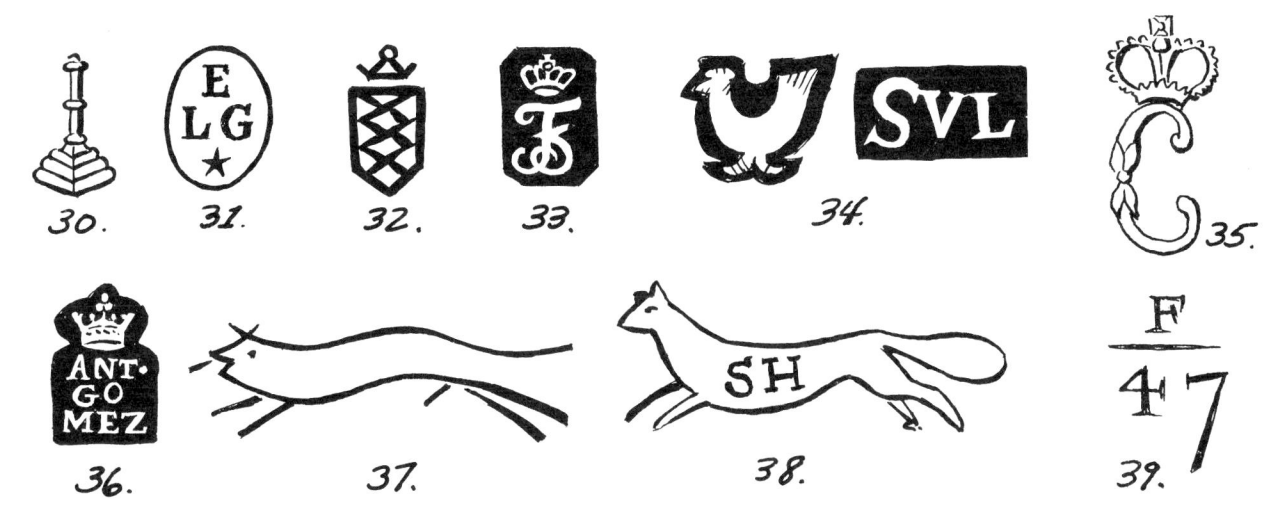

**TYPICAL WEAPON MARKINGS (Continued)**

inspector at St. Etienne. **(26)** The control stamp of Lilien. **(27)** Date stamp; "67" indicates last two digits of manufacture date, that is, 1767. **(28)** A controller's mark (inspector); "B" is his initial. **OTHER EUROPEAN MARKINGS: (29)** Cipher of Frederick the Great of Prussia (Frederick II, 1740–1786). **(30)** Liege, Belgium; 1672–1810 and 1835 to the present. **(31)** Liege; 1810 to present (a crown was added in 1893). **(32)** Amsterdam control mark (on the barrel). **(33)** Denmark and Norway (circa 1746–1766). **(34)** The hen figure was used by the county of Henneberg; "SVL" was the mark for Suhl (Henneberg County, Germany). **(35)** Cipher for Duke Charles I of Brunswick (1735–1780). **(36)** Typical Spanish barrel marking. **(37)** Running wolf figure; originally Passau and Solingen (Germany); later copied across Europe (sword blades). **(38)** English running fox figure (sword blades); "SH" for maker (Samuel Harvey, Birmingham). **(39)** British "fraction" on government arms; the top indicates the unit, the bottom shows the weapon's rack number. **NOTE:** Gun markings believed used to identify some American state-owned arms during the Revolutionary War: "SC" Connecticut; "MB" Massachusetts; "P" and "PP" Pennsylvania; "CR" Rhode Island; "PS" and "JS" Maryland; "SP" New Jersey; "NH" New Hampshire; "SGF" State Gun Factory, Fredericksburg, Virginia.

the discipline and weaponry to stand against professional troops, militia provided the men who fought at Lexington and Concord and at Bunker Hill, as well as supplementary forces whenever danger threatened their locality. Moreover, throughout the war these units proved invaluable by providing an internal police force to counter Loyalist activity, guard key roads, garrison local fortifications and protect quartermaster stores, as well as to escort supply trains. Each individual was required to provide his own shoulder arm (often his hunting fowler) plus a bladed secondary weapon, for example a short sword, belt ax or bayonet. Many of these local units included mounted troops.

The Continental line or long term regiments were the backbone of the American army. Recruiting began among the militia assembled around Boston in 1775, but they mostly remained subject to state control throughout the war. Fearing a large central army, the states limited these early enlistments to a single year or less. By the end of 1776, however, Washington persuaded them to extend the period to three years or the duration.

The British experienced their own recruiting problems for the "American War," as many considered it to be "Englishmen fighting Englishmen." This was largely overcome after France actively entered the conflict in 1778. In the meantime England found little enlistment response from the Irish, who were enjoying a period of prosperity, but successfully raised several regiments in Scotland. The remaining gap was filled with mercenaries contracted from six German states (Hesse Cassel, Hesse Hanau, Brunswick, Waldeck, Anspach-Beyreuth and Anhalt Zerbst), which furnished close to 30,000 soldiers. In addition Americans who remained loyal to the Crown formed many of the most aggressive and reliable regiments in the Royal service.

This American struggle for freedom was one of passion, stubbornness, endurance and incredible valor by the combatants on both sides. Central to its understanding is a knowledge of the weapons and the all-important battlefield tactics they required. Identification of these arms is the objective of this book. Typical examples are illustrated in the following chapters covering shoulder and hand firearms, bayonets, swords and polearms.

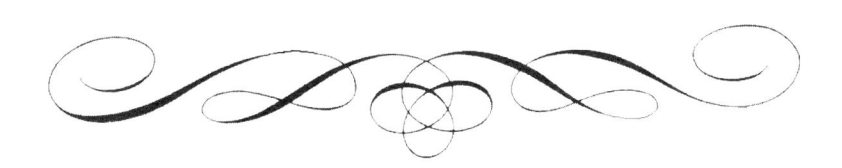

*Chapter 2: Weapons Determined the Tactics* **15**

# Chapter 3

# Smoothbore Shoulder Arms ...Up Close by Volley

## ENGLISH MILITARY MUSKETS

*1702–1713* — The new century began with the long and costly War of the Spanish Succession (or "Queen Anne's War," 1702–1713). At that time the private London Gunmakers' Company (charted in 1637) dominated most British firearm production, and they varied specifications according to the wishes of each regimental colonel, who also purchased competitive muskets offered by Continental makers. There was little uniformity beyond an official barrel length (46 inches) and bore size (.75 caliber). Thus at the conclusion of the war, Britain had an incredible mixture of different patterns of varying quality from domestic and foreign makers. At this point the Royal Board of Ordnance began to introduce a series of controls and manufacturing systems to bring about standard patterns of uniform quality.

*1714–1722* — The Board continued the established policy of relying on private makers. Beginning with a 1714 contract, however, new procedures were introduced. The Tower Armory would now accumulate and test all components from its suppliers (most barrels, locks and iron fittings from Birmingham and brass furniture plus "small" items from London). When arms were required, the Tower would issue individual guns as patterns ("sealed" muskets with a stamped wax seal on the buttstock) accompanied by the necessary components from its stockpiled inventory for assembly into complete guns by "rough stockers," or "setters up," primarily in the Minories section of London.

Birmingham would likewise assemble some finished arms, and foreign sources such as Holland, Liege and Germanic centers would still be considered in periods of high demand. New proofing and inspection with standard gauges were also instituted throughout the manufacturing process.

*1715–1720* — The doglock had begun to disappear during the century's first decade, and rounded lock plates with gooseneck hammers were now in use, as well as the handrail butt form (5.MM).

*Circa 1718* — "Pattern of the 10,000" was created for both

**A LOYALIST INFANTRYMAN RELOADS IN ACTION**
He has just torn open a cylindrical paper-wrapped cartridge with his teeth and primed the pan and is ramming the loose black powder and round bullet down the barrel (note the powder fouling smudges around his mouth). In proper fashion the smoothbore musket is at its half cock safety position for loading (the cock is vertical).

the land and sea services. Unlike the earlier 1714 contract, its furniture reverted to iron instead of brass.

*1722* — The announcement of a new "King's Pattern" musket received little acceptance, although each colonel was instructed to supply his troops with long arms equal to or better than these new specifications. He traditionally received a grant from the Crown to recruit and equip his regiment (including the selection of arms) and succeeded in keeping most of this control until the 1750s. During that period the regiment was usually identified by his name; this was changed to a numerical designation in 1751. Few colonels took the field with their troops, as most active campaigning was conducted by professional lieutenant-colonels.

Also in 1722 the first official 42-inch barreled musket was produced for dragoons, who were mounted but fought on foot.

*The Long Land Pattern 1730* — Manufacture of the new "King's Pattern" commenced in 1728. It was issued beginning in 1730 and is considered the first of the long land Brown Besses, having a 46-inch barrel (.75 caliber), wooden rammer, curved "banana" lock, brass furniture and a walnut stock (8.MM).

*1740–1741* — Following the outbreak of war in Europe, a wholesale rearmament of the army with the pattern 1730 was undertaken.

*The Long Land Pattern 1742* — This updated Brown Bess musket retained the 46-inch barrel (.75 caliber) and wooden ramrod but had modified brass furniture and a second bridle added to the banana lock (9.MM).

*1748* — Following King George's War, a conversion from wooden to steel rammers was begun and progressed slowly.

*1752* — All sea service muskets were now to be fitted with socket bayonets and sling swivels.

*1754–1763* — During the French and Indian War (also known as the Seven Years' War, 1756–1763), long land Brown Besses with wooden rammers (Patterns 1730 and 1742) were the basic weapons of the British infantry, but smaller bore (.65 caliber) carbines were issued to special units. Apparently some of the English light troops also carried captured French arms.

*The Long Land Pattern 1756* – This third Brown Bess version retained the 46-inch pinned barrel (.75 caliber) but introduced a straighter lock, steel rammer and a long, flared upper ramrod pipe. It is uncertain how much American service this musket had in the French and Indian War (10.MM).

*The Pattern 1756 Sea Service Musket* — Earlier naval arms were apparently of varied forms in "black" or "bright" finishes; they favored a flat three-screw lock with a ring-neck cock and simplified brass furniture similar to the Queen Anne period. This new pattern reduced the flat lock to two side screws and shortened its barrel to 37 inches (27.MM–29.MM).

*The Pattern 1756 Marine or Militia Musket* — Created for the marines, this design was first issued in 1757 with a wooden ramrod. It had a barrel reduced to 42 inches, as well as brass fittings that included a flat side plate and a top screw through a shortened butt tang (12.MM). An updated version (Pattern 1759 Marine or Militia) added a steel rammer with a long, flared upper rammer pipe but probably was not issued to the marines until 1768 (13.MM).

*1764* — Immediately following the French and Indian War, the practice of engraving the date of manufacture and the maker's name on the lock's tail was discontinued. It would now be marked "Tower" or "Dublin Castle."

*The Short Land Pattern 1768* — A new 42-inch barrel (.75 caliber) Brown Bess was approved in 1768 and issued beginning in 1769 as the new standard arm of the British army. The brass furniture was simplified (flat side plate, shorter butt tang) but retained the basic long land pattern, which itself continued in limited production until 1790 (14.MM).

*1775–1783, The American War for Independence* — Despite the new 1768 Short Land Pattern, long land Brown Bess muskets were apparently the principal weapon of the British army in America until 1777. Earlier long lands with wooden rammers remained in use by Loyalist units throughout the war and on occasion as replacements for German regiments.

*The Short Land Pattern 1777* — This revised 1768 pattern included a changed second ramrod pipe, which had an expanded upper end (with a straight line profile). Known as "Pratt's improvement" for the contractor, John Pratt, who created the form, it was intended to speed the return of the rammer. Evidence indicates it was already in use (15.MM).

In addition, to settle a serious supplier pricing problem, a less expensive lock (lock II) was substituted (15.MM). It was close to an established design in widespread use by private manufacturers, including the standard infantry pattern for the independent British East India Company Army (that is, the "India Pattern") (19.MM).

*1778* — With the entrance of France into the war as an active ally of the American Colonies, the English quickly expanded their arms production, including large orders for short land pattern muskets from Liege (at least 60,000) and various Germanic centers (16.MM–17MM).

*Sources* — Britain manufactured some 218,000 land service muskets during the American war and added more than 100,000 contract arms from abroad (re: Bailey, bib. 168). The Royal Proof Houses were at the Tower of London and Dublin Castle (which continued until the Irish rebellion of 1798). These cities provided most of the furniture and stocking. Birmingham, which did not gain a Royal proof house until 1813, supplied the majority of iron components plus numbers of finished arms.

## FRENCH MILITARY MUSKETS

The French were leaders in weapons development during our Colonial period. Their primary innovations included:

*Late 17th Century* — Introduction of the new plug bayonet followed by the socket version and the ultimate flintlock ignition system.

*1713* — Inheriting a disarray of arms after the War of the Spanish Succession (1702–1713), France, like England, pursued central control of weapons production and the development of official patterns.

*1717* — The first European standard firearm was introduced as the Model 1717, and three royal arms manufactories were operating under artillery supervision at St. Etienne, Charleville and Maubeuge. The Department of Marine did, however, continue to contract with the

**THE PENNSYLVANIA LINE AT MONMOUTH (New Jersey), June 1778**
Continental troops deliver a disciplined volley in their first battle after receiving indoctrination under a new unified manual by von Steuben at Valley Forge. Notice the second row, prepared to fire over the shoulders of the front line while the latter is reloading in order to deliver a continuing series of shocks against the enemy line.

independent armory at Tulle, which became an official royal manufactory in 1777. France also adopted a smaller bore than the British (.69 versus .75 caliber), plus a more slender stock to provide a lighter musket requiring less ammunition weight in the field.

*1728* — The Model 1728 introduced a banded instead of a pinned barrel to facilitate cleaning and maintenance.

*1741* — The steel rammer was mandated.

*1754* — Light muskets (*Fusils d' Officiers*) were ordered for grenadier officers.

*1762* — To correct weaknesses evident during the French and Indian War, the entire French army began a reorganization under the Duke de Choiseul, leading to the new Model 1763 musket series.

*1777* — A noncorrosive brass flashpan was introduced on the innovative Model 1777.

*1776–1783* — Over 100,000 muskets were included in the vast aid supplied to the American rebels during their War for Independence. In addition the honey-colored French gun flint, created by a unique knapping technique, was used extensively by the armies on both sides.

*1789* — Many surviving arms were destroyed in France to prevent capture by their own revolutionaries.

## French Arms Sources

For an understanding of the French arms used in North America during our period, it is important to appreciate that they came from two basic jurisdictions that favored different patterns: the French Naval Ministry (*Minist re de la Marine*), and the Department of the French Army. The French Naval Ministry not only oversaw the sailing navy but also provided and equipped the land forces that served in the North American colonies from the 1680s until 1755. These infantry units (*compagnies franches de la Marine*) were issued arms largely designed and produced by the private contractor at Tulle, although some were from St. Etienne.

Under the Department of the French Army, regular infantry (*troupes de terre*) was finally sent to Canada in 1755 at the beginning of the French and Indian War. Their weapons were the standard land service arms produced from the three royal manufactories. (Numbers of these patterns, however, were present in North America before that date.)

## French Pattern Systems

To best visualize these primary designs, the French muskets will be considered in three groups: Department of

*18    Chapter 3: Smoothbore Shoulder Arms*

the Marine (Colonial Land Service), Department of the Army, and Department of the Marine (Ocean Navy).

**Department of the Marine** (Colonial Land Service): Sources—Tulle, St. Etienne.

*Circa 1700* — Rounded lock, Roman nose stock, pinned barrel, forend to muzzle, wooden ramrod.

*Circa 1716* — Stock forend shortened for a socket bayonet, flat beveled lock.

*Circa 1724–1734* — (1) the Fusil Ordinaire (*fusil du soldat*), the ordinary soldier's musket with a flat lock, pinned barrel (46-3/4 inches, .66 caliber) and no sling swivels prior to 1729 (34.MM); (2) the Fusil Grenadier, like the Ordinaire but with side sling swivels, a center band and usually a shorter 44-3/4 inch, .66 caliber barrel (35.MM).

*Circa 1744* — The Fusil A Domino replaced the barrel pins with three bands and used a steel ramrod instead of wood (36.MM).

**Department of the Army**: Sources—St. Etienne, Charleville, Maubeuge.

*Model 1717* — The first standard pattern, it included a 46-3/4 inch barrel (.69 caliber). The flat lock had a unique vertical bridle, Roman nose butt profile, pinned barrel, side sling swivels, wooden ramrod and iron furniture (38.MM).

*Model 1728* — Three barrel bands were added, the flat lock's vertical bridle became horizontal, wooden rammer (39.MM).

*Model 1746* — The lock's exterior bridle was eliminated and a button-head steel ramrod added; the two side sling swivels remained (40.MM).

*Model 1754* — Its round sling swivels moved from the side down under the musket; a spring was added to the center barrel band (41.MM).

*Model 1763* — A 44-3/4 inch banded barrel (.69 caliber); a new flat lock had a ring cock and faceted pan; an unusual tunnel-like ramrod spring covered the channel between the top two barrel bands; its upper band retained a squared tail (42.MM).

*Model 1766* — Like the prior pattern but with a smaller lock and lighter furniture; the rammer spring was now inside; a tapered tail appeared on the upper band (43.MM).

*Circa 1768–1774* — Numerous earlier models were renovated in France, including a new rear spring added behind the bottom band on the Model 1766, which formed the pattern for the future United States Model 1795 (44.MM).

*Model 1770–1771* — A convex lock with a ring cock, a heavier barrel (still 44-3/4 inch) and a less-defined buttstock comb were introduced. The top band also added a curving edge between its two straps, as well as a brass sight. Rear springs held the two upper bands. Its top bayonet stud of 1769 reverted underneath in 1771.

*Model 1773* — Like the preceding pattern but with retaining springs behind all three bands, a straight edge between the upper band's straps and restoration of a top bayonet stud also to serve as the front sight (45.MM).

*Model 1774* — A rounded lock of the 1770s was included; the 44-3/4 inch banded barrel (.69 caliber) continued; a clip projecting out under the muzzle snapped over the rear ring on its bayonet (46.MM).

*Model 1777* — A typical 44-3/4 inch banded barrel (.69 caliber). This innovative pattern, which lasted through the Napoleonic Wars, included a sloped brass flashpan, a cheek rest cut into the butt, finger ridges on the trigger guard and an exterior screw retaining its top band, which was soon dropped (47.MM).

**Department of the Marine** (Ocean Navy): Sources—Tulle and the three royal manufactories.

Like most contemporary naval weapons, land service patterns were adopted with minor variations and usually given brass furniture in place of iron (54.MM–56.MM).

## DUTCH-GERMANIC MILITARY MUSKETS

The subdivision of the Holy Roman Empire during the 18th century into numerous small states epitomizes the gunmaking sources of central Europe. For example, Charleville (France), Maastricht (Holland) and Liege (a principality) were only a few miles apart and shared the Meuse River, as well as weapons components and contracts. Amsterdam, Maastricht, Liege, Solingen, Suhl, Potsdam–Spandau, Essen, Thuringen and other great arms making locations filled individual orders with a wide variety of patterns—making it difficult to identify "standard" models.

However a number of distinctive features are usually apparent in these Low Country–Germanic arms, including: brass furniture, thick heavy butts, flat/beveled locks, long irregular butt tangs (top screws), two large screw heads protruding from the butt plate, teardrop carving around the barrel tang, faceted ramrod pipes, a top front sight and bottom bayonet stud, an oval or shield escutcheon with pins or a top screw head, a frizzen spring screw from the inside, and raised carving around the lock and side plate (57.MM–70.MM).

## AMERICAN MILITARY MUSKETS

Like any young nation suddenly at war, the Americans reached out to acquire arms wherever available. As colonists they had been denied the right to build their own manufacturing sources and, in turn, received from England mostly obsolete, damaged and surplus weapons. The rebels, therefore, seized whatever existed in domestic arsenals or in the hands of Loyalists, and each state, as well as the Continental Congress, issued its own specifications for local production—which were seldom followed. The result was a broad mixture of doglocks, fowlers, rifles, muskets, trade or commercial guns, as well as shiploads of European castoffs purchased through independent agents. American ships, too, were forced to use a wide variety of small arms.

By 1777 large amounts of military weaponry, especially from France, finally began arriving to fill most needs of the Continental Line (71.MM–116.MM).

## OFFICERS' FUSILS

The fusil ("fuzee," "fusee") was a light, smoothbore shoulder arm of smaller size and caliber than the regular infantry weapon. It was also the French term for a full-size flintlock musket. Fusils began to replace the traditional spontoons of commissioned officers by the middle of the 18th century, as similar carbines were being issued to noncoms. Since they were usually purchased privately, patterns varied but remained close to the current official form.

## CARBINES

Today a carbine is considered a short-barreled, small caliber, light shoulder arm. During the 18th century, its barrel would vary in length; reduced bore size was the primary consideration. The English, in fact, had three official sizes, .75 musket, .65 carbine, and .56 pistol, although they were often interchanged. The principal carbine patterns considered in this work are listed below.

### English Carbines (Foot Troops)

*Circa 1740s* — For heavy dragoons who fought on foot; a 42-inch barrel (.75 caliber); long land pattern furniture; cut to mount a bayonet (117.MM).

*The Light Infantry Carbine Pattern 1760* — a 42-inch barrel (.65 caliber), brass furniture and bayonet, produced 1760–1762, full issue to new light companies in 1771 (123.MM).

*The Sergeant's Carbine Pattern 1770* — A 39-inch barrel (.65 caliber); similar to short land configuration with a steel rammer; issued to sergeants of grenadiers in line companies, fusiliers and guard regiments by 1771 (120.MM).

*The Artillery Carbine Pattern, circa 1756* — A 37-inch barrel (.65 caliber), wooden ramrod, steel ramrod and long upper pipe with a center ring added by the 1760s (121.MM).

*The Artillery Carbine Pattern, circa 1777* — A 37-inch barrel (.65 caliber) with the new Lock II approved on the 1777 Short Land musket, fourth thimble added, no raised ring on the upper pipe (122.MM).

### English Carbines (Light Horse)

*The Light Dragoon Carbine Pattern 1756* — A 37-inch pinned barrel, side bar/ring, stocked to the muzzle, wooden rammer (118.MM).

*The Light Dragoon Eliott #1 Pattern (1760)* — A 28-inch pinned barrel (.65 caliber), stocked to the muzzle, wooden ramrod, side bar/ring (124.MM).

*The Light Dragoon Eliott #2 Pattern (1773)* — A 28-inch pinned barrel (.65 caliber); a unique notched iron ramrod, mounted a bayonet, side bar/ring (125.MM).

*The Light Dragoon Royal Foresters Carbine Pattern 1776* — A 28-inch pinned barrel (.65 caliber), side bar/ring with a double outboard screw plate, slot keys replaced barrel pins, used a bayonet (126.MM).

### French Carbines (Cavalry)

France officially set a .69 caliber bore size for muskets and a .67 for carbines and pistols.

*The Carbine Model 1733* — A 31-inch pinned barrel, .67 caliber, stocked to the muzzle; flat Model 1728-type lock, side bar/ring, brass furniture (130.MM).

*The Carbine Model 1766* — A 31-inch banded barrel, .67 caliber, double strap center band, stocked to the muzzle, brass furniture, side bar/ring (131.MM).

*The Carbine Model 1777* — A 30-inch barrel, .67 caliber, eight inches of barrel unsupported, new Model 1777 rounded lock (brass pan), side bar/ring (132.MM).

### American Carbines

There were no official patterns for the American light horse. They employed various European weapons or cut down longarms.

## BLUNDERBUSSES

These shortened shoulder-stocked firearms had large bores and flared muzzles. Normally loaded with multiple small shot, they were very effective at close quarters. The form first became popular beginning in the mid-1600s as greater overland travel increased banditry on the European highways. Later studies established that the muzzle's flare had minimum influence on the shot pattern.

Most military employment was aboard ships at sea in crowded deck actions. The infantry found limited use for street control, sentry duty and as personal officer weapons (133.MM–141.MM).

## WALL OR RAMPART GUNS

Wall guns were heavy-barreled, large bore (smooth or rifled) semi-shoulder arms with a range well beyond the average infantry musket. They were usually employed at fortified positions—often mounted on swivels or projecting a bottom stud near the muzzle to hook over a parapet. Shorter versions were installed along the decks of ships or on longboats (142.MM–147.MM).

## FOWLERS AND TRADE GUNS

Fowlers were the civilian hunting guns. They could vary from a plain utility arm to an elaborate work of art and were traditionally stocked to the muzzle (although often cut back for militia bayonet requirements). Some were imported but the majority were apparently produced by local makers, often with reused or foreign components. The stocks were mostly walnut, maple, cherry or apple (100.MM–116.MM).

Trade and commercial guns in turn were usually created by private sources in Europe for sale in the American Colonies through the fur trade, frontier sutlers and established merchants (149.MM–160.MM).

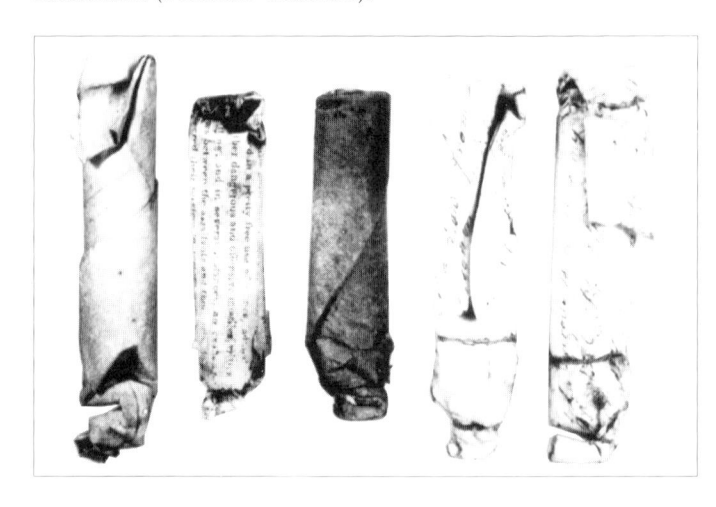

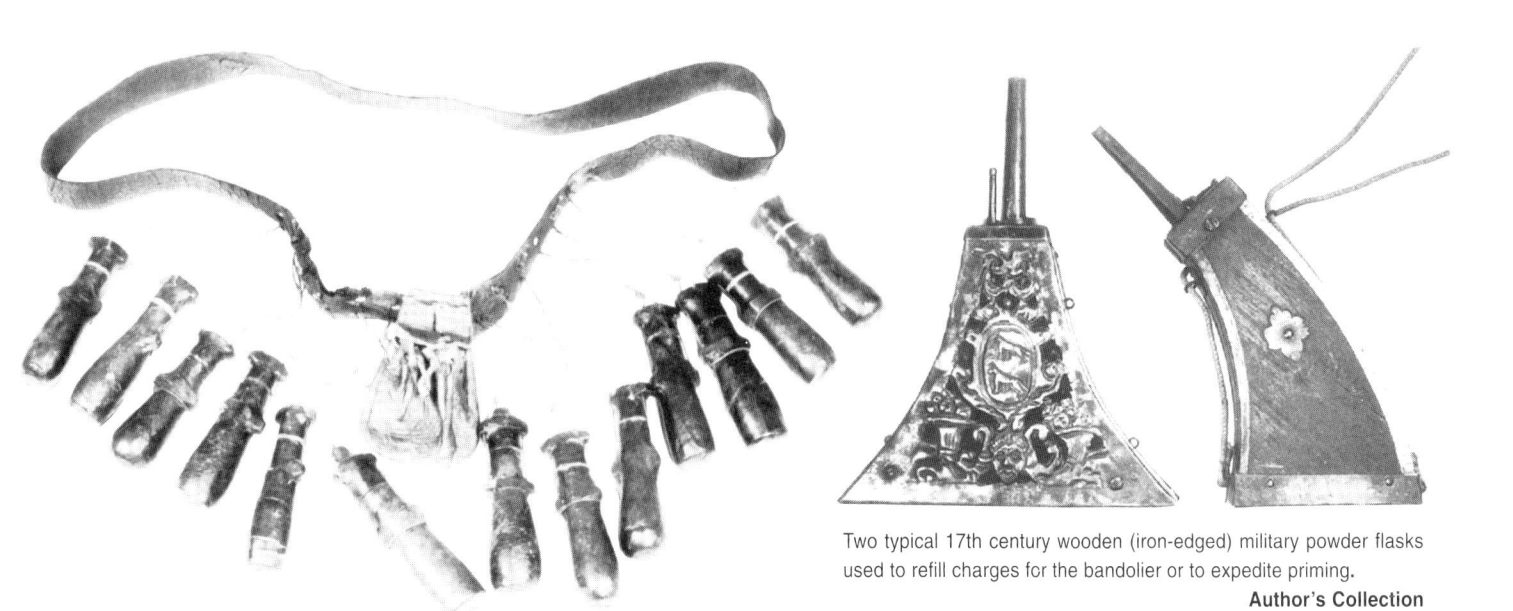

Two typical 17th century wooden (iron-edged) military powder flasks used to refill charges for the bandolier or to expedite priming.
**Author's Collection**

A 17th century musketeer's bandolier ("twelve apostles") consisting of leather-covered wooden cylinders, a separate priming container (center) and the bullet bag seen on the shoulder belt. Premeasured powder charges were carried in the dozen or more wooden cylinders.
**Author's Collection**

In 1689 French infantry was ordered to change to such pouches *("gibecieres")*, which held seven or eight of the new paper-wrapped cartridges and a leather-covered powder flask *("poire à poudre")*. These early pre-1700 accoutrements are included for the reader's reference. **Author's Collection**

**PAPER CARTRIDGES (facing page)**
Typical Revolutionary War paper cartridges containing loose black powder and one or more round lead bullets. The soldier tore them open with his teeth. As shown, Americans used whatever paper was available, including books, letters and newspapers.
**Author's Collection**

**BULLET MOLDS**
Single and multiple bullet mold forms, shown at right, include the early leaf type (16th century) at lower left and crude cavities cut into a two-piece soap stone unit at upper right.
**Author's Collection**

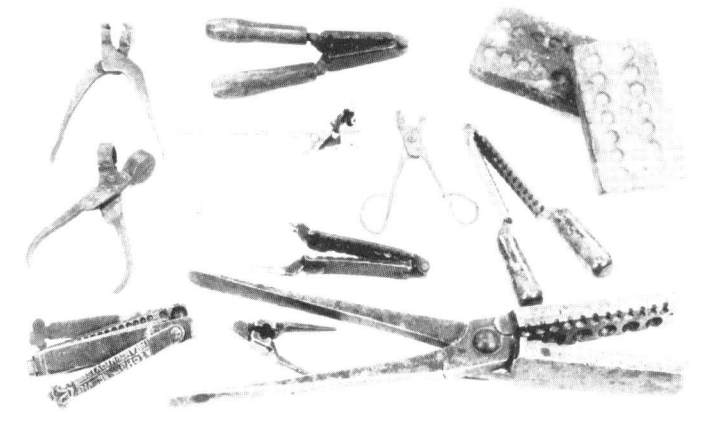

*Chapter 3: Smoothbore Shoulder Arms* **21**

**ENGLISH WAIST CARTRIDGE BOX**
The government issued each recruit a "stand-of-arms" that included this "belly box" form, a slightly curved wooden block with 18 holes (9, 9), two front waist belt loops (to hold it against the stomach) and a leather flap nailed along the rear edge (note the gold embossed "crown/ GR 3"). A larger hip pouch was later added at the regimental level. Block: 8-5/16" X 2" X 2-7/8".
George C. Neumann Collection, Valley Forge National Historical Park

**ENGLISH SHOULDER BOX**
In 1775 the waist belt box pattern was ordered converted to a shoulder strap by adding rear horizontal back strips plus squared iron buckles on the bottom (nailed to the block). The original front belt loops were removed (nail holes remain). It retained the 18 holes. Block: 8-5/8" X 2" X 3-1/4".
George C. Neumann Collection, Valley Forge National Historical Park

**ENGLISH LIGHT INFANTRY POUCH**
Larger pouches were supplied by each regiment from government funds. This was recovered after the Bunker Hill battle. Note the outer flap (6-3/4" X 8-1/4") and typical British shallow inner cover with end tabs (1-3/4" X 8"). The rear cross strip and bottom iron buckles hold its buff leather shoulder strap. A flat accessories pocket is sewn on the black calfskin body (7-5/8" X 4-7/8" X 1-3/4"). No block survives. Marks: "62 B" above the pocket.
J. Craig Nannos Collection

*Chapter 3: Smoothbore Shoulder Arms*

**BRUNSWICK GRENADIER CARTRIDGE BOX**

This Germanic box was retrieved from the Bennington Battlefield (Vermont, 1777). Only one of four (grenadier) flaming bombs (2-5/8" high) remains on the large outer flap in addition to the center brass plate (4-3/4" high) for Duke Charles I of Brunswick. Its thick leather body has leather strips sewn to cover all seams and inner edges, while remains of a circular pocket appear on the front (4-1/4" high X 4" wide). The wooden block is missing. Its front flap continues on to form the rear of the box; the sides and bottom are also one piece. The outer body measures 10 inches wide by 7-3/4 inches high. The flap is 13-1/4" X 9-1/4" (front only, maximum).
**New Hampshire Historical Society**

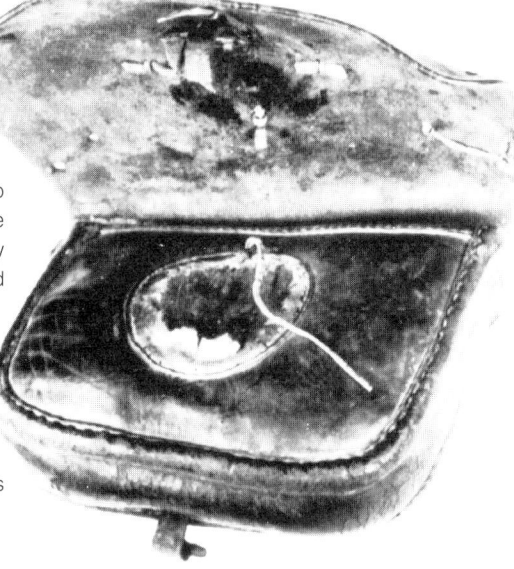

**ENGLISH CARTRIDGE POUCH**

The primary British cartridge container was a pouch worn on the right hip suspended by a 2-3/4" wide buff leather shoulder strap. Being purchased and issued by each regiment, its design varied in detail but was usually of black calfskin covering a wooden block with holes and space for 36 paper-wrapped cartridges. This unique variation from a William Rawle 1777 patent uses a block having 18 holes in both top and bottom. A side strap/cover lifts out the block to be reversed when the lower rounds are needed. The body measures 8-3/8" X 5-1/2" X 2-1/8" and includes a flat front accessories pocket plus a rear cross strip and bottom iron buckles to secure the shoulder strap.
**Former Edward Charol Collection**

*Chapter 3: Smoothbore Shoulder Arms*

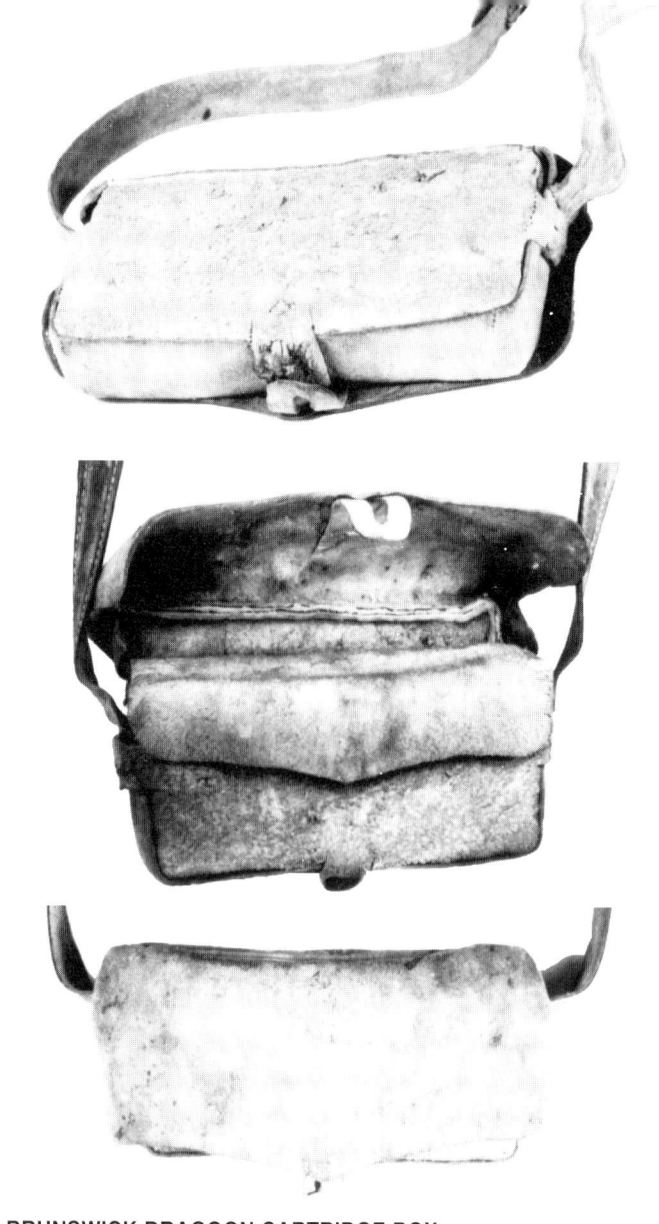

**FRENCH GRENADIER BOX (Circa 1770–1800)**
Note the gusseted accessory front pocket and 2-3/4" wide buff leather strap. The wooden block's two side cavities held packets of reserve cartridges; one of the six center holes often secured a vial of oil. Body: 8-3/4" X 4-1/2" X 2-3/4".
**George C. Neumann Collection, Valley Forge National Historical Park**

**BRUNSWICK DRAGOON CARTRIDGE BOX**
This Germanic pattern is all of buff leather with two flaps to protect a single row of ten cartridge holes in its wooden block. A buff shoulder strap (stitched along each edge) is held by loops to both ends of the body and continues along the bottom. Its front flap is joined to the back along an upper rear seam. The body is 9" X 4" X 1-3/4".
**J. Craig Nannos Collection**

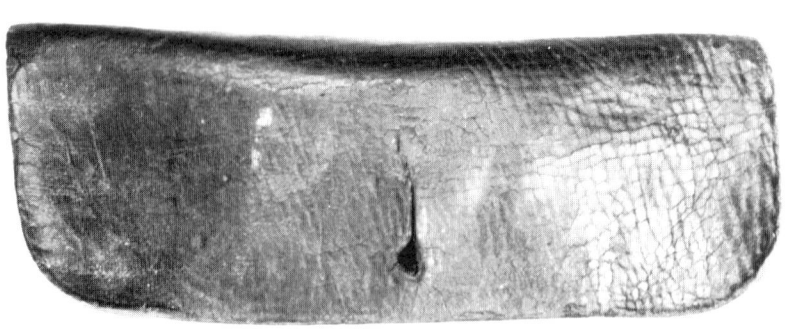

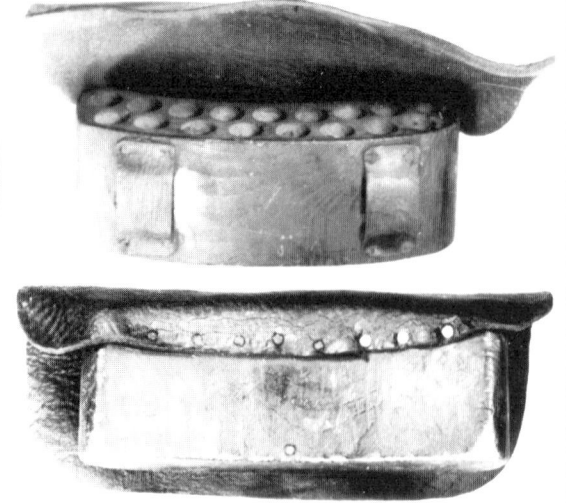

**AMERICAN WAIST BOX**
This American copy of the British belly box repeats the two front belt loops and nailed flap but limits the curved block to 17 holes (9, 8). It measures 8-3/4" X 2-1/8" X 2-7/8" high.
**George C. Neumann Collection, Valley Forge National Historical Park**

24  *Chapter 3: Smoothbore Shoulder Arms*

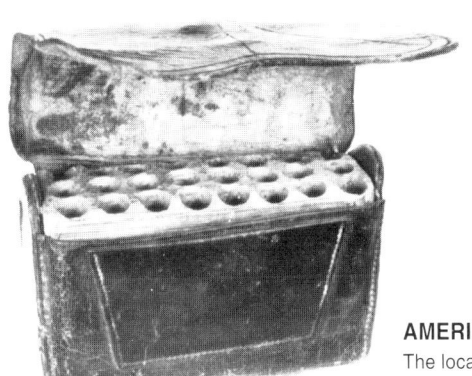

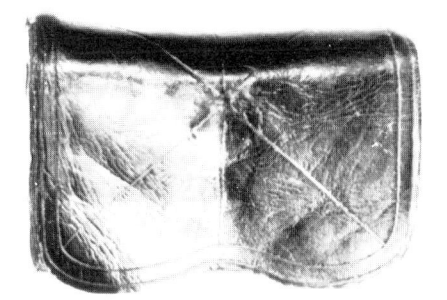

**AMERICAN SHOULDER BOX**
The locally made American boxes show individuality, for example this curving flap with incised ruled line decorations. Note also the 24-hole block (8, 8, 8) above a tray and the flat front pocket. Body: 7-3/4" X 2-1/4". **Author's Collection**

**AMERICAN SHOULDER BOX**
Many Colonists inserted the wooden block into a round-bottom leather pouch and added a flap, as seen here. The wood could be loose for removal in order to store accessories in the lower void or could be nailed permanently in position. This 17-hole (9, 8) block still holds two paper cartridges. A 1-3/4" wide buff leather shoulder belt (rectangular iron buckle) pierces the flap's rear seam and is nailed in place. Outer body: 9-3/4" X 4-3/4" X 2-1/2". **Author's Collection**

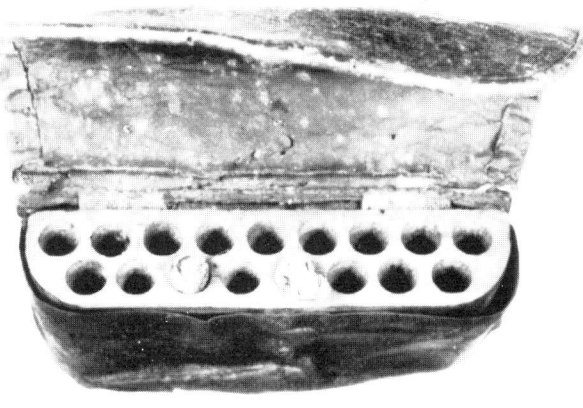

**AMERICAN SHOULDER BOX**
The ends of the original shoulder strap penetrated the rear flap seam of this leather-covered body. A replacement 1-1/2" wide buff strap was later nailed to the back. Its 17-hole (9, 8) block has been eased into the tight pocket-like covering. Body dimensions: 9-5/8" X 4-1/2" X 2-7/8".
**Author's Collection**

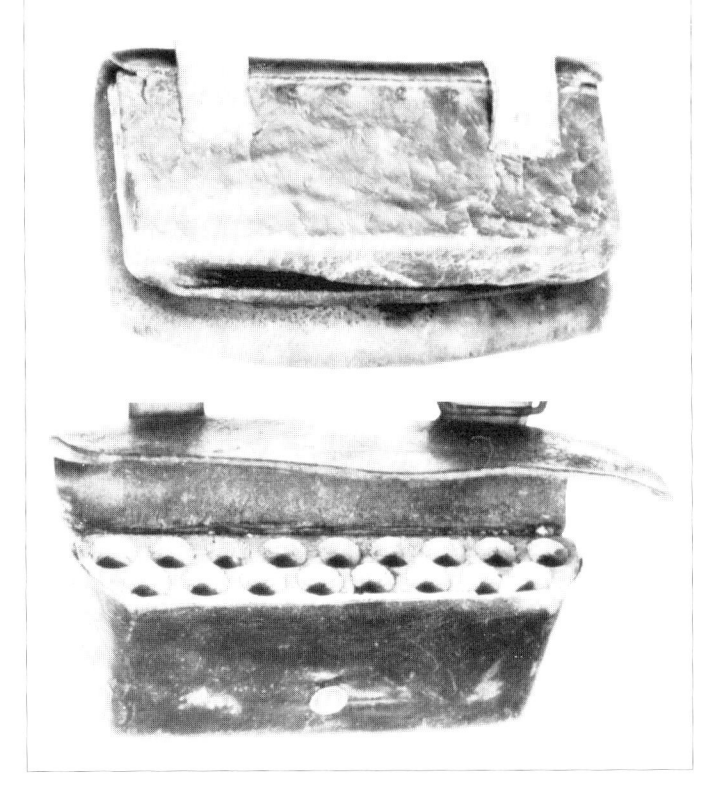

*Chapter 3: Smoothbore Shoulder Arms*

**AMERICAN MILITIA WAIST BOX**
The body's front, bottom and back are one piece. The flap's upper rear seam, in turn, secures the tops of two waist belt loops. Separate pieces cover both tapered ends of the 24-hole block (9, 8, 7). Body: 9-3/4" X 3-3/8" X 2-3/4".
**Author's Collection**

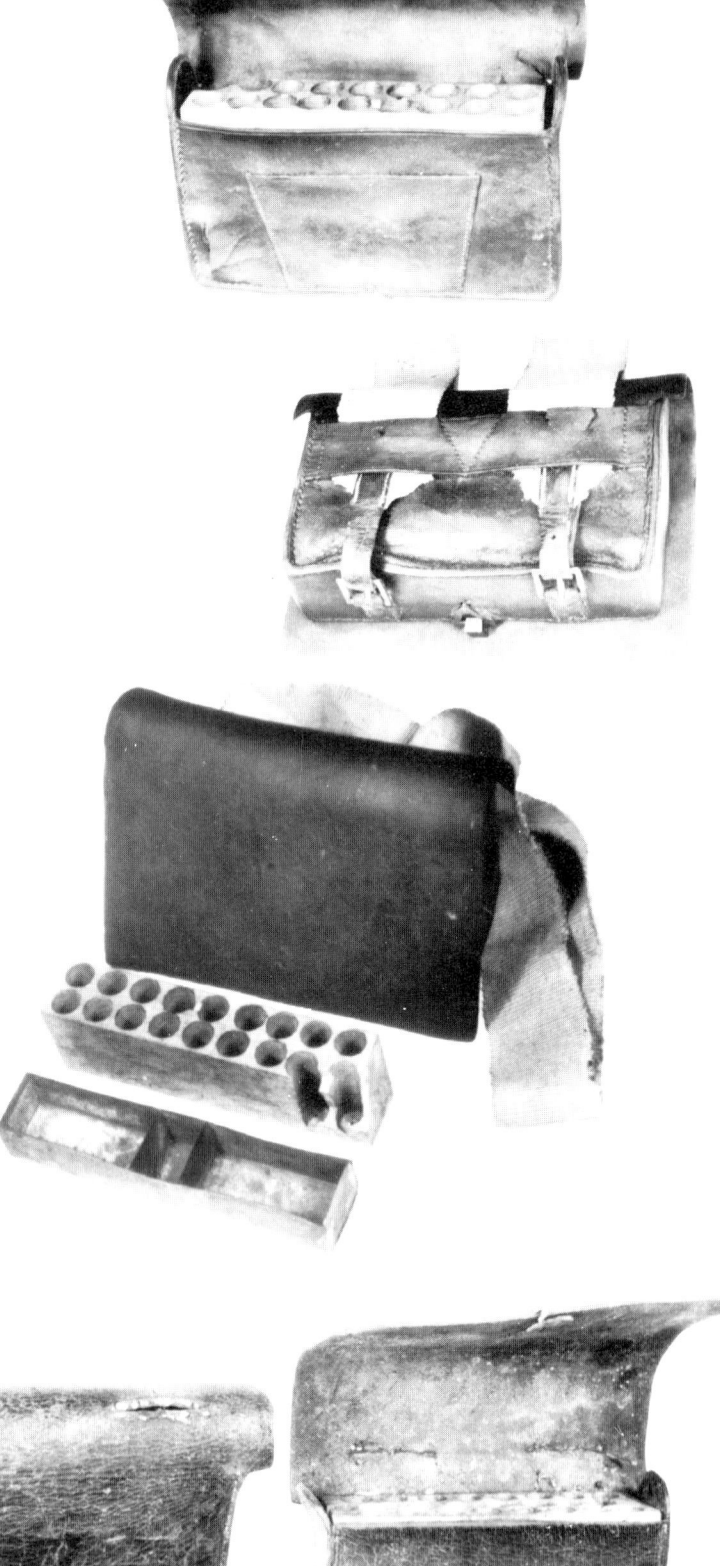

**AMERICAN SHOULDER BOX**
This was a popular American form: 18 holes (9, 9), a hand-woven 2-1/2" wide linen shoulder strap (secured by bottom iron buckles), a squared body and flap, plus a flat front pocket. A tinned iron tray for accessories rests under the removable pine block. The figure *8* is stitched into each of its leather end panels. Body size: 9-1/4" X 5-3/4" X 2-1/8".
**Author's Collection**

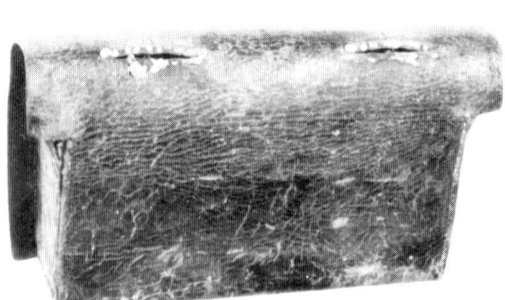

**AMERICAN SHOULDER BOX**
A wooden tray survives under this 24-hole block (8, 8, 8). The squared leather flap continues on to form the back, bottom and front of the body as a single piece; the ends are separate. Both shoulder strap ends pierced the upper flap as pictured. Outer body: 9-1/8" X 5-1/8" X 2-3/4".
**Author's Collection**

26  *Chapter 3: Smoothbore Shoulder Arms*

**AMERICAN SHOULDER BOX**
Note the deep flap on this pocket-shaped body (typical center end seam), the later end tabs (nailed), plus a flat inner flap to cover the 24 cartridge holes (9, 8, 7), as per the common American request for double flaps like the British to retard rain penetration. Outer body: 9-1/2" X 5-1/2" X 2-3/4".  **Author's Collection**

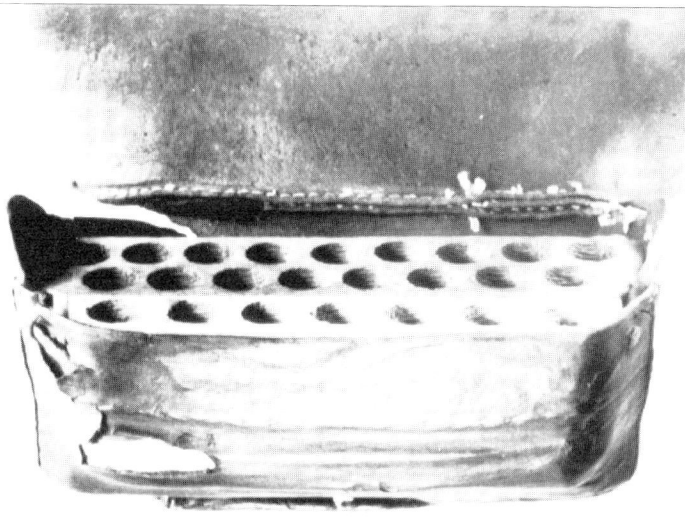

**AMERICAN SHOULDER BOX**
The flap of this pouch-type body has an embossed panel showing a light infantryman holding his musket in front of two tents plus a cannon and the inscription "THIS IS FAIR / LIBERTY" (tents and cannon were painted). A second block added seven holes to the original's 17. The leather strap was 1-5/8" wide. Body dimensions: 9-1/2" X 4-1/8" X 3-1/16" deep.
**Fort Ticonderoga Collection**

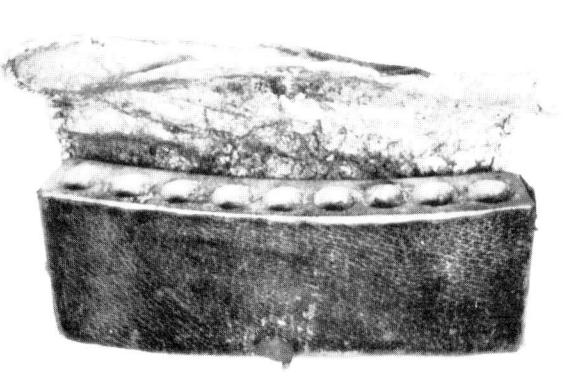

**FRENCH WAIST BOX**
A nine-hole (one row) pattern worn by France's *Troupes de la Marine* in Canada circa 1700. Note the rear belt loops and originally fur-covered flap. Similar nine-hole forms were used by horsemen and in some flank companies in the Revolutionary War. Its body measures 9-1/2" X 3-1/2" X 1-1/4".
**Author's Collection**

*Chapter 3: Smoothbore Shoulder Arms*   27

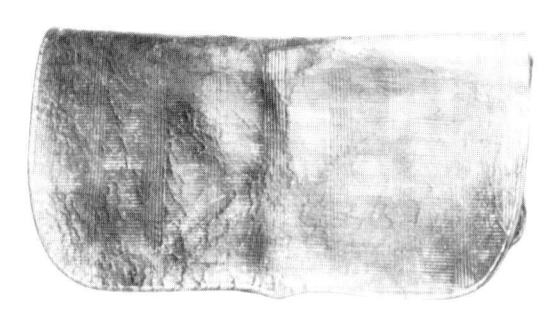

**AMERICAN SHOULDER BOX**
Right-angled crisscrossed incised lines decorate this front flap. The 26-hole (9, 8, 9) block is nailed into a leather cover that includes lined seams. Its original shoulder strap entered at the upper rear seam. Body: 9-1/2" X 4-1/4" X 2-7/8".
**Author's Collection**

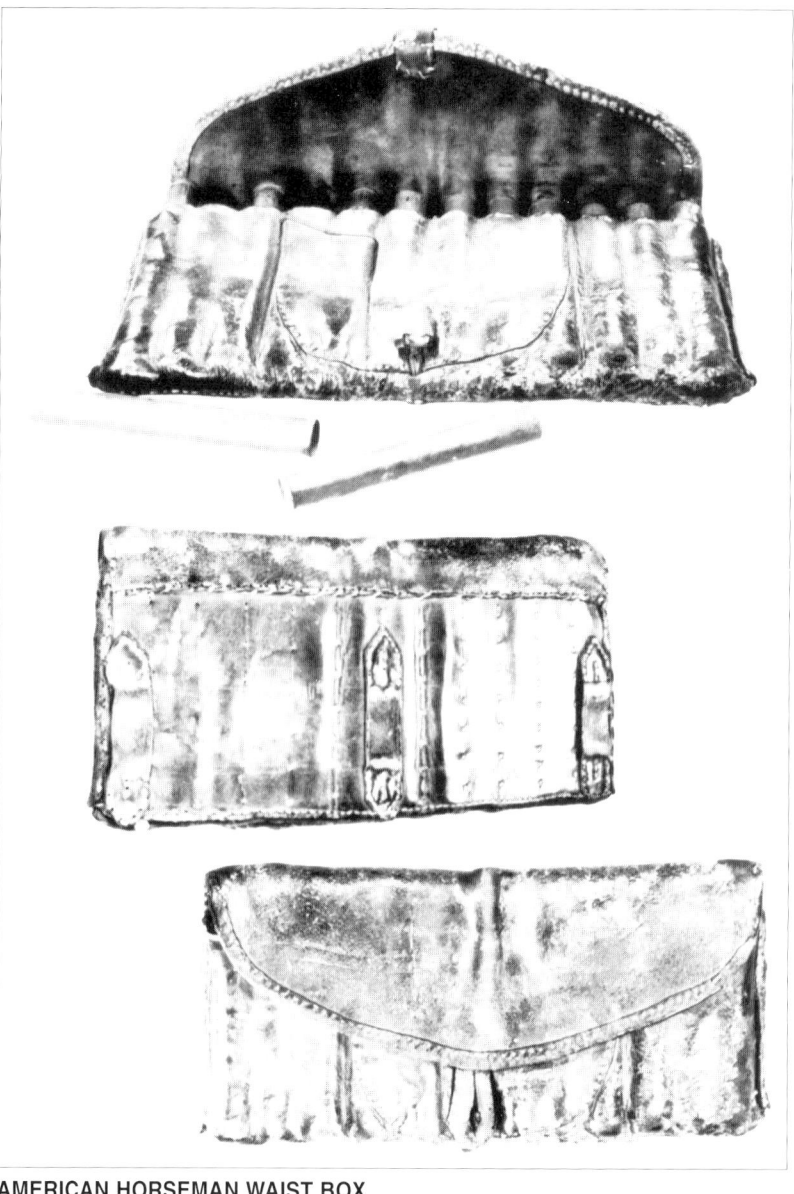

**AMERICAN HORSEMAN WAIST BOX**
Congress recommended a waist box for dragoons with 12 tin pipes in 1778. This variation has 12 removable pipes, each divided in the center to hold 24 cartridges. Body: 11-1/4" X 5-1/4" X 4-1/4" high.  George C. Neumann Collection, Valley Forge National Historical Park

**AMERICAN "NEW MODEL" BOX**
British infantry pouches captured at Saratoga were copied for the Continental Line beginning in 1777–1778. Called "New Model" or "New Construction" boxes, they had two forms: double (with a tin tray under the block), or single (lacking a tray). Note this large 29-hole block (10, 9, 10), front flat pocket, pointed flap (no inner one), and two-inch-wide buff leather strap (with a pick and brush). Body: 10" X 5-1/4" X 2-7/8".  J. Craig Nonnos Collection

28  *Chapter 3: Smoothbore Shoulder Arms*

### AMERICAN SHOULDER BOX
This large 30-hole maple block (11, 10, 9) rests in a deep leather pouch under a broad, rounded flap that is secured by an inner tab and squared leather button. Its dark leather two-inch-wide shoulder strap pierced the flap's rear seam (sewn in place). Body: 10-1/2" X 6" X 2-3/4".  **Author's Collection**

### AMERICAN CONVERTED POUCH
Many riflemen were changed to musketmen, and this was apparently a hunting bag altered to a cartridge box. The added 18-hole block (9, 9) is held by nails plus a heavy thread through both the leather and wood along its upper edge. An original bag-type drawstring remains. Note too the 1-3/4" wide strap painted with white lead and the pouch's earlier gathered bottom seam.
**George C. Neumann Collection, Valley Forge National Historical Park**

### AMERICAN TINNED BOX
To help overcome a shortage in the field, the Board of War recommended a tinned-iron canister as a substitute for leather boxes in 1778. It carried 36 cartridges in layers of four across and included a hinged lid plus three side shoulder strap attachments. Dimensions: 6-1/2" X 3-1/4" X 2-7/8".
**Author's Collection**

*Chapter 3: Smoothbore Shoulder Arms*    29

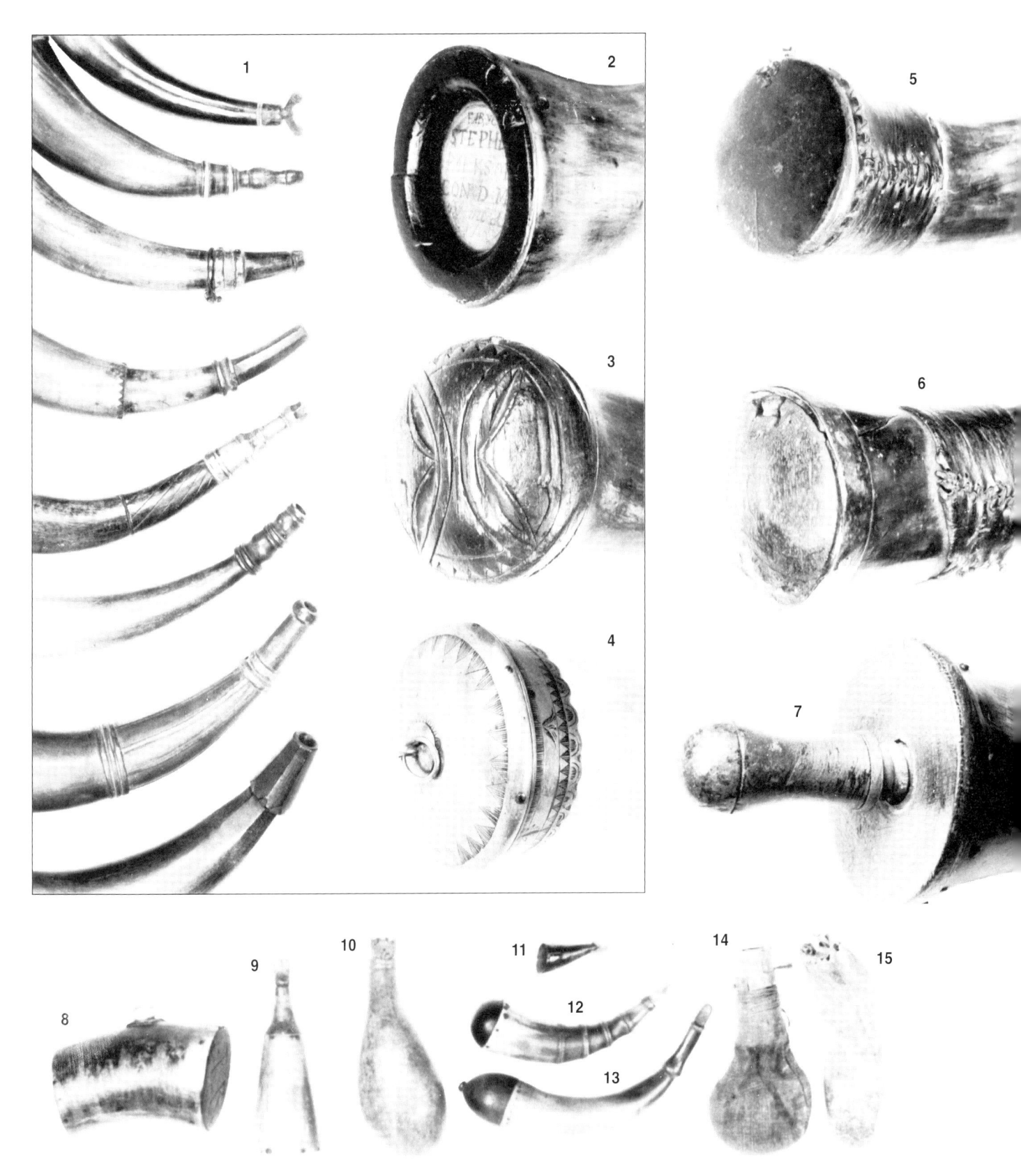

**POWDER HORN FORMS**
Cattle horns served as convenient containers as they were readily available, curved to fit the body, waterproof, easy to work and would not strike a spark against steel. **(1)** Being prepared at home and by numerous professional horn workers, they displayed a variety of spout designs. **(2)** A Massachusetts open end plug with a glass window and "FAB: YE BY STEPHEN PARKS: OF CONCD: MADE BY Dec 1745." **(3)** A raised hand-carved wooden plug. **(4)** Period engraving on a brass end cap. **(5,6)** Leather and brass band repairs to retard a horn split. **(7)** A rear wooden handle that unscrewed to refill (see 17). **(8)** A common truncated form. **(9)** A pocket priming powder horn. **(10)** A similar gourd primer. **(11)** A horn tip cut as a powder charge measure. **(12, 13)** Small priming horns. **(14)** A heavy linen (tow) shot bag with wooden spout. **(15)** A shot bag of deerskin.
**Author's Collection**

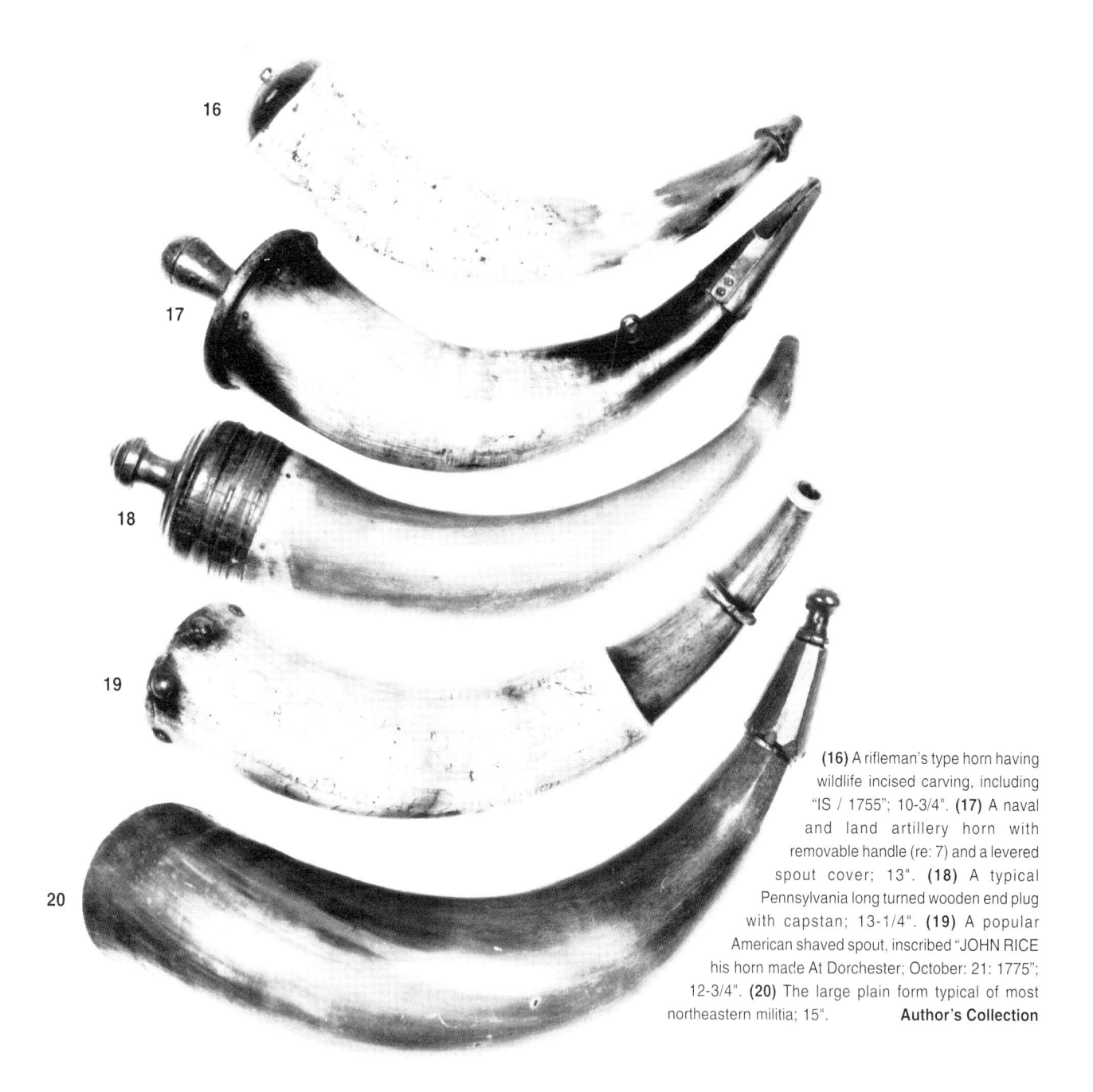

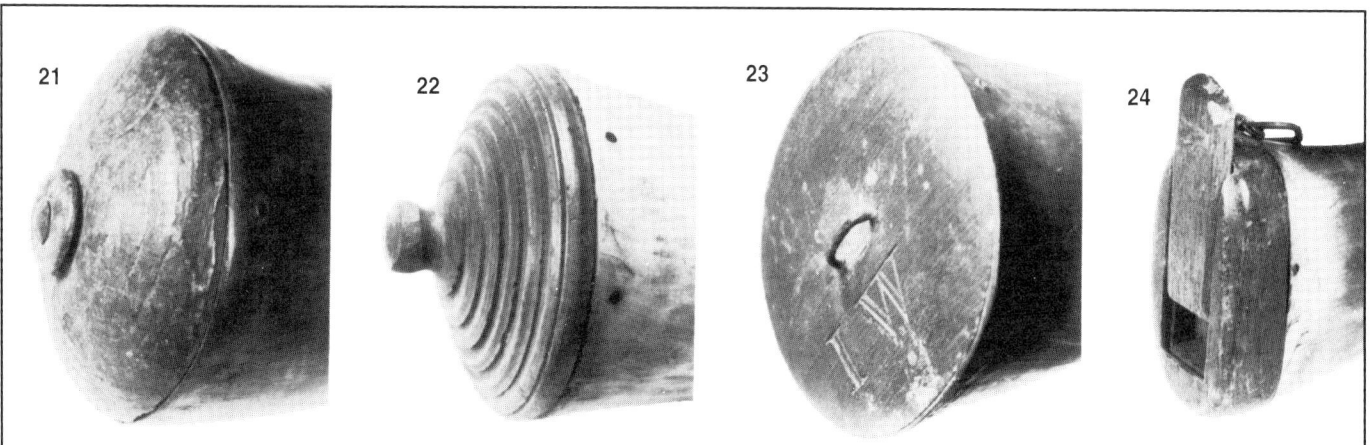

(16) A rifleman's type horn having wildlife incised carving, including "IS / 1755"; 10-3/4". (17) A naval and land artillery horn with removable handle (re: 7) and a levered spout cover; 13". (18) A typical Pennsylvania long turned wooden end plug with capstan; 13-1/4". (19) A popular American shaved spout, inscribed "JOHN RICE his horn made At Dorchester; October: 21: 1775"; 12-3/4". (20) The large plain form typical of most northeastern militia; 15". **Author's Collection**

(21) A simple leather washer for the shoulder cord attachment. (22) A concentric ringed plug. (23) Common flat end with iron staple; carried by John Williams (shown are his initials, "IW"; the letter *I* was also used for *J*) of Easton, Massachusetts, at Lexington–Concord alarm in 1775. (24) A sliding rear base cover for accessories.
**Author's Collection**

*Chapter 3: Smoothbore Shoulder Arms*

## CANTEENS

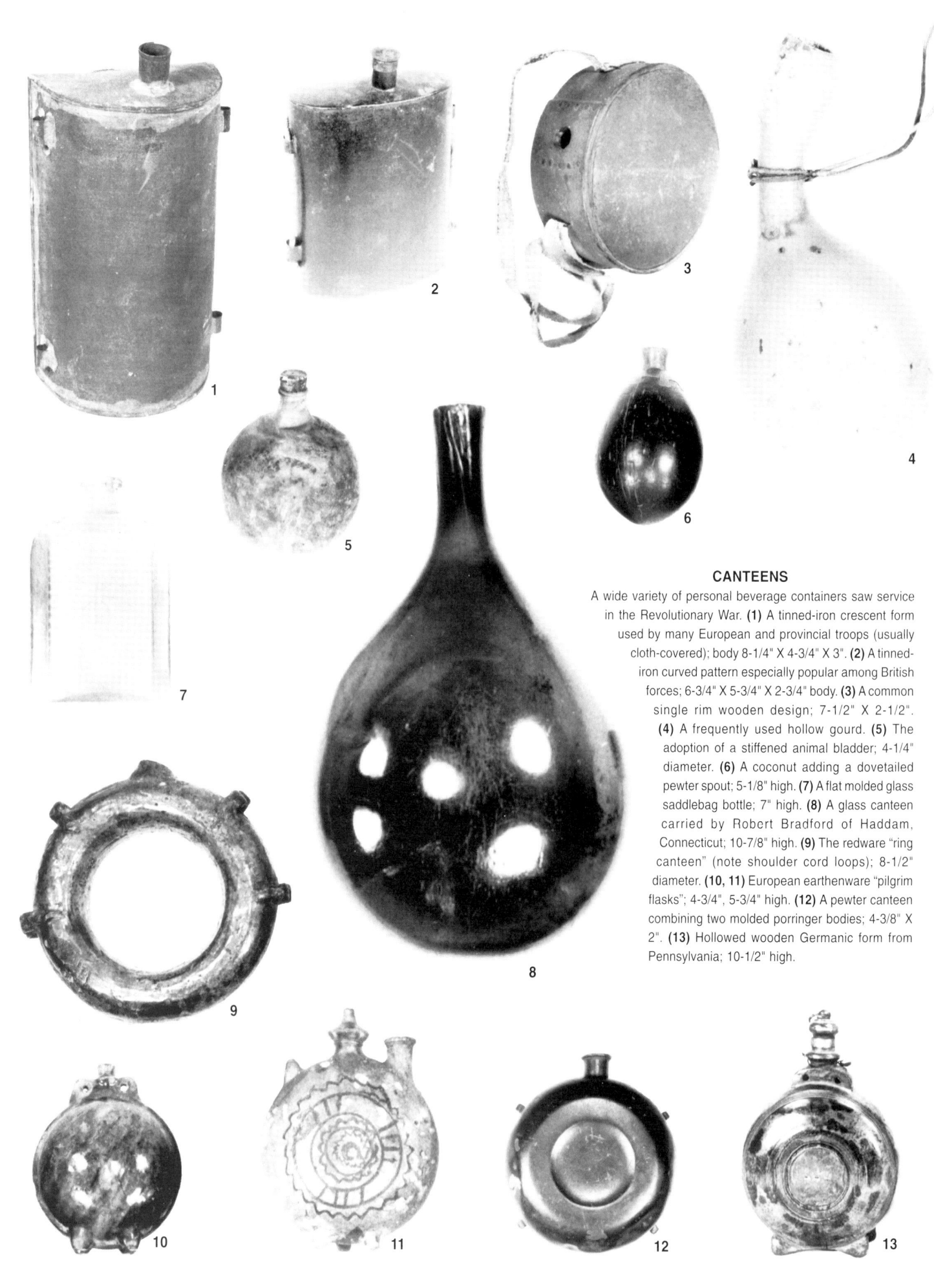

A wide variety of personal beverage containers saw service in the Revolutionary War. **(1)** A tinned-iron crescent form used by many European and provincial troops (usually cloth-covered); body 8-1/4" X 4-3/4" X 3". **(2)** A tinned-iron curved pattern especially popular among British forces; 6-3/4" X 5-3/4" X 2-3/4" body. **(3)** A common single rim wooden design; 7-1/2" X 2-1/2". **(4)** A frequently used hollow gourd. **(5)** The adoption of a stiffened animal bladder; 4-1/4" diameter. **(6)** A coconut adding a dovetailed pewter spout; 5-1/8" high. **(7)** A flat molded glass saddlebag bottle; 7" high. **(8)** A glass canteen carried by Robert Bradford of Haddam, Connecticut; 10-7/8" high. **(9)** The redware "ring canteen" (note shoulder cord loops); 8-1/2" diameter. **(10, 11)** European earthenware "pilgrim flasks"; 4-3/4", 5-3/4" high. **(12)** A pewter canteen combining two molded porringer bodies; 4-3/8" X 2". **(13)** Hollowed wooden Germanic form from Pennsylvania; 10-1/2" high.

*Chapter 3: Smoothbore Shoulder Arms*

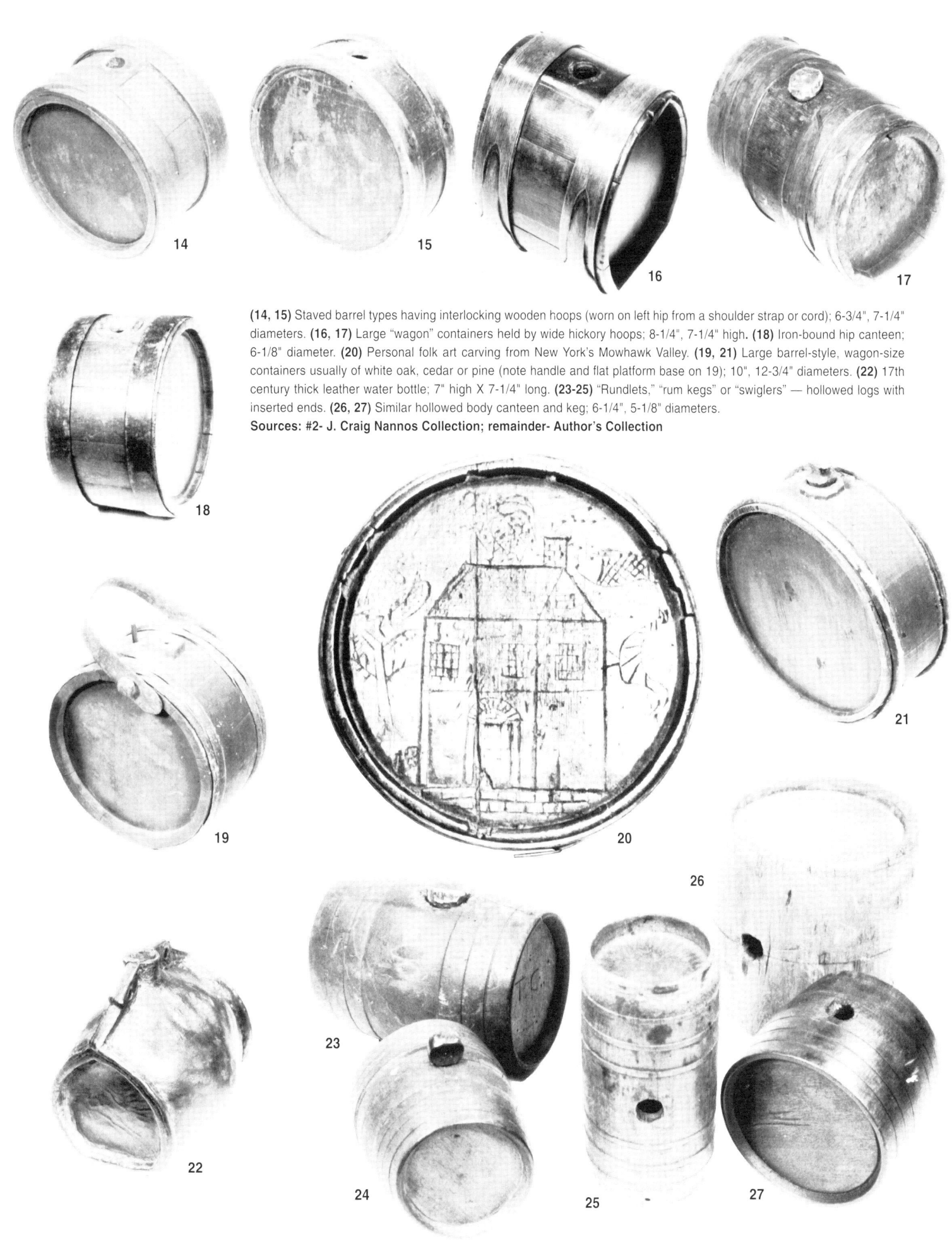

**(14, 15)** Staved barrel types having interlocking wooden hoops (worn on left hip from a shoulder strap or cord); 6-3/4", 7-1/4" diameters. **(16, 17)** Large "wagon" containers held by wide hickory hoops; 8-1/4", 7-1/4" high. **(18)** Iron-bound hip canteen; 6-1/8" diameter. **(20)** Personal folk art carving from New York's Mowhawk Valley. **(19, 21)** Large barrel-style, wagon-size containers usually of white oak, cedar or pine (note handle and flat platform base on 19); 10", 12-3/4" diameters. **(22)** 17th century thick leather water bottle; 7" high X 7-1/4" long. **(23-25)** "Rundlets," "rum kegs" or "swiglers" — hollowed logs with inserted ends. **(26, 27)** Similar hollowed body canteen and keg; 6-1/4", 5-1/8" diameters.
**Sources:** #2- J. Craig Nannos Collection; remainder- Author's Collection

Chapter 3: Smoothbore Shoulder Arms   33

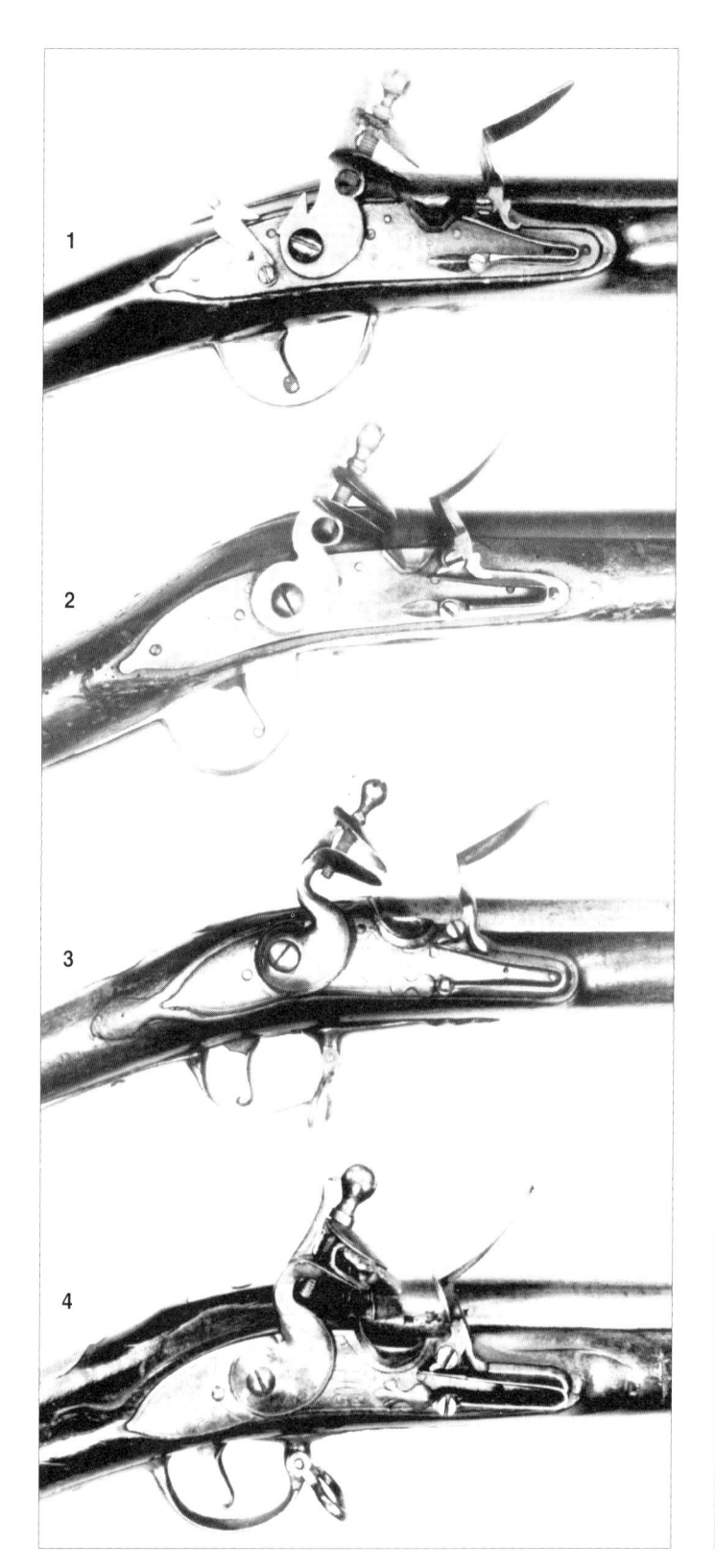

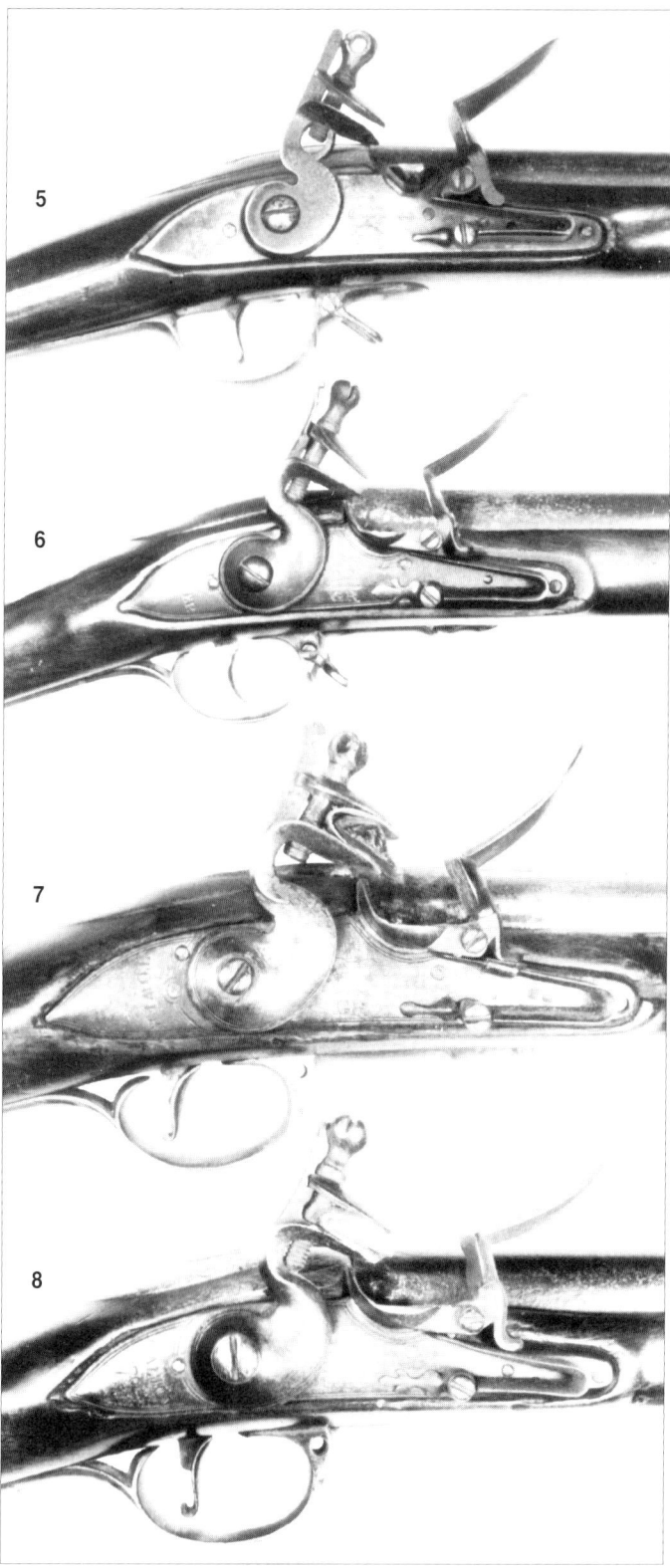

## FLINT GUNLOCK EVOLUTION

**ENGLISH LOCKS: (1)** Circa 1690–1710; doglock; flat plate and ringed cock; three side screws; see 1.MM, 3.MM. **(2)** Circa 1700–1713; dog latch eliminated; flat lock plus cock remain; banana-shaped plate, three side screws; see 2.MM. **(3)** Circa 1710–1720; evolving Dutch-type rounded banana lock framed in raised stock carving; no supporting bridle from pan to frizzen screw; early curled trigger; signed by maker, "W PREDDEN"; see 5.MM. **(4)** First official Long Land Brown Bess lock (Patterns 1730 and 1742); rounded banana plate; flat back post on convex cock; no exterior bridle until 1740; marked "TOWER" (the royal arsenal in the Tower of London); see 8.MM. **(5)** Circa 1750–1780; flat sea service lock and ringed cock; copied from earlier Queen Anne arms (refer to 1 and 2 above); plain cock upper post; no outside bridle; frizzen often squared; little stock carving; see 27.MM, 28.MM. **(6)** Circa 1750–1777; Long Land Pattern 1756 and early Short Land 1768–1777; rounded two-screw lock with straight bottom edge; exterior bridle included; see 10.MM–14.MM. **(7)** Circa 1777–1795; simplified commercial wartime variation ("Type II"); straight two-screw rounded plate, two screw ends now visible behind cock, a front notch in the cock's new squared upper post, a simple lobe frizzen spring finial, double border lines dropped from both the top jaw and frizzen's forward face; see 15.MM. **(8)** Circa 1756–1780; reduced size carbine lock that copies the Brown Bess (see 6) see 118.MM–123.MM.

*34      Chapter 3: Smoothbore Shoulder Arms*

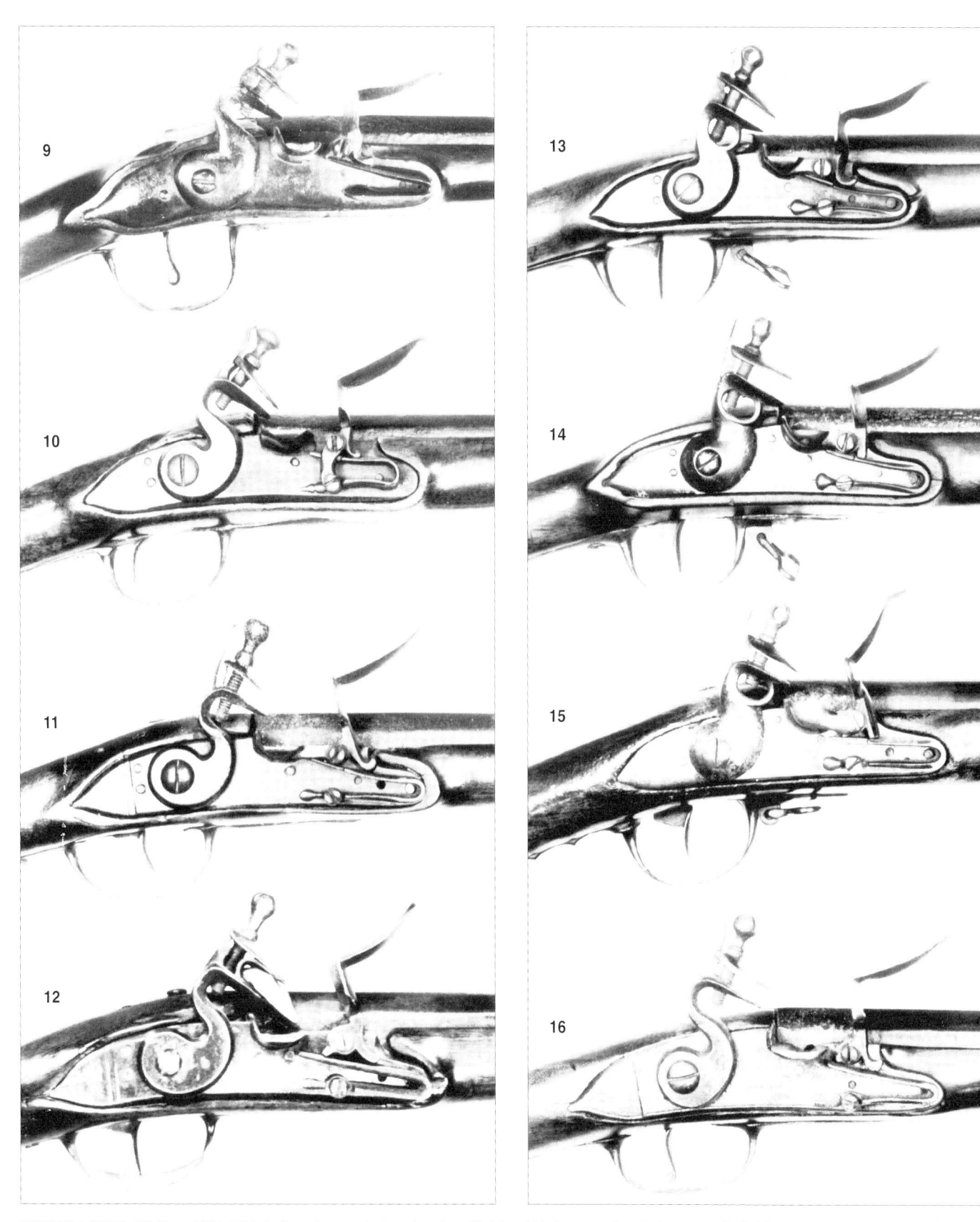

**FRENCH LOCKS: (9)** Circa 1697–1716; bulbous banana lock and cock on Ministry of Marine arms from Tulle; no exterior bridle; long rear tip; see 33.MM. **(10)** Model 1717; first standard French military pattern; flat plate with channeled tail and swansneck cock; distinctive vertical bridle; short frizzen spring; minimal raised carving; see 38.MM. **(11)** Model 1728; the two-screw flat plate and cock continue; bridle now horizontal; see 39.MM. **(12)** Model 1746; basic Model 1728 form with the bridle omitted; see 40.MM. **(13)** Model 1763 series; a flat beveled lock with ringed cock (plate shortened from 6-3/4" to 6-1/4" in Model 1766); faceted pan; outside bridle in place since Model 1754; see 42.MM–44.MM. **(14)** Circa 1770–1777; the plate and ringed cock are now convex; rounded iron pan with bridle; frizzen's front stud has become blunted; see 45.MM, 46.MM. **(15)** Model 1777; its rounded surfaces continue but with a sloping brass pan/bridle (no rear fence); top of frizzen is angled; see 47.MM. **(16)** Circa 1720–1740; an early flat pattern (like 11 above) with known naval use; see 55.MM.

*Chapter 3: Smoothbore Shoulder Arms*    **35**

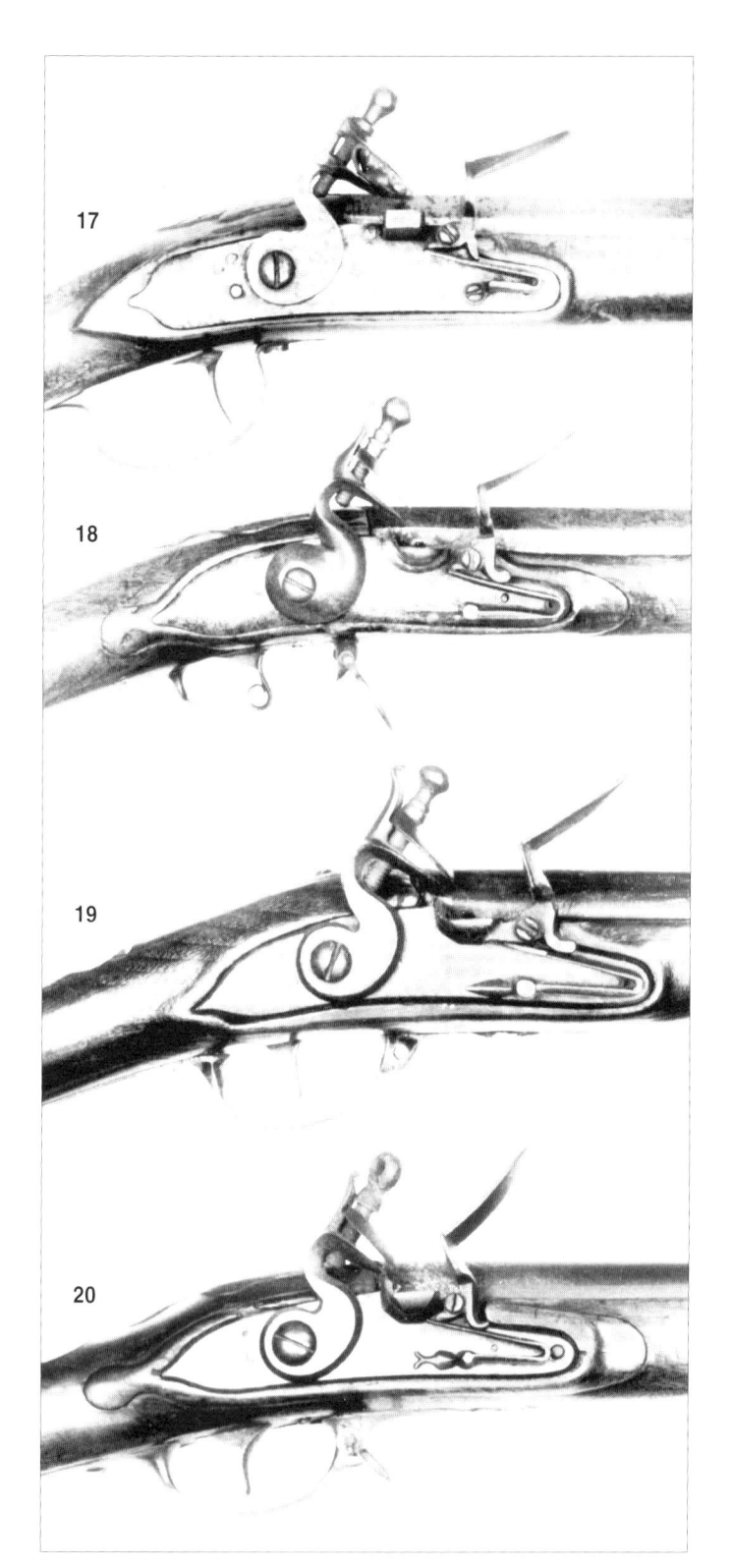

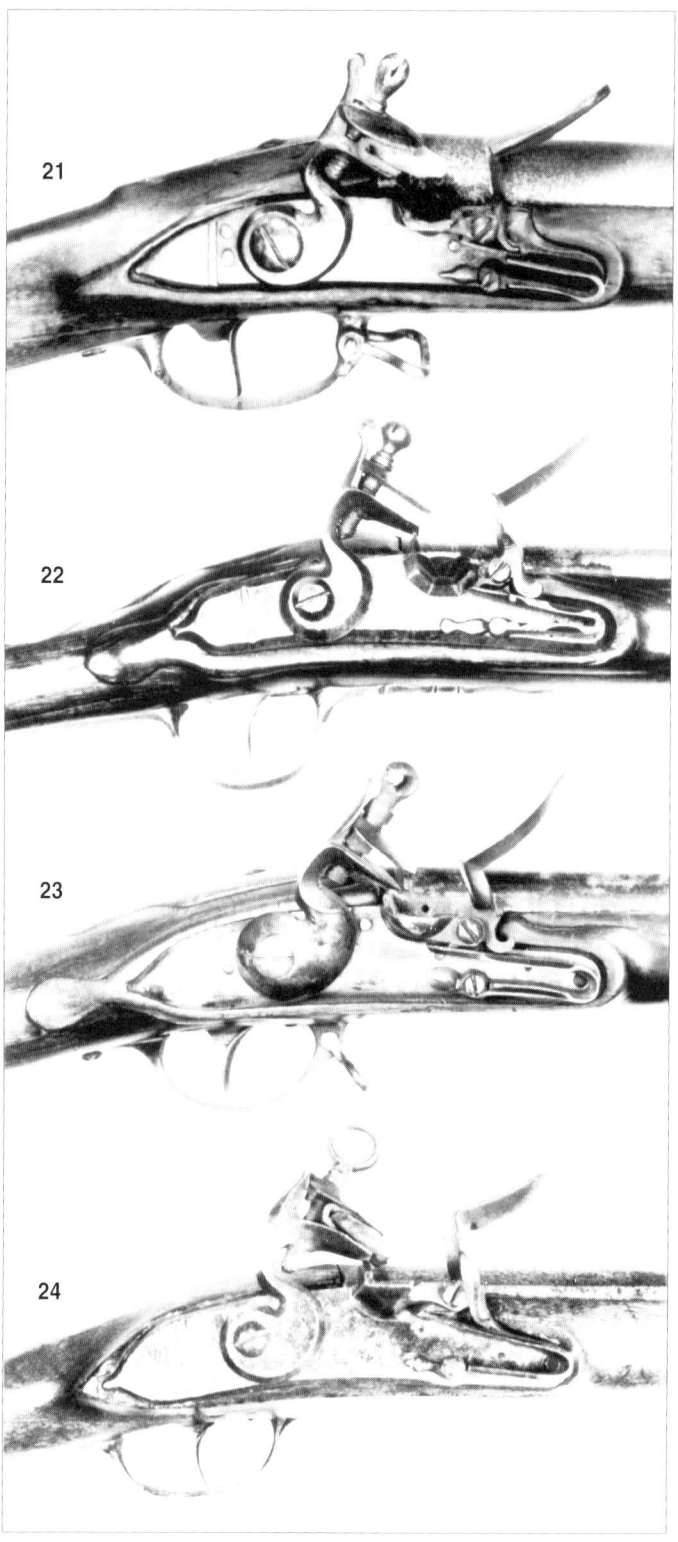

## FLINT GUNLOCKS (Continued)

**DUTCH-GERMANIC: (17)** Circa 1690; an early Dutch flat lock with its characteristic abrupt shouldered tail and plain swansneck cock; the squared pan still lacks the later outside bridle; see 57.MM. **(18)** Circa 1710–1740; the bulbous banana pattern of early century Dutch-German arms; note the cock's humpback upper post, the rounded pan without a bridle, curled trigger and raised stock carving; see 58.MM, 64.MM. **(19)** Circa 1720–1780; the popular flat/beveled form favored throughout central Europe for military arms and commercial exports in this period (early banana example); its faceted pan is found with or without a bridle; an inside screw typically holds its frizzen spring; see 59.MM–61.MM. **(20)** Circa 1777–1798; a later Dutch version of 19 (above) combining a shorter straight plate and traditional stock carving; see 62.MM. **(21)** Circa 1770–1780; one of the German interpretations of the flat/beveled form resembling the pre-Model 1763 French locks with a channeled tail, faceted pan and exterior bridle; the wood carving is also diminished. **(22)** Prussian Model 1740; its distinctive features include an undulating tail surface, faceted pan (no bridle), squared hammer and frizzen top, plus bulbous stock borders; marked "POTZDAM MAGAZ," for the Potsdam–Spandau manufactories; see 65.MM. **(23)** Circa 1771–1795; note the Dutch return to a rounded lock again in the 1770s, plus the straighter plate, rounded pan with bridle and renewed raised border carving; see 63.MM. **(24)** Spanish Models 1753 and 1757; similar to contemporary French styling, it also adds a distinctive humpback cock upper post and large ring jaw screw; see 51.MM.

*Chapter 3: Smoothbore Shoulder Arms*

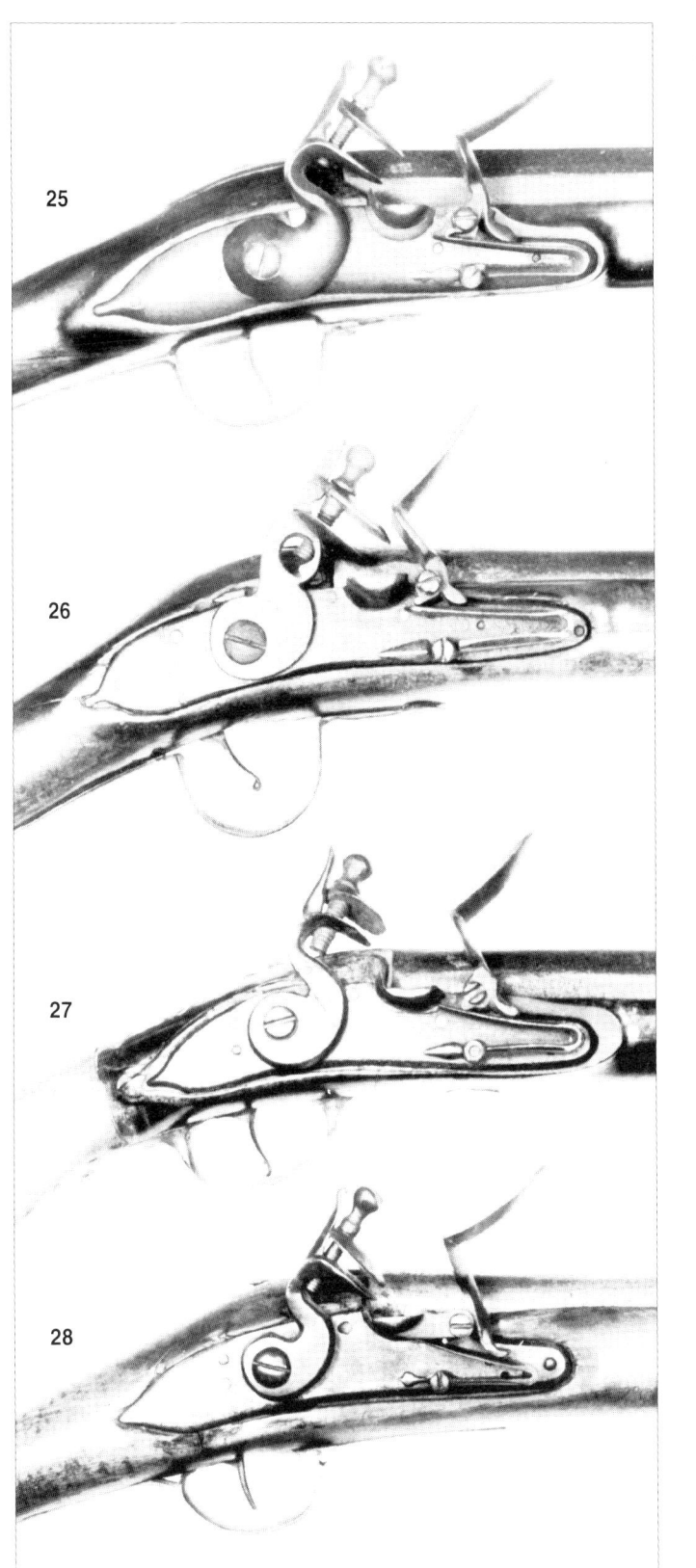

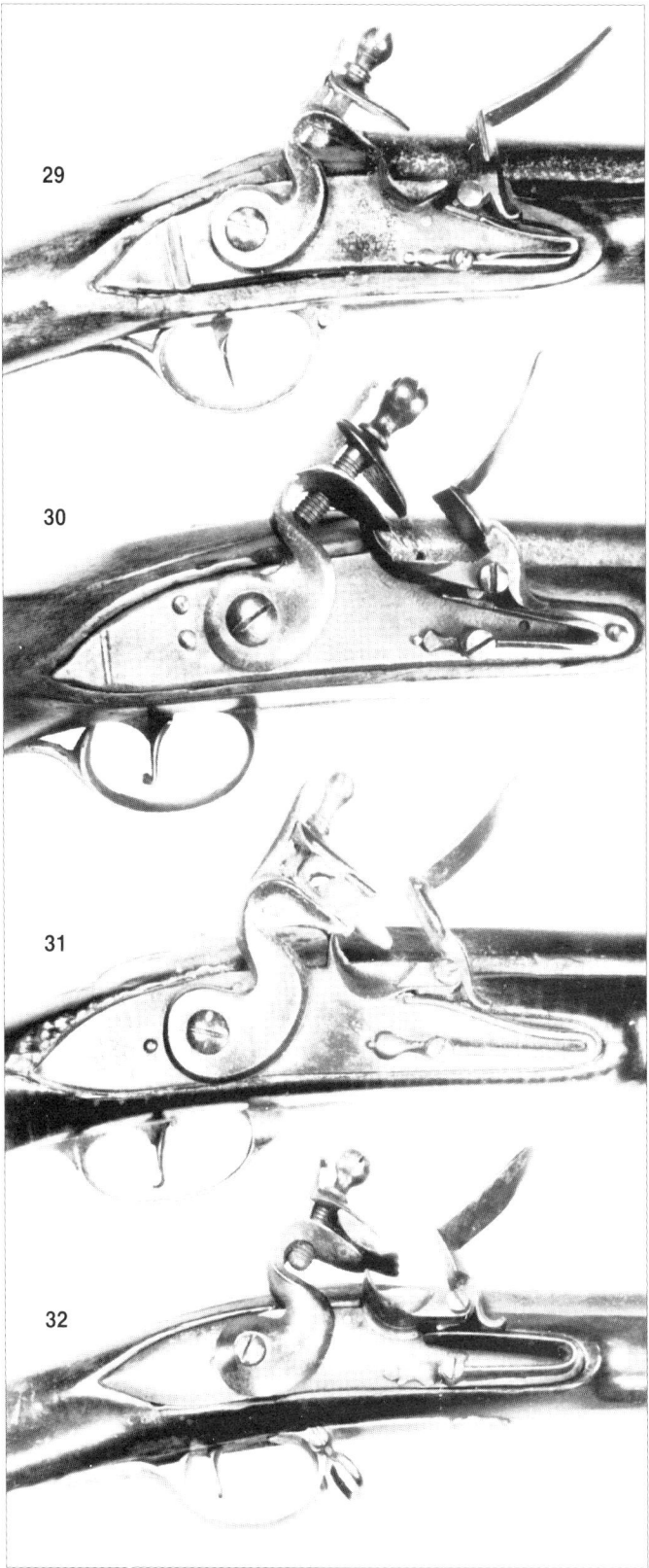

**AMERICAN LOCKS: (25)** Circa 1710–1730; an early long, rounded banana lock with three side screws and a swansneck cock; the round pan still lacks a bridle; a typical English pattern equally popular in the American Colonies; see 109.MM. **(26)** Circa 1720–1750; a provincial copy of the British Queen Anne flat plate and ringed cock; see 101.MM. **(27)** Circa 1720–1780; an American adaptation of the widespread European flat banana form (see 19); observe the de-emphasized Colonial stock carving; see 102.MM. **(28)** Circa 1770–1800; an additional provincial-interpreted flat/beveled lock (note its awkward plate dimensions); see 86.MM. **(29)** Circa 1775–1777; a flat lock that adds a rear tail, channel, faceted pan and lobed frizzen spring finial in French fashion; by the Connecticut maker Stephen Chandler; see 81.MM. **(30)** Circa 1775–1780; American lock from the Rappahannock Forge (Virginia) marked "RAPA FORGE" on the tail; see 38.PP. **(31)** Circa 1776; the flat pattern produced for Virginia's Fredericksburg arsenal; inscribed "FRED / 1776" at the rear; see 83.MM. **(32)** Circa 1750–1780; American copy of a mid-century British Brown Bess lock (see 6 above); note its rear point raised to the centerline level.

*Chapter 3: Smoothbore Shoulder Arms* 37

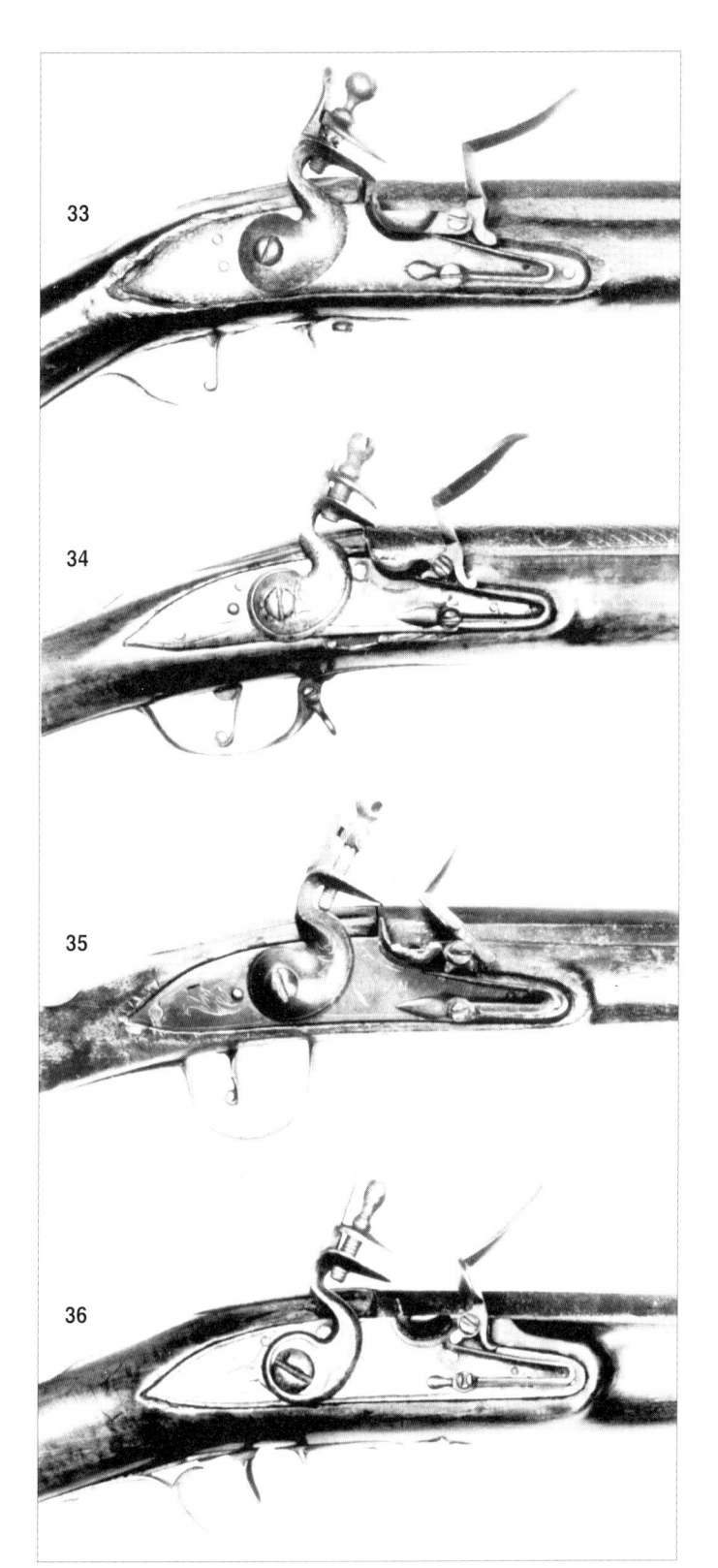

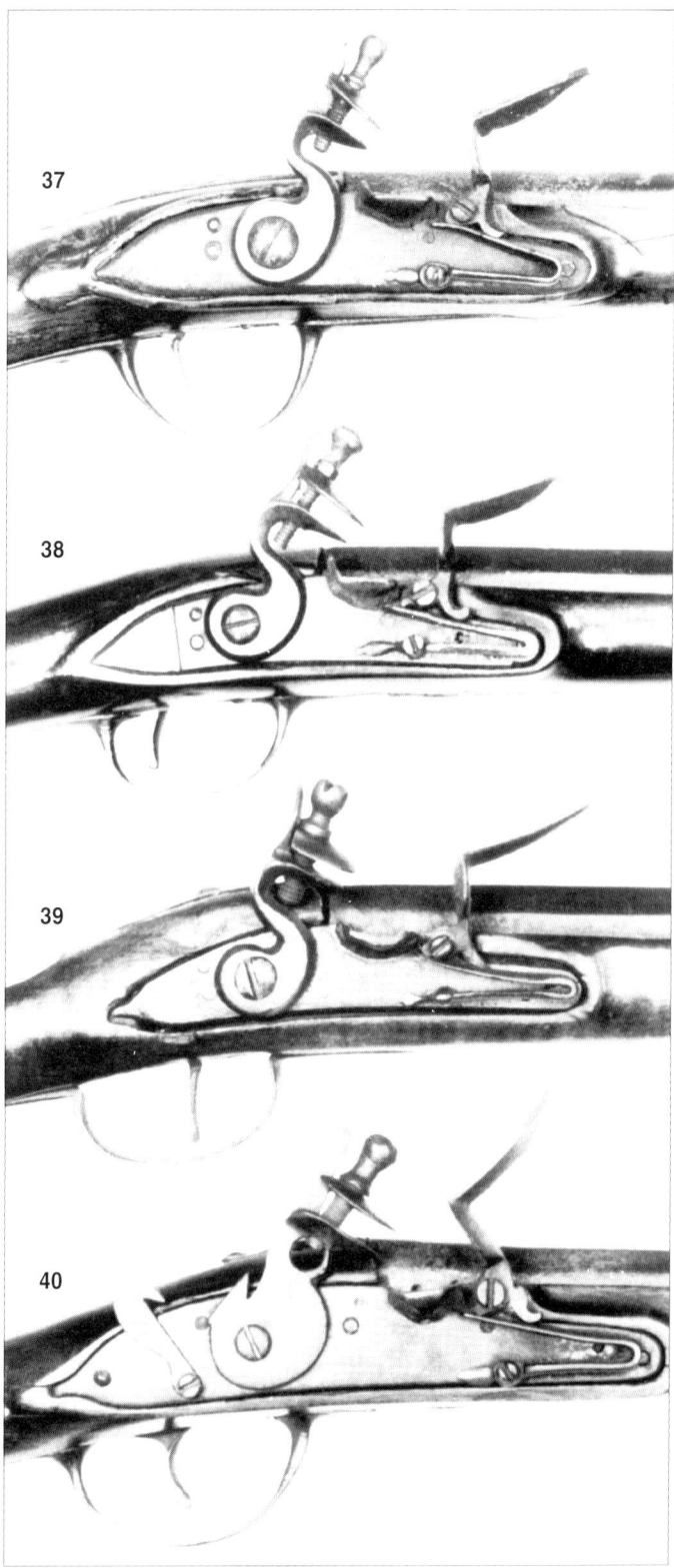

## FLINT GUNLOCKS (Continued)

**TRADE LOCKS**: **(33)** Circa 1700–1720; a long three-screw rounded lock found in early century British trade guns—similar to the evolving Brown Bess patterns (see 3); see 149.MM. **(34)** Circa 1770–1780; American version of a light hunting gun lock; note its disproportionate dimensions; signed "PAGE" on the plate; see 94.MM. **(35)** Circa 1730–1750; a common English trade form; observe the plain cock post, foliage engraving and the frizzen spring's spearpoint finial; signed by the London maker "WILSON"; see 152.MM. **(36)** Circa 1730–1760; another popular British trade lock that had a flat plate and single neck cock, plus an abrupt right angle at the upper base of the forward nose; a common military panoply is engraved on the tail; see 154.MM. **(37)** Circa 1730–1750; a typical French flat/beveled lock from Tulle found on Marine military and hunting guns for North America; notice the squared cock post (forward notch), faceted pan (no bridle) and raised carving; see 156.MM. **(38)** Circa 1740–1760; a French Model 1728-style (see 11) was adopted for this later hunting arm; see 159.MM. **(39)** Circa 1720–1740; a French trade lock remounted in a later American light fowler; note the flat plate, swansneck cock, faceted pan (no bridle) and inexpensive surface foliate designs; see 160.MM. **(40)** Circa 1715–1740; a continental European copy of England's Queen Anne-period doglock to compete in the North American fur trade; see 151.MM.

*38   Chapter 3: Smoothbore Shoulder Arms*

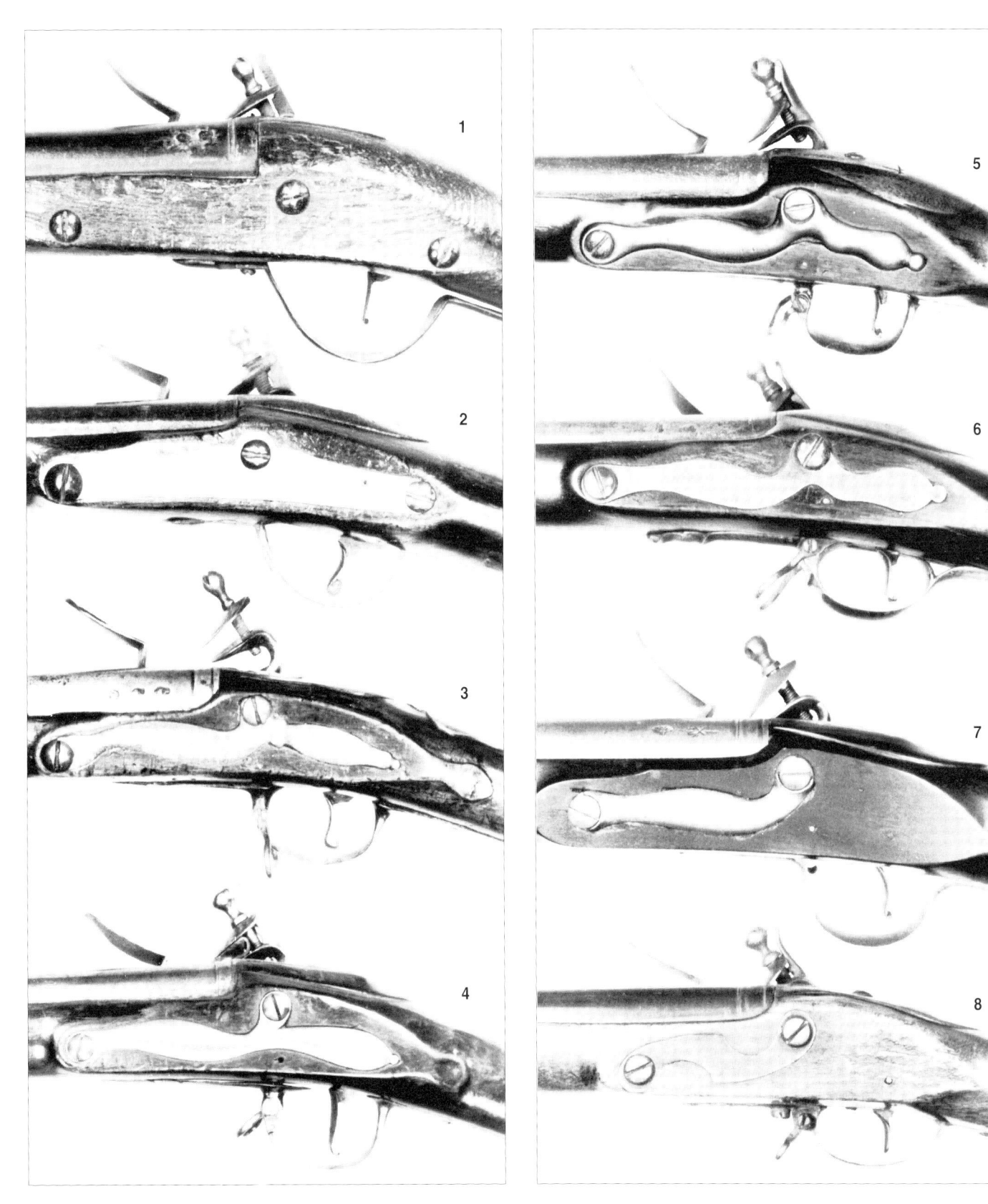

## SIDE PLATE EVOLUTION

**ENGLISH: (1)** Circa 1670–1710; the large early three-screw locks often omitted a formal side plate. **(2)** Circa 1690–1710; many Tower-issued muskets of this period had this flat semi-triangular three-screw side plate. **(3)** Circa 1710–1720; a modified two-screw form with a tail beginning to develop; see 5.MM. **(4)** Circa 1720–1728; further evolution toward the Brown Bess pattern is evident (iron); see 6.MM. **(5)** Circa 1730–1769; the two-screw rounded form for the famous Long Land Pattern Brown Besses; see 8.MM–11.MM. **(6)** Circa 1756–1793; Britain's flattened side plate initiated with the Marine or Militia 1756 pattern and continued through the Short Land series, plus naval muskets until circa 1793; see 12.MM–17.MM and 27.MM–30.MM. **(7)** *Not* considered a Revolutionary War weapon; circa 1775–1809; the privately produced convex India Pattern finally accepted for government use circa 1793; see 19.MM. **(8)** Circa 1755–1790; a semi-S, flat design used on English carbines and fusils plus Low Country light muskets; see 127.MM.

Chapter 3: Smoothbore Shoulder Arms    39

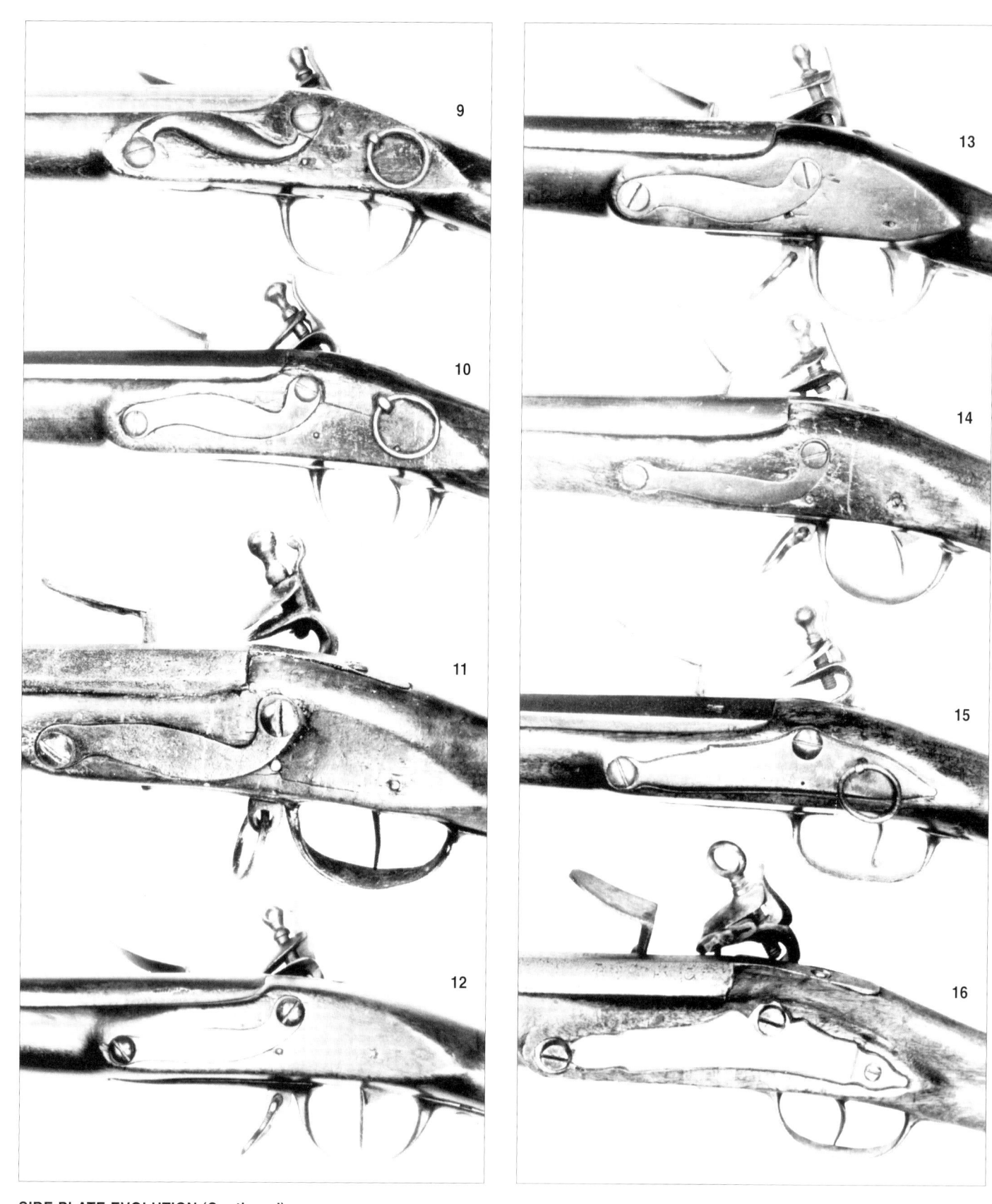

**SIDE PLATE EVOLUTION (Continued)**

**FRENCH: (9)** Circa 1697–1715; early rounded French S-form, plus a side shoulder strap ring indicating a grenadier musket. **(10)** Models 1717 and 1728; the traditional flat S-shape is established; see 38.MM, 39.MM. **(11)** Model 1754; France's basic S-plate continues, but the round, side shoulder strap ring is now positioned underneath the stock; see 41.MM. **(12)** Model 1766; the Model 1763 musket series S-contour is narrower and the sling swivels have become flattened; see 42.MM–44.MM. **(13)** Model 1774; the side plate continues to straighten; see 46.MM. **(14)** Model 1777; this S-plate is thinner and almost straight along the lower edge; see 47.MM. **(15)** Circa 1720–1740; a French commercial and naval triangular shape, including a penetrating military shoulder sling swivel; see 55.MM. **(16)** Spanish Models 1753 (iron) and 1757 (brass); note the rear wood screw as well as its similarity to both the French pattern (see 15) and the German (see 24); see 51.MM.

*40    Chapter 3: Smoothbore Shoulder Arms*

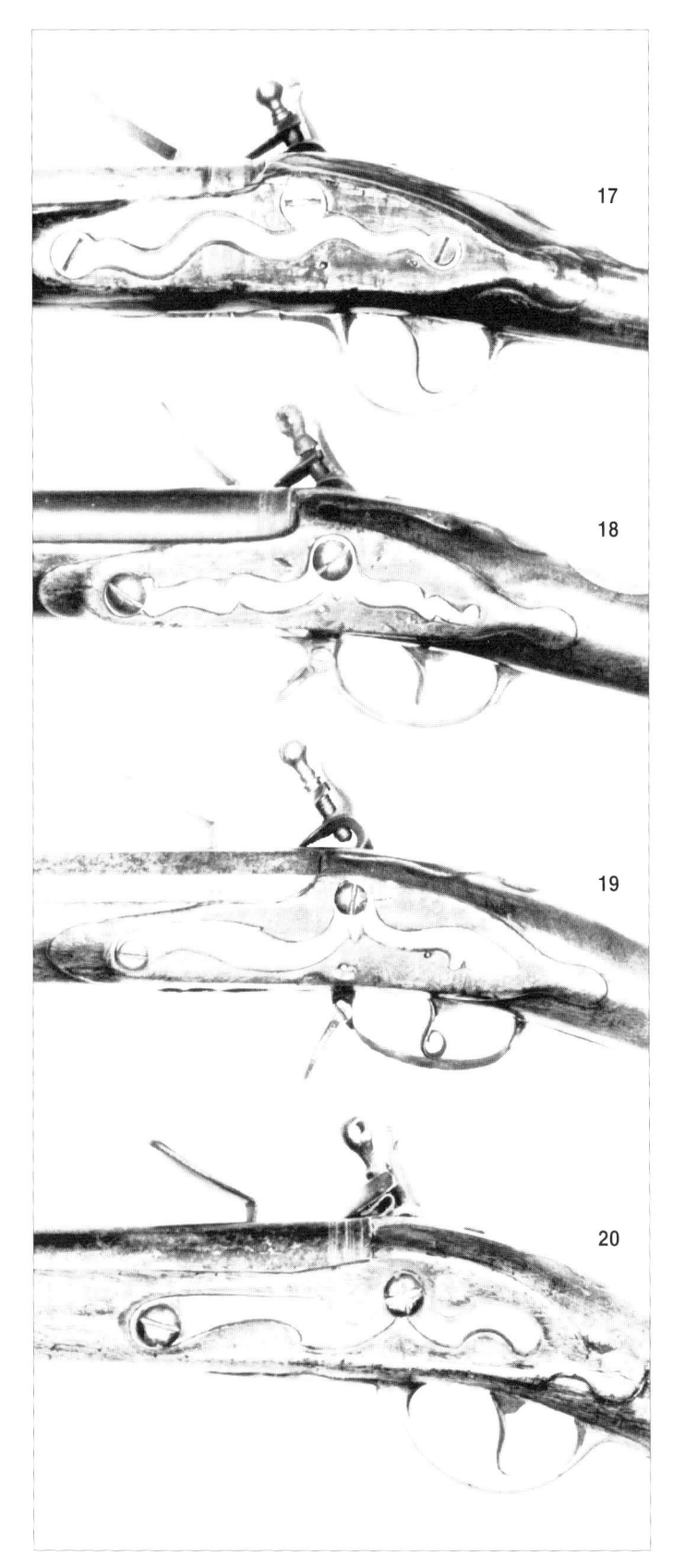

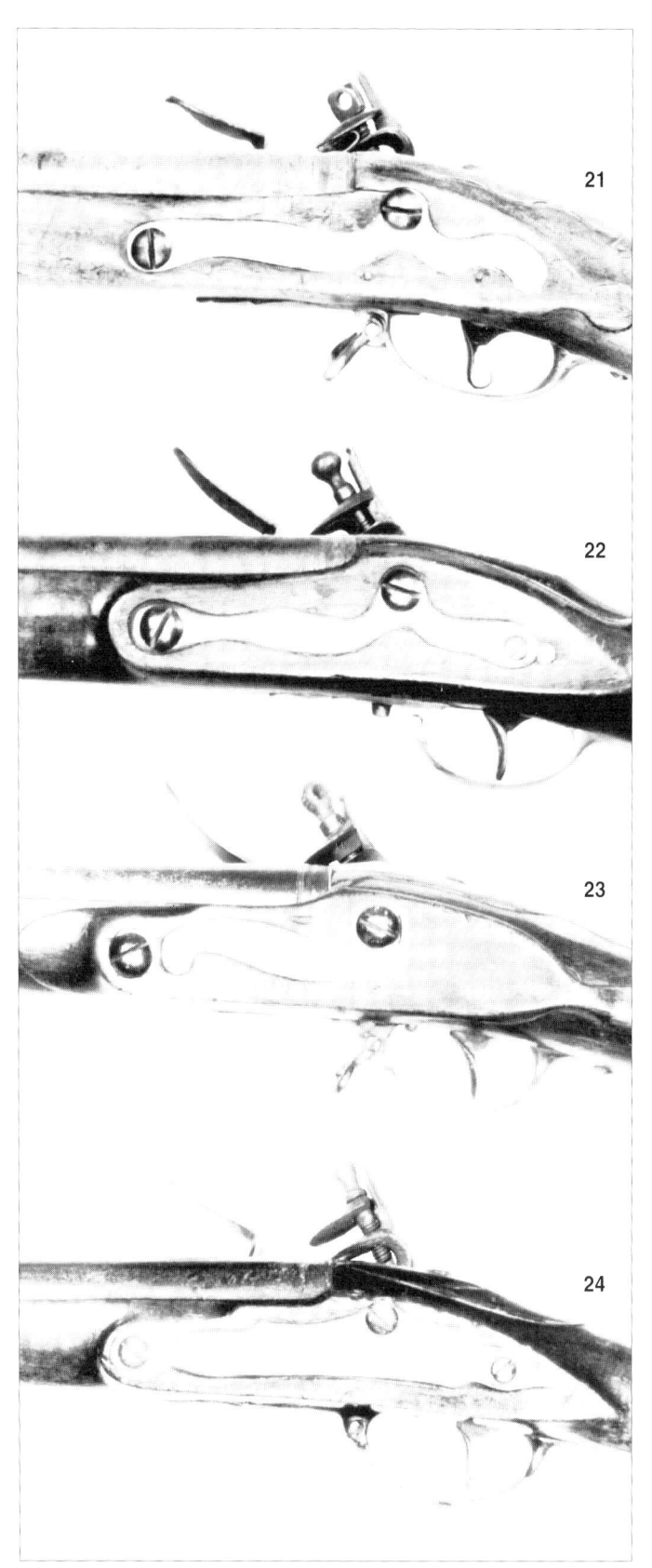

**DUTCH-GERMANIC: (17)** The Prussian "Potzdam Magaz" musket; circa 1740–1782; its distinctive wavy outline (note the rear wood screw) was frequently copied; see 65.MM. **(18)** Circa 1777–1798; a Dutch brass variation of the two-screw tailed form; 62.MM. **(19)** Circa 1720–1760; a popular Germanic–Low Country design especially on Suhl manufactured arms; see 64.MM. **(20)** Circa 1720–1770; a flattened adaptation found on early Dutch/Liege muskets supplied to American Colonists by Britain; note the raised outline carving; see 61.MM, 62.MM. **(21)** Circa 1760-1780; the Dutch "tailed" side plate continues to simplify, retaining a similarity to England's convex Long Land patterns. **(22)** Circa 1750–1775; a Holland contract musket copy of the British Brown Bess but with a wood screw added in the tail. **(23)** Circa 1771–1795; an abbreviated wartime rounded shape that drops the previous tail (to resemble the private English India Pattern); see 63.MM. **(24)** Circa 1740–1760; a Germanic flat brass plate similar to some French and Spanish designs (see 15 and 16 above).

*Chapter 3: Smoothbore Shoulder Arms*

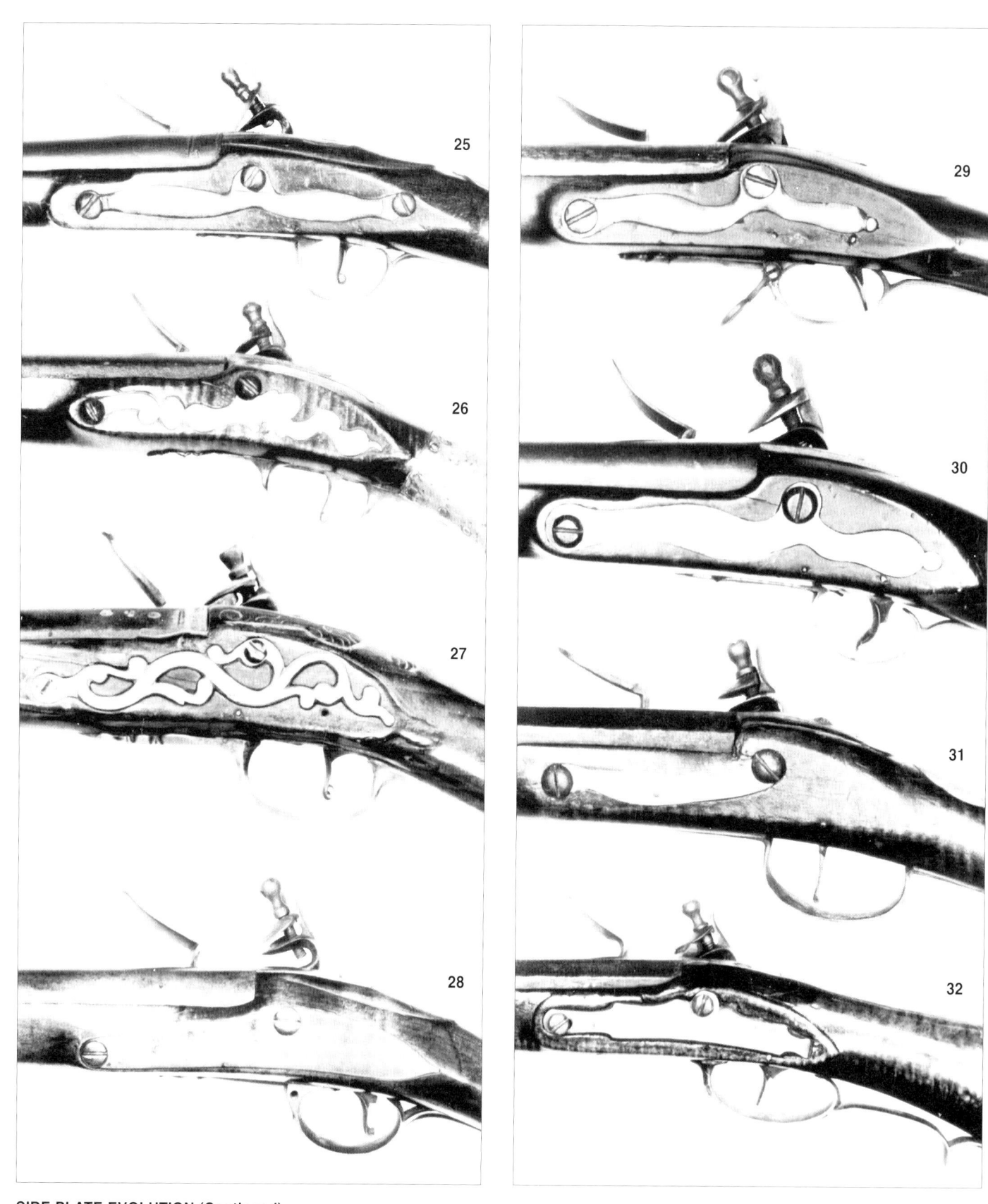

## SIDE PLATE EVOLUTION (Continued)

**AMERICAN: (25)** A three-screw convex double arm that resembles British Queen Anne styling (re: 2 above; see 77.MM). **(26)** Circa 1740–1760; a combination vine-cameo shape popular on European fowlers and copied for this American club butt; see 102.MM. **(27)** Circa 1730–1750; the European "open vine" cast brass plate often imitated by the Colonists (per this Hudson Valley fowler); see 110.MM. **(28)** Circa 1760–1790; a flat cast brass provincial form that often traced the lock plate outline; see 91.MM. **(29)** Circa 1760–1780; an American rounded shape imitating the British Long Land style. **(30)** Circa 1775–1785; a copy by the rebels of the English Short Land pattern. **(31)** Circa 1760–1780; a Colonist's sheet brass approximation of France's traditional S-design; see 160.MM. **(32)** Circa 1740–1800; the scalloped/blunt-ended shape found on many Pennsylvania long rifles; see 8.RR–11.RR.

*42    Chapter 3: Smoothbore Shoulder Arms*

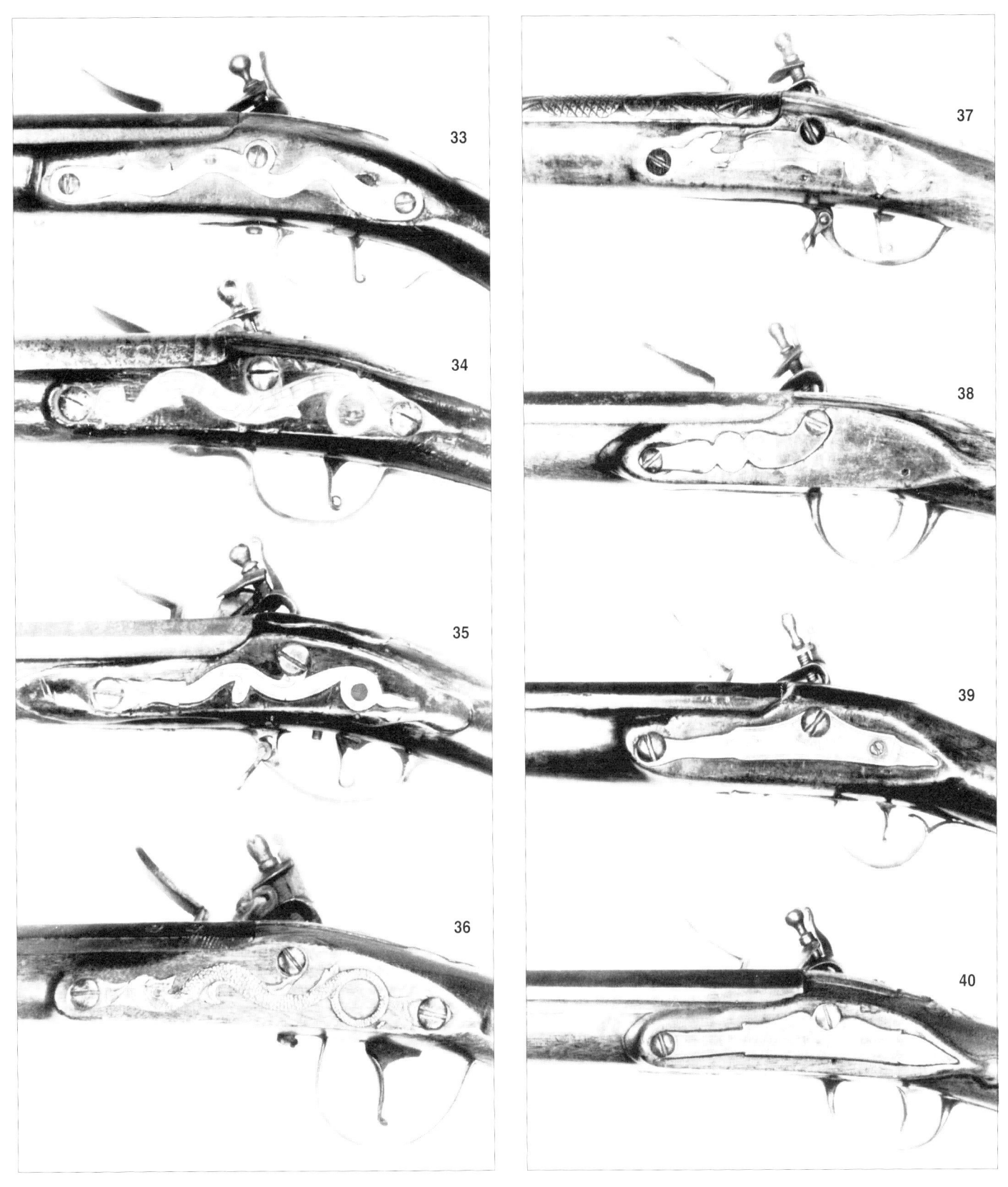

**COMMERCIAL / TRADE: (33)** Circa 1690–1720; an English three-screw commercial/trade gun; its early dragon outline contains no engraved details; see 149.MM. **(34)** Circa 1710–1730; a more detailed three-screw British/Germanic civilian dragon design; see 150.MM. **(35)** Circa 1730–1750; this less-detailed Germanic/Liege dragon plate is now adopted to a two-strew lock (used on both military and civilian arms); see 70.MM. **(36)** Circa 1750–1880; a definitive cast brass dragon side plate having raised details, which appeared on the famed English "Northwest" trade gun for over a century; see 155.MM. **(37)** Circa 1770–1780; a creative American interpretation of the dragon design for a light fowler; see 94.MM. **(38)** Circa 1720–1750; the flat center oval iron shape found on most Tulle manufactured Marine muskets and hunting guns used in New France; see 34.MM, 156.MM. **(39)** Circa 1730–1760; a typical British triangular commercial/trade gun brass form; note the rear wood screw and token engraving; see 154.MM. **(40)** Circa 1730–1750; the French three-sided pattern (iron) popular on their commercial and hunting arms; also observe its typical stock border carving; see 157.MM.

*Chapter 3: Smoothbore Shoulder Arms*

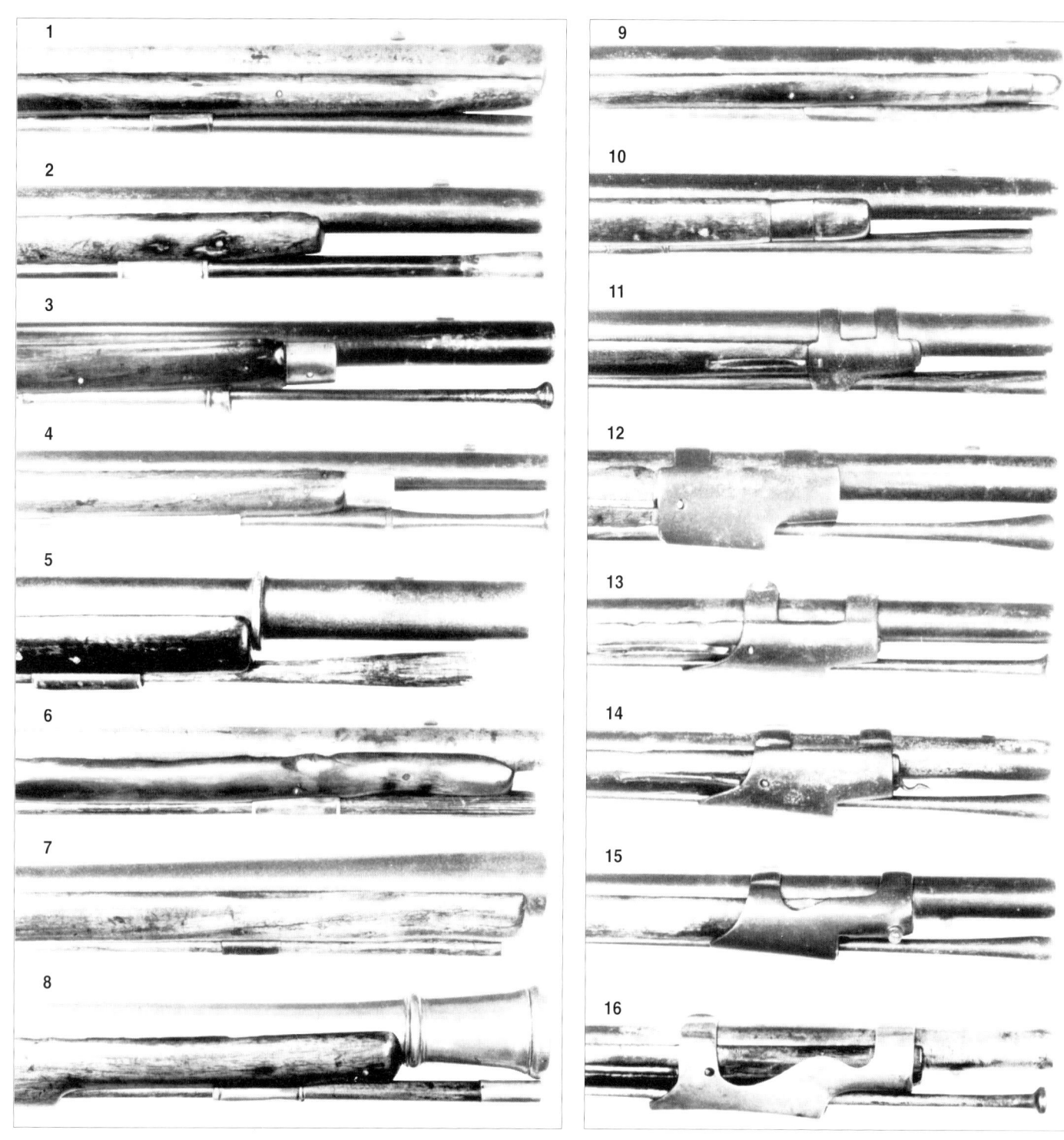

## MUZZLE COMPARISONS

**ENGLISH: (1)** Circa 1680–1715; muskets and fowlers stocked to the muzzle prior to the socket bayonet; wooden ramrod. **(2)** British Long Land Brown Bess Patterns 1730 and 1742; the walnut forend is reduced for a bayonet socket (requiring the traditional British top stud); its wooden rammer is brass-tipped; note the short but large diameter upper pipe; some nose caps were added by the regiments; see 8.MM, 9.MM. **(3)** English Long and Short Land muskets circa 1756–1793; note the steel button-head rod, long open-mouthed upper pipe and cast brass end cap; 10.MM–18.MM. **(4)** British Elliot #2 light dragoon carbine, circa 1773; a lower lip of the nose cap snaps into a groove encircling the swollen section of its steel ramrod; see 125.MM. **(5)** Circa 1747; a shortened Long Land Brown Bess with a barrel ring added below the muzzle to mount a grenade launching cup; see 31.MM. **(6)** An English sea service musket stocked to the muzzle before bayonets were approved in 1752; see 28.MM. **(7)** Circa 1680–1800; the blunderbuss (or musketoon) trumpet-shaped iron barrel; see 138.MM–140.MM. **(8)** Circa 1760–1790; a popular British blunderbuss brass "cannon" muzzle with the usual wooden rammer; see 137.MM. **FRENCH: (9)** Circa 1695–1716; an early century French musket typically stocked to the muzzle plus an iron nose band and wooden rammer (plug bayonet period). **(10)** French Model 1717; iron furniture, wooden rod, with the stock shortened for a socket bayonet; see 38.MM. **(11)** French Model 1728; three bands have replaced the previous barrel pins, including this double-strap straight-backed upper band; see 39.MM. **(12)** French Model 1763; the two-strap top band adds a top sight plus an iron ramrod cover extending back to the center band; a steel rammer was authorized in 1741; see 42.MM. **(13)** French Model 1766; its upper band has acquired a tail and drops the rear ramrod cover; the steel rod, in turn, is now button-beaded, while the bayonet stud moves under the barrel; see 43.MM. **(14)** French Model 1774; a unique clasp extends from the forend to snap over a rear ring on the bayonet; see

*44    Chapter 3: Smoothbore Shoulder Arms*

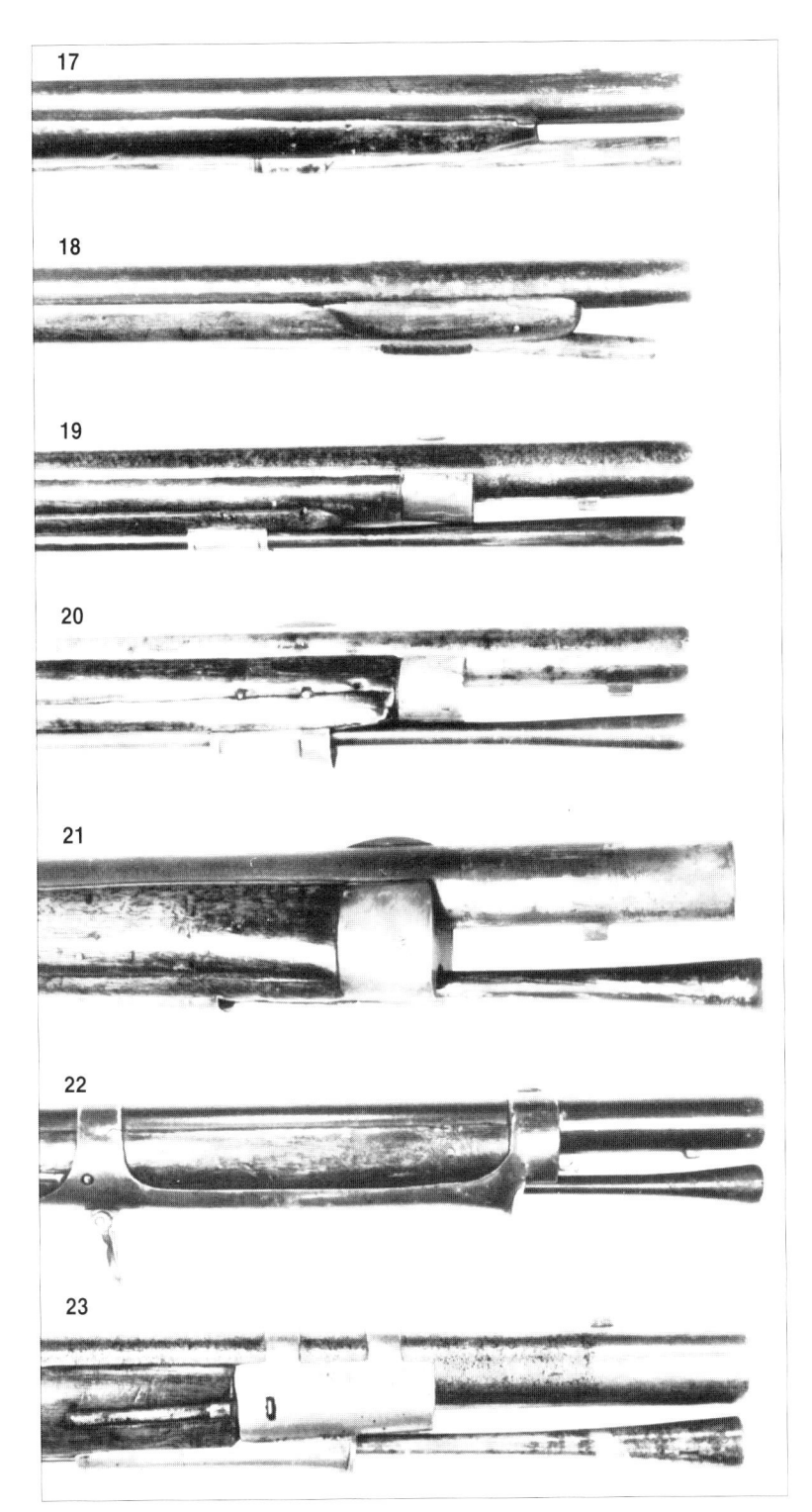

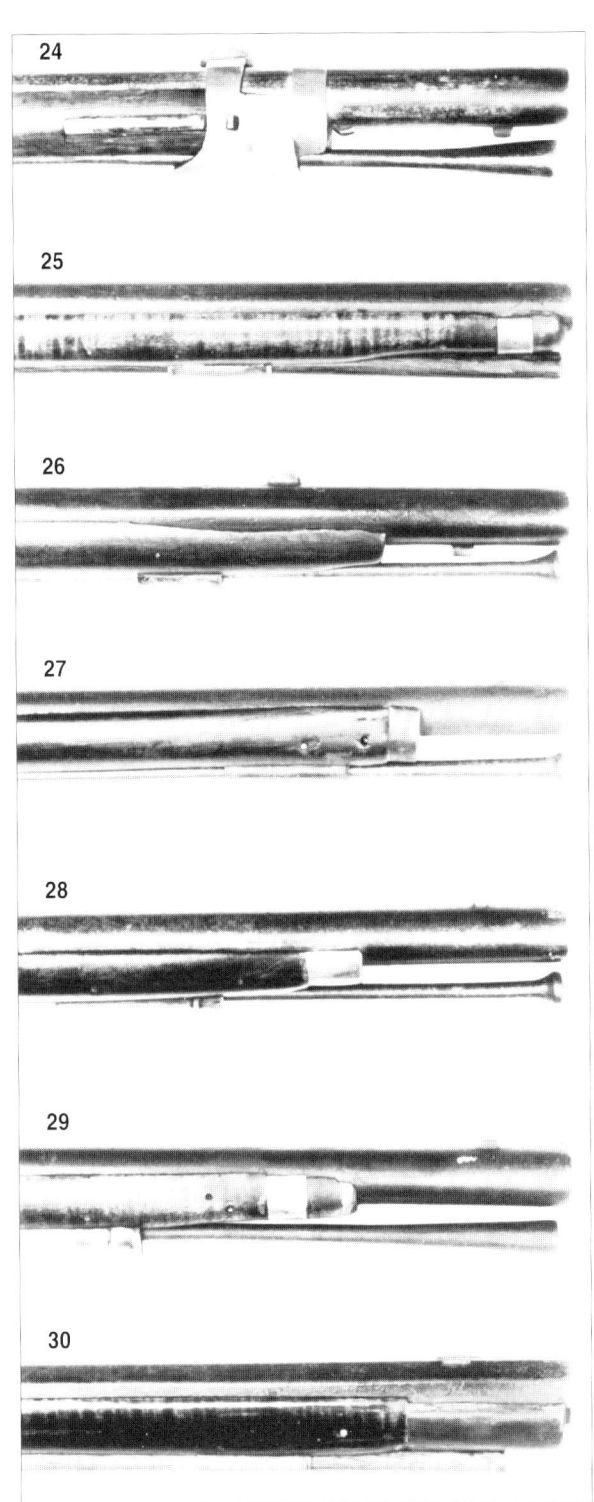

46.MM. **(15)** French Model 1777; an exterior screw anchors the top barrel band, which also adds a wavy edge between its straps; see 47.MM. **(16)** French Dragoon Model 1772; note the unique stretched brass upper band (its center band is also two straps but in iron); see 129.MM. **(17)** French "Marine" musket circa 1729–1734; there is no upper cap on the bayonet-shortened stock; see 34.MM, 35.MM. **(18)** Circa 1730–1750; French hunting gun *(fusil de chasse)* omits any bayonet accommodation and mounts a blade sight; see 156.MM. **DUTCH-GERMANIC: (19)** Circa 1720–1740; a typical Germanic pinned musket with a top sight, bottom stud, sheet brass nose band, faceted pipe and wooden rod; see 64.MM. **(20)** Prussian Model 1740; note its thickened trumpet ramrod held in a flare-mouth faceted thimble; see 65.MM. **(21)** A Brunswick musket, circa 1760–1777; from the Bennington, Vermont, battlefield (1777); observe the unusual forend brass cap having a front ramrod hole; see 69.MM. **(22)** Circa 1771–1780; Dutch light musket that uses a long two-strap upper barrel band plus a small bayonet clip in its forend; see 127.MM. **(23)** Spanish Models 1753 (iron) and 1757 (brass furniture); its top band includes a lower pipe for the steel rammer; see 51.MM. **(24)** Circa 1771–1795; this later Dutch wartime musket's band is reduced but continues the short bayonet clip; see 63.MM. **AMERICAN: (25)** Circa 1680–1785; common American fowler or pre-bayonet musket stocked to the muzzle. **(26)** Circa 1750–1785; a Colonist's fowler with its wood cut back and a bottom bayonet stud added. **(27)** Circa 1740–1780; a provincial musket bearing a thin inexpensive end band; see 74.MM. **(28)** Circa 1760–1780; an American copy of the British Brown Bess (rammer thimble shortened). **(29)** Circa 1775–1785; the common Colonial brass strip used to secure the forend versus a cast brass nose cap; see 84.MM. **(30)** Circa 1740–1800; the popular long sheet brass forend cover under the octagonal barrel of an American long rifle.

*Chapter 3: Smoothbore Shoulder Arms*

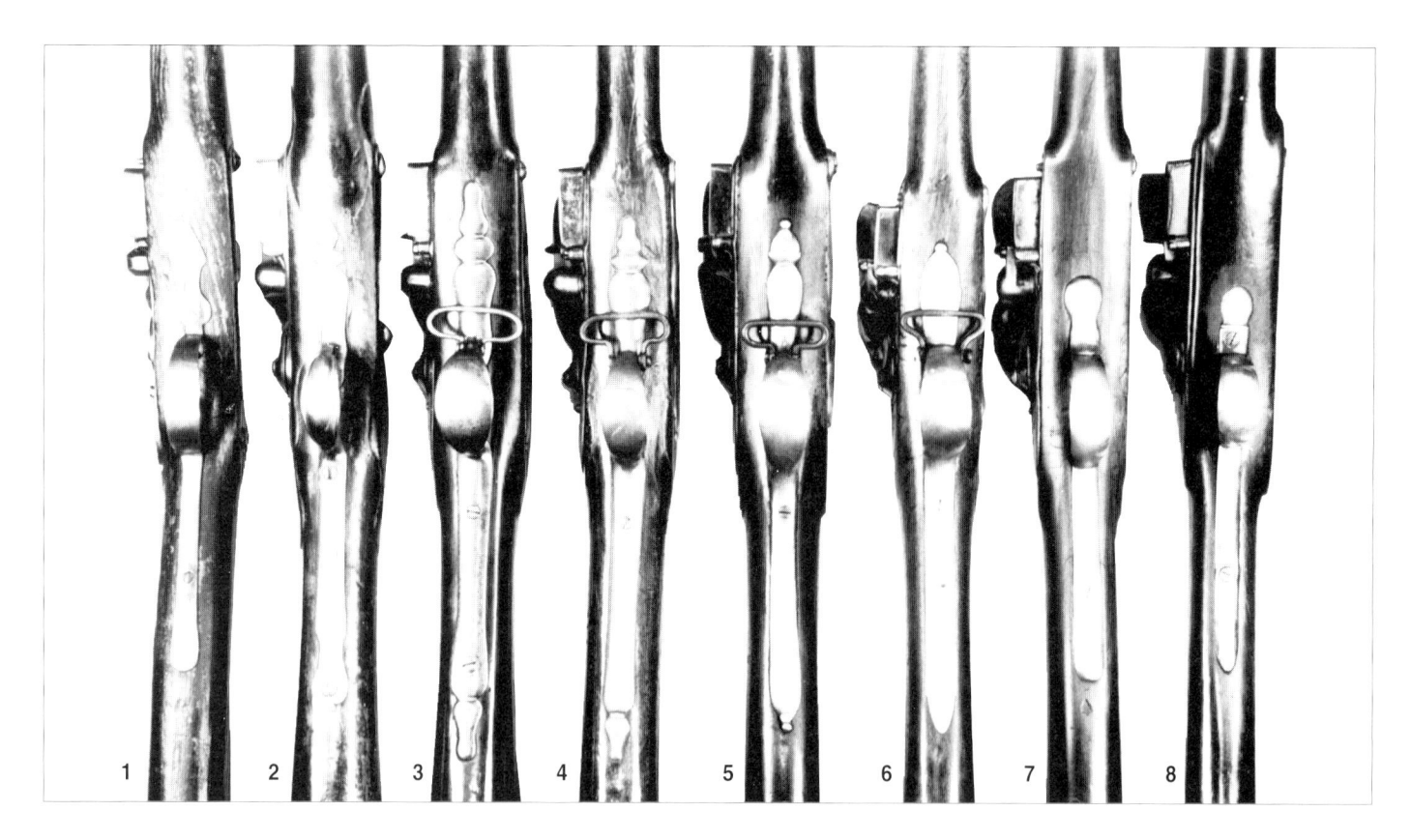

## TRIGGER GUARD PATTERN EVOLUTION

**ENGLISH:** English "land pattern" trigger guards were mostly pinned. The single rear screw penetrated the stock's wrist to hold the escutcheon. **(1)** Circa 1700; a regimental contract musket; sheet brass. **(2)** Circa 1710; an iron-mounted pre-standardized pattern. **(3)** Circa 1720; iron; shows Dutch design influence. **(4)** The new Long Land Brown Bess Pattern 1730; brass. **(5)** Circa 1742–1793; typical of Long and Short Land muskets during this period; brass. **(6)** Circa 1760; a light infantry carbine and fusil variation. **(7)** Circa 1750–1790; sea service longarms. **(8)** Circa 1755–1790; a common commercial and sea service variation. **FRENCH:** Note the steady shortening and use of two rear screws (most infantry in iron, naval in brass). **(9)** Model 1717. **(10)** Model 1728. **(11)** Model 1754; the rounded sling swivel now moves from the far side of the stock to a stud just forward of the trigger bow. **(12)** 1763 series; the swivel is now flattened. **(13)** Model 1774; its forward end has been reduced. **(14)** Model 1777; note the rounded lower end and raised finger ridges (only one screw remains). **(15)** Model 1733 cavalry carbine (brass). **(16)** Spanish Models 1753 (iron) and 1757 (brass). **DUTCH-GERMANIC:** Most of these were brass, using two rear screws and often channels in the trigger loop. **(17)** Dutch, circa

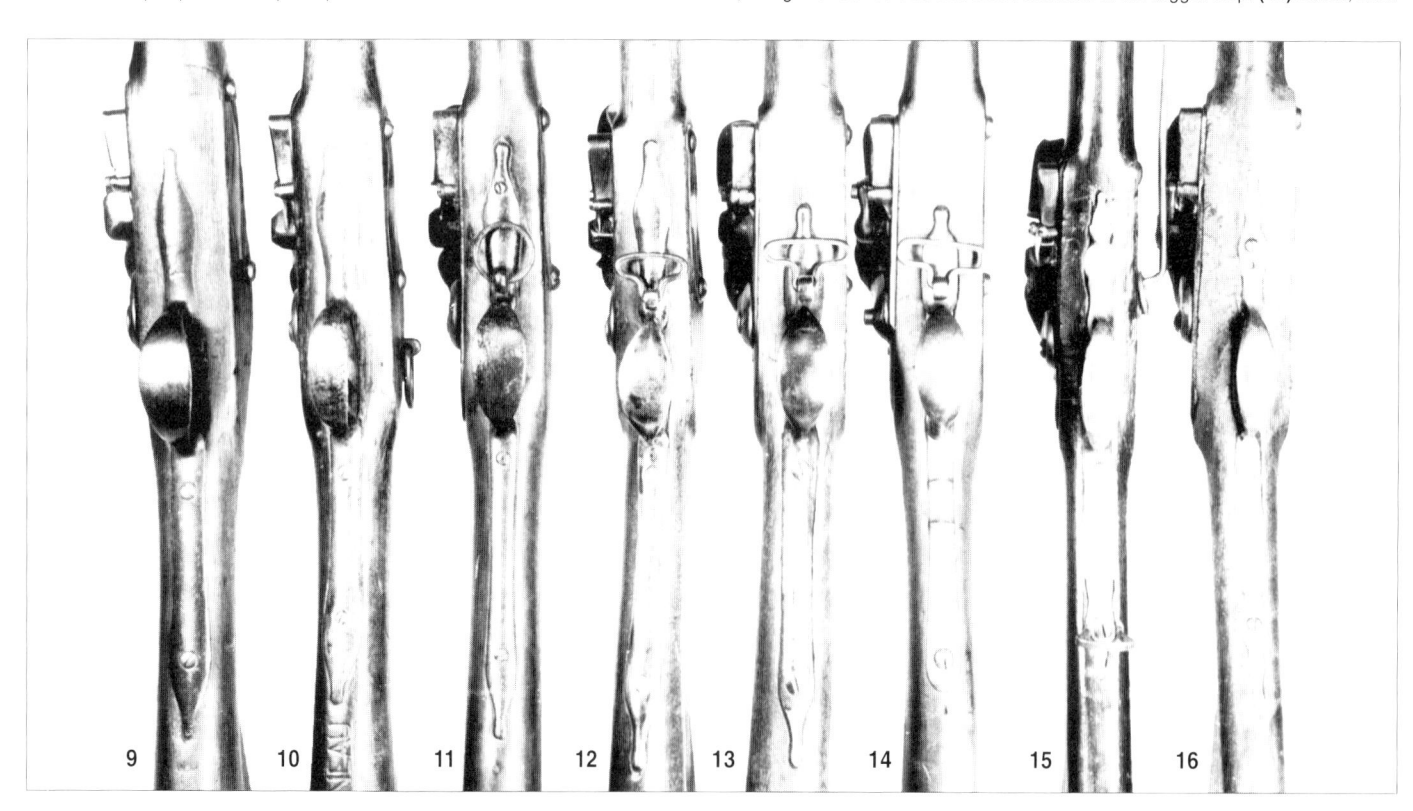

46  *Chapter 3: Smoothbore Shoulder Arms*

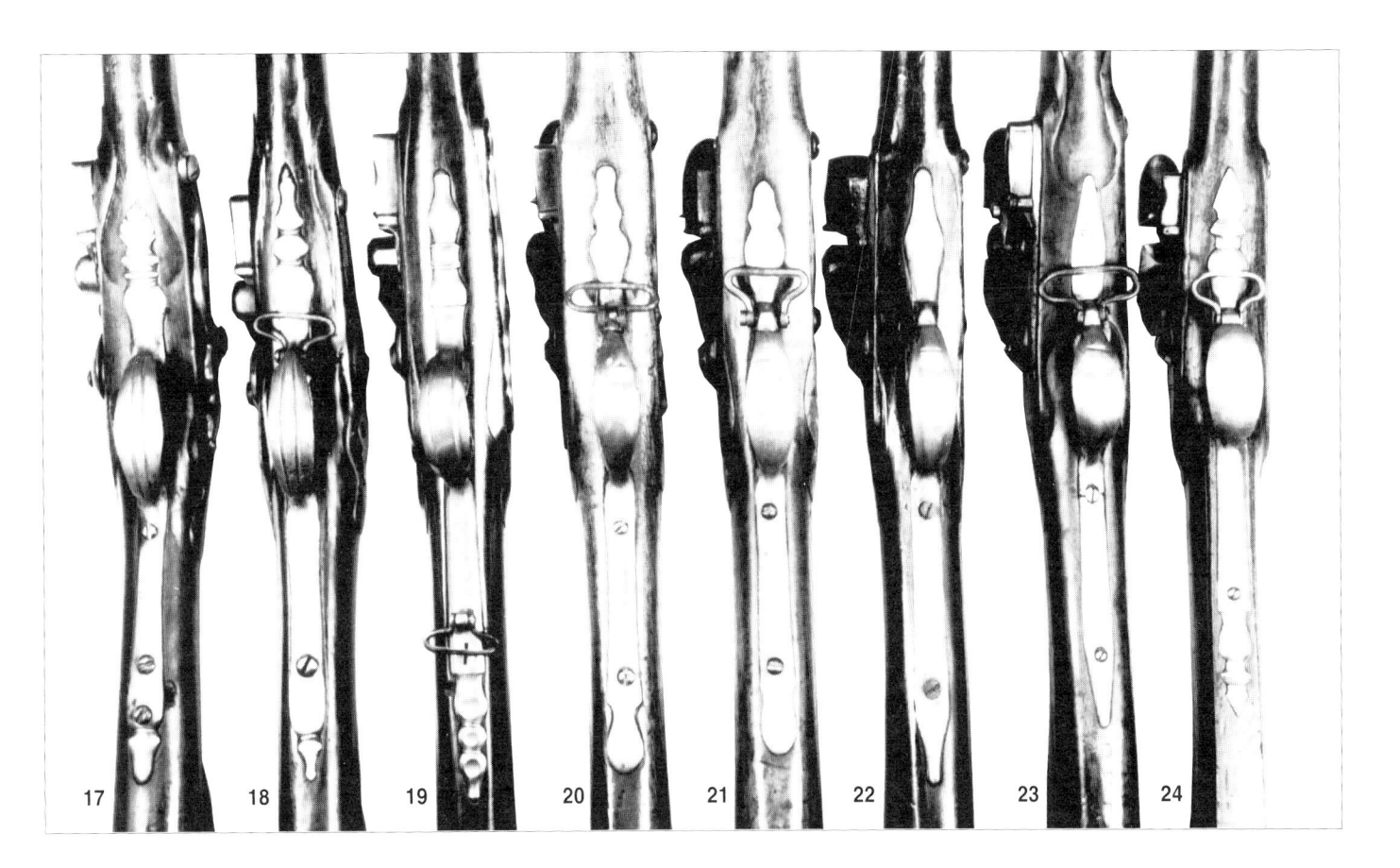

1710–1720. **(18)** Germanic, circa 1710–1730. **(19)** Prussian Model 1740 ("Potzdam Magaz"). **(20)** Dutch-Germanic, circa 1720–1770. **(21)** Dutch-Germanic, circa 1740–1760. **(22)** Dutch-Germanic, Circa 1765–1780; note the progressive simplification of design. **(23)** Dutch, circa 1771–1795; observe the further simplification to meet wartime demands. **(24)** Circa 1720–1760; the popular Germanic arrowpoint styling. **AMERICAN: (25-29)** Various interpretations of the British Brown Bess design; most Americans omitted the lower screw that the English used to pierce the stock wrist and secure an escutcheon plate, which the Colonials often did not provide (or substituted a short screw/nail from the top); all brass; circa 1750–1783. **(30)** Circa 1760–1770; an uneven brass casting with crude incised decoration. **(31)** Circa 1770–1800; a copy of the popular British civilian acorn front terminal. **(32)** Circa 1760–1785; a brass version of the French pattern.

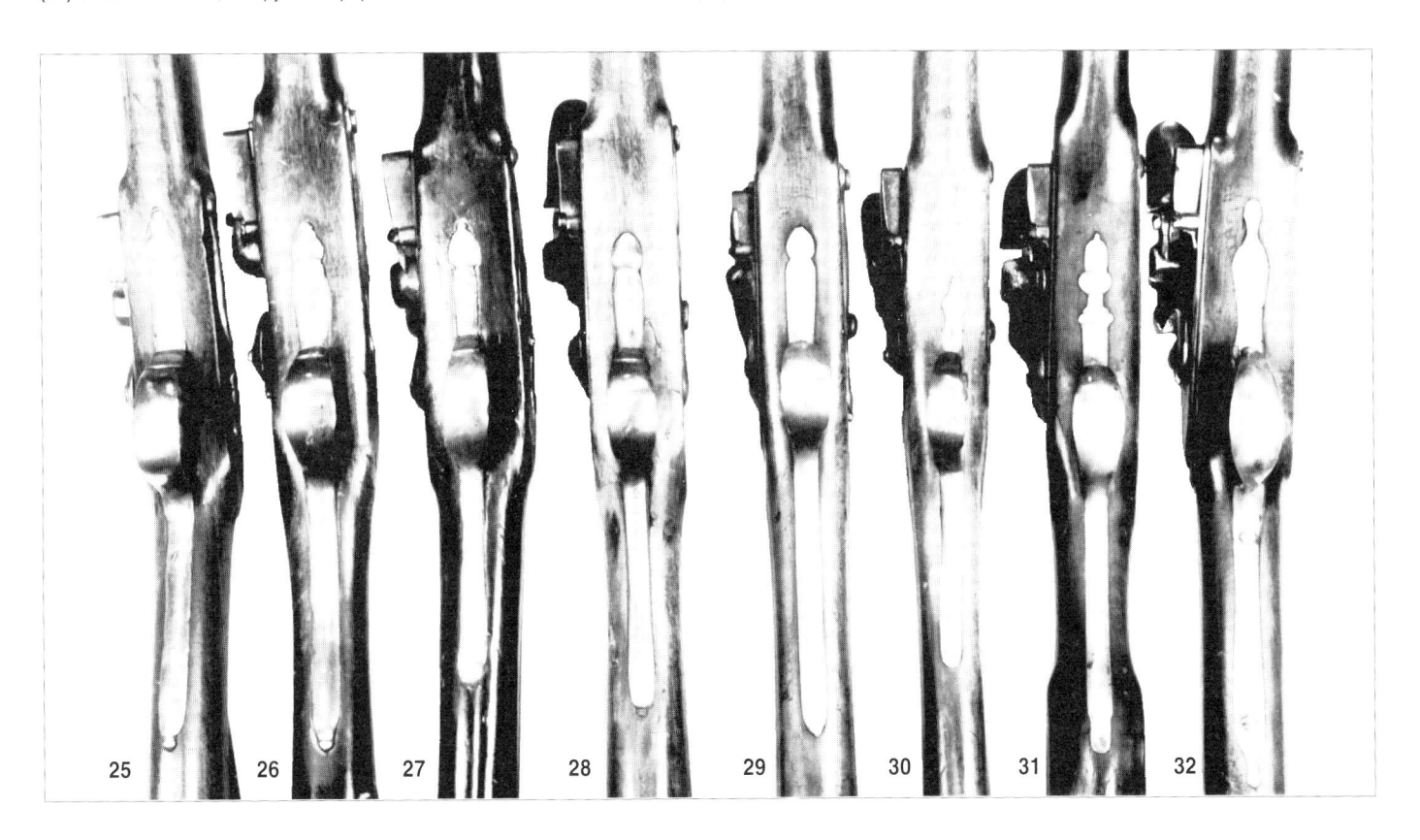

*Chapter 3: Smoothbore Shoulder Arms* 47

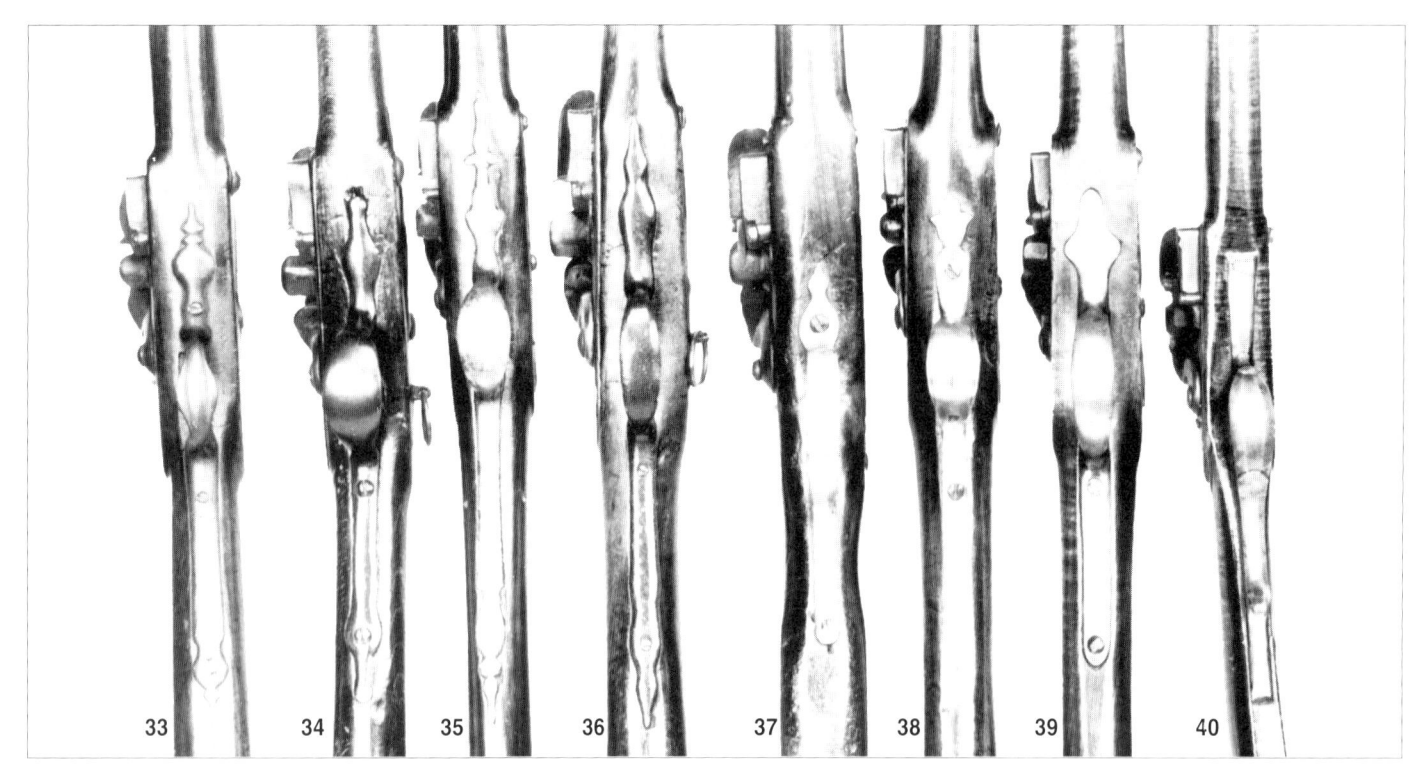

**TRIGGER GUARD PATTERN EVOLUTION (Continued)**

(**33**) Circa 1697–1715; the early baluster French Tulle pattern. (**34**) Circa 1700–1717; the evolving French army's double-pointed form. (**35**) Circa 1720–1760; a popular French commercial trigger guard. (**36**) Circa 1720–1740; French, with known naval use (55.MM). (**37**) Circa 1700–1720; an English economical brass trade gun guard. (**38**) Circa 1730–1760; the common British commercial tulip front terminal. (**39**) Circa 1760–1785; an improvised Colonist pattern. (**40**) Circa 1750–1800; the squared-end shape popular on American long rifles.

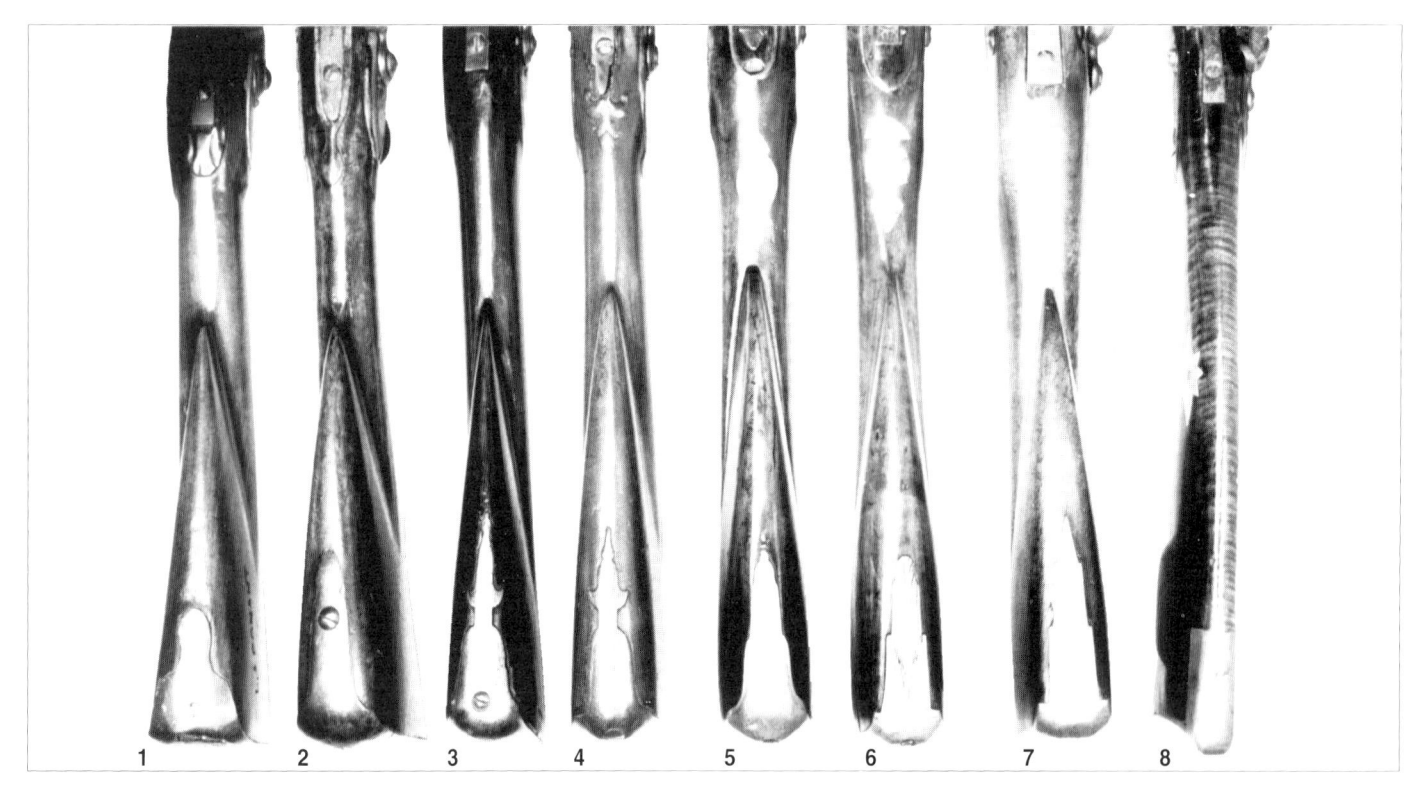

**BUTT STYLING EVOLUTION**

(**1**) Circa 1697–1715; French "Marine" lobed shape; manufactured at Tulle. (**2**) Circa 1720–1750; Tulle-made muskets and hunting guns (iron); note the pear-like finial and top screw. (**3**) Circa 1730–1750; the three-pointed French military and commercial form. (**4**) Circa 1730–1750; an engraved three-pointed tang on a French hunting gun *(fusil fin de chasse)*; 158.MM. (**5**) Circa 1730–1760; an English "stepped" commercial fowler engraved tang. (**6**) Circa 1770–1780; an American adaptation of the British form (5 above). (**7**) Circa 1770–1780; a simplified Colonist's copy of the Brown Bess musket pattern. (**8**) Circa 1750–1800; the squared and faceted brass butt found on many American long rifles.

*48    Chapter 3: Smoothbore Shoulder Arms*

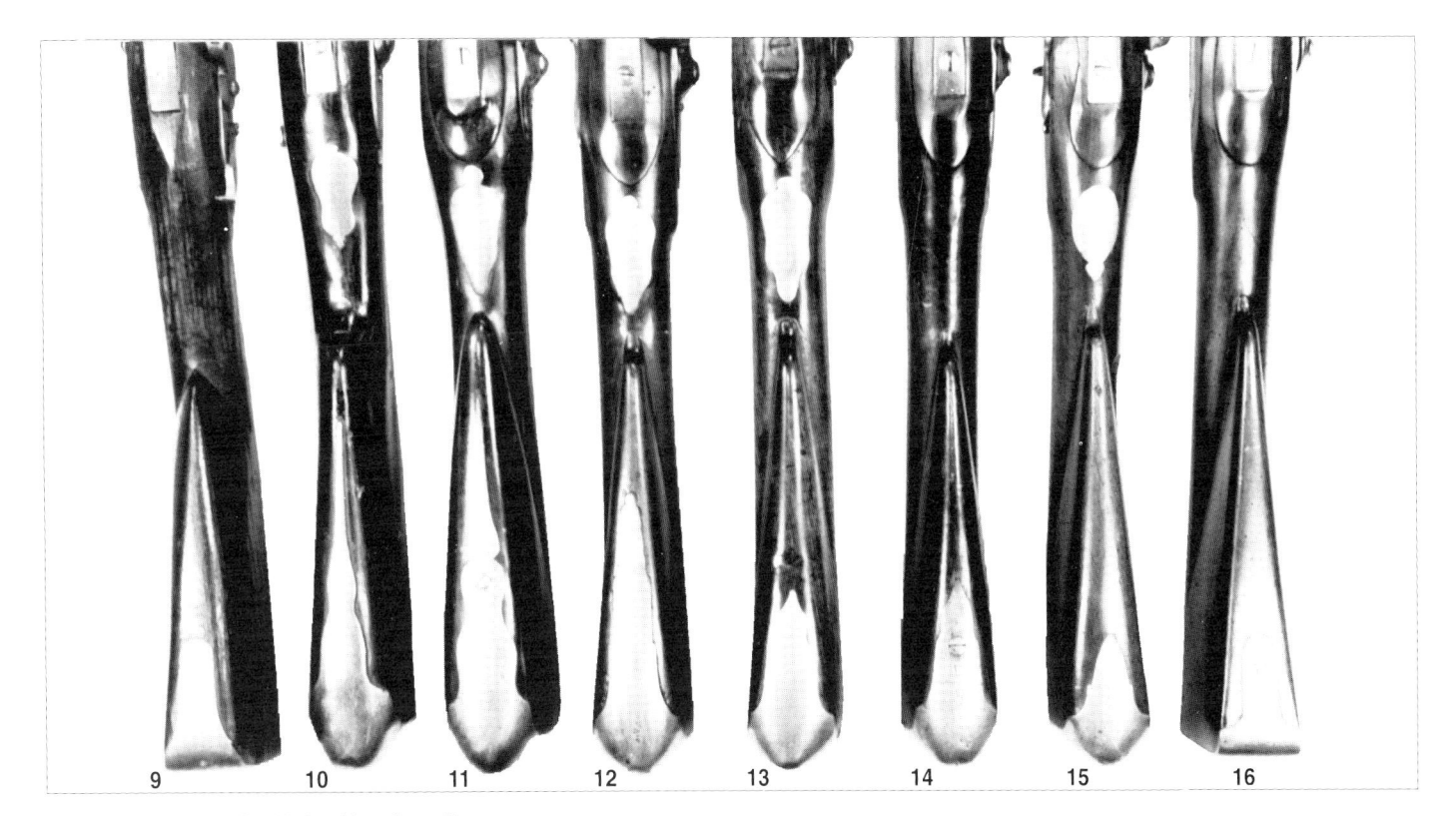

## BUTT STYLING EVOLUTION (Continued)

**ENGLISH: (9)** Circa 1700; flat brass. **(10)** Circa 1710–1720; iron. **(11)** Circa 1720; iron; note Dutch influence and the rare top screw. **(12)** Circa 1730–1768; Long Land Brown Besses; brass. **(13)** Circa 1768–1793; Short Land Brown Besses; brass. **(14)** Circa 1756–1769; the Marine or Militia patterns; note their distinctive screw head (British army military butt tangs were traditionally pinned—with screws in the rear of the butt plate). **(15)** Circa 1760; a light infantry carbine design; brass. **(16)** Circa 1750–1790; the flat sea service form (copied from the earlier 9 at left).

**FRENCH: (17)** Model 1717; iron. **(18)** Model 1728 iron. **(19)** Model 1746; iron. **(20)** Models 1763–1777; iron; observe the steady butt tang shortening. **(21)** Circa 1750–1760; an officer's fusil; brass. **(22)** Circa 1760; an engraved fusil tang. **(23)** Carbine Model 1733; the French three-pointed form (also 3); brass. **(24)** Spanish Model 1757; note its two screws and French styling influence (re. 23); brass.

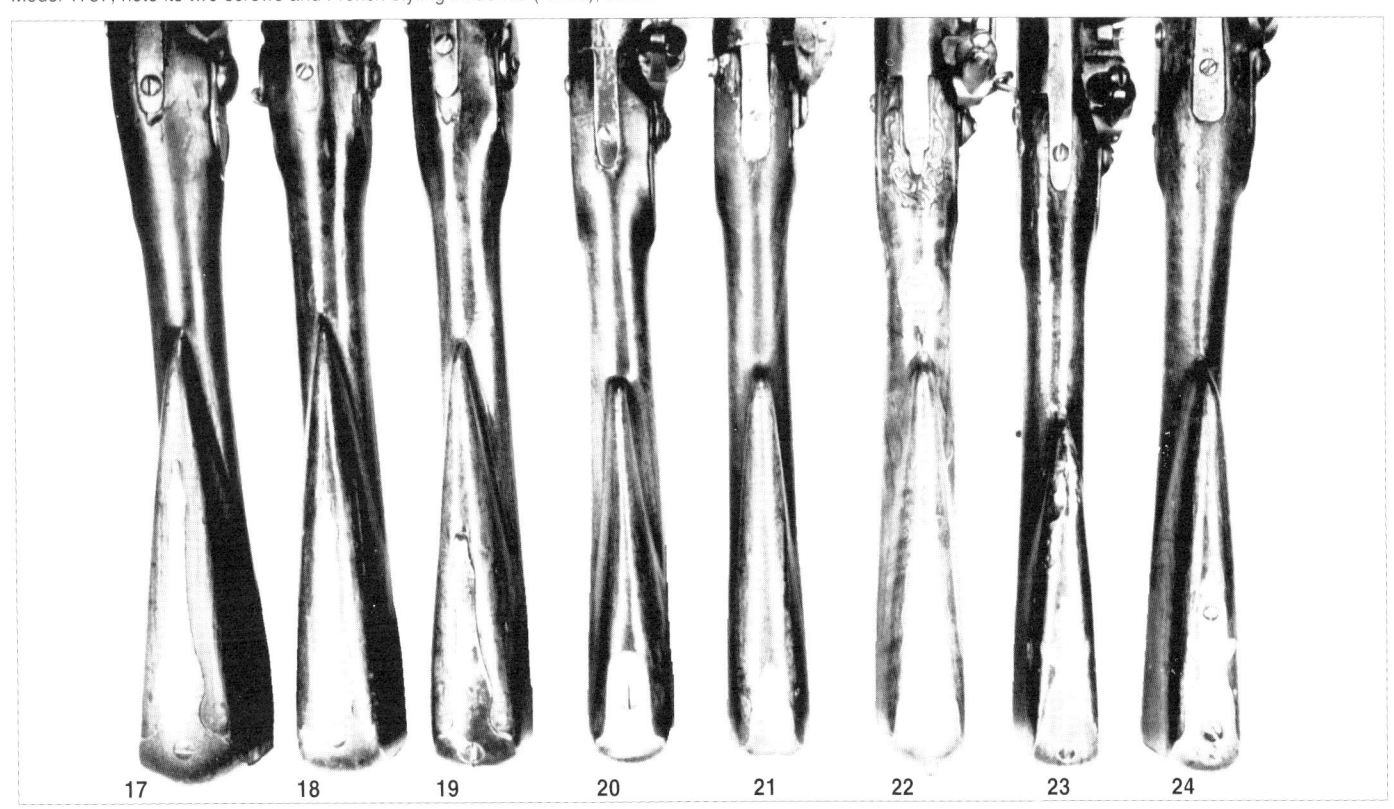

Chapter 3: Smoothbore Shoulder Arms   49

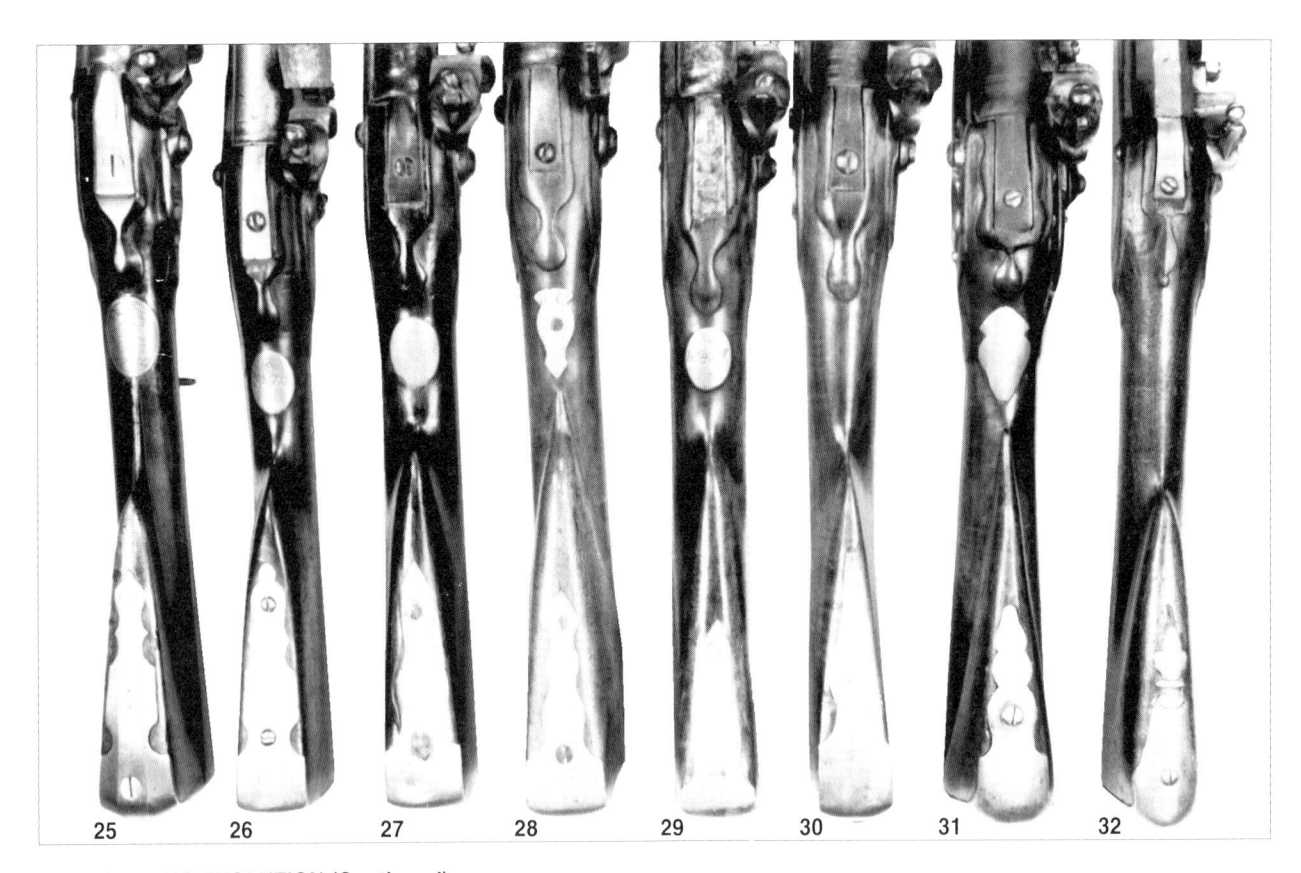

**BUTT STYLING EVOLUTION (Continued)**
**DUTCH-GERMANIC: (25)** Circa 1740–1782; Prussian "Potzdam Magaz" form; note the three top screws, oval escutcheon and teardrop barrel tang carving. **(26)** Circa 1760–1780; a later and plainer Dutch–German pattern. **(27)** Circa 1750–1770; Dutch–Germanic; a further simplified form. **(28)** Circa 1760–1780; Dutch; many of their escutcheons were held by a top screw. **(29)** Circa 1770–1780; Dutch; observe the wartime reductions plus two pins used here in its oval escutcheon. **(30)** Circa 1720–1770; an early long Dutch single screw configuration. **(31)** Circa 1710–1720; Dutch; brass. **(32)** Circa 1740–1780; Dutch–Germanic; a rare escutcheon omission. **AMERICAN: (33-38)** Variations of butt plates copied from British patterns. **(39, 40)** Circa 1730–1760; early Dutch influence as found on Hudson Valley fowlers.

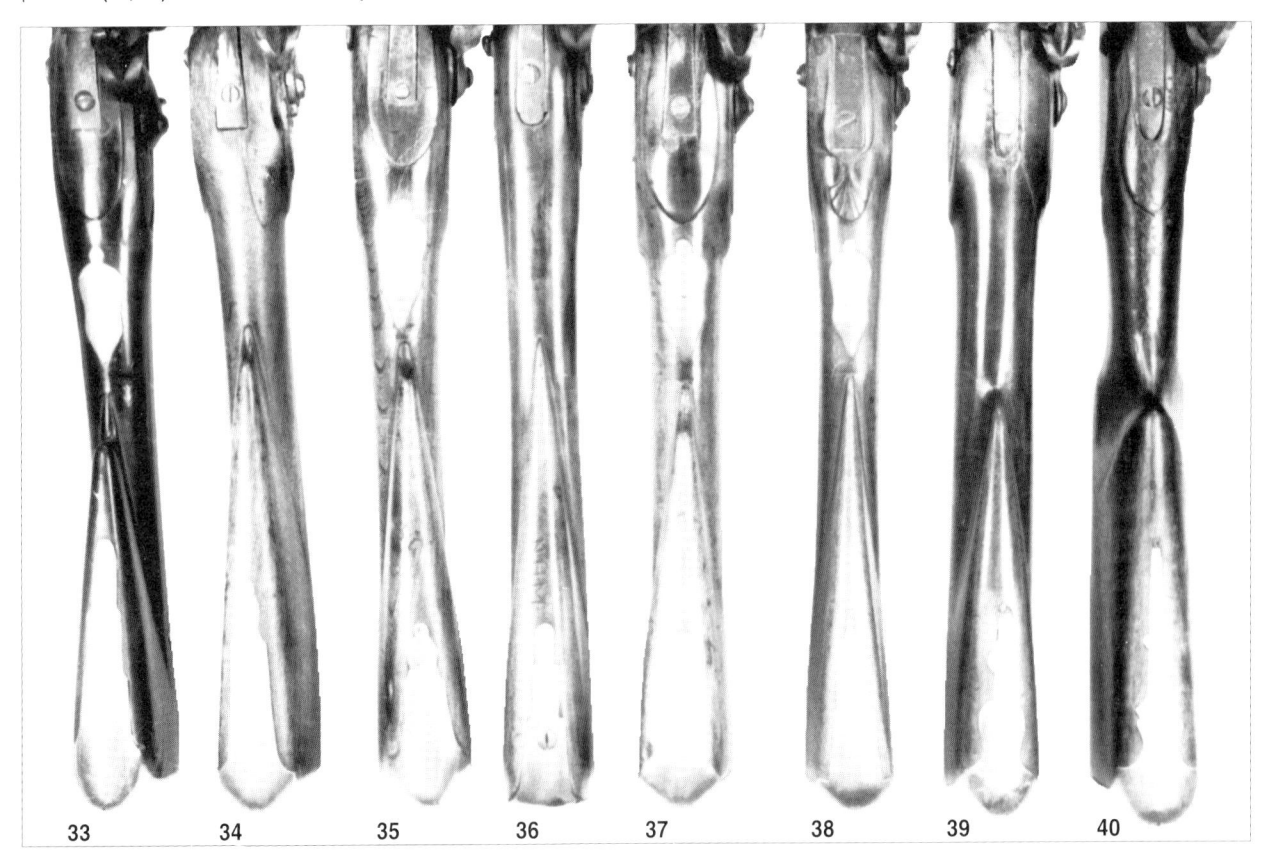

50    *Chapter 3: Smoothbore Shoulder Arms*

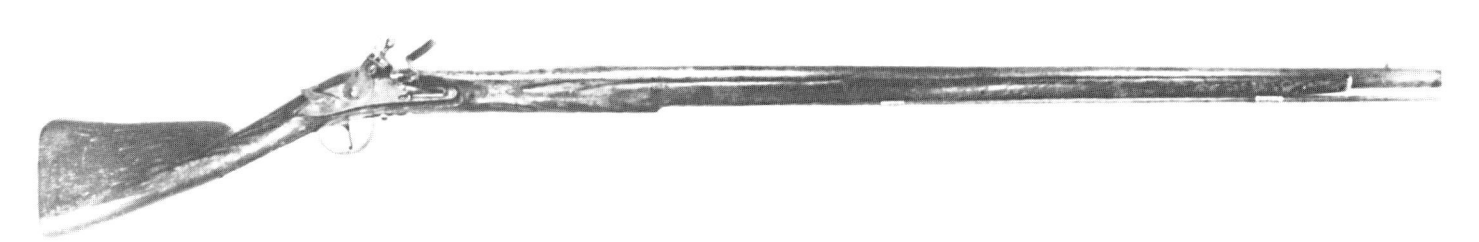

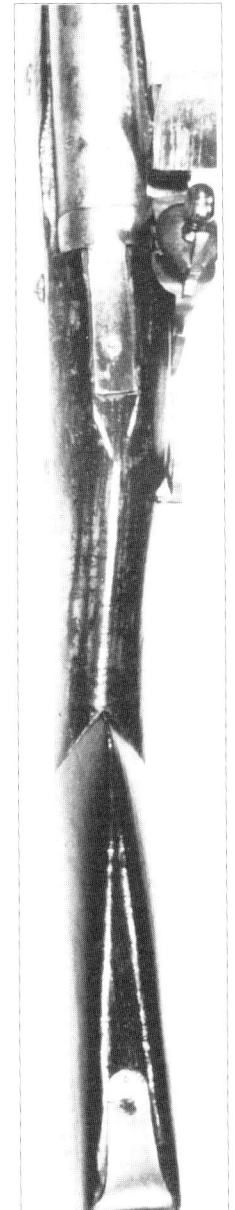

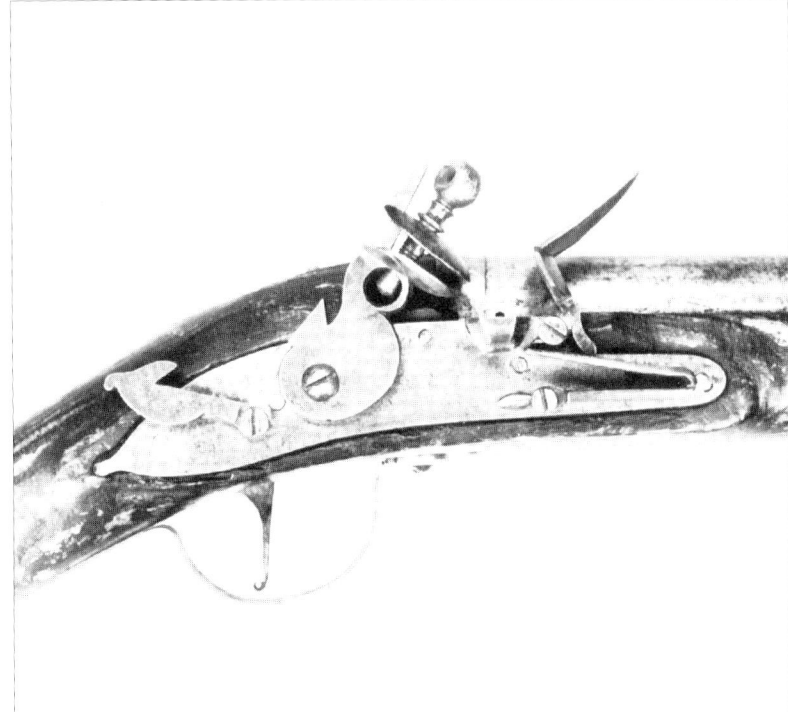

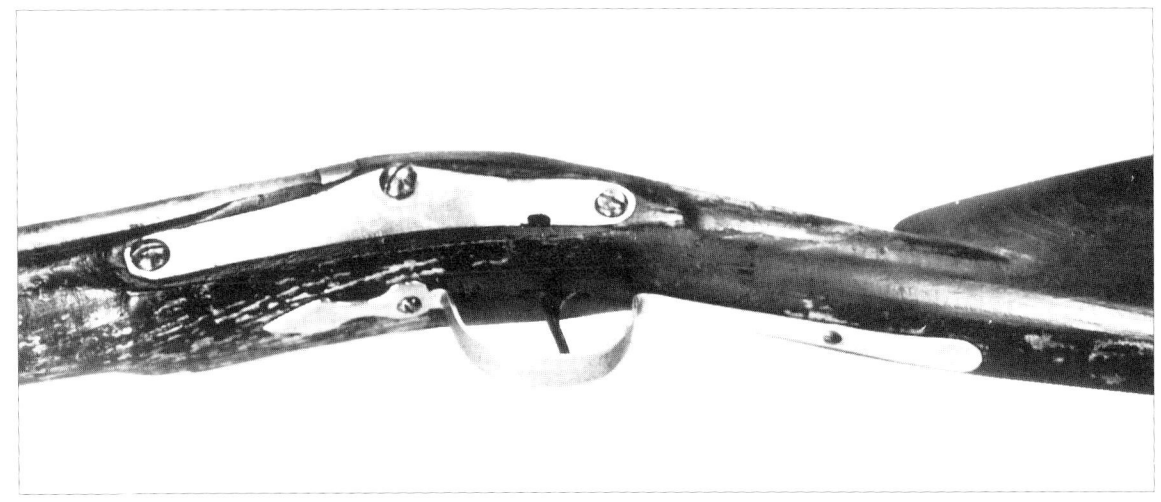

**1.MM  ENGLISH DOGLOCK MUSKET**                                                                                 Circa 1690–1710

This late doglock infantry arm is typical of the inexpensive weapons purchased by many regimental colonels during the late 17th and early 18th centuries. Given a grant by the Crown to raise and equip a regiment, the colonel—bound only by a specified barrel length (46") and bore size (.75 caliber)—too often bought marginal arms from private domestic or Continental contractors and kept the profit. Notice the absence of raised carving, as well as the elimination of a tail pipe and escutcheon. Its three-screw doglock (squared frizzen) has a notched tumbler without an interior or external bridle. The brass furniture, in turn, is limited to a thin triangular side plate, elementary flat trigger guard, ribbed rammer pipes and a rudimentary lobed butt plate (nailed). Its original full-length forend was cut back later to mount a socket bayonet. The barrel breech is stamped "crown / P" and "15" and is secured by a bottom screw reaching to its rear tang.

| | | | |
|---|---|---|---|
| Length: 61-1/2" | Lock: 7" X 1-1/4" | Butt Tang: 2-3/4" | Furniture: Brass |
| Barrel: 46-1/8", .79 cal. | Trigger Guard: 9-5/8" | Side Plate: 6-5/8" | Weight: 8.9 lbs. |

**George C. Neumann Collection, Valley Forge National Historical Park**

*Chapter 3: Smoothbore Shoulder Arms*

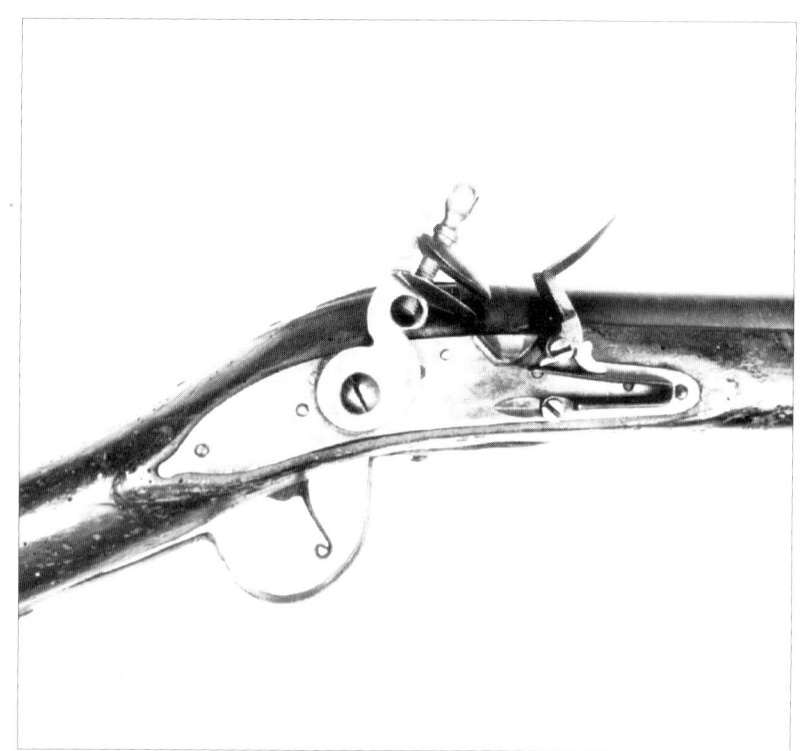

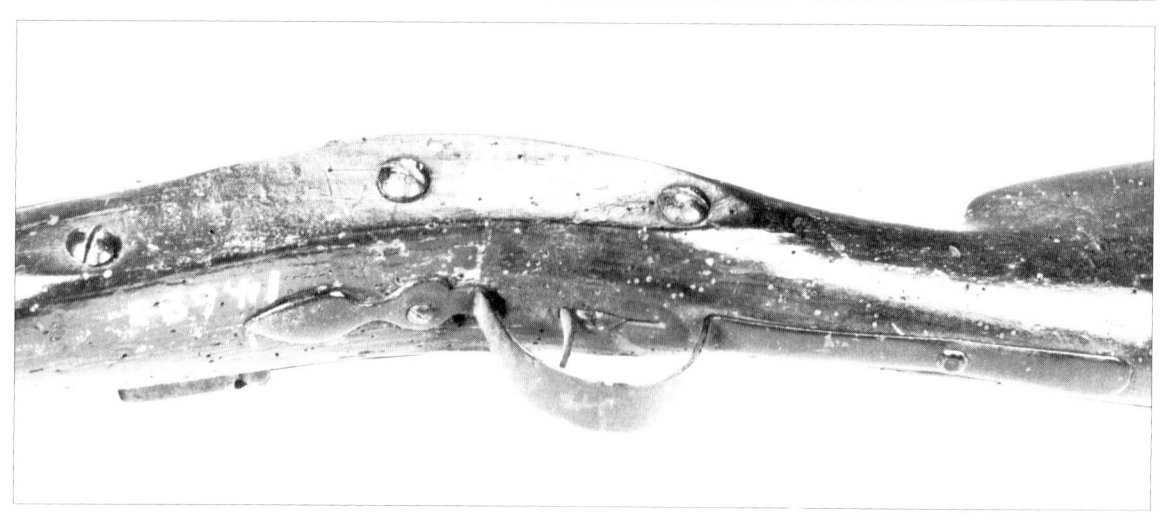

**2.MM ENGLISH INFANTRY MUSKET**  Circa 1700–1713

A comparison with the preceding longarm illustrates the trend to eliminate the lock's "dog," which had secured the cock from premature ignition. Beyond that its overall pattern remains basically the same—further illustrating the minimum quality of many arms purchased by the individual regiments during the War of the Spanish Succession (1702–1713). The three-screw lock has characteristics typical of this period: a reinforced cock, faceted flash pan without a bridle, a squared frizzen top, and a frizzen spring ending short of the side screw tip and having a leaf finial. The flat lobed butt plate is fastened by seven square-headed nails, while two rounded screws hold the simple flat trigger guard. A bottom rammer pipe, escutcheon and side plate are absent, probably to reduce cost. Two Birmingham-type proofs, "P" and "V" under crowns, and "13" are visible on the breech. Its barrel tang is held by a screw from underneath (head just forward of the trigger). Note, too, that the forend was later shortened to hold a socket bayonet. The wooden rammer (no metal tip) is typical.

| | | | |
|---|---|---|---|
| Length: 61-1/4" | Lock: 7" X 1-1/8" | Butt Tang: 3-1/4" | Furniture: Brass |
| Barrel: 46-1/2", .76 cal. | Trigger Guard: 9-1/2" | Weight: 8.1 lbs. | |

**West Point Museum Collection**

*Chapter 3: Smoothbore Shoulder Arms*

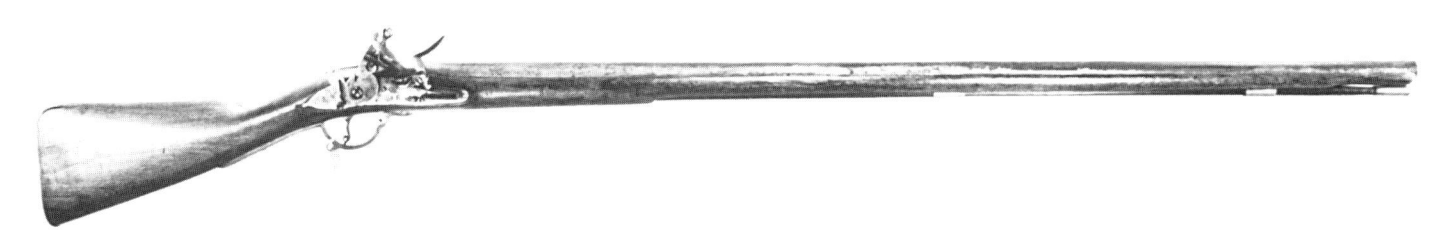

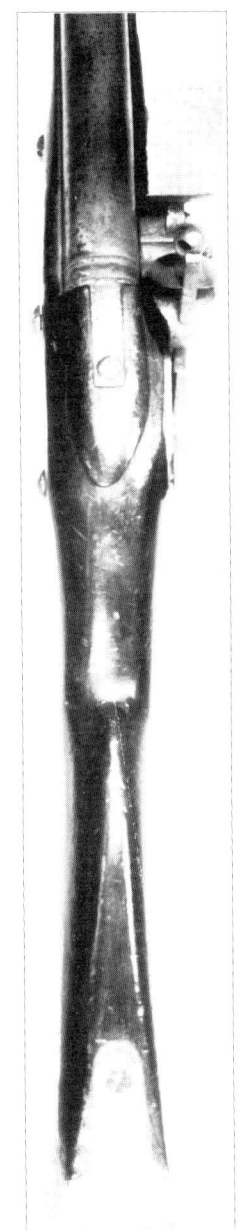

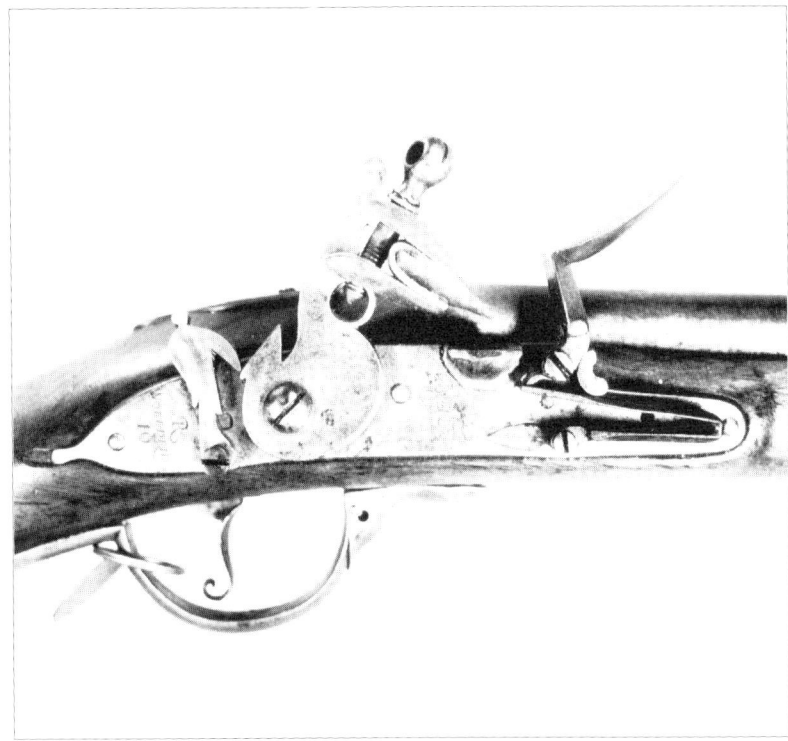

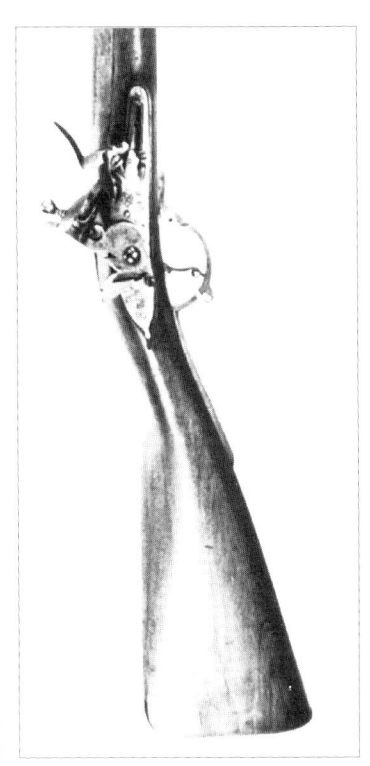

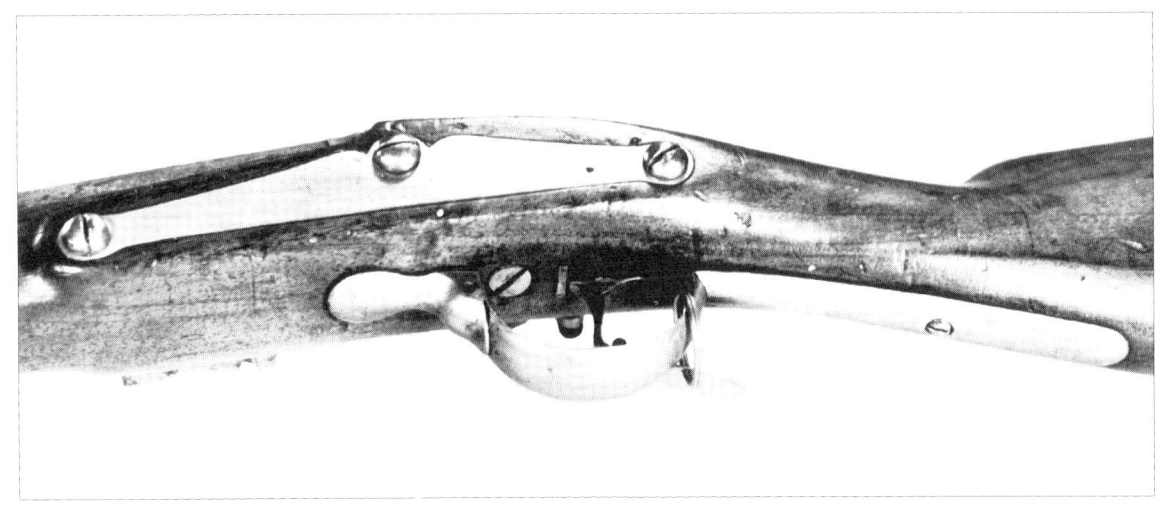

**3.MM ENGLISH INFANTRY MUSKET**  Circa 1710–1714

This gun is more substantial than the two preceding examples and more representative of England's better issued arms during the War of the Spanish Succession (1702–1713). Its forend extends to the muzzle of a 46", .75 caliber barrel (thus still restricted to a plug bayonet), and the butt stock does not yet incorporate the emerging handrail form. The straight three-screw flat doglock includes a typical notched ring-cock, bridleless yet faceted flash pan, squared frizzen top, and a frizzen spring leaf finial. Its tail is marked "R WOLLDRIDG" (Richard Wooldridge at the Tower Armory) and "10" (that is, manufactured in 1710). A "crown / AR" under the pan, as well as "AR / crown / crossed scepters" barrel proofs indicate a government-issued musket during Queen Anne's reign (1702–1714). Other period features include: a flat nailed butt plate, the trigger guard's rounded front terminal, a triangular side plate, a bottom screw to hold the barrel tang (no trigger plate), and only two pipes for the wooden rammer (tail pipe omitted). (Note: the top view shown is from a later arm with top screws now holding the barrel tang and butt tang.)

| | | | |
|---|---|---|---|
| Length: 61-1/2" | Lock: 7-3/8" X 1-1/4" | Butt Tang: 2-7/8" | Furniture: Brass |
| Barrel: 45-7/8", .78 cal. | Trigger Guard: 9-3/16" | Weight: 9.0 lbs. | |

**Former Jac Weller Collection**

Chapter 3: Smoothbore Shoulder Arms   53

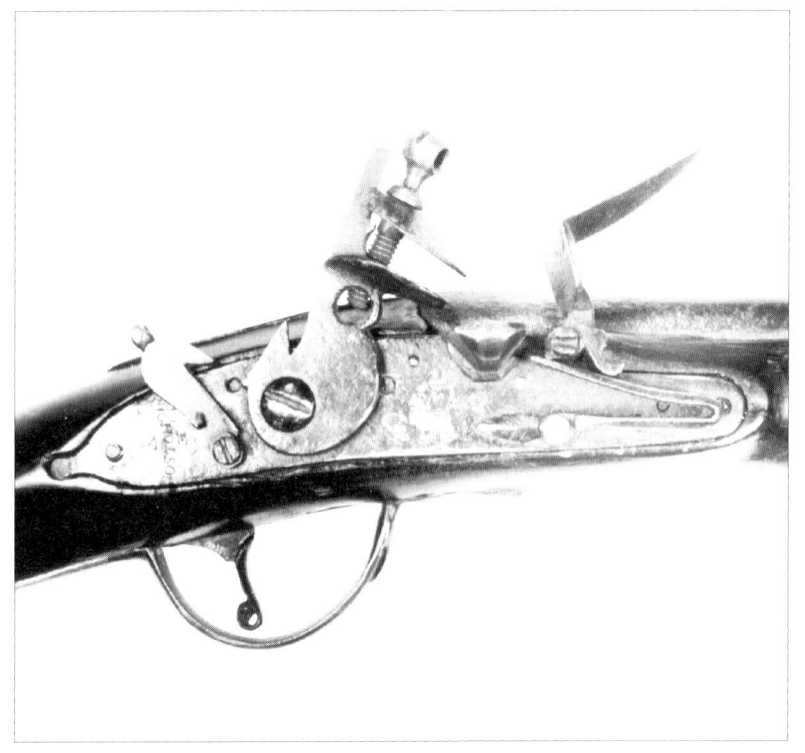

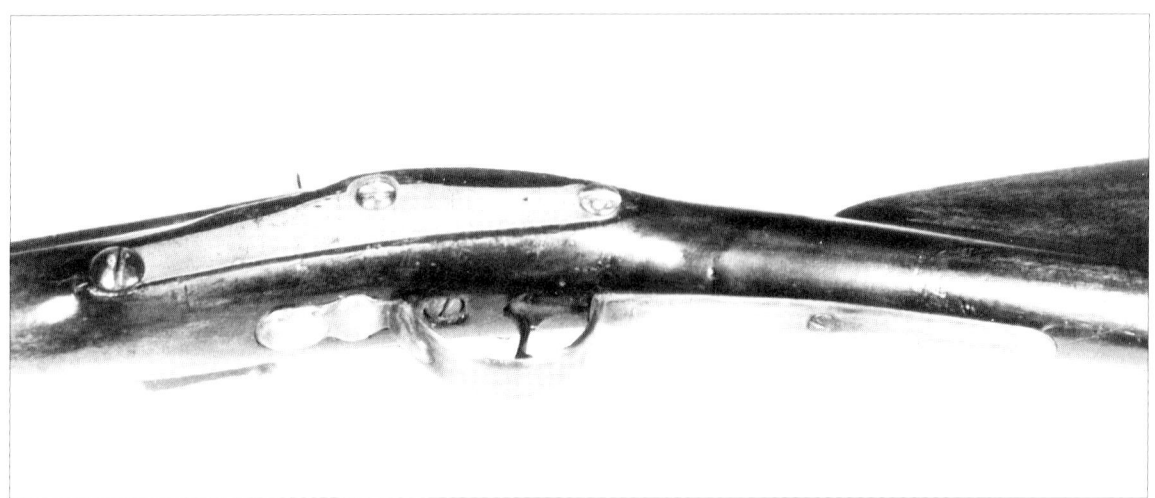

**4.MM ENGLISH INFANTRY MUSKET**                                                                                **Circa 1712–1720**

Continuing evolution of British land arms in this period is further evident here. Like the preceding example, this pattern mounts a straight flat three-screw government-proofed doglock, a nailed butt plate (lobed tang), rounded trigger guard terminal, a bottom screw retaining the tang of a 46" pinned barrel and a flat triangular side plate, but without an escutcheon, raised border carving or sling swivels. Note however that the walnut stock now includes a handrail butt pattern with a more pointed toe and three sheet-brass ramrod pipes for a brass tipped wooden rammer. The forend is cut back 3-1/4 inches to mount a socket bayonet (top stud). On the lock's tail is engraved "E NICHOLSON / 8," identifying its maker, Edward Nicholson of London, and the date of manufacture, 1708. Crown marks above Queen Anne's "AR" cypher and a broad arrow (government ownership) appear under the flash pan. The breech has two Tower "AR" proofs and Nicholson's stamp, "EN," between them.

| | | | |
|---|---|---|---|
| Length: 61-3/8" | Lock: 7-3/8" X 1-1/4" | Butt Tang: 3-3/4" | Furniture: Brass |
| Barrel: 45-7/8", .79 cal. | Trigger Guard: 11" | Side Plate: 7-1/8" | Weight: 9.6 lbs. |

**Author's Collection**

*54  Chapter 3: Smoothbore Shoulder Arms*

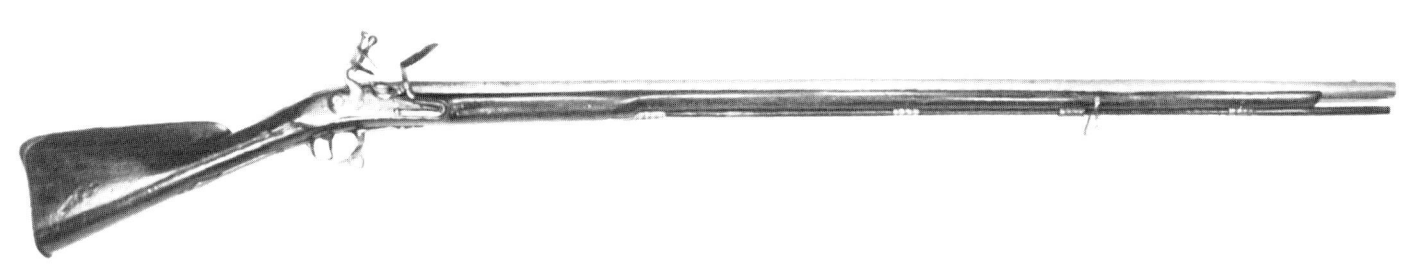

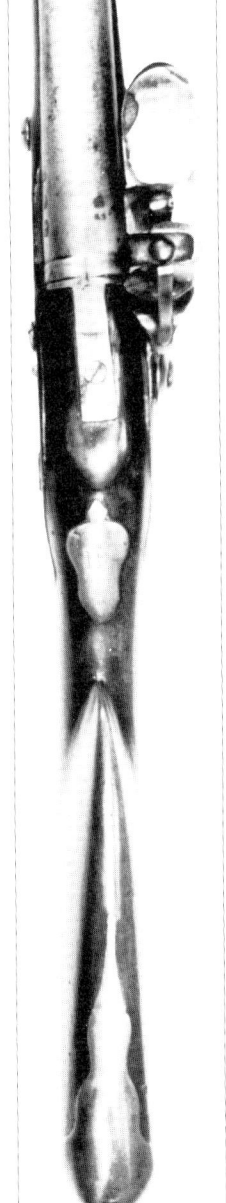

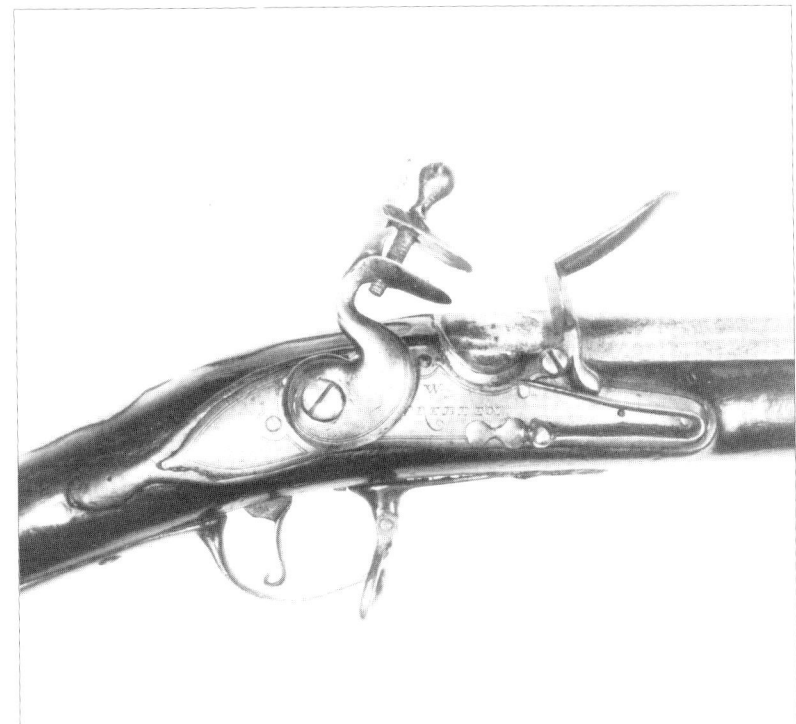

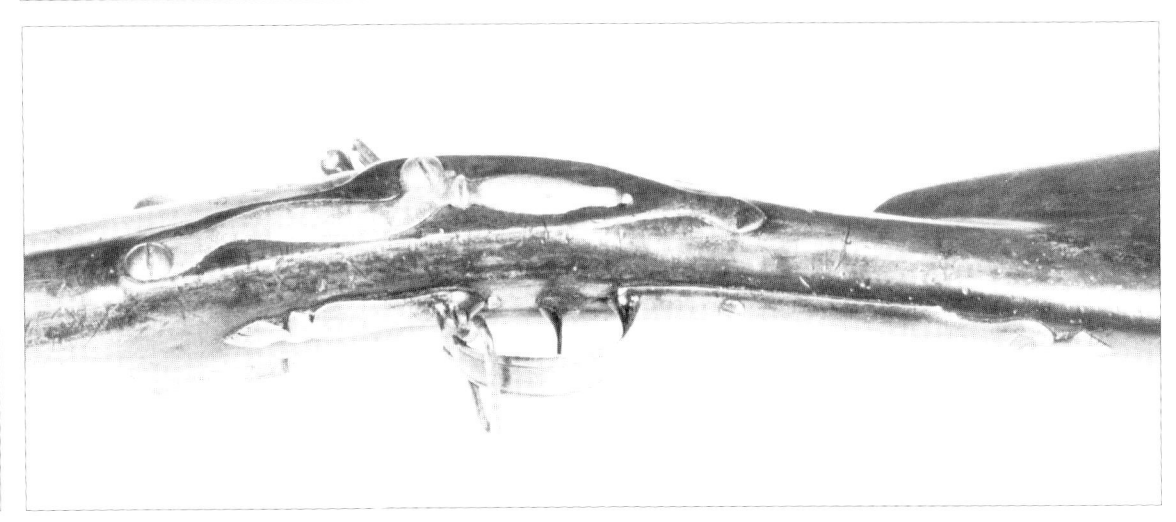

**5.MM ENGLISH INFANTRY MUSKET**                                                                                        **Circa 1715**

The Dutch influence in Britain's developing musket pattern is evident in this private contract iron-mounted musket, including: a new two-screw rounded banana-curved lock having a gooseneck cock and double incised border lines; a convex side plate with a tail; bulbous raised stock carving behind the lock, side plate and barrel tang; a double-pointed trigger guard incorporating two recessed lines (Germanic) in the bow; a long bulging 5-3/4" butt tang; and a shield-like escutcheon. Four baluster sheet-iron thimbles hold a wooden rammer. The standard round 46" barrel has a .75 caliber bore (which would increase from wear and powder fouling erosion). Notice that the frizzen spring now extends forward to cover the side screw tip and is secured by an inside screw next to a bulbous finial. Sling swivels have also been added. The private contract maker is identified under the lock's rounded pan, "W (William) PREDDEN," and by his overlapped "WP" stamp above two 1702-type London Gunmakers Company proofs at the breech. Regimental markings, "EARLE OF DUNMORE" (3rd Rgt. of Foot Guards) and a large "Crown / GR" (George I, 1714–1727), appear on the barrel. The escutcheon is engraved "18."

| | | | |
|---|---|---|---|
| Length: 62" | Lock: 6-1/4" X 1-3/8" | Butt Tang: 5-3/4" | Furniture: Iron |
| Barrel: 45-3/4", .77 cal. | Trigger Guard: 11-1/2" | Side Plate: 6-1/2" | Weight: 9.3 lbs. |

**Author's Collection**

*Chapter 3: Smoothbore Shoulder Arms*     55

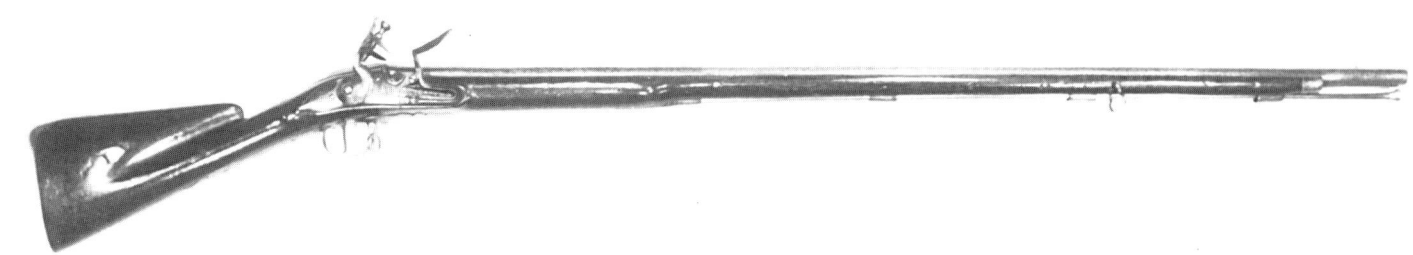

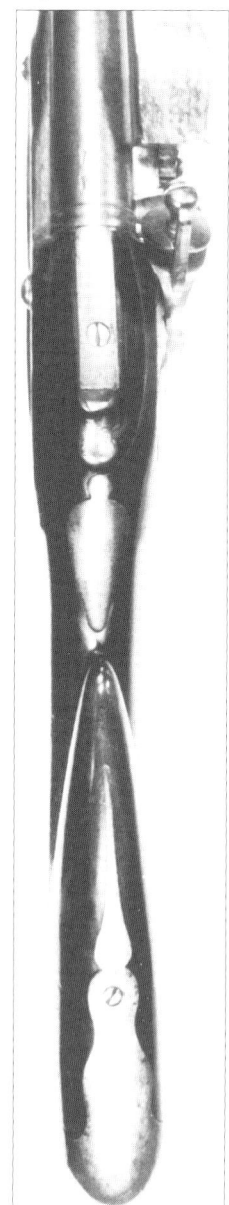

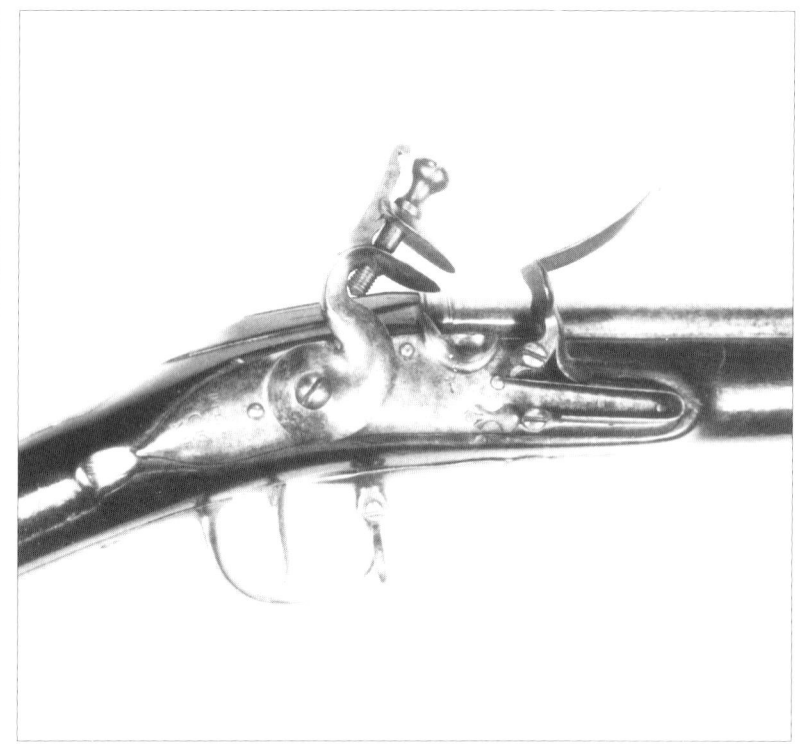

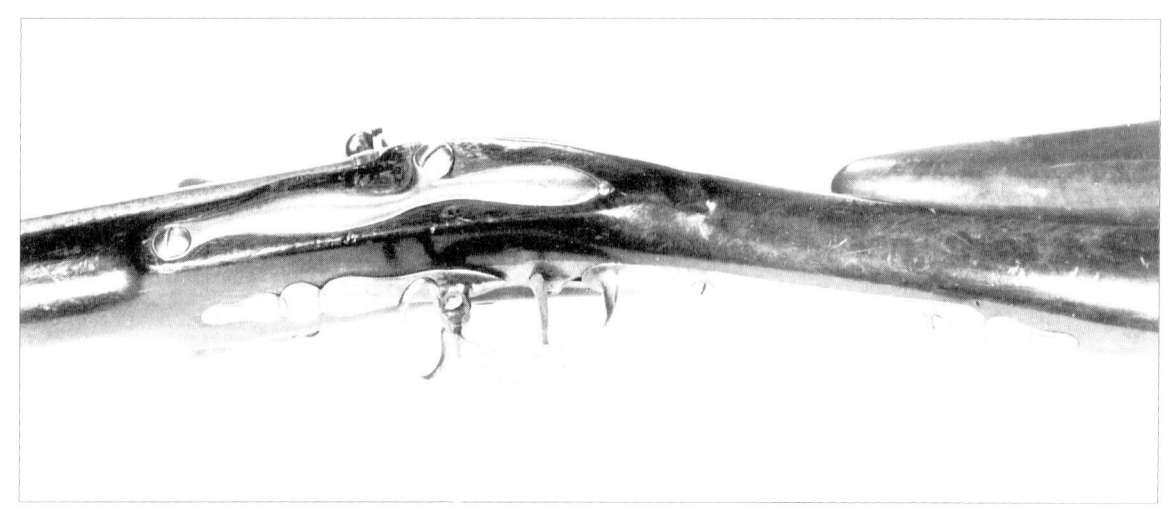

**6.MM ENGLISH INFANTRY MUSKET**                                                                                                **Circa 1720–1728**

Although the colonels jealously clung to their control over regimental arms, the advance toward a final Long Land Pattern continues in this iron-furniture musket from Col. Hawley's (33rd) Regiment in the 1720s. The bulbous-ended trigger guard, long bulging butt tang, rounded banana lock and raised walnut stock carving bordering the lock and side plate still evidence a strong Dutch influence, but the more graceful side plate, shield escutcheon, "beaver-tail" at the barrel tang, baluster breech ring, stock swelling opposite the tail pipe, three-fingered frizzen spring finial and sling swivels testify to the evolving forces at work. The lock still lacks an exterior bridle but mounts a cock with a notched rectangular upper post and a wraparound top jaw. The tail is marked by the maker, "WILSON" (London), above "C 10" (10th company) and "N 21" (rack number 21). The colonel's name, "HAWLEY," appears on the barrel, while a three-pointed crown over "T" is stamped on the lock plate (under the pan), the barrel tang and twice at the breech. A steel rammer and flat iron nose cap may have been part of an innovative period in the mid-1720s when several contracts included them (see following musket).

| | | | |
|---|---|---|---|
| Length: 62" | Lock: 7" X 1-1/4" | Butt Tang: 7-3/4" | Furniture: Iron |
| Barrel: 46", .75 cal. | Trigger Guard: 12-1/4" | Side Plate: 6-1/4" | Weight: 10.0 lbs. |

**Robert Nittolo Collection**

*56    Chapter 3: Smoothbore Shoulder Arms*

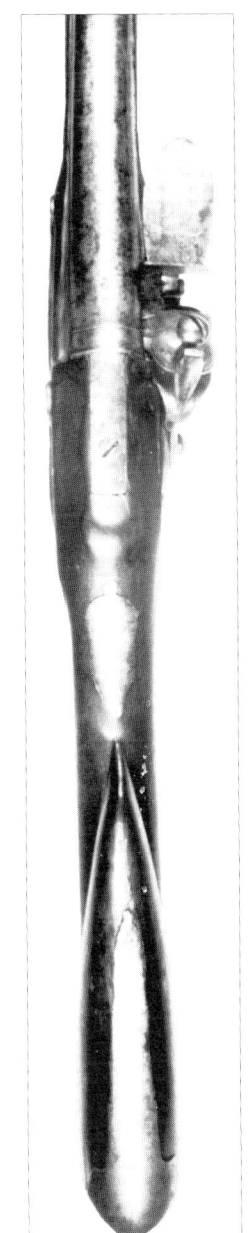

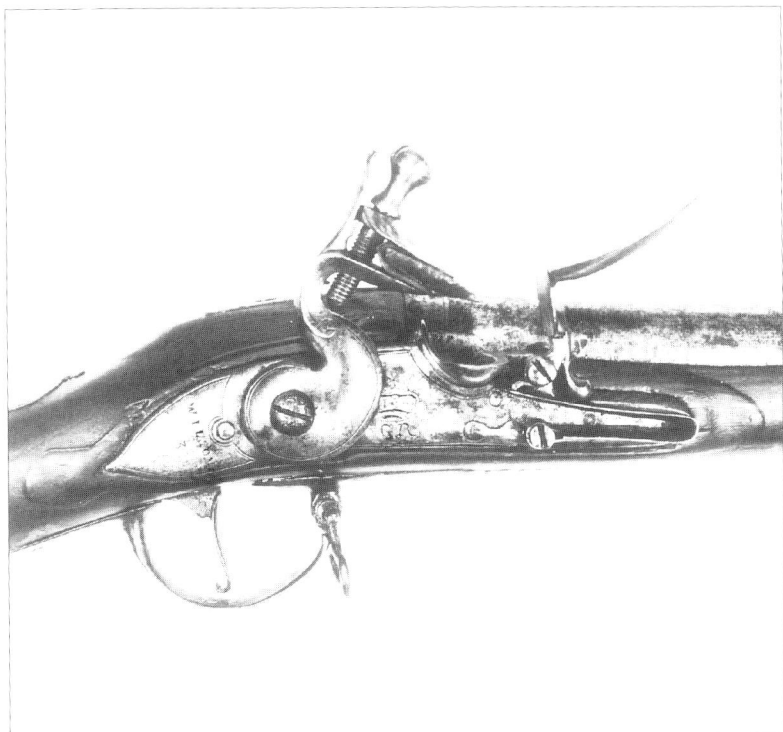

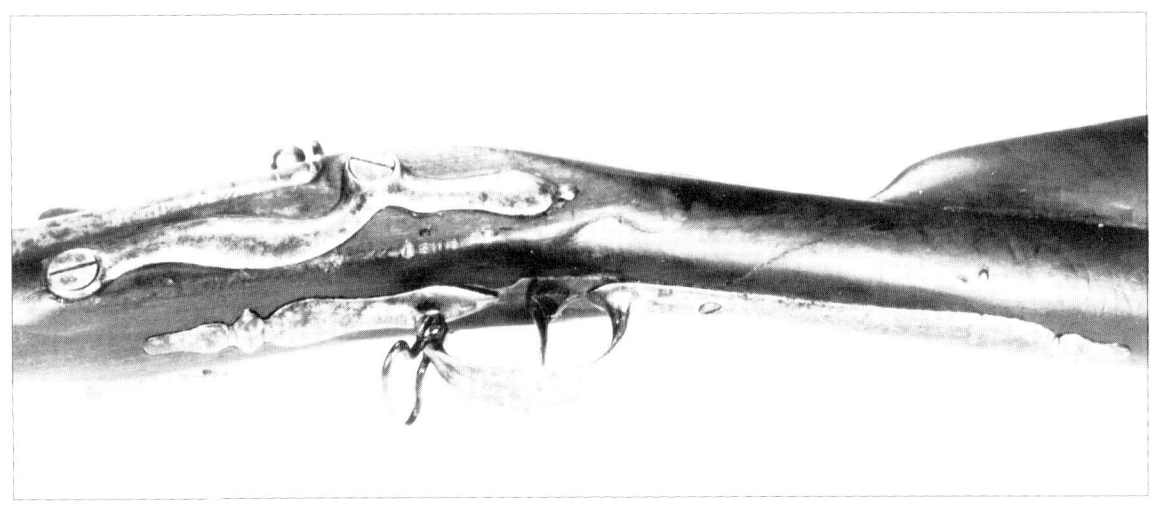

**7.MM ENGLISH INFANTRY MUSKET**                                                                     **Circa 1726**

The King's Pattern announced in 1722 led to the Long Land design finally issued in 1730 (8.MM). This musket produced by Wilson (London) for Col. Pocock's 8th or "King's Regiment" is very close to that final form but was iron-mounted (iron fittings were still in use as late as 1736). Its trigger guard with bulbous ends and incised lines in the trigger bow, as well as a rounded frizzen spring finial, are earlier features. A steel ramrod and iron nose cap are also present. Some troops in Ireland were supplied with muskets having steel rods in 1726 and it is believed that this regiment received these arms at that time. The lock is marked "WILSON" above "3" (3rd company) and "24" (the rack number) on the tail, with a crown above "GR" (King George) under the pan (but not the usual crown/broad arrow stamp denoting formal government ownership). Most regiments were known by the colonel's name until 1751 (when numerals were assigned), thus the barrel is engraved "POCOCK C 3, No 24," supplemented by two crown proofs. Notice how the final Brown Bess form is already apparent in the straight walnut butt stock with a hand rail and round wrist, the swelling behind the tail pipe, and the round 46" barrel.

Length: 61-7/8"                    lock: 6-7/8" X 1-1/4"                    Butt Tang: 6-1/4"                    Furniture: Iron
Barrel: 45-7/8", .77 cal.            Trigger Guard: 12-1/8"                 Side Plate: 6-1/4"                   Weight: 9.0 lbs.

**West Point Museum Collection**

*Chapter 3: Smoothbore Shoulder Arms*     **57**

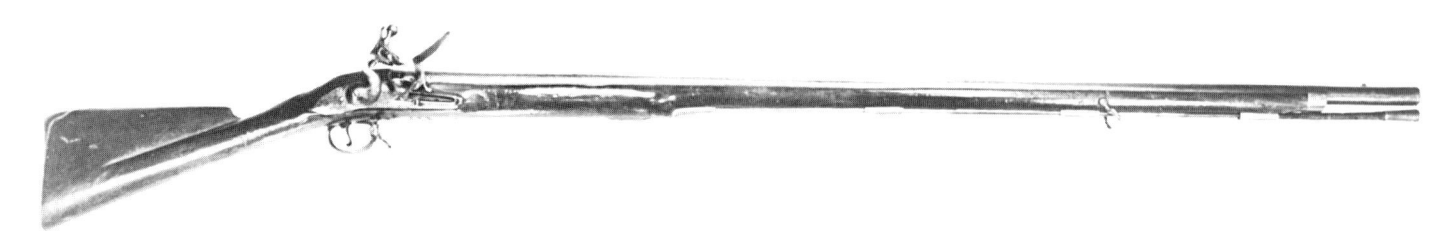

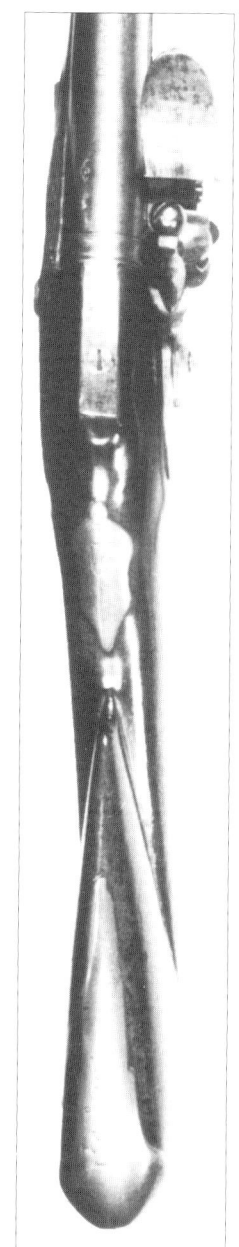

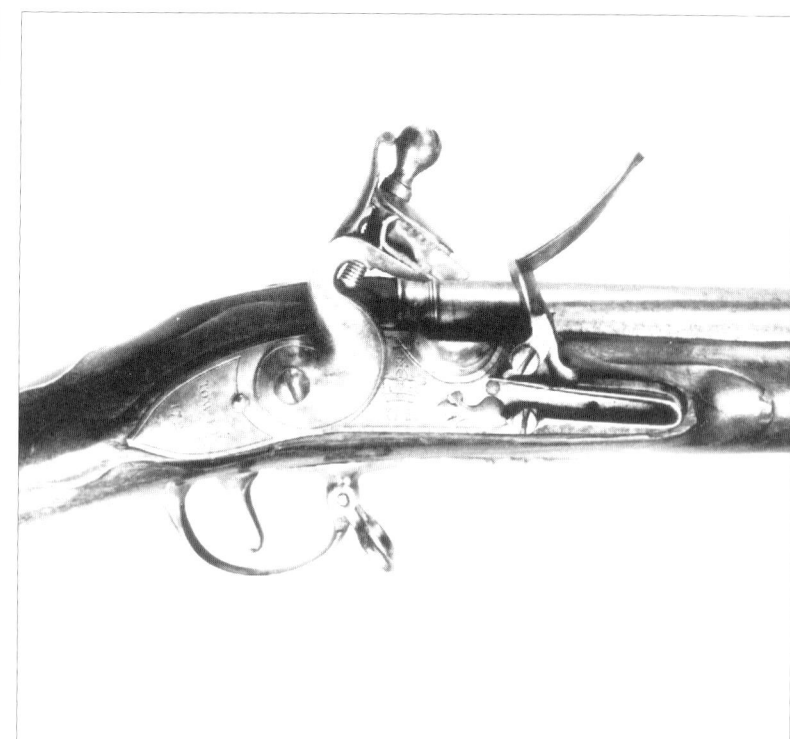

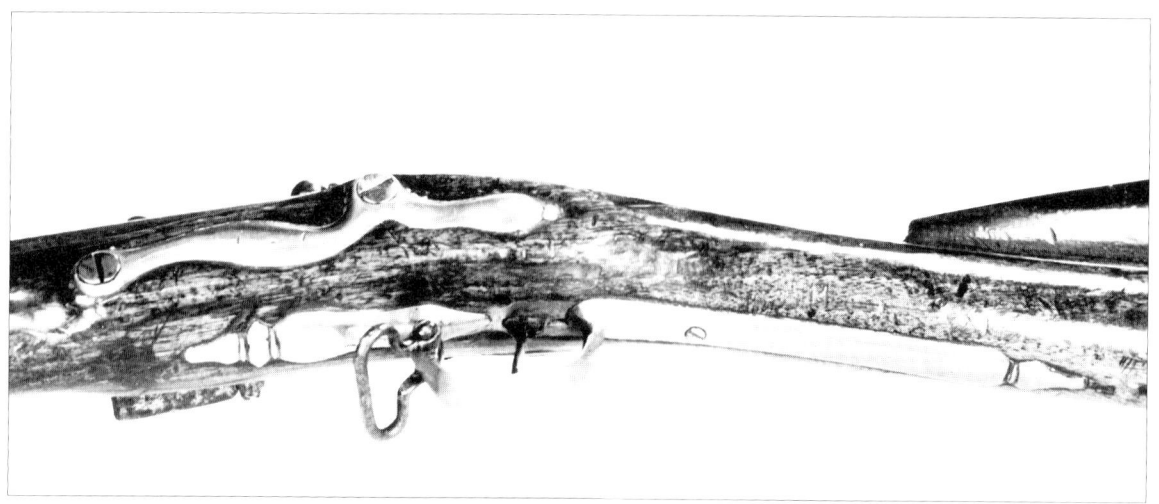

**8.MM ENGLISH LONG LAND PATTERN 1730 MUSKET**                                                                           Circa 1728–1730

Following the 1722 submission of a new King's Pattern, full production commenced in 1728. This first Long Land Brown Bess pattern was issued in 1730. Its new standard form mounted brass furniture, a rounded two-screw banana lock (no exterior bridle), a gooseneck cock with a flat-backed upper post, a three-fingered claw frizzen spring finial, a long three-step butt tang (six inches), a shield escutcheon (held by a screw from below), an old Dutch-style lobed trigger guard, a rounded side plate with a tail, four ramrod pipes for a wooden rammer, and a pinned 46", .75 caliber, round barrel (top bayonet stud). The black walnut stock included a handrail butt, raised undulated carving around the barrel tang, bulbous carving surrounding the lock and side plate, and a swelling behind the tail pipe ("hand hold"). The original pattern lacked a nose cap (often added by the regiments). The lock plate is marked "TOWER 1728" (Tower of London Armory, 1728 lock manufacture). Its breech has Tower proofs and "ROYAL WELSH" (23rd Royal Welsh Fusiliers). The inscription "Lt. Col. Waite" on the butt tang places this arm in his (2nd) company. The escutcheon reads "B / N 9."

| | | | |
|---|---|---|---|
| Length: 62-1/8" | Lock: 6-3/4" X 1-1/4" | Butt Tang: 6" | Furniture: Brass |
| Barrel: 46", .77 cal. | Trigger Guard 11-1/2" | Side Plate: 6-1/8" | Weight: 9.4 lbs. |

**George C. Neumann Collection, Valley Forge National Historical Park**

58    *Chapter 3: Smoothbore Shoulder Arms*

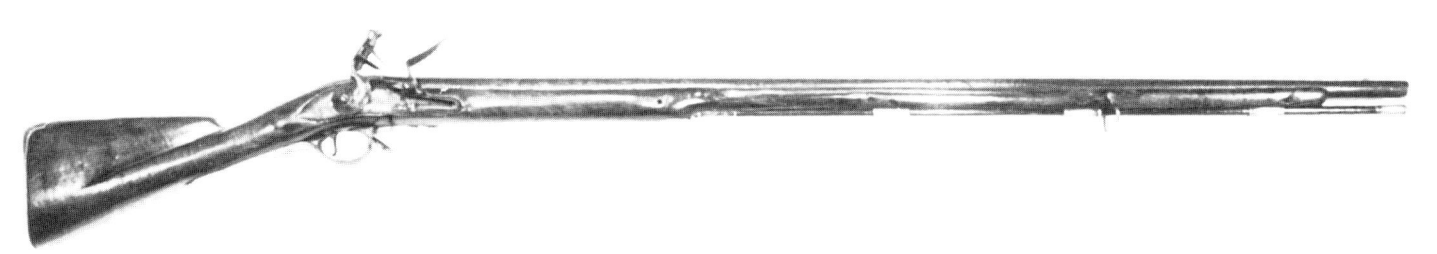

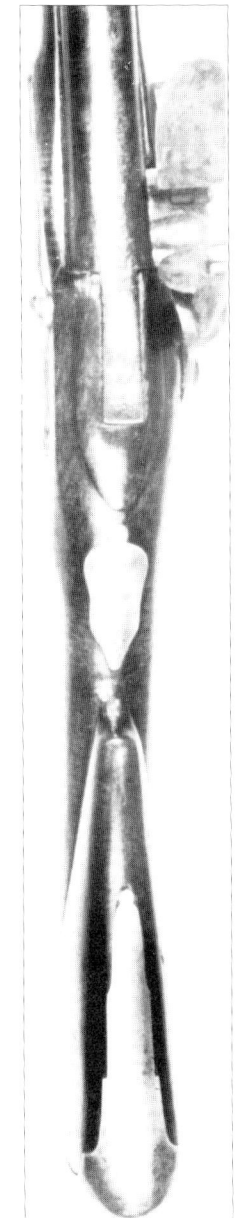

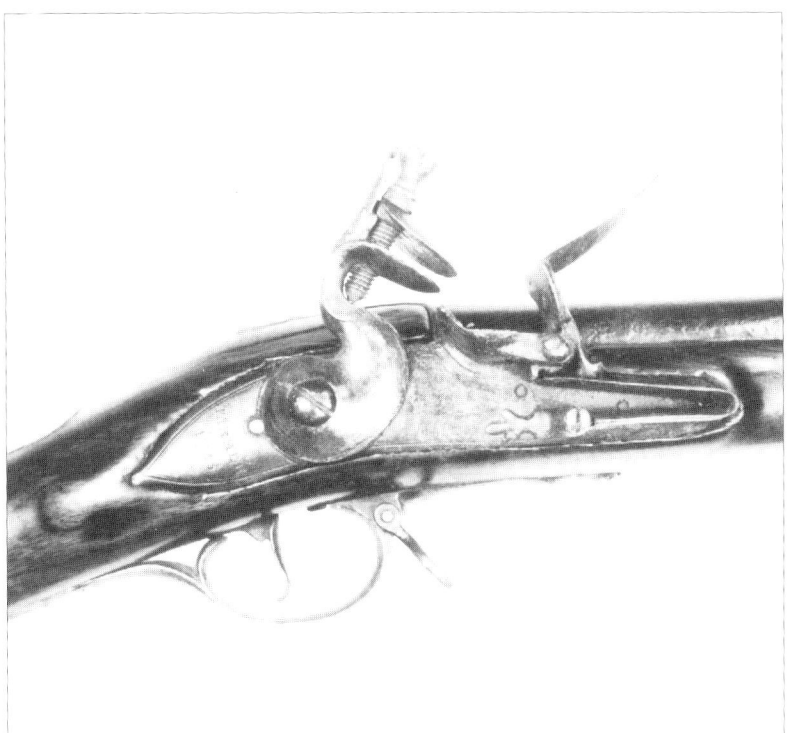

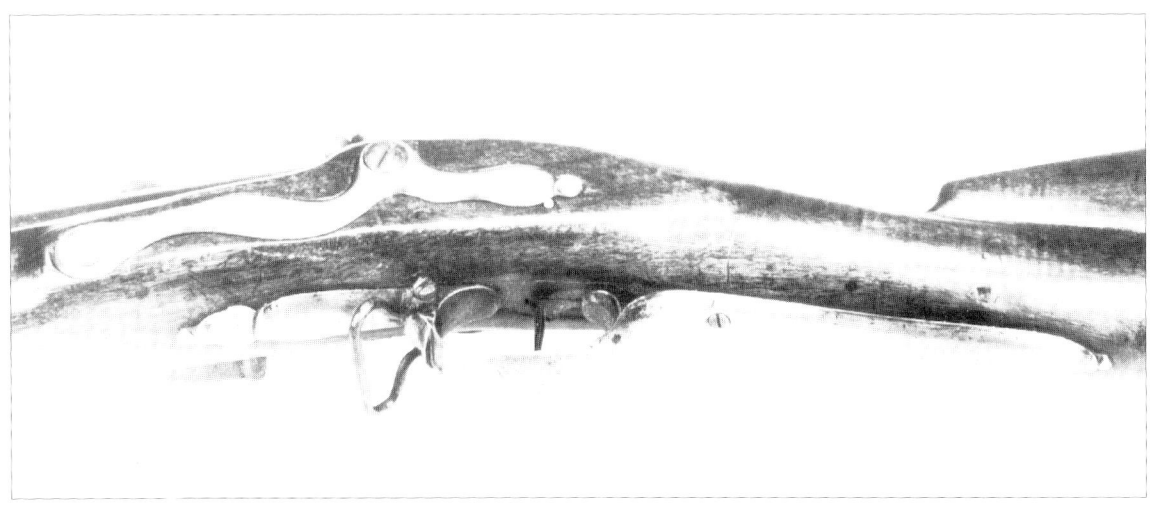

**9.MM  ENGLISH LONG LAND PATTERN 1742 MUSKET**  Circa 1745

Following the major rearming of the British army with the Long Land Pattern 1730 in 1740–1741, this updated design was adopted in 1742. It includes several changes from the previous configuration: an exterior bridle and shallower pan, reduced carving bordering its lock and side plate (although a raised beaver-tail now appears around the barrel tang), a "hazelnut" front end on the trigger guard, and a split of the trigger bow's rear post to create a forward curl. The .75 caliber, 46" round barrel remains—pinned to a black walnut stock above four equal barrel-shaped pipes for the wooden rammer (no nose cap, although often added by the regiments). The fully developed banana lock also includes a flat upper post and round top jaw on the cock, as well as a rounded top frizzen with its spring ending in three "fingers" and projecting forward to reach the side screw tip. Double engraved lines outline most of the lock plate, cock, top jaw and frizzen's forward face. The lock's tail is marked "FARMER / 1745" (the maker), while its side plate reverse shows "H" (for the brass contractor, Thomas Hollier) and a broad arrow. These Long Land Brown Bess Patterns 1730 (8.MM) and 1742 were the primary muskets for royal forces in the French and Indian War.

| | | | |
|---|---|---|---|
| Length: 61-3/4" | Lock: 6-7/8" X 1-1/4" | Butt Tang: 6" | Furniture: Brass |
| Barrel: 45-3/4", .77 cal. | Trigger Guard: 11-1/4" | Side Plate: 6-1/4" | Weight: 8.6 lbs. |

**Author's Collection**

*Chapter 3: Smoothbore Shoulder Arms*

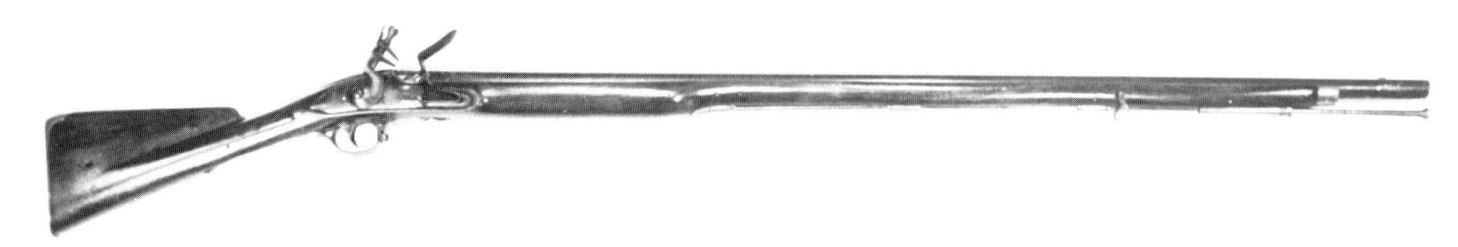

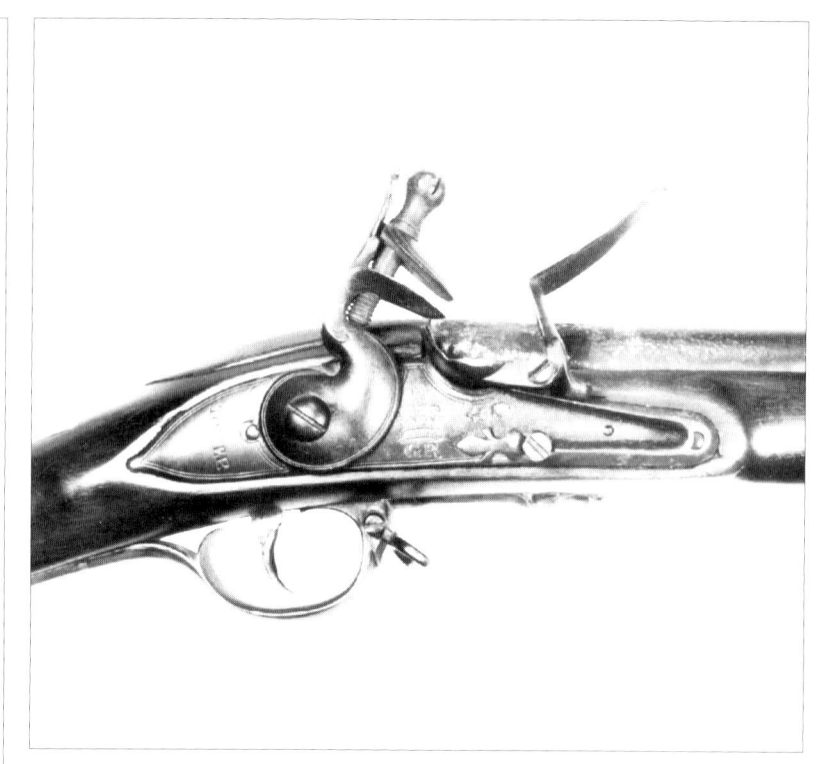

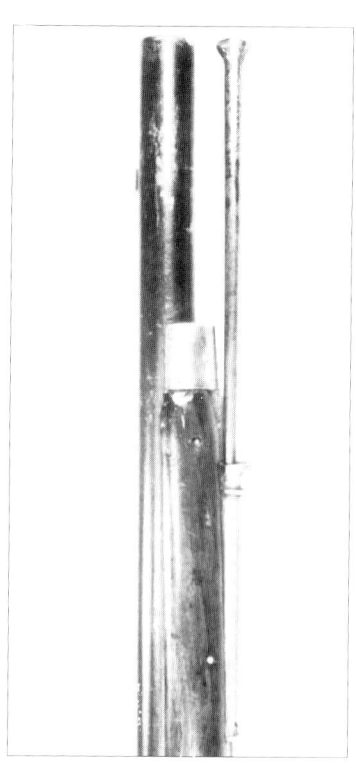

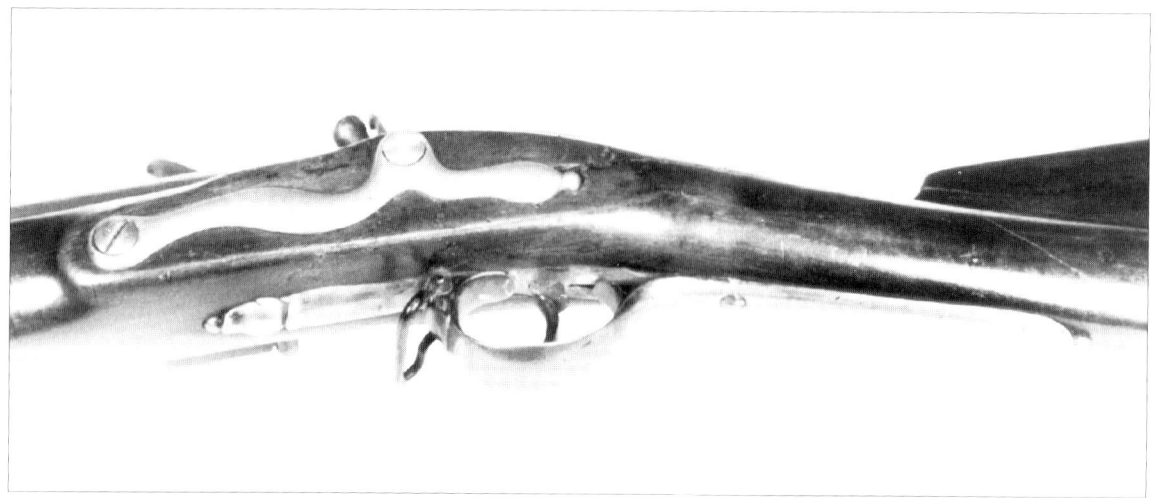

**10.MM ENGLISH LONG LAND PATTERN 1756 MUSKET**  Circa 1764

This third version of the Long Land Brown Bess retained the basic furniture from the 1742 Pattern (9.MM) but incorporated some differences: the double-bridled lock now has an almost straight bottom edge (versus the earlier banana form); a button-headed steel rammer has replaced the previous wooden rod (conversions began about 1748); the four ramrod pipes have a smaller diameter as well as a longer top pipe with a flared mouth; and the frizzen spring now ends just short of the side screw tip. A cast brass nose cap has also become a standard component. A slimmer walnut stock abandons the raised carving around both the lock and side plate in favor of a simple ridge form and reduces the hand hold swelling behind the tail pipe. Sling swivels on these Long Land muskets were broad, with a typical inside width of 1-3/4 inches (bottom swivel) and two inches (top). This example is estimated circa 1764 or later, as the maker and date of manufacture were dropped from the lock's tail in that year and replaced with "TOWER." The breech bears a maker's stamp, "RE," under a flower-like symbol. This pattern saw most of its North American service during the American Revolution.

| | | | |
|---|---|---|---|
| Length: 61-7/8" | Lock: 7" X 1-1/4" | Butt Tang: 5-3/4" | Furniture: Brass |
| Barrel: 46", .78 cal. | Trigger Guard: 11-1/4" | Side Plate: 6-1/8" | Weight: 10.5 lbs. |

**Author's Collection**

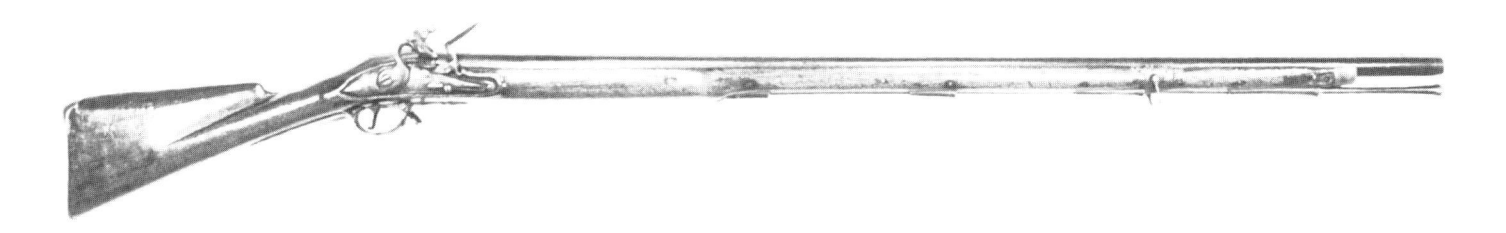

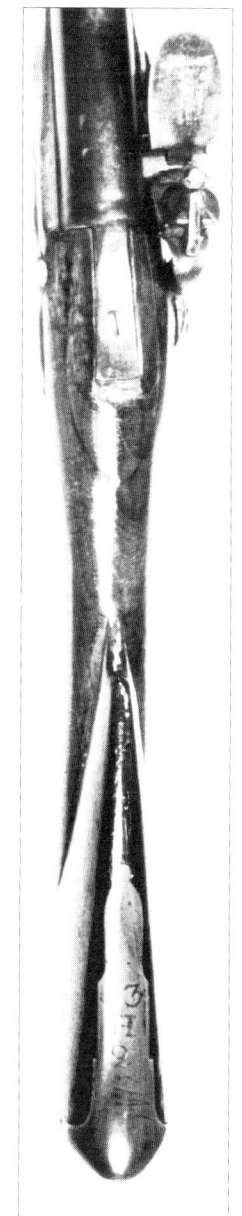

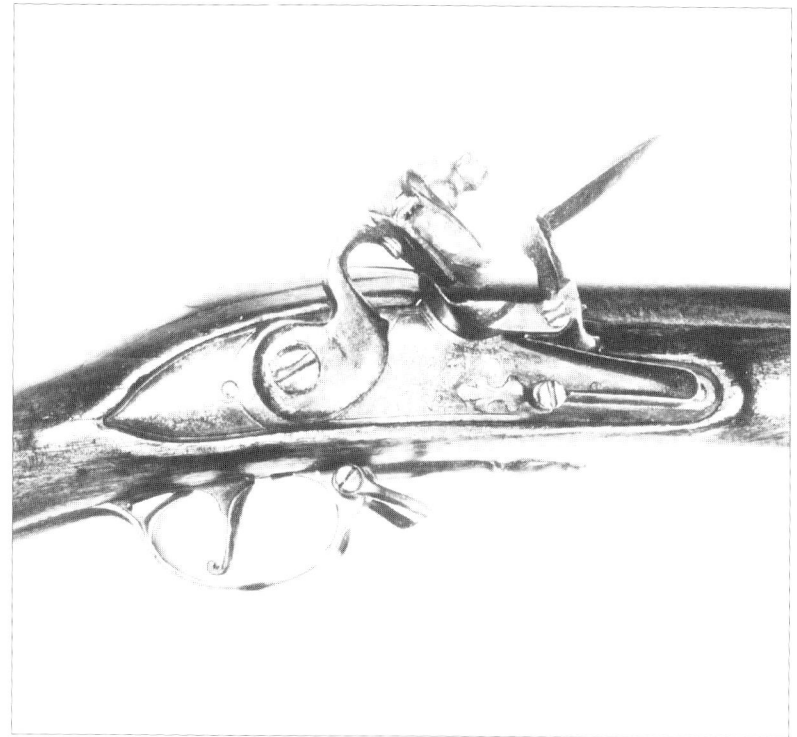

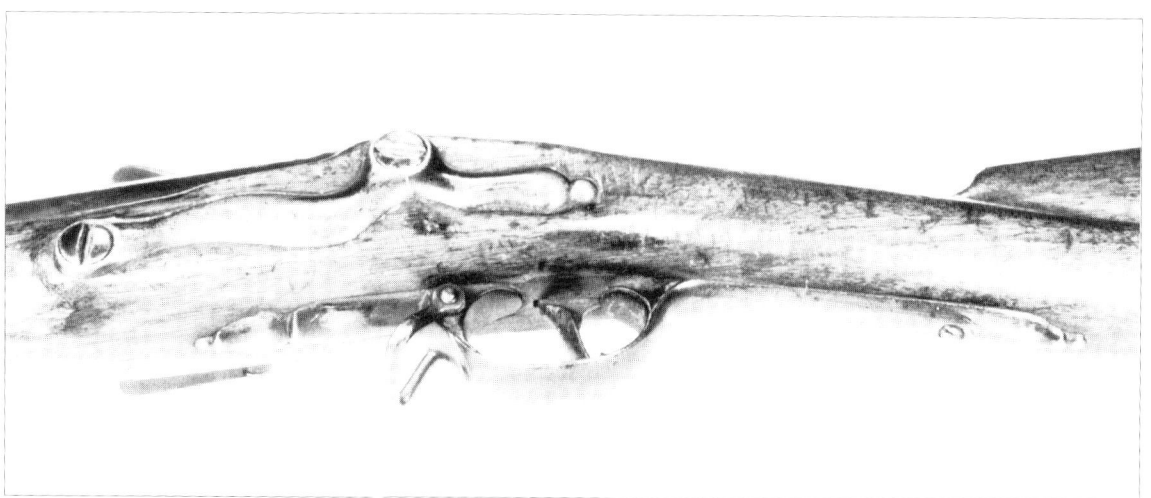

**11.MM ENGLISH LONG LAND MUSKET**                                                                           **Circa 1768**

Under wartime pressure specification variations are to be expected, and this modified Long Land Brown Bess is an example. It copies the Pattern 1756 (10.MM), but all components are proportionately scaled down in size (not cut) with the escutcheon plate omitted. The barrel is reduced from 46 inches to 43-1/2 inches; the lock from seven inches to 6-3/8 inches, etc. The objective was apparently to reduce cost. Inscriptions on the lock include the normal "crown / GR / broad arrow" plus "POWELL / 1762," a known contractor to Dublin Castle for troops in the Irish Establishment (at least two similar arms are known—"F LORD / 1762" and "I TRULOCK 1762"). All three muskets have three rows of butt tang marks, in this case, "53 / H / 2." The "53" identifies the 53rd Regiment (part of Burgoyne's 1777 invasion force); "H" places the arm in the "H" or 8th company under Capt. Baird, which was captured at Fort Ticonderoga during Col. John Brown's raid on Sept. 18, 1777; "2" is the gun's rack number. Later repairs to the captured weapon by the patriots include the crude cock and three flared copper tube rammer thimbles (re: Ahearn, bib. 165-6).

Length: 59-5/8"            Lock: 6-3/8" X 1-1/4"            Butt Tang: 5-3/4"            Furniture: Brass
Barrel: 43-1/2", .79 cal.        Trigger Guard: 9-3/8"            Side Plate: 5-5/8"            Weight: 9.7 lbs.
**Bill Ahearn Collection**

*Chapter 3: Smoothbore Shoulder Arms*

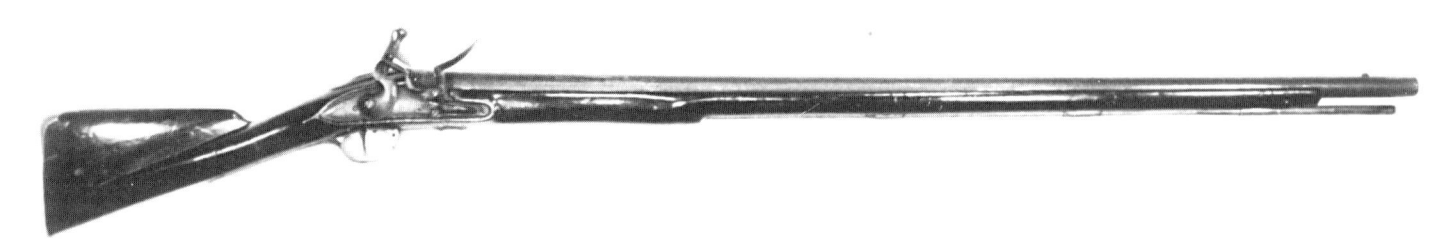

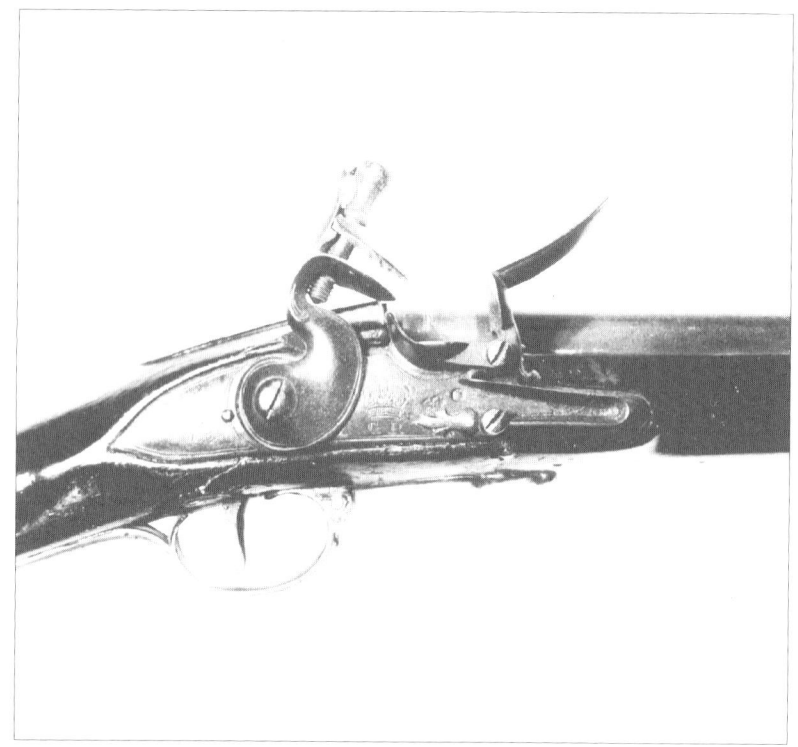

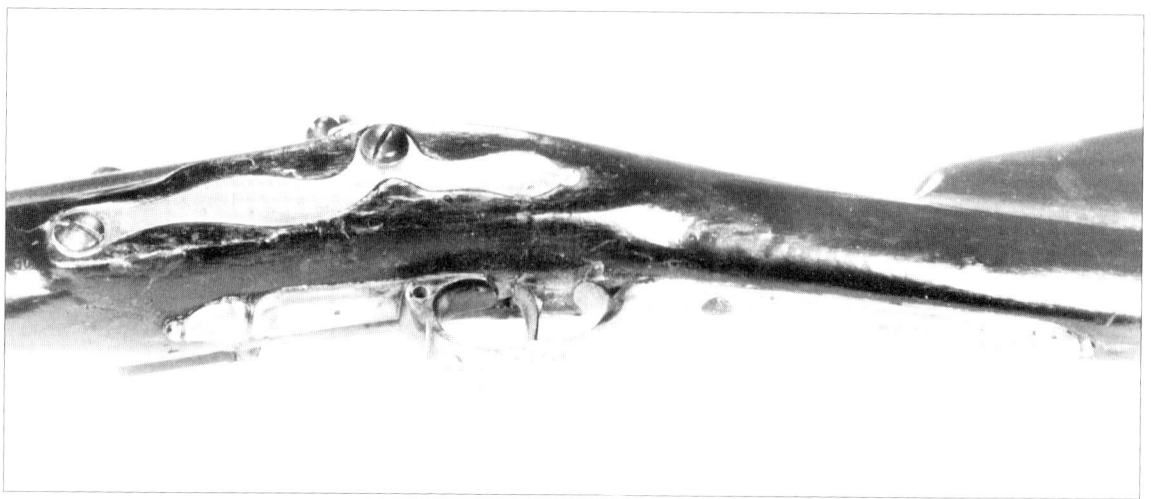

**12.MM ENGLISH MARINE OR MILITIA PATTERN 1756 MUSKET**  Circa 1758

To help answer demands from the French and Indian War, a lower cost 42" barreled musket was approved in 1756 for issue to the marines and the domestic militia. It included a wooden ramrod and three equal barrel-shaped thimbles, yet lacked a tail pipe and nose cap. The escutcheon was also eliminated. While the side plate retained the outline of the established Long Land patterns, it was now flat instead of convex. Perhaps the most apparent brass furniture change was the shortening of its butt tang and the use of a visible wood screw to anchor it from the top (versus the traditional side pin). This straight-edged double-bridled lock includes the usual "crown / GR" and broad arrow (signifying government ownership) markings, plus the maker and date of manufacture, "EDGE / 1758." "ABD / 28" appears on the butt tang. An ordnance storekeeper's stamp remains in the outboard buttstock. Its 42" barrel bears two Tower proofs and has a top stud for a regulation four-inch bayonet socket.

| | | | |
|---|---|---|---|
| Length: 57-3/4" | Lock: 7" X 1-1/4" | Butt Tang: 3-3/4" | Furniture: Brass |
| Barrel: 41-3/4", .75 cal. | Trigger Guard: 11-1/4" | Side Plate: 6-1/4" | Weight: 9.6 lbs. |

**Robert Nittolo Collection**

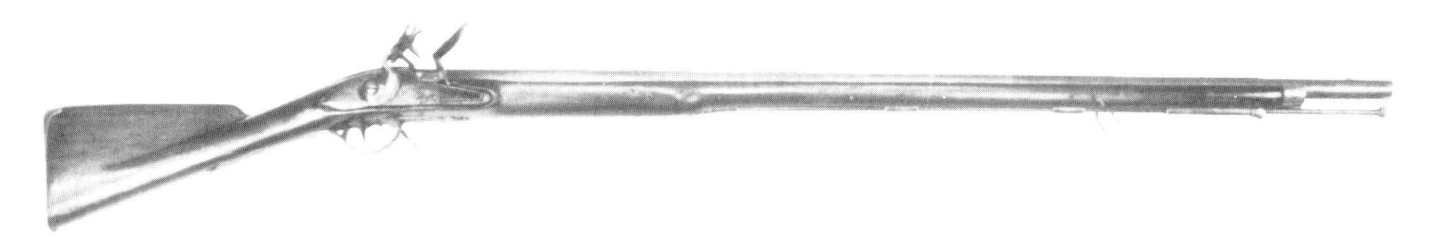

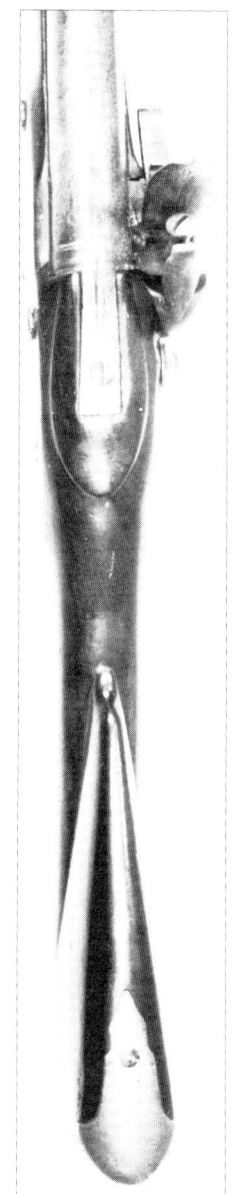

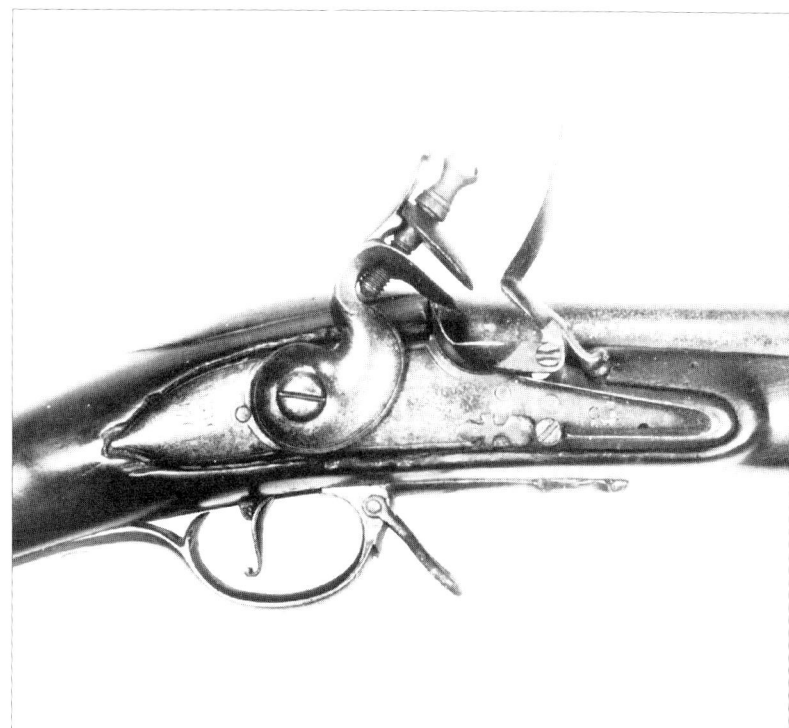

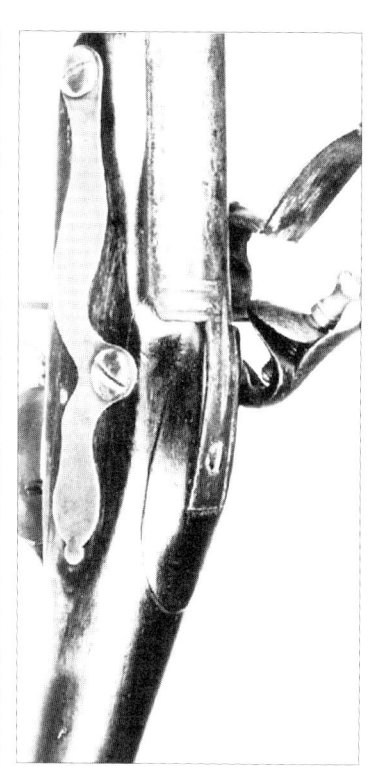

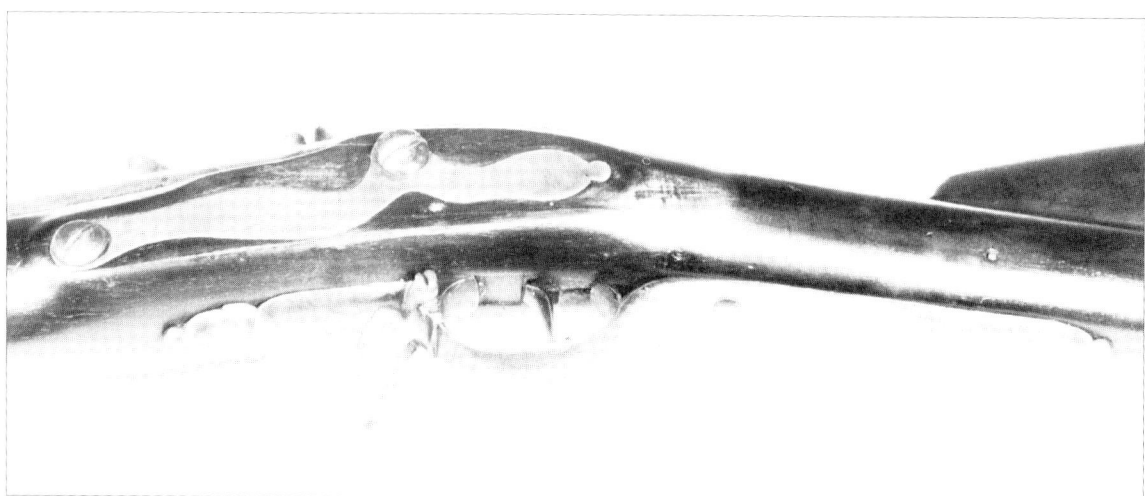

### 13.MM ENGLISH MARINE OR MILITIA PATTERN 1759 MUSKET                                                    Circa 1761

This improved Marine or Militia design in 1759 retained the basics of the original pattern (vs. 12.MM) with its 42" barrel, flat side plate, screw anchored short butt tang and absence of an escutcheon. But the rammer was now of steel (button head) and a bottom ramrod thimble, long flared upper pipe and nose cap were also added. Typical lock markings include the "crown / GR / broad arrow," as well as its maker and date, "GRICE / 1761" (William Grice, Birmingham). Inside the lock plate are the stamps "WG" and a crown above "2" (the inspector's or viewer's mark). Tower proofs and "IC" (under an asterisk) are on the barrel breech. Apparently this improved pattern was not generally distributed to the marines until circa 1768. Production ceased in 1776 although the arms were issued throughout America's War for Independence. This barrel length measures 41-1/2 inches versus a specified 42 inches, illustrating the constant filing down of musket muzzles as the steel rammer's action wore the edges sharp (which cut the hand while ramming).

| | | | |
|---|---|---|---|
| Length: 57-3/8" | Lock: 7" X 1-1/4" | Butt Tang: 3-3/4" | Furniture: Brass |
| Barrel: 41-1/2", .79 cal. | Trigger Guard: 11-1/4" | Side Plate: 6-3/8" | Weight: 10.0 lbs. |

**Author's Collection**

Chapter 3: Smoothbore Shoulder Arms   63

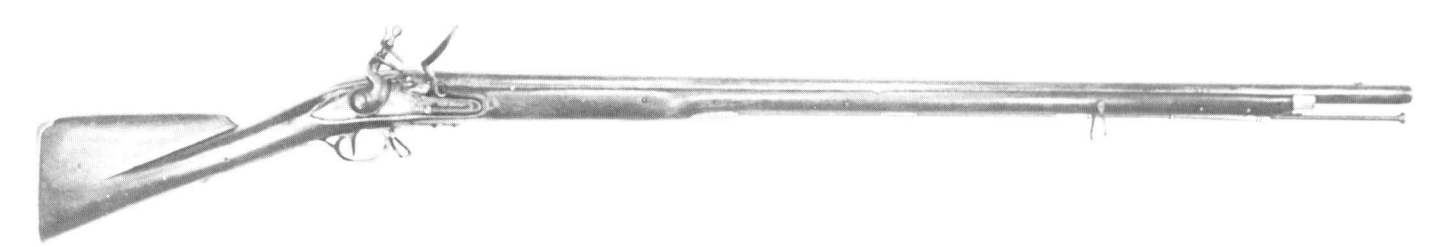

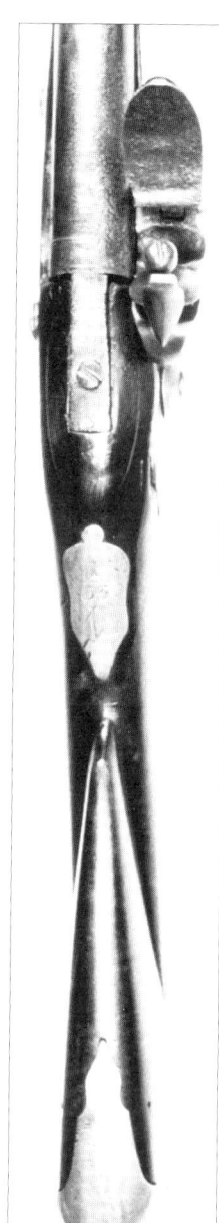

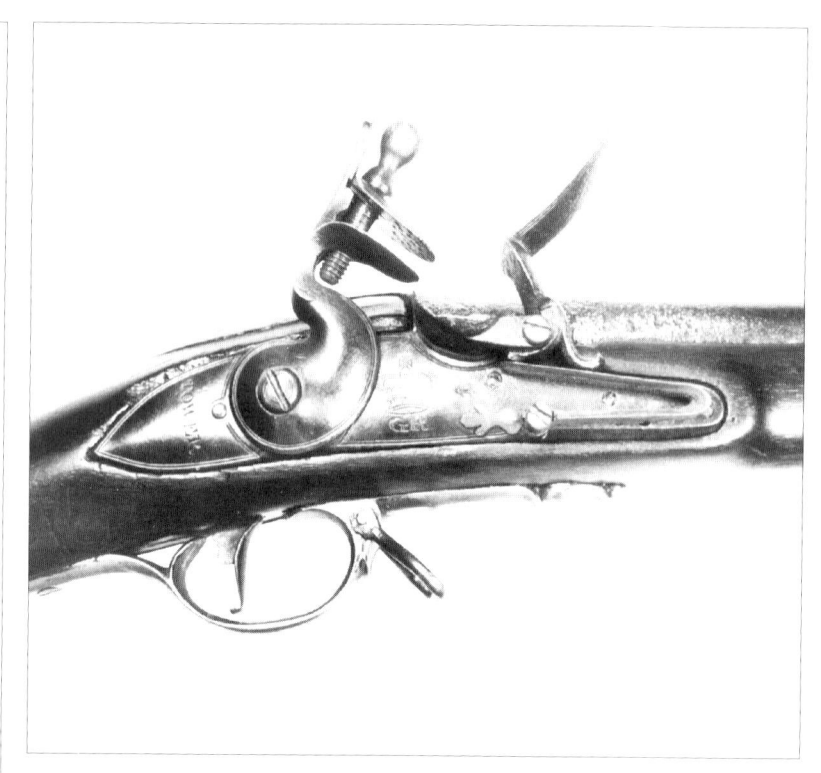

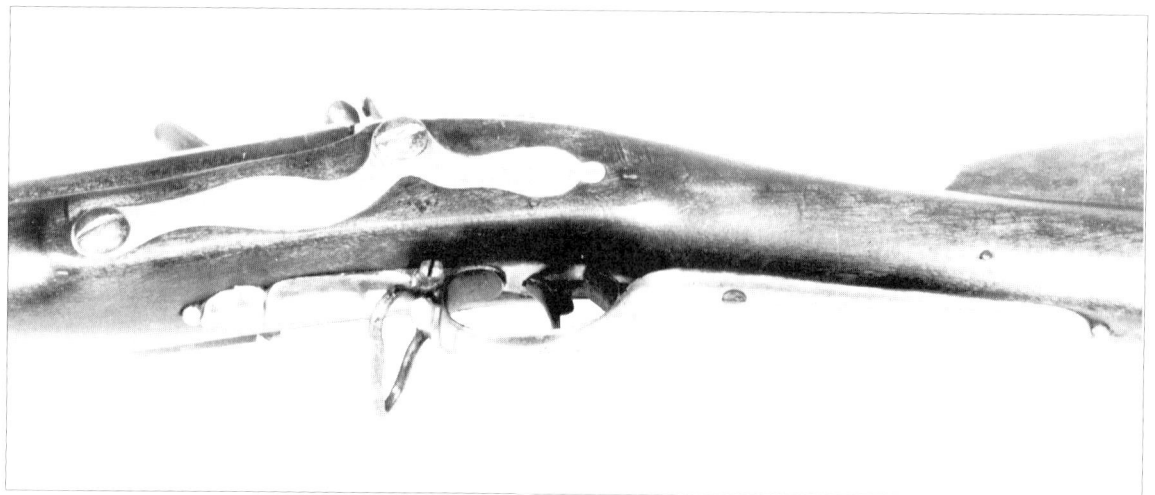

**14.MM ENGLISH SHORT LAND PATTERN 1768 MUSKET**            Circa 1769

Primarily because of the ease and mobility of the shortened Marine or Militia musket (12.MM, 13.MM), this 42" barreled pattern was adopted in 1768 for all infantry regiments and issued beginning in 1769. Compared to the then-current Long Land configuration (10.MM), which remained in limited production until 1790, this new design retained the straight double-bridled lock, four ramrod pipes (including the long flared top one), the cast nose cap, a steel rammer, the escutcheon, a hazelnut trigger guard, plus the established walnut stock form. The innovations (many copied from the Marine or Militia design) were a 42" (.75 caliber) barrel, a flat side plate, a shortened butt tang (no top screw), and reduced stock carving around the lock and side plate. It continued the regulation four-inch socket bayonet (17" blade). "TOWER" stamped on the lock's tail reflects the decision to drop a maker's name and date in 1764. This breech is marked "71 REGT 1T B," for Fraser's 71st (Highland) Regiment of Foot (1775-1783), which numbered 2,340 troops in two battalions and served in more battlefield engagements during the American Revolution than any other British unit.

| | | | |
|---|---|---|---|
| Length: 58" | Lock: 7" X 1-1/4" | Butt Tang: 3-3/4" | Furniture: Brass |
| Barrel: 42", .77 cal. | Trigger Guard: 11-1/4" | Side Plate: 6-1/4" | Weight: 10.2 lbs. |

**Author's Collection**

64    *Chapter 3: Smoothbore Shoulder Arms*

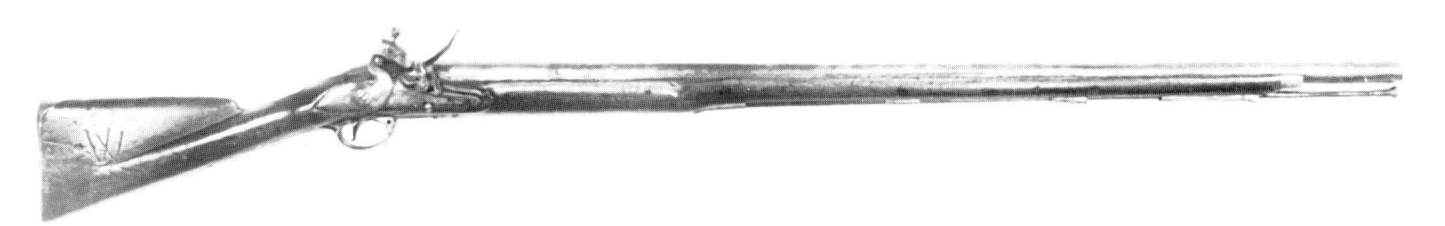

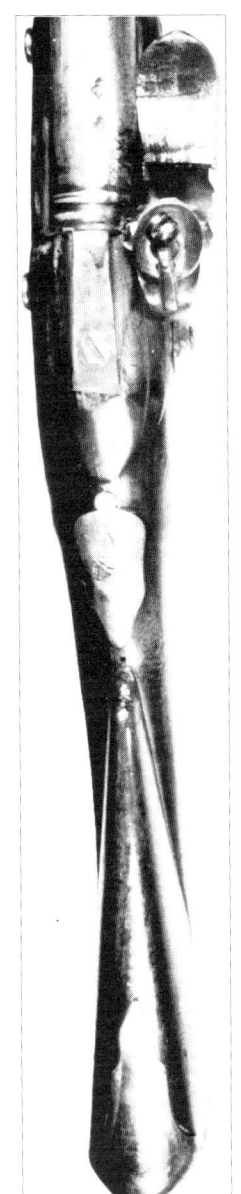

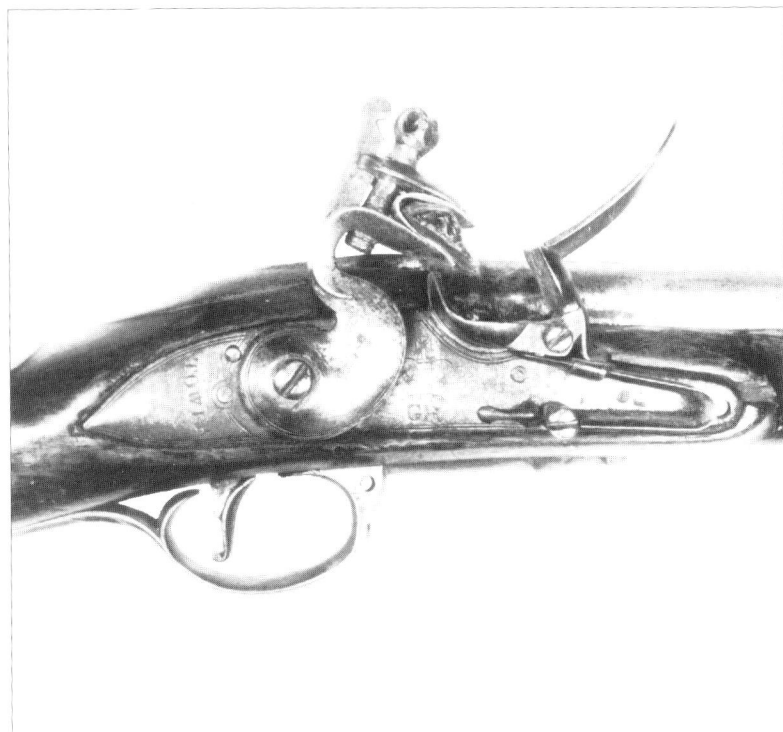

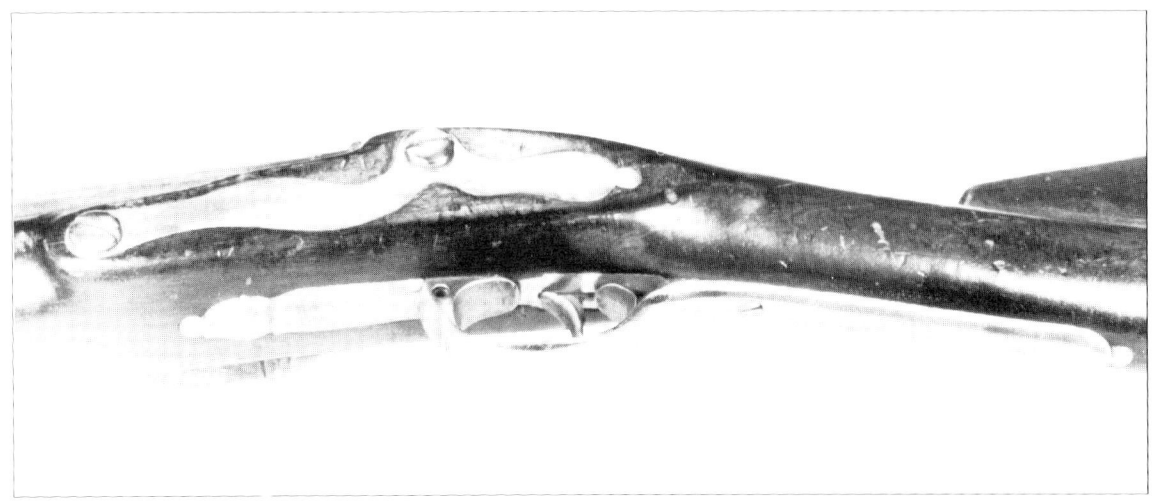

**15.MM ENGLISH SHORT LAND PATTERN 1777 MUSKET**  Circa 1777

As the realities of war developed, changes occurred in the Short Land Musket. By 1777 two basic alterations were acknowledged: a revised lock, and a reshaped ramrod pipe. The demand for locks forced acceptance of a less expensive design already in production by non-government contractors—including longarms for the East India Company's private army (19.MM). In this new lock, Lock II, two screw ends instead of one appear behind the cock, the cock's upper post is no longer flat but a rectangular shape with a notched forward edge (primary difference from the India Pattern), the top jaw is now oval (previously round) and projects around both sides of the post, its slotted jaw screw adds a lateral hole, the frizzen spring acquires a lobed finial (previously three fingers) and ends well short of the side screw tip, and engraved borders are dropped from the top jaw and frizzen's forward face. The second ramrod pipe ("Pratt's Improvement," already in limited use) slopes forward to an enlarged mouth (see 18.MM). This barrel is marked "QUEENS RANGERS," an outstanding Loyalist regiment under Col. John Simcoe during the American Revolution.

| | | | |
|---|---|---|---|
| Length: 58" | Lock: 6-7/8" X 1-1/4" | Butt Tang: 3-3/4" | Furniture: Brass |
| Barrel: 42", .78 cal. | Trigger Guard: 11-1/4" | Side Plate: 6-1/2" | Weight: 10.0 lbs. |

**Fort Ticonderoga Collection**

*Chapter 3: Smoothbore Shoulder Arms*

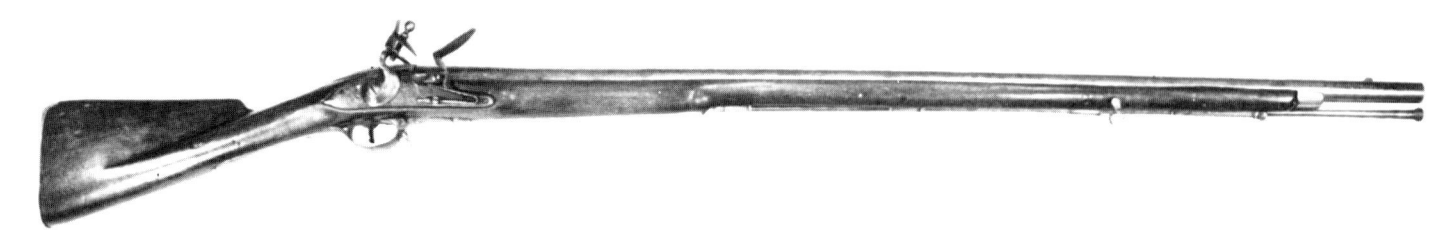

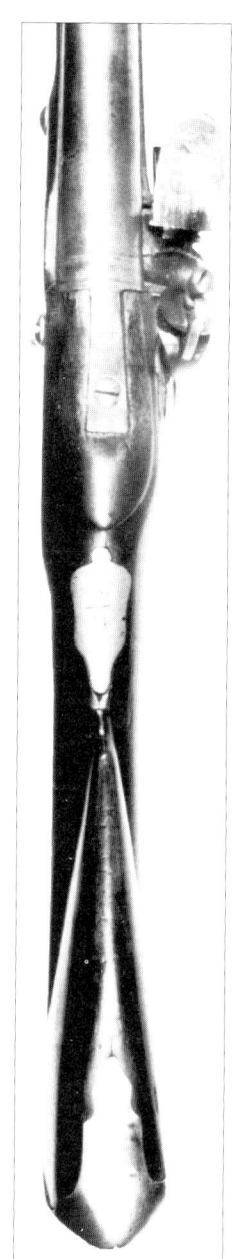

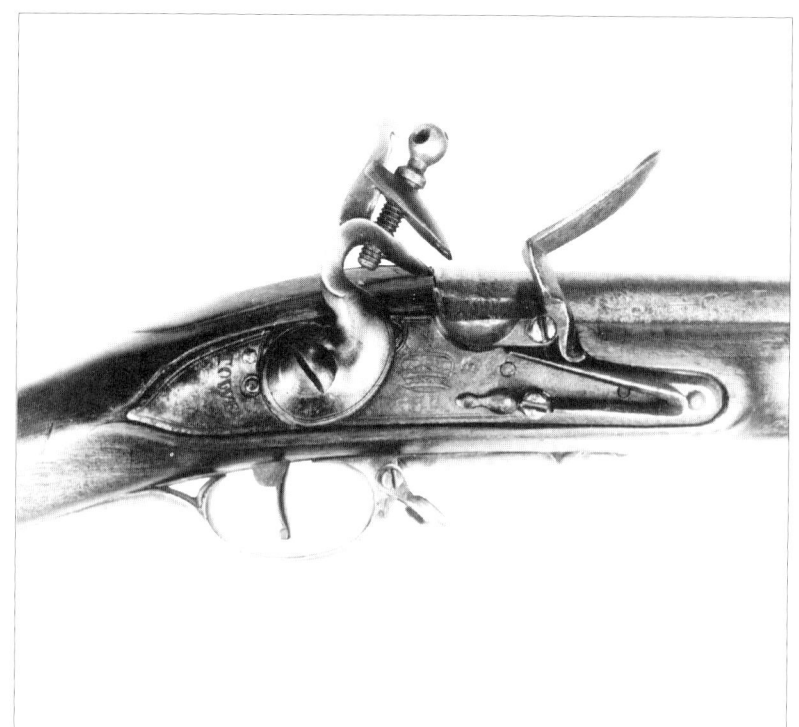

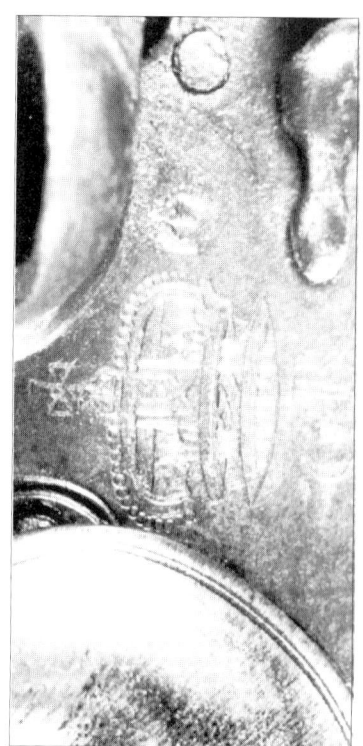

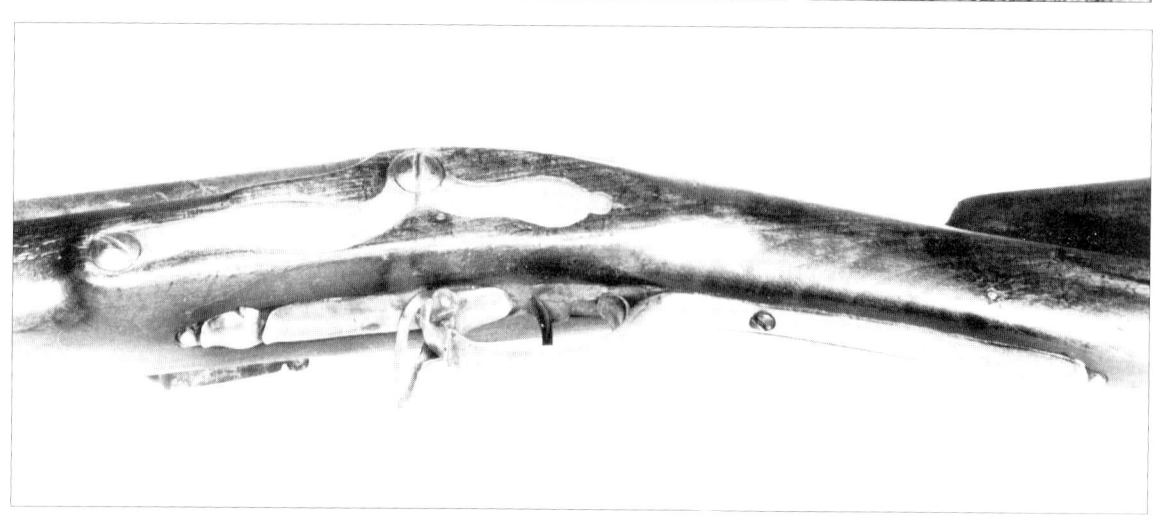

**16.MM ENGLISH SHORT LAND MUSKET, LIEGE CONTRACT**                                                                                           **Circa 1778**

When France actively joined the Americans in 1778, the Colonial rebellion became a global war. Britain expanded its domestic weapons production and contracted for more than an additional 100,000 longarms from European manufactories. Among these were orders for 60,000 from Liege, the largest independent arms producing center on the Continent (comprised of 70 to 80 private gunmakers). This is believed to be one of those muskets. It follows the Short Land Pattern 1777 with the new simplified Lock II and Pratt's second ramrod pipe. However unlike the English-made version (15.MM), these lock plate markings show a crown above the "GR" that is wider and fuller in the "shoulders," there is no broad arrow beneath the small crown stamp and the double border lines discontinue under the pan. Moreover the "TOWER" engraved on its tail has unusual open shaded letters. (Note: Other known Liege examples copied the pre-1777 pattern lock but included the same marking variations.) This butt tang is 3/8" shorter than normal. The walnut stock, in turn, retains a storekeeper's stamp. Other marks include: "NS" inside the lock; "IR" under the breech; Tower barrel proofs; and "B / 14" on the escutcheon, barrel tang and ramrod.

| | | | |
|---|---|---|---|
| Length: 57-3/4" | Lock 6-7/8" X 1-1/4" | Butt Tang: 3-3/8" | Furniture: Brass |
| Barrel: 42", .78 cal. | Trigger Guard: 11-1/4" | Side Plate: 6-1/4" | Weight: 10.0 lbs. |

**Author's Collection**

66     *Chapter 3: Smoothbore Shoulder Arms*

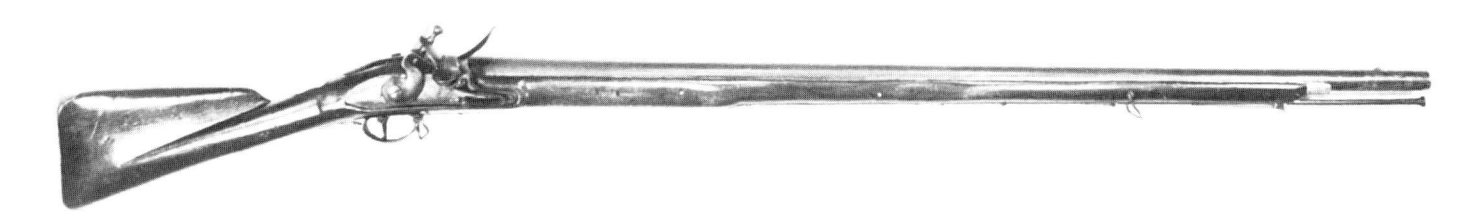

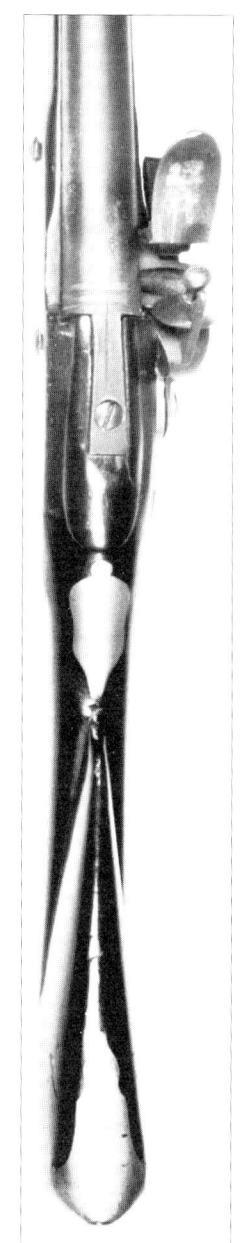

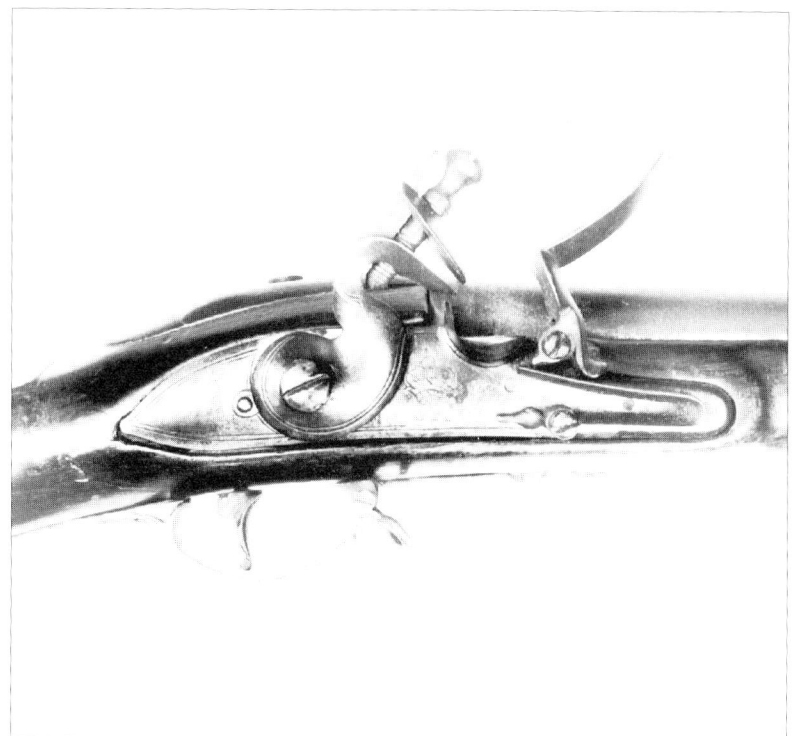

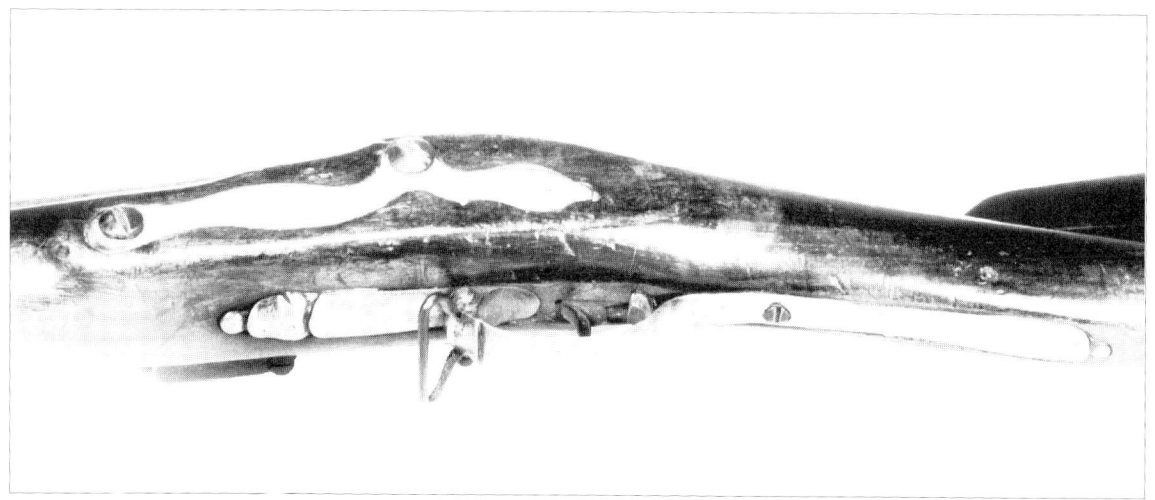

**17.MM  ENGLISH SHORT LAND MUSKET, GERMANIC CONTRACT**  Circa 1778

In addition to Liege, German sources (probably including Solingen) also supplied England with contract arms. While this example follows the basic Short Land Pattern 1777 (15.MM), there are variances in its lock and markings. The large crown above the "GR" is distinctly Germanic and, as with the Liege musket, omits both the broad arrow under the small crown and the engraved border lines beneath the flash pan. "TOWER," engraved on the tail, also has the shaded letter strokes. The lock itself omits an outside bridle, while its unusual double border lines are wide apart and recessed from the edge. Notice too that this version of the simplified British Lock II shows only one screw end behind the cock instead of two, and the trigger guard is flatter than normal. Markings include: "HC" inside the lock plate, a cross in a cartouche and a crown above crossed scepters under the breech, regular Tower barrel proofs, and a storekeeper's stamp on the walnut buttstock. In addition the raised beaver-tail carving around the barrel tang is narrower than normal, and the flat side plate measures 1/4" undersize.

| | | | |
|---|---|---|---|
| Length: 58" | Lock: 7" X 1-1/4" | Butt Tang: 3-5/8" | Furniture: Brass |
| Barrel: 42", .79 cal. | Trigger Guard: 11" | Side Plate: 6" | Weight: 10.3 lbs. |

**Author's Collection**

*Chapter 3: Smoothbore Shoulder Arms*   67

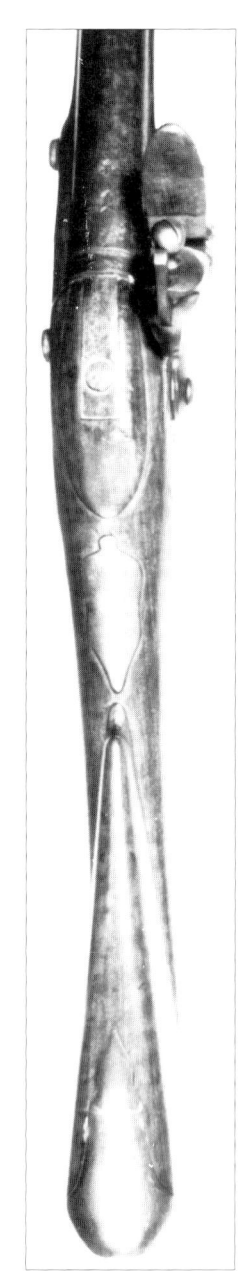

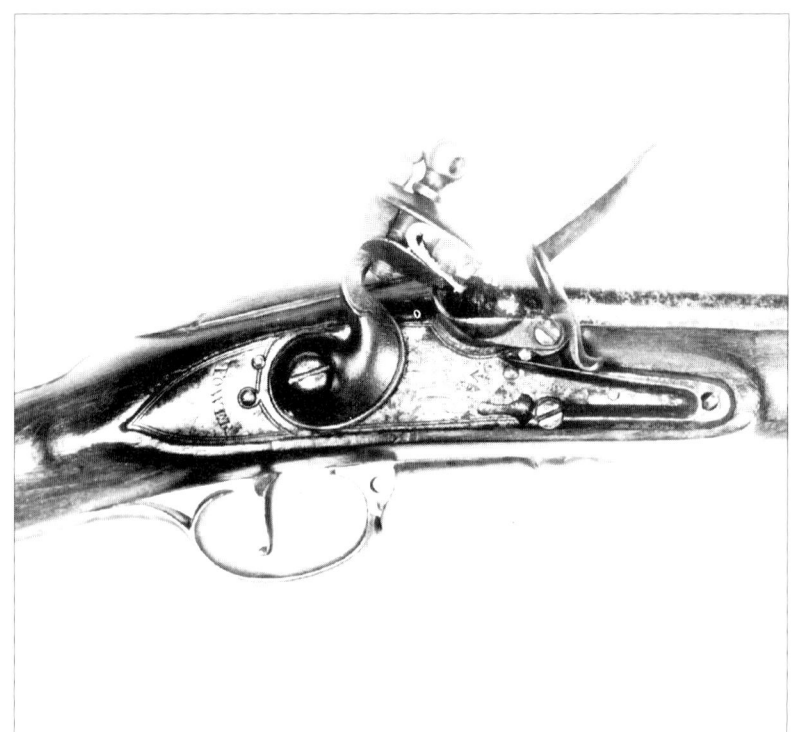

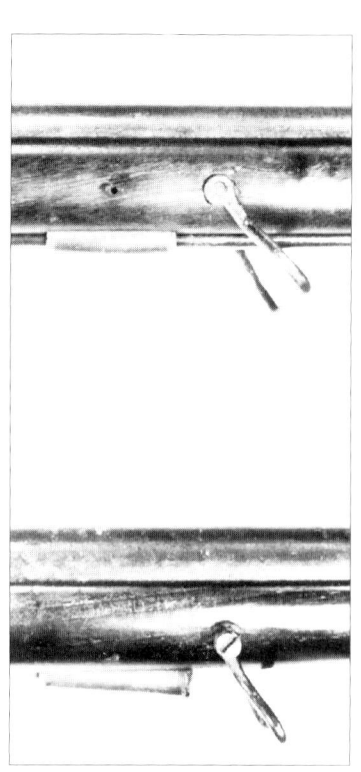

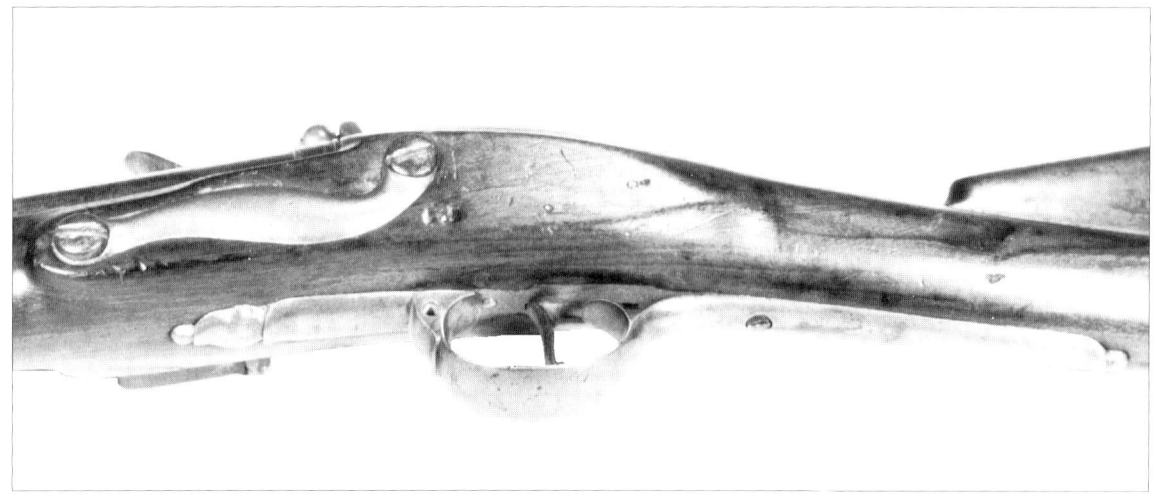

**18.MM  ENGLISH SHORT LAND MUSKET (Variation)**  Circa 1779

During the great emphasis on increasing production after France's active entry as America's ally in 1778 (followed by Spain and Holland in successive years), the disciplined system installed by the Board of Ordnance had to be relaxed in some instances. Several thousand firearms were accepted as final weapons from contractors without complete Tower-issued components or interim inspections, allowing the independent gunmakers to include their own barrels, locks and brass furniture. This example of a Short Land Pattern 1777 Brown Bess bears the mark of John Pratt, a leading "rough stocker" of London, in its ramrod channel. It was one of 2000 he delivered in 1779. The official form is followed, but an S-shaped convex side plate without a tail was substituted, which was the design in use on the India Pattern Musket (19.MM) being manufactured at the time for the British East India Company. Normal markings including Tower barrel proofs are present, as well as a brand in the outboard walnut buttstock, "1st R / CBM," possibly from Canadian usage during its active life. Both sling swivels are missing (often removed by American Colonists and later owners). Note the sloped "Pratt's Improvement" rammer thimble below the earlier form and the cock's humpback post profile now gaining acceptance.

| | | | |
|---|---|---|---|
| Length: 58" | Lock: 7" X 1-1/4" | Butt Tang: 3-7/8" | Furniture: Brass |
| Barrel: 42", .78 cal. | Trigger Guard: 11-1/4" | Side Plate: 4-1/2" | Weight: 10.2 lbs. |

**The Benninghoff Collection**

*68   Chapter 3: Smoothbore Shoulder Arms*

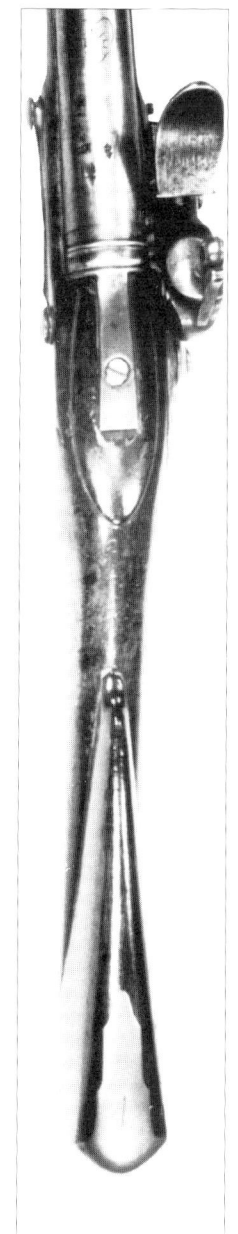

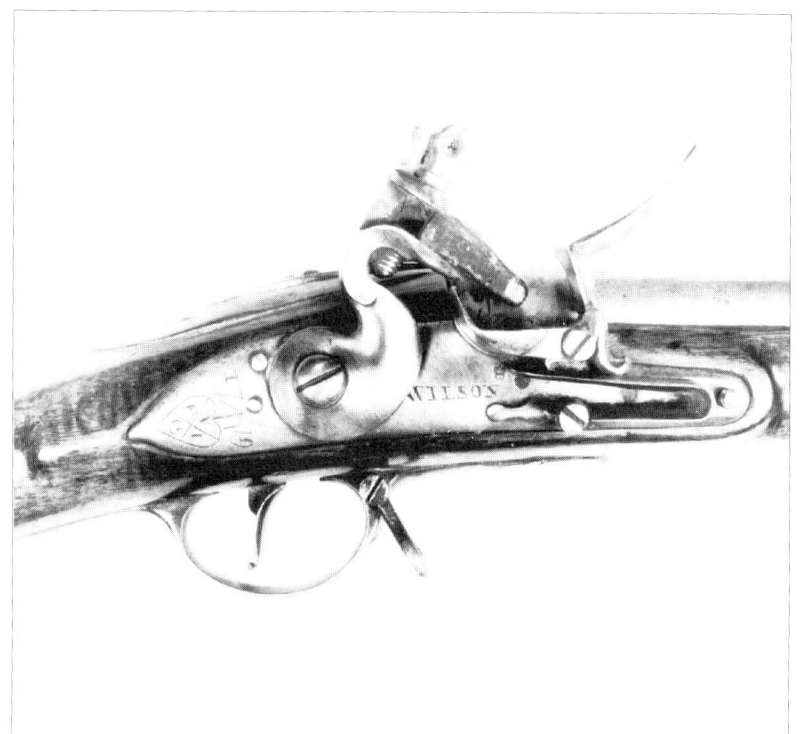

**19.MM  ENGLISH INDIA PATTERN MUSKET**                                                                                                                                  Circa 1779

**This is *not* considered a weapon of the American Revolution.** It is illustrated to identify the pattern—incorrectly called the "3rd Model Brown Bess" by some modern collectors. The form was being produced in this period by independent English gunmakers under non-government contracts for the private army in India of the British East India Company. It resembles the Crown's Short Land Pattern but with economies: the barrel is only 39 inches (.75 caliber); the lock is the form just copied by the Board of Ordnance for its Pattern 1777 (15.MM) yet lacks the latter's notched cock post; two of the three ramrod pipes have flared mouths; its butt tang is narrower; the escutcheon is gone; and an S-shaped convex side plate omits a tail. Moreover the trigger guard adopts a simplified forward end, a single rear trigger bow support and two rear screws. This lock and barrel are marked with the E. I. C. "heart" symbol, "WILSON" (the maker, Richard Wilson, of London) and "1779." London Gunmakers Company proofs are on the breech. Facing war with Revolutionary France, the British government began acquiring this pattern in 1793 and adopted it as the new standard infantry musket in 1797. A ring cock was added in 1809.

| | | | |
|---|---|---|---|
| Length: 54-3/4" | Lock: 6-1/2" X 1-1/8" | Butt Tang: 3-3/4" | Furniture: Brass |
| Barrel: 39", .75 cal. | Trigger Guard: 10-7/8" | Side Plate: 4-1/4" | Weight: 9.2 lbs. |

**George C. Neumann Collection, Valley Forge National Historical Park**

*Chapter 3: Smoothbore Shoulder Arms*   **69**

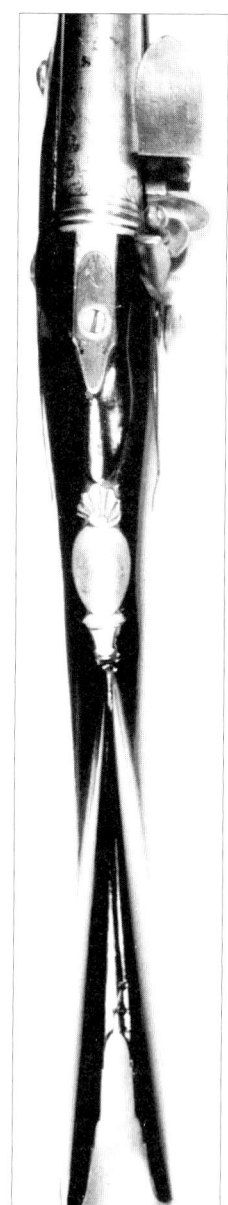

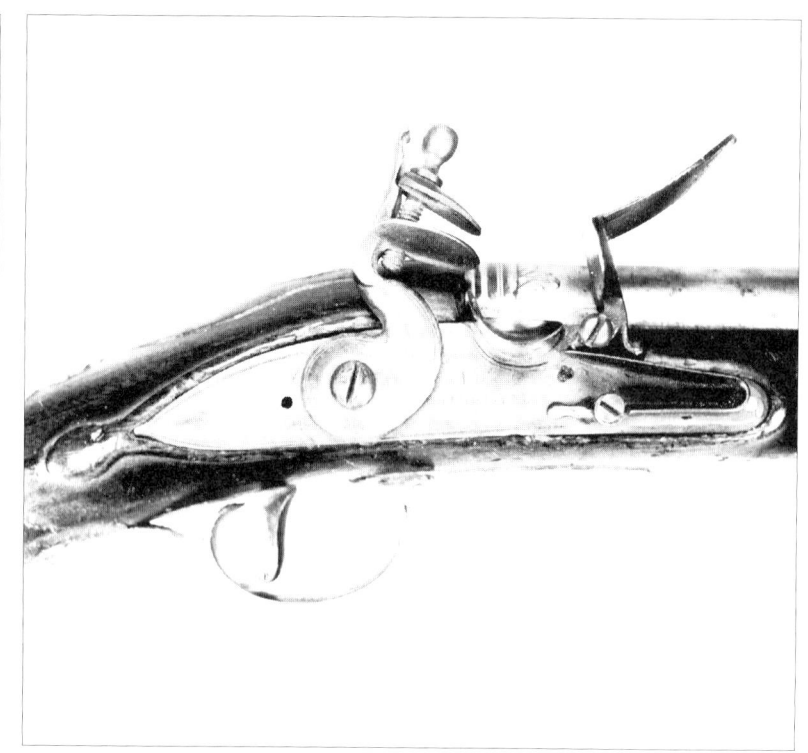

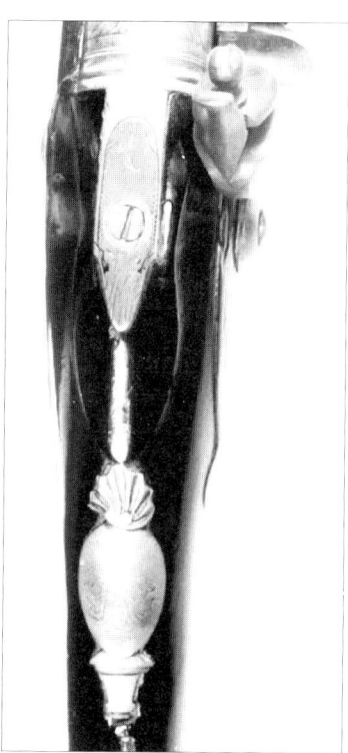

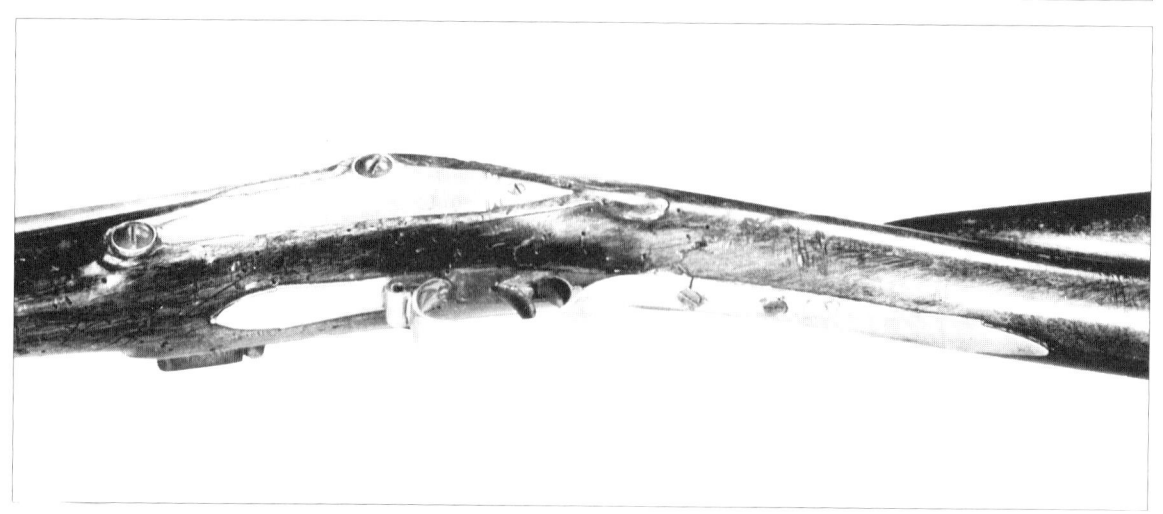

**20.MM ENGLISH OFFICER'S FUSIL**                                                                                              Circa 1744–1755

Although European pikes were obsolete by 1700, polearms continued in use (spontoons and halberds) by officers and sergeants for identification and symbols of rank well into the 19th century. During the 1740s and 1750s, Royal warrants suggested that officers replace them with light, short, smaller bore muskets ("fusils," "fusees") that mounted a bayonet. ("Fusil" was also the French term for a regular musket.) Commissioned officers usually purchased these arms privately, selecting their own pattern—often with elaborate decoration. This example shows transitional characteristics, that is, earlier large bulbous raised carving around the lock, side plate and barrel tang. It also includes a single-bridled lock, an escutcheon and a pointed butt tang—typical of the 1740-period English private patterns. The side plate plus trigger guard, in turn, are more indicative of the 1750s (see 4.PP). Three equal pipes suggest an original wooden rammer. Its barrel is engraved by the maker, "COLLUMBELL LONDON NO 2"; "I LUDLAM" appears on the lock plate.

| | | | |
|---|---|---|---|
| Length: 52-5/8" | Lock: 5-3/4" X 1" | Butt Tang: 4-1/8" | Furniture: Brass |
| Barrel: 37-1/8", .68 cal. | Trigger Guard: 10-1/8" | Side Plate: 5-1/2" | Weight: 6.5 lbs. |

**George C. Neumann Collection, Valley Forge National Historical Park**

*70    Chapter 3: Smoothbore Shoulder Arms*

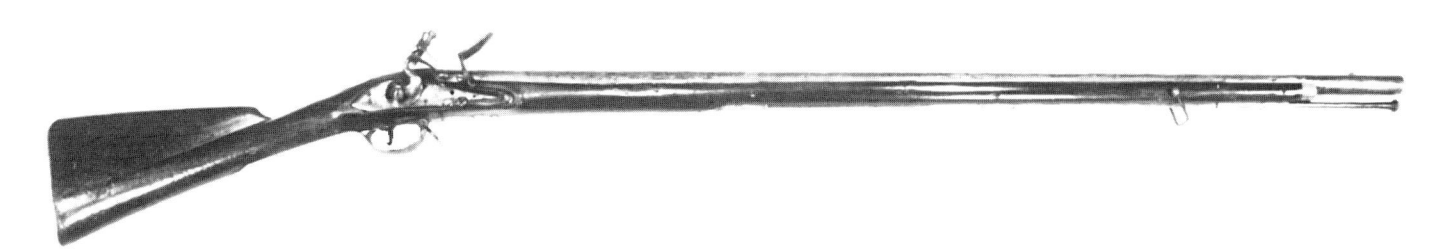

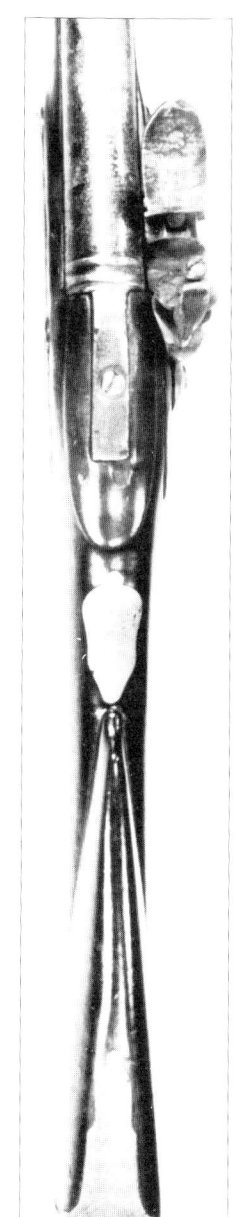

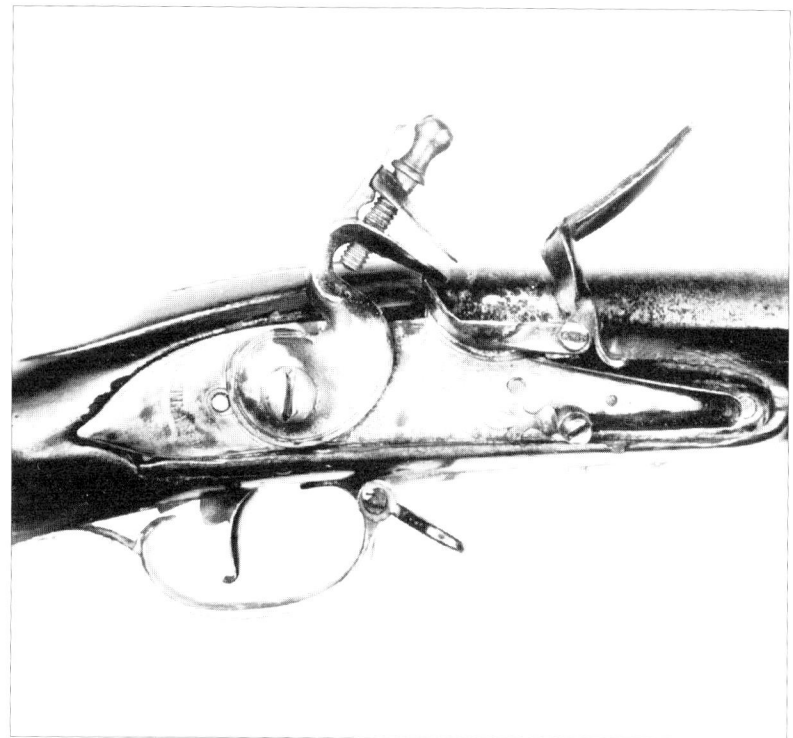

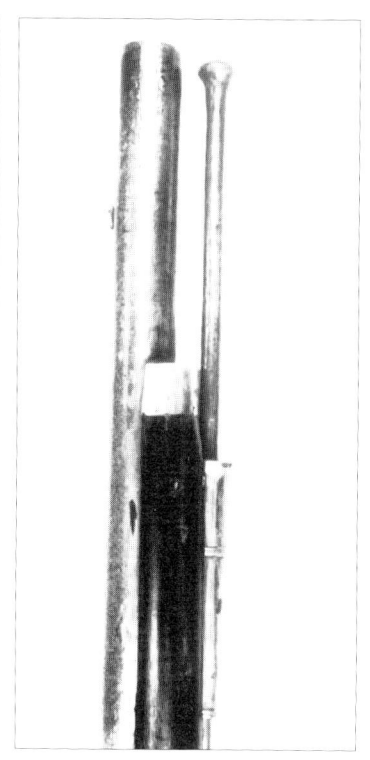

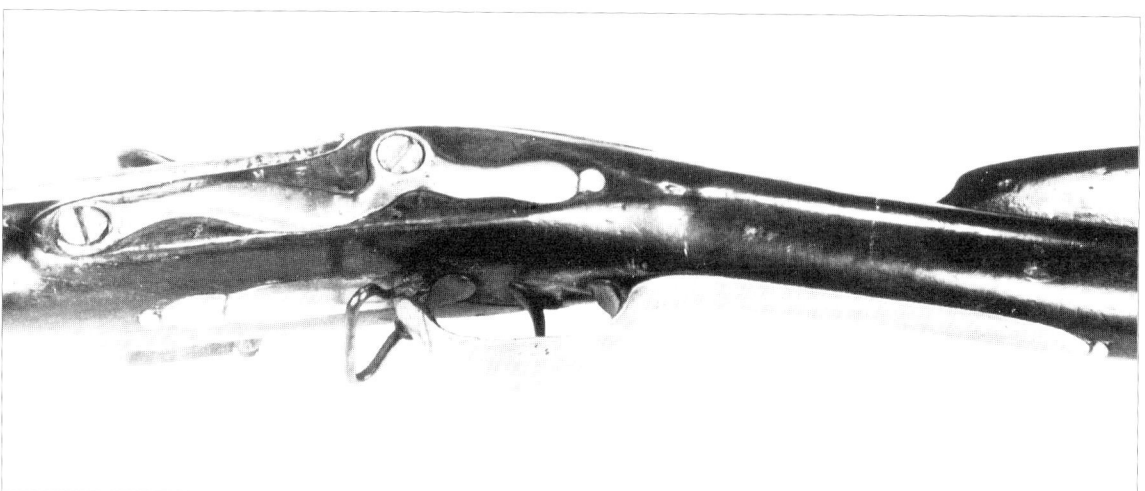

### 21.MM ENGLISH OFFICER'S FUSIL
Circa 1760–1768

The name of the famous Birmingham/London gun- and lock-making family, Ketland, appears on the lock's tail of this British fusil. It also bears a large "crown / GR" under the flash pan, but not the broad arrow, which would have indicated government instead of personal ownership. Two private London Gunmakers Company proofs were struck on the breech. The fusil's double-bridled lock and most of the scaled-down furniture follow the Long Land infantry design. Yet the two-tier butt tang adds a button tip, the rear screw is omitted from the trigger guard and the uppermost of the three ramrod pipes is flared, with a center raised ring. Its 40" pinned barrel, in turn, has the usual top bayonet stud (a consistent English practice) and a .74 caliber bore. Both sling swivels remain on the walnut stock. The total weight differential at 6.7 pounds versus the usual standard musket's 10 to 11 pounds would prove meaningful in the field.

| | | | |
|---|---|---|---|
| Length: 55-3/4" | Lock: 6-1/4" X 1-1/8" | Butt Tang: 3-3/4" | Furniture: Brass |
| Barrel: 40", .74 cal. | Trigger Guard: 10-3/4" | Side Plate: 5-7/8" | Weight: 6.7 lbs. |

**Author's Collection**

*Chapter 3: Smoothbore Shoulder Arms* 71

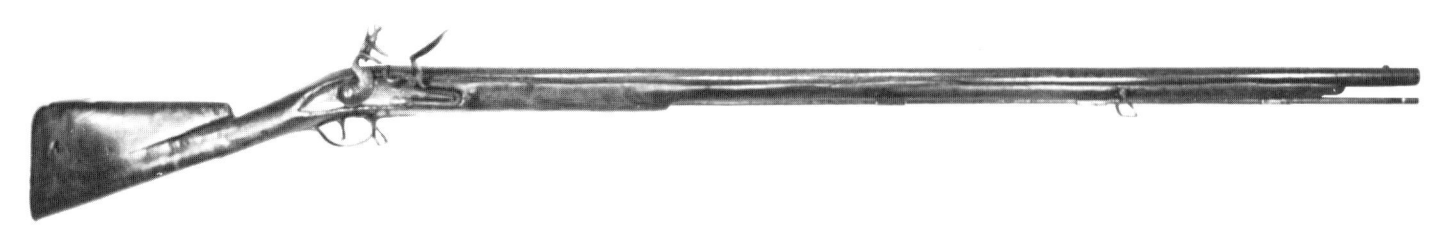

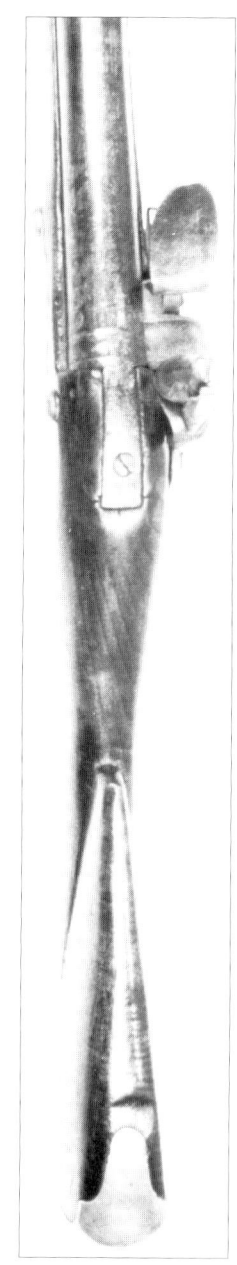

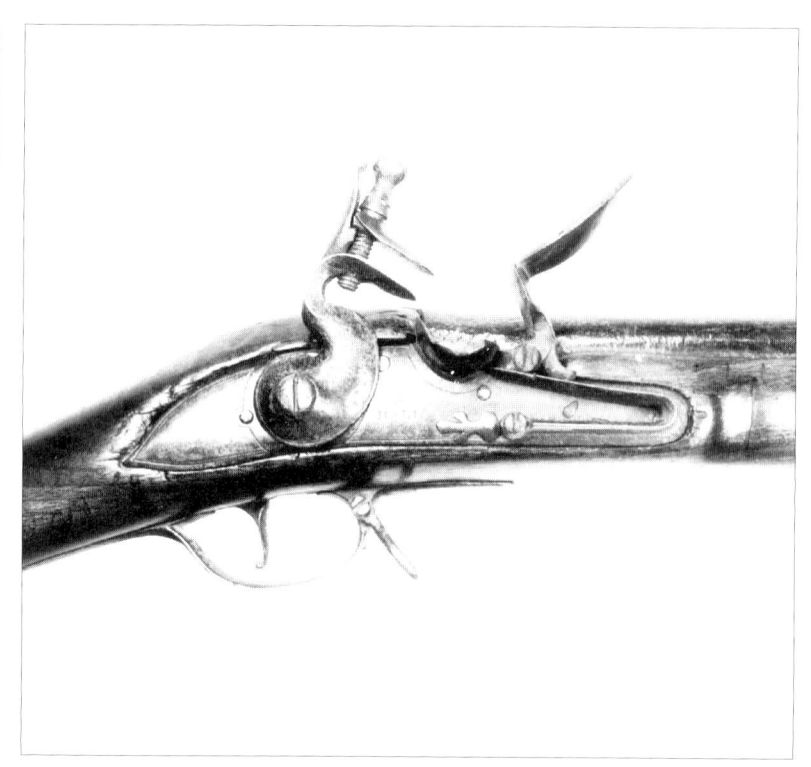

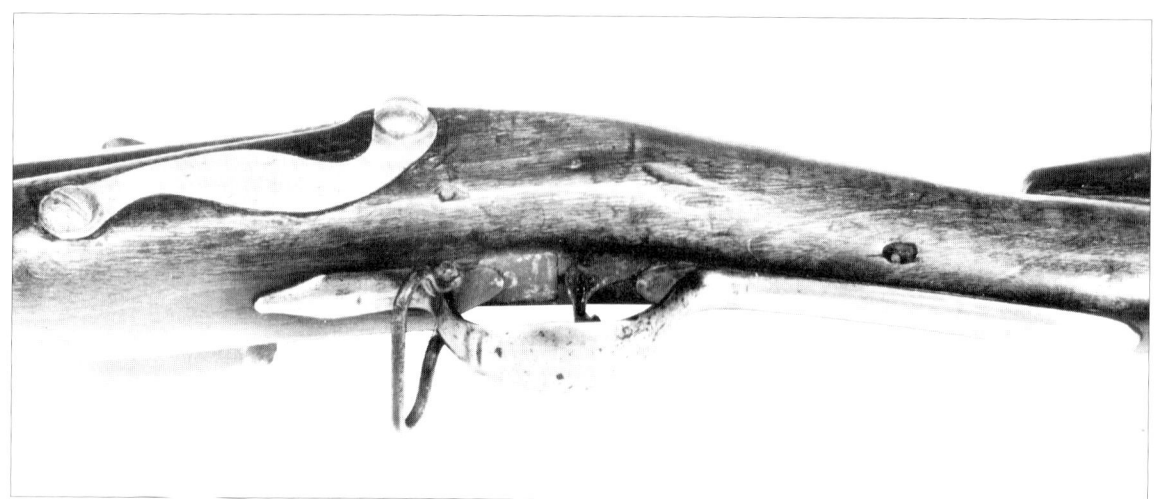

**22.MM ENGLISH COMMERCIAL LONG LAND MUSKET**  Circa 1738–1746

In addition to the controlled production of government arms issued to royal troops, a parallel industry of weapons manufacture existed among the private contractors who supplied individual regimental colonels and regional defense units, as well as customers in the cities, colonies and local militias of North America. Such weapons usually followed the basic Tower patterns but incorporated changes whenever possible to remain competitive in price. This example resembles the contemporary Long Land Pattern 1742 (9.MM) in profile, with a quality 46", .75 caliber barrel and banana lock (although omitting the exterior bridle). However its less important elements were economized: a low grade walnut stock and wooden rammer; an abbreviated trigger guard, side plate and butt tang; sheet-brass (versus cast) ramrod pipes; a lack of border carving; plus omission of the tail pipe, escutcheon and nose cap. Markings: the maker, "J HALL," on the lock (1736–1746); London Gunmakers Company proofs; and "IH" at the breech. "I BUTTALL," a London brass foundryman (1738–1754), is cast inside the flat side plate.

| | | | |
|---|---|---|---|
| Length: 61-3/8" | Lock: 7" X 1-1/4" | Butt Tang: 2-1/2" | Furniture: Brass |
| Barrel: 45-1/4", .78 cal. | Trigger Guard: 8-7/8" | Side Plate: 4" | Weight: 9.1 lbs. |

**Author's Collection**

Chapter 3: Smoothbore Shoulder Arms

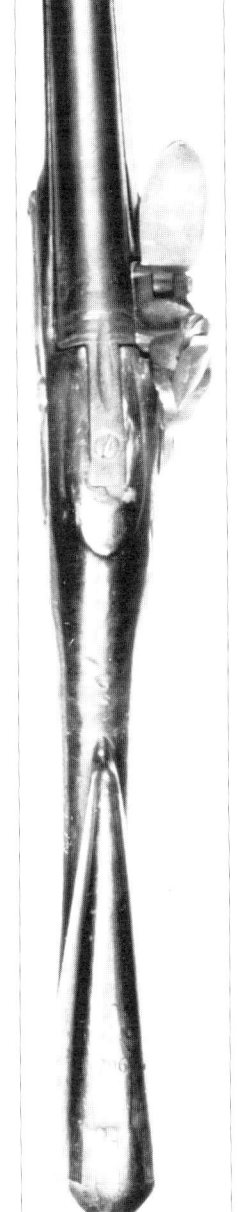

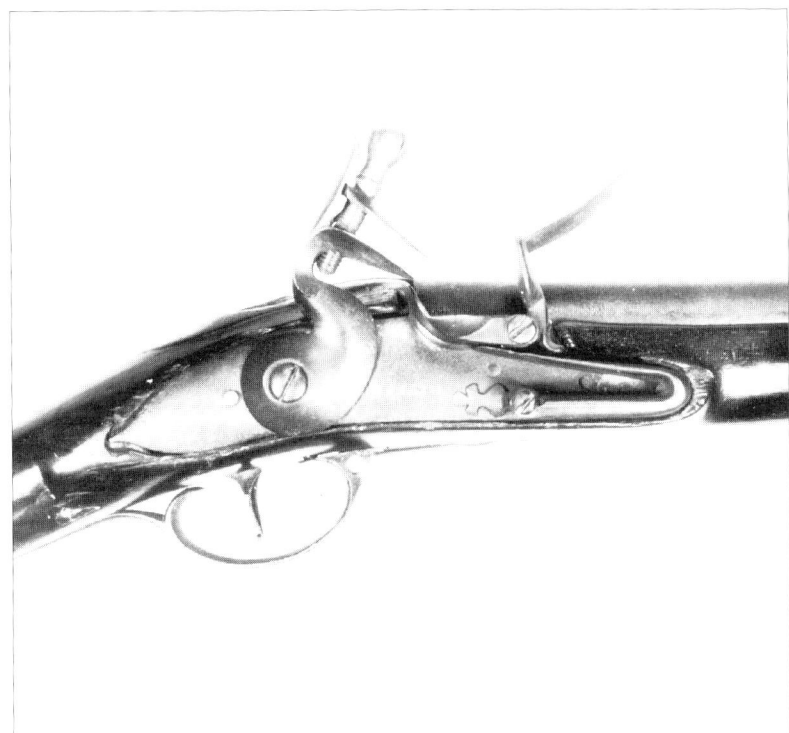

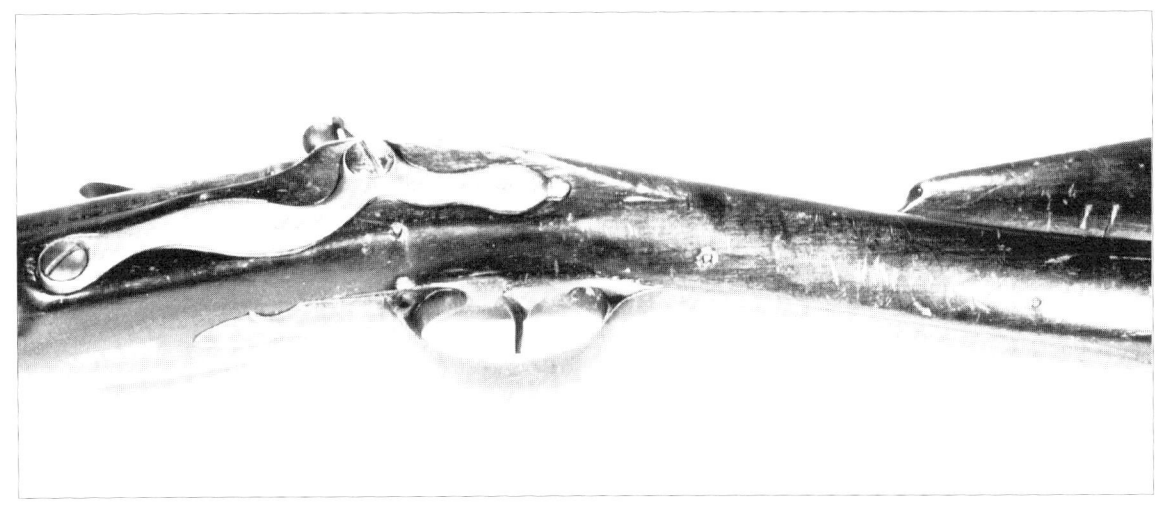

**23.MM ENGLISH COMMERCIAL LONG LAND MUSKET**                                                          **Circa 1755**

In 1755 the City of New York purchased 1,000 privately produced muskets from Britain for local defense. They sold them to the Province of New York in 1758 to aid General Abercrombie's expedition against Fort Ticonderoga, then purchased at least another 550 that year from Richard Wilson of London. In 1775 they were seized by the Americans and later issued to the 1st and 3rd New York Regiments for the Quebec campaign. Originally this arm was based upon the contemporary Long Land design (double-bridled banana lock, 46" barrel) but had its barrel shortened to the Short Land's 42" length probably during the Revolution. At that time the long front rammer pipe was pushed back and the original second pipe removed. Its outboard walnut buttstock is branded "N-Y / I. REG." Note the Long Land-style side plate, the modified trigger guard, three-step butt tang and absence of an escutcheon. The breech is marked "LONDON." "WILSON," the maker, appears on the lock. Its rack number, "796," plus the initials "LB" are visible on the butt tang (re: Mulligan, bib. 225).

| | | | |
|---|---|---|---|
| Length: 57-1/8" | Lock: 7" X 1-1/4" | Butt Tang: 4-1/4" | Furniture: Brass |
| Barrel: 41-1/2", .78 cal. | Trigger Guard: 11-3/8" | Side Plate: 6-1/8" | Weight: 8.9 lbs. |

**West Point Museum Collection**

*Chapter 3: Smoothbore Shoulder Arms*

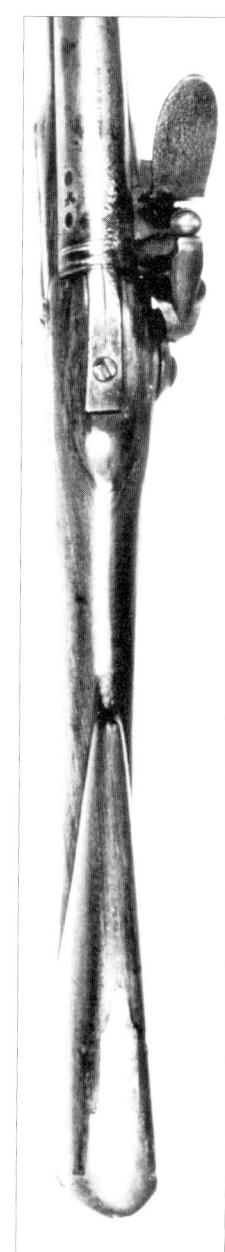

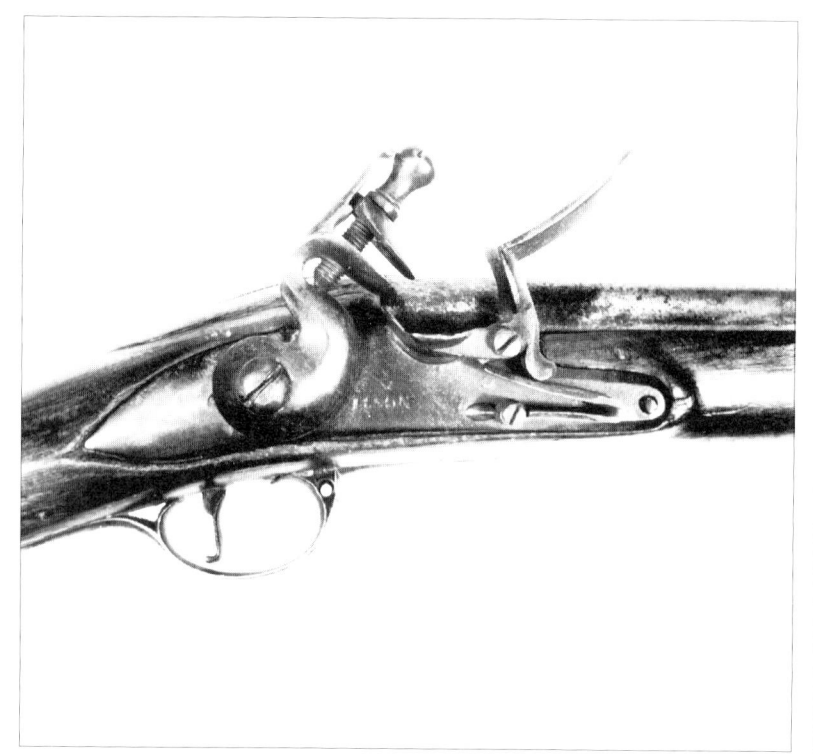

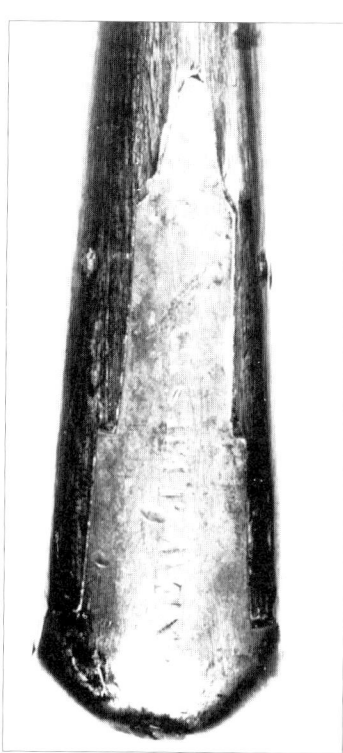

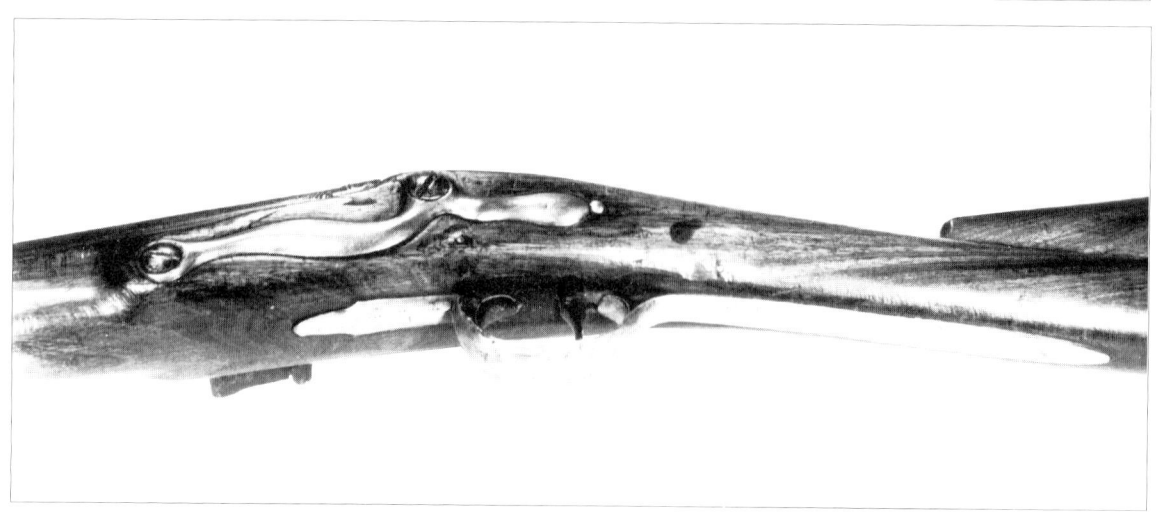

### 24.MM ENGLISH COMMERCIAL LONG LAND MUSKET
**Circa 1755**

Like other Colonies at the beginning of the French and Indian War, New Jersey ordered privately made military muskets for 500 of its state troops. This example typically followed the contemporary Long Land's pinned 46", .75 caliber barrel, wooden rammer, double-bridled banana lock and convex side plate. Yet the opportunities to economize are also evidenced by the elimination of the tail pipe and escutcheon, a marginal quality walnut stock, plus an abbreviated three-step butt tang and simple trigger guard. The barrel tang's beaver-tail is present, however no carving appears around the lock or side plate. "NEW JERSEY" is engraved on the butt tang; its breech has 1702 London Gunmakers Company proofs, "LONDON" and the maker's "R*W" strike, as well as "WILSON" on the rounded lock (Richard Wilson, a major supplier of these commercial arms). The rear sling swivel is missing. Note that a nose cap was also added to protect its forend from splitting.

| | | | |
|---|---|---|---|
| Length: 61" | Lock: 6-1/2" X 1-1/4" | Butt Tang: 4-1/8" | Furniture: Brass |
| Barrel: 46", .75 cal. | Trigger Guard: 10-1/4" | Side Plate: 5-3/4" | Weight: 7.6 lbs. |

**Robert Nittolo Collection**

*Chapter 3: Smoothbore Shoulder Arms*

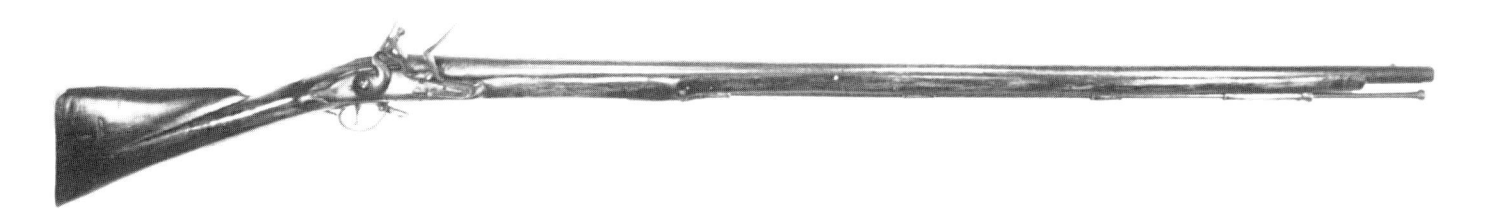

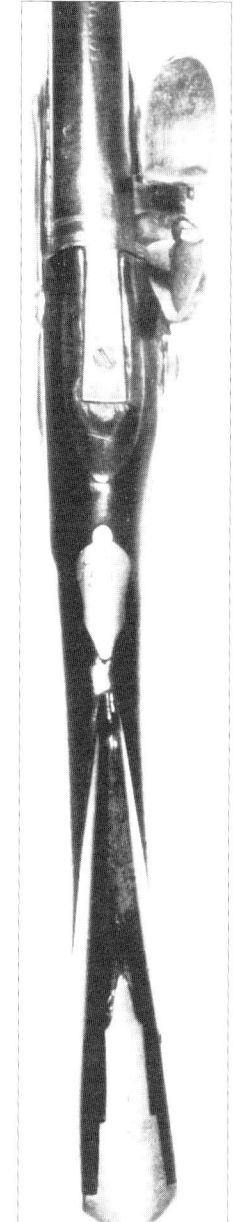

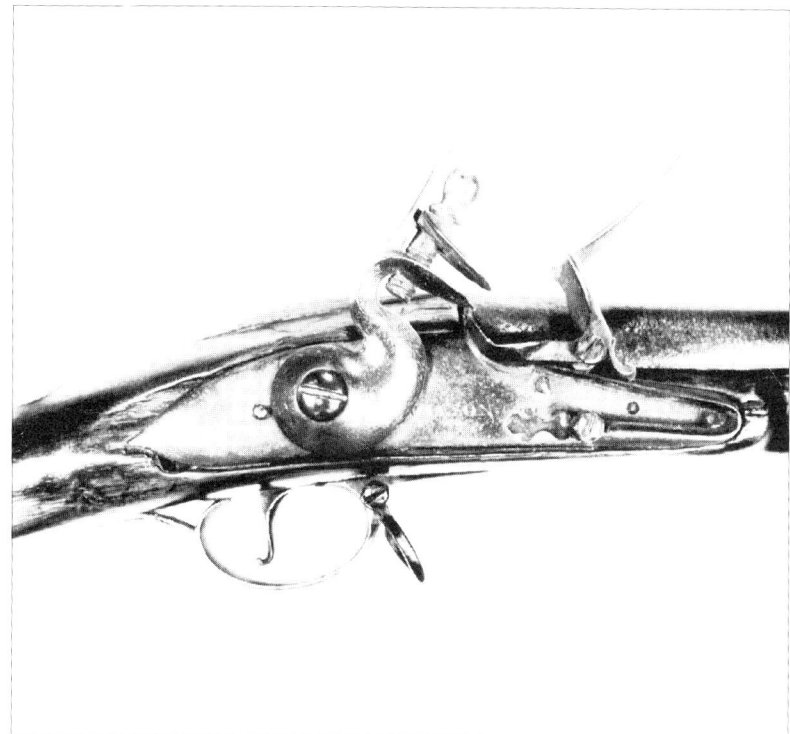

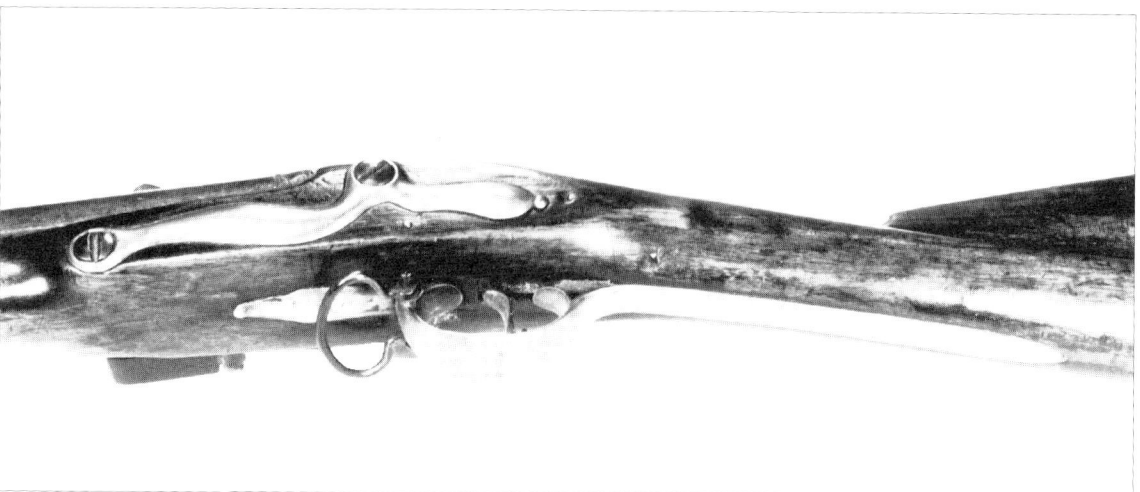

### 25.MM ENGLISH COMMERCIAL LONG LAND MUSKET

**Circa 1770–1774**

This privately purchased musket from England by New Jersey is from a later contract than the preceding example of French and Indian War vintage. It was probably acquired in the early 1770s and approximates Britain's later Long Land Pattern 1756 (10.MM) with its 46" barrel (later shortened here), straighter double-bridled lock, steel rammer, escutcheon plate, beaver-tail barrel tang carving, rounded side plate, top bayonet stud and four cast brass ramrod thimbles (upper one long and flared). The usual economies in these commercial arms, however, are also present, primarily in the simple trigger guard (no rear screw to secure the escutcheon), a plain three-step butt tang and a second-level quality walnut stock. The barrel is marked "LONDON." It also bears both Gunmakers Company proofs with "R*W" between them—identifying the maker, Richard Wilson, whose name ("WILSON") is also on the rounded lock under the pan. "NEW JERSEY" is engraved on the butt tang; its escutcheon bears "Q / 95." Such a musket would have been issued by the state to its troops at the beginning of the War for Independence.

| | | | |
|---|---|---|---|
| Length: 60" | Lock 6-1/2" X 1-1/4" | Butt Tang: 4-1/4" | Furniture: Brass |
| Barrel: 44-3/4", .70 cal. | Trigger Guard: 10-1/4" | Side Plate: 5-3/4" | Weight: 8.5 lbs. |

**Robert Nittolo Collection**

Chapter 3: Smoothbore Shoulder Arms  75

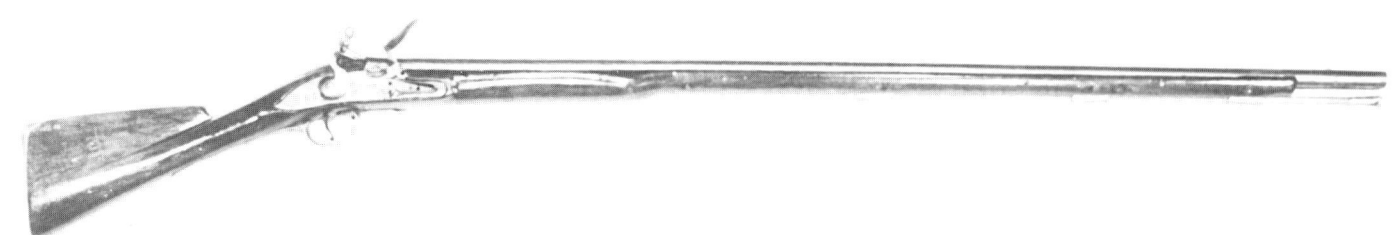

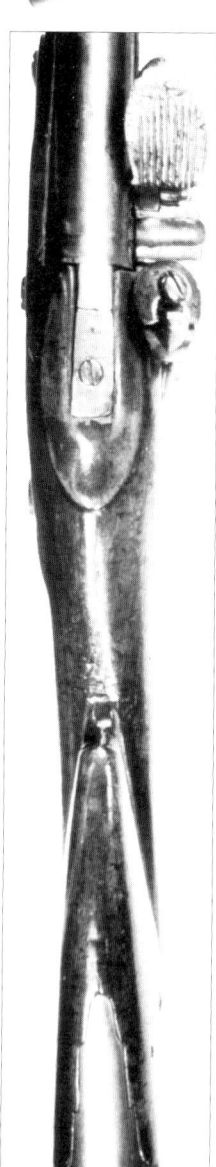

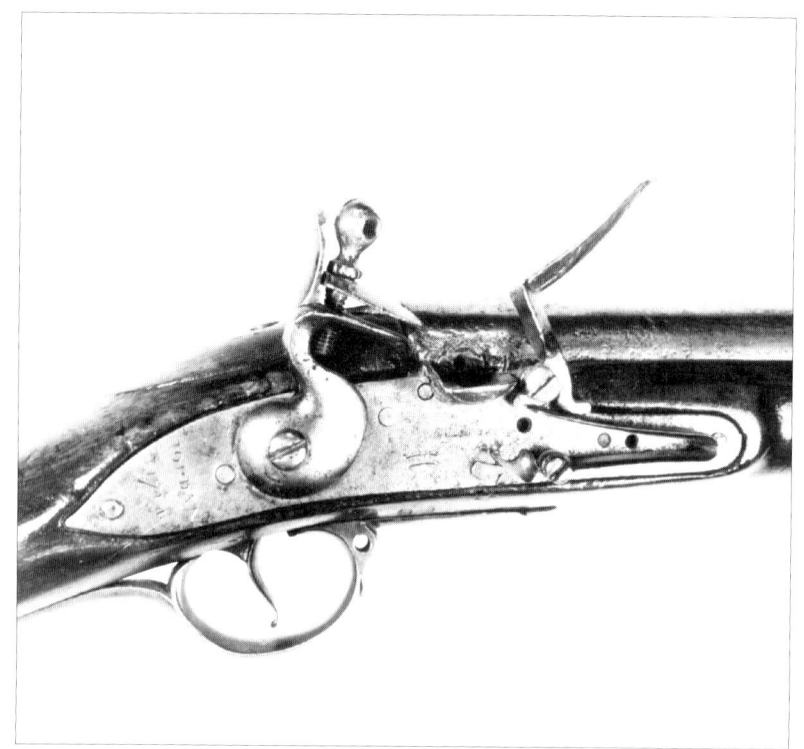

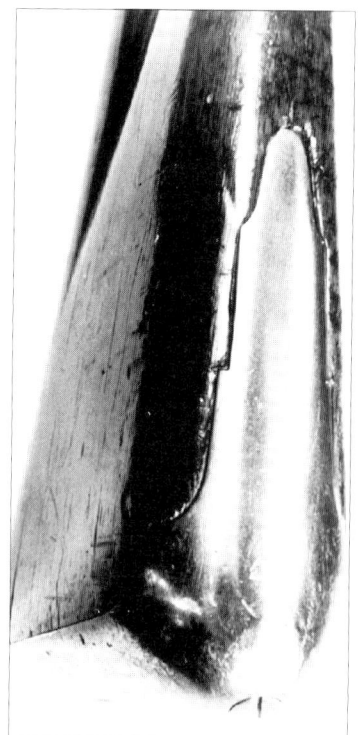

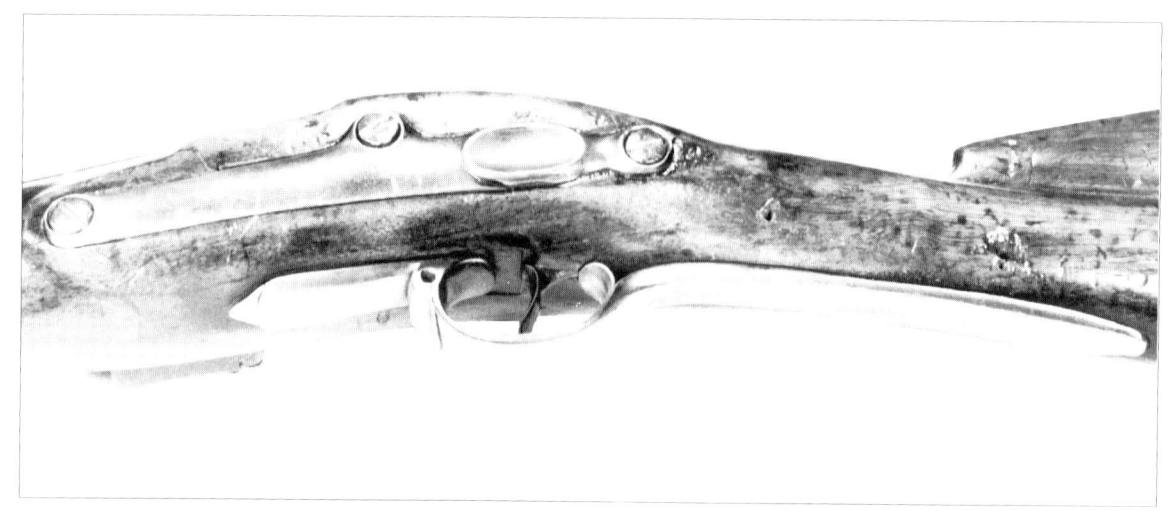

**26.MM  ENGLISH LONG LAND/SEA SERVICE PATTERN 1746**                                                                                      Circa 1746

During the first half of the 18th century, British sea service muskets were a mixed variety. This unusual short-lived design was found at Fort Ticonderoga, as well as three of its butt plates—one of which came from Amherst's ship, Boscowen, sunk in the 1760s. Two are marked on the inside by a broad arrow and "1746" (possibly from contracts in 1738 and 1746, see Fox, bib. 199). It was apparently designed for both land and sea services with a pinned 46" barrel (.75 caliber) and a flat naval-type banana lock inscribed "IORDAN / 1744" (J was then written as I). The three-screw lock has obviously had its cock (originally flat and ringed), frizzen and spring replaced (18th century rule: flat cock on flat lock, round on round). A three-step butt tang resembles commercial arms of that period (24.MM) and is larger than the similar India Pattern (19.MM). Its convex side plate, in turn, includes a unique oval thumb depression, probably for a proper manual position. A pointed trigger guard is another innovation. Naval influence is further apparent in the absence of an escutcheon, trigger plate and tail pipe (iron rammer).

| Length: 61-1/8" | Lock: 7-1/2" X 1-1/4" | Butt Tang: 4-1/2" | Furniture: Brass |
| Barrel: 45-1/4", .78 cal. | Trigger Guard: 11" | Side Plate: 7-1/2" | Weight: 9.3 lbs. |

**Fort Ticonderoga Collection**

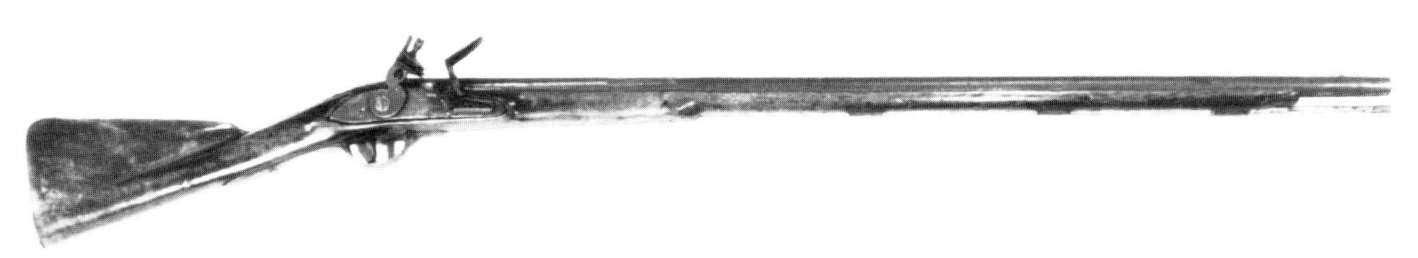

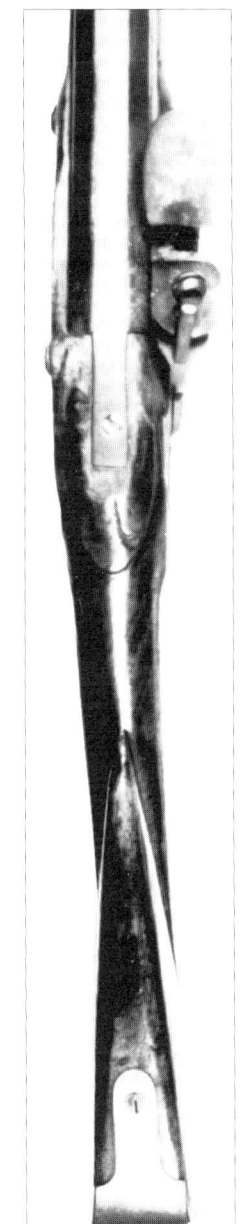

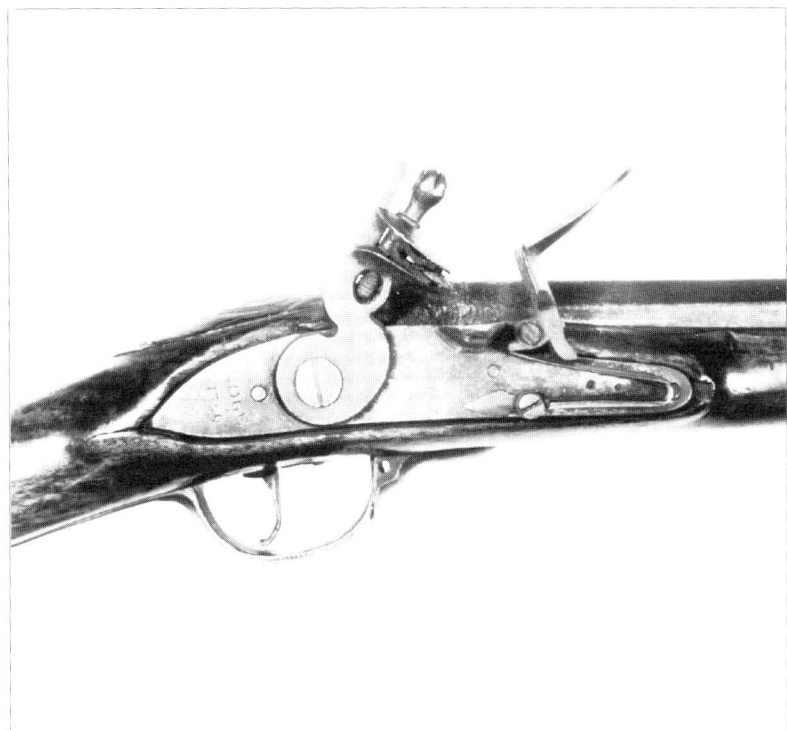

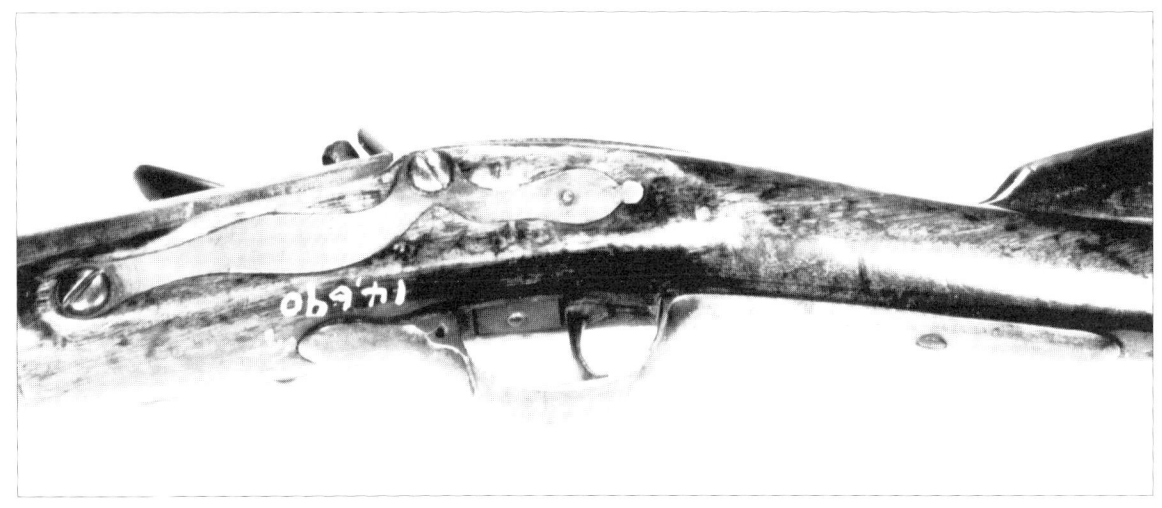

### 27.MM  ENGLISH SEA SERVICE ("LONG") MUSKET PATTERN 1757
Circa 1759

By the mid 1700s, distinct sea service musket characteristics had evolved. The arms were classified according to two barrel lengths: 37 inches (short) and 40–46 inches (long) in either "black" (entirely painted with black paint) or "bright" finishes. In 1752, bayonets and sling swivels were ordered. The lock and furniture, however, continued to follow early Queen Anne period styling (see 4.MM) including a flat lock and ring cock, a flat butt plate with a simple lobed tang, a wooden ramrod, a flat side plate, a rounded trigger guard front terminal, plus the absence of both a tail pipe and escutcheon. This "long" example mounts a reused 42" barrel having an octagonal breech (8", and rings at 11" and 14"). The established sea service flat lock (with ringed cock, leaf-ended frizzen spring, faceted pan and no outside bridle) is marked "crown / GR / broad arrow" and "EDGE / 1759" (two-screw locks with rounded frizzens were officially approved by this date). The cast brass trigger guard is drilled for a swivel (none mounted). Its thick walnut stock, in turn, includes the British handrail plus raised beavertail carving around the barrel tang.

| | | | |
|---|---|---|---|
| Length: 57-5/8" | Lock: 7-1/4" X 1-1/4" | Butt Tang: 3-1/4" | Furniture: Brass |
| Barrel: 41-7/8", .80 cal. | Trigger Guard: 9-1/2" | Side Plate: 6-3/4" | Weight: 9.6 lbs. |

**West Point Museum Collection**

*Chapter 3: Smoothbore Shoulder Arms*

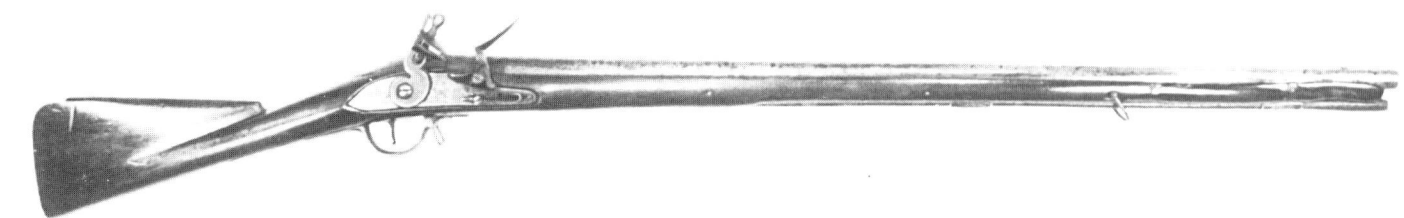

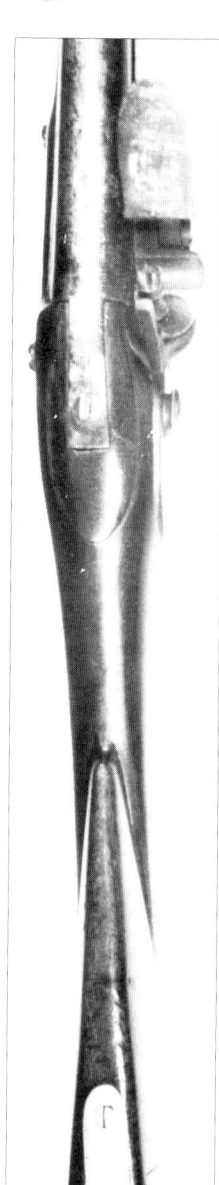

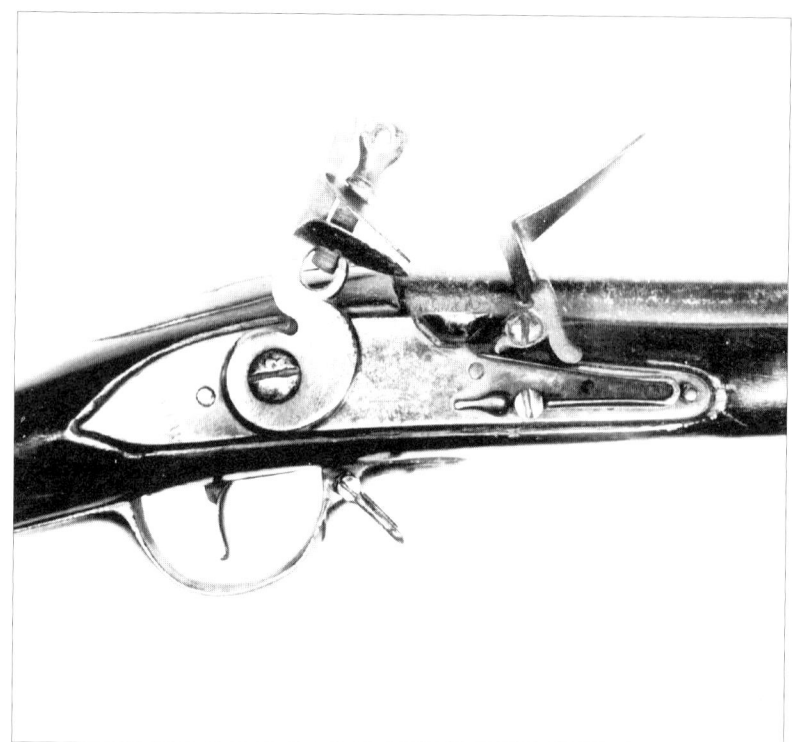

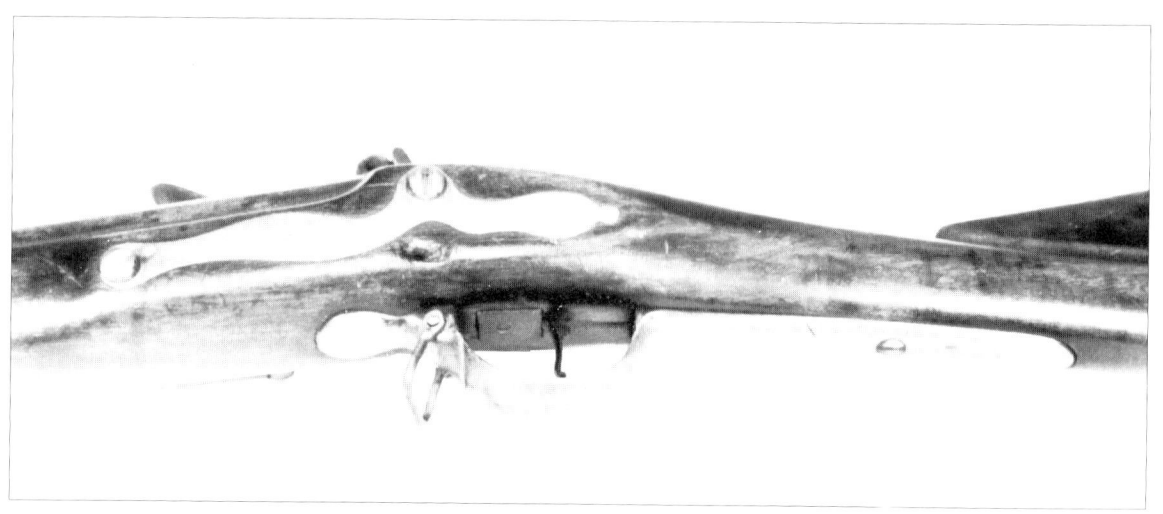

**28.MM ENGLISH SEA SERVICE ("SHORT") MUSKET PATTERN 1757**  Circa 1764

Although British naval musket specifications were in place by the 1750s, there continued to be considerable variances. This weapon, for example, mounts the official ("short") 37" barrel (.75 caliber) and sling swivels ordered in 1752, but it is stocked to the muzzle despite the bayonet authorization of that same date. It also has a lock stamped "TOWER" (although maker and date markings were normal until 1764). On the whole however the standard sea service pattern of this period is observed: a flat brass butt plate with a simple lobed tang (three flush screws); an omitted trigger plate and escutcheon; two barrel-shaped thimbles (both 1-5/8" long) for the wooden rammer (no tail pipe); a flat side plate (like the Marine or Militia 13.MM); plus a bulbous, rounded front terminal on the brass trigger guard. Standard features of the flat lock include the ringed cock, rectangular upper post (no forward notch), a round top jaw with side projections, a slotted/pierced jaw screw, no outside bridle, a rounded frizzen top, and a frizzen spring short of the forward side screw tip and ending in a teardrop finial.

| | | | |
|---|---|---|---|
| Length: 53" | Lock: 7-1/4" X 1-1/4" | Butt Tang: 3-1/4" | Furniture: Brass |
| Barrel: 37", .79 cal. | Trigger Guard: 9-1/2" | Side Plate: 6-1/2" | Weight: 8.2 lbs. |

**Author's Collection**

Chapter 3: Smoothbore Shoulder Arms

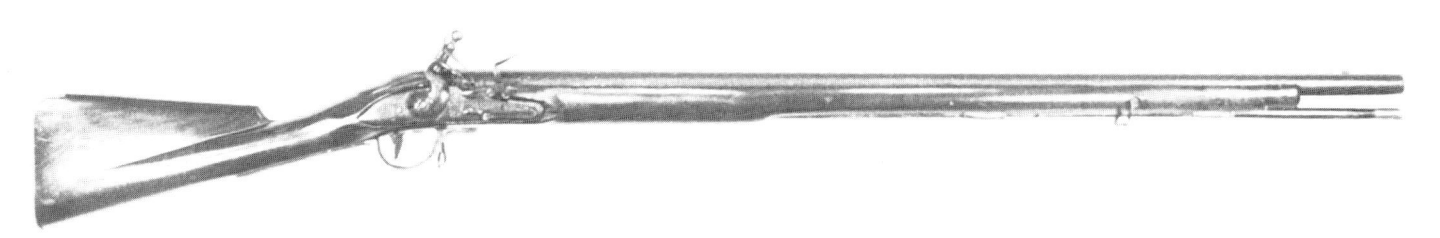

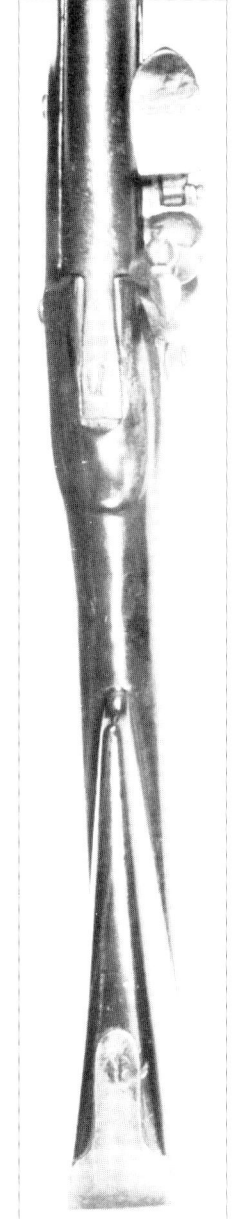

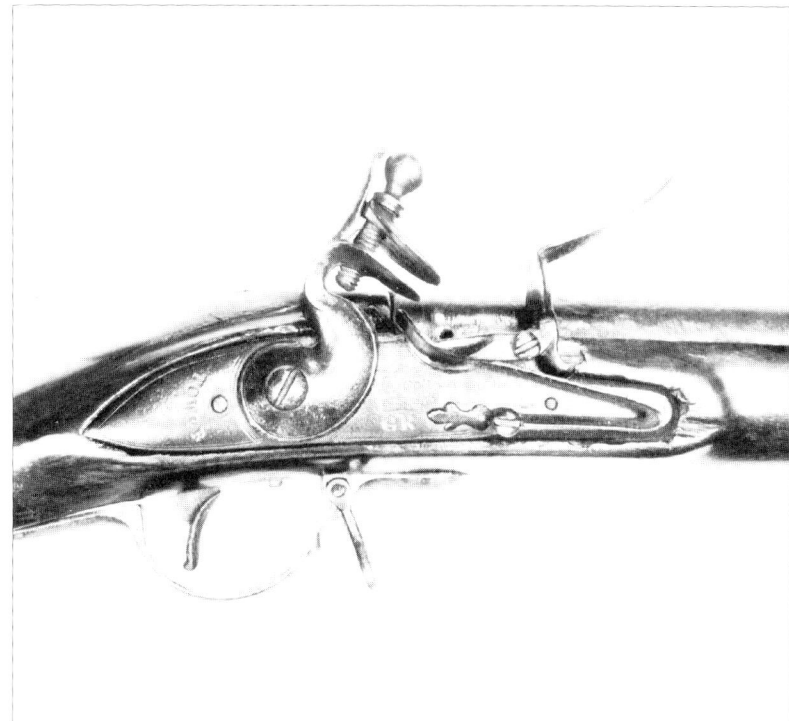

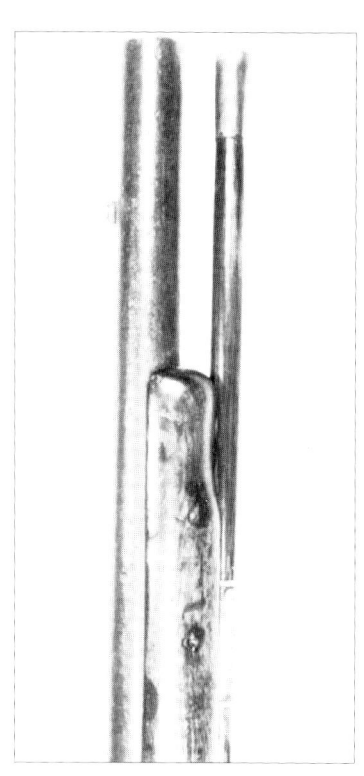

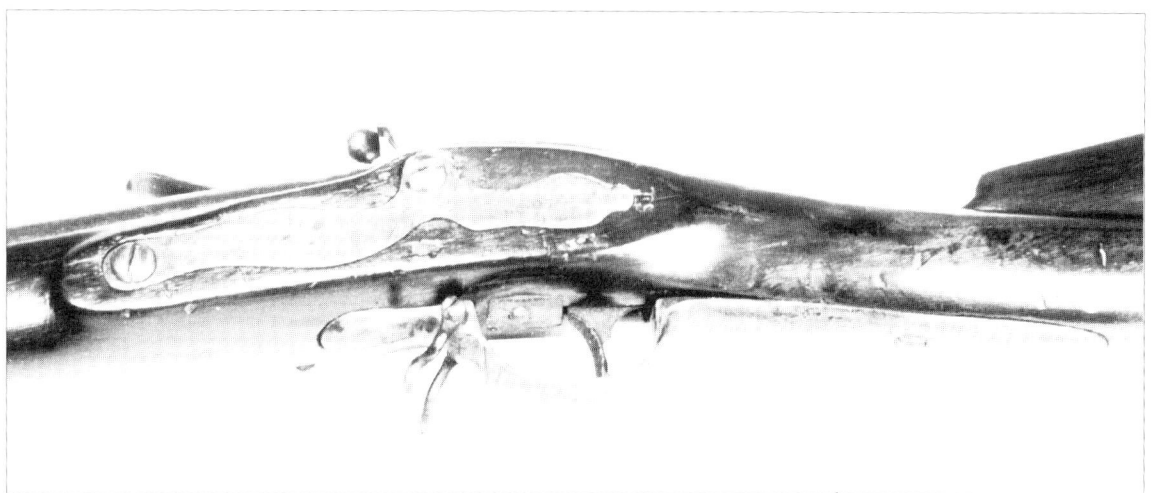

**29.MM ENGLISH SEA SERVICE ("SHORT") MUSKET**  Circa 1770–1780

A few rounded locks were mounted on naval longarms in the 1750s but they were used most often after 1762, including on some 16,000 muskets fitted with Land Service locks because of shortages during the American Revolution (re: Bailey, bib. 168). This 37" barreled example (.75 caliber) received a round pre-1777 infantry two-screw lock with double bridles (marked "TOWER"). It also has the forend shortened to take the standard four-inch bayonet socket (top stud). Of the two barrel-shaped thimbles (no tail pipe) for the brass-tipped wooden ramrod, the upper pipe is now 7-1/8 inches below the muzzle, versus a four-inch distance on the prior arm, which was stocked to the muzzle (28.MM). Also note the continuing characteristics of naval arms: the flat butt plate and tang; a thick walnut stock with a handrail and beaver-tail but no nose cap; a flat side plate; omission of an escutcheon; plus a cast brass trigger guard headed by a raised round terminal and including a sling swivel. Its barrel bears a broad arrow at the breech, while the top tang screw extends down to a rectangular iron nut before the trigger (no plate).

| | | | |
|---|---|---|---|
| Length: 53" | Lock: 6-7/8" X 1-1/4" | Butt Tang: 3-1/4" | Furniture: Brass |
| Barrel: 37", .76 cal. | Trigger Guard: 9-1/2" | Side Plate: 6-1/4" | Weight: 8.6 lbs. |

**Author's Collection**

*Chapter 3: Smoothbore Shoulder Arms*

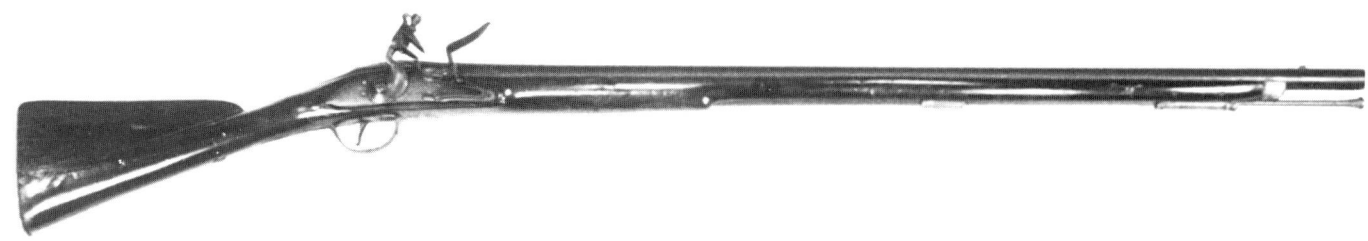

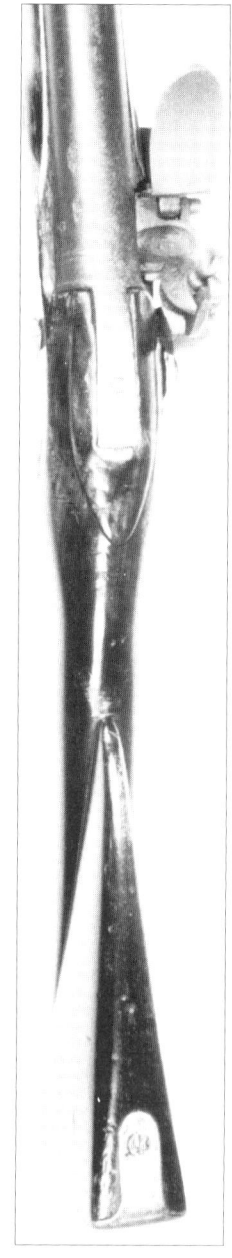

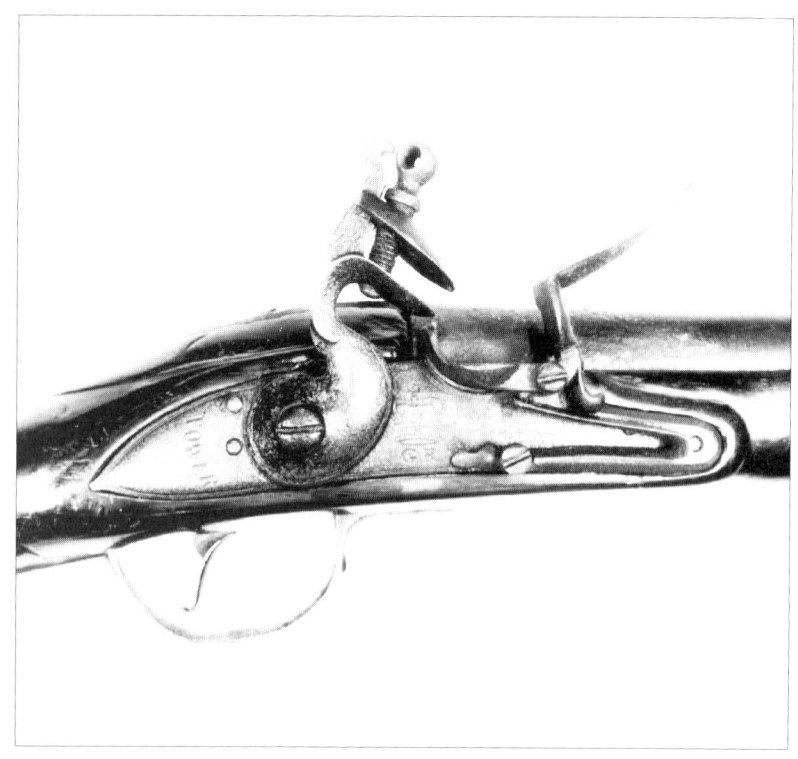

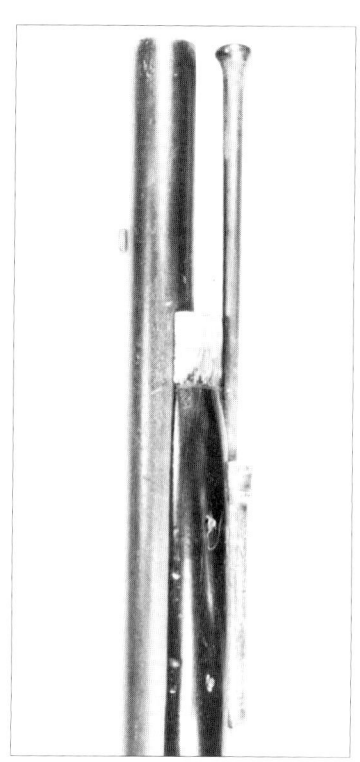

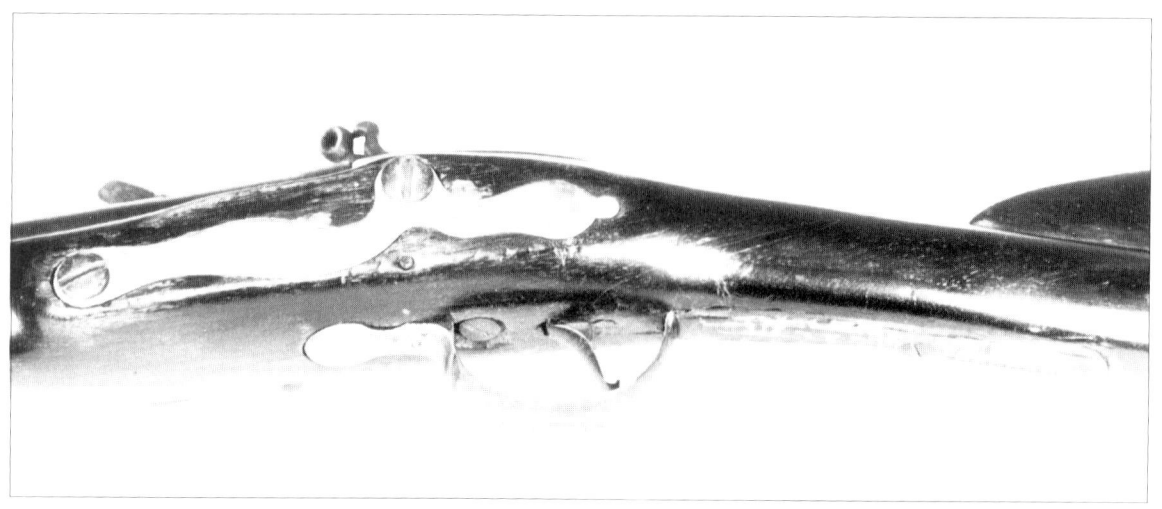

**30.MM ENGLISH COMMERCIAL SEA SERVICE MUSKET**  Circa 1777–1790

In addition to naval vessels, virtually every merchant ship carried racks or chests of small arms. They would usually obtain these weapons from private manufacturers. This musket uses a Lock II adopted for the Short Land Pattern in 1777, which was being sold to non-government sources prior to that time. It is marked "TOWER" plus "crown / GR," yet omits the small crown/broad arrow under the pan signifying the King's property. Moreover the breech has London Gunmakers Company private proofs. The gun does however include much of the contemporary official sea service pattern, that is, a flat butt plate with a simple tang, the flat military side plate, a trigger guard with a rounded front terminal, and the absence of both a tail pipe and escutcheon. Several differences are also apparent: the barrel measures 38-7/8 inches (.75 caliber); the two ramrod pipes are heavy cast brass (upper one long and flared); and the button-head rammer is steel. No sling swivels are present, but a nose cap has been added. Its walnut stock is of marginal quality and secures the barrel tang by the early practice of projecting a screw up from in front of the trigger (no plate).

| | | | |
|---|---|---|---|
| Length: 54-5/8" | Lock: 6-3/4" X 1-1/8" | Butt tang: 2-1/8" | Furniture: Brass |
| Barrel: 38-7/8", .78 cal. | Trigger Guard: 9" | Side Plate: 6-1/8" | Weight: 8.6 lbs. |

**Author's Collection**

*Chapter 3: Smoothbore Shoulder Arms*

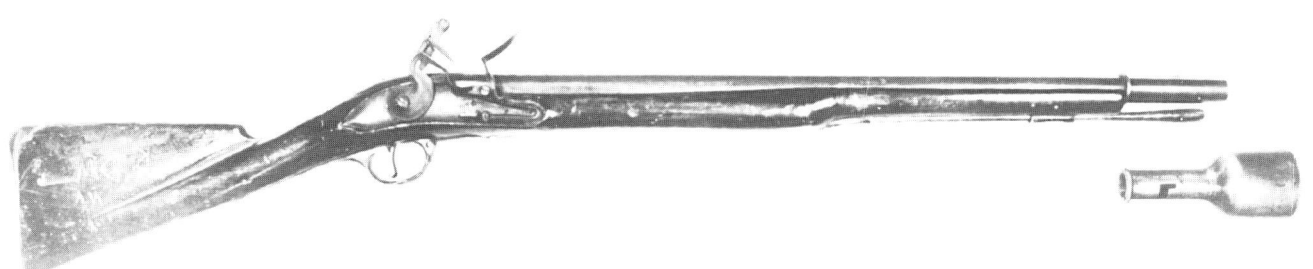

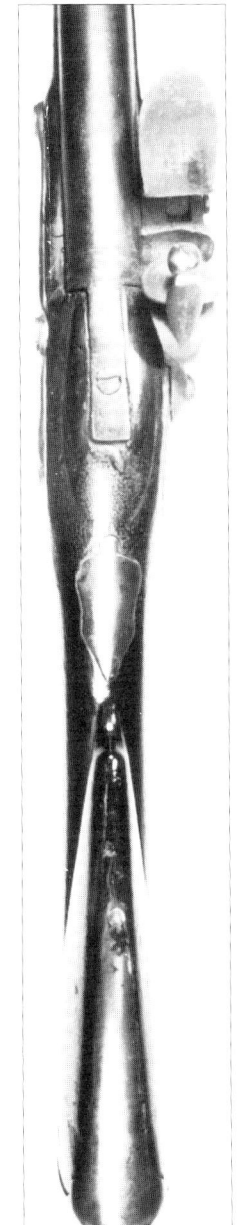

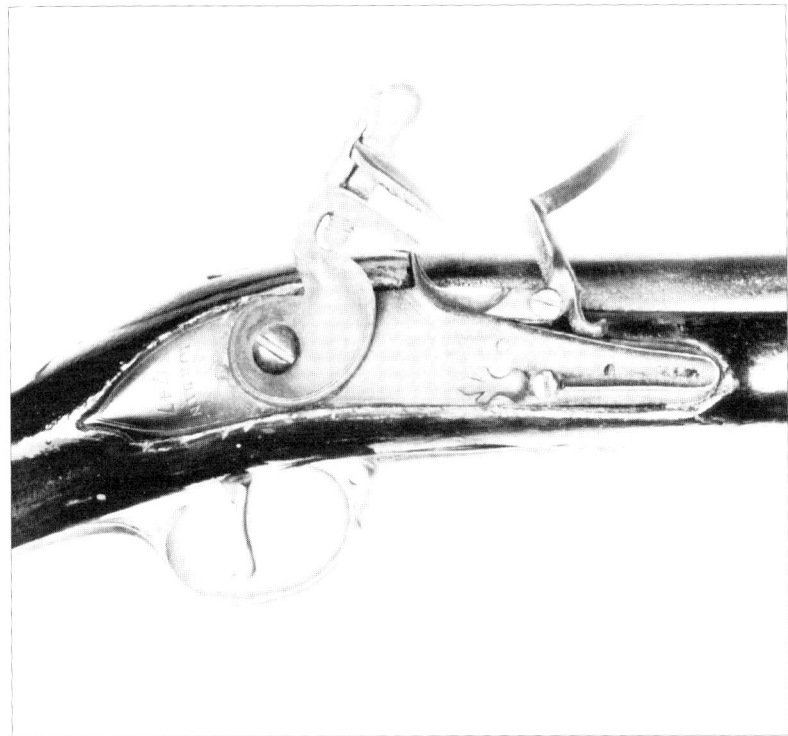

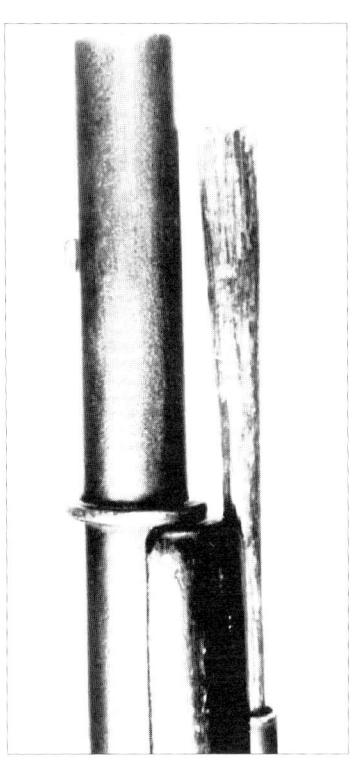

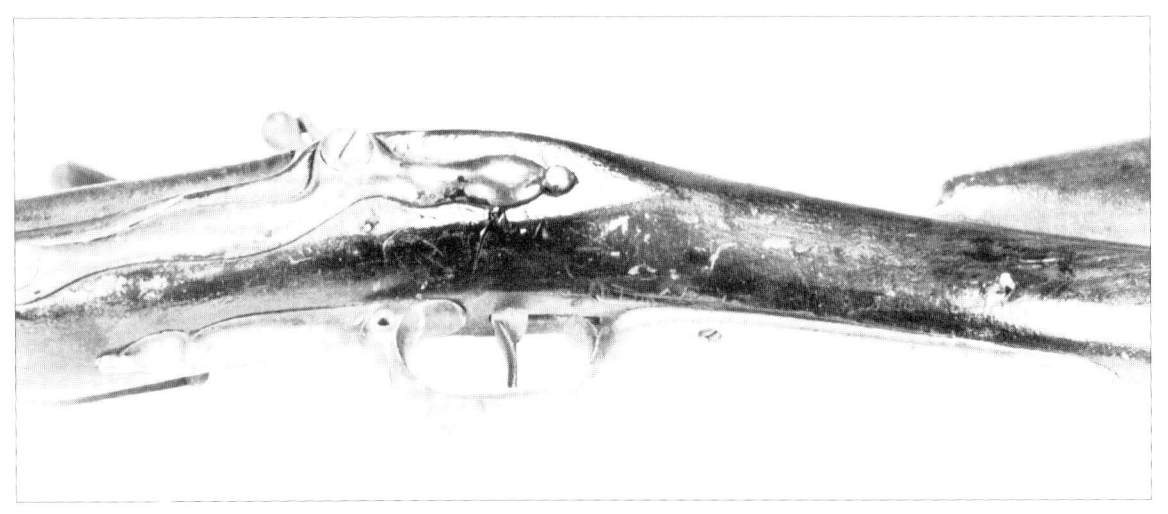

**31.MM  ENGLISH GRENADE LAUNCHING MUSKET**                                                               **Circa 1747**

Hand grenades were small round shells filled with powder and a projecting fuse. Initially they were ignited and thrown by grenadiers (created in 1678). Later, to expand their range, special steel cups (shaped like period rum bottles) were designed to act as mortar tubes and fit over the end of shortened shoulder arms. This example is a British Long Land musket with a typical banana lock (marked "IORDAN / 1747") and brass furniture. Its regular barrel however has been shortened to 28-1/2 inches, with a raised 3/16" collar mounted 3-7/8 inches below the muzzle. The grenade cup had an end neck ring plus penetrating slots like a bayonet socket and slid onto the muzzle in the same manner (note the top barrel stud). After the musket was loaded with a powder charge, the grenade was placed in the cup with the fuse away from the muzzle. When fired, the ignition not only launched the grenade but also at the same time sent flame around its surface to light the fuse. Quadrant sights were often fitted to the side plate. Britain's sea service used similar arms. (Also see shoulder mortar 148.MM.)

| | | | |
|---|---|---|---|
| Length: 44-1/2" | Lock: 6-7/8" X 1-1/4" | Butt Tang: 5-7/8" | Furniture: Brass |
| Barrel: 28-1/2", .77 cal. | Trigger Guard: 11-3/8" | Side Plate: 6-1/4" | Weight: 8.0 lbs. |

*Chapter 3: Smoothbore Shoulder Arms*

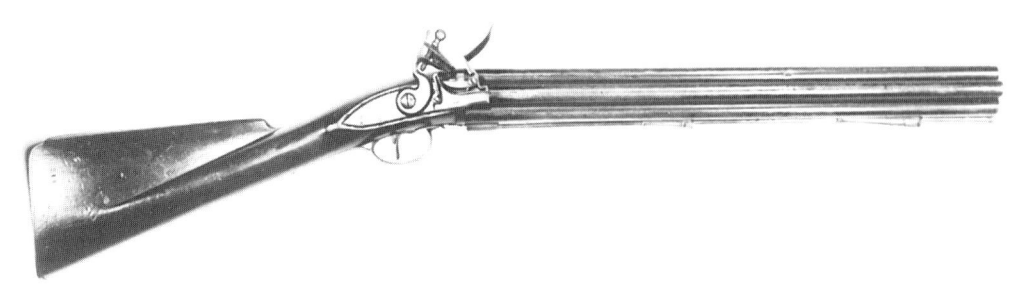

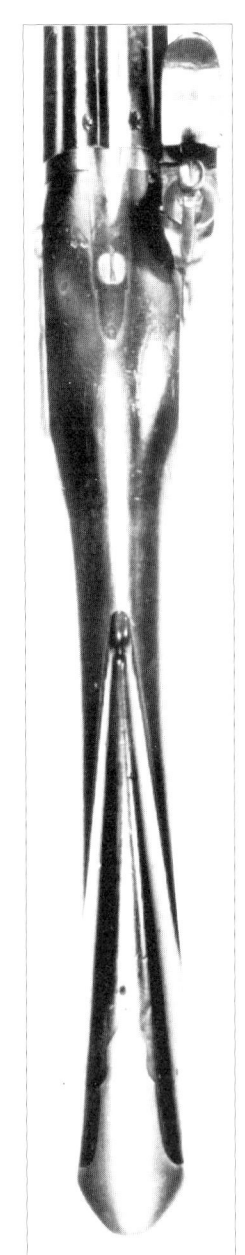

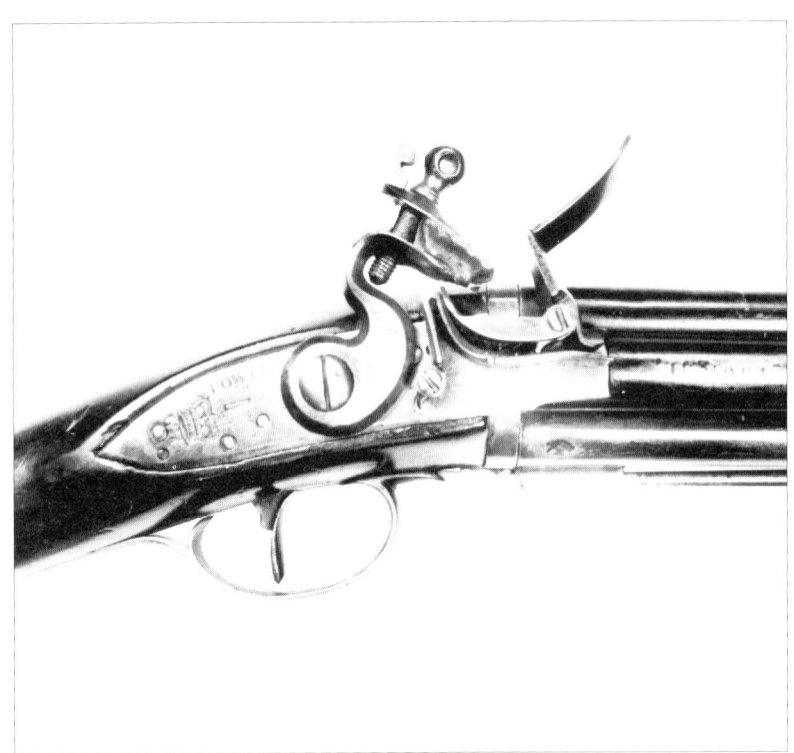

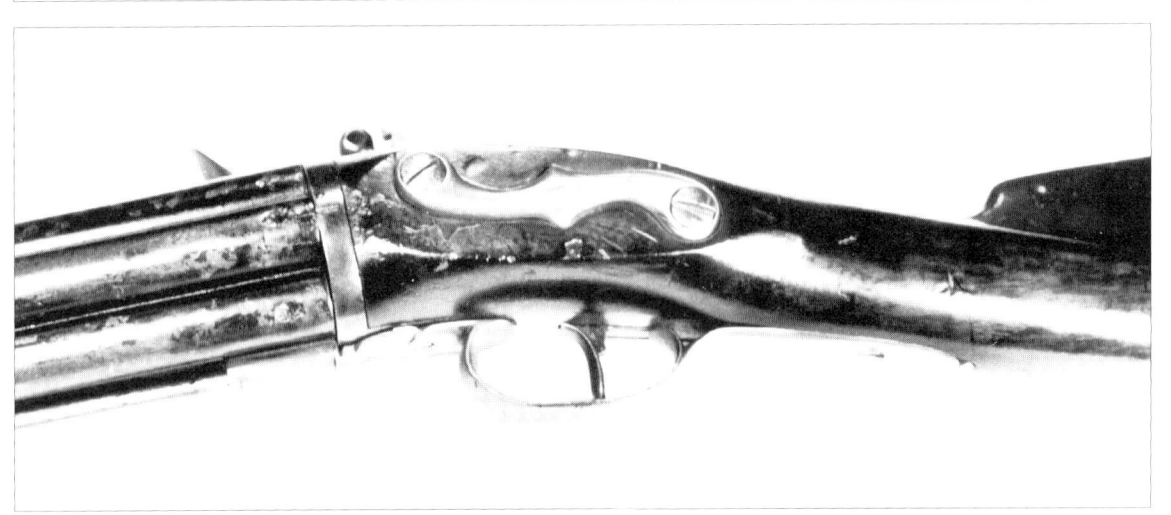

**32.MM  ENGLISH SEA SERVICE "NOCK" VOLLEY GUN**  Circa 1779

It is not known if the volley gun saw actual service here during the American Revolution, but it is included for reference. The arm clusters six barrels around a center barrel, and all fired together for devastating effect—usually from a ship's "tops." The design was created by James Wilson; 500 were produced by London gunmaker Henry Nock in 1779 (another 155 made by 1788 had a shorter lock and a reversed outer spring). All of the smoothbore barrels were brazed together (with a breech plug in each). The center barrel screwed into a plug that housed a bell-like chamber that when fired through the touch-hole also ignited each of the other barrels by individual channels. The long flat back-action lock is marked "TOWER" above "crown / GR" on its tail (also "crown/broad arrow" under the pan). The cock's upper post is notched, and a tipped L-shaped frizzen spring is behind the bridled pan. Its brass butt tang resembles the Short Land Pattern 1768 (14.MM). Board of Ordnance private proofs were struck on each breech, and "H NOCK" is engraved along the outboard side barrel. The butt is stamped "215."

| | | | |
|---|---|---|---|
| Length: 37-1/8" | Lock: 5-3/8" X 1-1/8" | Butt Tang: 4" | Furniture: Brass |
| Barrel: 20", .52 cal. | Trigger Guard: 6-7/8" | Side Plate: 3-3/8" | Weight: 12.0 lbs. |

**Richard Ulbrich Collection**

82    *Chapter 3: Smoothbore Shoulder Arms*

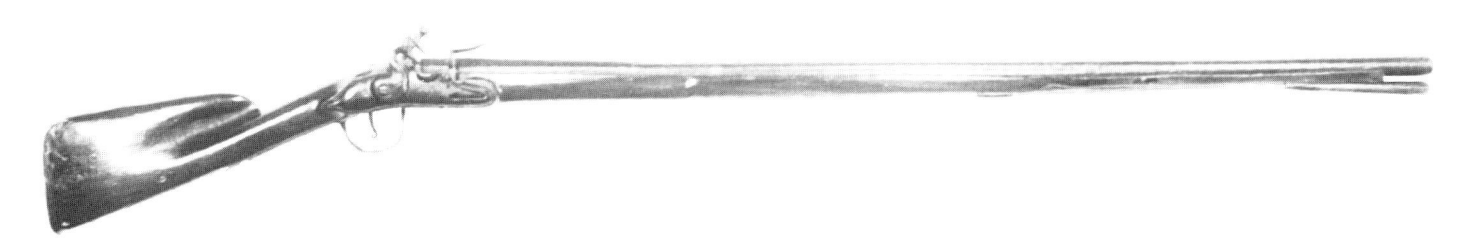

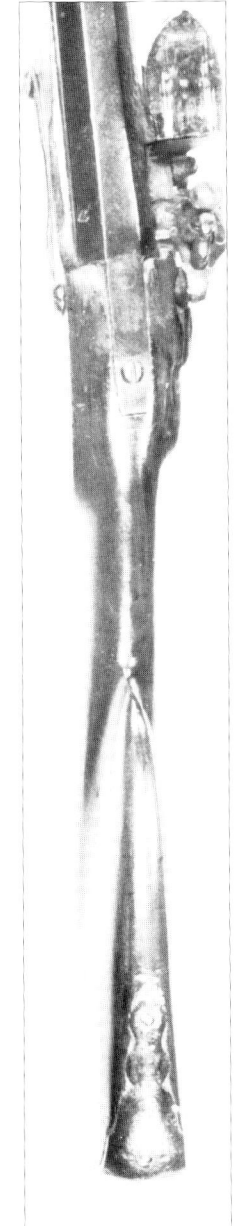

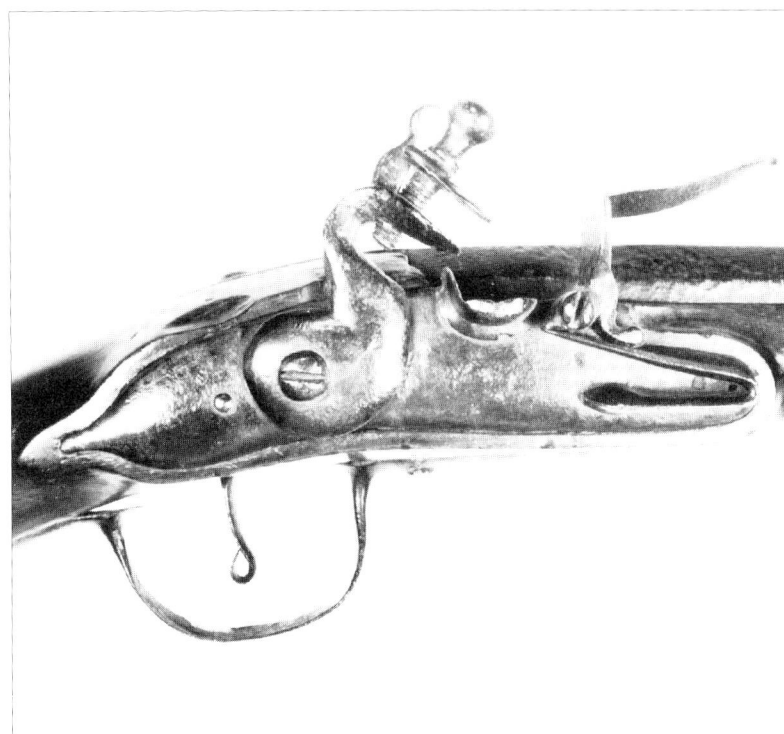

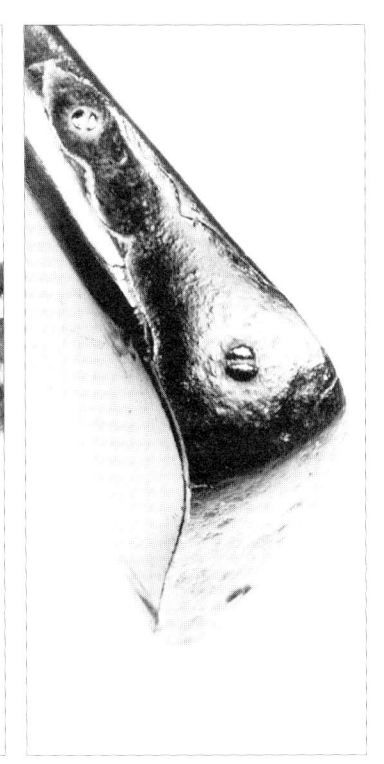

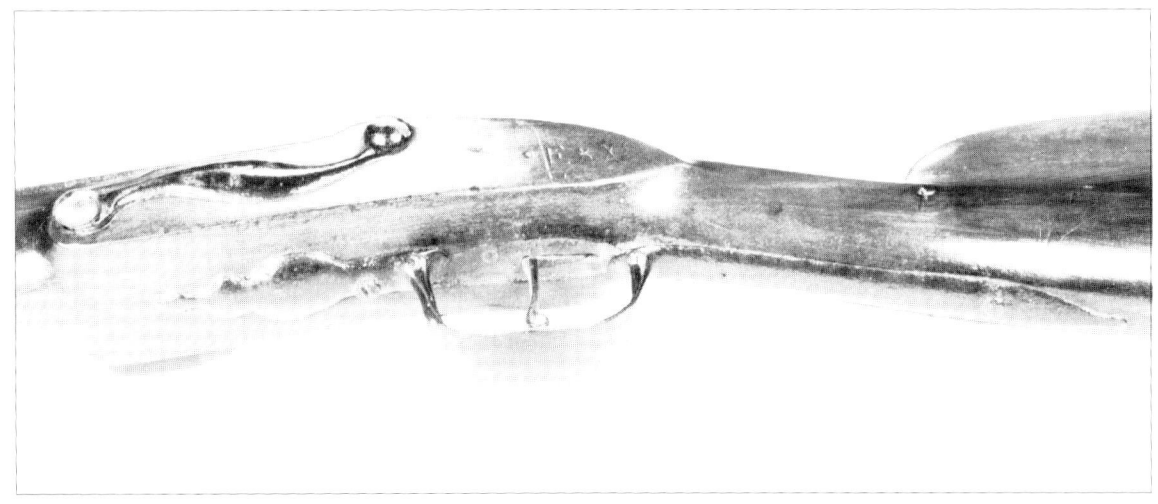

**33.MM FRENCH INFANTRY MUSKET**                                                                                                                               **Circa 1695–1716**

Very few French military longarms dating at the beginning of the 1700s have survived. Yet, iron components from a musket of that period are shown above — possibly in a later restocking (most had a Roman nose buttstock). Notice the early bulbous rounded lock (no external bridle), curled trigger tip, and deep bow. The complete trigger guard (three screws) displays the bulging segmented forward outline of that era (also see 74.MM), plus the emerging pointed rear end which characterized later patterns. An already established S-type side plate remains convex at this time. Its breech, in turn, is octagonal for nine inches, while two sheet iron pipes hold a wooden rammer (no tail pipe). The muzzle has probably been shortened from about 46-3/4 inches. A fleur-de-lis in a diamond cartouche is stamped into the breech, and a small fleur-de-lis above "C" appears on the cock. Its inboard butt bears the brand "ARR 17". An undulating, iron butt tang with a top end screw also reflects the lack of uniformity in those years prior to the first standard model of 1717 (38.MM). France was continually refurbishing earlier arms usually for their Colonial and auxiliary forces.

| | | | |
|---|---|---|---|
| Length: 58-3/4" | Lock: 6-1/2" X 1-1/4" | Butt Tang: 4" | Furniture: Iron |
| Barrel: 43-1/2", .72 cal. | Trigger Guard: 11-1/4" | Side Plate: 4-1/8" | Weight: 7.7 lbs. |

**George C. Neumann Collection, Valley Forge National Historical Park**

*Chapter 3: Smoothbore Shoulder Arms*    **83**

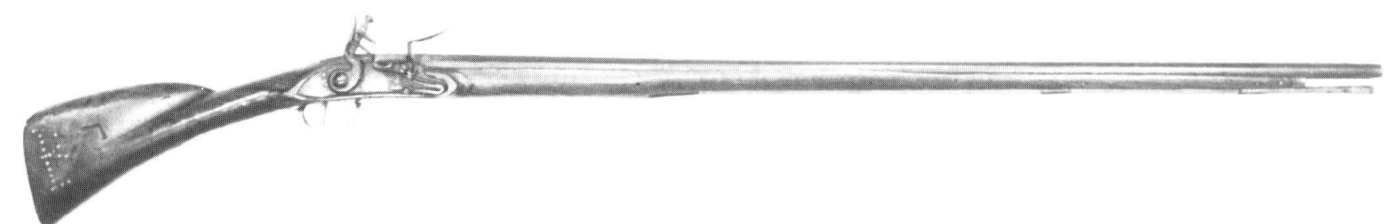

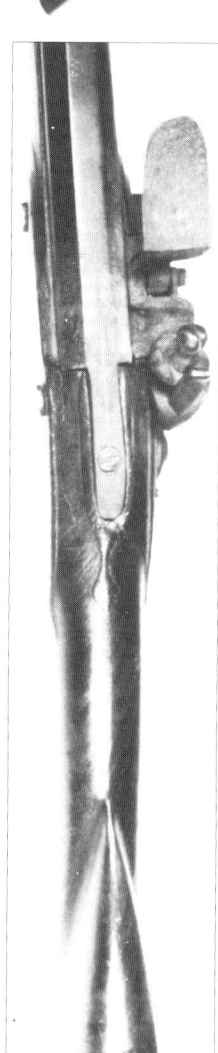

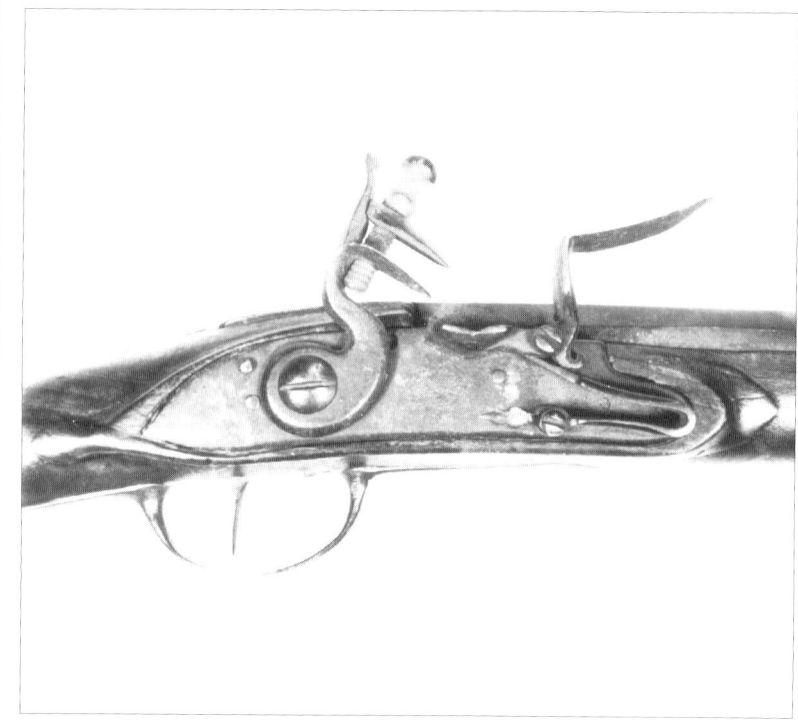

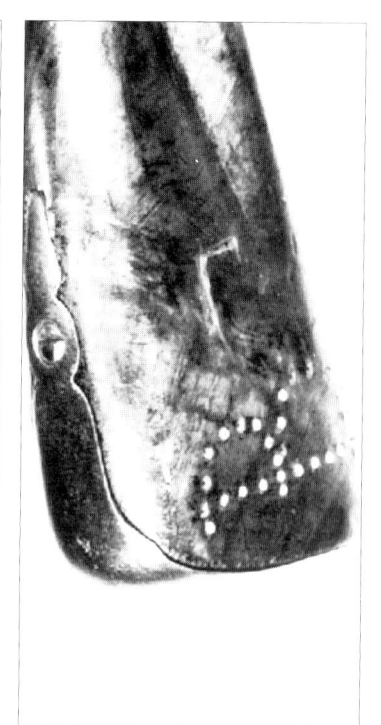

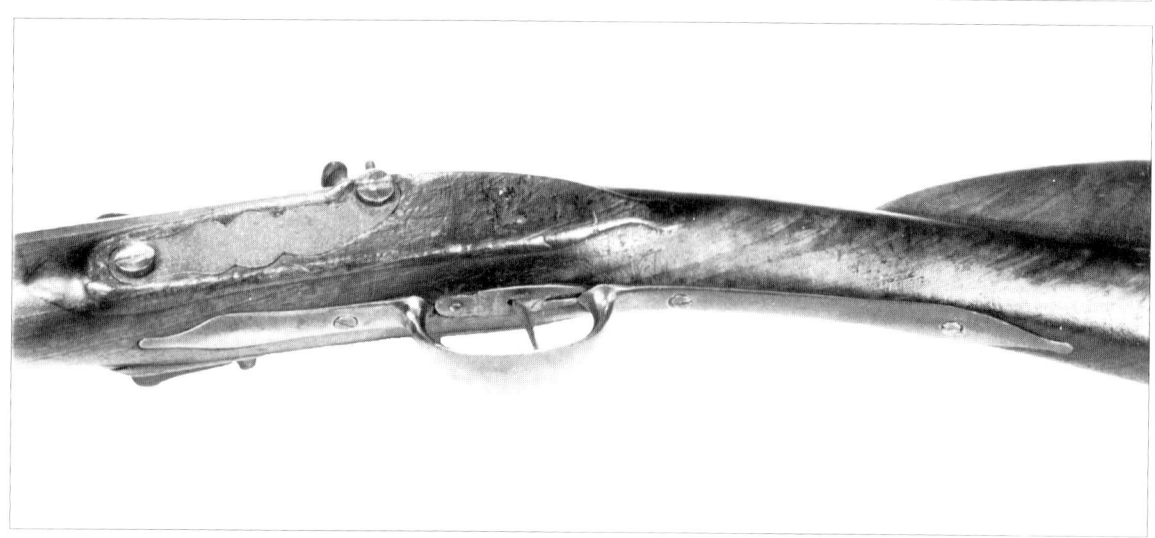

### 34.MM  FRENCH MARINE INFANTRY MUSKET (*Fusil Ordinaire*)　　　　　　　　　　　　　　　　　　　　　　　　　　　　　　　　　　　　　　　　Circa 1729–1734

Early muskets of this period produced at Tulle for the Department of Marine's *Compagnies Franches* in North America (France's only regular troops here until 1755) were grouped as either *ordinaire*, with a long 46-3/4", .66 caliber barrel and no sling swivels, or *grenadier*, having a shorter 44-3/4", .66-caliber barrel plus two oval side swivels (see 35.MM). This example of the former has the typical configuration of these Tulle arms: a curving Roman nose butt; a flat beveled lock showing two screw ends behind the cock, a faceted pan with bridle and a swans-neck hammer; raised teardrop carving around the side plate, lock and barrel tang; a double-pointed French military trigger guard; a long butt tang with a pear-shaped end held by a wood screw; and a flat S-shaped side plate that included an upright center oval. The pinned barrel is a form adopted by Tulle about 1720, which has an octagonal breech (ten inches here), followed by a section of 16 flats (1-3/4") and a multiple ring. There are three sheet-iron thimbles (the fourth is missing) for its wooden ramrod. No sling swivels are present, but they were approved for this pattern in 1729. The letter *B* is formed in the walnut stock by the insertion of small beads (later owner).

| | | | |
|---|---|---|---|
| Length: 60-1/2" | Lock: 6-3/8" X 1-1/4" | Butt Tang: 4" | Furniture: Iron |
| Barrel: 45-3/8", .69 cal. | Trigger Guard: 12-1/2" | Side Plate: 4" | Weight: 7.0 lbs. |

**Robert Nittolo Collection**

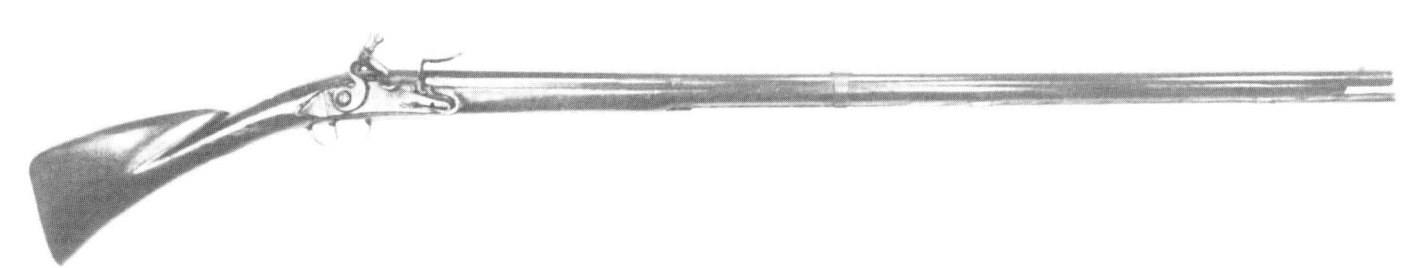

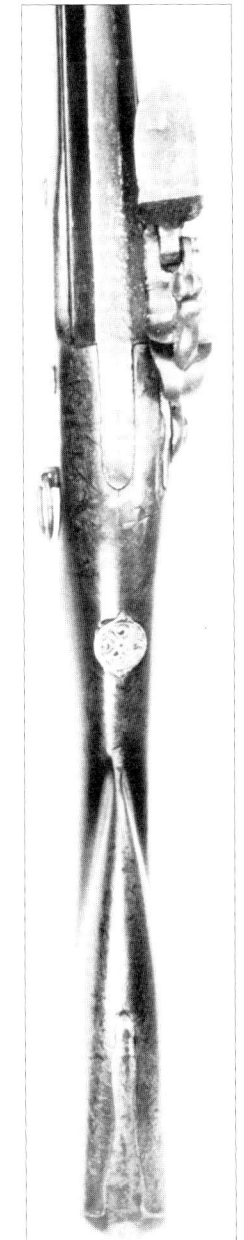

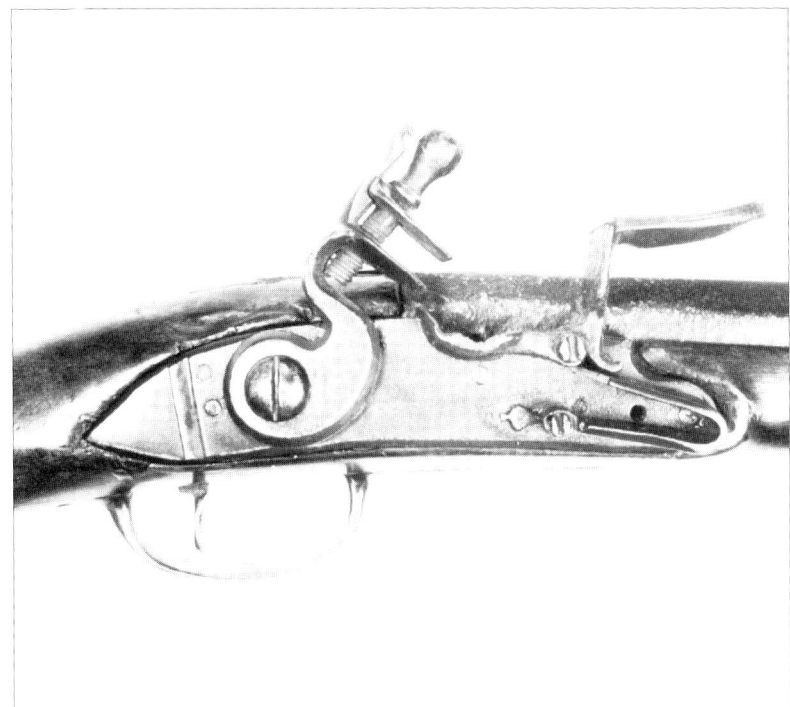

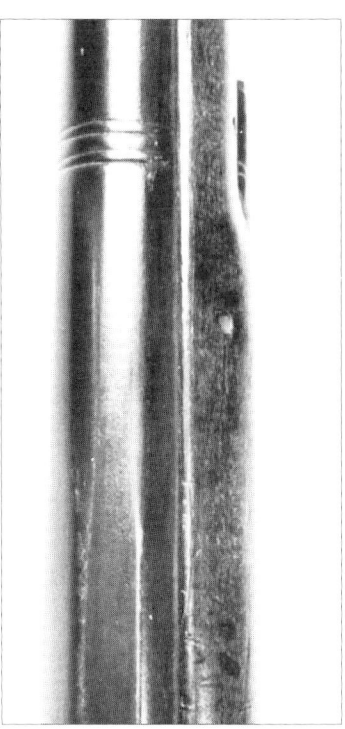

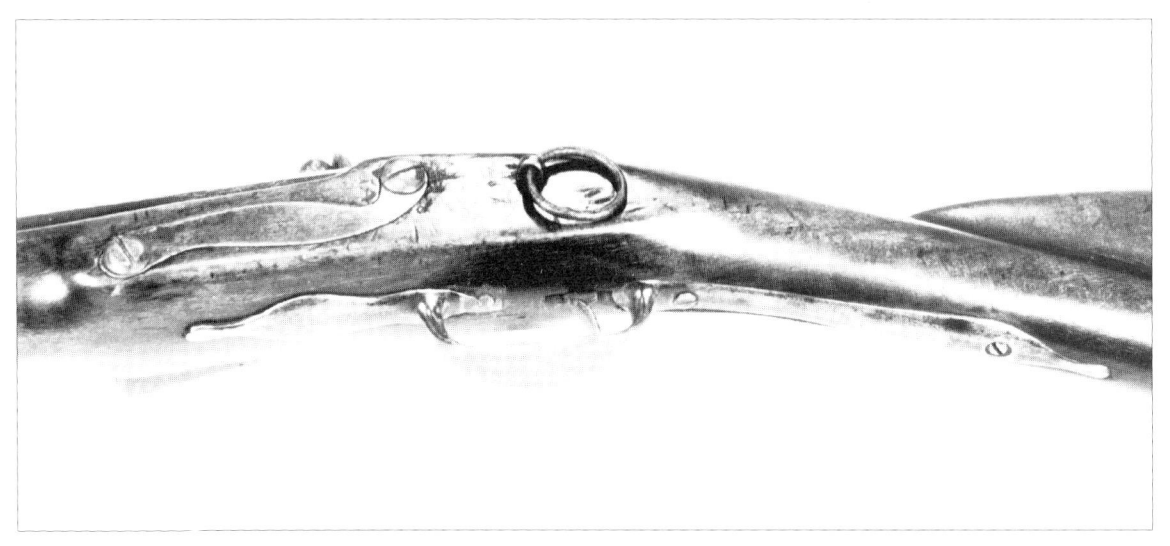

**35.MM FRENCH MARINE INFANTRY MUSKET (*Fusil Grenadier*)**  Circa 1729–1734

This is a *grenadier* pattern, versus the *ordinaire* version in the preceding illustration, because its .66 caliber barrel was two inches shorter (44-3/4 inches) and two oval sling swivels were mounted at the side—one anchored to a stud on the far side of its single barrel band and the other held by a post behind the side plate. Although most of the marine infantry muskets for Canada were made at Tulle, by the 1720s increased demand led to additional contracts at St. Etienne. The lock plate is stamped by a crown above "S-E" for that manufactory, which followed the basic dimensions but used some iron furniture patterned after the contemporary regular army muskets. Thus this longarm includes component forms from the army's Model 1728 (39.MM): the flat lock with a rear channel, a simple flat S-shaped side plate, the double-pointed trigger guard, a long narrow butt tang, and the absence of border carving. The Tulle type of barrel, however, is present (octagonal 10-1/4 inches and a 16-flats section for 2-1/4 inches to a multiple ring). Three sheet-iron pipes and the single center band secure the wooden rammer. The round escutcheon is a later private addition.

| | | | |
|---|---|---|---|
| Length: 59-3/4" | Lock: 6-1/2" X 1-1/4" | Butt Tang: 4-3/4" | Furniture: Brass |
| Barrel: 44-1/2", .71 cal. | Trigger Guard: 11-1/2" | Side Plate: 4" | Weight: 7.8 lbs. |

**Author's Collection**

*Chapter 3: Smoothbore Shoulder Arms*

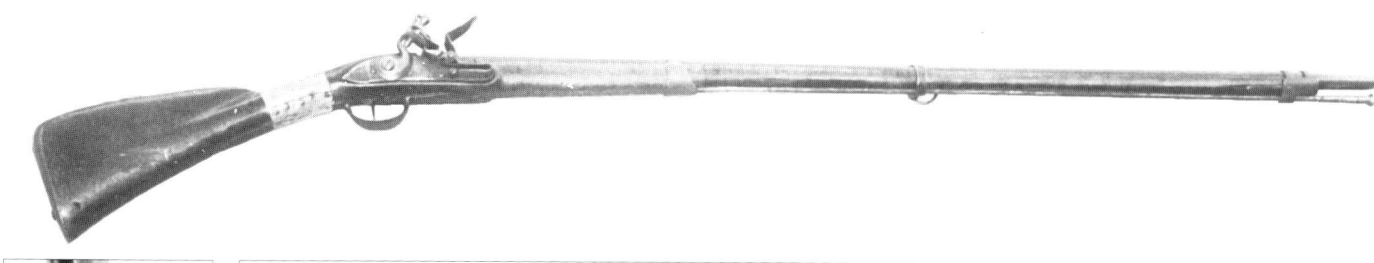

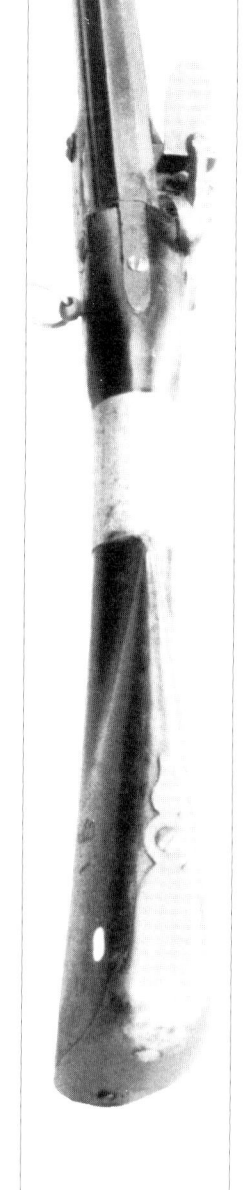

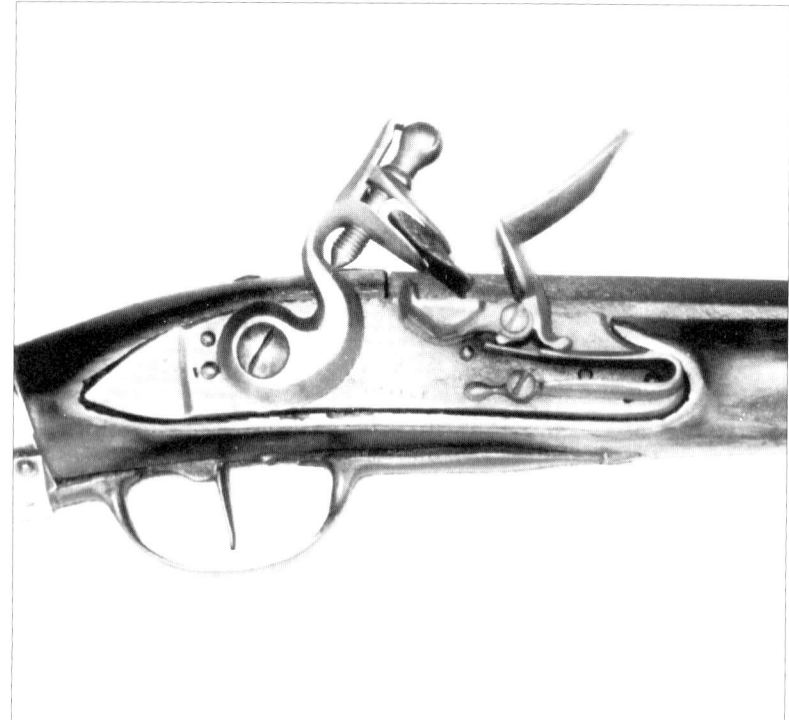

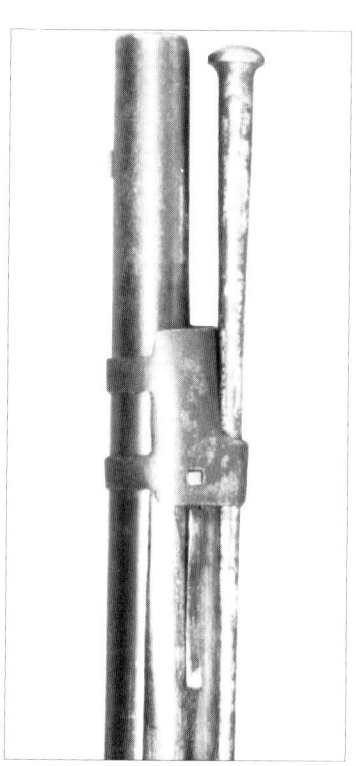

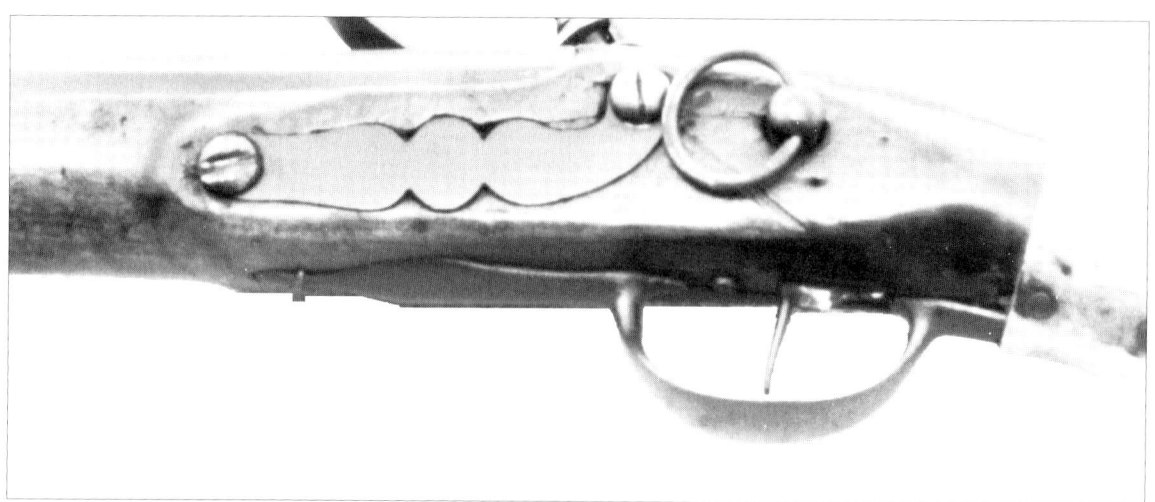

**36.MM FRENCH MARINE INFANTRY MUSKET (*Fusil A Domino*)**  Circa 1744

In the mid 1740s, during King George's War (1744–1748), the current Tulle pattern for the Department of Marine's Canadian troops had three bands added to replace the previous barrel pins. This new *A Domino* model also eliminated raised carving around the lock, side plate and barrel tang, as well as the 16-flat section on the barrel, which now flowed smoothly from octagonal to round. The flat/beveled lock with its indented tail and faceted/bridled pan is marked "A TVLLE" (the *V* became a full *U* in 1745). That armory's traditional styling also continues in the flat S-shaped side plate with a center oval, the long butt tang tipped by a pear-shaped finial (and wood screw) plus the curved Roman nose butt (note the period sheet-brass wrist repair). Its new barrel bands match the current army's Model 1728 (39.MM), while an iron button-head ramrod (approved by the army in 1741) also appears. The two grenadier side sling swivels continue. Other markings include "769" on the breech and a fleur-de-lis behind the trigger guard.

| | | | |
|---|---|---|---|
| Length: 60-1/2" | Lock: 6-3/8" X 1-1/8" | Butt Tang: 4-1/2" | Furniture: Iron |
| Barrel: 45", .70 cal. | Trigger Guard: 12" | Side Plate: 4" | Weight: 9.0 lbs. |

**Robert Speelman Collection**

*Chapter 3: Smoothbore Shoulder Arms*

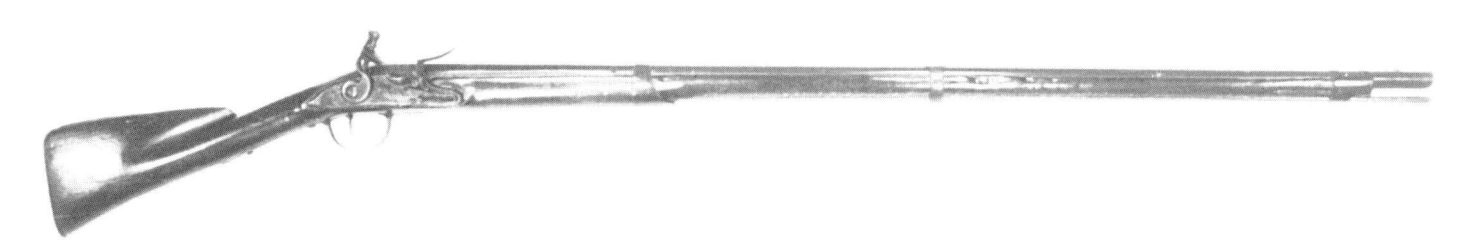

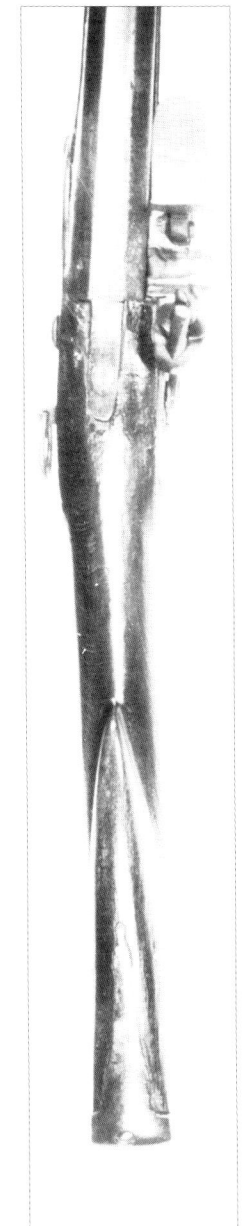

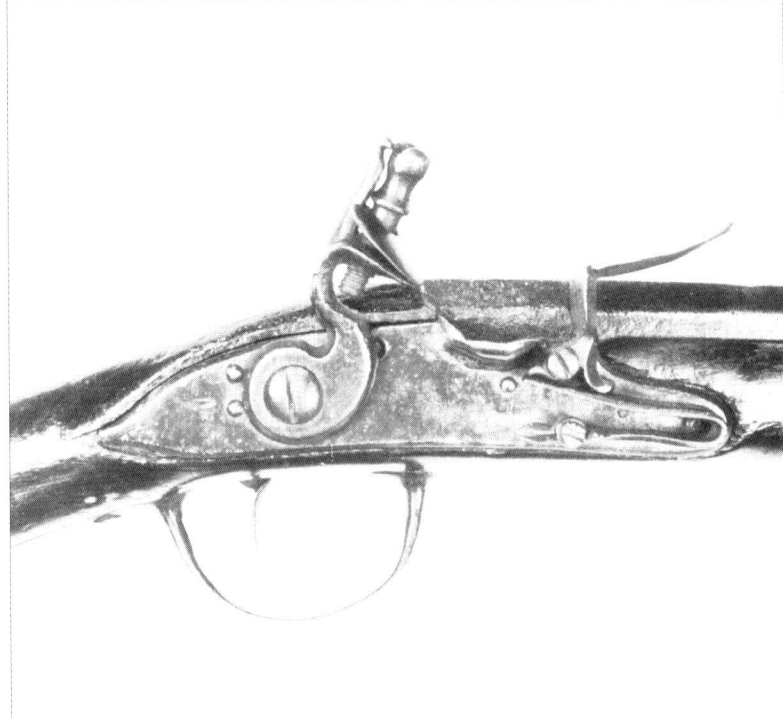

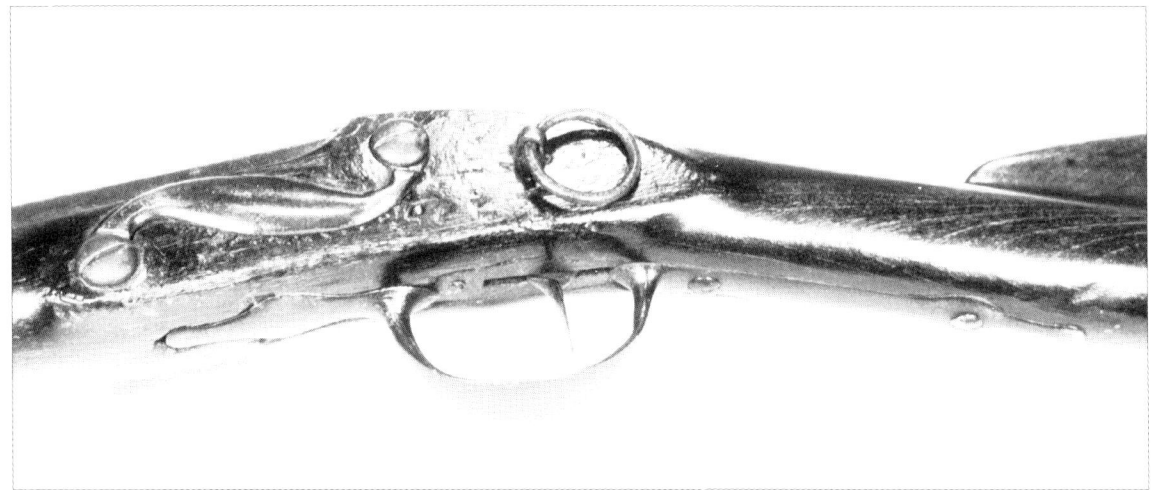

**37.MM FRENCH RESTOCKED MARINE INFANTRY MUSKET**                                                  **Circa 1740–1755**

Although students prefer to judge arms as complete models, great numbers of these muskets were constantly being reassembled with surplus or salvaged components and reissued. This restocked example includes parts of a marine Tulle-made musket from early in the century, including: a flat/beveled lock marked "A TVLLE" and no internal or external bridles, a deeply bowed and bulbous double-pointed trigger guard, and a convex S-shaped side plate—combined with three barrel bands, a long narrow butt tang and rounded side sling swivels associated with the army's Model 1728 pattern. The stock profile, however, has lost its Roman nose, which suggests the later dating. Many of the Tulle marine arms were acquired by Americans at Louisbourg in 1745 and during the French and Indian War. This gun could have been assembled in North America using available parts or from remains after the great Quebec City arsenal fire of 1754, but use of beechwood suggests restocking in France. The barrel is of the Tulle circa 1720 pattern: octagonal for 9-3/4 inches behind a 1-1/2" section of 16 facets. A "crown / fleur-de-lis" and an anchor (meaning the Department of Marine's *Compagnies Franches*) are struck into the breech.

| | | | |
|---|---|---|---|
| Length: 60-1/2" | Lock: 6-5/8" X 1-1/4" | Butt Tang: 4-1/2" | Furniture: Iron |
| Barrel: 45-5/8", .71 cal. | Trigger Guard: 10-1/8" | Side Plate: 4" | Weight: 8.0 lbs. |

**Author's Collection**

*Chapter 3: Smoothbore Shoulder Arms*     87

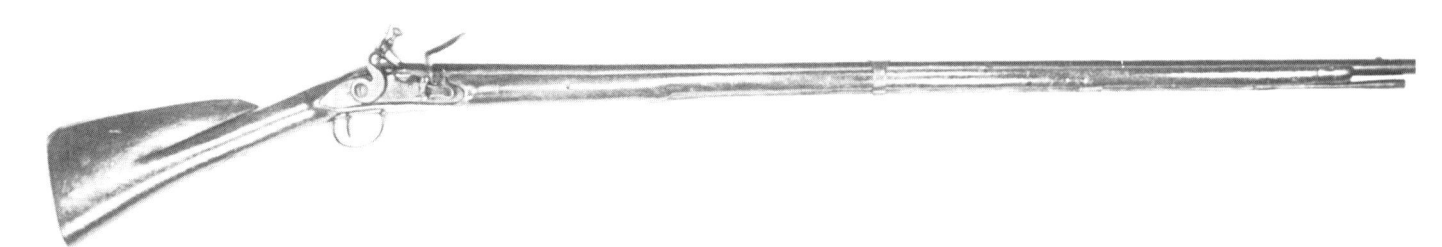

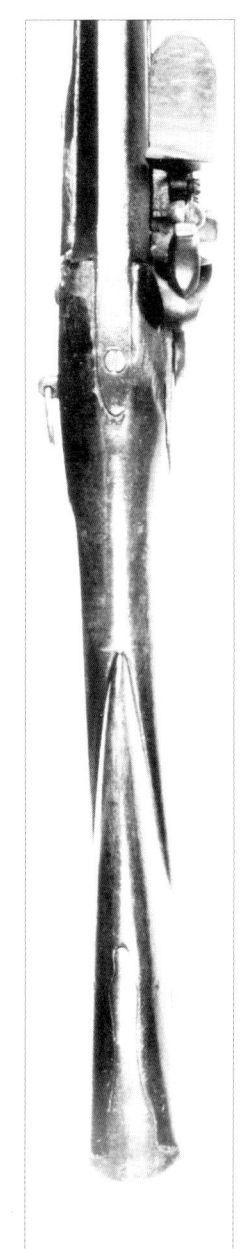

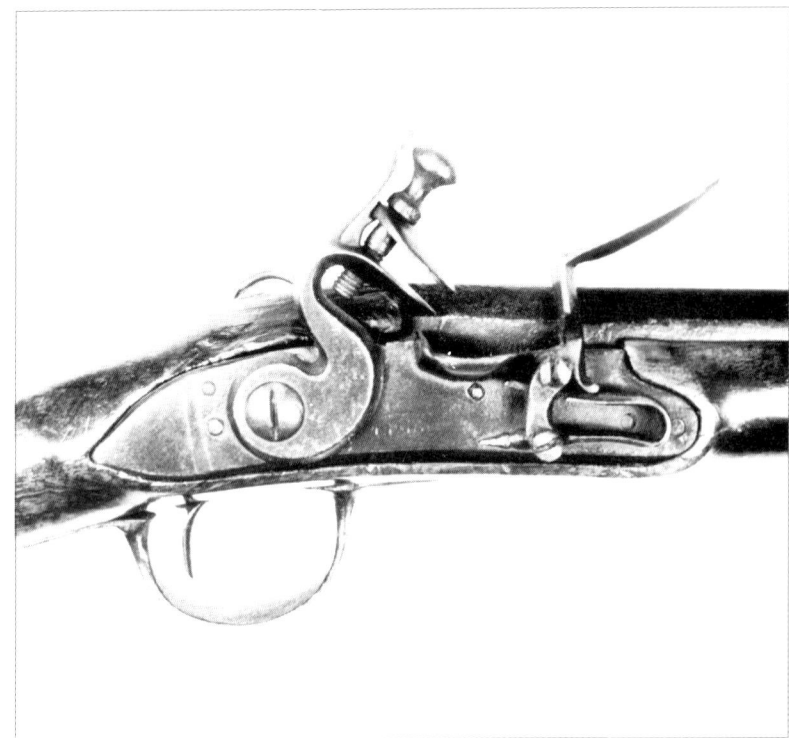

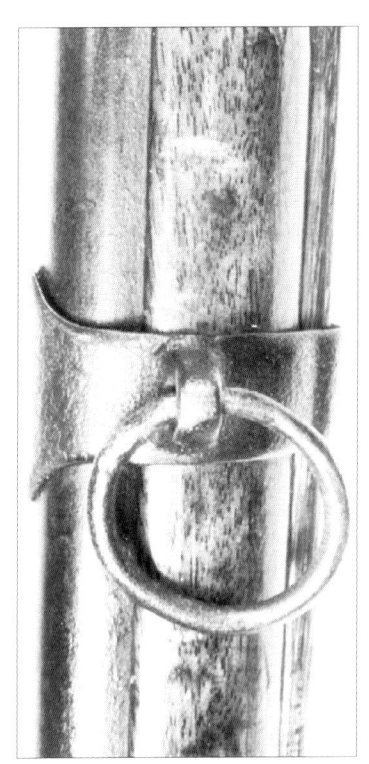

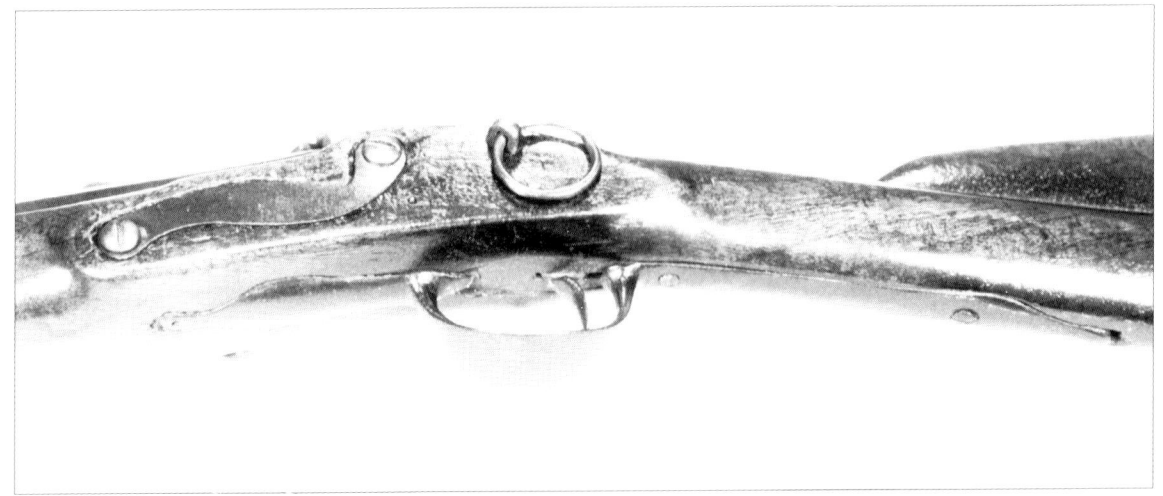

**38.MM FRENCH MODEL 1717 MUSKET**  Circa 1717

This Model 1717 was the first standard infantry musket adopted for the French army. Its distinctive elements were the vertical (slightly curved) bridle between the frizzen and frizzen spring screws, the pinned barrel (46-3/4", .69 caliber), long butt tang, and side sling swivels mounted to a stud on the inboard side of the single barrel band and to a post behind the rear side plate screw. The Roman nose walnut stock mounts three 1-1/8" iron pipes (plus the center band) to hold a wooden ramrod and adds a 3/4" iron strip one inch from the forend tip. Its flat/beveled lock plate is stamped "crown / SE" (St. Etienne manufactory). Note also the swans-neck cock (with a flat-backed top jaw and slotted screw), plus a frizzen spring ending short of the upper side screw tip. An octagonal breech, in turn, continues a flat panel along the barrel top to the bayonet lug. All three royal manufactories produced some 48,000 of this model. Although the French army did not relieve the Ministry of Marine troops in Canada until 1755, artifacts and local restocked arms indicate the pattern's presence prior to 1750.

| | | | |
|---|---|---|---|
| Length: 63-1/4" | Lock: 6-1/2" X 1-1/4" | Butt Tang: 4-3/4" | Furniture: Iron |
| Barrel: 47", .72 cal. | Trigger Guard: 11-1/2" | Side Plate: 3-7/8" | Weight: 7.8 lbs. |

**Author's Collection**

88  *Chapter 3: Smoothbore Shoulder Arms*

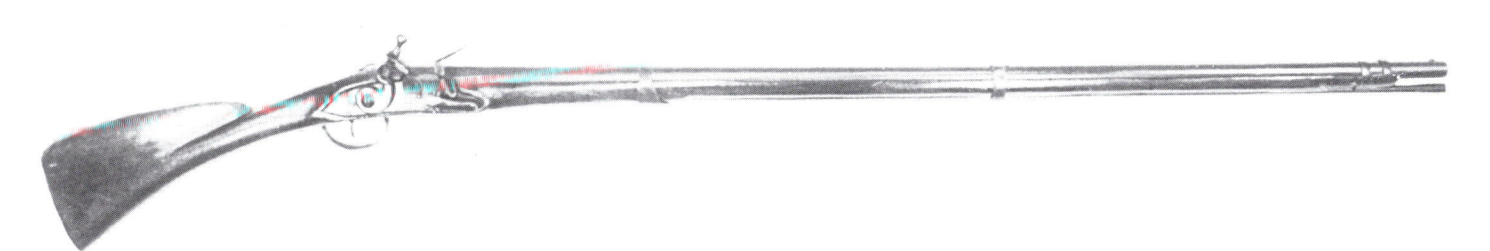

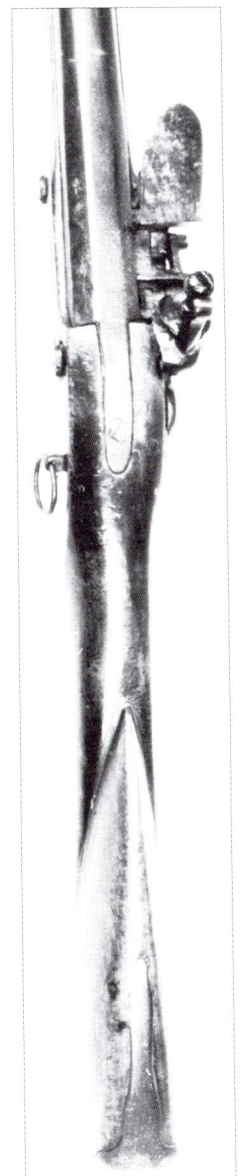

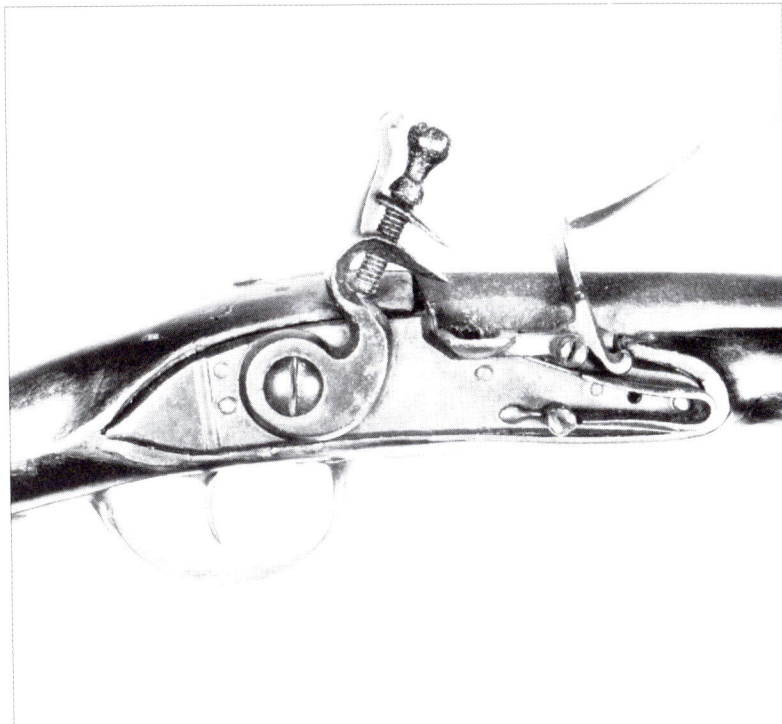

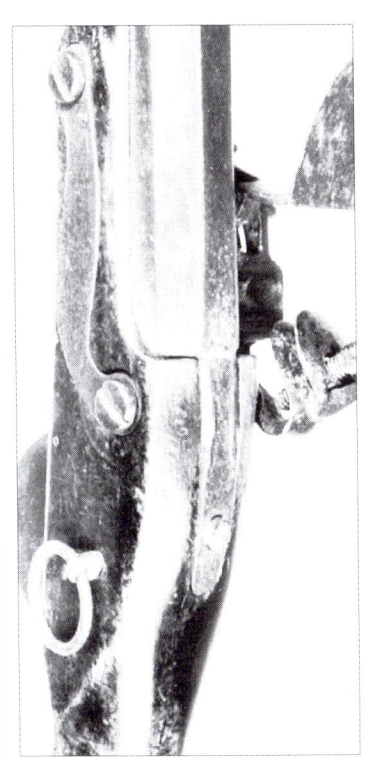

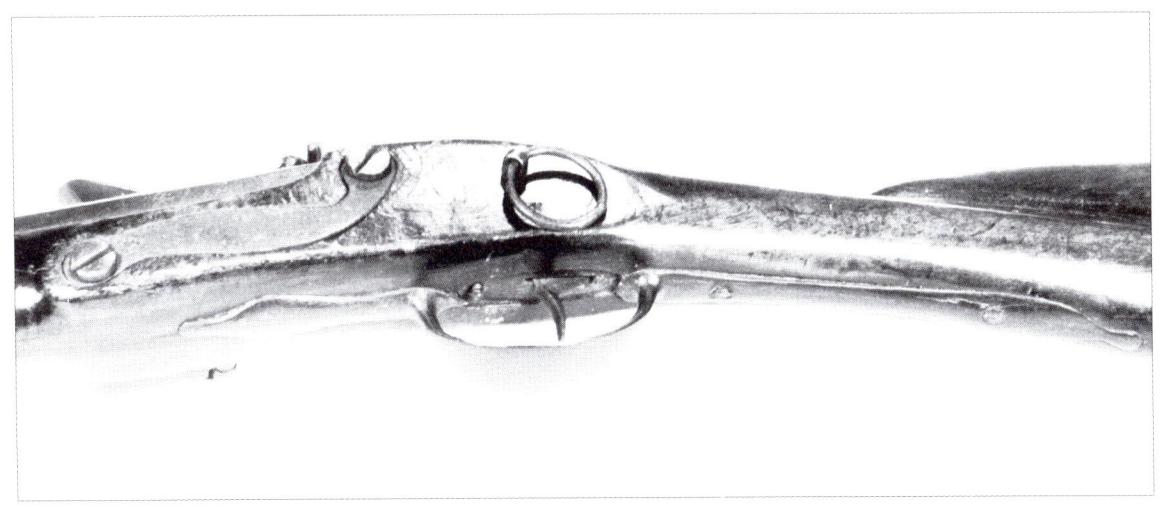

### 39.MM  FRENCH MODEL 1728 MUSKET

**Circa 1728**

As successor to the 1717 Pattern (38.MM), this Model 1728: switched to a horizontal exterior lock bridle; added three bands to replace the pinned barrel (upper band had a rear spring, others held by friction); lengthened the lobe-ended frizzen spring to cover the side screw tip; and installed an oval rear-notched jaw on the cock. Yet it retained the prior 46-3/4", .69 caliber barrel, flat S-shaped side plate, round-ended barrel tang, double-pointed trigger guard, long butt tang and circular sling swivels. The latter are attached to a lug on the far side of the middle barrel band and to a post behind the rear side screw (which threads into a square nut inside the walnut stock). Notice too the continued Roman nose butt, wooden rammer and typical French absence of raised decorative carving. An octagonal breech still continues the top flat panel that now ends five inches below the muzzle. Marks: on the lock, "SE" (St. Etienne manufactory) and "CG"; on the barrel, "crown / LL / heart" (control stamp of Lilien), plus "crown / CN" (Inspector Nicholas Carteron). This model was also supplementing the Tulle pattern longarms of the *Compagnies Franches de la Marine* in Canada by the 1730s. About 375,000 were produced.

| | | | |
|---|---|---|---|
| Length: 62" | Lock: 6-1/2" X 1-1/4" | Butt Tang: 4-3/4" | Furniture: Iron |
| Barrel: 45-7/8", .72 cal. | Trigger Guard: 11-3/4" | Side Plate: 4-1/8" | Weight: 8.2 lbs. |

**Author's Collection**

*Chapter 3: Smoothbore Shoulder Arms*  **89**

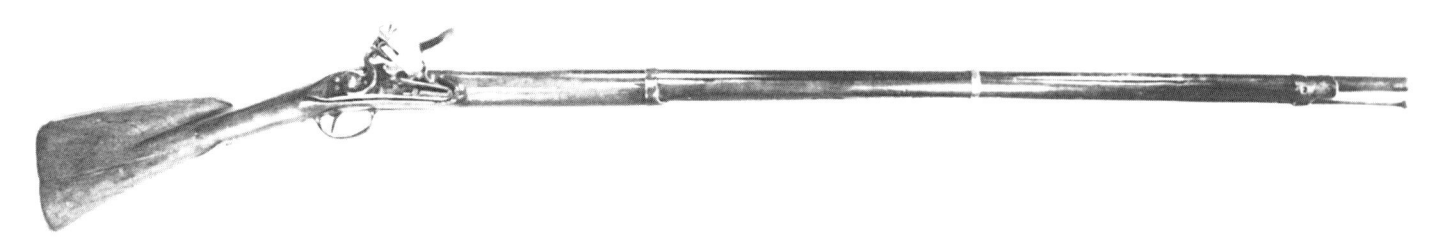

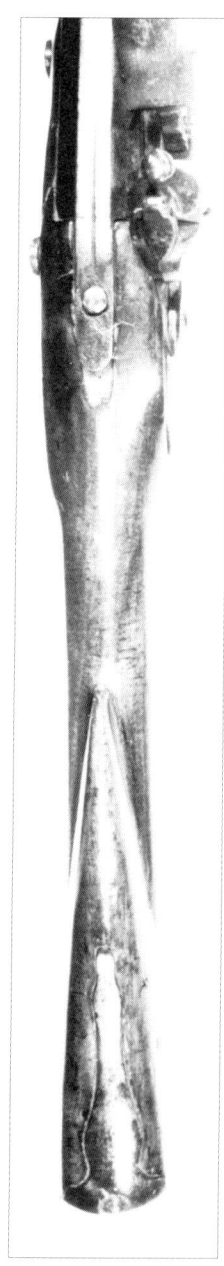

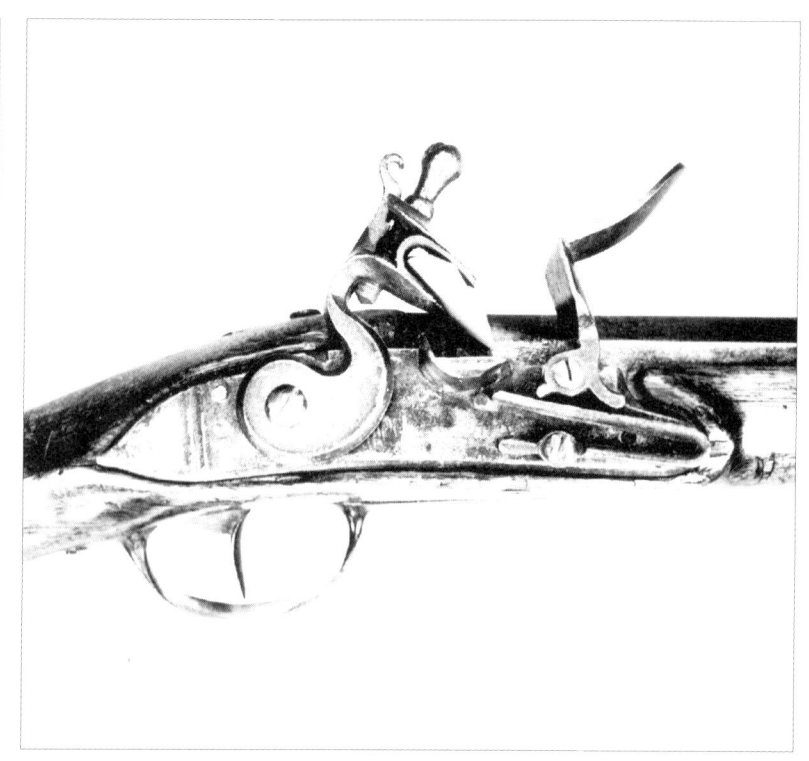

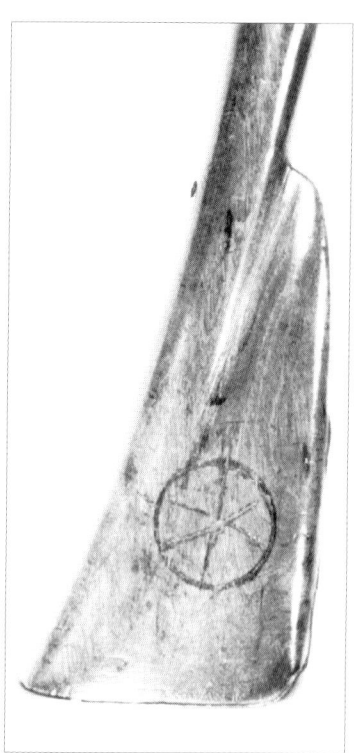

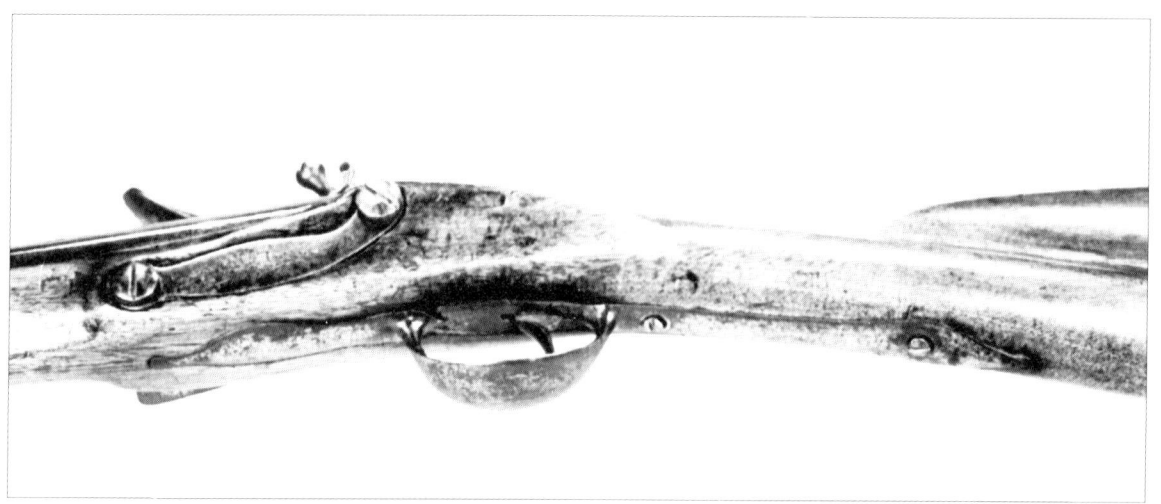

**40.MM FRENCH MODEL 1746 MUSKET**  Circa 1746

The basic form of the 1717 and 1728 Models continued here with further modifications. Its three primary changes were: elimination of the horizontal bridle between the flash pan and frizzen spring screw; a flattening of the middle of the three barrel bands (and elimination of its front and rear center-points); and the addition of a steel button-headed ramrod (authorized in 1741). About 248,000 were manufactured. The Roman nose butt, long undulating butt tang, flat side plate and double-pointed trigger guard continue. As before, its two lower bands are held by friction and there is no escutcheon or raised outline carving. The original side sling swivels are missing from this example. Note the typical French round-ended barrel tang and the straight incised line that extends onto the breech. This usually served as a crude rear sight (to line up with the bayonet stud), as well as an indication that the breech plug was screwed tight. The wheel form butt carving was from a later owner. Many of the earlier wooden rammers were changed to steel here during the French and Indian War.

Length: 62-1/4"  Lock: 6-1/2" X 1-1/4"  Butt Tang: 5"  Furniture: Iron
Barrel: 46-1/2", .72 cal.  Trigger Ward: 11-3/4"  Side Plate: 4"  Weight: 8.8 lbs.

**George C. Neumann Collection, Valley Forge National Historical Park**

*Chapter 3: Smoothbore Shoulder Arms*

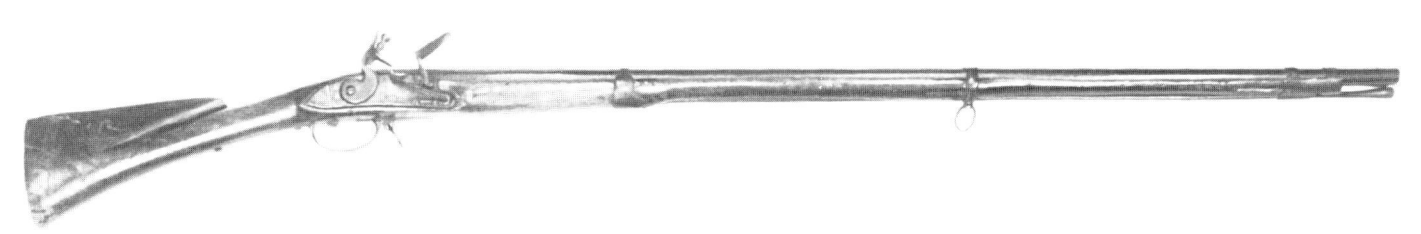

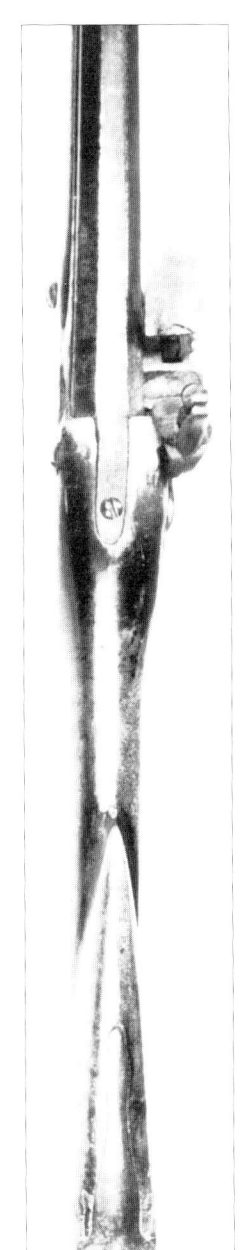

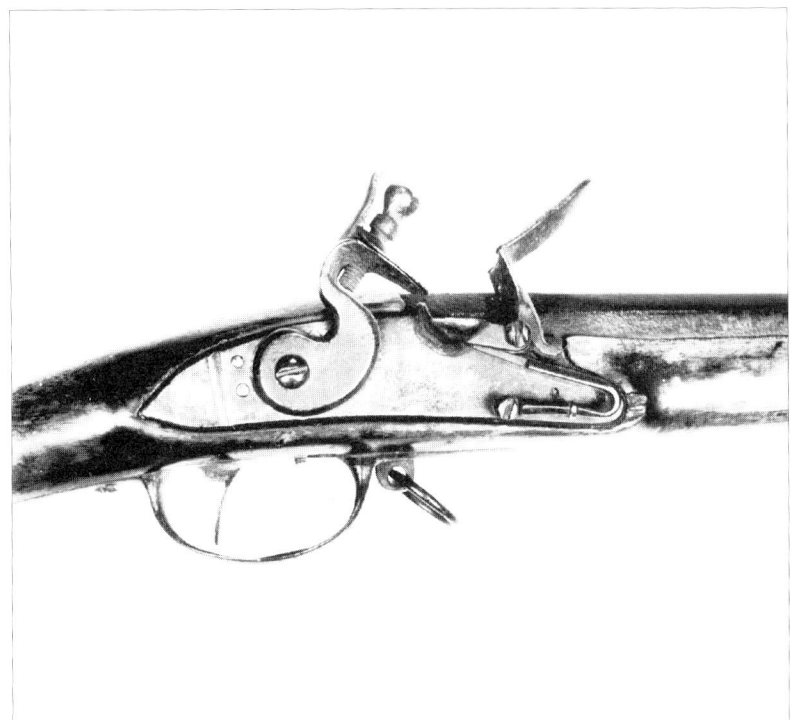

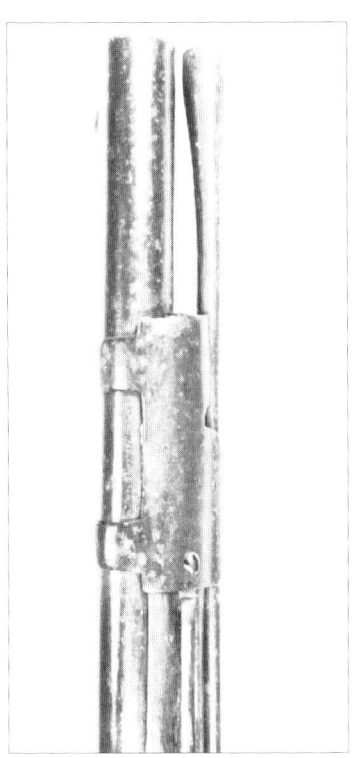

**41.MM FRENCH MODEL 1754 MUSKET**          Circa 1754

The Model 1754 is considered the last of this Model 1717 series, as it begins the transition toward the coming Model 1763 system. The important changes it introduced are: moving both sling swivels (still circular in shape) from the side to positions under the stock attached to the bottom of the middle of the three bands and to a stud projecting through the front section of the trigger guard; reappearance of the horizontal exterior lock bridle from the faceted pan to the frizzen screw; and a rear retaining spring on the middle band as well as upper one. The butt tang, in turn, is slightly shorter, while the steel ramrod has evolved from the previous button head to a trumpet shape. Some 208,000 of these were manufactured at the three royal manufactories (St. Etienne, Charleville and Maubeuge). Its walnut stock's Roman nose is still in place but with a reduced curve. Markings on the barrel are "RC B N54" and a "fleur-de-lis / HL." Note that the frizzen spring finial is missing from this example.

| | | | |
|---|---|---|---|
| Length: 61" | Lock: 6-1/4" X 1-3/8" | Butt Tang: 4-3/4" | Furniture: Iron |
| Barrel: 45-1/2", .75 cal. | Trigger Guard: 12-1/4" | Side Plate: 3-7/8" | Weight: 8.3 lbs. |

**Robert Nittolo Collection**

*Chapter 3: Smoothbore Shoulder Arms*

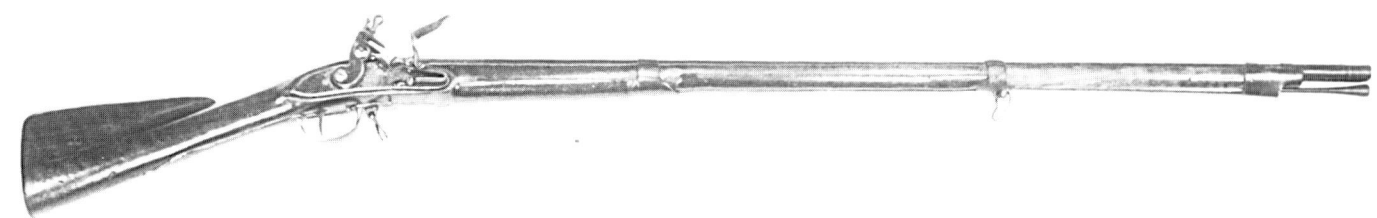

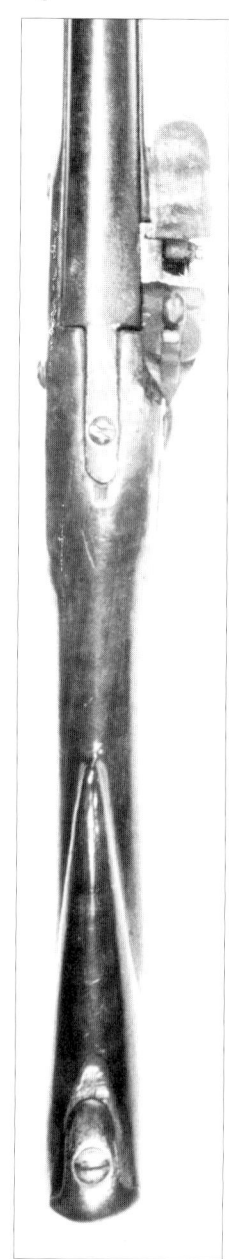

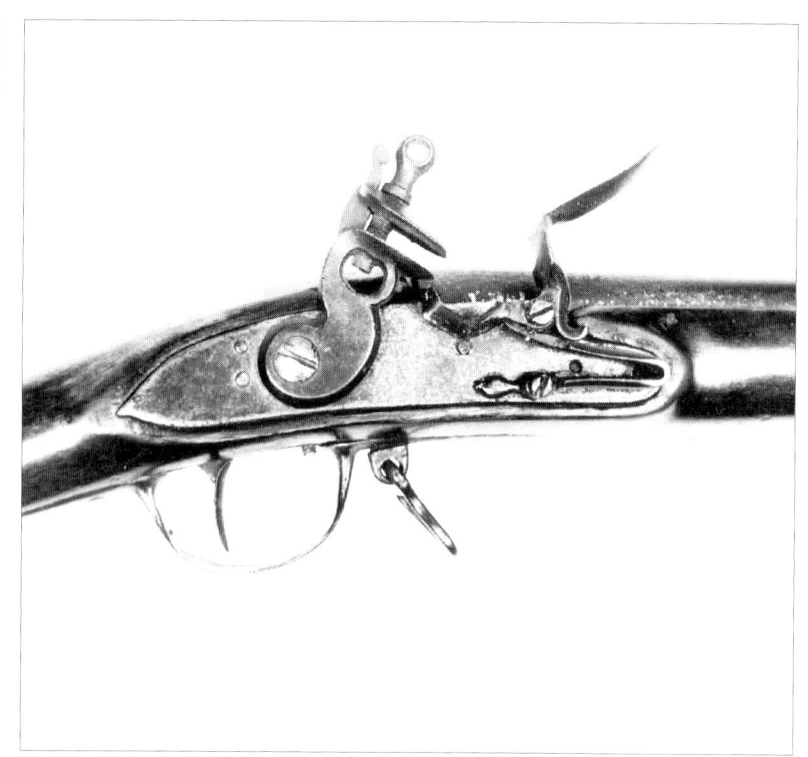

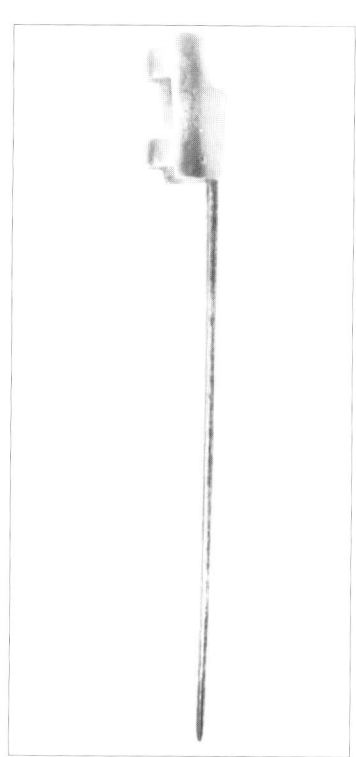

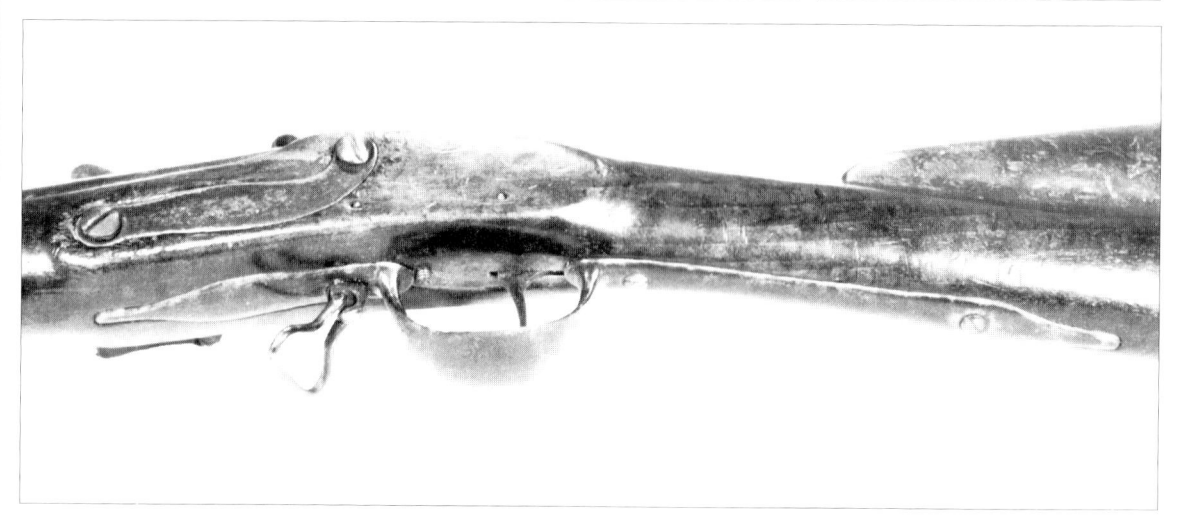

**42.MM FRENCH MODEL 1763 MUSKET**  Circa 1763

This flintlock with a straighter stock profile introduced a new series that would continue into the 1770s. It was part of the complete reorganization of French forces that began at the end of the French and Indian War. A heavier barrel retains the .69 caliber bore but is shortened to 44-3/4 inches and replaces the old octagonal breech with a rounded form (flat sides). A longer flat lock, in turn, mounts a new ring cock having a front-notched upper post, a wraparound oval top jaw, plus a hole added to the slotted jaw screw. A detachable faceted pan supports a horizontal bridle. Only on this model the uppermost of three barrel bands has a long U-shaped iron strip riveted to its underside that extends back to cover the ramrod channel (as a spring) all the way down to the middle band, which secures it under a front lip. This revised design still keeps the S-shaped flat side plate and double-pointed trigger guard but introduces a simple lobed butt tang (large top screw) and bell-shaped sling swivels. Eighty-eight thousand were produced. Marks: crossed quill pens on the breech (St. Etienne), and a fleur-de-lis over "SB" on the inboard buttstock.

| | | | |
|---|---|---|---|
| Length: 60-1/4" | Lock: 6-3/4" X 1-1/4" | Butt Tang: 2-1/2" | Furniture: Iron |
| Barrel: 44-3/4", .72 cal. | Trigger Guard: 13-1/4" | Side Plate: 4" | Weight: 9.2 lbs. |

**Author's Collection**

92   *Chapter 3: Smoothbore Shoulder Arms*

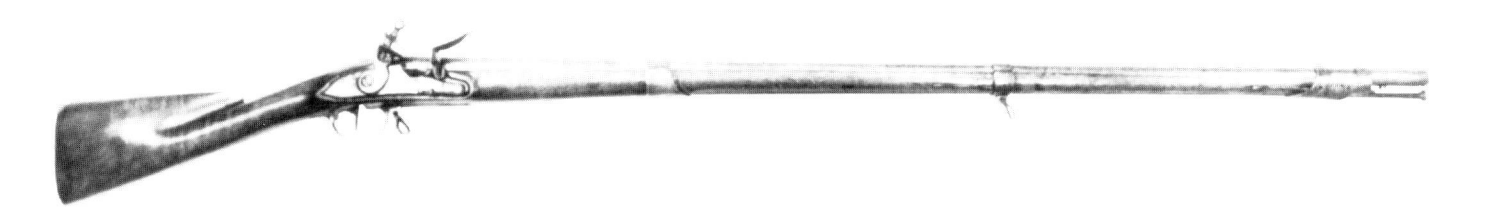

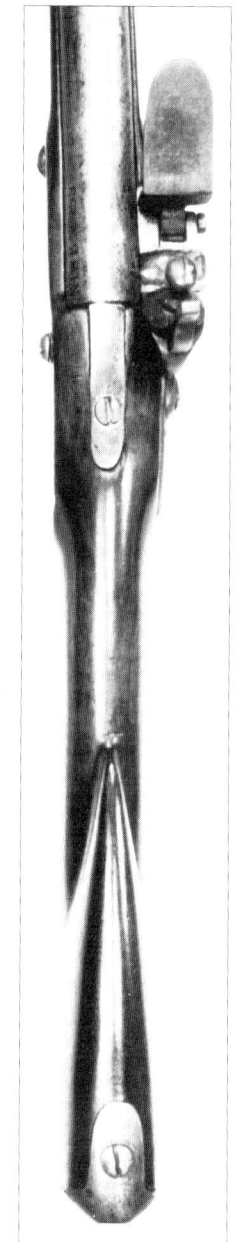

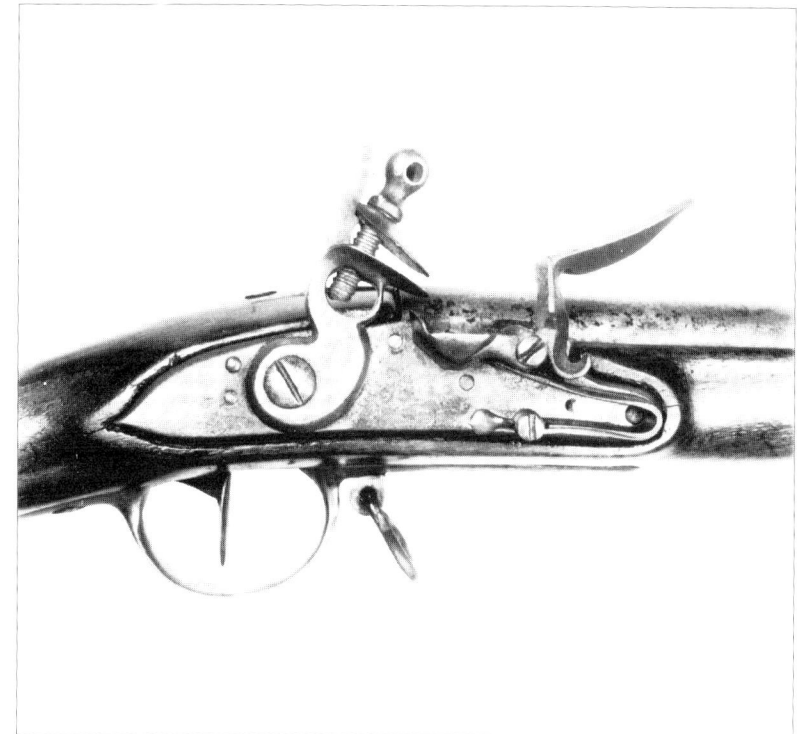

### 43.MM FRENCH MODEL 1766 MUSKET

**Circa 1766**

The Model 1763 was quickly found to be too heavy. This revised 1766 Pattern kept that basic configuration but reduced its original weight: the similar lock is now 1/2" shorter, its walnut stock is slimmer and the long iron ramrod cover has been replaced by a pinned spring under the breech. A narrower walled barrel, in turn, keeps the 44-3/4" length (.72 caliber) and smooth-rounded breech with two flat sides. A brass front sight appears on the rear of the two straps of the upper band, which also has abandoned the previous straight rear edge for a sloping tail. Friction holds the bottom band; the other two have outboard rear springs. One hundred forty thousand were produced. Note also that the previous trumpet-shaped iron ramrod is now a button head. Many of this model were among the 37,000 long arms arriving from France during the spring of 1777 at Portsmouth, New Hampshire. That state appropriated some of those weapons for its own regiments and identified them on the left side of the breech as shown above ("NH 3B No 228"). Most of these marked muskets observed have Maubeuge manufactory locks. Such Portsmouth shipments were important in arming the American forces at Saratoga in October 1777.

Length: 60-1/4"  
Barrel: 44-3/4", .72 cal.  
Lock: 6-1/4" X 1-1/4"  
Trigger Guard: 12-3/4"  
Butt Tang: 2-1/2"  
Side Plate: 3-7/8"  
Furniture: Iron  
Weight: 8.5 lbs.

**Author's Collection**

*Chapter 3: Smoothbore Shoulder Arms*

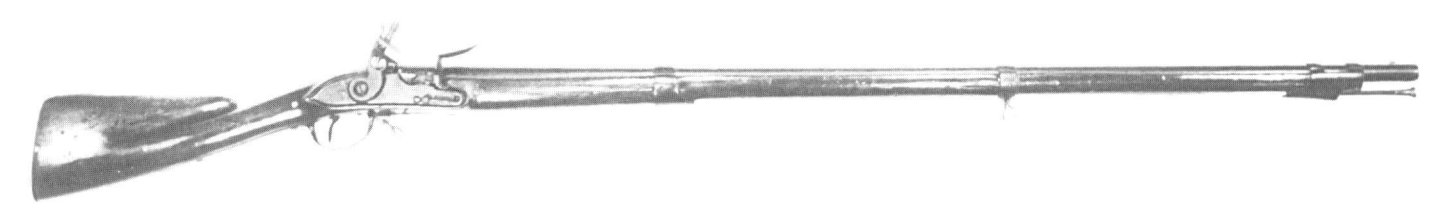

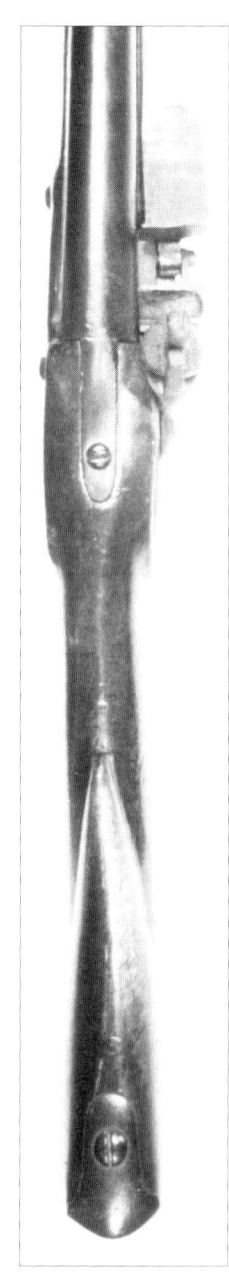

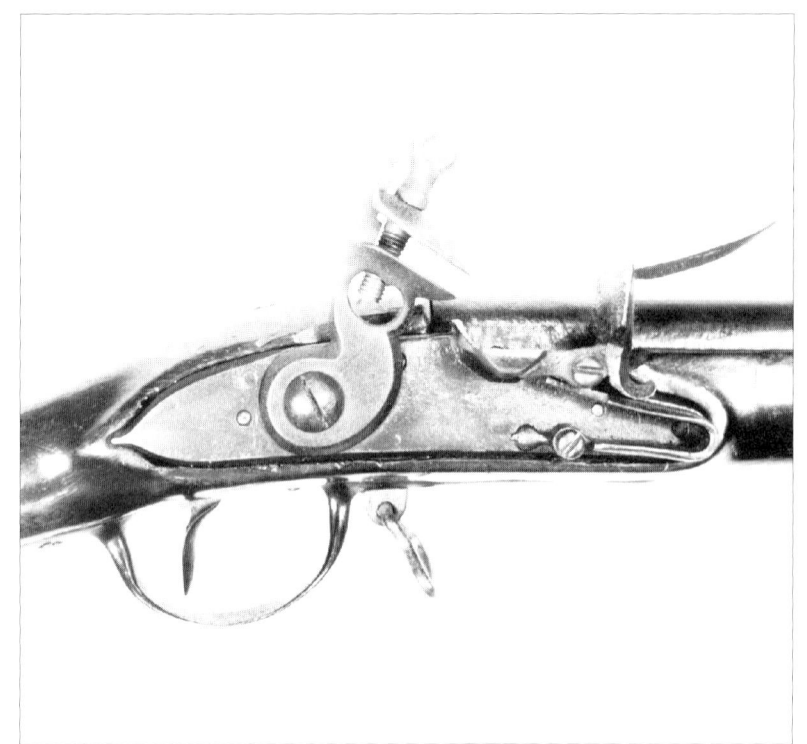

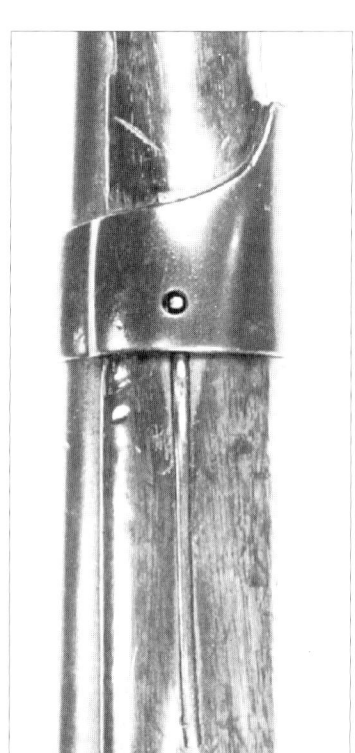

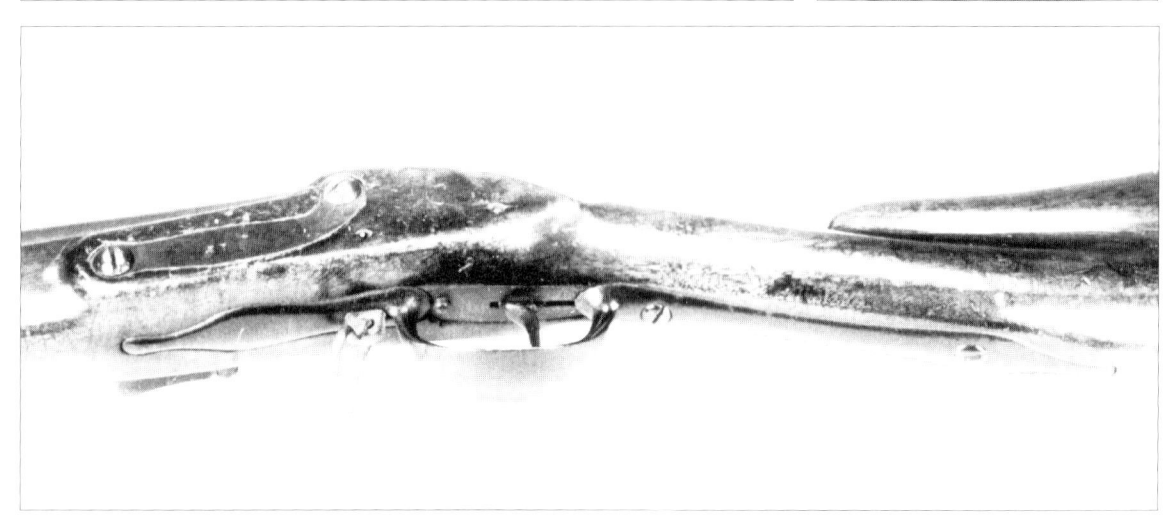

**44.MM FRENCH INFANTRY MUSKET**                                                             **Circa 1768–1773**

This pattern is mistakenly called the Model 1768 by many American collectors. It was actually the product of a massive French upgrading of earlier weapons undertaken from circa 1768 to 1773. The arm is a basic Model 1766 (43.MM) that at this time was altered primarily by the addition of a side retaining spring to the bottom barrel band, similar to the ones already in place on the upper two. Because the Model 1766 and this revised version were a major portion of the more than 100,000 arms sent as French aid during the American Revolution, the design was chosen as the first official United States musket produced after the war—our Model 1795. The example shown includes most Model 1766 features: the 44-3/4" (.69 caliber) round barrel (bayonet stud now on top), a flat lock with a ring cock, the double-pointed trigger guard, a lobed butt tang, button-head steel rammer, an S-shaped side plate, three barrel bands, bell-shaped sling swivels, plus the anti-twist lug under the barrel      4-1/4 inches below the muzzle. Marks: "Charleville" on the lock plate; "E" and "D" in the buttstock.

| | | | |
|---|---|---|---|
| Length: 59-3/4" | Lock: 6-1/4" X 1-1/4" | Butt Tang: 2-3/4" | Furniture: Iron |
| Barrel: 44-3/4", .73 cal. | Trigger Guard: 12-3/4" | Side Plate: 3-5/8" | Weight: 8.4 lbs. |

**Author's Collection**

*94    Chapter 3: Smoothbore Shoulder Arms*

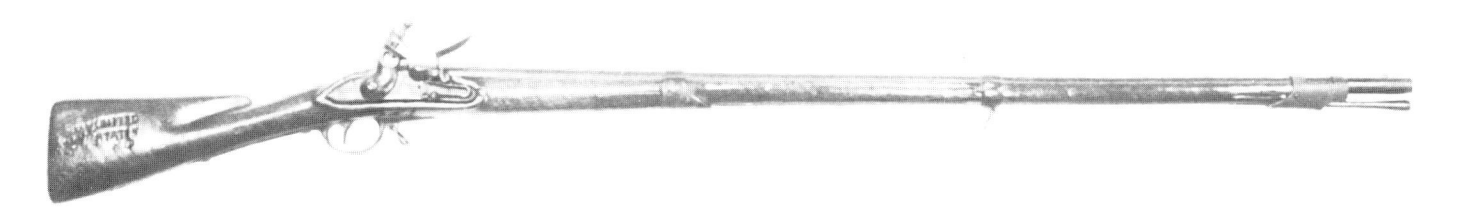

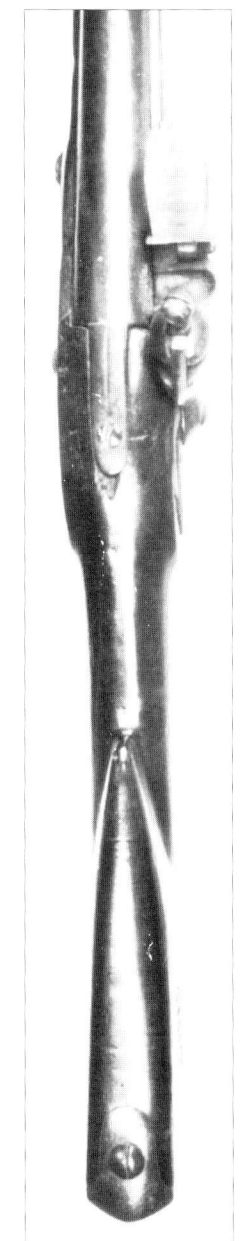

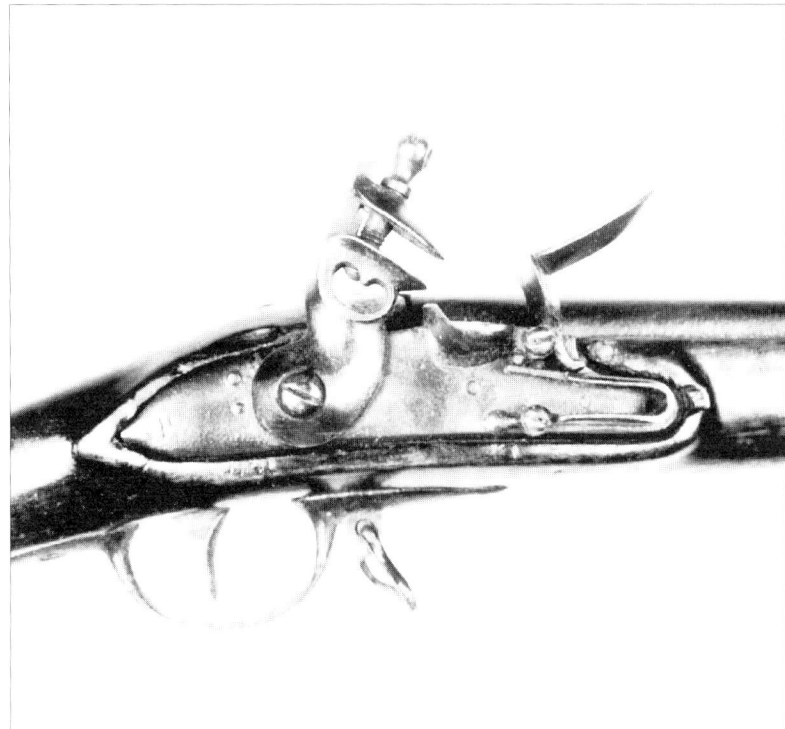

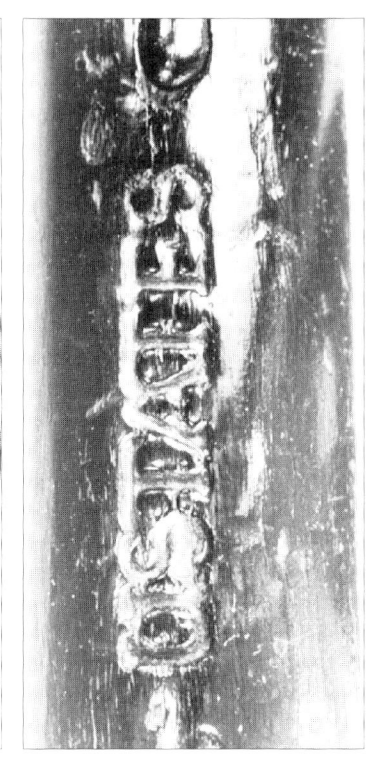

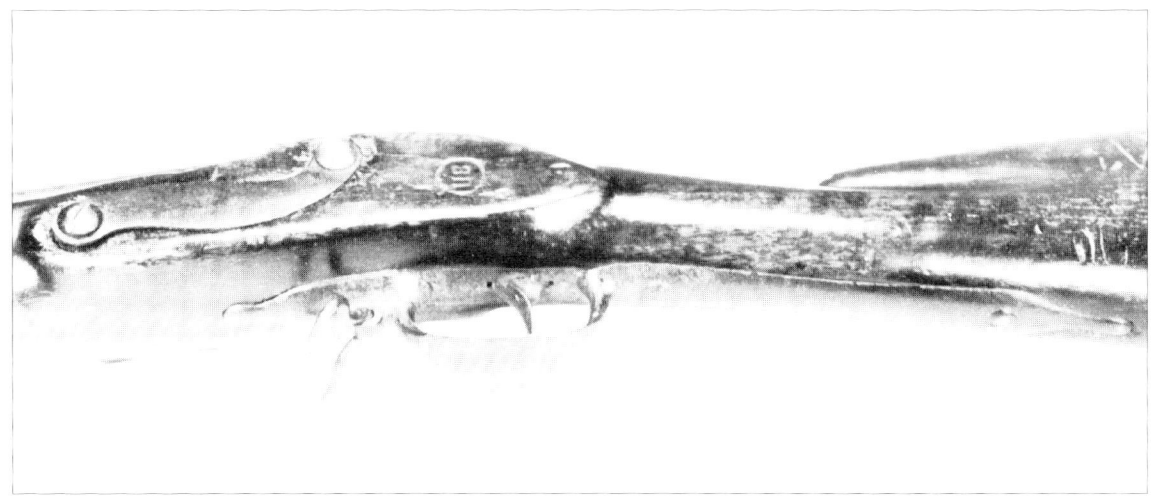

**45.MM FRENCH MODEL 1773 MUSKET**  Circa 1773–1774

France upgraded its arms with the Model 1770–1771, which introduced a rounded lock, heavier barrel (still 44-3/4", .69 caliber) and a reduced walnut stock's handrail contour. Most of these innovations continued in this short-lived Model 1773 (29,000 produced). Note that the convex lock includes a rounded pan, a ring cock (heart-shaped opening), a plain squared upper post, plus a wraparound top jaw. A further unique change in this particular model has the lock plate's squared shoulder now visible in front of the frizzen's curled tip. The bottom barrel band also adds a rear spring (2-5/8 inches) like the two above, while the previous blade sight is omitted, as the bayonet lug returns to the top (moved below in 1771). Its button ramrod, in turn, has assumed a trumpet shape (to remain through the Model 1777). Most of the iron furniture still reflects the 1760s, with a lobed butt tang, flat S-shaped side plate and double-pointed trigger guard, although this example's shortened front section is transitional to the Model 1774. Both lock and breech here are surcharged "US"; the buttstock is branded "UNITED STATES" (twice), "U:STATES," "US" and "IP" (Joseph Perkins).

Length: 60"   Lock: 6-1/4" X 1-1/4"   Butt Tang: 2-1/4"   Furniture: Iron
Barrel: 44-3/4", .72 cal.   Trigger Guard: 11-3/8"   Side Plate: 3 7/8"   Weight: 8.2 lbs.
**Author's Collection**

*Chapter 3: Smoothbore Shoulder Arms*

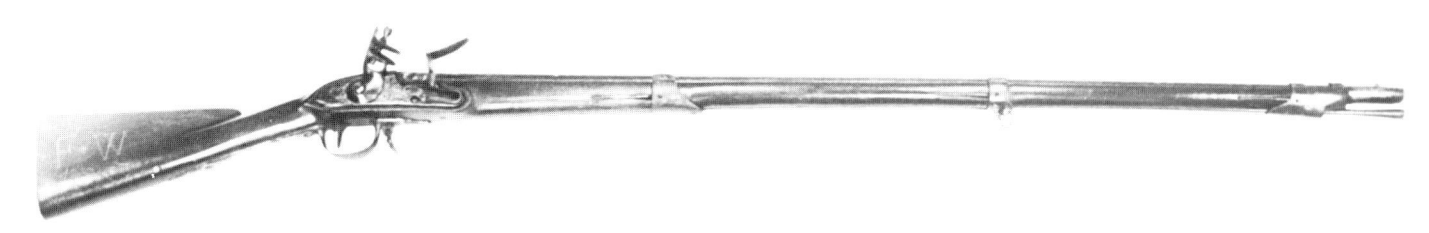

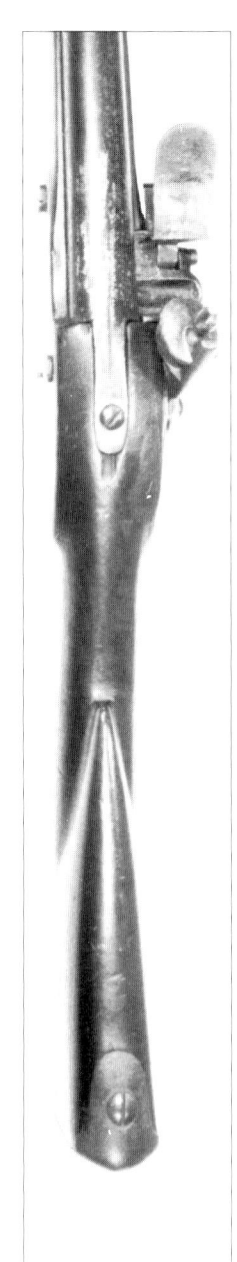

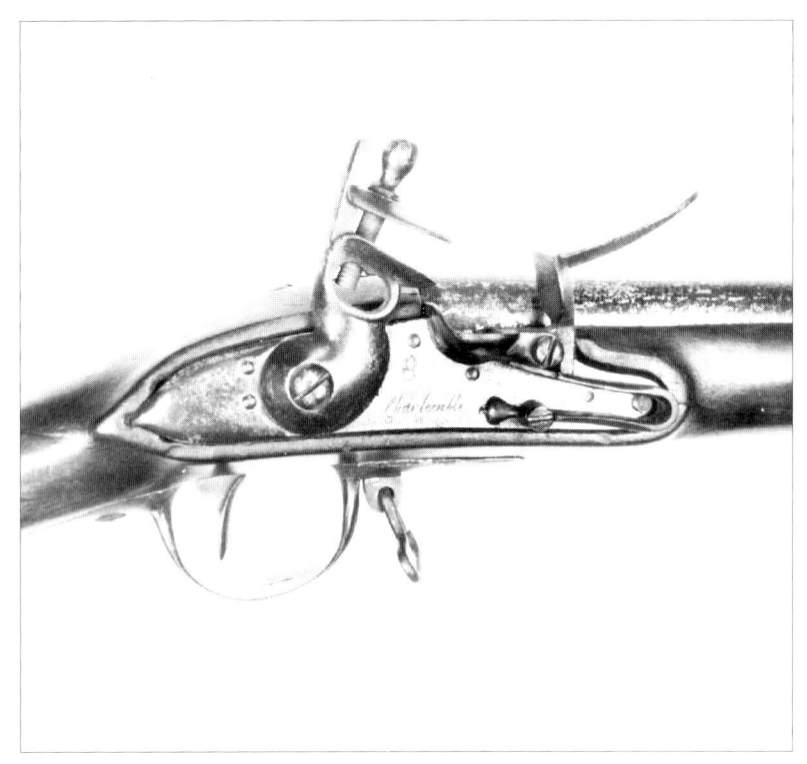

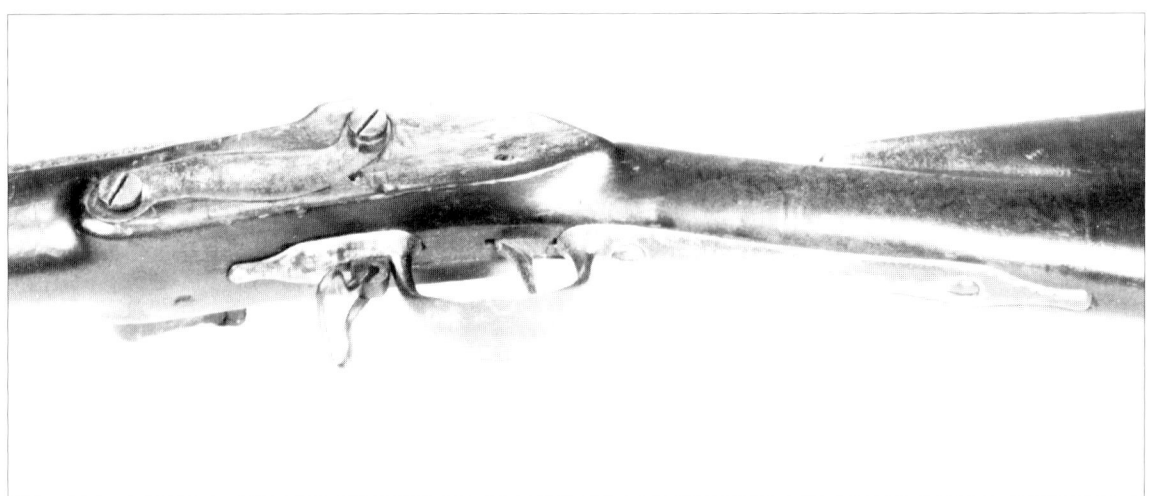

**46.MM FRENCH MODEL 1774 MUSKET**  Circa 1776

This was the newest French musket prior to the American Revolution. Yet its parts have been found on rebel campsites as early as Valley Forge (1777–1778), indicating that France's best models were included among the vast variety of arms shipped here. The 1774 pattern adds several innovations: a spring catch (pinned to a bottom barrel lug) projects out from the forend to snap over the rear ring on a newly designed bayonet (34.BB); the trigger guard forward of the bow is shortened to two inches; the lock's frizzen has a blunt front end versus a previous curled tip; and the walnut stock's indented comb is disappearing. Of the three barrel bands, the lowest now shows a bottom convex screw head that holds an internal two-inch ramrod spring; the center band adds a frontal lip; and a forward blade sight returns to the upper band's rear strap (despite a top bayonet stud). All of these bands, however, do have rear springs. Only 70,000 were manufactured. Marks: "Charleville" and "crown / D" on the lock plate; and the buttstock shows "MAI / DV / 76" (the last two digits of the year produced, that is, 1776).

| | | | |
|---|---|---|---|
| Length: 60" | Lock: 6-1/4" X 1-1/4" | Butt Tang: 2-3/8" | Furniture: Iron |
| Barrel: 44-3/4", .72 cal. | Trigger Guard: 11-1/4" | Side Plate: 3 7/8" | Weight: 9.0 lbs. |

**Author's Collection**

*Chapter 3: Smoothbore Shoulder Arms*

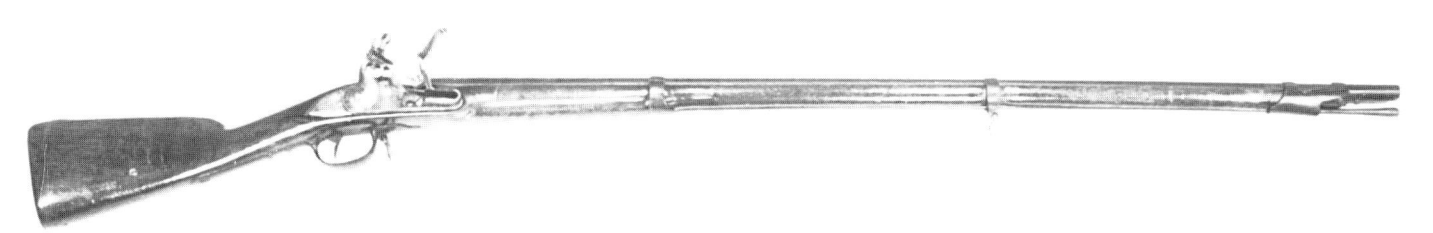

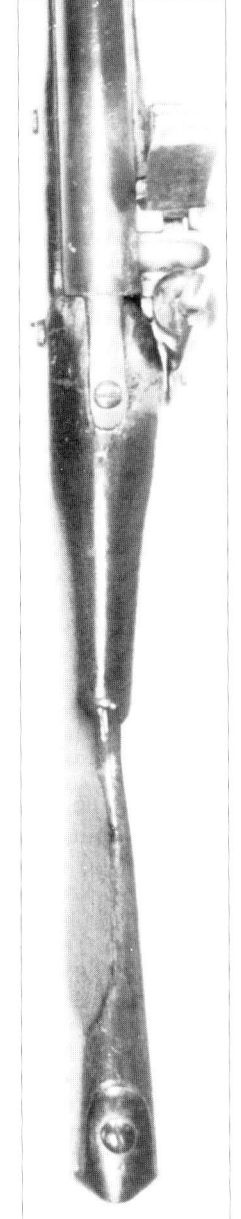

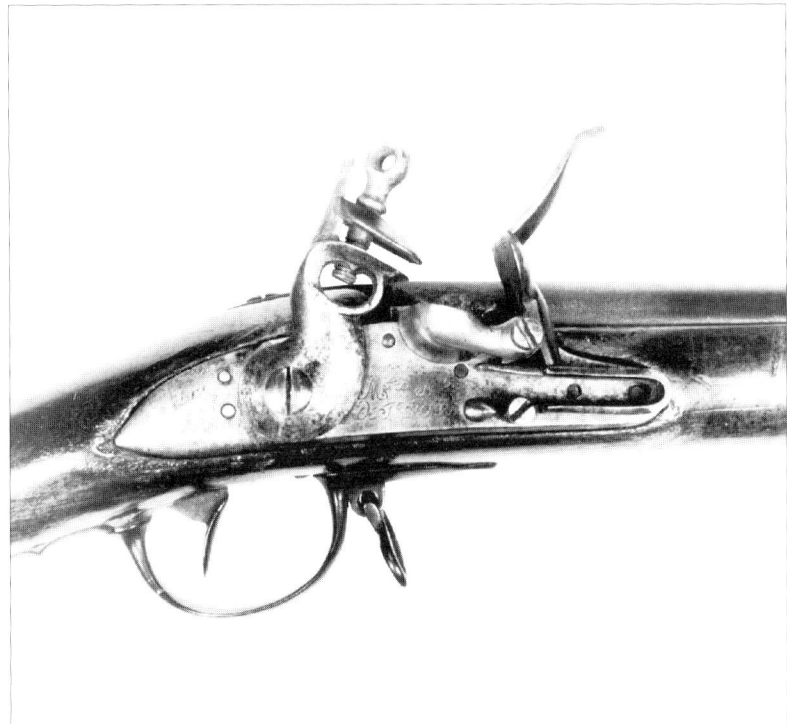

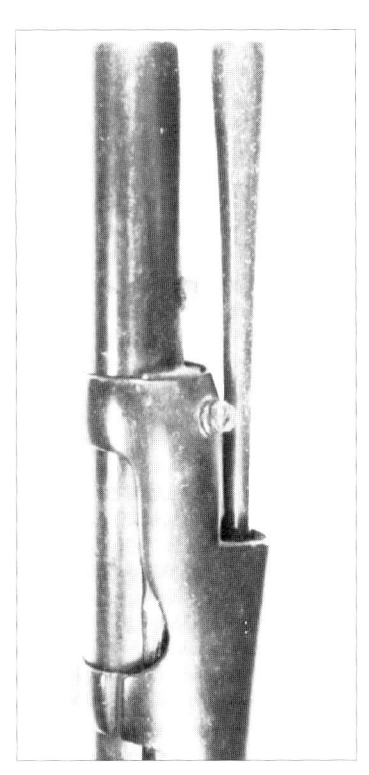

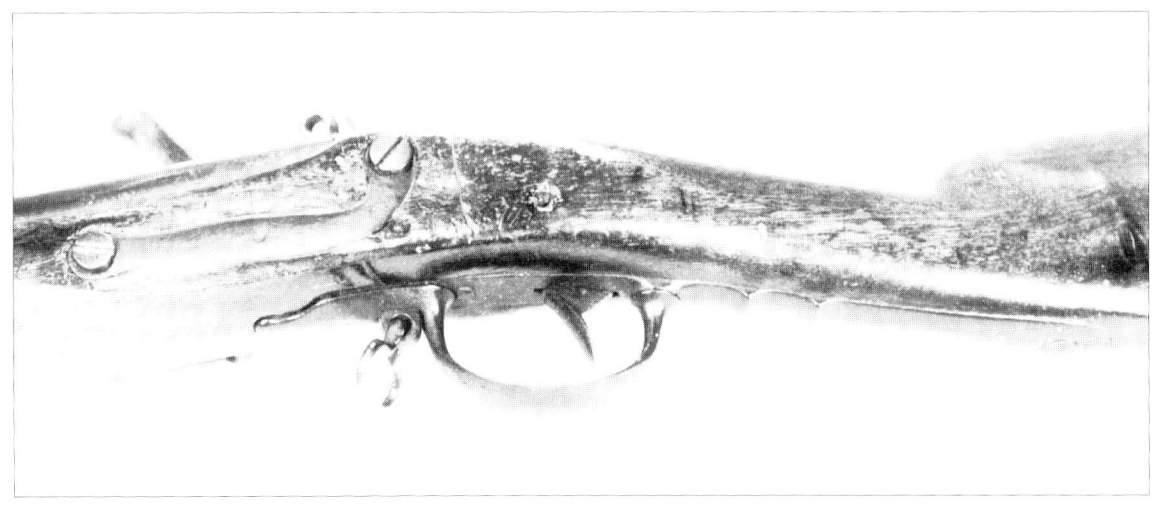

**47.MM FRENCH MODEL 1777 MUSKET**                                                                                                           **Circa 1779**

The Model 1777 was a major advance in flintlock design and would continue through the Napoleonic Wars. Those first produced were issued to General Rochambeau's troops coming to America in 1780. Certain indicators help to identify these early versions of the model contemporary with our Revolutionary War, that is: a visible screw head in a raised collar on the lower front side of the top band (which locks the band against the barrel's anti-twist lug (see 50.MM); a narrow middle band tightened by a bottom cross-screw that secures the sling swivel (no rear spring); a two-inch flat on each side of the round breech; and barrel markings that include the last two digits of the production year (this one, "ST / S / 79," that is, 1779). Other innovations include: a slanted brass pan (no fence) and bridle; the upper frizzen's forward bend; two rear finger ridges and an even shorter front end on the trigger guard; a cheek rest recessed into the stock's reverse side; plus a forward spring stud holding the bottom band against a rear stock ridge. The lock is marked "St. Etienne."

| | | | |
|---|---|---|---|
| Length: 60" | Lock: 6-1/4" X 1-1/4" | Butt Tang: 2-1/4" | Furniture: Iron |
| Barrel: 44-3/4", .73 cal. | Trigger Guard: 9-7/8" | Side Plate: 3-7/8" | Weight: 8.7 lbs. |

**Author's Collection**

*Chapter 3: Smoothbore Shoulder Arms*

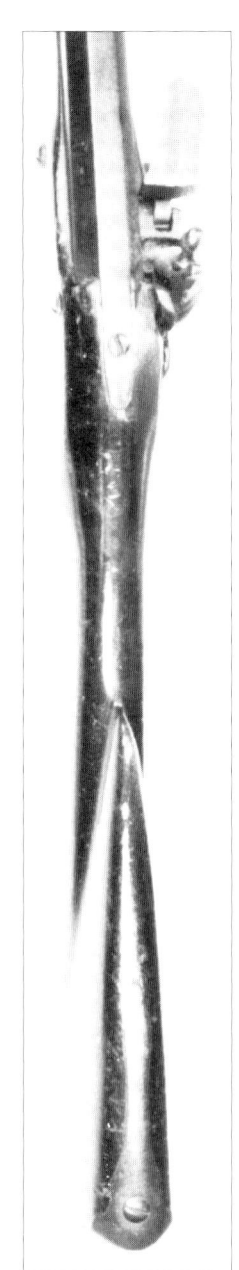

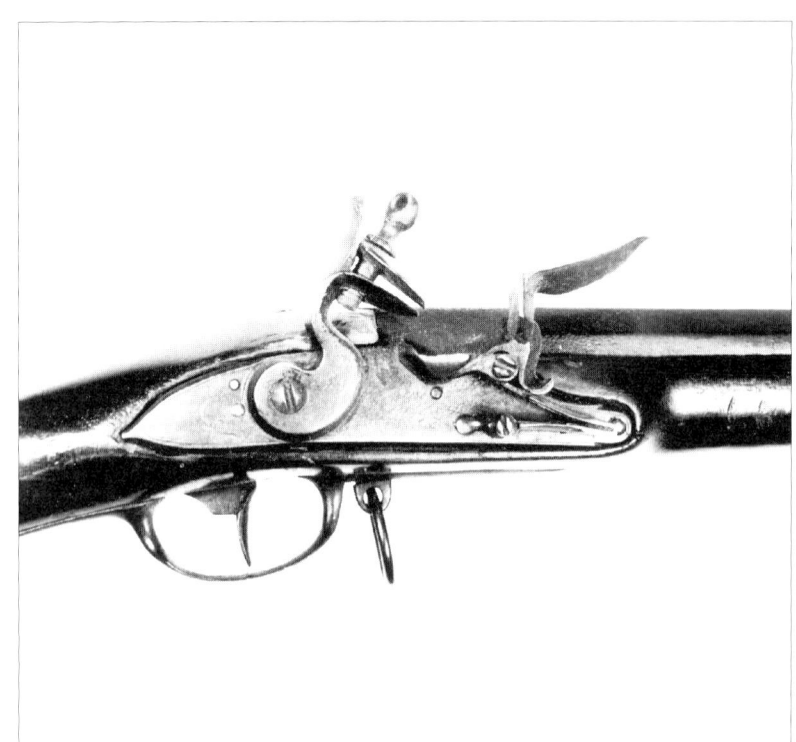

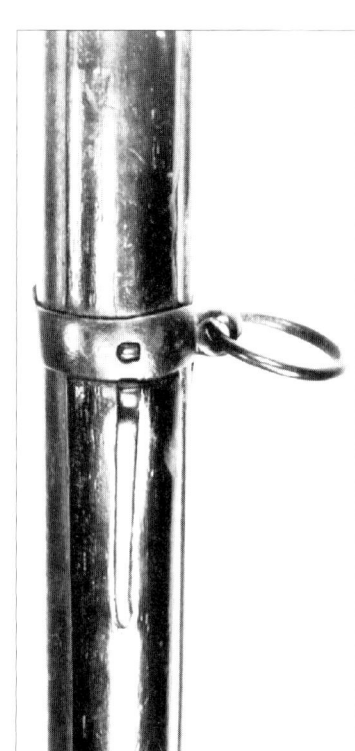

**48.MM FRENCH OFFICER'S FUSIL**                                                                                                                                                   Circa 1754

The word *fusil* (or *fusee*), meant a full-size musket in France but is used here in the manner of the English and Americans to designate a lighter longarm often with a reduced bore that was for use by an officer. The first French design appeared about 1754 to replace the spontoon. A fusil was usually purchased privately by the commissioned officer and reflected his personal taste within the official specifications. This early example has a typical flat/beveled lock of the period but lacks the usual slash across the tail. Incised decorations cover the plate and cock. The remainder of the arm follows the Model 1754 (41.MM) with scaled-down components, that is, the curved Roman nose on the walnut butt, round sling swivels under the stock, a long butt tang, springs behind the two upper barrel bands (third held by friction), the double-pointed trigger guard, flat S-shaped side plate and an iron ramrod. This shortened barrel includes an octagonal barrel breech for 8-1/2 inches.

| | | | |
|---|---|---|---|
| Length: 58-1/2" | Lock 5-1/2" X 1" | Butt Tang: 5" | Furniture: Iron |
| Barrel: 42", .72 cal. | Trigger Guard: 10-1/2" | Side Plate: 3-3/8" | Weight: 6.3 lbs. |

**Robert Nittolo Collection**

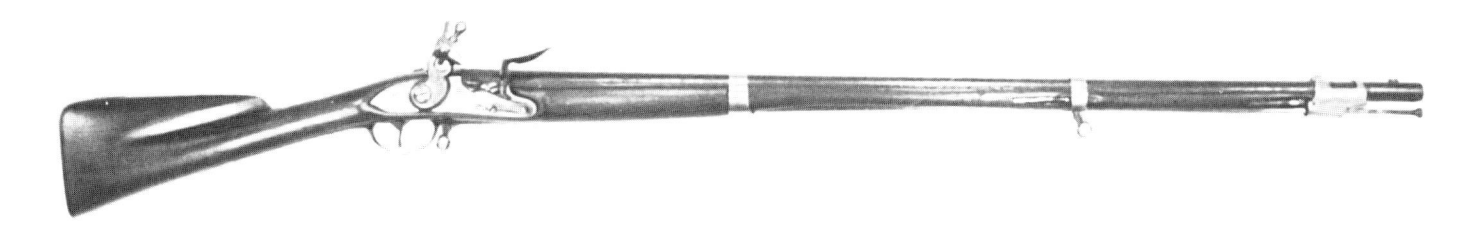

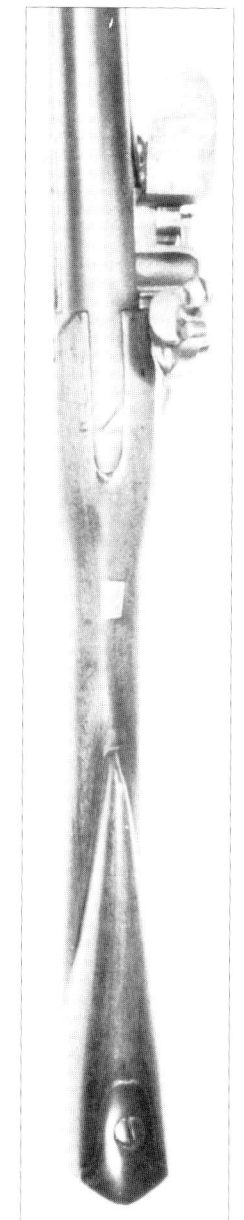

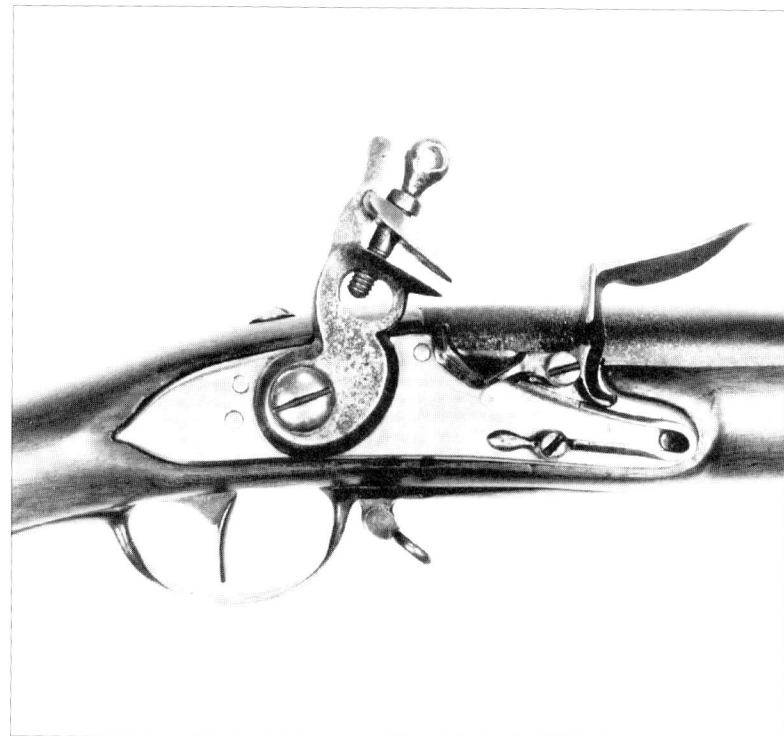

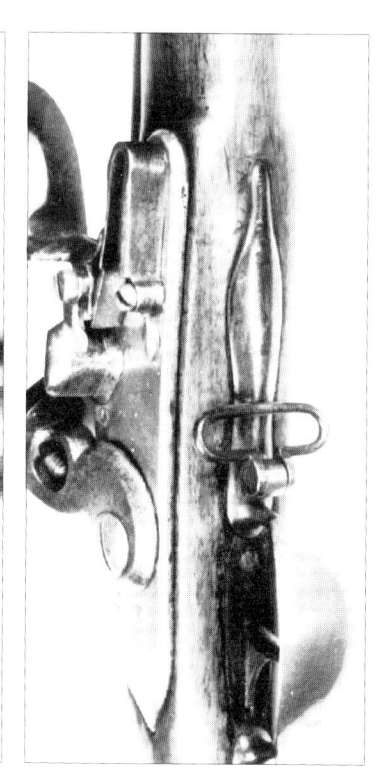

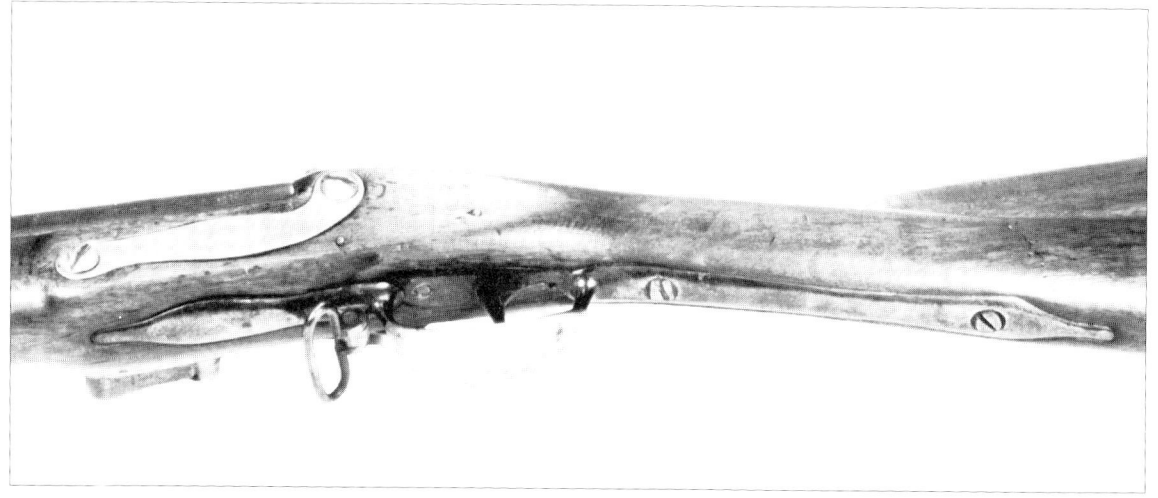

**49.MM FRENCH OFFICER'S FUSIL**  Circa 1767

This unusual arm follows the basic pattern of the Model 1766 infantry musket (43.MM) but with reduced length (38-3/8", .69 caliber barrel) and sheet brass applied over the iron base of many of its components. Naval arms of this period generally followed the army styling but substituted brass for much of the iron furniture, as did some special land units. This selective application of brass to certain elements, however, suggests a unique officer's fusil. Those areas covered are the lock plate, the cock's top jaw, both frizzen screw heads, the outer trigger loop, the head of the barrel tang screw, all three barrel bands and the side plate with the heads of both side screws. Each of the flattened sling swivels is held by a cross-rivet. Its upper band includes a blade sight despite a top bayonet stud, and the tail was cut off at one time. A small rectangular silver escutcheon was a later owner's addition. The iron rammer, in turn, has a typical button head. Its only marking is "PG" inside the lock plate.

| | | | |
|---|---|---|---|
| Length: 53-3/4" | Lock: 6-1/4" X 1-1/4" | Butt Tang: 2-1/2" | Furniture: Iron/Brass |
| Barrel: 38-3/8", .72 cal. | Trigger Guard: 12-3/4" | Side Plate: 3-7/8" | Weight: 7.5 lbs. |

**Author's Collection**

Chapter 3: Smoothbore Shoulder Arms    99

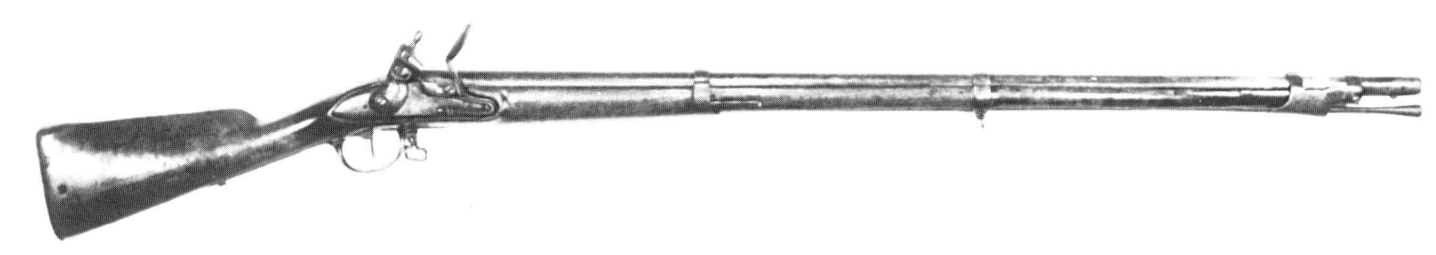

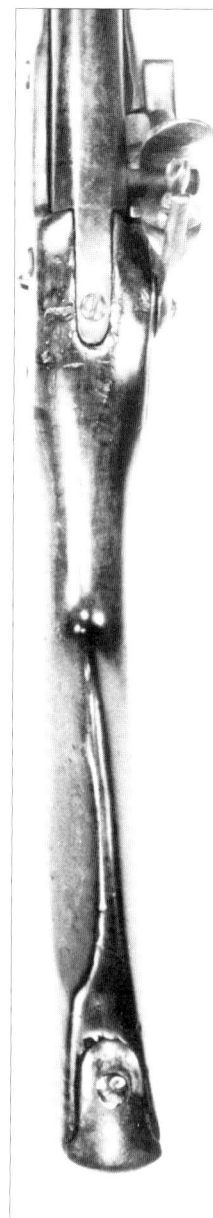

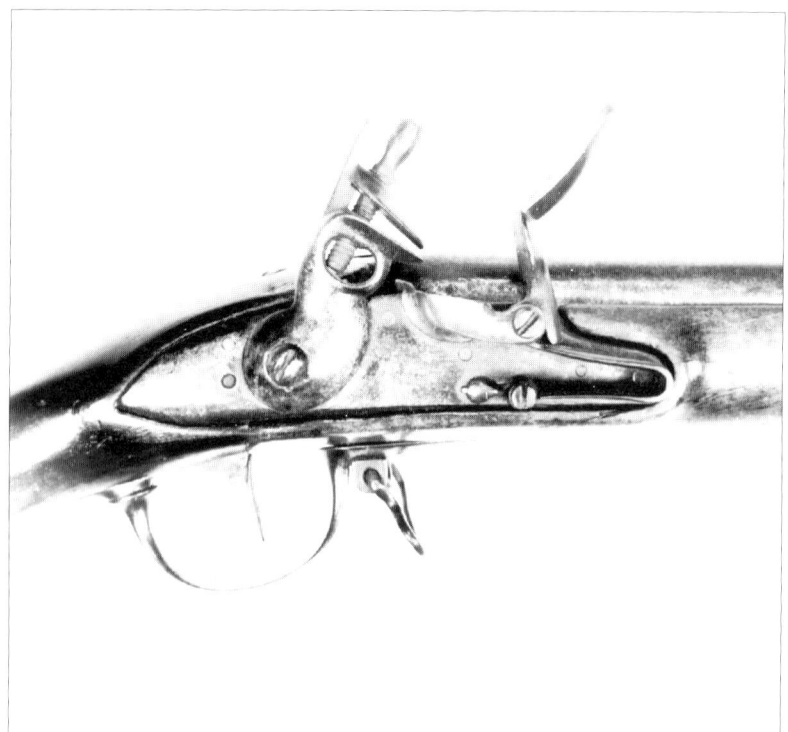

**50.MM FRENCH OFFICER'S FUSIL MODEL 1777**  Circa 1777

The impressive innovations of the Model 1777 (47.MM) led to its being adopted into numerous sizes and modifications by land, horse and naval units throughout France's armed forces. The example in this case combines a shortened 39-1/4" barrel (still .69 caliber) with scaled down standard 1777 musket components except for elimination of the two finger ridges on the rear trigger guard. The firearm is believed to be a junior officer's fusil, which was also the form carried by the regiment's *cadet gentilhomme*. Note the exterior head of the screw on its upper band that locked onto the barrels anti-twist lug, the rounded lock having a ring cock and tilted brass pan/bridle, its walnut buttstock's cheek rest cut into the inboard comb, a middle band held by friction, the forward spring's stud locking its bottom band, and a stubby front section on the trigger guard (including this pattern's unusual trigger loop's attachment). The only visible mark is "P" on the side plate. Over 16,000 regular French troops served on American soil during the Revolutionary War (mostly at Savannah, Newport and Yorktown).

| | | | |
|---|---|---|---|
| Length: 54" | Lock: 6-1/4" X 1-3/8" | Butt Tang: 2-1/4" | Furniture: Iron |
| Barrel: 39-1/4", .71 cal. | Trigger Guard: 9-7/8" | Side Plate: 4" | Weight: 8.0 lbs. |

**Author's Collection**

*100    Chapter 3: Smoothbore Shoulder Arms*

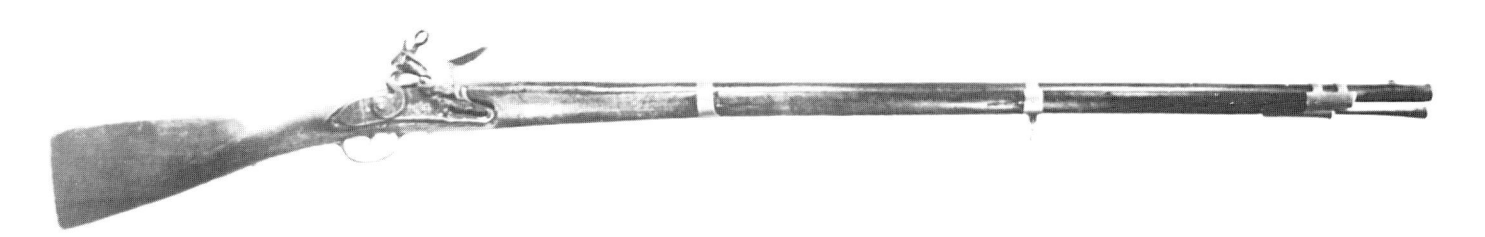

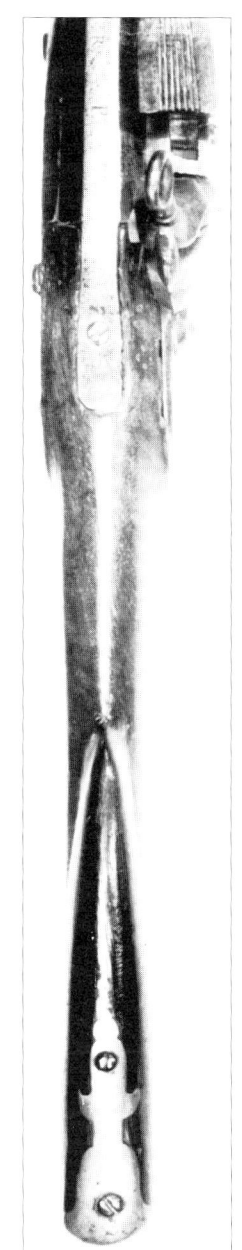

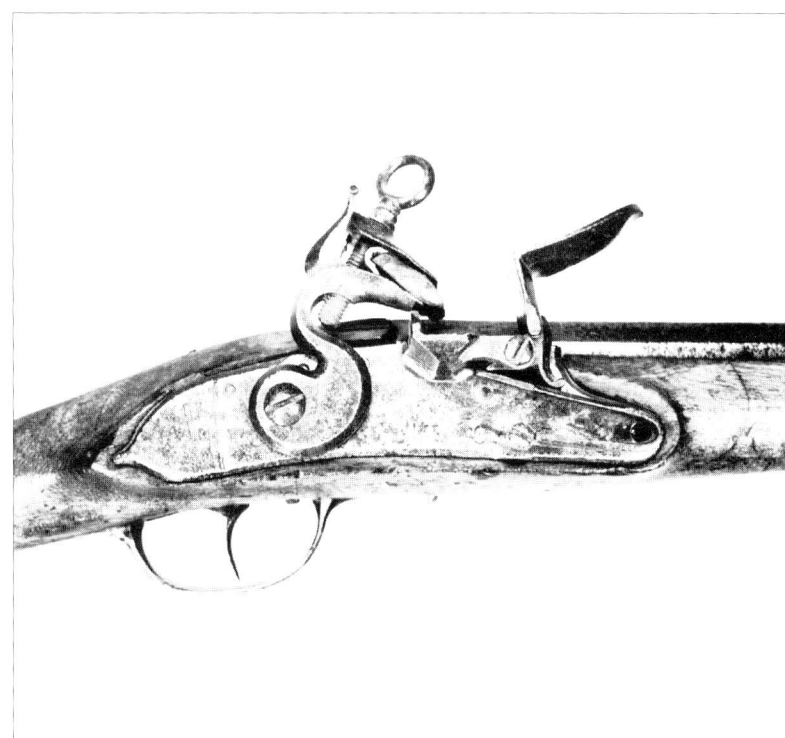

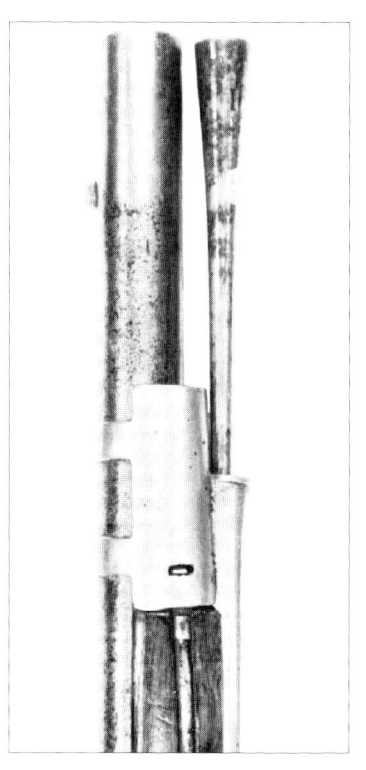

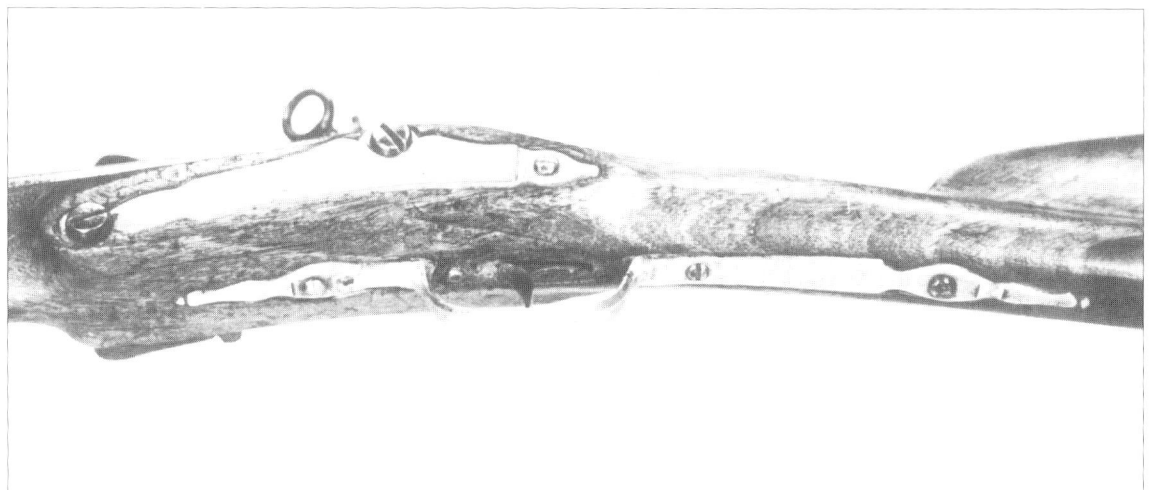

**51.MM  SPANISH MODEL 1757 MUSKET**  Circa 1757

Spanish military muskets favored the miquelet lock prior to 1718 and after 1789. In the interim they were greatly influenced by the French, adopting a flat lock similar to theirs with a cock that added a flared upper post and a distinctive top ring on the jaw screw. This three-banded pattern appeared in 1753 having iron furniture, which changed to brass in this updated Model 1757. It was their standard infantry musket during the French and Indian War and American Revolution. Note the distinctive thin trigger guard (three screws), triangular side plate (with a rear wood screw), the French-style three-arm butt tang (two top screws) and the French form of upper barrel band that adds an integral long tapered ramrod pipe underneath. The steel ramrod replaced wood in 1755. Its rear sling swivel was located behind the trigger guard. These muskets reached the American Revolution from the earlier 1762 Havana expedition, the West Indies trade, aid from New Orleans to the Western frontier and with the troops of Bernardo de Galvez in his 1779–1781 Gulf of Mexico campaign.

| | | | |
|---|---|---|---|
| Length: 59-5/8" | Lock: 6-3/4" X 1-3/8" | Butt Tang: 4-1/4" | Furniture: Brass |
| Barrel: 43-1/2", .72 cal. | Trigger Guard: 11-1/4" | Side Plate: 6-1/2" | Weight: 8.6 lbs. |

**George C. Neumann Collection, Valley Forge National Historical Park**

*Chapter 3: Smoothbore Shoulder Arms*

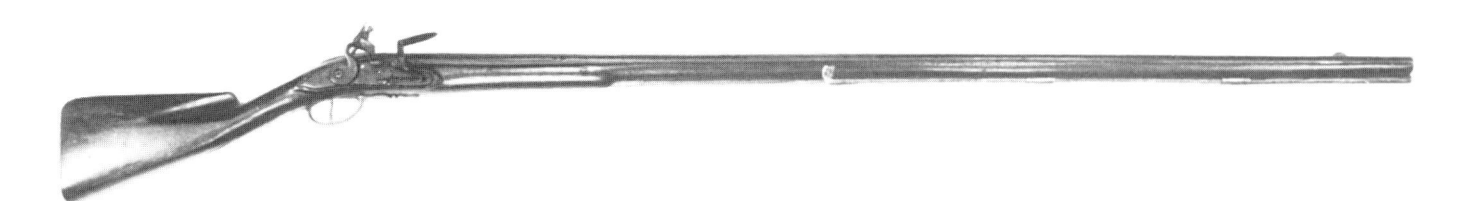

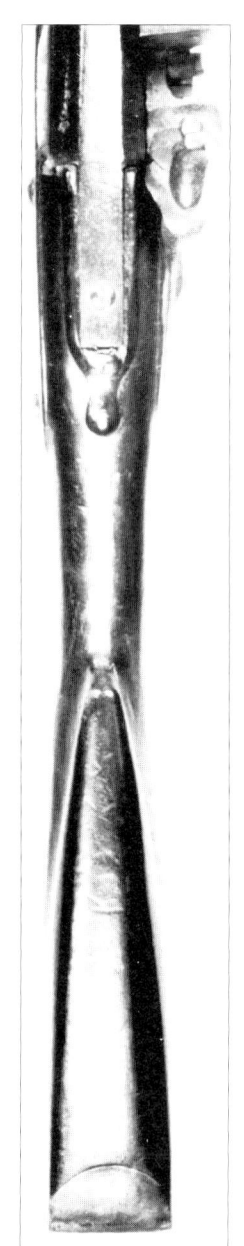

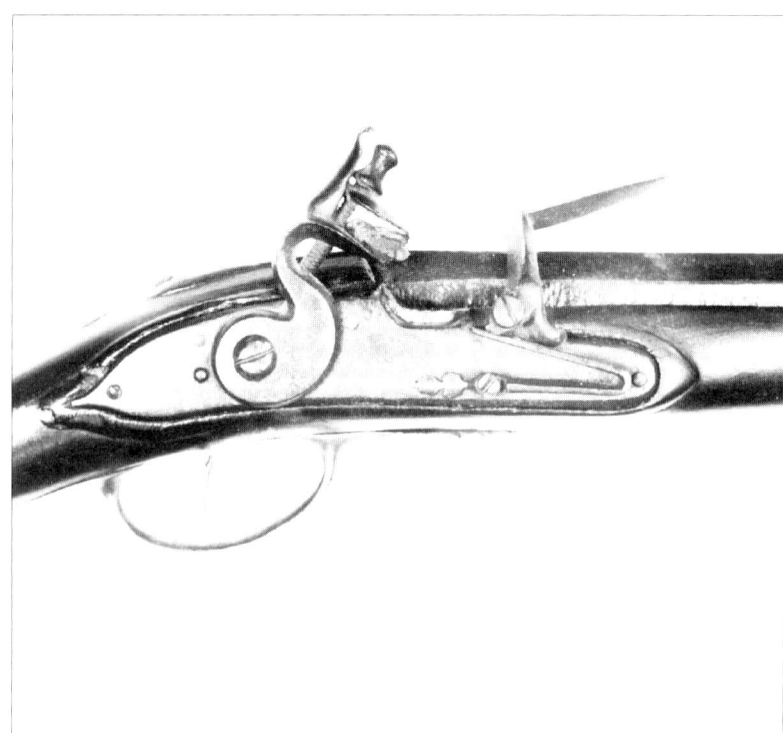

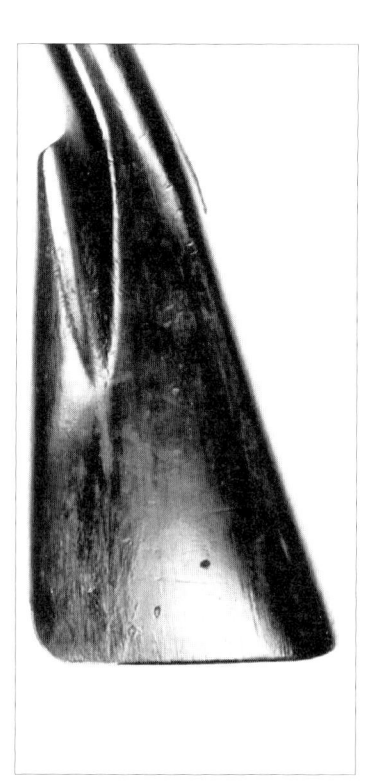

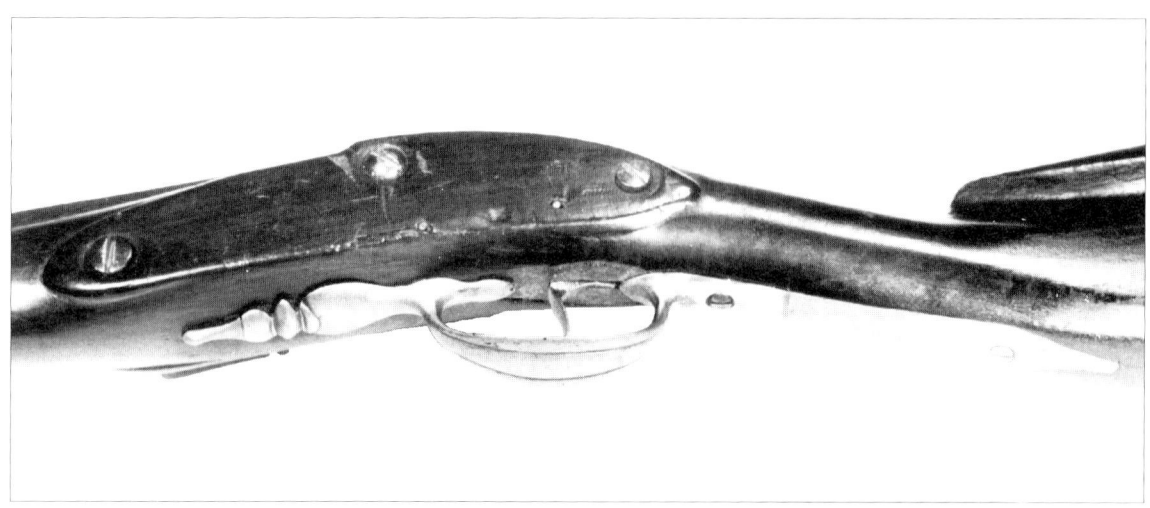

**52.MM FRENCH BUCCANEER NAVAL MUSKET**  Circa 1700–1710

Perhaps the most romantic longarm in French naval service at this time was the *fusil bucanier*. It continued in use from the late 1600s through the 18th century. The weapon had two visual distinctions: a long smoothbore pinned barrel (usually 50" to 60"), plus a large club butt. Originating in the West Indies, the buccaneer form spread throughout the New World—not only aboard French sea service and civilian vessels, but also at land fortifications and as a commercial item, including the slave trade. It had numerous variations, yet few survive. This early example includes the popular flat/beveled three-screw lock, a brass segmented trigger guard, semi- teardrop barrel tang carving plus a short rounded butt tang. There is no side plate (usually triangular). A broad fuller creases the thick butt comb on the walnut stock that in turn extends to the muzzle and holds four sheet-brass thimbles (wooden ramrod, no sling swivels). The long 56" barrel (originally .69 caliber) is octagonal at the breech for 20 inches. It is stamped "crown / F," (probably Toussaint or Victor Fournier).

| | | | |
|---|---|---|---|
| Length: 72-1/8" | Lock: 7" X 1-1/4" | Butt Tang: 1" | Furniture: Brass |
| Barrel: 56", .72 cal. | Trigger Guard: 11-1/2" | Weight: 9.5 lbs. | |

**The Benninghoff Collection**

*102    Chapter 3: Smoothbore Shoulder Arms*

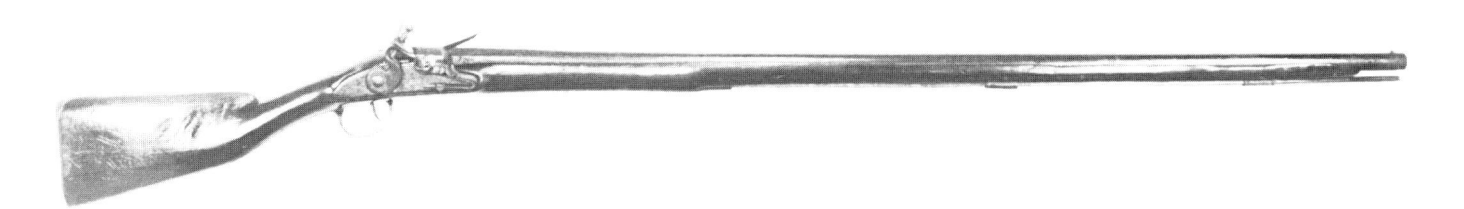

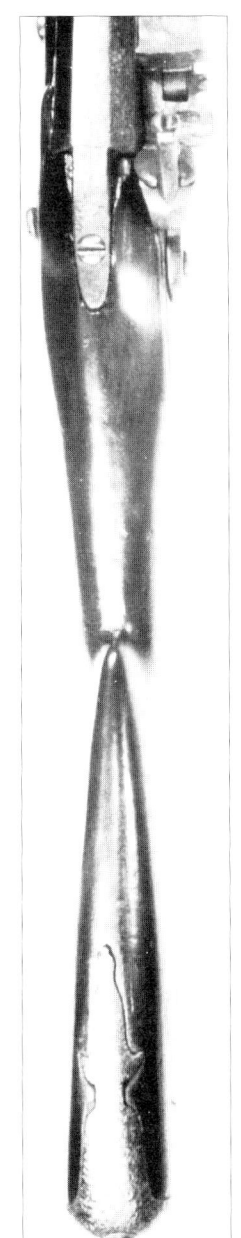

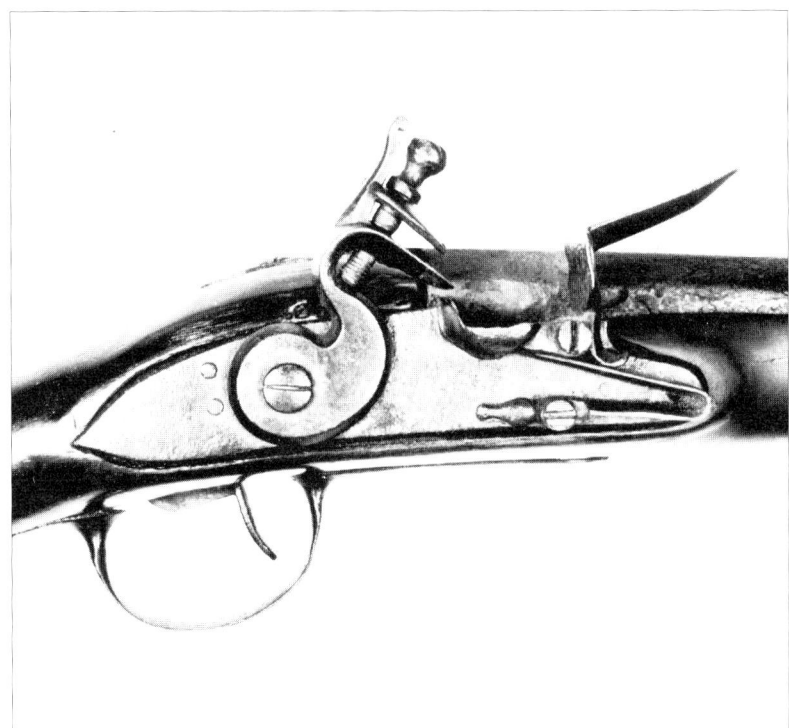

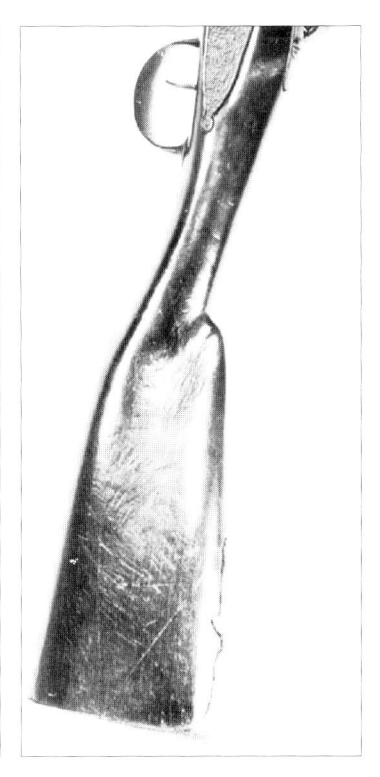

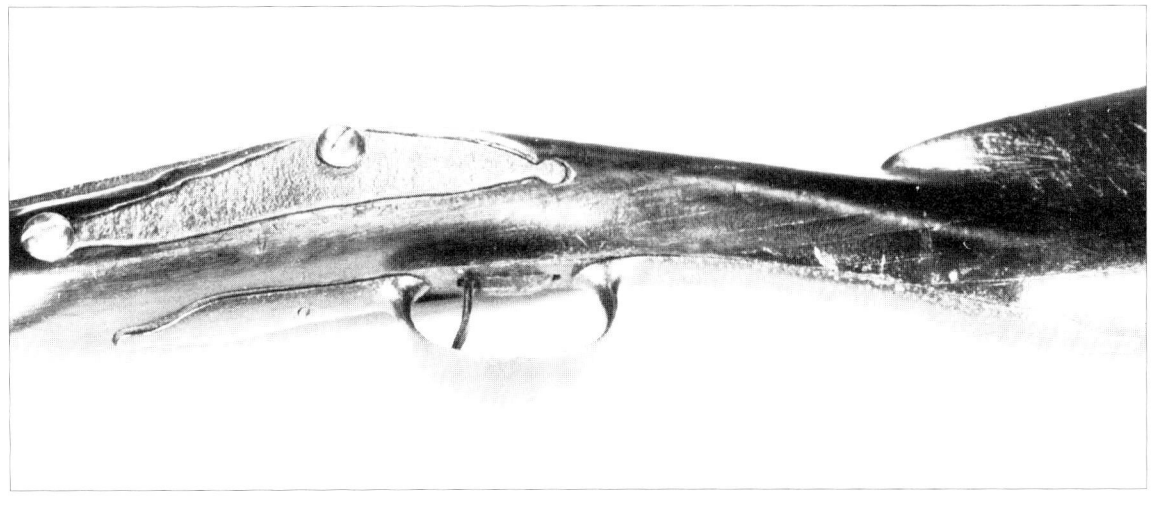

**53.MM FRENCH BUCCANEER NAVAL MUSKET**  Circa 1740–1760

French arsenal inventories list several variations of the buccaneer musket including a "demi-buccaneer" of reduced barrel length (closer to 48 inches). The even shorter pattern illustrated here (45-3/4" barrel—probably shortened at least one inch) has a club butt profile but a minimum recessed area in the comb's sides. It is believed to be a further simplification, possibly dating closer to mid century. Included are a double-pointed military-type trigger guard, the three-arm French iron butt tang, a two-screw flat/beveled lock (double-bridled) and a triangular side plate. The breech bears a stamp, "E / fleur-de-lis / C" (a Charleville mark), and is octagonal for six inches. There is no provision for sling swivels. The walnut stock, in turn, holds a pinned barrel (front blade sight—possibly a filed down bayonet stud), plus three typical sheet-iron ramrod pipes (1-1/2 inches). Its rammer is wooden (no metal tip), while the forend terminates 2-3/8 inches below the muzzle. The club butt form was established in 17th century Europe, but the French buccaneer's popularity here enhanced its use on the long fowlers of the New English Colonists (for example, 113.MM–116.MM).

| | | | |
|---|---|---|---|
| Length: 62-1/8" | Lock: 6-3/8" X 1-1/4" | Butt Tang: 4-5/8" | Furniture: Iron |
| Barrel: 45-3/4", .74 cal. | Trigger Guard: 11-3/4" | Side Plate: 6" | Weight: 8.9 lbs. |

**Author's Collection**

*Chapter 3: Smoothbore Shoulder Arms* **103**

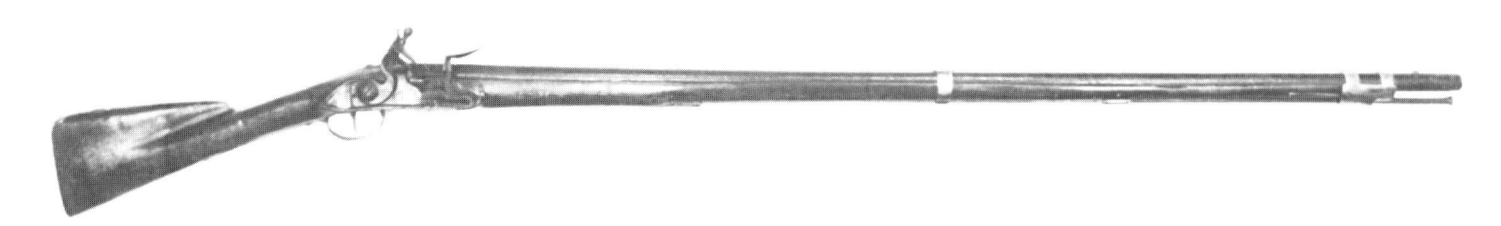

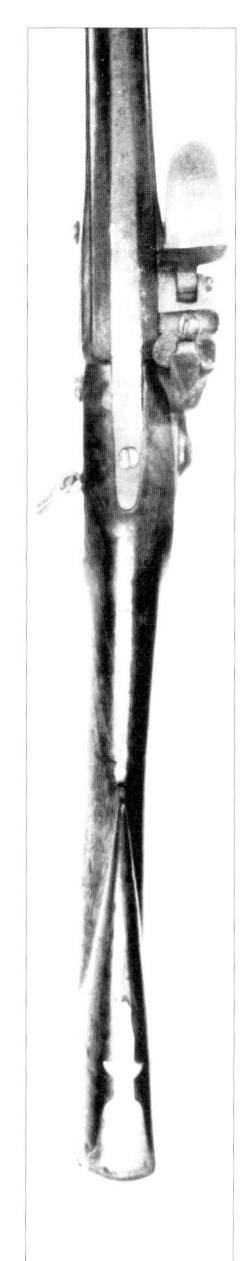

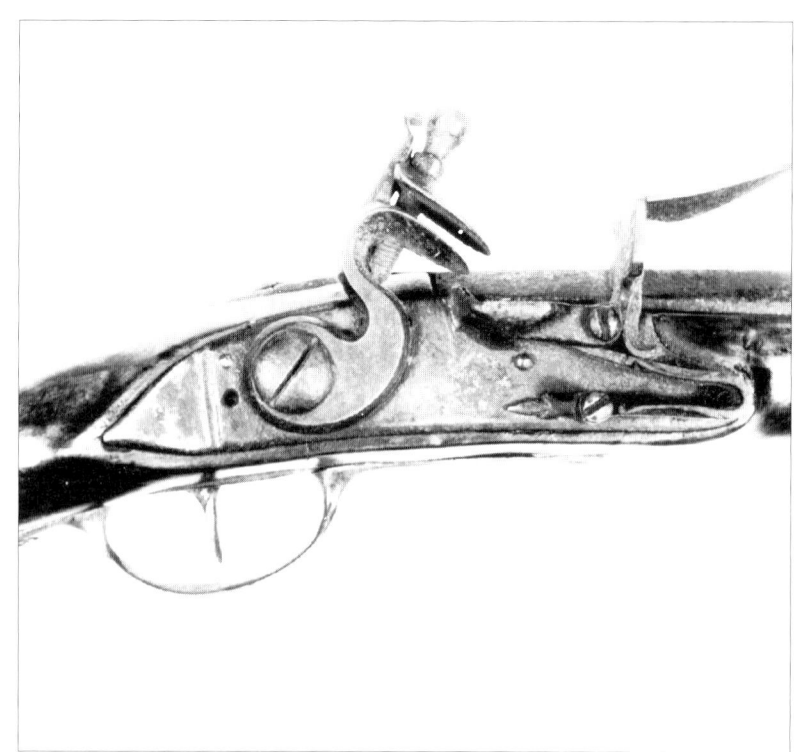

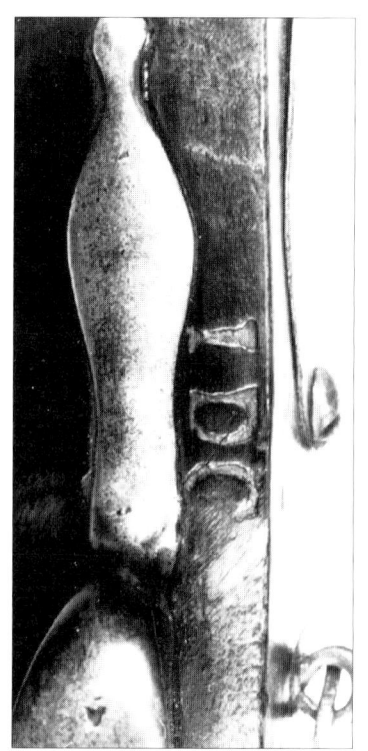

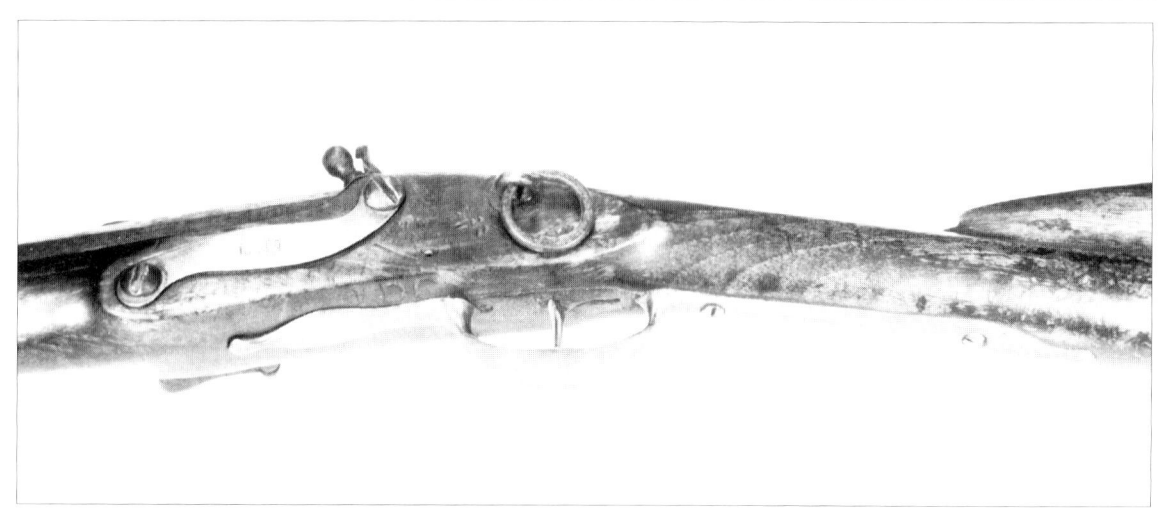

**54.MM FRENCH NAVAL/COMMERCIAL MUSKET**  Circa 1720–1745

A number of these muskets are known, several of which are branded "IDC," as in this case. Notice that the brass furniture and pattern reflect the iron-mounted French Model 1728 infantry arm (39.MM) but supplement the two barrel bands with a pair of rammer pipes. The 46-1/2" (.69 caliber) military-type barrel is octagonal at the breech for five inches and continues a top flat panel to the bayonet stud. The brass fittings and three-arm butt tang suggest naval use, a special pattern for a regimental colonel or a private commercial contract. It also illustrates typical configurations of this period, that is: a walnut stock shaped with a modified Roman nose and handrail, a flat S-shaped side plate, a double-pointed trigger guard, iron side sling swivels (anchored behind the side plate and on the inboard side of the middle band) plus a button-headed steel rammer (a later conversion).

| | | | |
|---|---|---|---|
| Length: 62-1/2" | Lock: 6-5/8" X 1-1/2" | Butt Tang: 4-1/2" | Furniture: Brass |
| Barrel: 46-1/2", .69 cal. | Trigger Guard: 12" | Side Plate: 4" | Weight: 8.0 lbs. |

**Robert Nittolo Collection**

*104    Chapter 3: Smoothbore Shoulder Arms*

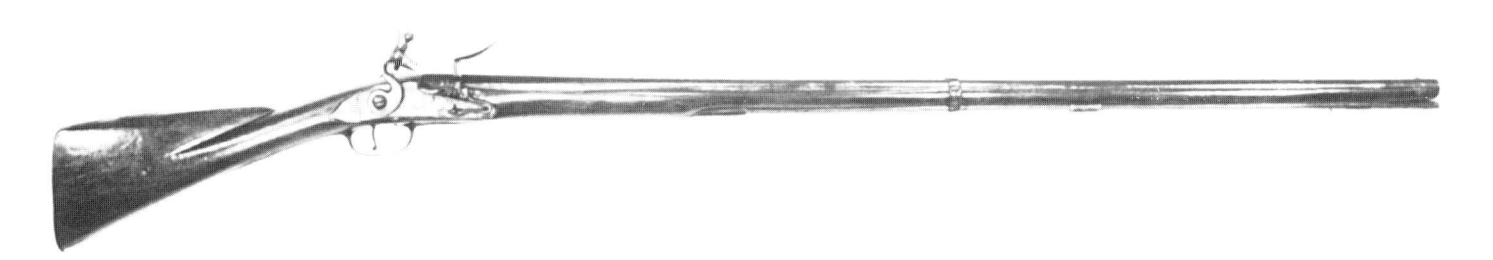

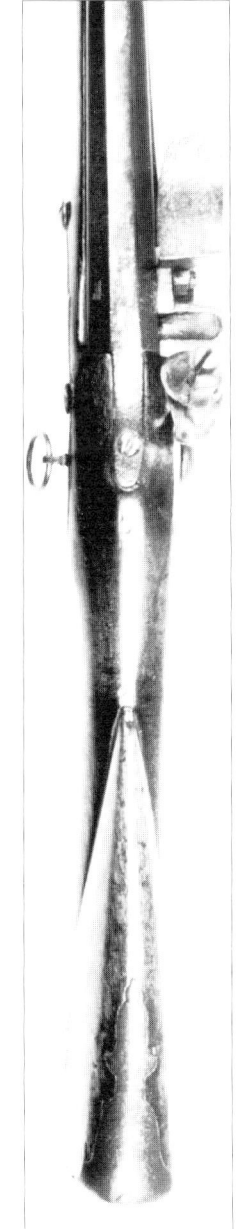

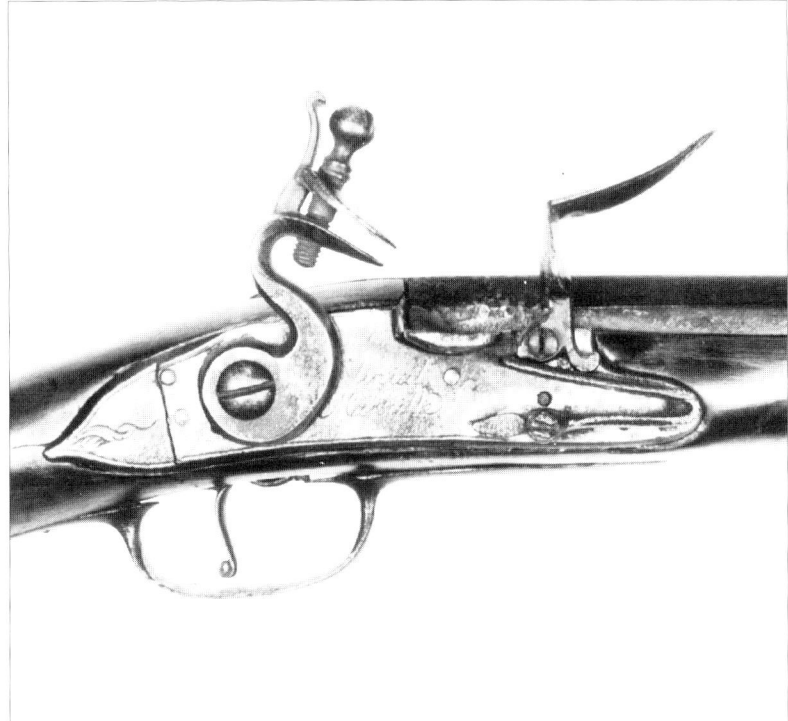

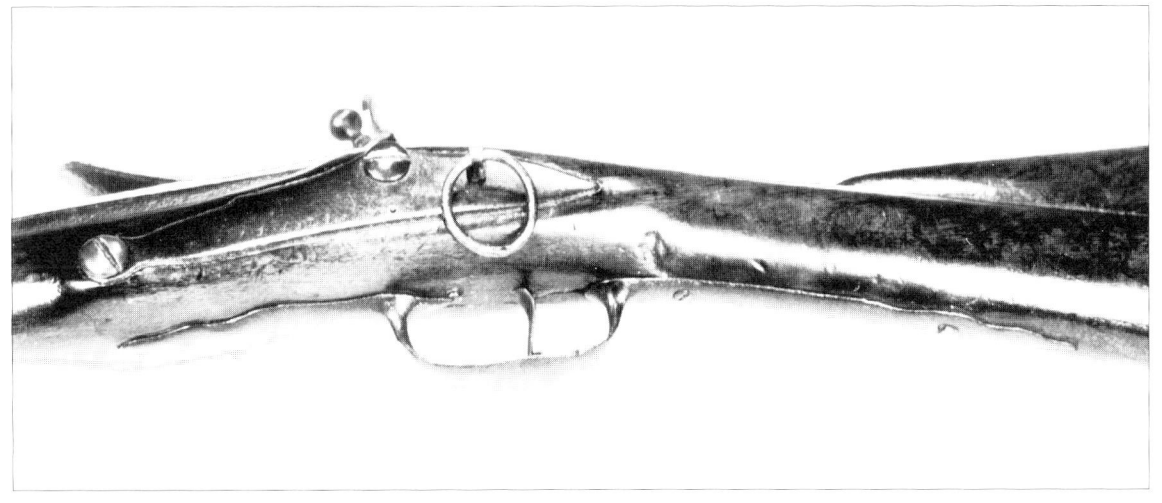

**55.MM FRENCH NAVAL MUSKET**                                                           **Circa 1720–1740**

This longarm's iron furniture matches the brass components found on muskets from the wreck of the French frigate *Le Machault*, sunk in Canada during 1760 (re: Sullivan, bib. 144). Like those recovered artifacts, which had the ship's name branded into the reverse butt face, this stock is similarly marked "DGRASSE" (3/8" high), possibly referring to the admiral of the French fleet at Yorktown, one of his family or a ship bearing their name. The musket includes a large flat lock lacking an exterior bridle, the popular three-arm butt tang, a triangular side plate, a wavy trigger guard and sling swivels secured to side studs through the side plate and on the center barrel band. A walnut stock, in turn, stretches to the muzzle (that is, no socket bayonet) and holds three sheet-iron pipes for a wooden rammer. Its 46-1/4" barrel has a 6-3/4" octagonal breech plus a flat top panel extending for 40-1/2 inches. The visible markings are: "Vinial/Marseille" (probably a contractor) on the lock plate; and "S*E" (St. Etienne) and "No 667" on the breech. This weapon may have been used in the old "galley navy" that disbanded in 1748, when its small arms were distributed to the ocean fleet (re: Katsianos, bib. 216).

| | | | |
|---|---|---|---|
| Length: 62" | Lock: 7" X 1-3/8" | Butt Tang: 4-1/2" | Furniture: Iron |
| Barrel: 46-1/4", .73 cal. | Trigger Guard: 12" | Side Plate: 6-1/4" | Weight: 7.6 lbs |

**Author's Collection**

*Chapter 3: Smoothbore Shoulder Arms*    **105**

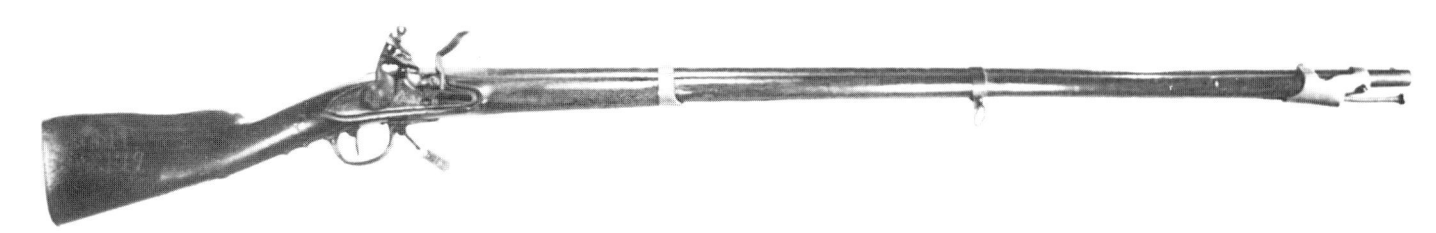

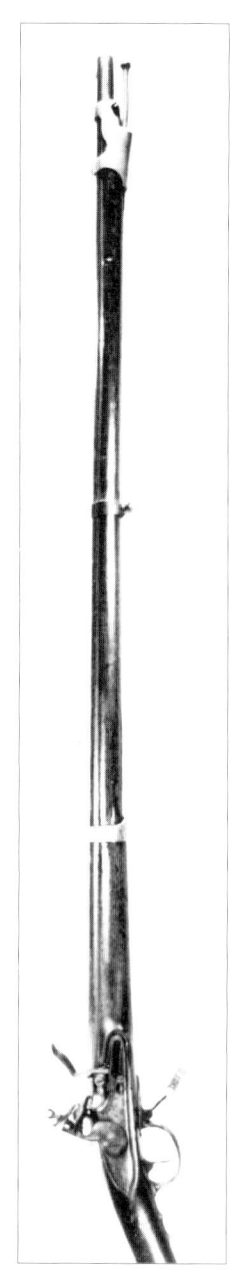

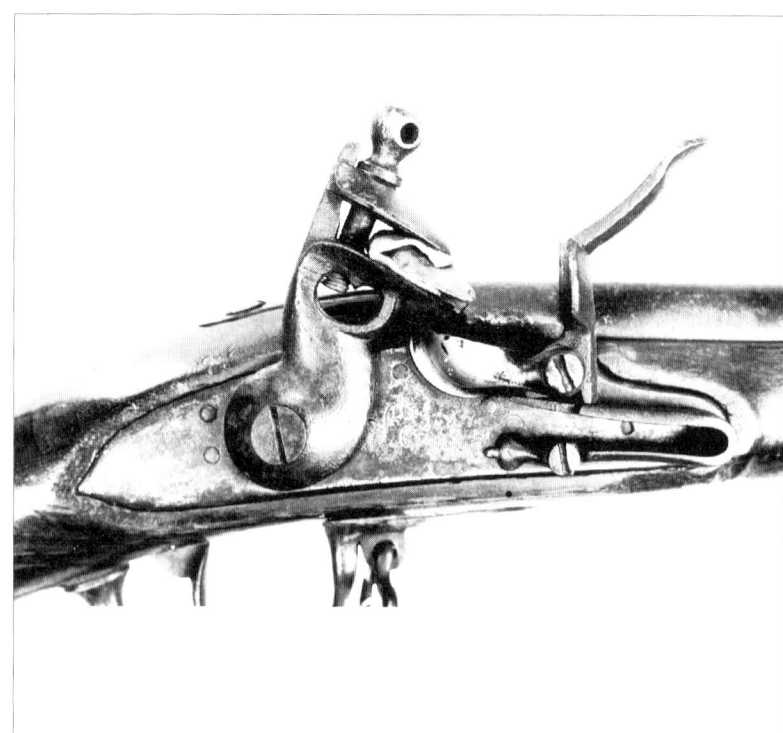

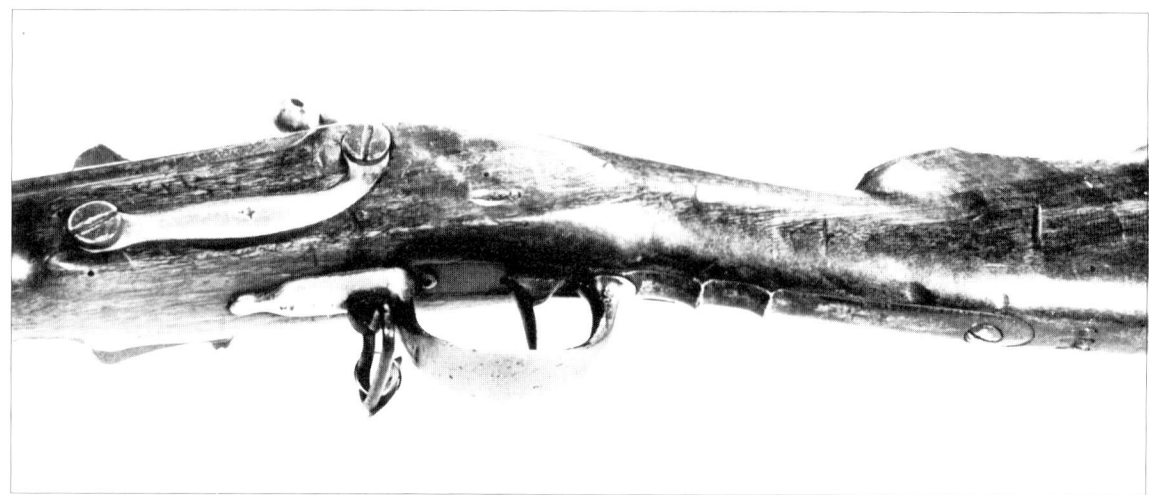

**56.MM FRENCH NAVAL MODEL 1777 MUSKET**                                                                                                              Circa 1779

When the innovative French Model 1777 infantry arm (47.MM) was approved, the pattern was adopted by most of the other services as well. Among them was its selection as the first standard naval pattern, the Fusil de Marine Model 1777. This musket copied the army's basic configuration except for the substitution of brass furniture in place of iron. Most land service features, however, remained: a rounded lock with its ring cock (heart-shaped opening) and sloped brass pan, a trigger guard having a stubby front extension plus two raised finger ridges at the rear, a recessed cheek rest in the inboard butt comb, a short lobed butt tang, and the visible head of a locking screw on the outboard side of the top barrel band (which was set against a curved anti-twist lug under the barrel; also see 50.MM). Its bottom band is secured by a front stud spring, while the center band is friction fitted. Unlike the flat S-shaped side plate on the land service model, this one is convex. Markings on the lock plate are "St. Etienne" and "crown / EL." Its outboard buttstock is branded "BB 11 / 1779." Some 15,500 were produced.

| | | |
|---|---|---|
| Length: 59-1/2" | Lock: 6-1/4" X 1-1/4" | Furniture: Brass |
| Barrel: 44-1/4", .71 cal. | Trigger Guard: 10-1/8" | Weight: 9.7 lbs. |

*Chapter 3: Smoothbore Shoulder Arms*

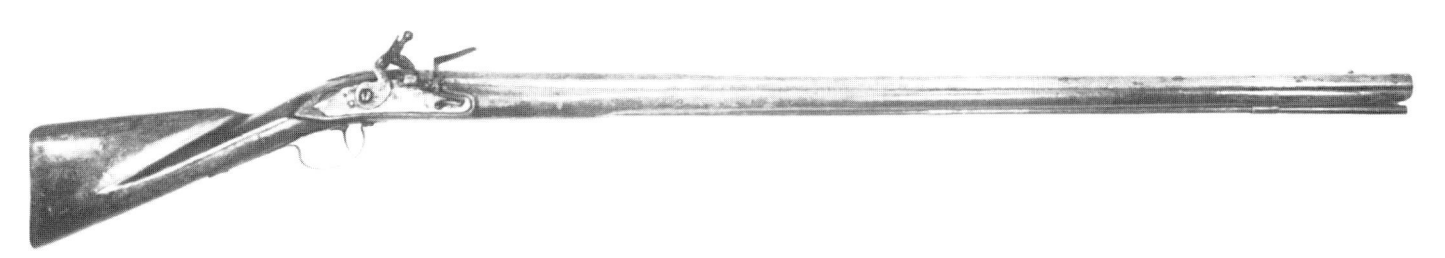

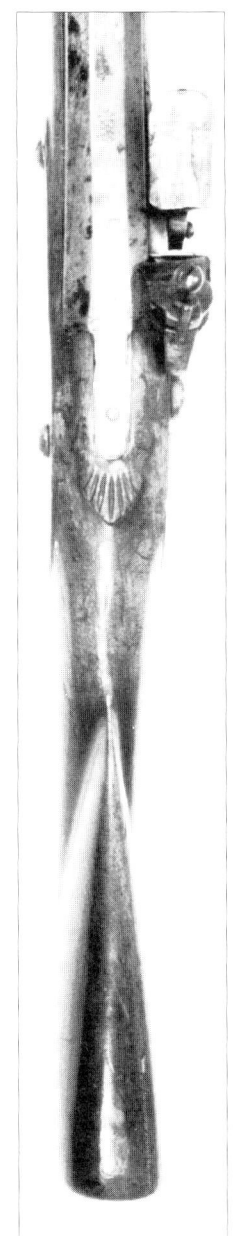

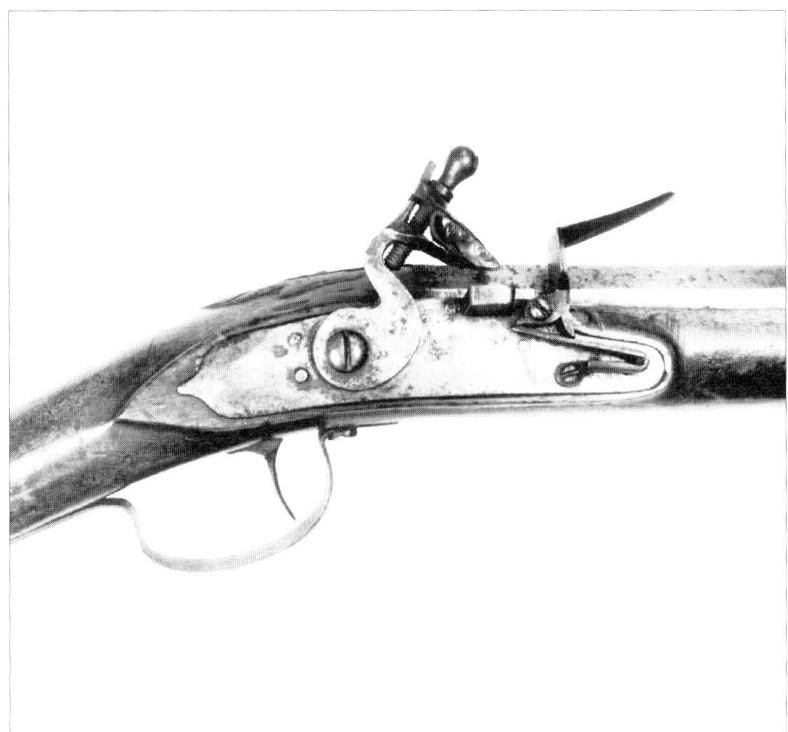

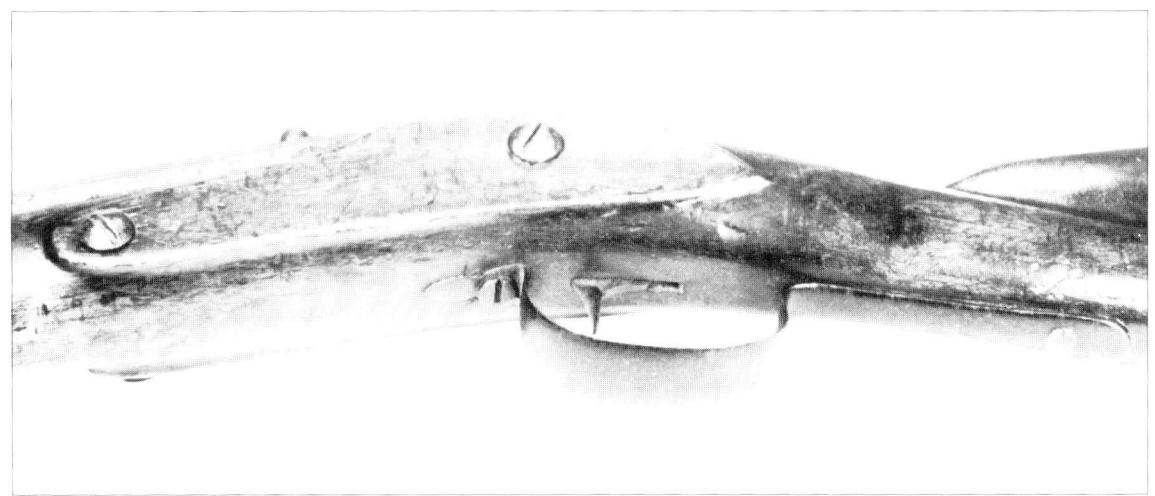

### 57.MM DUTCH INFANTRY MUSKET

**Circa 1680–1700**

The Dutch were the leading world traders of the 17th and 18th centuries, and their firearms of this period are found throughout the known world—including the American Colonies. They were apparently manufactured not only in the Netherlands (for example, Amsterdam, Rotterdam, Maastricht), but also contracted from Liege, Suhl, Solingen, Zella and others. This late 1600s musket bears the Amsterdam city strike. Its early two-screw Dutch lock includes a squared tail, rectangular pan (no bridles), a rounded frizzen top, plus a short frizzen spring without an end finial. The elementary iron strap trigger guard, in turn, is also typical. A walnut stock extends to the flared muzzle (requiring a plug bayonet). It supports two sheet-brass rammer pipes for the wooden rod. Because of economic or wartime demands, the butt plate, bottom ramrod pipe, escutcheon and side plate are omitted. The octagon-to-round barrel's tang (note the shell carving) is held by a screw from underneath, which also anchors the trigger guard's front end (no trigger plate).

Length: 59-1/4"
Barrel: 44-3/8", .79 cal.
**Author's Collection**

Lock: 6-1/2" X 1-1/4"
Trigger Guard: 7-3/4"

Furniture: Brass/Iron
Weight: 9.0 lbs.

Chapter 3: Smoothbore Shoulder Arms  **107**

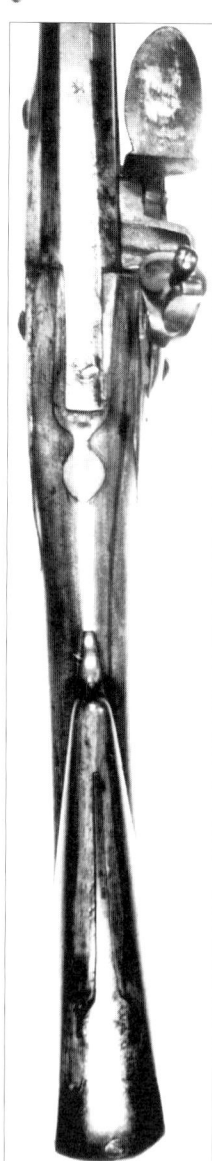

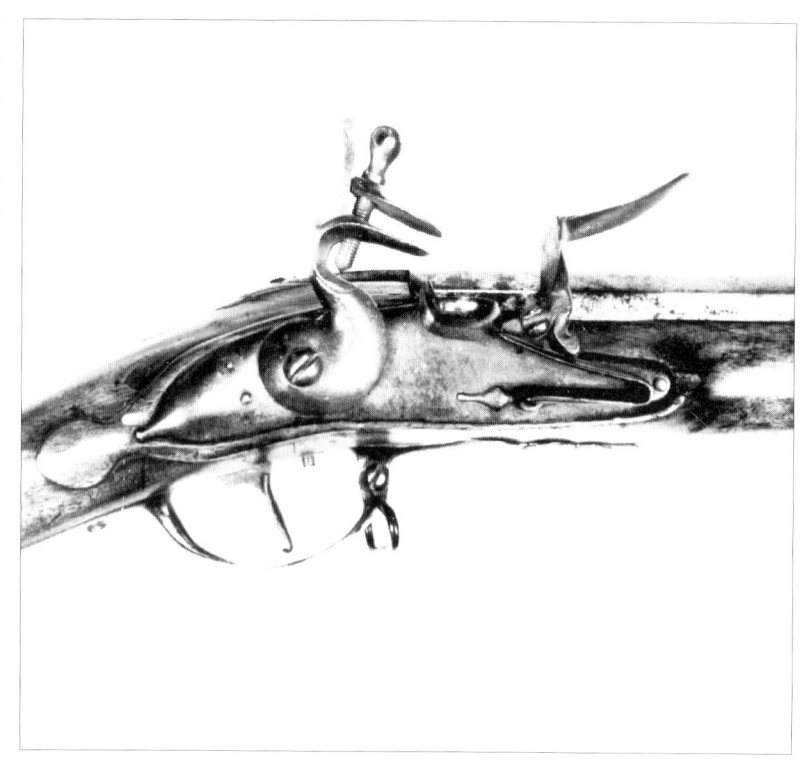

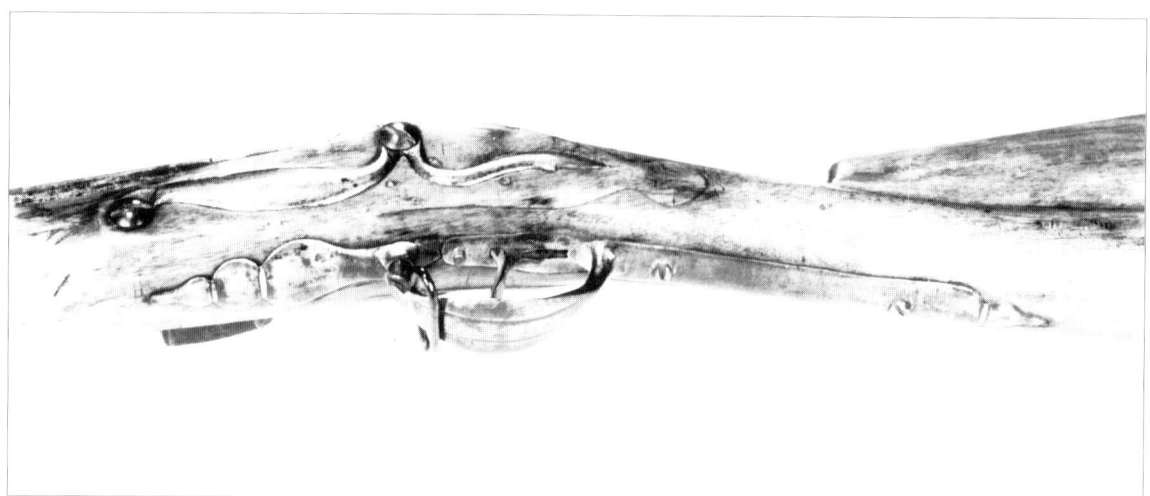

**58.MM DUTCH INFANTRY MUSKET**                                                                        **Circa 1710–1720**

Comparing this Dutch longarm with early 18th century British muskets illustrates how much Holland's weapon patterns influenced England's developing Brown Bess design. Dutch arms of this form were also purchased directly by Britain for their own use, as well as their colonies. Notice the similarity between this example and the English muskets 5.MM to 8.MM, for example the two-screw rounded banana lock (no exterior bridle); raised teardrop carvings surrounding the lock, barrel tang and side plate; the bulbous segmented trigger guard (with Germanic lines in this bow); rounded side plate including a curved tail; the extended butt tang; four early baluster-shaped ramrod pipes; and wooden rammer. Its 44-1/2" (.80 caliber) barrel has an octagon breech for 11-1/4 inches (2-3/4 inches to a second ring), as well as a top stud for a socket bayonet. The walnut stock includes a handrail butt plus a hand-hold swelling behind the tail pipe. The breech shows a rough lion rampant strike and "CJ."

| | | | |
|---|---|---|---|
| Length: 60" | Lock: 6-5/8" X 1-3/8" | Butt Tang: 7-1/8" | Furniture: Iron |
| Barrel: 44-1/2", .80 cal. | Trigger Guard: 12-3/8" | Side Plate: 6-7/8" | Weight: 10.0 lbs. |

**Robert Nittolo Collection**

*Chapter 3: Smoothbore Shoulder Arms*

### 59.MM DUTCH INFANTRY MUSKET

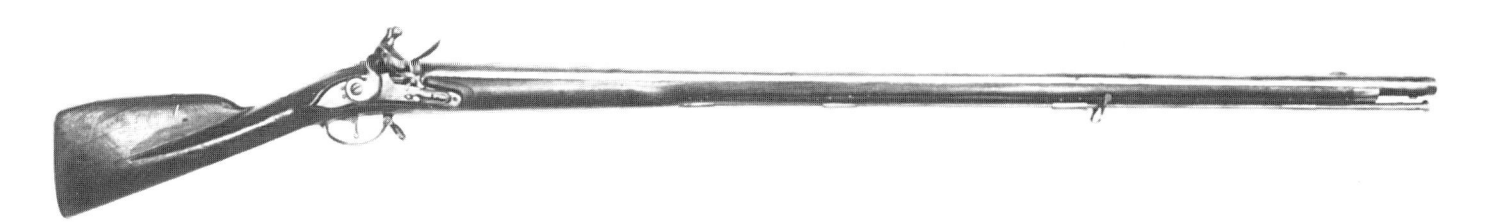

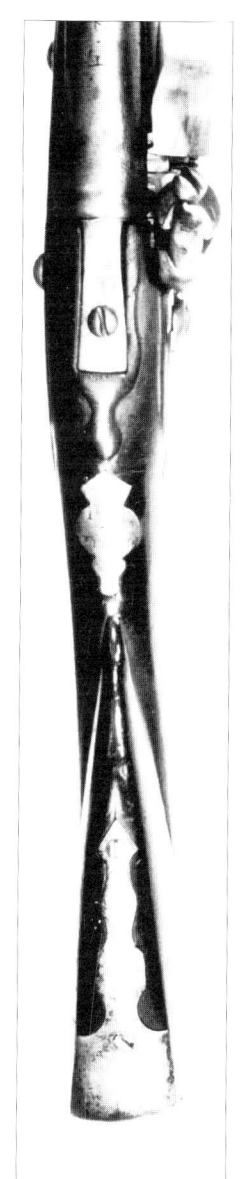

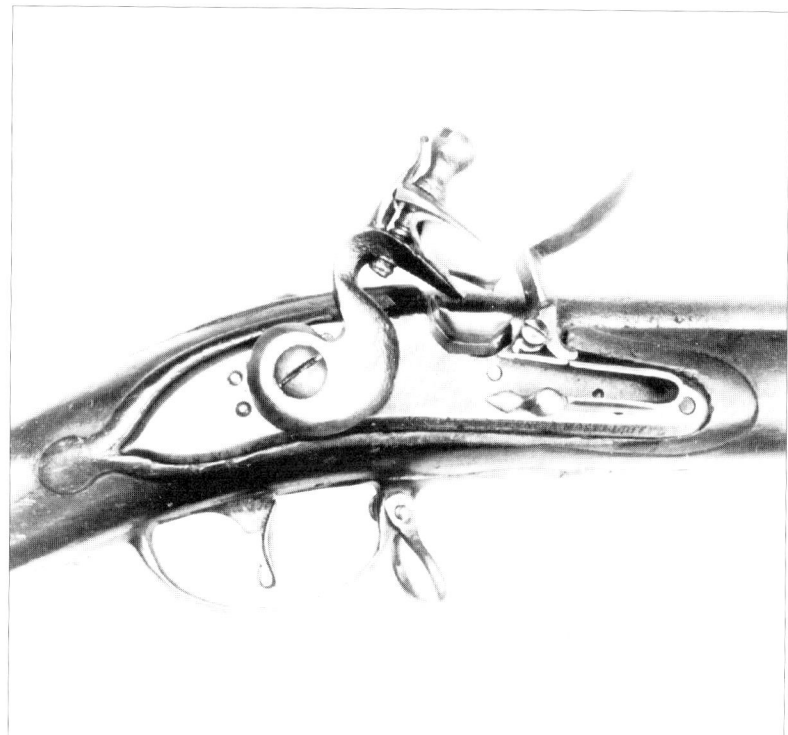

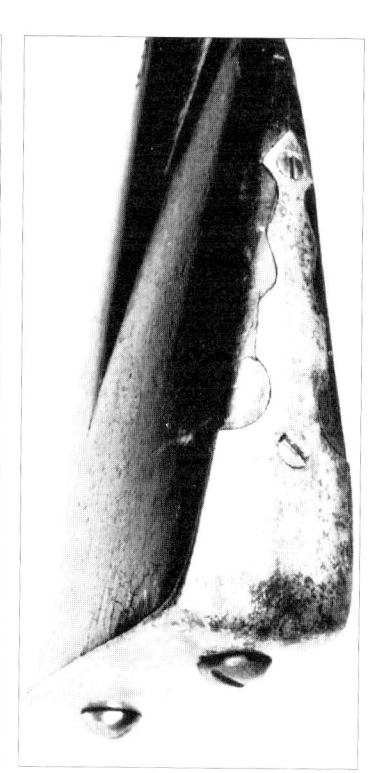

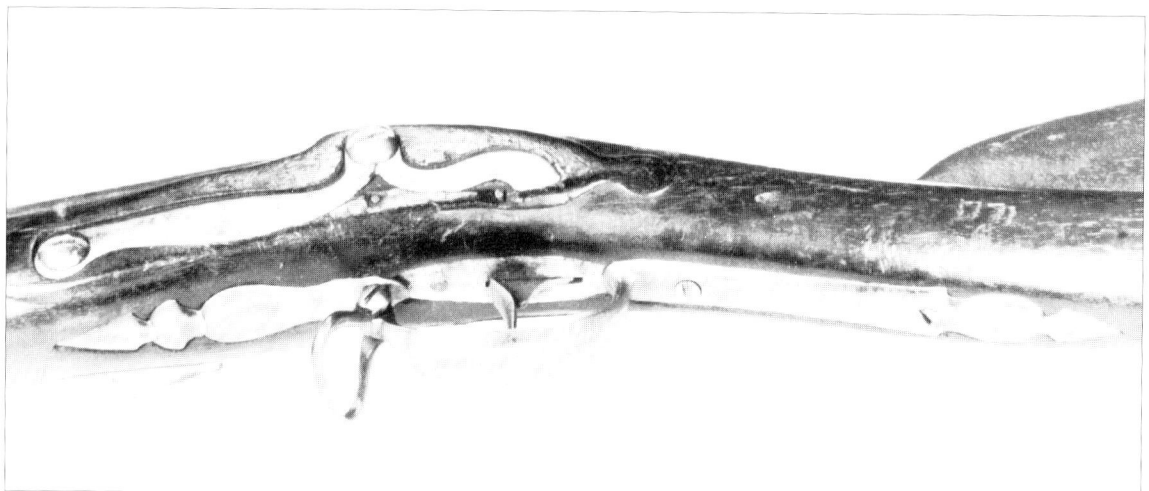

**Circa 1720–1745**

The flat beveled edge lock became popular in continental Europe beginning about 1720, and it continued in most Dutch/Germanic muskets until the 1770s. Notice this flat cock, faceted pan (no exterior bridle), squared frizzen top and spear-like frizzen finial. Another example of this pattern is marked "SO CAROLINA." They are believed to have been part of the 18,000 Dutch muskets purchased by England in 1741, of which at least 4,500 were shipped to the North American colonists during the French and Indian War. Typical Dutch/Germanic styling is apparent here in the long arrowhead butt tang, convex butt plate rear screws, double-pointed trigger guard with a beveled edge trigger loop, the shield escutcheon held by a top screw, teardrop carvings, a tail-ended side plate, the top blade sight, a bottom bayonet stud, plus a sheet-iron forend nose band. The iron rammer probably replaced a wooden rod. Its lower lock bevel reads "CORBAV LE IEVNE A MASTRICHT" (Godefroi Corbau the Younger, Maastricht 1717–1750). Other marks: "F:366" and "CONSTANT" in a banner display at the breech; "LT COLL MESTRAL" on the escutcheon.

| | | | |
|---|---|---|---|
| Length: 60-3/4" | Lock: 6-3/8" X 1-1/4" | Butt Tang: 5-7/8" | Furniture: Iron |
| Barrel: 45-1/4", .77 cal. | Trigger Guard: 12-1/4" | Side Plate: 5-7/8" | Weight: 9.7 lbs. |

**Kit Ravenshear Collection**

*Chapter 3: Smoothbore Shoulder Arms*

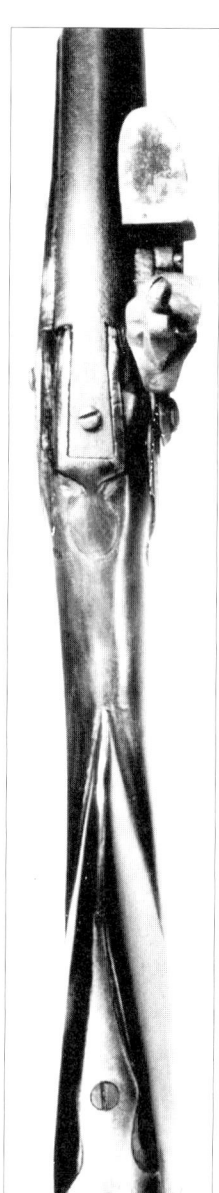

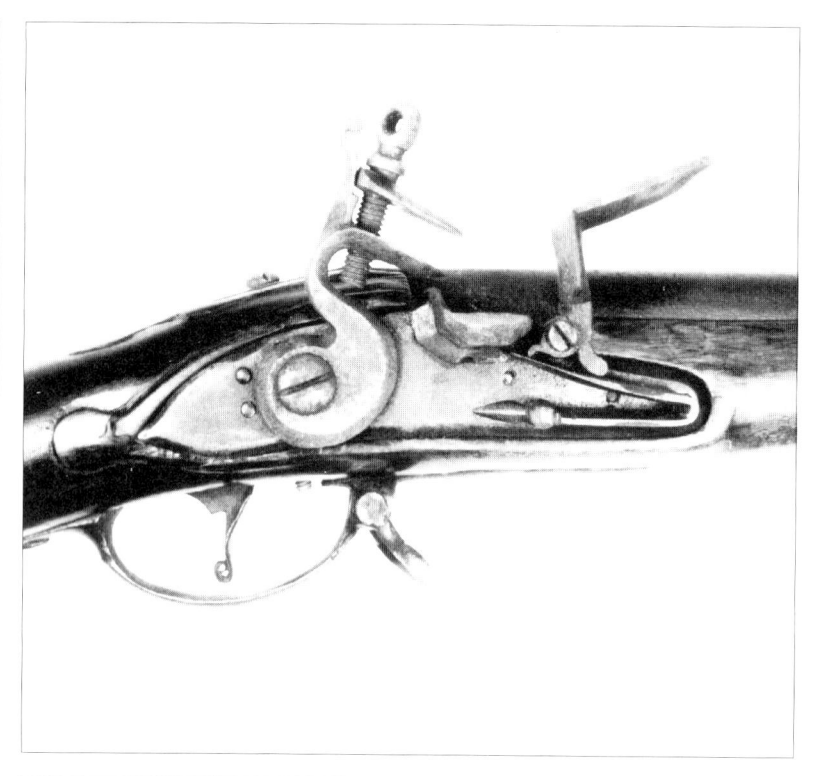

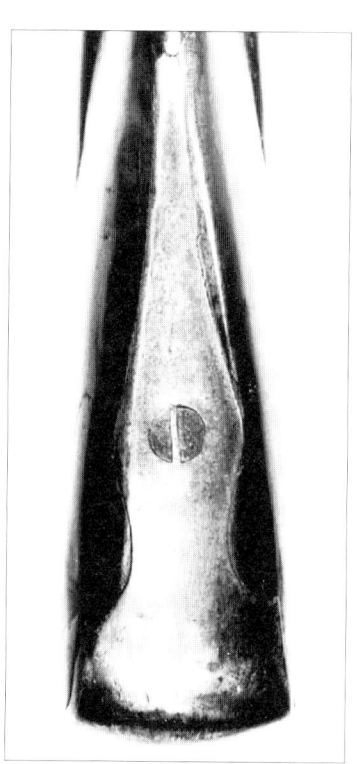

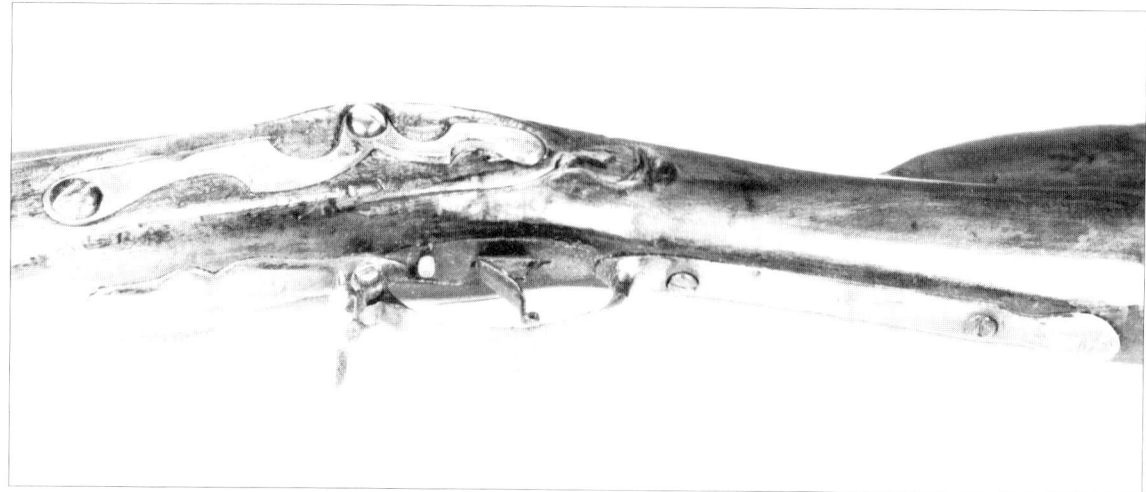

**60.MM DUTCH INFANTRY MUSKET**  Circa 1720–1745

This long pinned pattern is also believed to be among the Dutch arms supplied to American provincials during the French and Indian War. Its features are evolving from earlier forms (59.MM), for example the popular flat/beveled lock with an unbridled faceted pan, rounded frizzen, spearpoint frizzen spring finial (inside screw), vase-like trigger guard terminal, long smooth-sided butt tang (top screw), a sharp shouldered side plate, four faceted rammer pipes (wooden rod), a front sight (plus lower bayonet stud), a brass nose band, a sloping comb ridge, and raised teardrop stock carving surrounding the lock, side plate, and barrel tang (top screw). Many of this pattern were later converted to shorter barrels with bands and shaved butts (see 61.MM). The only mark here is a small "NR" (faint) in a rectangular cartouche under its pan.

Length: 61-1/2"
Barrel: 45-3/4", .78 cal.
**Author's Collection**

Lock: 6-1/8" X 1-1/4"
Trigger Guard: 12-1/4"

Butt Tang: 5-7/8"
Side Plate: 5-3/4"

Furniture: Brass
Weight: 9.8 lbs.

*Chapter 3: Smoothbore Shoulder Arms*

**61.MM  DUTCH INFANTRY MUSKET**                                              Circa 1750–1770

A number of this design have survived—easily identified by the high comb, brass bands and relatively short barrel (41"). Apparently they were originally muskets of the preceding pattern (60.MM) refurbished to create a new configuration (possibly in America). The round barrel was shortened by five inches to 41 inches, three or four brass bands were added (all but the upper one friction-fitted; note, old pin holes and spaces for the earlier rammer pipes are still visible in the stock), and its butt has been thinned from 2-1/4 inches wide to 1-1/2 inches wide (compare preceding example). Moreover the pre-existing stock handrail form has been lost and the stock comb shortened by this narrowing. However the remaining lock, trigger guard, side plate, butt tang (thinned) and stock carving remain in their earlier shape—supplemented by a new steel trumpet ramrod. Markings: breech, "No. 463"; lock, "NIB" (small rectangular cartouche); side plate (inside), "RN"; stock, "DR"; butt tang, "H." One should remember that the rebuilding and mixing of parts from earlier weapons was a constant 18th century practice across Europe, as well as in America.

| | | | |
|---|---|---|---|
| Length: 56" | Lock: 6-3/8" X 1-1/4" | Butt Tang: 6-1/2" | Furniture: Brass |
| Barrel: 41", .77 cal. | Trigger Guard: 12-1/4" | Side Plate: 5 7/8" | Weight: 8.8 lbs. |

**Author's Collection**

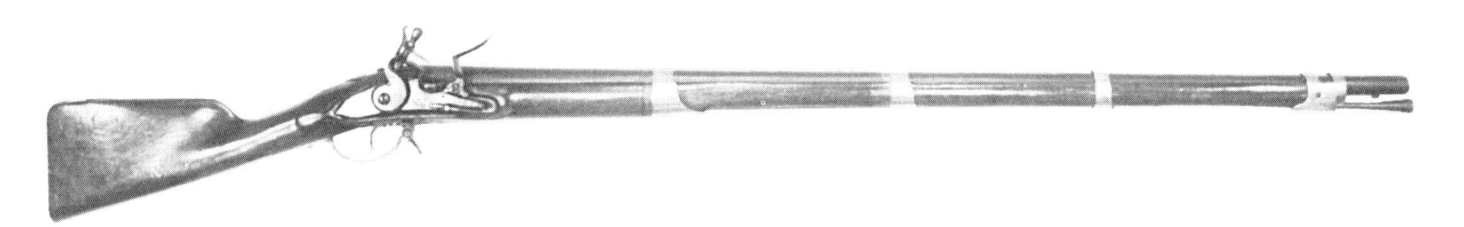

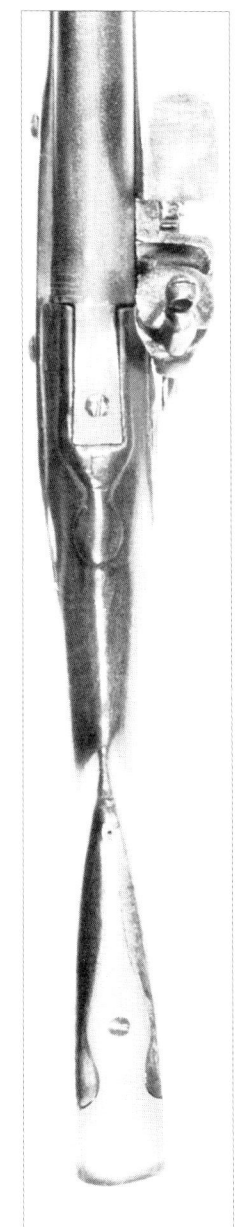

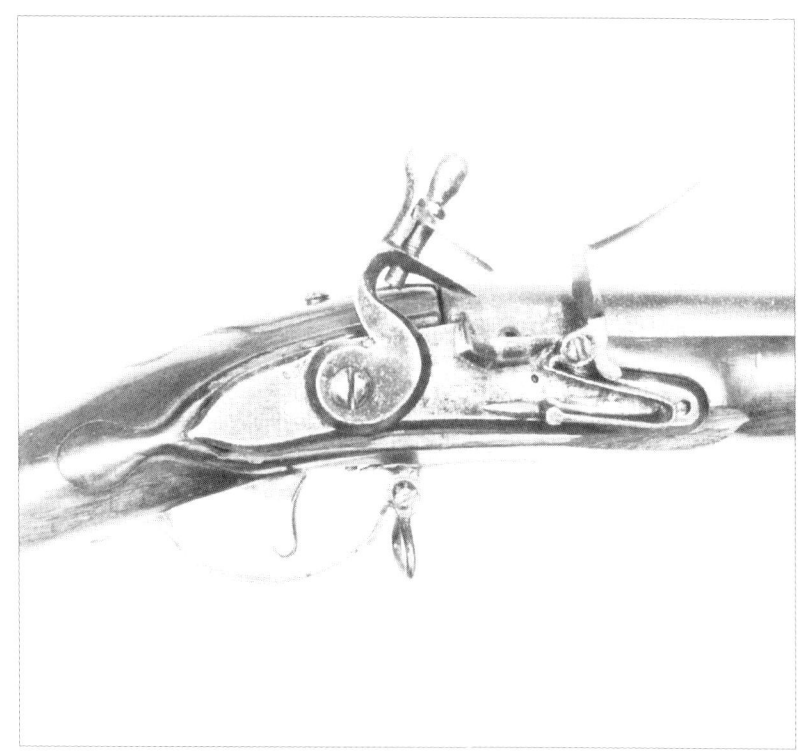

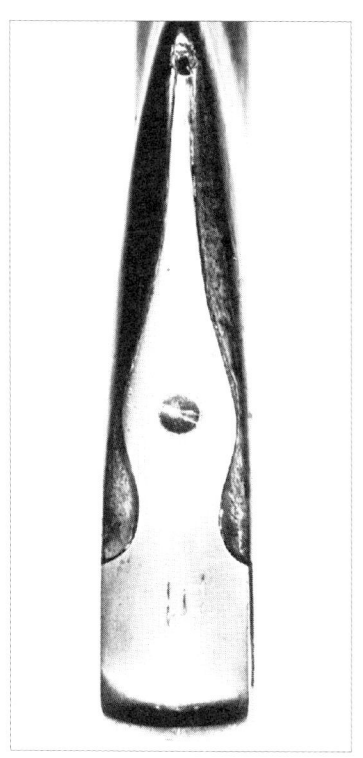

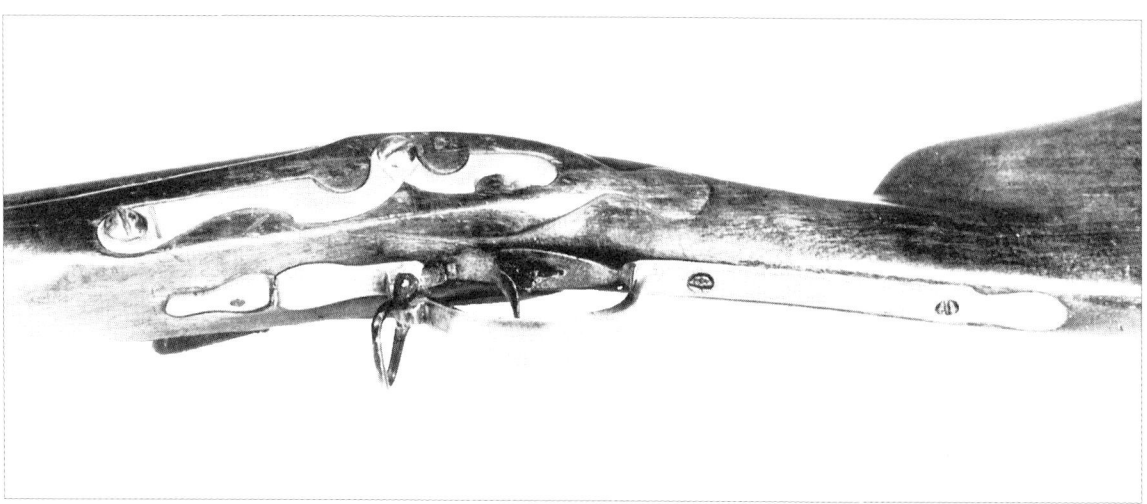

*Chapter 3: Smoothbore Shoulder Arms*     **111**

### 62.MM DUTCH INFANTRY MUSKET

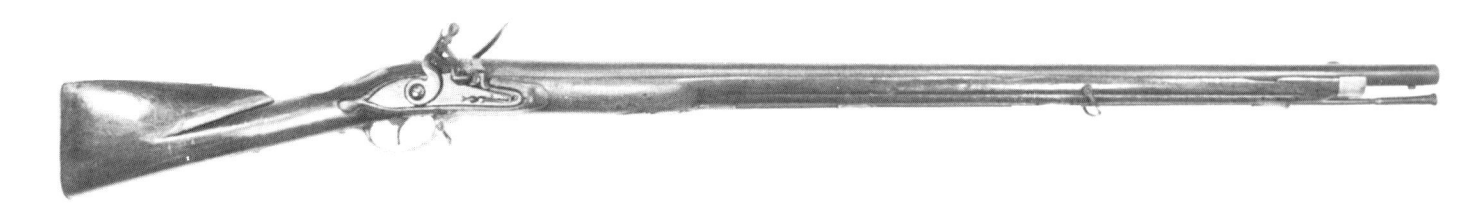

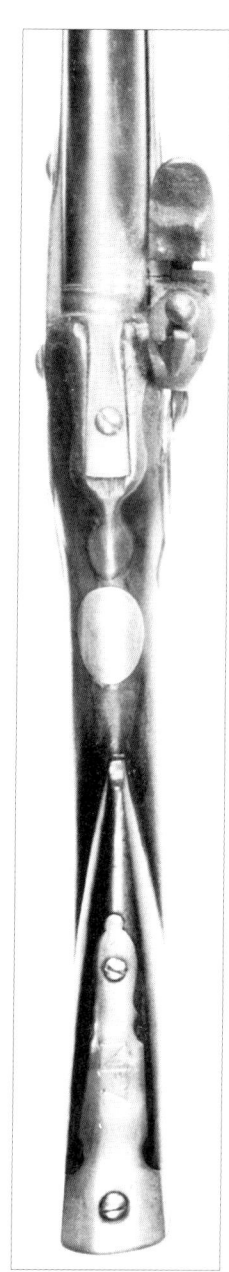

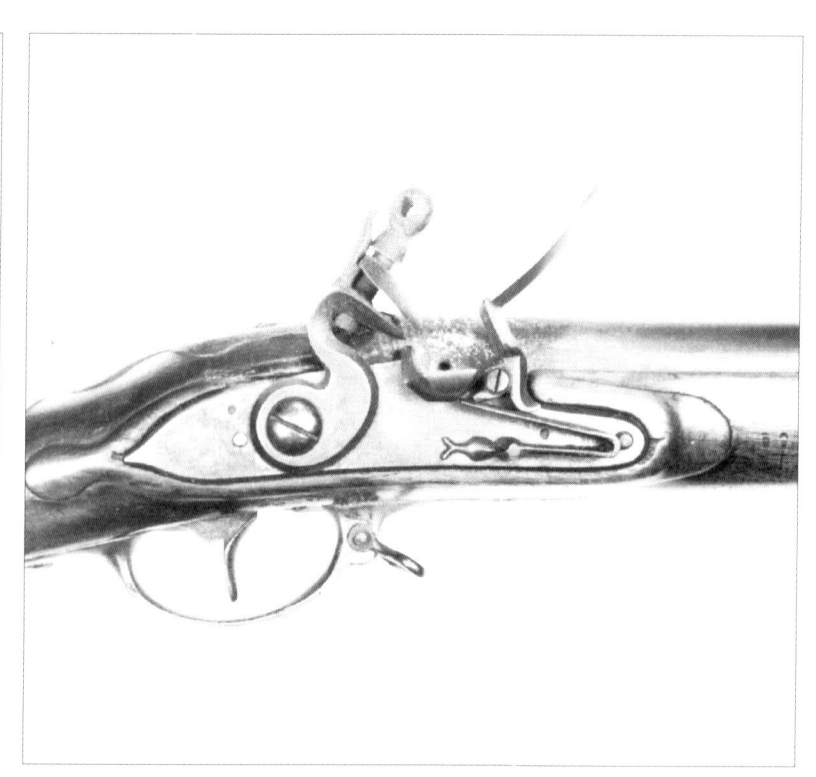

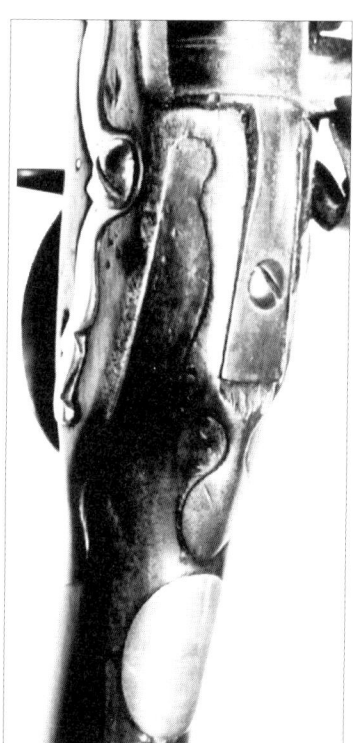

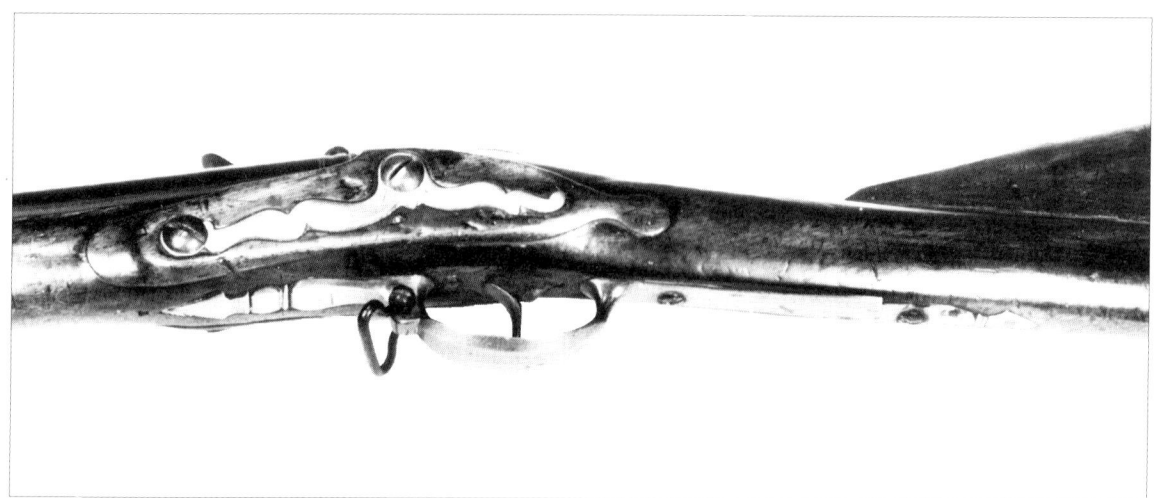

**Circa 1777–1798**

A number of this straight profile pattern are known, and some are marked "KULENBURG" on the lock plate for the Culemborg manufactory in Amsterdam. Because of its short barrel (38-7/8", .75 caliber), it might have been designed for light troops or as an officer's fusil. Yet like so many muskets from this Low Country/German region with its myriad production sources, a mixture of Germanic component forms are apparent: an arrowhead trigger guard; an undulating long butt tang (two top screws); a pinned barrel; and a raised stock ridge parallel to the rammer channel. Commonly shared characteristics of central Europe are also present: bulbous teardrop carved borders, large convex screwheads on the rear butt plate; an oval escutcheon; four faceted ramrod thimbles (two at top have flared mouths); a flat swirled side plate; a brass band on the walnut forend; and both a front sight and a bottom bayonet stud at the muzzle. The popular flat lock with beveled edges is now straight; it includes a faceted pan (no outside bridle), a rounded frizzen top and a fishtail frizzen spring finial. A flat cock, in turn, supports a wide upper post, a flat-backed top jaw, plus a slotted and pierced jaw screw.

| | | | |
|---|---|---|---|
| Length: 54" | Lock: 5-3/4" X 1-1/8" | Butt Tang: 5-5/8" | Furniture: Brass |
| Barrel: 38-7/8", .75 cal. | Trigger Guard: 12-1/4" | Side Plate: 5-1/2" | Weight: 8.5 lbs. |

**Author's Collection**

### 63.MM  DUTCH INFANTRY MUSKET
**Circa 1771–1795**

By the 1770s Holland once again began to favor the rounded lock that had been replaced by the flat design earlier in the century. This new musket pattern is marked "KULENBURG" (Amsterdam's Culemborg manufactory) on the lock plate and "GENERALITEIT" at the breech (that identified government ownership). Its brass furniture has been simplified with a plain narrow trigger guard, a convex side plate lacking a tail, a shortened butt tang (two top screws), and four (often three) brass barrel bands, of which the lower three are held by friction. The walnut stock too is straighter with a lower comb. Yet several earlier features have been retained: the teardrop raised stock carving; two large protruding rear butt plate screws; an oval escutcheon (held by two pins); plus a front blade sight on the two-strap upper barrel band. A small spring catch attached to the stock protrudes from the forend to latch over the rear ring on a bayonet socket (like France's Model 1774, 46.MM). This was the principal pattern when Holland actively joined America's rebelling colonies in 1780.

Length: 59-5/8"
Barrel: 43-1/4", .76 cal.
**Author's Collection**

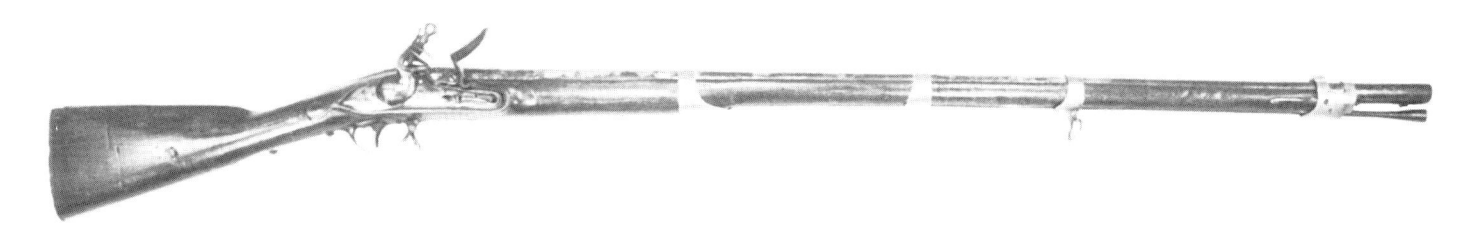

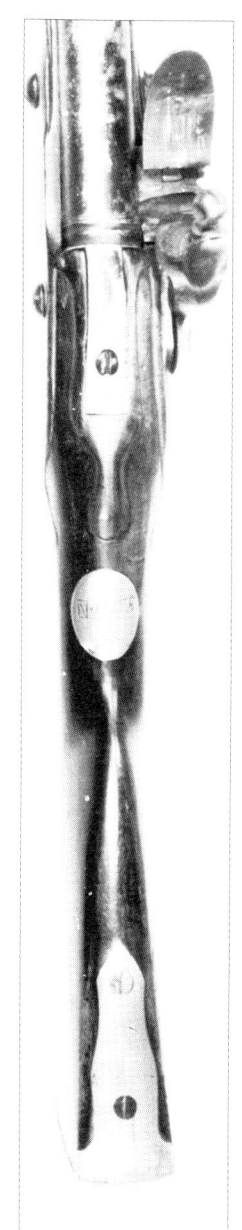

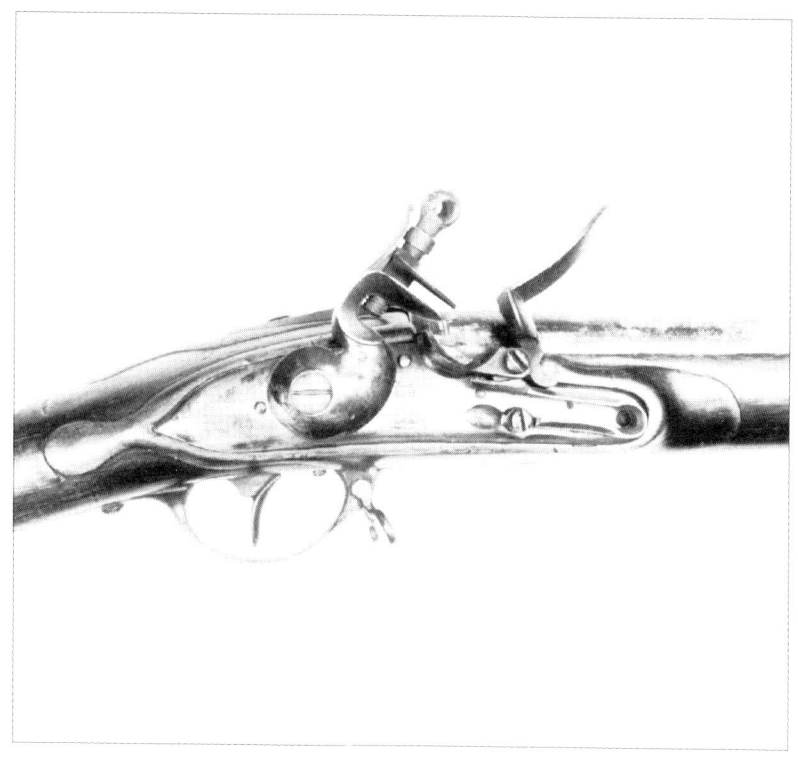

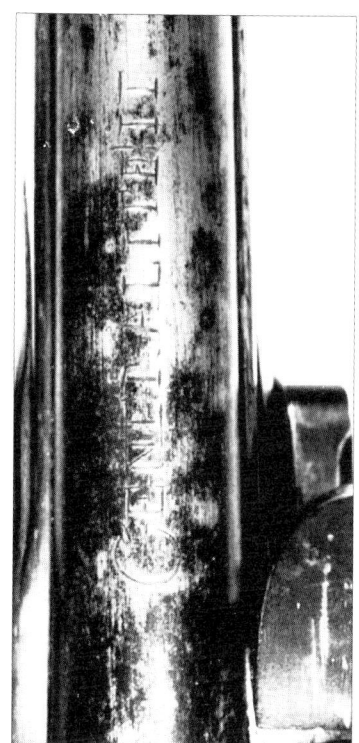

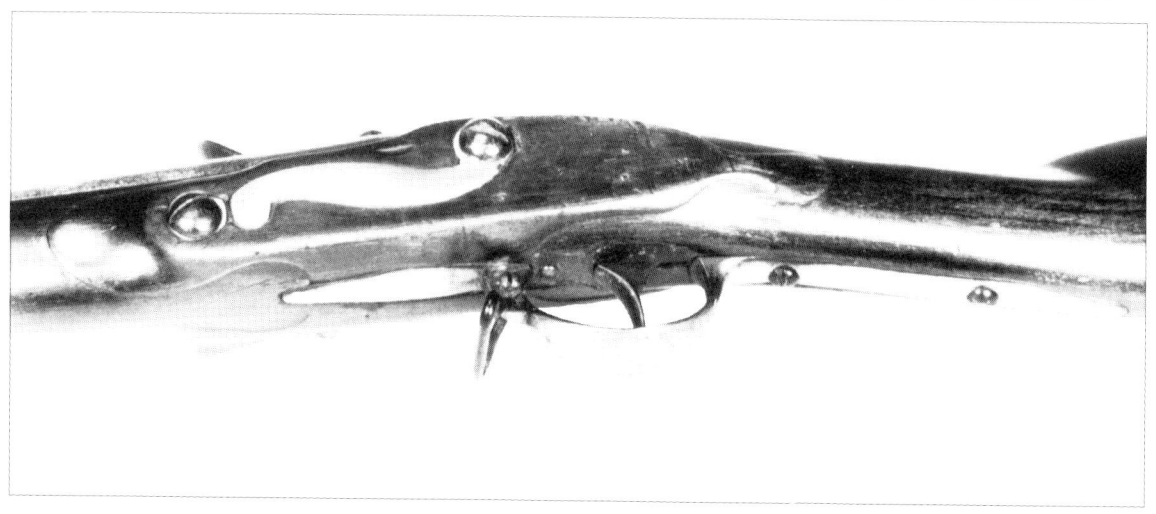

Lock: 6-3/4" X 1-3/8"
Trigger Guard: 10-3/4"

Butt Tang: 4-3/8"
Side Plate: 4-1/4"

Furniture: Brass
Weight: 9.6 lbs.

*Chapter 3: Smoothbore Shoulder Arms*  113

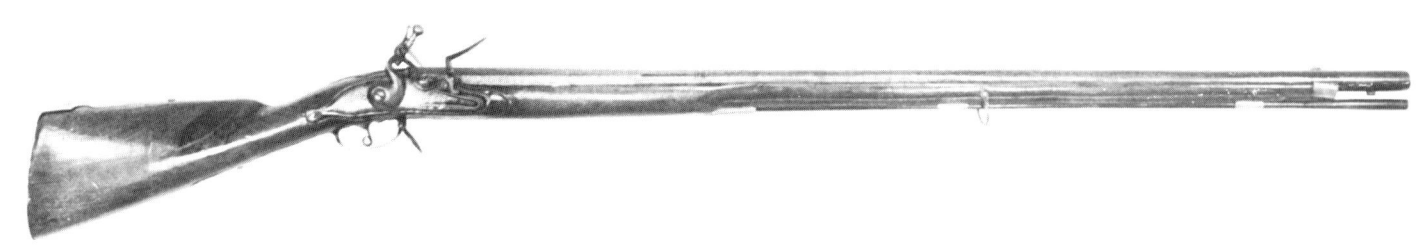

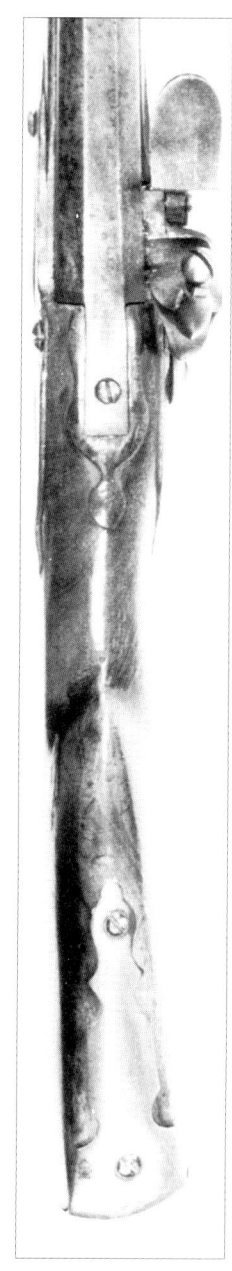

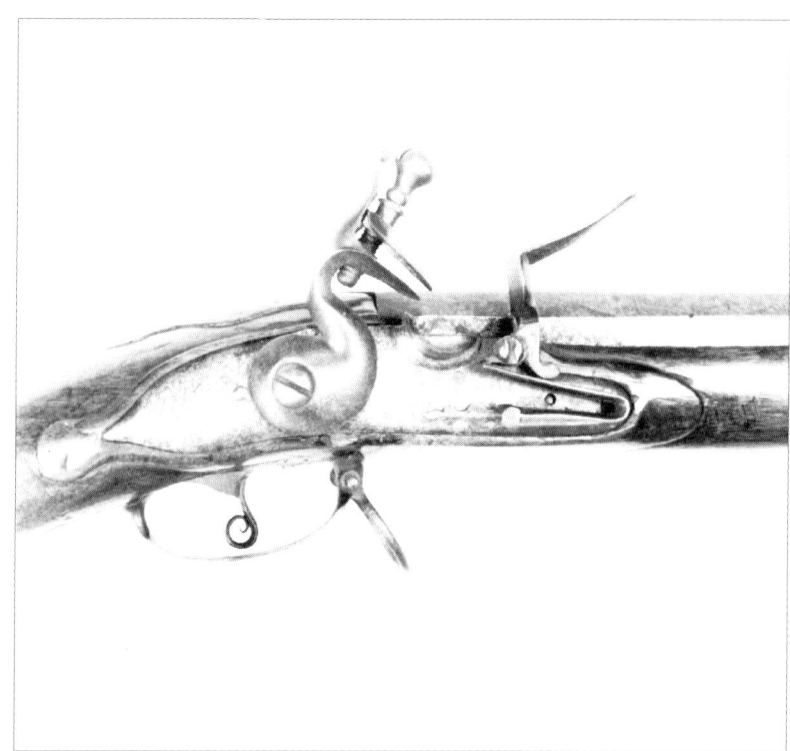

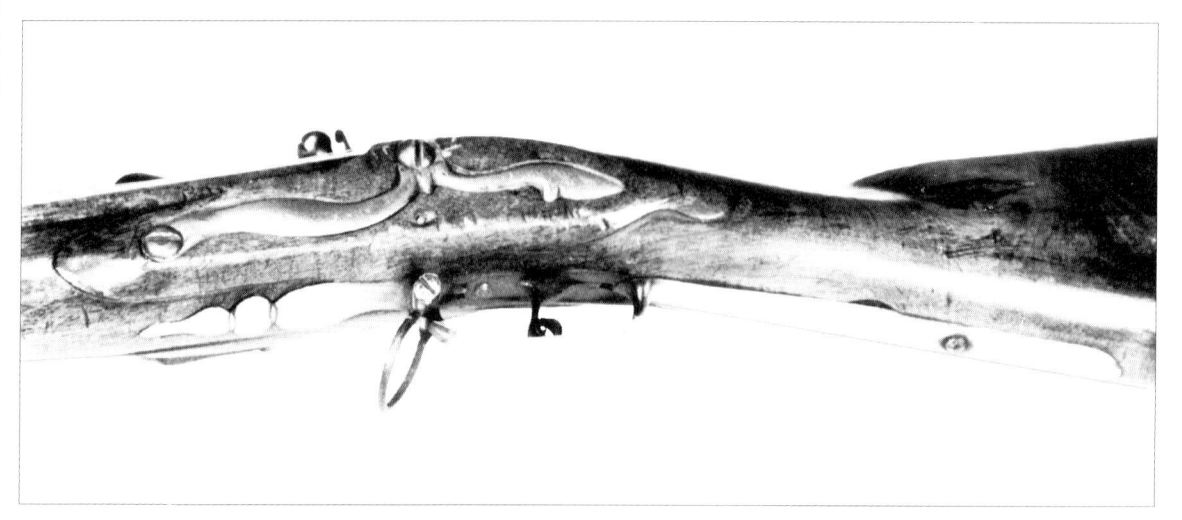

**64.MM GERMANIC INFANTRY MUSKET**  Circa 1720–1740

A common modern fallacy tries to assign a pattern to each of the large arms-making centers of Europe, forgetting that they were, in fact, contractors who manufactured each group of firearms according to the specifications of that buyer. The situation was further complicated by their production of components for sale to other suppliers. This musket for example has the "SVL" and "chicken" stamps on its breech of Suhl (German) which, like Liege (Low Countries) and St. Etienne (France), was not a single source but dozens of independent makers who often applied bogus proofs. The Germanic musket in this case has a lower-than-normal profile, yet exhibits the early rounded lock (no exterior bridle), segmented trigger guard, raised teardrop carving and the convex side plate often seen on Dutch arms, for example 58.MM and 59.MM. It also includes typical German characteristics: a thick butt (2-3/8" wide), a long undulating butt tang, two large protruding end screws, three faceted rammer pipes (wooden rod), a top blade sight, and a bottom bayonet lug. The stock is stamped "US" in a small cartouche.

| | | | |
|---|---|---|---|
| Length: 54-3/4" | Lock: 6-1/8" X 1-1/4" | Butt Tang: 5-1/2" | Furniture: Brass |
| Barrel: 40-1/8", .68 cal. | Trigger Guard: 12" | Side Plate: 5-3/4" | Weight: 8.5 lbs. |//
**Author's Collection**

*114    Chapter 3: Smoothbore Shoulder Arms*

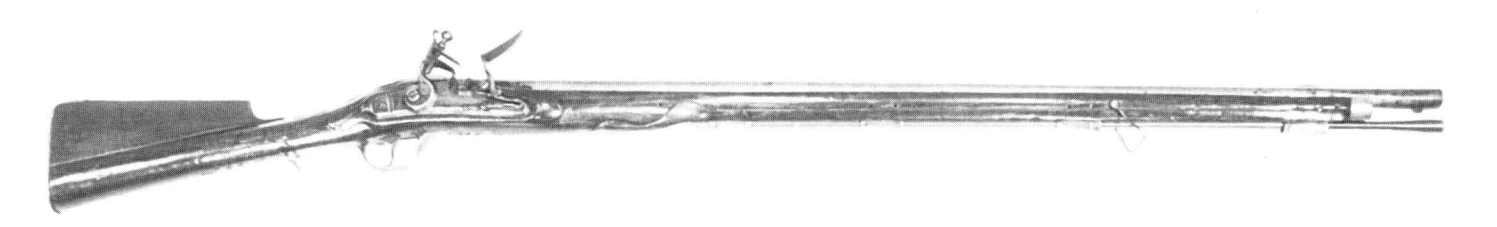

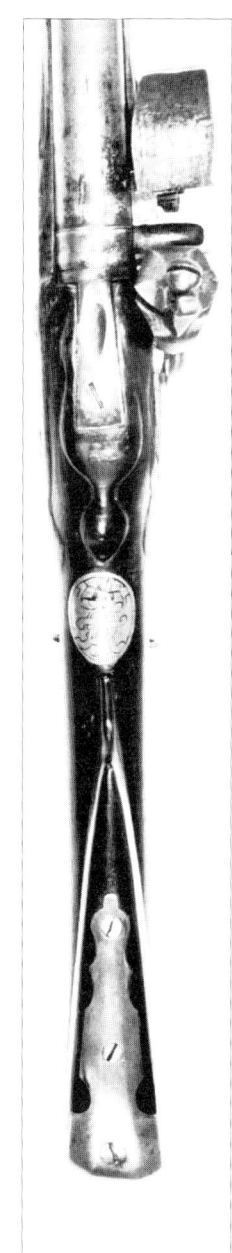

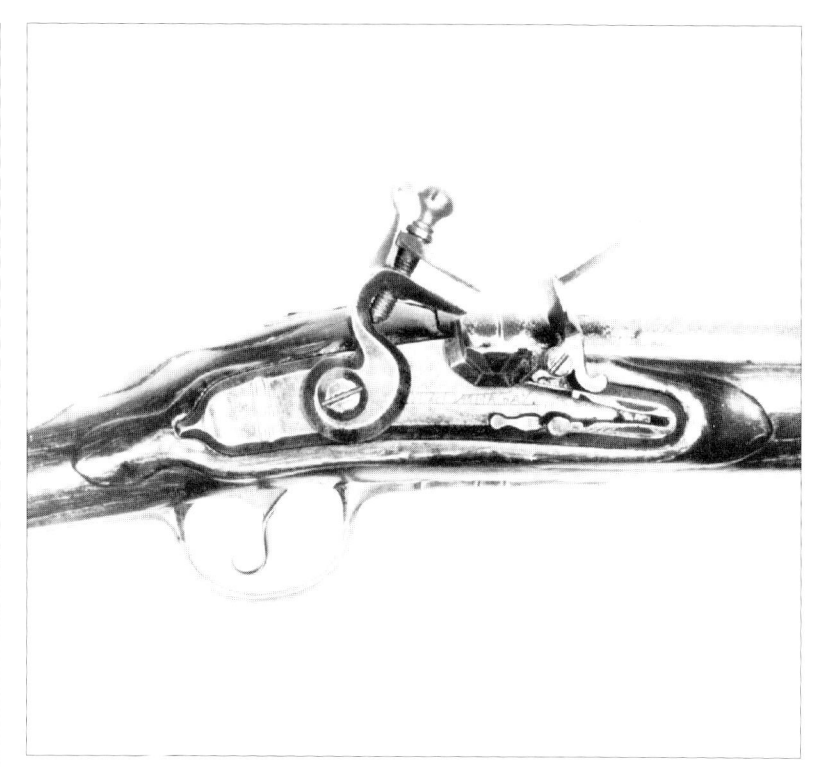

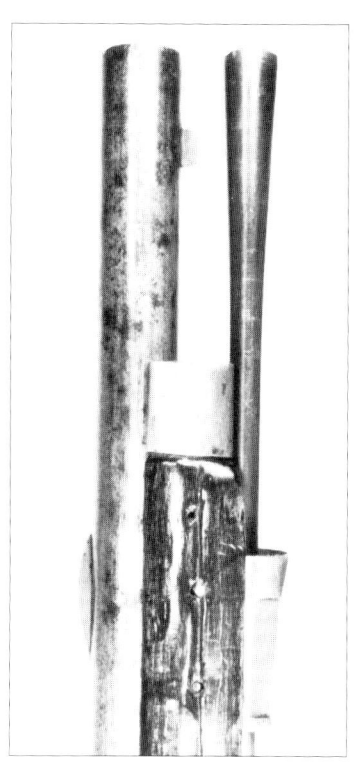

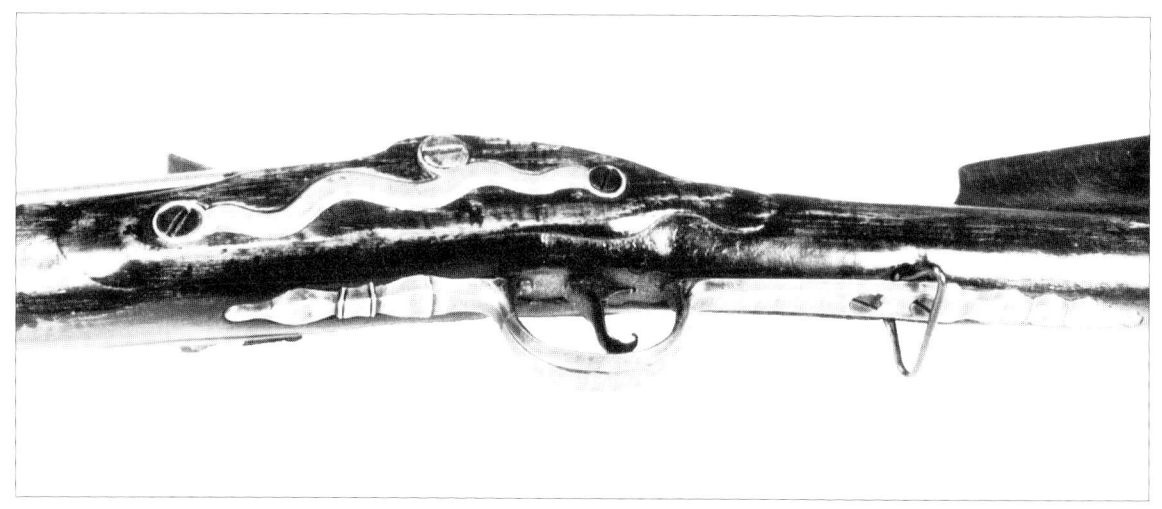

### 65.MM PRUSSIAN INFANTRY MUSKET MODEL 1740
### Circa 1775–1780

The unique Prussian Model 1740 was made in Berlin at the joint Potsdam (locks) and Spandau (barrels, furniture, assembly) manufactories. Prussia's Frederick the Great shunned American aid, and questions exist whether any of his muskets were used in our Revolution. However, given the continual wars of that century with the accumulation of captured, damaged, abandoned, surplus and private contract arms in every country—plus American agents acquiring a wide variety from used weapons dealers as well as our allies—it is assumed that most basic Continental patterns arrived in the thirteen rebelling colonies. This distinctive musket includes the Potsdam lock form marked "POTSDAM MAGAZ" and "DSE" (the maker's principals 1775–1795; if inscribed "S&D," the dating is 1723–1775). Notice its unusual undulating tail surface, large squared upper jaw and frizzen top, faceted pan and decorated frizzen spring edge. Also unique are the wavy flat side plate, lobed trigger guard, raised carving, high comb and long irregular butt tang (three top screws). The heavier faceted pipes plus the thickened ramrod were 1773 modifications. Frederick's "FR" is on the oval escutcheon.

| | | | |
|---|---|---|---|
| Length: 57-3/8" | Lock: 6-5/8" X 1-1/4" | Butt Tang: 5-5/8" | Furniture: Brass |
| Barrel: 41-1/4", .76 cal. | Trigger Guard: 12-1/4" | Side Plate: 6-1/8" | Weight: 10.7 lbs. |

**Author's Collection**

*Chapter 3: Smoothbore Shoulder Arms* **115**

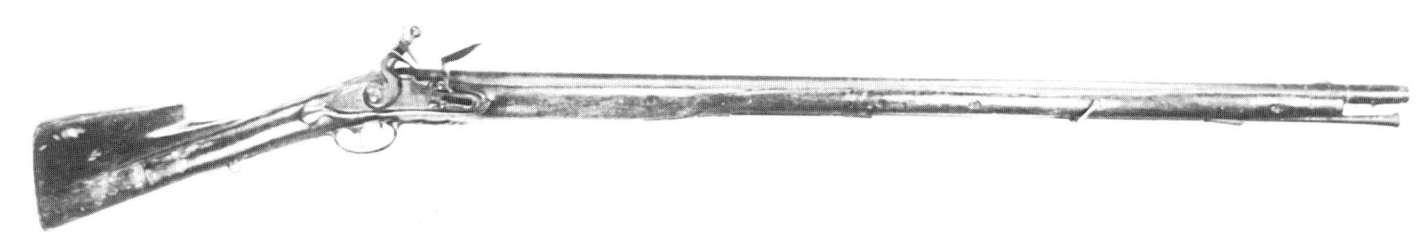

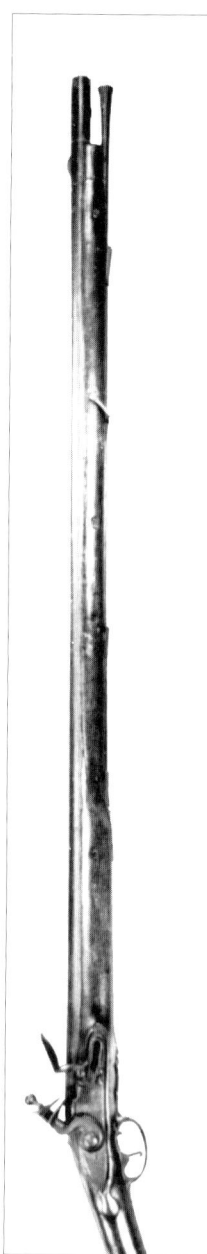

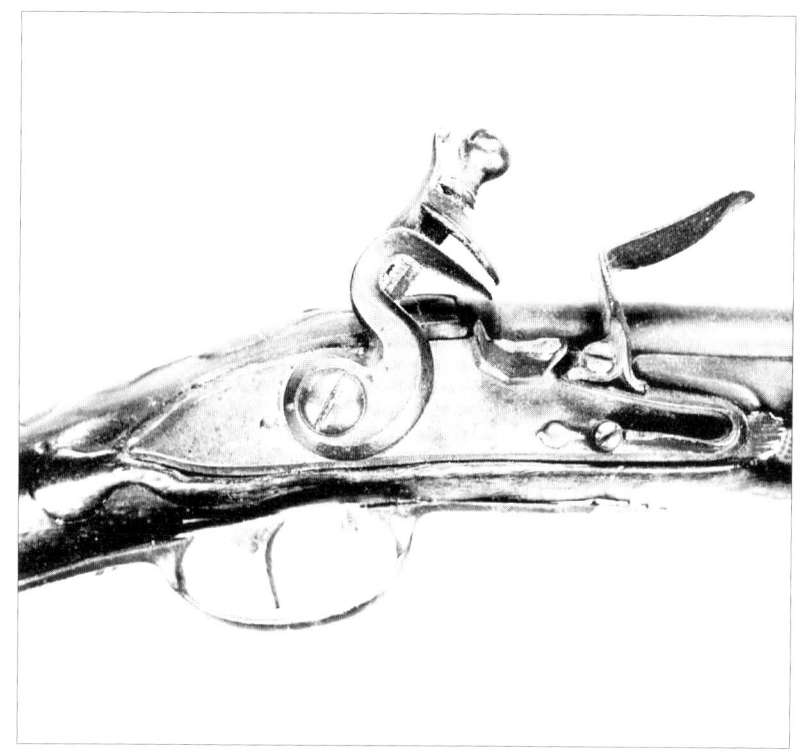

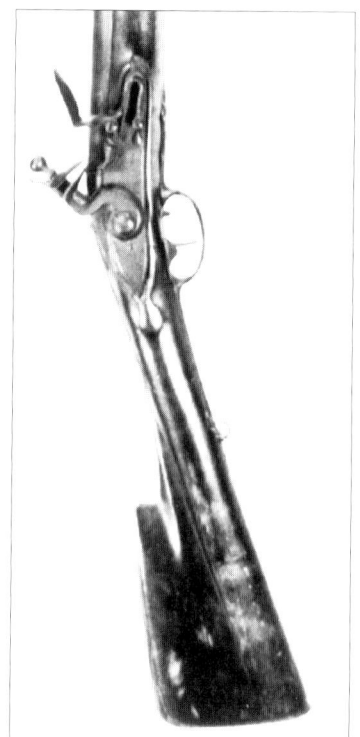

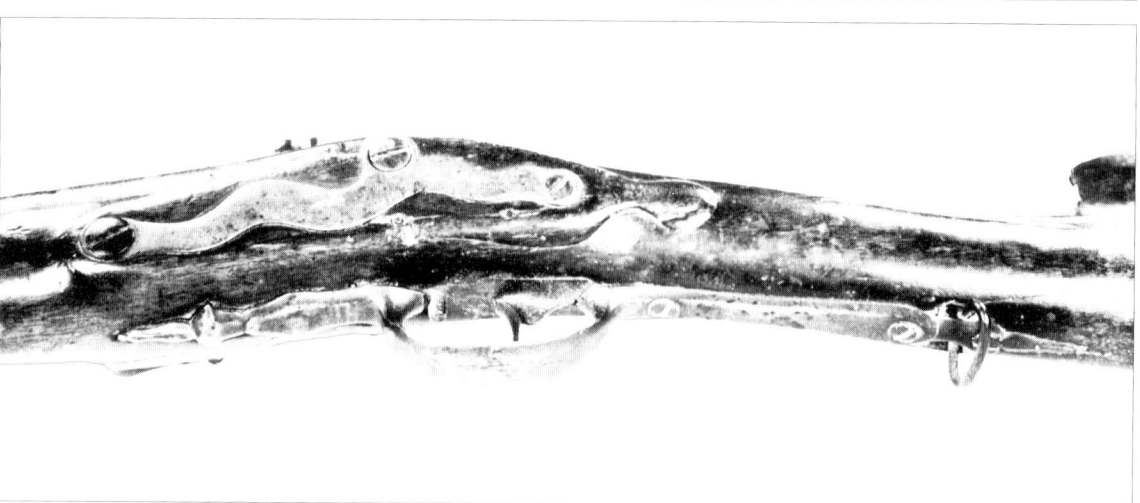

**66.MM  GERMANIC INFANTRY MUSKET**                                                        **Circa 1730–1750**

The success of Prussia's army induced many German states to adopt features from their muskets (see 65.MM). This example includes a distinctive shortened cliff-like butt comb similar to the Prussian cow's-foot shape. It also copies the flat wavy side plate (although wider) with its rear wood screw, as well as the Model 1740's thick forend (and sheet-brass nose band). The earlier curved banana profile is gone from this common flat/beveled two-screw lock (no exterior bridle), while raised teardrop carving surrounds the barrel tang, side plate and lock. Three conical thimbles, in turn, secure a trumpet-head steel rammer. The double-pointed trigger guard (with its beveled-edge trigger bow), however, resembles earlier Low Country designs (59.MM). In Germanic tradition the round pinned barrel (baluster breech) mounts a brass front sight at the muzzle and a bayonet stud underneath.

| | | | |
|---|---|---|---|
| Length: 59" | Lock: 6-1/2" X 1-1/4" | Butt Tang: 5" | Furniture: Brass |
| Barrel: 43", .79 cal. | Trigger Guard: 12" | Weight: 10.5 lbs. | |

*116*    *Chapter 3: Smoothbore Shoulder Arms*

**67.MM GERMANIC INFANTRY MUSKET**  Circa 1730–1745

In most contracted patterns, various design influences were combined according to the customer's wishes. In this case a number of Germanic features are apparent: a wavy Prussian-type side plate; the flat/beveled three-screw banana lock with its frizzen spring's German spear-like finial and incised designs along the spring's edges; a clipped upper end on the frizzen; arrowhead terminals on the brass trigger guard (plus a beveled loop); four faceted rammer pipes (wooden rod); teardrop raised carving surrounding its barrel tang; and a sheet-brass forend band. The long plain butt tang, however, resembles Low Country styling (and the rear screws are flush). Note also the absence of raised stock carving around the lock and side plate, as well as the escutcheon. Its long (47") barrel is octagonal at the breech for 12-5/8 inches, ending in a double ring. The top bayonet stud, in turn, is unusual for German arms. No proof marks are visible, but its inboard butt is branded "CAP. Et COMP / De ST VALLERY / LXX."

Length: 62-3/8"  
Barrel: 47", .70 cal.  
**Author's Collection**

Lock: 6-1/8" X 1-1/4"  
Trigger Guard: 10-1/2"

Butt Tang: 6-1/4"  
Side Plate: 6-1/4"

Furniture: Brass  
Weight: 8.8 lbs.

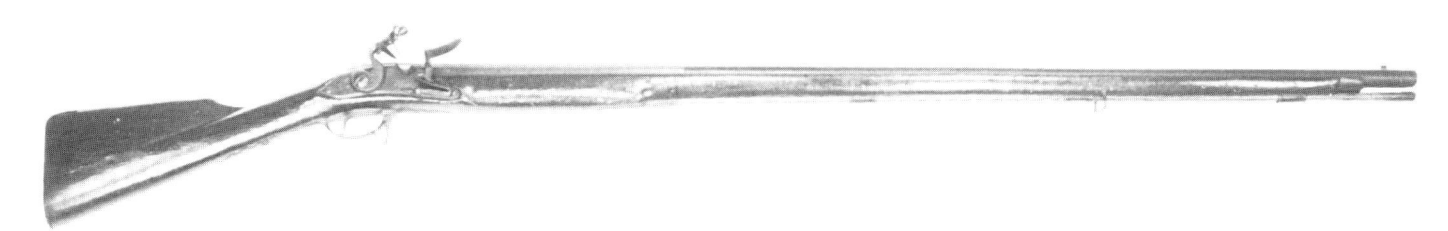

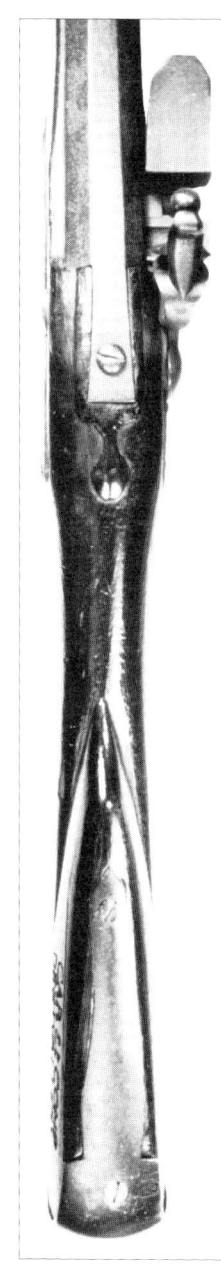

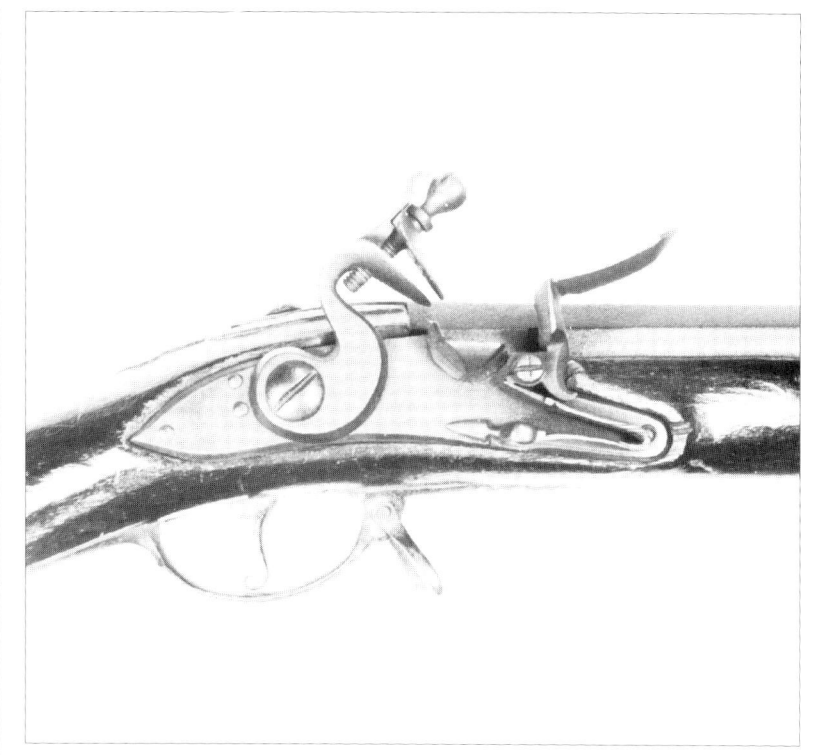

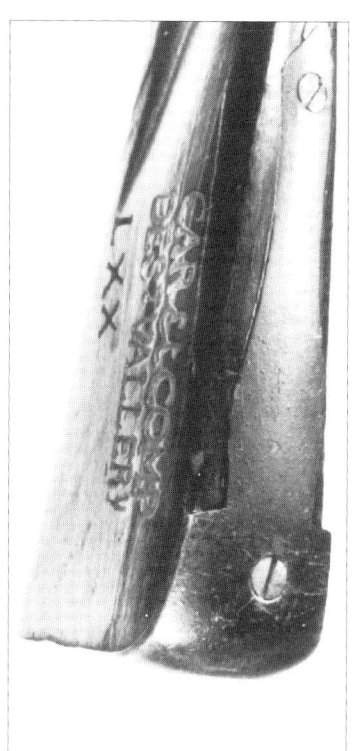

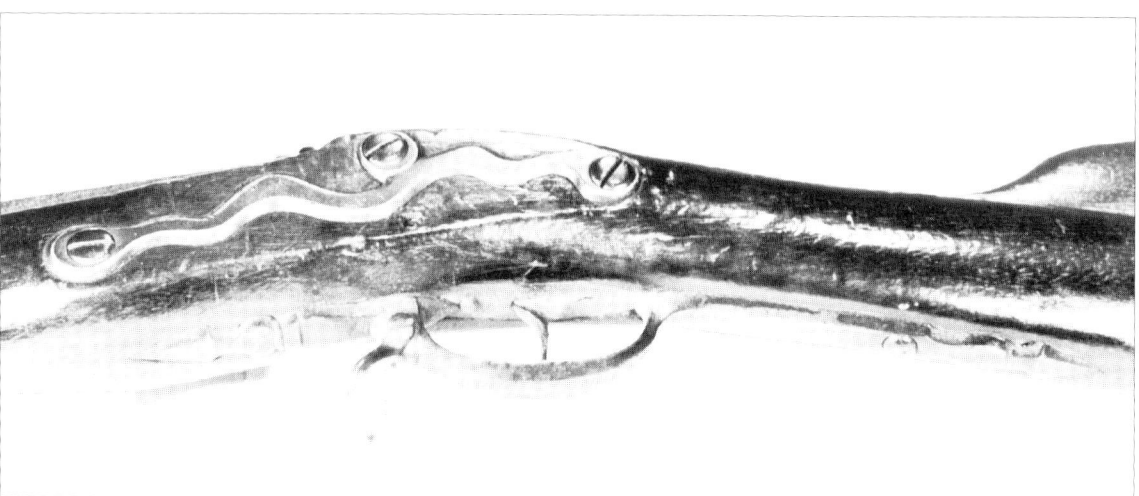

*Chapter 3: Smoothbore Shoulder Arms*   **117**

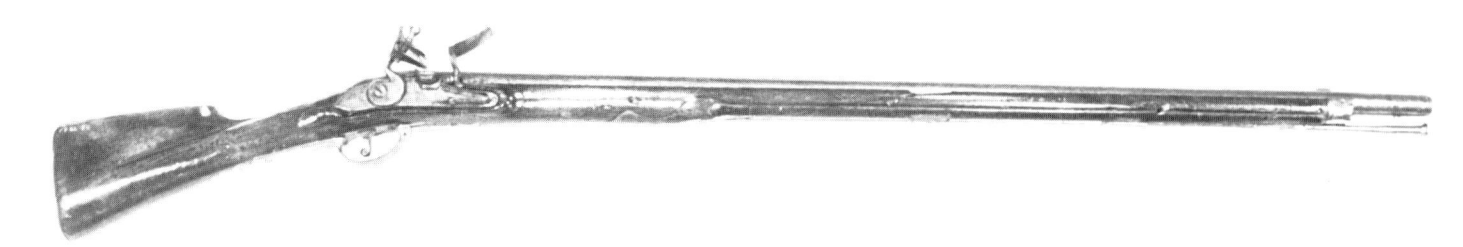

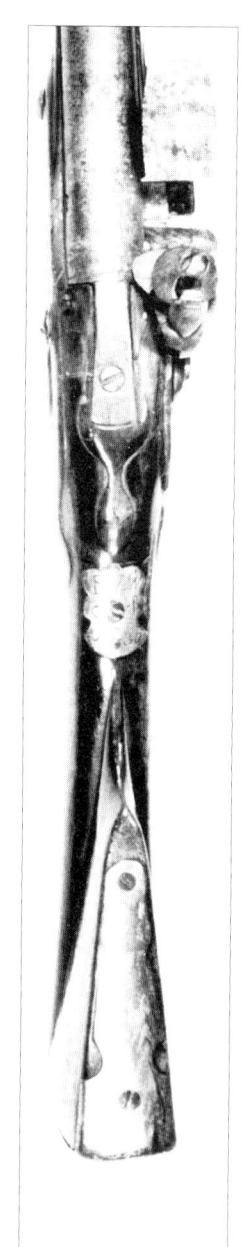

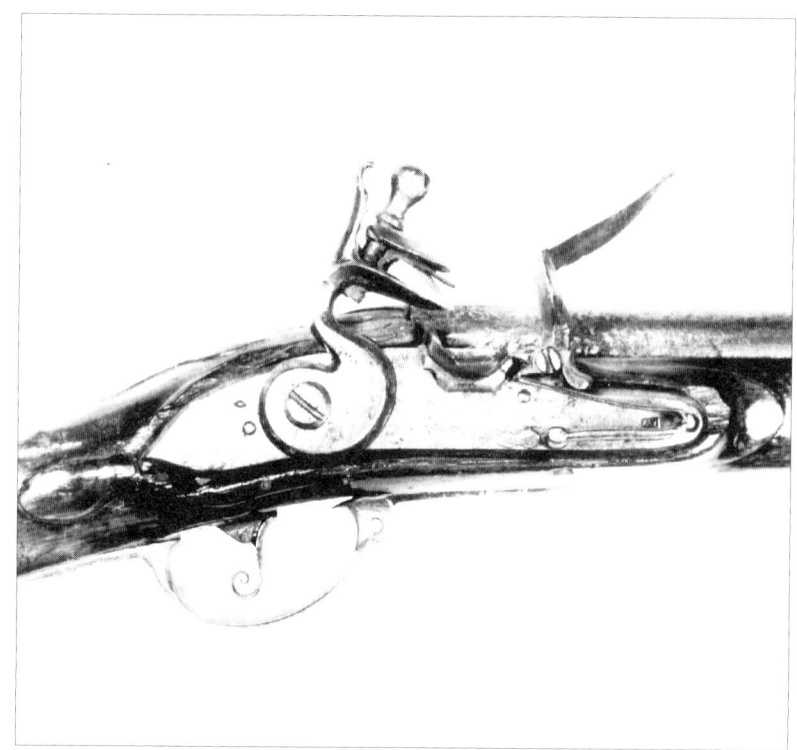

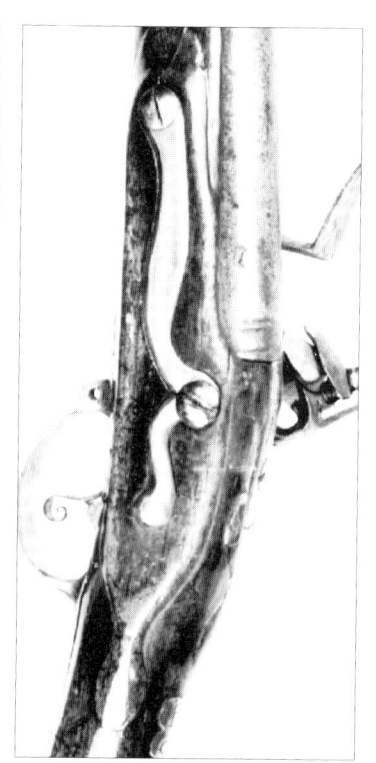

### 68.MM GERMANIC INFANTRY MUSKET
### Circa 1740–1765

A map of 18th century Germany resembles a colonial patchwork quilt, as it depicts the breakup of the Holy Roman Empire, dissolving into multiple small principalities, each with its own army. They, in turn, ordered a variety of gun patterns using a mixture of available components from different manufactories. The difficulty of identifying which specific ones saw service in America during the Revolutionary War is compounded not only by the varied firearms brought by England's mercenary forces, but also by the shiploads of odd captured and obsolete weapons obtained by America's European agents. This example, plus the two following, illustrate many of their common characteristics. Note here that the flat/beveled lock is like France's Model 1728 (39.MM), yet includes a squared frizzen and inside frizzen spring screw, as well as a plain side plate similar to Dutch patterns. The lobed trigger guard, plus a round pinned barrel (baluster breech) and irregular butt tang (two screws) are similar to Prussia's Potsdam muskets (65.MM). A center screw holds the scalloped escutcheon plate that is inscribed "RVW / GB / No 30." "LW" appears in a squared cartouche on the lock plate.

| | | | |
|---|---|---|---|
| Length: 56-3/4" | Lock: 6-3/4" X 1-1/4" | Butt Tang: 5-3/4" | Furniture: Brass |
| Barrel: 41-3/4", .79 cal. | Trigger Guard: 11-3/8" | Side Plate: 5-3/4" | Weight: 9.0 lbs. |

**Fort Ticonderoga Collection**

*Chapter 3: Smoothbore Shoulder Arms*

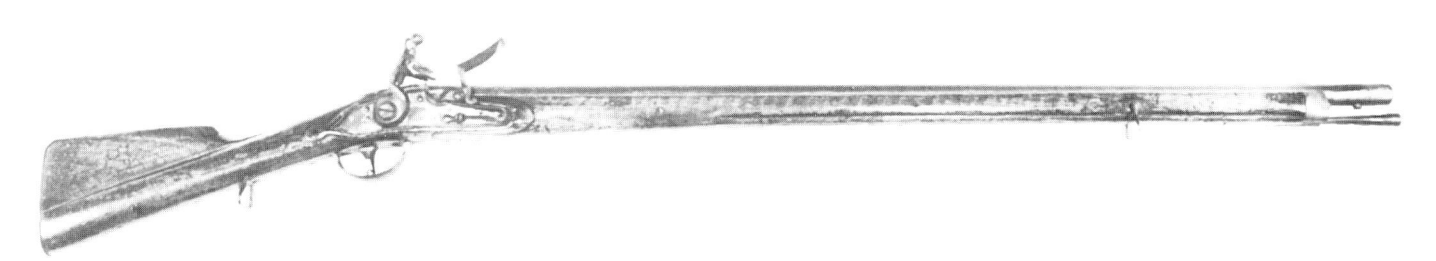

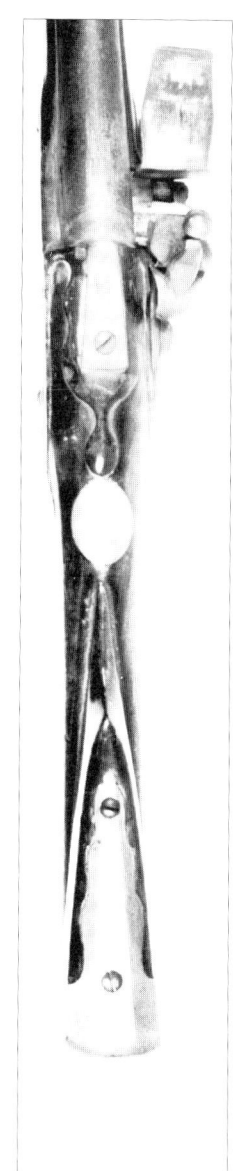

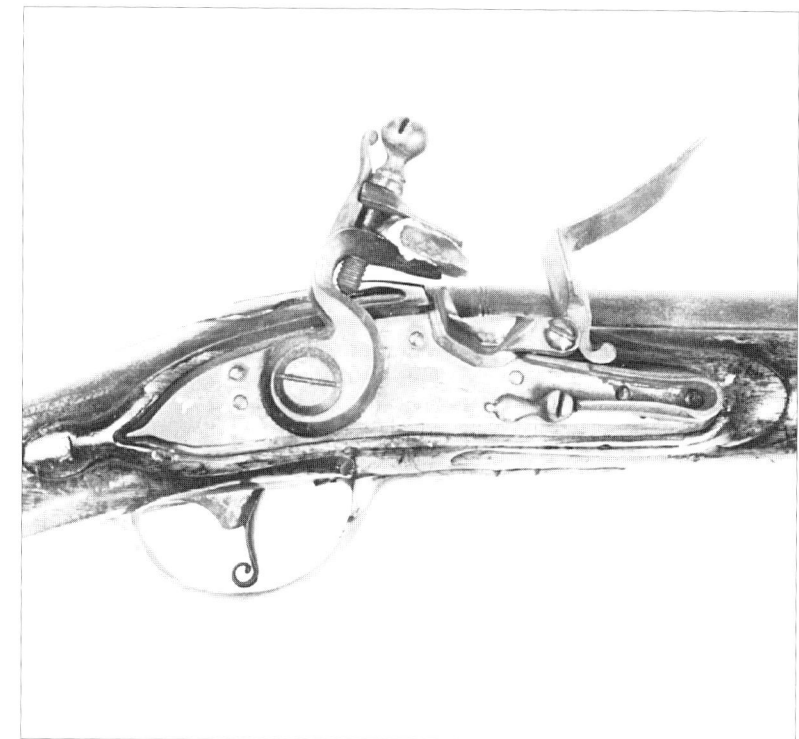

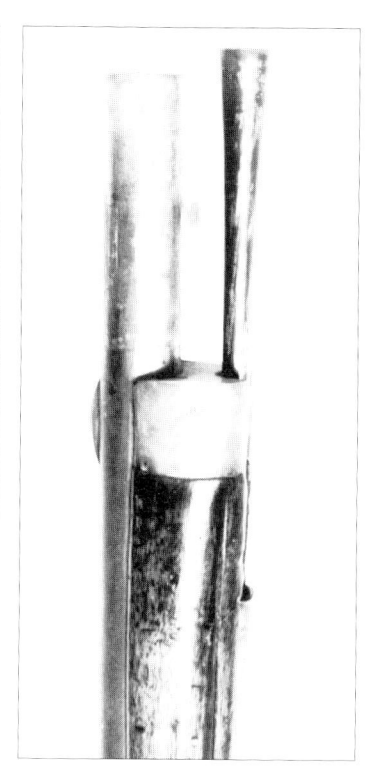

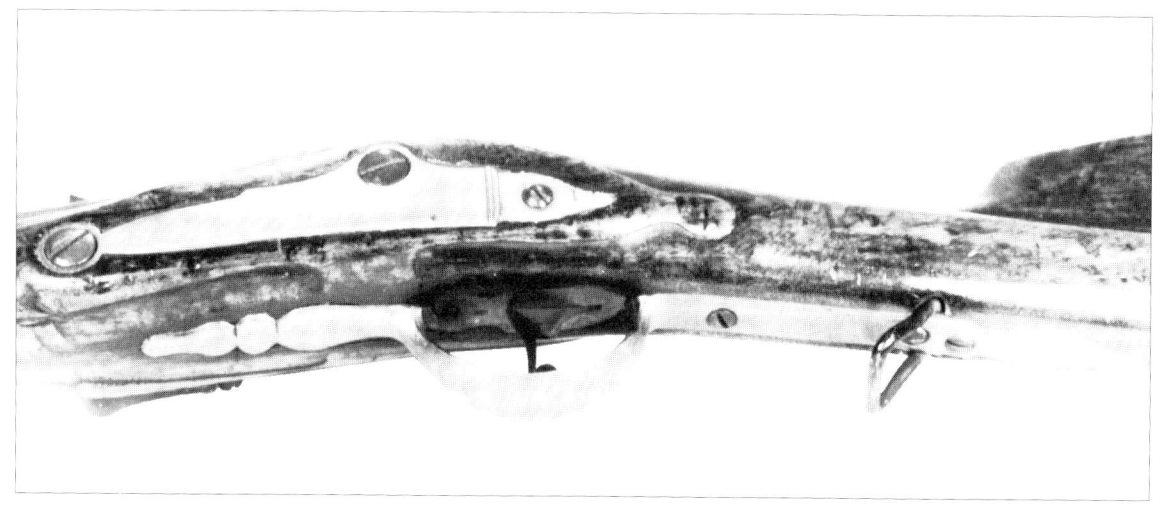

**69.MM GERMAN BRUNSWICK MUSKET**  Circa 1760–1777

Two detachments of Brunswick troops from General Burgoyne's invasion force were defeated at Bennington, Vermont, by New Hampshire's General Stark on August 16, 1777. Stark sent several captured trophies to Massachusetts. This musket is one of those items (also see 137.SS). Like most Germanic longarms at that time, it was not a common pattern. Moreover it is not known if the gun was carried by Brunswick's dismounted dragoons, grenadiers, light infantry or artillery. The long undulating butt tang (two top screws), oval escutcheon (unmarked), bulbous raised carvings, sling swivel placement and baluster breech/round barrel show influence of the Prussian Model 1740 (65.MM) but other features vary. The Germanic flat/beveled two-screw lock, for example, includes an exterior bridle, squared frizzen and outside frizzen spring screw. A unique triangular side plate (with a rear wood screw) has three grooves across the tail, while the lobed trigger guard follows Low Country form. Its walnut stock, in turn, ends in an unusual deep nose cap that provides a hole in the face to insert the steel trumpet ramrod (held by four faceted and flared pipes; see 21 on page 45). Marks: a crown above "C" (unclear) in a shield on the breech.

| | | | |
|---|---|---|---|
| Length: 56" | Lock: 6-7/8" X 1-3/8" | Butt Tang: 5-5/8" | Furniture: Brass |
| Barrel: 41-1/4", .75 cal. | Trigger Guard: 11-7/8" | Side Plate: 6-3/4" | Weight: 11.0 lbs. |

**Commonwealth of Massachusetts Archives**

*Chapter 3: Smoothbore Shoulder Arms*

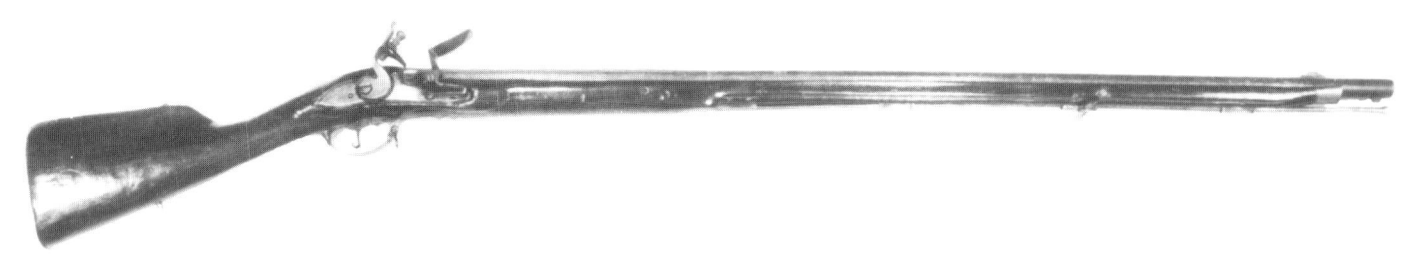

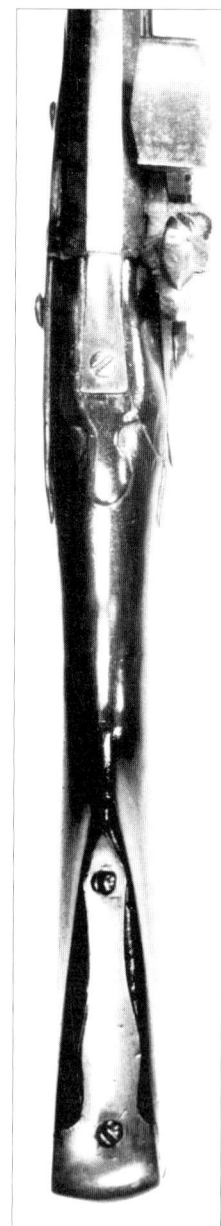

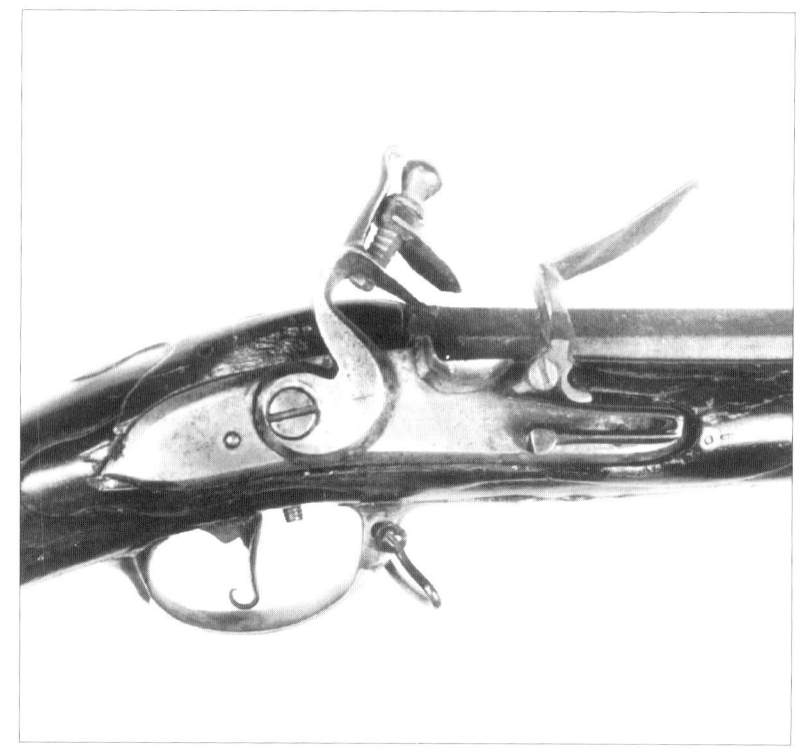

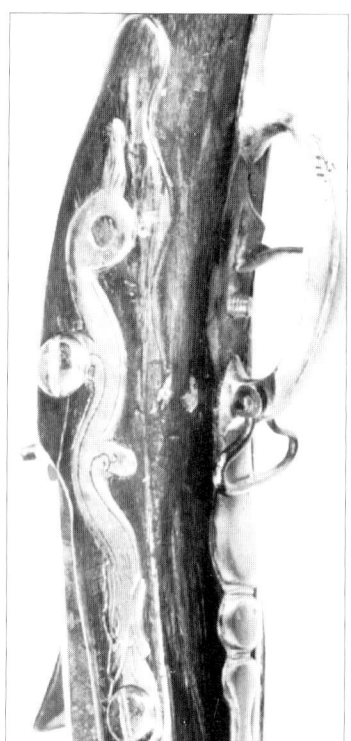

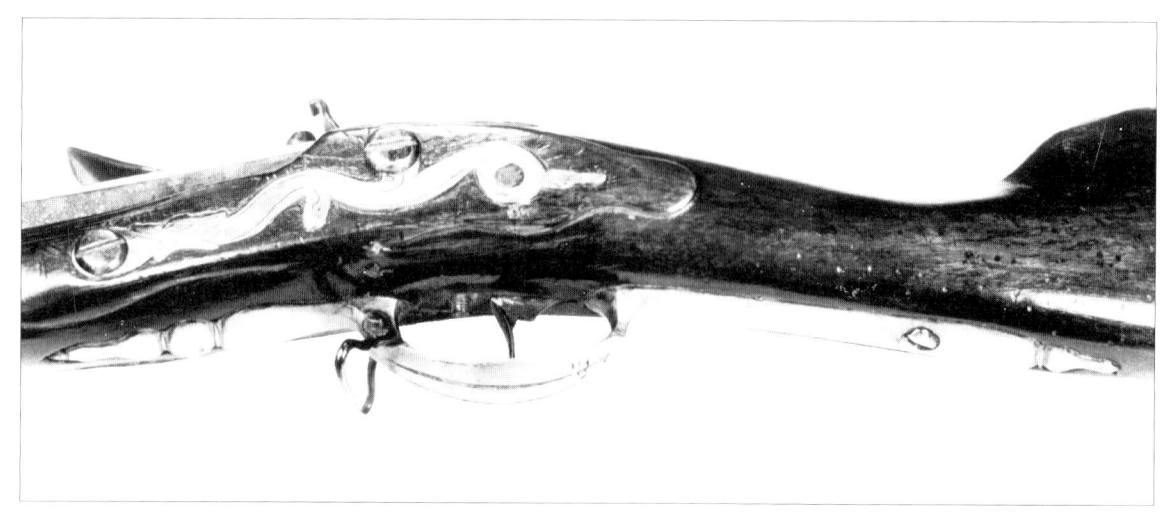

**70.MM  LOW COUNTRY/GERMANIC INFANTRY MUSKET**  Circa 1740–1750

The Principality of Liege (in modern Belgium) was the major independent weapons-making center for most of Europe. It was actually composed of many small producers (70 to 80 in 1788) who, as was their usual practice, supplied arms to both sides during America's War for Independence (see 16.MM). This popular flat/beveled Germanic lock form is marked by a Liege maker, "I. I. BEHR" (note the squared frizzen and inside frizzen spring screw). Such locks were also shipped worldwide to other manufacturers. Typical of the Liege contractors, who could furnish a mixed variety of components, the arm shown here has a Dutch-type long butt tang (two top screws), a thick butt and a lobed trigger guard with incised lines on the bow. German influence is apparent in the elementary dragon side plate, faceted rammer pipes and brass front sight and bottom bayonet stud at the muzzle. Other features of both regions include two rear convex screw heads on the butt plate, teardrop carving around the barrel tang and raised borders outlining the side plate and lock. Its breech is octagonal for 10-3/4 inches.

| | | | |
|---|---|---|---|
| Length: 57" | Lock: 6-1/8" X 1-1/8" | Butt Tang: 6-1/4" | Furniture: Brass |
| Barrel: 42-1/4", .75 cal. | Trigger Guard: 12-1/8" | Side Plate: 5-7/8" | Weight: 8.7 lbs. |

**George C. Neumann Collection, Valley Forge National Historical Park**

*120    Chapter 3: Smoothbore Shoulder Arms*

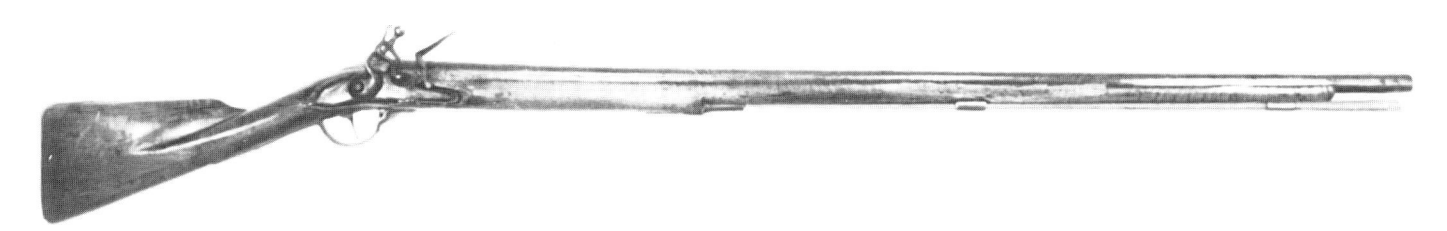

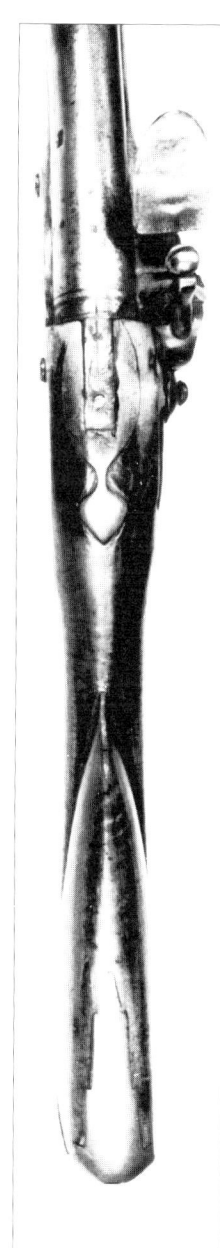

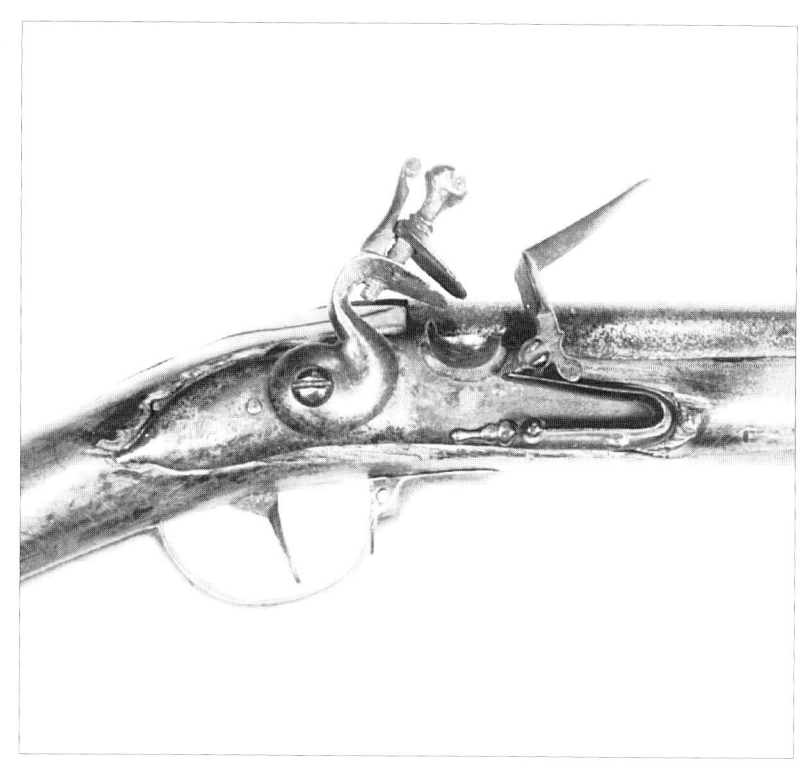

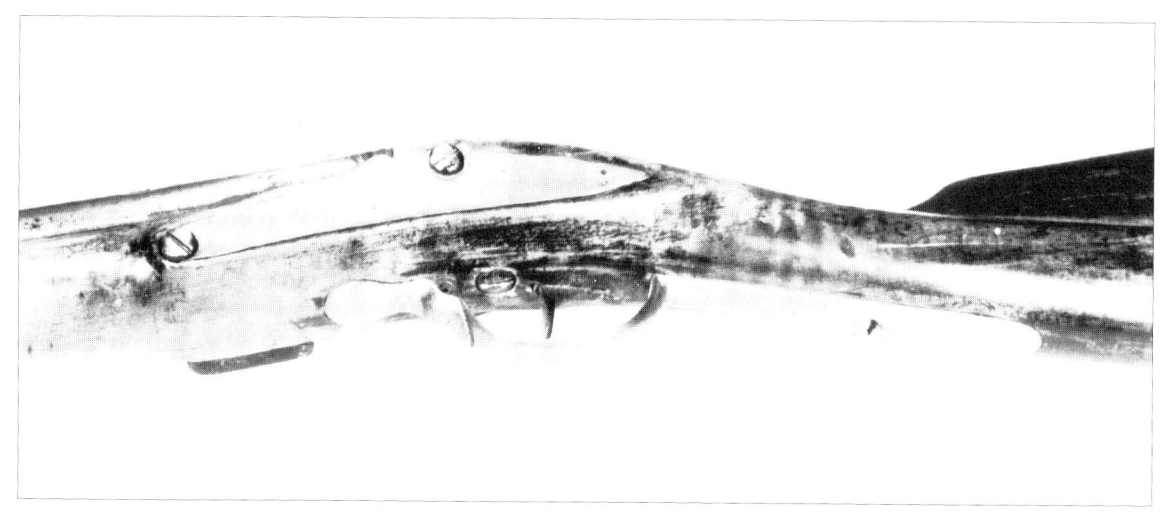

**71.MM AMERICAN MUSKET**                                                         **Circa 1730–1740**

By English law the provincials were not permitted to create sizable manufacturing capabilities. Their role was as a source of raw materials to the mother country and as a customer for her final products. Britain reserved the production of most goods for herself. Thus, although the Americans were allowed gunmakers and craftsmen for local needs, they had to use and reuse many manufactured items from Europe. This is evident in most of their firearms up through the Revolutionary War. In the above weapon, a round banana-shaped, Dutch-style lock (no outside bridle), a 46" Queen Anne English barrel (proofed "crown / AR / broad arrow") and trigger guard (typical rounded front) have been combined with an American side plate and hefty maple stock. The forend was cut back to accommodate a bayonet (top stud) and combines a cast brass English rammer pipe with two provincial sheet-brass examples (wooden rod). Note too the popular three-step British butt tang form, bottom barrel tang screw and the French Tulle-type tang carving (see 34.MM).

| | | | |
|---|---|---|---|
| Length: 61-1/4" | Lock: 6-1/2" X 1-1/4" | Butt Tang: 4-1/4" | Furniture: Brass |
| Barrel: 46", .82 cal. | Trigger Guard: 9-1/2" | Side Plate: 6-3/8" | Weight: 8.8 lbs. |

**Robert Nittolo Collection**

*Chapter 3: Smoothbore Shoulder Arms*     **121**

### 72.MM AMERICAN MUSKET

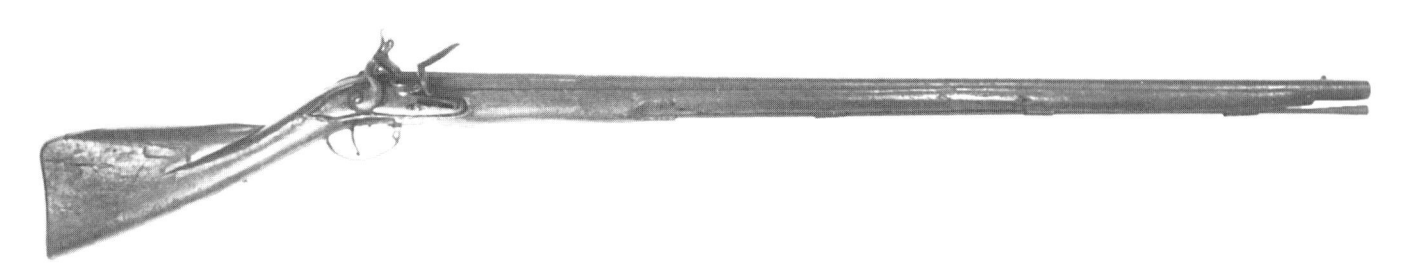

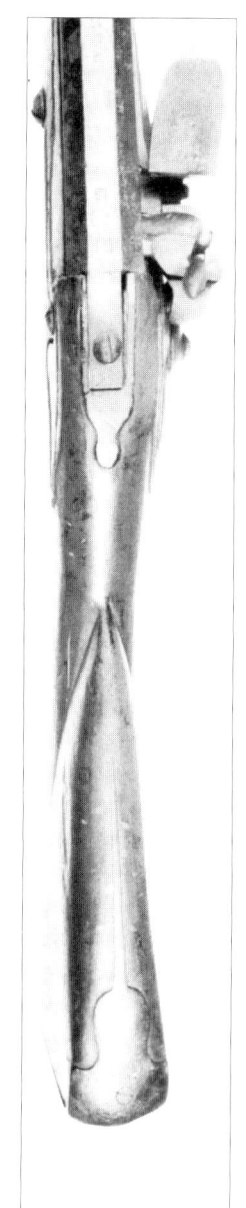

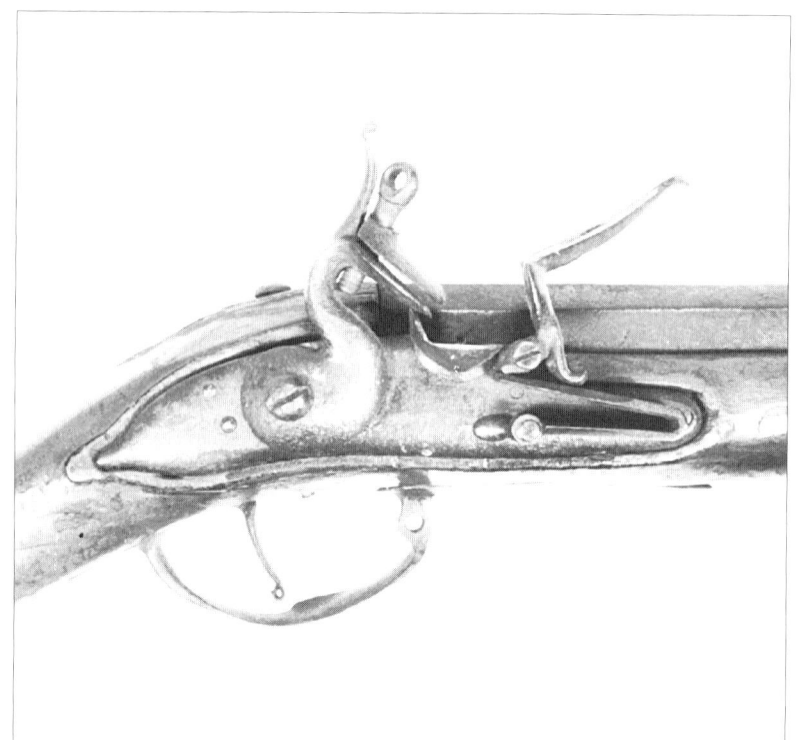

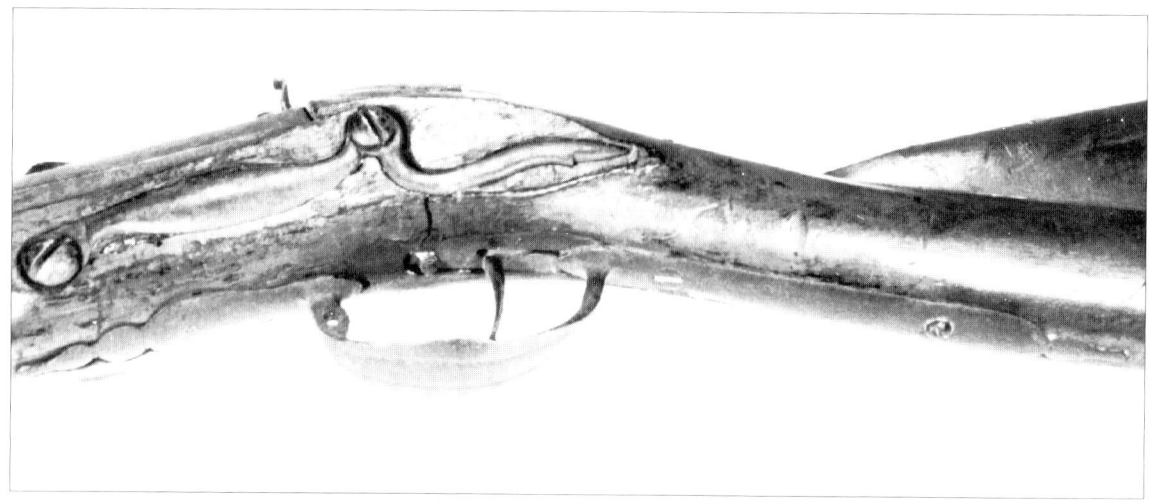

**Circa 1730–1740**

This rather gaunt profile shows considerable service and a coating at one time of the ubiquitous colonial brick-red paint. The two-screw round banana lock (no exterior bridle), convex side plate with a tail and bulbous trigger guard (including incised lines on the bow) are early Dutch features. The barrel has an octagonal breech for nine inches (plus rings at 11-1/2 inches and 14-1/4 inches) as well as typical Netherland markings, "Co=14" (breech) and "No=684" (top of muzzle). Its needle-like iron butt tang is a known circa 1700 European form. The barrel, in turn, is inscribed "SO CAROLINA," suggesting that this may have been among the old 4,500 Dutch muskets sent to the provincials by the English during the French and Indian War or possibly contracted directly by the colony (59.MM). The upper two of four ramrod thimbles are early replacements; they hold an iron rammer which probably was added in place of an original wooden rod. Because of the unusual butt form and crude raised border carving, this stock appears to be of American origin.

| | | | |
|---|---|---|---|
| Length: 60-1/2" | Lock: 6-3/4" X 1-3/8" | Butt Tang: 7-1/4" | Furniture: Iron |
| Barrel: 45", .79 cal. | Trigger Guard: 13" | Side Plate: 7" | Weight: 10.2 lbs. |

**West Point Museum Collection**

*Chapter 3: Smoothbore Shoulder Arms*

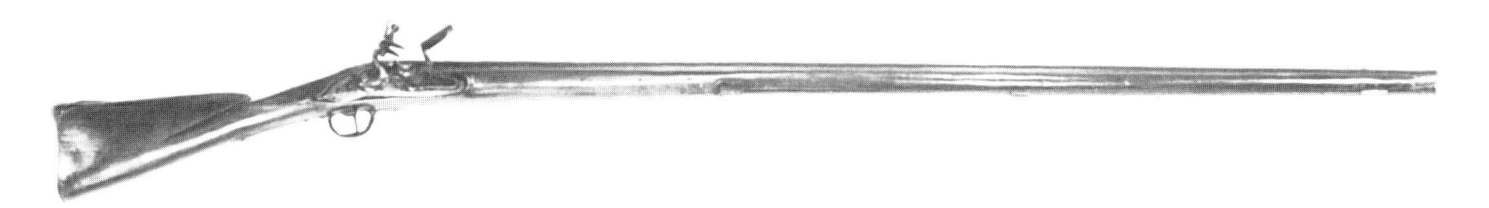

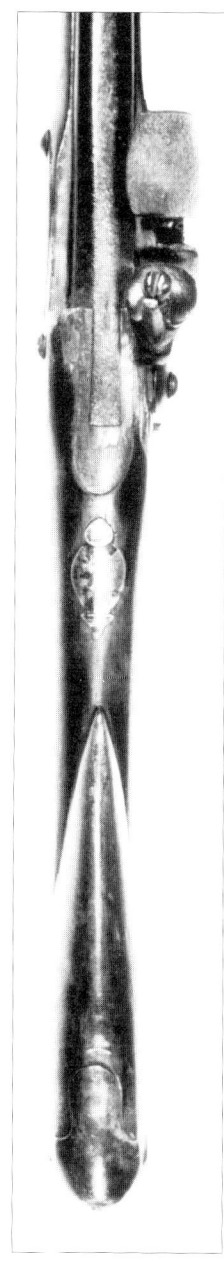

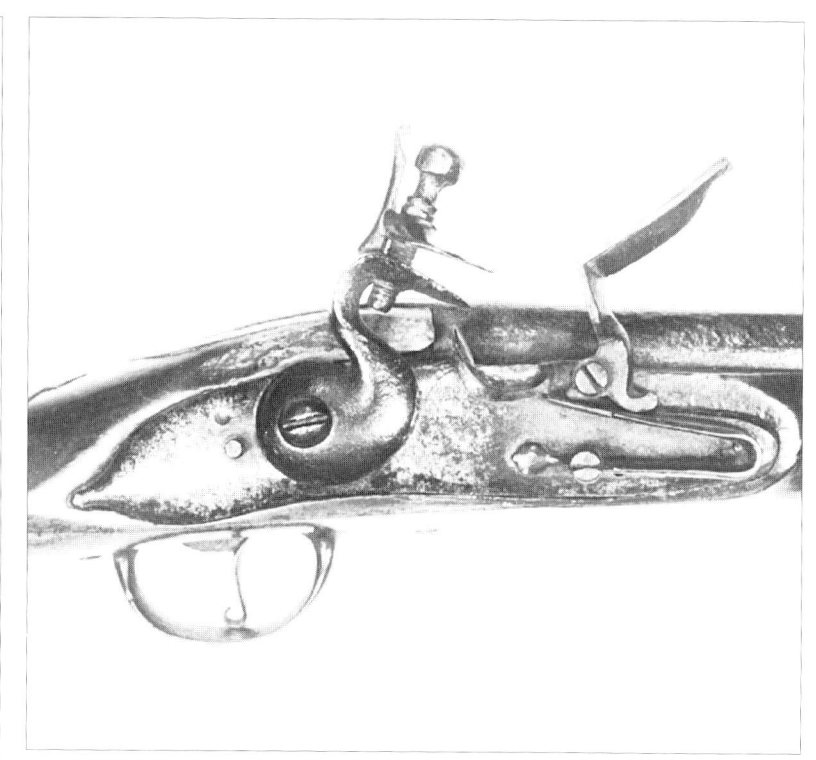

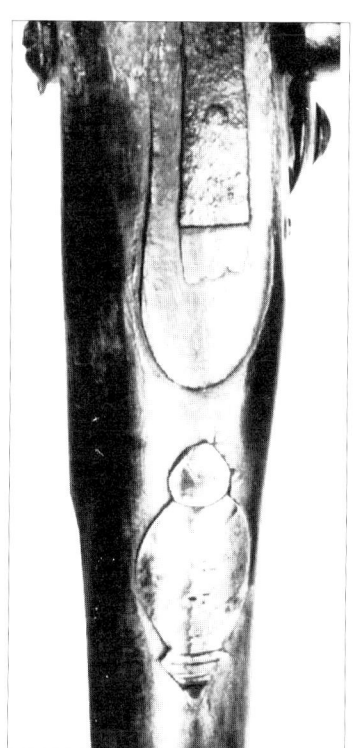

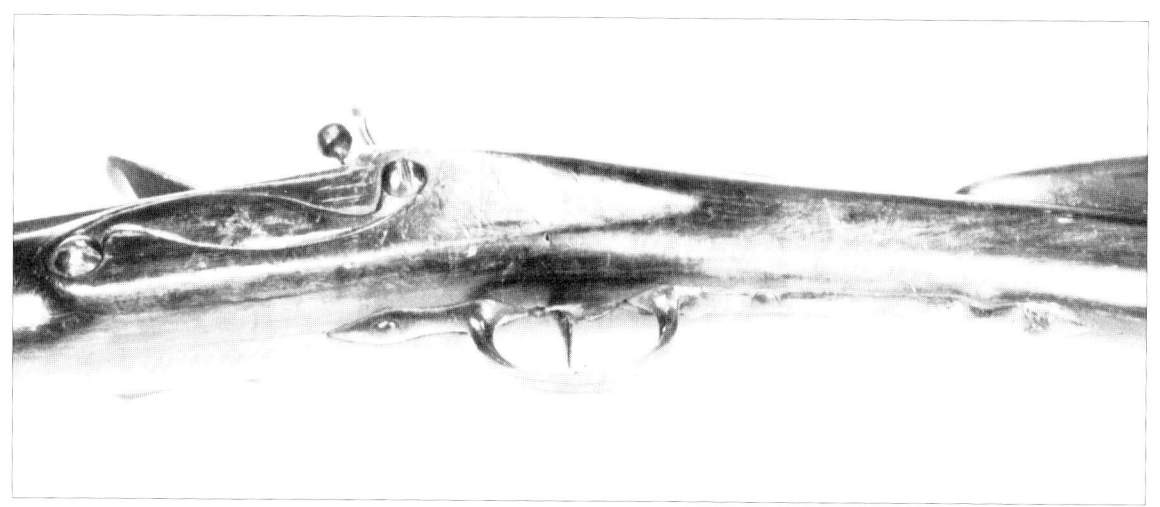

**73.MM AMERICAN MUSKET**                                                              Circa 1740–1775

Jacob Man of Wrentham, Massachusetts, carried this musket as a Minuteman at Lexington–Concord and as a member of Col. Joseph Read's 13th Continental (Massachusetts) Regiment through the New York and Trenton–Princeton campaigns of 1775–1777, as well as during later service at the Battle of Rhode Island. It is a typical provincial flintlock assembled from available parts, for example an early rounded Dutch-type lock (squared frizzen), a cut-down butt tang (probably British), a convex French S-shaped side plate, an English trade pattern escutcheon and an American crudely cast brass trigger guard (held by four nails). The French barrel (octagonal breech), in turn, has its rear tang secured by a long screw from below (no trigger plate). Three sheet-brass pipes hold a hand-forged iron rammer (bottom pipe ribbed, the others plain). Note that despite service in a line regiment for two years at the beginning of the war, the cherry stock was never cut back to mount a socket bayonet—reflecting their severe lack of proper weapons. A blade sight is 3-1/2 inches below the muzzle, while the forend terminates in a 1-1/4" brass band.

Length: 67-1/4"                      Lock: 6-3/4" X 1-3/8"            Butt Tang: 2-7/8"             Furniture: Brass/Iron
Barrel: 51-1/8", .71 cal.          Trigger Guard: 8-5/8"           Side Plate: 4-1/8"            Weight: 7.8 lbs
**Author's Collection**

Chapter 3: Smoothbore Shoulder Arms     123

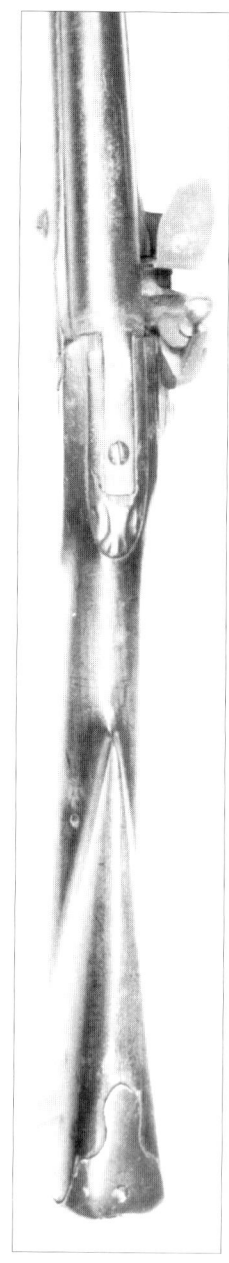

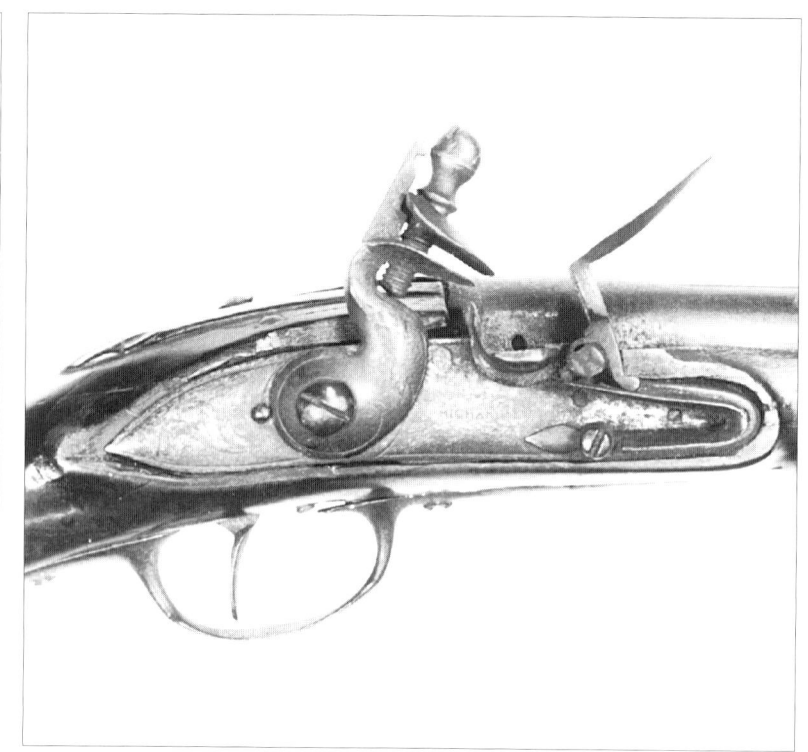

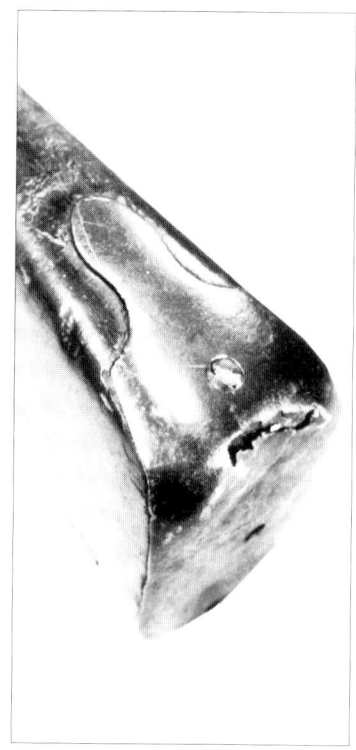

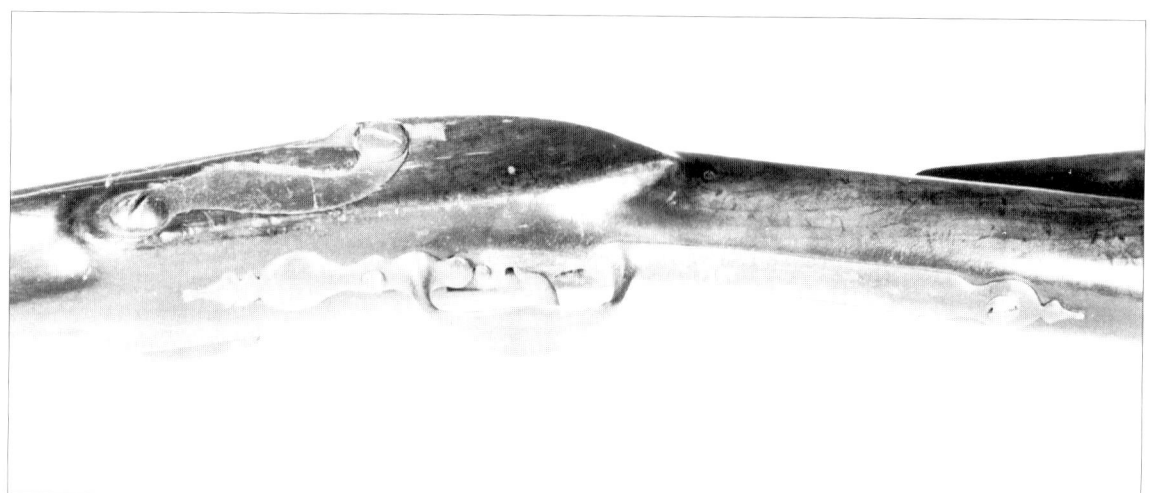

**74.MM AMERICAN MUSKET**                                                                                                 **Circa 1760–1780**

An owner's name, "L. A. CONANT," is branded into both sides of the thick cherry buttstock of this musket from Massachusetts. In keeping with the Colonial practice of assembling odd available components, the arm mounts an American-made barrel (44-1/4") and a British trade lock stamped "RICHARDS" under the pan. Its unique attraction, however, is inclusion of a bulbous iron trigger guard and butt plate from an early French circa 1697 Tulle musket (re: Bouchard, bib. 21) reflecting the accumulation of French weapons in the northeastern English Colonies from constant border attacks, trade, the Louisbourg 1745 expedition and the French and Indian War before the large shipments of aid from that country during the Revolution. The flat S-shaped side plate may be from a later source. Notice the elementary raised carving surrounding the barrel tang, as well as a thin nose band (1/2") securing the forend. In keeping with the Colonists' English tradition, the round barrel is pinned to the stock, which also holds three sheet-iron rammer pipes (iron button-head rod).

| | | | |
|---|---|---|---|
| Length: 60" | Lock: 5-3/4" X 1-1/8" | Butt Tang: 2-3/4" | Furniture: Iron |
| Barrel: 44-1/4", .70 cal. | Trigger Guard: 10-1/4" | Side Plate: 3-5/8" | Weight: 7.7 lbs. |

**Author's Collection**

124    *Chapter 3: Smoothbore Shoulder Arms*

**75.MM AMERICAN MUSKET**                                                                 **Circa 1770–1778**

Parts from a French Model 1717 infantry musket (38.MM) furnished most of the components for this American longarm. The flat lock is a rare banana form of that pattern; it includes an early replaced vertical bridle and is marked with a "fleur-de-lis / I.F.C" under the faceted flash pan (Jean Baptiste Fournier at the Charleville manufactory). The iron double-pointed trigger guard, long butt tang (4-3/4"), S-shaped side plate and 47" barrel (octagonal breech 5-1/4") apparently also originated on that same weapon. Its breech is stamped "DMC" (with a crown above the "C," a Charleville mark). The two lower barrel bands are of French Model 1728 form, while the double strap upper band matches a Model 1763 French musket. The Americans added a cherry stock with their familiar raised splay carving behind the barrel tang and a long iron cone-shaped upper rammer pipe brazed to the bottom of the forward band (as seen on some Dutch and Spanish arms). Its bayonet stud is on top. A locally forged iron rammer has a button head. The weapon was found in Connecticut.

| | | | |
|---|---|---|---|
| Length: 63" | Lock: 6-1/2" X 1-3/8" | Butt Tang: 4-3/4" | Furniture: Iron |
| Barrel: 47", .70 cal. | Trigger Guard: 12-5/8" | Side Plate: 4-3/8" | Weight: 9.2 lbs. |

**Author's Collection**

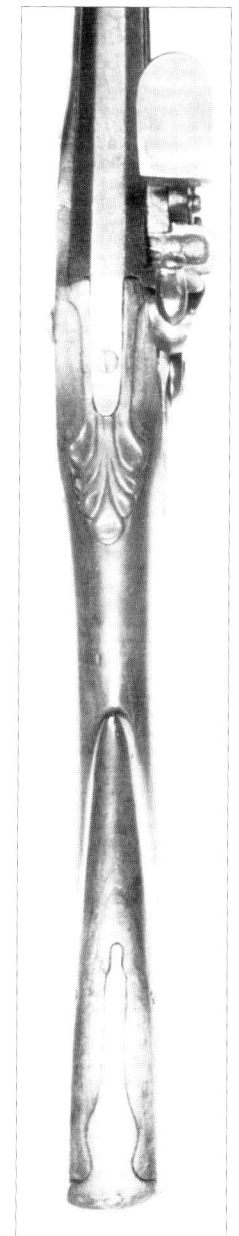

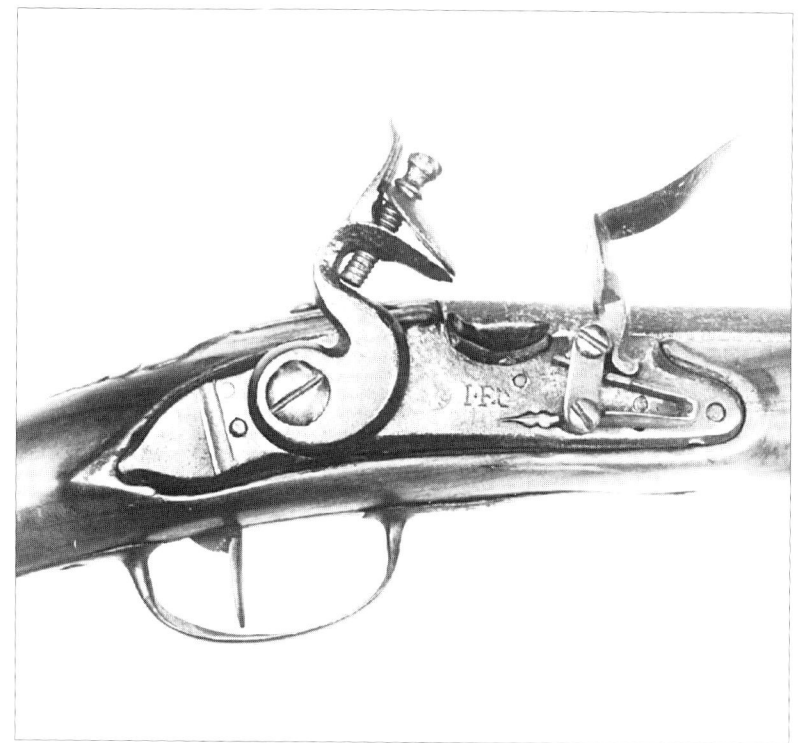

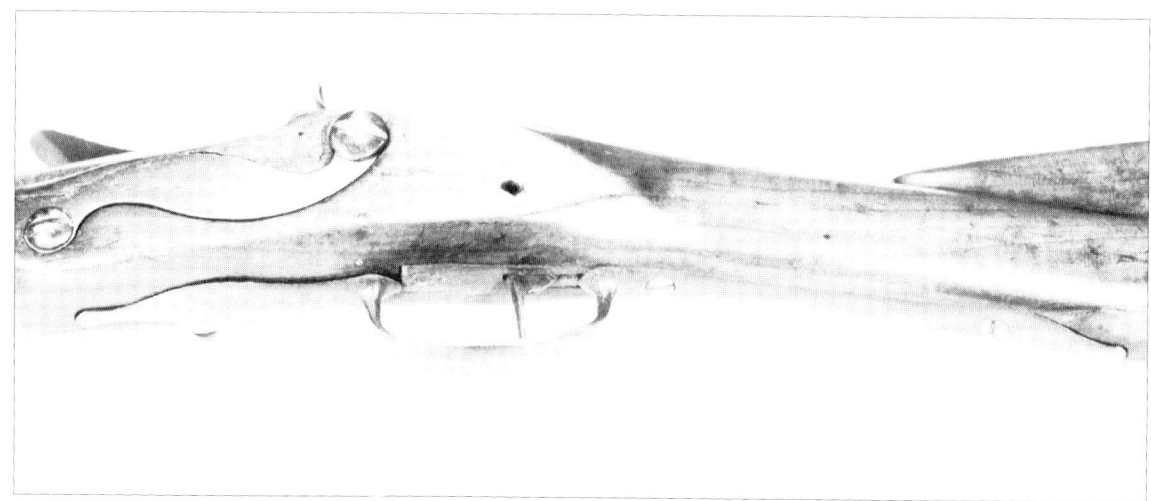

*Chapter 3: Smoothbore Shoulder Arms*     **125**

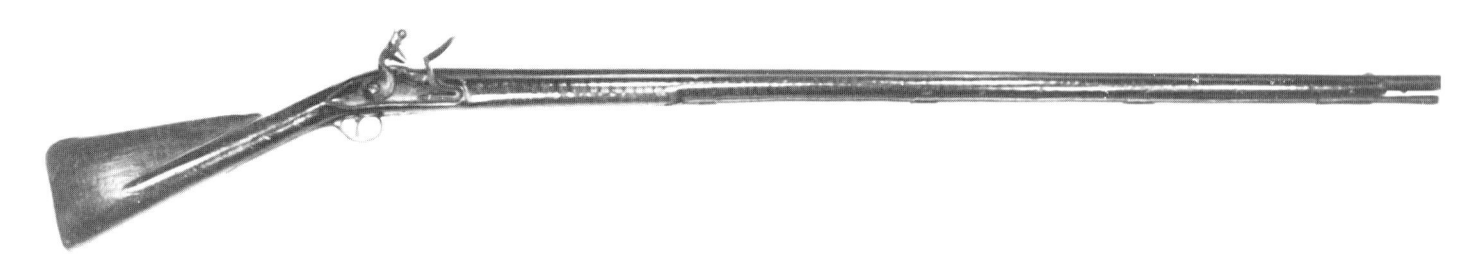

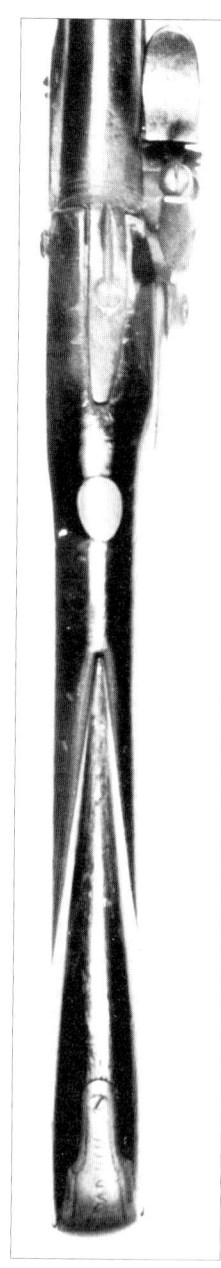

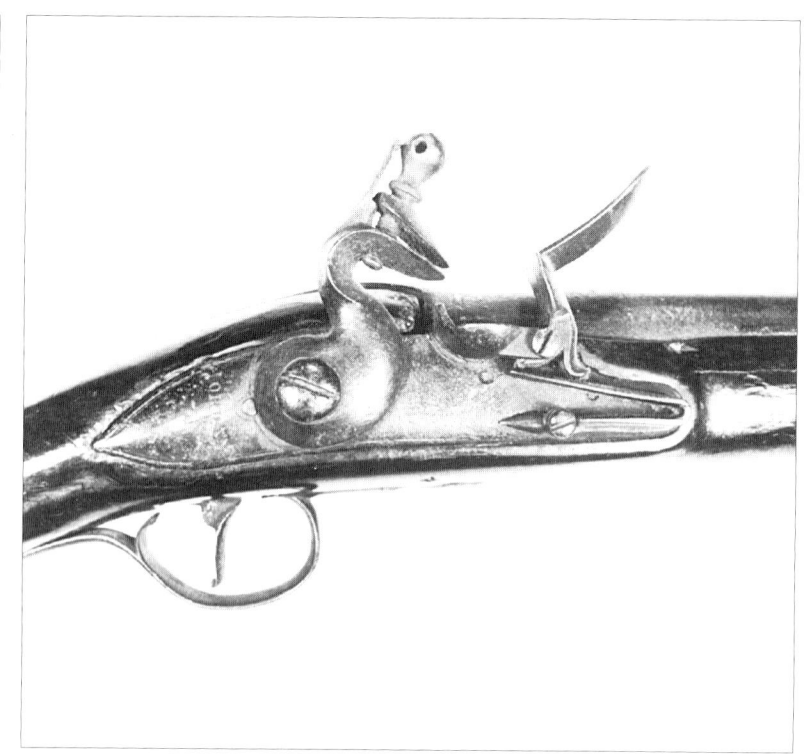

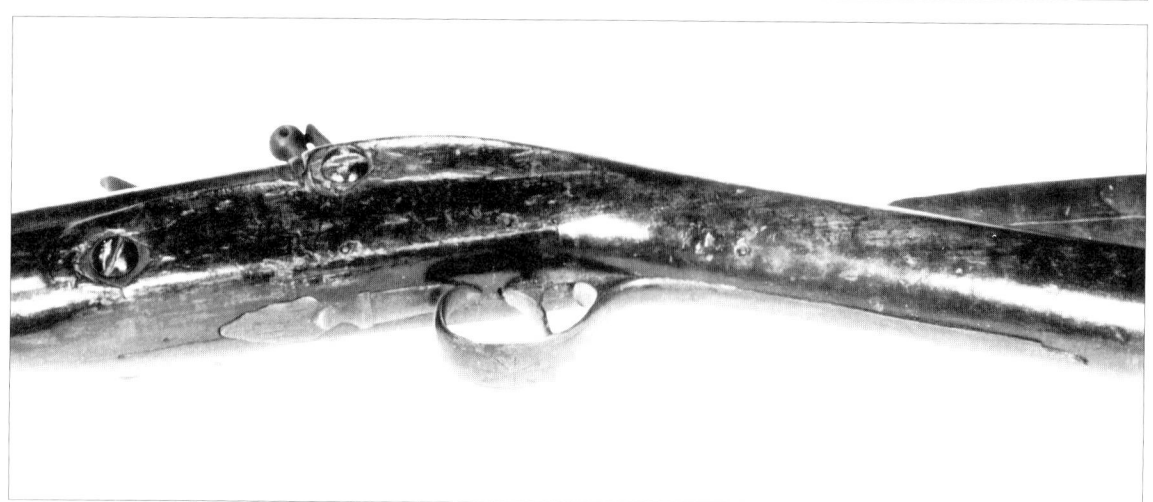

**76.MM AMERICAN FOWLER/MUSKET**                                                        Circa 1770–1780

Medad Hills was born the son of gunsmith Benoni Hills in 1729 at Durham, Connecticut. They moved to Goshen, Connecticut, in 1740, which was a busy center of arms making. Medad and his brother, John, are well-remembered today because of their pre-War practice of signing the butt tang and putting the customer's name on the side plate (re: Mayer, bib. 222). Medad became a lieutenant colonel of militia in 1777 and contracted arms for the local Committee of Safety. Most of his work contains reused components in the economical mode practiced by the settlers. This long hunting fowler has the remains of his name, "_EDAD HILLS," inscribed on a typical butt tang. The maple stock, in turn, was later cut back to allow space for a socket bayonet, thus showing both a bladed front sight plus a bottom bayonet stud. The rounded lock is from a British Brown Bess ("JORDAN / 1747" on its tail and a later spear-point frizzen spring finial). Expanded four-pointed washers under the side screw heads replace the normal side plate, while an arrow-like trigger guard appears to be American. Note also the four sheet-brass thimbles, oval escutcheon and thin nose band (3/8").

| | | | |
|---|---|---|---|
| Length: 60-1/2" | Lock: 5-3/4" X 1-1/8" | Butt Tang: 3" | Furniture: Brass |
| Barrel: 45", .59 cal. | Trigger Guard: 9-5/8" | Weight: 7.5 lbs. | |

**Robert Nittolo Collection**

*Chapter 3: Smoothbore Shoulder Arms*

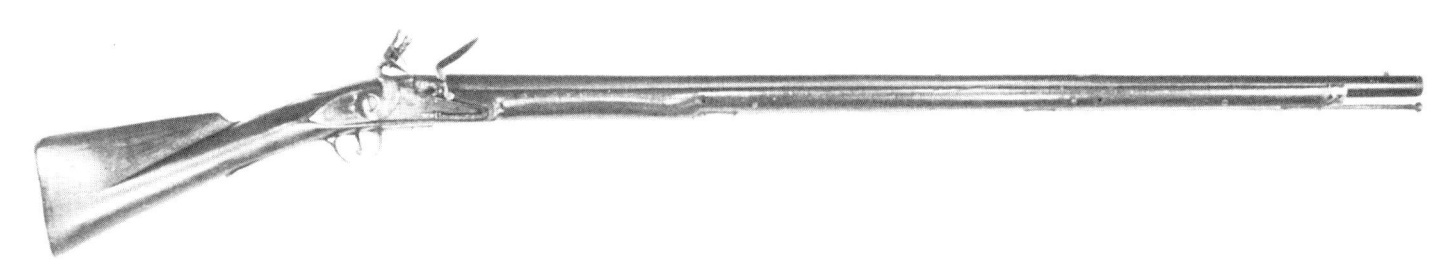

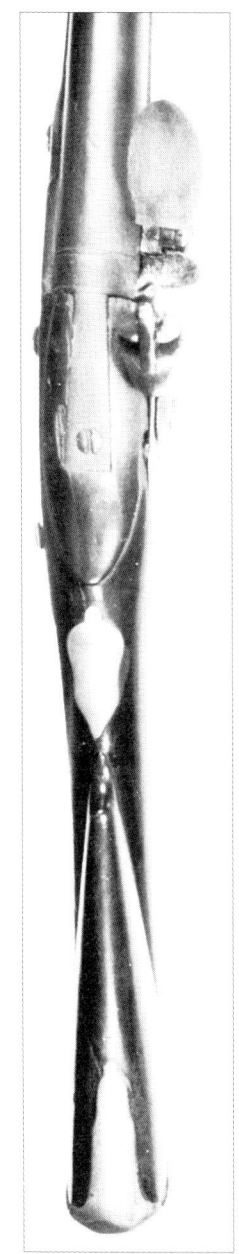

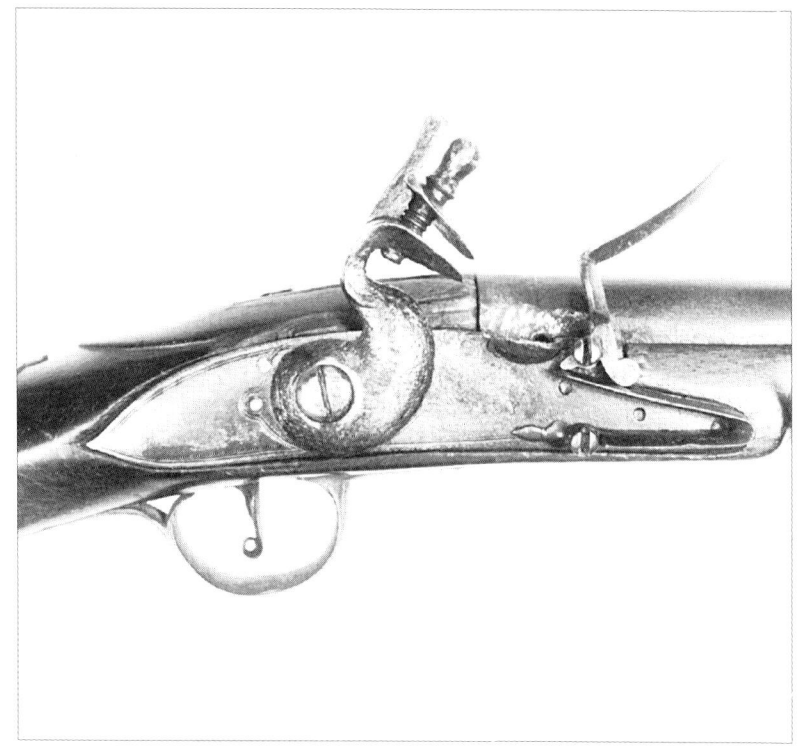

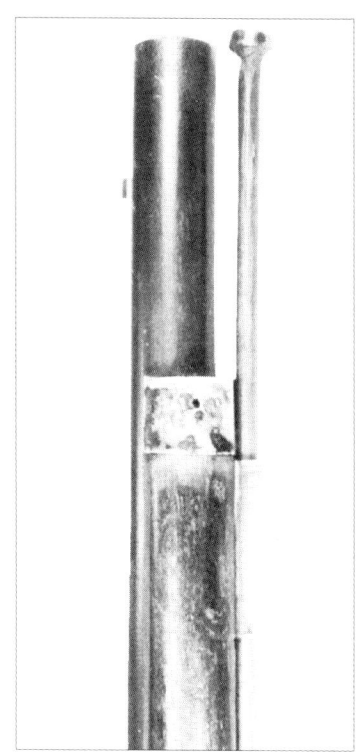

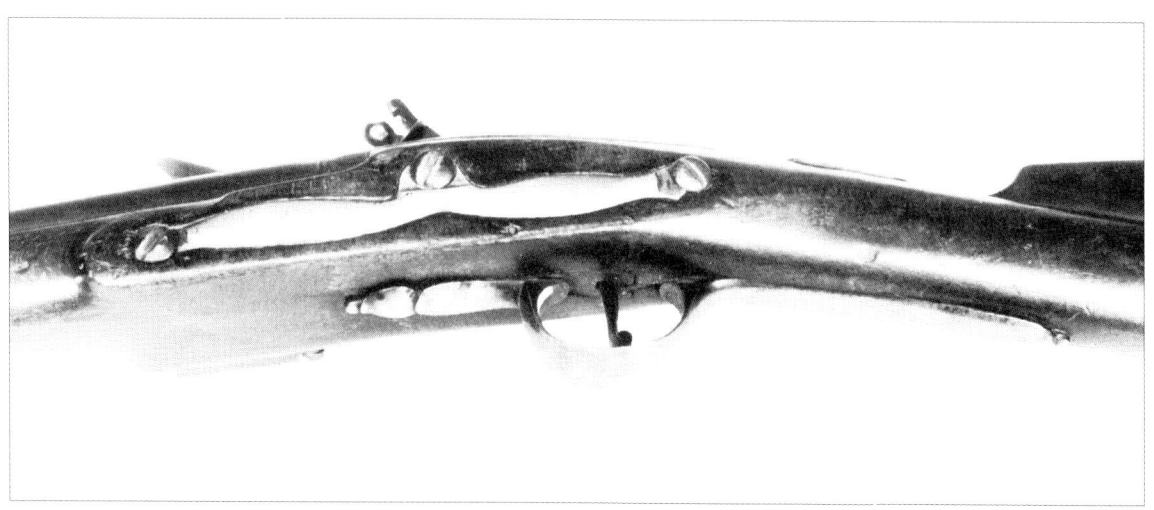

**77.MM AMERICAN MUSKET**                                                                               **Circa 1760–1780**

The mother country's influence on North American Colonial weaponry is obvious here. Its former British barrel bears faint private proofs from the Tower of London (double scepter strikes). In addition the early 18th century rounded lock has a narrow permanent flash pan (no exterior bridle; the "HADLEY" marking below it is a later addition). The shortened American two-step butt tang, shield escutcheon and beaver-tail barrel tang carving further reflect English patterns—as with the three-screw double arm side plate in the Queen Anne tradition (3.MM). A provincial's copy of the Brown Bess trigger guard is smaller than normal, yet it is held with pins (no screw) and omits a hole for the rear sling swivel. A 3/4" brass strip, in turn, binds the tip of the forend, while the three American sheet-brass thimbles hold a crude button-head iron rammer. Its muzzle mounts a top bayonet stud. The arm was discovered in New England.

| | | | |
|---|---|---|---|
| Length: 57" | Lock: 7-1/8" X 1-1/4" | Butt Tang: 3-3/8" | Furniture: Brass |
| Barrel: 41-3/8", .75 cal. | Trigger Guard: 8-3/4" | Side Plate: 5-7/8" | Weight: 8.9 lbs. |

**Author's Collection**

*Chapter 3: Smoothbore Shoulder Arms*    **127**

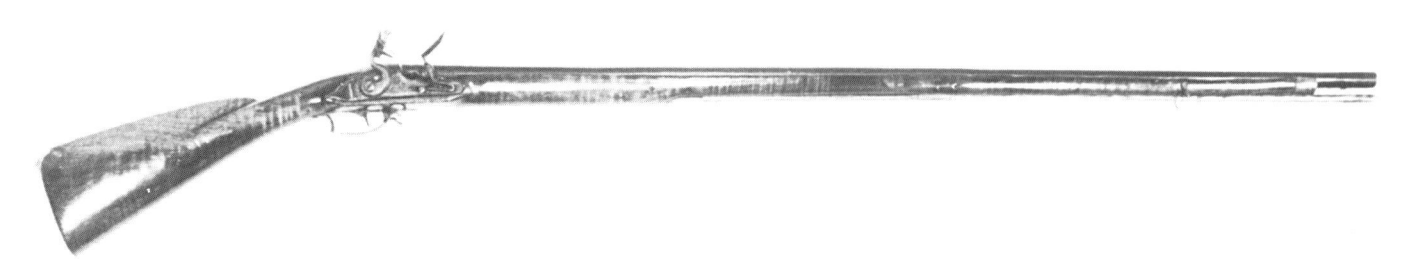

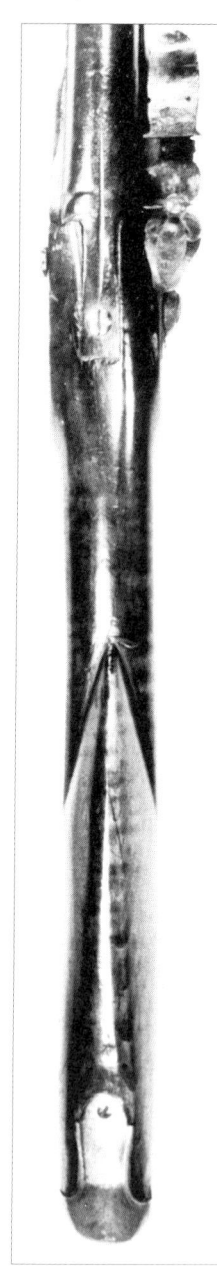

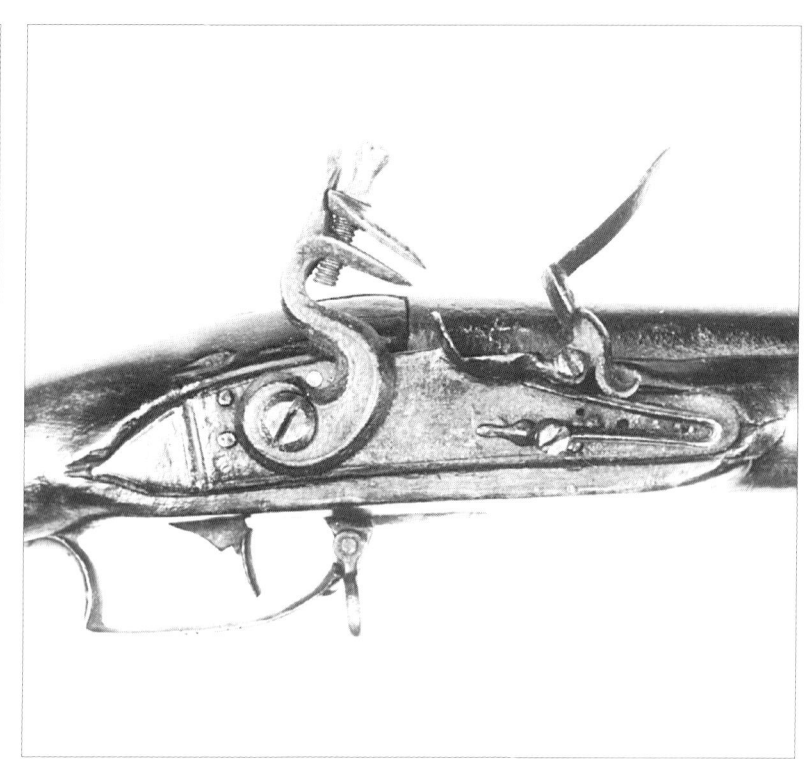

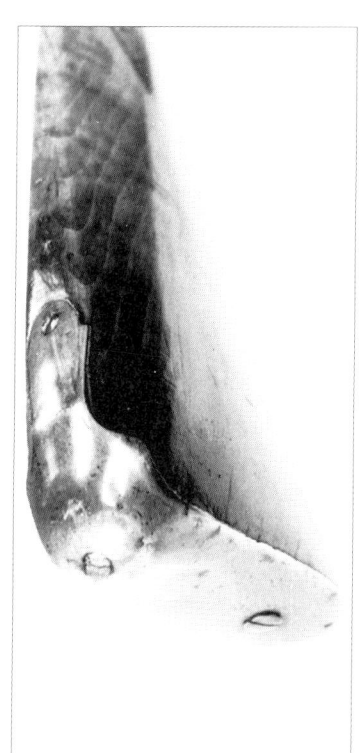

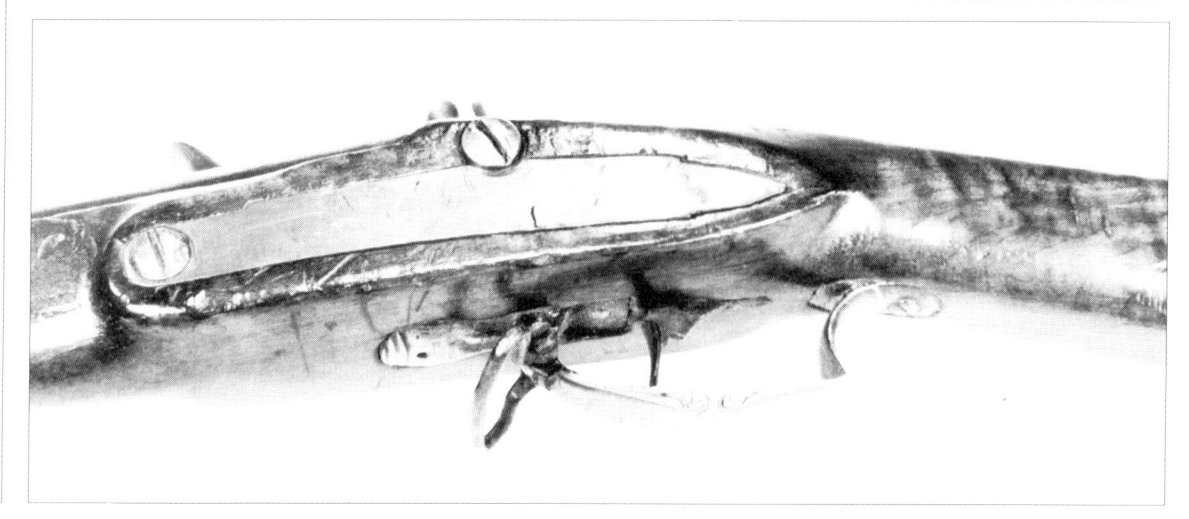

**78.MM AMERICAN MUSKET**                                                                                                          **Circa 1776–1780**

This musket has an association with the arms-making town of Goshen, Connecticut—perhaps created by Medad Hills (see 76.MM) or other local gunsmiths such as John Doud, Ebenezer Norton, Elisha Childs or Benjamin Cargill. (The town employed as many as 28 blacksmiths forging components during the Revolution). The striped maple stock with an angled butt profile as seen here was popular in that area. Notice however the reused parts, omission of an escutcheon and lack of raised carving and trigger plate plus the 44" barrel (the length specified by Connecticut, October 1776)—all suggesting wartime production. In addition, its stubby butt tang has been shortened, as with the former straight-backed European fowler trigger guard (which has both ends cut off). The flat lock is from an English fowler of the period. A brass sheet was used to create the American side plate. Also included are three simple sheet-brass rammer pipes, a one-inch nose band, two sling swivels and a wooden ramrod, as well as a bottom bayonet stud. The common incised line along the barrel tang and breech served as a makeshift rear sight, as well as a mark to align a reinstalled breech plug.

| | | | |
|---|---|---|---|
| Length: 60-1/2" | Lock: 5-3/4" X 1" | Butt Tang: 3" | Furniture: Brass |
| Barrel: 44", .67 cal. | Trigger Guard: 4-5/8" | Side Plate: 5-3/8" | Weight: 7.0 lbs. |

**Author's Collection**

*128    Chapter 3: Smoothbore Shoulder Arms*

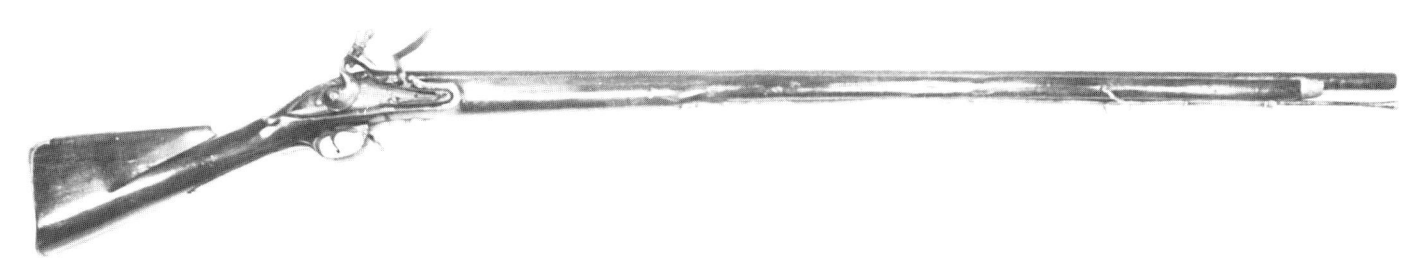

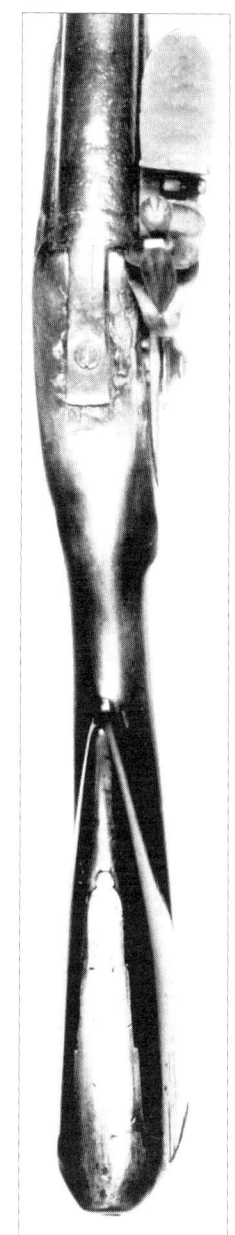

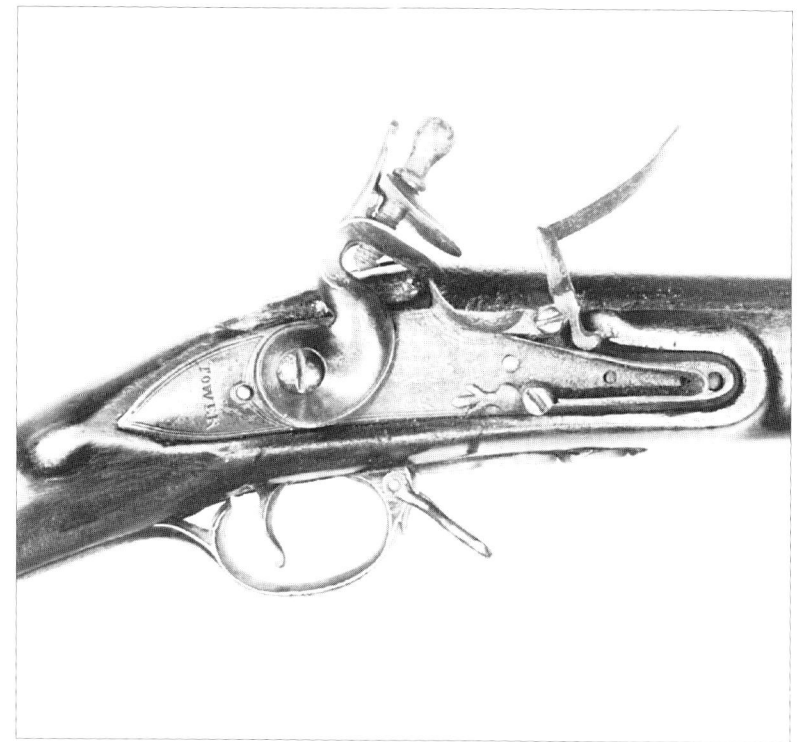

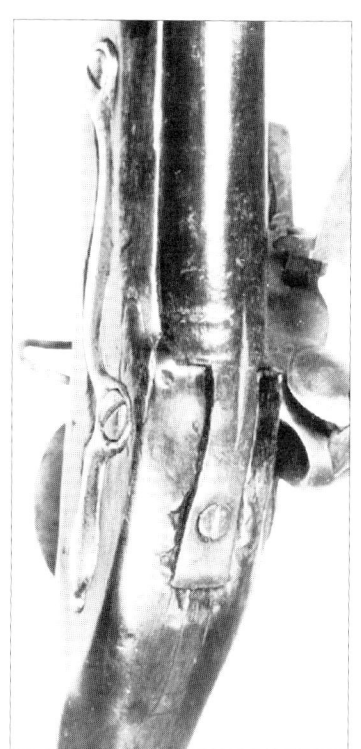

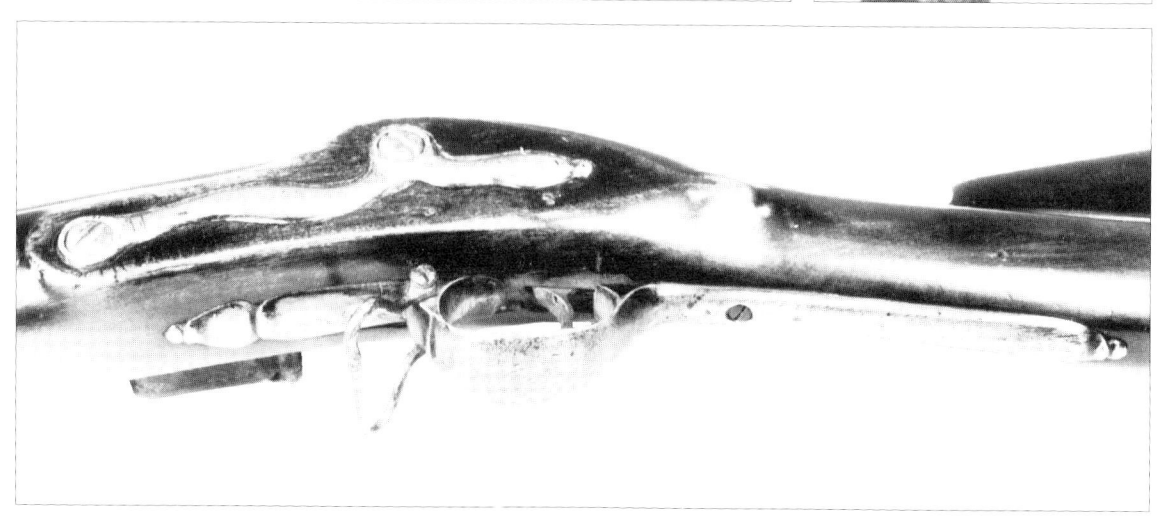

**79.MM AMERICAN MUSKET**                                                                  **Circa 1775–1783**

An English Long Land Brown Bess Pattern 1756 (10.MM) furnished most metal components for the American infantry musket shown here. The Colonists even kept the top edge of its butt comb parallel with the barrel in British fashion. Yet the stock is maple instead of walnut and thicker at the barrel tang/lock area (most vulnerable to breaking) with the carved beaver-tail eliminated. Its escutcheon and fourth rammer pipe from the English weapon were also omitted by the restocker. The straight Brown Bess lock has "TOWER" cast into the tail, indicating manufacture after 1764 (when maker names and dates were discontinued). The trigger guard, long butt tang, pinned round barrel, ramrod thimbles, nose cap and side plate (inset deeper than normal) are all transfers from the Long Land musket, which was still the primary weapon for English land troops early in the War for Independence. Its iron rammer has a thicker-than-normal button head. The barrel was originally 46 inches in length, but like most period longarms, constant iron rammer use thinned the muzzle walls to razor sharpness, requiring the barrel to be shortened to protect the rammer's hand.

| | | | |
|---|---|---|---|
| Length: 60-5/8" | Lock: 7" X 1-1/4" | Butt Tang: 5-3/4" | Furniture: Brass |
| Barrel: 45-3/8", .77 cal. | Trigger Guard: 11" | Side Plate: 6-1/8" | Weight: 10.3 lbs. |

**Author's Collection**

*Chapter 3: Smoothbore Shoulder Arms*     129

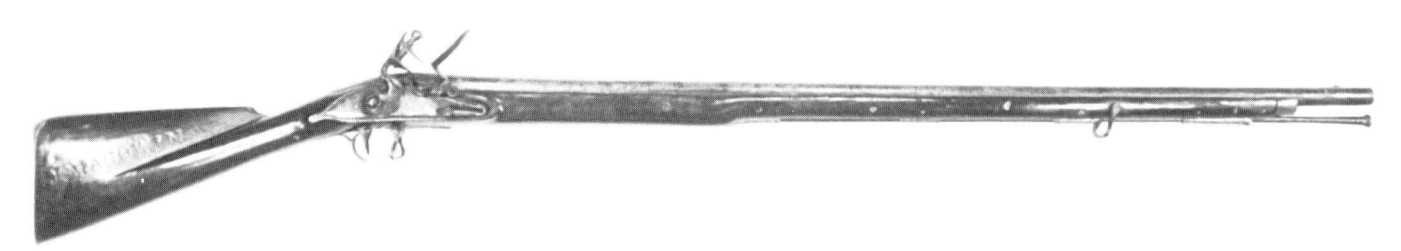

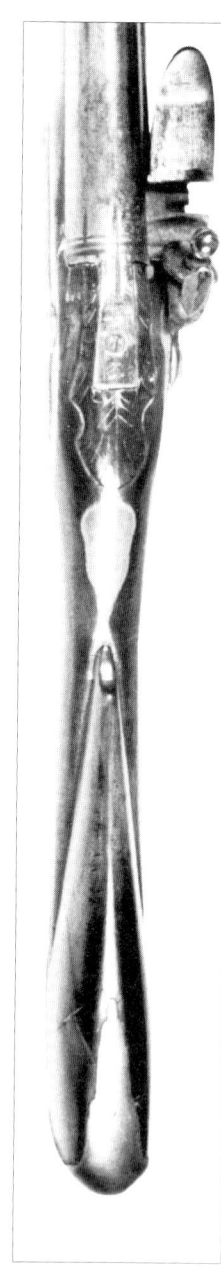

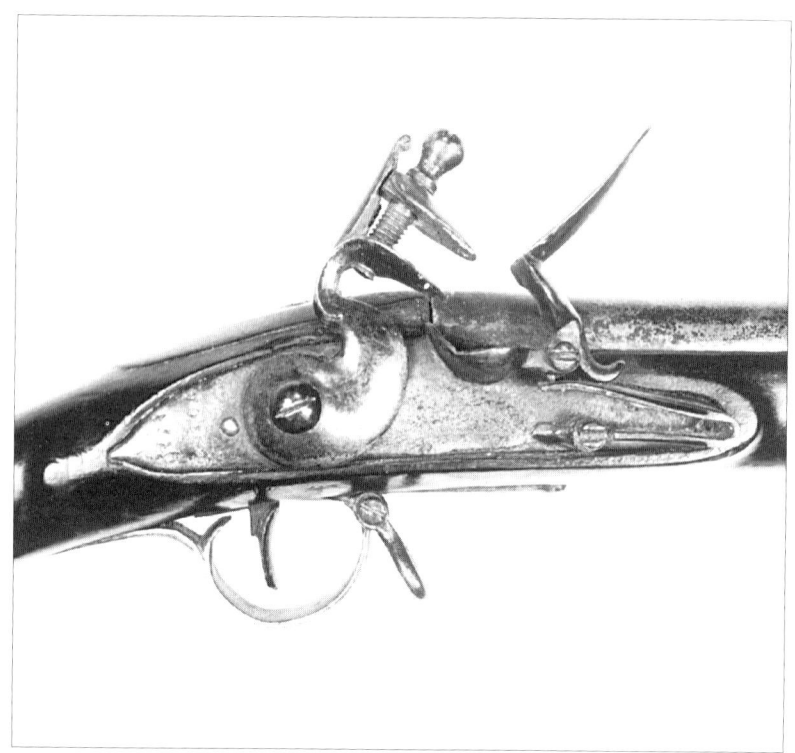

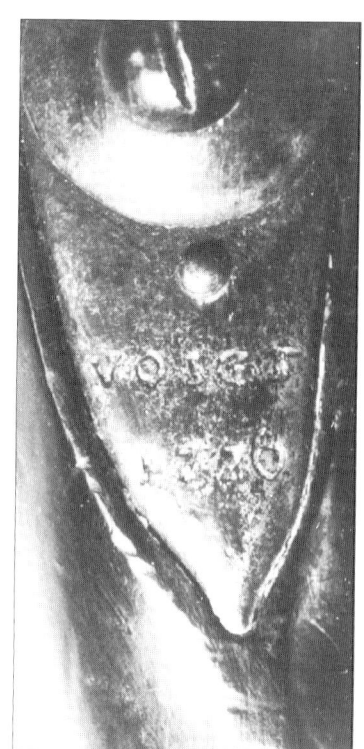

**80.MM AMERICAN MUSKET**  Circa 1776

Although some states specified it, very few gunmakers added their names to the firearms they manufactured for the Revolutionary cause. One of those who did was the Philadelphia locksmith Henry Voigt. His name and date, "VOIGT / 1776," appear on this lock's tail. Whether he produced the entire musket is not known (at least two similar locks dated 1775 and 1776 exist). The English influence is apparent in the pinned barrel, handrail buttstock, rounded double-bridled lock (despite a simplified frizzen spring finial), shield escutcheon and two-step butt tang (although shortened). Nevertheless, American innovations are already apparent at this early date, for example a slimmed trigger guard, a flat triangular side plate incorporating two channels on the tail, a shorter barrel (37-5/8", .70 caliber) and flared forward ends on the upper two of four ramrod thimbles (top one long and conical like the British). Raised leaf-like carving surrounding the barrel tang is also unusual. An owner of the musket branded the outboard buttstock "J MAGOWIN."

| | | | |
|---|---|---|---|
| Length: 53" | Lock: 6-1/4" X 1-1/4" | Butt Tang: 3-3/8" | Furniture: Brass |
| Barrel: 37-5/8", .70 cal. | Trigger Guard: 8-3/4" | Side Plate: 5-1/2" | Weight: 7.3 lbs. |

**James D. Forman Collection**

*130   Chapter 3: Smoothbore Shoulder Arms*

**81.MM AMERICAN MUSKET**                                                           **Circa 1775–1777**

Stephen Chandler is listed as a Committee of safety gunmaker in Connecticut. He was apparently located near Hartford, and his name appears on the lock plate of this weapon. The arm is a light musket (42" barrel) having a carbine-size bore of .67 caliber. Its flat/beveled lock with a faceted pan (no exterior bridle), lobed frizzen spring finial and slashed tail resemble the current Low Country/Germanic form. The rounded side plate and trigger guard, on the other hand, are close copies of the Brown Bess pattern, while a three-stepped butt tang adopts English fowler/trade gun styling. Also of interest is an original diamond-shaped wooden patch plugged into the inboard buttstock to replace a knot (see 105.MM). An escutcheon is omitted from the wrist, although the carved beaver-tail remains. All four rammer pipes are cast in the European fashion (versus the Colonists' usual formed sheet brass), and the long upper pipe includes a raised center ring similar to some British carbines of this period. A bottom barrel bayonet stud appears just forward of a brass nose band. Note also the American preference for a slightly sloped butt comb ridge (British muskets were more horizontal).

| | | | |
|---|---|---|---|
| Length: 58" | Lock: 5-3/4" X 1-1/8" | Butt Tang: 4" | Furniture: Brass |
| Barrel: 42", .67 cal. | Trigger Guard: 10-1/4" | Side Plate: 5-3/8" | Weight: 9.4 lbs. |

**James D. Forman Collection**

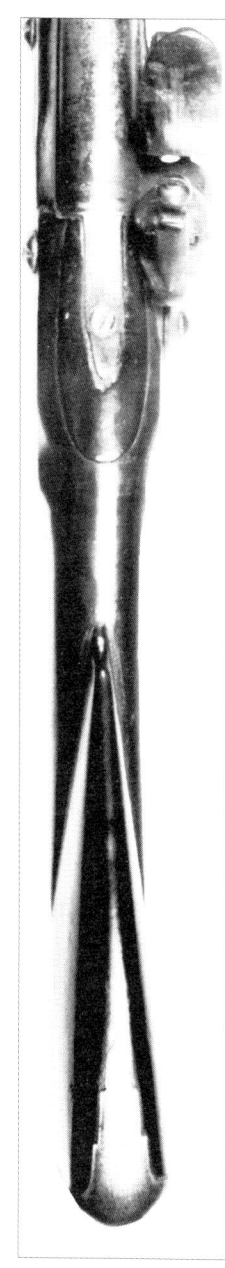

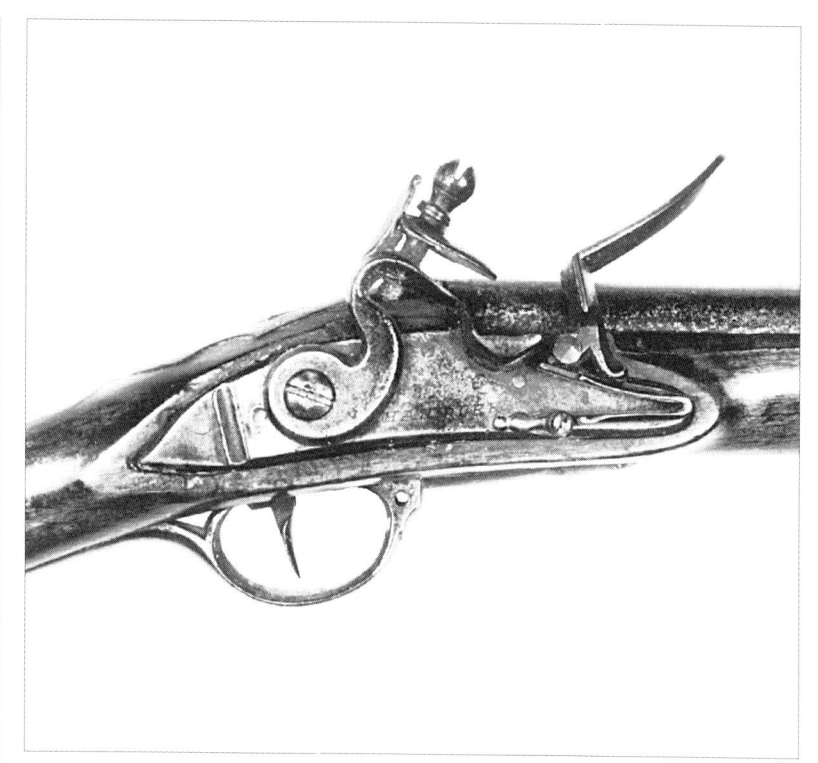

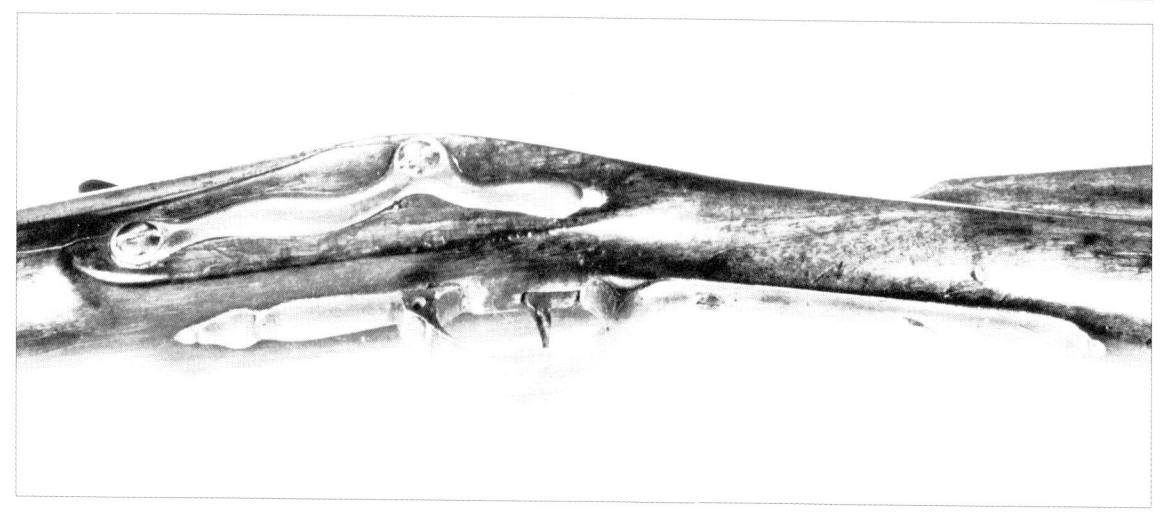

*Chapter 3: Smoothbore Shoulder Arms*    **131**

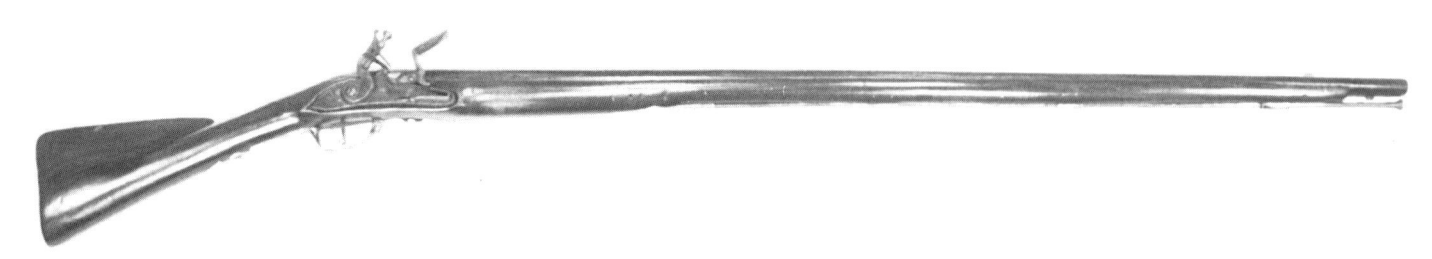

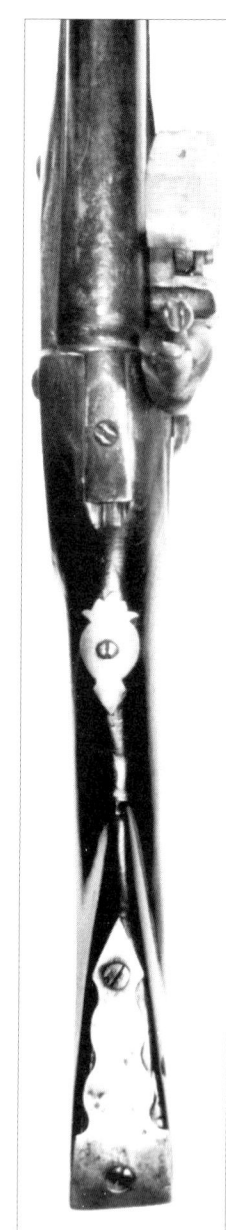

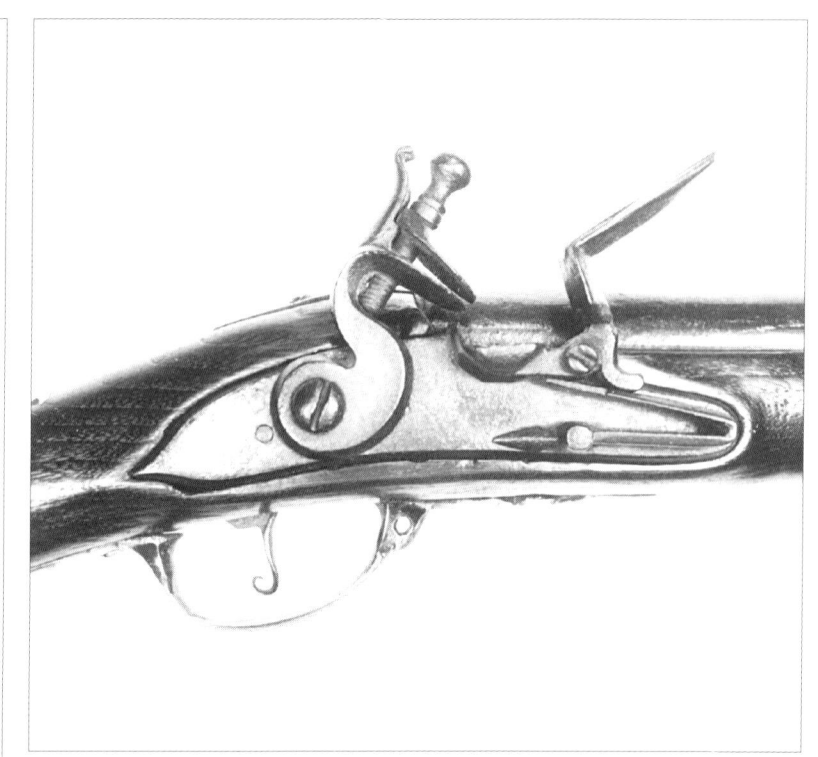

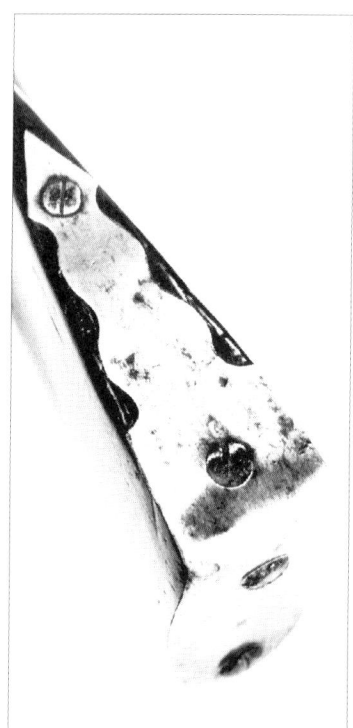

**82.MM AMERICAN MUSKET**                                                                  **Circa 1776–1785**

The American provincials created this longarm by remounting parts from a wide butt German musket on a heavy chestnut stock. Typical Germanic features are apparent in the flat/beveled banana lock, including its spearpoint finial and internal screw on the frizzen spring, a faceted flash pan with bridle and a squared top on the frizzen. Its broad flat butt plate (2-1/8" across) hosts the usual two protruding convex screw heads at the rear, yet secures the pointed tang with a pair of flush screws. (Note: a butt plate of this form was found in a cache of burned military artifacts near Crown Point.) The spearheaded trigger guard (beveled bow), pointed escutcheon (center screw), long round barrel (having a baluster breech), top front sight and bottom bayonet stud are also typical Germanic features. The Americans did however improvise a plain sheet-brass side plate, omit the traditional German teardrop carving around the barrel tang and supplement an original faceted tail pipe with three plain sheet-brass thimbles above it. The iron rod has a button head.

| | | | |
|---|---|---|---|
| Length: 61-1/8" | Lock: 6-1/2" X 1-1/4" | Butt Tang: 5-3/4" | Furniture: Brass |
| Barrel: 45-3/4", .78 cal. | Trigger Guard: 10-7/8" | Side Plate: 4-3/8" | Weight: 9.9 lbs. |

**Author's Collection**

*132    Chapter 3: Smoothbore Shoulder Arms*

### 83.MM AMERICAN MUSKET

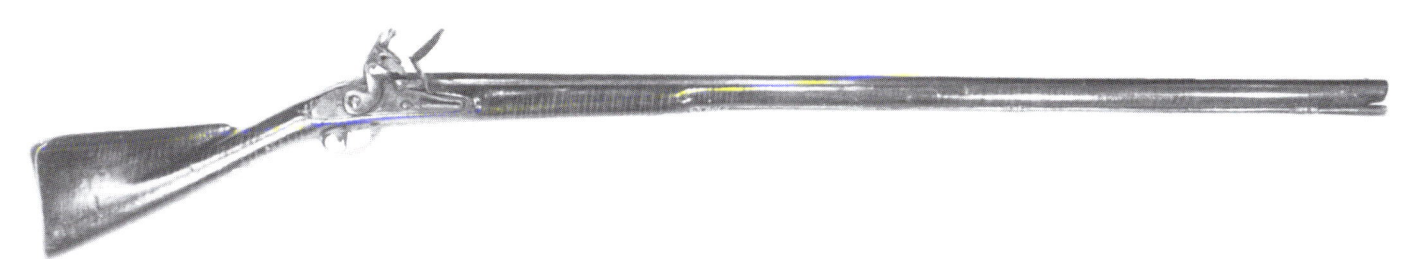

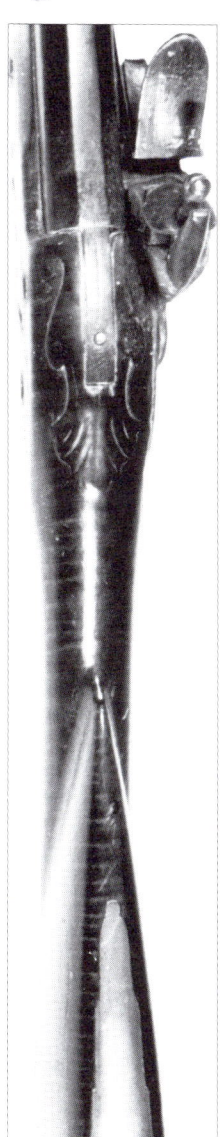

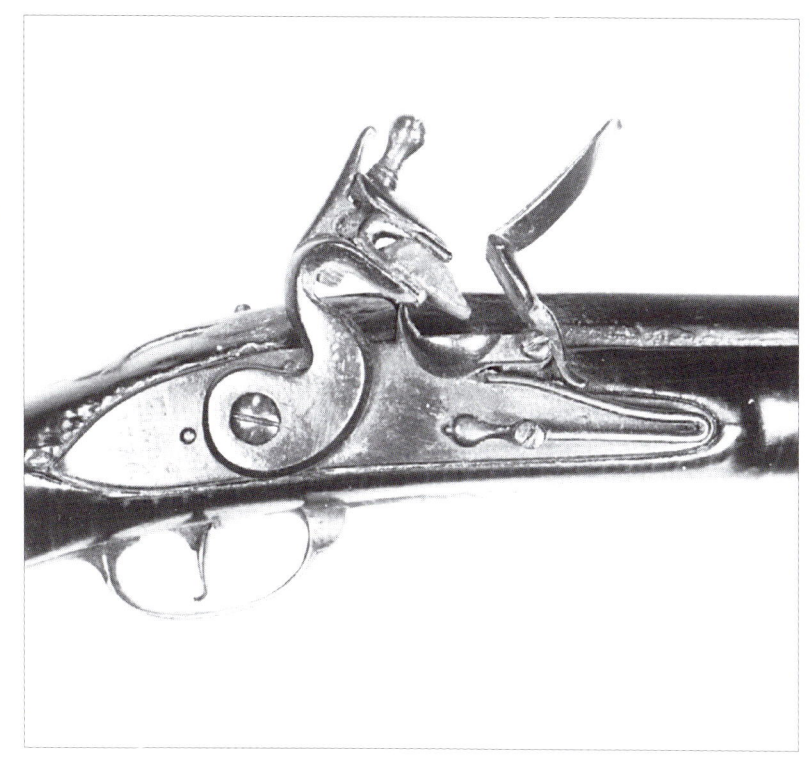

**Circa 1776**

In 1775 Virginia authorized an arms factory at Fredericksburg to fabricate complete small arms. It continued through the war, but the few surviving weapons identified with it exhibit a wide variety of sizes and patterns. The lock design however remains consistent. The one in this longarm illustrates the typical flat lock plate and cock, with a rounded pan/bridle and a lobed finial on the frizzen spring. Its tail is engraved "FRED / 1776." Inside the lock "WG" was stamped by William Grady, master armorer. Although this striped maple stock extends to the muzzle, its final 28 inches is an early replacement—possibly added after the war for use as a fowler when a bayonet was no longer needed. The arm's mixed brass furniture displays a reused British Long Land butt tang, a unique American spear-headed trigger guard, the early European form of dragon side plate, three ribbed rammer pipes, a carved splay around the butt tang, plus a pre-1763 French-type barrel (octagonal for 10 inches). The escutcheon, nose band and sling swivels are omitted. The barrel's tang, in turn, is held by a screw from below the stock (no trigger plate).

| | | | |
|---|---|---|---|
| Length: 61-1/2" | Lock: 7" X 1-1/4" | Butt Tang: 5-3/4" | Furniture: Brass |
| Barrel: 45-1/8", .70 cal. | Trigger Guard: 10" | Side Plate: 6-1/4" | Weight: 9.3 lbs. |

**James D. Forman Collection**

*Chapter 3: Smoothbore Shoulder Arms* **133**

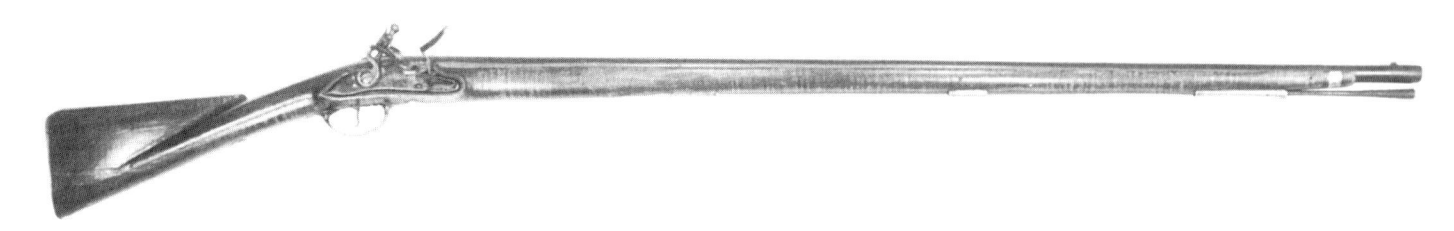

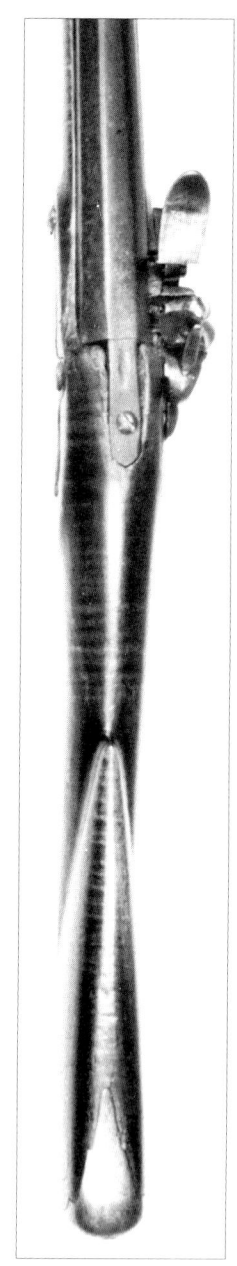

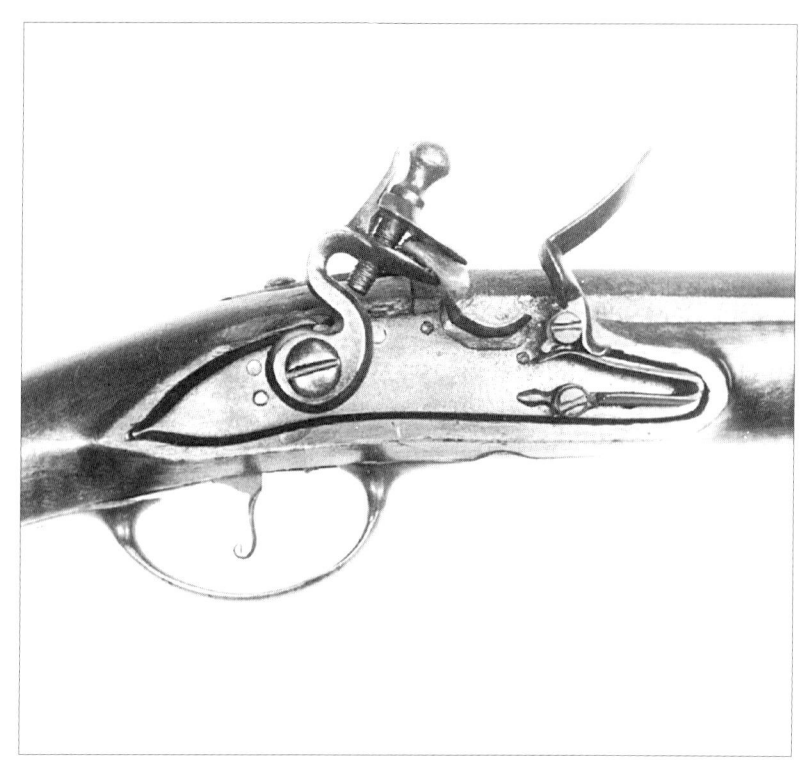

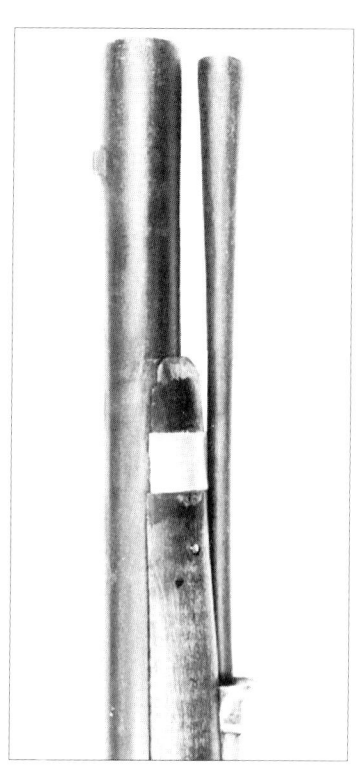

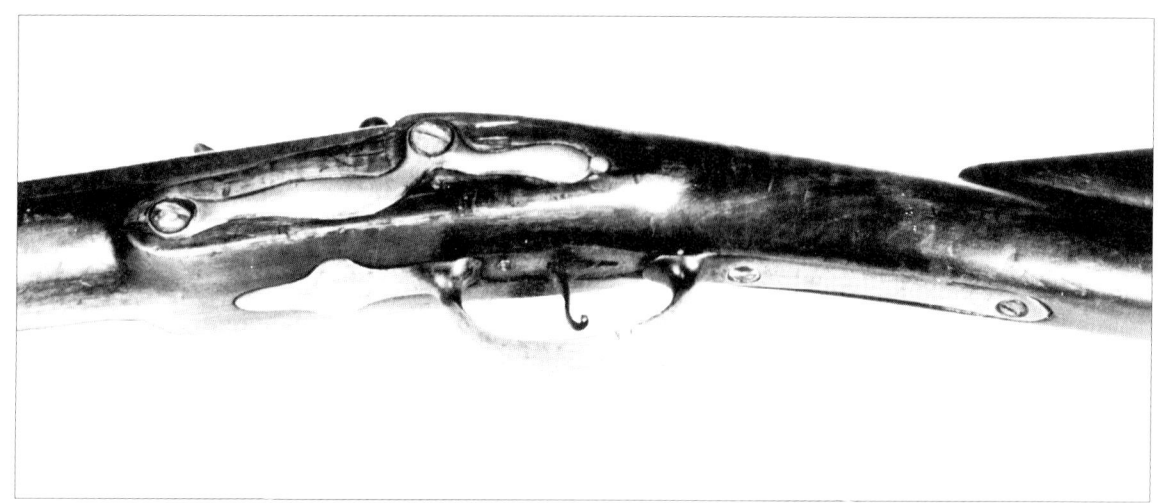

**84.MM AMERICAN MUSKET**                                                                                                              Circa 1775–1785

Although many of the American muskets mounted a wide variety of components from available sources, they fired a multiple load or undersized ball, so the primary requirement was not bore size but a reliable ignition system. The unbalanced lock plate in this firearm has a low-tapered tail that suggests local manufacture. Moreover, the replaced cock, being too tall, was apparently reshaped into a crouch profile to fit the action. The colonists also created an interesting triple-pointed bulbous trigger guard and reproduced a small version of a British Long Land side plate. The short engraved butt tang was taken from an English fowler/trade gun, while three cast brass rammer pipes in the slender striped maple stock appear to have originated in a Brown Bess. Also note the common Colonial practice of inserting a brass strip below the muzzle as a pseudo nose cap to retard splitting.

| | | | |
|---|---|---|---|
| Length: 60-1/2" | Lock: 5-3/4" X 1" | Butt Tang: 2-7/8" | Furniture: Brass |
| Barrel: 45", .68 cal. | Trigger Guard: 9-3/8" | Side Plate: 5-1/4" | Weight: 8.0 lbs. |

**Author's Collection**

*Chapter 3: Smoothbore Shoulder Arms*

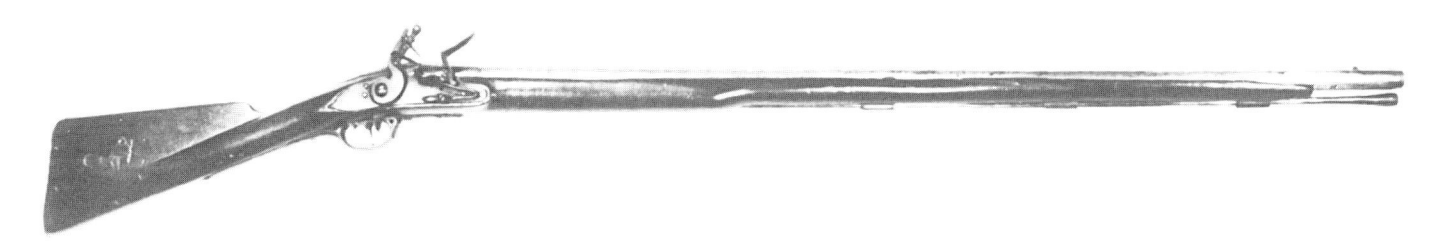

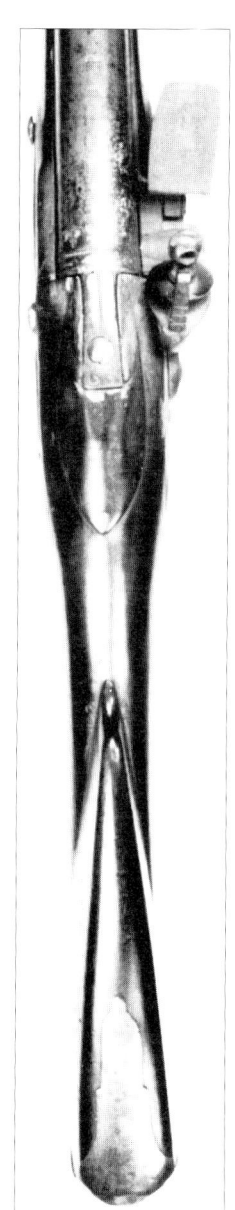

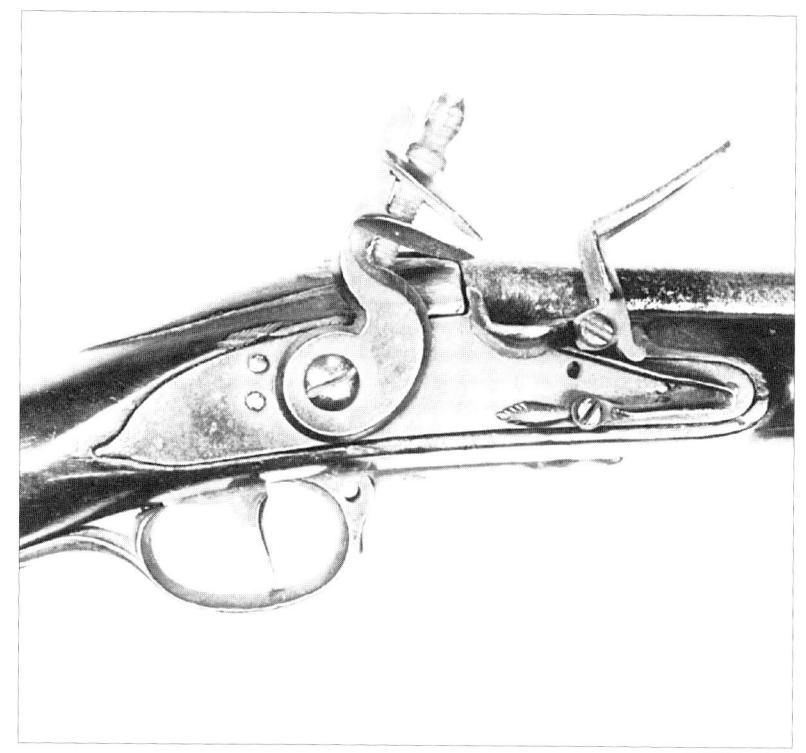

**85.MM AMERICAN MUSKET**  Circa 1776

Reflecting its strong pacifist Quaker influence, Pennsylvania had no official militia organization until June 30, 1775. A Committee of Safety under Benjamin Franklin promptly met the following month to specify the needed weapons. On October 27, 1775, the committee's muskets were ordered to show a "P" proof mark; a March 2, 1776, directive then authorized a "PP" stamp. This musket bears "PP" marks on the breech's left side and in the stock flanking the head of its trigger guard. A single "P" appears on the barrel one third of the distance above the breech. In typical fashion, despite the official specification for a 44" barrel, the length here is 41-3/4 inches. Its pattern reflects the British Brown Bess form with a stepped butt tang, beaver-tail tang carving, a convex side plate, a hazelnut trigger guard and a pinned round barrel. The flat American lock includes a plain rectangular post on the cock and a leaf-shaped frizzen spring finial having incised edges. Additional markings: "63" (number of the arm) in the barrel tang, and a hand-carved Masonic formula on the butt (later owner; re: Bazelon and Trussell, bib. 171).

| | | | |
|---|---|---|---|
| Length: 57-5/8" | Lock: 6-5/8" X 1-1/8" | Butt Tang: 24-1/8" | Furniture: Brass |
| Barrel: 41-3/4", .73 cal. | Trigger/ Guard: 11-3/8" | Side Plate: 5-3/4" | Weight: 10.6 lbs |

**Pennsylvania Historical and Museum Commission**

*Chapter 3: Smoothbore Shoulder Arms* 135

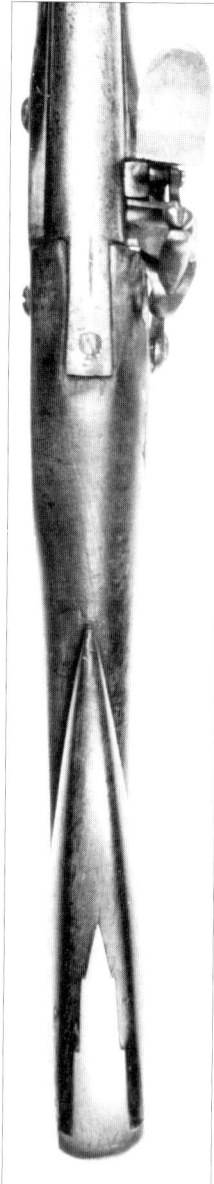

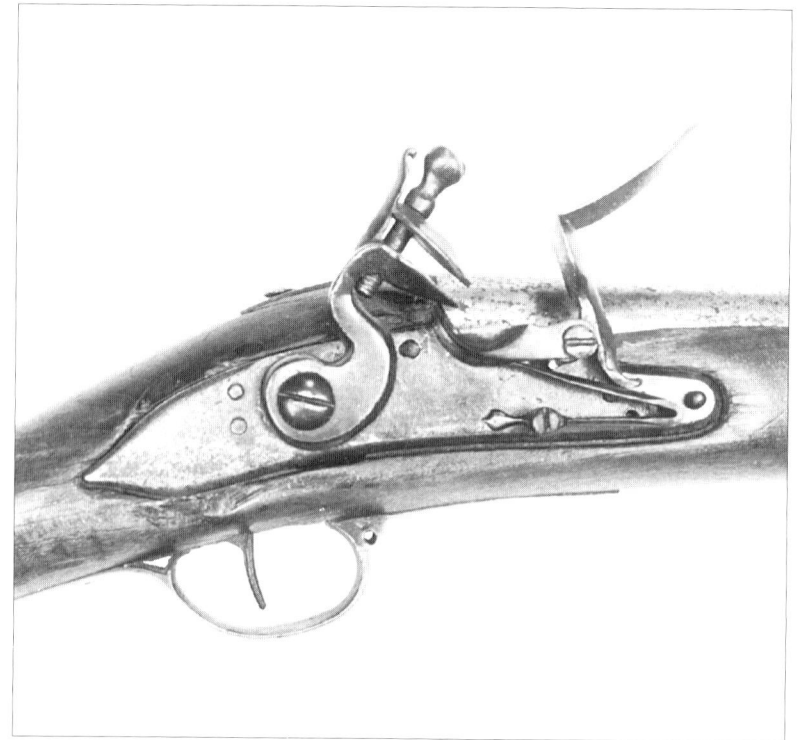

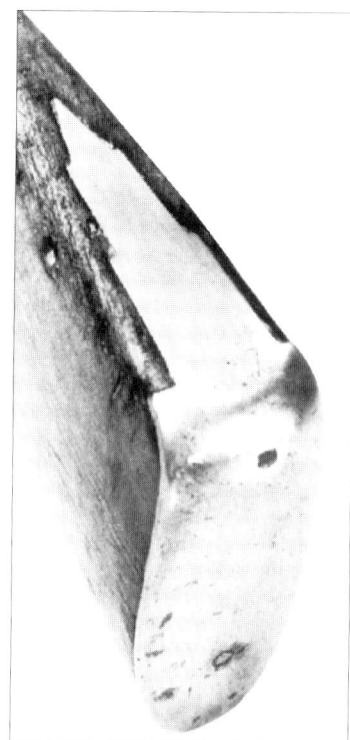

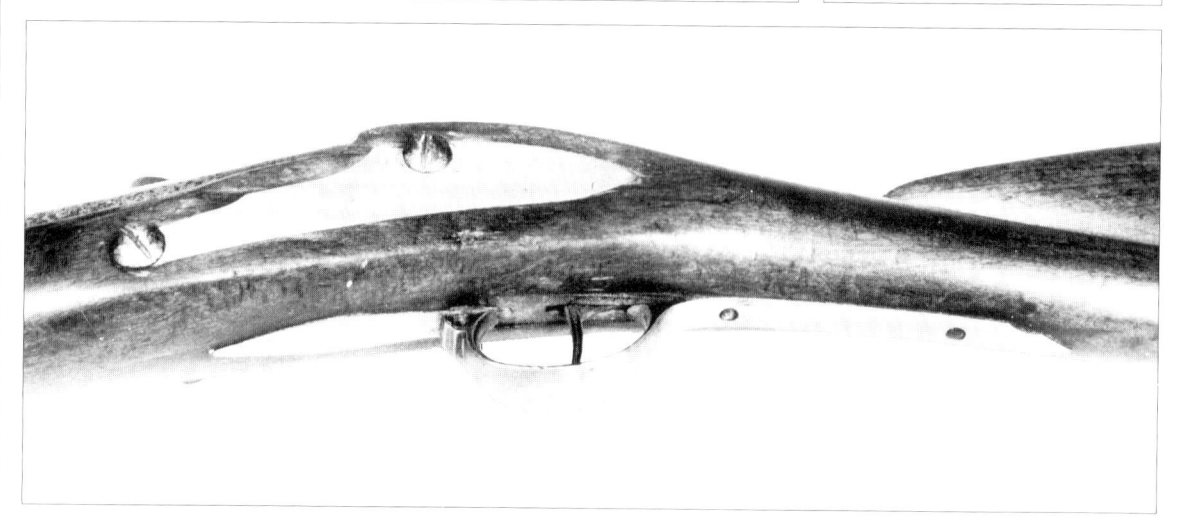

**86.MM AMERICAN MUSKET**    Circa 1770–1800

The heavy round barrel on this weapon is stamped at the breech "NEW HAMPSHIRE MILITIA" (probably an individual's marking). It appears to have been constructed entirely in America—durable and practical without embellishments. Notice the bulky profile, for example, with an unusually thick stock around the lock area, where its cavity plus the barrel breech and side screw intrusions make it vulnerable to breakage. The popular Low Country/Germanic flat/beveled lock pattern was copied, yet the extended tail and rounded pan (with bridle) identify local craftsmanship. Its brass furniture also is simple and severe, for example the rigid two-step butt plate tang (two nails in rear), pointed trigger guard and flat brass triangular side plate. An escutcheon and all stock carving are omitted. The walnut stock ends in a 1/2" nose band, while a button-head iron ramrod is held in three sheet-brass thimbles (the long upper one copies the Brown Bess). Its butt tang is engraved "7."

| Length: 59-3/4" | Lock: 6-3/4" X 1-1/4" | Butt Tang: 4-3/8" | Furniture: Brass |
| Barrel: 44", .75 cal. | Trigger Guard: 10" | Side Plate: 7-1/8" | Weight: 10.0 lbs. |

**Author's Collection**

*Chapter 3: Smoothbore Shoulder Arms*

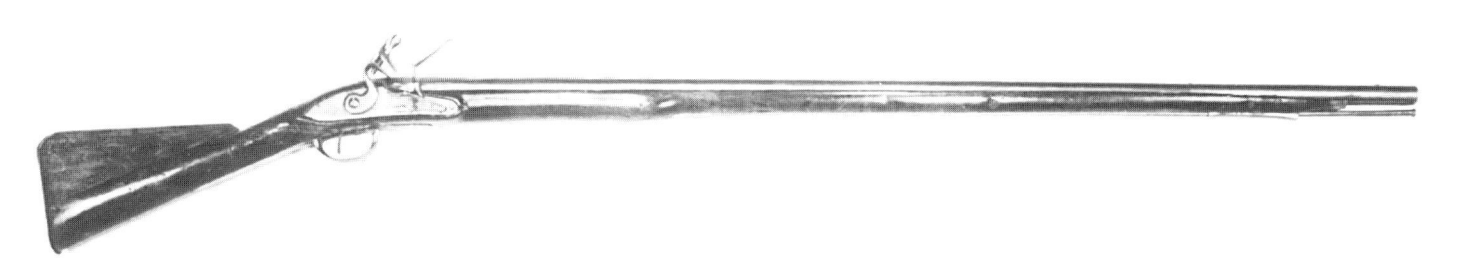

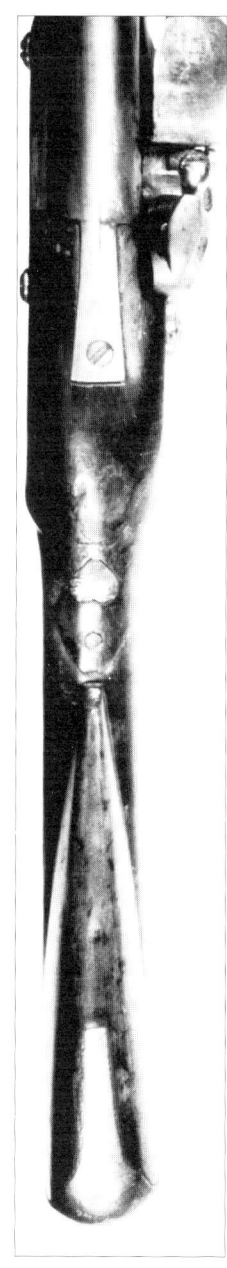

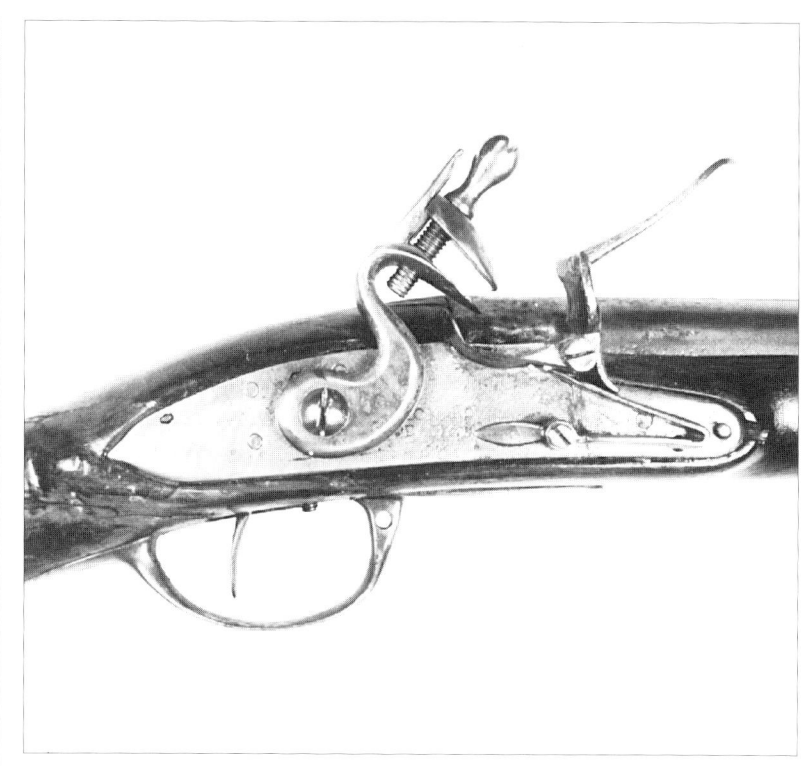

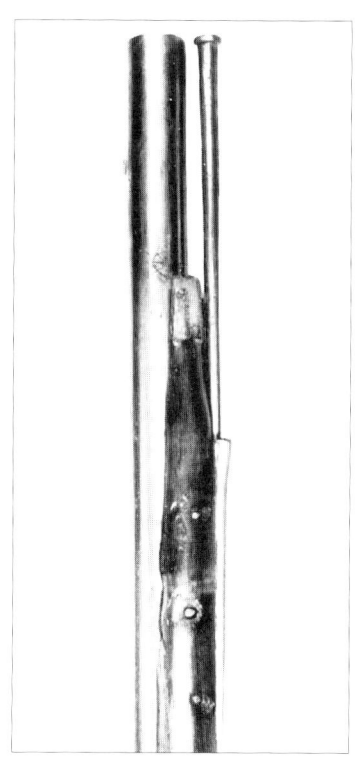

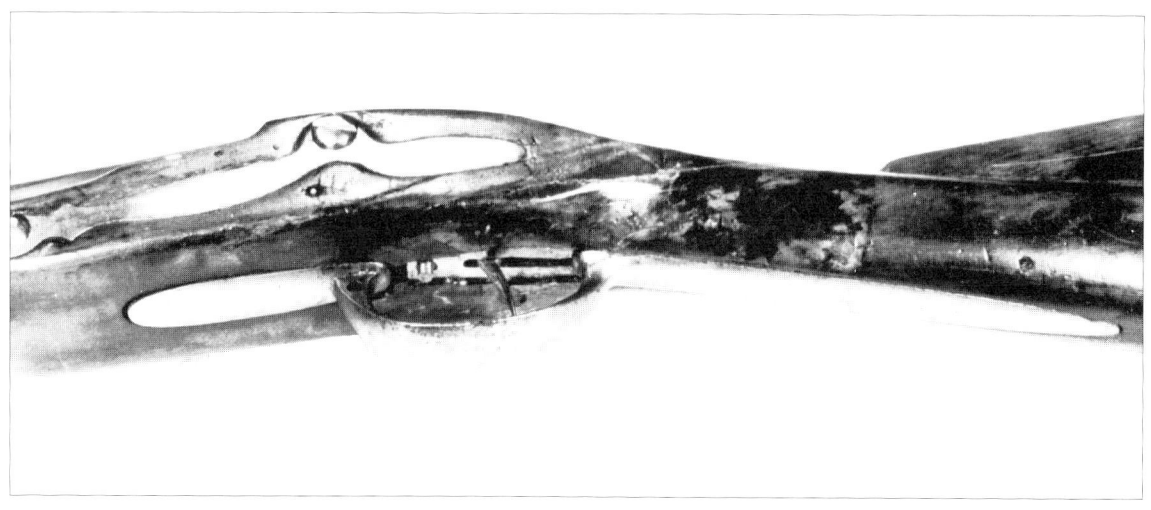

**87.MM AMERICAN MUSKET**                                                           **Circa 1776**

For an obvious reason, few of the arms ordered by the rebellious Committees of Safety in the early years of 1775–1776 were identified by their makers. This unusual longarm is signed on the lock plate by one of those contractors, "Eliphalet Leonard," of Easton, Massachusetts, plus the date, "1776" (although in a different hand). His family had a long history in the iron business and he is reported to be one of the first to attempt steel manufacture in this country. It appears that Leonard made every part of the musket. He adhered to the established British practice of a round pinned barrel in a walnut stock with a handrail butt. Yet the iron furniture is simplified and its ends are blunted. The flat French-style lock mounts an undersize swansneck cock (possible replacement), a very shallow pan with bridle and a flattened frizzen spring finial. Its Brown Bess-type side plate, in turn, is very plain—as with the elementary trigger guard, squared end butt plate and reverse-heart escutcheon. The unusual top two rammer pipes (three total) flare gradually toward the front. A broken stock wrist has been repaired by dowel pins.

| | | | |
|---|---|---|---|
| Length: 64-1/4" | Lock: 7" X 1-1/4" | Butt Tang: 3-7/8" | Furniture: Iron |
| Barrel: 48", .80 cal. | Trigger Guard: 11-1/4" | Side Plate: 6-1/4" | Weight: 12.0 lbs. |

**Fort Ticonderoga Collection**

*Chapter 3: Smoothbore Shoulder Arms*    **137**

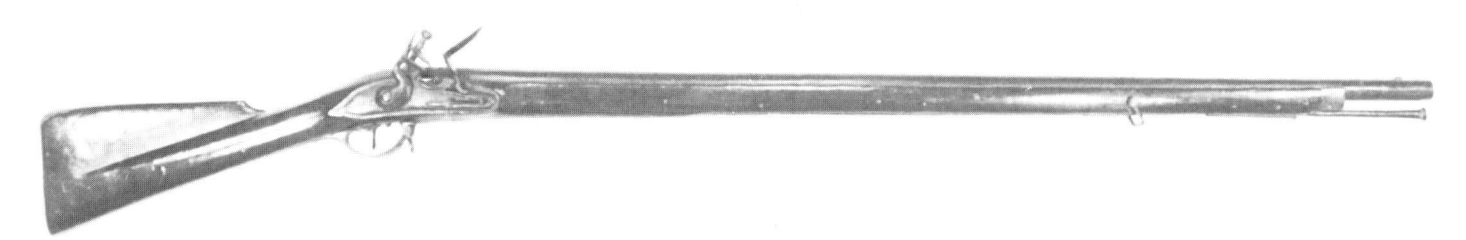

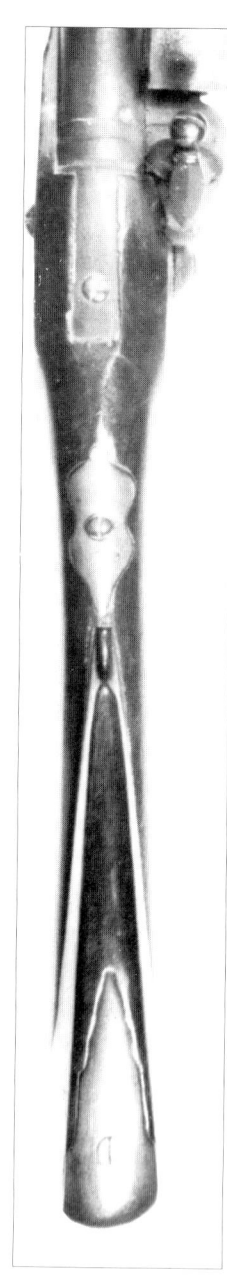

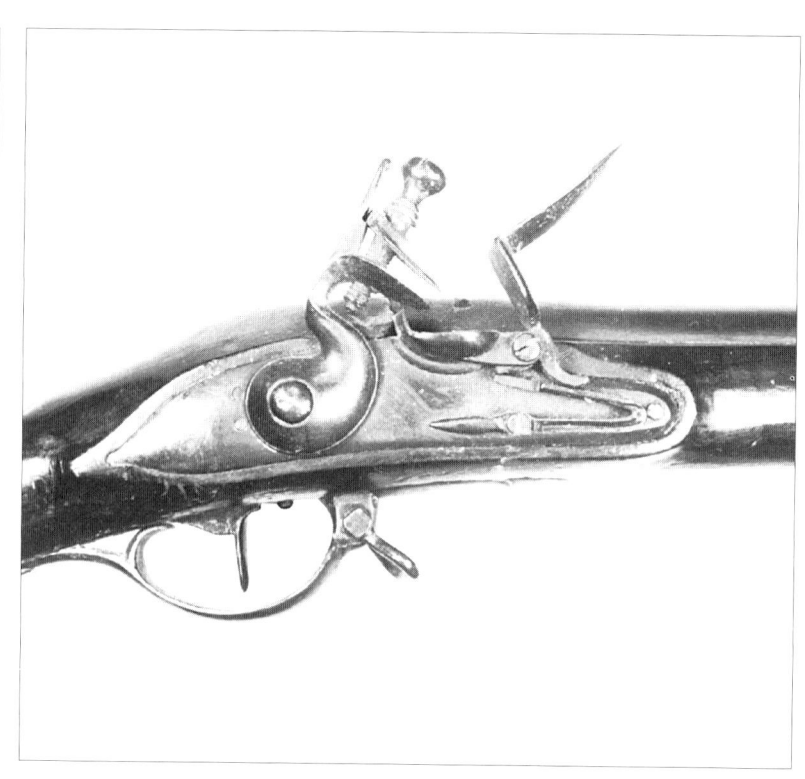

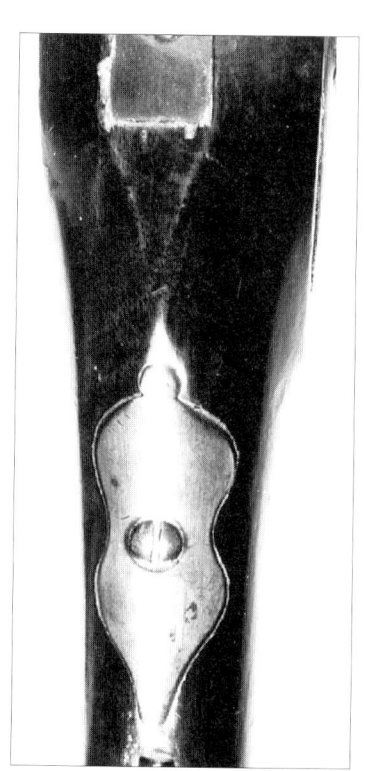

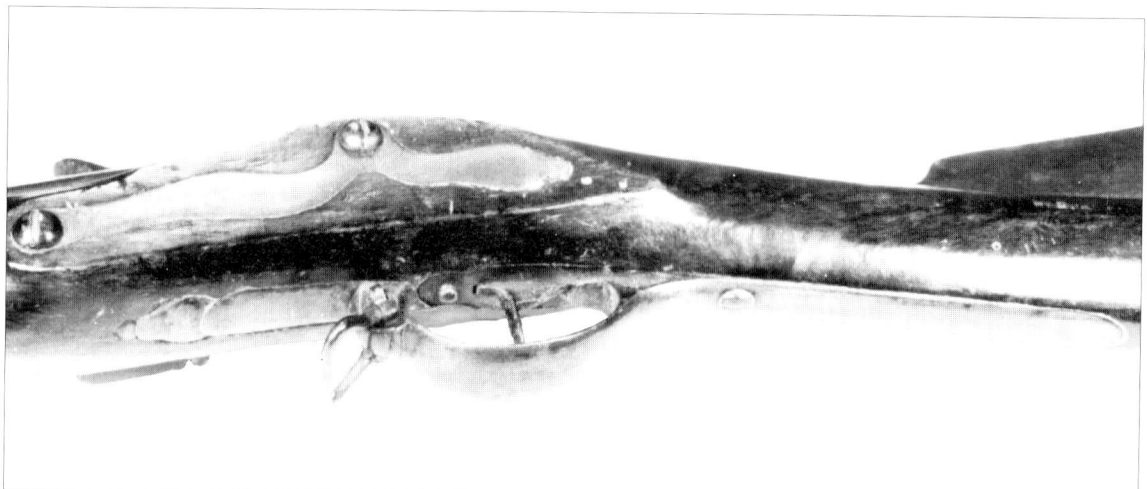

**88.MM AMERICAN MUSKET**   Circa 1775–1780

Several of this pattern exist. Although lacking official markings, they are associated with arms produced by Maryland. In August 1775 that state specified the manufacture of muskets that followed the existing British Short Land Brown Bess (14.MM), for example using a 42", .75 caliber pinned barrel, a double-bridled lock, a black walnut or maple stock and brass furniture. The configuration here approximates these guidelines but with a number of variations: the pointed butt tang adds a top screw, a rounded screw also appears in the escutcheon plate, the frizzen spring has a long spear-like tip, beaver-tail carving is omitted, and the use of sheet-brass, not cast, ramrod thimbles. It does, however, include the 42", .75 caliber barrel, bridled lock, flat English side plate and a close copy of their trigger guard. Several surviving examples of this model have parts bearing foreign type marks; one barrel includes a German Nuremberg stamp on its underside. However it is documented that as shortages developed, Maryland purchased locks and barrels in 1776 from Europe.

| | | | |
|---|---|---|---|
| Length: 57-1/2" | Lock: 6-1/2" X 1-1/4" | Butt Tang: 4-1/4" | Furniture: Brass |
| Barrel: 41-3/4", .77 cal. | Trigger Guard: 11" | Side Plate: 5-7/8" | Weight: 9.6 lbs. |

**James D. Forman Collection**

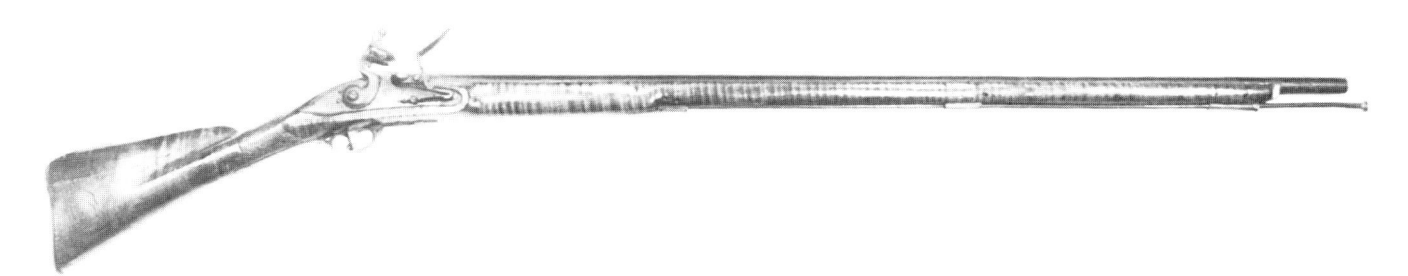

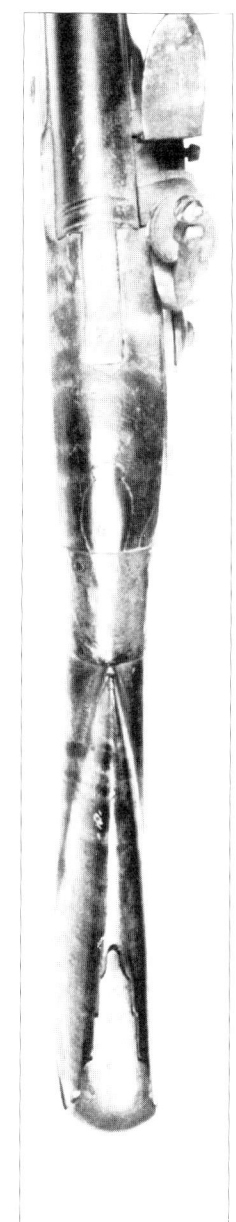

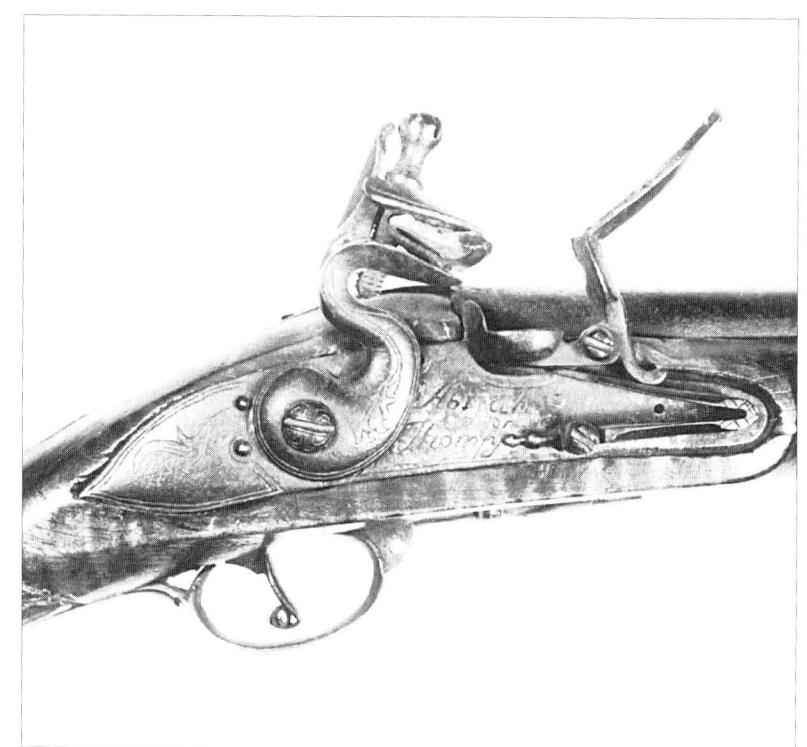

### 89.MM AMERICAN MUSKET

**Circa 1775–1776**

This musket was created by Abijah Thompson of Woburn, Massachusetts, in 1775–1776 and signed by him on the lock under its flash pan. In addition to service as a Minuteman in the Lexington–Concord alarm, he was also listed as a master armorer in Continental service during 1775. The longarm may have been produced under a Committee of Safety contract. Except for the reused British musket barrel (faint Tower proofs, length cut from 46 inches to 44 inches), the remainder of the weapon appears to be locally made. Note that he followed the pinned barrel pattern favored in the Brown Bess but added the slanted buttstock preferred by many Colonists. English influence is also seen in the three-step butt tang and rounded lock form, as well as an escutcheon and crude copy of the acorn trigger guard design used on their private arms. Wrapped around the wrist is a nailed band of brass—a common cure for a stock fracture. Its triangular flat side plate is typically American, as are the three sheet-brass rammer thimbles. In keeping with the pressures of wartime production, raised carving on its striped maple stock is omitted.

| | | | |
|---|---|---|---|
| Length: 59-1/2" | Lock: 7" X 1-1/4" | Butt Tang: 4" | Furniture: Brass |
| Barrel: 44", .77 cal. | Trigger Guard: 9-1/8" | Side Plate: 6-1/2" | Weight: 9.0 lbs. |

**William H. Guthman Collection**

*Chapter 3: Smoothbore Shoulder Arms*

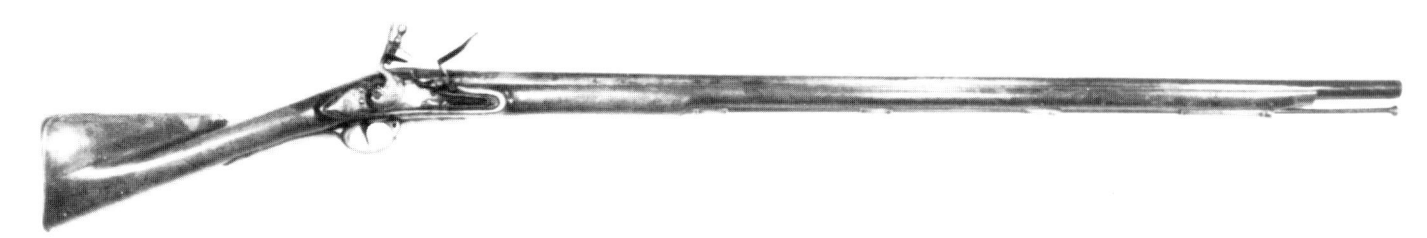

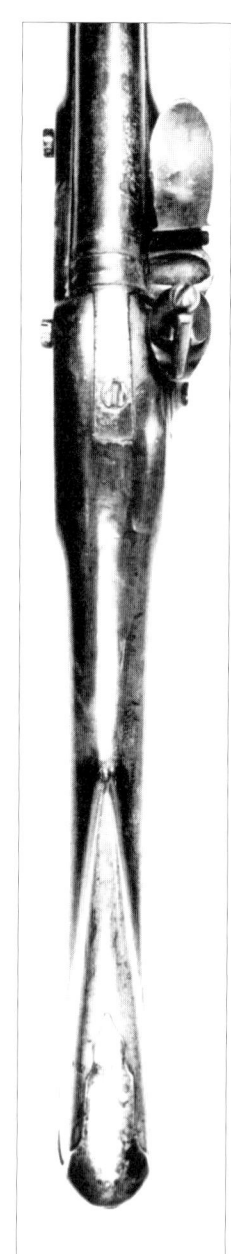

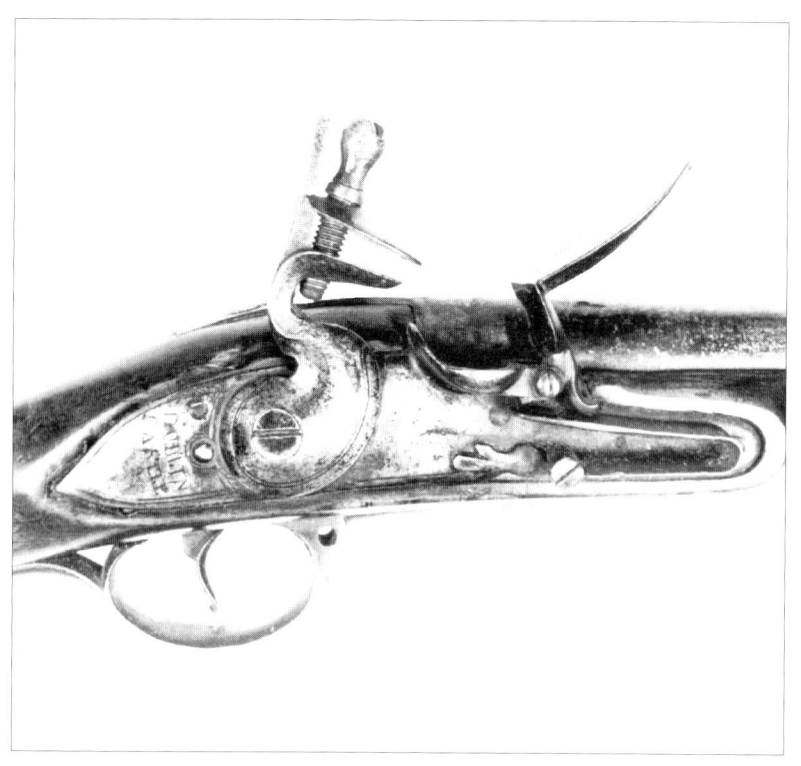

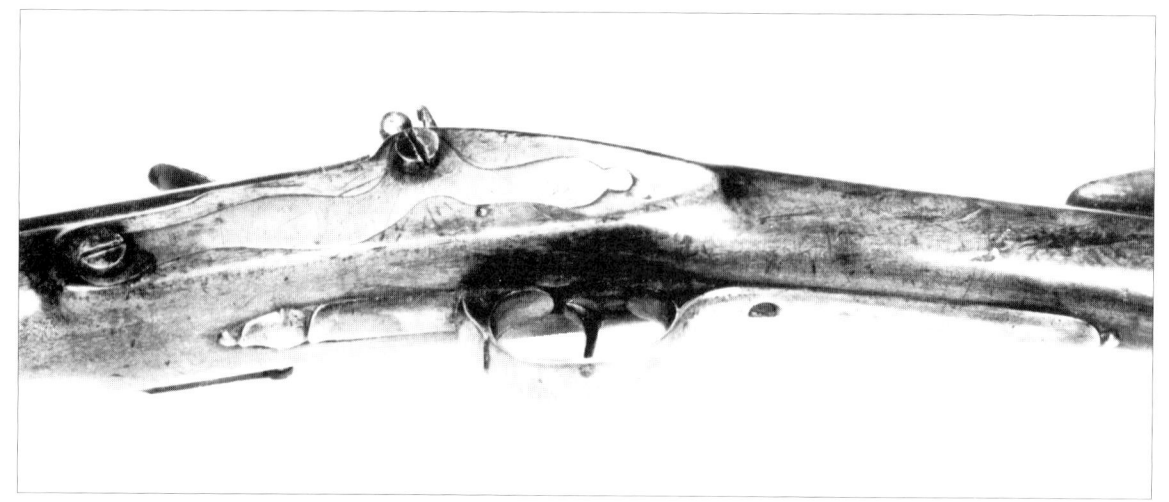

**90.MM AMERICAN MUSKET**      Circa 1779–1783

Components from a British Short Land Pattern 1777 musket (15.MM) were reused to create this American arm. It was found in Virginia and is stocked in maple. The lock reads "Dublin Castle" on the tail, although all original Royal markings forward of the cock were removed — possibly by the Colonists. In addition, the three-fingered frizzen spring appears to be an American replacement. Partial Tower proofs remain visible on the breech of its 42-1/8" barrel, while the top bayonet stud was eliminated in later use. Notice, too, the buttstock form typical of mid-18th century styling with a slender round wrist and long handrail crease alongside the comb. The escutcheon and beaver tail carving were omitted in restocking. Beyond a surviving hole in the reused Brown Bess trigger guard bow, there were no provisions for sling swivels (typical of many restocked American longarms).

| | | | |
|---|---|---|---|
| Length: 58" | Lock: 7" X 1-1/4" | Butt Tang: 3-3/4" | Furniture: Brass |
| Barrel: 42-1/8", .78 cal. | Trigger Guard: 10-3/8" | Side Plate: 6-1/4" | Weight: 9.3 llbs. |

**Author's Collection**

140    *Chapter 3: Smoothbore Shoulder Arms*

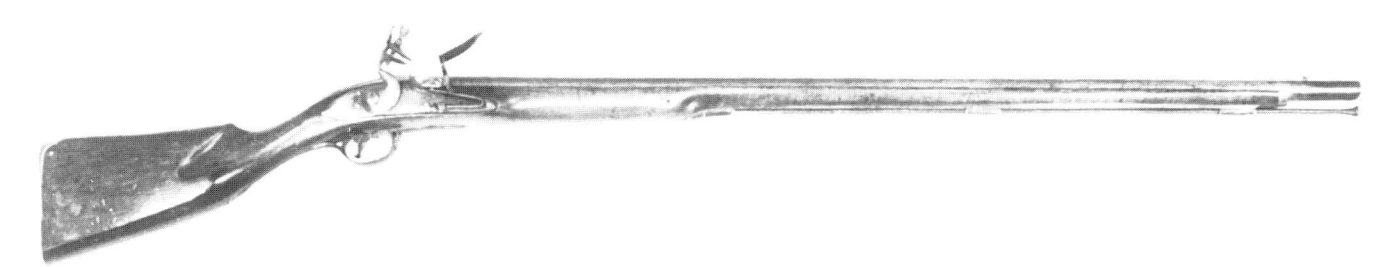

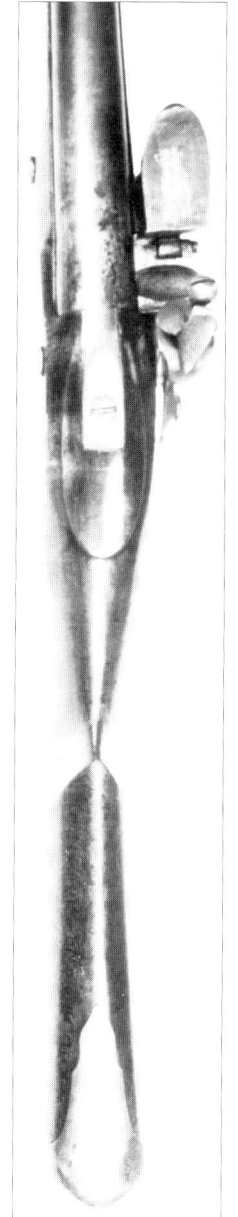

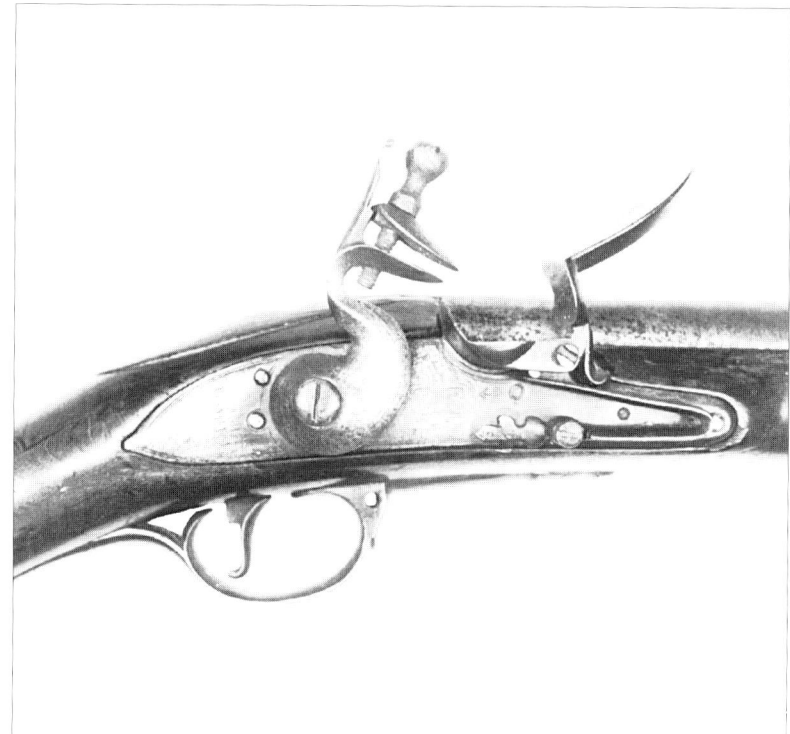

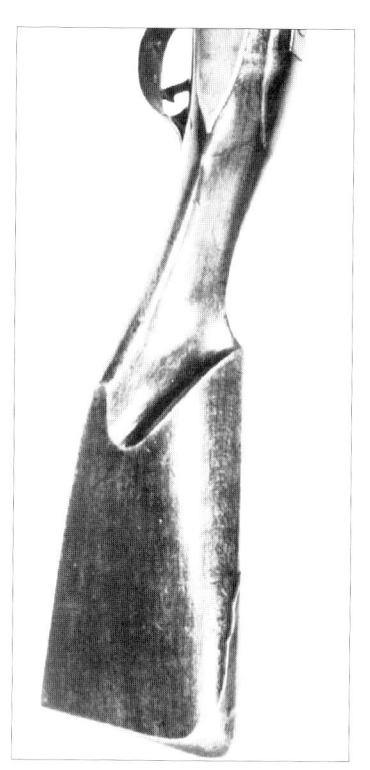

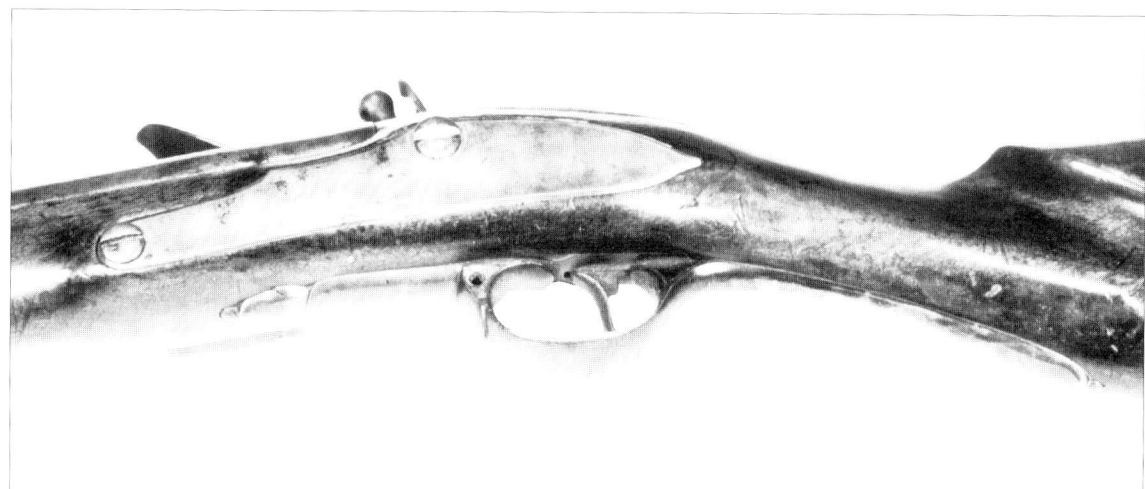

**91.MM  AMERICAN CLUB BUTT MUSKET**  Circa 1778–1783

The club butt was popular in Colonial North America—influenced by the French "buccaneer" naval musket (52.MM) and similar civilian fowlers from Europe. This example of a club butt infantry musket, which has its forend cut back to mount a bayonet, is unusual. It includes a restocked British Short Land butt plate and lock. The latter appears to be in the transition period between its Type I form (goose-neck cock with a flattened upper post and a three-fingered frizzen spring finial) and the Type II adopted in 1777 (two screw ends visible behind the cock, a lobed frizzen spring finial, and no engraved borders on the frizzen's forward face). The American trigger guard also follows the Brown Bess design, including the drilled hole for a sling swivel, but has no provision for the rear screw that usually pierced the wrist to anchor an escutcheon. This walnut stock has an interesting concave contour along both sides of the forend to create a ridge that traces the rammer channel (three cast British pipes). The flat triangular brass side plate is a common provincial form.

| | | | |
|---|---|---|---|
| Length: 54-7/8" | Lock: 7" X 1-1/4" | Butt Tang: 3-3/4" | Furniture: Brass |
| Barrel: 39-1/8", .77 cal. | Trigger Guard: 10-3/4" | Side Plate: 7" | Weight: 9.2 lbs. |

**Author's Collection**

*Chapter 3: Smoothbore Shoulder Arms*

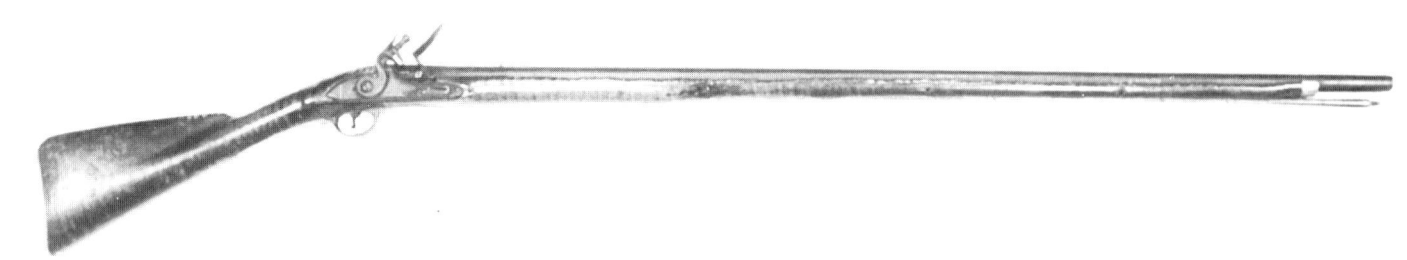

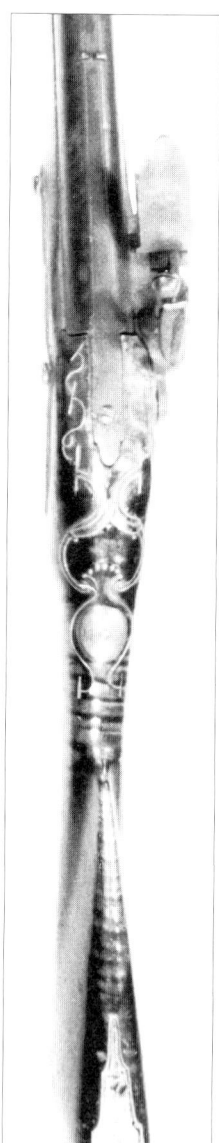

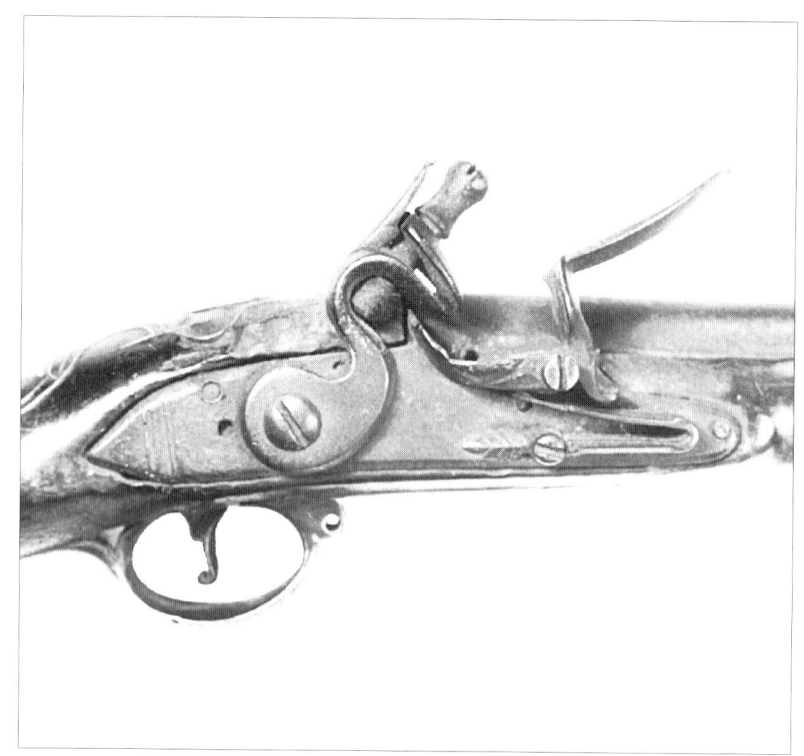

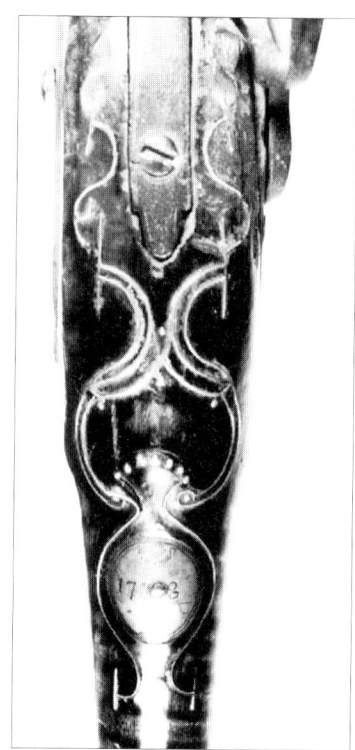

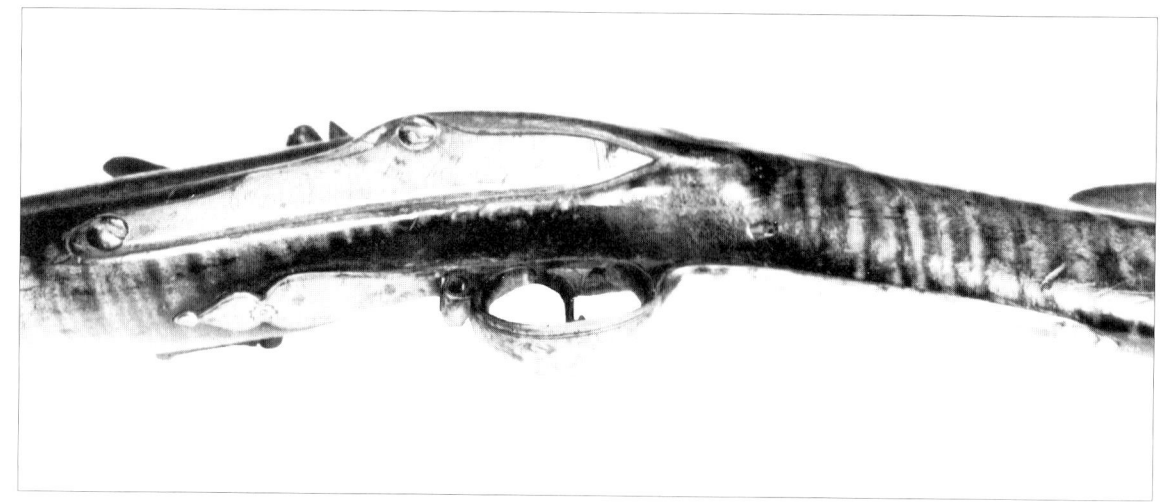

**92.MM  AMERICAN FOWLER/FUSIL**  **Circa 1778**

This impressive and uniquely American personal hunting gun/fusil is stamped on the butt tang "DOUD & NORTON." Located in Goshen, Connecticut, Doud had apprenticed under arms maker Benoni Hills (see 76.MM) and with Norton fulfilled militia contracts during the Revolutionary War. The triangular two-screw butt plate is inscribed by an owner, "Lieut. Jannah Churchel" (reported Connecticut location). Its brass wire inlay plus an oval silver escutcheon (center silver pin) are attractive additions to the striped maple stock—as with the engraved bulbous trigger guard and two-step butt tang. The year 1778 appears on the escutcheon. Its barrel mounts both rear and front sights (no bayonet stud survives). An American flat/beveled lock (two bridles) includes double channels across the tail and a feather-like frizzen spring finial. Five pipes (long top one 4-5/8") hold a wooden ramrod. Western Connecticut makers at that time usually favored striped maple stocks as seen here.

Length: 57-1/4"  
Barrel: 41-7/8", .60 cal.  
Lock: 5-1/8" X 1-1/8"  
Trigger Guard: 9-1/2"  
Butt Tang: 4-1/8"  
Side Plate: 5-7/8"  
Furniture: Brass  
Weight: 7.2 lbs.

**Richard Ulbrich Collection**

142    *Chapter 3: Smoothbore Shoulder Arms*

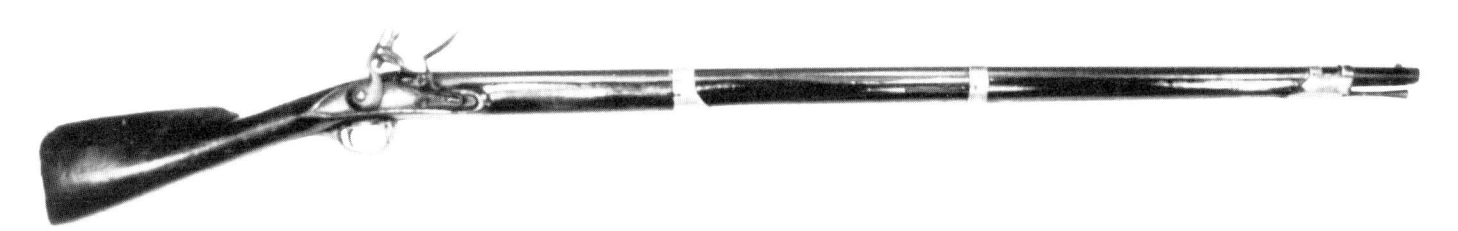

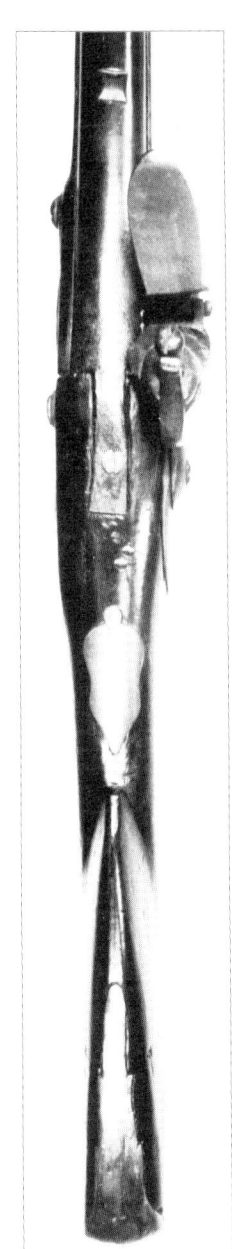

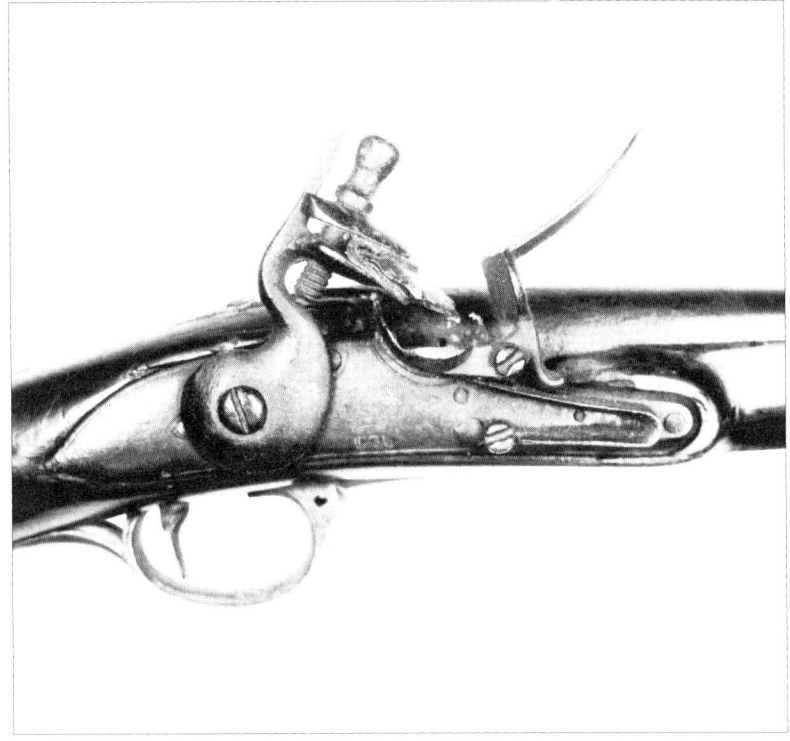

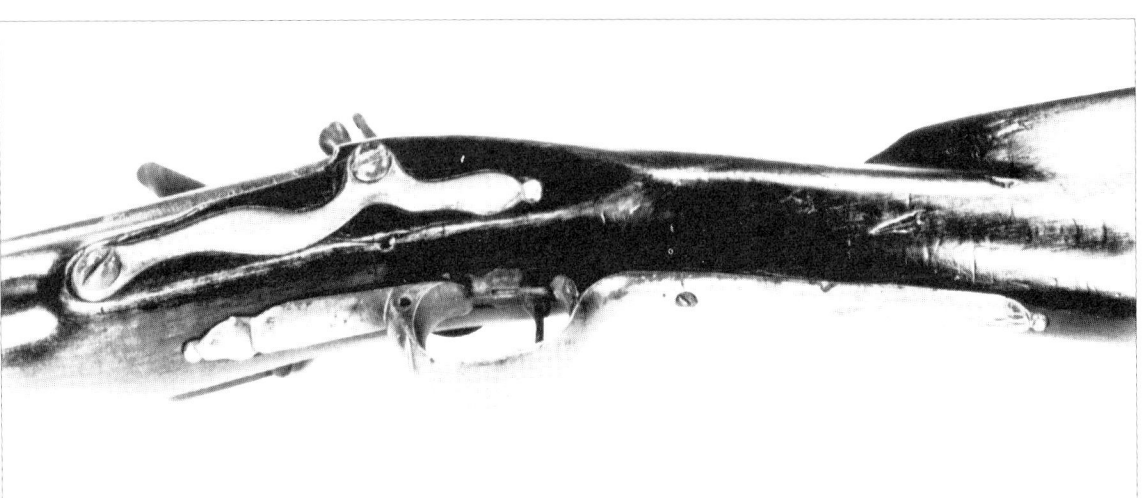

**93.MM AMERICAN MUSKET**　　　　　　　　　　　　　　　　　　　　　　　　　　　　　　　　　　　　　　　　　　　　　　　　　　　　　　　　Circa 1777–1783

An English Long Land musket furnished the lock (marked "EDGE 1756"), trigger guard, side plate, escutcheon and barrel (shortened to 44-1/2") for this American assembled arm. Note also the three colonist-manufactured brass bands with rear side springs of a pattern that denotes French influence, thus suggesting its stocking after the Revolution had begun. The sturdy chestnut stock forms a slightly sloping rear profile which supports a narrow, two-step butt tang. Raised carving around the lock and side plate is minimal; none exists at the barrel tang. Of special interest is the American, hand-forged, replaced cock still holding a broad (1-3/8" across) oval flint of the kind knapped by a private individual in contrast to the smaller rectangular military form. All "three fingers" have been lost from the original Brown Bess frizzen spring finial. Use of this musket as a hunting weapon after the war is indicated by a narrowing of the upper bayonet stud to create a front sighting blade, accompanied by a later dovetail near the breech that secured a rear sight. Like many rebel longarms, there are no sling swivels.

| | | | |
|---|---|---|---|
| Length: 60-1/2" | Lock: 7" X 1-1/4" | Butt Tang: 5-1/2" | Furniture: Brass |
| Barrel: 44-1/2", .78 cal. | Trigger Guard: 11-3/8" | Side Plate: 6-1/4" | Weight: 9.5 lbs. |

**Author's Collection**

Chapter 3: Smoothbore Shoulder Arms　　**143**

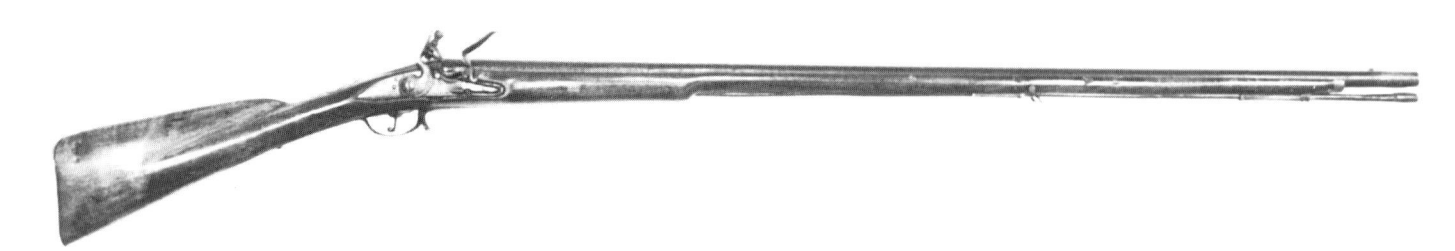

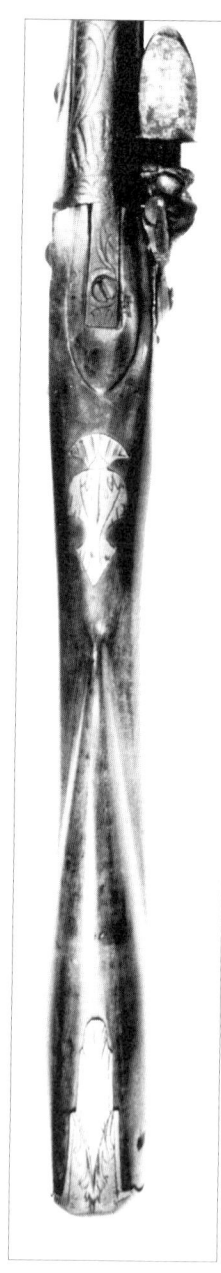

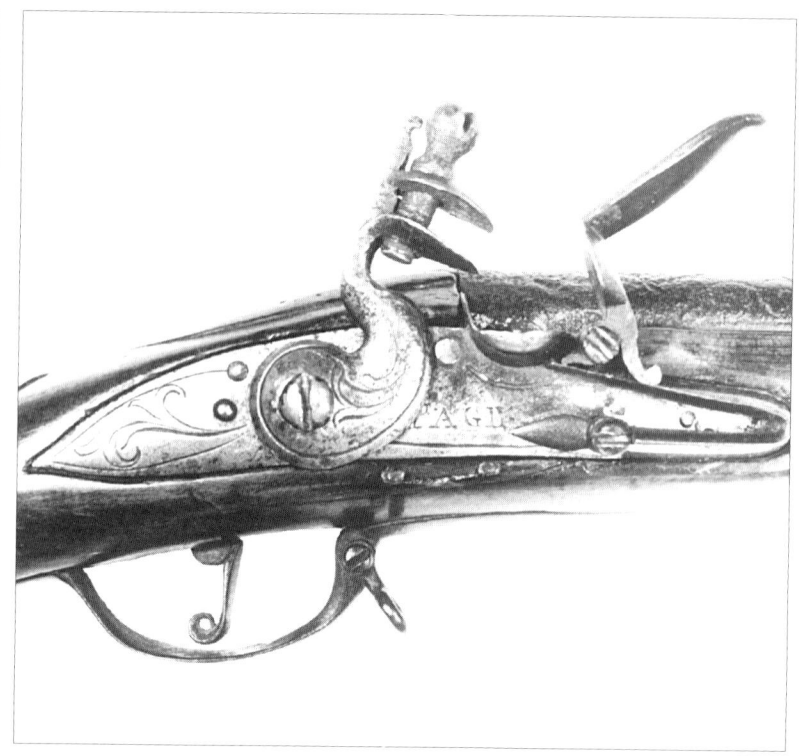

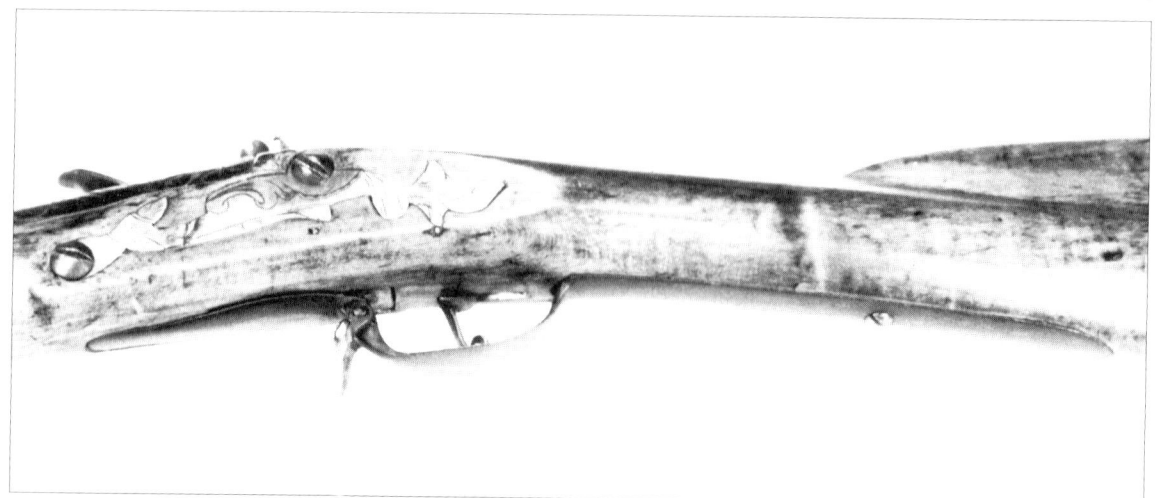

**94.MM AMERICAN FOWLER/FUSIL**             Circa 1770–1780

The light hunting weapon illustrated here has had the forend cut back to mount a bayonet (top stud) in the common practice of adopting a family "meat" gun to satisfy militia requirements. It is marked "PAGE" on the lock plate and is attributed to John Page of Preston, Connecticut, who supplied locks to the Committee of Safety in 1777. This lock, the furniture and even the barrel's breech bear profuse but simplistic Colonial incised designs. A plain French-influenced trigger guard is iron; the remaining furniture is brass. Its unique side plate, in turn, has adopted a crude, almost primitive dragon form, while the escutcheon and blunt-ended two-step butt tang reflect British trade arm styling. Eighteenth century diamond checkering (with the usual center dots) is included in a floral decorative panel (8-1/2") on the barrel breech. The slender apple stock contains a variation of the English beaver-tail barrel tang carving, ends in a brass forend band and holds two elongated rammer thimbles (no tail pipe) for a wooden rod. Also note the use of an early curled trigger form.

| | | | |
|---|---|---|---|
| Length: 57-5/8" | Lock: 5-7/8" X 1" | Butt Tang: 3-3/4" | Furniture: Brass/Iron |
| Barrel: 41-1/4", .60 cal. | Trigger Guard: 11-3/4" | Side Plate: 5-1/8" | Weight: 6.0 lbs. |

**Author's Collection**

*Chapter 3: Smoothbore Shoulder Arms*

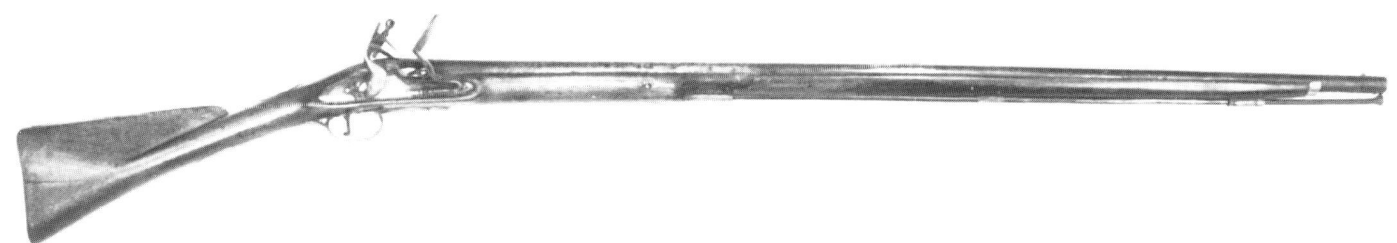

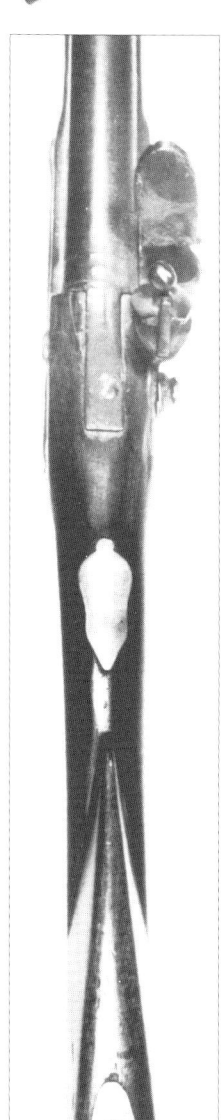

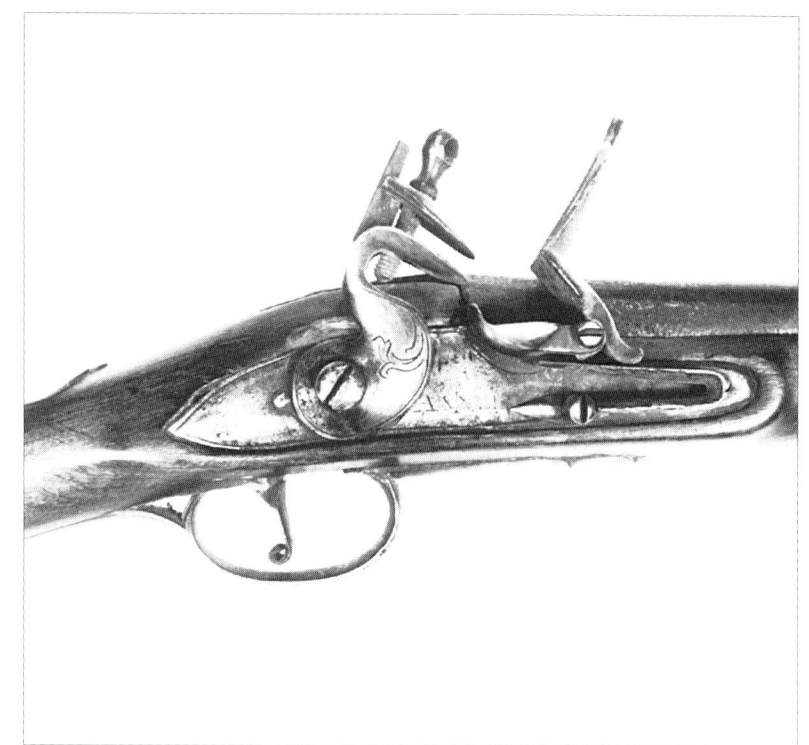

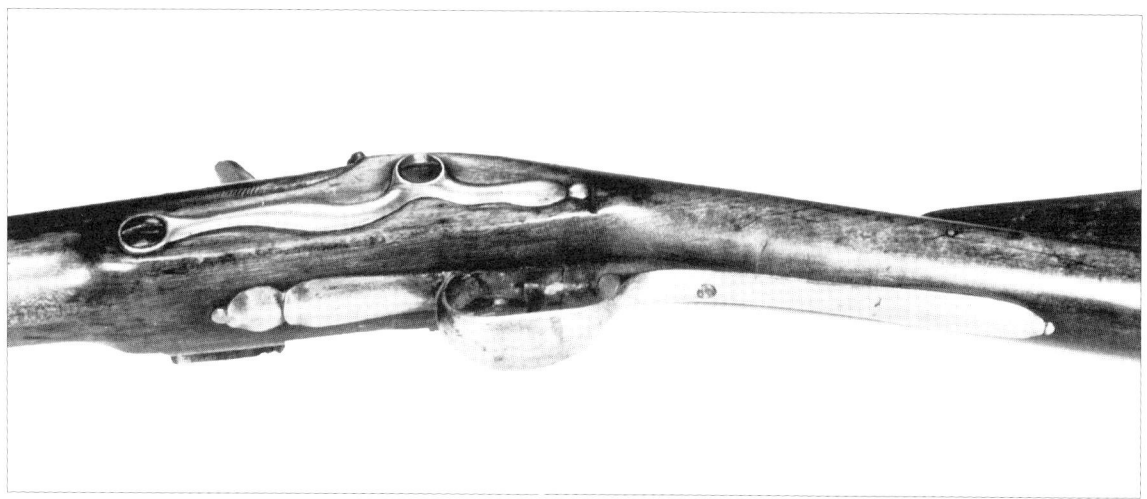

### 95.MM AMERICAN FUSIL
**Circa 1775–1777**

Edward Annely (I) was a gunsmith in New York City and then worked with Thomas Annely in Trenton, New Jersey, from 1770–1777, where they also served as armorers to that colony. (Thomas is later listed in Philadelphia and New York City.) This light musket is believed to have been produced early in the Revolution at Trenton. It is marked "ANNELY" under the lock's pan. The breech's stamp, "P," is possibly a Philadelphia proof, as New Jersey purchased components from Pennsylvania during the War. Brown Bess pattern influence is apparent here in the pinned barrel, rounded lock, shield escutcheon, convex side plate and hazelnut trigger guard. The stubby butt tang, in turn, favors the French form, yet also relates to the Pattern 1760 English light infantry carbine (123.MM). London proofs remain on the old British barrel, and raised carving (a convenience of peacetime) is missing from the maple stock. Also visible is the American simplification of the lock form—using a plain rectangular post on the cock, plus a spearhead frizzen spring tip.

| | | | |
|---|---|---|---|
| Length: 56-3/4" | Lock: 6-1/8" X 1-1/8" | Butt Tang: 2-3/4" | Furniture: Brass |
| Barrel: 41-1/4", .65 cal. | Trigger Guard: 10-3/4" | Side Plate: 5-3/4" | Weight: 7.5 lbs. |

**Robert Nittolo Collection**

*Chapter 3: Smoothbore Shoulder Arms* **145**

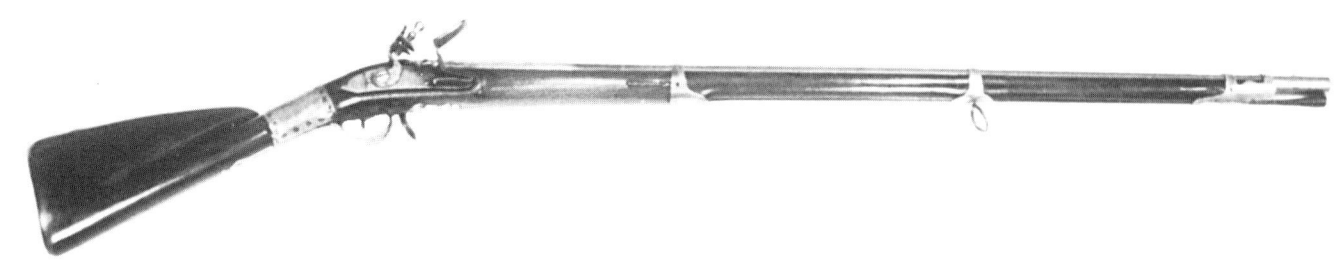

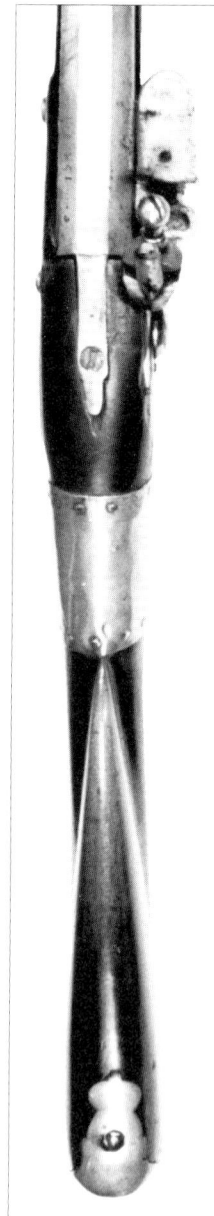

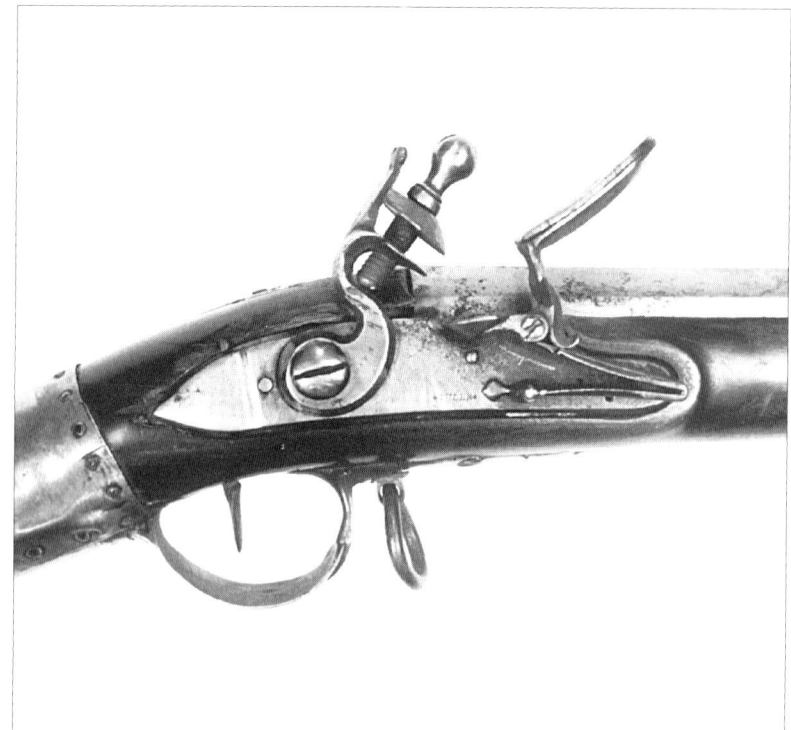

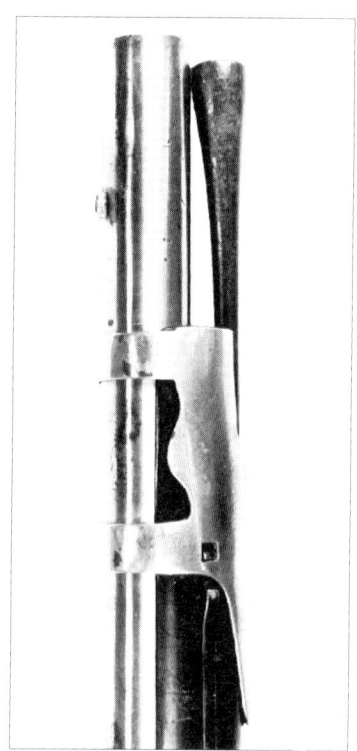

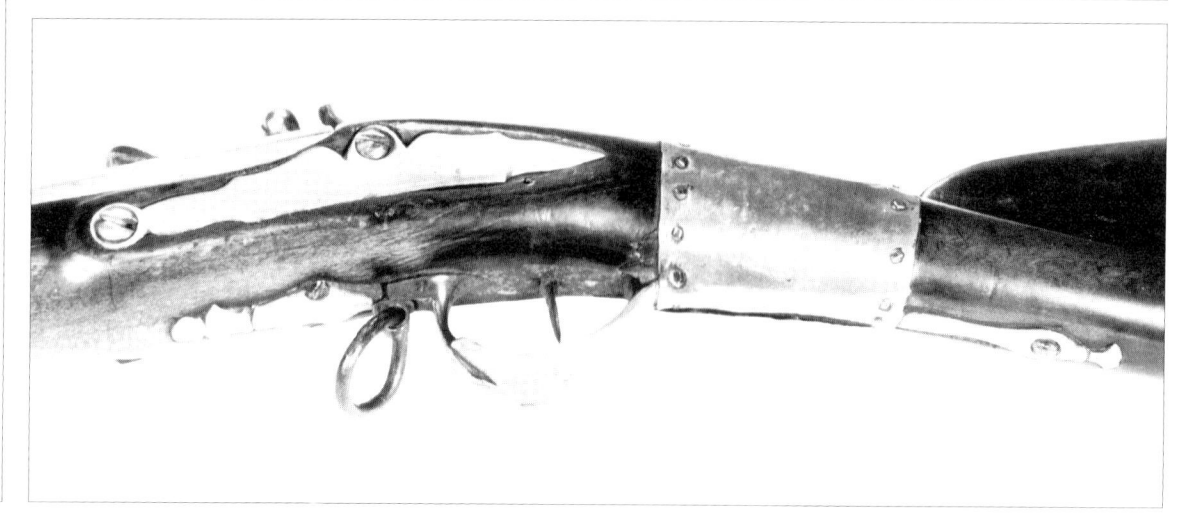

**96.MM AMERICAN FUSIL**  Circa 1755–1765

The reduced-size lock and barrel in this arm are both marked "TULLE," the private manufactory that supplied most of France's marine troops in Canada until 1755. The remainder of the weapon, however, appears to be a restocking of mostly mid-century French brass parts to create a light fusil, probably in North America by the English colonists. Its high comb buttstock follows French styling, but it is cherry and includes a typical sheet-brass repair on the wrist. In addition the original tips of the brass butt tang and trigger guard were cut off before restocking. The barrel tang is partially replaced and the crude sling swivels are round. Rear retaining springs exist for the top and bottom barrel bands (the middle one is held by friction). The flat Tulle lock includes a slash across the tail, a bridled flash pan and a cut-back replaced upper cock jaw. Its octagon breech measures 6-3/4 inches (no raised rings).

| | | | |
|---|---|---|---|
| Length: 54-1/2" | Lock: 5-1/2" X 1" | Butt Tang: 2-5/8" | Furniture: Brass |
| Barrel: 38-3/4", .72 cal. | Trigger Guard: 10" | Side Plate: 5-1/4" | Weight: 7.2 lbs. |

**Author's Collection**

146  *Chapter 3: Smoothbore Shoulder Arms*

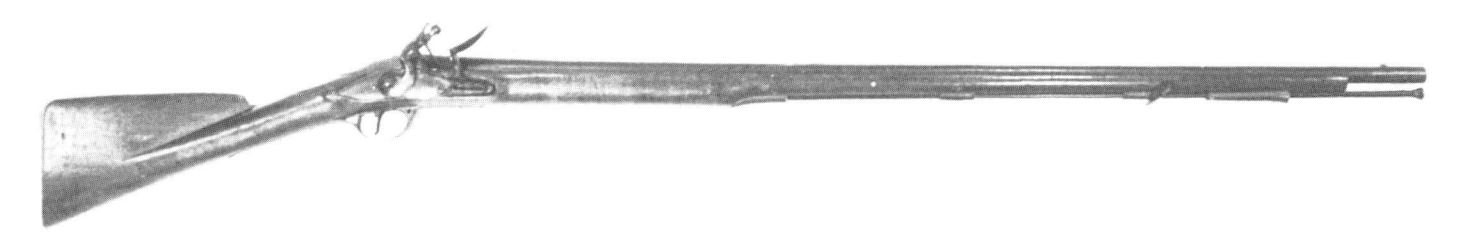

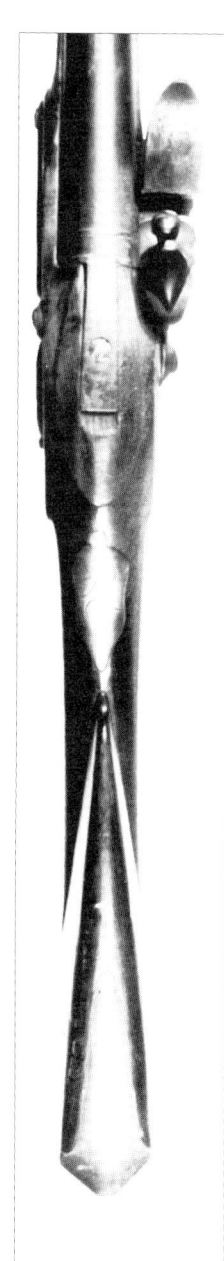

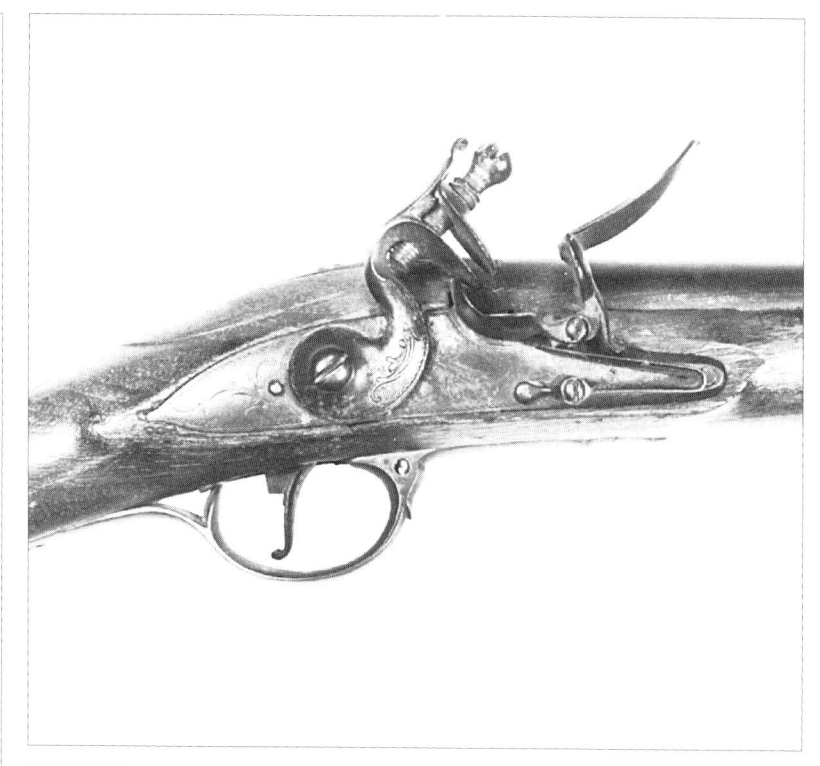

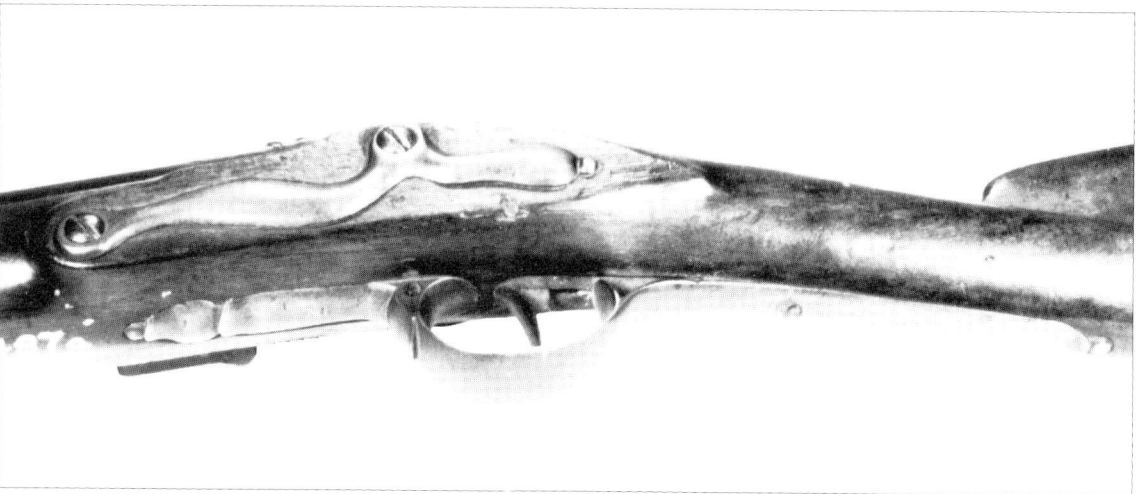

**97.MM AMERICAN FUSIL**  Circa 1774–1780

"NICHOLSON PHILADA" is engraved along the breech of this American officer's fusil, which has adopted a scaled-down English Long Land musket pattern (10.MM). John Nicholson is listed as a Philadelphia gunsmith from 1774 to 1799 who had Committee of Safety contracts. Partial private British proofs remain on the barrel, while American copies of the hazelnut trigger guard, convex side plate, beaver-tail carving, shield escutcheon, three-step butt tang, walnut stock configuration and four rammer thimbles also establish influence from the former mother country. The rounded two-screw lock includes double bridles and a thick teardrop tip on the frizzen spring. Vine engraving in the lock plate and cock are similar to British commercial trade locks of that period. The original bayonet still accompanies this firearm (3-1/4" socket, 14-3/8" blade, 18-1/2" overall; English pattern). Its rear sling swivel is missing.

| | | | |
|---|---|---|---|
| Length: 56" | Lock: 6" X 1-1/8" | Butt Tang: 4-3/8" | Furniture: Brass |
| Barrel: 40-1/4", .62 cal. | Trigger Guard: 10-1/4" | Side Plate: 5-1/2" | Weight: 7.5 lbs. |

**West Point Museum Collection**

*Chapter 3: Smoothbore Shoulder Arms*

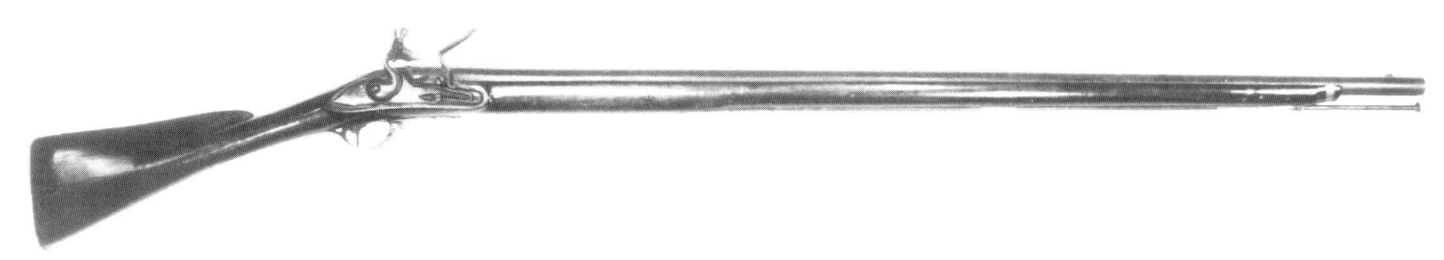

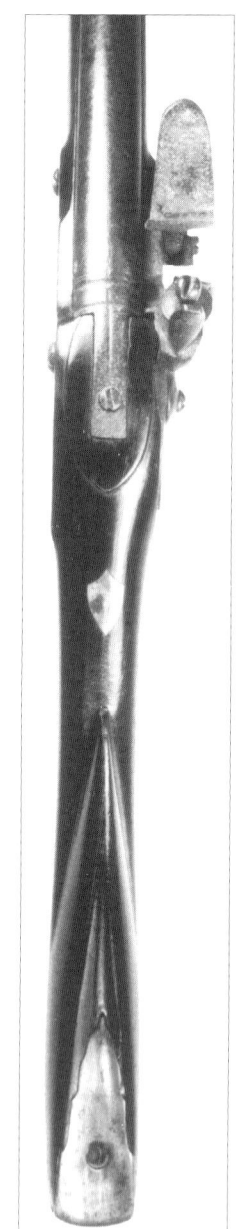

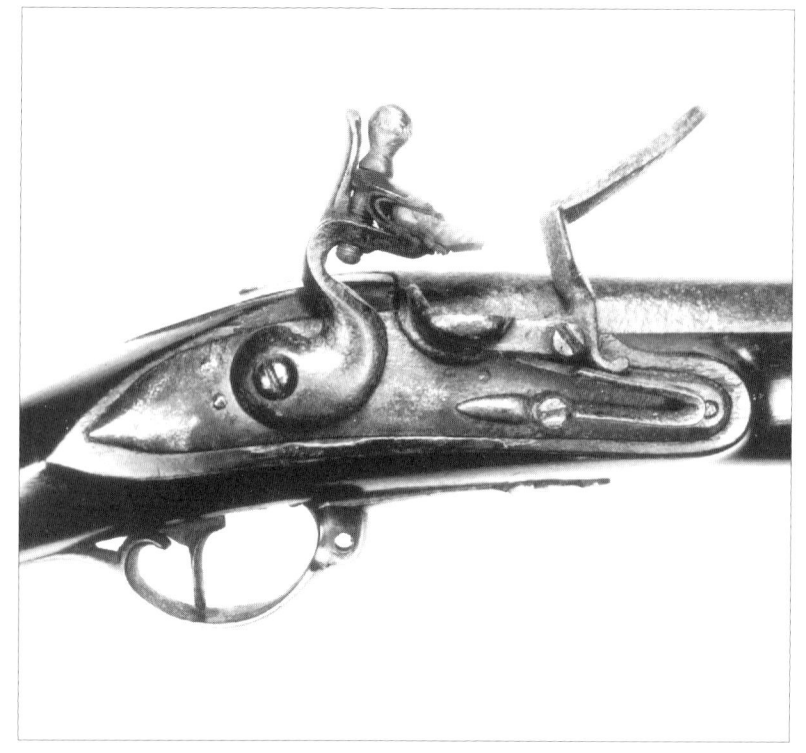

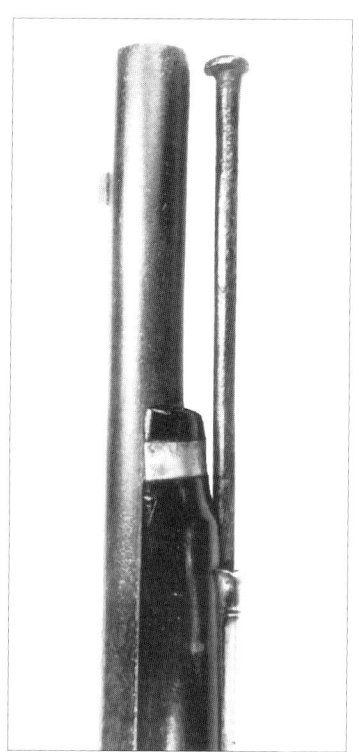

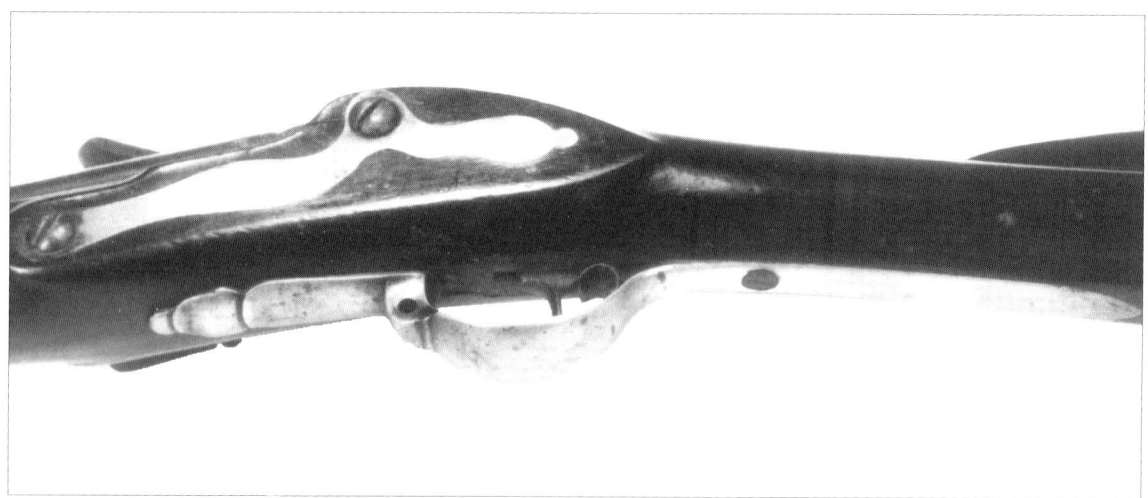

**98.MM  AMERICAN MUSKET**  Circa 1775–1783

The established English pinned barrel pattern is evident here, but variations suggest that all of it is probably of American manufacture. Even the lock, which approximates a common British commercial form, has a squat cock and expanded frizzen spring finial more typical of provincial sources. The arm is attributed to Phineas Sawyer, a gunsmith in Harvard, Massachusetts, from 1772 to 1800 (also see 114.MM), where he was producing military firearms at least by February 1775. This 44" barrel includes baluster breech rings yet adds two non-British type adjacent lines and a squared breech tang, as well as the initials "PS" (no proof marks). Notice also the American pointed butt tang with a top retaining screw plus the flattened side plate—both similar to England's marine or militia musket (12.MM, 13.MM). Its pointed beaver-tail carving and brass hazelnut trigger guard, in turn, are Colonial copies of the Brown Bess pattern, while the three ramrod thimbles of sheet brass hold a button-head rammer. As seen on many American muskets, there is no forward hole for a sling swivel and a narrow brass strip binds the end of its maple stock. The shield escutcheon of bone is a later private owner's addition.

Length: 60-3/8"  
Barrel: 44", .74 cal.  
Lock: 6-1/4" X 1-1/4"  
Trigger Guard: 10-1/2"  
Butt Tang: 4-1/8"  
Side Plate: 6"  
Furniture: Brass  
Weight: 9.8 lbs.

**Douglas Neumann Collection**

*148     Chapter 3: Smoothbore Shoulder Arms*

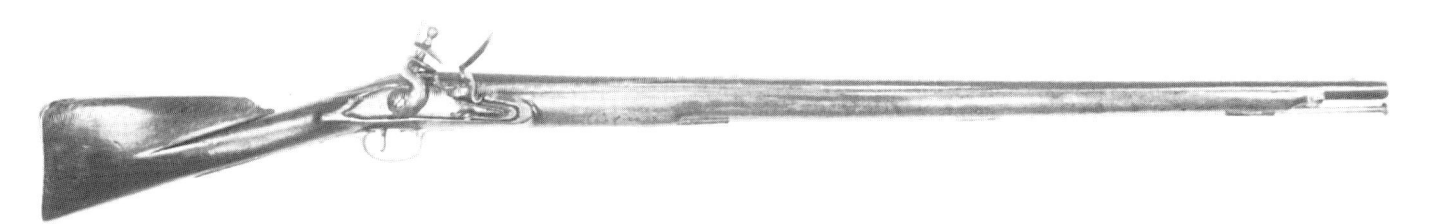

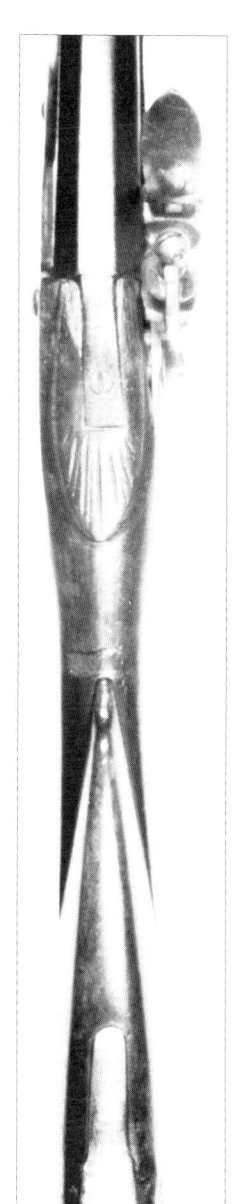

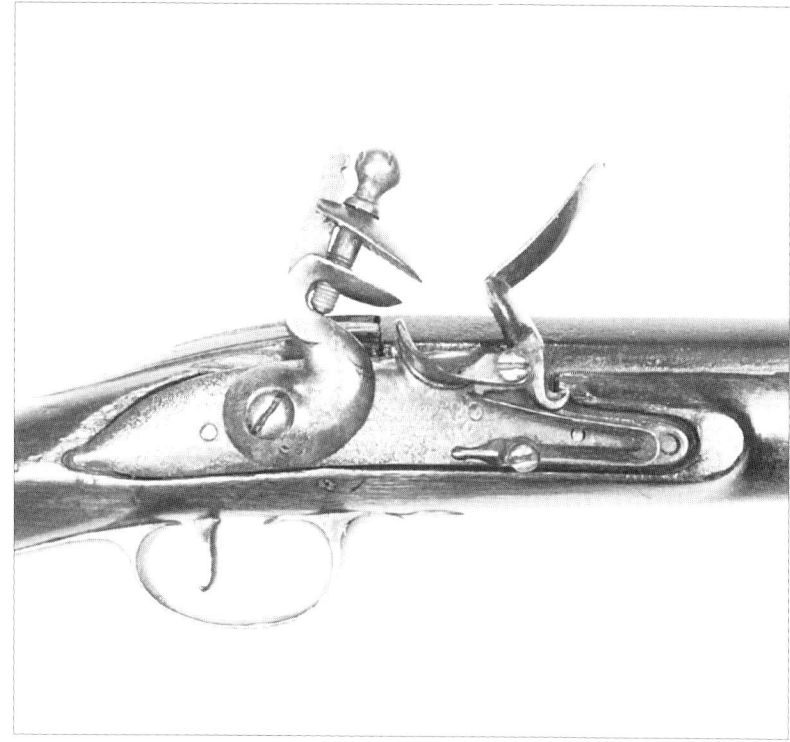

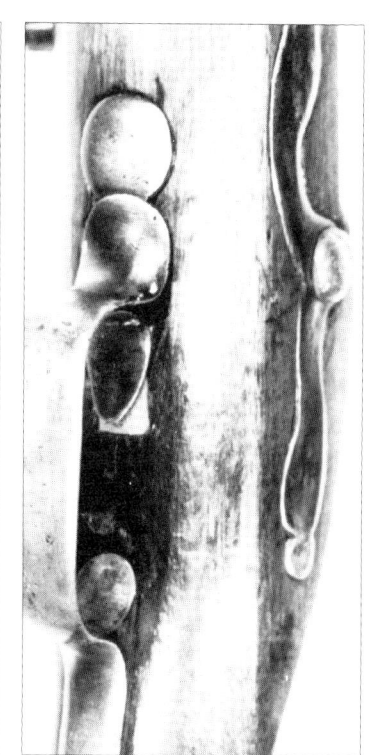

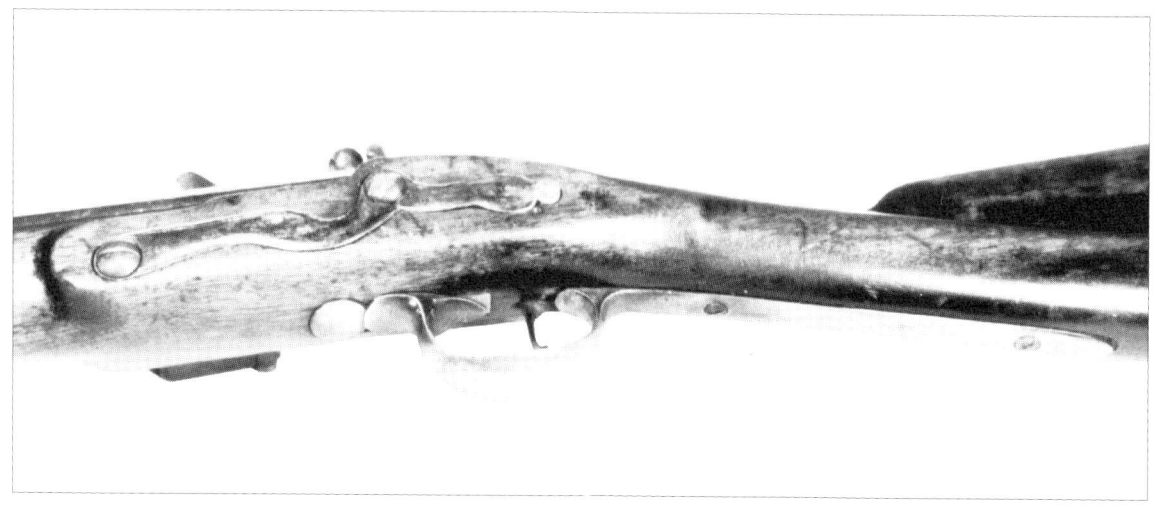

**99.MM  AMERICAN (NAVAL) MUSKET**                                                                                                                                                      **Circa 1775–1783**

The rounded lock illustrated here with its forward notch on the hammer's upper post and narrow frizzen spring tip is typical of many of the commercial patterns made by English gunmakers for private use in the 1770s. The remainder of this short-barreled musket appears to be of Colonial origin, possibly for use aboard ship. Its ball-shaped trigger guard terminal is naval in form, and the absence of an escutcheon, the straightened version of Britain's flat sea service side plate, the omission of a trigger plate, plus the lobe-ended butt tang reinforce that possibility (see 29.MM). The short 39-5/8" barrel has a full musket size bore (.76 caliber) as well as a top stud for the bayonet. Judging by the width of the breech (1-1/2 inches across; octagonal for 10-3/4 inches), it might have been cut down from a long fowler. The familiar beaver-tail carving has had radiating lines added. There was no formal American naval musket pattern, as their limited commissioned ships and privateers relied on whatever was obtainable.

| | | | |
|---|---|---|---|
| Length: 55-3/4" | Lock: 6-7/8" X 1-1/4" | Butt Tang: 4" | Furniture: Brass |
| Barrel: 39-5/8", .76 cal. | Trigger Guard: 10-3/4" | Side Plate: 6" | Weight: 10.2 lbs. |
| Author's Collection | | | |

Chapter 3: Smoothbore Shoulder Arms

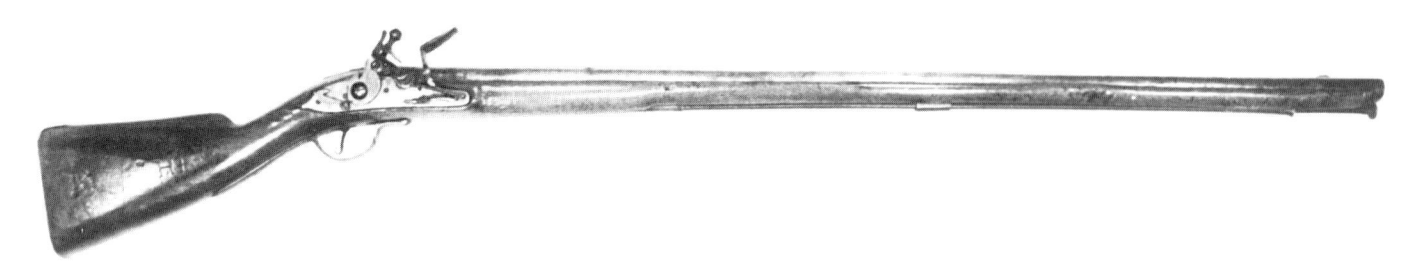

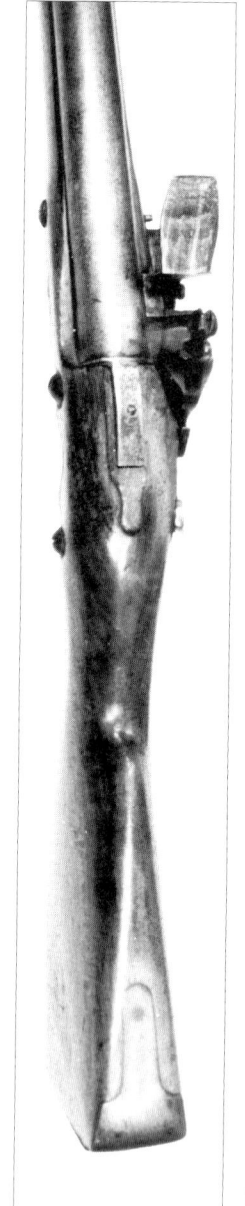

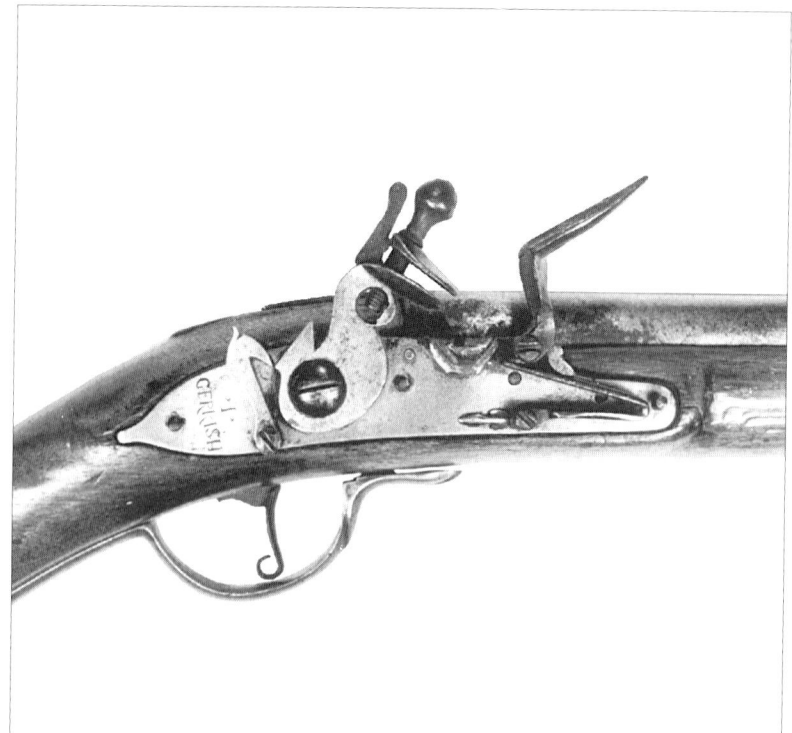

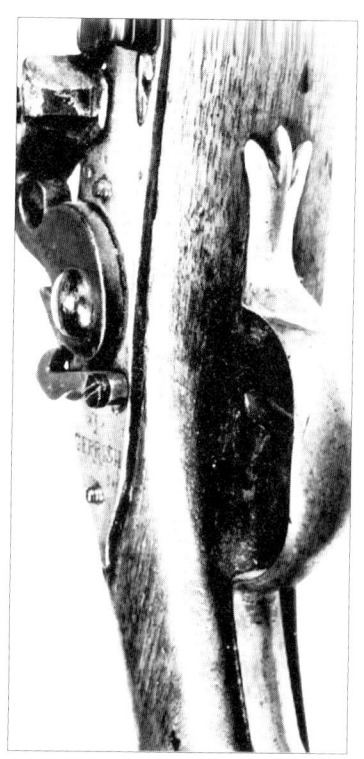

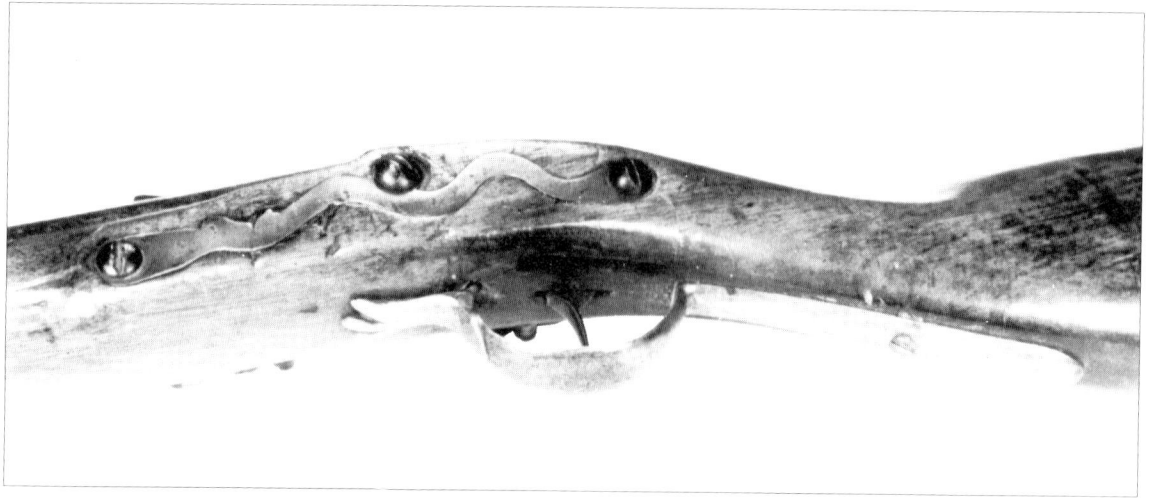

### 100.MM  AMERICAN FOWLER
**Circa 1710**

This is an American version of the traditional English fowler at the beginning of the 18th century. It was a heavily stocked form developed to fire a large load of multiple shot with a weak powder charge at water birds on the surface, from a flat-bottomed punt (boat) or a stationary shore location. The locally cast brass three-fingered trigger guard is unusual, but its three-screw flat doglock (squared frizzen, ring cock, no external bridle) and flat nailed butt plate are typical of this Queen Anne period. A flat undulating side plate shaped in an early dragon outline without engraved features also appears on contemporary trade arms (for example, 149.MM). The thick walnut stock, in turn, continues to the muzzle, ending in a sheet-brass nose band. Its barrel mounts both front and rear fixed sights, while a bottom screw reaches up to hold the breech tang. A crudely forged ramrod rests in three plain thimbles. The rifled bore is a rarity at this early date, especially in New England. "I GERRISH" (John Gerrish, a prominent Boston businessman) is engraved on the lock's tail.

| | | | |
|---|---|---|---|
| Length: 58-1/4" | Lock: 7-1/8" X 1-1/4" | Butt Tang: 3-1/2" | Furniture: Brass |
| Barrel: 43-1/2", .80 cal. | Trigger Guard: 9-3/8" | Side Plate: 7" | Weight: 10.5 lbs. |

**Robert Nittolo Collection**

*Chapter 3: Smoothbore Shoulder Arms*

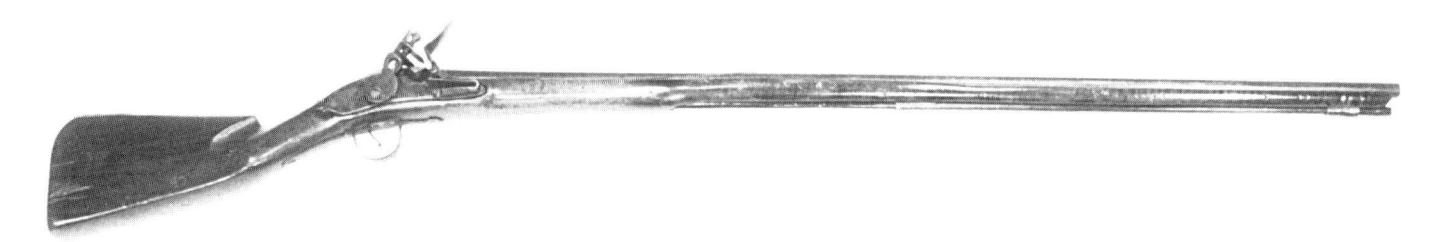

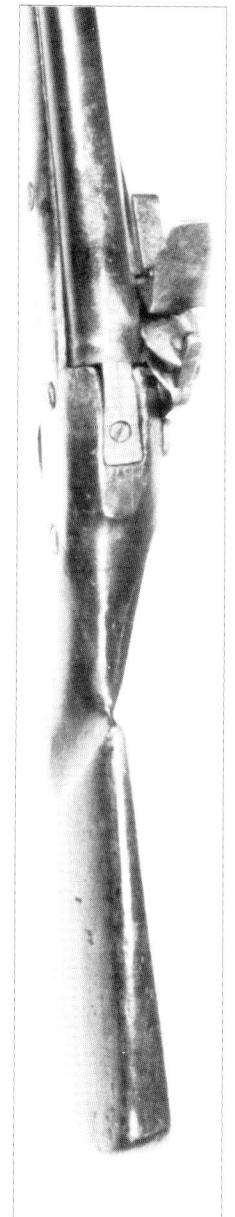

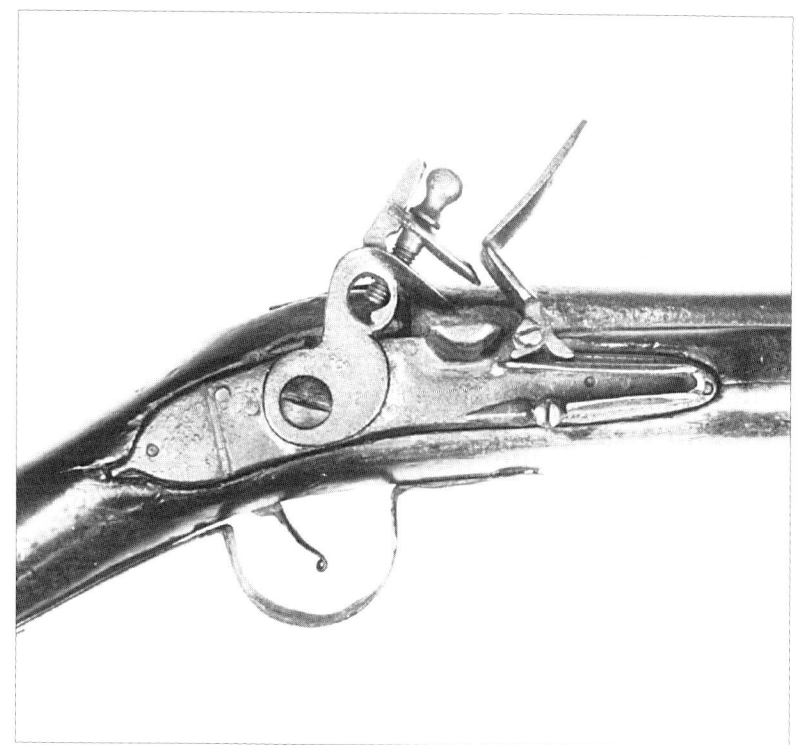

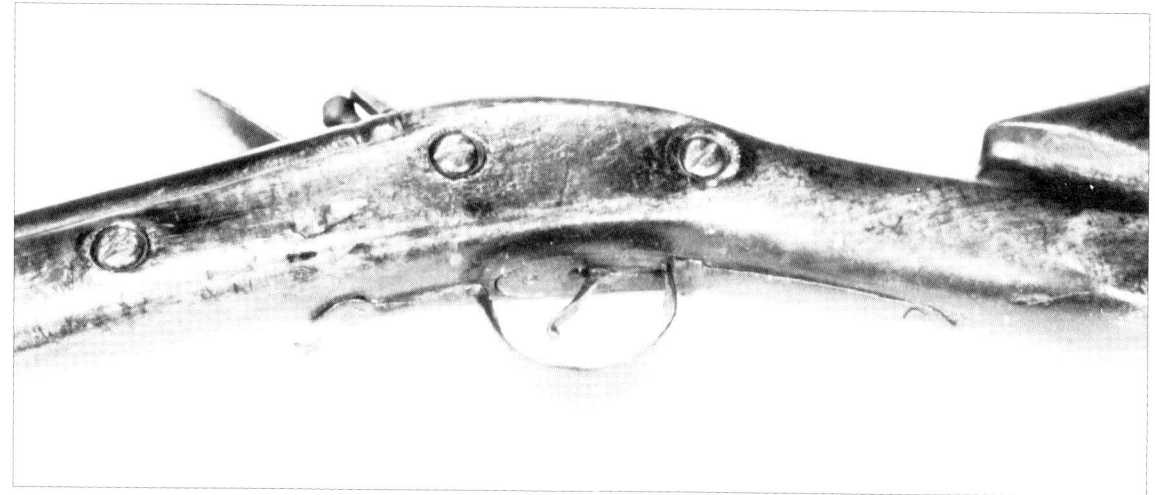

**101.MM  AMERICAN CLUB BUTT FOWLER**  Circa 1720–1750

The early colonists brought European weapons with them and continued a number of those patterns in the arms produced here. Among the popular forms was the heavy club butt. Unlike most of the well-crafted hunting arms of the Old World, many of the provincials' creations were sturdy and unadorned "meat" guns intended only to feed poor farming families. Thus this fowler is stocked to the muzzle in maple but dispenses with all but the very basic components—omitting a butt plate, side plate and raised carving. The spear-headed iron strap trigger guard is locally forged, and its flat lock with a ringed cock and enlarged tail appears to be an American product following the English pattern just after the dog latch was dropped (2.MM). Its round barrel (baluster breech ring) includes an early replaced breech plug. Two plain sheet-brass pipes secure a wooden rod. "CB," carved twice in the buttstock, is probably an owner's initials. Family hunting guns such as this saw considerable military service with the militia throughout the Revolutionary War.

Length: 60"  
Barrel: 45", .70 cal.  
Lock: 7" X 1-1/8"  
Trigger Guard: 7-1/8"  
Furniture: Iron/Brass  
Weight: 7.5 lbs.

**Author's Collection**

*Chapter 3: Smoothbore Shoulder Arms*  **151**

**102.MM AMERICAN CLUB BUTT FOWLER**                                                  Circa 1755–1780

The club butt fowler illustrated here has a Boston, Massachusetts, association. Like most American arms created in the Colonial period, mixed components were employed when available. This flat/beveled banana lock (probably American, with an early pinned repair in the cock's neck) shows contemporary French–Low Country influence. Its ornamental trigger guard reflects Dutch exposure, and the butt plate plus three rammer thimbles are reused from a British Long Land Brown Bess musket. The side plate is a period European design. A common sheet-brass (nailed) patch to repair a damaged wrist covers most of the escutcheon. Note, too, the splayed carving behind the barrel tang, which is typical of many New England gunmakers. Its long striped maple stock, in turn, reaches to the muzzle (1/2" brass nose band). Fowlers of such length and weight were normally employed for firing at waterfowl from a fixed position. The long 48-1/2" barrel (round, ringed at 12-1/2 inches) supposedly allowed time for the slow burning black powder to exert its full thrust. As the century progressed, barrel length was reduced as experience proved otherwise.

| | | | |
|---|---|---|---|
| Length: 64-1/2" | Lock: 6-5/8" X 1-1/2" | Butt Tang: 5-3/4" | Furniture: Brass |
| Barrel: 48-1/2", .75 cal. | Trigger Guard: 9-1/2" | Side Plate: 6-1/4" | Weight: 10.4 lbs. |

**Author's Collection**

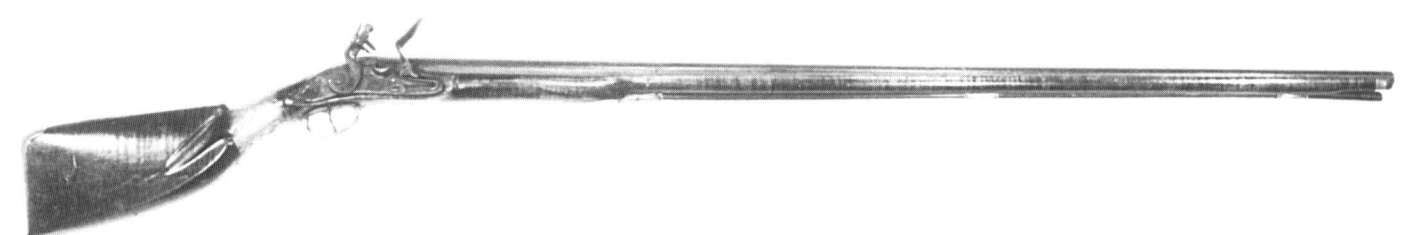

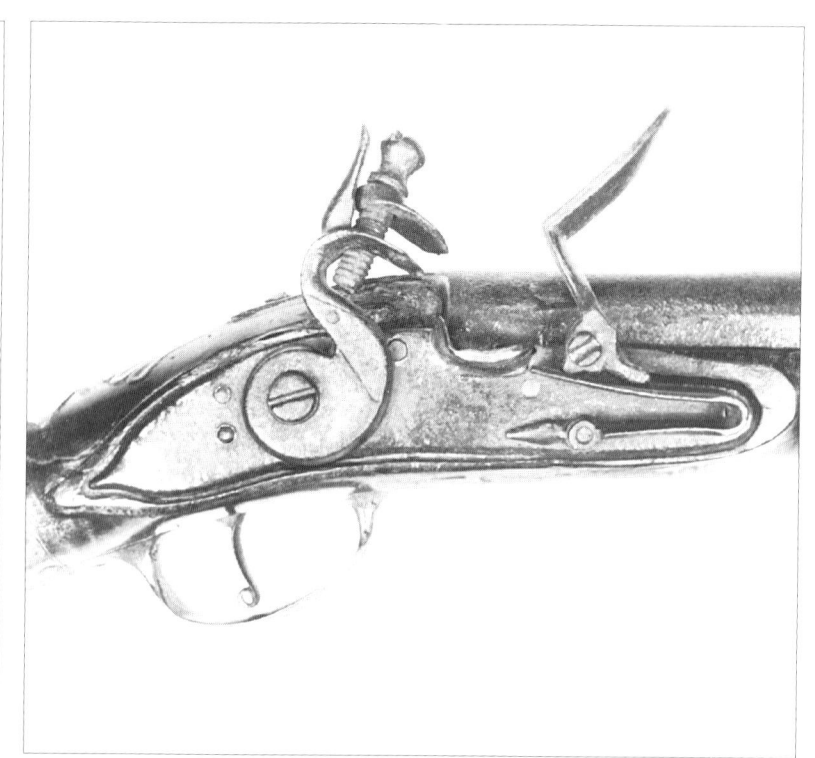

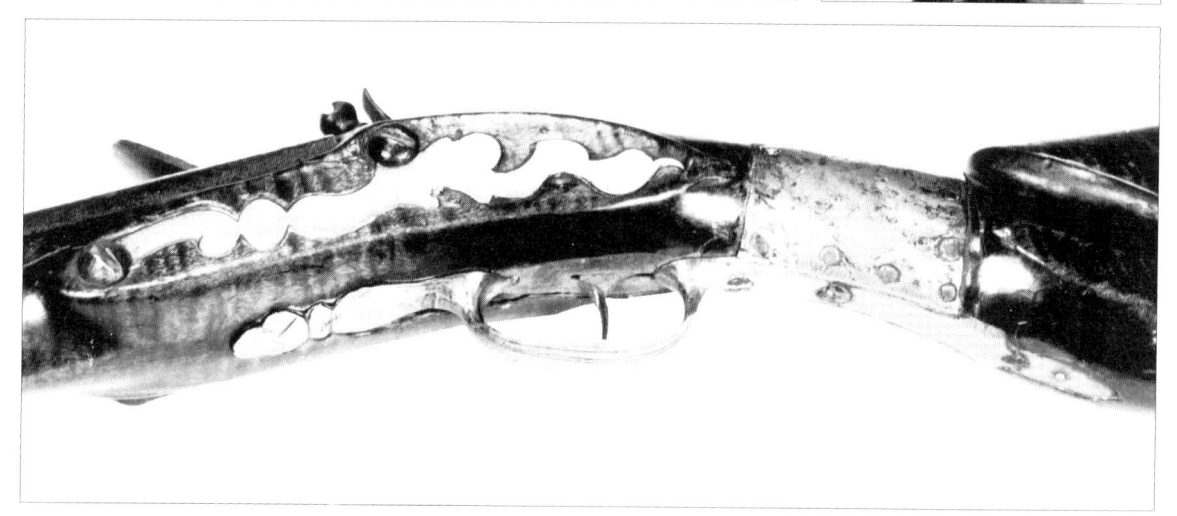

*Chapter 3: Smoothbore Shoulder Arms*

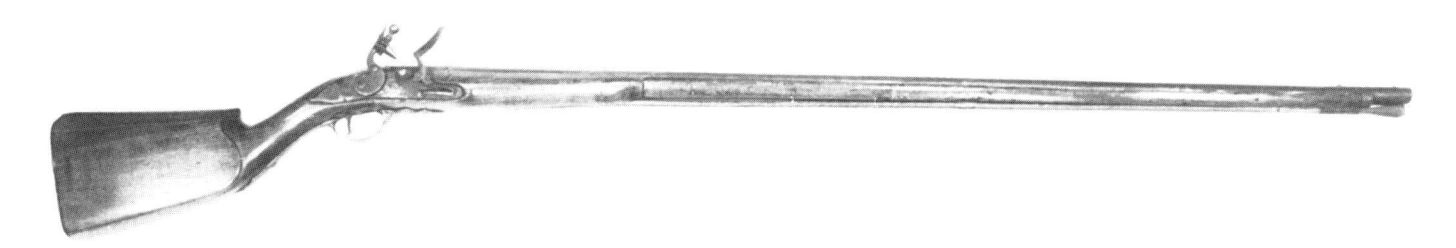

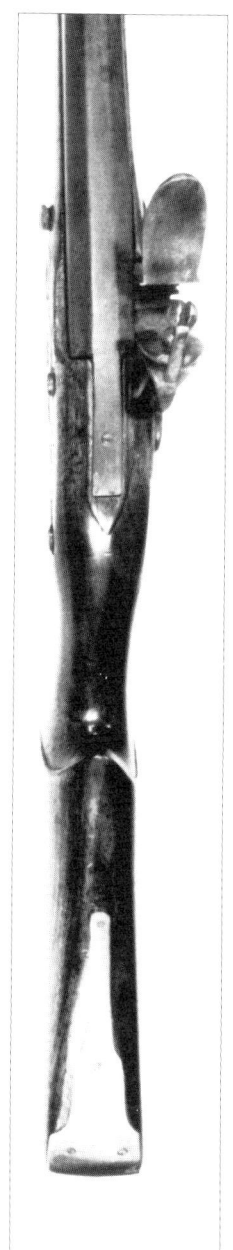

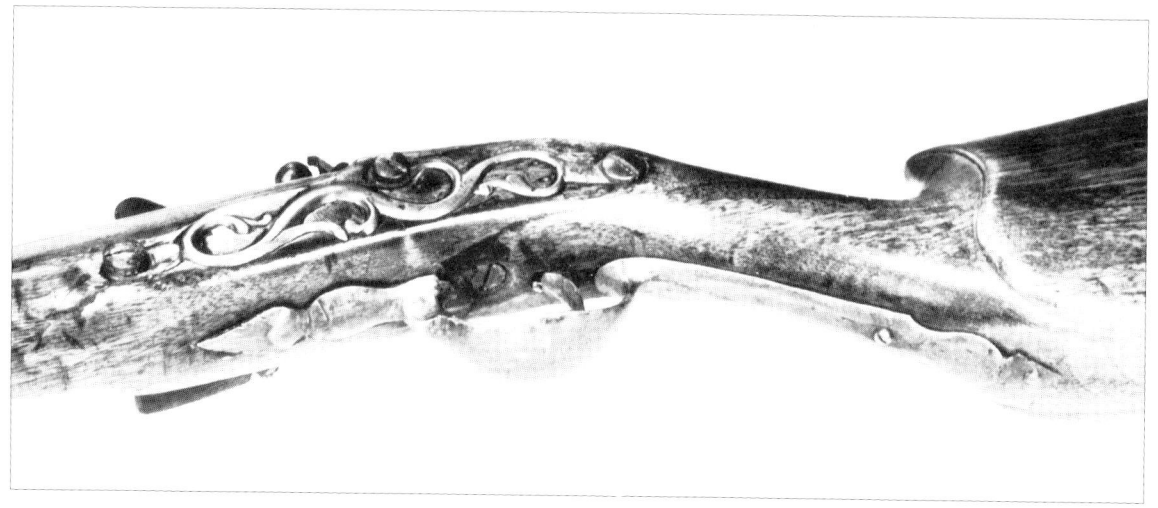

**103.MM AMERICAN CLUB BUTT FOWLER**  Circa 1760–1770

Edward Annely was a gunsmith in New York City before moving to Trenton, New Jersey, in 1770, where he worked with Thomas Annely (see 95.MM). This club butt fowler is believed to date during his New York period. Although the butt form is conservative with virtually no raised carving, its long butt tang (nailed), open vine form side plate and bulbous trigger guard show Dutch influence, which was present there and in the Hudson Valley. Notice, too the locally made, flat three-screw lock that shows a period patch on the neck of its cock, omission of both an outer bridle and frizzen spring finial, and the line engraving decorating the tail and adding a foliage design under the pan with his name, "E ANNELY." The walnut stock apparently had a section removed above the ramrod entry, and the remaining forend moved backward to create space at the muzzle for a socket bayonet (both a front sight and a top bayonet stud survive). Two plain thimbles hold a wooden rammer, while a bottom screw pierces the stock to secure the barrel tang. There is no trigger plate.

| | | | |
|---|---|---|---|
| Length: 62-1/2" | Lock: 6-3/4" X 1-1/4" | Butt Tang: 5-1/4" | Furniture: Brass |
| Barrel: 47-1/4", .75 cal. | Trigger Guard: 10-3/4" | Side Plate: 6-1/2" | Weight: 7.8 lbs. |

**Robert Nittolo Collection**

*Chapter 3: Smoothbore Shoulder Arms*    153

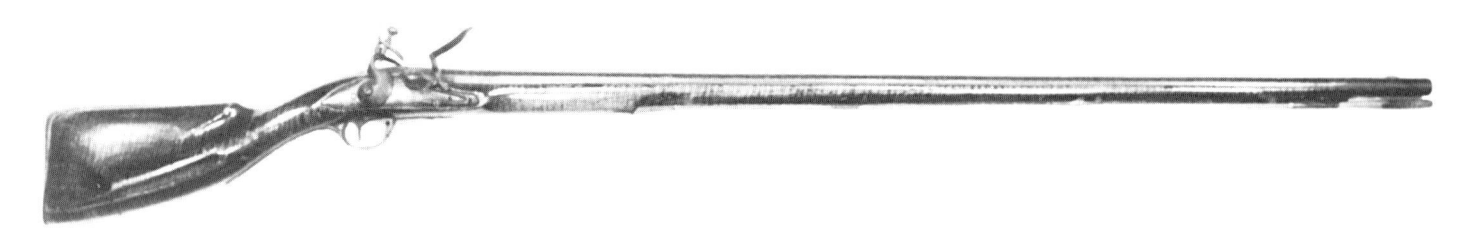

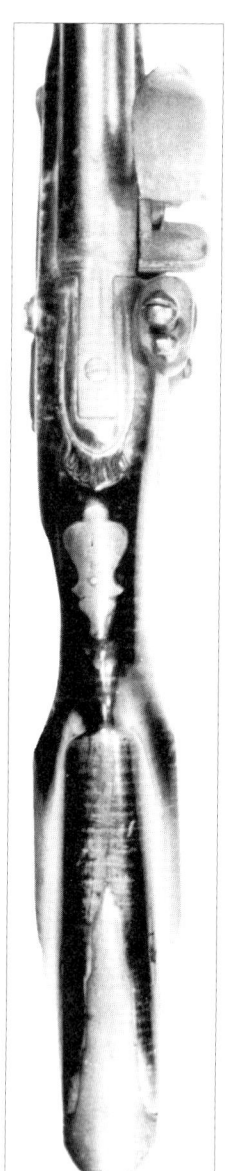

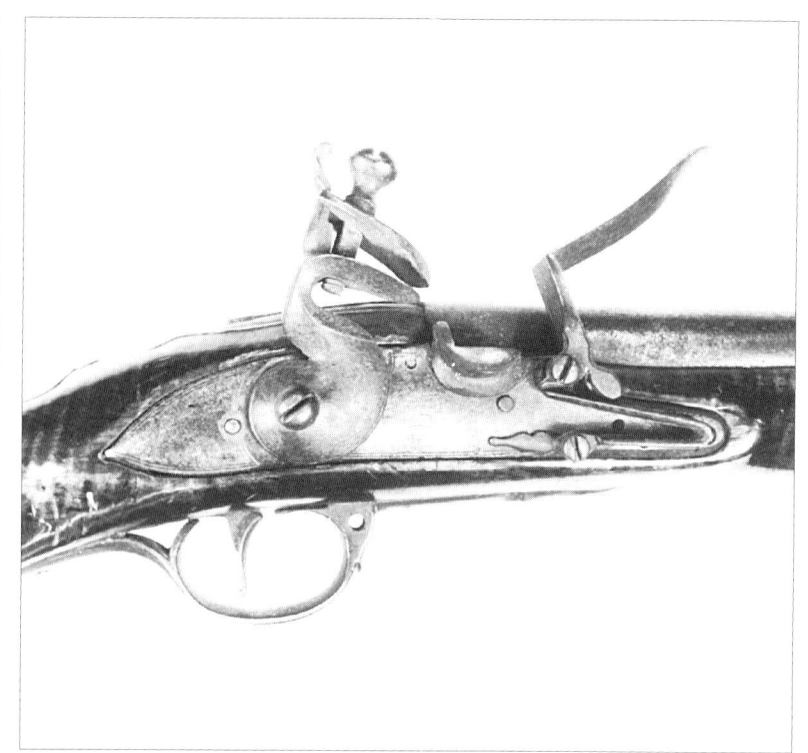

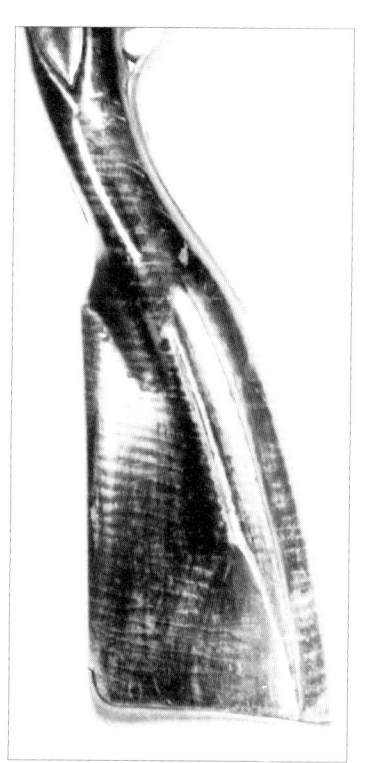

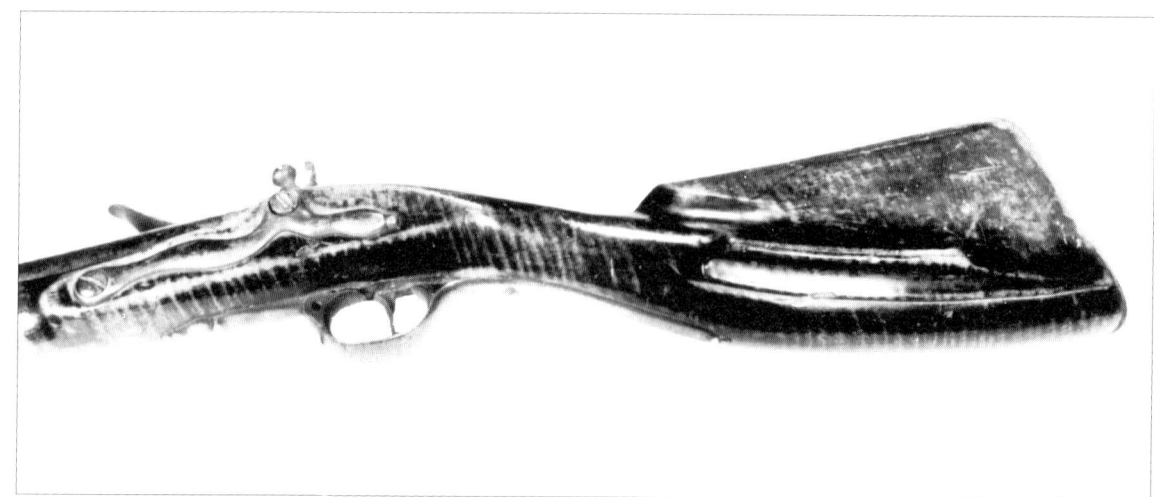

**104.MM  AMERICAN CLUB BUTT FOWLER**  Circa 1760–1785

English Long Land muskets furnished most of the components for this Massachusetts club butt. Its British 48" barrel (two inches longer than standard) is marked "Ks OWN REGT" (4th Regiment, "the King's Own"), while "XV / C / 53" (that is, 15th Regiment, 3rd company, gun number 53) appears on the trigger guard bow. Both units served in North America during the Revolution. The convex side plate, trigger guard and three-step butt tang also originated on a King's musket. Its straight British Brown Bess lock, in turn, has replaced the original cock. An impressive Colonial striped maple club butt includes substantial cheek projections on both sides. Note also the relief cape carving above an attractive scalloped escutcheon that was held by a center pin and inscribed with a British fraction, "E / 12." Its stock ends four inches below the muzzle, which mounts a front blade sight. The absence of a bayonet stud suggests this exposed muzzle space permitted an easier grip and withdrawal of the wooden ramrod, especially when covered with powder fouling (four thimbles present).

| | | | |
|---|---|---|---|
| Length: 64-3/4" | Lock: 7-1/8" X 1-1/4" | Butt Tang: 5-3/4" | Furniture: Brass |
| Barrel: 48-1/8", .78 cal. | Trigger Guard: 11-1/4" | Side Plate: 6-1/8" | Weight: 11.0 lbs. |

**Richard Ulbrich Collection**

*Chapter 3: Smoothbore Shoulder Arms*

### 105.MM AMERICAN FOWLER

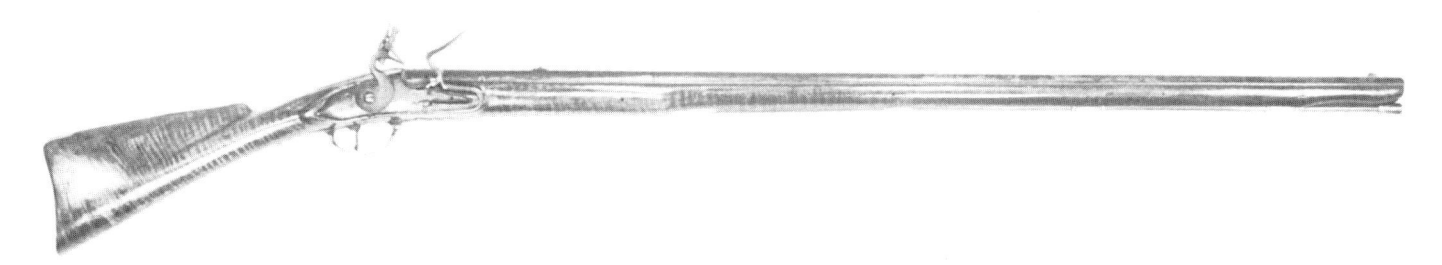

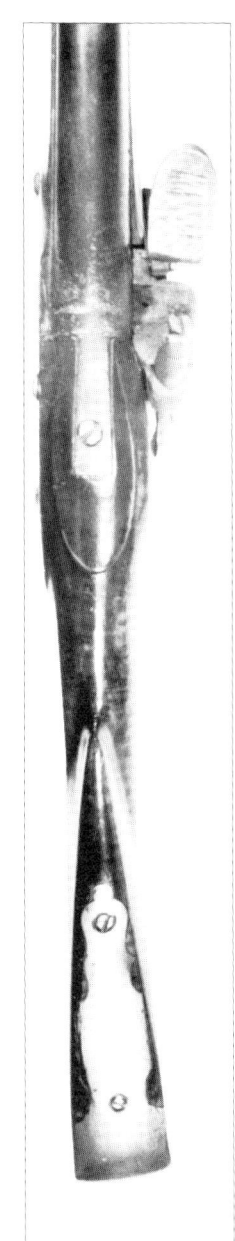

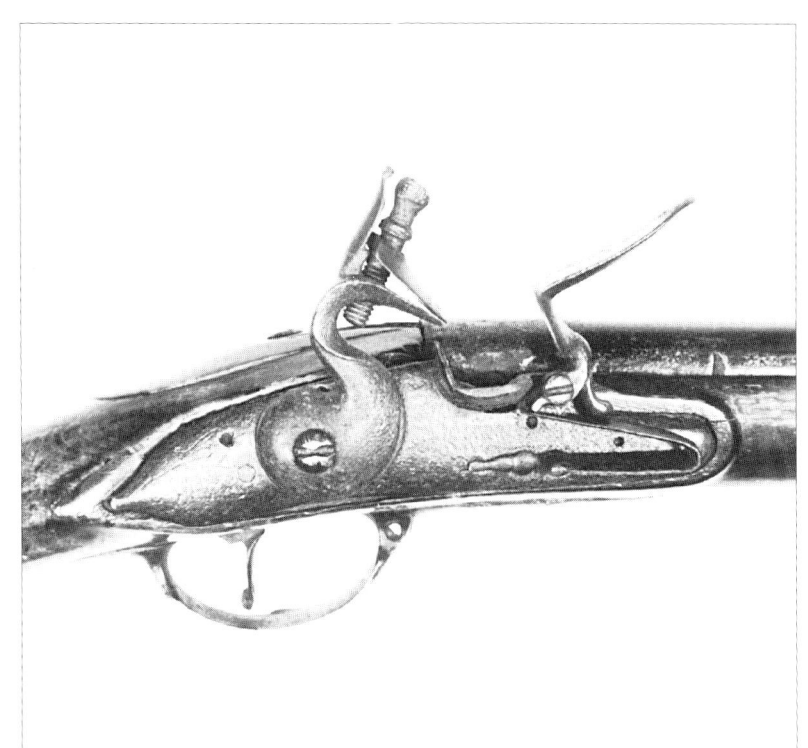

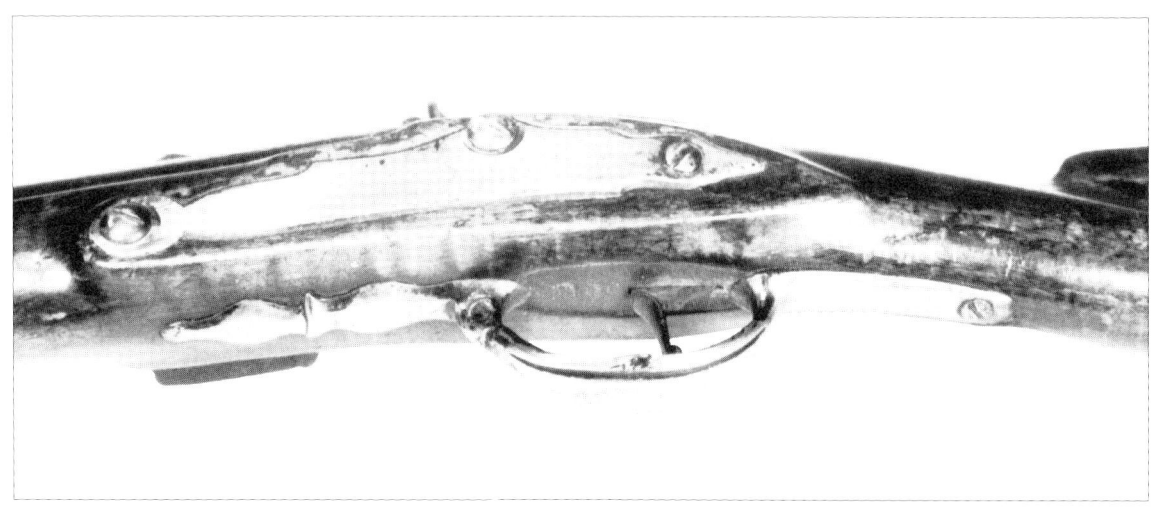

Circa 1760—1790

Some believe the only Germanic military muskets that reached the New World prior to the end of the Revolutionary War came with the German mercenaries. Throughout the colonial period, however, a mother country's colonies were the dumping grounds for her obsolete, damaged and surplus arms—as well as the numerous unwanted captured weapons and battlefield pickups from the continual 18th century wars. Moreover, the American Colonies and local sources purchased mixed cargos of arms direct from agents across Europe. This fowler, for example, has a striped maple American stock bearing the English beaver-tail tang carving but completes the gun with a Germanic infantry musket's components, including the early rounded lock (old coat of arms still on its tail), the triangular side plate (rear short wood screw), a wide scalloped butt tang (two top screws) and a trigger guard with its end cut off (probably damaged or to minimize inletting work). The heavy barrel mounts two sights; its forend extends to the muzzle. Also notice the original butt patch added to replace a knot.

| | | | |
|---|---|---|---|
| Length: 57-1/4" | Lock: 6-1/2" X 1-1/2" | Butt Tang: 5-3/4" | Furniture: Brass |
| Barrel: 42-3/8", .73 cal. | Trigger Guard: 8-1/8" | Side Plate: 6-1/4" | Weight: 8.4 lbs. |

**Author's Collection**

Chapter 3: Smoothbore Shoulder Arms  **155**

### 106.MM  AMERICAN FOWLER  Circa 1760–1790

To most farmers the hunting gun was simply a utilitarian means to help feed and protect the family. Therefore it was not necessary to invest large amounts of time or expense to create a showpiece. The two important components were a reliable lock and a barrel. As illustrated in this fowler, the owner reused a flat lock from a French Model 1728 musket (marked "crown / SE," that is, St. Etienne) and an old large-bore barrel (octagonal breech 10-1/2", .82 caliber). He created the remainder of the weapon from a sturdy striped maple stock, a home-forged simple iron trigger guard (front held by a bottom screw that penetrates up to the barrel tang) and two plain sheet-brass rammer thimbles. The wooden rod includes a crude 2-1/4" pewter head. A side plate, escutcheon, butt plate and stock carving were not considered necessary. Although this was a basic hunting gun, it undoubtedly also served as the man's militia arm. The forend is not cut for a bayonet, but most units allowed a choice for the secondary weapon, for example a belt axe, short sword or socket bayonet.

Length: 61-7/8"
Barrel: 45-3/4", .82 cal.
Lock: 6-5/8" X 1-1/4"
Trigger Guard: 10-1/4"
Furniture: Iron/Brass
Weight: 8.7 lbs.

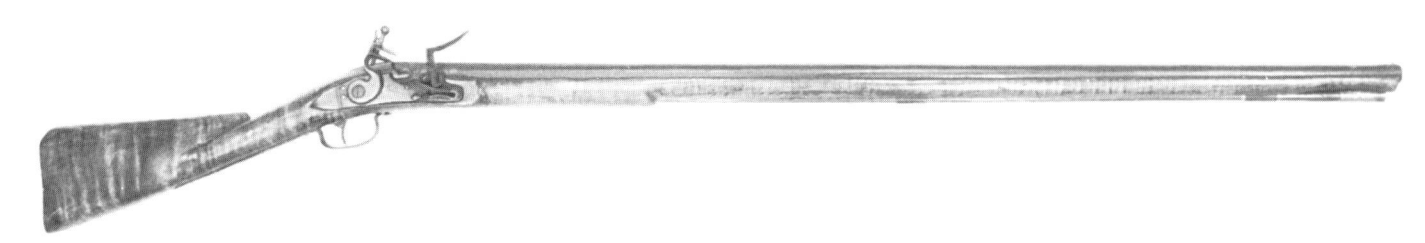

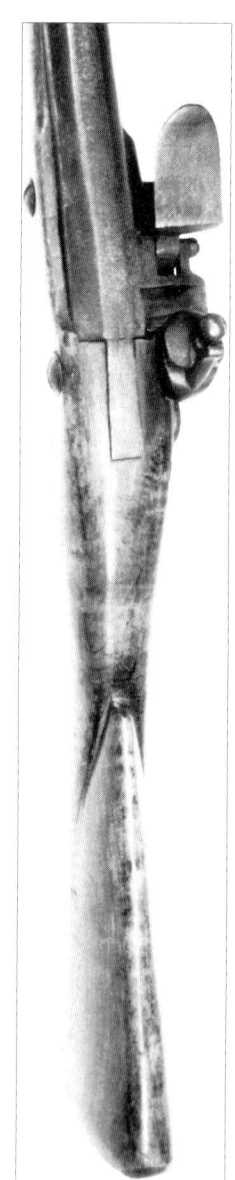

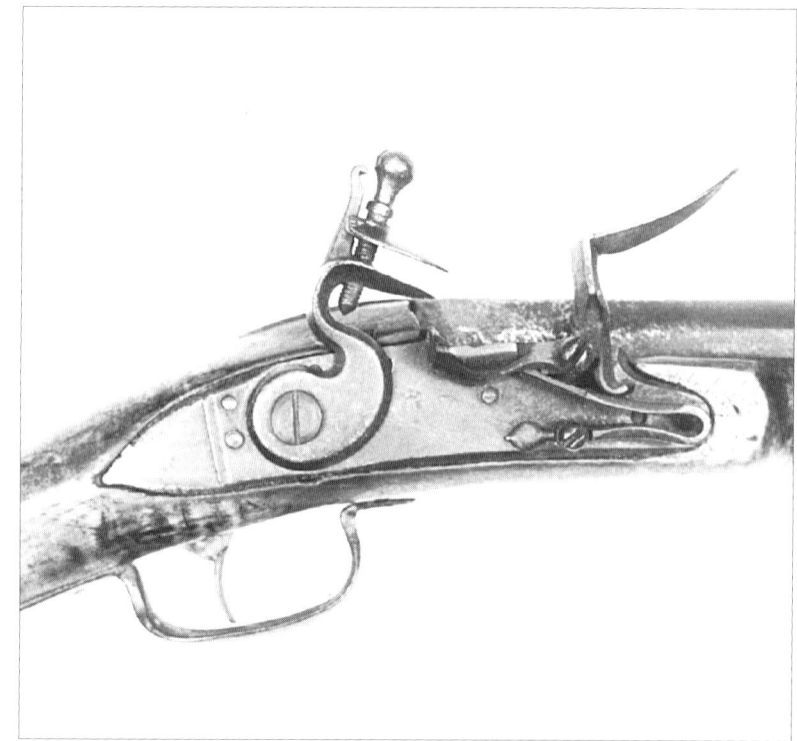

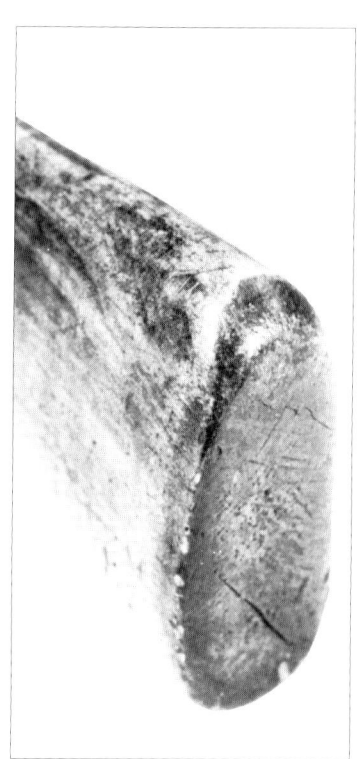

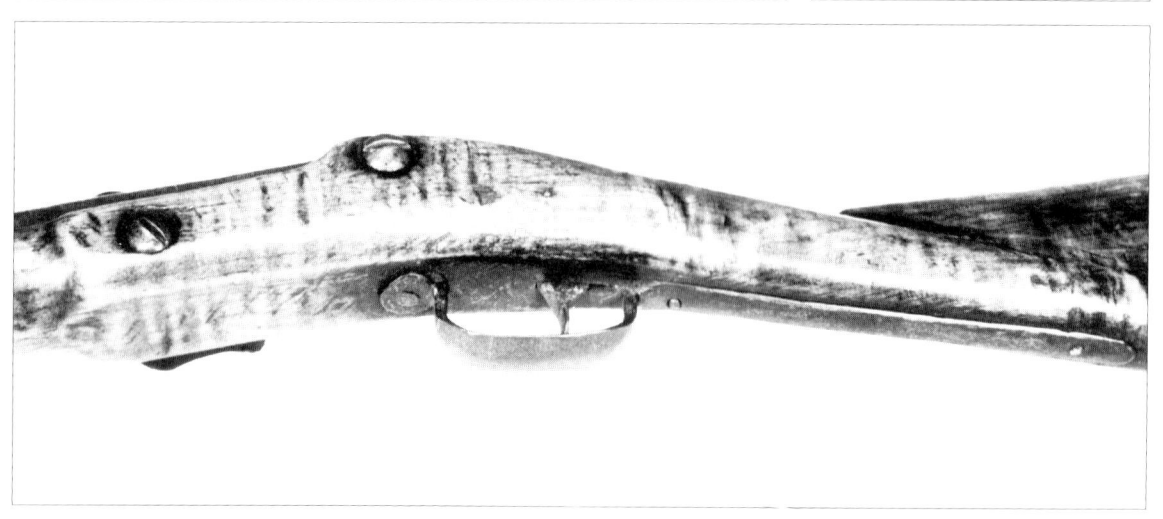

**Author's Collection**

*Chapter 3: Smoothbore Shoulder Arms*

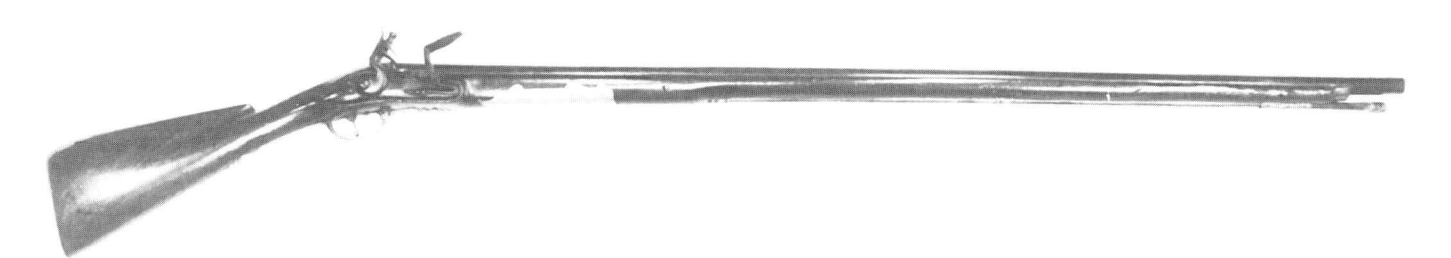

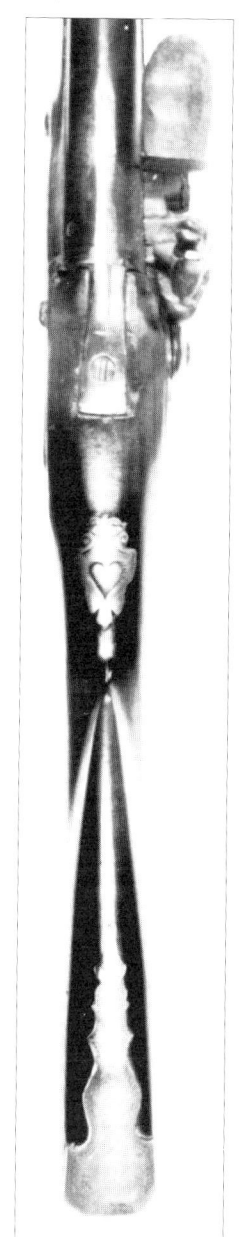

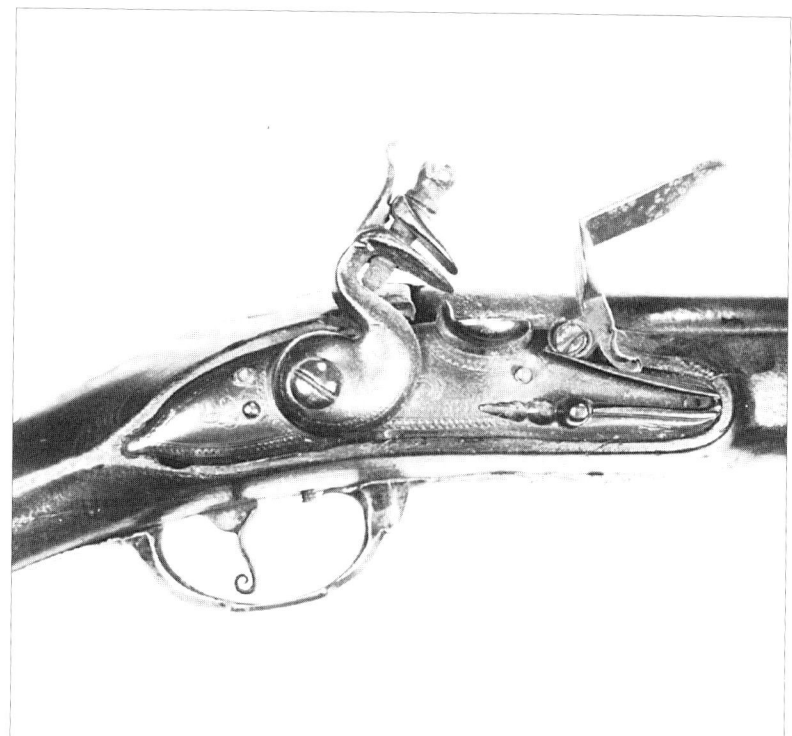

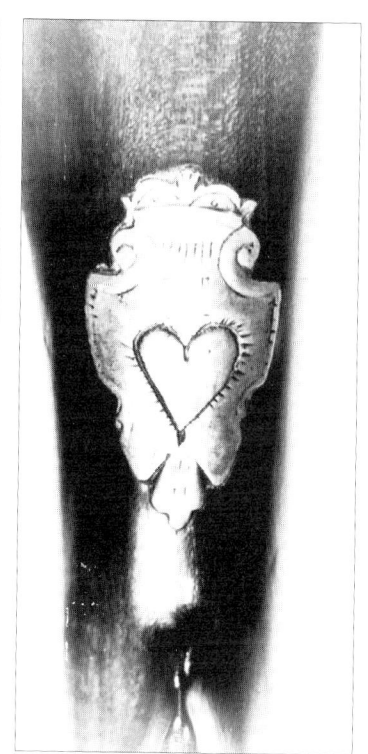

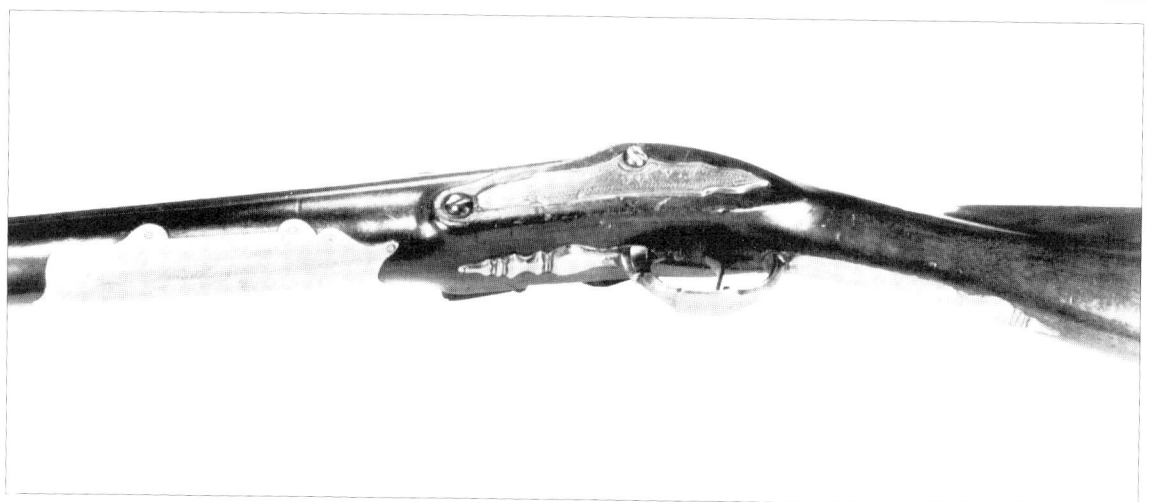

**107.MM AMERICAN FOWLER**                                                                                                                   **Circa 1740–1760**

The personal attraction between this Pennsylvania–Dutch area longarm and its owner is apparent in its many embellishments, for example the stippled border design on the rounded lock, the popular heart figure of that region in the elaborate escutcheon, outline frills encompassing the long butt tang and triangular side plate, as well as the scalloped brass plate nailed to the stock at the hand-hold position. Its structured trigger guard and three faceted rammer pipes (wooden rod, pewter tip) also testify to the Germanic influence of that area. Although the forend has been shortened to create space for a bayonet (that is, a militia fowler/musket), the sharp-angled drop in the stock profile and personal enhancements described above have classified it here as more typical of an honored family fowler than a campaign musket. It is interesting, however, that the cherry stock bears no raised carving. Sling swivels were never attached.

Length: 60"  
Barrel: 44-1/2", .78 cal.  
**Robert Nittolo Collection**

Lock: 5-7/8" X 1-1/8"  
Trigger Guard: 10-1/2"

Butt Tang: 5-1/2"  
Side Plate: 5-3/4"

Furniture: Brass  
Weight: 8.1 lbs.

*Chapter 3: Smoothbore Shoulder Arms*

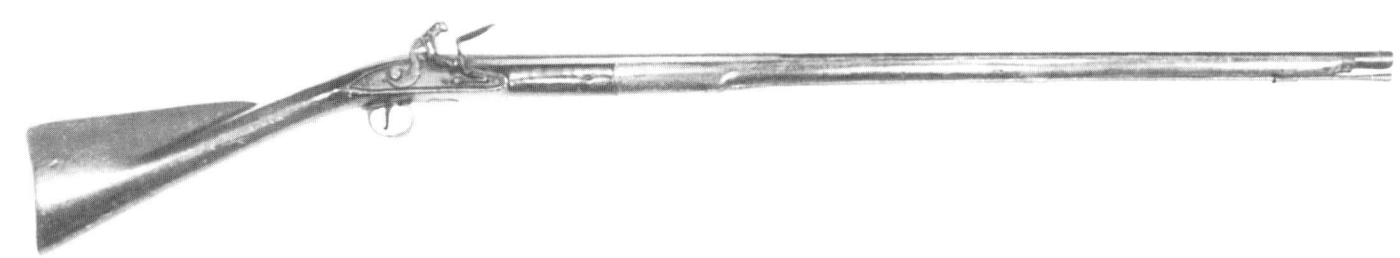

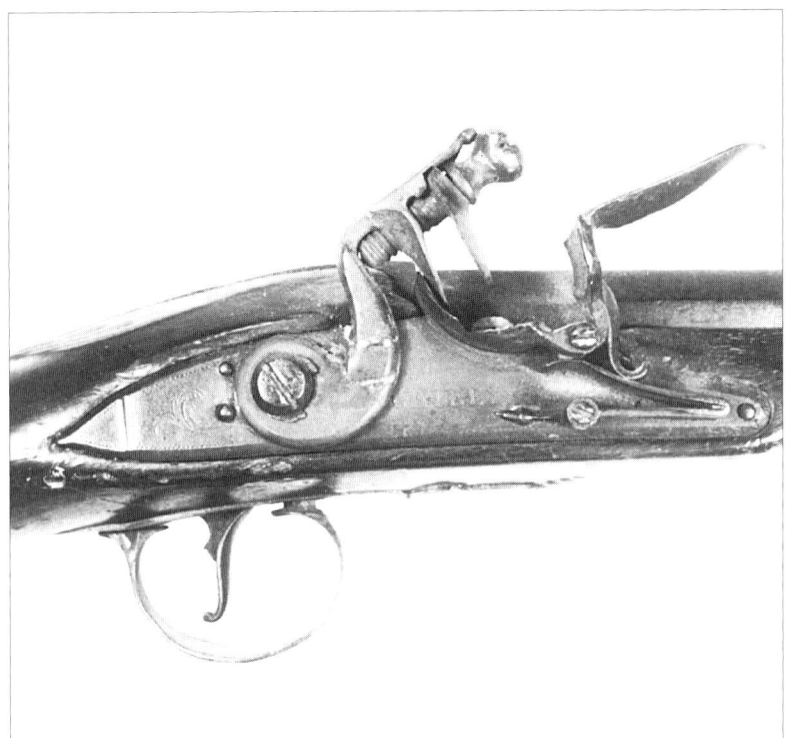

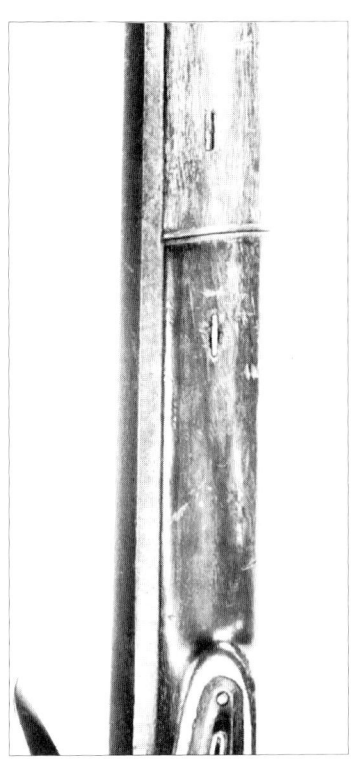

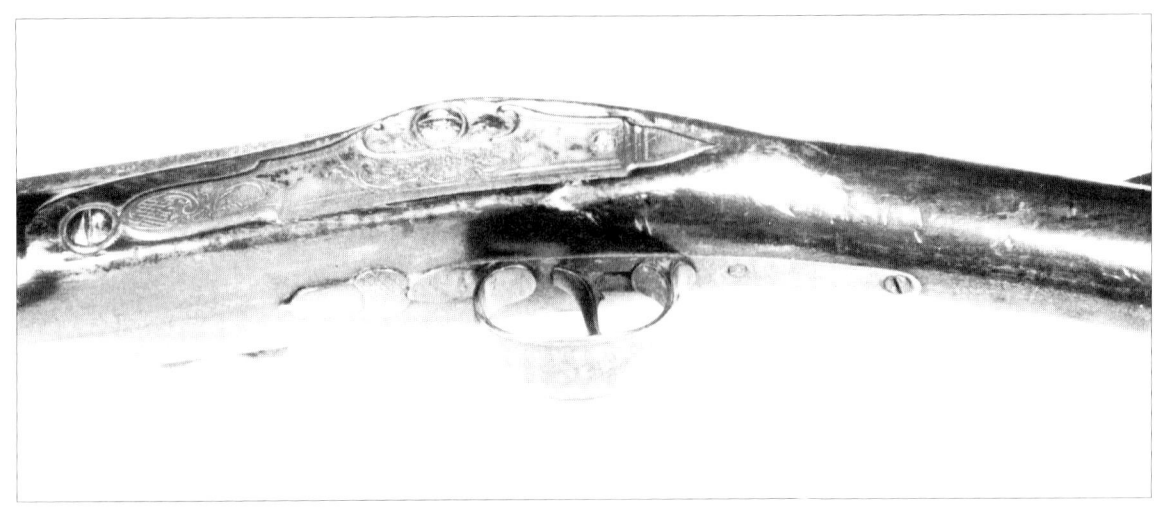

### 108.MM  AMERICAN "TAKE-DOWN" FOWLER                                                                                                   Circa 1770–1790

A new form of private light hunting gun gaining acceptance among the well-to-do Colonists after 1750 was the "take-down" design illustrated here. The slender stock was originally cut 4-1/2 inches forward of the flat lock so that with the barrel removed all three parts could be stored or transported in a shorter package. Also of interest is its post-1750 English private styling, which includes the trigger guard's acorn-shaped forward terminal, a rounded profile trigger bow, a narrower and flatter flash pan and bridle, plus four flat "slot keys" that secured the barrel (more easily removed than the previous pins). Most of this furniture is of German silver and appears to be imported. The British barrel has double scepter strikes, which are private proofs done at the Tower. Its octagonal breech extends 14-1/2 inches to a double ring and has a decorative touch-hole bushing. A functional rear sight was created by a raised channel on the barrel tang. "WATKEYS NEW YORK" is stamped on the breech and "WATKEYS" in the lock face. Henry Watkeys worked in New Windsor, New York, during the 1770s and in New York City as late as 1801.

| | | | |
|---|---|---|---|
| Length: 55-3/4" | Lock: 5-3/4" X 1" | Butt Tang: 2-1/2" | Furniture: German Silver |
| Barrel: 39-1/2", .67 cal. | Trigger Guard: 6" | Side Plate: 6" | Weight: 5.5 lbs. |

**William H. Guthman Collection**

*Chapter 3: Smoothbore Shoulder Arms*

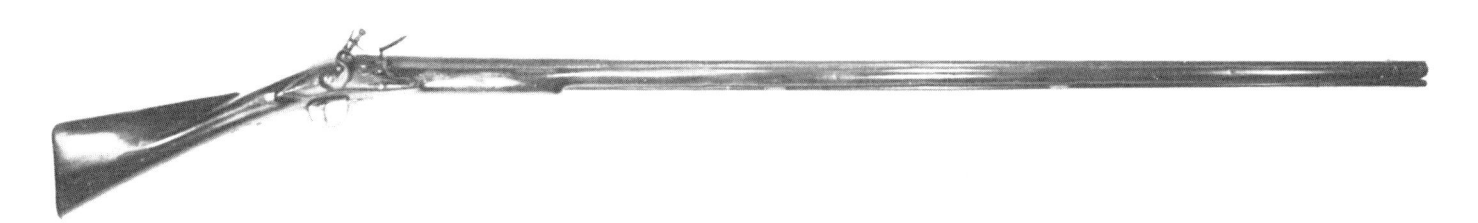

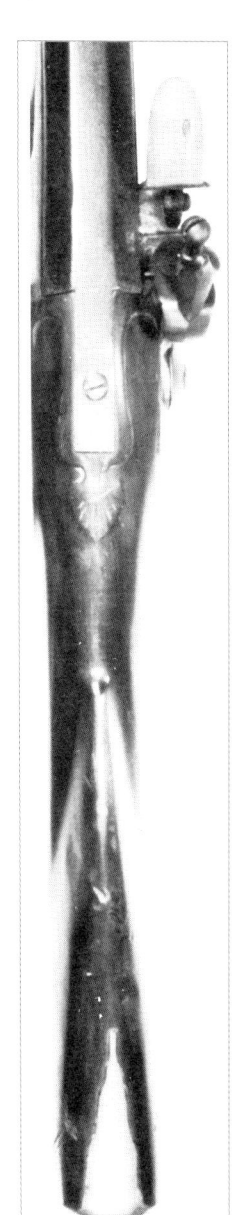

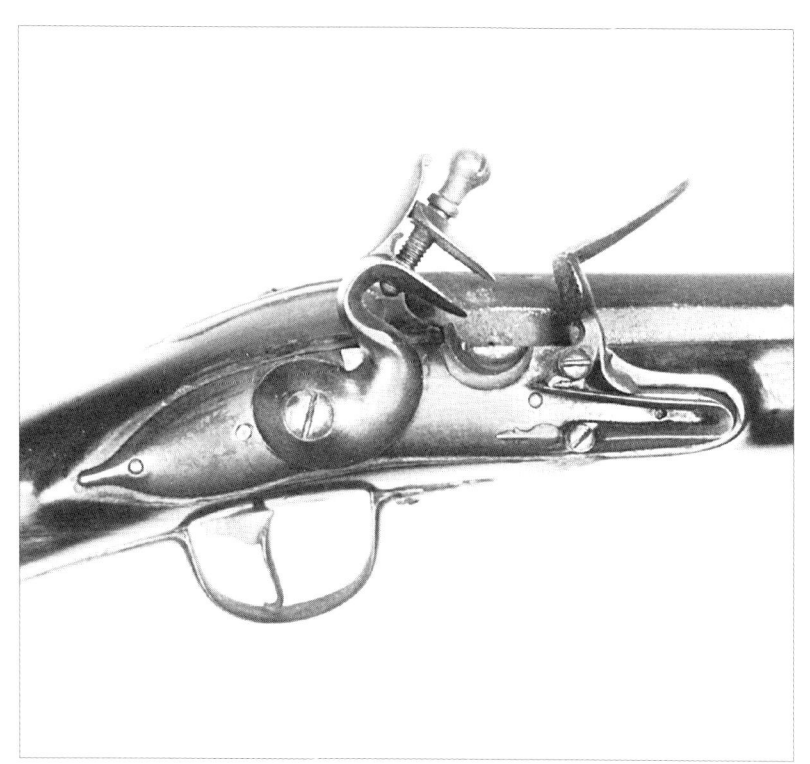

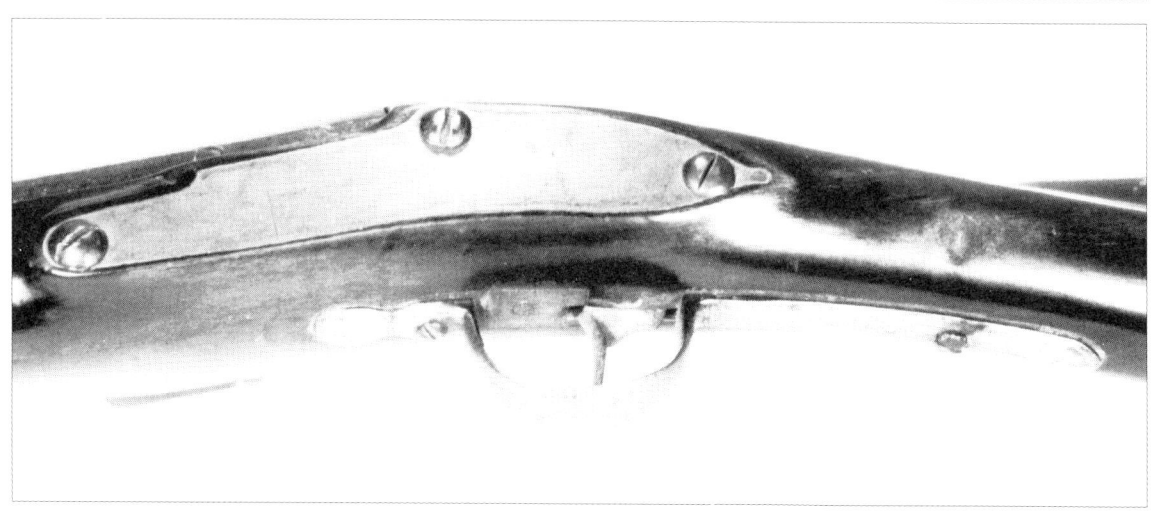

**109.MM AMERICAN FOWLER**  Circa 1730–1750

Most early North American forests had such a dense overhead tree cover that the low brush we encounter today was largely absent—permitting the use of light, well-balanced hunting guns with long barrels. Yet some fowlers were created with an exceptional length, as in this case. The European-made barrel is 65-1/4 inches long with a large .88 caliber bore. It has an octagonal breech for five inches, a 16-faceted section (4") and two forward rings. Arms of this magnitude were intended as "set" pieces, positioned to fire multiple shot from a fixed position in a boat or on shore—usually at waterfowl. The long cherry stock has a marked drop to its butt and extends forward to the muzzle. In typical American practice, mixed components were used: an early English-style rounded three-screw banana lock (circa 1710–1730), raised carving below the barrel tang, a stepped British butt tang pattern, a Queen Anne-period ball terminal trigger guard and a common provincial flat cast brass side plate (with an outline probably traced from the lock plate). Three sheet-brass thimbles hold the wooden ramrod above the bare entry hole.

| | | | |
|---|---|---|---|
| Length: 82-1/2" | Lock: 7-1/2" X 1-1/4" | Butt Tang: 4-1/2" | Furniture: Brass |
| Barrel: 65-1/4", .88 cal. | Trigger Guard: 8-1/2" | Side Plate: 7-1/2" | Weight: 14.6 lbs. |

**Author's Collection**

Chapter 3: Smoothbore Shoulder Arms

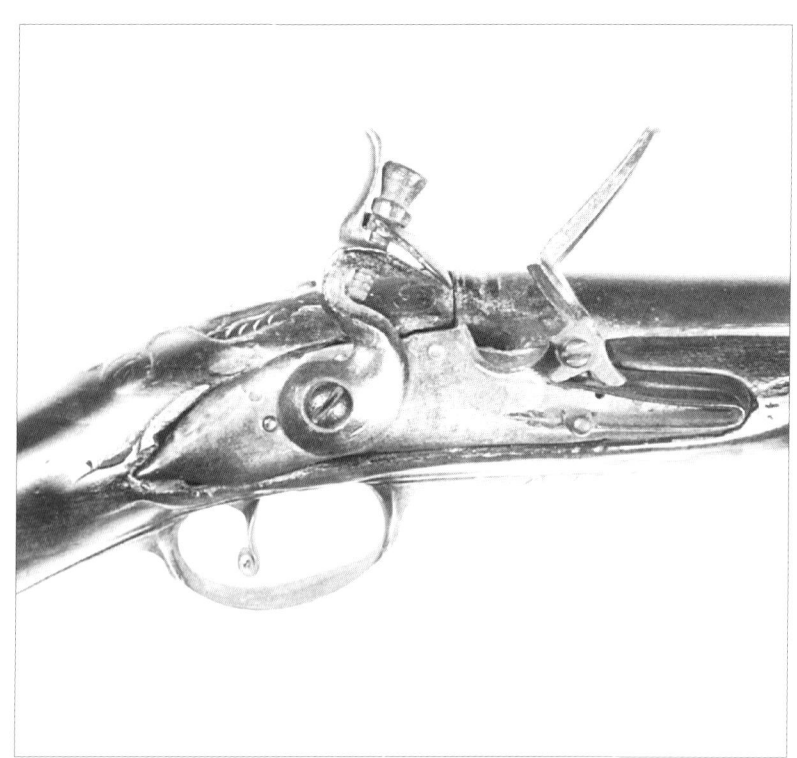

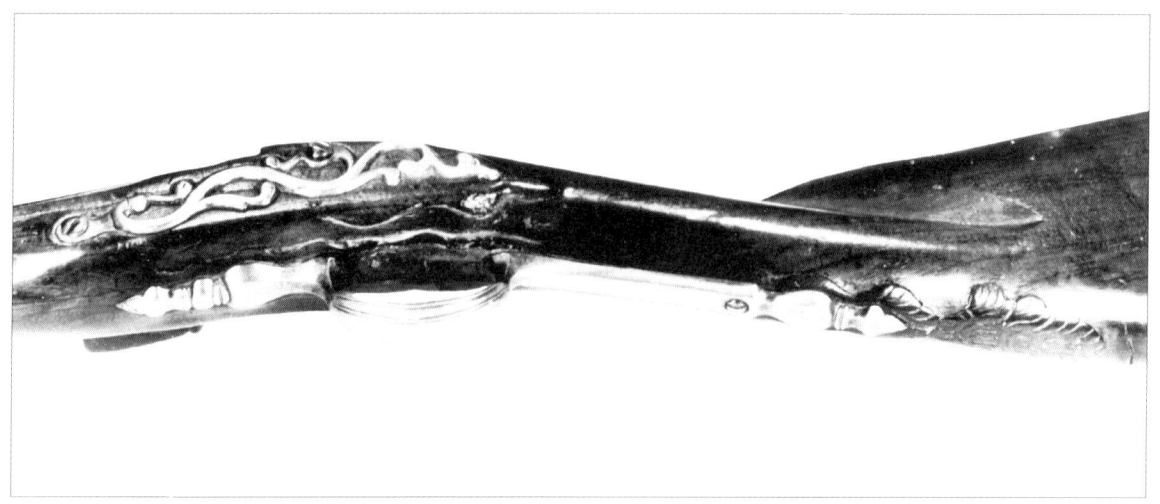

**110.MM AMERICAN "HUDSON VALLEY" FOWLER**  Circa 1730–1740

One of the American Colonies' distinctive regional patterns was developed in the Dutch-dominated New York Hudson River Valley during the late 17th and early 18th centuries. These long hunting guns usually employed imported locks and barrels, as well as Dutch-style furniture on elaborately carved stocks of native American wood. This example has a 59" English barrel marked by two London Gunmakers Company proofs with its maker's stamp, "R*W" (Richard Wilson), between them. Low Country influence is evident in the rounded banana lock, a thick arrow-headed trigger guard with incised lines on its bow, a long bulbous butt tang (top screw) and ribbed rammer pipes (wooden rod). The open vine-like side plate is typical of early century European fowlers. Another common characteristic of that region was decorative raised carving as seen on this cherry stock around the trigger guard, barrel tang, lock and side plate. Fowlers of such length were usually employed against waterfowl.

| | | | |
|---|---|---|---|
| Length: 75" | Lock: 6-1/4" X 1-1/8" | Butt Tang: 5-1/4" | Furniture: Brass |
| Barrel: 59", .71 cal. | Trigger Guard: 6-1/8" | Side Plate: 6-1/8" | Weight: 10.3 lbs. |

**George C. Neumann Collection, Valley Forge National Historical Park**

*Chapter 3: Smoothbore Shoulder Arms*

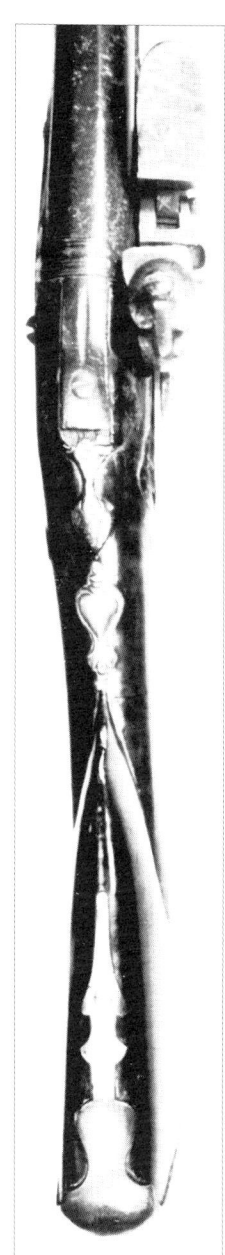

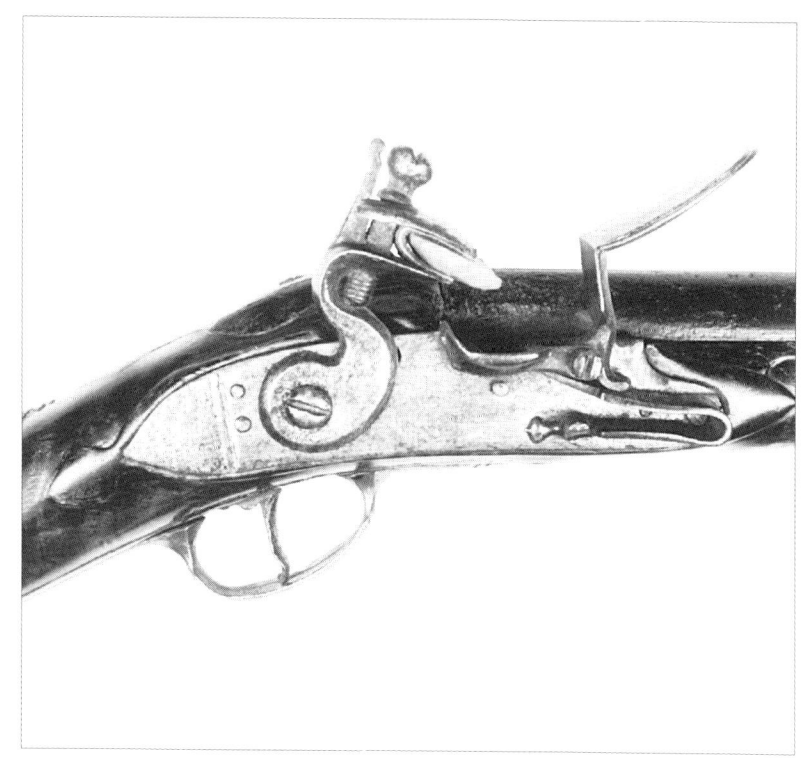

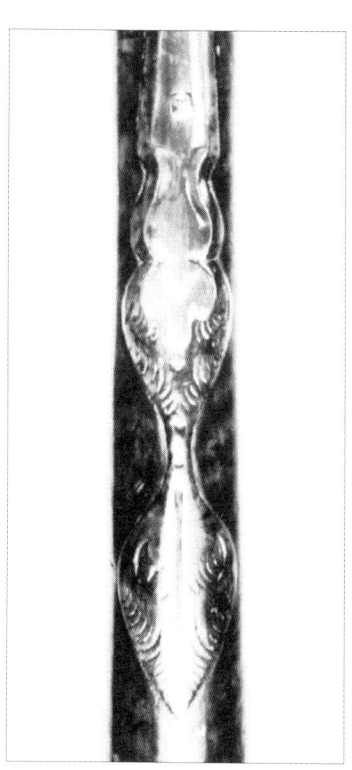

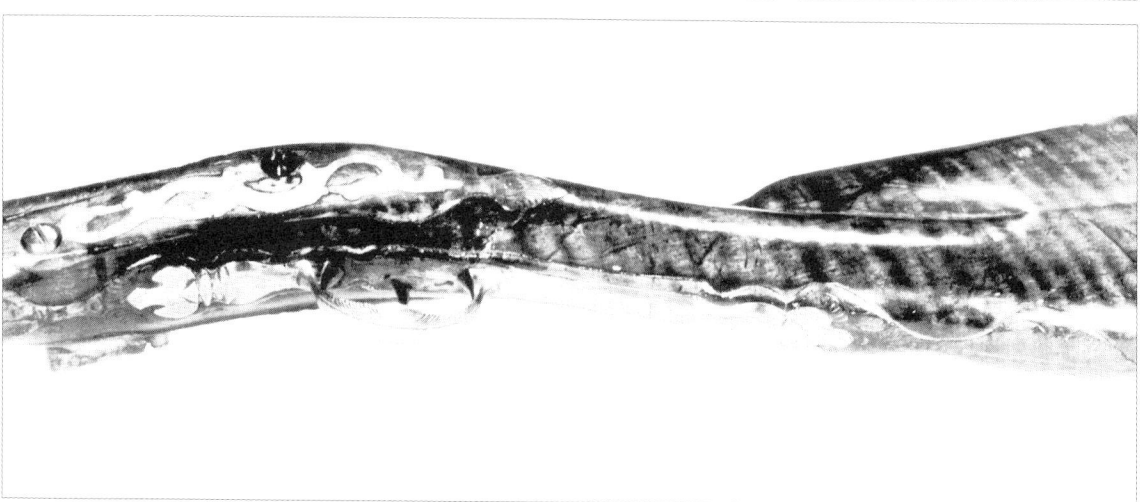

### 111.MM AMERICAN "HUDSON VALLEY" FOWLER
### Circa 1740

The typical Hudson Valley profile is apparent here with the heavy handrail-shaped striped maple butt (note comb ridge is parallel to barrel) and a thin forend stocked to the muzzle. A French Model 1728-style musket lock was reused. The 60" barrel, in turn, bears London Gunmakers Company proofs. Since the open vine-pattern side plate was apparently broken or lost at an early date, pewter was poured into the original cavity and filed flat (a period practice). As with the prior fowler, Dutch styling is evident in the heavy trigger guard's bow and three-pointed terminals, the long structured butt tang (top screw), the ornate escutcheon and the elaborate raised carving surrounding the barrel tang, trigger guard, lock, side plate and each of the ramrod thimbles. The barrel has a flat-topped breech for eight inches and ends in a flared muzzle. There is a rear sight guide notch filed into the barrel tang, while a front blade rests six inches from the muzzle. Although cumbersome, many of these arms saw service with the American militia, especially during the early years of the Revolution.

| | | | |
|---|---|---|---|
| Length: 75-3/4" | Lock: 6-1/2" X 1-1/4" | Butt Tang: 6-1/4" | Furniture: Brass |
| Barrel: 60", .65 cal. | Trigger Guard: 10-1/4" | Side Plate: 6" | Weight: 10.7 lbs. |

**George C. Neumann Collection, Valley Forge National Historical Park**

*Chapter 3: Smoothbore Shoulder Arms* **161**

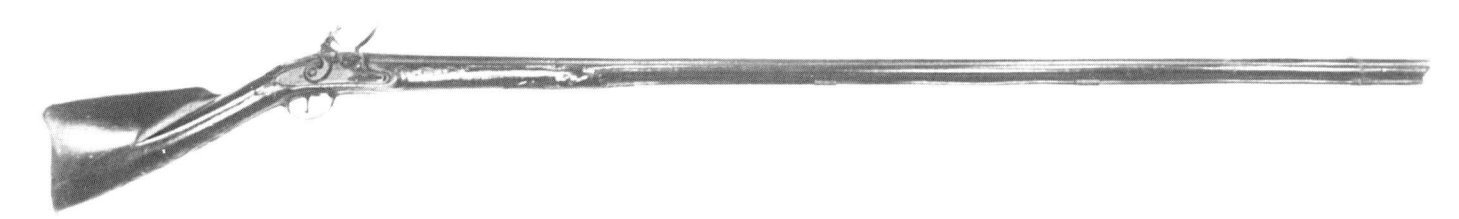

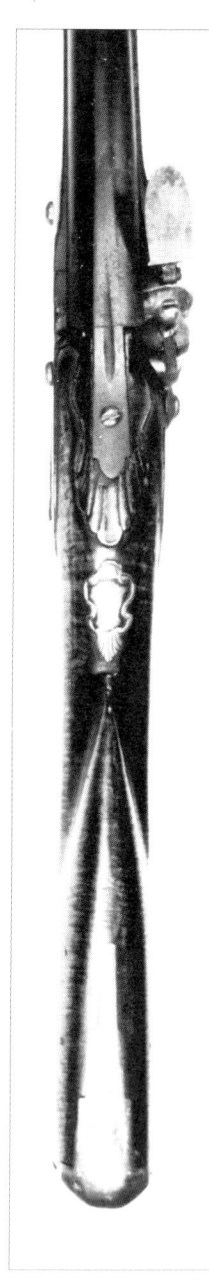

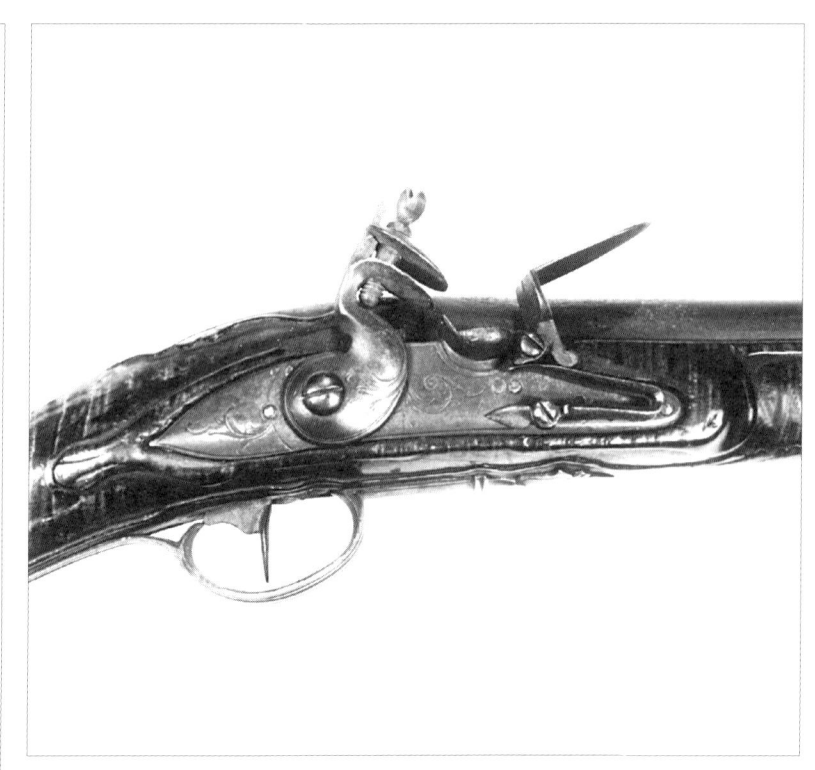

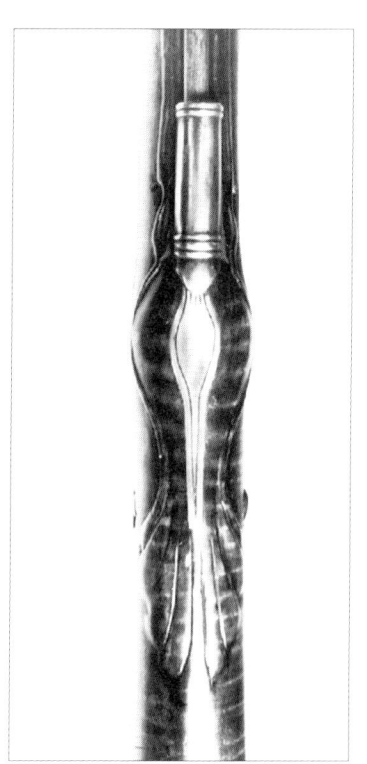

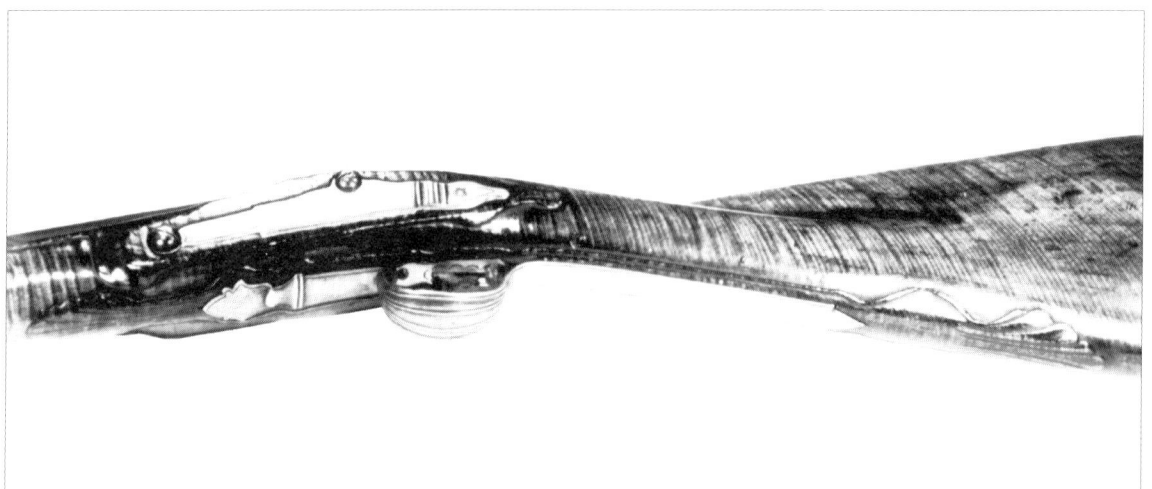

**112.MM AMERICAN "HUDSON VALLEY" FOWLER**  Circa 1775

The Hudson Valley tradition of long fowlers with thick butts, pinned barrels, Dutch brass furniture and elaborate raised carving continues in this impressive striped maple example. The furniture by this date is more subdued and the workmanship more precise. Its 60" barrel shows Birmingham proofs, and the rounded lock with foliage engraving is a typical English commercial pattern circa 1760 (stamped inside "B HOMER"). The triangular side plate, long trigger guard, decorated escutcheon and rammer pipes (multiple end rings) continue to reflect Dutch styling, but further British influence is visible in the stepped butt tang. More dignified carving traces the entire ramrod channel and outlines the barrel tang, trigger guard, lock and side plate. Four cast pipes hold the wooden rammer. The butt was marked by its owner, "RICHARD VARICK, ESQ.," who was from New York. During the Revolutionary War, he served as aide-de-camp to Generals Schuyler and Arnold, as well as confidential secretary to Washington.

Length: 75"  Lock: 5-7/8" X 1"  Butt Tang: 5-3/8"  Furniture: Brass
Barrel: 60", .67 cal.  Trigger Guard: 11-1/4"  Side Plate: 6"  Weight: 9.5 lbs.
**Robert Nittolo Collection**

*162   Chapter 3: Smoothbore Shoulder Arms*

### 113.MM AMERICAN "NEW ENGLAND" FOWLER

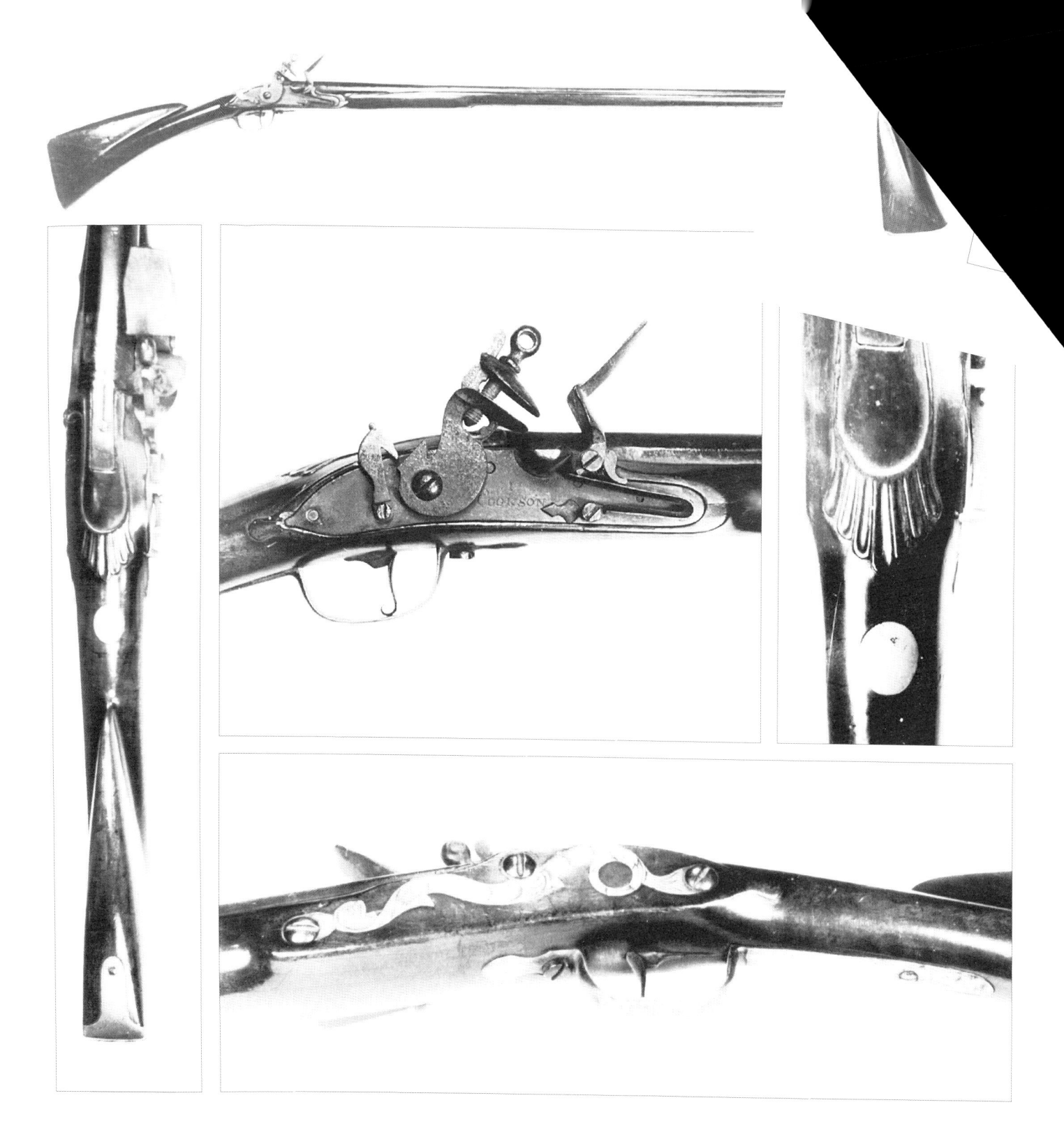

**Circa 1750**

The New England fowler evolved by the mid-1700s and is considered probably the most graceful of the regional Colonial arms. It normally had a curved Roman nose handrail butt, slim round wrist and long unadorned narrow forend to the muzzle. In this case components typical of the century's early years are mounted on a cherry stock form of the 1750 period. A three-screw flat doglock (squared frizzen top), dragon side plate, ball terminal trigger guard, flat stubby butt plate and bottom screw securing the barrel tang are all of the Queen Anne era. The English barrel, in turn, is octagonal for eight inches, faceted for 2-1/2 inches and 3-5/8 inches to a second ring. "I COOKSON" is engraved on the lock plate beneath the flash pan. Cookson was a Boston gunmaker, circa 1701–1762. Yet the gently curving stock with its petal carving below the barrel tang, oval silver escutcheon and incised rammer pipes is more indicative of mid-century, suggesting a later stocking or restocking of the earlier parts. This arm also has a front blade sight 3/4 inch behind the muzzle, a rear sight guide channel filed into the breech tang and a wooden ramrod.

| | | | |
|---|---|---|---|
| Length: 67-3/4" | Lock: 7-1/4" X 1-1/4" | Butt Tang: 2-3/4" | Furniture: Brass |
| Barrel: 51-1/2", .70 cal. | Trigger Guard: 8-1/2" | Side Plate: 7" | Weight: 9.0 lbs. |

**Richard Ulbrich Collection**

*Chapter 3: Smoothbore Shoulder Arms*

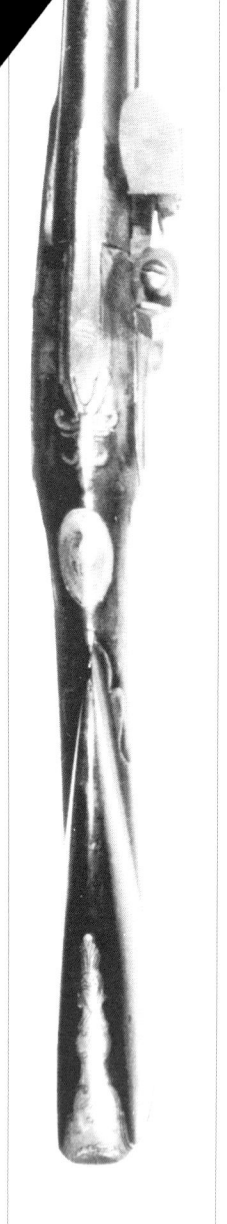

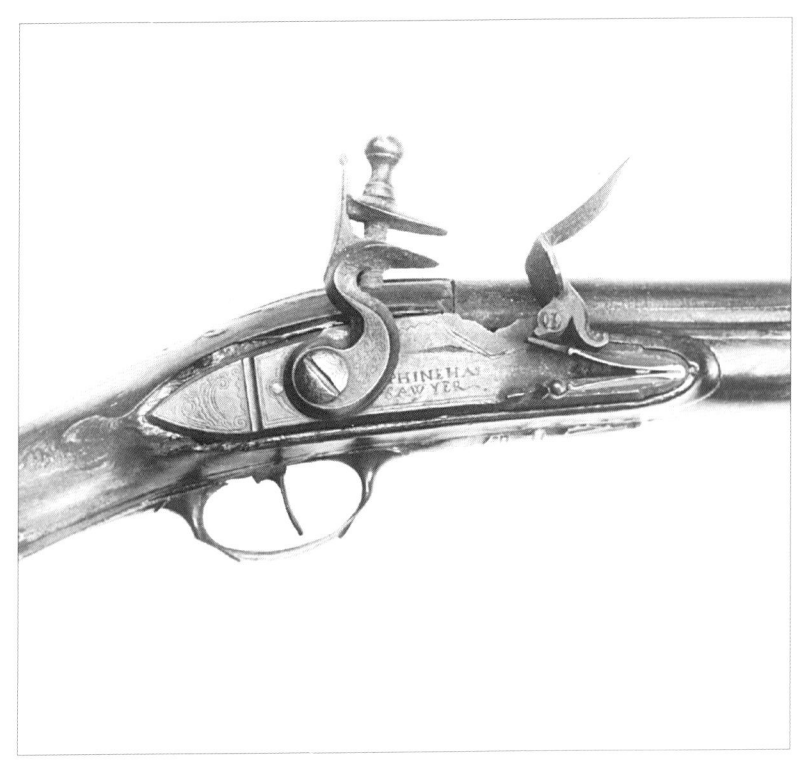

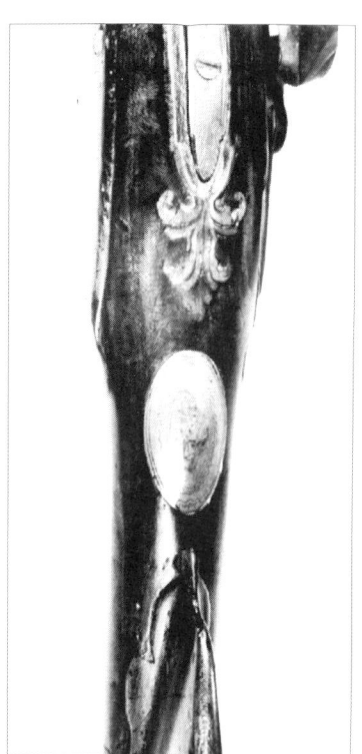

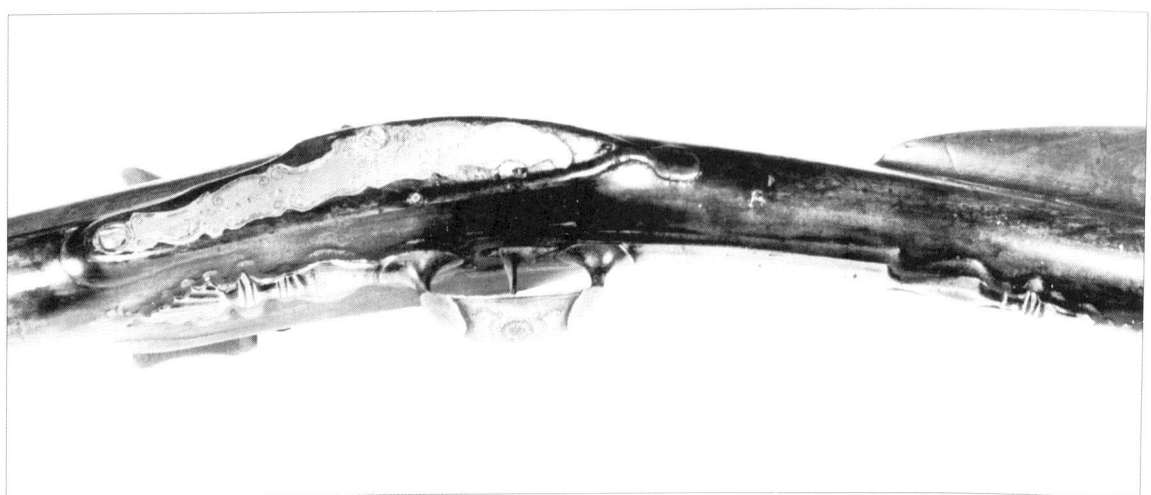

**114.MM AMERICAN "NEW ENGLAND" FOWLER**　　　　　　　　　　　　　　　　　　　　　　　　　　　　　　　　　　　　　　　　　　　　　　　　　　Circa 1772–1780

It is believed that the flowing contours of the New England fowler's Roman nose butt and thin forend came to England with the French Huguenots in the late 1600s and then to America. This pleasing eastern Massachusetts example adds gentle raised carving behind the barrel tang, at the comb's forward end and bordering the trigger guard, lock and side plate. Floral patterns are engraved near the breech and on the lock's tail and trigger bow. The name "PHINEHAS SAWYER," a gunmaker at Harvard, Massachusetts, from circa 1772 to 1800, appears on the lock. "IONATHAN PUFFER," the owner, from Lancaster, Massachusetts, who participated in the Lexington Alarm and the 1776 Canada Expedition, is inscribed on the side plate. Note that the arm's furniture is an interesting gathering of sources, that is: a Germanic lock form that uses an internal frizzen spring screw (note that the flash pan has been lost), an attractive trigger guard that includes French-type struts on the trigger bow, and American provincial artistry evident in the irregular side plate and butt tang. An oval silver escutcheon is marked "1776." Five long thimbles in the walnut stock support an iron trumpet-headed ramrod.

| | | | |
|---|---|---|---|
| Length: 75" | Lock: 5-3/4" X 1-1/8" | Butt Tang: 5" | Furniture: Brass |
| Barrel: 59-1/4", .58 cal. | Trigger Guard: 5-3/8" | Weight: 9.2 lbs. | |

**Richard Ulbrich Collection**

*164　Chapter 3: Smoothbore Shoulder Arms*

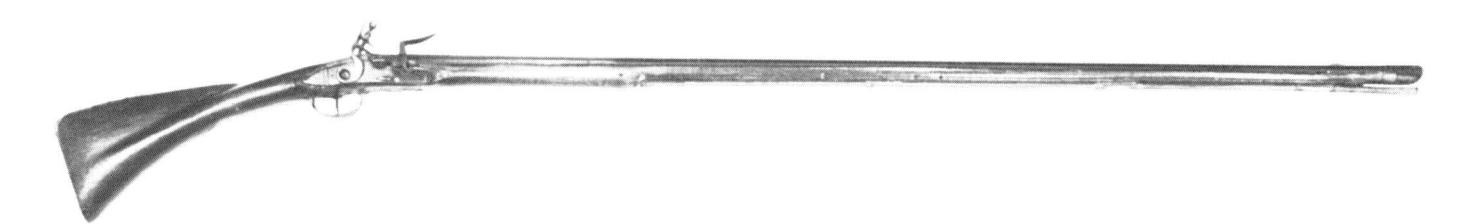

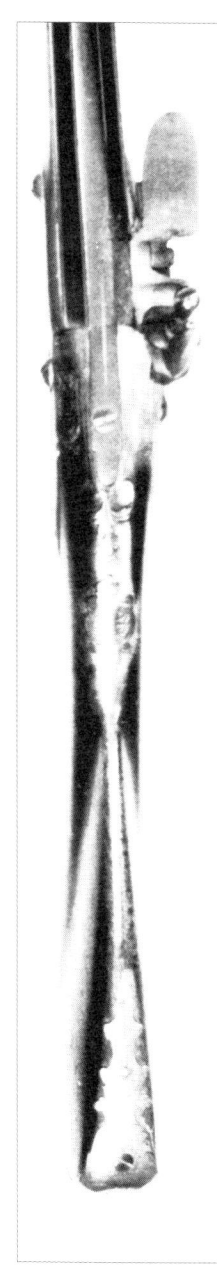

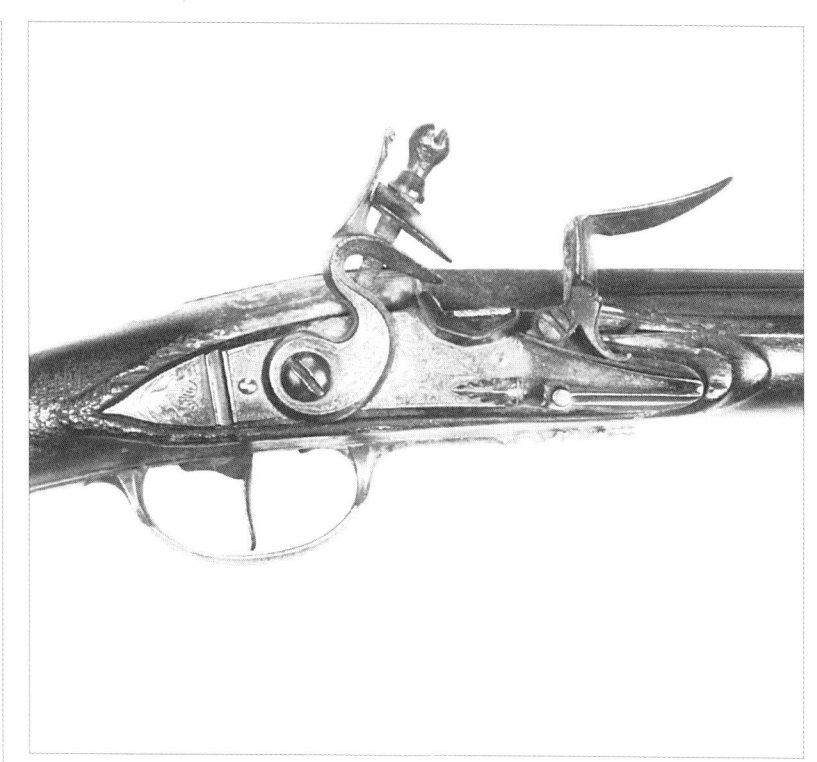

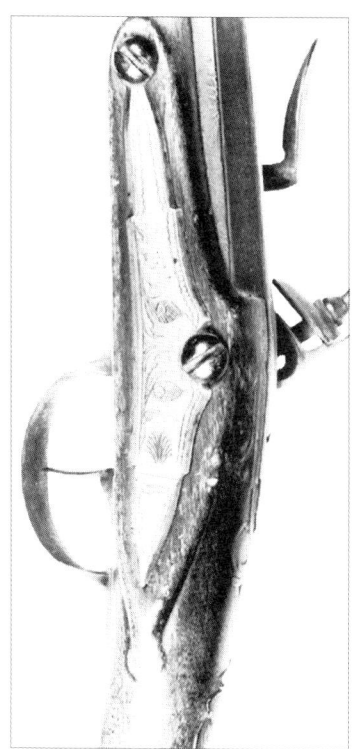

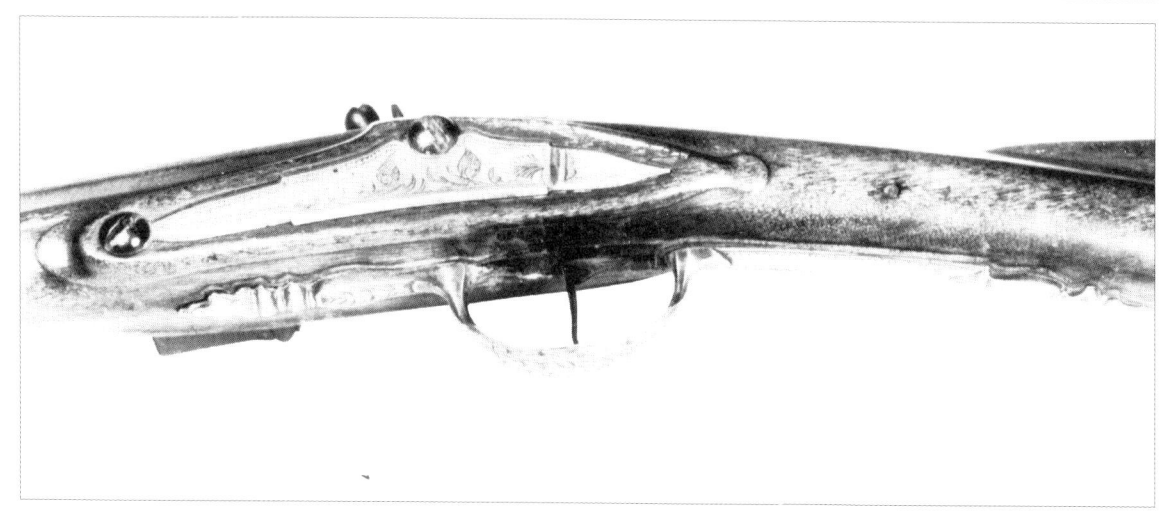

### 115.MM AMERICAN "NEW ENGLAND" FOWLER

Circa 1750–1760

Although these early fowlers might appear overly long and too deep at the buttstock to use in the forest, they were well balanced to carry, with a lightness and fit to the shooter's shoulder and eye that testify to the gifted realities of their designers. This handsome arm has a sharply curved walnut stock that achieves an extremely delicate grace in profile. It is attributed to Joseph Chapin, a gunsmith near Windsor, Connecticut, as the pattern matches another signed example. Notice his crisp workmanship in the flat/beveled Germanic-style lock with its channeled tail, "pine tree" frizzen spring finial and interior holding screw, the lack of an exterior bridle, and the decorative foliate pattern covering the entire plate and cock. Its triangular side plate follows a mid-century French outline yet introduces a tail groove plus local pine cone incised designs. The richly decorated butt tang and trigger guard further speak for his abilities. Raised carving borders the lock, barrel tang and side plate and traces the forend's rammer channel. Four pipes hold a wooden ramrod. The 51" barrel is octagonal for 11-1/8 inches and provides a top flat panel to 3-3/4 inches below the muzzle.

Length: 66-1/4"
Barrel: 51", .66 cal.
Lock: 6" X 1-1/8"
Trigger Guard: 11"
Butt Tang: 4-3/4"
Side Plate: 5-3/4"
Furniture: Brass
Weight: 7.2 lbs.

**Richard Ulbrich Collection**

*Chapter 3: Smoothbore Shoulder Arms*

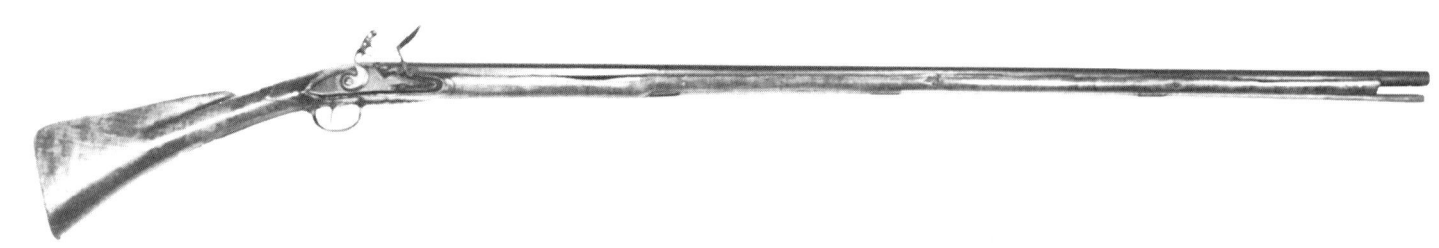

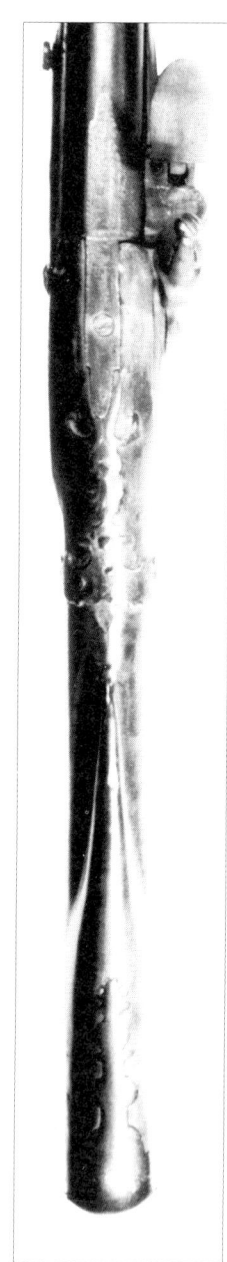

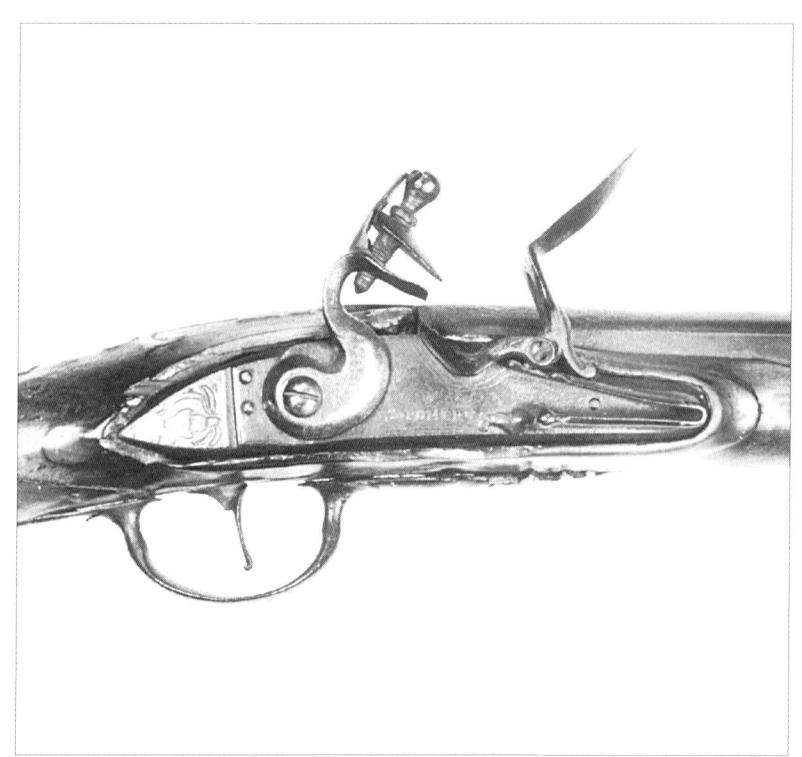

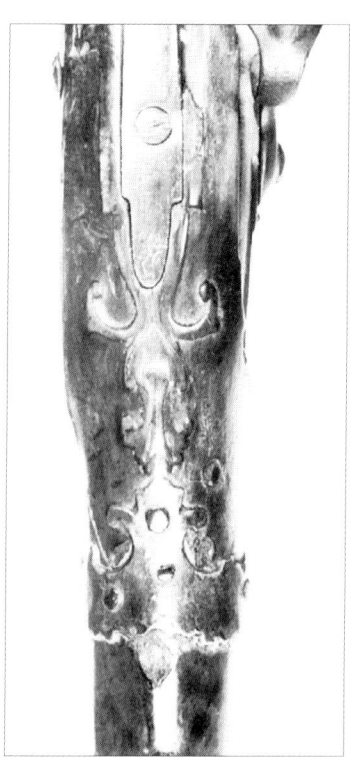

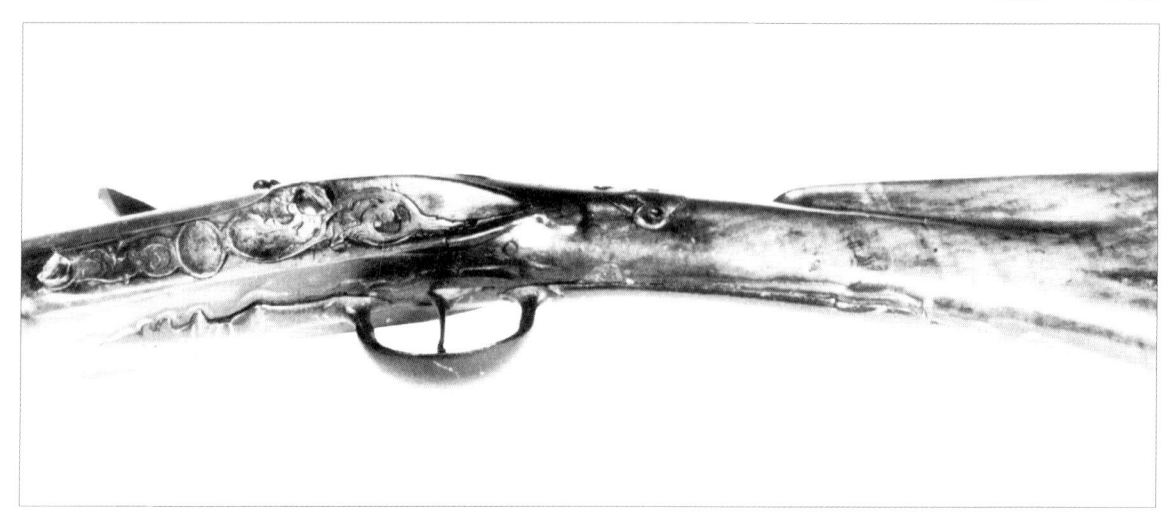

**116.MM AMERICAN "NEW ENGLAND" FOWLER**                                                                **Circa 1750–1760**

"Seth Pomeroy" appears on this lock plate as the gunmaker. He worked in Northampton, Massachusetts, (1706–1777) and was an early enthusiast for freedom, serving as an officer at Louisbourg in 1745, the 1755 Battle of Lake George, and as a 69-year-old private at Bunker Hill. This gently curving cherry stock adds a raised "antler" design behind the barrel tang, as well as surrounding borders for the segmented trigger guard, lock plate and forward comb area. An unusual contemporary scalloped brass repair (nailed) remains on the wrist. The flat/beveled lock has an improvised design on the tail behind a vertical channel, while the faceted pan provides an exterior bridle (its cock appears to be an early replacement). The butt tang is an interesting Yankee pattern, however the side plate follows the French vine/cameo design. A flat panel along the top of this barrel (popular on New England fowlers) reaches to 11 inches below the muzzle. Also note that the forend is cut back, probably to add a bayonet for militia requirements, although such stock reductions were also done on hunting arms the better to grip a ramrod coated with powder fouling and jammed into the thimbles.

| | | | |
|---|---|---|---|
| Length: 64" | Lock: 6" X 1-1/8" | Butt Tang: 4-7/8" | Furniture: Brass |
| Barrel: 48-1/4", .63 cal. | Trigger Guard: 11-1/2" | Side Plate: 5-1/2" | Weight: 7.8 lbs. |

**Richard Ulbrich Collection**

*166    Chapter 3: Smoothbore Shoulder Arms*

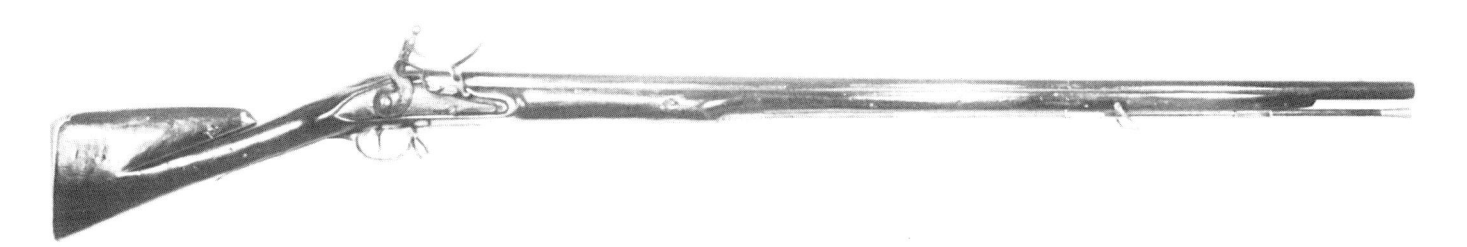

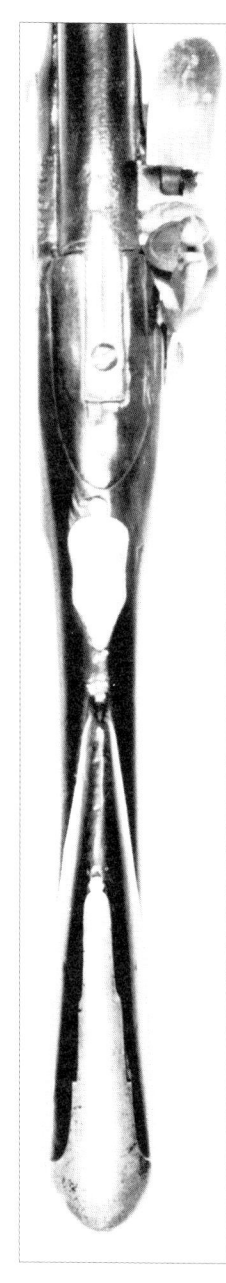

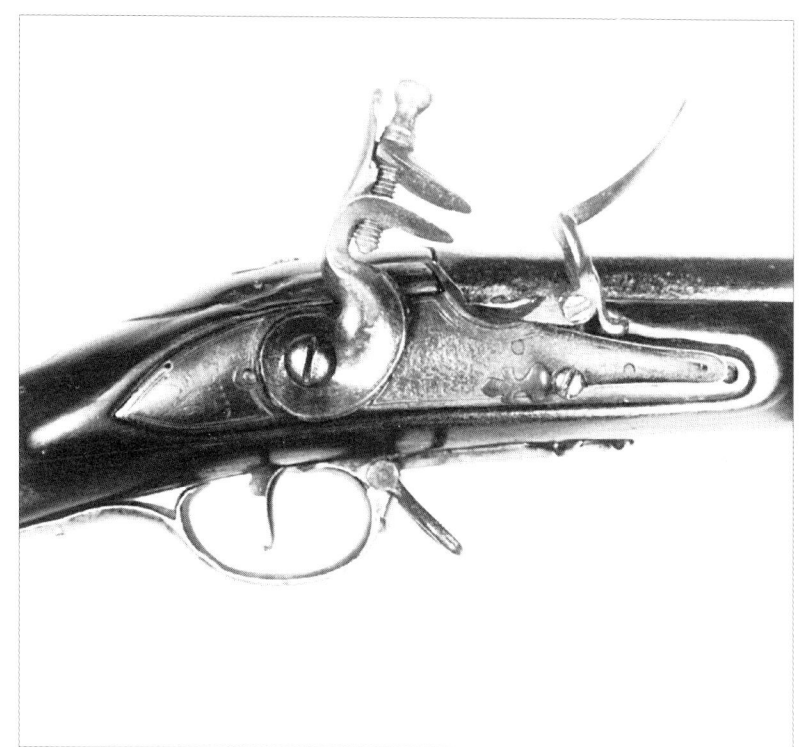

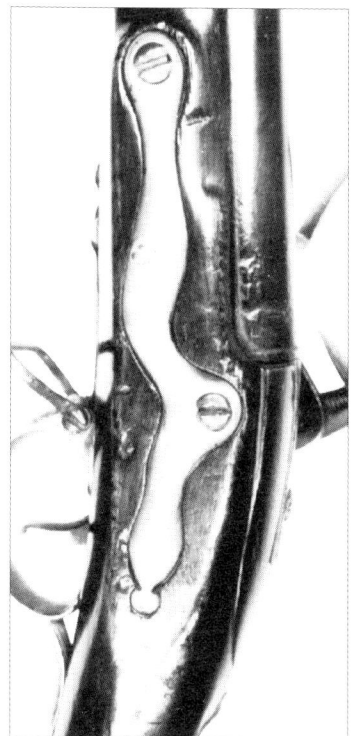

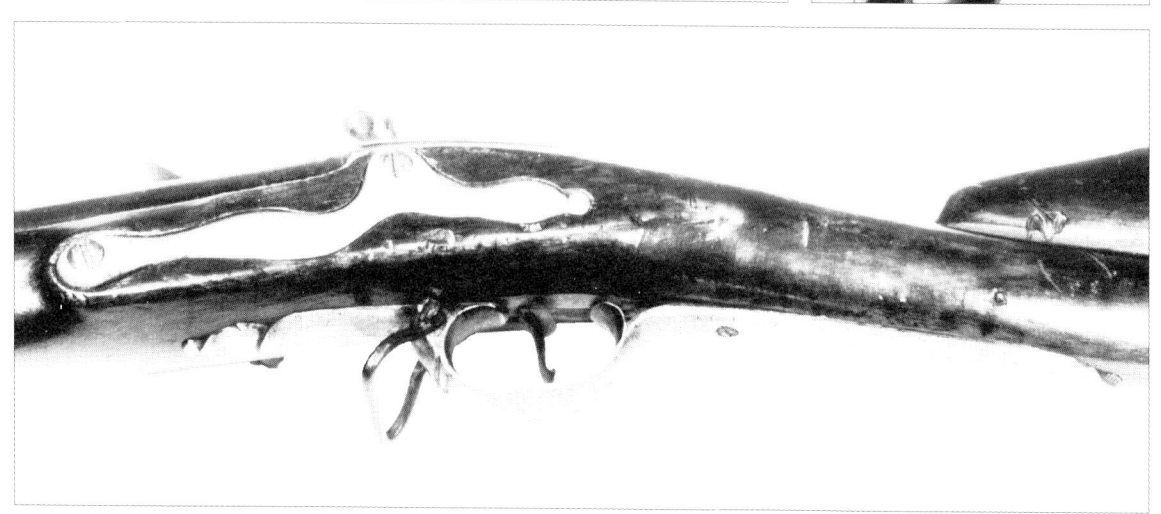

### 117.MM  ENGLISH DRAGOON MUSKET/CARBINE PATTERN 1744
**Circa 1757–1770**

During the 1700s firearm barrels were steadily shortened to reduce weight and bulk—with little loss in range. The British military transition from a standard 46 inches to 42 inches in length reportedly began with the dragoons. They were mounted troops who moved on horseback yet fought dismounted with an infantry-type musket. It appears that some 42" barreled arms were issued to them as early as 1722, and from circa 1740 to 1770 that length appeared on their musket/carbines that adopted this Brown Bess styling. The gun includes a wooden rammer, four equal barrel-shaped thimbles and two sling swivels, yet omitted a nose cap. The remaining brass furniture copies the Long Land Pattern 1742 (9.MM). Note however that a more primitive form of the rounded side plate lacks the normal cavities for the side screw heads. Its double-bridled straight lock is engraved "STAMPS / 1756." The muzzle accepted a regular four-inch bayonet socket (top stud). Unusual wear in this example's stock between the lock and tail pipe suggests prolonged use resting across a saddle. Steel rammers were often added beginning about 1757 (when the banana lock was straightened); this pattern was replaced by a lighter carbine in 1770.

Length: 57-3/4"  
Barrel: 42", .79 cal.  
**Author's Collection**

Lock: 7" X 1-1/4"  
Trigger Guard: 11-1/4"

Butt Tang: 6"  
Side Plate: 6-1/4"

Furniture: Brass  
Weight: 8.3 lbs.

*Chapter 3: Smoothbore Shoulder Arms*

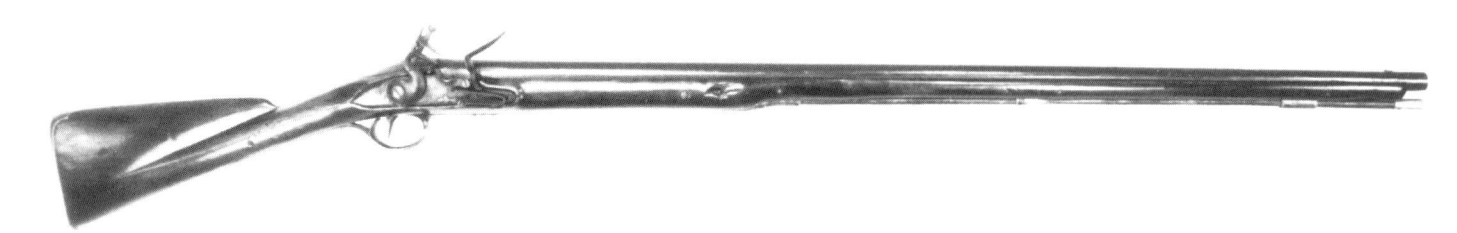

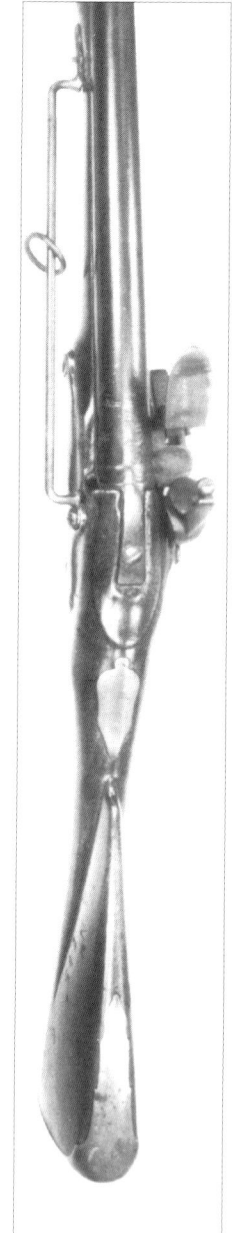

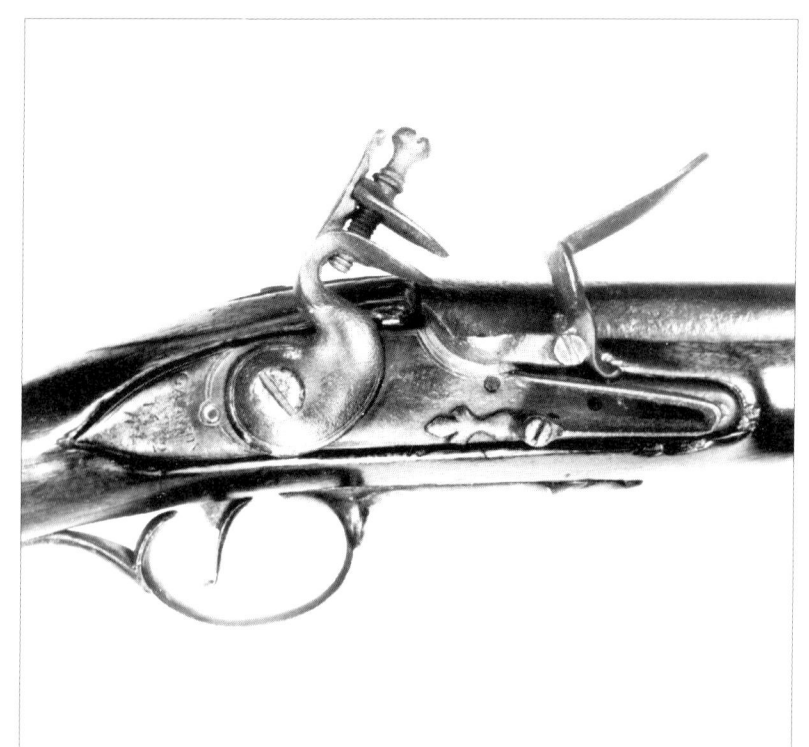

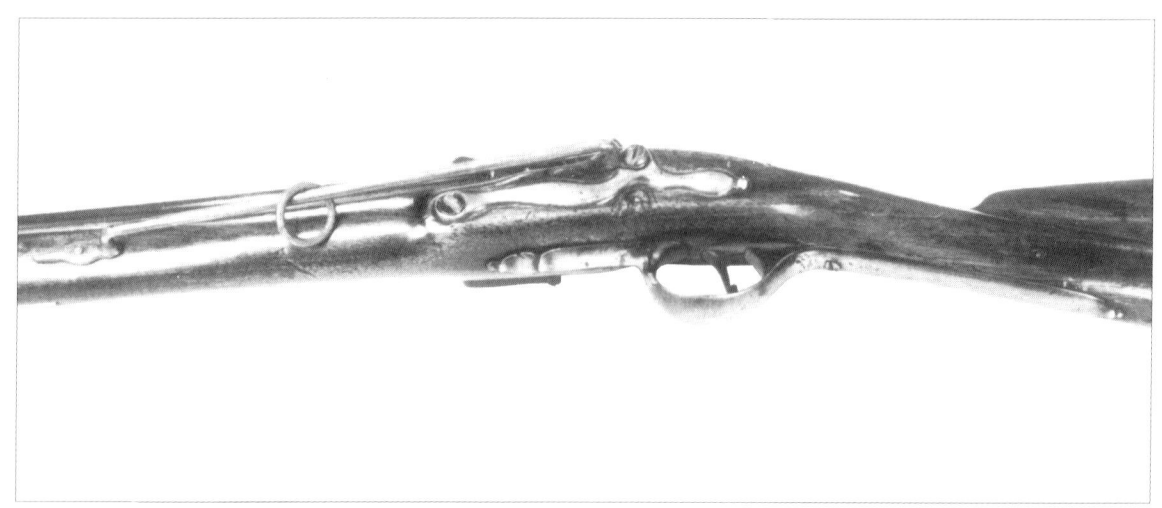

**118.MM  ENGLISH LIGHT HORSE CARBINE PATTERN 1756**  Circa 1762

Impressed with the success of light cavalry in Eastern Europe, Britain issued a warrant in 1756 to establish light dragoons who fought from the saddle. This was their new carbine. It mounted a 37" barrel (.65 caliber) on a slight walnut stock that reached to the muzzle. Three equal thimbles held a wooden ramrod (brass tip). A side bar, in turn, had a sliding ring that attached to a shoulder belt clip (to drop after firing, permitting a change to the sword or pistol). Its reduced-size Long Land brass furniture includes a convex side plate, shield escutcheon and long three-step butt tang. The trigger guard, however, introduces an unusual pinched front post on its bow (no sling swivels). The double-bridled lock is marked "GALTON / 1762," while "FG" and Tower proofs are on the breech. Its butt is carved "4 NO 145 Cl." Many of this pattern were issued without the side bar (some forends were also cut for bayonets) to arm light companies of foot in the French and Indian War. It saw service during the American Revolution (mostly in original form), primarily with Loyalist mounted units. Also note the carbine's ditinctive side plate slot cut for the bar forward of the rear screw head.

| | | | |
|---|---|---|---|
| Length: 52-1/4" | Lock: 6" X 1-1/8" | Butt Tang: 4-5/8" | Furniture: Brass |
| Barrel: 36-3/4", .68 cal. | Trigger Guard: 11" | Side Plate: 5-3/8" | Weight: 6.3 lbs. |

**Author's Collection**

*Chapter 3: Smoothbore Shoulder Arms*

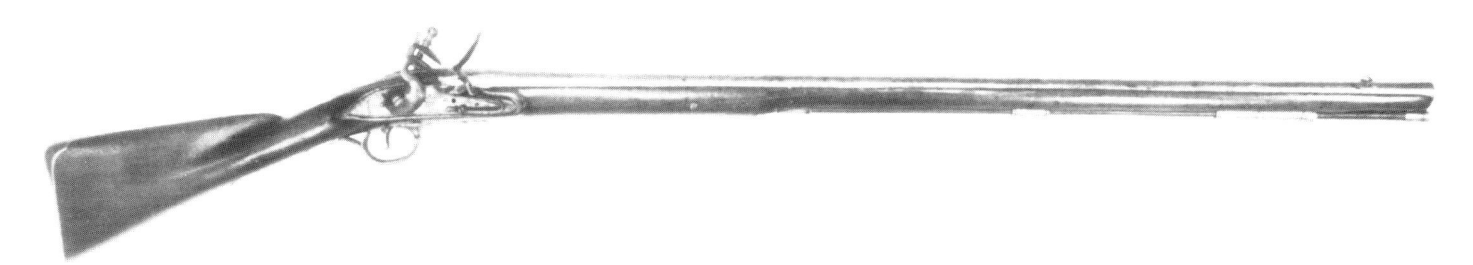

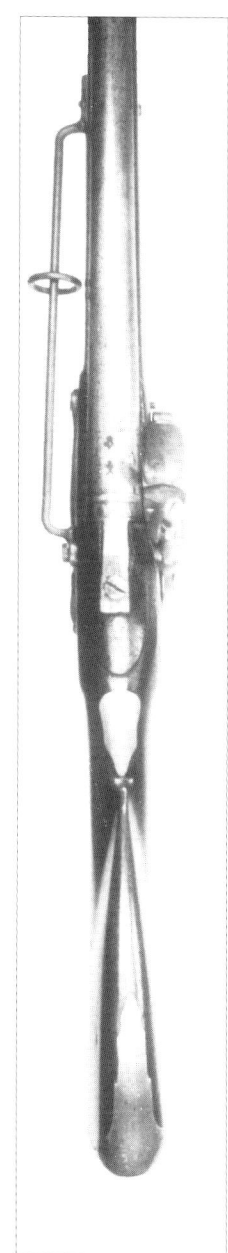

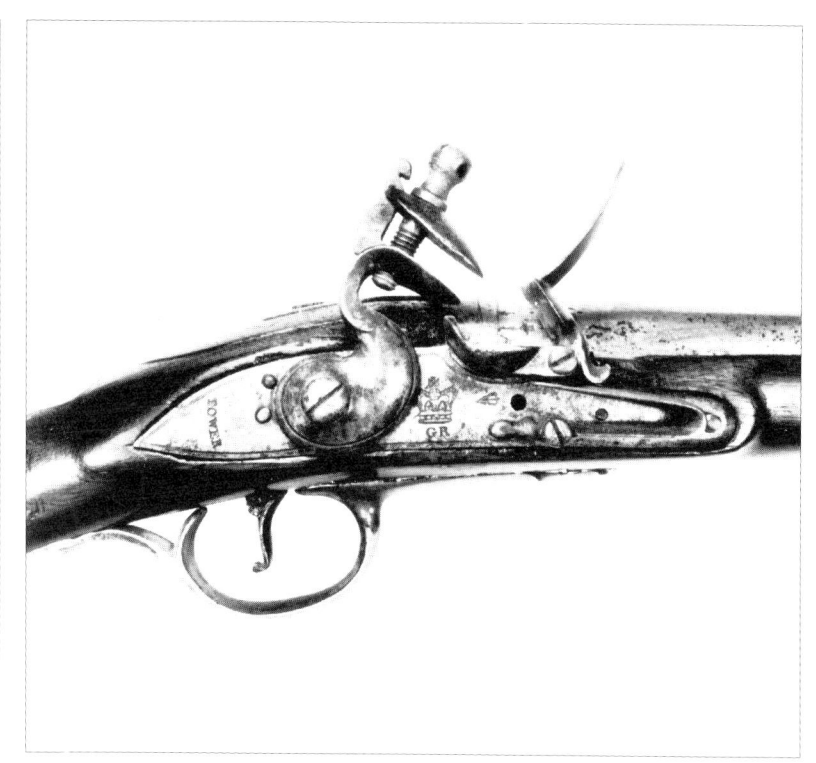

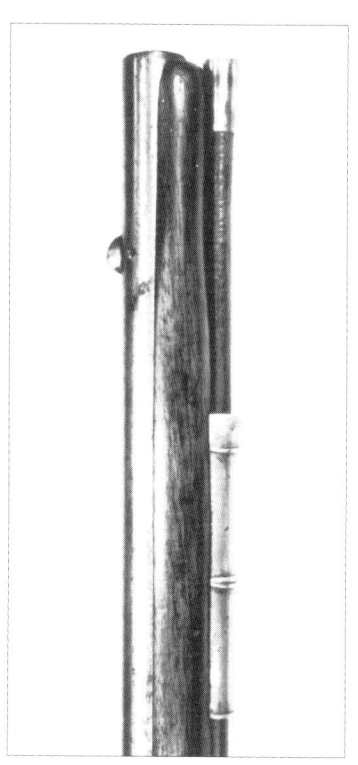

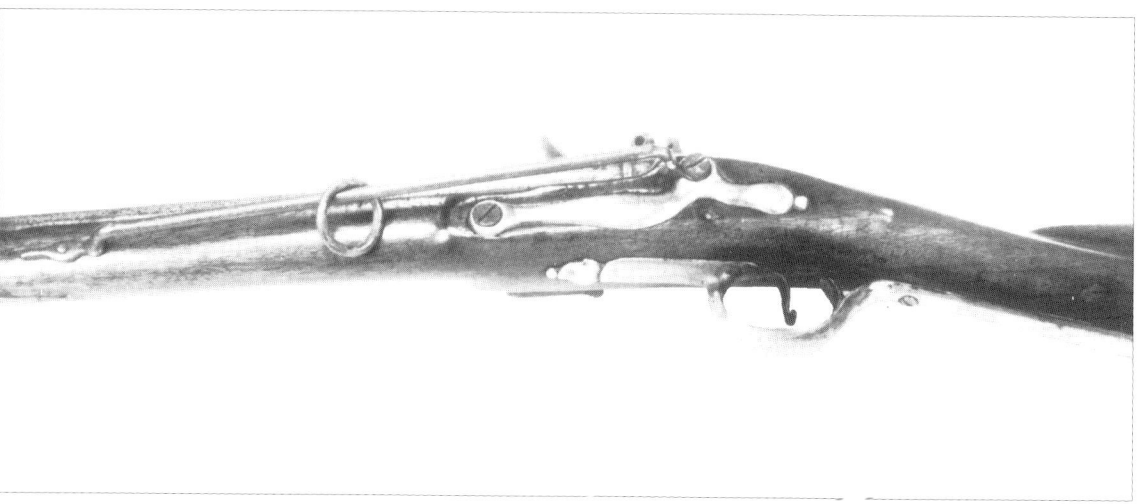

### 119.MM ENGLISH LIGHT HORSE CARBINE PATTERN 1779

**Circa 1779**

This upgraded version of the Light Dragoon 1756 Carbine (118.MM) continues the 37" barrel (.65 caliber), a side bar/ring, stocking to the muzzle (no bayonet), plus a wooden rammer (brass tipped). Its primary difference is adoption of the Type II lock like that chosen for the Short Land infantry musket in 1777 (15.MM). Notice the two screw ends now visible behind its swansneck cock and the lobe-like finial on the frizzen spring, as well as a forward notch in the newly squared post on the cock plus the wraparound extension of its top jaw. The other major change is a longer (3-3/4") upper ramrod pipe that incorporates both a flared forward mouth and a double raised ring at midpoint in the manner of the artillery carbine (121.MM) and 1760 Eliott pattern (124.MM). Visible on the lock plate are "crown / GR / broad arrow" markings under the flash pan, accompanied by "TOWER" on the tail. Like the preceding example, during the American Revolution this carbine was mostly issued to Britain's Loyalist mounted troops, especially in the South. The cock's humpback post form is also now appearing.

Length: 52-3/4"
Barrel: 37-1/4", .68 cal.
Lock: 6-1/4" X 1-1/8"
Trigger Guard: 10-1/2"
Butt Tang: 4-7/8"
Side Plate: 5-1/2"
Furniture: Brass
Weight: 7.1 lbs.

**Author's Collection**

*Chapter 3: Smoothbore Shoulder Arms*  169

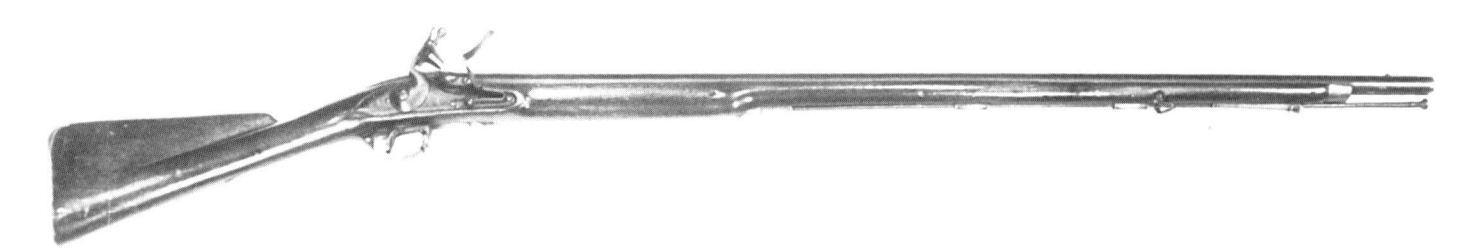

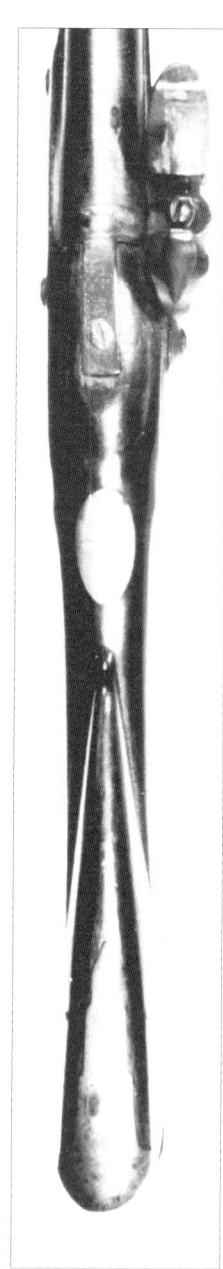

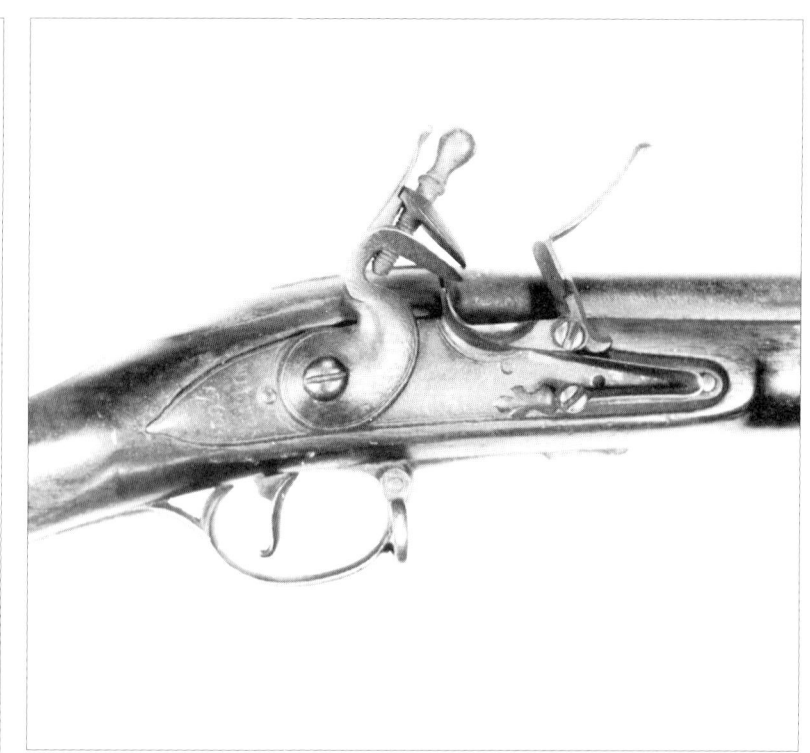

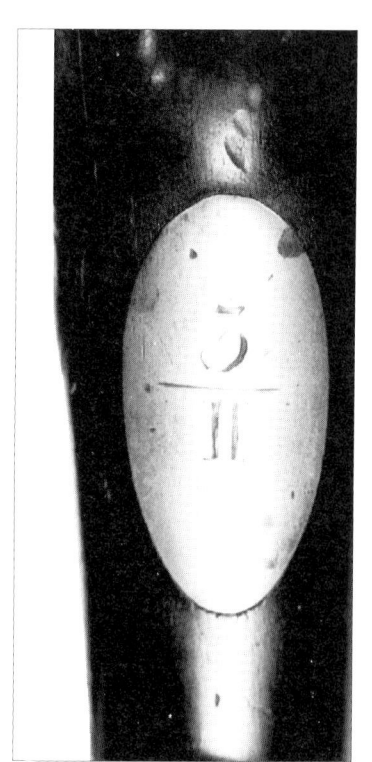

**120.MM ENGLISH CARBINE PATTERN 1770 (SERGEANTS OF GRENADIERS)**　　　　　　　　　　　　　　　　　　　　　　　　　　　　　Circa 1770

Just as fusils were replacing the commissioned officers' spontoons, carbines were beginning to take the place of noncoms' halberds in the line regiments following the French and Indian War. This 39" barreled pattern (.65 caliber) was accepted in 1770 for sergeants of grenadiers and began distribution in 1771 (including fusilier and guard regiments). It is essentially a scaled-down copy of the Long Land 1756 musket with an iron ramrod, four pipes, a nose cap, a straight double-bridled lock and beaver-tail carving around the barrel tang. Yet it changes to an oval escutcheon (versus the usual shield) and a flat horizontal S-shaped side plate design popular on light weapons at this time. The barrel is marked "ROYL NB FUZILIERS" (Royal North British Fusiliers, 21st Regiment of Foot—participants in the 1777 Saratoga campaign with Burgoyne). The lock's tail is inscribed "WILLETS / 1762" (the lock maker and date of manufacture). Such components were usually accumulated by the Board of Ordnance for later assembly, thus the earlier date. "WG" (William Grice) and Tower of London proofs are on the breech; its escutcheon is marked "3/11," that is, the British "fraction" (the unit or company above; the arm's rack number below).

| | | | |
|---|---|---|---|
| Length: 54-3/8" | Lock: 6" X 1-1/8" | Butt Tang: 4-5/8" | Furniture: Brass |
| Barrel: 39", .68 cal. | Trigger Guard: 10-1/2" | Side Plate: 3-7/8" | Weight: 7.2 lbs. |

**Don Troiani Collection**

170　　Chapter 3: Smoothbore Shoulder Arms

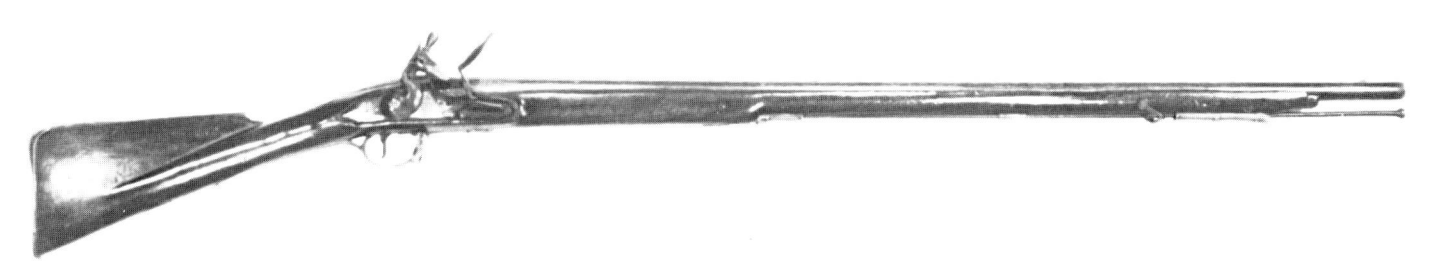

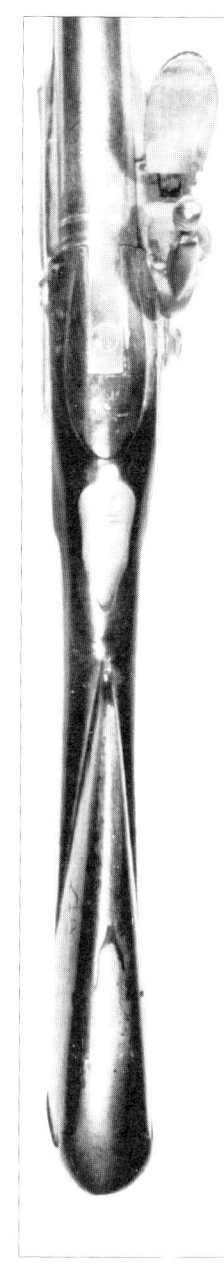

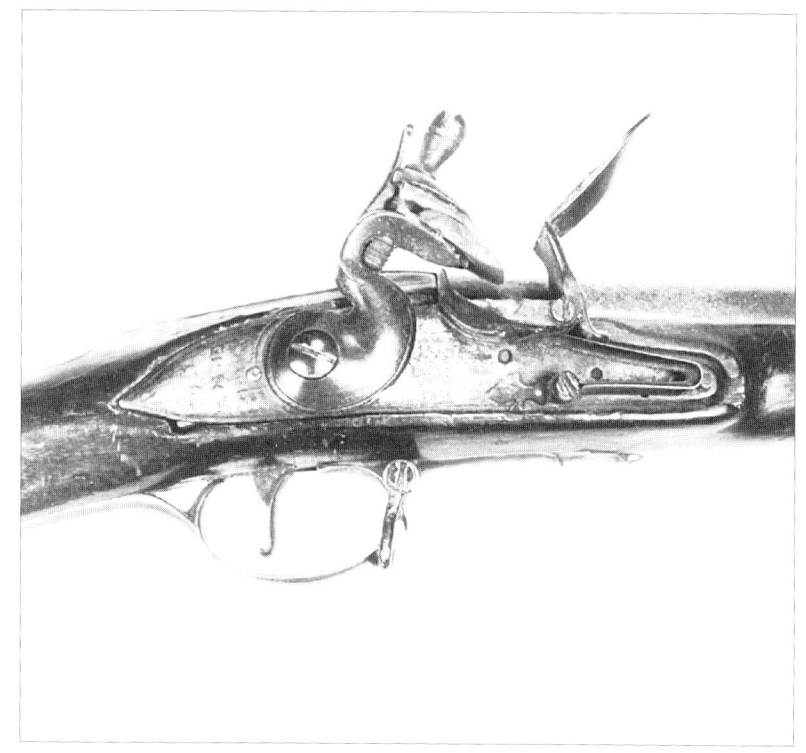

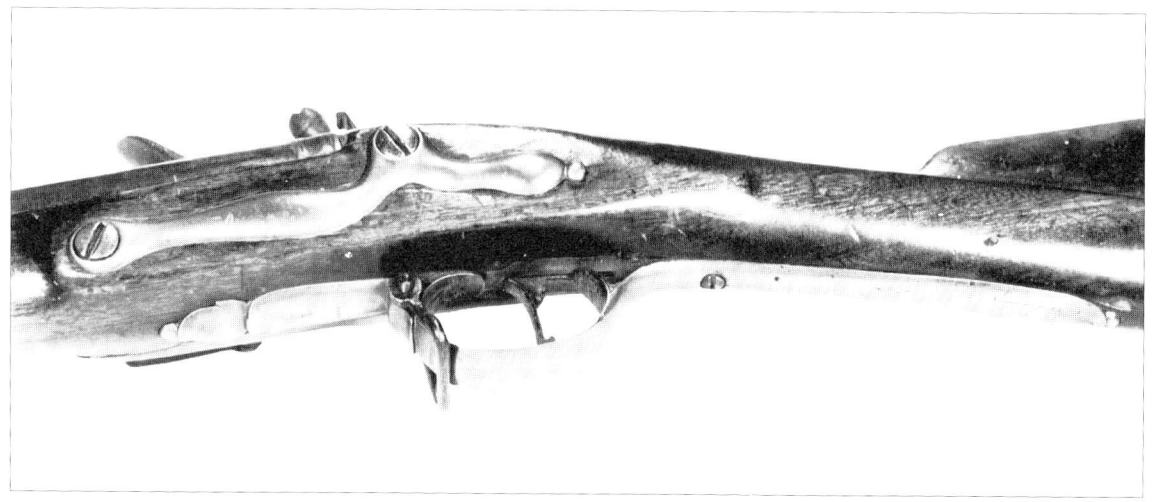

**121.MM ENGLISH CARBINE PATTERN CIRCA 1756 (ARTILLERY #1)**  Circa 1765–1770

Artillery carbines were issued to gunners for defense of their cannon and support equipment. In the mid 1750s, a pattern with a 37" barrel (.65 caliber) and wooden ramrod was authorized. Some were probably issued to new light infantry companies in 1758. Yet most of these carbines were converted to steel rammers with a long flared upper pipe having a raised center double ring (as seen here) beginning in the late 1760s. Overall styling reflects the 1756 Long Land Pattern in reduced size, for example a long two-step butt tang, shield escutcheon, carved beaver-tail at the breech, convex side plate, hazelnut trigger guard, sling swivels, pinned barrel and straight double-bridled lock. This barrel is engraved "ROYL ARTILLERY IB" and stamped with both Tower proofs. Lock markings include the standard "crown / GR / broad arrow" beneath the pan, plus the maker, "GRICE / 1762," on its tail. (Date stamping was discontinued in 1764.) "D / 17" is on the escutcheon. Note, too, that raised carving around the lock and side plate is now minimal. Also see 122.MM.

Length: 52-1/8"  
Barrel: 37", .66 cal.  
Lock: 6-1/8" X 1-1/4"  
Trigger Guard: 10-1/2"  
Butt Tang: 4-5/8"  
Side Plate: 5-1/2"  
Furniture: Brass  
Weight: 7.2 lbs.

**Don Troiani Collection**

Chapter 3: Smoothbore Shoulder Arms  171

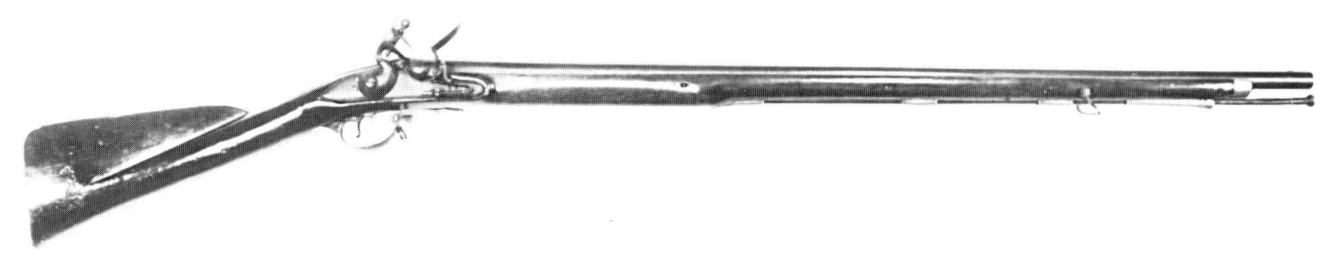

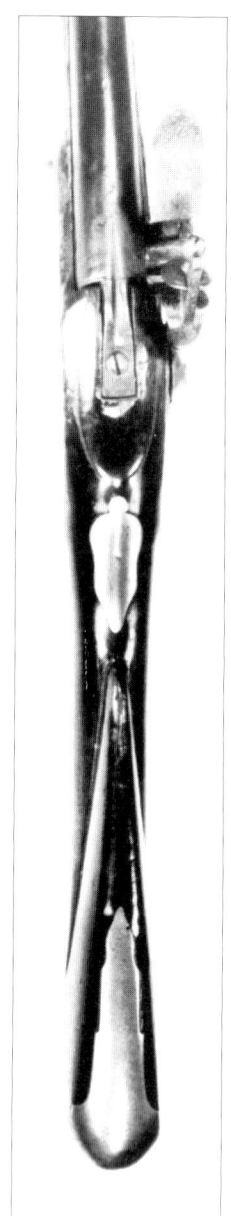

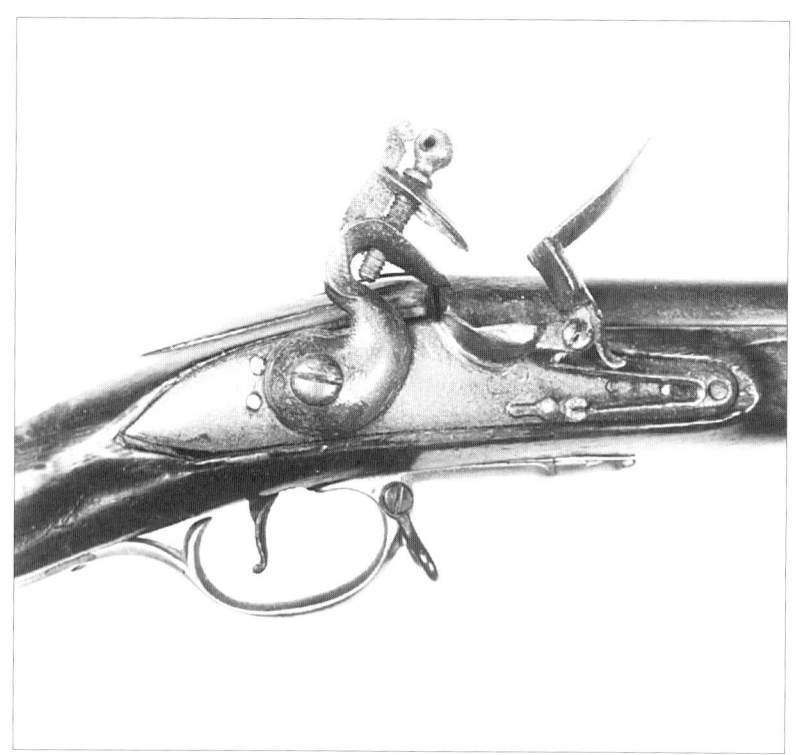

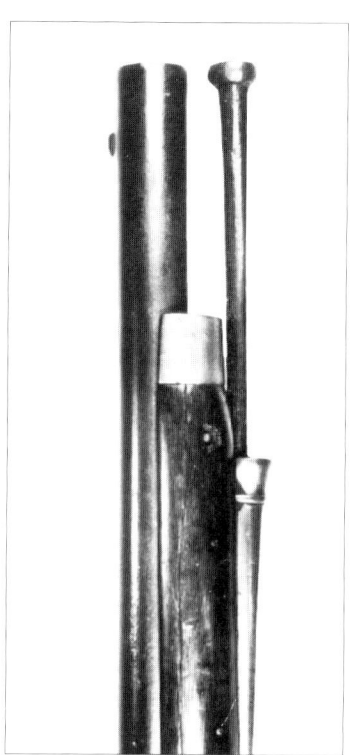

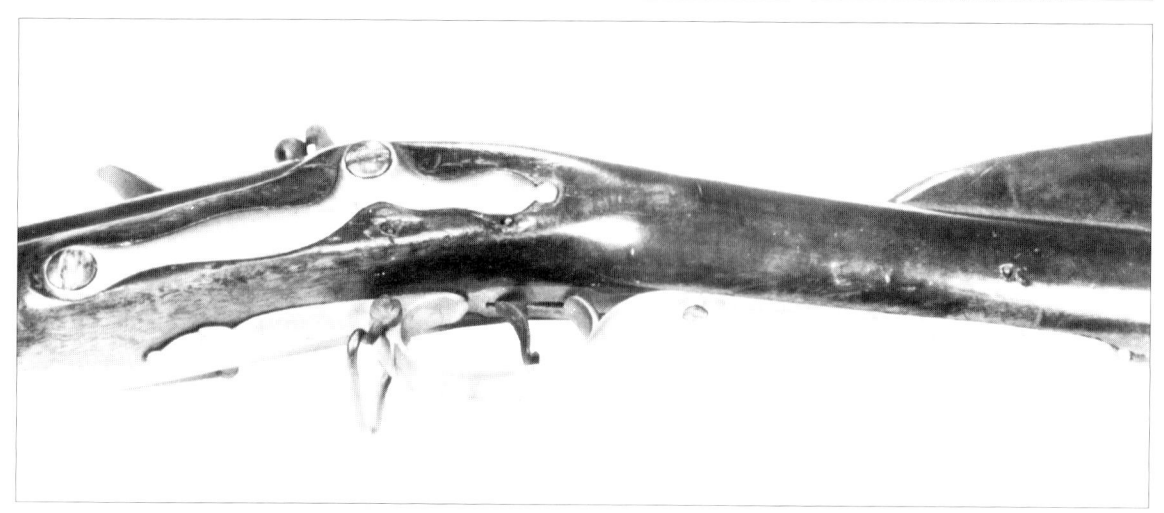

**122.MM  ENGLISH CARBINE PATTERN 1776 (ARTILLERY #2)**  Circa 1777

A revised artillery pattern made with a steel ramrod appeared about 1776. This example includes the revised Lock II adopted for the Short Land Brown Bess in 1777, with its notched hammer post, two screw ends behind the cock and lobed frizzen spring finial. A fourth rammer pipe has also been added, as well as a long flared upper pipe that now omits its raised center rings (see 121.MM). The basic brass furniture from the earlier Long Land Patterns persists in reduced size, for example the three-step butt tang, rounded side plate, shield escutcheon, nose cap and hazelnut trigger guard. Its walnut stock also maintains the established Brown Bess profile with the pinned 37" (.65 caliber) barrel. As with most of these smoothbores, the barrel length measures slightly less than the specifications, the result of periodically dressing the muzzle as the steel ramrod's rubbing action wore down and sharpened the edge of its walls. The lock is marked "TOWER" at the tail and has both Tower proofs on the breech. A storekeeper's stamp is also visible on the outboard buttstock.

| | | | |
|---|---|---|---|
| Length: 51-1/2" | Lock: 6" X 1-1/8" | Butt Tang: 4-3/4" | Furniture: Brass |
| Barrel: 36-3/8", .68 cal. | Trigger Guard: 10-5/8" | Side Plate: 5-1/2" | Weight: 6.7 lbs. |

**Author's Collection**

*Chapter 3: Smoothbore Shoulder Arms*

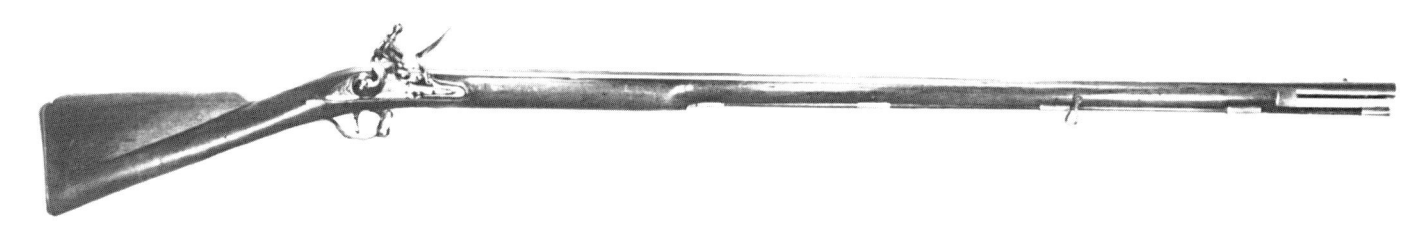

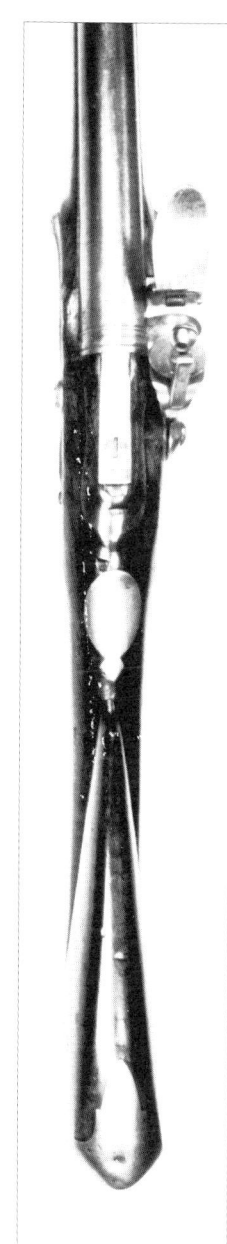

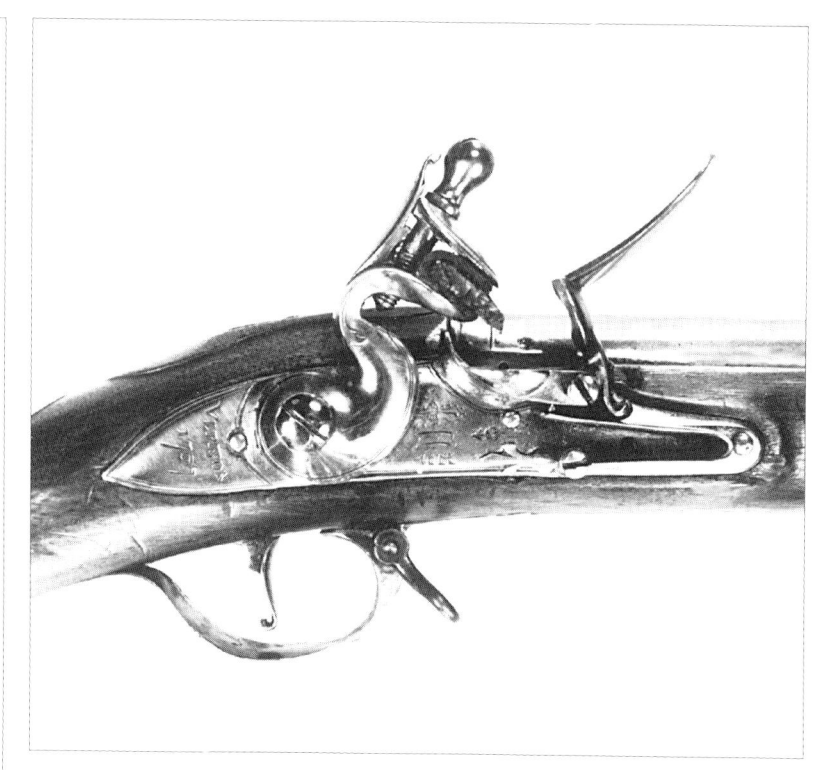

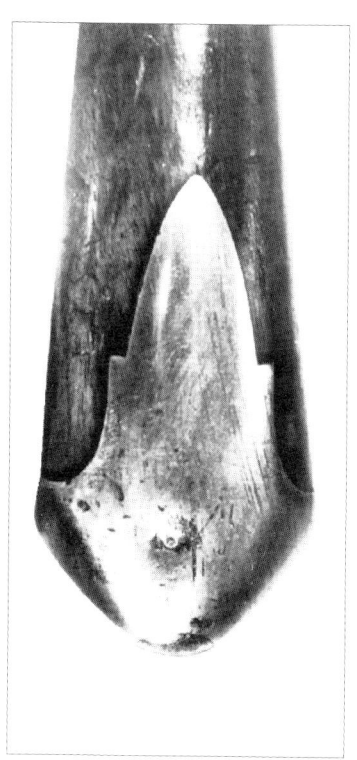

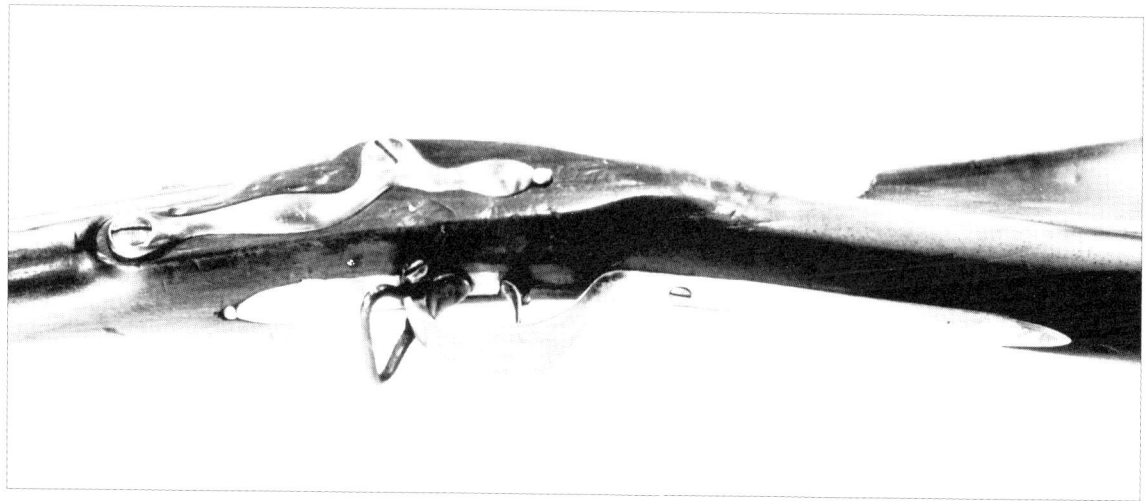

**123.MM  ENGLISH LIGHT INFANTRY CARBINE PATTERN 1760**  Circa 1760

This graceful design combines the Short Land musket's 42" barrel and form with a smaller carbine bore (.65 caliber) and abbreviated brass furniture. It was originally developed for the newly organized light infantry companies here during the French and Indian War. Previously thought to have been issued in large quantities to them at that time, recent research (re: Bailey, bib. 168) indicates that although manufactured circa 1760–1762, the majority remained stored until being issued to the recreated light infantry companies (disbanded in 1763) during 1771, to be carried by them through the American Revolution. This example held a bayonet (18.BB, top stud) and supported a wooden rammer in four equal pipes. Many are found with steel ramrods. Its slender walnut stock includes a scaled-down Long Land side plate, nose band and sling swivels, but the oval/arrow escutcheon, trigger guard and pointed butt tang are innovations. The straight double-bridled lock is marked "VERNON / 1757" on the tail; its breech has Tower proofs.

| | | | |
|---|---|---|---|
| Length: 57-1/2" | Lock: 6-1/8" X 1-1/8" | Butt Tang: 2-1/2" | Furniture: Brass |
| Barrel: 42", .65 cal. | Trigger Guard: 10-1/2" | Side Plate: 3-5/8" | Weight: 7.1 lbs. |

**George C. Neumann Collection, Valley Forge National Historical Park**

*Chapter 3: Smoothbore Shoulder Arms*

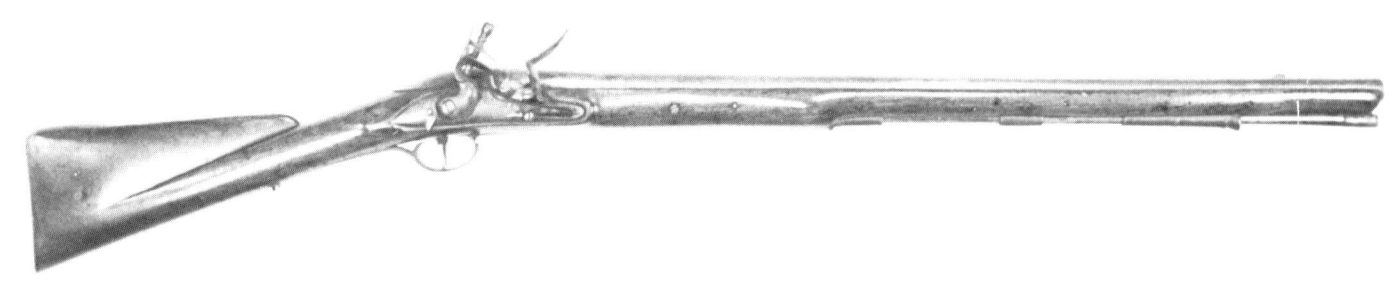

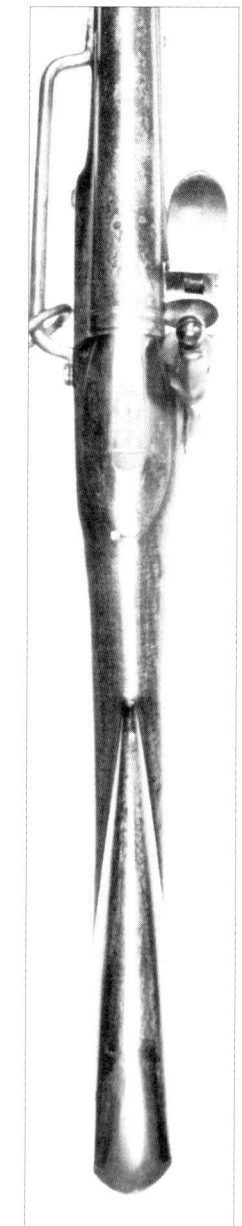

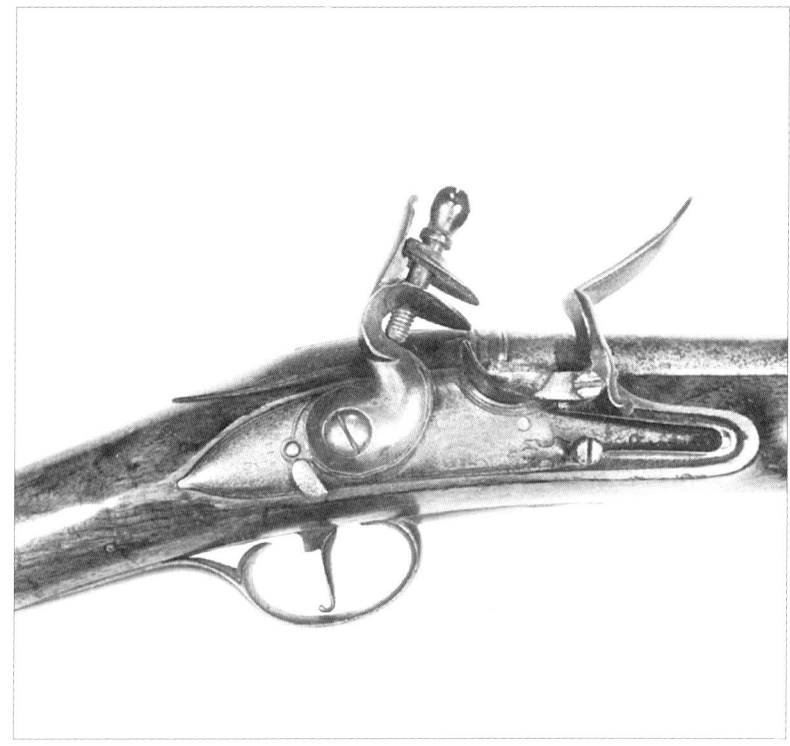

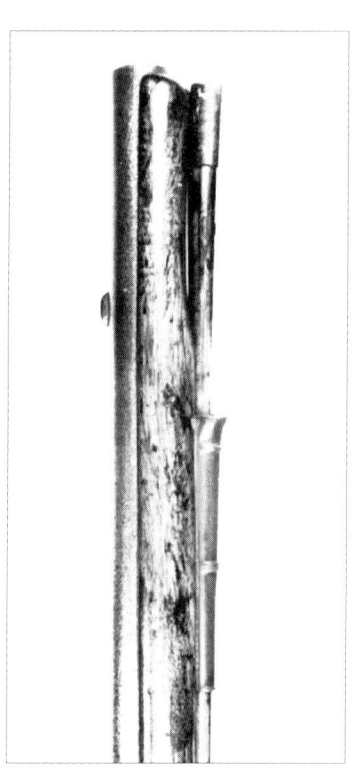

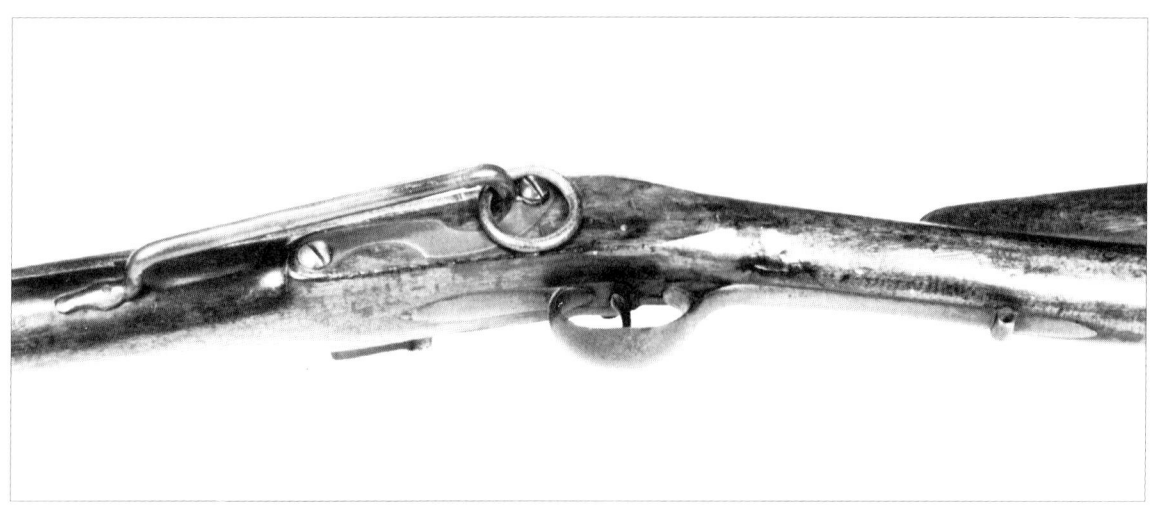

**124.MM  ENGLISH ELIOTT LIGHT HORSE CARBINE PATTERN 1760**                                                                                                                    Circa 1764

Col. George A. Eliott raised the 15th Light Dragoons in 1759 and designed this new carbine for them by 1760. Its subsequent refinements led to a new standard "Eliott" for all light horse regiments by 1773 (125.MM). This rare example of his first pattern has a pinned, short 28" barrel of carbine bore (.65 caliber) that is stocked to the muzzle and provides for sling swivels. The uppermost of its three rammer pipes is long with a flared mouth plus a double-raised ring at midpoint; the wooden rod mounts a brass tip. A 7-1/8" long bar (having a sliding ring that attaches to a shoulder belt's clasp) is anchored by both the rear side screw and a screw that passes through the walnut stock just forward of the lock. This military lock includes a safety catch opposite the lower left corner of its cock. The Birmingham maker's name, "WILLETS / 1764," appears on the tail. Tower proofs are at the breech and a storekeeper's stamp remains in the outboard buttstock. Notice also the currently popular bulbous trigger guard and S-type side plate. There is no escutcheon.

| | | | |
|---|---|---|---|
| Length: 43-1/2" | Lock: 6-1/8" X 1-1/8" | Butt Tang: 2-3/4" | Furniture: Brass |
| Barrel: 28-1/4", .68 cal. | Trigger Guard: 10-1/4" | Side Plate: 3-7/8" | Weight: 5.8 lbs. |

**Robert Nittolo Collection**

*174    Chapter 3: Smoothbore Shoulder Arms*

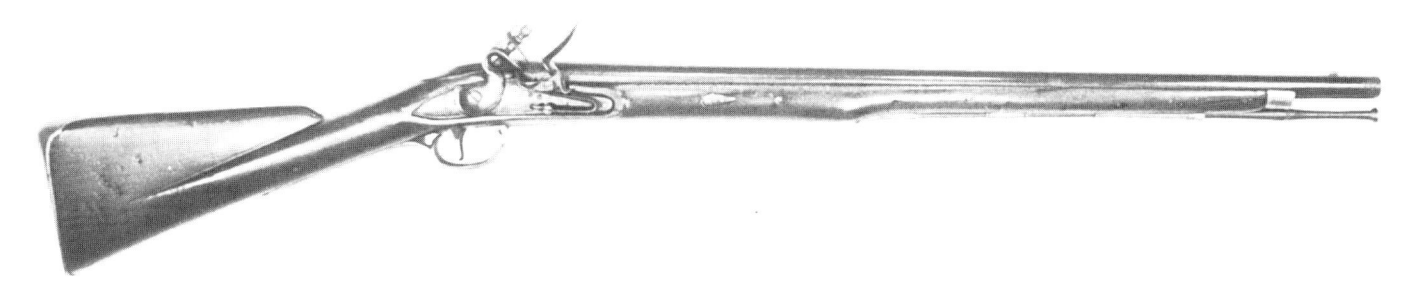

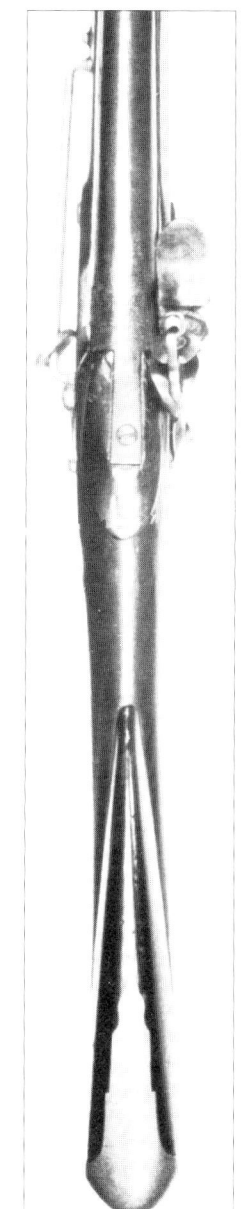

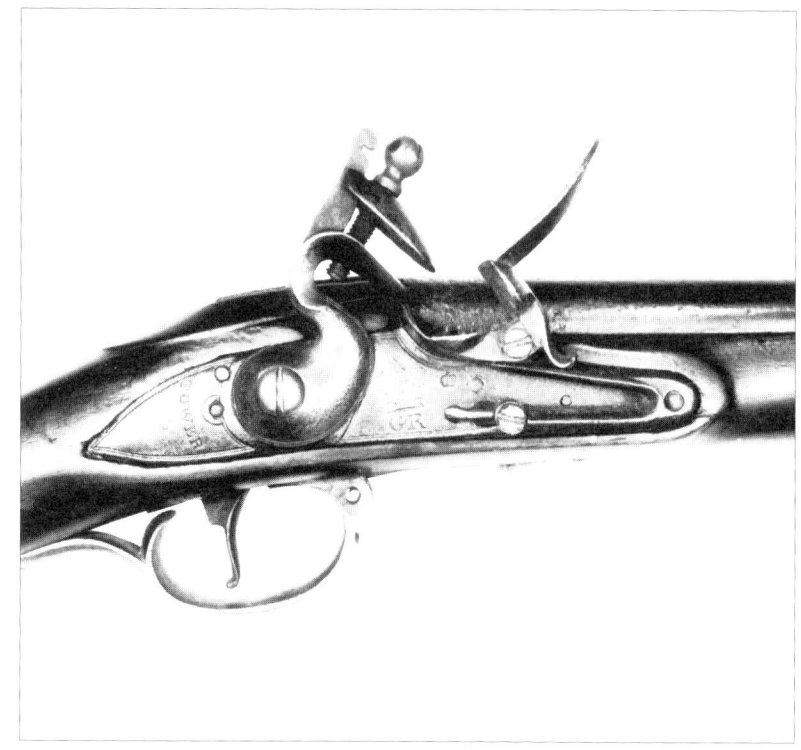

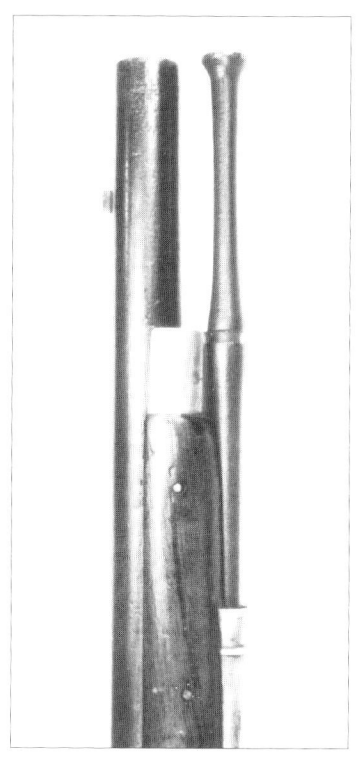

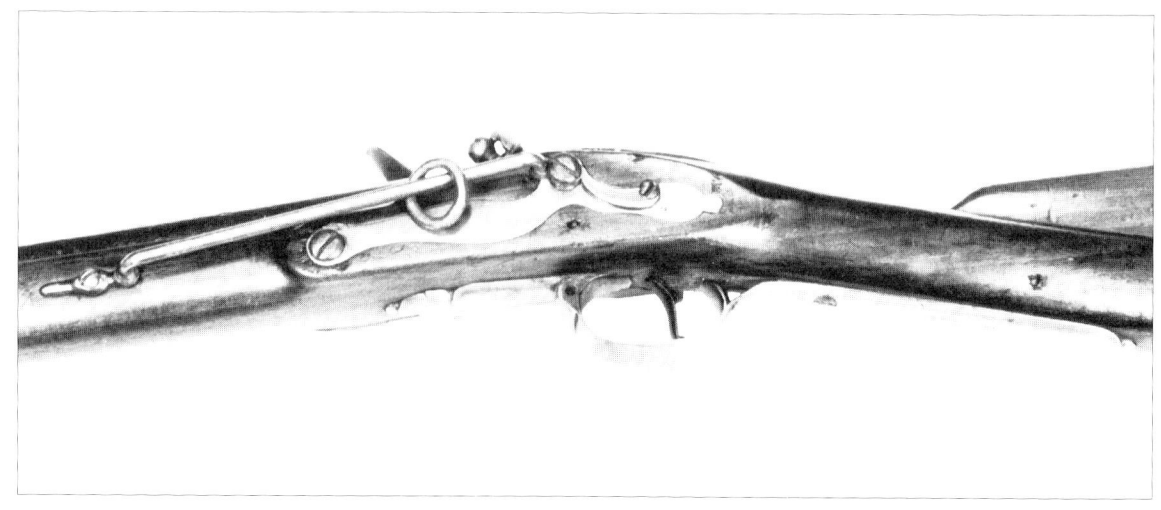

**125.MM  ENGLISH ELIOTT LIGHT DRAGOON CARBINE PATTERN 1773**                                                                    **Circa 1777**

The second Eliott pattern (vs. 124.MM) was accepted in 1773 as the standard longarm for all British light dragoons to succeed the 1756 Pattern (118.MM) then in general use. Its pinned 28" barrel (.65 carbine bore) mounts a socket bayonet (top stud, see 19.BB), while a side bar with ring is on the inboard side. The new form Tower lock and flat side plate copy the Pattern 1777 Short Land musket (15.MM). A three-step butt tang, hazelnut trigger guard and beaver-tail carving, in turn, reflect the earlier Long Land series. An escutcheon is omitted and no sling swivels were apparently attached—despite a drilled hole in the trigger loop. Three pipes (uppermost long and flared) hold the steel rammer in a manner unique to these Eliotts, that is the cast brass nose cap projects a front lip downward to snap into a grooved ring cut in a swollen section of the ramrod. Also note the teardrop-shaped nut for the forward side bar screw in this example. The barrel is stamped "WG" (William Grice, Birmingham), and "RE" is branded twice into the walnut stock. It is believed that Eliott Patterns served with the British 17th Light Dragoons during the American Revolution.

| | | | |
|---|---|---|---|
| Length: 43-1/2" | Lock: 6-1/8" X 1-1/8" | Butt Tang: 4-5/8" | Furniture: Brass |
| Barrel: 27-7/8", .69 cal. | Trigger Guard: 10-5/8" | Side Plate: 5-3/4" | Weight: 6.7 lbs. |

**Author's Collection**

*Chapter 3: Smoothbore Shoulder Arms*     175

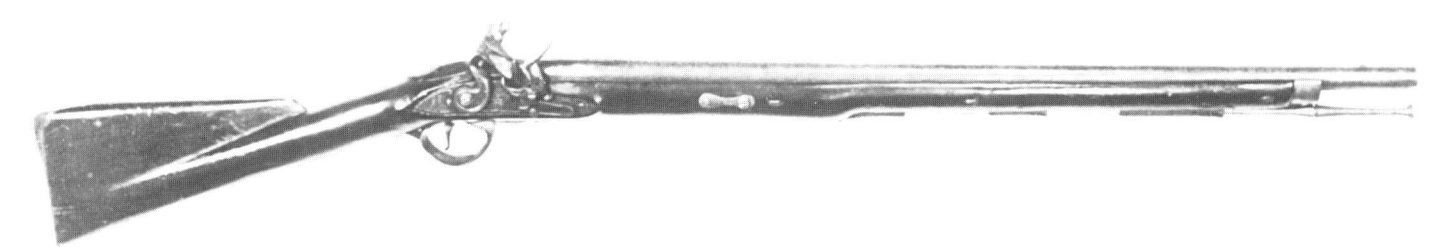

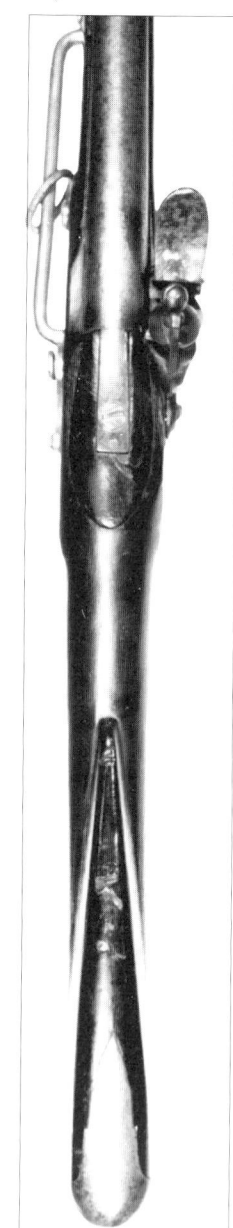

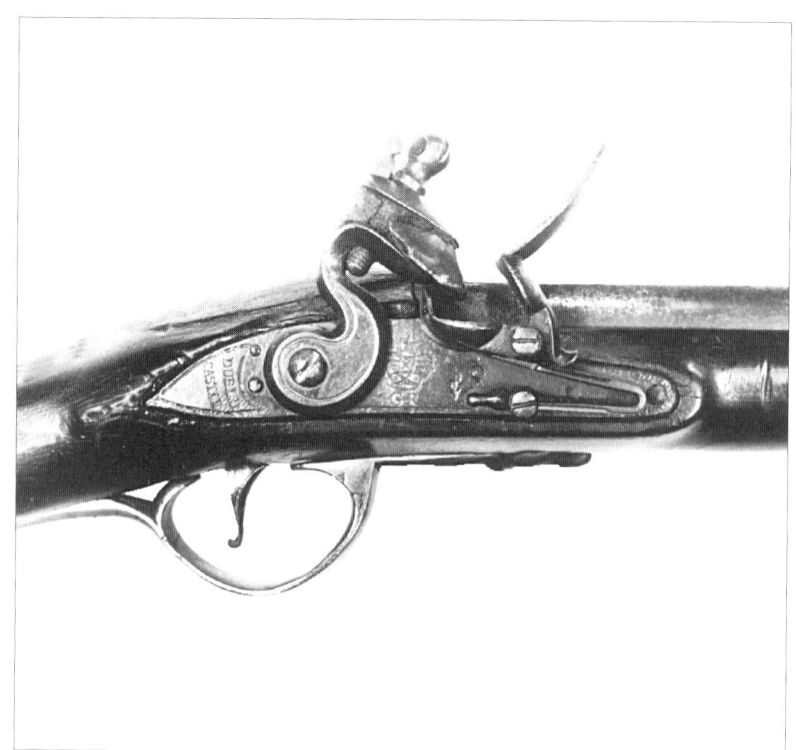

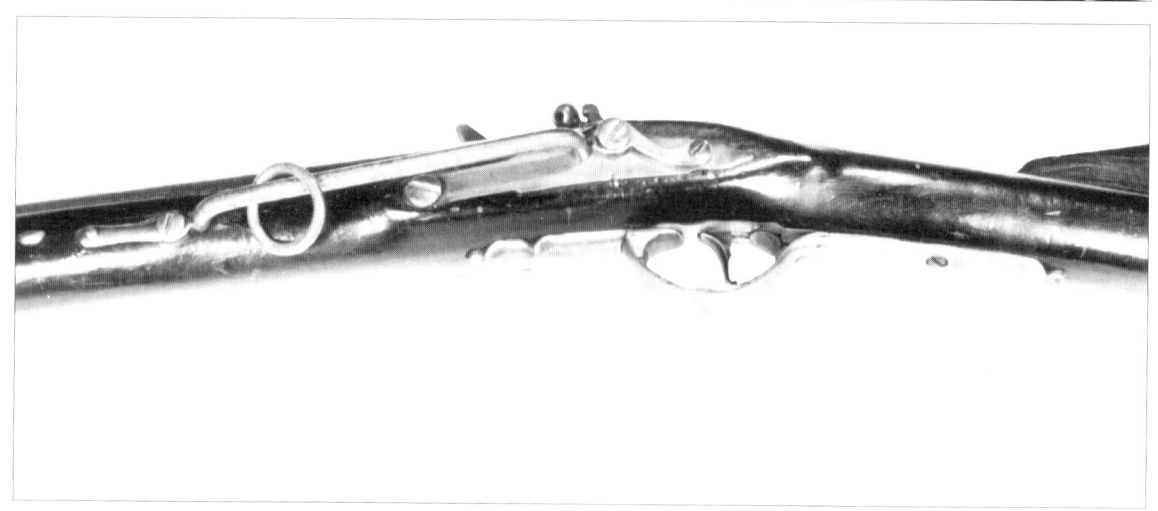

**126.MM  ENGLISH "ROYAL FORESTER" CARBINE PATTERN 1776**                                                                                             Circa 1776

This near relative of the Eliott carbine (125.MM) was carried by Britain's 16th Light Dragoons when they reached America in 1776 from Ireland. It embraces the basic Eliott pattern but includes several distinct differences: the lock is now flat and bears the usual "crown / GR / broad arrow" under the pan, as well as "DUBLIN CASTLE" on its tail (the Irish Establishment armory circa 1740–1798); the standard 28" barrel (.65 caliber) is secured by three flat keys instead of pins and mounts a bayonet; its side bar and ring are held at the rear by both a lock screw and wood screw against a flat triangular side plate, plus two forward screws that penetrate through the stock to a unique double-lobed outboard plate. Of the three rammer pipes, both the first and second have a flared mouth. Some earlier Eliott characteristics do persist however: the iron notched-ring ramrod, raised beaver-tail carving, three-step butt tang and absence of an escutcheon. There is no indication of sling swivels.

| | | | |
|---|---|---|---|
| Length: 43-1/8" | Lock: 5-3/8" X 1" | Butt Tang: 3-1/2" | Furniture: Brass |
| Barrel: 28-1/8", .68 cal. | Trigger Guard: 8-3/4" | Side Plate: 5-1/4" | Weight: 6.5 lbs. |

**The Benninghoff Collection**

176   *Chapter 3: Smoothbore Shoulder Arms*

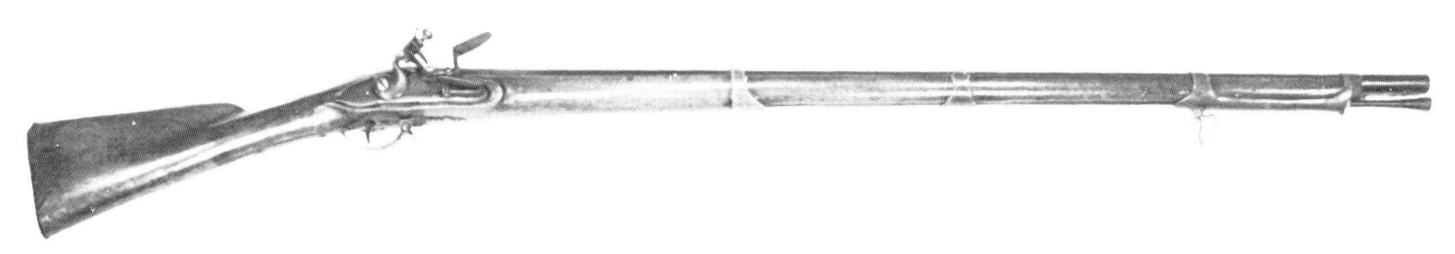

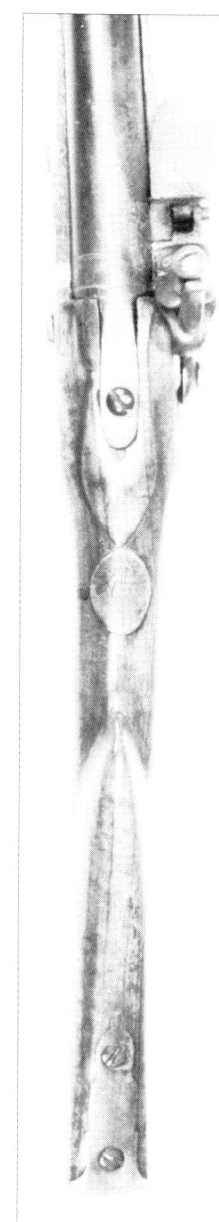

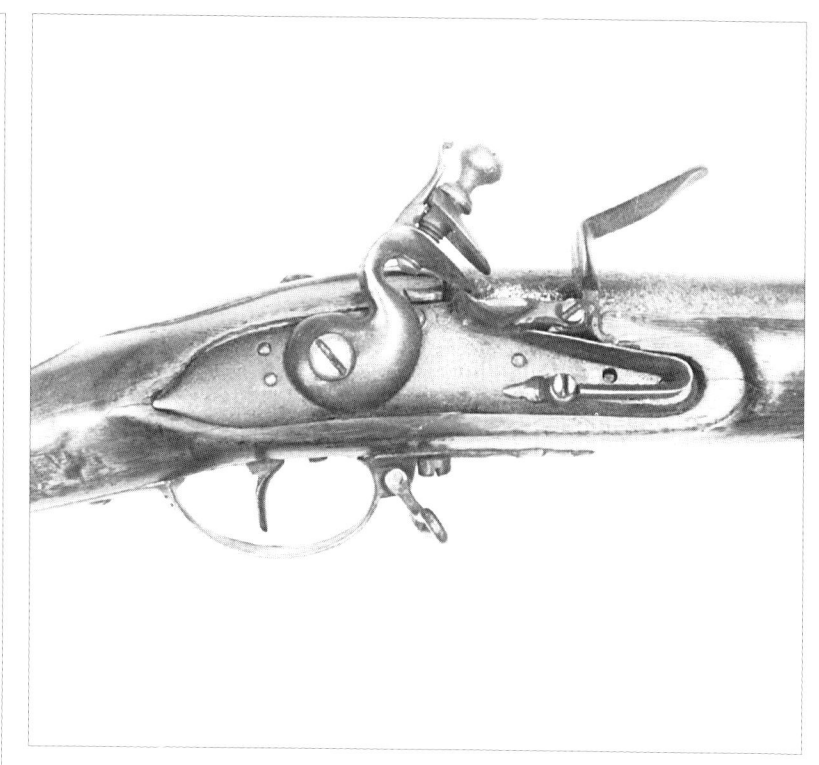

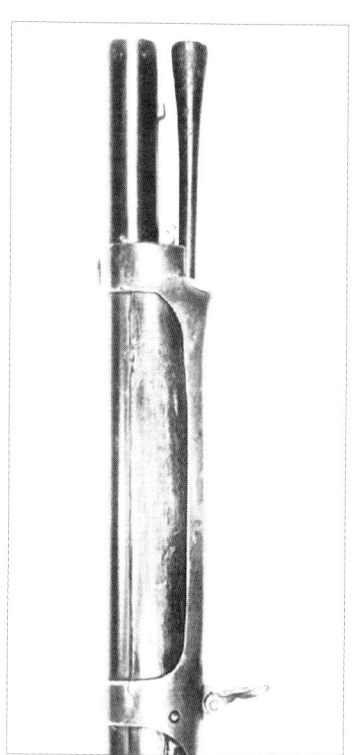

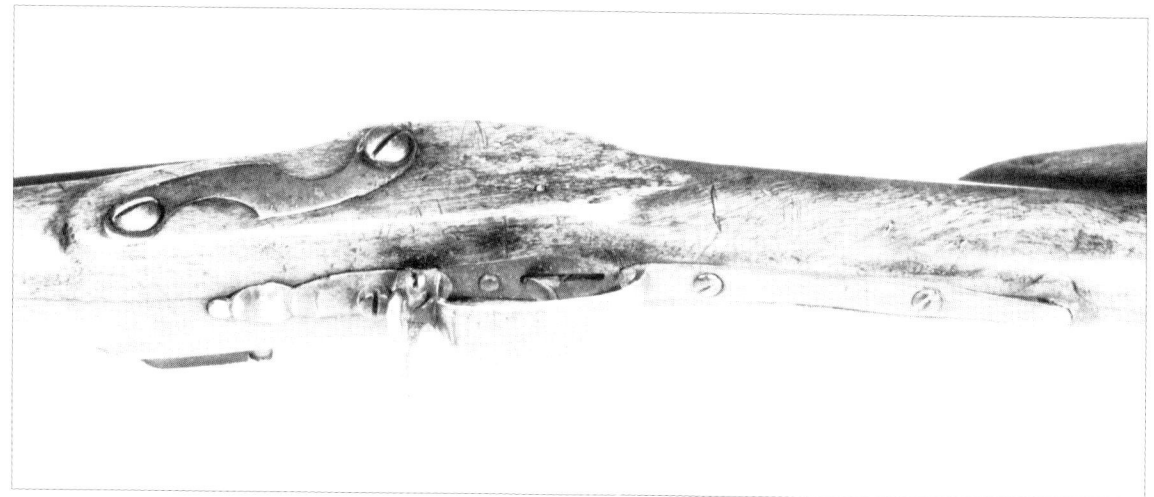

### 127.MM DUTCH MUSKET/CARBINE
**Circa 1771–1800**

Because of the number of this pattern found today, it is now considered a more widely used carbine or light musket rather than a fusil. The most distinctive feature is its elongated upper barrel band (7-1/2"), which is held by a rear side spring. Both of the other bands are friction-fitted (four bands are also encountered). Holland's influence on British styling is apparent in this trigger guard's hazelnut front terminal, baluster breech and S-type side plate. Note also the oval escutcheon (marked "N=3") plus the innovative barrel tang carving that is a variance of the Germanic teardrop form. Of further interest is the clasp projecting out of the forend to snap over the rear ring of a socket bayonet (see similar arrangement on French Model 1774, 46.MM). The typical thin Dutch butt plate continues its two large projecting screw heads at the back, as well as flush heads in the three-stepped tang. The steel rammer has a trumpet head. An Amsterdam control mark is stamped into the rounded breech of the 40" (.72 caliber) barrel. The stock is walnut.

Length: 55-1/4"   Lock: 5-3/4" X 1-1/8"   Butt Tang: 3-1/2"   Furniture: Brass
Barrel: 40", .72 cal.   Trigger Guard: 9-1/2"   Side Plate: 3-1/2"   Weight: 8.1 lbs.

**Author's Collection**

*Chapter 3: Smoothbore Shoulder Arms* 177

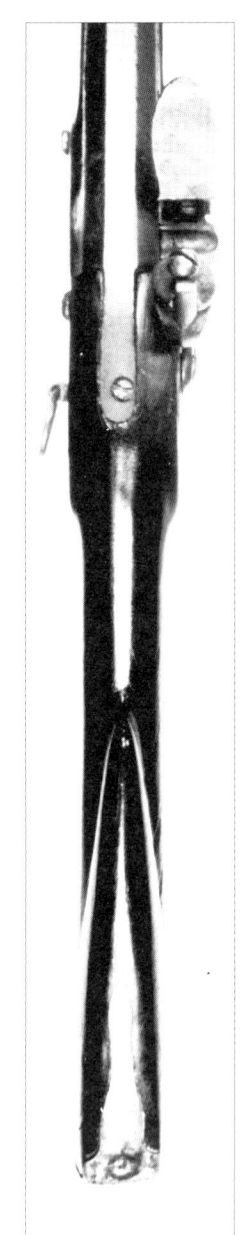

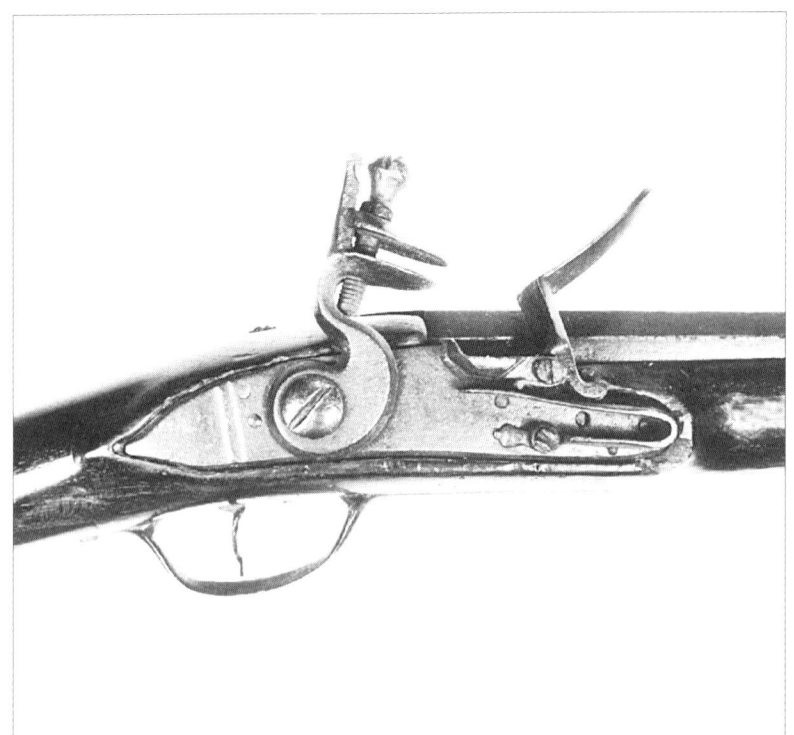

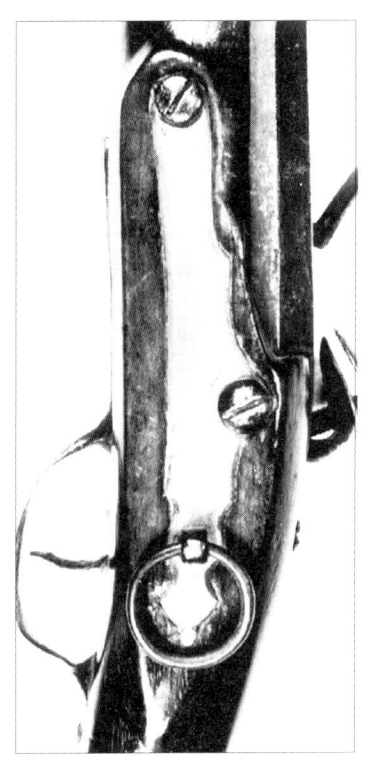

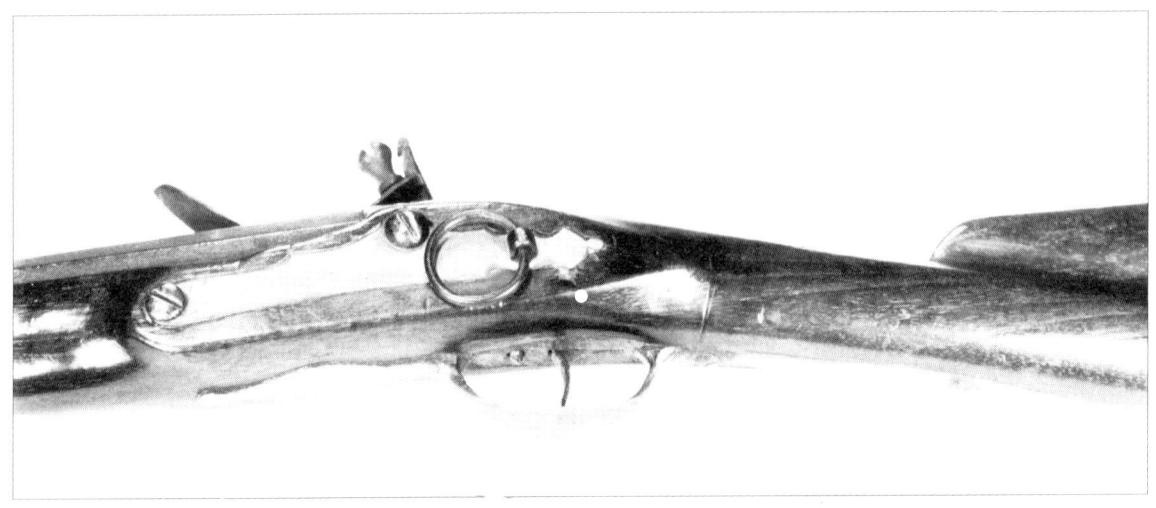

**128.MM  FRENCH DRAGOON MUSKET MODEL 1733**  Circa 1733

Like their British counterparts, French dragoons moved on horseback but fought as infantry with muskets and bayonets. Their longarms traditionally mixed iron and brass components (129.MM) and, especially in the early patterns, closely followed the regular army patterns. This Model 1733 is strongly influenced by the army Model 1728 (39.MM) with the exception of adding brass furniture and a distinctive side plate, which appears on both the horseman's pistol (21.PP) and cavalry's carbine (130.MM) in 1733. The original dragoon specifications listed an iron center barrel band, but all here are brass. The Roman nose walnut stock, two side sling swivels, pointed end trigger guard, long thin butt tang, three barrel bands and flat double-bridled lock reflect the Model 1728 land service configuration. Its barrel, however, is slightly smaller—45-1/4 inches (.67 caliber, octagonal breech for 7-1/2 inches). Six thousand were made. Although France's heavy dragoons did not officially serve here during the Revolutionary War, the more than 100,000 arms supplied as aid to the Americans included patterns from all of their services.

| | | | |
|---|---|---|---|
| Length: 60-3/4" | Lock: 6-1/4" X 1-1/4" | Butt Tang: 4" | Furniture: Brass |
| Barrel: 45-1/8", .68 cal. | Trigger Guard: 11" | Side Plate: 5-1/2" | Weight: 8.5 lbs. |

**Robert Nittolo Collection**

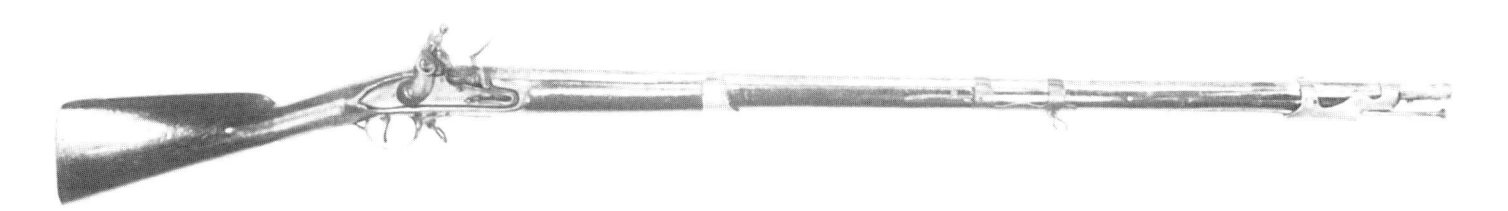

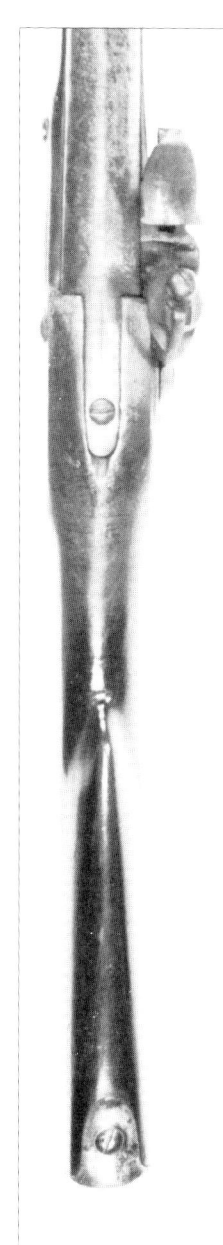

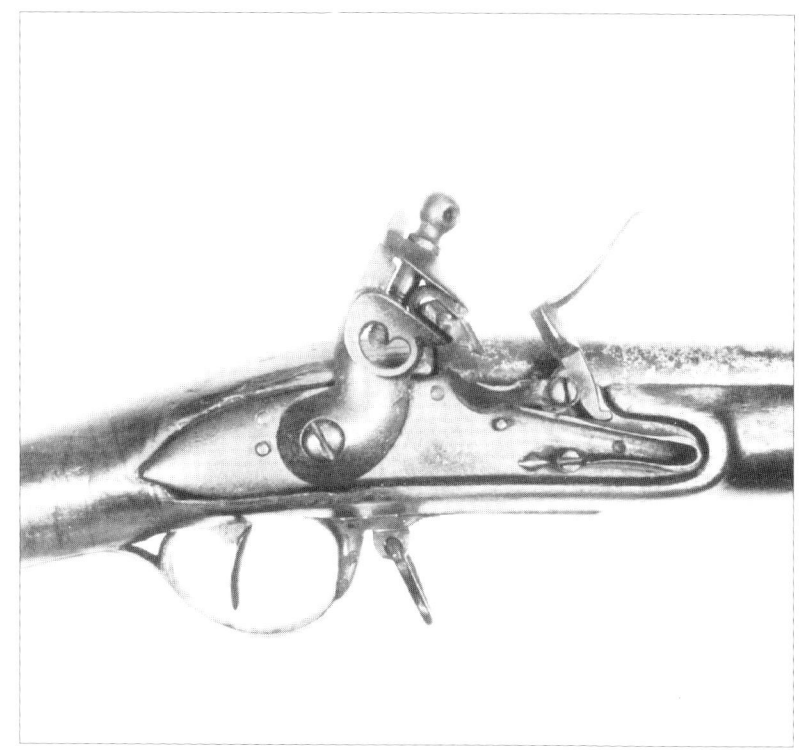

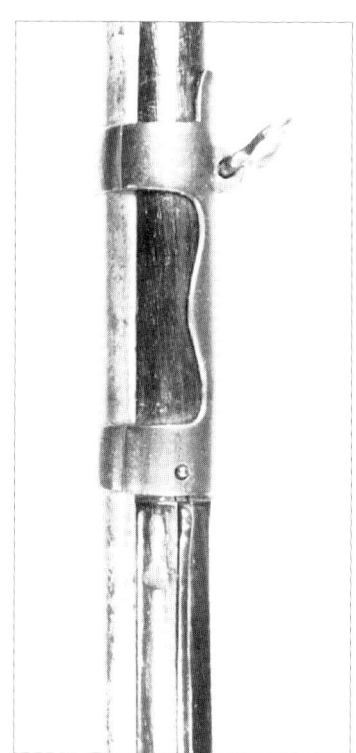

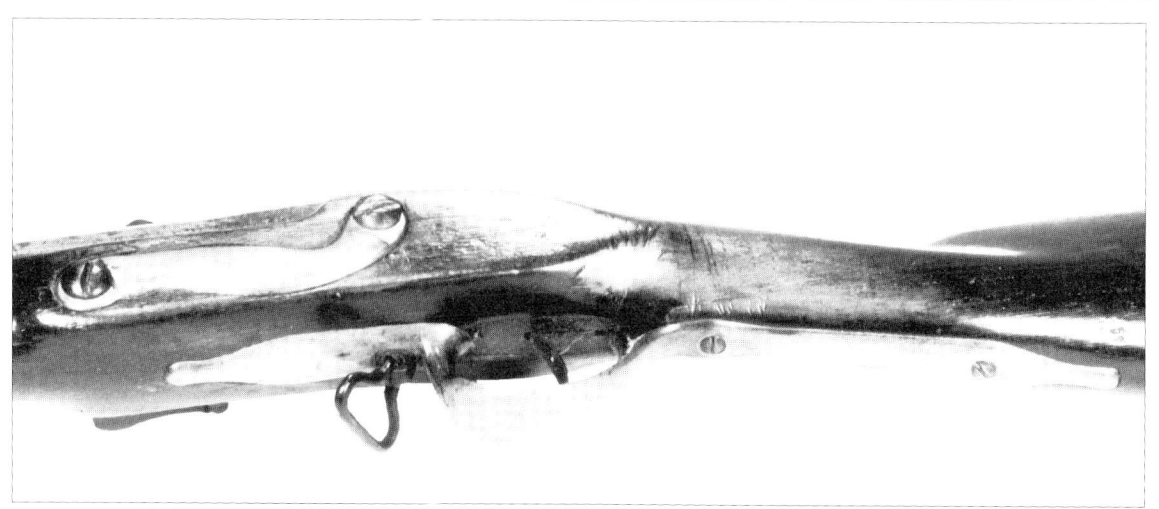

### 129.MM FRENCH DRAGOON MUSKET MODEL 1770–1771
**Circa 1772**

Successive French dragoon musket patterns continued to follow a tradition of mixed iron and brass furniture. Since 1754 their preference also included a long brass upper barrel band of two straps (4-7/8 inches here; undulating side edge) and an iron double strap center band (4-5/8 inches), with a lock matching the standard infantry pattern. This example has a rounded circa 1770 lock ("St. Etienne") and a 42" barrel (original .67 bore, rounded breech, side flats). Most components are brass, including the two-screw buttplate (lobed tang), double-pointed trigger guard, convex S-shaped side plate and the top and bottom barrel bands. The distinctive two-strap iron center band displays a forward lip, as well as a bell-shaped swivel. Both upper bands are secured by long (2-1/8", 2-3/4") rear side springs (lowest held by friction). The trigger bow, in turn, adds a forward spur to the rear post, while the bayonet stud—uniquely on the right side of previous models—is now directly beneath the barrel. About 5,000 were manufactured. This particular musket has a family history of American use during the Revolutionary War.

| | | | |
|---|---|---|---|
| Length: 57-1/4" | Lock: 6-1/8" X 1-1/8" | Butt Tang: 2" | Furniture: Brass/Iron |
| Barrel: 42", .72 cal. | Trigger Guard: 10-1/2" | Side Plate: 3-7/8" | Weight: 8.0 lbs. |

**Author's Collection**

*Chapter 3: Smoothbore Shoulder Arms*

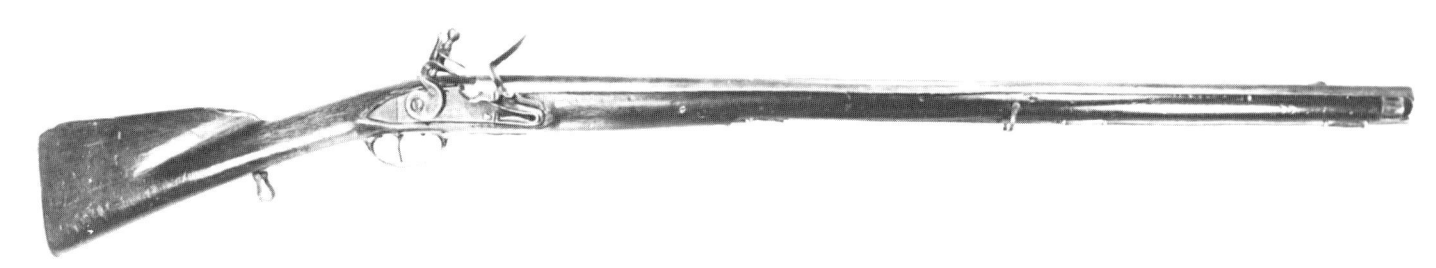

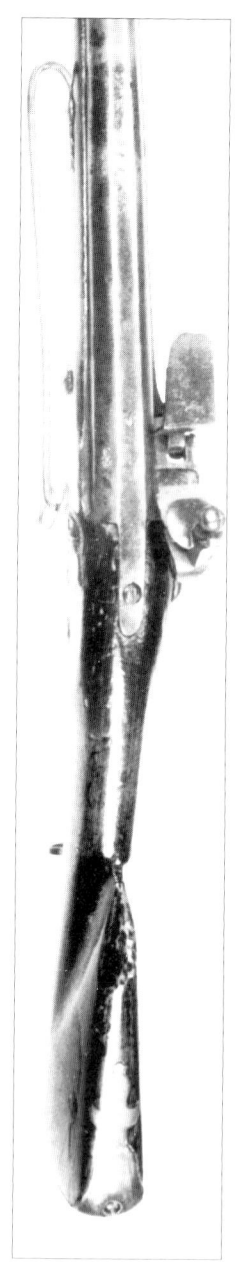

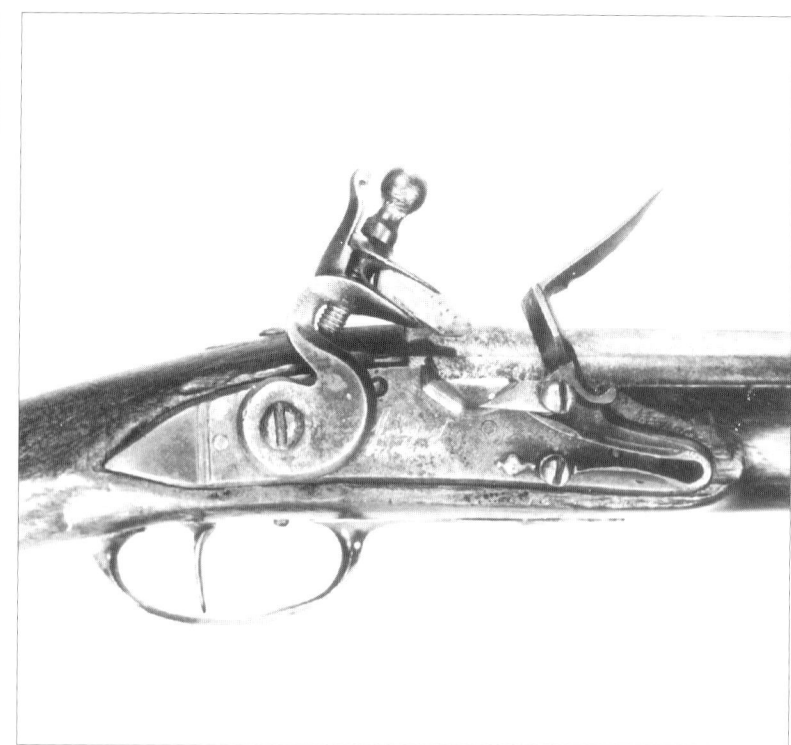

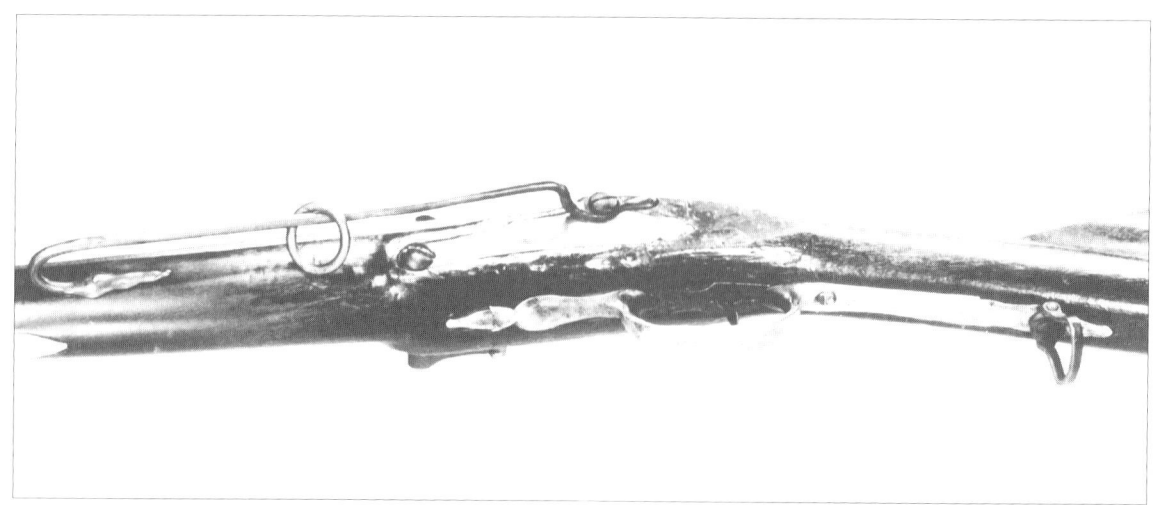

**130.MM  FRENCH CAVALRY CARBINE ("MUSKETOON") MODEL 1733**                                                                                                              Circa 1733

Carbines for France's light cavalry (mousquetons de cavalerie), who fought from horseback, were smaller and of less weight than the "heavy" dragoon muskets (used dismounted with a bayonet, see 129.MM). Yet these scaled down cavalry arms were still influenced by the dragoon patterns. (Note: British terms were "light dragoons" and "carbines"; the French were "cavalry" and "musketoons.") This early model includes a scaled-down flat lock ("Charleville") like the Dragoon's Model 1733 (128.MM) but mounts some unusual brass furniture, which includes a triple branch butt tang, a bud-shaped trigger guard terminal, as well as a unique side plate associated with 1733 arms patterns (also see 21.PP). A side bar (note the reversed forward end) holds a ring that hooked onto a cross belt clip. Two sling swivels are also present, of which the rear one is attached by a screw at the end of the trigger guard. Its short, .67 caliber barrel (octagon breech) is stocked to the muzzle (thin brass nose band). About 25,000 were produced, plus 1,100 with rifling beginning eight inches below the muzzle. This pattern is considered among the arms supplied by France to the American rebels.

| | | | |
|---|---|---|---|
| Length: 45" | Lock: 5-3/4" X 1-1/8" | Butt Tang: 3-3/4" | Furniture: Brass |
| Barrel: 30-3/4", .67 cal. | Trigger Guard: 10" | Side Plate: 4-3/8" | Weight: 6.0 lbs. |

**George C. Neumann Collection, Valley Forge National Historical Park**

180     *Chapter 3: Smoothbore Shoulder Arms*

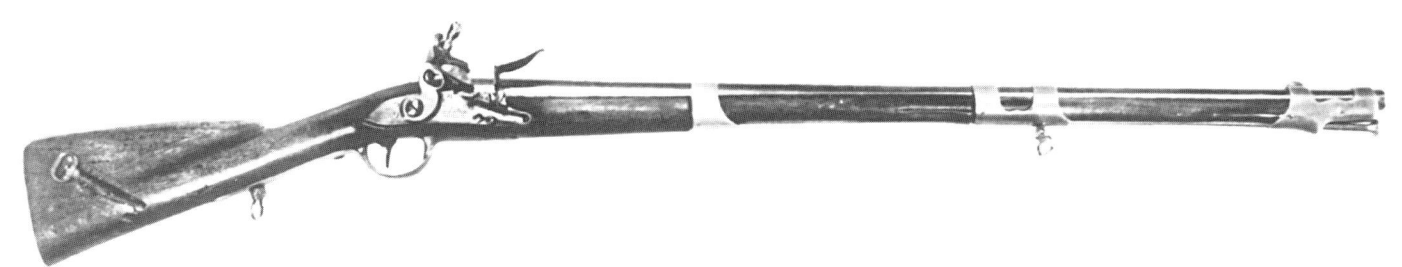

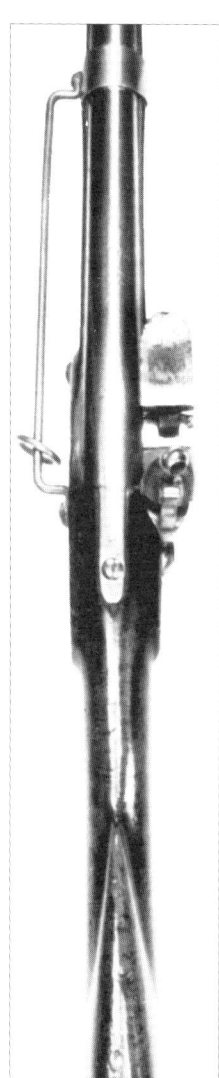

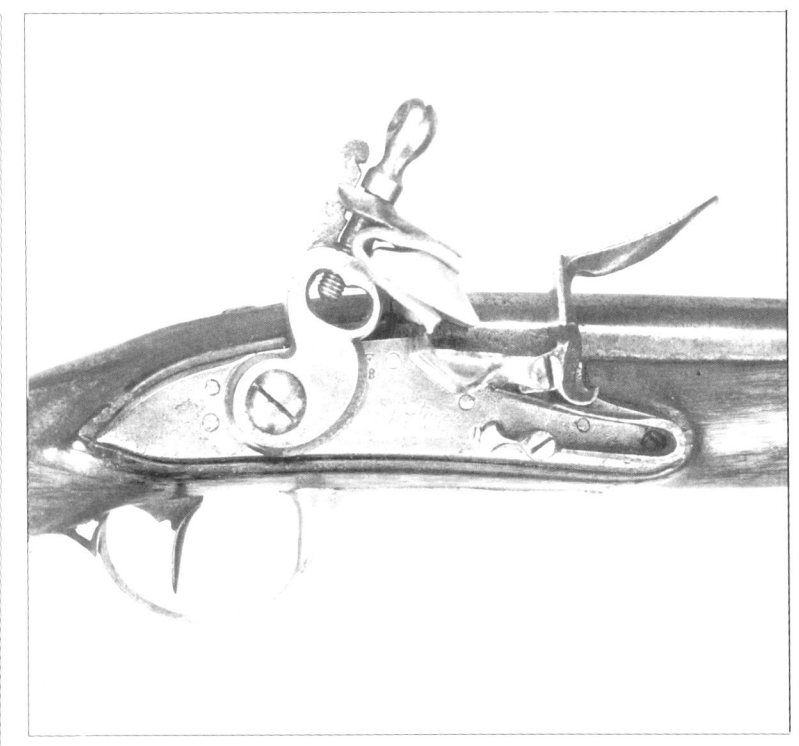

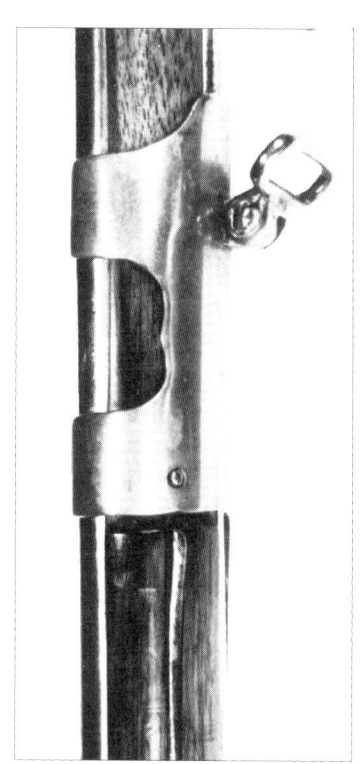

**131.MM FRENCH CAVALRY CARBINE ("MUSKETOON") MODEL 1766**  Circa 1766

This light horseman's carbine has a scaled-down version of the flat/ringed cock lock favored on infantry muskets during the 1760s (see 43.MM). Its brass furniture, in turn, shows influence from the larger heavy dragoon musket (129.MM), that is, the unique center band has a double strap, as does the long upper band with its curved side edge. The S-shaped side plate is convex. A top wood screw secures the blunt butt plate tang, while its cavalry-type side bar has the forward end anchored to the bottom barrel band. A walnut stock extends to the muzzle (button-head steel ramrod). The sling swivels are attached to the center band and a screw at the rear of the trigger guard. About 6,400 were produced. "Manufacture de Charleville" appears on this lock plate. Later Model 1766s made at St. Etienne during the early 1770s usually have the convex lock of that period. The key-shaped stock brand was probably for identification in later use.

Length: 45"
Barrel: 31", .68 cal.
Lock: 5-1/2" X 1-1/8"
Trigger Guard: 10-1/4"
Butt Tang: 2"
Side Plate: 3-1/2"
Furniture: Brass
Weight: 6.1 lbs.

**George C. Neumann Collection, Valley Forge National Historical Park**

*Chapter 3: Smoothbore Shoulder Arms*  **181**

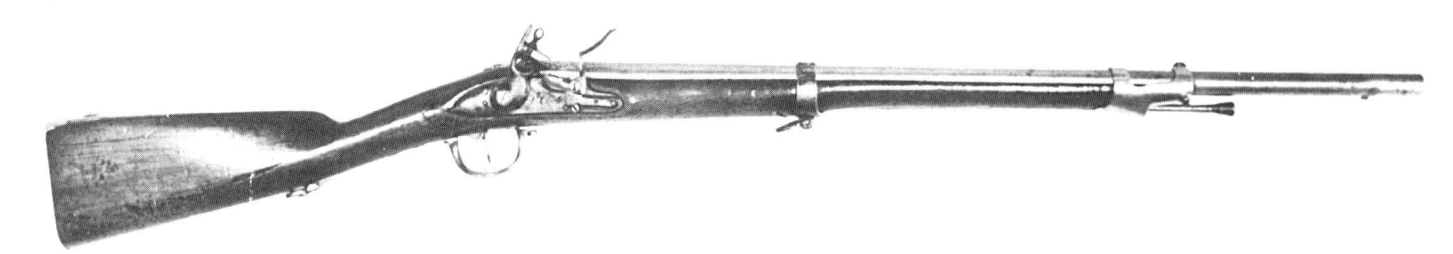

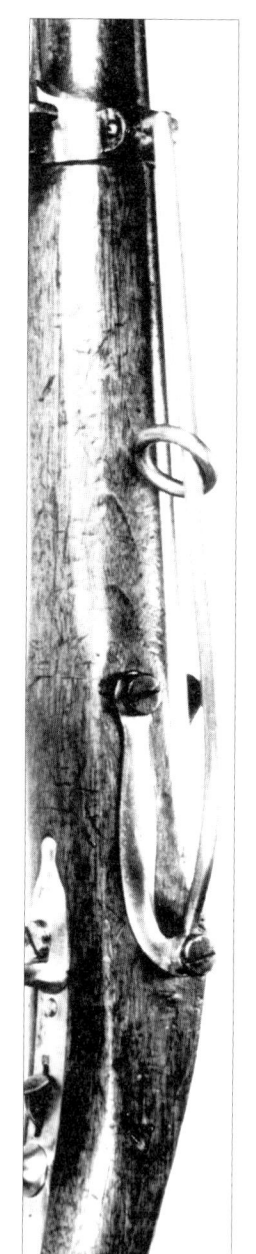

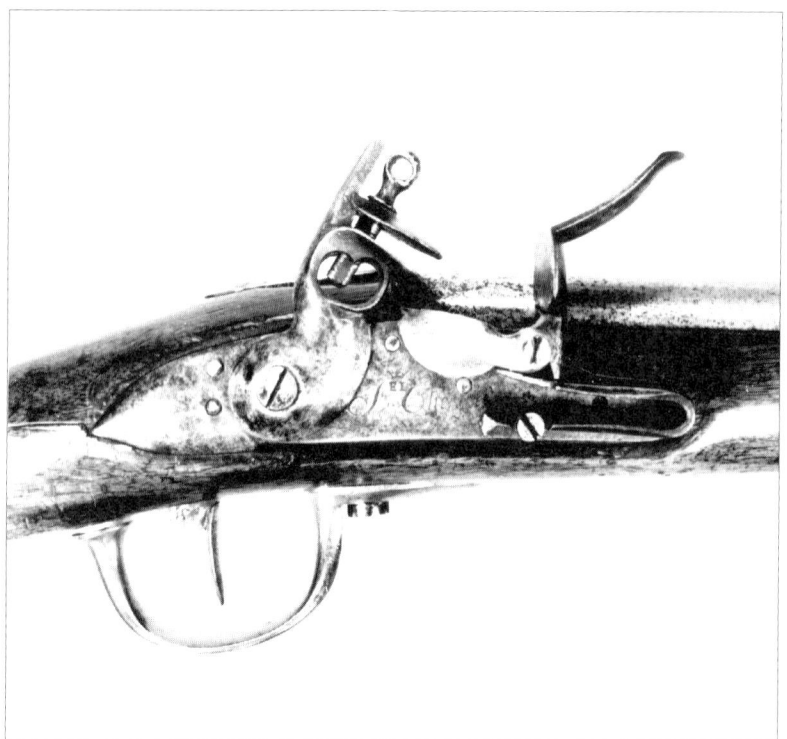

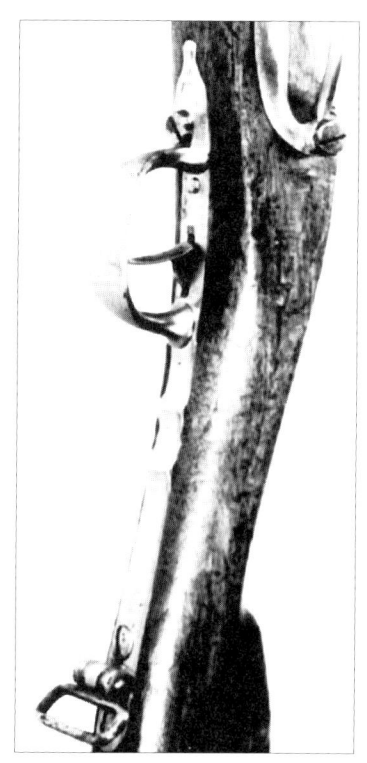

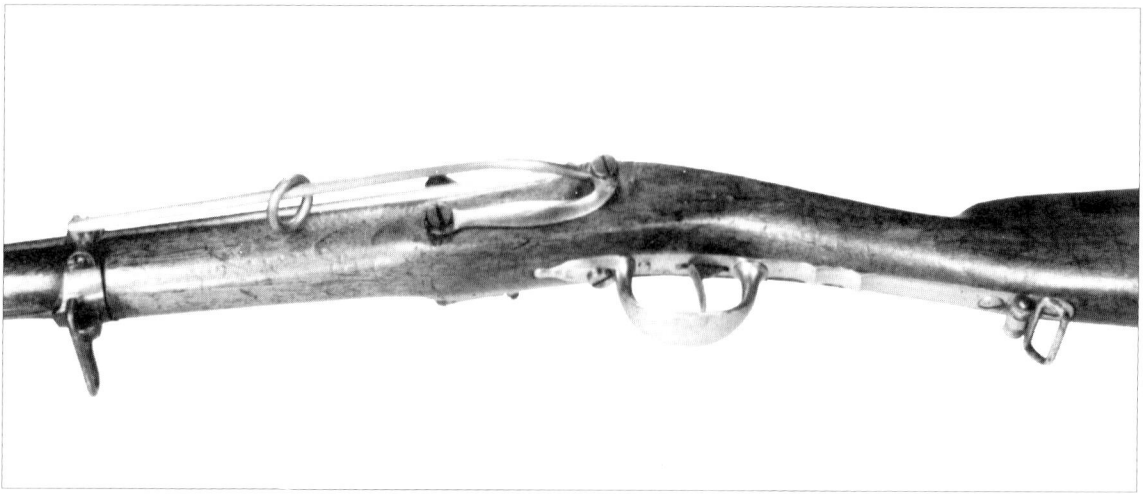

**132.MM FRENCH HUSSAR CARBINE ("MUSKETOON") MODEL 1777**  Circa 1777

A similar pattern with an exposed barrel preceded the previous French Hussar carbine during the 1760s. This later adaptation has added Model 1777 musket (47.MM) components in a reduced scale, although in brass. They include: the rounded lock with its slanted brass pan/bridle (no fence); the short-nosed brass trigger guard having two rear finger ridges; the inboard buttstock's recessed cheek rest; and a short lobed butt tang. Note also that its double strap upper barrel band displays the early Model 1777's unusual visible screw head that extends inside against the barrel's anti-twist stud, while the lower band is anchored by the forward end of the cavalry side bar. The side plate, like most French carbines, has a convex S-form. The 30" (.67 caliber) barrel is rounded at the breech (two side flats); it mounts a bottom bayonet stud. Sling swivels, in turn, are found under the lower band and at the rear of the trigger guard. "Crown / El" and "St. Etienne" appear on the lock. Similar exposed barrel musketoons were issued to the navy—produced at Tulle, which became an official royal manufactory in 1777.

| | | | |
|---|---|---|---|
| Length: 45-1/2" | Lock: 5-5/8" X 1-1/4" | Butt Tang: 2" | Furniture: Brass |
| Barrel: 29-1/2", .67 cal. | Trigger Guard: 9-1/2" | Side Plate: 3-3/4" | Weight: 6.0 lbs. |

*182  Chapter 3: Smoothbore Shoulder Arms*

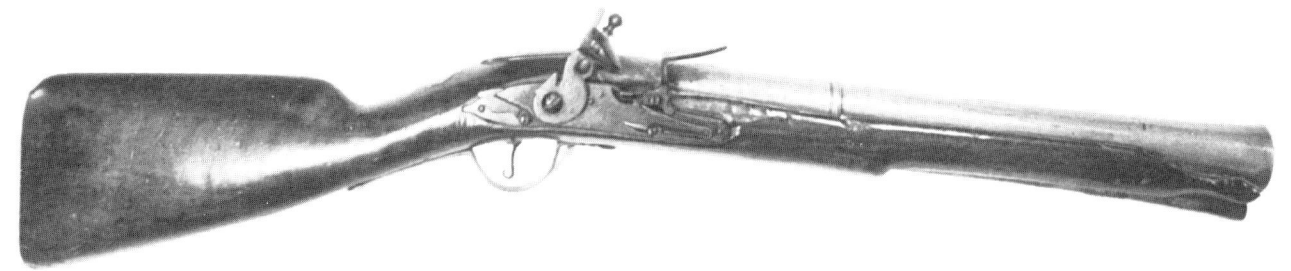

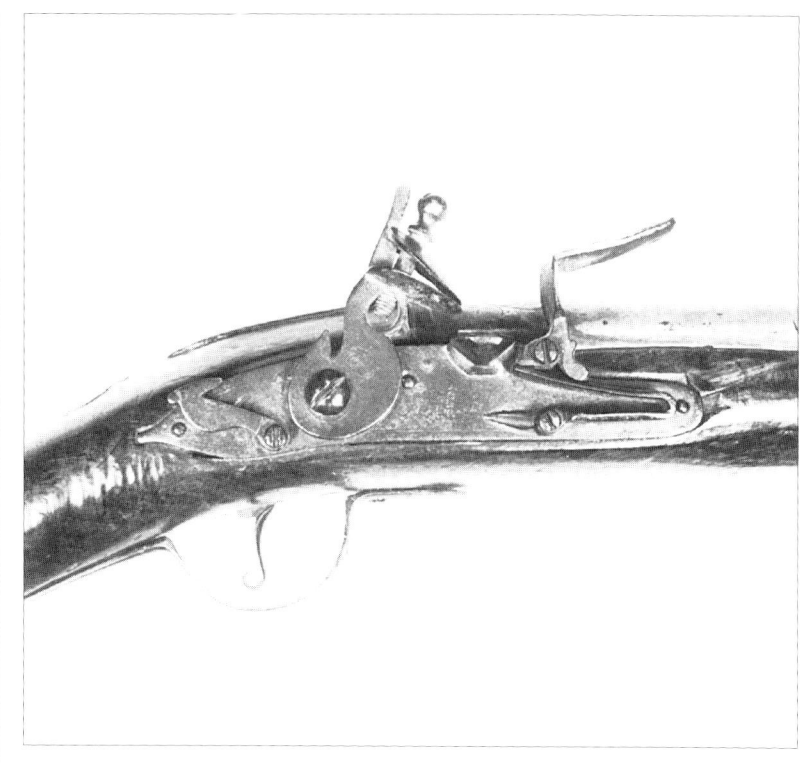

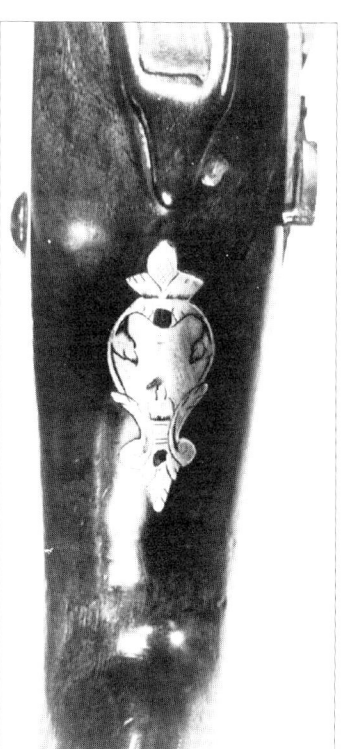

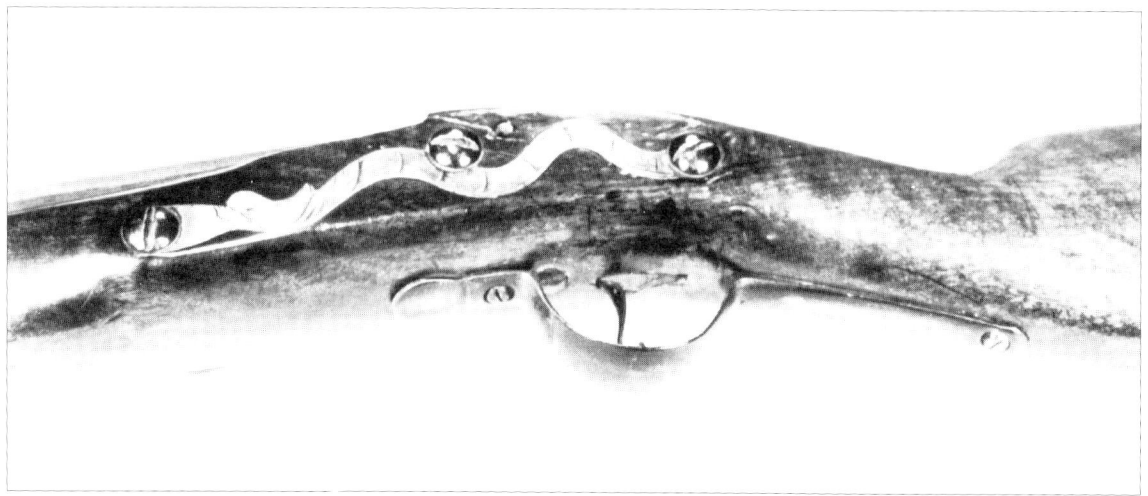

### 133.MM ENGLISH BLUNDERBUSS  Circa 1710

Britain used the terms *blunderbuss* and *musketoon* interchangeably to describe these firearms having a short barrel, a large bore and an expanded muzzle. They became popular in England during the last third of the 17th century for protection as roads improved and coach travel proliferated. The weapon fired a multiple load with devastating impact at close quarters, yet the advantage of the wide mouth was apparently to facilitate loading as subsequent tests established that the muzzle form had little influence on shot dispersion. Most blunderbusses were used by civilians for travel, protection of property or safety in crowded situations. This Queen Anne-era example, marked "J HALL" on the lock (a London maker), illustrates that period's styling: the early trumpet-shaped muzzle on a large round barrel (ring 6-1/4 inches above breech), a heavy walnut buttstock still lacking the evolving handrail form, a flat three-screw doglock including a ringed cock, rounded front terminal on the trigger guard, and a flat dragon side plate. Its thin butt plate and tang (six nails), as well as the pointed escutcheon and ribbed single rammer pipe are also contemporary.

| | | | |
|---|---|---|---|
| Length: 33" | Lock: 6-3/4" X 1-1/8" | Butt Tang: 1-5/8" | Furniture: Brass |
| Barrel: 18", 1-1/4" bore | Trigger Guard: 7-1/4" | Side Plate: 6-5/8" | Weight: 8.2 lbs. |

**Robert Nittolo Collection**

*Chapter 3: Smoothbore Shoulder Arms*

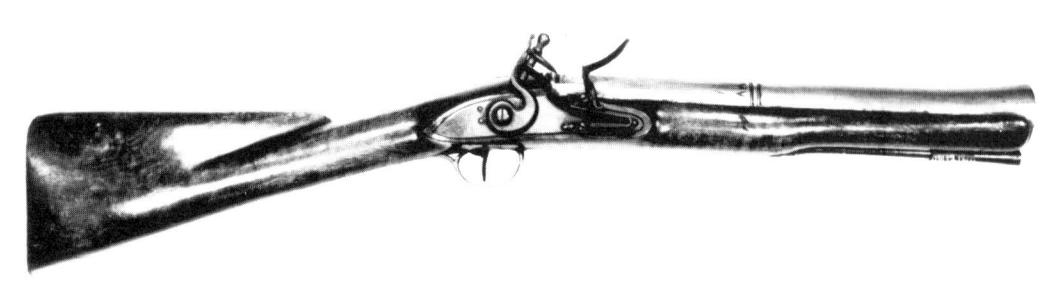

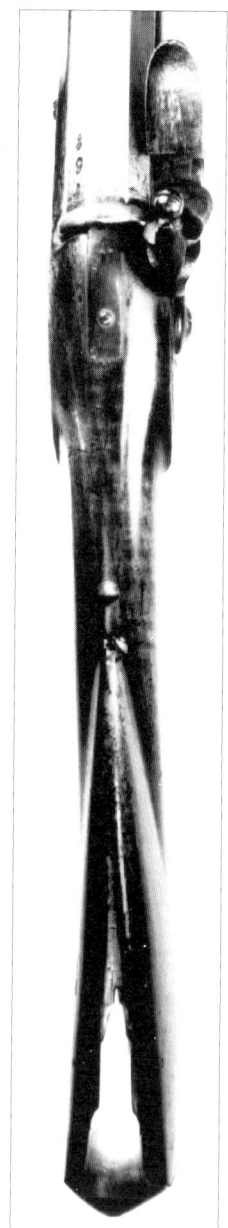

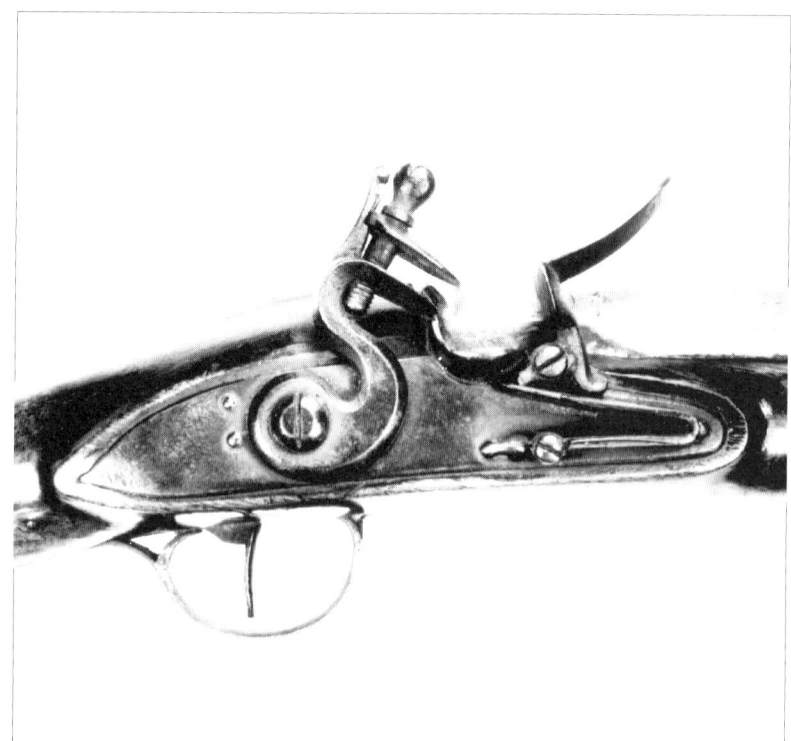

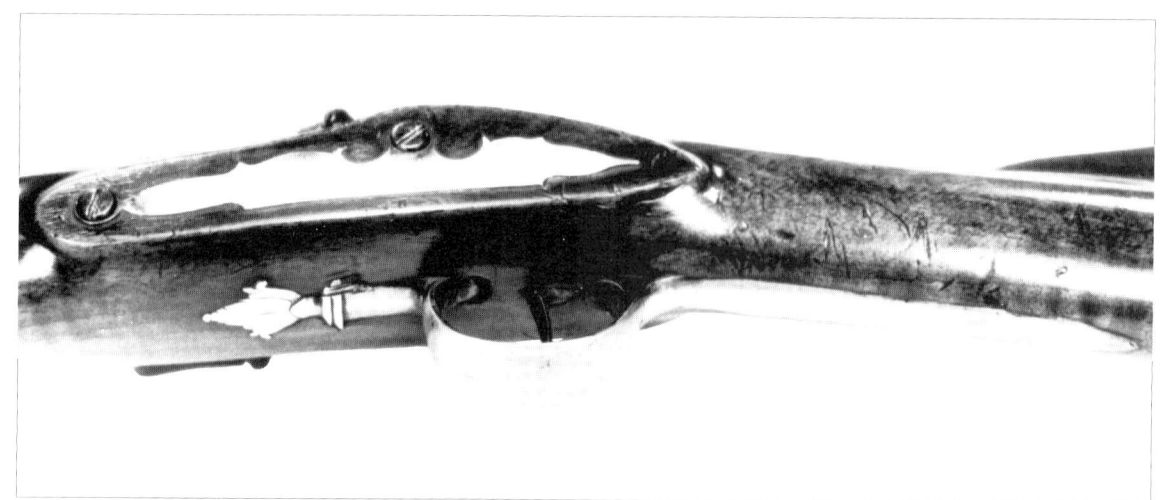

**134.MM ENGLISH BLUNDERBUSS**                                                                                           **Circa 1730–1760**

Blunderbuss styling followed the evolving longarm patterns in England during the century's second quarter. This interesting commercial example combines an earlier circa 1700–1715 period blunderbuss brass barrel and ribbed upper rammer pipe with a later stocking that includes a handrail buttstock and brass furniture typical of private arms closer to the mid-1700s. Observe the early barrel's raised base ring (1/4" wide; 3/16" high, only applied above the stock), plus a 3-1/2" octagonal engraved breech that changes to a two-inch faceted section (and 1/4" band) leading to the round/flared muzzle. It is marked "I SIBLEY" (London maker). An iron barrel tang is held by a bottom screw (no trigger plate). Conversely, the later stepped butt tang, scalloped side plate, cast tail pipe and pedestal/vase-headed trigger guard are all devoid of incised decoration, reflecting the economizing of many utility arms. The name "FARMER" appears below the rounded pan. Note also the common use of a broad brass tack head to cover the wooden ramrod's tip.

| | | | |
|---|---|---|---|
| Length: 29-1/4" | Lock: 5-7/8" X 1" | Butt Tang: 3-7/8" | Furniture: Brass |
| Barrel: 13-3/4", 1-3/8" | Trigger Guard: 9-1/8" | Side Plate: 5-3/8" | Weight: 5.9 lbs. |

**Author's Collection**

184    *Chapter 3: Smoothbore Shoulder Arms*

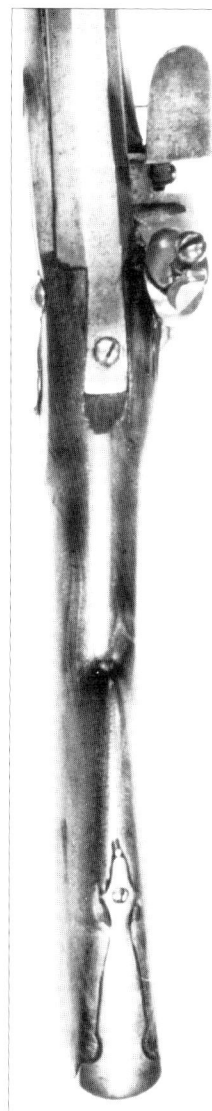

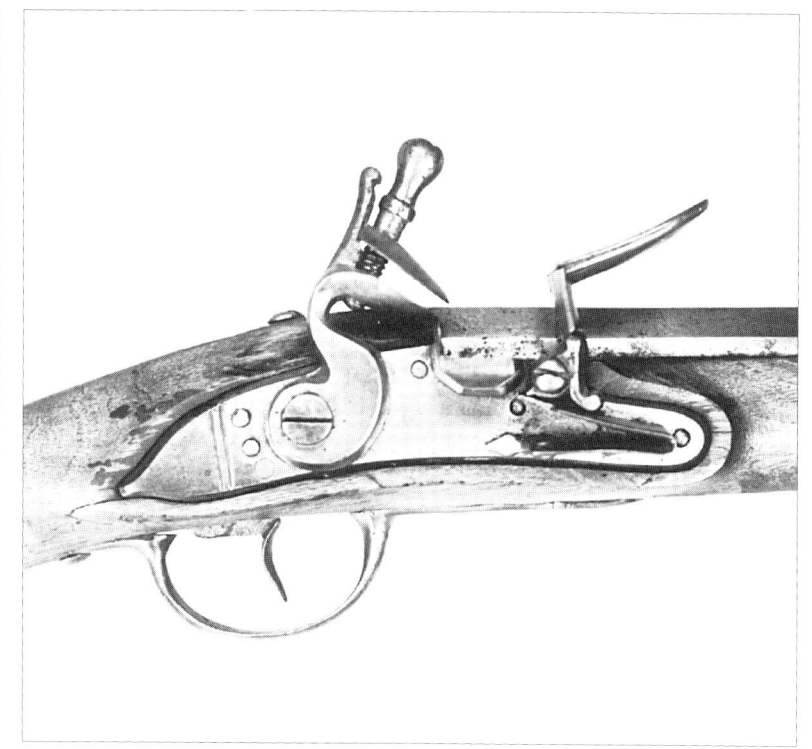

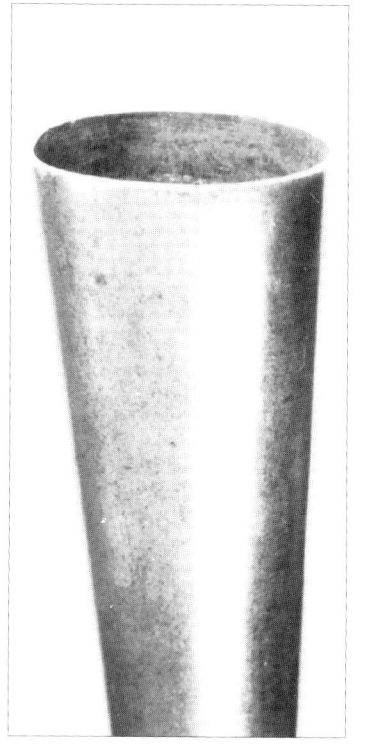

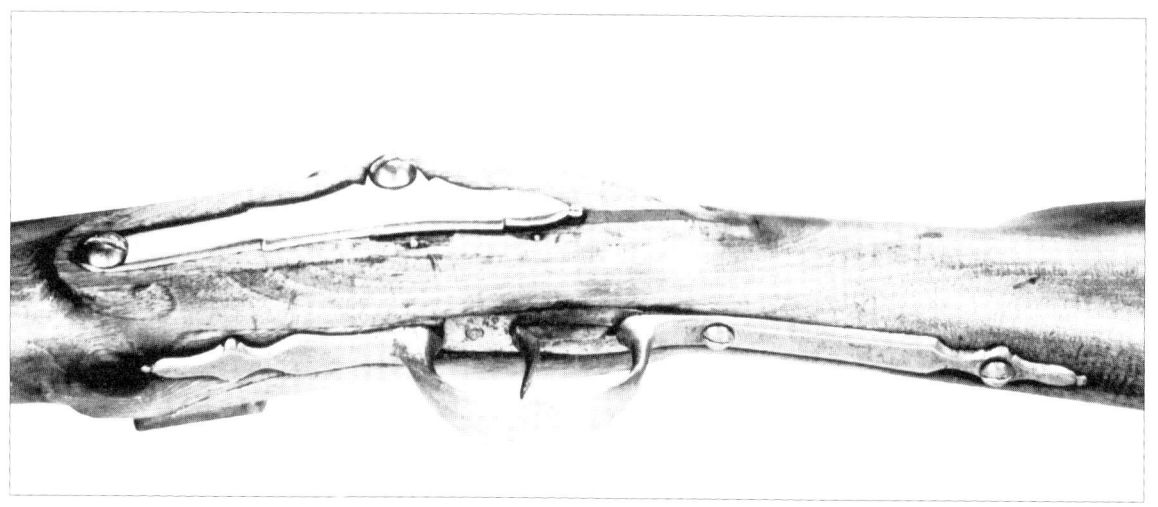

### 135.MM EUROPEAN BLUNDERBUSS
**Circa 1730–1750**

Just as the blunderbuss proliferated in England and America, similar weapons evolved in continental Europe, reflecting their own current patterns. One of the interesting variations they produced was a flaring oval muzzle as illustrated above. Because of the barrel's early swelling at the sides, the stock forend terminates considerably short of the muzzle (negating the need of a pipe for its wooden ramrod). The flat/beveled lock (with typical slashes across the tail and an omitted external bridle), plus the triangular two-screw side plate, tapered butt tang and narrow trigger guard, show French/Low Country influence, suggesting Liege as a possible source. Its breech, in turn, is octagonal for 10 inches, ending in an incised ring. Raised carving and an escutcheon were probably omitted for the usual private manufacture economies. A trigger plate, however, is included to anchor the barrel tang screw from above. All furniture is iron; no marks are visible.

| | | | |
|---|---|---|---|
| Length: 41-1/8" | Lock: 6-1/8" X 1-1/4" | Butt Tang: 5-1/8" | Furniture: Iron |
| Barrel: 26", 1-3/4" X 1-1/8" | Trigger Guard: 10-1/2" | Side Plate: 5-1/2" | Weight: 8.0 lbs. |

**George C. Neumann Collection, Valley Forge National Historical Park**

*Chapter 3: Smoothbore Shoulder Arms*

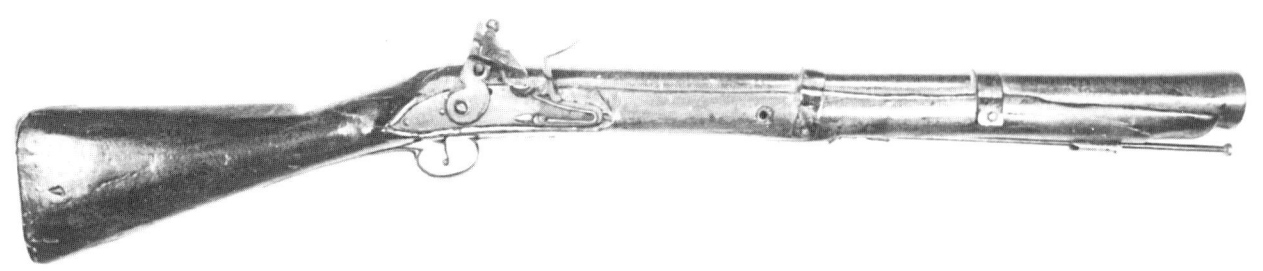

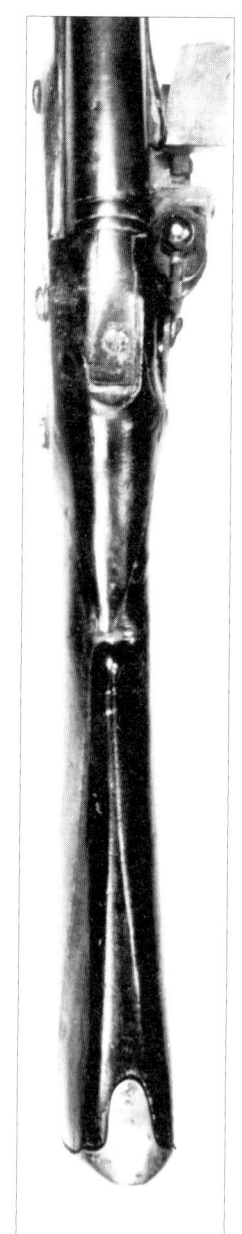

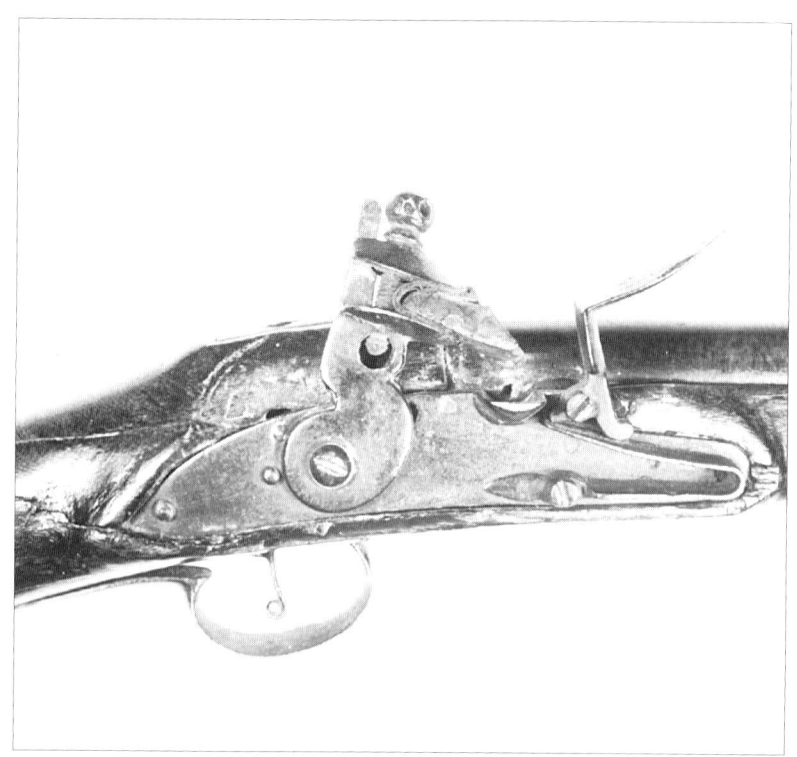

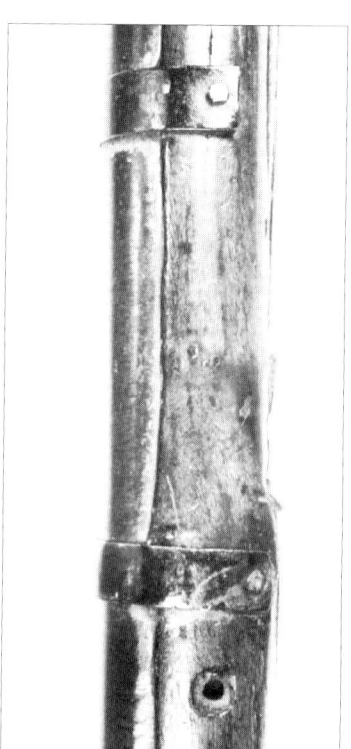

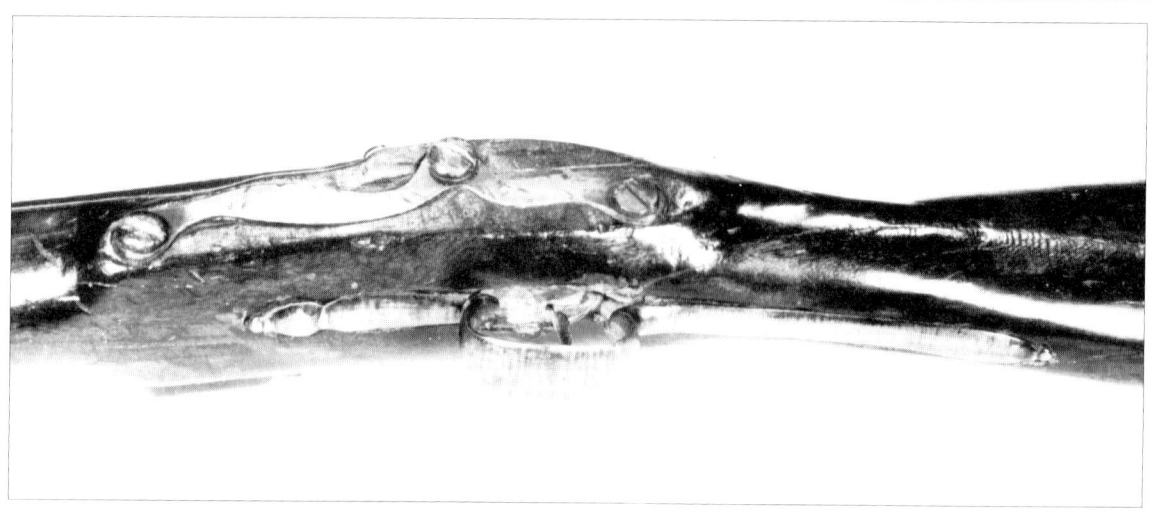

**136.MM AMERICAN SEA SERVICE BLUNDERBUSS**                                                                Circa 1750–1780

Just as the rebellious American Colonists used a wide assortment of commissioned ships and privateers at sea, they also armed them with whatever weapons were available—from established European models to firearms assembled from odd components, as in this case. Its three-screw, flat Queen Anne-pattern lock, with a ring neck cock and squared frizzen top, is the form copied for many Royal navy muskets through mid-century. The brass trigger guard, in turn, is a provincial's Brown Bess duplication that omits both the bow's rear post spur and a hole for the screw leading up to the escutcheon (also absent). A flat three-screw side plate includes two branches similar to the Queen Anne style, while the stubby butt tang appears to be from a cut-down English land pattern musket. Two nailed iron straps help to secure the typical naval trumpet-mouthed barrel (2" outside diameter; faint British proofs on breech). Its utilitarian walnut stock omits all but token carving yet shows a side hole forward of the lock, identifying its one-time use on a Y-yoke as a swivel gun.

| Length: 39-1/4" | Lock: 6-1/2" X 1-1/4" | Butt Tang: 2-1/8" | Furniture: Brass |
| Barrel: 23-1/4", 1-5/8" bore | Trigger Guard: 9-7/8" | Side Plate: 6-1/2" | Weight: 10.0 lbs. |

**George C. Neumann Collection, Valley Forge National Historical Park**

*186     Chapter 3: Smoothbore Shoulder Arms*

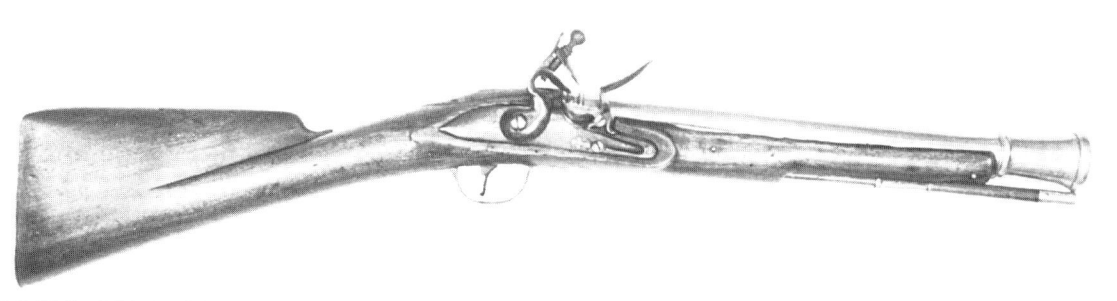

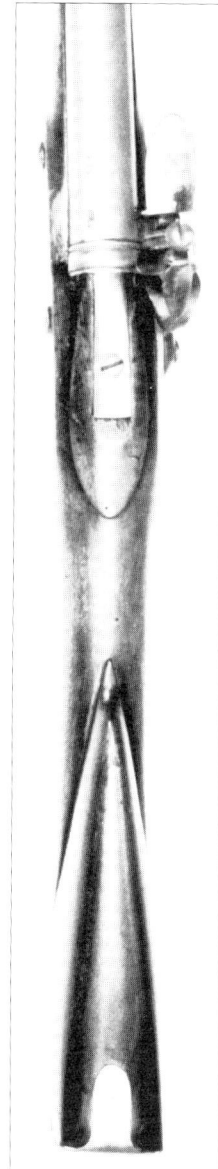

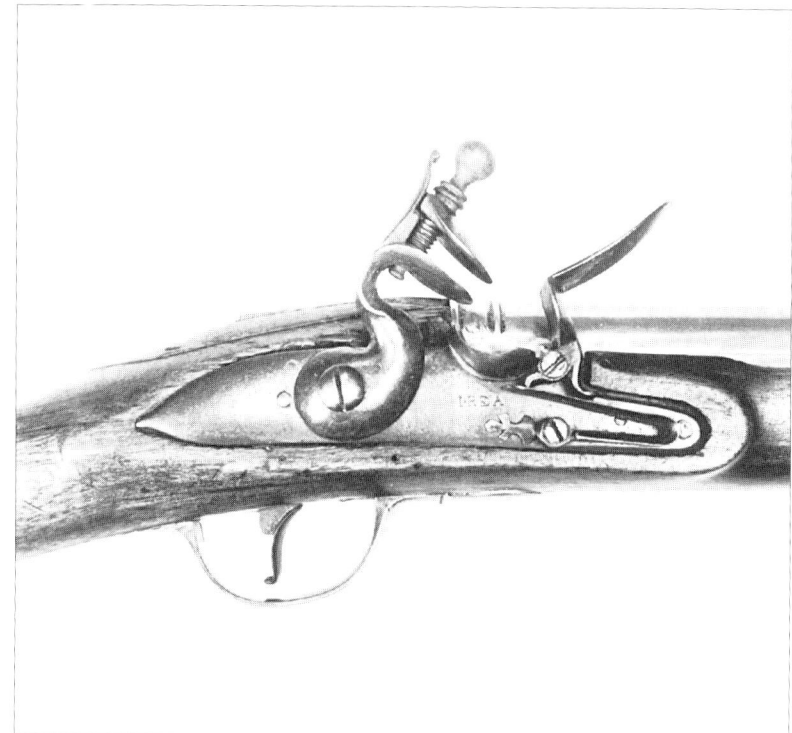

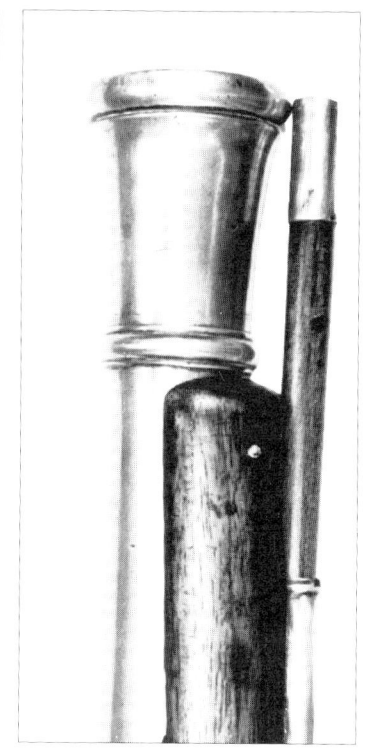

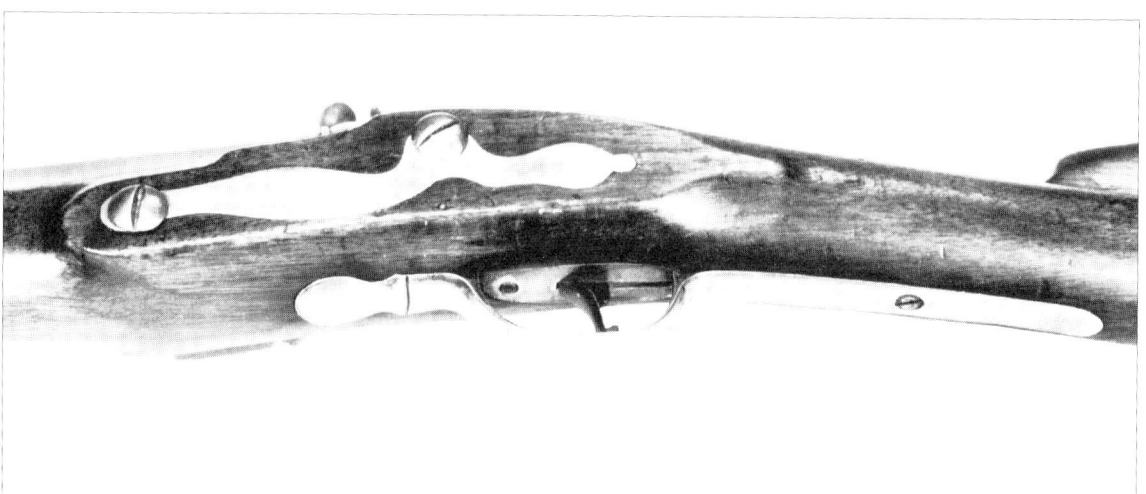

### 137.MM ENGLISH BLUNDERBUSS                                                                                                    Circa 1774–1785

At the time of the American Revolution, this turned brass "cannon" muzzle form was popular for both land and maritime usage. The lock plate is stamped "I REA" (for John Rea of London). Since private ships as well as Royal Navy vessels carried stands of arms, these multiple load weapons, which were so effective when fired from aloft onto a crowded deck or face-to-face against boarding parties, saw considerable use at sea. Thus military—especially naval—styling was popular and is apparent here, that is: a thin brass butt plate with a simple lobed tang (held by seven nails); the flat Short Land side plate; a rounded forward terminal trigger guard; the convex Brown Bess lock form; and beaver-tail barrel tang carving. Its walnut stock, which displays a military butt profile, adds an abbreviated forend to leave the double-ringed brass cannon muzzle exposed. A single sheet-brass pipe, in turn, holds the wooden rammer (tipped by a brass band). The two usual London Gunmaker Company proofs are stamped into the left side of the breech.

| | | | |
|---|---|---|---|
| Length: 30-5/8" | Lock: 6-1/8" X 1" | Butt Tang: 1-3/4" | Furniture: Brass |
| Barrel: 15-1/2", 1-3/8" bore | Trigger Guard: 8-3/8" | Side Plate: 5-3/8" | Weight: 6.0 lbs. |

**Author's Collection**

*Chapter 3: Smoothbore Shoulder Arms*     **187**

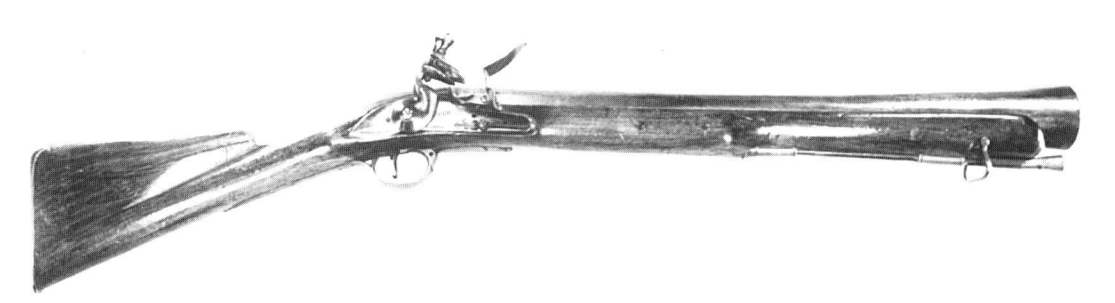

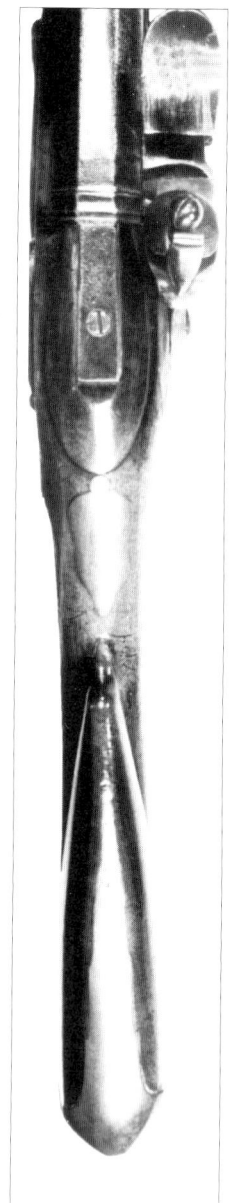

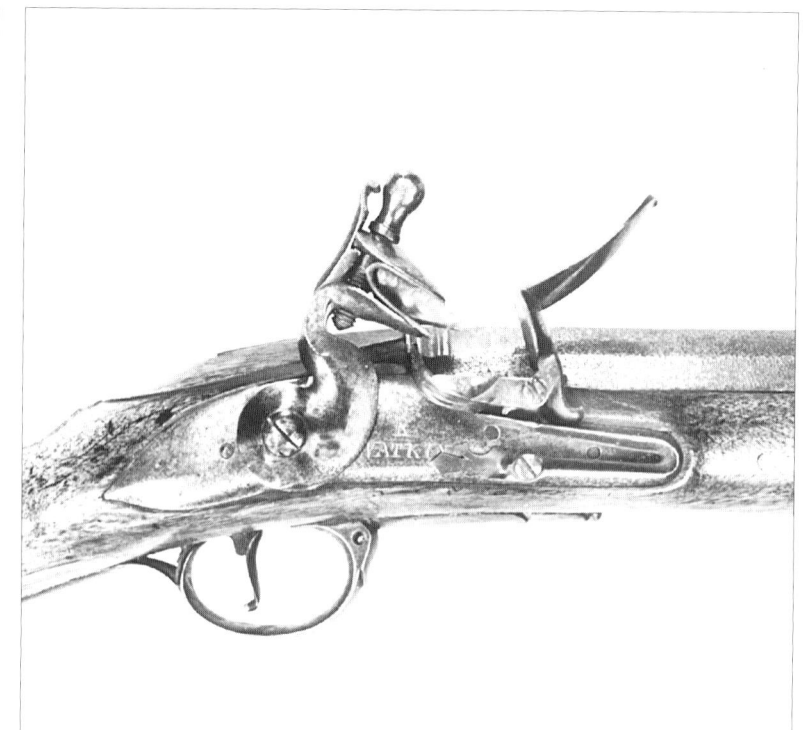

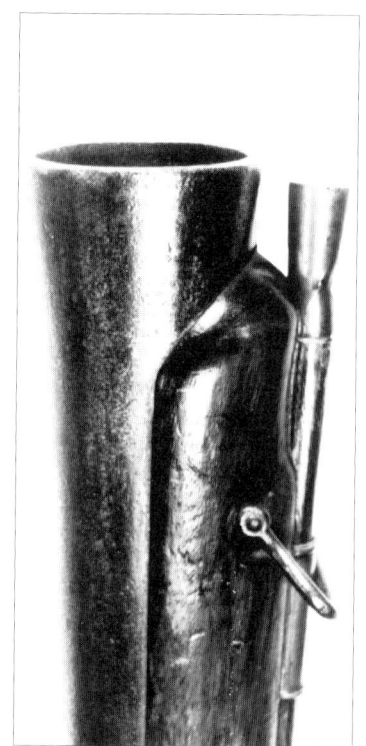

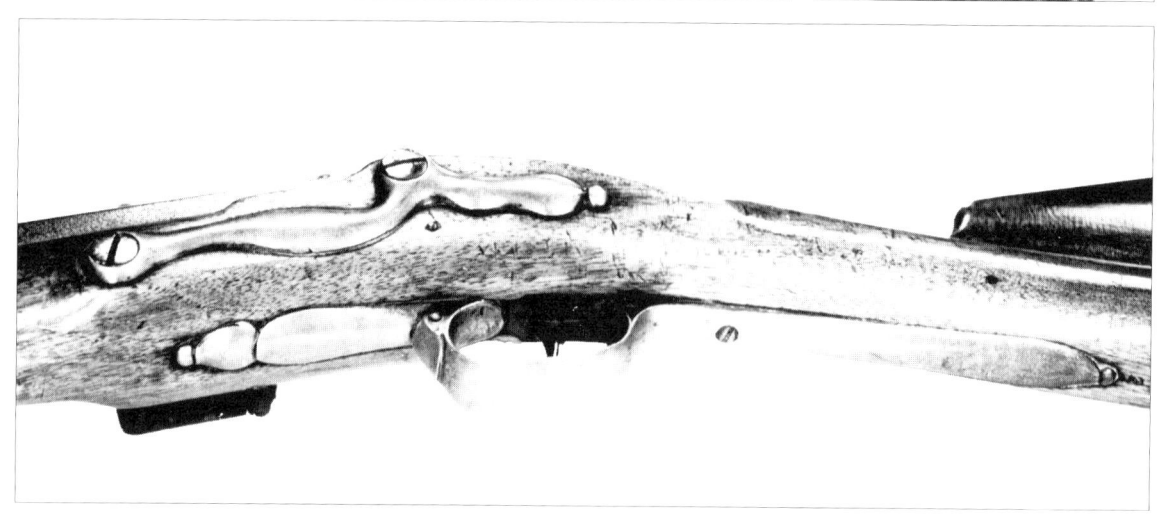

**138.MM  ENGLISH BLUNDERBUSS**  Circa 1740–1750

Although the sea service is primarily associated with British blunderbuss designs, this large military-size weapon closely follows the Long Land Brown Bess Pattern 1742 (9.MM), even though manufactured under a private contract. Its typical land service banana lock form is marked "R WATKIN" (the maker) under the pan. Note that the government's "crown / GR / broad arrow" and double border lines are absent. The long stepped butt tang, shield escutcheon, beaver-tail tang carving, convex side plate and hazelnut trigger guard also copy official styling. Even sling swivels were provided (rear one missing). The heavy trumpet-ended iron barrel is octagonal for 8-1/2 inches from the breech (muzzle has a 2-3/8" outside diameter); it also bears two Birmingham proofs on the left side. There is no end cap. A pair of cast brass thimbles hold a brass-tipped wooden ramrod. Land forces usually employed such arms for guard duty, crowd control, signaling and close quarter situations.

| | | | |
|---|---|---|---|
| Length: 39" | Lock: 6-3/4" X 1-1/4" | Butt Tang: 5-3/4" | Furniture: Brass |
| Barrel: 22-7/8", 2" bore | Trigger Guard: 11-1/4" | Side Plate: 6-1/8" | Weight: 10.1 lbs. |

**George C. Neumann Collection, Valley Forge National Historical Park**

188    *Chapter 3: Smoothbore Shoulder Arms*

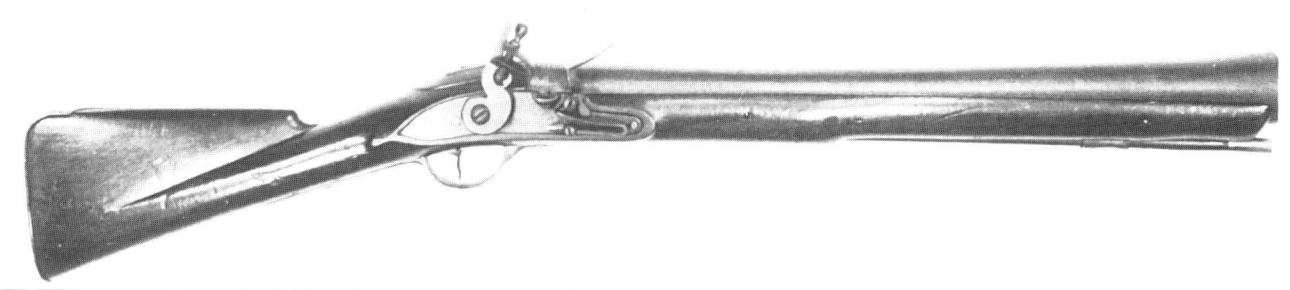

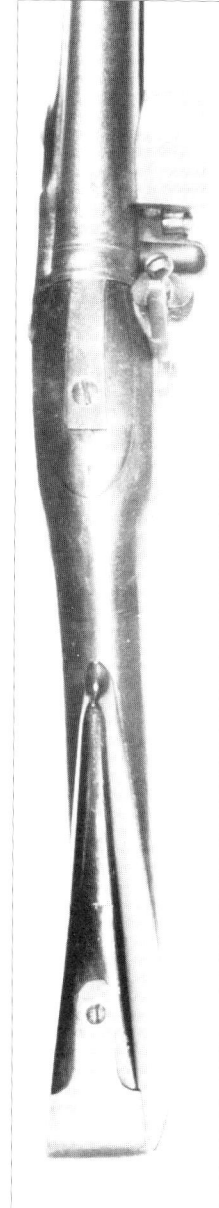

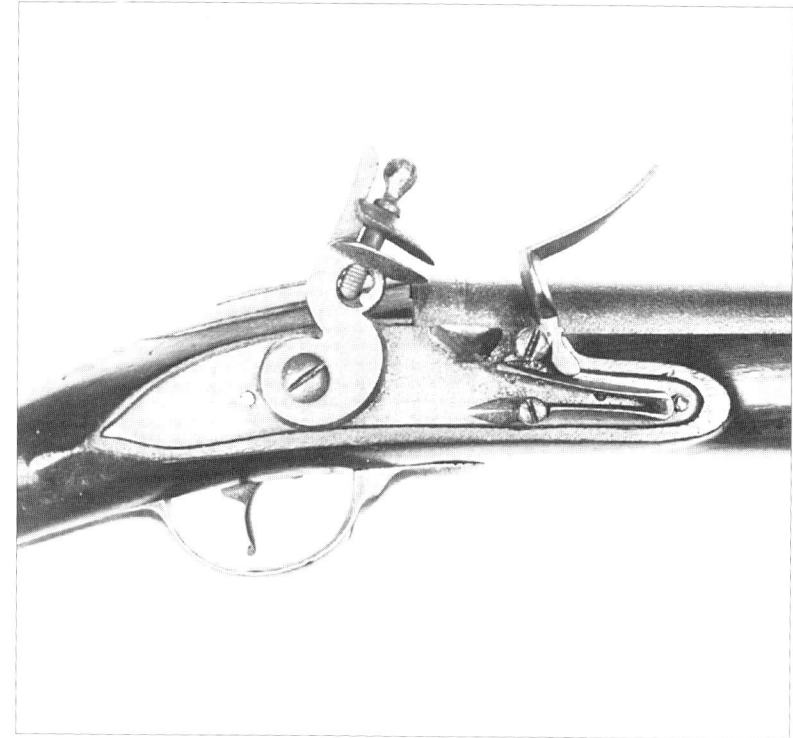

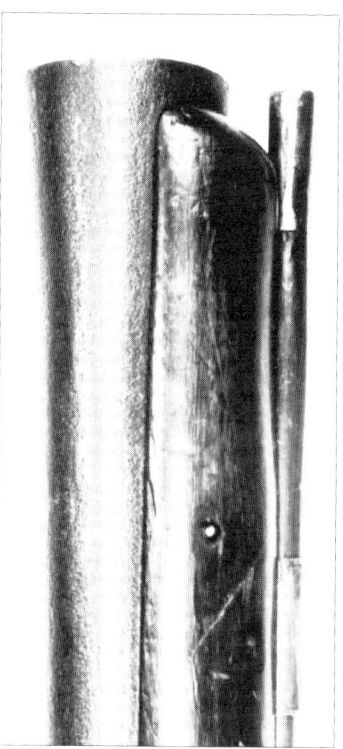

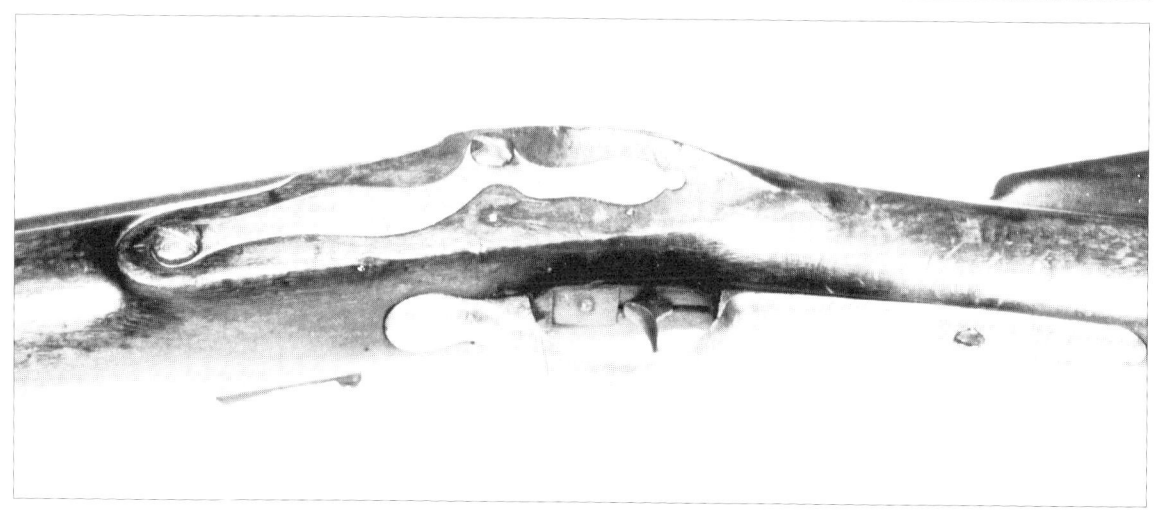

### 139.MM  ENGLISH SEA SERVICE BLUNDERBUSS
**Circa 1750–1760**

Few mid-century Royal sea service blunderbusses have survived. Yet this large example follows the contemporary naval musket pattern (28.MM) and bears official government markings, that is, Tower proofs on the breech, "crown / GR / broad arrow" below the lock's flash pan, a viewer's mark, "crown / 8" (inspector number 8) behind the trigger guard, and "crown / EI" under the barrel. The typical flat banana naval lock with its ring cock, squared frizzen top, faceted pan and leaf-shaped frizzen spring finial omits both inside and outside bridles. A flat butt plate ending in a simple lobed tang is held by three screws. A ball-shaped trigger guard terminal, flat side plate, beaver-tail carving and omitted escutcheon complete the usual sea service configuration. A heavy duty walnut butt (2-1/4 inches across) reaches to the trumpet-shaped iron muzzle (2-3/8" outside diameter) and neglects a nose band. The military brass tip heads its wooden rammer. Such a weapon would have been extremely effective aboard ship in crowded deck fighting.

| | | | |
|---|---|---|---|
| Length: 40-1/8" | Lock: 7-1/2" X 1-1/4" | Butt Tang: 3-1/2" | Furniture: Brass |
| Barrel: 24-1/8", 2" bore | Trigger Guard: 9-5/8" | Side Plate: 6-5/8" | Weight: 10.9 lbs. |

**Author's Collection**

*Chapter 3: Smoothbore Shoulder Arms*

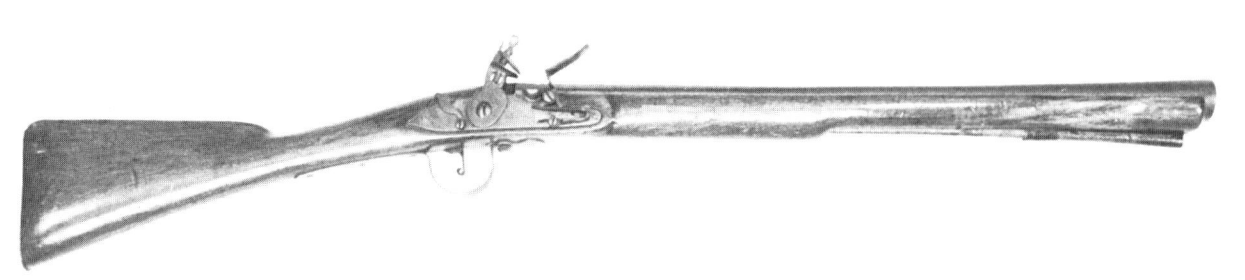

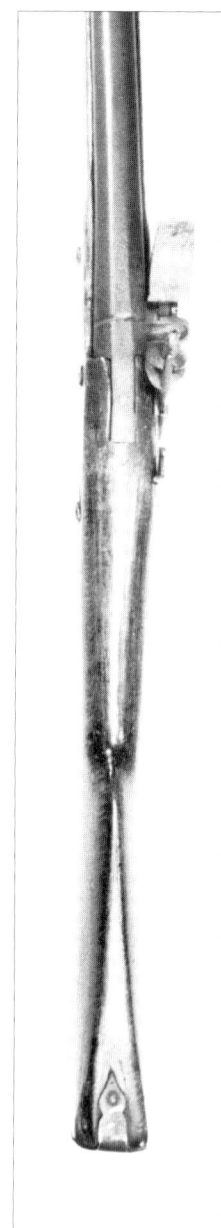

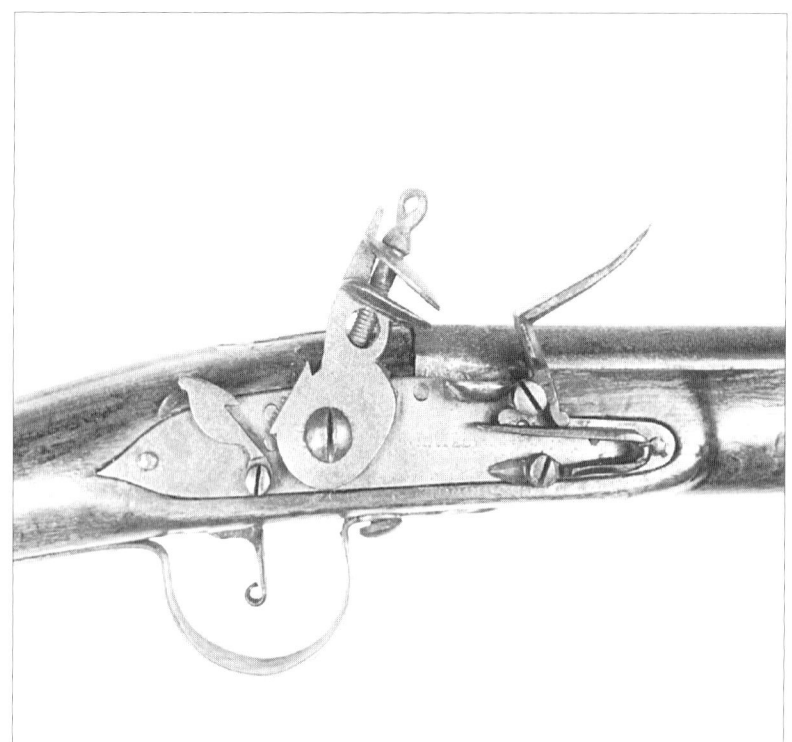

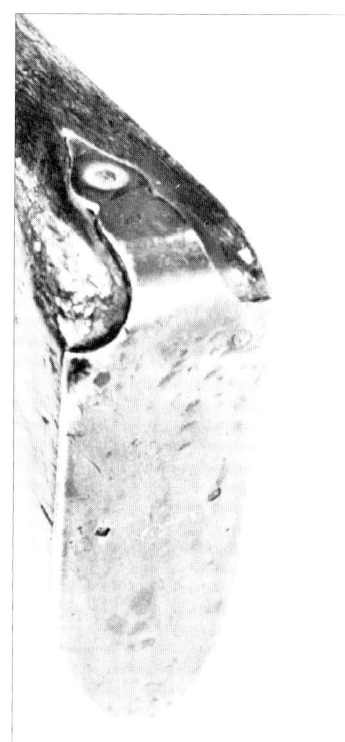

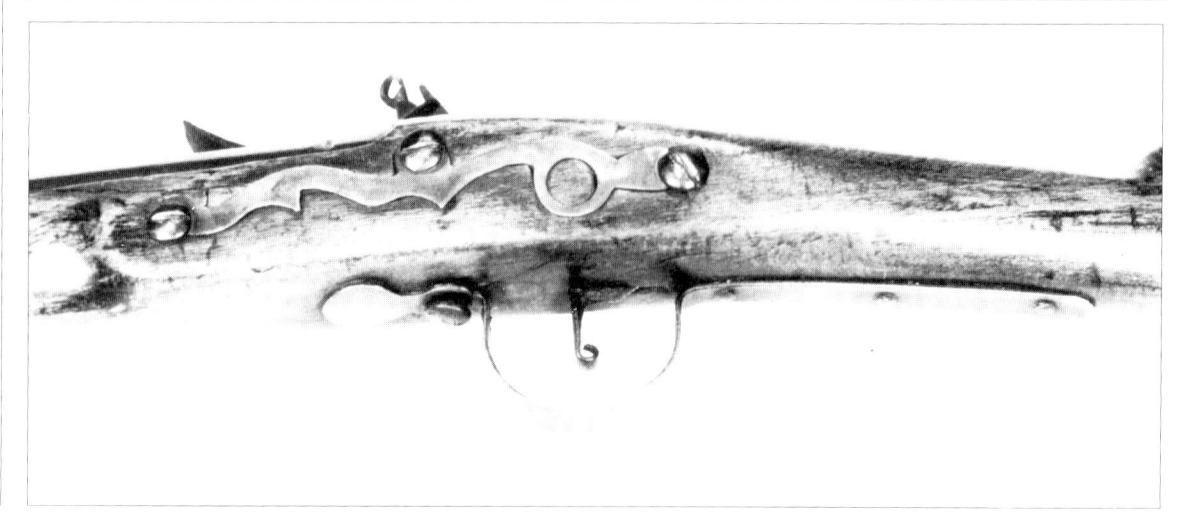

**140.MM  ENGLISH TRADE BLUNDERBUSS**  Circa 1750–1800

The lock and brass furniture on this blunderbuss are patterned from early Queen Anne styling, yet their light construction and surface mountings suggest an inexpensive commercial arm of the type offered to remote markets such as the slave trade or North American Indians. The three-screw flat doglock, for example, has an early profile but is very thin and bears the name "WHATELEY"—probably the English gunmaking family of that name during the post-1750 period. Its non-engraved dragon outline side plate is also drawn from prior years (149.MM), as with the fragile butt plate (six nails) and round-headed sheet-brass trigger guard (which includes a traditional deep bow favored on trade pieces, supposedly to permit firing with a gloved hand). Note also that the trigger guard is not inlaid but nailed to the stock to effect economies. In addition the barrel tang is secured by a screw from below that at the same time anchors the trigger guard's forward section. A single pipe holds its wooden ramrod. The pinned trumpet-mouthed barrel is octagonal for seven inches. There are no other marks.

| | | | |
|---|---|---|---|
| Length: 37" | Lock: 5-7/8" X 1" | Butt Tang: 1-3/4" | Furniture: Brass |
| Barrel: 21-3/4", .90 cal. | Trigger Guard: 7-3/4" | Side Plate: 5-5/8" | Weight: 4.7 lbs. |

**Author's Collection**

*Chapter 3: Smoothbore Shoulder Arms*

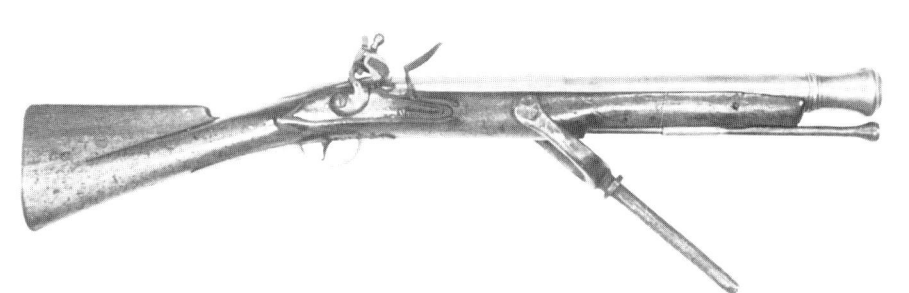

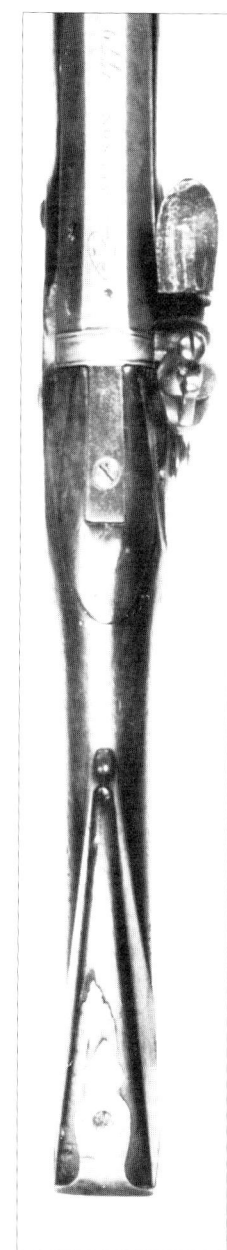

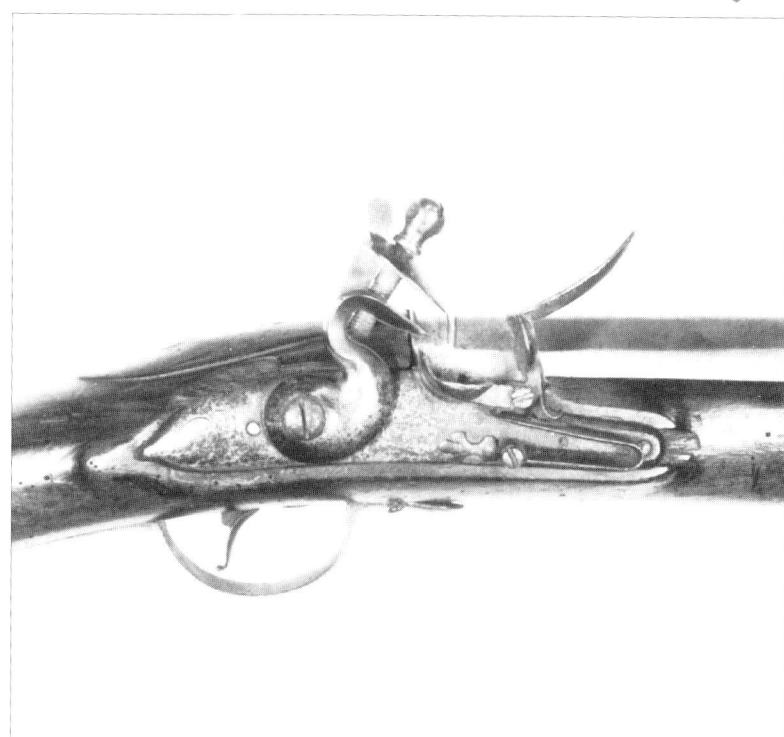

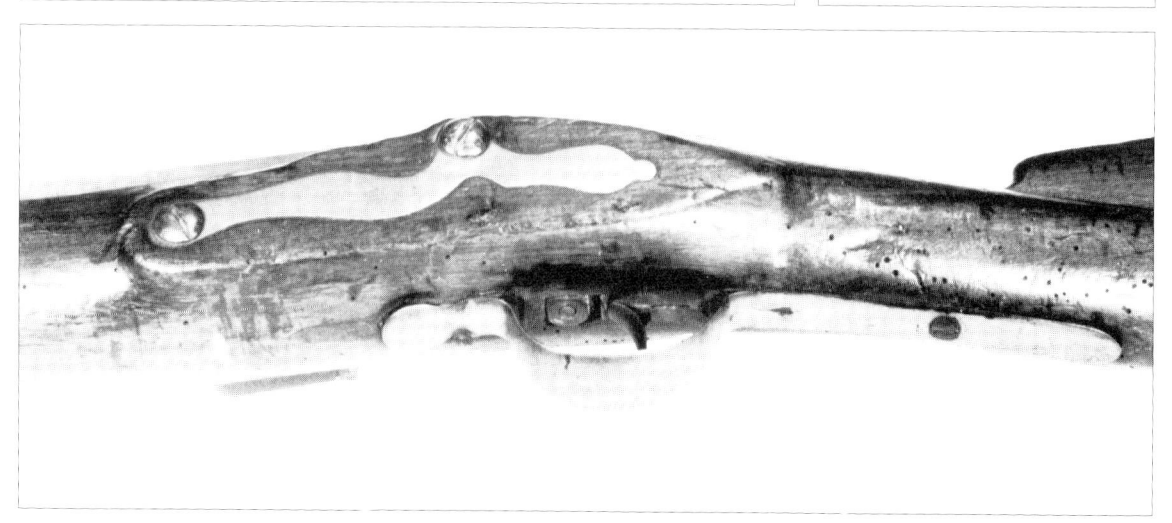

**141.MM  ENGLISH SWIVEL-MOUNTED BLUNDERBUSS**  Circa 1779

The octagonal breech of this impressive heavy blunderbuss is engraved "WILSON 1779" plus the East India Company symbol. The latter identifies it as purchased for their private armed forces in India, which could not have participated in America's War for Independence. Yet it does illustrate a popular pattern being produced for countless merchant ships and commercial sources at that time. Notice the turned brass cannon muzzle form and its Y-yoke still attached for use as a swivel weapon. The ball-ended trigger guard, flat side plate and beaver-tail barrel tang carving typically reflect the contemporary Royal sea service designs. A rounded military type lock, however, includes a plain upper post on its cock (that is, not notched) that did not receive government authorization until the 1790s. A sheet-brass butt plate is held by two flat screws at the back plus a third through its short upper tang. The hefty walnut buttstock, in turn, imitates the accepted land pattern profile although with thicker proportions. Both London Gunmakers Company proofs are struck into the breech's left side, as well as the maker's personal stamp between them, "R*W" (Richard Wilson).

| | | | |
|---|---|---|---|
| Length: 38-3/8" | Lock: 7" X 1-1/4" | Butt Tang: 3-1/4" | Furniture: Brass |
| Barrel: 22-1/4", 1-1/2" bore | Trigger Guard: 9-1/4" | Side Plate: 6-1/8 1/8" | Weight: 14.4 lbs. |

**The Benninghoff Collection**

*Chapter 3: Smoothbore Shoulder Arms*   **191**

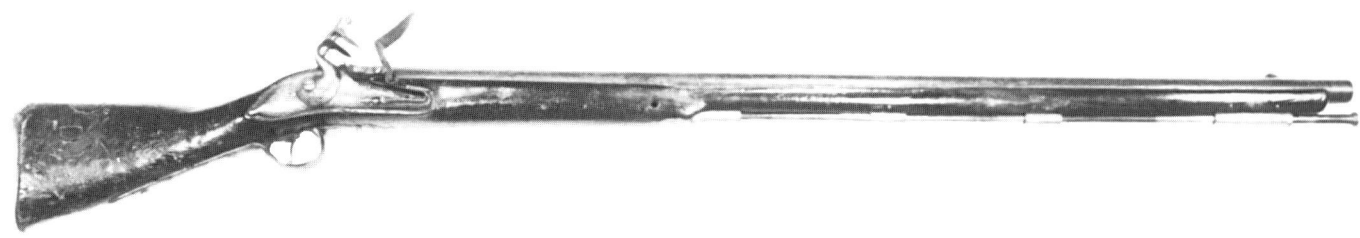

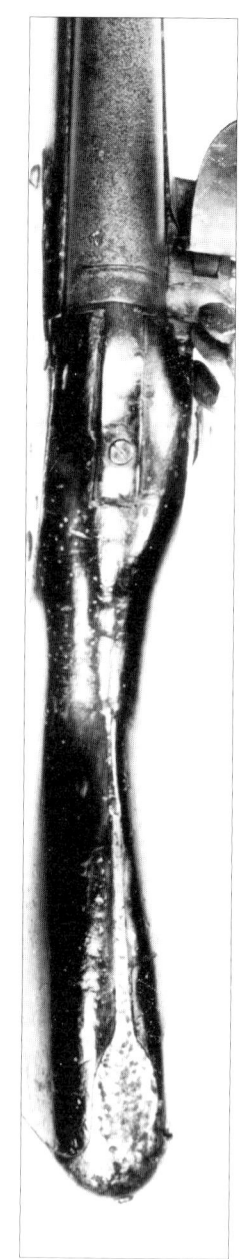

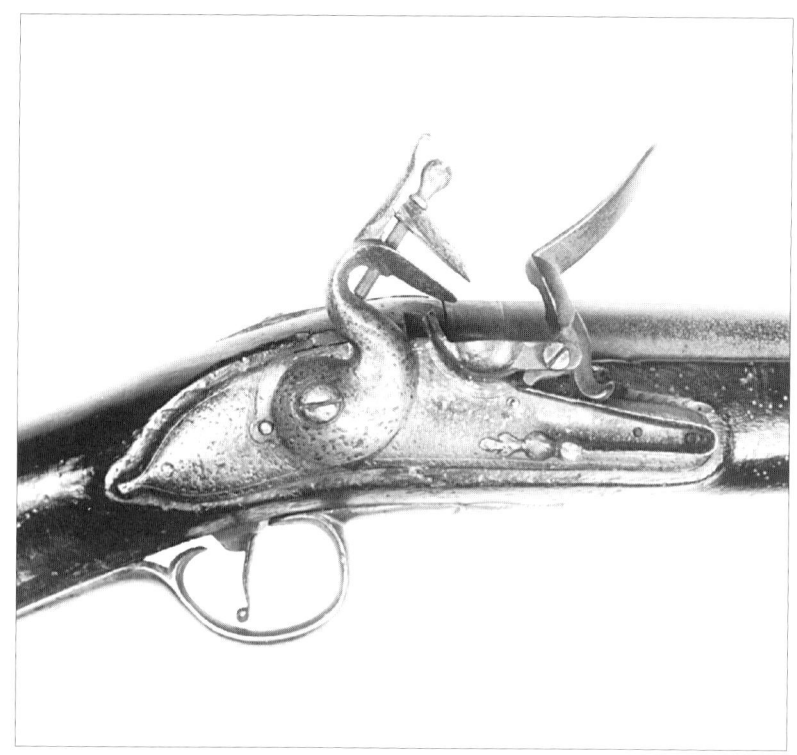

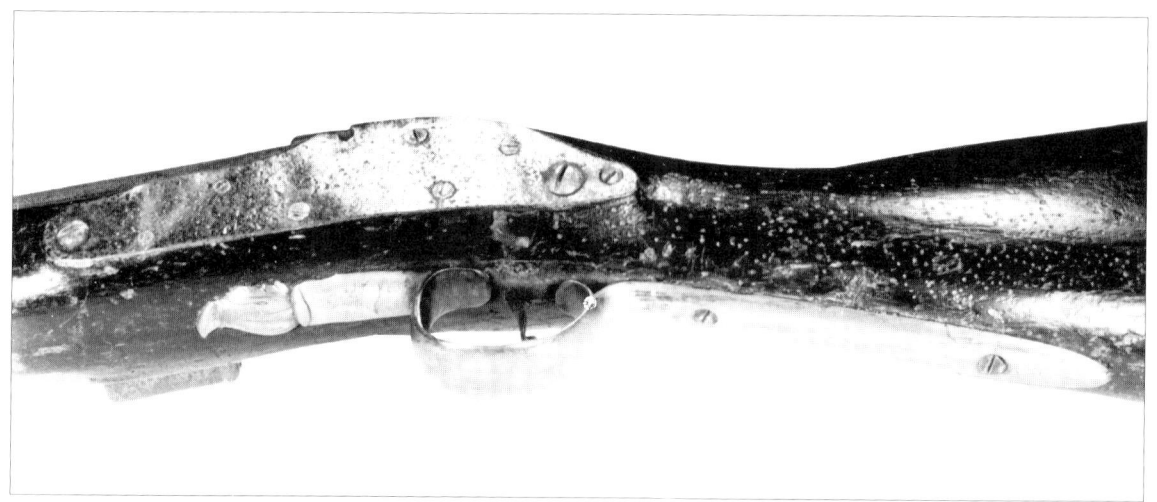

**142.MM  ENGLISH WALL GUN ("RAMPART GUN," "AMUSETTE")**  Circa 1735–1750

Wall guns were upsized longarms created to shoot a larger ball for greater distances. They were usually fired from fortified positions to keep attackers back beyond musket range. This extended reach and portability gave them even more importance in the New World at inland forts and waterways that could not easily be reached by artillery. Many also served at sea—effective at distances beyond the normal swivel gun. This sizable British smoothbore weighs 32 pounds yet includes many features of contemporary Long Land muskets. The side plate has been replaced by a flat iron patch. Its trigger guard, in turn, is headed by a flame-shaped finial. Included on the rounded banana lock plate (9-3/8 inches long) is "I TITTENSOR," a first quarter gunmaker whose dates match the needle-like iron butt tang. Their combination with later features, however, such as the lock's external bridle, a spur on the trigger bow's rear post and a flared forward rammer pipe for the 1/2" diameter steel rod, suggest assembly closer to 1750. Other English wall guns (circa 1738–1778) had flat locks and ring cocks.

| | | | |
|---|---|---|---|
| Length: 72" | Lock: 9-3/8" X 2" | Butt Tang: 8" | Furniture: Brass/Iron |
| Barrel: 54", 1.05 cal. | Trigger Guard: 15-1/8" | Side Patch: 9-3/4" | Weight: 32.0 lbs. |

**George C. Neumann Collection, Valley Forge National Historical Park**

192   *Chapter 3: Smoothbore Shoulder Arms*

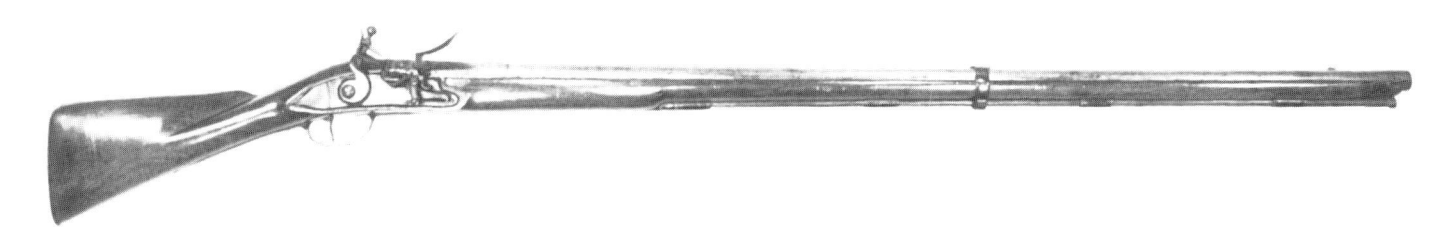

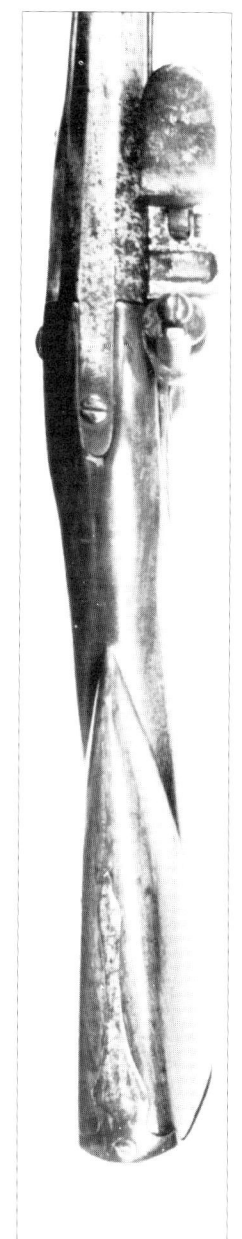

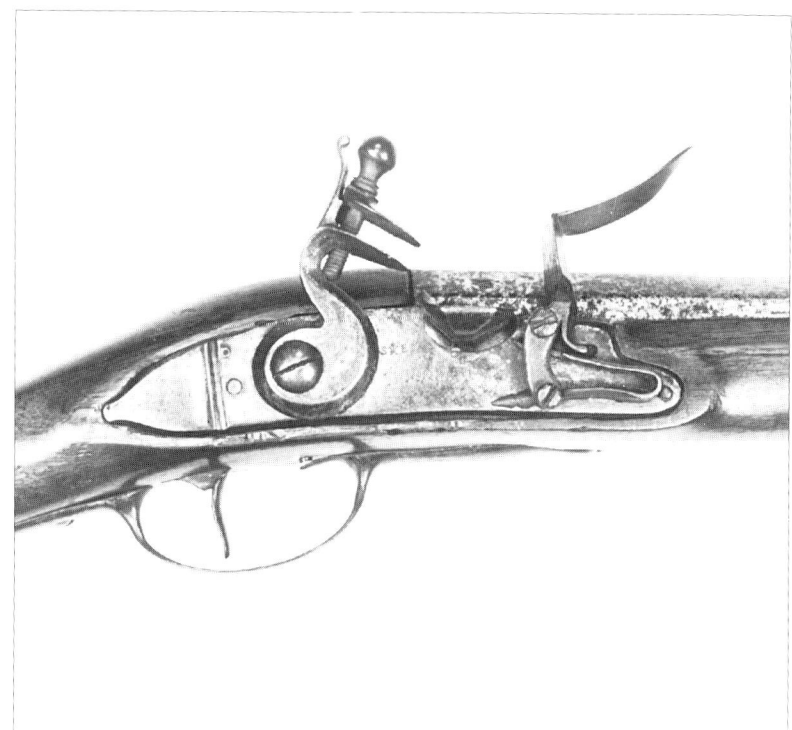

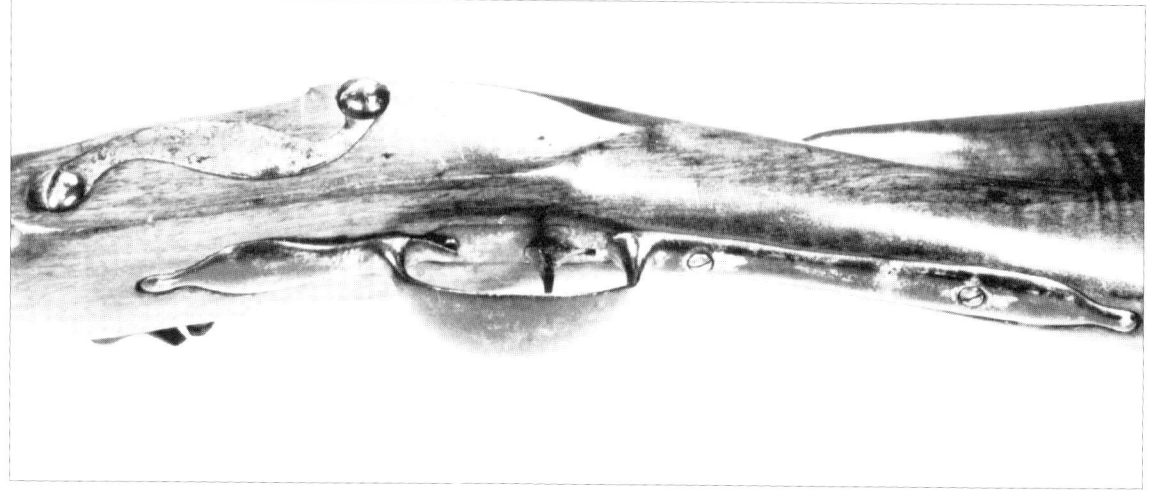

**143.MM FRENCH WALL GUN MODEL 1717**             Circa 1717–1725

During the 18th century, French ordnance authorized only two official rampart guns, the Models 1717 and 1728. They followed the basic infantry musket patterns of those dates but with some variances as seen in this Model 1717 (versus the musket 38.MM). Its hefty walnut stock now assumes a straighter butt and reaches to the muzzle (that is, no bayonet). Although the same length as the standard arm, its pinned barrel has a larger bore (.78 versus .69 caliber) and a wider breech to permit the higher powder charge. All iron components copy the regular infantry configuration yet in slightly larger sizes, including the Model 1717's distinctive lock form with a vertical bridle. This lock plate is 7-1/4" long (3/4 inch more than the musket). Typical sheet-iron French rammer pipes secure a wooden rod. Note, too, the single middle band (no sling swivels here). Markings for St. Etienne, "S / fleur-de-lis / E," appear on the lock, breech and buttstock. A total of 40,000 were manufactured. Some of this model have been found refitted to mount a bayonet for use by infantry, where its power could be effective beyond musket range—especially against field artillery.

| | | | |
|---|---|---|---|
| Length: 62-3/4" | Lock: 7-1/4" X 1-3/8" | Butt Tang: 5-3/4" | Furniture: Iron |
| Barrel: 47-1/8", .78 cal. | Trigger Guard: 12-3/4" | Side Plate: 4-5/8" | Weight: 10.4 lbs. |

**Author's Collection**

Chapter 3: Smoothbore Shoulder Arms    193

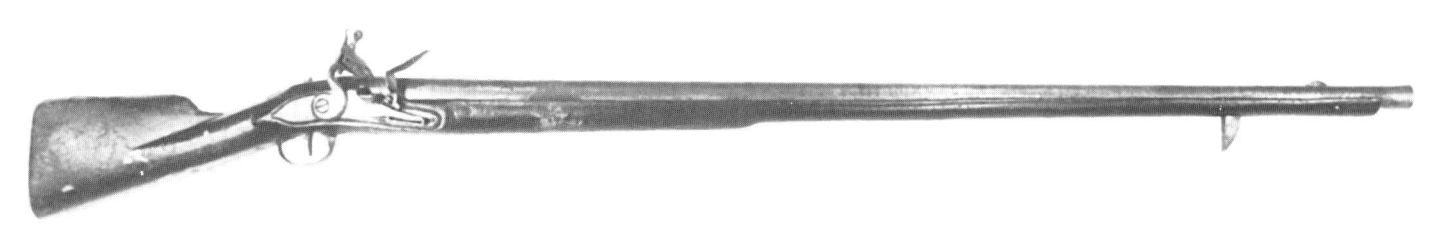

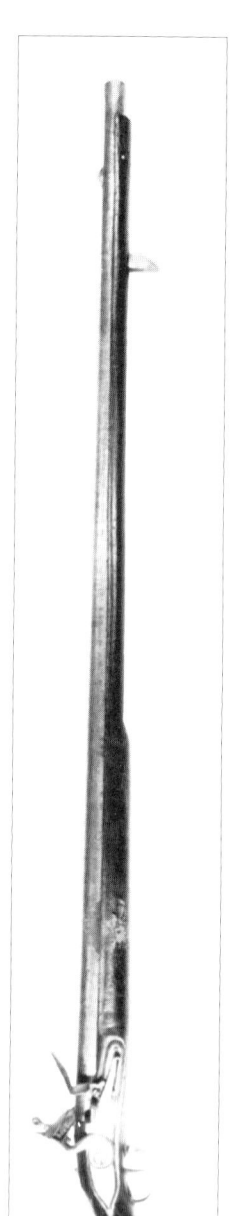

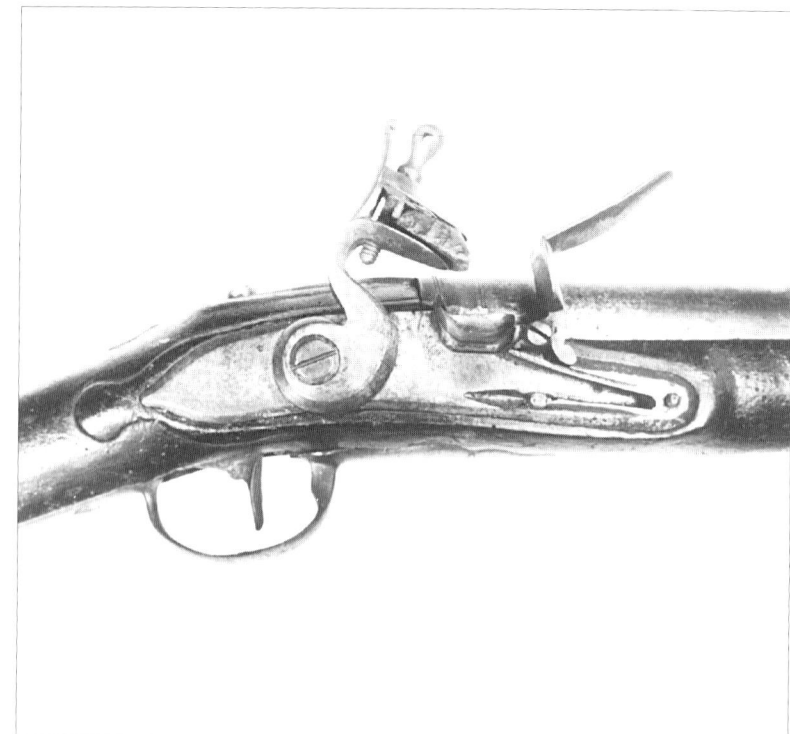

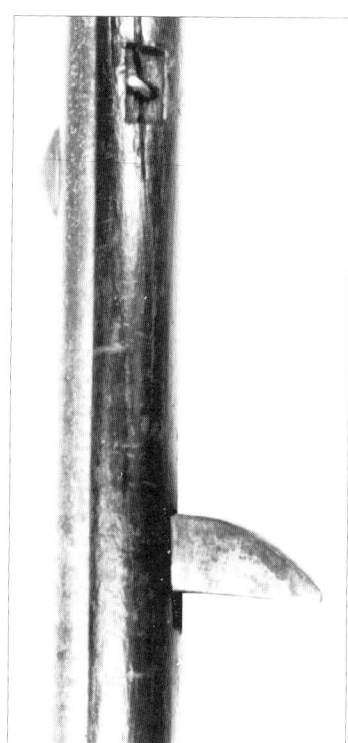

**144.MM DUTCH/GERMANIC WALL GUN**  Circa 1750–1775

Germanic/Low Country features are present on this European rampart gun. Essentially an oversized smoothbore musket, the arm includes a pointed iron stud welded to the barrel and projecting down through a thick stock 9-1/2 inches behind the flared muzzle. It was intended to hook over a fortified wall or to anchor the forend in the soft earth of entrenchments. Although stretched to 8-3/4 inches in length, the flat/beveled lock, with an unbridled faceted pan and squared frizzen top, retains the proportions of this popular central European pattern. A vase-like trigger guard terminal, two-screw curved tail side plate and 7-1/2" curving butt tang held by a top screw also conform to this configuration. Typical bulbous raised carving surrounds the lock and side plate. Such a weapon would have been among the sizable inventories of wall guns received by the American Colonists during the Revolutionary War. The lock is marked "ICR" under the breech; "FR / 1775" in a circle has been stamped into the side of the butt.

| | | | |
|---|---|---|---|
| Length: 73" | Lock: 8-3/4" X 1-1/2" | Butt Tang: 7-1/2" | Furniture: Iron |
| Barrel: 55-1/2", .94 cal. | Trigger Guard: 13-5/8" | Weight: 18.2 lbs. | |

**The Benninghoff Collection**

*194    Chapter 3: Smoothbore Shoulder Arms*

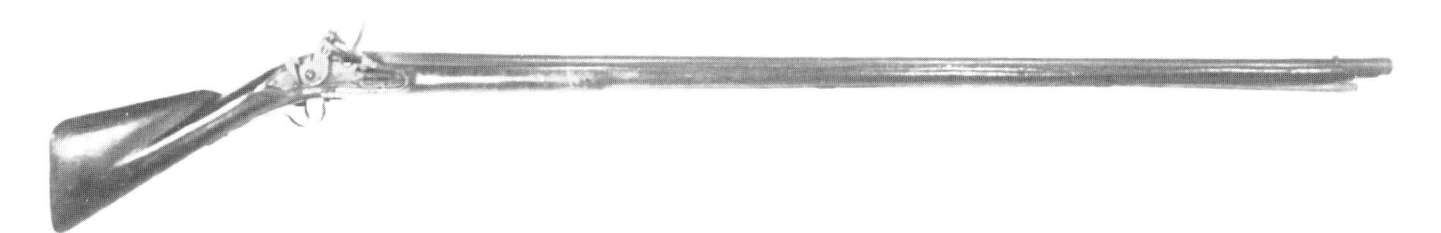

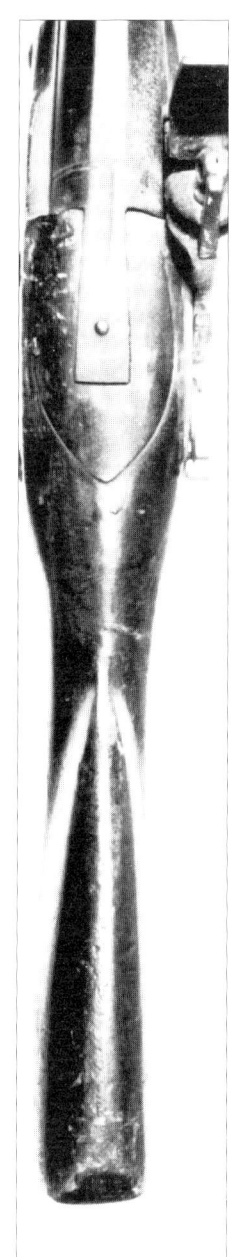

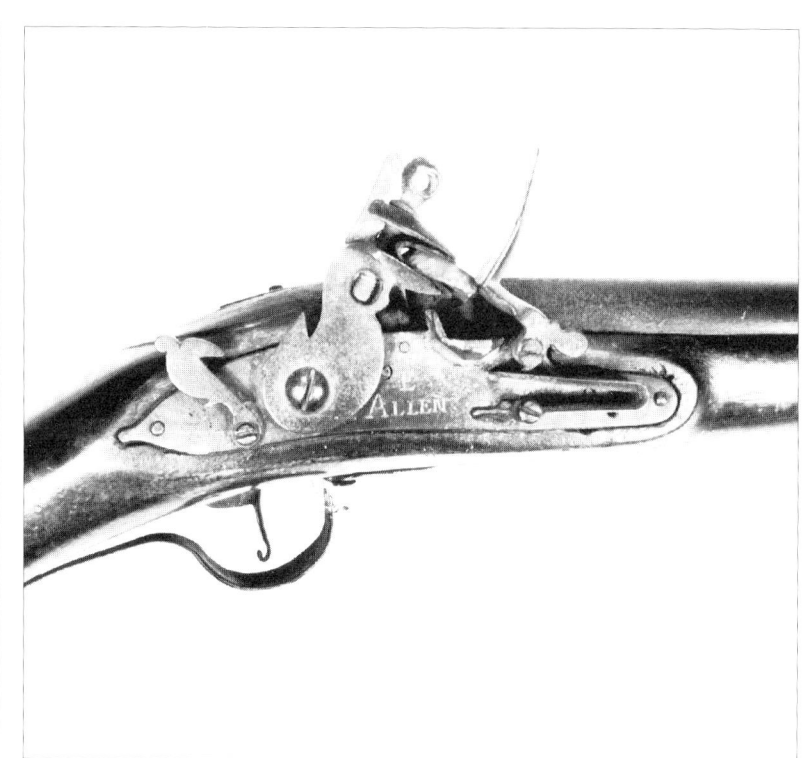

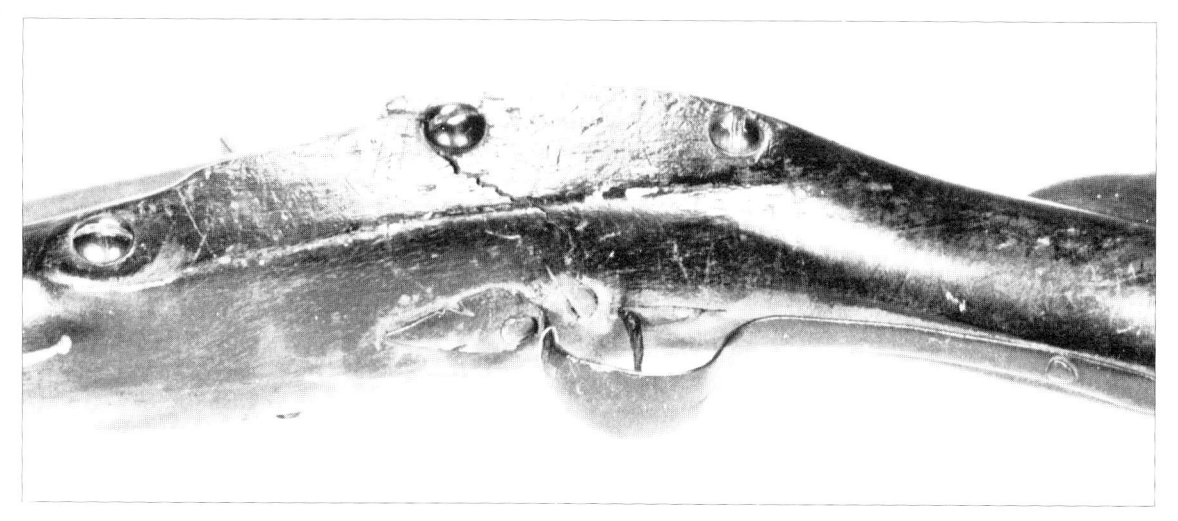

**145.MM AMERICAN FOWLER/WALL GUN**                                   Circa 1705–1720

This heavy long barreled flintlock may have been used as a set-piece fowler, but it would also serve admirably as a military wall gun. The three-screw flat doglock (marked "E / ALLEN") is a common English pattern of this period (ring cock, squared frizzen), but the remainder of the arm appears to be pure American. Yankee thrift probably decided the absence of a butt plate, side plate and escutcheon. Even the trigger guard is a simplistic flat strip with a nail holding the "partisan-shaped" forward terminal. A sharp drop to its butt is characteristic of many provincial longarms. The impressive mass of the butt is apparent in the topside illustration—as well as the breadth of its barrel (which ends in a swamped muzzle). Typical of many early century guns, a long screw originating just before the trigger passes up through the stock to reach the breech tang. A rectangular piece of flint is shown in normal position between the cock's upper jaws. It was usually wrapped in a strip of leather or sheet lead to help remain in place.

Length: 76-1/4"  
Barrel: 59-3/4", .82 cal.  
Lock: 7-1/8" X 1-1/4"  
Weight: 15.5 lbs.  
Furniture: Iron

**West Point Museum Collection**

*Chapter 3: Smoothbore Shoulder Arms*     **195**

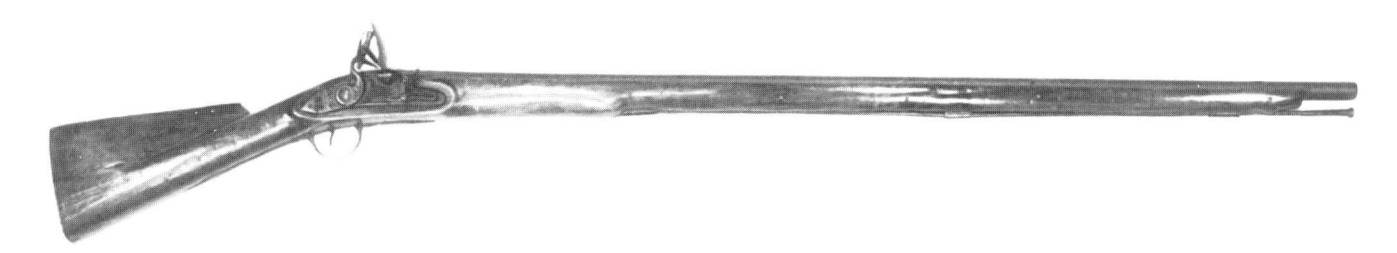

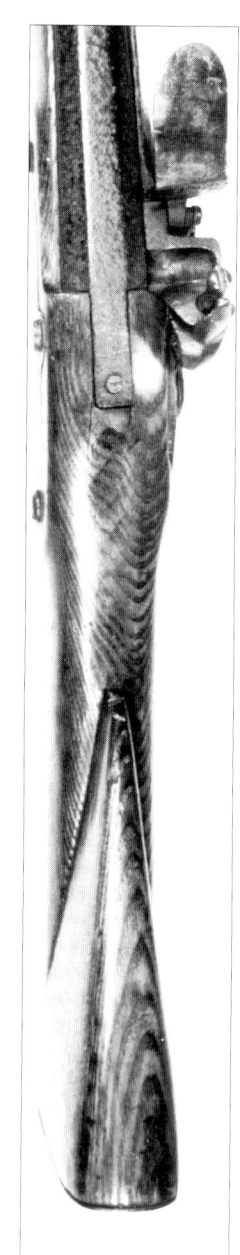

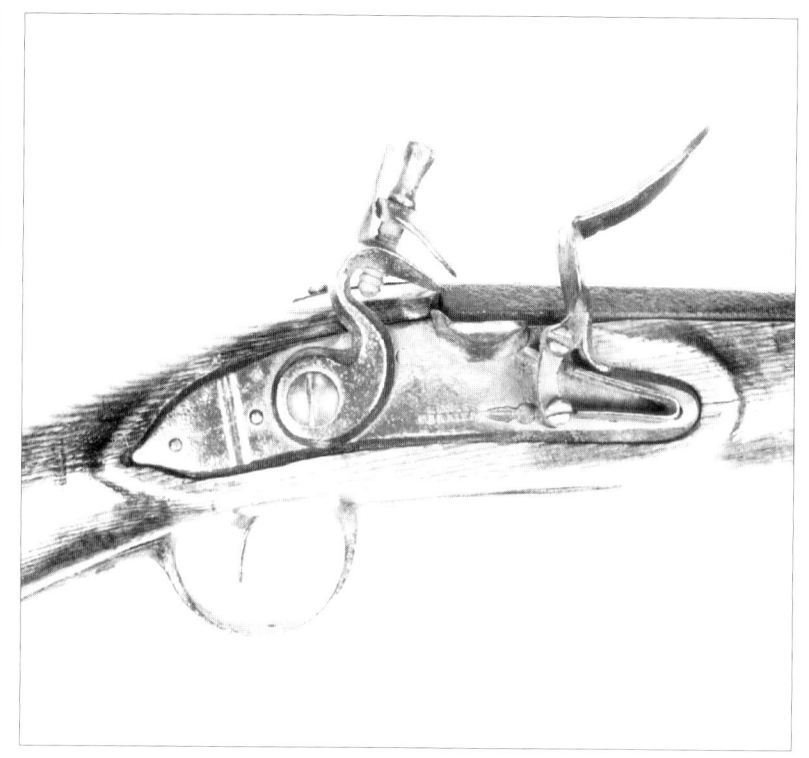

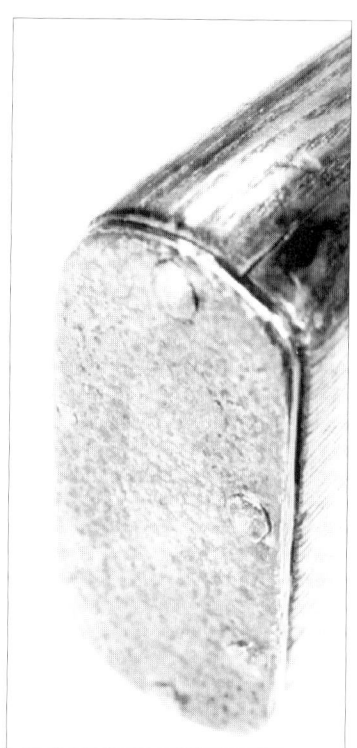

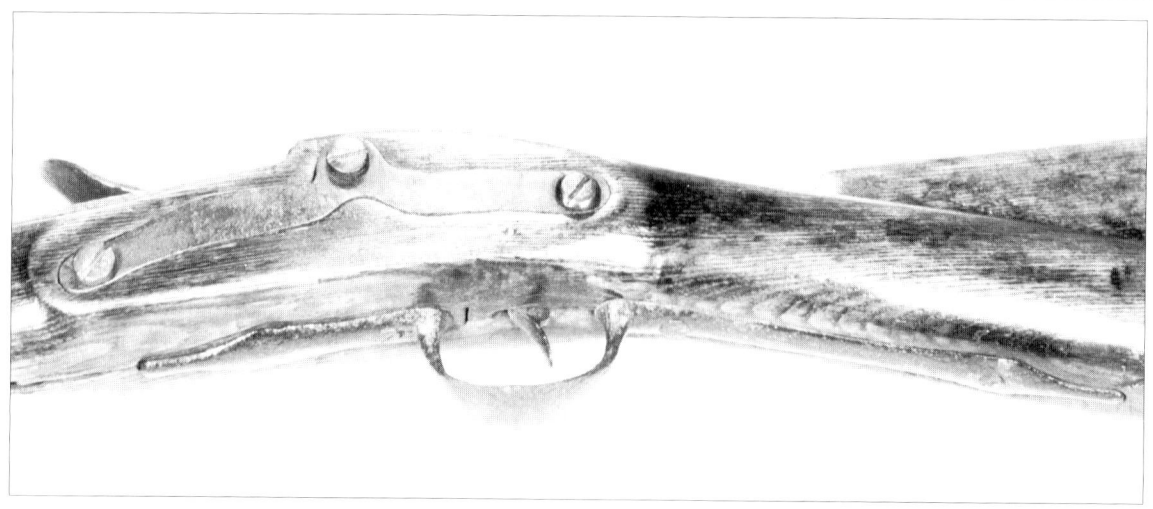

**146.MM  AMERICAN WALL GUN**                                                                                          Circa 1760–1780

Just as the American Colonists restocked a wide variety of parts to create their muskets, the same scarcities controlled their wall gun production. An original French Model 1717 rampart gun's components were reused in this case (see 143.MM). Its long flat/beveled lock with the unique vertical bridle is marked "S / fleur-de-lis / E" (St. Etienne) and "LOVIS / CARRIER" (the barrel maker and manufactory superintendent). Note that a third side screw was later added to its tail. The thick ash stock omits unnecessary elements beyond a crude iron buttplate (six large nails; no tang), an improvised double-arm side plate (three screws), the reused French double-pointed trigger guard and three sheet-brass rammer thimbles (wooden rod). There is no nose cap. The old French rampart's barrel, in turn, has that pattern's octagonal breech and flat top strip reaching almost to the muzzle. The original Model 1717 might have been captured by the Colonists in the French and Indian War or might have arrived in unusable condition among the arms sent as aid during the American Revolution.

Length: 63-1/4"                    Lock: 7" X 1-3/8"                    Furniture: Iron/Brass
Barrel: 47", .77 cal.              Trigger Guard: 12-3/4"               Side Plate: 7"                    Weight: 11.4 lbs.
**Author's Collection**

196     *Chapter 3: Smoothbore Shoulder Arms*

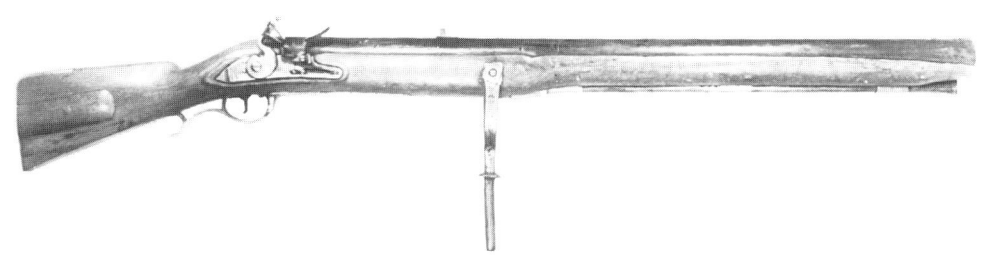

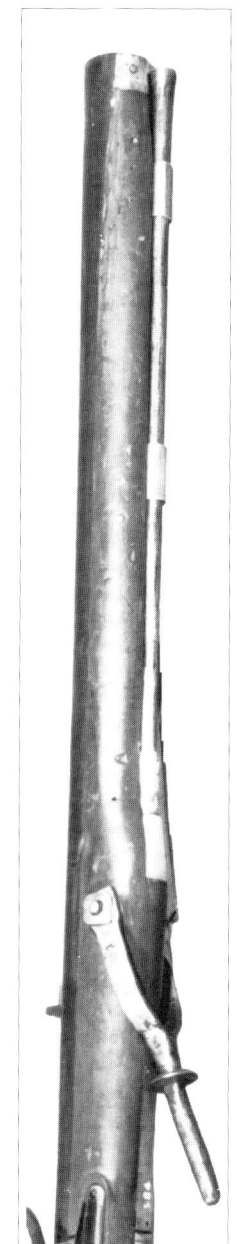

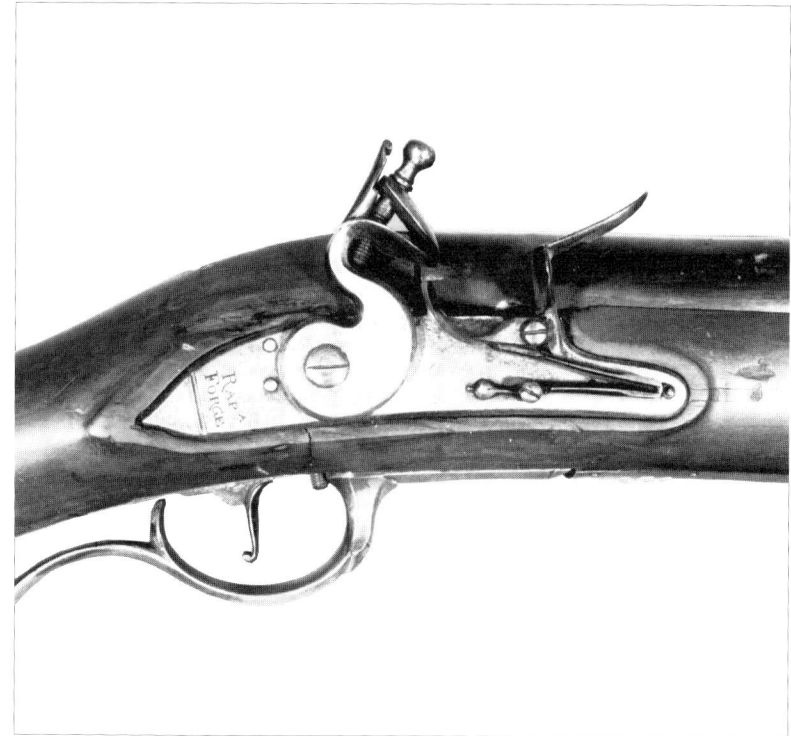

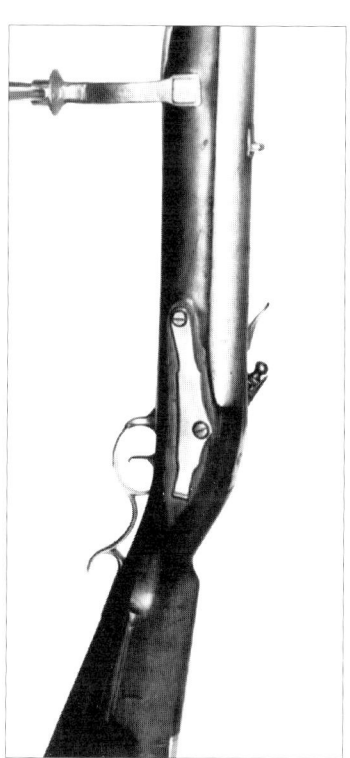

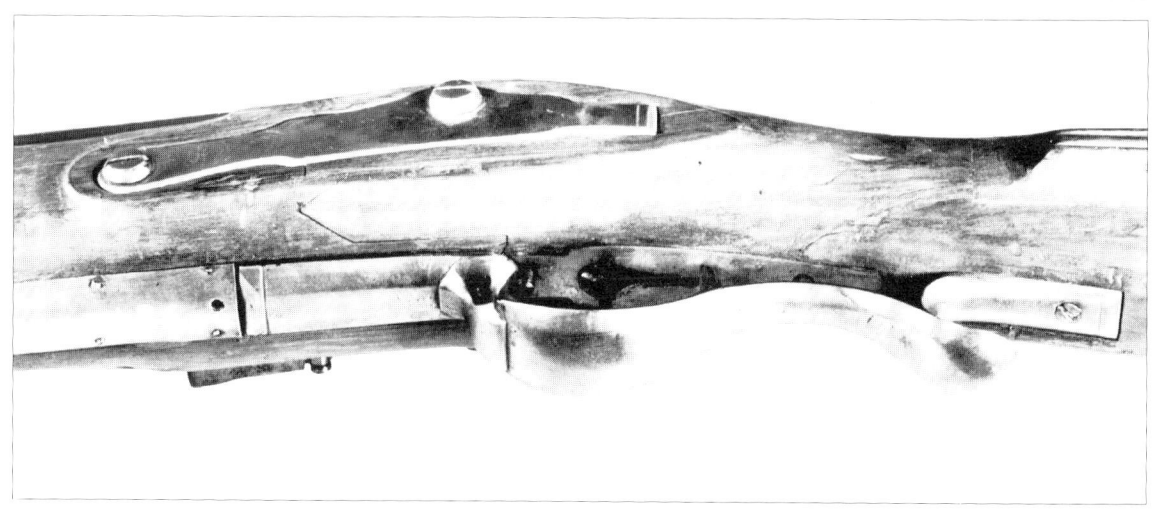

**147.MM AMERICAN RIFLED WALL GUN**  Circa 1776

Drawing upon their experience with rifled barrels, the American rebels developed a "rifle amusette" at James Hunter's Rappahannock Forge in Virginia. Not only does it have a rifled 1-1/8" bore (12 grooves), but also related characteristics such as the butt's wooden patch box, extended trigger guard strut, a raised cheek piece and a flat-ended side plate. The heavy (53.5 lbs.) arm was mounted on a Y-shaped yoke that permitted controlled rotation and elevation. It was intended to fill the gap between a musket and light cannon—with a rifle's precision over long distances. One report testifies to its surprising accuracy at 500 yards. The flat lock is marked across its tail "RAPPA / FORGE." Four of this pattern survive, of which one (at the Smithsonian) includes "I HUNTER" (James Hunter) on the breech (also see 38.PP). Notice, too, that the barrel mounts front and rear fixed sights. Its flared muzzle is cradled in a wide forend terminating at a brass nose band. Three pipes hold the ramrod, while a sheet metal repair is visible just forward of the trigger guard. (Note: the reverse side close-up is from the Smithsonian's wall gun.)

| | | | |
|---|---|---|---|
| Length: 61-1/4" | Lock: 7-7/8" X 1-1/2" | Butt Tang: 3-7/8" | Furniture: Brass |
| Barrel: 44-1/4", 1-1/8" bore | Trigger Guard: 11-3/8" | Weight: 53.5 lbs. | |

**West Point Museum Collection**

*Chapter 3: Smoothbore Shoulder Arms*   **197**

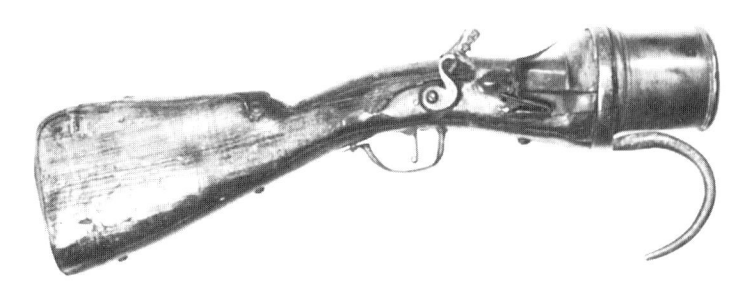

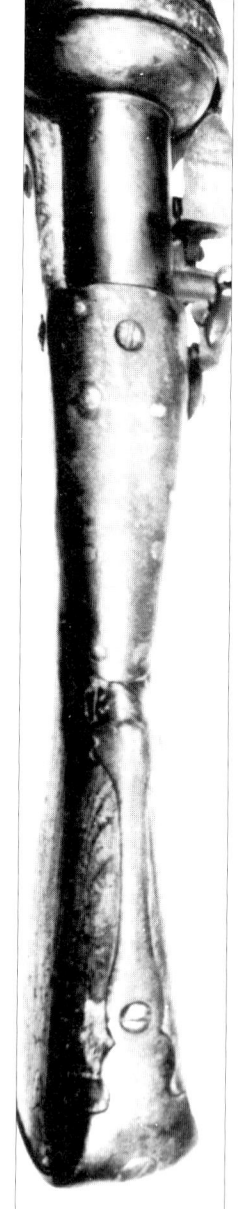

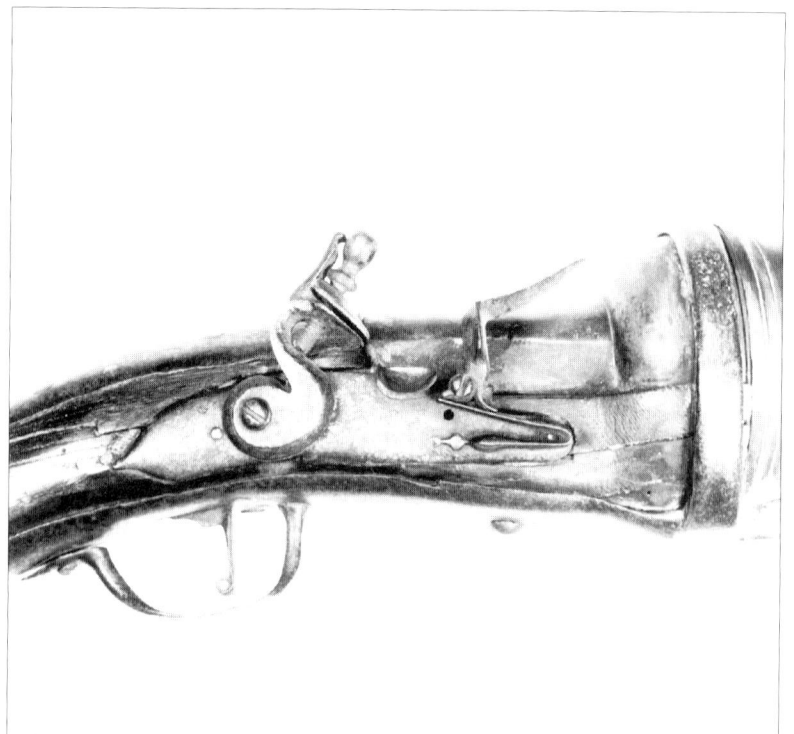

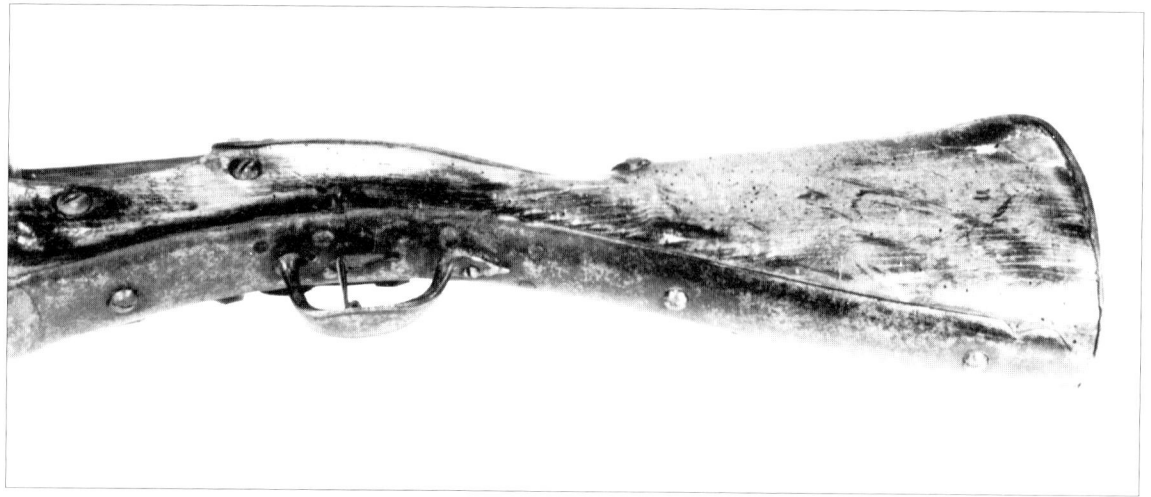

### 148.MM  DUTCH MORTAR SHOULDER ARM
**Circa 1700–1710**

The mortar was a short wide-bore barrel that fired an exploding round shell (or grenade) in an arching low velocity high trajectory—usually to drop into the center of a fort or entrenched camp. From circa 1670 to the 1750s, European armies adopted small mortar barrels to musket-type shoulder stocks for shooting hand grenades beyond arm throwing range. This sturdy Dutch example has a nine-inch-long cast brass mortar barrel with a three-inch bore and a 4-1/2" rear tube, which contained the propelling charge. It is secured to the oak stock by heavy forged straps above and below, plus a thick breech ring. In addition a crude half circle hook/handle projects down under the muzzle. Its stock, in turn, mounts a normal type lock and trigger guard. The round grenade (about a 2-1/2" diameter in this case) was filled with black powder and placed in the barrel with the protruding unlit fuse away from the muzzle. Firing the lock in the normal manner set off the propelling charge, which launched the shell after igniting the fuse by its blast of flame around the projectile's surface. (For a similar musket launcher, see 31.MM.)

Length: 24"  
Barrel: 9", 3" bore  
Lock: 6" X 1-1/8"  
Trigger Guard: 2-1/2"  
Butt Tang: 8-1/4"  
Weight: 16.8 lbs.  
Furniture: Iron

**Robert Nittolo Collection**

Chapter 3: Smoothbore Shoulder Arms

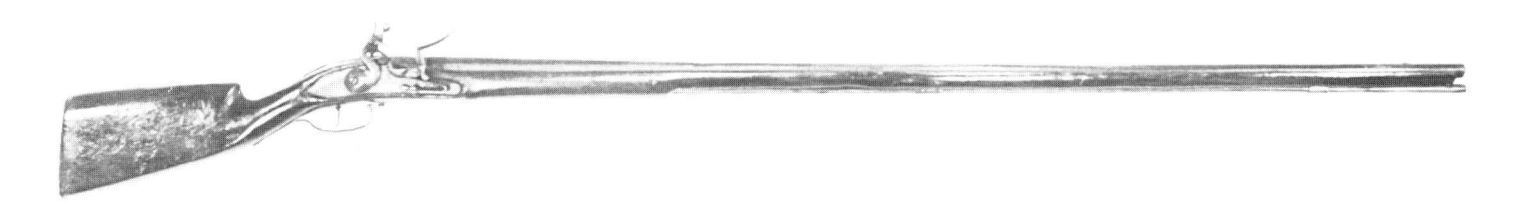

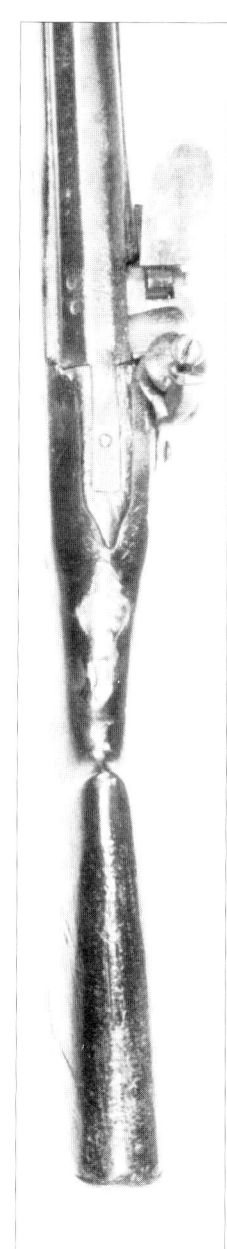

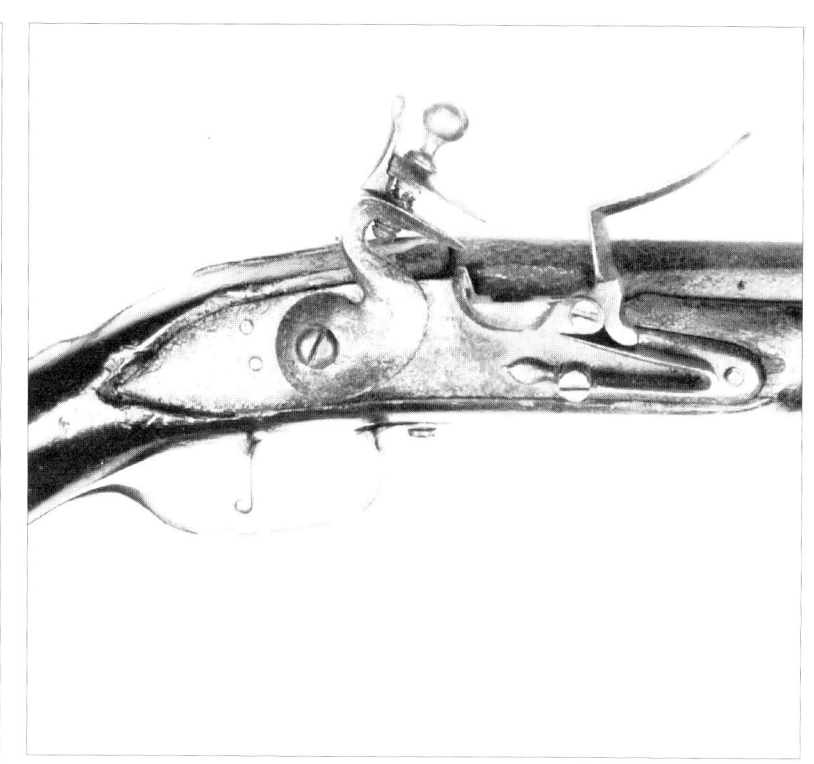

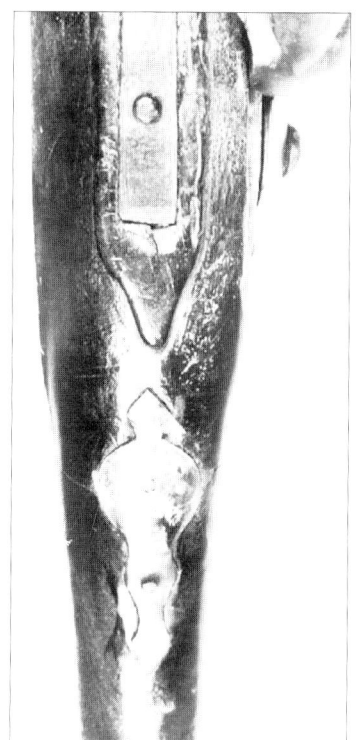

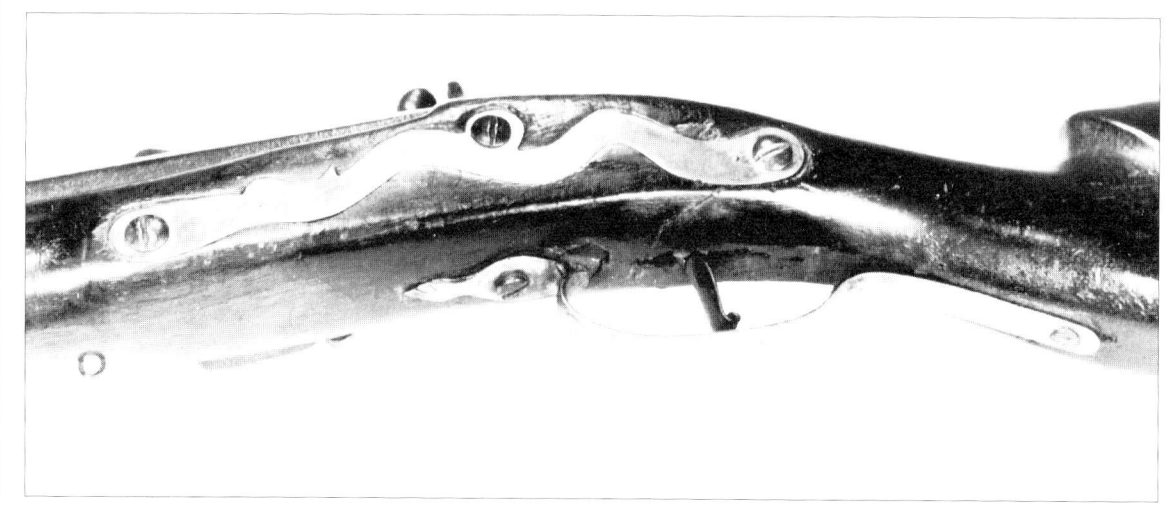

**149.MM ENGLISH COMMERCIAL HUNTING/TRADE GUN**                                                                         **Circa 1700–1720**

Most historians favor the military muskets of the American Colonial period, yet a vast business also existed in commercial arms for the civilian market, especially hunting guns and inexpensive patterns in the rich fur trade. English merchants had the freedom to select firearms to fit their customers' needs and ordered a wide range of configurations direct from private weapons makers. Through the late 1600s to early 1700s, these guns followed the long barreled, large bore fowler and musket patterns of Europe. This example illustrates many of the typical English trade components of that era, for example, the big three-screw lock, a plain flat dragon-outline side plate (no details), and a heavy walnut club butt (like the contemporary competitive French "buccaneer"; see 52.MM). The cost savings of private business are also apparent: a flat iron buttplate (six nails); a simple brass trigger guard (the first of two screws also secures the barrel tang); crude barrel tang border carving; and an early British escutcheon (two nails). The 53-1/4" barrel (circa 1702 London Gunmakers Company proofs) is octagonal for 10 inches. Two one-inch cast brass thimbles (no tail pipe) hold a wooden ramrod.

| | | |
|---|---|---|
| Length: 68-1/8" | Lock: 7-1/4" X 1-3/8" | Furniture: Brass/Iron |
| Barrel: 53-1/4", .73 cal. | Trigger Guard: 7-1/2" | Side Plate: 7-1/2"      Weight: 8.7 lbs. |

**Author's Collection**

*Chapter 3: Smoothbore Shoulder Arms*

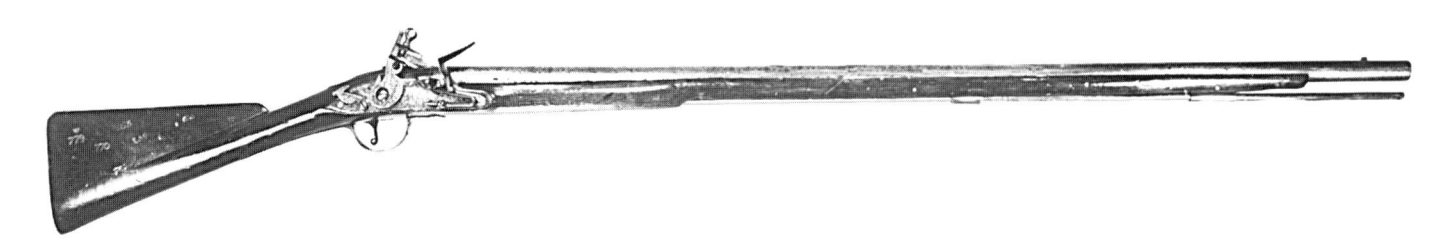

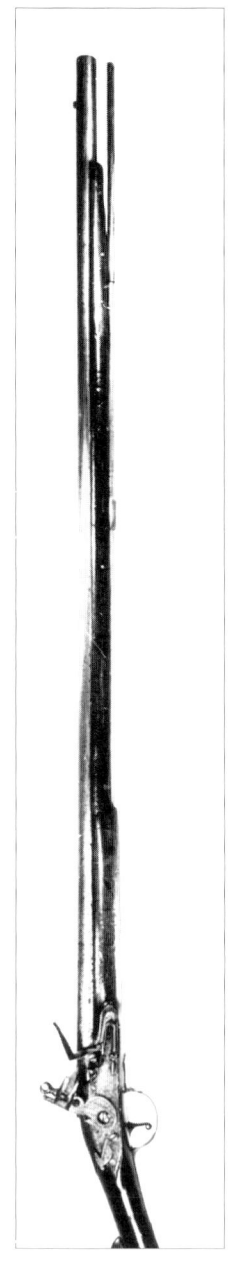

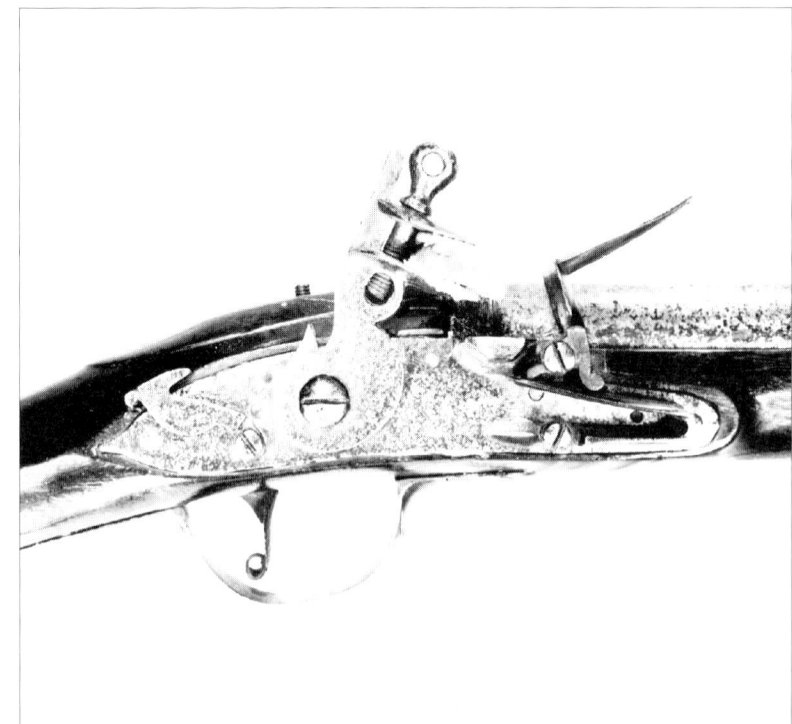

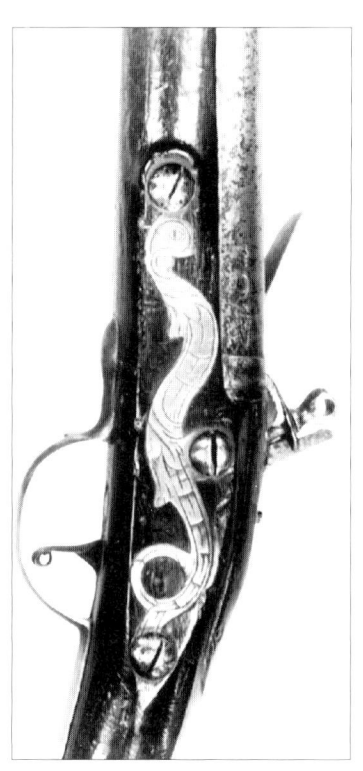

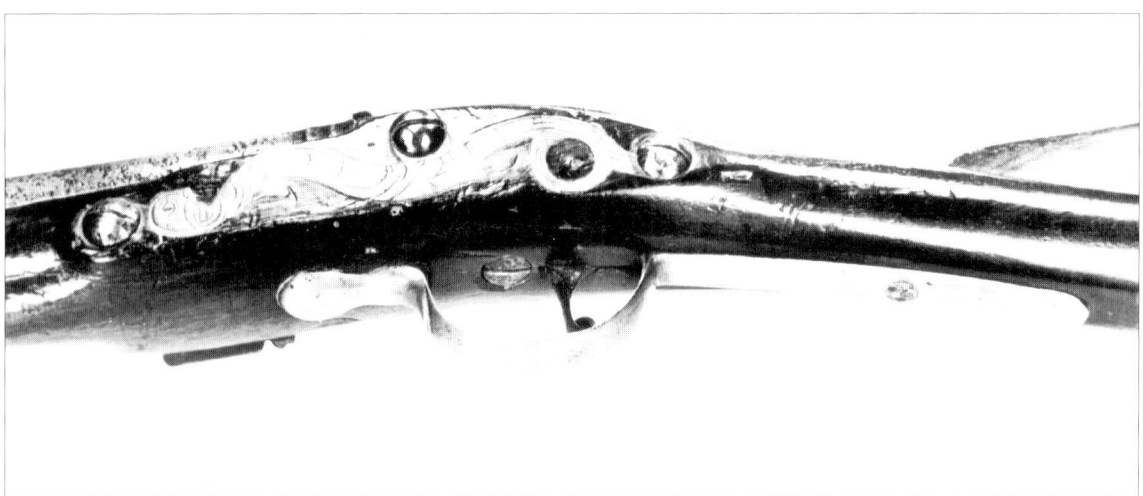

**150.MM  ENGLISH UTILITY/TRADE GUN**                                                                                **Circa 1710–1730**

In addition to the fowler trade patterns during the initial 1700s (see 149.MM), surplus or obsolete European muskets were shipped to the North American Colonies not only for military capability, but also to their civilian merchants for the lucrative hunting and trapping business. This Queen Anne-period pattern had its barrel shortened (the base for its original forward loop remains under the present muzzle), apparently to convert it into a trade or general utility hunting arm for the provincials. The flat three-screw lock with ring cock and squared frizzen is typical of that period. Other contemporary features seen here became established with the Indians and were carried forward into the evolving fur trade patterns of the late 1700s (see 140.MM, 155.MM). These include: a flat nailed butt plate with a short lobe-ended tang; a three-screw dragon side plate having incised features; a plain trigger guard headed by a round terminal; a bottom screw to secure the barrel tang; and simple sheet-brass rammer thimbles for a wooden rod. This particular arm had its forend cut back at one time to mount a bayonet (no end cap). Its lock is marked "WALKER" for a London gunsmith.

| | | | |
|---|---|---|---|
| Length: 57-5/8" | Lock: 6-3/4" X 1-1/4" | Butt Tang: 2-3/4" | Furniture: Brass |
| Barrel: 42", .77 cal. | Trigger Guard: 9" | Weight: 8.1 lbs. | |

*Chapter 3: Smoothbore Shoulder Arms*

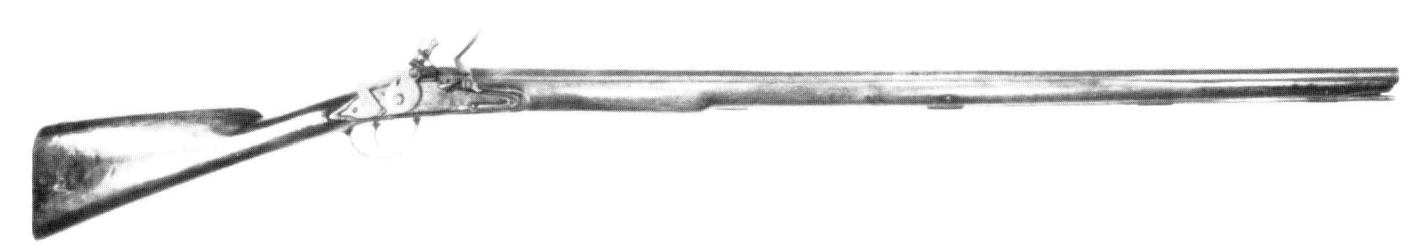

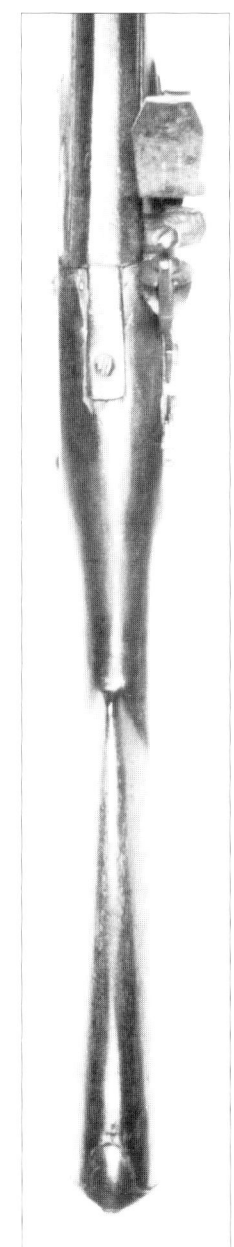

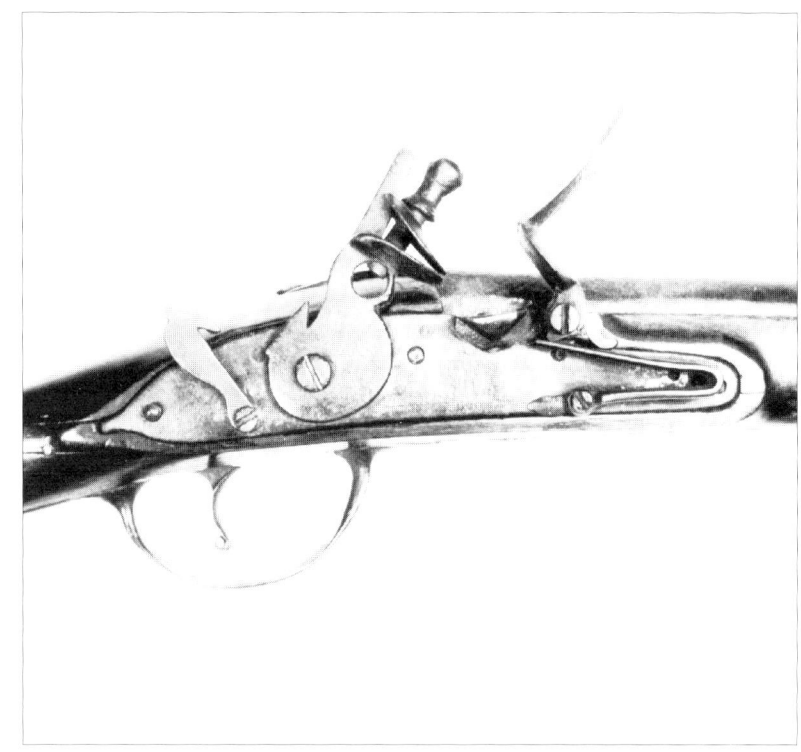

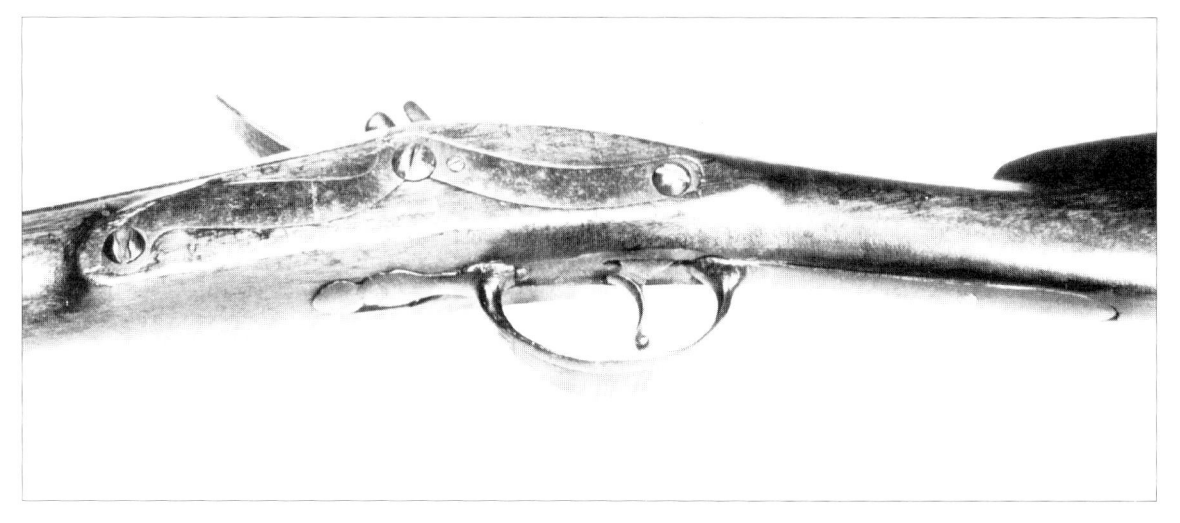

**151.MM EUROPEAN UTILITY/TRADE GUN**  Circa 1715–1740

When compared to a typical obsolete English musket included among early North American trade arms (see prior example), it is interesting in this case to see how European private contractors copied its basic features for customer acceptance, yet introduced economies where possible to remain cost competitive. The three-screw doglock resembles the English form but has a thinner lock plate and cock (no bridles); iron furniture replaces brass; a simple double arm side plate approximates the dragon shape; a convex butt plate and stubby tang resemble the flat Queen Anne style; raised carving is eliminated; and four plain sheet-iron pipes support a wooden rammer. The trigger guard, in turn, is headed by a lobed terminal not unlike the rounded end on the British pattern. Its shape and the incised lines on the trigger bow, however, suggest a French or Low Country source—possibly Liege, which manufactured guns of all forms for military and private contracts worldwide. A durable walnut stock extends to the muzzle. Note also that economies achieved here do not detract from the reliability of its essential components, that is, the lock, stock and barrel.

| | | | |
|---|---|---|---|
| Length: 57-1/8" | Lock: 7-1/4" X 1-1/4" | Butt Tang: 1-1/2" | Furniture: Iron |
| Barrel: 40-3/8", .73 cal. | Trigger Guard: 9-5/8" | Side Plate: 7" | Weight: 8.2 lbs. |
| Author's Collection | | | |

*Chapter 3: Smoothbore Shoulder Arms*

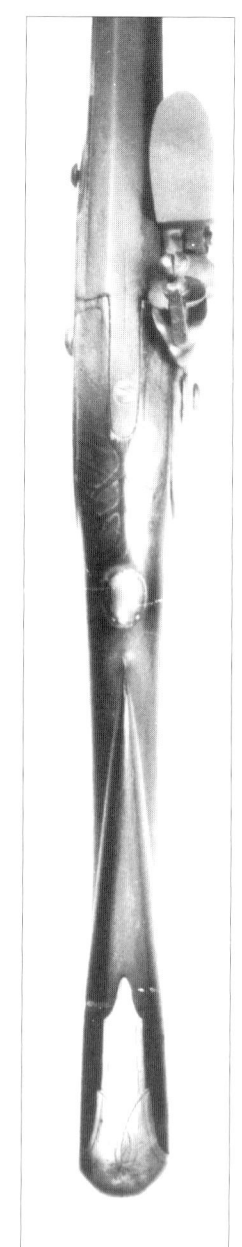

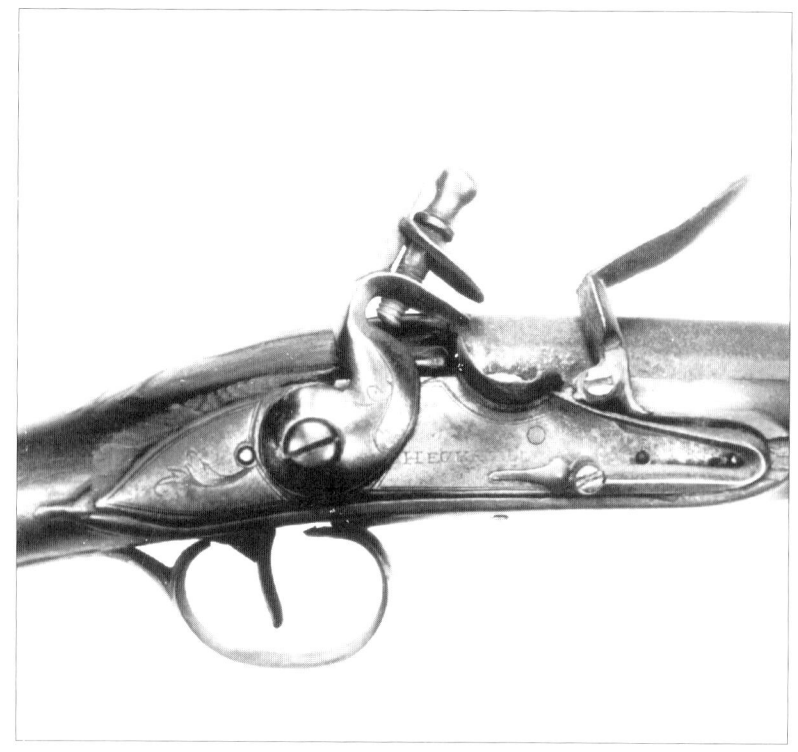

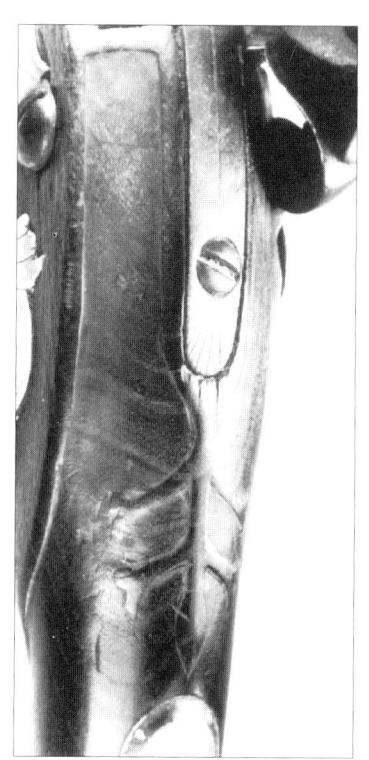

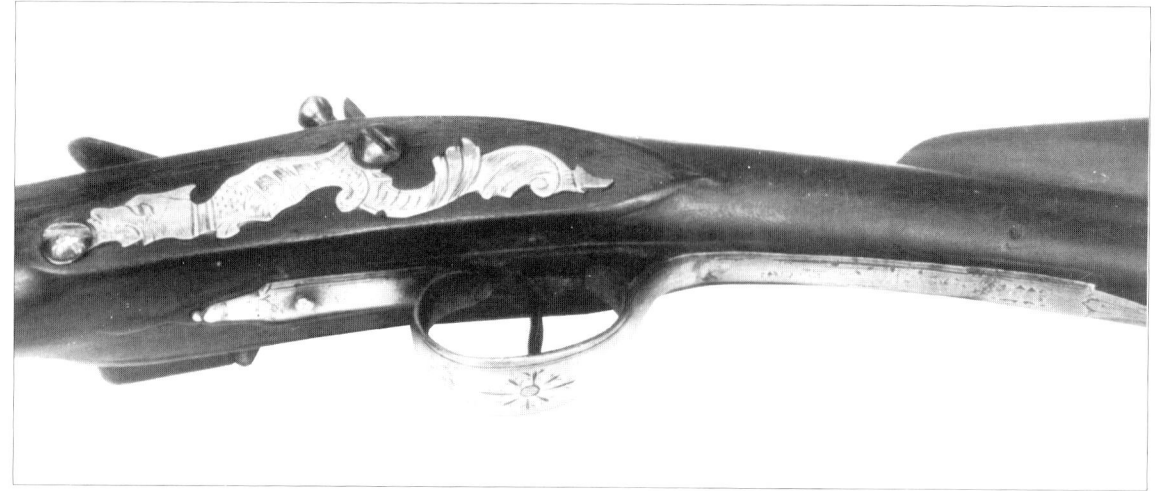

**152.MM ENGLISH COMMERCIAL HUNTING/TRADE GUN**                                                Circa 1730–1760

By 1730 Britain's commercial arms became more responsive to customer preferences for lighter, better balanced and more utilitarian patterns. This slender example, with its Roman nose buttstock and pinned barrel, copies the French "fusil de chasse" (see 156.MM), probably in an effort to compete with that popular hunter's weapon. Notice the two-screw rounded trade lock marked by its London maker, "HECKSTALL," and incorporating the economies of only token floral decoration, a plain cock post and omission of an outer bridle. Elementary stock carving includes a period "tree" form behind the barrel tang (the silver escutcheon was added later), while a dragon side plate, stepped butt tang and double-pointed trigger guard are typical British commercial patterns. Its walnut forend reaches to 1-3/4 inches below the muzzle and provides three brass thimbles for the wooden rammer. A 46-3/8 inch (.69 caliber) pinned barrel, in turn, is octagonal for 8-1/2 inches. The single "crossed scepters" stamp suggests "private" Tower proofing only for the barrel (probably to save the maker money and time).

| | | | |
|---|---|---|---|
| Length: 61-1/2" | Lock: 6" X 1-1/8" | Butt Tang: 4-1/4" | Furniture: Brass |
| Barrel: 46-3/8", .69 cal. | Trigger Guard: 9-3/4" | Side Plate: 5-1/2" | Weight: 6.8 lbs. |

**Author's Collection**

202    *Chapter 3: Smoothbore Shoulder Arms*

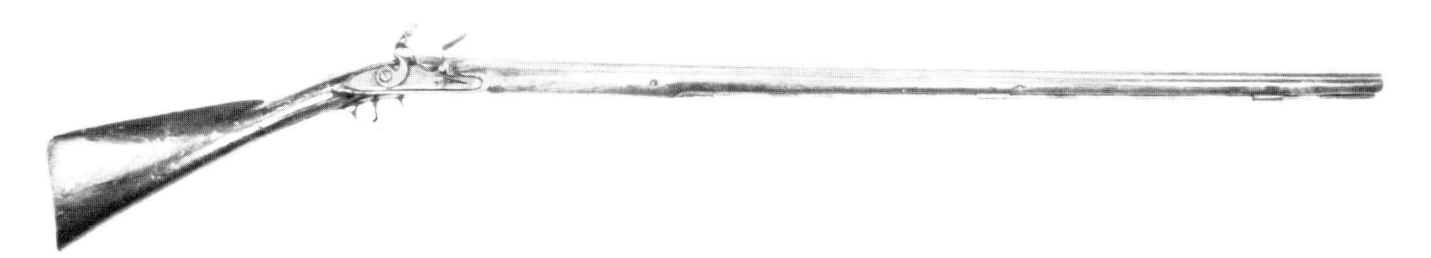

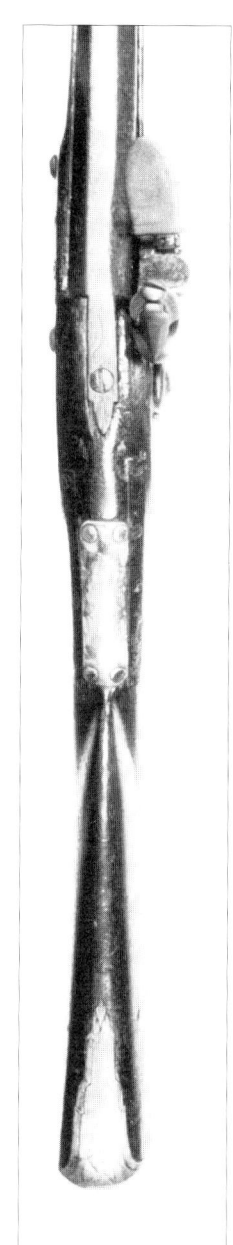

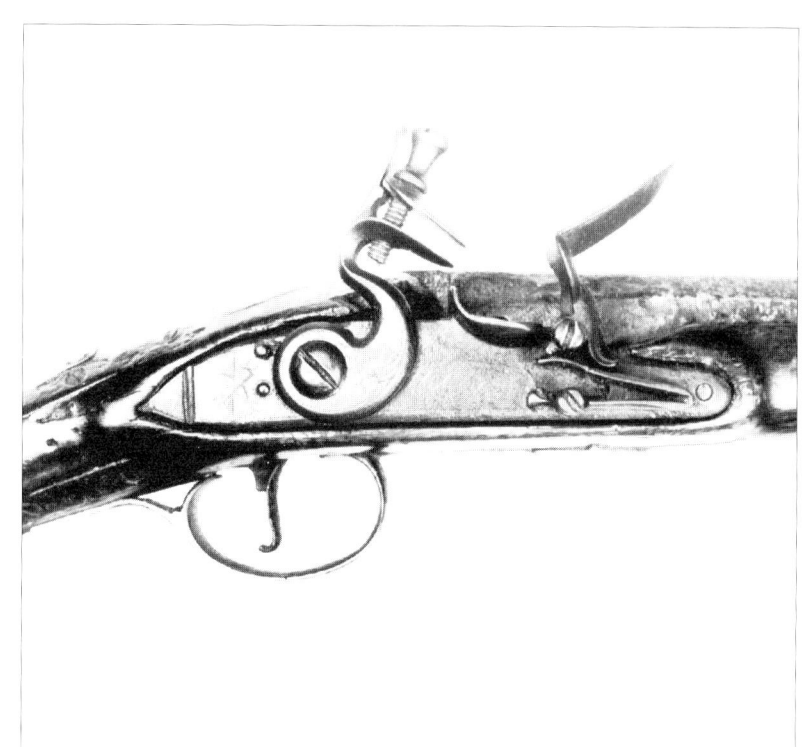

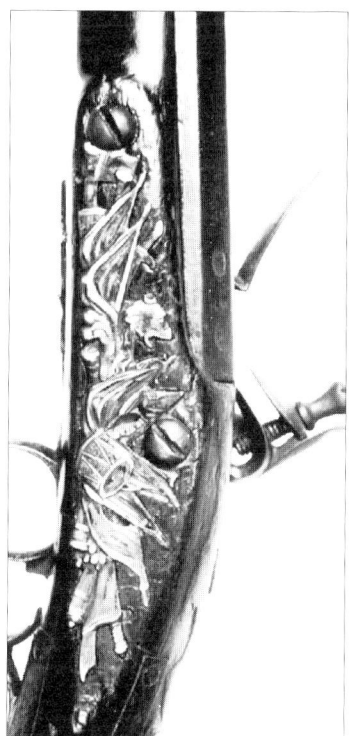

### 153.MM ENGLISH COMMERCIAL HUNTING/TRADE GUN

**Circa 1735–1750**

Several of the continuing changes in these English commercial arms toward more standardized patterns are evident here. The impressive panoply-of-arms side plate and cast brass furniture identify it at the level targeted to attract the established trappers and hunters or as a gift to Indian leaders. It had its narrow wrist broken and repaired by four iron straps and a brass patch. Yet notice the typical British trade stepped butt tang, quiver/bow engraving on the flat lock's tail, the tulip-like terminal and rear post spur on its trigger guard, and the shorter small bore barrel (42", .62 caliber, octagonal 7-1/4 inches). When this flintlock is picked up, it is immediately apparent why the reduced weight, shortened barrel and comfortable balance appealed to the woodsman. Moreover the lesser bore still permitted a lethal ball size but required less powder. In normal practice, sling swivels were never included. A front blade is 2-1/8 inches behind the muzzle (no rear sight). Its breech and lock bear Richard Wilson's stamps, plus "MINORIES LONDON" along the barrel (the primary gunmaking section near the Tower).

| | | | |
|---|---|---|---|
| Length: 57-3/8" | Lock: 5-1/2" X 1" | Butt Tang: 4" | Furniture: Brass |
| Barrel: 42", .62 cal. | Trigger Guard: 11-1/8" | Side Plate: 5-1/2" | Weight: 5.7 lbs. |

**Author's Collection**

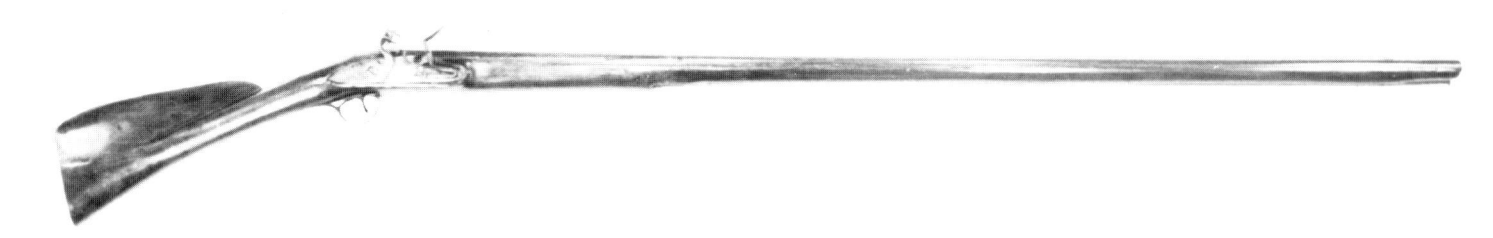

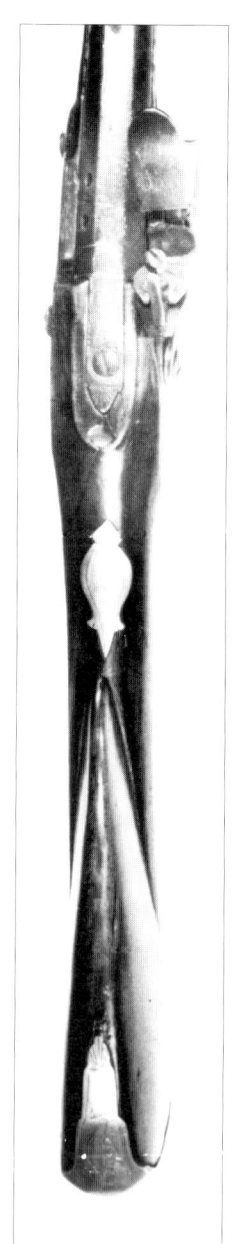

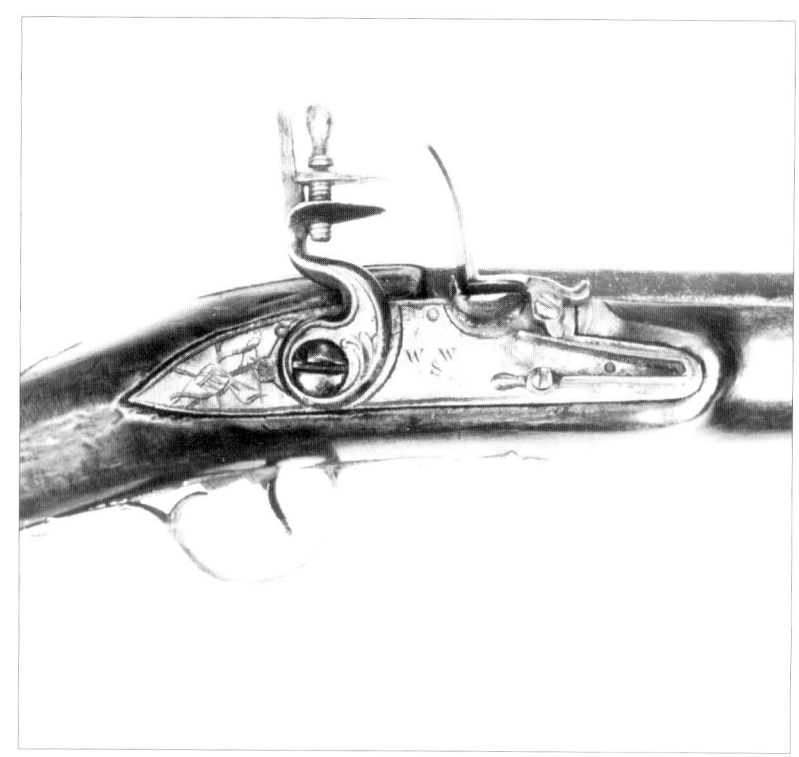

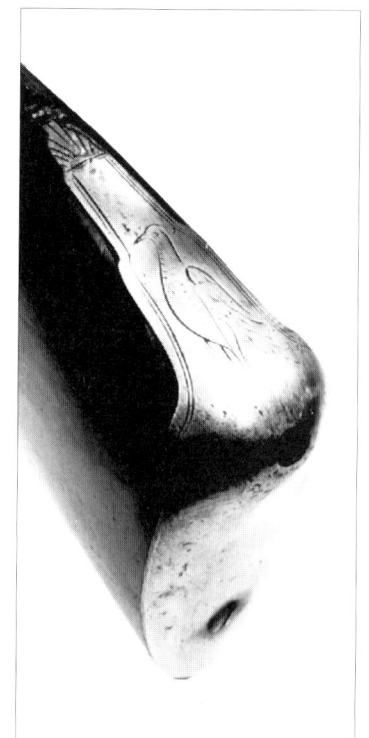

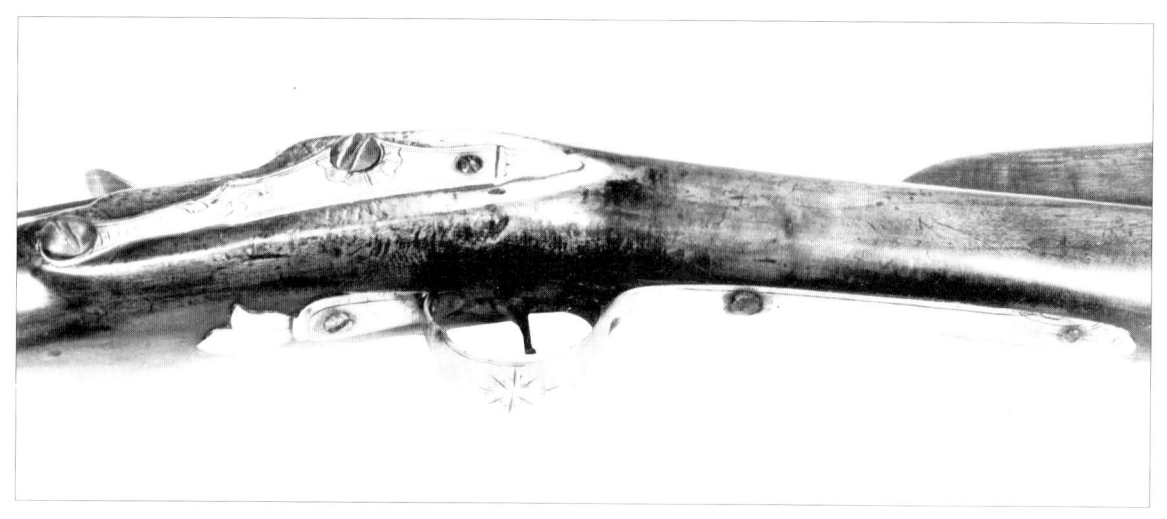

**154.MM ENGLISH/AMERICAN HUNTING/TRADE GUN**   Circa 1730–1760

One of the common British trade locks had the typical flat plate and cock but installed a distinctive right angle at the upper rear end of its forward nose (above illustration is at half-cock to make it visible). In addition to importing complete firearms, many parts were ordered separately for assembling and repairing guns locally. This full-size fowler, having a Roman nose and a substantial cherry stock, was apparently created here by a provincial who preferred that form or by a merchant possibly in competition with established French traders. Its real importance, however, is the period's typical British trade components that it displays, that is, a wild turkey engraved on the two-step butt tang, an arms panoply at the lock's tail, the trigger guard's "tulip" forward terminal, its decorated triangular side plate (rear wood screw), a double-pointed escutcheon, and a pinned .67 caliber barrel (octagonal for 9-1/2 inches). The breech has circa 1702 London Gunmakers Company proofs with Richard Wilson's strike, "R*W," between them.

| | | | |
|---|---|---|---|
| Length: 66-3/4" | Lock: 6" X 1-1/8" | Butt Tang: 4" | Furniture: Brass |
| Barrel: 50-3/4", .67 cal. | Trigger Guard: 10" | Side Plate 5-3/4" | Weight: 8.3 lbs. |
| **Author's Collection** | | | |

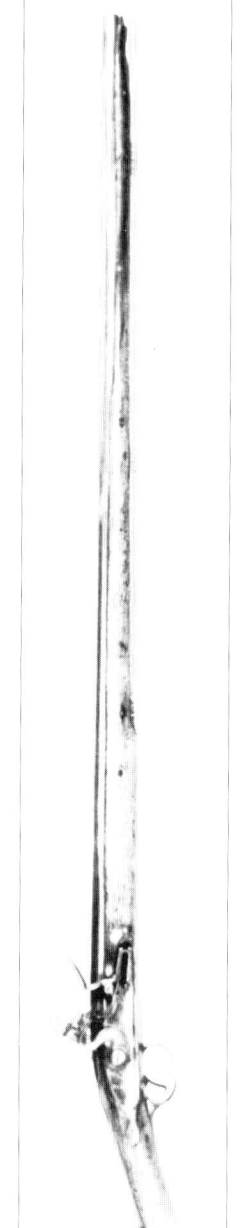

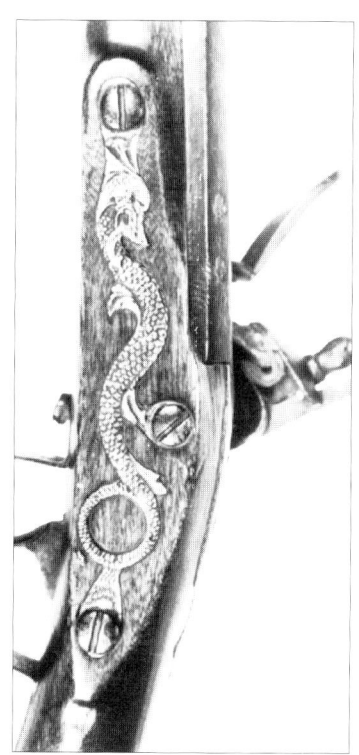

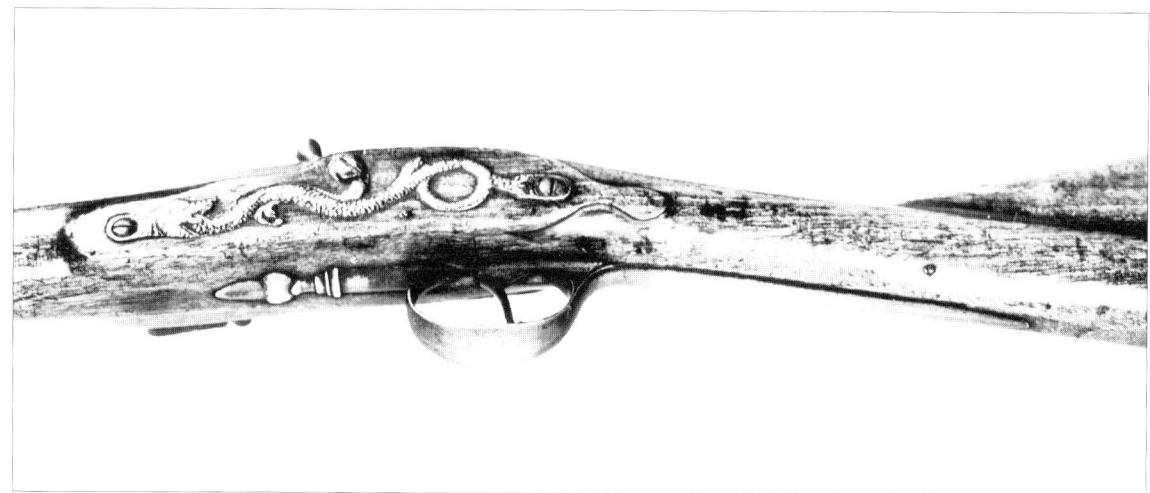

**155.MM ENGLISH "NORTHWEST" TRADE GUN**                                   Circa 1770–1800

At the end of the French and Indian War, France was eliminated from the North American fur trade and the English became dominant. To replace the established French designs, they developed by the 1770s a short durable and economical trade pattern. It became known as the "Northwest gun" (also "Hudson's Bay fuke" or "Mackinaw gun") and continued its basic configuration with great success until the late 1800s. This new inexpensive pattern, as seen here in early form, was a hunter's weapon having a short barrel (convenient in rough terrain and to load in a crouch); a simple flat trigger guard (two screws—one reaching up to the butt tang); a deep bow to accommodate a gloved hand; a new cast brass dragon side plate with raised scales (above photo from a similar gun); a light convex three-screw lock (often without bridles); border carving around the lock, side plate and barrel tang; plus a nailed lobe-ended flat buttplate. The two ramrod pipes are ribbed sheet brass (the original wooden rod had a brass tip). "WILSON" is marked at the lock's tail and "RW" on the breech. The Indians often removed trigger guards, butt plates and such for use as hide scrapers or domestic tools.

Length: 51-3/4"       Lock: 6" X 1"       Butt Tang: 2-1/4"       Furniture: Brass
Barrel: 35-3/4", .60 cal.       Trigger Guard: 10-5/8"       Weight: 5.1 lbs.

**Foster Tallman Collection**

*Chapter 3: Smoothbore Shoulder Arms*

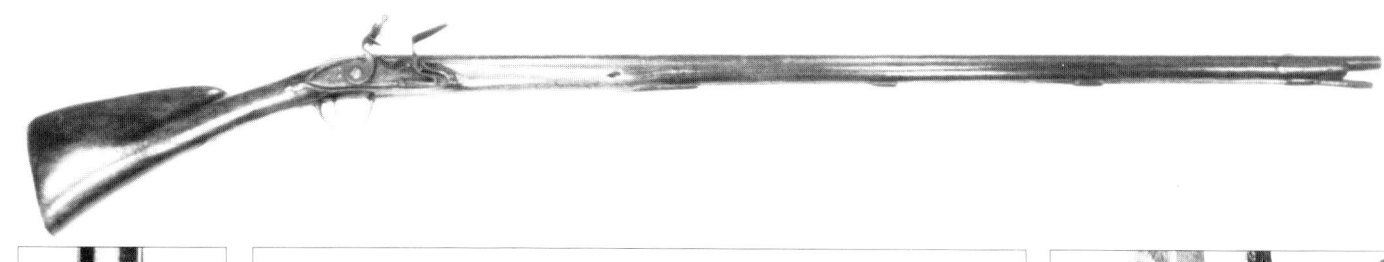

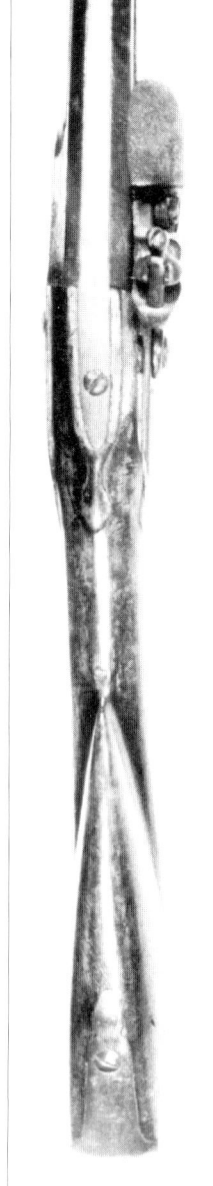

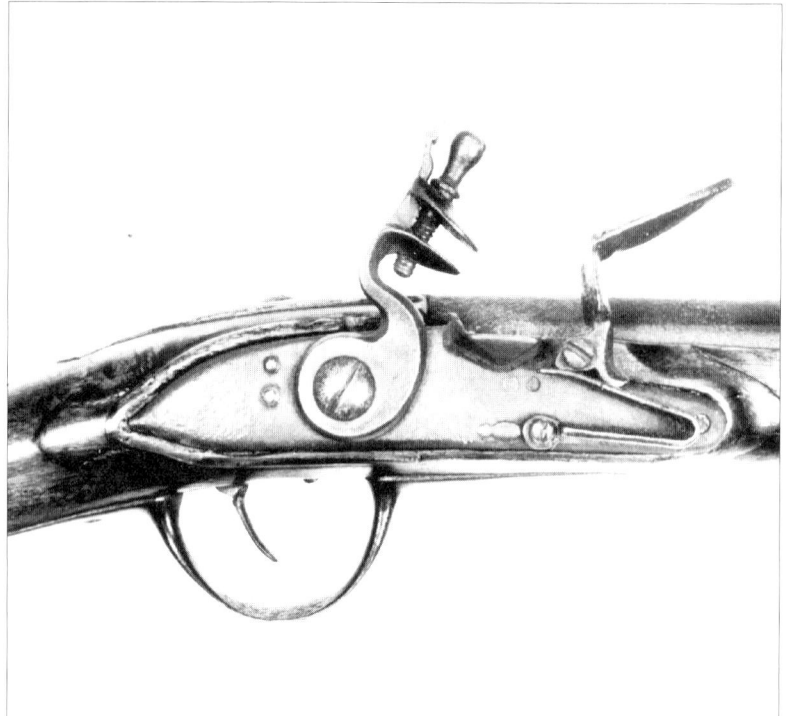

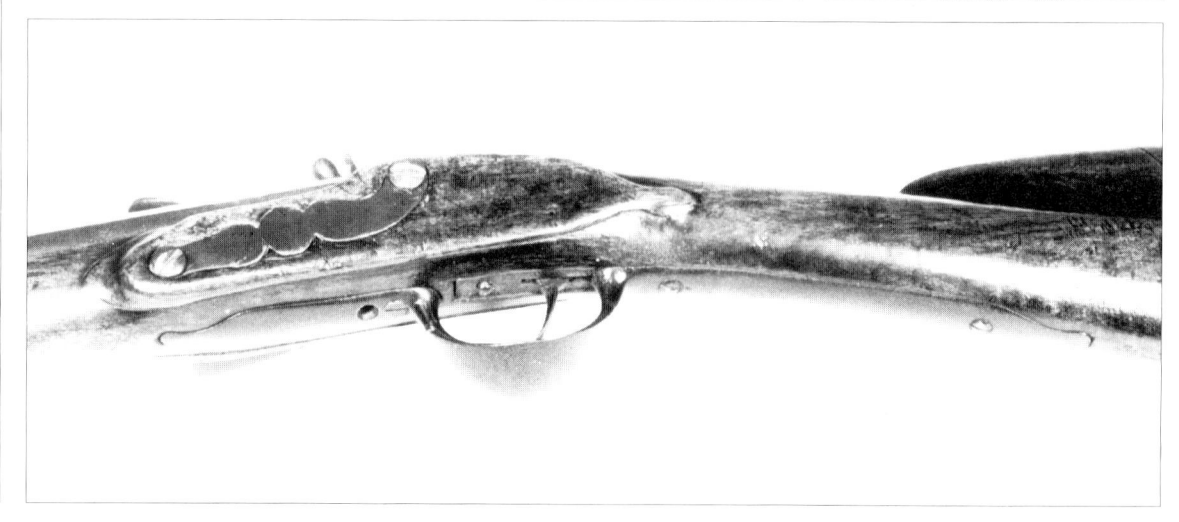

**156.MM FRENCH COMMERCIAL HUNTING GUN *(FUSIL DE CHASSE)***                  Circa 1730–1750

The importation and distribution of civilian firearms into French Canada—as with their military forces—was controlled by the Ministry of Marine until circa 1760. Such commercial weapons were usually classified as either hunting guns *(fusils de chasse)* or trade arms *(fusils de traite)*. This pattern was apparently the most common hunting form, which was primarily offered to French woodsmen, Indian partisans and some local militia. The trade guns, in turn, were relegated to the Indian fur trade (see 160.MM). Tulle produced most of these arms, although some were supplied from St. Etienne (157.MM). Notice how close this civilian design matches Tulle's contemporary military *fusil ordinaire* (34.MM), for example: a Roman nose walnut stock; an octagonal breech (9-1/4") plus a 16-flat section (two inches) and ring on the barrel; the blunted-spear stock carving around the lock, side plate and breech tang; a pear-like butt tang tip; a flat S-shaped side plate with a center oval; and a double-ended trigger guard. They differ mostly in this pattern's shortened flat lock that omits the tail groove, yet includes a longer nose, a smaller bore (.62 caliber) and no provision for a bayonet. "Fleur-de-lis / L" is stamped behind the trigger guard.

| | | | |
|---|---|---|---|
| Length: 59-3/4" | Lock: 6" X 1-1/4" | Butt Tang: 3-7/8" | Furniture: Iron |
| Barrel: 44-1/8", .62 cal. | Trigger Guard: 11-3/4" | Side Plate: 3-5/8" | Weight: 6.9 lbs. |

**Author's Collection**

206     *Chapter 3: Smoothbore Shoulder Arms*

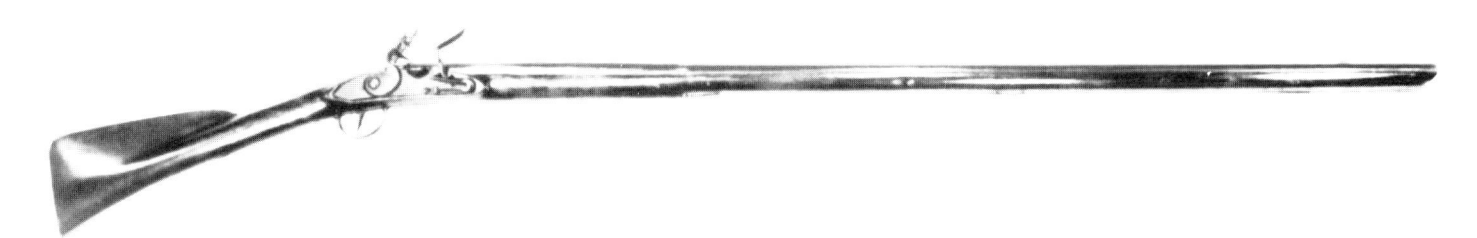

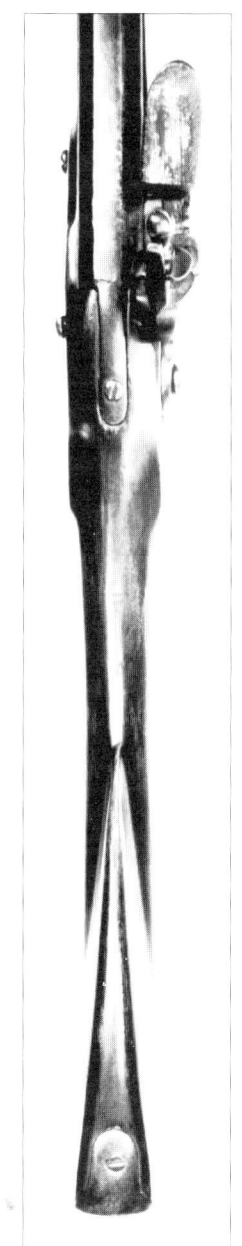

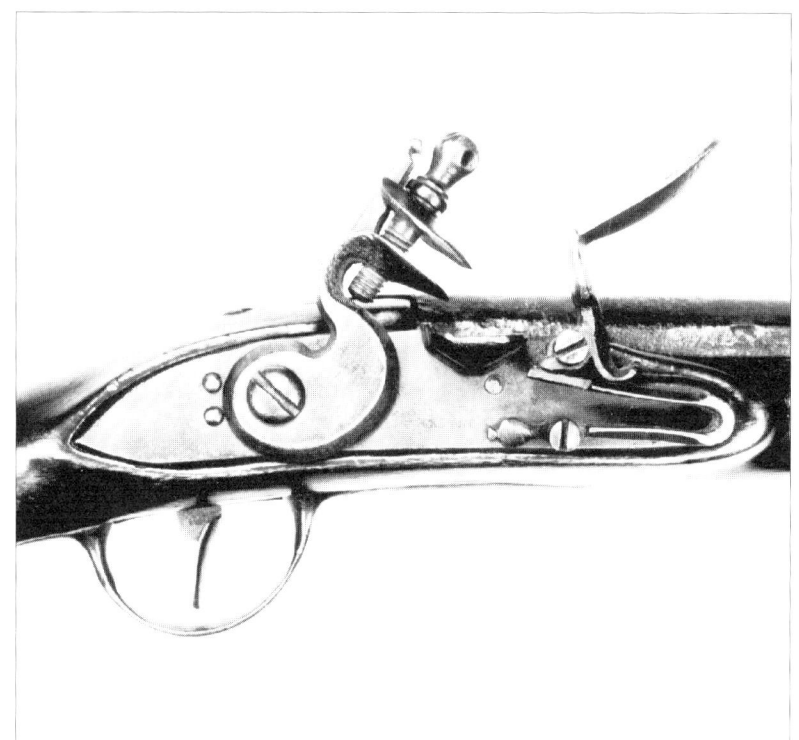

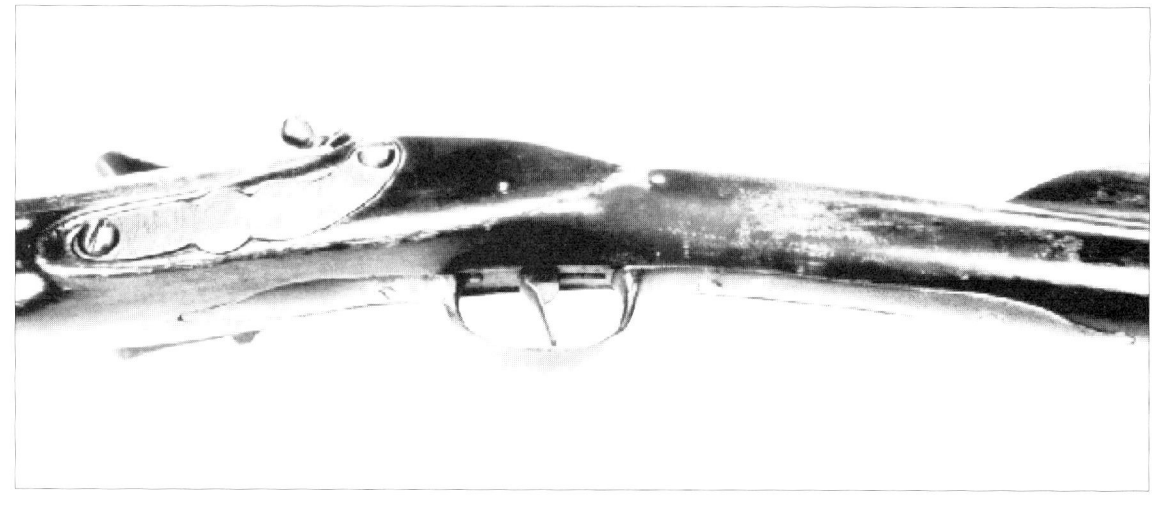

**157.MM FRENCH COMMERCIAL HUNTING/TRADE GUN *(FUSIL DE CHASSE)***           Circa 1730–1750

Compared to the Tulle-made hunting arms, similar patterns from St. Etienne were usually considered inferior (re: Bouchard bib. 176). This example of the latter follows the Tulle configuration with a similar flat lock (St. Etienne marking; no bridles) yet mounts a thinner Roman nose walnut stock that extends to the muzzle (single front sight) and omits carved finials behind the lock, side plate and barrel tang. In addition, the iron butt tang is reduced to a simple lobe (top screw), while the double-pointed trigger guard is 1-1/4 inches shorter. Its flat side plate continues the oval center design but in a less-defined outline. The 44-3/8" barrel, in turn, retains Tulle's octagonal base (9-3/4" here) and a faceted section (1-3/4") plus ring, yet narrows across the breech (1" versus 1-1/8"), reflecting thinner walls surrounding the .62 caliber bore. Three sheet-iron thimbles (versus Tulle's four) hold a wooden rammer. Although this weapon's lightness and balance are well-adopted for woodland use, its lower level of durability compared to the more substantial Tulle product is apparent.

| | | | |
|---|---|---|---|
| Length: 60-1/4" | Lock: 6" x 1-1/8" | Butt Tang: 2" | Furniture: Iron |
| Barrel: 44-3/8", .62 cal. | Trigger Guard: 10-1/2" | Side Plate: 3-5/8" | Weight: 6.5 lbs. |

**Author's Collection**

*Chapter 3: Smoothbore Shoulder Arms*    **207**

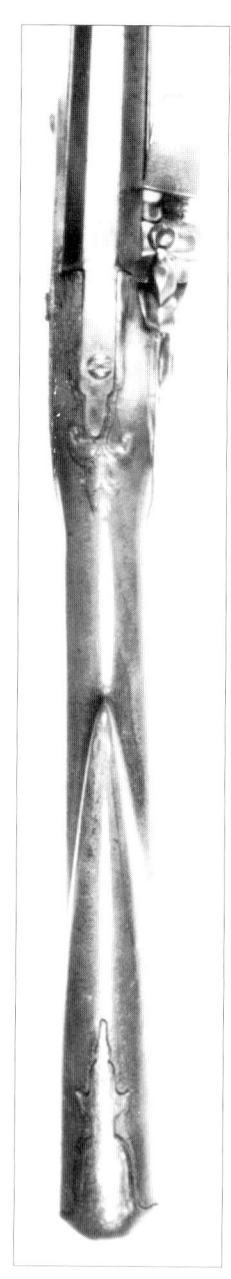

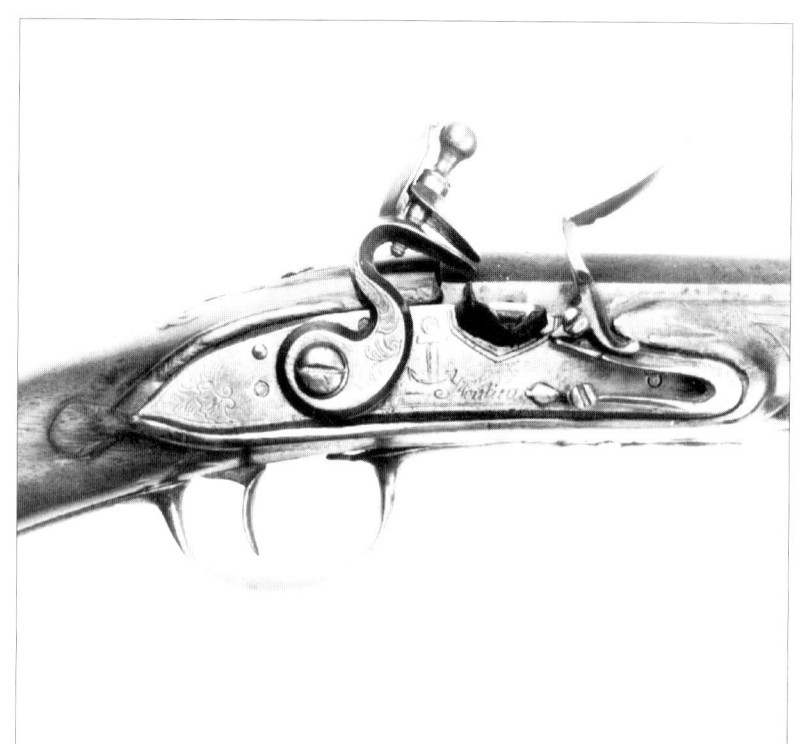

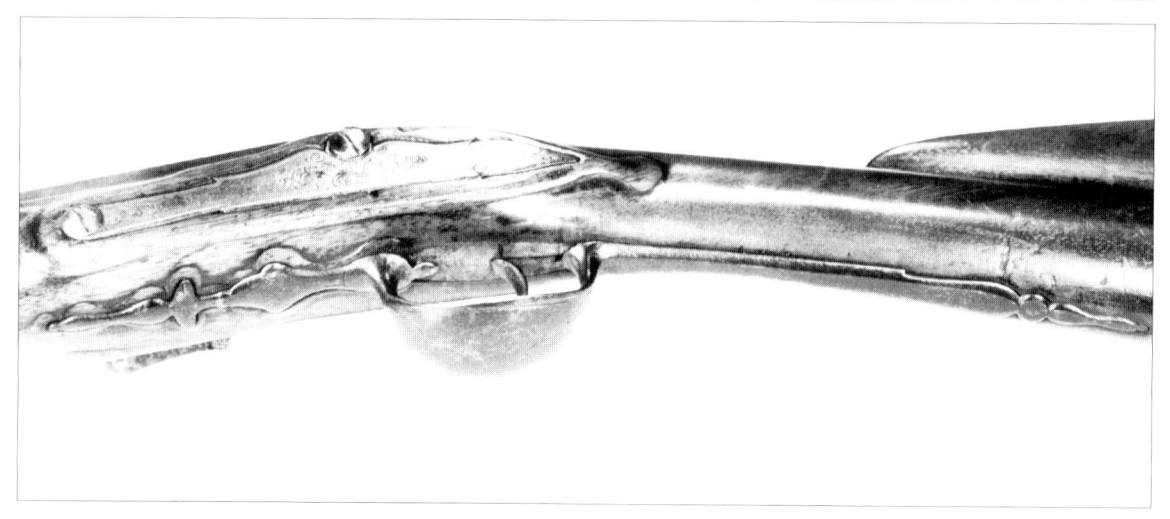

**158.MM  FRENCH COMMERCIAL HUNTING GUN *(FUSIL FIN DE CHASSE)***                        Circa 1730–1750

In addition to the regular hunting gun (156.MM), higher quality patterns were produced for more important settlers and even presentation pieces to Indian Chiefs. They included finer furniture and more decorative enhancements, as seen here. Notice the typical long-nosed French flat/beveled lock (no exterior bridle) that now adds floral engraving on its surface plus an anchor (probably to identify with the Ministry of Marine) and "MONLIEU," an agent in Nantes. It also mounts iron furniture in currently popular French civilian configurations: the thin segmented trigger guard; triangular side plate; three-pointed butt tang; and narrowed barrel tang tip. Raised carving provides a foliage design behind the barrel tang and adds the familiar blunted-spear at the rear of lock and side plate borders. In addition, double lines trace the edge of the walnut stock's forend alongside the barrel and also below—parallel to the ramrod channel. Four sheet-iron thimbles secure a wooden rammer having a two-inch wrapped pewter tip. Its barrel is octagonal for eight inches and extends a top flat panel to the front blade (no rear sight). Most of these arms were manufactured at Tulle.

| | | | |
|---|---|---|---|
| Length: 65-1/8" | Lock: 5-7/8" X 1-1/8" | Butt Tang: 4-1/4" | Furniture: Iron |
| Barrel: 49-1/2", .65 cal. | Trigger Guard: 12-3/8" | Side Plate: 5-3/4" | Weight: 6.8 lbs. |

**Author's Collection**

*Chapter 3: Smoothbore Shoulder Arms*

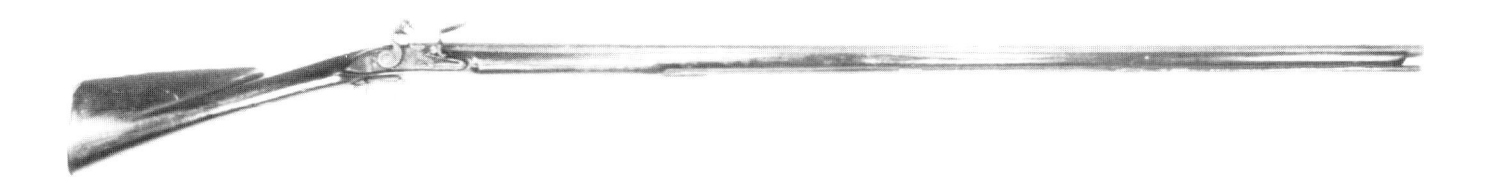

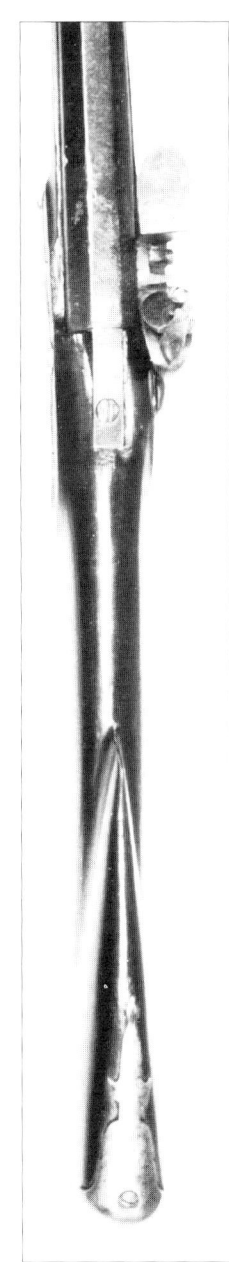

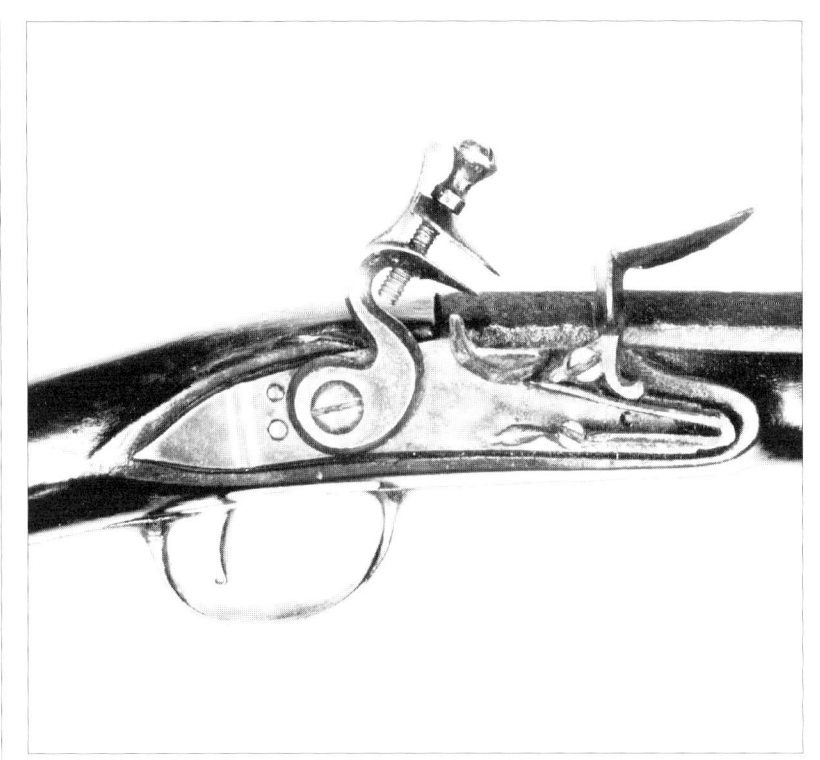

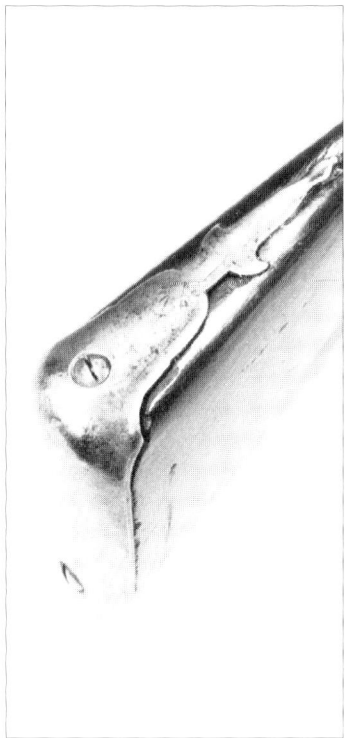

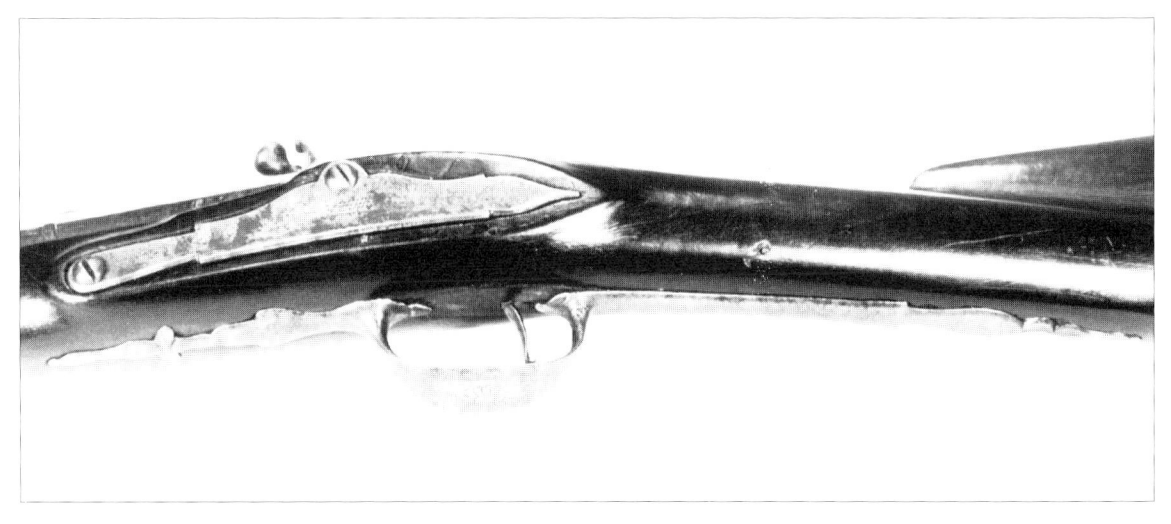

**159.MM FRENCH COMMERCIAL HUNTING GUN *(FUSIL DE CHASSE)***                    Circa 1740–1760

By the mid-1700s, French commercial arms were evolving. This longer length hunting gun, for example (50-7/8", .62 caliber barrel) retains: the established flat/beveled lock (with a military-type grooved tail and omitted outer bridle); the thin segmented trigger guard; triangular side plate; three-pointed butt tang; wooden ramrod (four pipes); and a forend reaching to the muzzle. However all decorative raised carving and borders are eliminated. The stock's previous Roman nose butt profile has also been modified (compare with 158.MM). A "crown / NC" (Nicholas Carteron, St. Etienne) is stamped on the breech, which is octagonal for 10-1/2 inches and continues a flat top panel to the muzzle. Many of these long barrels were cut down individually for easier use in rough country. By 1763 the French and Indian War ended and England assumed control of the vast fur trade of New France, leading to a transition from these graceful French patterns to the shorter and more practical Northwest gun (see 155.MM).

| | | | |
|---|---|---|---|
| Length: 66-7/8" | Lock: 5-1/2" X 1" | Butt Tang: 4-1/2" | Furniture: Iron |
| Barrel: 50-7/8", .62 cal. | Trigger Guard: 12-1/2" | Side Plate: 5-5/8" | Weight: 7.2 lbs. |

**Author's Collection**

*Chapter 3: Smoothbore Shoulder Arms*

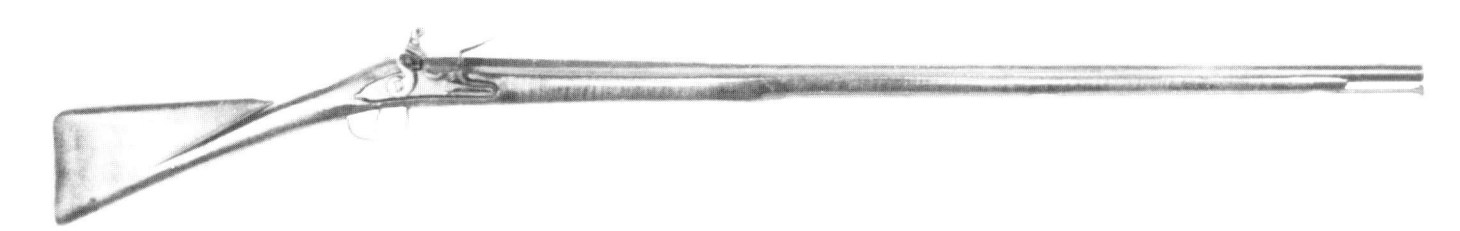

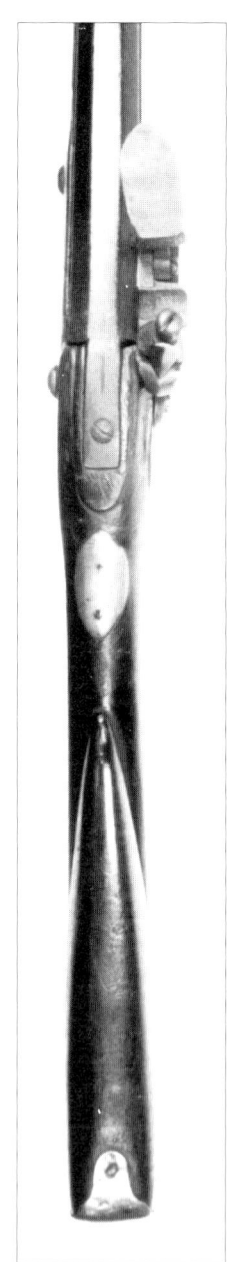

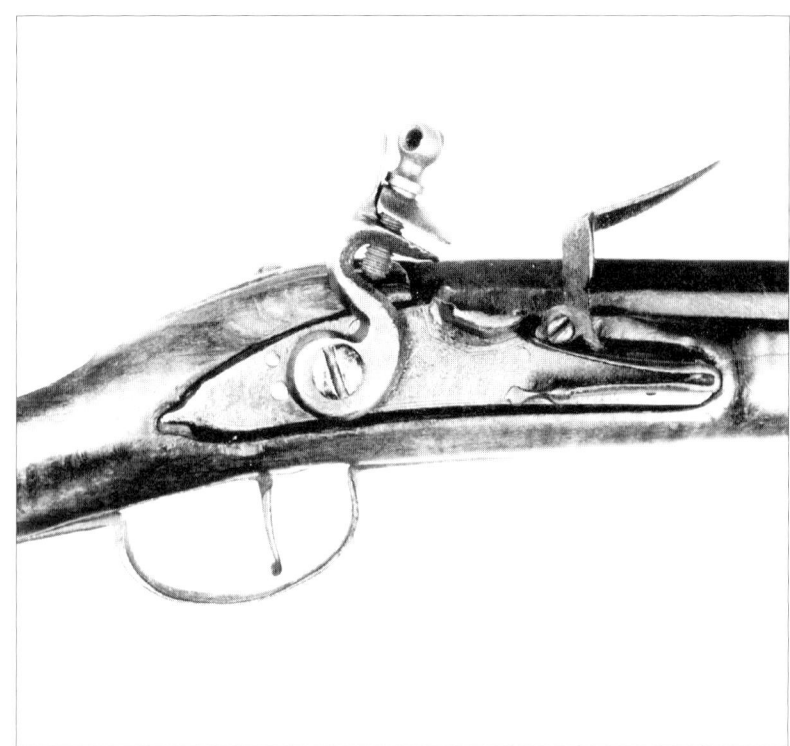

**160.MM  RESTOCKED FRENCH TRADE GUN**　　　　　　　　　　　　　　　　　　　　　　　　　　　　　　　　　　　　　　　　　　　　　　　　　　　　　　　　**Circa 1760–1780**

In addition to their durable hunting guns (156.MM, 157.MM), close to 200,000 lesser quality arms *(fusils de traite)* were developed specifically for the fur trade and distributed by the French to their Indian allies from circa 1650 to 1760. Yet little more than fragments and artifacts have survived—a testimony to those light well-balanced arms that were so well-adapted to the forests that they continued until worn out. This American light fowler, found in southern Connecticut, is believed to include an early (circa 1720–1740) French trade lock and barrel. The lock (squeezed tail, no bridles, floral engraving) is cheap but functional; the small pinned barrel (40-1/8", .63 caliber) follows the Tulle form with an octagonal breech for nine inches plus a 2-1/2" section of 16 flats and a raised ring. There is a forward blade sight, yet typically none at the rear. An economical American restocked these components with a thin brass butt plate (five nails), escutcheon (two pins), a reproduced French side plate, a crude home-forged iron trigger guard, plus three odd rammer pipes (iron rod). The evenly spaced "maple stripes" suggest the provincial practice of wrapping nitrate-treated cord around the stock and burning it to achieve that appearance.

| | | | |
|---|---|---|---|
| Length: 55-1/8" | Lock: 5-5/8" X 1" | Butt Tang: 1-1/2" | Furniture: Brass/Iron |
| Barrel: 40-1/8", .63 cal. | Trigger Guard: 10-3/4" | Side Plate 4" | Weight: 6.3 lbs. |

**Author's Collection**

*210*　　*Chapter 3: Smoothbore Shoulder Arms*

# Chapter 4

# *Rifles... The Precision Weapon*

The advantage of cutting spiraled grooves inside a barrel to spin the ball for greater distance and accuracy was known in Europe a century before Jamestown and Plymouth were settled in the New World. Those early gunsmiths also found that wrapping the round ball in a greased patch of cloth or thin leather helped it to better grip the rifling, as well as to loosen powder fouling from previous rounds.

## THE JAEGER HUNTING RIFLE

The rifle that developed in central Europe was a big game weapon designed to hunt the large horned animals, wild boar and bear in their thick forests. It is called the "jaeger" today (the word for "hunter" in German) and achieved a fully developed form shortly before 1700 as a short, large-bore, heavily stocked shoulder arm. The octagonal barrel most often measured 28 to 30 inches in length (.60 to .70 caliber). A typical buttstock, in turn, displayed a raised inboard cheekpiece, an outboard patchbox with a sliding wooden cover and decorative relief carving. For aiming, it mounted a front blade plus a rear open or folding leaf sight. Most furniture was brass, including a raised trigger guard extension. Total weight averaged seven to eight pounds. This was the pattern that accompanied the German, Swiss and French Huguenot gunmakers arriving in Pennsylvania beginning about 1710 and became the basis for the new American rifle.

## THE AMERICAN LONGRIFLE

The need for greater accuracy over longer distances in the New World beyond the range of a smoothbore or jaeger led to development of a new American rifle by 1760. Its evolution began about 1720 in Pennsylvania and expanded initially along the frontiers of Maryland, Virginia and the

**MORGAN'S RIFLE CORPS AT SARATOGA, October 1777**
The American longrifle with its impressive accuracy was not effective against bayonets in the open. But in wooded or irregular terrain its fire was deadly at unheard-of distances—as these men proved against Fraser's advancing troops near Bemis Heights.

*Chapter 4: Rifles*

**HUNTING BAGS**
Such typical leather pouches were favored by American riflemen and woodsmen to carry firearm accessories and personal items. These early forms were usually unpretentious and functional—often with a powder horn, patch-cutting knife or pick and brush attached to the shoulder strap.

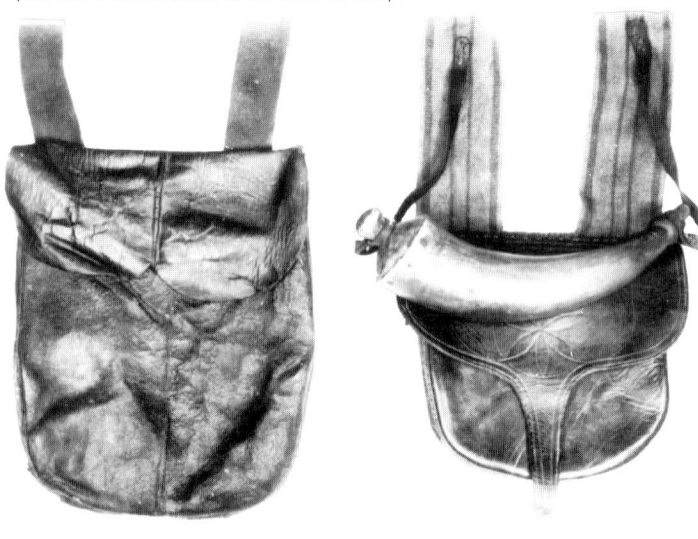

Carolinas. (The Northeast adopted the rifle after the Revolution.) This longer weapon introduced a smaller caliber, slower rifling twist and higher ratio of powder charge versus bullet size to attain the flatter trajectory needed for hunting in North American terrain. Most had octagonal barrels measuring 40 inches or more with bore diameters of .40 to .65 caliber, seven to eight grooves and mounted fixed open sights with an average weight of eight pounds.

The rifling approached one turn in 60 inches compared to a jaeger's normal one in 48 inches. This slower twist permitted a higher ratio of powder to ball size, such as three- or four-to-one (i.e. 100 grains of powder for a 300-grain bullet) versus a five- or six-to-one relationship for a jaeger.

Thus a new rifle pattern emerged in young America with a longer barrel (to consume more of the powder charge and create an increased aiming span), a smaller bore to reduce weight and the lead required, a slimmer stock for better balance in the hand and the higher ratio of powder to ball for greater distance. The earlier jaeger heritage continued in the patchbox, cheekpiece, raised trigger guard extension, relief carving and the use of a patched ball. Such popular terms as the "Kentucky" or "Pennsylvania" rifle were not acquired until the early 1800s.

These arms record amazing accuracy at distances of 200 to 300 yards (versus the smoothbore's limitations beyond 60 yards). Yet it should be remembered that the critical ingredient for such performance was the marksman. Using fixed open sights, he had to know the intricacies of his weapon to hold his sighting point off-target to allow for the black powder, which varied in quality, changed its pattern depending on the air's humidity, and, being a very hot powder, quickly heated the barrel causing heat waves to obscure sighting. Crosswinds were also a major factor at long distances.

The American longrifle gave an impressive performance during the Revolutionary War. On the open battlefield, however, it was soon replaced among the Continental regiments. Being a civilian arm, it was slower to load, fired a smaller bullet with less stopping power, did not mount a bayonet, used a smaller lock (less durable), was expensive to produce and had a thin stock that broke easily when used as a club in hand-to-hand fighting. The rifle, however, did perform extremely well in wooded conditions and in the hands of light troops or frontiersmen, as well as the militia (especially in the South; 3.RR–13.RR).

## THE ENGLISH RIFLES

A few hundred rifled carbines were placed in the hands of select British light companies in America during the French and Indian War. They were probably made in Germany. The provincials, in turn, provided their own locally made rifles.

In response to the American riflemen during the Revolution, England ordered 1000 of a new Pattern 1776 (800 in Birmingham; 200 from Hanover), all of which saw action with various regular companies of light infantry, light dragoons and even select Loyalist units in the northern and southern campaigns. This British arm had a 28-1/2 inch octagonal barrel (.65 caliber) stocked to the muzzle, with a fixed pivoting front swivel for the steel rammer (15.RR).

The 100 famed Ferguson Rifles, with their vertical breech loading action, were used by Ferguson's special force during the Brandywine Campaign. This unit was apparently disbanded to allow his men to return to their original light infantry companies after Ferguson's wounding (16.RR–17.RR).

The above rifles issued to British troops were supplemented by the short Germanic rifles in the hands of more than 4000 jaegers in America during the War for Independence (14.RR).

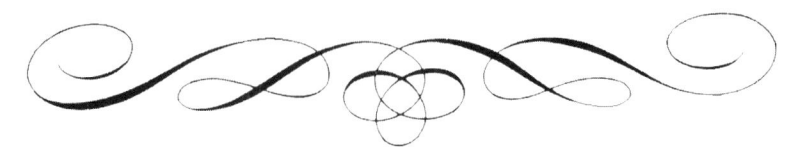

212   Chapter 4: Rifles

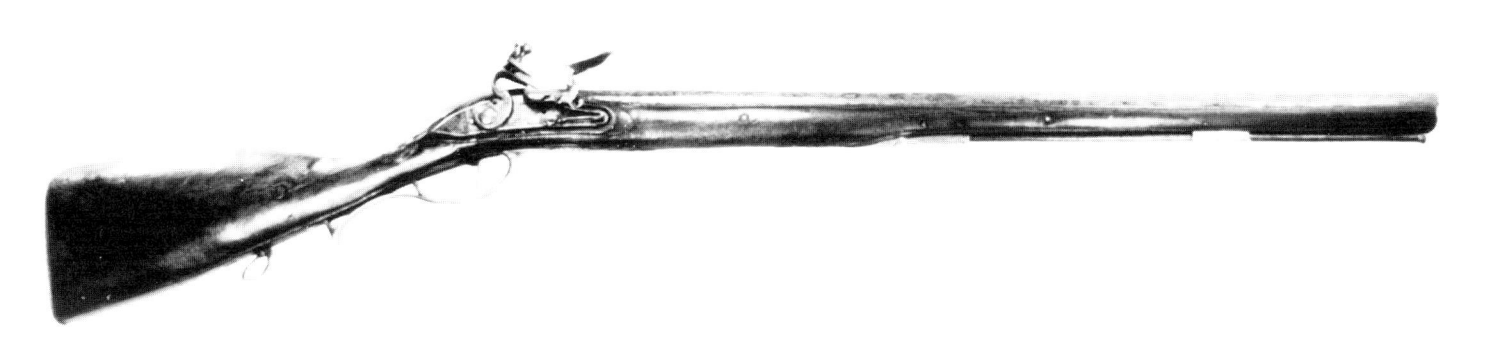

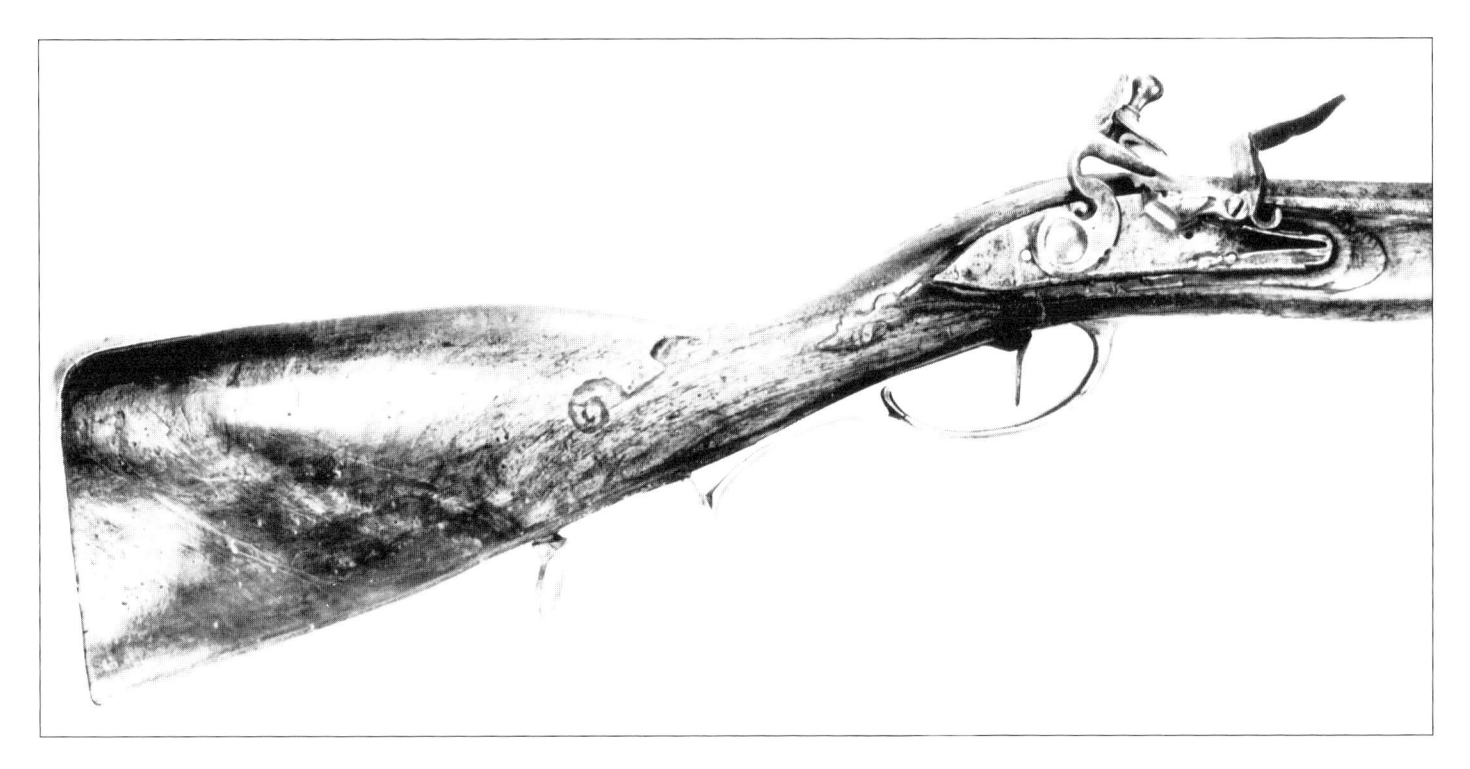

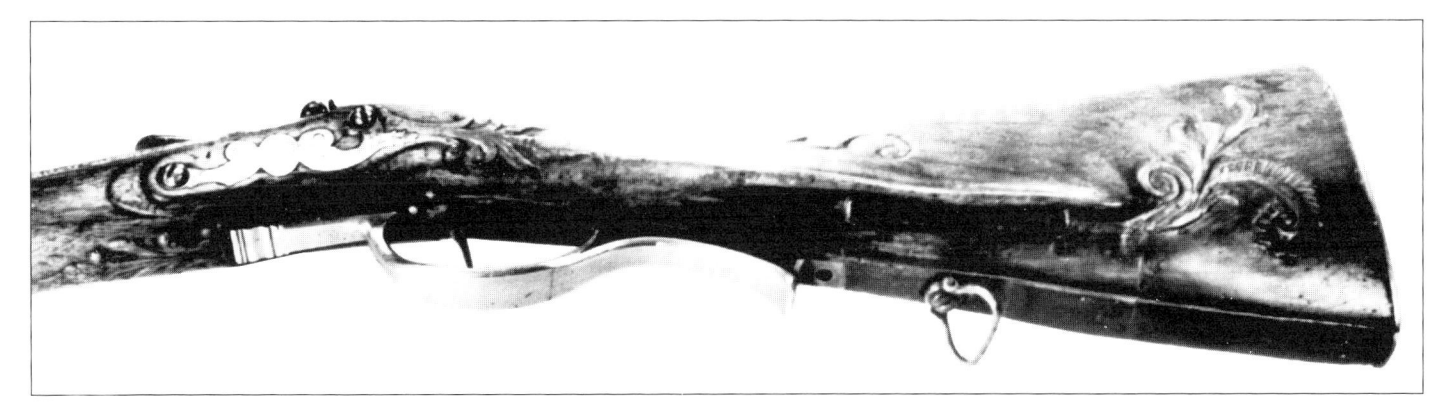

**1.RR GERMAN JAEGER HUNTING RIFLE**  Circa 1730–1740

Short-barreled hunting rifles such as this accompanied the German settlers coming into Pennsylvania beginning about 1710 and became the predecessor of America's new longrifle. The example here omits the usual patchbox but retains the thick butt (2-3/8" across) found on early patterns. Decorative raised carving brackets the comb's front end and borders the lock and side plate, as well as the trigger guard's squared tip and inboard butt face. Its typical flat/beveled Germanic lock includes a tail groove, two bridles, the usual faceted flash pan and an internal screw for the frizzen spring. A rear sling swivel remains in the buttstock's flat underside behind the raised trigger guard extension. A decorative 3-1/2" butt tang and side plate (with a centre oval), in turn, are contemporary European patterns. Notice also the two wire loops under the cheekpiece—often installed to hold a quill or pick to clean powder fouling from the flash pan and touch-hole. This short octagonal barrel (29", eight grooves) mounts a front blade, as well as a rear sight with a folding leaf 5-3/4 inches from the breech.

| | | | |
|---|---|---|---|
| Length: 44" | Lock: 5-1/2" X 1-1/8" | Butt Tang: 3-1/4" | Furniture: Brass |
| Barrel: 29", .51 cal. | Trigger Guard: 9" | Weight: 7.8 lbs. | |

**George C. Neumann Collection, Valley Forge National Historical Park**

*Chapter 4: Rifles* 213

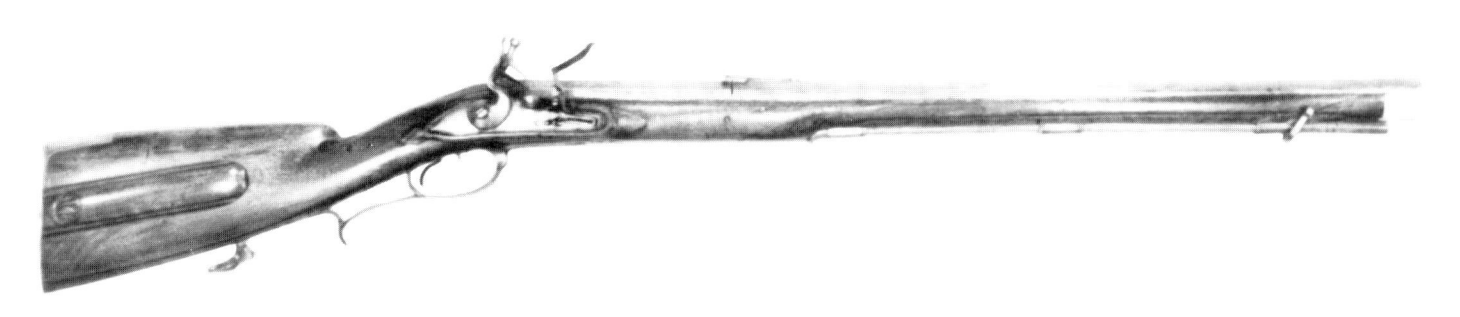

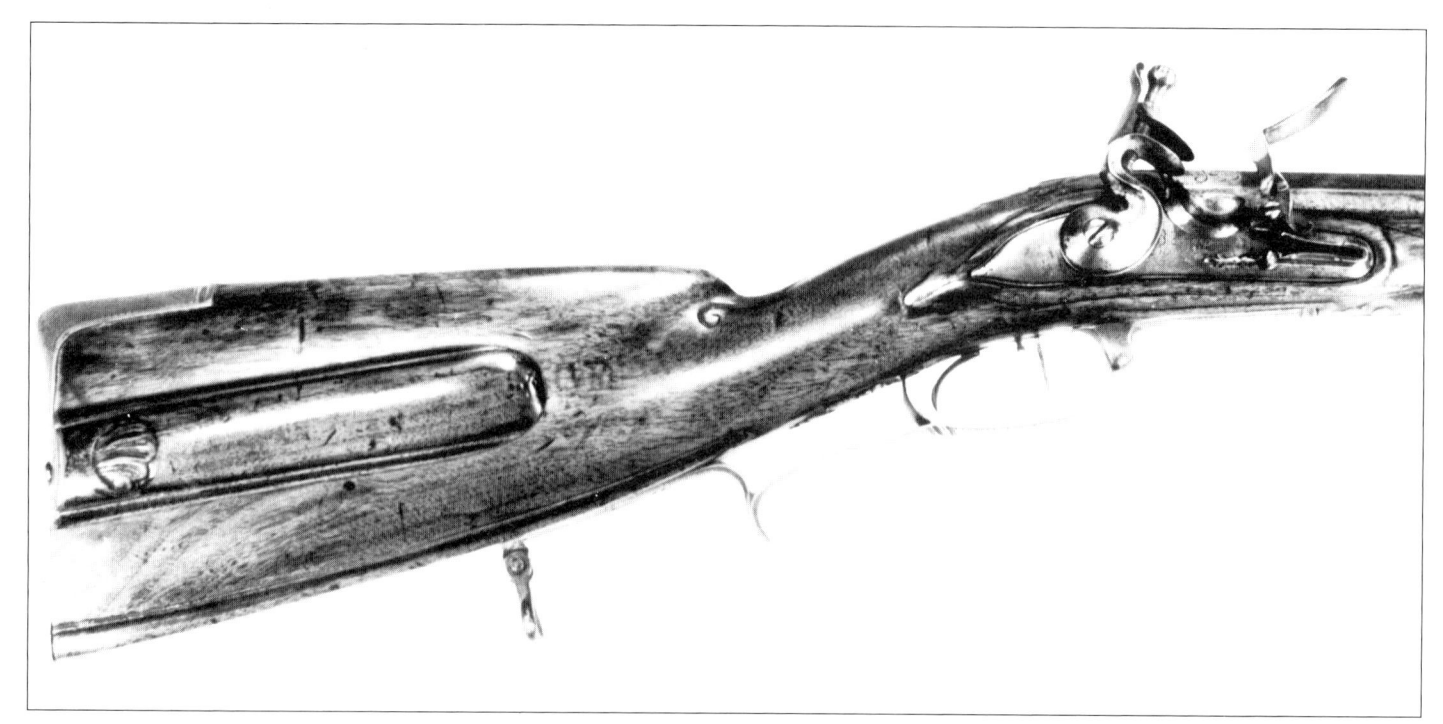

## 2.RR JAEGER HUNTING RIFLE
Circa 1760

The basic jaeger pattern continued with little change in Europe until the 1820s. However, being a civilian arm, it acquired small personal embellishments over the years. Here for example can be seen the popular six-pointed star (inlayed bone), as well as channeled border carving along the traditional sliding patchbox cover, cheekpiece and buttstock's flattened bottom edge. Relief borders also outline its triangular side plate, rounded lock and barrel tang. The thick walnut stock extends to a swamped muzzle (bone nose cap) with an incised line tracing the rammer channel (three faceted thimbles plus a wooden rod having a bone tip). The 28" octagonal barrel holds a fixed front blade, joined by a spring-adjusted, open rear sight. Note also the additional set ("hair") trigger, adjusted by a small adjacent screw. A Germanic inside frizzen spring screw and rounded frizzen (no outside bridle) are part of the convex lock. It is marked by its maker under the flash pan, "B MAY / MANNHEIM." Such short rifles were developed for the thick forests of central Europe, which required close-range accuracy and maximum stopping power.

| | | | |
|---|---|---|---|
| Length: 43" | Lock: 5-1/4" X 1" | Butt Tang: 2-3/8" | Furniture: Brass |
| Barrel: 28", .65 cal. | Trigger Guard: 9-3/4" | Side Plate: 4-3/4" | Weight: 7.6 lbs. |

**Robert Nittolo Collection**

214  *Chapter 4: Rifles*

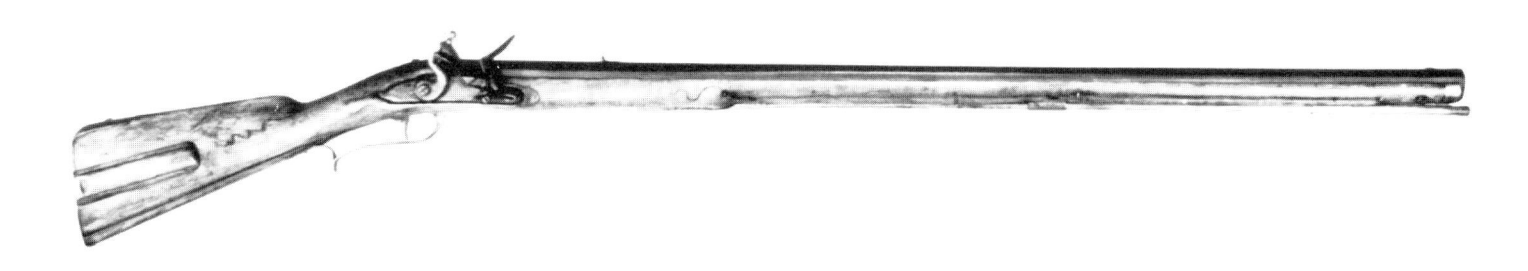

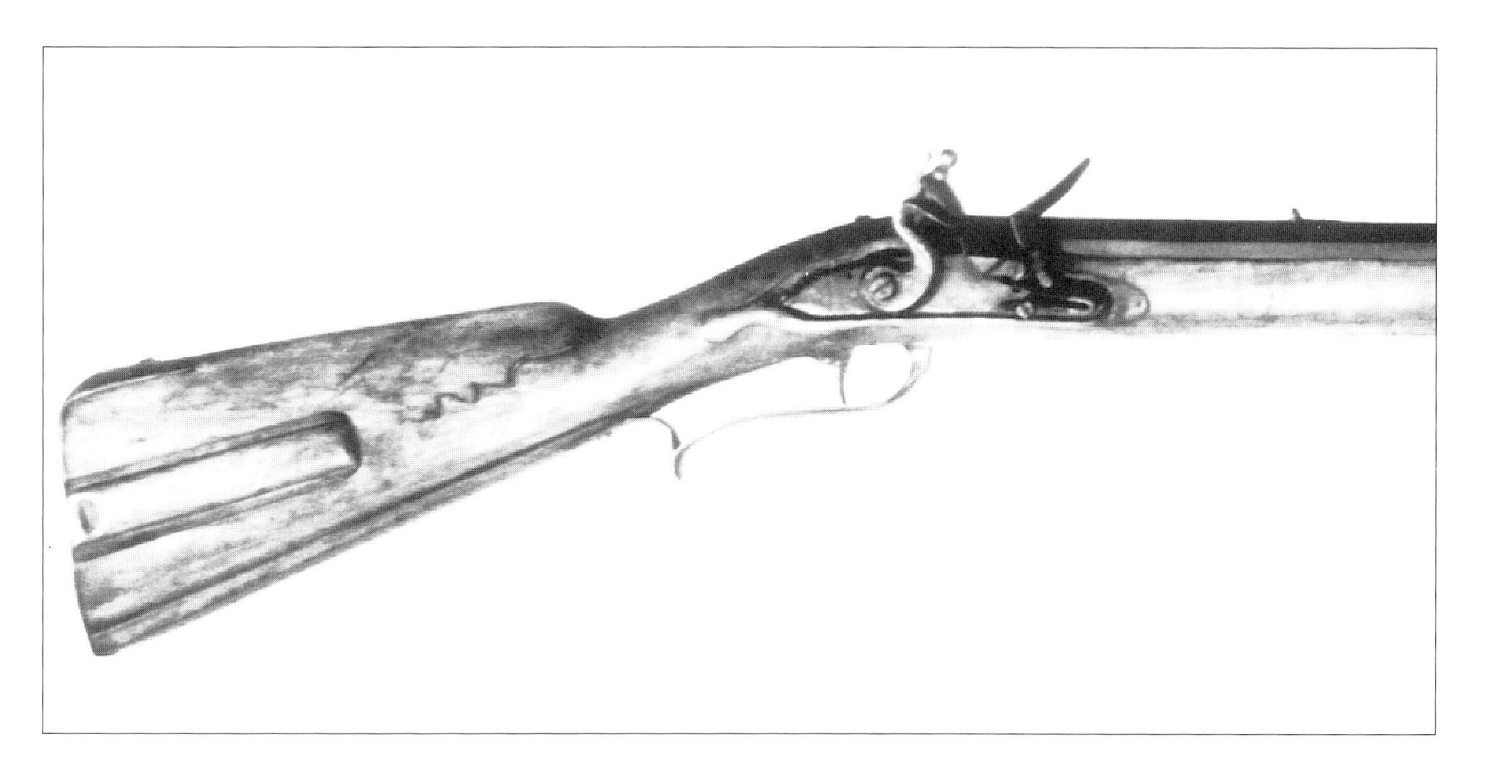

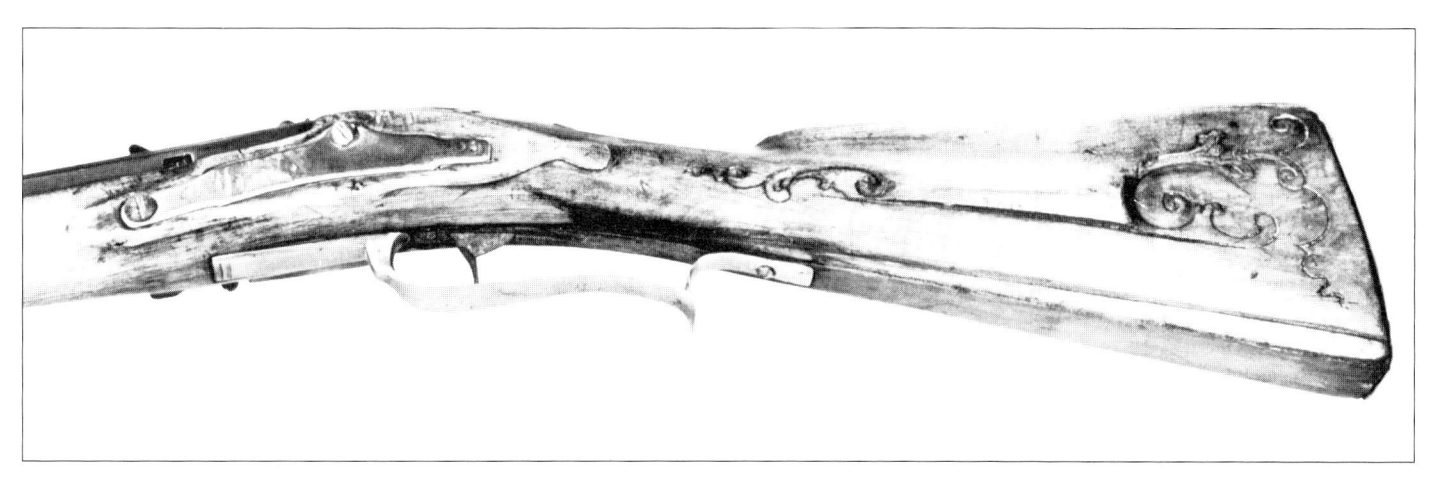

**3. RR AMERICAN RIFLE**                                                                                                                 **Circa 1730–1750**

About 1720, evolution began from the short jaeger rifle to a longer and more slender American form better suited to the local terrain. This rare transitional example retains many of the earlier Germanic characteristics, including the thick squared butt profile, sliding wooden patchbox cover, trigger guard extension, flattened lower edge of the buttstock, octagonal pinned barrel and forend extending to its swamped muzzle. Yet the barrel is now lengthening, the side plate is acquiring a triangular shape, more elementary brass furniture is apparent, and the carving on the maple stock is less ornate. Note the simple incised lines tracing the comb's forward end, behind the tail pipe, both ends of the cheekpiece and the wooden ramrod's channel. Most of these early pattern changes came from eastern Pennsylvania (especially the Reading–Lancaster–York area) before spreading west and south along the frontier to the Carolinas. This barrel is marked with the initials "G.S." and a pair of open shears in an recessed square. It is believed to be the product of George Schroyer when working in Reading, Pennsylvania (re: Kindig, bib. 82). His favored three-petal flower is carved below the barrel tang.

| | | | |
|---|---|---|---|
| Length: 53-3/4" | Lock: 5-1/4" X 1" | Butt Tang: 2-1/2" | Furniture: Brass |
| Barrel: 38-3/4", .59 cal. | Trigger Guard: 8-1/2" | Weight: 9.8 lbs. | |

**The Kindig Collection**

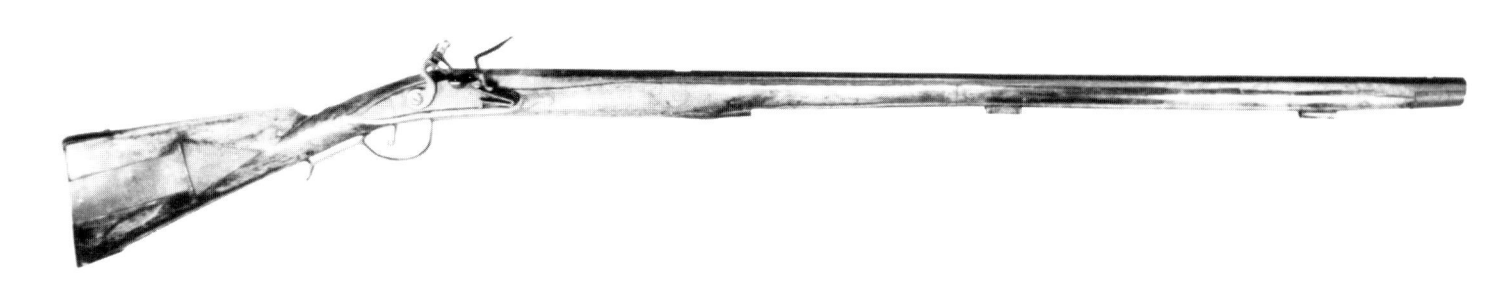

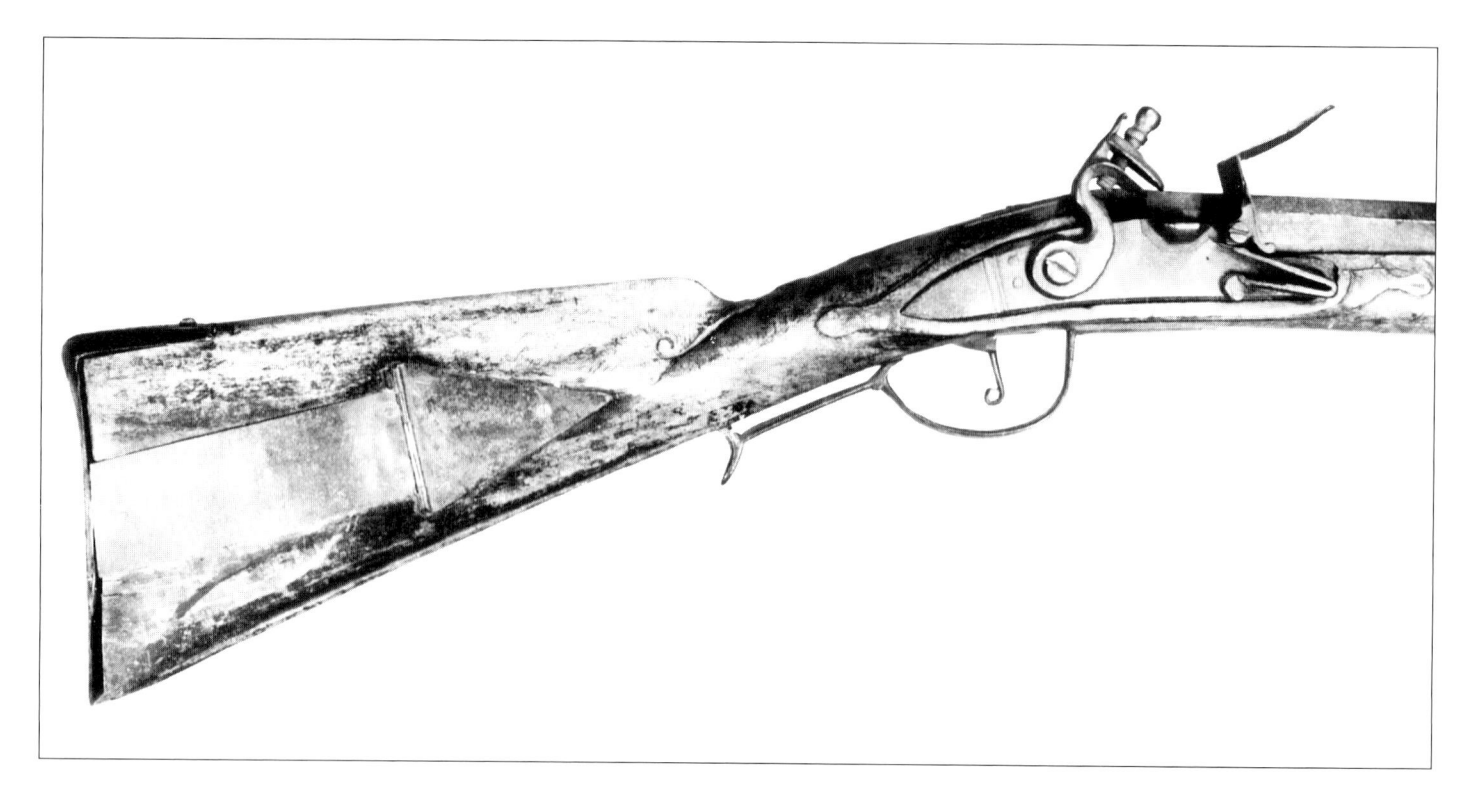

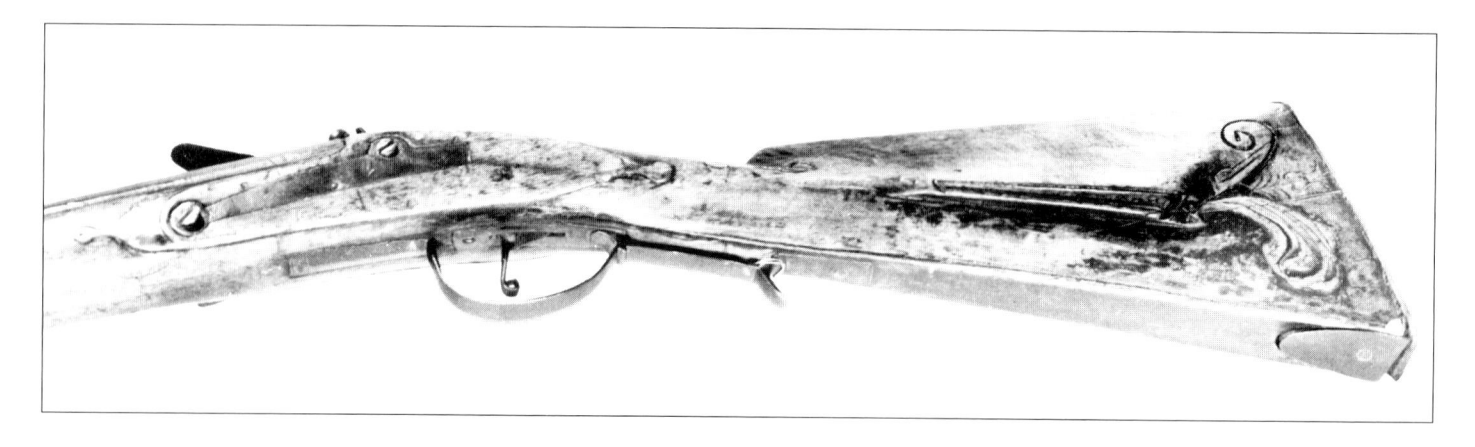

### 4.RR AMERICAN RIFLE

**Circa 1735–1750**

Here is another example of the transition period to the American rifle. It reflects those early years (before the ornate "Golden Age," circa 1783–1820) in which the focus was on little more than the fundamental components needed to accomplish the primary priority of feeding and protecting the owner and his family. This straight maple stock profile, vertical butt, high comb and sparse crude carving all indicate the emerging Pennsylvania form (probably a Lancaster County product). All of the fittings are iron and of American origin. Note, for instance, the elementary pointed patchbox, flat tapered lock, locally forged trigger guard, abbreviated side plate and simple cheekpiece. The 40-1/4" octagonal barrel (.57 caliber) now has a smooth bore, possibly worn from long use or the later practice of reaming the barrel for conversion to the multiple loads needed against fowl and small animals after the larger game had migrated westward. The original ramrod, secured by three plain sheet-iron pipes, is not present.

Length: 55-1/2"  
Barrel: 40-1/4", .57 cal.  
Lock: 6" X 1-1/8"  
Trigger Guard: 8-3/4"  
Butt Tang: 2-1/8"  
Weight: 8.4 lbs.  
Furniture: Iron

**The Kindig Collection**

216   *Chapter 4: Rifles*

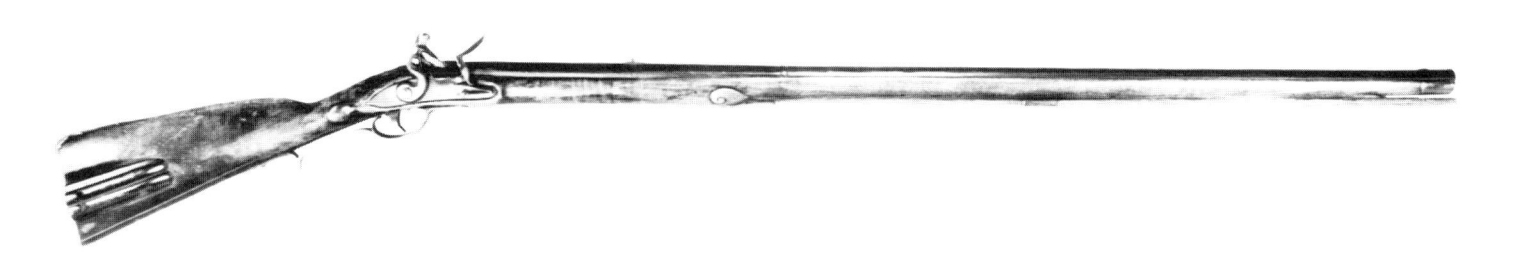

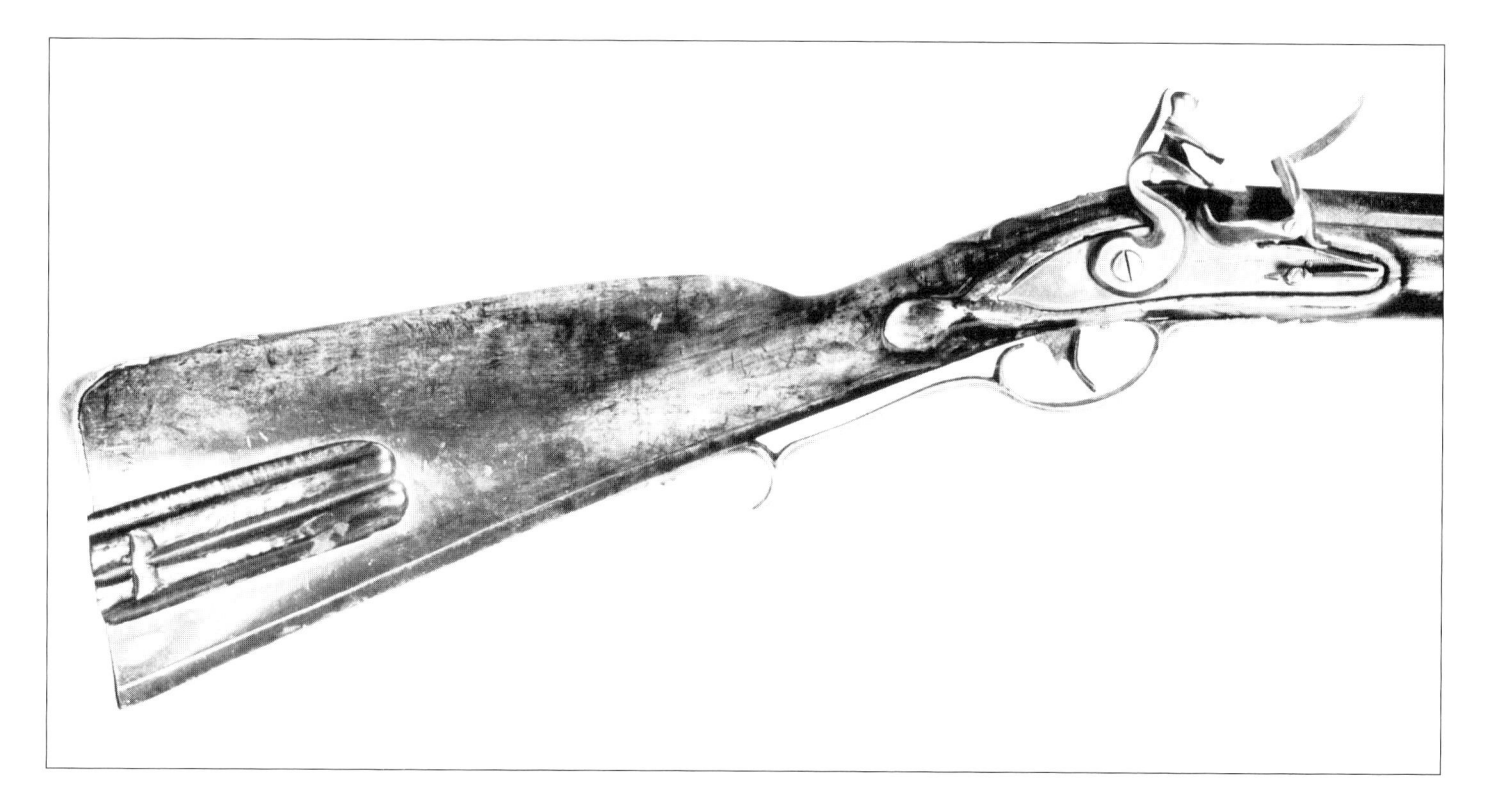

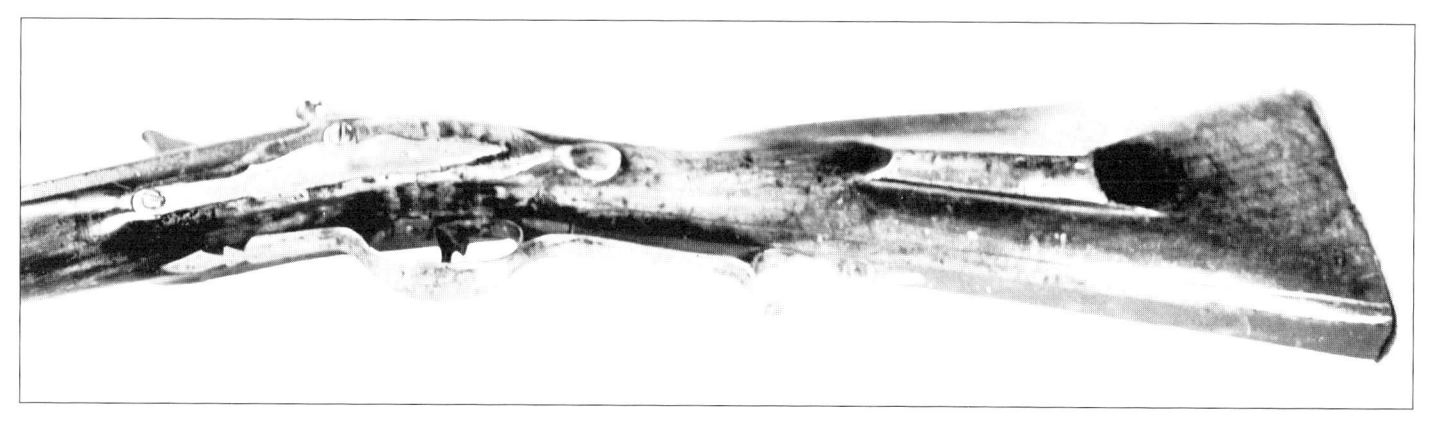

**5.RR AMERICAN RIFLE**                                                                           **Circa 1770–1780**

The lack of elaborate relief carving on this rifle again demonstrates the utilitarian priority of these early patterns. The stocker did however add small touches of primitive elegance with parallel channels in the sliding wooden patchbox cover, raised borders surrounding the lock and triangular side plate, an interesting scroll behind the tail pipe, plus incised lines tracing the rammer channel (three faceted pipes; wooden rod). Its maple stock forend terminates in a typical sheet-brass nose cap. The now fully lengthened octagonal barrel (42-3/8"), in turn, survives without visible rifling and mounts two open fixed sights. The barrel tang is typically anchored by a screw from the top to an iron plate forward of the trigger. Most established riflemakers had their apprentices and hired work force specialize in the manufacture of separate components. Initially this included making their own locks, but inexpensive yet reliable imports from Germany, the Low Countries and England were more economical and are found on most rifles by this period.

| | | | |
|---|---|---|---|
| Length: 58" | Lock: 5-1/4" X 1" | Butt Tang: 3-7/8" | Furniture: Brass |
| Barrel: 42-3/8", .66 cal. | Trigger Guard: 11" | Weight: 7.7 lbs. | |

**The Kindig Collection**

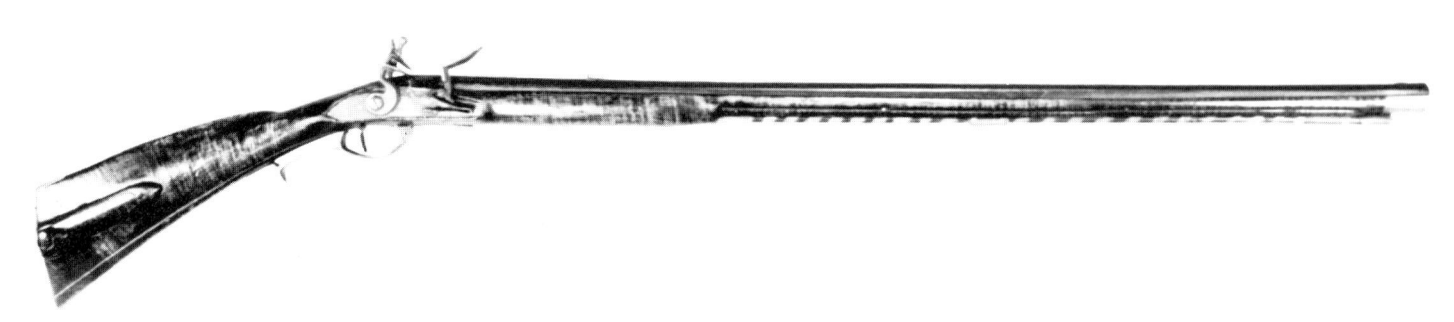

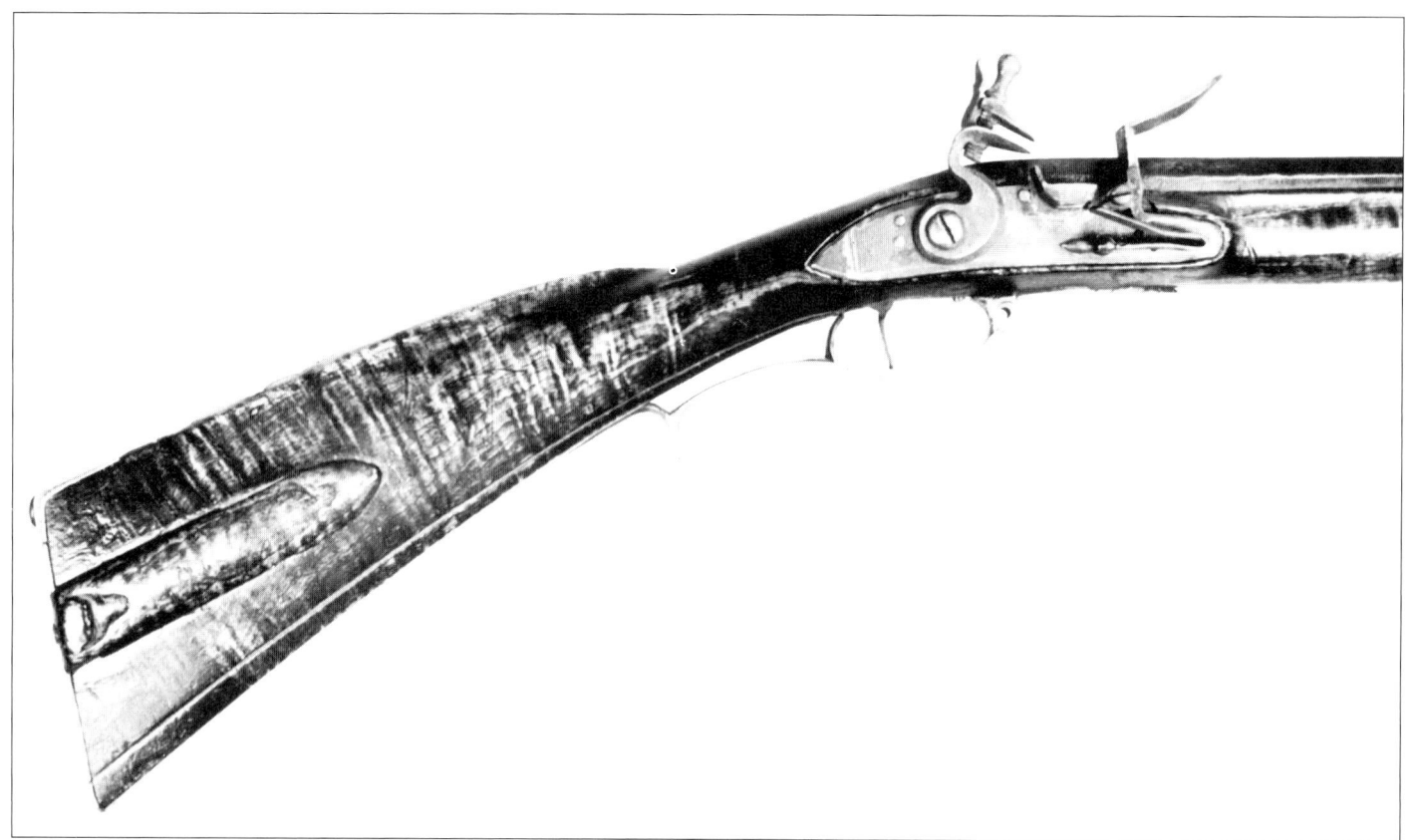

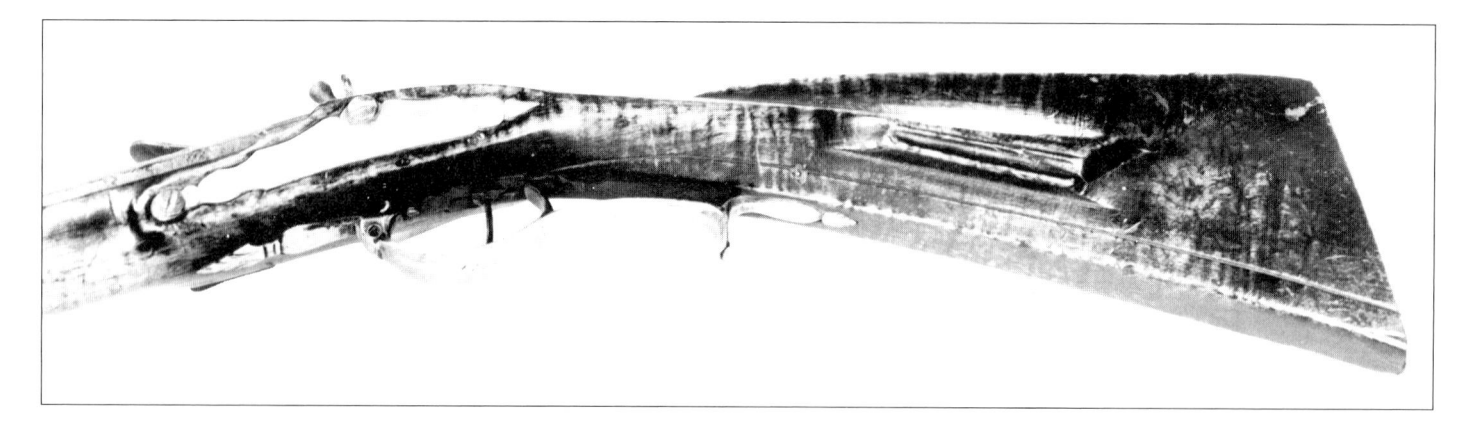

### 6.RR  AMERICAN RIFLE
**Circa 1770–1780**

The squared end and straight bottom edge of this buttstock are consistent with the new American rifle pattern. Yet its sharp drop anticipates the Roman nose—already established on early French arms plus many New England fowlers—destined to gain popularity on rifles following the Revolutionary War. It should be remembered that most of these guns were custom-made and incorporated individual features requested by the buyer. The riflemaker, in turn, also added his own special touches. This sliding wooden lid covers a typical hollowed compartment in the butt, which held greased bullet patches, flints and accessories. The inboard butt however includes the short straight American cheekpiece (many from Europe were curved) but omits the common relief carving. Note also the use of an embellished triangular side plate and decorative trigger guard (with a rare hole for a sling swivel), as well as the established preference for striped maple stocks. Its 38-1/2" octagonal barrel is slightly shorter than normal (original length); the rod is probably a replacement.

| | | | |
|---|---|---|---|
| Length: 53-1/4" | Lock: 5-3/4" X 1-1/8" | Butt Tang: 5-1/4" | Furniture: Brass |
| Barrel: 38-1/2", .65 cal. | Trigger Guard: 9-7/8" | Weight: 8.1 lbs. | |

**The Kindig Collection**

Chapter 4: Rifles

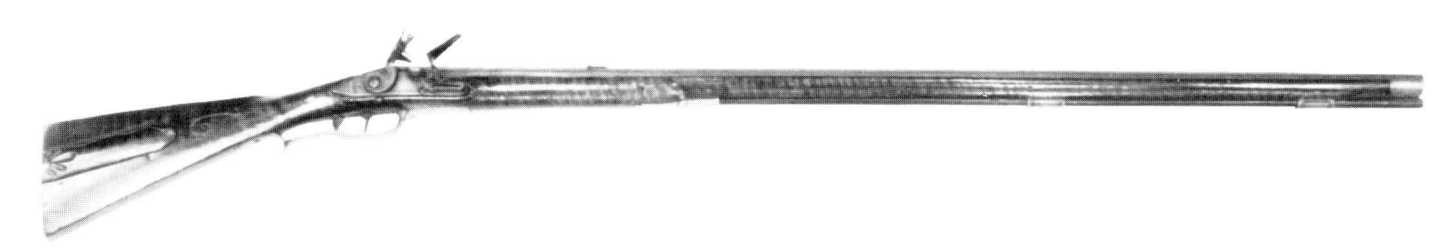

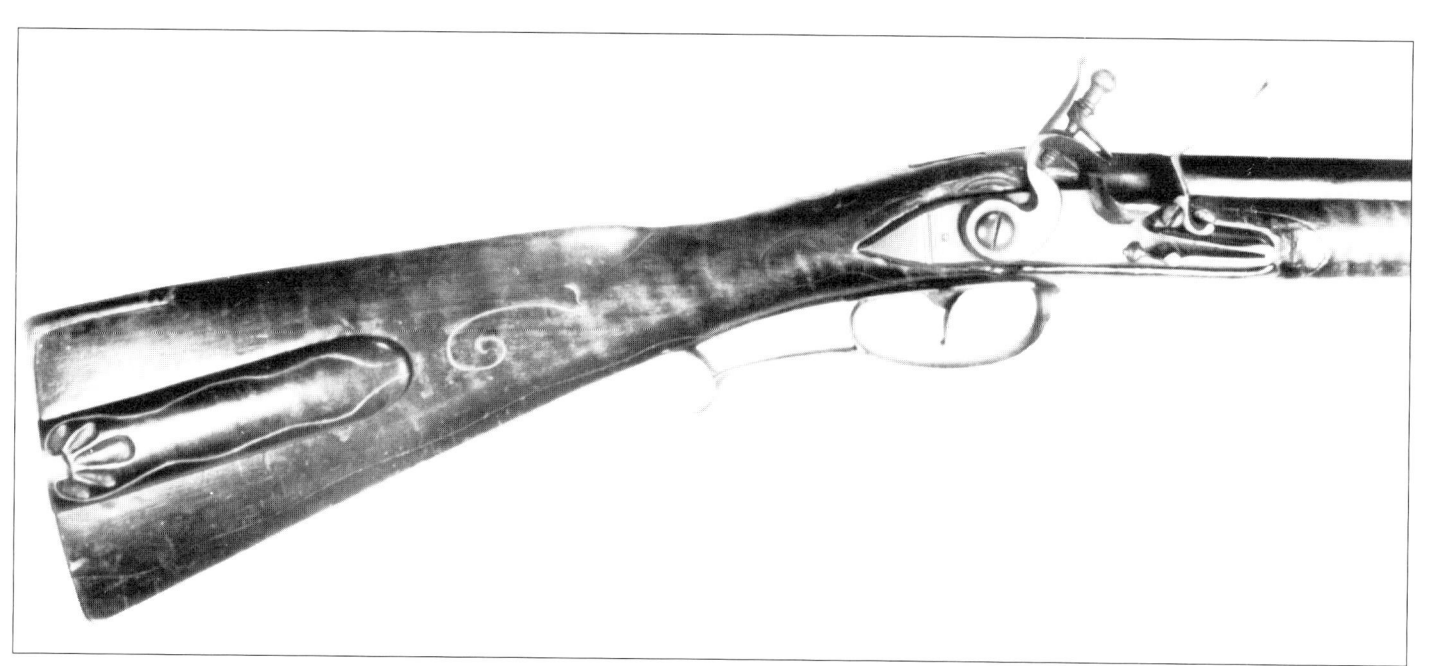

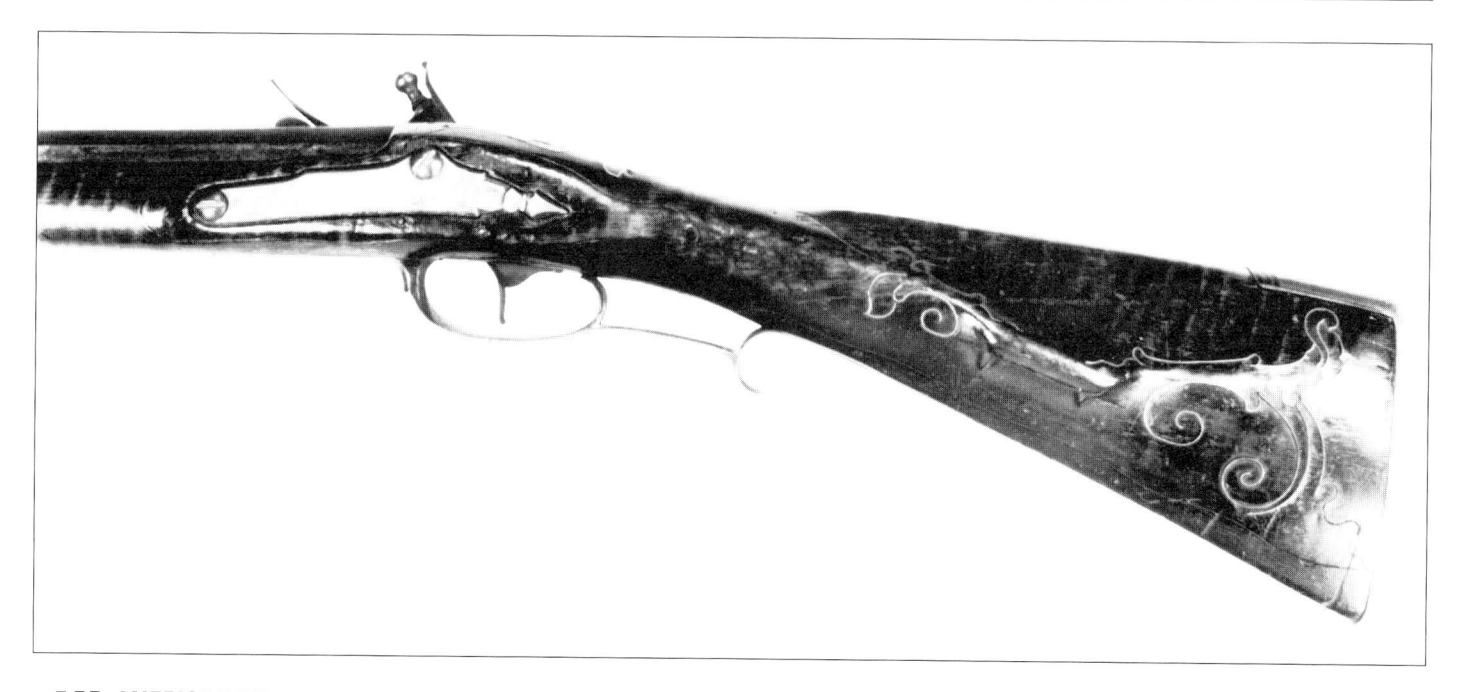

### 7.RR AMERICAN RIFLE
**Dated 1774**

This weapon was signed and dated on the barrel by Christian Oerter, a Moravian gunsmith of Christian Springs, Pennsylvania, in 1774. By this time, on the eve of the Revolutionary War, the American rifle's evolved basic features are apparent: a graceful comb has replaced the earlier squared pattern; a striped maple stock is now preferred; the square-ended trigger guard and butt tang have been established; and the octagonal barrel measures over 40 inches (41" here, .58 caliber, seven grooves). The traditional sliding patchbox cover continues but has an inlaid brass wire decoration that also appears in curved designs on both sides of the butt and below the barrel tang. A narrow incised channel follows the upper edge of its forestock (which ends in the usual long plain brass nosecap). Three faceted thimbles hold the wooden rammer. In the tradition of the earlier jaegers, two loops under the short cheekpiece probably held a quill or pick to clear powder fouling at the touch-hole. The side plate, lock and patchbox cover are accurate restorations.

Length: 56"
Barrel: 41", .58 cal.
**The Benninghoff Collection**

Lock: 5-1/2" X 1"
Trigger Guard: 9-5/8"

Butt Tang: 2-1/2"
Side Plate: 5-1/4"

Furniture: Brass
Weight: 7.6 lbs.

*Chapter 4: Rifles*

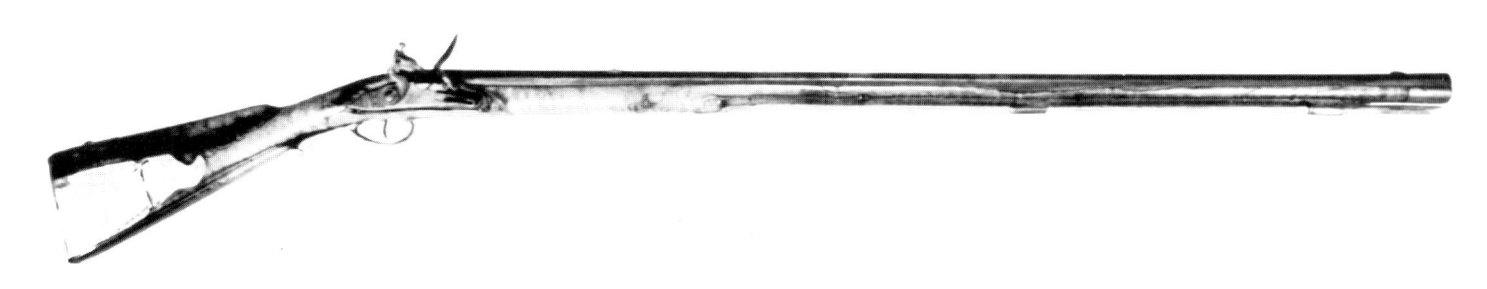

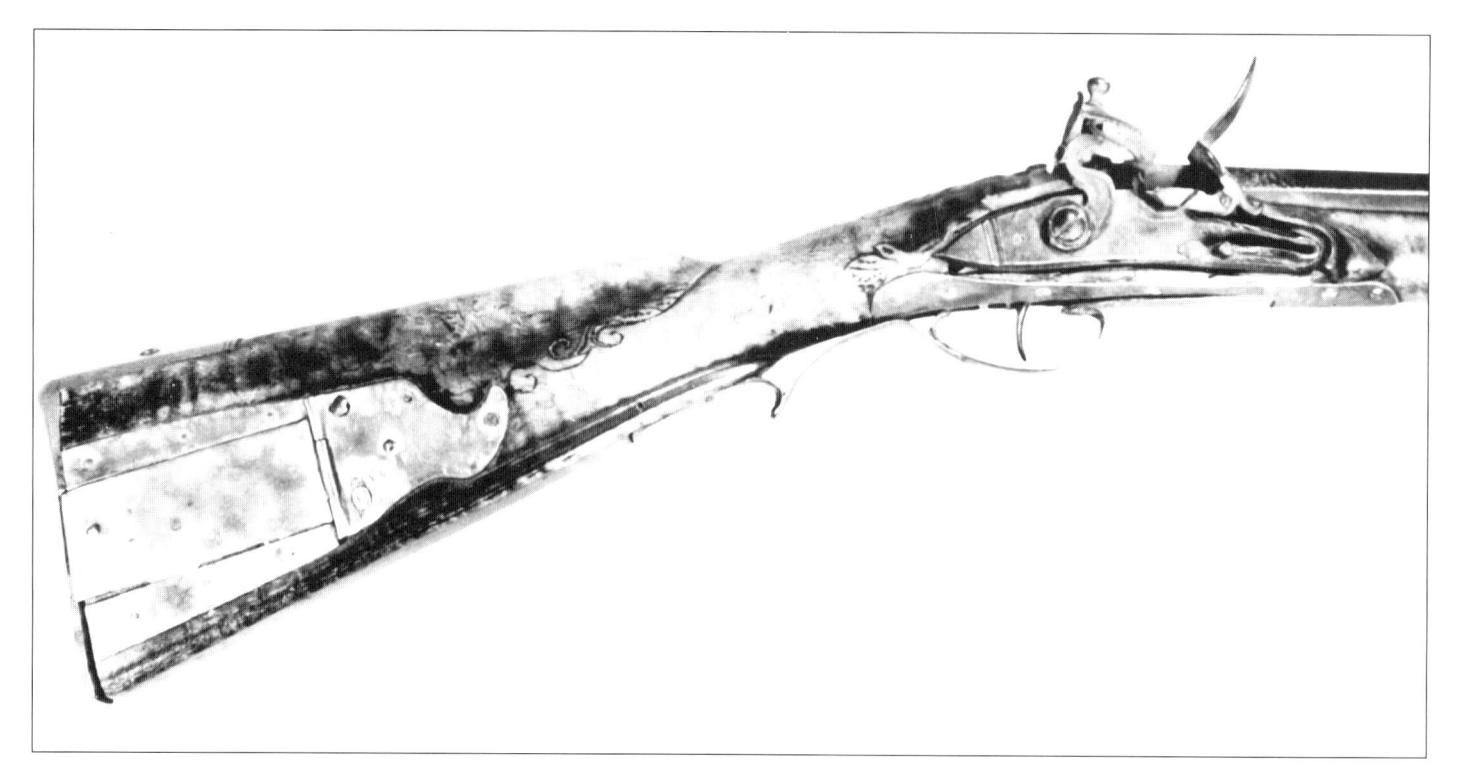

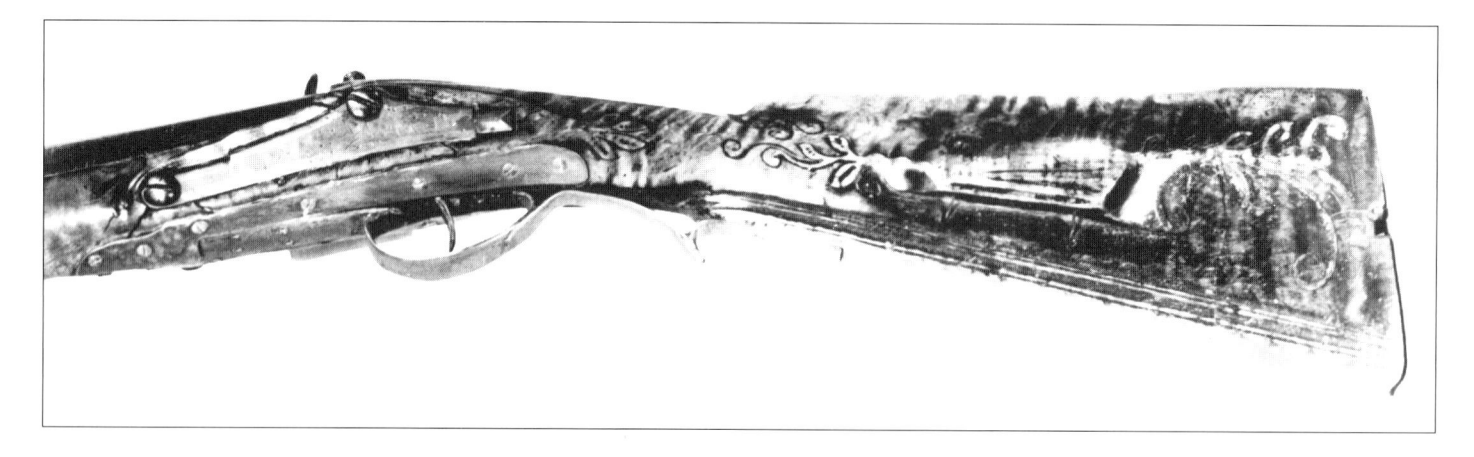

**8.RR  AMERICAN RIFLE**                                                                                                                                           Circa 1765–1780

The most visible feature of America's evolved rifle pattern beyond its greater length was the substitution of a hinged brass patchbox cover to replace the traditional sliding wooden form. This early example lacks the decorative edges and piercings of later periods as it borders the rectangular lid with plain side strips and an innovative simple bird head (all held by hand-wrought nails). The flat/beveled lock plate is typical for these Pennsylvania rifles, yet the cock is a replacement during its working life, as evidenced by its early 19th century characteristics: a rearward curl of the post's upper tip; a near-squared shoulder on the goose-neck; and a round bottom diameter smaller than the lock plate. Notice the floral carving around the lock and side plate, as well as the inboard buttstock. Incised line designs, in turn, mark the comb's forward slope and trace the forend's rammer channel (typical wooden rod; three faceted pipes). This arm was probably made in Lancaster County near Reading, Pennsylvania. Iron strap repairs are visible under the lock and side plate.

| | | | |
|---|---|---|---|
| Length: 54-1/2" | Lock: 5-3/8" X 1" | Butt Tang: 2-3/4" | Furniture: Brass |
| Barrel: 39-3/4", .52 cal. | Trigger Guard: 9" | Weight: 8.8 lbs. | |

**The Kindig Collection**

Chapter 4: Rifles

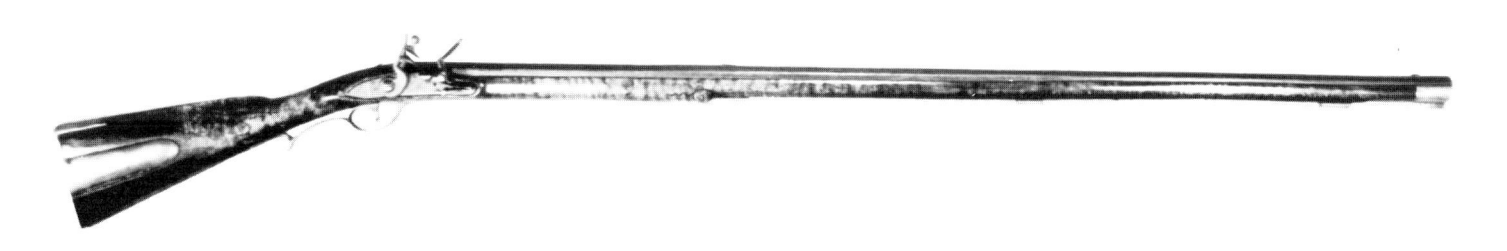

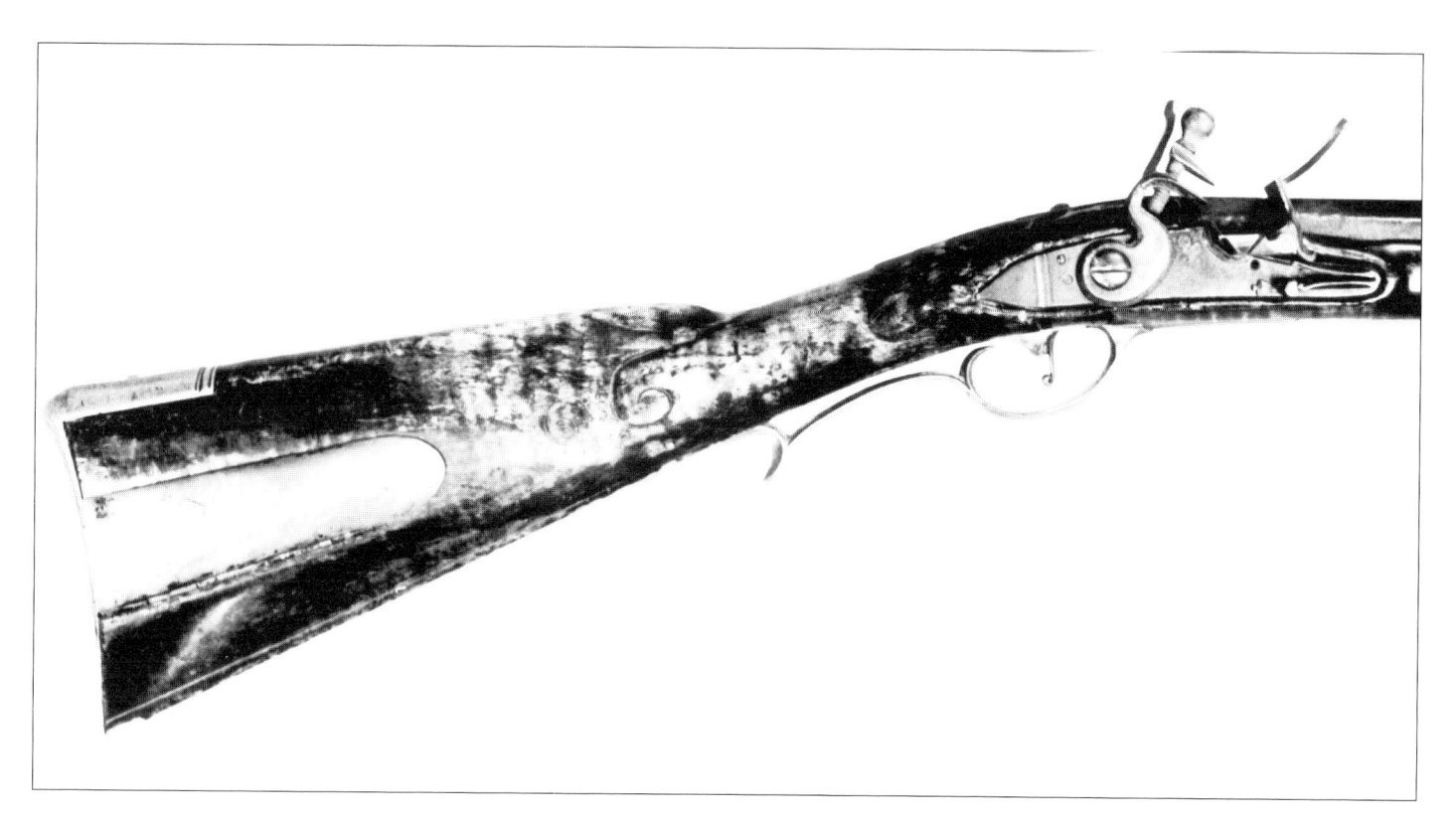

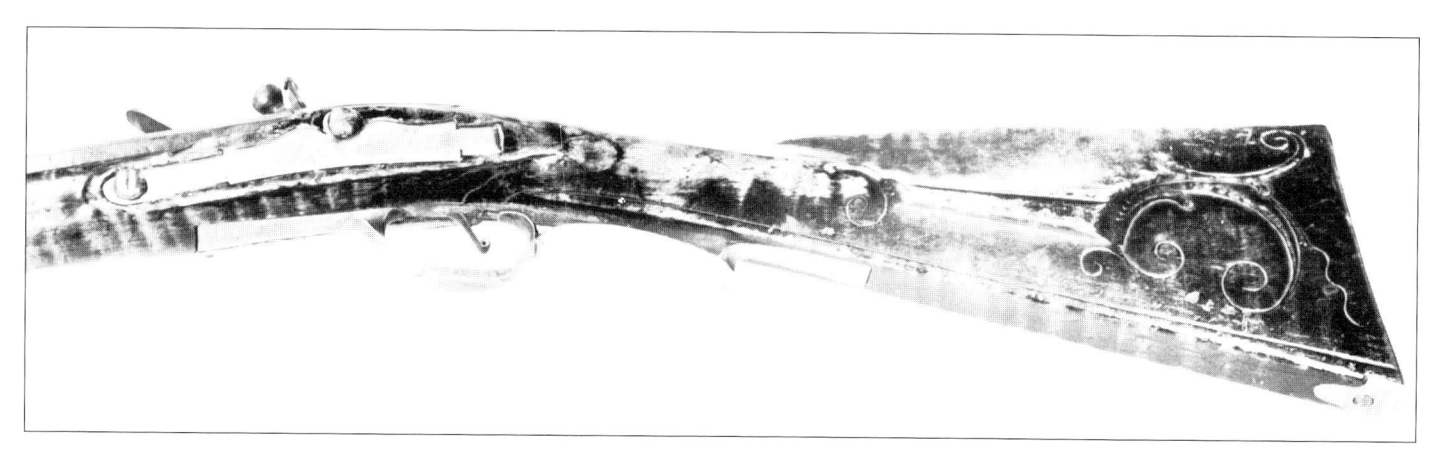

### 9.RR AMERICAN RIFLE
**Circa 1770–1790**

The true grace and flow of the American longrifle form are apparent in the above pattern, which had developed by the beginning of the Revolutionary War. Its brass patchbox cover is still plain and, in this case, hinged at the bottom. Note also the typical furniture that has evolved: the square-ended side plate and trigger guard with an extended rear bar; the right-angled and faceted butt tang; a short, straight inboard cheekpiece; the flat-bottomed buttstock; attractive scrolled carving and raised borders on the curly maple stock; three faceted rammer pipes; and large plain brass nose cap. Incised lines appear behind the tail pipe and parallel to the wooden ramrod. Its long (45-1/2", .59 caliber) octagonal pinned barrel mounts fixed open sights and is marked on the top "J DICKERT" (Jacob Dickert, the famous Lancaster, Pennsylvania, riflemaker). The flat/beveled lock follows the contemporary Germanic pattern, however its gradual tail taper and centered rear tip suggest American manufacture (double bridled).

| | | | |
|---|---|---|---|
| Length: 61-3/8" | Lock: 5-1/2" X 1" | Butt Tang: 2-1/2" | Furniture: Brass |
| Barrel: 45-1/2", .59 cal. | Trigger Guard: 9-1/2" | Weight: 8.8 lbs. | |

**The Kindig Collection**

*Chapter 4: Rifles* **221**

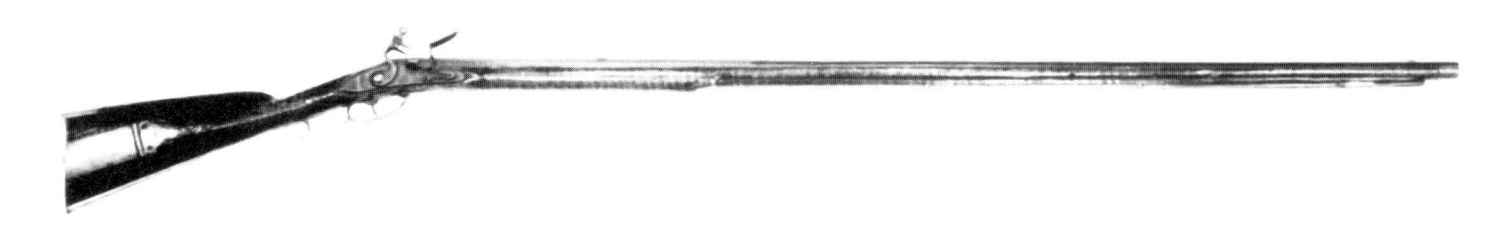

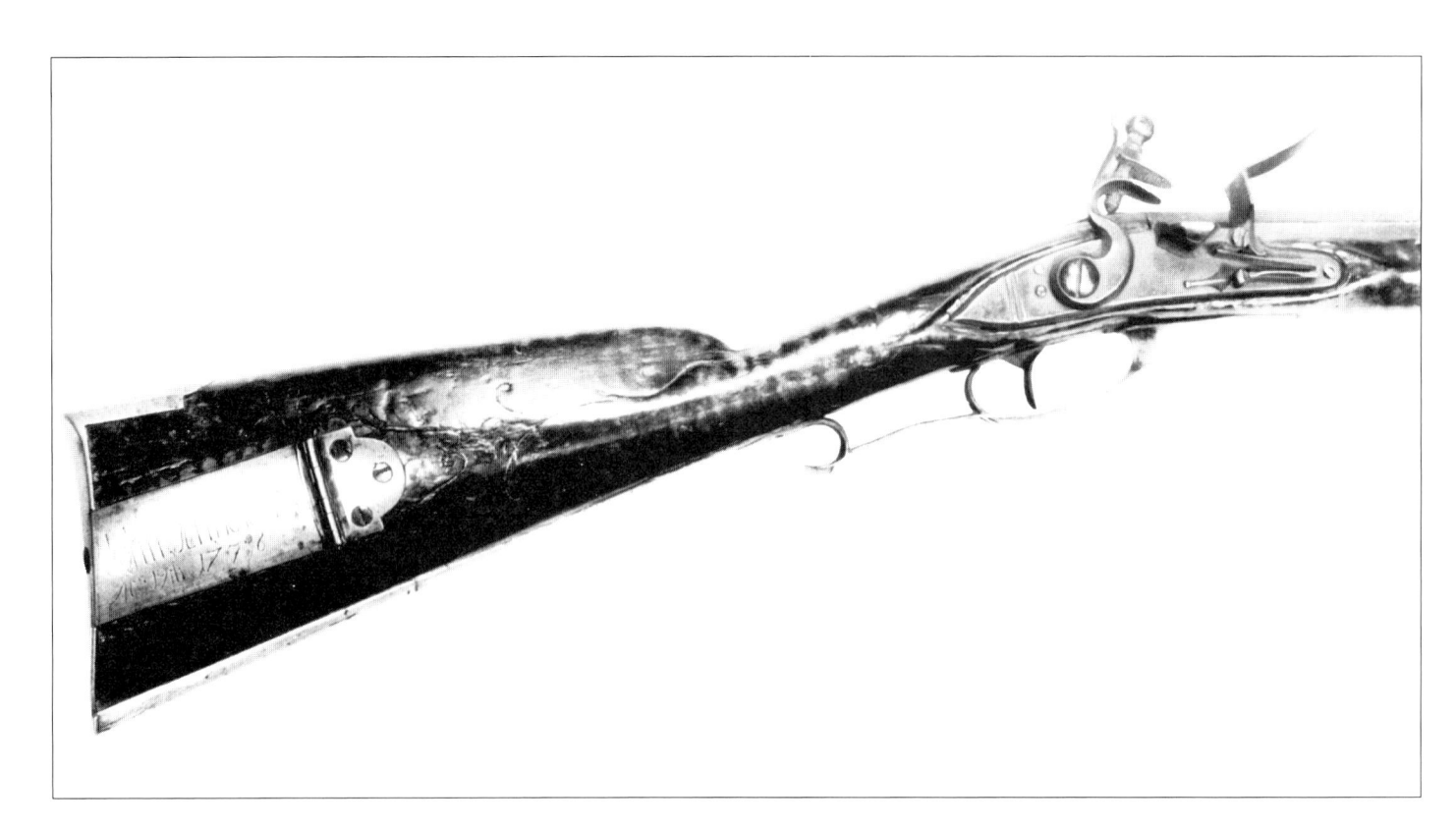

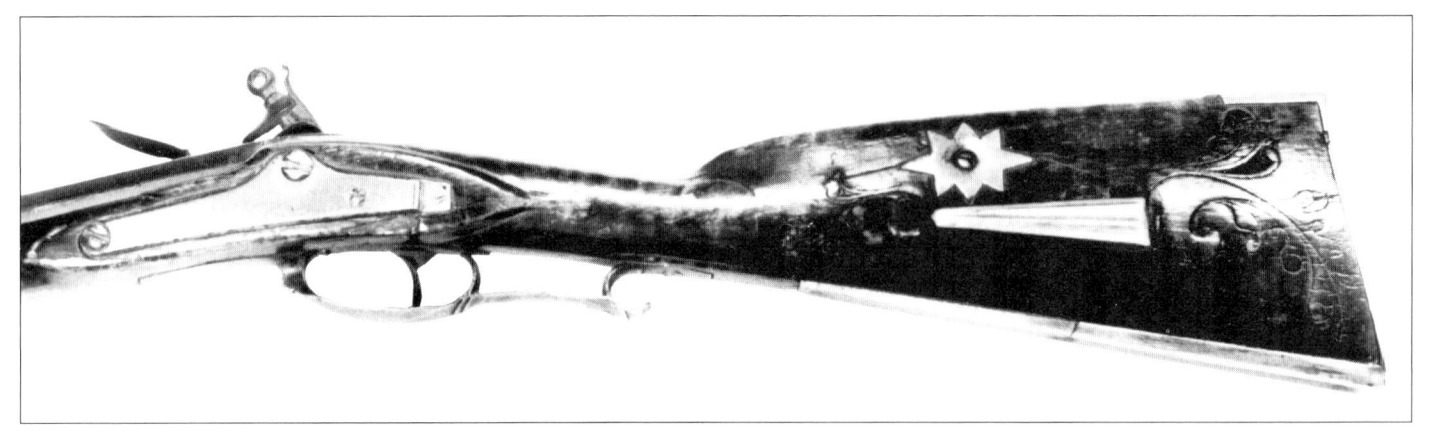

**10.RR  AMERICAN RIFLE**  Circa 1776

The early brass patchbox covers were of simple design, as in this case, which mounts a rounded three-screw head hinged to a rectangular lid (release button at rear). The arm's attractive configurations, however, do not follow many of the traditional features of contemporary Pennsylvania rifles. It has been attributed to Berks or Lebanon Counties in that state, but is probably of Virginia origin. Note, for example, the bowed trigger guard profile, simplified side plate, thumbnail finial on the short butt tang, bone inlays in the cheekpiece and along the toe plate, plus a six-pointed pewter star (center screw). Incised designs bracket the comb's front end and appear on the breech, while relief carvings on the maple stock are seen at the inboard butt, below the barrel tang, and around the lock and side plate. Its long barrel (47-1/2", .58 caliber, stocked to the muzzle) is octagonal (15-1/4 inches) to round. Four round thimbles secure a wooden rammer. A brass patchbox cover inscription reads "John Schneider" (unknown, probably an owner) and "Mr 18th 1776" (engraved by a different hand).

| | | | |
|---|---|---|---|
| Length: 62-7/8" | Lock: 5-1/2" X 1" | Butt Tang: 2-1/4" | Furniture: Brass |
| Barrel: 47-1/2", .58 cal. | Trigger Guard: 8" | Side Plate: 5" | Weight: 6.0 lbs. |

**Richard Ulbrich Collection**

222   *Chapter 4: Rifles*

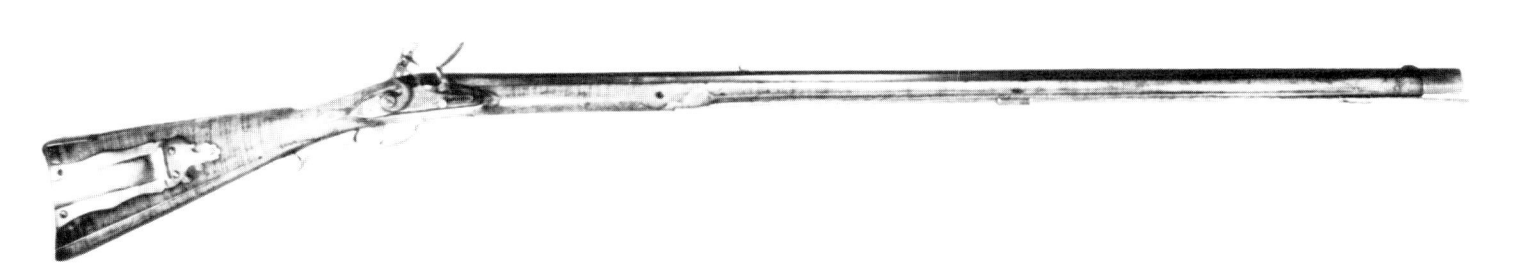

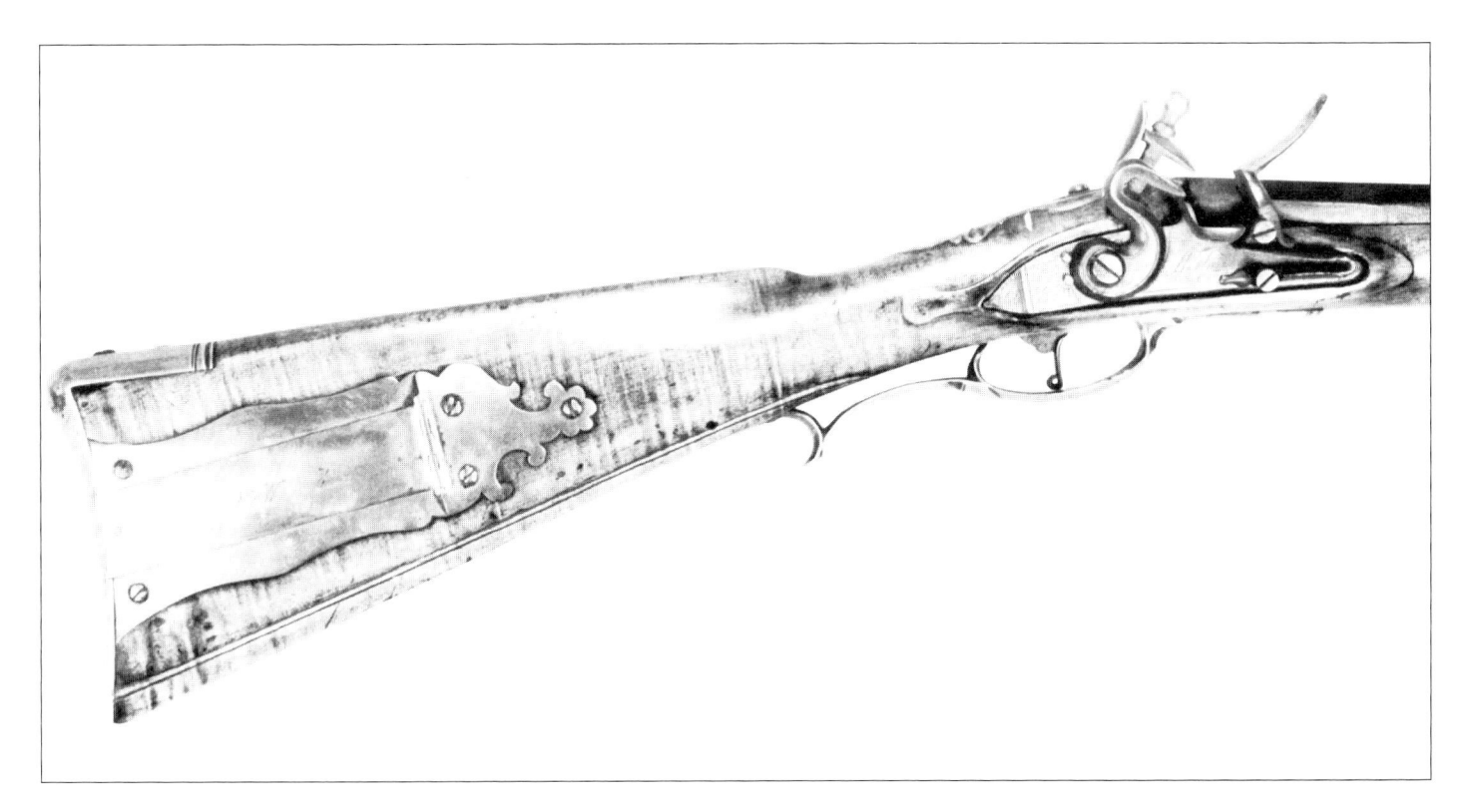

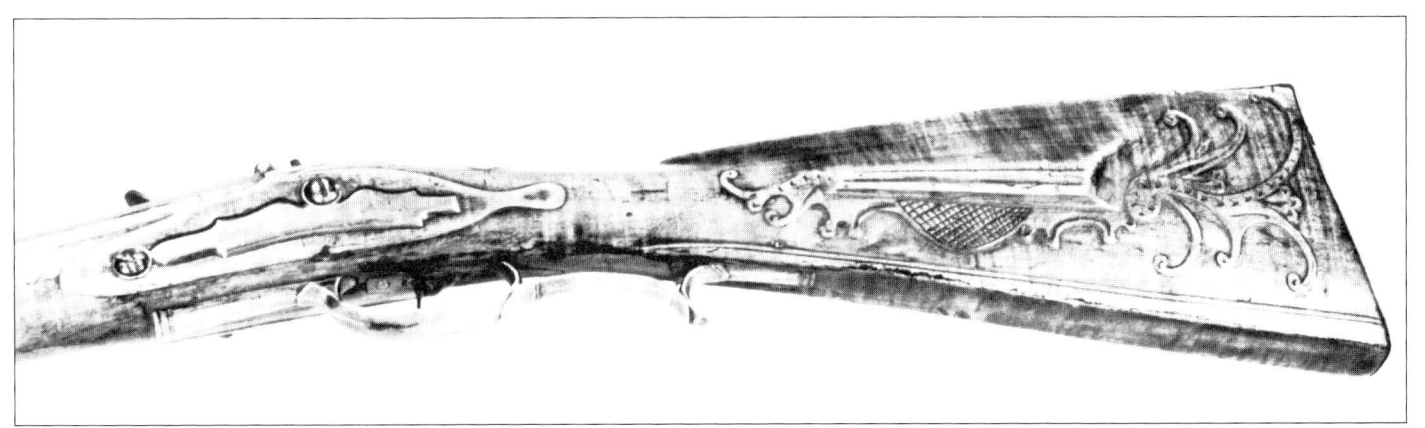

**11.RR AMERICAN RIFLE**  Circa 1770–1785

Being a civilian arm with a strong personal attachment to its owner, the American rifle gradually acquired decorative features once the basic pattern had been established. Moreover the individual characteristics of each county and gunmaker, especially in Pennsylvania, became apparent—leading to the ornate rifles of the "Golden Age," which followed the Revolutionary War (circa 1783–1820). The brass patchbox cover here is an early version of the "daisy-headed" pattern that became popular in Lancaster County, Pennsylvania. Its design shows a gentle curve on the lid's two borders and a five-petal daisy terminal (five screws). Additional raised carving on the attractive striped maple butt is also present, that is, scrolls and cross-hatching around the inboard cheekpiece, as well as behind the barrel tang; borders, too, surround the lock and square-ended side plate, as well as below the tail pipe and along the rammer channel (three pipes). Its flat/beveled lock (no exterior bridle) is a standard imported design marked by the prolific English maker, "KETLAND."

| | | | |
|---|---|---|---|
| Length: 59-1/2" | Lock: 5-3/8" X 1" | Butt Tang: 2-1/2" | Furniture: Brass |
| Barrel: 43-1/2", .64 cal. | Trigger Guard: 9-1/4" | Weight: 10.4 lbs. | |

**The Kindig Collection**

Chapter 4: Rifles   223

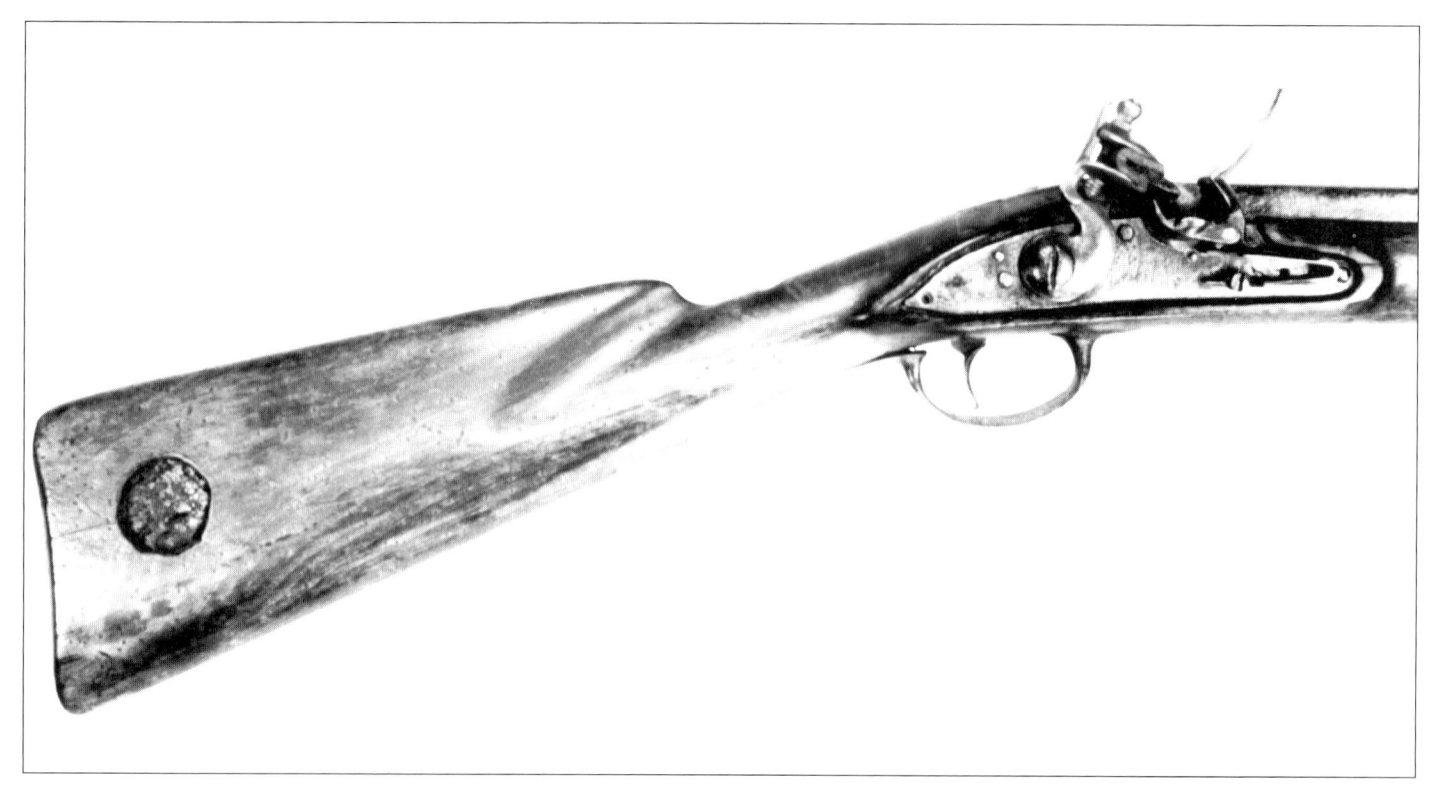

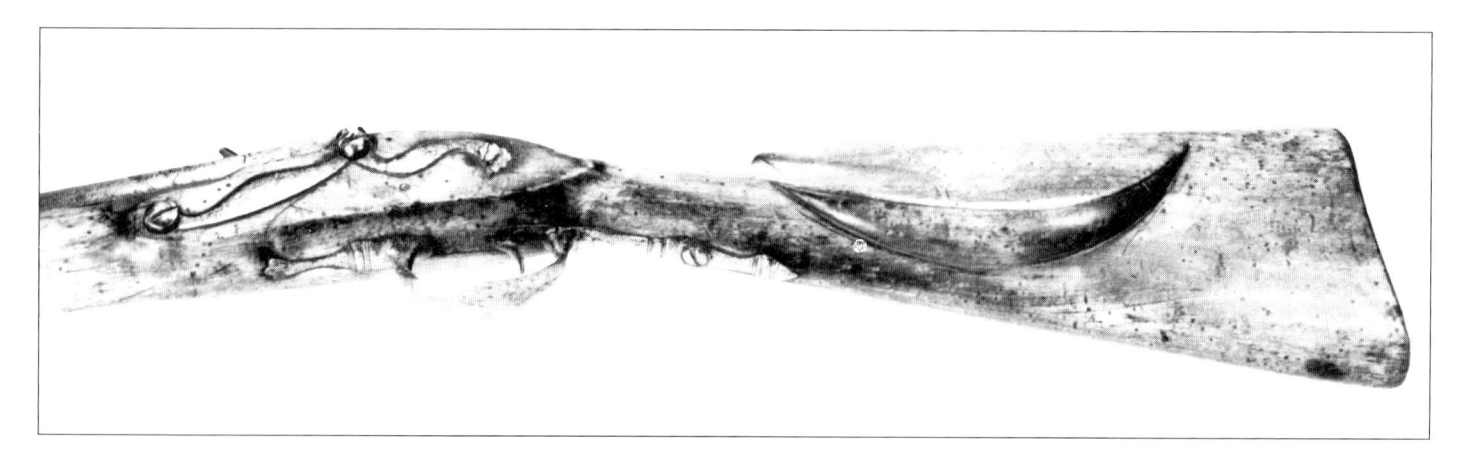

**12.RR AMERICAN RIFLE**                                                                                              Circa 1760–1770

Although development of the American rifle is generally credited to the Pennsylvania gunsmiths, it also became popular in the South—through Maryland, Virginia, the Carolinas and Georgia—with many fine patterns produced there. This early example is a crude "mountain gun" of the utilitarian type created in the back country of the South. The round opening in its butt is a "greasehole," which held thick grease used to rub into the cloth and leather bullet patches. Notice also the absence of all but the essential features required for hunting and personal protection, including elimination of a butt plate and tail pipe. The early iron furniture demonstrates European influence (also indicated by the curved cheekpiece). A three-screw lock, in turn, has been reconverted (incorrect round cock on a flat plate; also a later narrow waterproof flash pan). The unusual breech is squared for nine inches behind two fixed open sights. Its large bore has eight grooves. Rifles were a primary arm among the Southern militia in that theater's hard fighting during the War for Independence.

Length: 54-1/2"            Lock: 6-1/8" X 1-1/8"            Furniture: Iron
Barrel: 39-1/4", .66 cal.  Trigger Guard: 8"                Weight: 7.1 lbs.

**George C. Neumann Collection, Valley Forge National Historical Park**

224    *Chapter 4: Rifles*

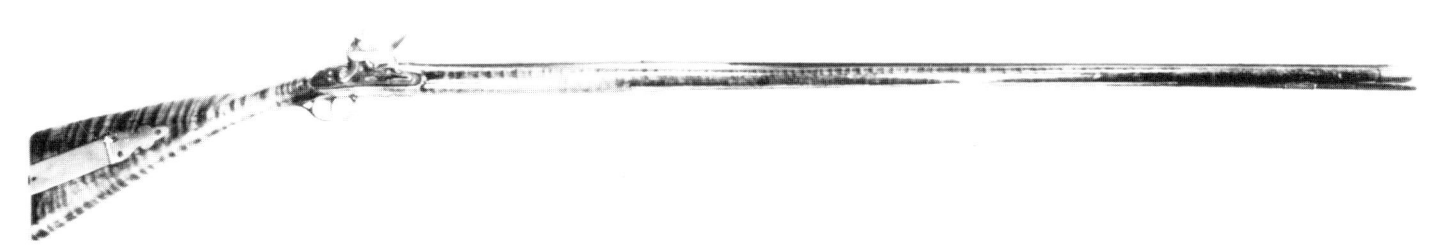

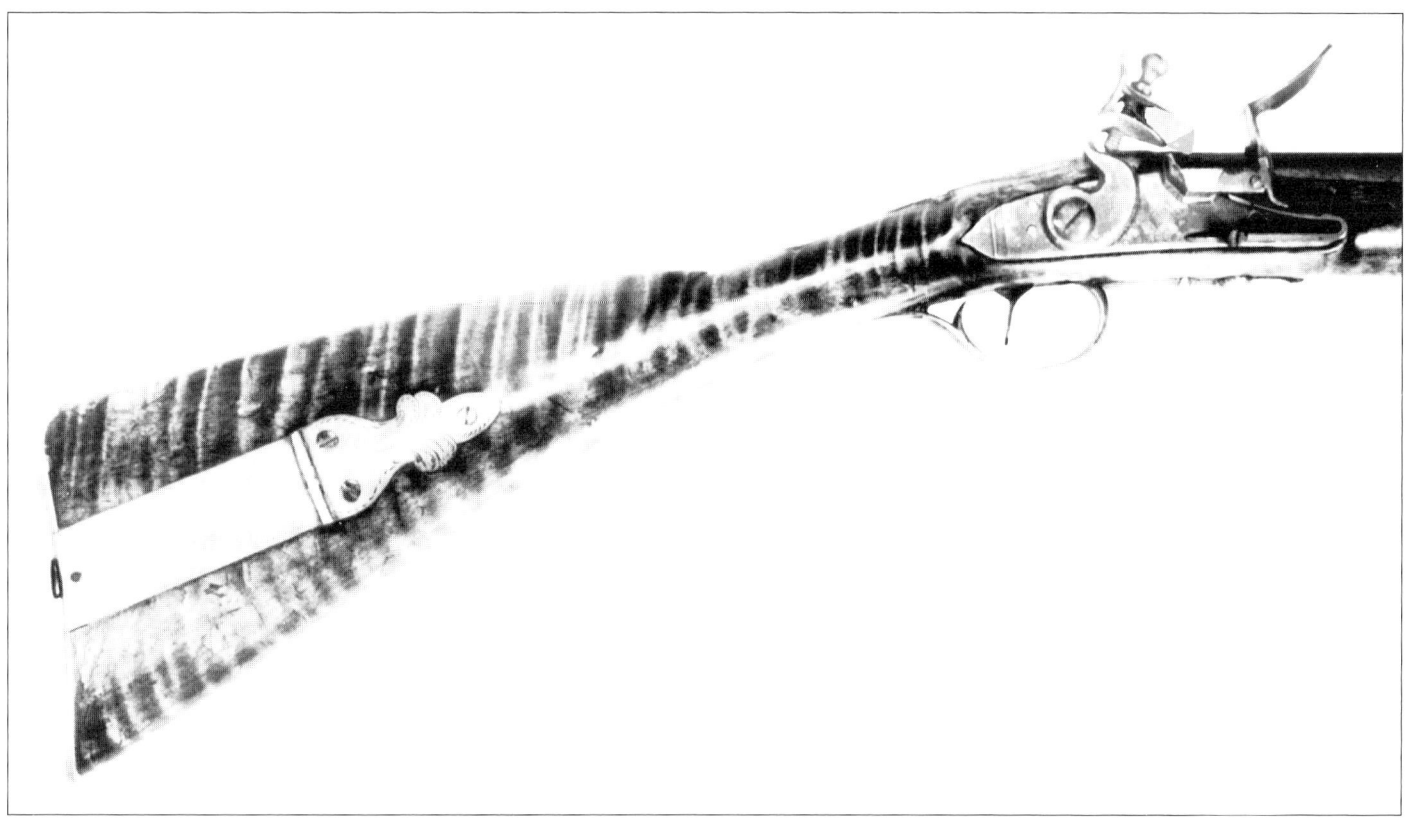

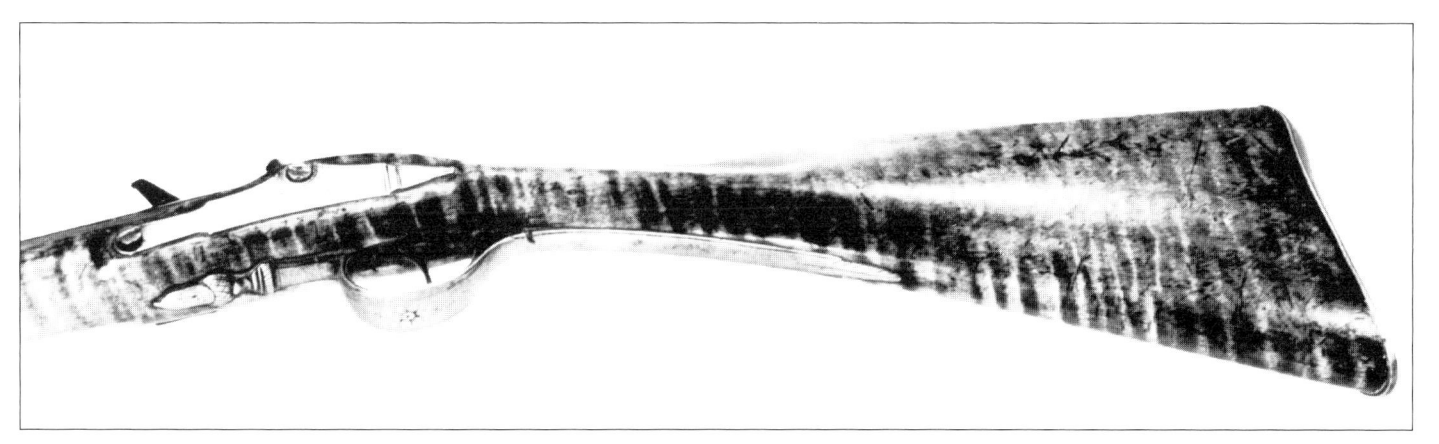

**13.RR  AMERICAN RIFLE**                                                                         **Circa 1770–1790**

Many of the rifles of this period were produced locally and did not follow the traditional Pennsylvania patterns. Although numerous rifled bores were "shot smooth" from use or reamed out by the early 1800s to adapt to fowl and smaller game, others were originally manufactured as smoothbores to fire a patched ball (with surprising accuracy) as in this case. The graceful weapon incorporates a rifle profile for its striped maple stock and includes a brass patchbox cover with an elementary head (three screws) plus a rectangular hinged lid. The remaining furniture, however, shows features of the English fowler, that is, a long trigger guard (omitting the rear bar extension) and headed by an acorn finial, a triangular-type side plate, and a long stepped butt tang—without a cheekpiece or raised carving (except behind its barrel tang). Most of the brass fittings have a typical 1770's stippled decoration made by striking a series of single stampings. The thin forend supports a pinned octagon-to-round barrel mounting two fixed open sights, as well as three rammer thimbles (wooden rod) and a nose cap.

| | | | |
|---|---|---|---|
| Length: 62-1/4" | Lock: 5" X 1" | Butt Tang: 3-1/2" | Furniture: Brass |
| Barrel: 47", .50 cal. | Trigger Guard: 10-3/4" | Weight: 5.5 lbs. | |

**George C. Neumann Collection, Valley Forge National Historical Park**

*Chapter 4: Rifles*     **225**

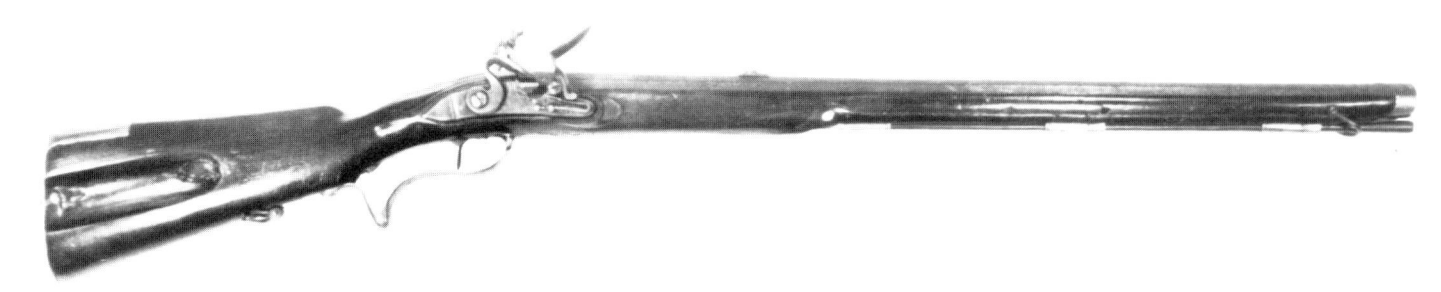

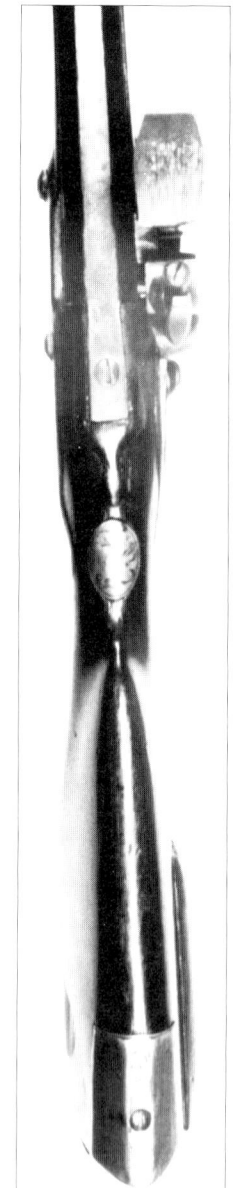

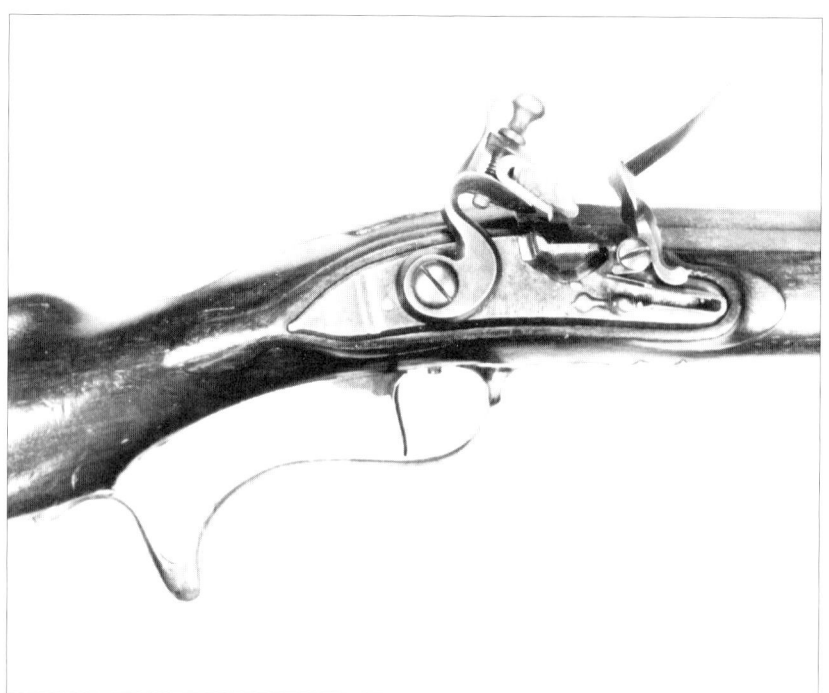

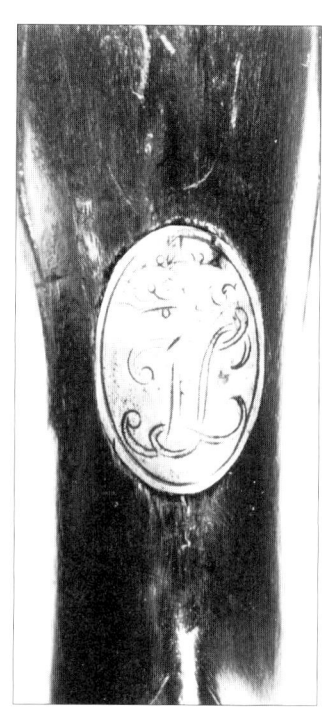

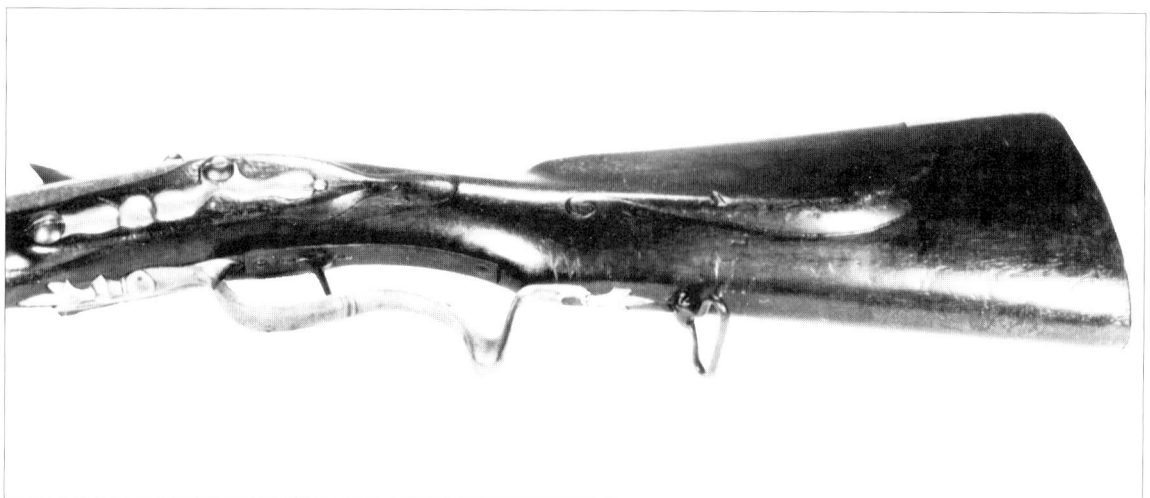

**14.RR  GERMANIC JAEGER MILITARY RIFLE**  Circa 1760–1780

An estimated 4,000 short rifles accompanied the jaeger troops during our Revolutionary War. Some came as personal weapons and others were standard military models. This German-issue rifle was found in America and is marked on the lock plate "T W PISTOR," (Thomas Wilhem Pistor, manager at Schmalkalden). He apparently supplied similar patterns to Hesse Cassel, Anhalt-Zerbst and probably other jaeger corps for use here. Its oval escutcheon reads "crown / FL" for Landgraf Frederick of Hesse Cassel, who provided 500 riflemen. Note the many traditional Germanic rifle features: a curved cheekpiece, the open trigger guard, a wooden patchbox lid, and a short octagonal barrel (28-5/8", .63 caliber, seven grooves). In addition, the flat/beveled lock includes a squared frizzen, no outside bridle, an inside screw and outer edge decoration on the frizzen spring. The upper two of three thimbles have flared mouths (iron trumpet rod); "N 206" appears on the squared butt tang. The side plate and trigger guard are also typical of these Pistor rifles. (Compare with civilian jaegers 1.RR, 2.RR.)

| | | | |
|---|---|---|---|
| Length: 43-5/8" | Lock: 5-3/8" X 1" | Butt Tang: 2-7/8" | Furniture: Brass |
| Barrel: 28-5/8", .63 cal. | Trigger Guard: 10-1/2" | Side Plate: 4-3/4" | Weight: 8.0 lbs. |

**West Point Museum Collection**

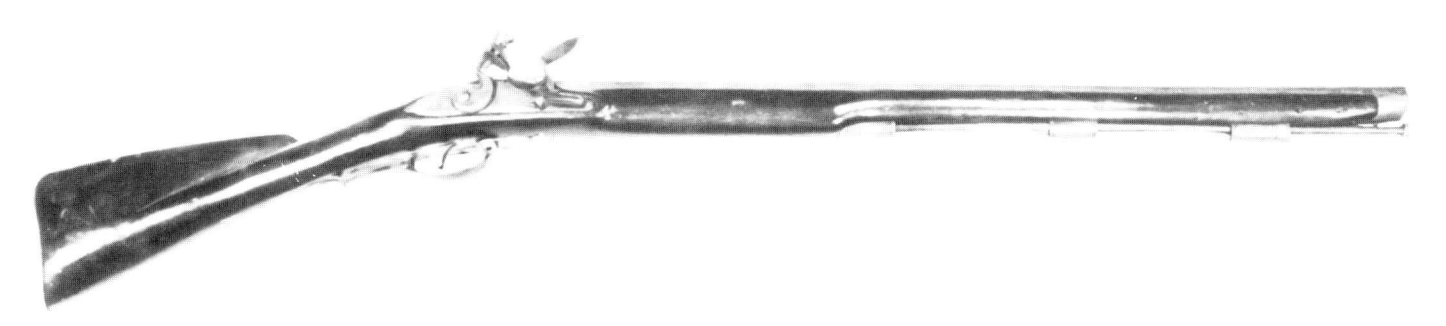

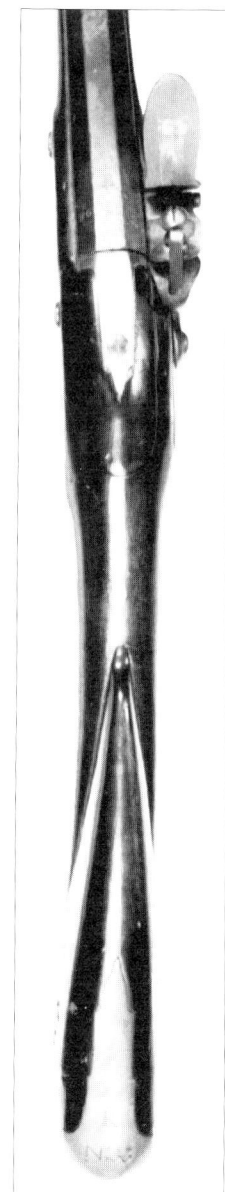

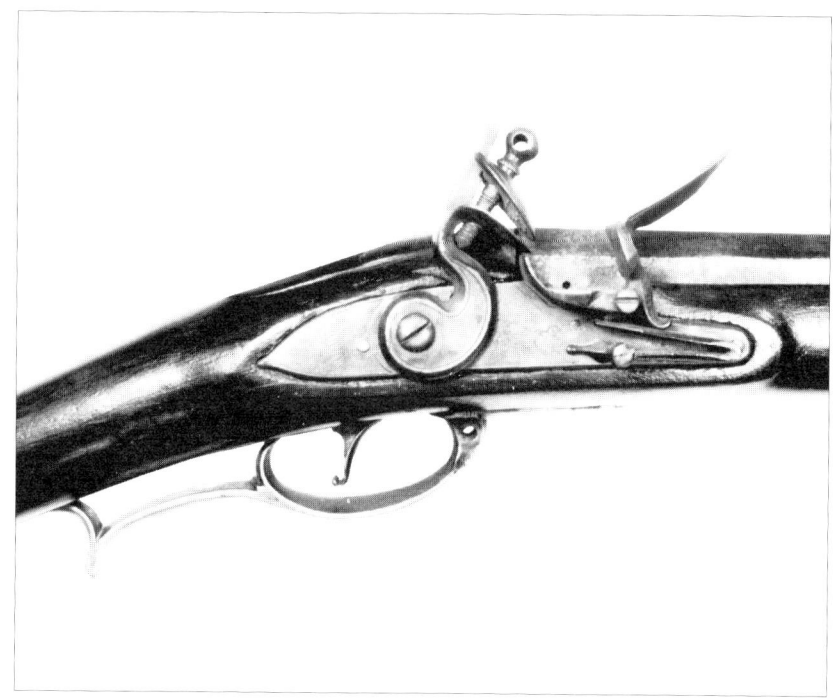

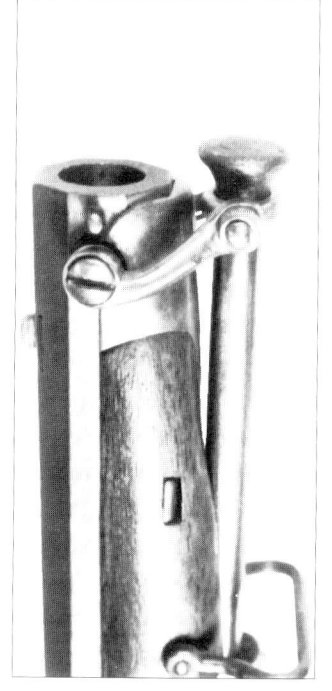

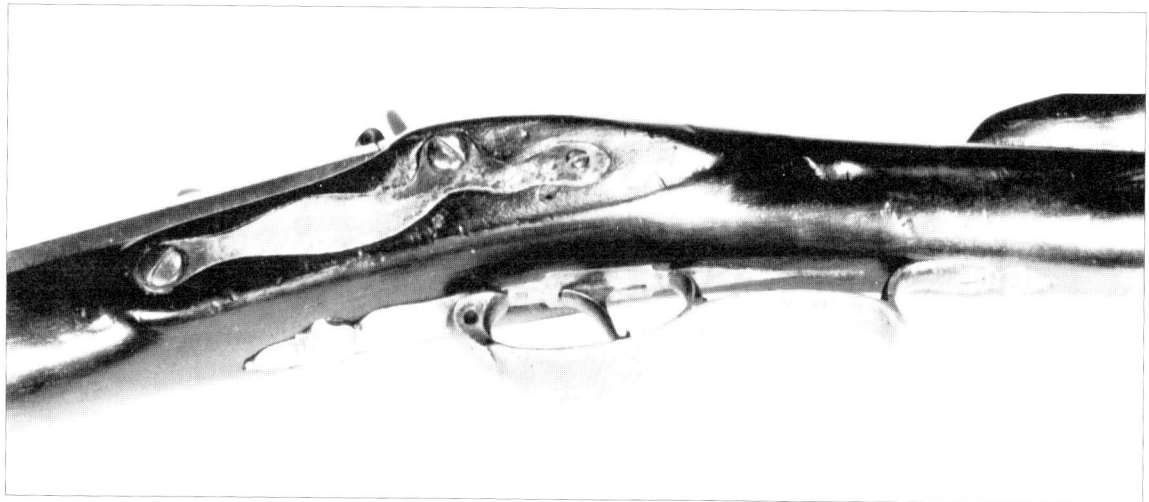

**15.RR ENGLISH RIFLE PATTERN 1776**                                                                                                                                    Circa 1776

To counter the American rifle, the British Board of Ordnance ordered 1,000 of a new short rifle pattern in 1776 (200 from Hanover; 800 from Birmingham, that is, 200 each from B. Willets, M. Barker, Galton & Son and Grice & Son). Apparently by 1777 they were all in America for use by various light infantry line companies and Loyalist units. It is a blend of German and English styling with an octagonal 28" barrel (.65 caliber, eight grooves) having three mounting keys and a rear leaf sight. A walnut stock extends to the muzzle (large iron nose cap, no bayonet provision). An unusual permanent swivel, in turn, held the iron ramrod's upper end (a reproduction is illustrated as no original survives on the available examples). Also note the three large barrel-shaped rammer pipes, the Short Land flat side plate (plus tail screw), and a trigger guard having both a Germanic rear extension and an English acorn forward terminal. An escutcheon was omitted, but a long stepped butt tang is marked "R / No 33." The flat English lock has "TOWER" on the tail and "crown / GR / broad arrow" under the pan. Its breech bears Tower proofs and "W*G" (William Grice).

| | | | |
|---|---|---|---|
| Length: 43-1/2" | Lock: 5-7/8" X 1" | Butt Tang: 4-1/4" | Furniture: Brass/Iron |
| Barrel: 27-3/4", .70 cal. | Trigger Guard: 9" | Side Plate: 5-1/8" | Weight: 7.0 lbs. |

**The Benninghoff Collection**

*Chapter 4: Rifles*   227

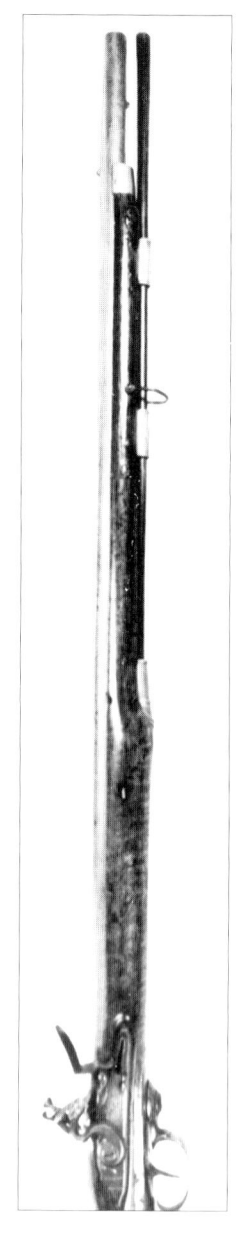

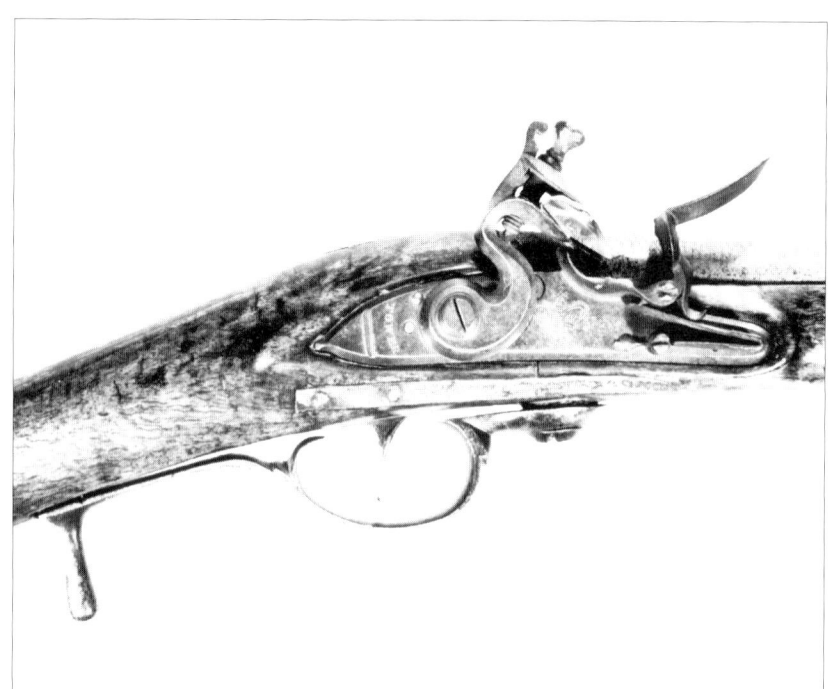

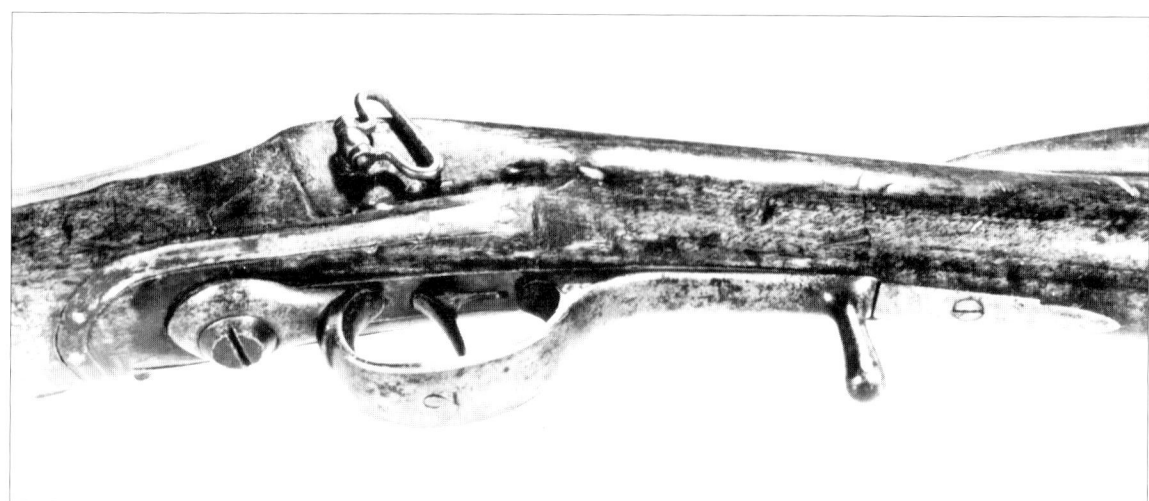

**16.RR  ENGLISH FERGUSON RIFLE**                                                                                                                    Circa 1776–1778

In addition to the 1,000 Pattern 1776 rifles (15.RR), another 100 of the famed Ferguson Model were issued here to British troops. This unique breechloader, developed by Capt. Patrick Ferguson, improved on a late-17th century concept by attaching the front end of its trigger guard to a vertical threaded cylinder that passed up through the breech of the barrel. Rotating the trigger guard's rear handle sideways (3/4 turn) lowered the screw to gain entrance from the top into a chamber for loading. It could reportedly sustain five rounds per minute even when lying down (versus the American rifle's two to three rounds per minute). The walnut stock supports a    34-1/8" (.65 caliber; eight grooves) barrel that is octagonal for 5-1/2-inches and held by three lateral keys. Three thimbles housed a wooden rammer. The bayonet stud, in turn, appears under the muzzle, while the rear sling swivel was mounted on the side. These were carried by a picked corps of 100 under Ferguson during the Brandywine campaign. His wounding led to its breakup and the members apparently returned to their separate units—each with his own rifle. Marks: "TOWER / crown / GR" on the lock; "2" on the barrel tang, trigger loop and butt tang. (Also see 17.RR.)

| | | | |
|---|---|---|---|
| Length: 49-3/8" | Lock: 5-1/8" X 1" | Butt Tang: 4-1/4" | Furniture: Brass |
| Barrel: 34-1/8", .65 cal. | Trigger Guard: 10-3/8" | Weight: 6.9 lbs. | |

**Morristown (New Jersey) National Historical Park**

Chapter 4: Rifles

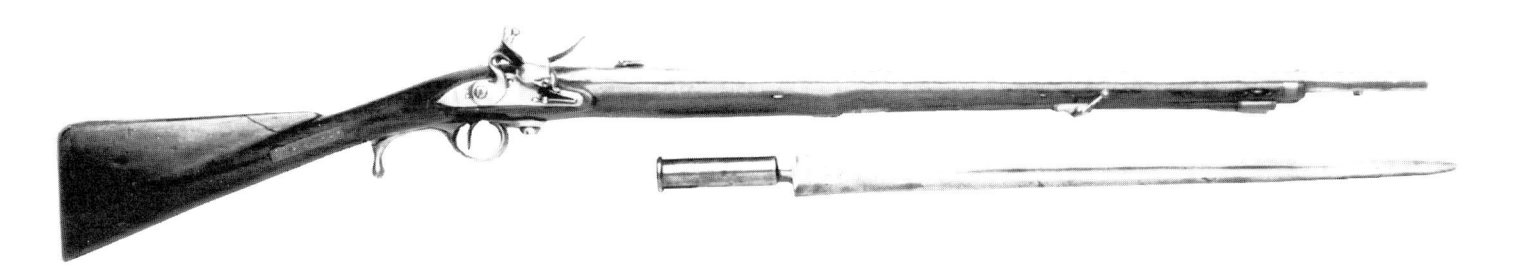

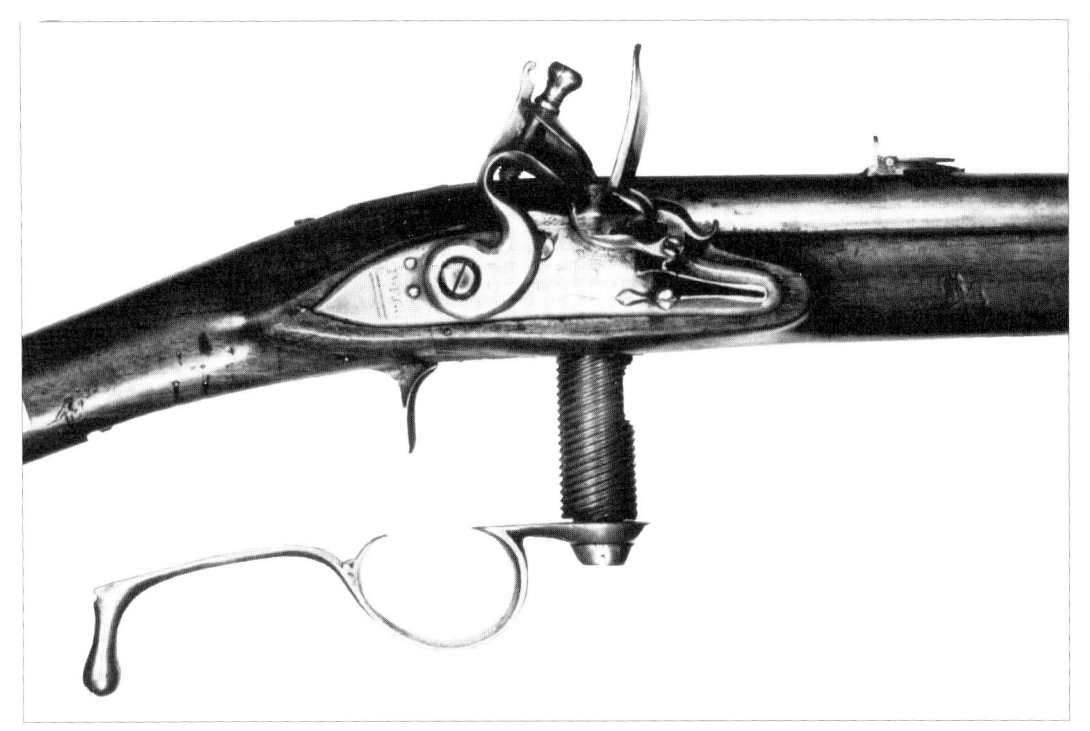

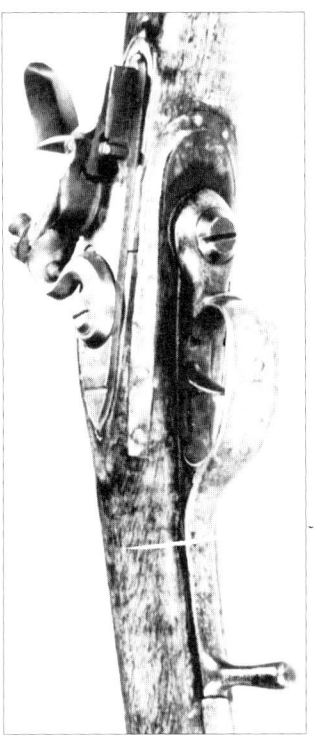

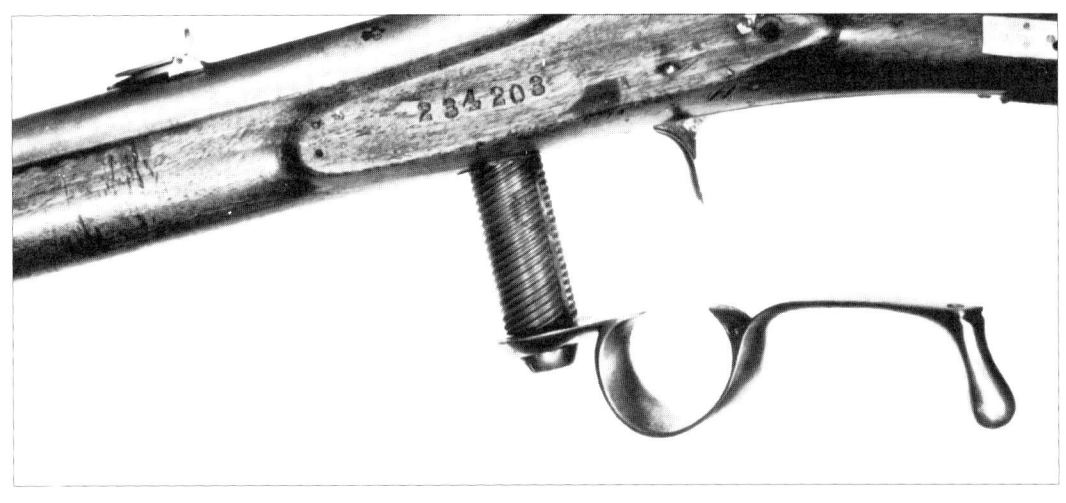

### 17.RR  ENGLISH FERGUSON RIFLE FUSIL

Circa 1775–1778

This officer's version of the Ferguson rifle was presented by the inventor to Capt. Frederic de Peyster. The enlisted man's pattern (16.RR) was made by Mathias Barker and John Whatley ("MB & IW" on barrel); this one is signed on the lock's tail, "D EGG," plus "D. EGG LONDON" on the breech (Durs Egg, who made many of the private Fergusons). In this case a brass strip replaced the issued model's nose cap, but its 43" octagon-to-round barrel (.69 caliber, eight grooves) is still held by three keys. Ferguson's patent added cut-out pockets in the vertical plug to accumulate the troublesome powder fouling residue. Unfortunately this did not stop clogging of the loading action, which, with frequent breakage of the walnut stock (at the hollowed lock/breech area), were its major problems. Note for example the U-shaped iron repair beneath the lock in the photo at right from the prior Ferguson. An interesting rear open sight has a folding leaf added with a V and an aperture. A special long bayonet was designed for this weapon (25-1/2" flat blade, 20.BB). It was slotted to position the blade under the muzzle (not at the normal right side) because of its breech-loading capability.

Length: 49-7/8"  
Barrel: 43", .69 cal.  
Furniture: Brass  
Weight: 7.2 lbs.

**The Smithsonian Institution Collection**

# Chapter 5

# Pistols... One Shot, Man-to-Man

The smoothbore pistol had limited range and accuracy. It did however possess a large bore size (.50 to .75 caliber) to deliver a ball of considerable stopping power at close quarters. Like most firearms the barrel length of handguns steadily shortened during the 18th century while retaining a sturdy stock with a bulbous butt.

Pistols were mostly considered standard military arms for horsemen, seamen and officers. Civilians commonly carried pocket-size patterns for protection whenever traveling. The typical examples presented here are grouped into four categories: cavalry, holster, naval, and civilian.

## CAVALRY PISTOLS

*English:* At the beginning of the 1700s, most British mounted troops carried pistols with a round pinned barrel measuring twelve inches or more. By the time of the American War for Independence, it had been reduced to nine inches. The stock was usually of walnut with heavy brass furniture. Bore size was either pistol (.56) or carbine (.65) caliber (1.PP–6.PP).

*French:* There were few specifications for France's military pistols until the Model 1733 (21.PP), which attempted to establish an official pattern following the success of the first standard infantry musket in 1717. Although it included a twelve-inch pinned barrel plus brass furniture, the later Model 1766 adopted a shorter nine-inch barrel held by a double strap band and furniture of iron to match the current army practice (22.PP). The unique design introduced in 1777 ended all relationship with prior configurations and was later copied as the United States' first official pistol after the Revolution (the North & Cheney). (See 23.PP).

*Dutch–Germanic:* As with the Dutch–Germanic longarms, the multiple manufacturers and various states of central Europe created a variety of military pistols. They traditionally had thick stocks mounting substantial brass furniture and long pinned barrels with bore sizes often in excess of .75 caliber (29.PP–31.PP).

*American:* Lacking the necessary manu-facturing facilities, the rebellious Colonies appropriated whatever was available—whether by capture, import or assembly of assorted parts. As might be expected, British patterns predominated early in the war; French designs, during the later years (32.PP–44.PP).

**PRIVATEERS BOARD A BRITISH VESSEL**
Close deck fighting aboard ship was usually conducted by a mixture of hand firearms and bladed weapons. An American boarding party is shown attacking an English seaman using a naval pistol and battling a Royal marine with pikes.

## HOLSTER PISTOLS

This military form was mostly carried by officers thrust under a belt or in leather holsters forward of the saddle (usually in pairs). Since they were purchased privately from independent gunsmiths, their configuration displayed a wide range of personal preferences and ornamentation. Yet most reflected the contemporary cavalry pistols (7.PP–9.PP; 25.PP–26.PP; 43.PP).

## NAVAL PISTOLS

The majority of sea service handguns followed the existing cavalry pattern but with some alterations. England's issued arm during the Revolutionary War (like its naval musket) used a flat lock, ringed cock, long belt hook and minimum brass furniture (18.PP); France, in turn, normally copied their cavalry designs, with brass replacing iron components (21.PP–22.PP). The Americans, relying largely on independent privateers, had no standard form.

## CIVILIAN PISTOLS

The dangers of travel in America and Europe required the presence of personal small arms for protection—normally pistols of reduced size to fit into a coat pocket. Many also accompanied officers serving in the American Revolution (10.PP–12.PP).

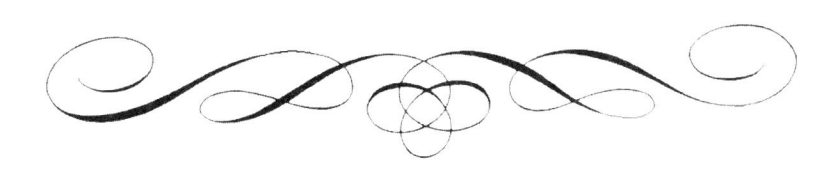

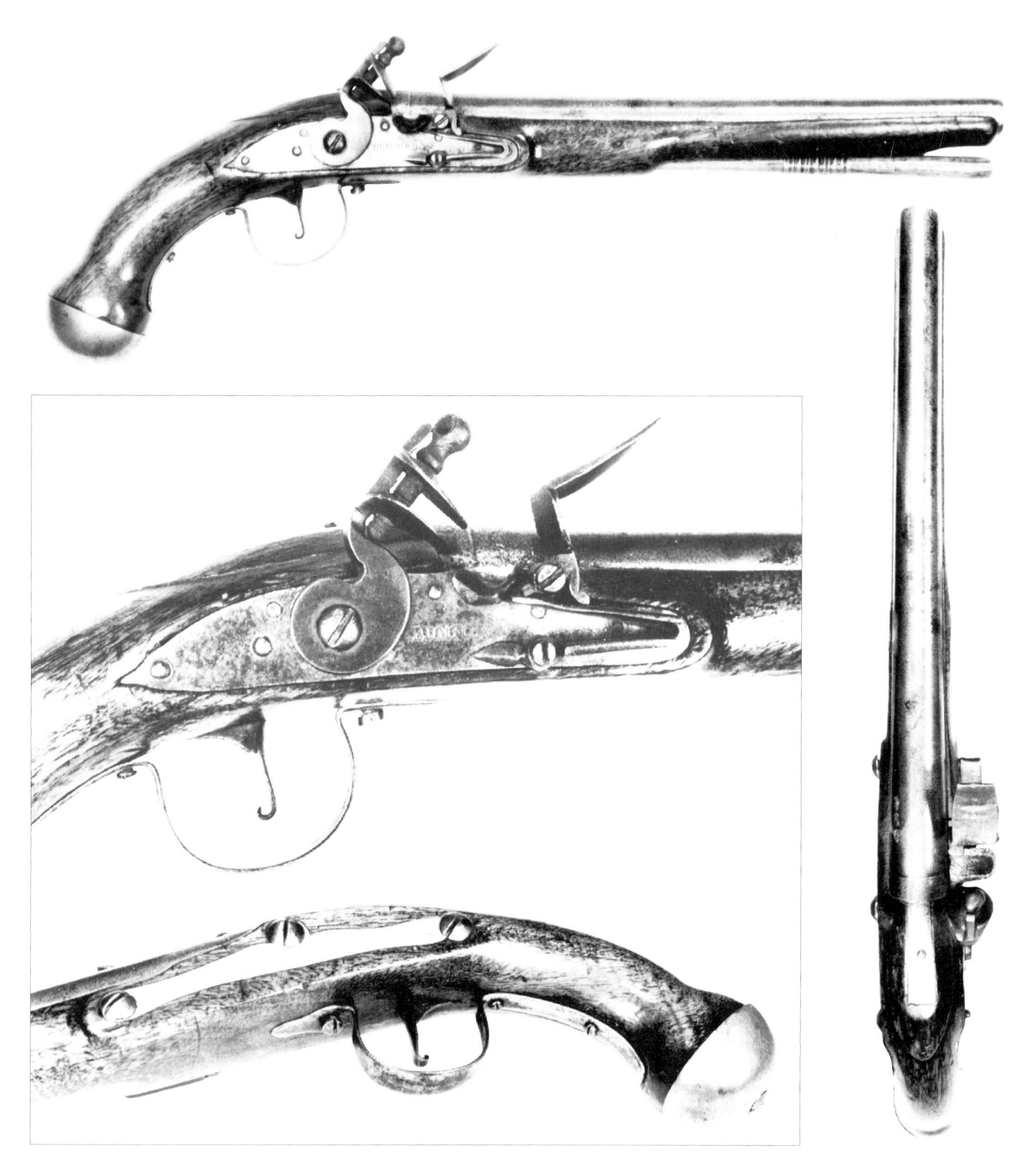

### 1.PP  ENGLISH HORSEMAN/SEA SERVICE PISTOL

**Circa 1710–1720**

This inexpensive pattern incorporates many of the features of early 18th century British longarms, for example: a flat three-screw lock omitting both internal and exterior bridles (squared frizzen), a stubby iron trigger guard surface-mounted with three screws, a straight-edged simple brass butt cap of 17th century form, the flat double-arm side plate, a single ribbed rammer thimble (no tail pipe; wooden ramrod), a bottom screw to secure the barrel tang, and the absence of raised carving except for the beaver tail at the breech. The maker's name, "I BUMFORD" (John Bumford), appears on the lock and his initials are in the breech, as well as London Gunmakers Company proofs. Because of these inexpensive features and the stamping (instead of engraving) of his name on the lock plate—a naval practice—this may have been issued to both cavalry and sea service. The pinned round barrel was originally 12 inches long with a .56 caliber bore. The sturdy walnut stock testifies to its effective use as a club at close quarters after firing.

| | | | |
|---|---|---|---|
| Length: 19" | Lock: 5-3/8" X 7/8" | Side Plate: 5-1/4" | Furniture: Brass/Iron |
| Barrel: 11-3/4", .58 cal. | Trigger Guard: 5-3/4" | Weight: 2.3 lbs. | |

**Robert Nittolo Collection**

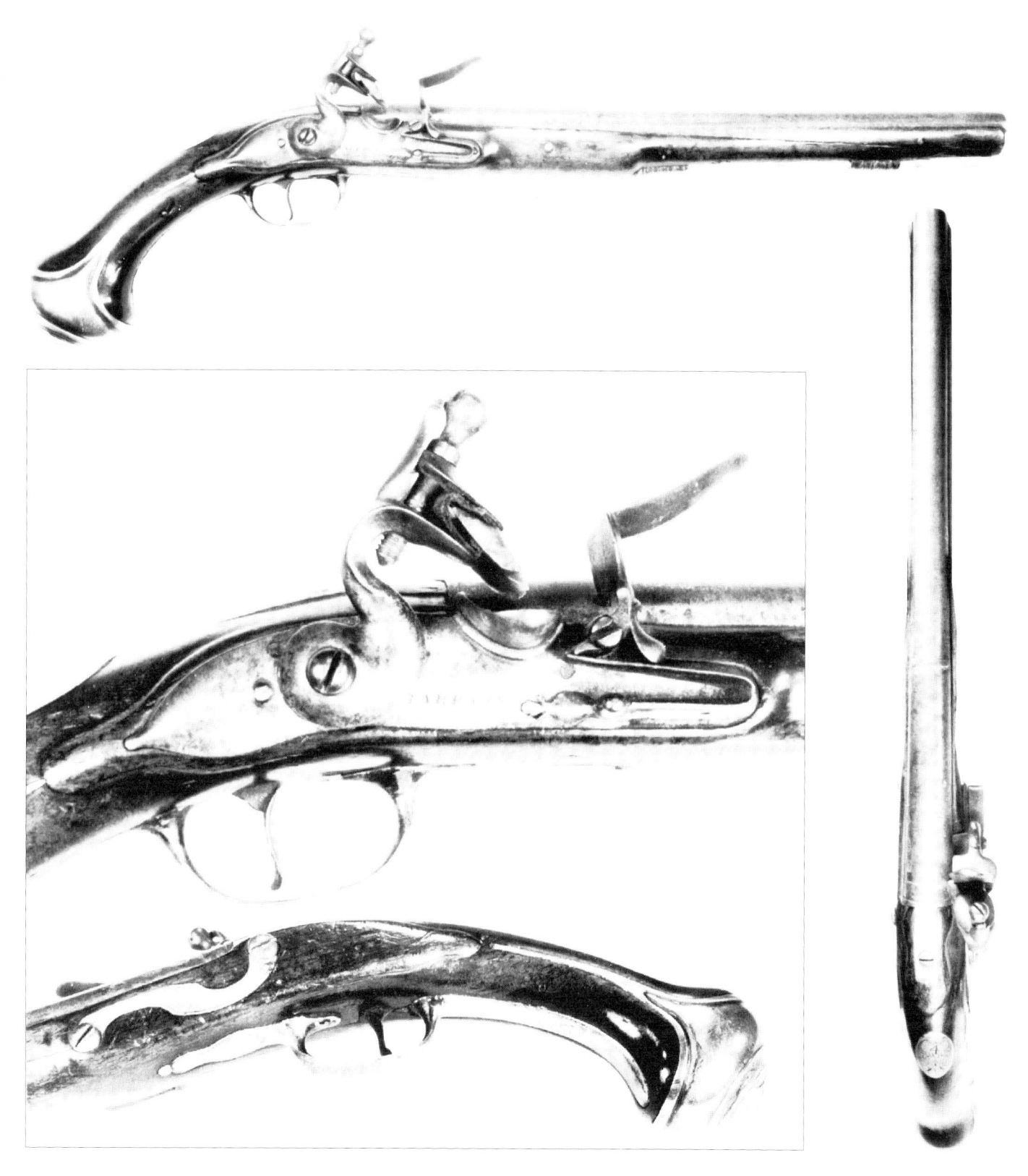

### 2.PP  ENGLISH HORSEMAN PISTOL

**Circa 1715–1725**

At the beginning of the 1700s, Britain had both "horse" (cavalry who fought from their saddle) and dragoons (who traveled mounted but engaged on foot like infantry). In 1746 the former were changed into dragoons yet kept the title "guards." Both groups carried pistols, swords and longarms (horse with a carbine, dragoons with a short large-bore musket). Their handguns, however, (carried singly or in pairs) usually had long pinned barrels such as this 14" example (originally .56 caliber pistol bore). Note the rounded banana lock without a bridle, the brass grotesque masked butt cap having side straps, two ribbed thimbles holding a wooden ramrod, and the long walnut stock that bears an oval escutcheon, as well as raised carving surrounding the lock, side plate and barrel tang. Its S-form side plate and tapered trigger guard would reappear again in the 1750s. Markings on the lock, "CLARKSON"; breech, London Gunmakers Company proofs and the maker's diamond-shaped "IC" stamp (Joseph Clarkson, London); barrel, "crown / Hartford" (colonel of 2nd Troop of Life Guards 1715–1740); escutcheon, "4 / WR."

Length: 21"  
Barrel: 14", .60 cal.  
Lock: 5" X 7/8"  
Trigger Guard: 7-3/4"  
Side Plate: 3-1/8"  
Weight: 2.5 lbs.  
Furniture: Brass

**William H. Guthman Collection**

*Chapter 5: Pistols*  233

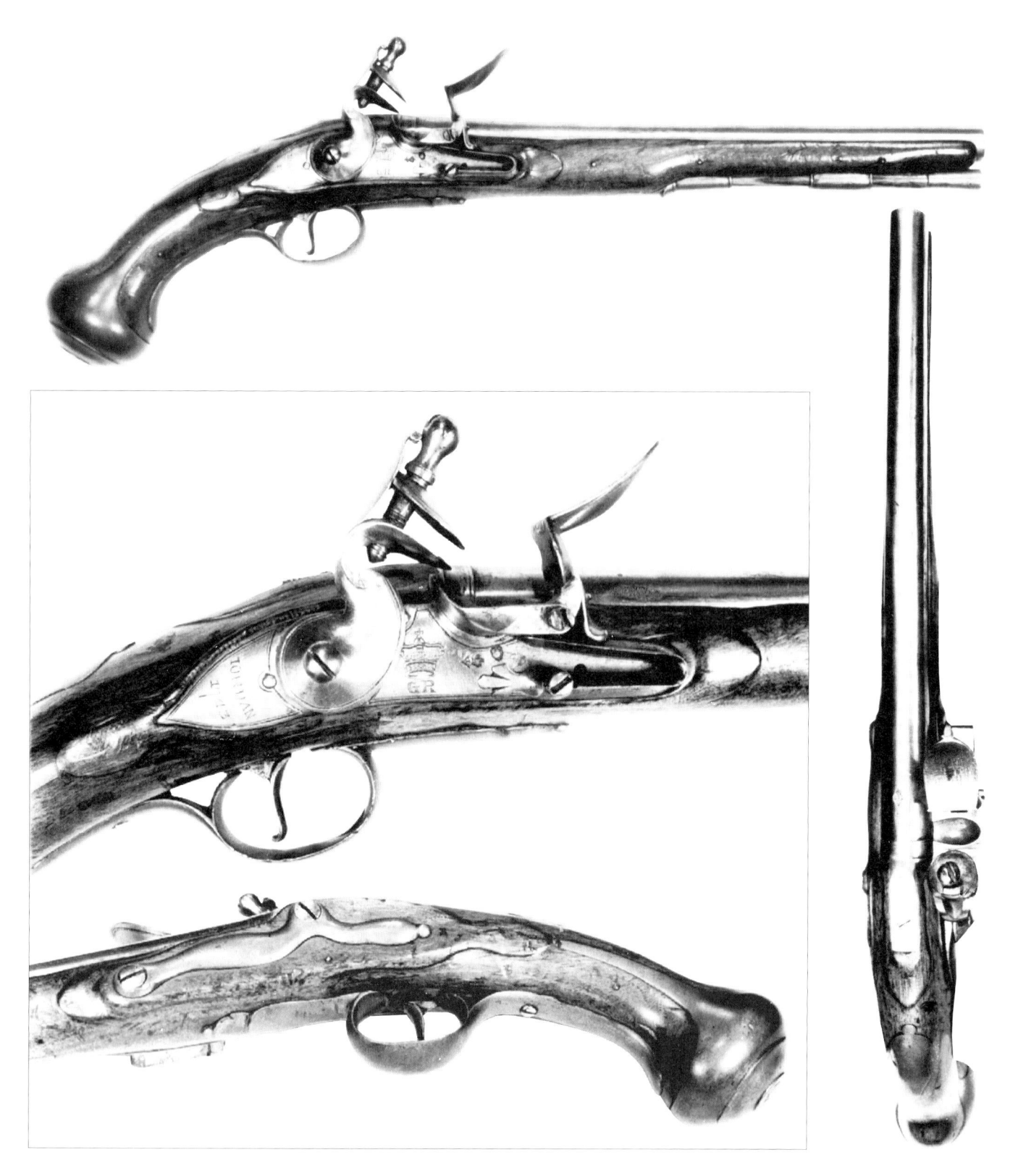

### 3.PP  ENGLISH DRAGOON PISTOL PATTERN 1738
**Circa 1743**

This 12-inch-barreled horseman's pistol (.56 caliber pistol bore) was developed shortly after the Long Land musket pattern and continued in use for several decades. Note how most of its features are scaled-down features of the Brown Bess, for example: the rounded banana lock including both bridles and an oval top frizzen; the convex side plate; a cast brass trigger guard incorporating a hazelnut front end and the split rear post on its bow; a shield escutcheon; bulbous raised carving on the walnut stock bordering the lock, side plate and barrel tang; two cast brass barrel-type rammer thimbles (wooden rod with brass tip); and an all-round barrel (no sights) ending in a baluster breech. A heavy ridged butt cap extends side straps along the grip. Although Britain's heavy dragoons did not serve here during the War for Independence, many of their weapons were acquired and used. Markings: lock, "IORDAN / 1743," "crown / GR / broad arrow"; breech, Tower proofs plus "IF" (Joseph Farmer, the barrel maker). Like the Long Land muskets, by 1756 the lock was straightened and the border carving reduced.

| | | | |
|---|---|---|---|
| Length: 19-1/2" | Lock: 5-1/2" X 1" | Side Plate: 4-3/4" | Furniture: Brass |
| Barrel: 12", .58 cal. | Trigger Guard: 7-1/4" | Weight: 2.8 lbs. | |

**Robert Nittolo Collection**

234  *Chapter 5: Pistols*

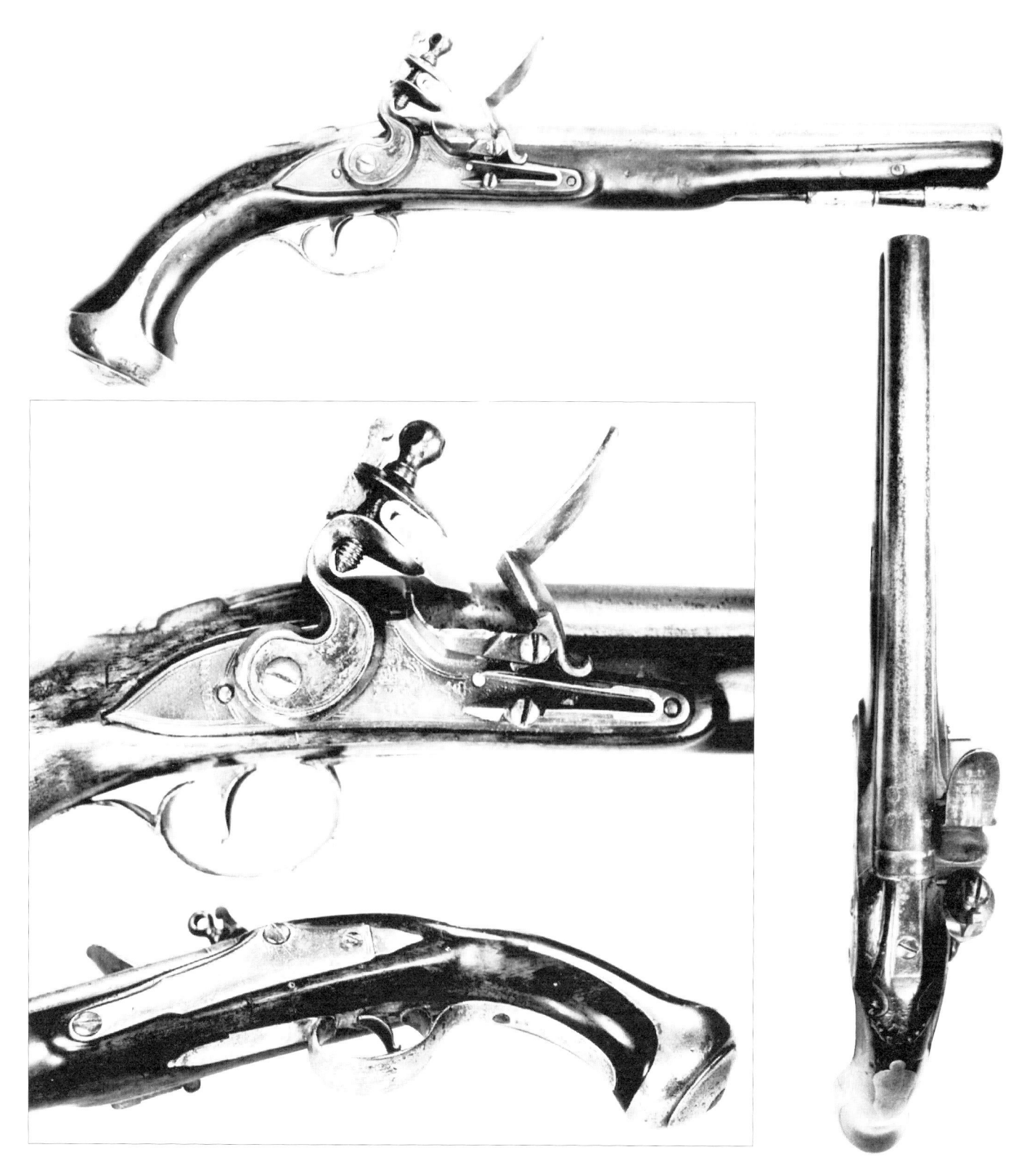

**4.PP  ENGLISH ROYAL FORESTERS LIGHT DRAGOON PISTOL PATTERN 1760/1778**  Circa 1765–1775

In 1756 a warrant established new light dragoons who would fight from the saddle with lighter carbines, pistols and swords. It also specified a 10" barreled pistol that was superseded by a nine-inch pattern in 1759. The 10" barrel form continued for special units, such as this Royal Foresters pattern which served in the Revolution with Britain's 16th Lt. Dragoons. The flat/beveled lock includes both bridles, a notched front in the cock's upper post (and a wraparound top jaw), plus an arrowhead frizzen finial. Its side plate (triangular with a rear wood screw) and pointed trigger guard are also seen on contemporary fusils and carbines. A ridged butt cap retains the long side straps of earlier patterns, while two cast brass pipes secure the wooden ramrod (brass tip). The grip, in turn, includes a shield escutcheon just below raised splay carving at the barrel tang. Its 10" round barrel (no sights) has been enlarged to a .65 caliber bore to permit sharing ammunition with the trooper's carbine. "TOWER" and "crown / GR / broad arrow" appear on the lock plate.

| | | |
|---|---|---|
| Length: 16-3/4" | Lock: 5-1/4" X 1" | Furniture: Brass |
| Barrel: 10", .65 cal. | Trigger Guard: 6-3/4" | Weight: 2.5 lbs. |

Chapter 5: Pistols   235

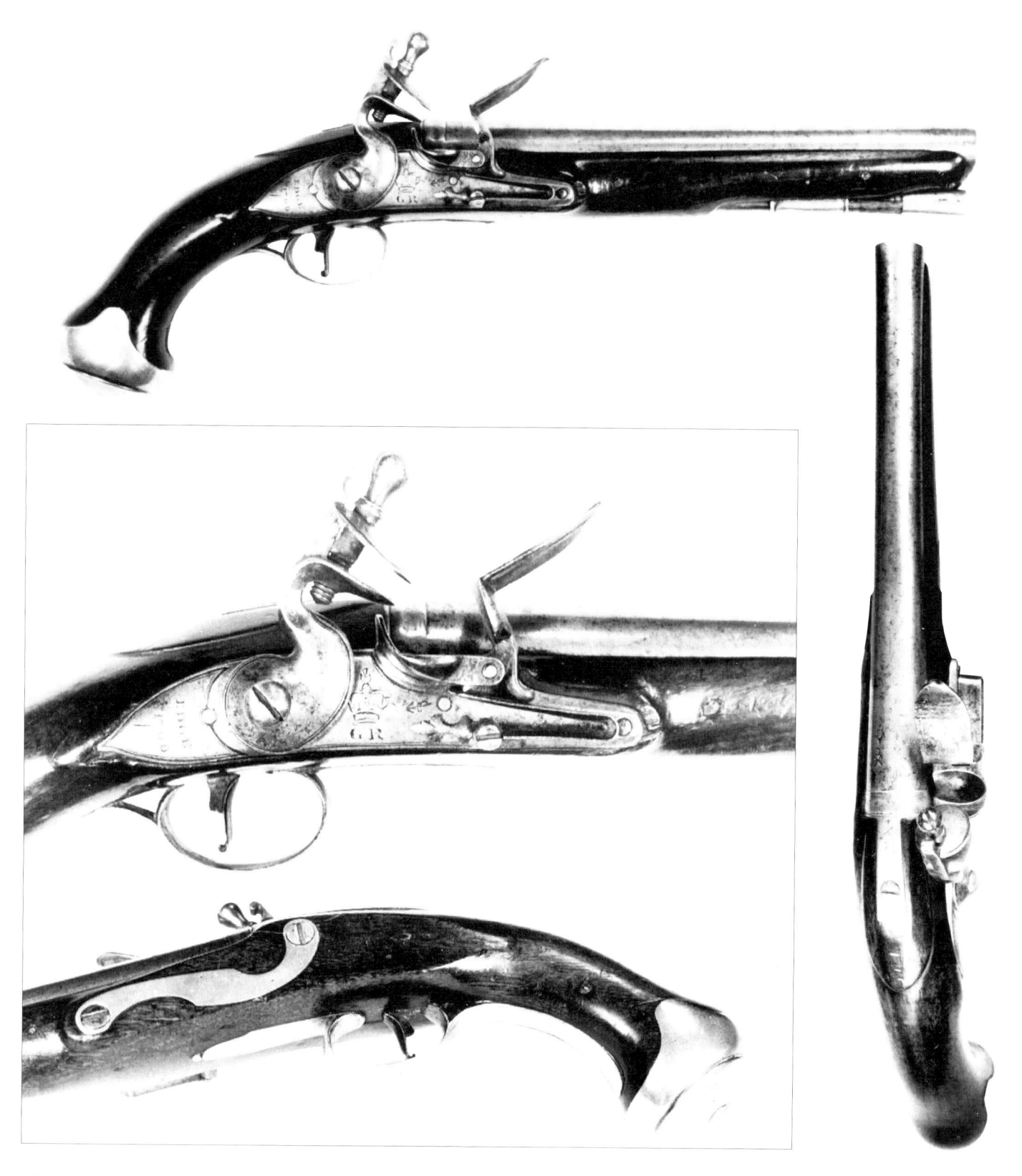

**5.PP  ENGLISH LIGHT DRAGOON PISTOL PATTERN 1759**                                                                                                                    Circa 1760

Based on the successful performance of the new light dragoon units created in 1756, full regiments were authorized in 1759. At that time a revised nine-inch barrel (.65 caliber) pistol pattern was also adopted for them (replacing the 10" as seen in 4.PP), based on a design by Col. Eliott. The model remained in use as their standard handgun through the American Revolution, where it was carried by Britain's 16th and 17th Light Dragoons. Note the innovations this pattern includes: a simple butt cap with the prior long straps removed; a flat S-form side plate and pointed trigger guard; a straight rounded lock having both bridles and incorporating a forward notch on the cock's rectangular upper post (some had flat posts); elimination of the escutcheon; a single cast thimble for the wooden rod (brass tip); and raised beaver-tail carving around the barrel tang of the walnut stock. The lock is marked on its tail by the maker, "EDGE / 1760," plus "crown / GR / broad arrow" under the pan. Its barrel bears both Tower proofs and "crown / crossed scepters" on the tang.

| Length: 15-5/8" | Lock: 5-1/4" X 1" | Side Plate: 3-3/8" | Furniture: Brass |
|---|---|---|---|
| Barrel: 9", .66 cal. | Trigger Guard: 6-1/2" | Weight: 2.3 lbs. | |

**The Benninghoff Collection**

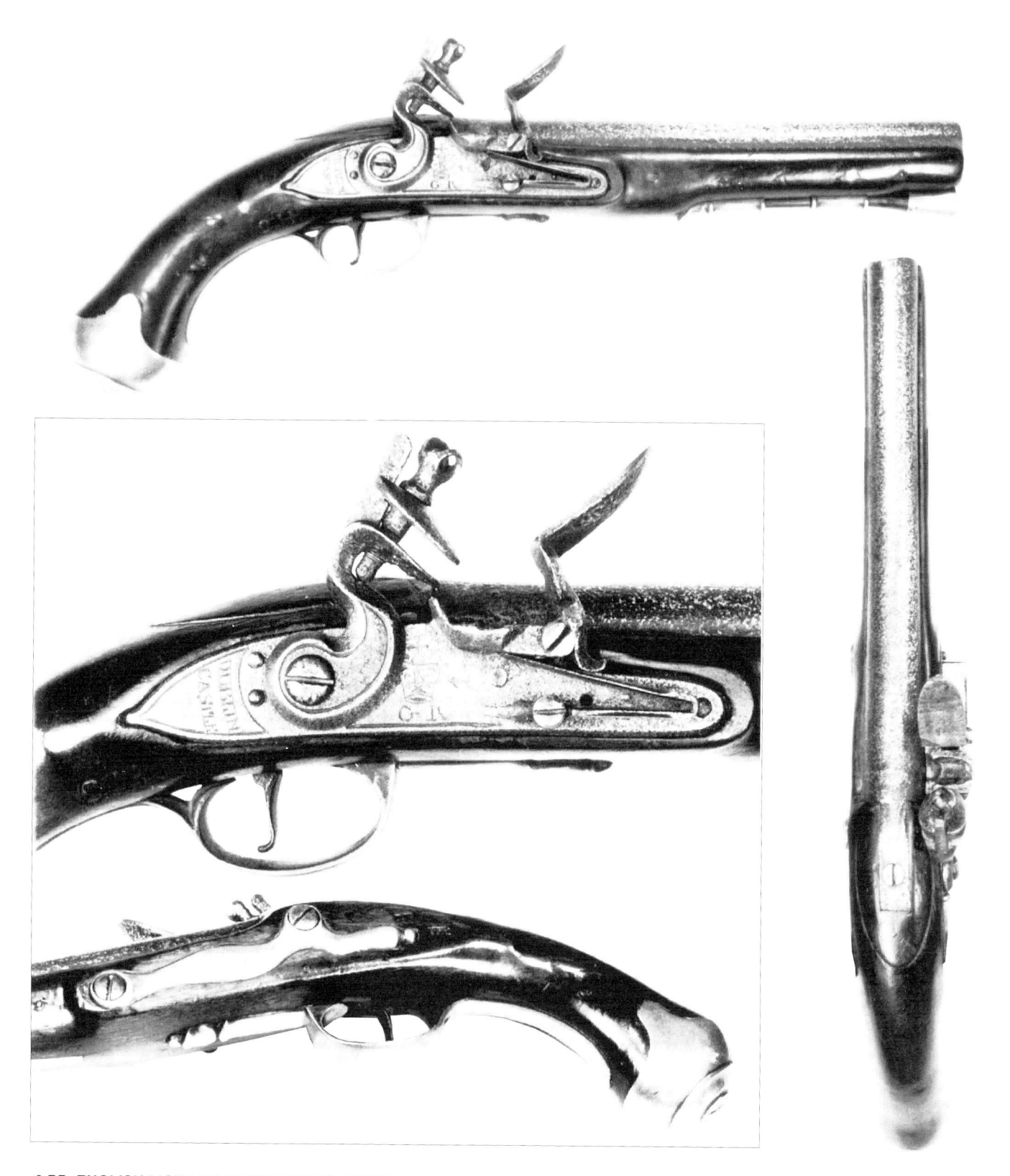

### 6.PP  ENGLISH LIGHT DRAGOON PISTOL PATTERN 1759/1778

Circa 1760

The Dublin Castle manufactory produced arms for troops serving in the Irish Establishment. They followed the basic British official patterns but often took liberties in their interpretations. In this case, for example, the current nine-inch barrel (.65 caliber), stubby eared butt cap and beaver-tail carving around the barrel tang were observed. However variations are apparent (see 5.PP) in the flat/beveled lock (no notch in the cock's upper post), the use of two high border rammer thimbles (wooden rod, brass tip), plus a convex side plate and hazelnut trigger guard that follow the current Long Land musket pattern. As with most English-issued pistols, the round barrel has no sights and adds a baluster ring at the breech. Of further interest is the later layer of hardened steel attached to the frizzen's face after repeated flint strikes had worn the original surface (that is, the flints were harder than the metal—the sparks at ignition are pieces of flaming steel). This lock is inscribed "DUBLIN / CASTLE" on the tail and "crown / GR / broad arrow" beneath the pan. Stamps in the stock include "RT" and "crown / 5" (an inspector's viewer's mark).

| | | | |
|---|---|---|---|
| Length: 16" | Lock: 5-1/2" X 1" | Side Plate: 4-7/8" | Furniture: Brass |
| Barrel: 9", .63 cal. | Trigger Guard: 7-1/4" | Weight: 2.4 lbs. | |

**Author's Collection**

*Chapter 5: Pistols*   237

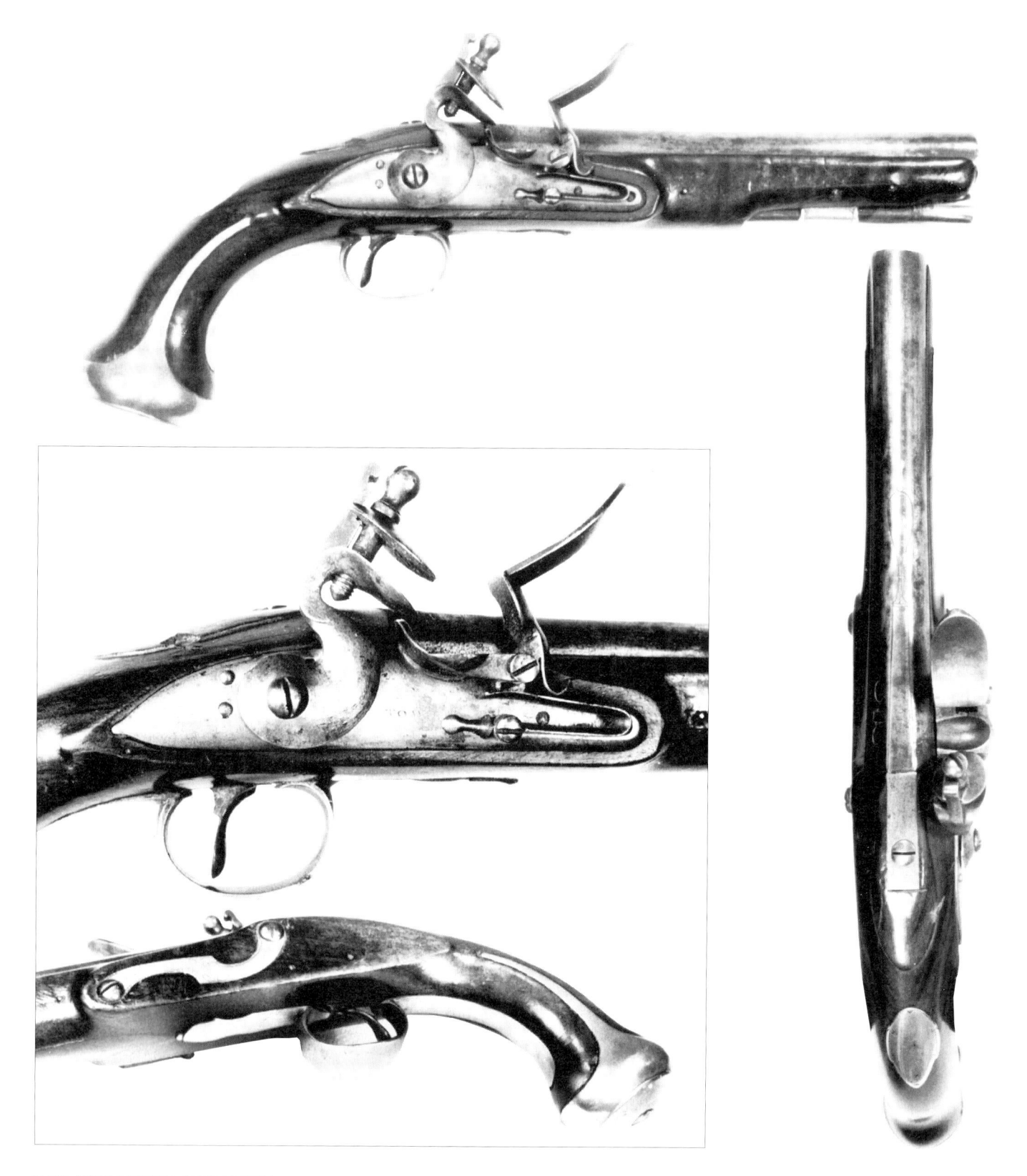

**7.PP  ENGLISH HOLSTER PISTOL**                                        **Circa 1775–1785**

The above is a privately made officer's pistol of a form popular with both British and American participants in the War for Independence. Although the slightly flared pinned barrel has been reduced to seven inches (.56 caliber originally), many features of the contemporary light dragoon pistol (5.PP) are included: a tapered trigger guard, flat S-shaped side plate, a single cast ramrod thimble, and a beaver-tail barrel tang carving in the walnut stock. Its maker, however, did indulge in an earlier butt cap form with long side straps, inset a semi-oval escutcheon and omit the military split spur in the trigger bow's rear post. He also added a simple line design along the barrel, as well as a stippled pattern outlining its side plate. The rounded lock is the pattern already in use by private gunsmiths when later adopted by the British Board of Ordnance for the Short Land muskets in 1777 (15.MM). London Gunmakers Company proofs are on the breech; the escutcheon is engraved "3."

| | | | |
|---|---|---|---|
| Length: 13" | Lock: 4-1/2" X 7/8" | Side Plate: 2-3/4" | Furniture: Brass |
| Barrel: 7", .59 cal. | Trigger Guard: 6" | Weight: 1.7 lbs. | |

**Author's Collection**

238     *Chapter 5: Pistols*

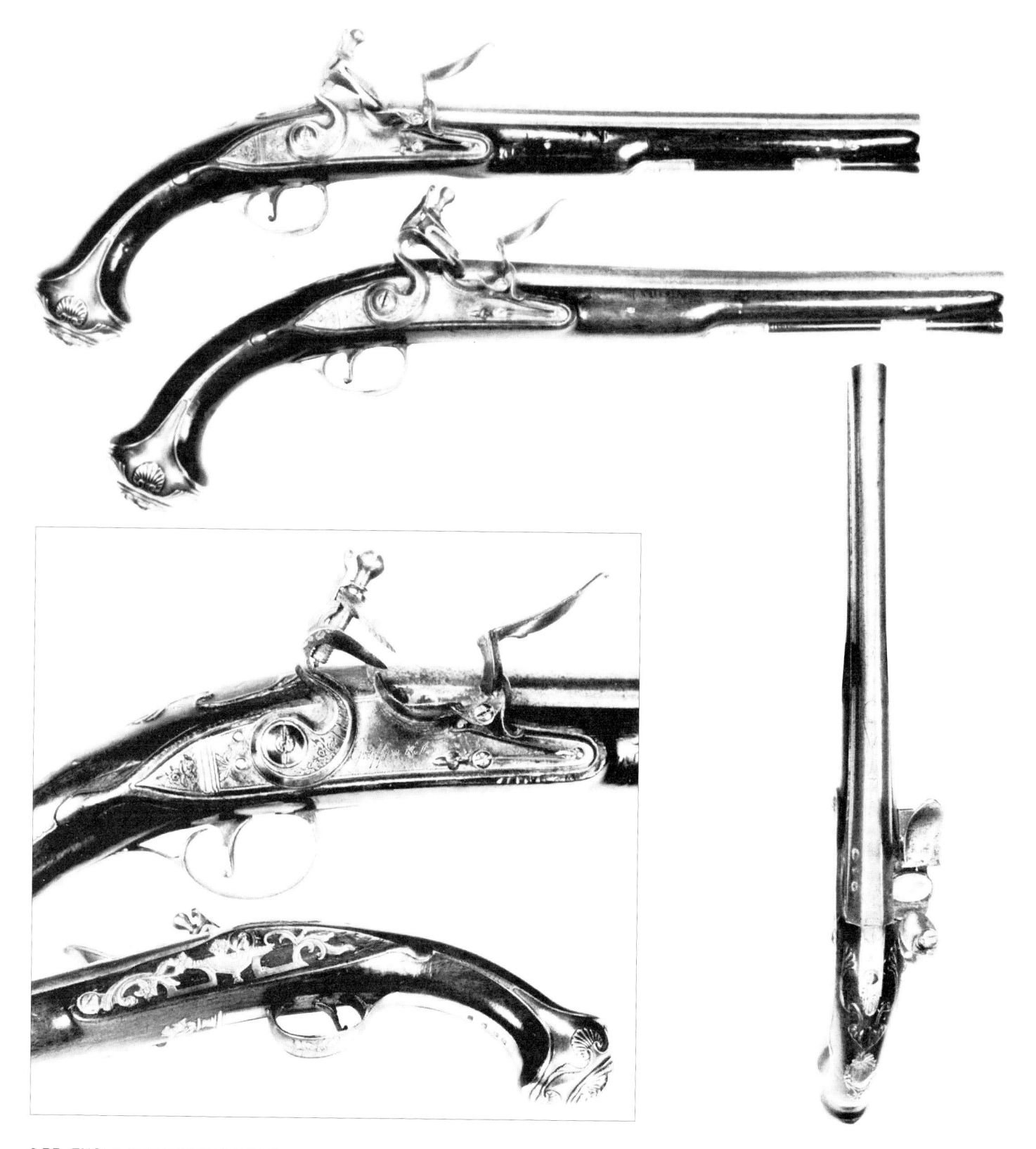

**8.PP  ENGLISH HOLSTER PISTOLS**                                                                                               Circa 1772–1778

This pair of elaborately decorated silver-mounted pistols illustrates the capabilities of England's private makers in this period. They are marked "Griffin & Tow" (the London gunsmiths Joseph Griffin and John Tow). Grotesque masked butt caps include raised scallop shell rococo motifs and extended side straps along the grips. Their trigger guards are headed with an acanthus leaf design, floral engraving is included on the bow, and silver hallmarks are opposite the handles. Foliage and vase-like features compose a delicate open side plate, while floral patterns plus a stippled edging enhance the ornate flat/beveled locks. Incised patterns and both London Gunmakers Company proofs appear on the slightly flared barrels (octagon breech), as well as the numbers 2400 and 2401. Horn tips (hollowed centers) complete the wooden ramrods, each of which is held in two pipes. Elaborate raised carving surrounds the barrel tang, lock and side plate. Such silver-embellished weapons were prized possessions and accompanied many well-to-do officers here in America.

| Length: 17-3/4" | Lock: 5-1/8" X 7/8" | Side Plate: 4-3/4" | Furniture: Silver |
|---|---|---|---|
| Barrel: 11", .63 cal. | Trigger Guard: 6-3/4" | Weight: 1.9 lbs. | |

**James D. Forman Collection**

*Chapter 5: Pistols*   239

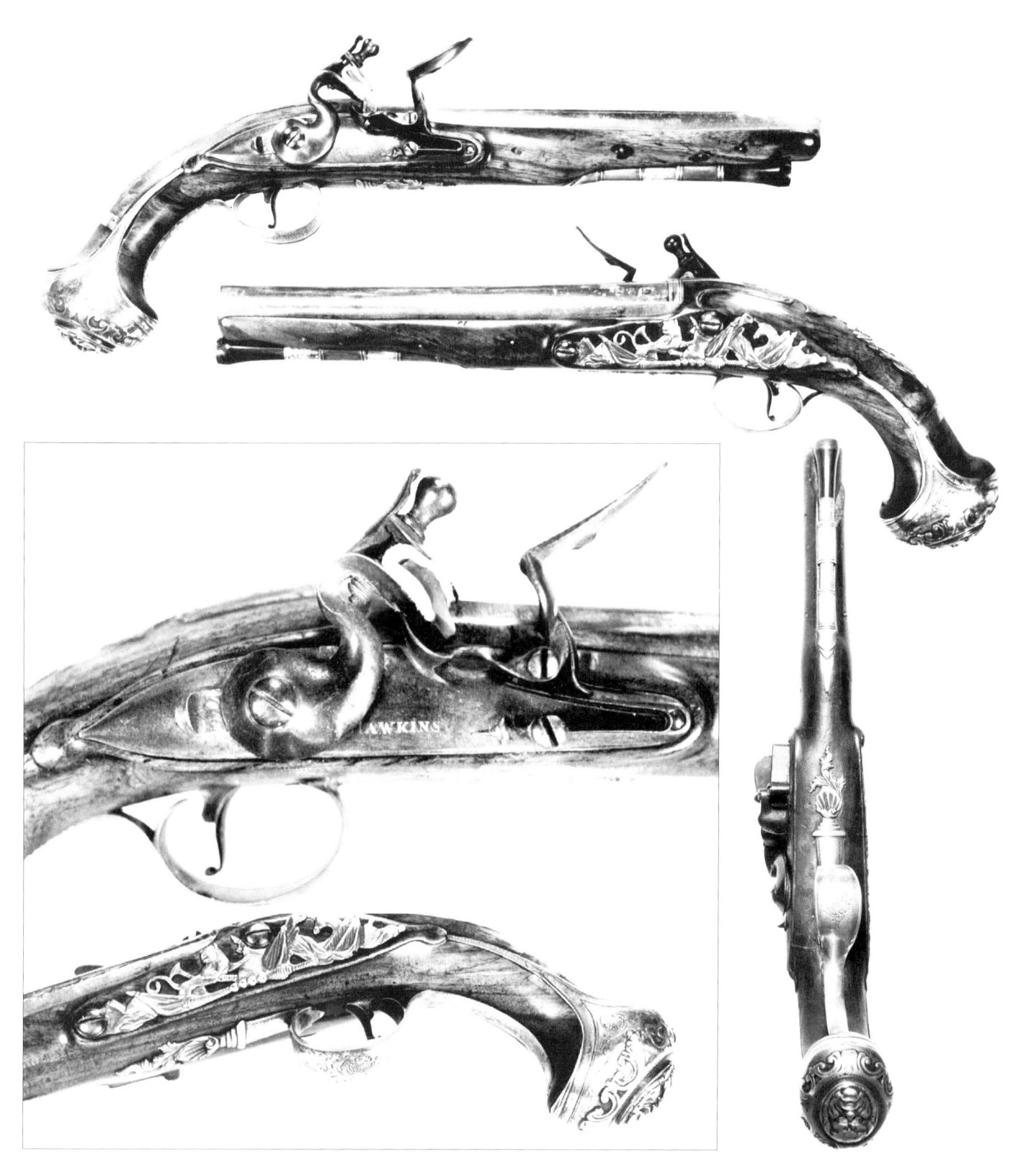

**9.PP  WASHINGTON'S HOLSTER PISTOLS (ENGLISH)**                                                                                                        Circa 1748–1760

Well-to-do American officers also appreciated fine English handguns. This silver-mounted pair is marked by the London maker "HAWKINS" on the lock and "RW" (R. Wilson, barrelmaker) on the breech. The hallmarked dates are 1748–1749. They were given to George Washington by a Virginia neighbor, Thomas Turner, prior to the Revolution. The eight-inch brass barrels have two short flats on the breech plus slightly flared muzzles. The impressive silver furniture includes an elaborate grotesque mask butt cap with long side straps, an open panoply-of-arms side plate featuring the British lion and unicorn in a military motif, as well as an elaborate trigger guard and escutcheon. A silver band spans the upper half of each handle, reading "Gen. Geo. Washington" (later additions). The English walnut stocks add a delicately carved splay behind both barrel tangs and raised borders surrounding the locks and side plates. Sliding safety latches can be seen behind the cocks, while the pans have a high-backed rain gutter at the rear (pierced for drainage). Incised designs appear on the barrels, plus "LONDON" and both Gunmakers Company proofs.

Length: 14"                                    Lock: 4-5/8" X 3/4"                                Furniture: Silver
Barrel: 8", .66 cal.                           Trigger Guard: 6-5/8"

**The West Point Museum Collection**

*Chapter 5: Pistols*

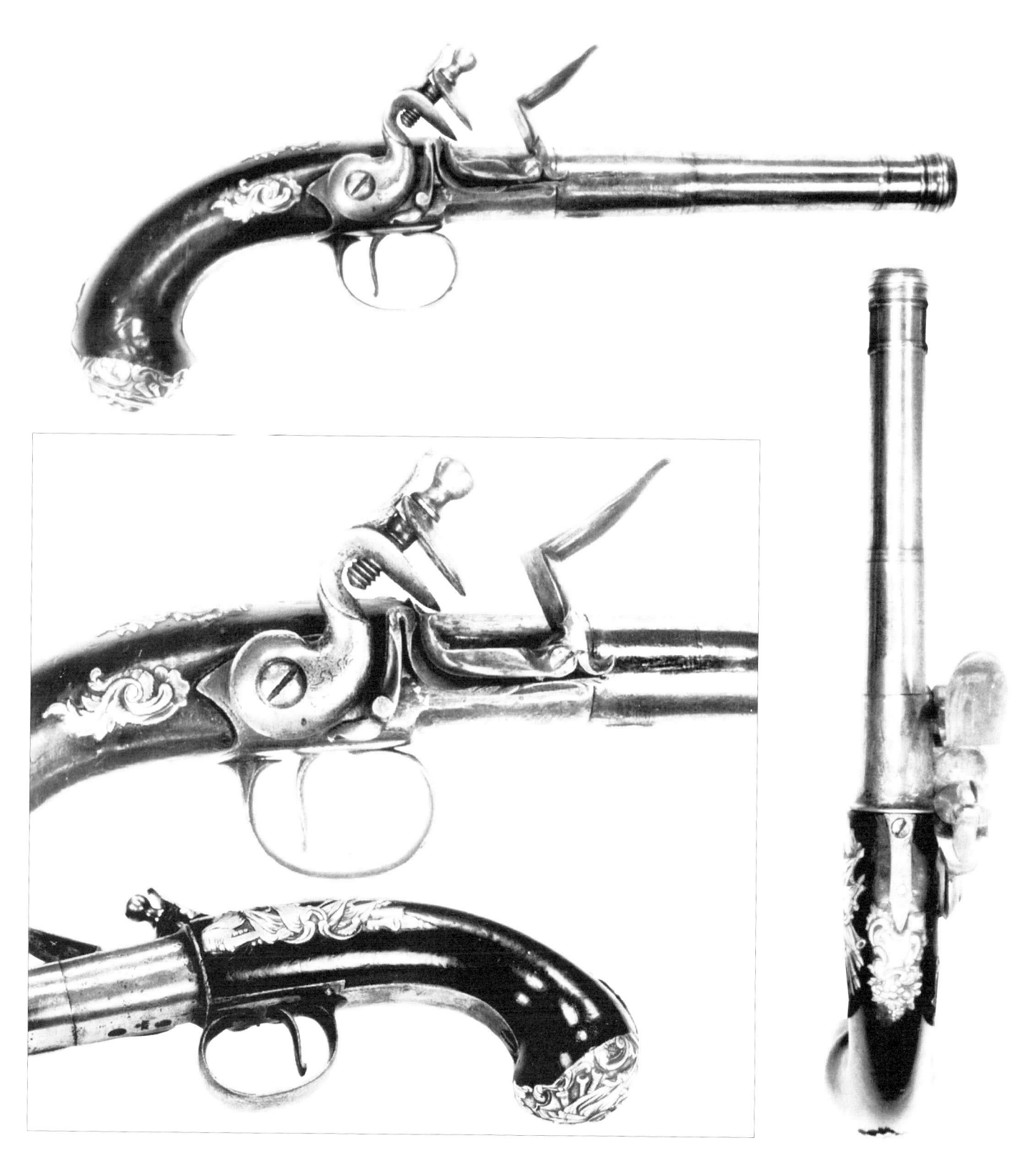

**10.PP ENGLISH SCREW-BARREL PISTOL**  Circa 1730–1750

Known as the cannon barrel, screw barrel, turnoff or Queen Anne pistol (it gained popularity during her reign, 1702–1714), this unique form was probably the best-known civilian handgun of 18th century England. Because loading required unscrewing the barrel, it had too slow a rate of fire for military issue, but it proved ideal for close-range personal protection and could be kept in a coat pocket. Note that the breech chamber and lock plate were formed as an integral part from one forging, while an L-shaped frizzen spring nestles under and behind the bridled flash pan. As an added safety precaution, the trigger guard slides forward to lock the hammer in the safe half-cock position. This round breech (earlier ones were octagonal, circa 1700–1720) is inscribed on the bottom "WILSON LONDON," plus both London Gunmakers Company proofs and his stamp, "R*W" (Richard Wilson). Military panoply designs appear on the silver butt cap and side plate, as well as on its breech and trigger bow. Raised silver foliage inserts provide decorations behind the barrel tang and lock housing.

| | | | |
|---|---|---|---|
| Length: 12" | Lock: 3-1/4" X 7/8" | Side Plate: 2-3/4" | Furniture: Silver/Steel |
| Barrel: 5-1/2", .65 cal. | Trigger Guard: 3-7/8" | Weight: 1.5 lbs. | |

**Author's Collection**

*Chapter 5: Pistols*   241

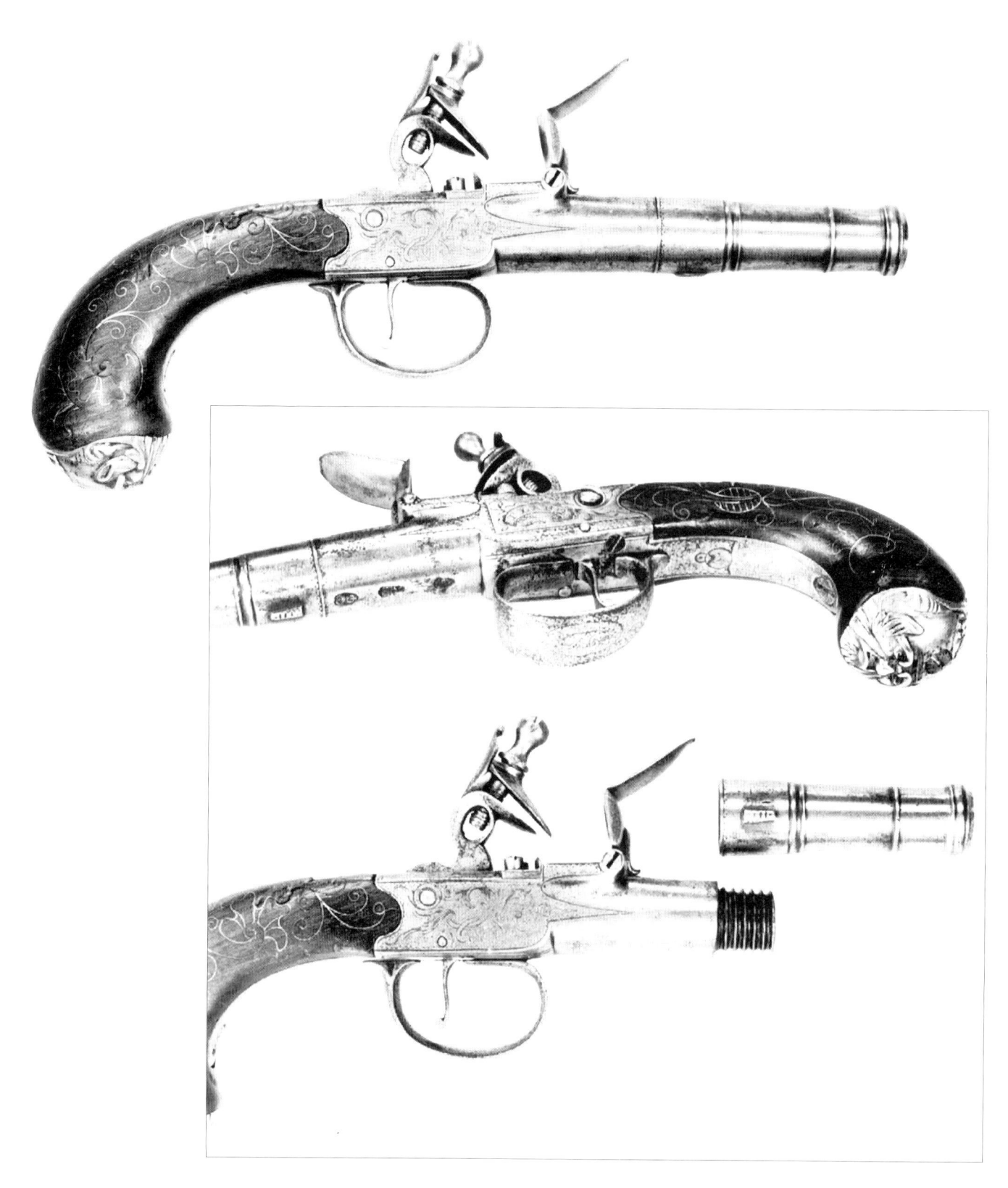

**11.PP ENGLISH SCREW-BARREL PISTOL**  Circa 1765–1780

By mid-century, the cock, frizzen and flashpan were moved from the side to the middle of the chamber block. Although this interfered with sighting, it reduced the chance of being caught in a pocket. In addition the cock and tumbler were now forged as one piece. This slightly later example has evolved from a rounded breech to flat sides and has added a supporting ring to the cock. As shown, the barrel was unscrewed from the breech by means of an open notched wrench that gripped the visible barrel lug or with a key that slid into grooves at the muzzle (see 12.PP). Powder was inserted into the breech's chamber and a slightly oversized ball placed in the recess above it. Reattaching the barrel locked the load in place. This method created a powerful and accurate breech-loading weapon for self protection. Many officers in America's Revolutionary War carried them as personal arms. This pistol is marked "T LANE" (maker), with London Gunmakers Company proofs, plus a "foreigner's" mark (that is, a non-member). Note also the popular silver wire stock inlay. After 1780 most of these handles became squared and omitted a butt cap.

Length: 8"  Lock: 3" X 3/4"  Furniture: Silver
Barrel: 2-1/4", .44 cal.  Trigger Guard: 7-3/8"  Weight: 0.8 lbs.

242     *Chapter 5: Pistols*

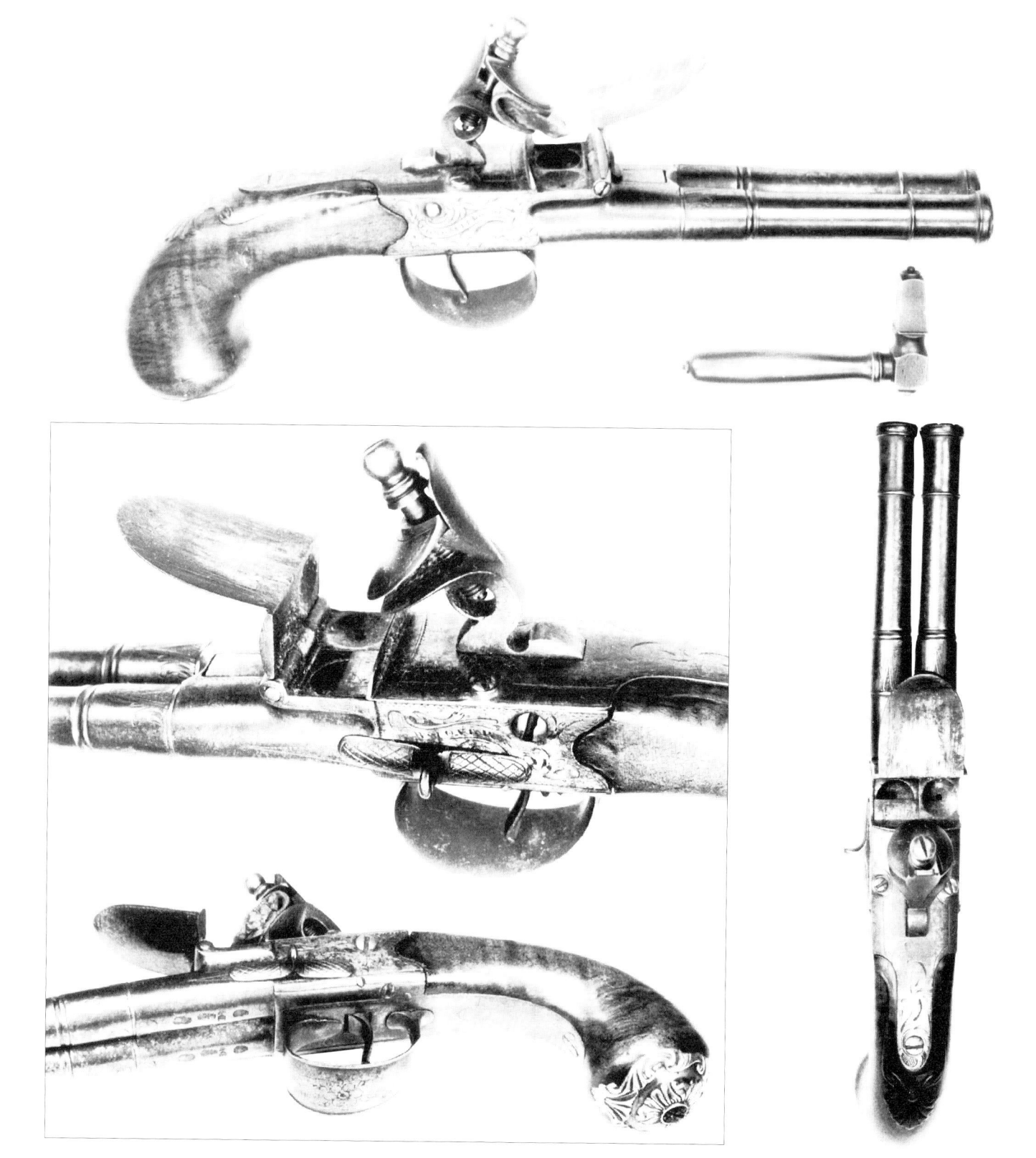

**12.PP  ENGLISH DOUBLE SCREW-BARREL PISTOL**                                                                              Circa 1775–1777

The reliability of these civilian screw-barreled handguns led to different adaptations, including a double-barreled version by the 1770s. As shown in 11.PP, a flat-sided "box lock" now positioned a ring cock in its center. This unique twin barrel arrangement fires by means of a single cock and two flash pans (instead of double locks). To achieve separate barrel firings, the frizzen showers sparks on both pans. For the first shot, ignition occurs in the right barrel, which offers an exposed flash pan, while the second charged pan at the left is covered by a sliding shutter. To fire the second barrel, the lock's side lever retracts the pan cover exposing its priming powder to a second flint ignition. Both of these "cannon" barrels were unscrewed from the breech for loading by a key (reproduction shown) that fitted into eight grooves cut 1/2 inch into each muzzle. Note that the maple handle includes raised fan carving below the lock tang and a cast silver butt cap. The box lock, in turn, is marked "W JOVER / LONGACRE LONDON" (the maker); its chamber bears Gunmakers Company proofs plus a foreigner's mark.

| | | |
|---|---|---|
| Length: 11" | Lock: 1-7/8" X 3/4" | Furniture: Steel/Silver |
| Barrel: 3-3/4", .45 cal. | Trigger Guard: 4-1/4" | Weight: 1.4 lbs. |

**Kenneth Peterson Collection**

*Chapter 5: Pistols*  243

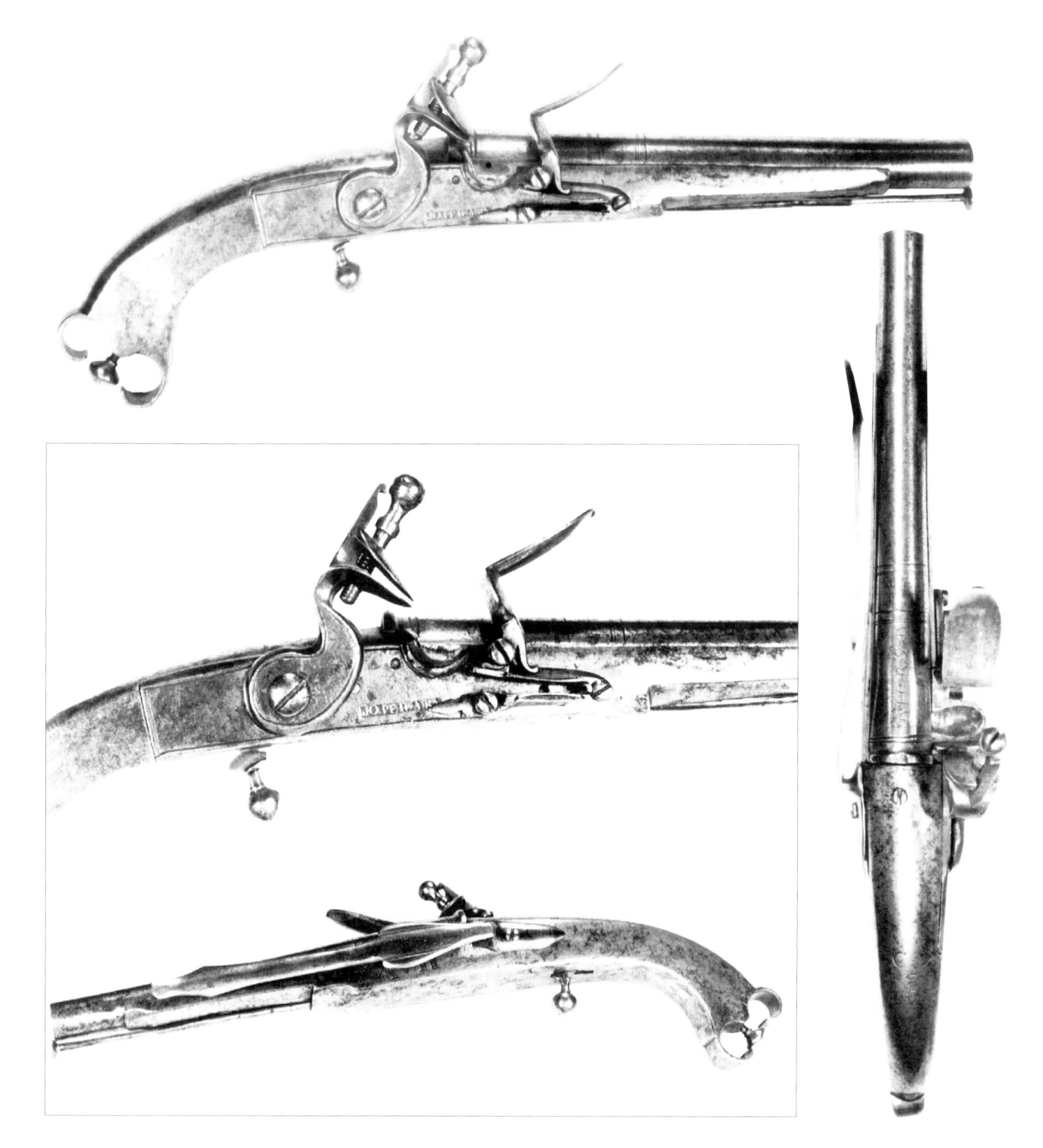

**13.PP  SCOTTISH REGIMENTAL PISTOL**  Circa 1758–1763

Scottish regiment enlisted men were the only soldiers in the British army to be issued pistols during the 18th century. These unique arms were entirely of metal and appeared as two basic patterns used in North America. The more popular is shown above (the other is 15.PP). Most of this form were manufactured by Issac Bissell of Birmingham, but the example here was made in Scotland, contracted directly by Lord John Murray (colonel) for the Royal Highland Regiment ("Black Watch") in 1758 (that is, not issued from the Tower). Note the distinctive all-steel body with its traditional features: a ram's horn (or scroll) butt that includes a center removable touch-hole pick (oval head matches the trigger); absence of a trigger guard; a square-ended flat lock (no outer bridle), and a slightly flared round barrel with a raised breech ring. The long belt hook on the inboard side slipped over a strap hanging under the left arm. Its lock is stamped "JO. PETCAIRN" (John Pitcairn, Scottish maker). The barrel markings are "RHR 2n B" (second battalion raised in 1758, disbanded 1763). "C5 / N 11" appears on the grip's upper face and "XXVII" under the belt hook.

| | | |
|---|---|---|
| Length: 12-3/4" | Lock: 4-7/8" X 7/8" | Furniture: Steel |
| Barrel: 7-1/4", .56 cal. | Belt Hook: 7-1/8" | Weight: 1.7 lbs. |

**Don Troiani Collection**

*Chapter 5: Pistols*

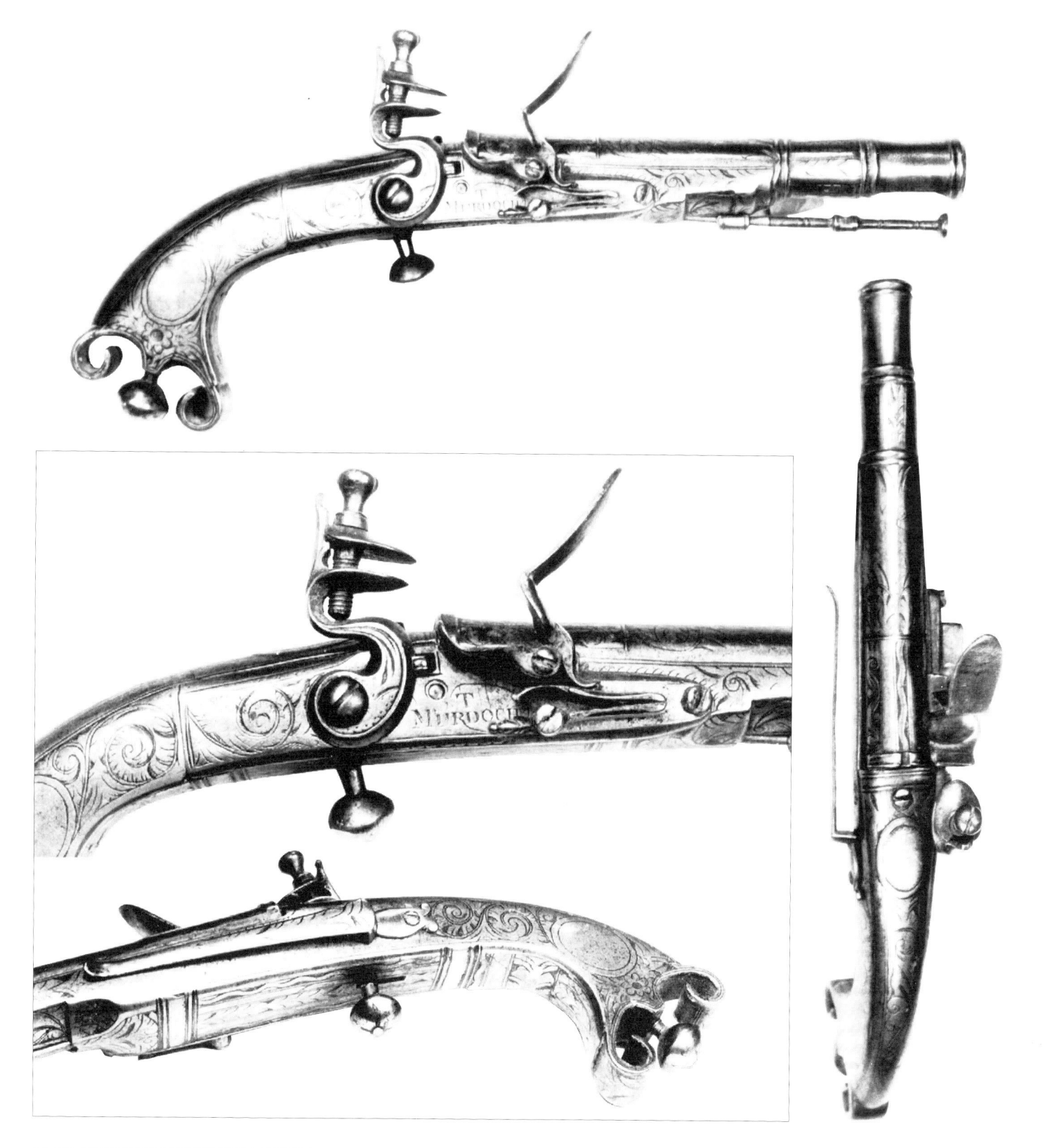

**14.PP SCOTTISH REGIMENTAL PISTOL**　　　　　　　　　　　　　　　　　　　　　　　　　　　　　　　　　　　　　　　　　　　　　　　　　　　　　　　　　　　Circa 1775

The traditional Scottish pattern illustrated in the preceding example continues here but with embellishments of the type found on pistols carried by noncoms and junior officers. The round stepped barrel has the raised breech band plus three forward double rings, including one at the flared muzzle. Its steel body ends in the established ram's horn butt with a center knob for the touch-hole pick (unscrews) and a lateral sear in the lock that projects out to secure the hammer at half-cock (its tumbler omits a second notch). Incised floral engravings cover all areas of the pistol and belt hook, with the popular oval form on each side of the handle. Its square-ended flat lock plate is engraved "T / MURDOCH" (maker in Doune), while the oval escutcheon reads "Sergeant / LT / 42 Regt." (Royal Highland Regiment, the Black Watch). Note also the Scottish preference for a button-head turned ramrod, the matching of both the lobed trigger tip and touch-hole pick handle, plus absence of a trigger guard.

Length: 10-1/2"  
Barrel: 5-3/4", .59 cal.  
Lock: 4-1/8" X 3/4"  
Weight: 0.8 lbs.  
Furniture: Steel

**James D. Forman Collection**

*Chapter 5: Pistols* **245**

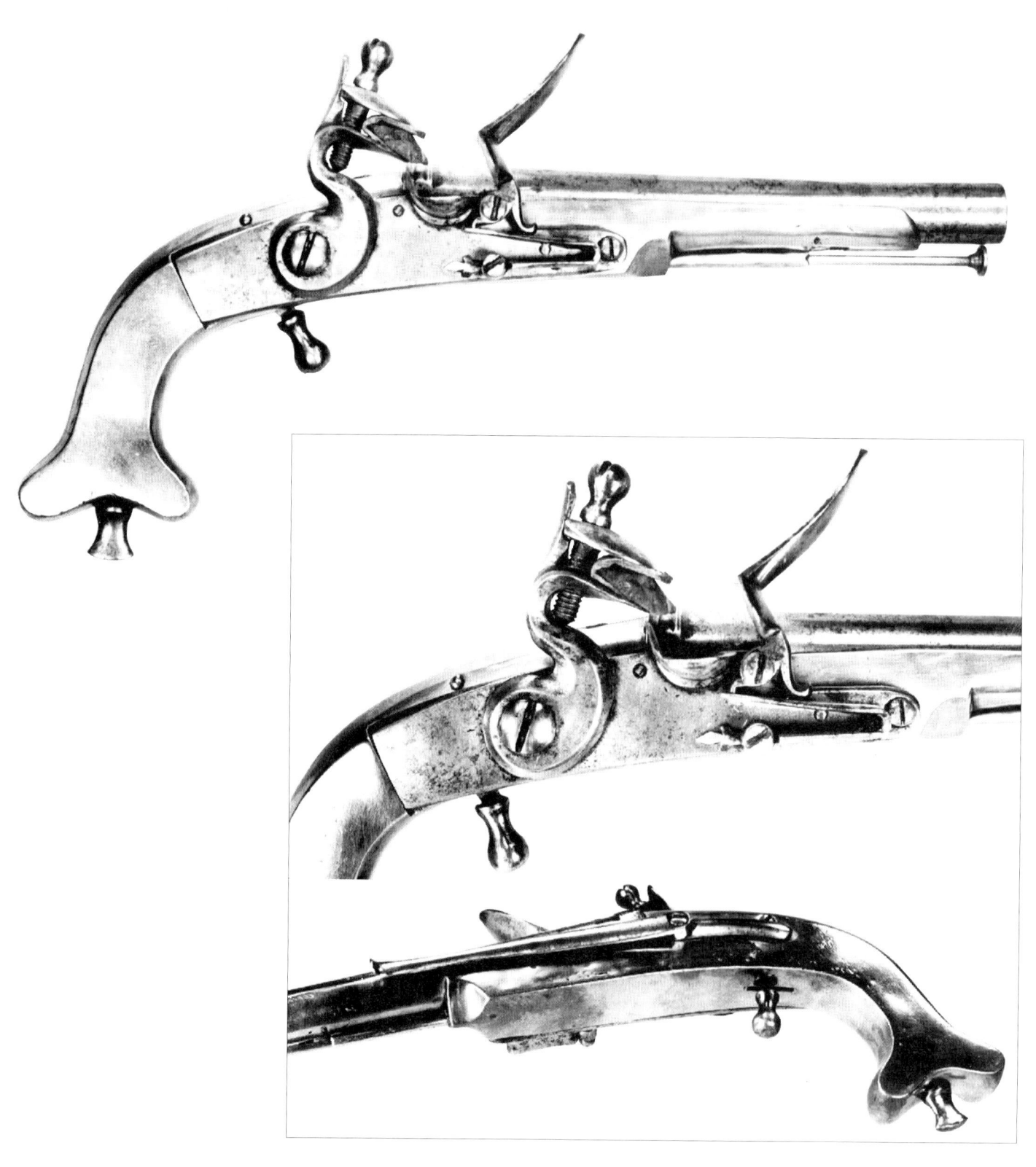

**15.PP SCOTTISH REGIMENTAL PISTOL**  Circa 1760–1776

The second basic pattern of pistols issued to Highland Regiments is shown here. It resembles the other form (see 13.PP) but is stocked in brass-like gun metal with a more abrupt handle profile that now terminates in a kidney-shaped butt. Not all of this design included a removable touch-hole pick as seen above. The plain configuration retains the traditional flat square-ended lock that includes a lateral sear to hold the hammer at half-cock (that is, no second notch on the inside tumbler) and lacks an exterior bridle. The usual side plate, button-head rammer, omitted trigger guard and round barrel (baluster breech ring) complete this utilitarian pattern. Highland troops in America were officially ordered to discard their broadswords and pistols in 1776, yet subsequent reports verify later use in battle by these forces, as well as by Scottish settlers. Most of this model were manufactured by John Waters of Birmingham and London. London Gunmakers Company proofs appear on the barrel. The colonel of a Scottish regiment would normally purchase such pistols for his men with a grant from the Crown.

Length: 11-5/8"  
Barrel: 6-7/8", .57 cal.  
Furniture: Gun Metal  
Weight: 1.6 lbs.

*Chapter 5: Pistols*

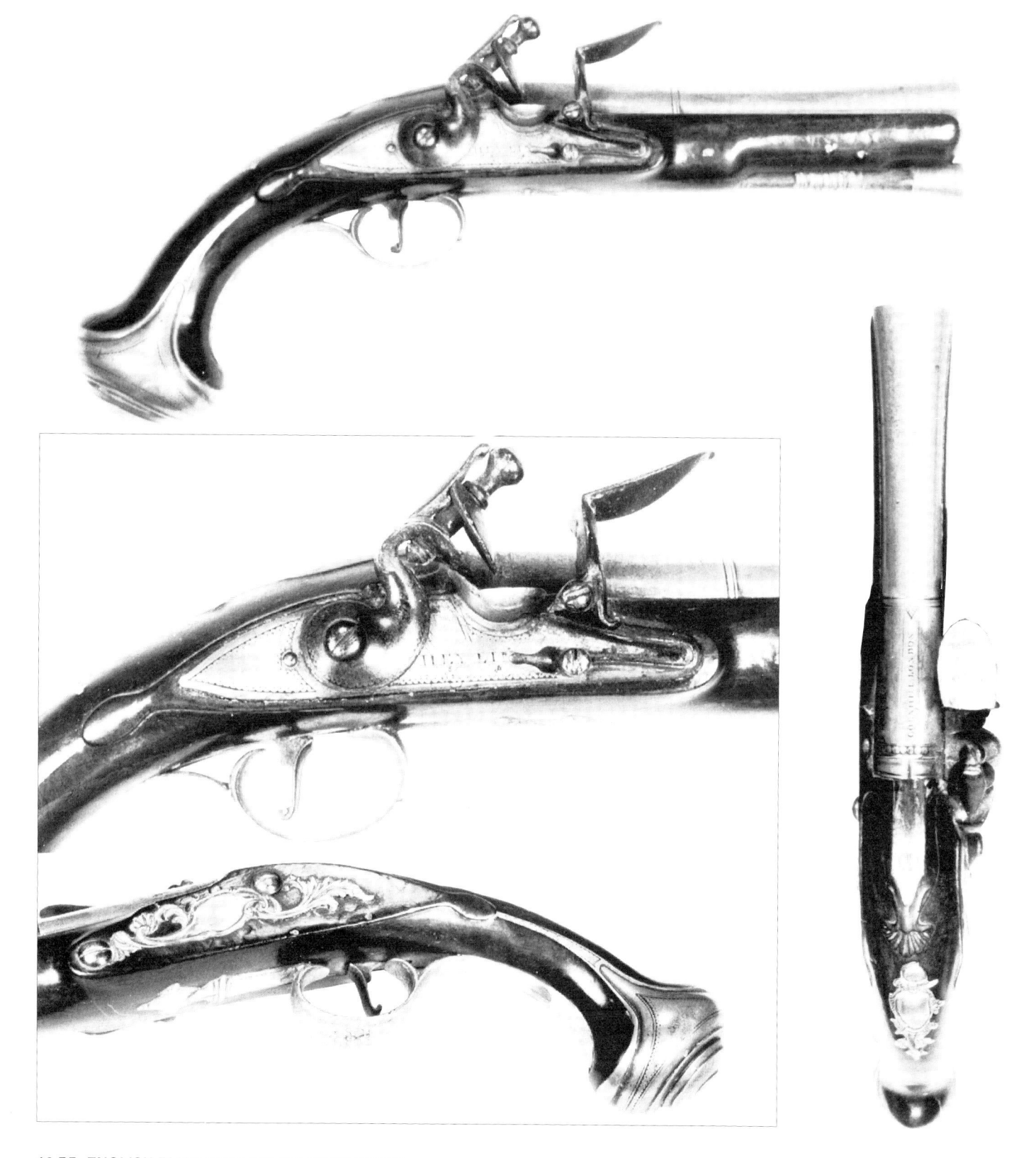

### 16.PP  ENGLISH BLUNDERBUSS HOLSTER PISTOL

Circa 1765

The constant need for personal protection on the roads or in the cities of England led to a revival of the intimidating wide-mouthed blunderbuss pistols at mid-century. This is a typical pattern by Joseph Heylin of Cornhill, London, who popularized the style during the 1760s and 1770s. Its trumpet-nosed barrel and furniture are brass (including the lock plate). In addition, a substantial butt cap bears a conservative stippled design and long side straps, while the rococo side plate has a center panel and scrolled floral branches. A less-elaborate trigger guard ends in a modest three-point terminal, as the bow displays a flower design and rear post spur. Raised carving on the walnut stock borders the lock plus side plate and adds a splay under the barrel tang above an elaborate neoclassical escutcheon. A single ribbed thimble supports the wooden ramrod (brass tip with a hollow center). Marks: "HEYLIN" on the brass lock plate; "crown / IH," "CORNHILL LONDON," and Gunmakers Company proofs on the barrel.

| | | |
|---|---|---|
| Length: 12-1/4" | Lock: 4-1/4" X 3/4" | Furniture: Brass |
| Barrel: 6-1/8", .88 cal. | Trigger Guard: 6-3/8" | Weight: 1.4 lbs. |

**James D. Forman Collection**

*Chapter 5: Pistols*   247

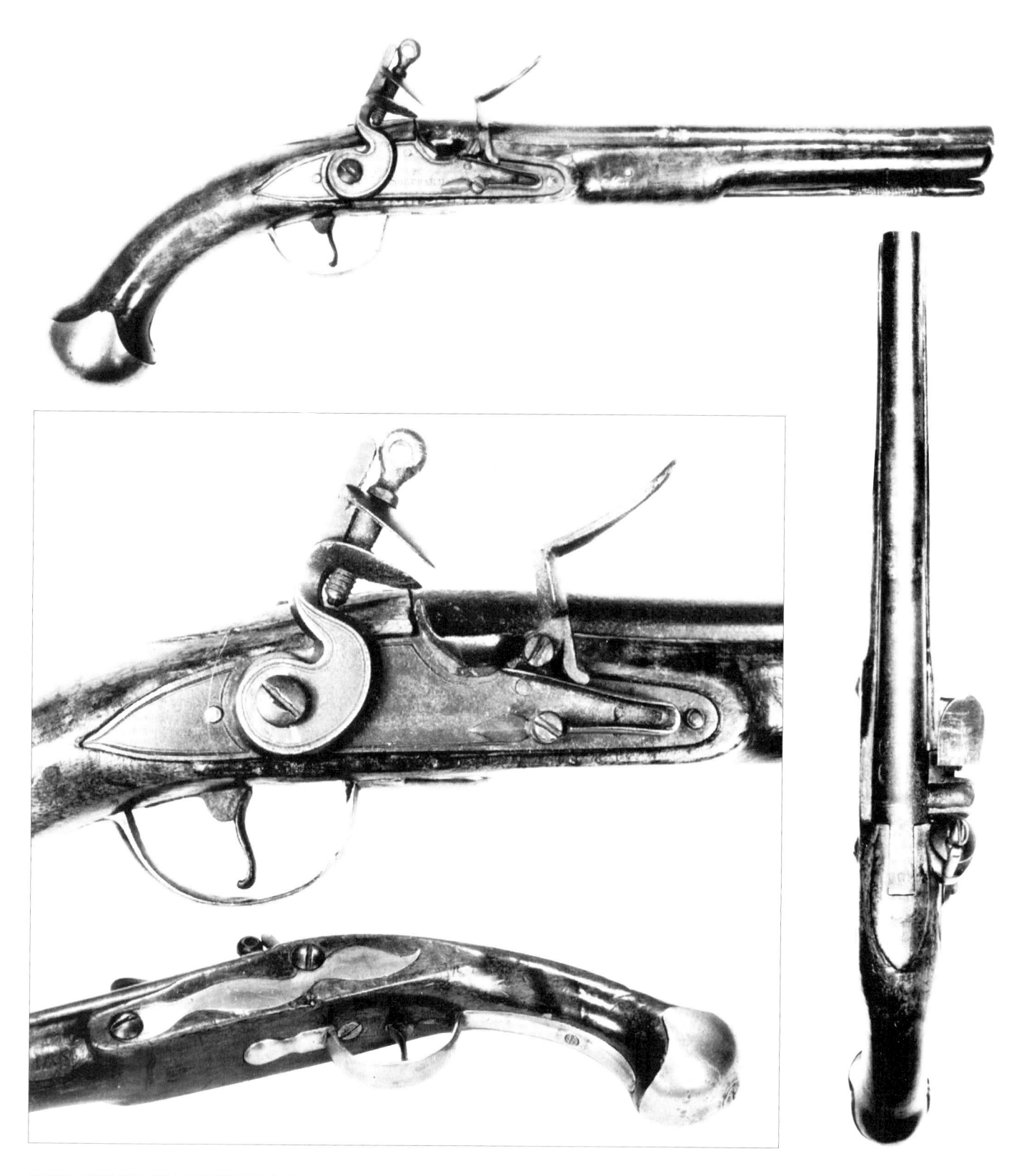

**17.PP  ENGLISH SEA SERVICE PISTOL**　　　　　　　　　　　　　　　　　　　　　　　　　　　　　　　　　　　　　　　　　　　　　　　　　　　　　Circa 1730–1740

A basic sea service pattern was established in 1718 with a flat lock, ringed cock and a 12" barrel (see 18.PP). As in this example, its basic features were also adopted for many of the private handguns produced for commercial vessels. Note, for instance, the two-screw flat lock with a faceted pan that omits both bridles, a single ribbed thimble supporting a crude wooden ramrod, the barrel tang held by a screw from below (no trigger plate), and the brass trigger guard that still omits a spur on the bow's rear post. Further emerging sea service characteristics include: a plain butt cap without side straps, the trigger guard's rounded front terminal, a flat lock plate, omission of an escutcheon, plus a simple beaver-tail carving around the barrel tang. This round pinned barrel (flared muzzle) measures 10-1/2 inches (originally .56 caliber) and shows London Gunmakers Company proofs. Its lock plate bears double-incised border lines plus the gunsmith's name, "SHEPPARD."

| Length: 17-1/2" | Lock: 5-1/2" X 1" | Side Plate: 4-7/8" | Furniture: Brass |
|---|---|---|---|
| Barrel: 10-1/2", .58 cal. | Trigger Guard: 6-3/8" | Weight: 2.2 lbs. | |

**Author's Collection**

248　　*Chapter 5: Pistols*

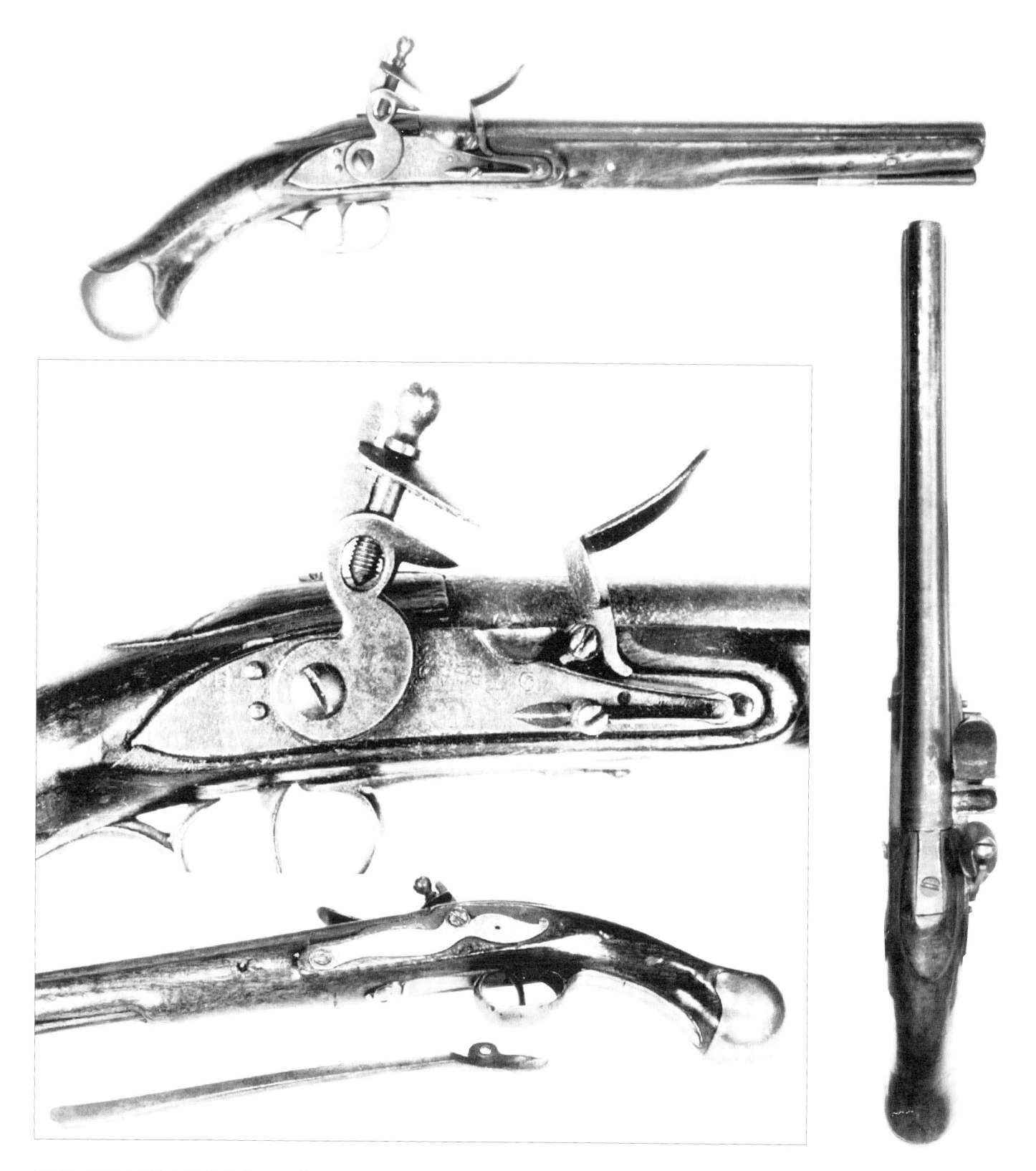

**18.PP ENGLISH SEA SERVICE PISTOL PATTERN 1756/1777**                                         Circa 1777
This basic form was adopted by the British Navy as its Pattern 1756. The example shown is Pattern 1756/1777, having an improved lock added at the later date (that is, two screw ends visible behind the cock and no date below "TOWER" on the tail), plus a new rounded pan. The basic characteristics however remain the same as the original 1718 version of this design: a 12" pinned barrel (.56 caliber); a flat lock with a ring cock; a narrow pan (no fence); the absence of both bridles; a single cast rammer pipe (wooden rod); the land service-type hazelnut trigger guard that adds a rear spur in the bow; a walnut stock providing beaver-tail carving at the barrel tang; a simple butt cap; and no nose band. A hole visible in the typical flat side plate tail anchored a stud on the belt hook's base—held, in turn, by a lengthened rear side plate screw (the hook is shown separately here). A top screw secures the barrel tang; there is no trigger plate. Tower proofs are struck into the breech, while both "TOWER" and "crown / GR / broad arrow" are on the lock. These plain but sturdy pistols were often thrown or used as clubs after firing during close deck action.

Length: 19-1/4"       Lock: 5-3/8" X 1"       Side Plate: 5"       Furniture: Brass
Barrel: 12", .56 cal.       Trigger Guard: 7-1/2"       Weight: 2.7 lbs.

**Author's Collection**

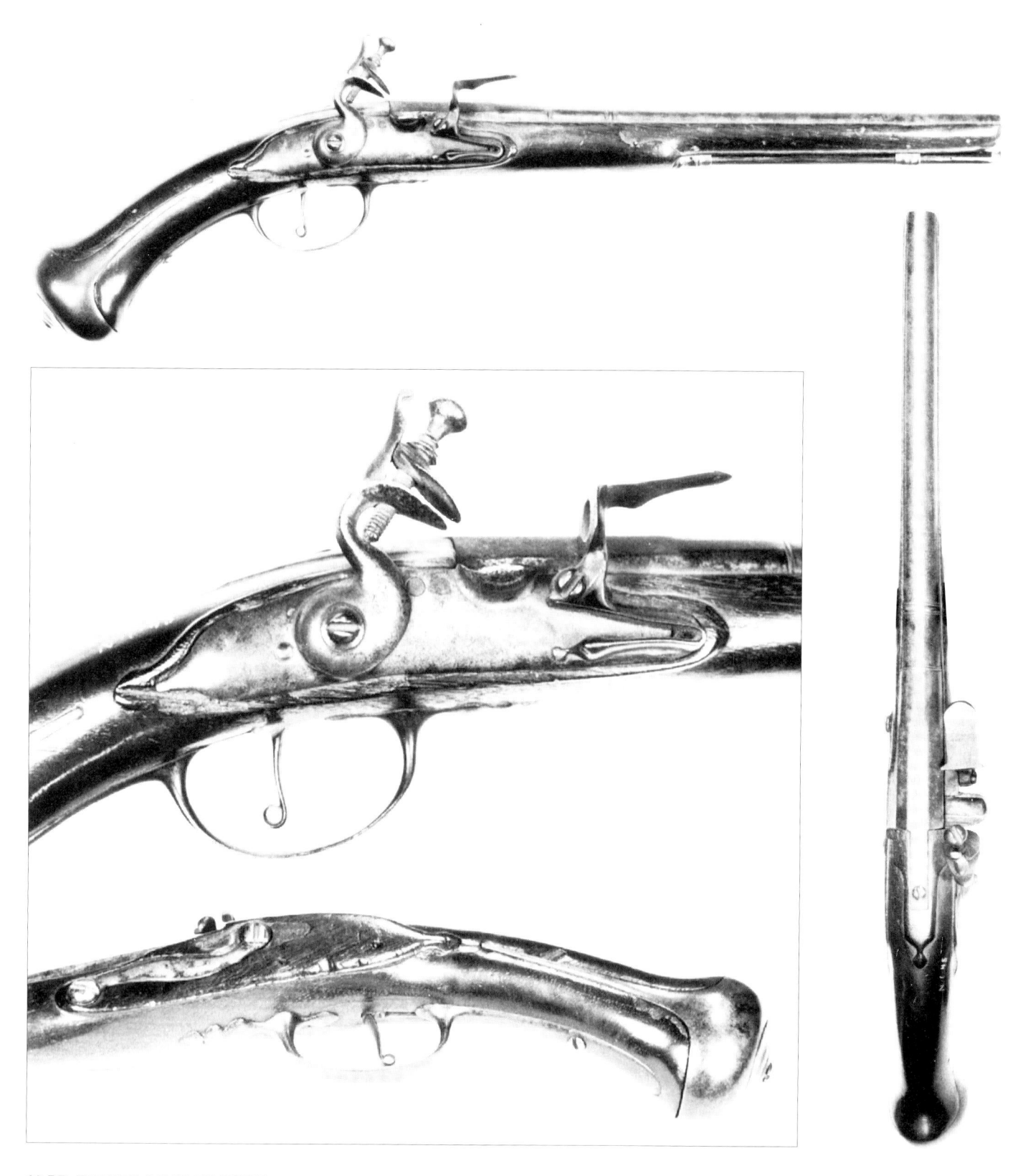

**19.PP FRENCH CAVALRY PISTOL**             **Circa 1690–1715**

The long-barreled profile and extended grip of this French pistol pattern associate it with their cavalry of this period. Yet a number of features are also found on early longarms made at Tulle for Department of Marine use in French Canada (see 33.MM). These features include: raised carving around the lock, side plate, and barrel tang; a pointed baluster-like front end on its trigger guard; a pinned round barrel having an octagonal breech (two inches), a section of 16 flats (one inch), and a further ring (one inch); a convex S-form side plate; and a round lock lacking an outside bridle. Two short ribbed thimbles, in turn, hold a plain wooden rammer (iron disk tip). The flattened iron butt cap, with thin side straps reaching almost to the lock, is typical of other early century French handguns. An interesting raised ridge is carved into the stock along the ramrod channel and rises behind the tail pipe. There are no visible marks. Similar pistols with cut-down barrels have been found in North America, indicating use of this form also in the civilian trade.

| | | | |
|---|---|---|---|
| Length: 18-1/2" | Lock: 4-3/4" X 7/8" | Side Plate: 2-3/4" | Furniture: Iron |
| Barrel: 11-1/2", .51 cal. | Trigger Guard: 6-1/2" | Weight: 1.6 lbs. | |

**Tom Wnuck Collection**

*Chapter 5: Pistols*

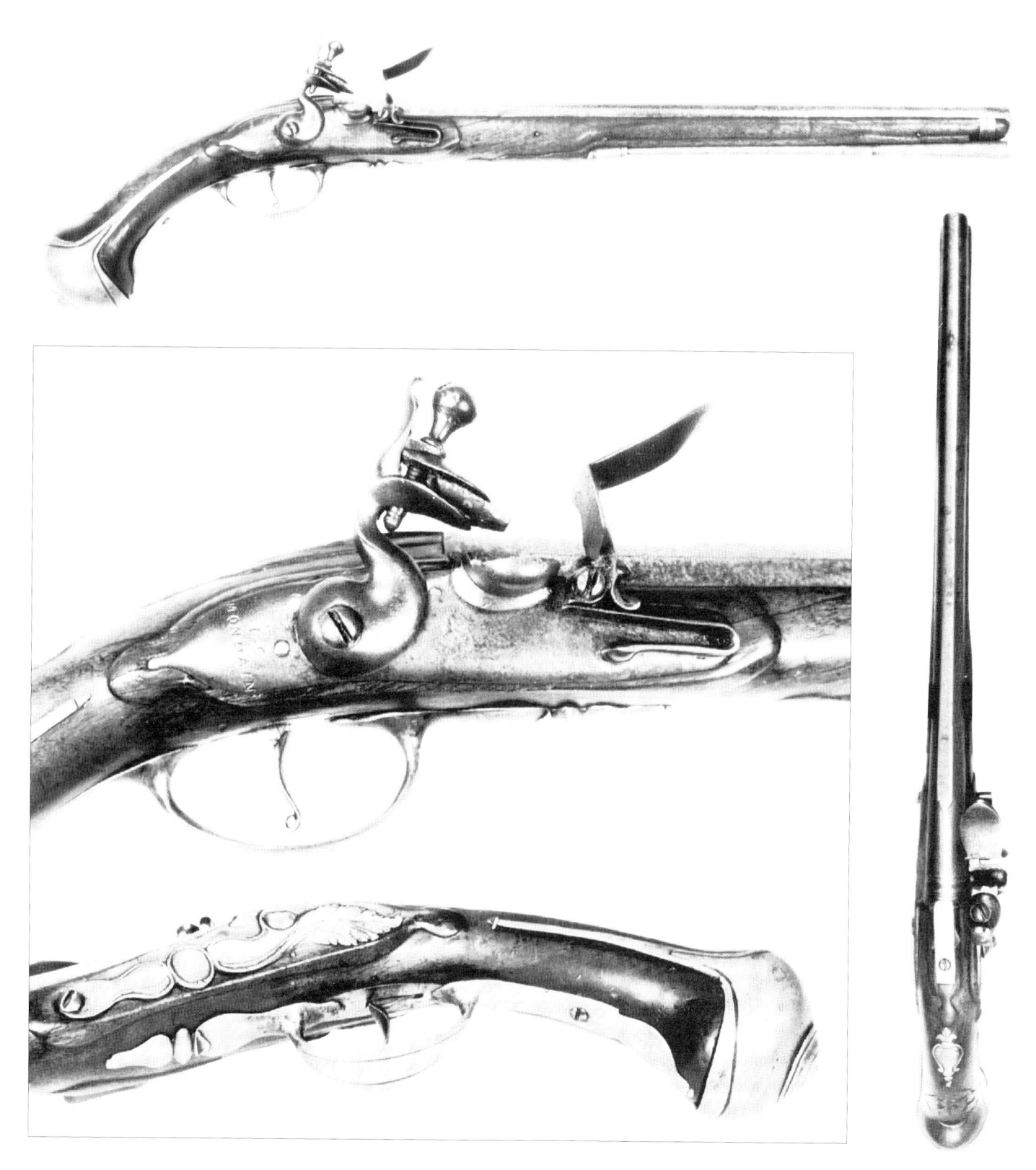

**20.PP FRENCH CAVALRY PISTOL**　　　　　　　　　　　　　　　　　　　　　　　　　　　　　　　　　　　　　　　　　　　　　　　　　　　　　　　　　　　　　　　　　　　　　Circa 1715–1730

This long-barreled (16-1/2", .55 caliber) horseman's pistol illustrates the transition period from the century's early patterns (19.PP) to France's first standard Model 1733 (21.PP). Notice that it continues raised carving around the lock, side plate and barrel tang; the rounded lock excludes an outside bridle; and two plain thimbles service a wooden rammer. Yet Low Country influence is also apparent in the bulbous-tipped trigger guard with incised lines in its bow, a large brass butt cap that extends long side straps, and a heavy central European-type side plate. An interesting barrel form has a baluster band and flat sides at the breech, plus a top panel beginning 2-1/2 inches forward and reaching to the muzzle. The stylized escutcheon, in turn, is topped by an acanthus leaf finial. A narrow nose band secures the forend tip, while a raised stock ridge parallels the ramrod channel before proliferating below the tail pipe. "I+C / MONMAIN" is inscribed on the lock's tail.

Length: 24"  
Barrel: 16-1/2", .55 cal.  
Lock: 5-1/4" X 1"  
Trigger Guard: 8-1/2"  
Side Plate: 4-5/8"  
Weight: 2.8 lbs.  
Furniture: Brass

**West Point Museum Collection**

*Chapter 5: Pistols*　251

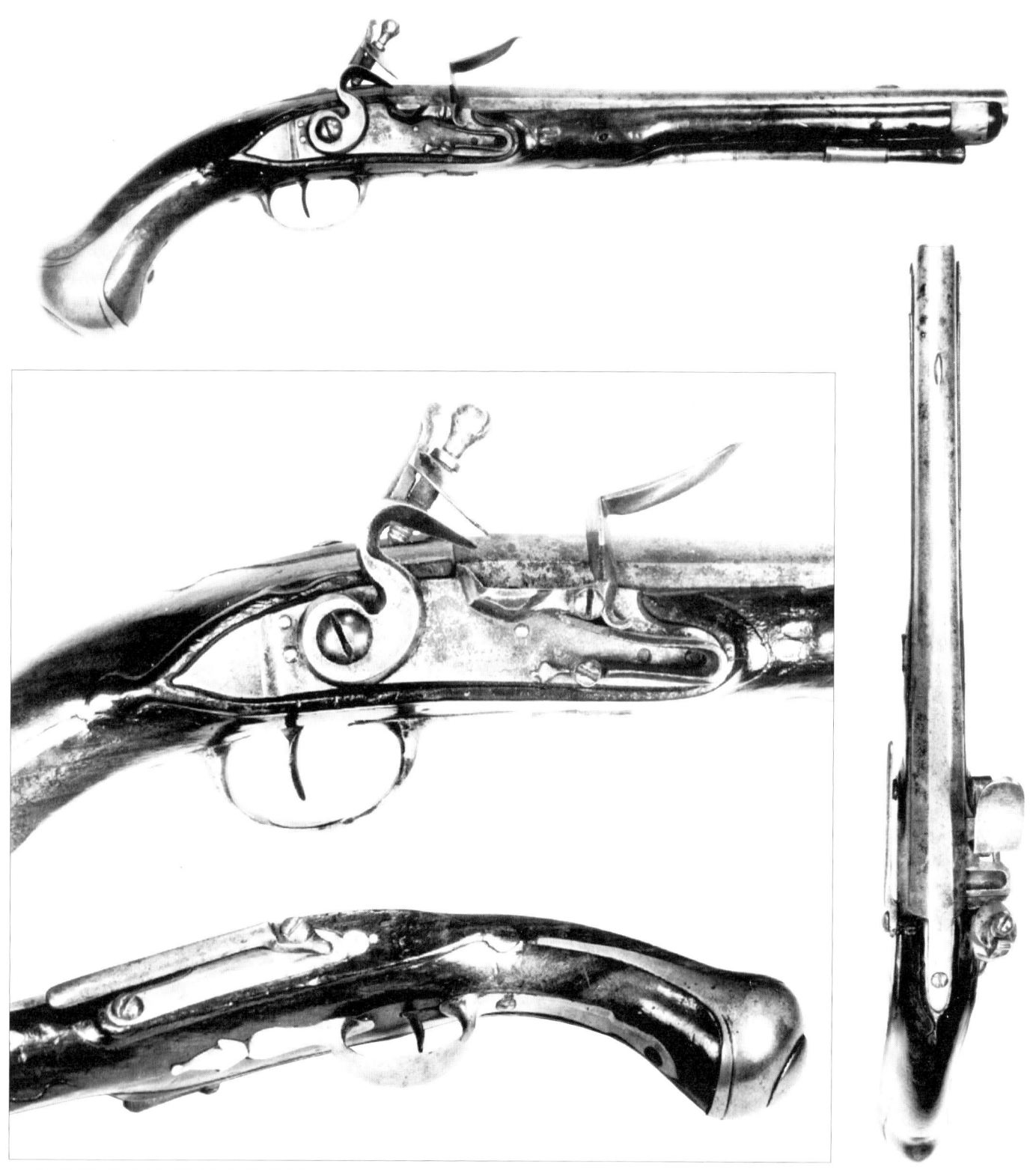

**21.PP FRENCH CAVALRY PISTOL MODEL 1733**　　　　　　　　　　　　　　　　　　　　　　　　　　　　　　　　　　　　　　　　　　　　Circa 1733

Following introduction of a standard army musket in 1717, this first official cavalry/dragoon pistol pattern appeared as the Model 1733 and continued as such until superseded in 1763. Its flat/beveled lock, showing a groove across the tail and an outside bridle on the faceted pan, is a reduced version of the then-standard army musket (Model 1728, 39.MM). However a distinctive solid triangular side plate and three-pointed trigger guard terminal are new forms that were adopted in France's revised cavalry carbine (130.MM) and dragoon musket (128.MM), both authorized at the same time (also as Models 1733). A short four-inch belt hook secured to the side plate's rear screw was usually attached for dragoons and naval use. Its 12-1/4" (.67 caliber) barrel is octagonal for 4-1/2 inches and supports an elliptical front sight. Teardrop raised carving surrounds the side plate, lock and barrel tang, while the modified brass butt cap has a low and plain screw cover. The walnut stock, in turn, supports two rammer thimbles (wooden rod) and a flat nose band. Notice also the raised ridge bordering the rammer channel that continues below the entry pipe. "GIRARD" appears on the lock (gunsmith, St. Etienne).

| Length: 19-5/8" | Lock: 5-1/4" X 1" | Side Plate: 3-7/8" | Furniture: Brass |
|---|---|---|---|
| Barrel: 12-1/4", .67 cal. | Trigger Guard: 7-3/4" | Weight: 2.7 lbs. | |

**Robert Nittolo Collection**

252　　*Chapter 5: Pistols*

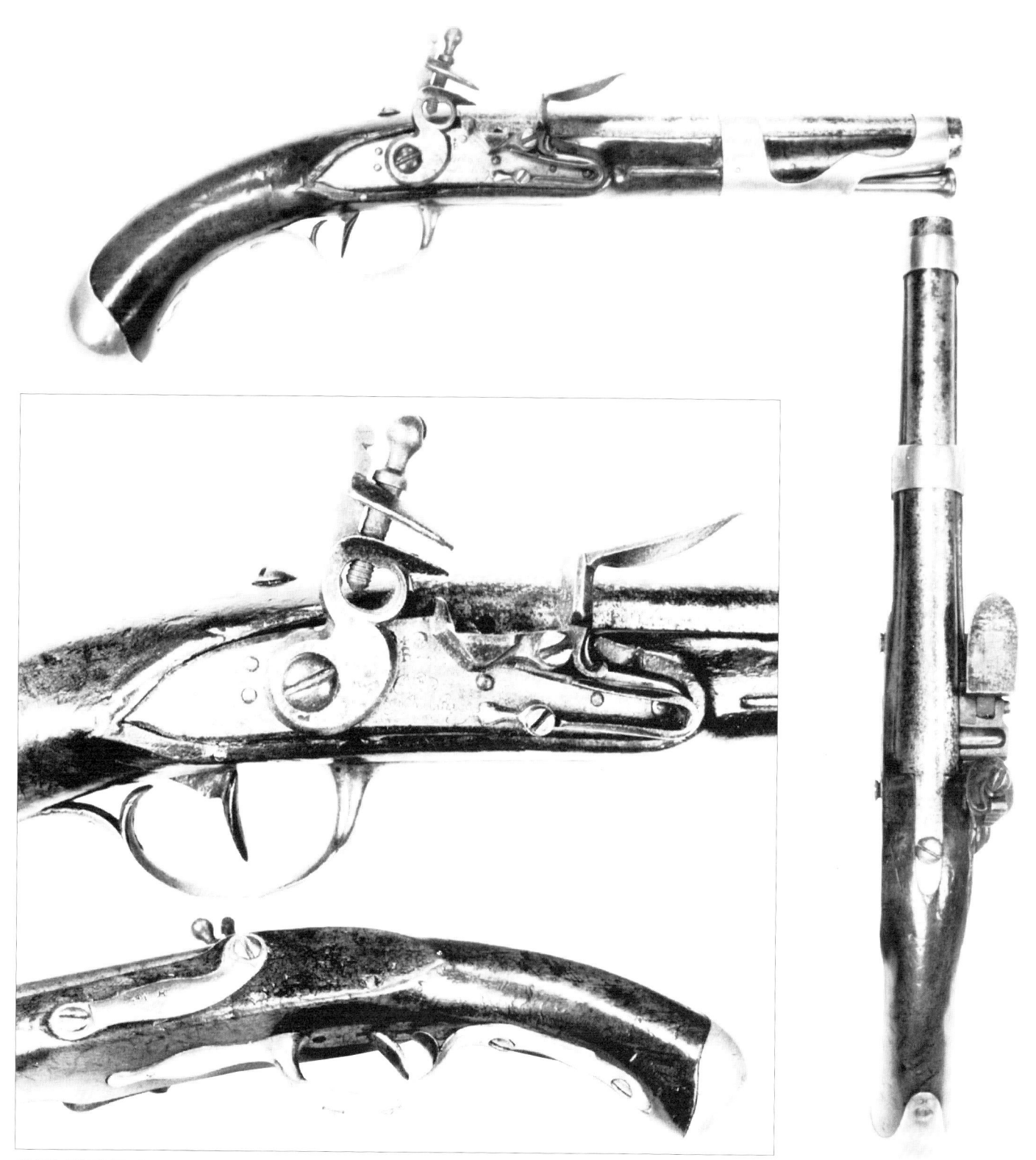

### 22.PP  FRENCH CAVALRY PISTOL MODEL 1763/1766
**Circa 1766**

As part of the restructuring of France's armed forces after the French and Indian War, significantly different longarm and pistol patterns were introduced in 1763—both mounting a new flat/beveled lock with a ring cock, faceted pan and exterior bridle. The original Model 1763 pistol introduced a 12" barrel, two barrel bands and a birds-head butt cap shape. Being overly long and clumsy, that first version promptly had its barrel cut to nine inches and adopted a single double strap band to create the Model 1766 illustrated here. It was probably the most common style of handgun supplied to the American rebels by France. The majority had iron furniture, although brass-mounted examples, as in this case, were produced for some cavalry, special units and the navy. Notice the unique long band (with its rear spring) securing the nine-inch round barrel (.67 caliber), the slenderized walnut stock profile, convex S-form side plate, birds-head butt cap, steel button rammer and rounded trigger guard that includes the military front tip as well as a spur at the bow's rear post. Its markings read "M de Maubeuge" (the manufactory) and "fleur-de-lis / B" on the lock, "H / 14" in the trigger bow; plus "H / I.P" at the side plate.

Length: 16-3/8"  
Barrel: 9", .70 cal.  
Lock: 5" X 1"  
Trigger Guard: 7-3/4"  
Side Plate: 3"  
Weight: 2.7 lbs.  
Furniture: Brass

**Author's Collection**

*Chapter 5: Pistols*

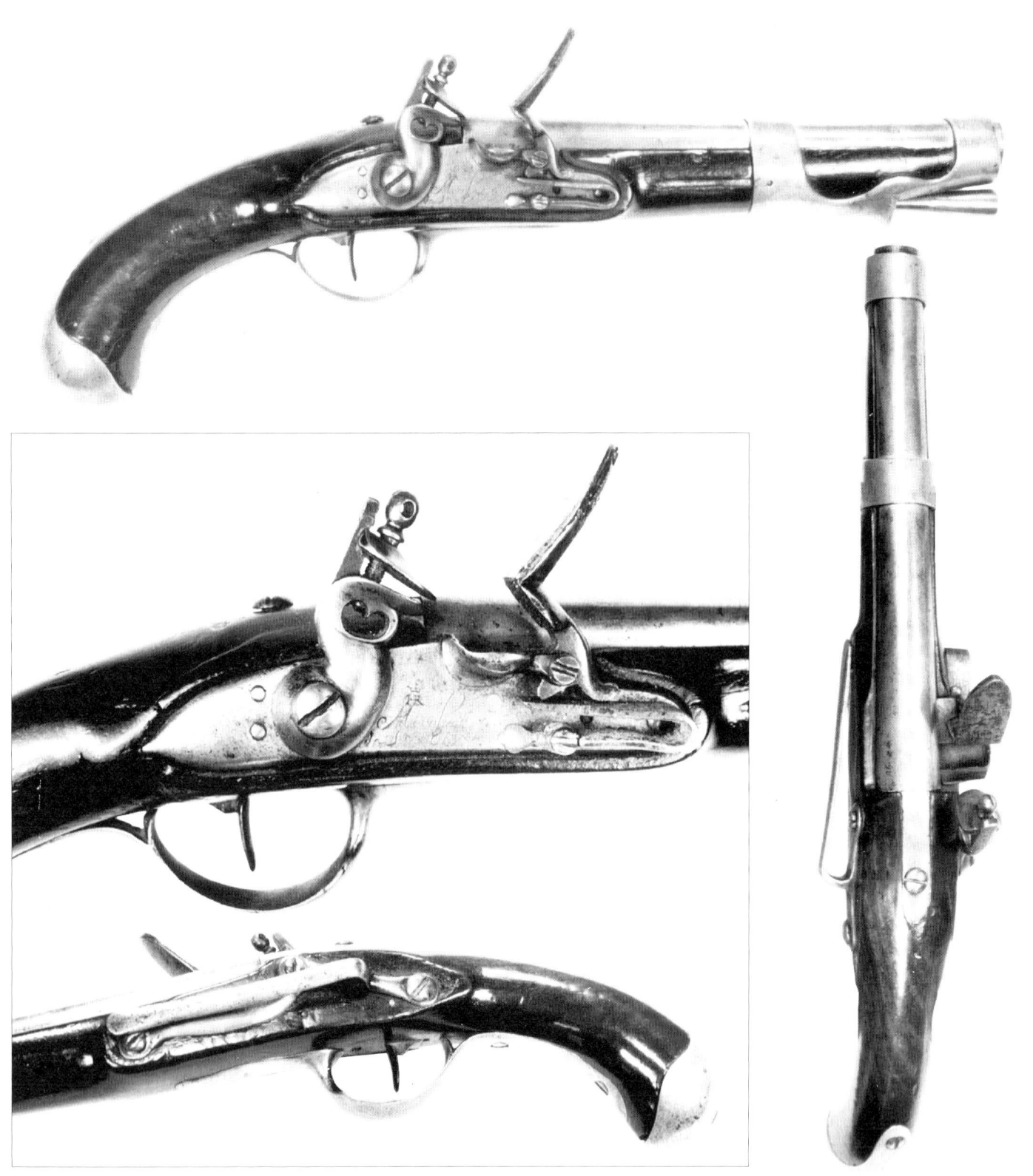

**23.PP  FRENCH CAVALRY PISTOL MODEL 1773**                                                            Circa 1773

Like the army's musket models, the pistol patterns showed few basic variations from 1766 through the first half of the 1770s, except for the adoption of a convex lock (circa 1770) having a rounded pan and bridle, plus a ring cock (heart-shaped opening) that introduced a straight rectangular upper post and notched rear top jaw. The round nine-inch barrel (.67 caliber) continues in this Model 1773, but the steel ramrod has evolved from the button head to a trumpet shape. Its long double strap barrel band (rear spring), pointed trigger guard, birds-head butt cap, convex S-form side plate and low profile walnut butt have all been retained from the Model 1766 pattern (22.PP). Notice, too, the brass furniture here, which was attributed to some cavalry, special units and the sea service (iron was standard). Of further interest is the 4-1/8" belt hook with its diagonal mounting bracket (2-5/8", two screws). Lock markings are "crown / IR" and "Manufacture de St. Etienne" (one of three Royal manufactories; others were Charleville and Maubeuge). Its breech is stamped "76" for the year of its proofing. Typical of French-issued arms in this period, there is no raised carving.

| | | | |
|---|---|---|---|
| Length: 16-1/8" | Lock: 5-1/8" X 1" | Side Plate: 3-1/8" | Furniture: Brass |
| Barrel: 9", .71 cal. | Trigger Guard: 7-5/8" | Weight: 2.8 lbs. | |

**Author's Collection**

254    *Chapter 5: Pistols*

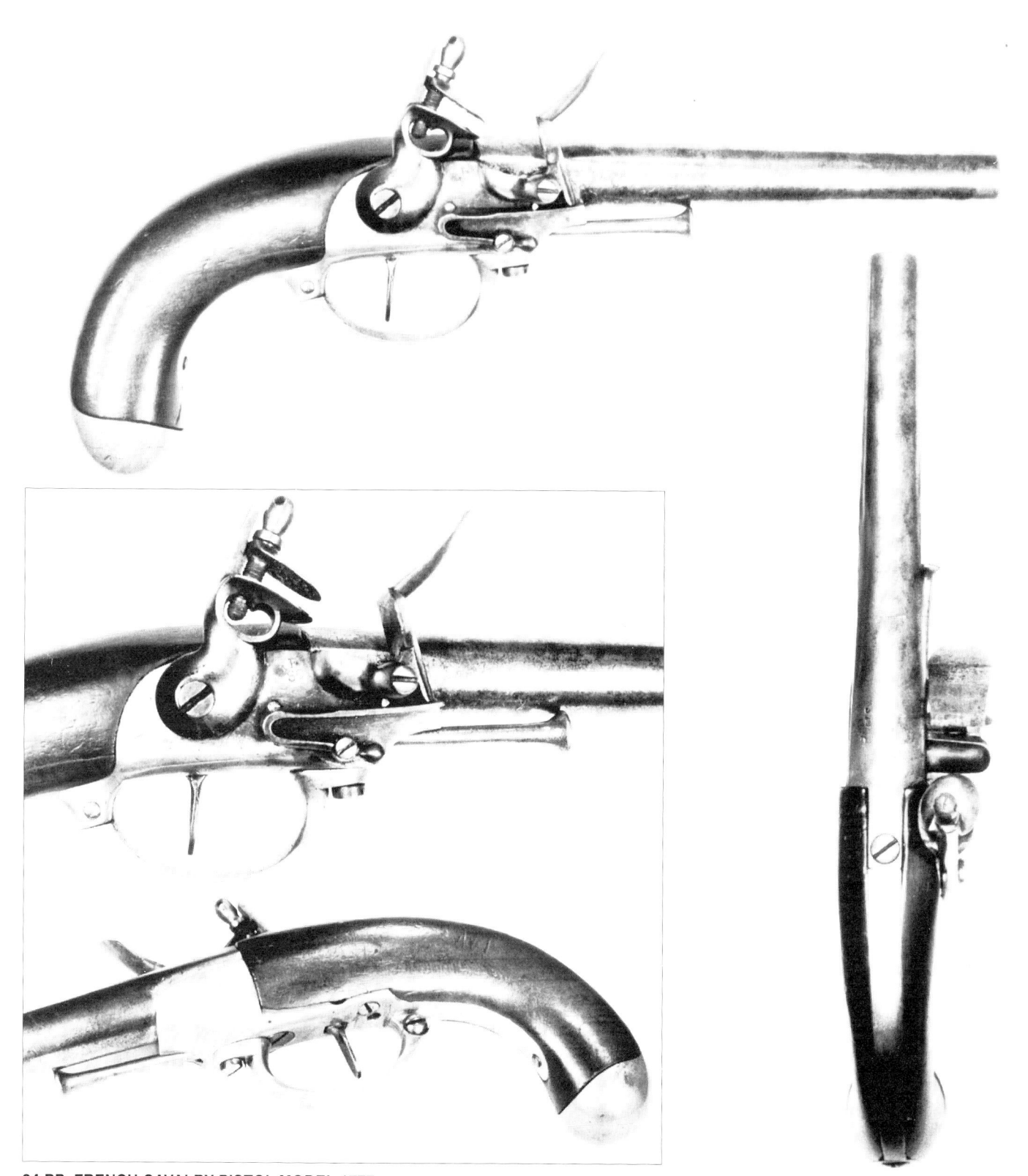

**24.PP  FRENCH CAVALRY PISTOL MODEL 1777**                                                                                        Circa 1777

In 1777 France introduced a significant new longarm design (47.MM) and the even more radical cavalry pistol shown above. A unique brass housing secured a short button-head steel rammer plus a tapered round 7-1/2" (.67 caliber) barrel without a supporting stock forend. While its cock, frizzen and inverted frizzen spring are of steel, the round slanted flash pan (with bridle) was cast as part of the brass housing. An iron strip, in turn, continues from the integral barrel tang along the back of its curved walnut handle to the spur of a plain oval butt cap. In addition the unusual trigger bow is attached by vertical (front) and horizontal (rear) screws. Breech markings include "F 33" and "S 79" (1779, the proofing date), while its tang identifies the model, Model 1777. "F / 80" behind the pan indicates an inspection date of **1780.** This pattern saw service with regular French troops in America during the Revolutionary War and was copied by the United States as its first postwar pistol (the North and Cheney contract).

| | | |
|---|---|---|
| Length: 13-1/2" | Lock: 3-5/8" X 1-1/4" | Furniture: Brass/Iron |
| Barrel: 7-1/2", .68 cal. | Trigger Guard: 5-7/8" | Weight: 2.9 lbs. |

**Author's Collection**

*Chapter 5: Pistols*

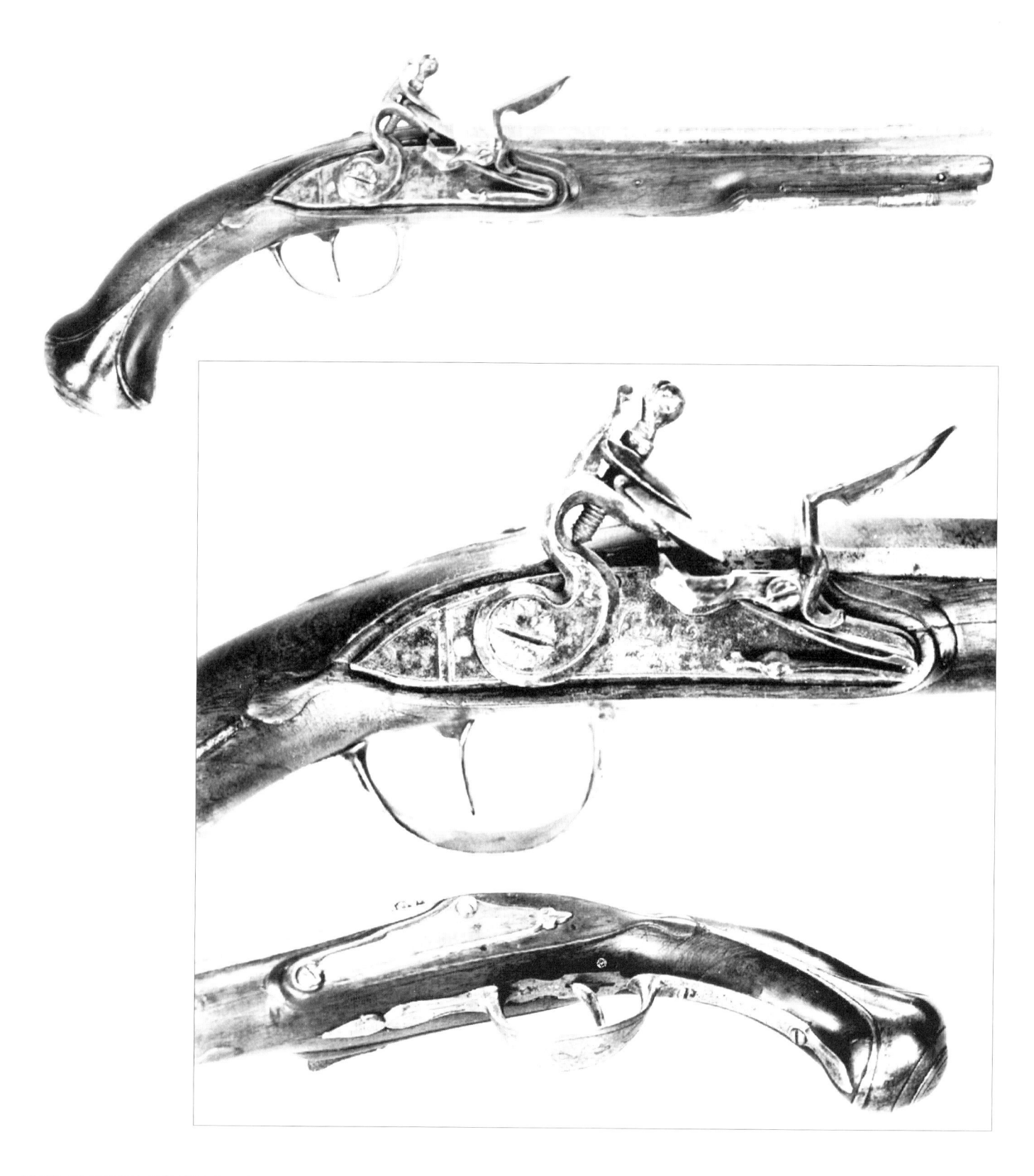

**25.PP  FRENCH CAVALRY OFFICER'S PISTOL**                                                                                                                   Circa 1733–1763

The iron furniture of this holster pistol is a close scaled-down copy of the Model 1733 cavalry issue (21.PP). Its shorter barrel and finer workmanship indicate ownership by an officer. Notice the typical features of this period's French handguns: the solid triangular side plate; three-pointed trigger guard terminal; conservative butt cap with long side straps; raised teardrop carving around the lock, side plate and barrel tang; two rammer pipes (wooden rod, horn tip); and a flat/beveled lock that includes a faceted pan, exterior bridle and a decorated screw head on the gooseneck cock. Two incised lines trace the rammer channel of the walnut stock (no nose band). "CHEVAUX REGT" (horse regiment) is marked on the barrel and "COIGNEL LE LIEUNOIS" on the lock plate beneath the pan. There is no escutcheon plate. Its 9-1/2" (.64 caliber) barrel is octagonal for four inches before blending into a round shape that leads to a front blade sight.

| | | |
|---|---|---|
| Length: 15-7/8" | Lock: 4-5/8" X 7/8" | Furniture: Iron |
| Barrel: 9-1/4", .64 cal. | Trigger Guard: 7-7/8" | Weight: 1.9 lbs. |

256   *Chapter 5: Pistols*

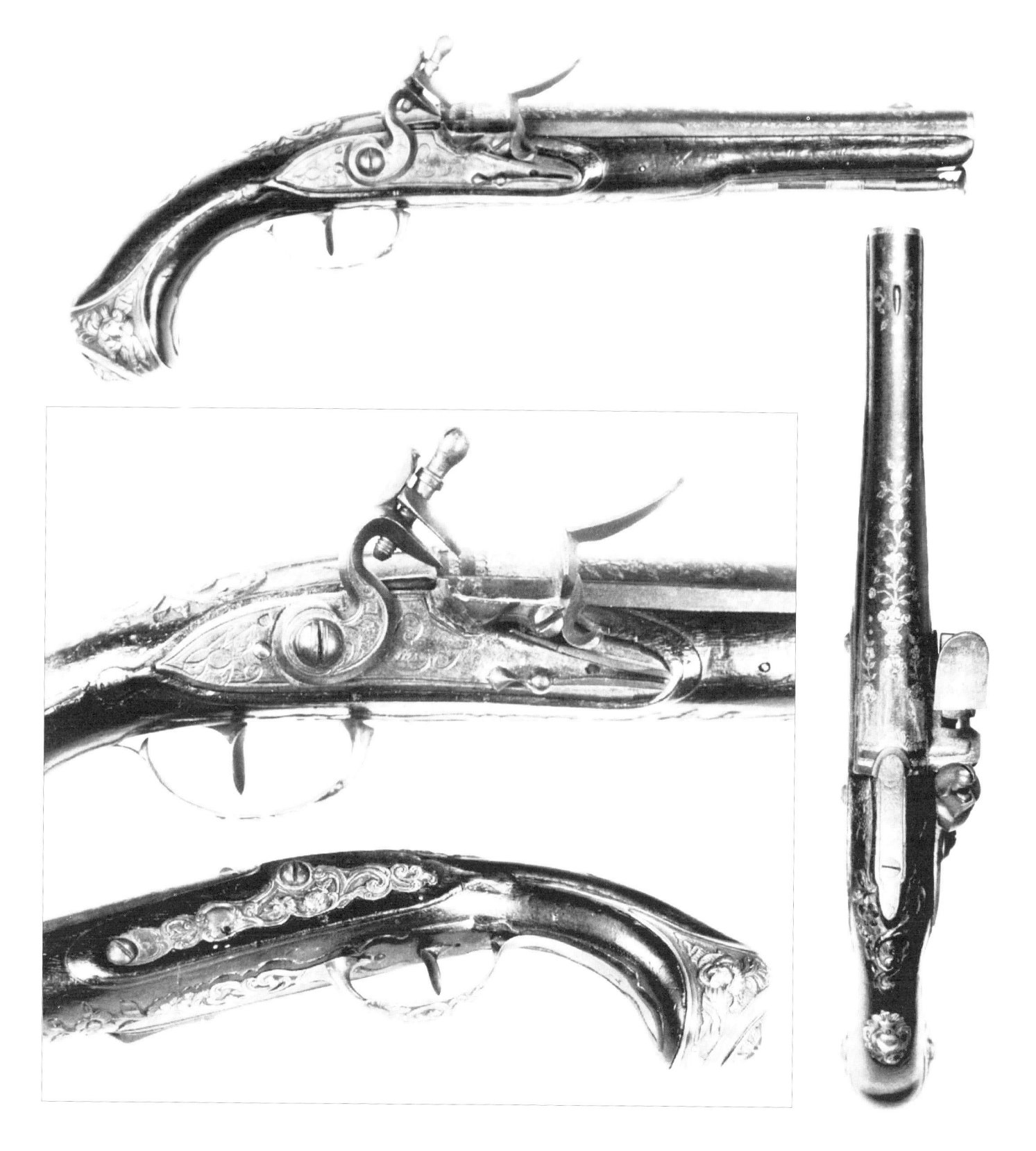

**26.PP  FRENCH OFFICER'S HOLSTER PISTOL**                                                                                                                    Circa 1750–1770

Obvious elegance has been added to this silver-mounted side arm, yet it maintains the sturdiness needed for use by an officer in the field. One of a pair is illustrated. Although created as a private weapon, several basic French features are apparent: the flat/beveled lock mounting a gooseneck cock, faceted pan/bridle, plus a frizzen spring with a bulbous finial and inside screw; a narrow rod-like post on the trigger bow; the reduced tip of its barrel tang; and teardrop borders around the lock and side plate. Raised rococo and neoclassical designs dominate its silver butt cap, triangular side plate and tapered trigger guard—which are enhanced by floral designs of gold inlay on the barrel and elaborate stock carving below the breech, as well as a multi-detailed escutcheon. The wooden rammer (in two pipes) adds an iron end disk. "LOUIS THOMAS" (a St. Etienne maker) is engraved on the lock plate, which bears further incised designs on its tail and cock.

Length: 13-3/8"  
Barrel: 7-5/8", .58 cal.  
Lock: 4-1/4" X 7/8"  
Trigger Guard: 6-1/2"  
Side Plate: 3-3/4"  
Weight: 1.3 lbs.  
Furniture: Silver

**The Benninghoff Collection**

*Chapter 5: Pistols*   257

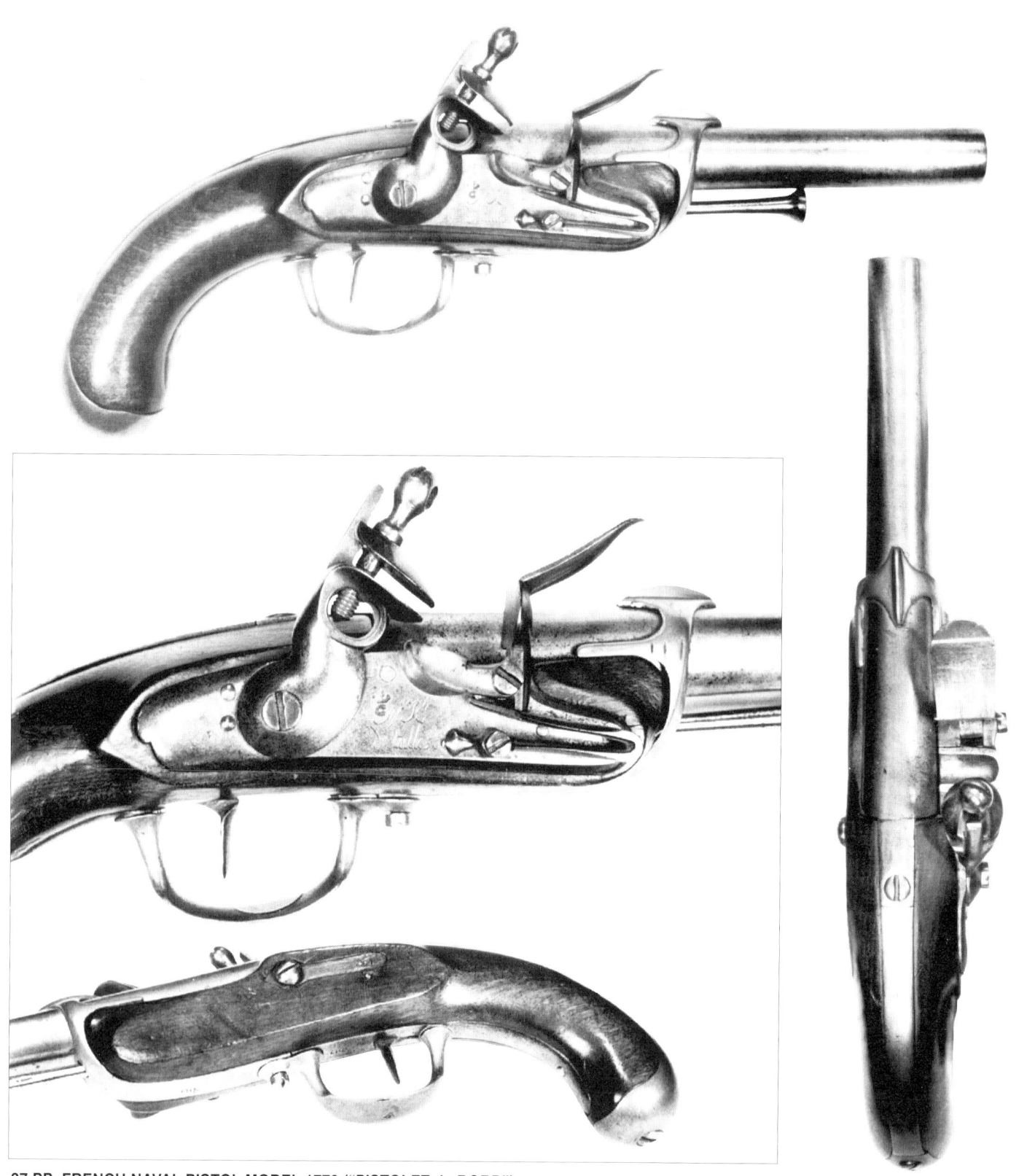

**27.PP  FRENCH NAVAL PISTOL MODEL 1779 ("PISTOLET de BORD")**                                                                                                Circa 1779

As a supplement to three Royal manufactories (Charleville, St. Etienne and Maubeuge), the independent producer at Tulle supplied arms almost exclusively for the navy and offshore colonies. In 1777 Tulle was nationalized to become the Crown's fourth official source. Its first major sea service contract included 6,700 of this new Model 1779—the first pistol design created specifically for the navy. Notice that the overall profile reflects influence from the cavalry's Model 1777 (24.PP), but the final arm is distinctly different. Its broad lock includes a unique clipped tail (changed to a conventional pointed shape in the model's Type II revision of 1783). The tapered 7-1/2" barrel (.67 caliber) is held by a solid band that provides a front sight and covers the entire forward end of the walnut half stock. An iron backstrap along the handle's upper edge reaches from the short barrel tang to a plain round butt cap. Also note the rounded ring cock, sloped brass pan/bridle (no rear fence), and squared frizzen tip — all typical of this period. An innovative lug anchoring the trigger bow's rear post is not visible. The short two-inch side plate is missing. Marks: on lock plate, "MR / De Tulle" and "crown / C" (an inspector).

| | | | |
|---|---|---|---|
| Length: 13-1/2" | Lock: 4-7/8" X 1-1/8" | Side Plate: 2" | Furniture: Brass/Iron |
| Barrel: 7-1/2", .69 cal. | Trigger Guard: 6-1/8" | Weight: 2.2 lbs. | |

**Robert Nittolo Collection**

*Chapter 5: Pistols*

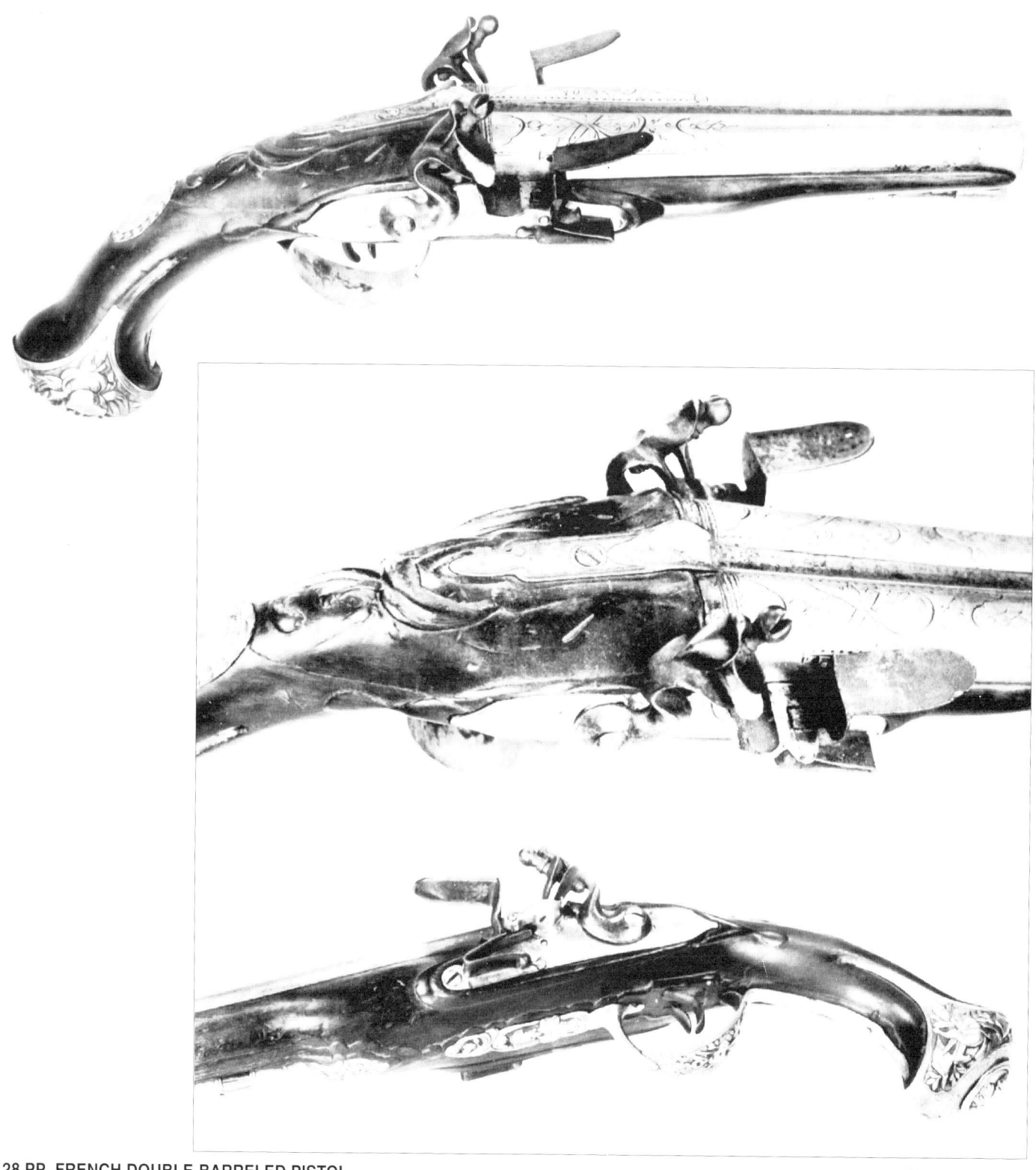

**28.PP  FRENCH DOUBLE-BARRELED PISTOL**                                                                                                                   Circa 1768–1780

This double-barreled silver mounted pistol displays the quality level of arms carried by many French officers in land and sea service. Both barrels are brass, as well as the two lock plates and flash pans. Decorative rococo raised designs cover its butt cap, trigger guard, oval escutcheon and tail pipe extension. Further embellishment adds incised patterns on both barrels plus entwined raised carving below the single barrel tang. A pair of triggers allows separate ignitions. Of further interest are the single wooden ramrod (horn tip), French-style narrow forward trigger loop strut and raised carving bordering the lock, trigger guard and rammer channel. Both of the frizzens and their springs are held by inside screws. "JEROME BLACHON" (the maker) is inscribed under one pan, "ST ETIENNE" beneath the other. There are no sights—only a channel between the barrels. One of the butt cap's side straps is missing.

Length: 13"  
Barrel: 6-3/4", .60 cal.  
Lock: 4" X 3/4"  
Trigger Guard: 7"  
Furniture: Silver  
Weight: 1.8 lbs.

*Chapter 5: Pistols*

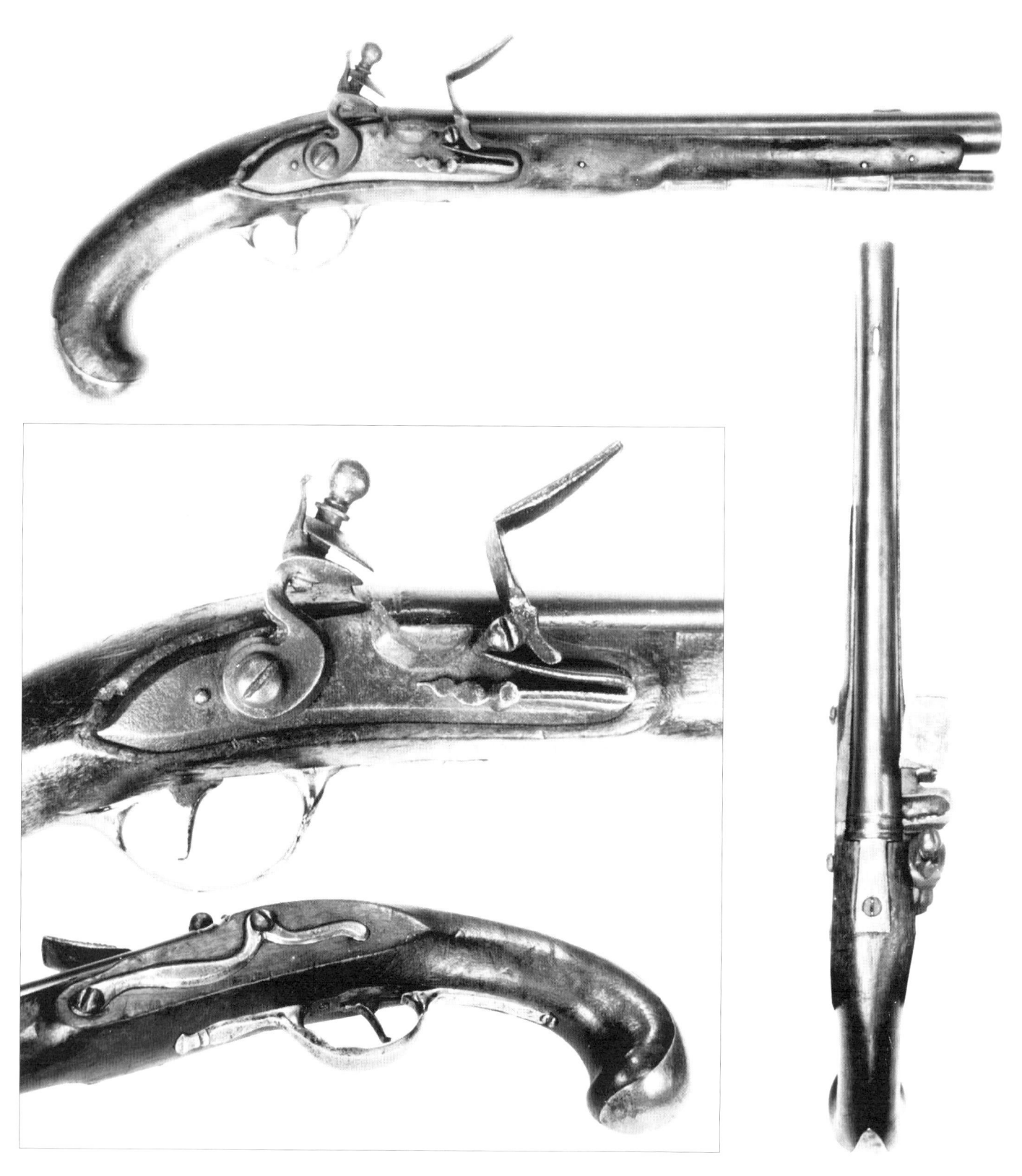

**29.PP  DUTCH HORSEMAN PISTOL**  Circa 1750–1770

The Dutch supplied many of the long and short arms used by the American rebels and most of their handguns reflected the long-barreled, heavily stocked, brass-mounted Germanic patterns. This plain horseman's example, however, suggests production in wartime or for private trade, as it eliminates the stock carving, the escutcheon and a nose band. Moreover, the curved handle—possibly a further evolution of Britain's screw barrel form (10.PP) or France's Model 1766 (22.PP)—ends in a hook-like butt that would later become popular on America's rifled pistols. Note also that the brass furniture includes a crude, tailed side plate, two faceted rammer thimbles (octagonal wooden rod), a blunted trigger guard and a plain butt cap with an extended rear tang. A faceted pan (no exterior bridle) and squared frizzen are typical of its flat/beveled lock design. The only mark is a Dutch rampant lion in a rectangular cartouche under the 11-1/4" barrel (.65 caliber), which mounts a front sight near the flared muzzle and adds a baluster ring at the breech.

| | | | |
|---|---|---|---|
| Length: 17-5/8" | Lock: 5" X 1" | Side Plate: 4-3/8" | Furniture: Brass |
| Barrel: 11-1/4", .65 cal. | Trigger Guard: 5-3/4" | Weight: 2.0 lbs. | |

**Author's Collection**

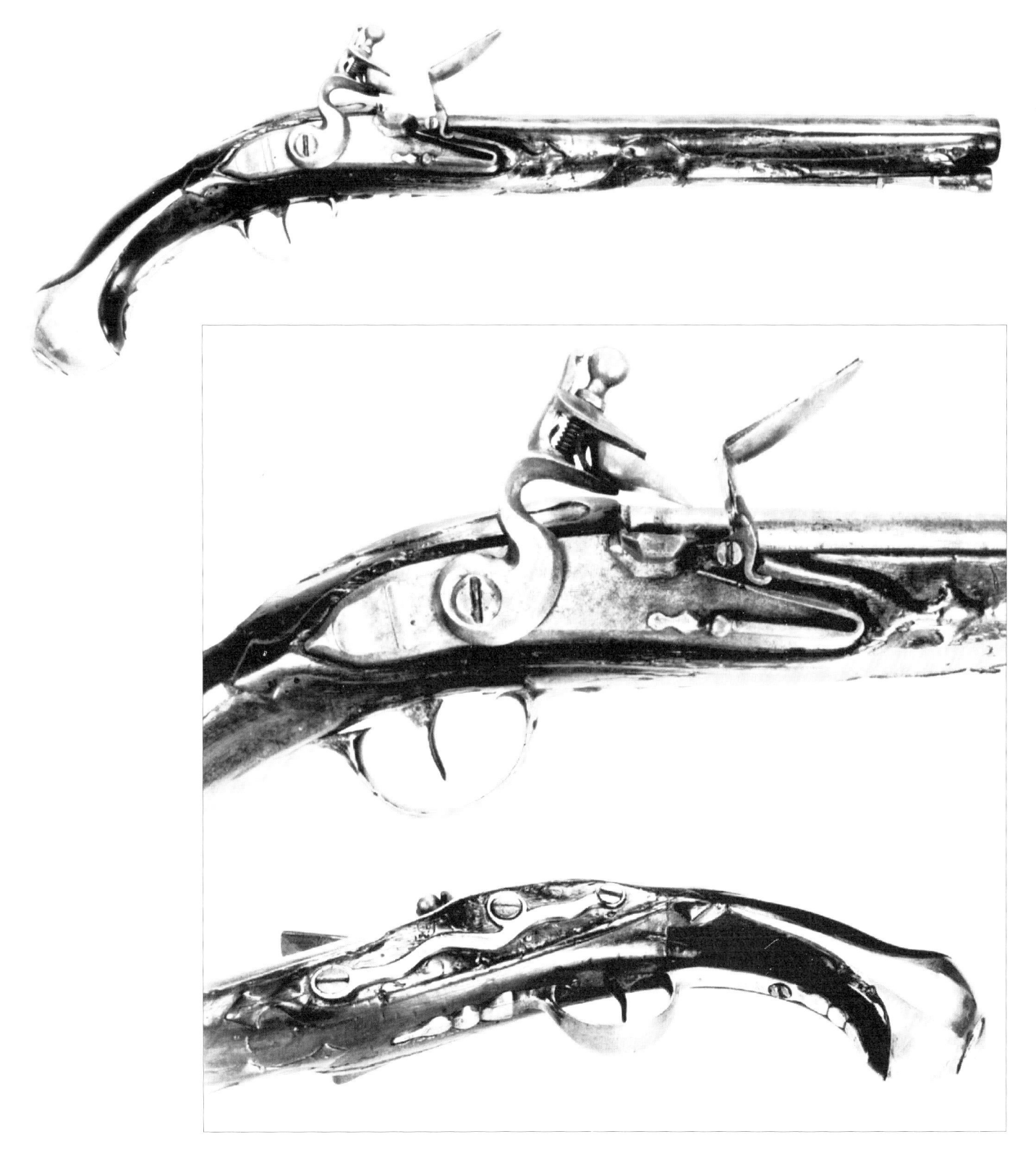

**30.PP  GERMAN HORSEMAN PISTOL**                                                                                                              Circa 1727–1731

There was a mixed variety of Germanic horseman pistols in America's Revolution—those that accompanied their mounted mercenaries and others acquired by the rebels through aid or purchase. These patterns were typically long and thickly stocked and had heavy brass furniture. It is impossible to detail all of the variations from the many available manufacturers, but the two basic Prussian "POTZDAM MAGAZ" forms that influenced most of the others are included here (the above and 31.PP). This 12-3/4" (.69 caliber) pinned barrel has been shortened almost two inches. Nevertheless the basic pattern remains: the flat/beveled lock with its undulating tail, faceted pan (no bridle), and squared frizzen; raised carving in the walnut stock that provides Germanic arrowheads at both ends of the lock and side plate, as well as below the barrel tang; a raised ridge outlining the two faceted rammer pipes (wooden rod); a deep flat-sided butt cap having long side straps; a segmented trigger guard; and the typical Potsdam–Spandau wavy three-screw side plate. Its oval escutcheon and round barrel are unmarked.

| | | |
|---|---|---|
| Length: 20-1/2" | Lock: 5-3/4" X 1-1/8" | Furniture: Brass |
| Barrel: 12-3/4", .69 cal. | Trigger Guard: 8" | Weight: 3.2 lbs. |

*Chapter 5: Pistols*   **261**

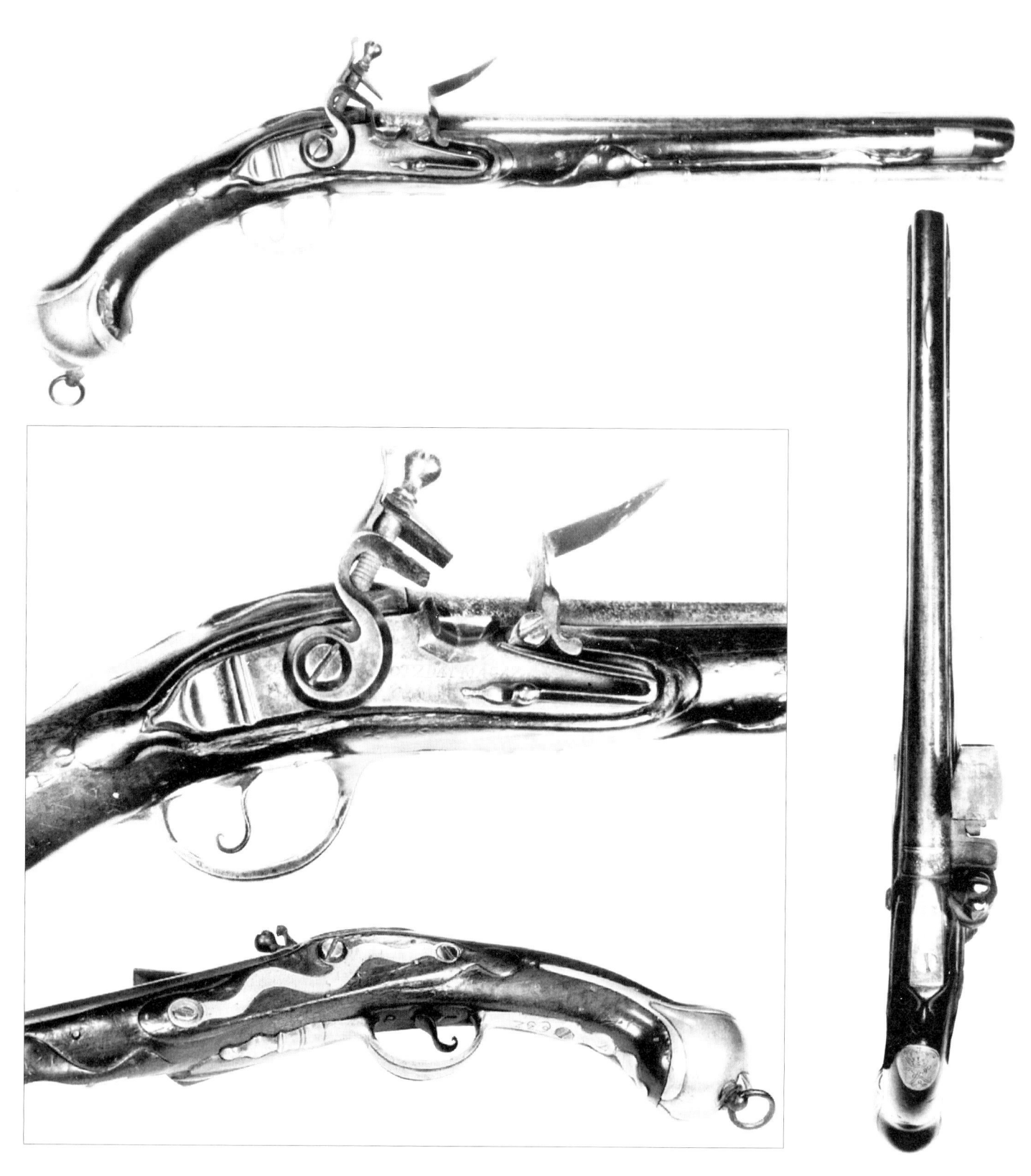

**31.PP  GERMAN HORSEMAN PISTOL**                                                                                         Circa 1742

The Prussian 1742 pattern developed for their mounted huzzars included a distinctive pierced iron stud and ring projecting from the butt cap for attachment to a trooper's lanyard. A 14-1/2" pinned barrel (.69 caliber) dominates its profile. The long walnut stock, in turn, has rounded its former arrowhead terminals bordering the lock and side plate (see 30.PP) and provided a teardrop form below the barrel tang as well as a decorative outline surrounding both smooth rammer thimbles (wooden rod). Its typical Potsdam–Spandau flat/beveled lock retains the characteristic undulating tail surface, faceted pan (no bridle) and squared frizzen—while the established wave-like side plate (plus a rear wood screw) and segmented trigger guard also continue. A raised diamond screw cover appears on the rounded butt cap, and the oval escutcheon is engraved "crown / FR" (Frederick Rex, Frederick the Great). The familiar "POTZDAM MAGAZ" arsenal marking remains under the flash pan.

| Length: 22-1/4" | Lock: 5-5/8" X 1" | Side Plate: 5-1/2" | Furniture: Brass |
|---|---|---|---|
| Barrel: 14-1/2", .69 cal. | Trigger Guard: 8-3/4" | Weight: 3.2 lbs. | |

**Robert Nittolo Collection**

262   *Chapter 5: Pistols*

**32.PP AMERICAN HORSEMAN PISTOL**  Circa 1730–1760

Most historians visualize the American Colonial militia as local bands of semi-military foot soldiers. In reality many of these units included mounted troops. As with the settlers' longarms, large numbers of these horsemen created their pistols by remounting earlier components. In this weapon associated with New York's Hudson Valley, iron components from an original Dutch cavalry handgun were reused on a provincial black cherry stock. Notice, for example, the almost abrupt angle of its handle when compared with the more graceful contours of contemporary European pistols. The earlier vintage of its Dutch iron components is apparent in the round two-screw lock (no exterior bridle), lobed trigger guard (typical channels in the bow), a ridged butt cap with long side straps, the convex side plate ending in a tail, plus a 14" barrel (.70 caliber) octagonal at the breech (3-5/8") and continuing a top flat panel to the slightly flared muzzle. Its shield-style escutcheon is secured with two nails. Both ramrod pipes appear to be local creations, as is the forend's nosecap, which is carved into the stock.

Length: 21"  
Barrel: 14", .70 cal.  
Lock: 5-1/2" X 1"  
Trigger Guard: 8-1/2"  
Side Plate: 5-1/8"  
Weight: 2.8 lbs.  
Furniture: Iron

**Robert Nittolo Collection**

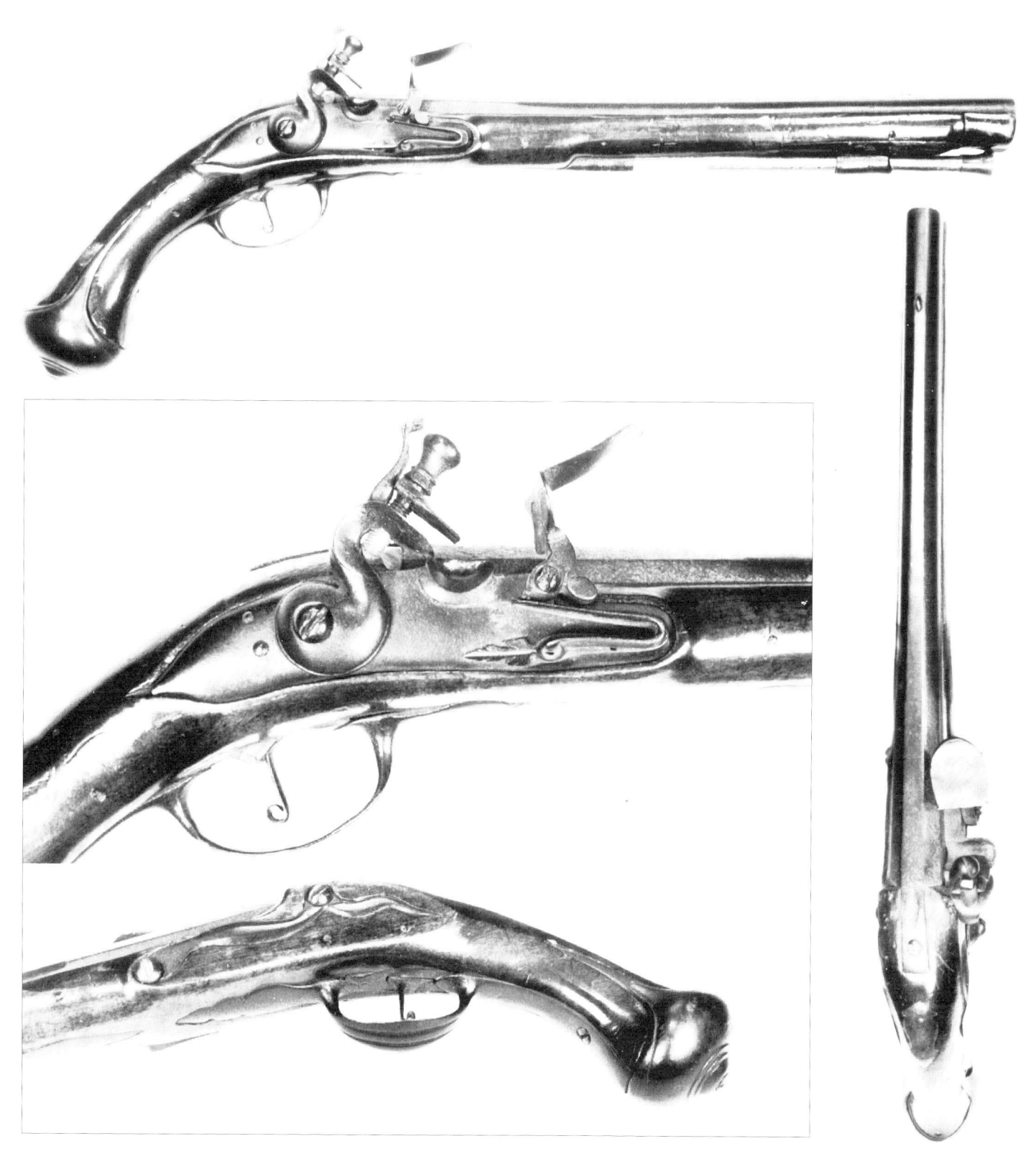

Chapter 5: Pistols  263

**33.PP AMERICAN HOLSTER PISTOL**  Circa 1750

This classic pistol of the Colonies is entirely American and identified on a panel along the barrel with the name "MATTHEW SADD," a Hartford, Connecticut, gunsmith. The attractive striped-maple stock mounts a straight-edged butt cap of circa 1700 form and provides bulbous raised carving around the lock, side plate and barrel tang. Notice the oddly proportioned flat banana lock edged by overly wide chamfers and including an off-center cock plus a narrow faceted pan and flat-topped frizzen. Its unique side plate and narrow trigger guard (incised lines on the bow) are obviously provincial. The 10-3/8" (.52 caliber) barrel remains octagonal for four inches to a decorative ring; simple channeled designs are also present and a front blade sight is visible. An elementary escutcheon, in turn, has top and bottom points. Two ring-bordered brass pipes hold a plain wooden rammer. Although lacking many of the configurations found in European pistols, this functional arm was endowed with all of the sturdiness and dignity required for surviving in a burgeoning America.

| | | | |
|---|---|---|---|
| Length: 16-1/2" | Lock: 5-1/4" X 1" | Side Plate: 5-1/8" | Furniture: Brass |
| Barrel: 10-3/8", .52 cal. | Trigger Guard: 7" | Weight: 2.7 lbs. | |

**Robert Nittolo Collection**

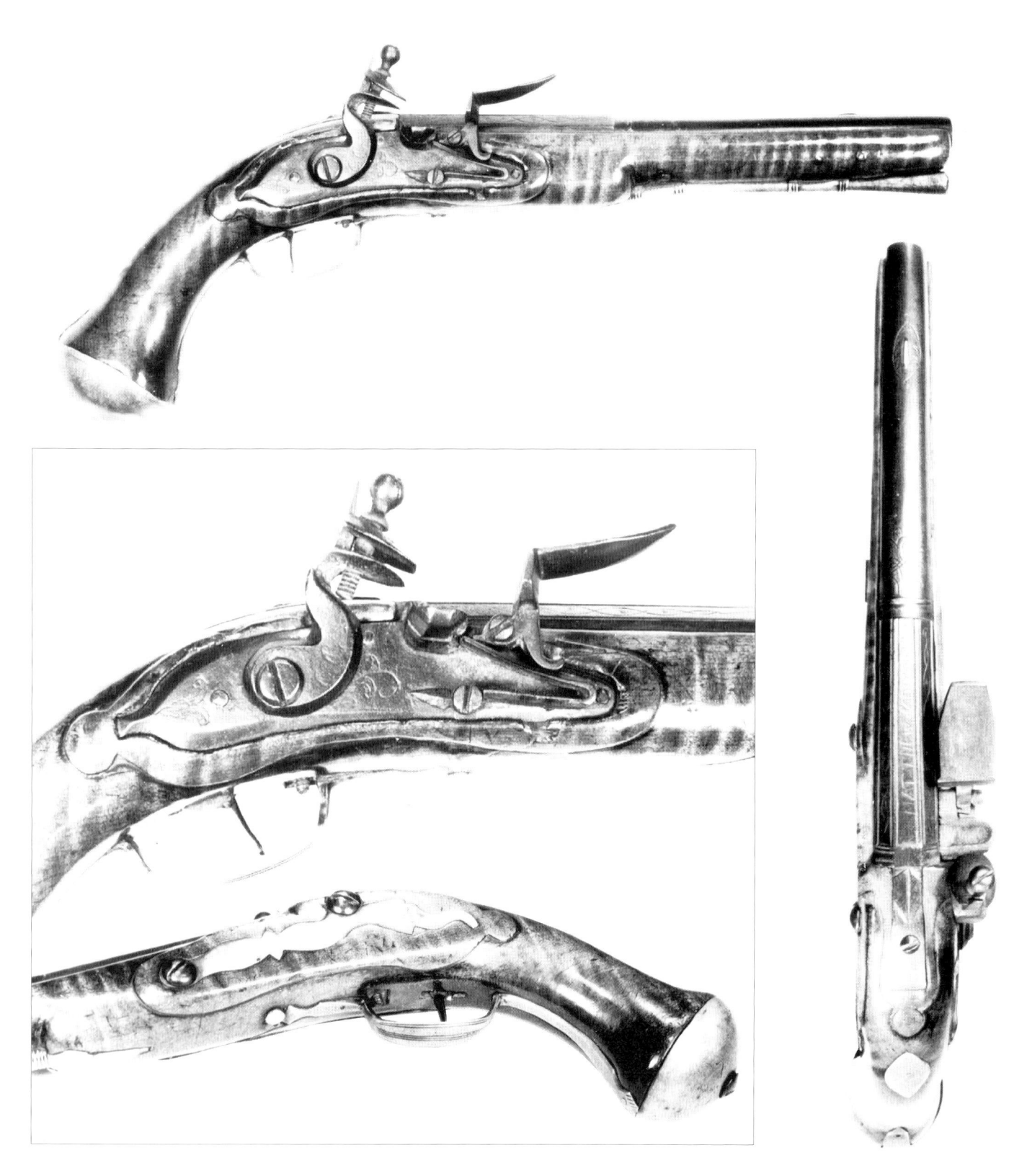

**34.PP AMERICAN HOLSTER PISTOL**                                                                                **Circa 1750–1775**

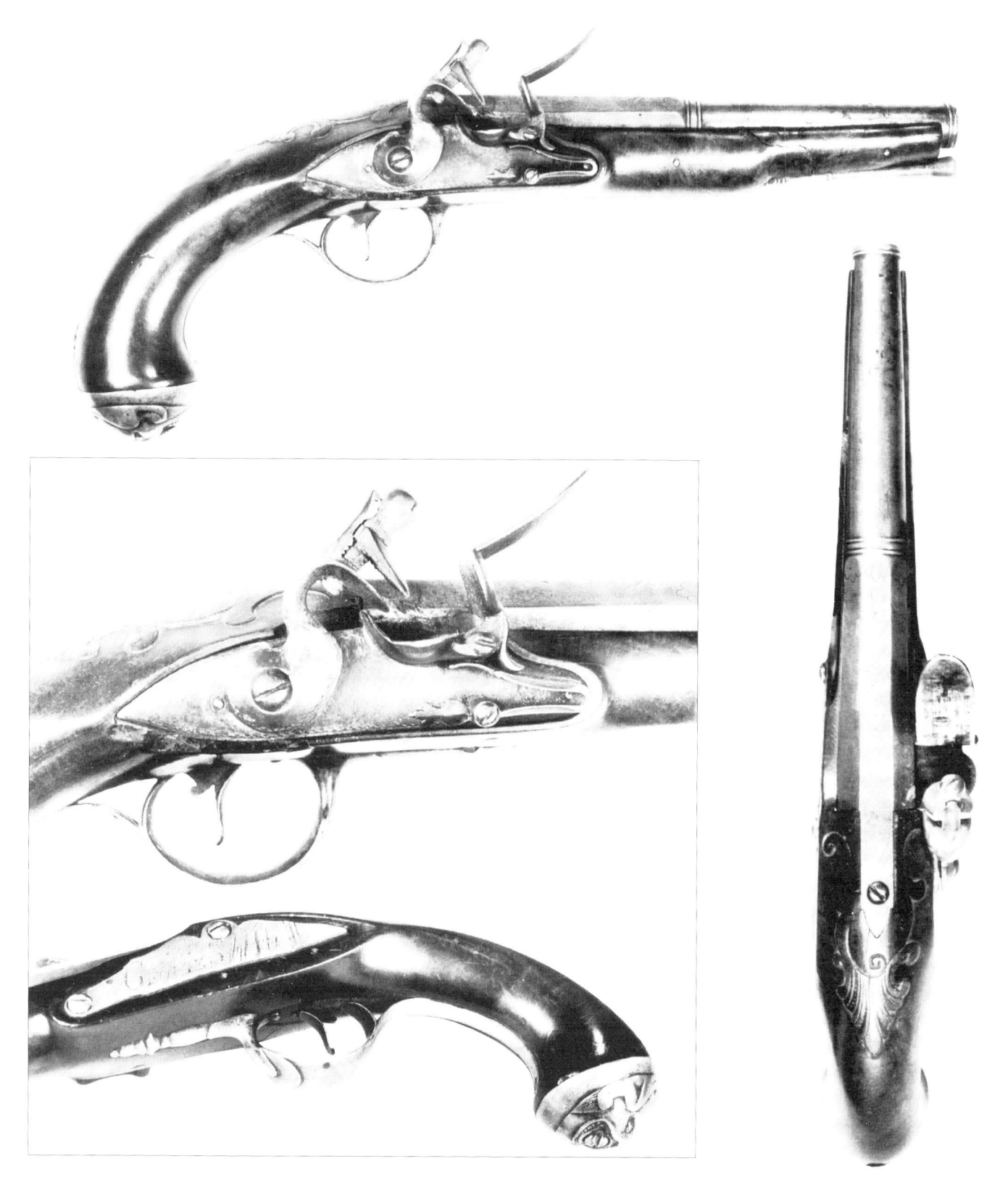

The interesting pinned brass barrel of this American handgun is octagonal for three inches to a double band and then round to a ringed cannon-type muzzle. It is signed along the top, "Wm Antes," a Philadelphia area gunsmith (and upper New York State at the end of the century). French influence appears in the trigger guard's modified arrow-like front finial, narrow forward strut on the bow and the straight-edged animal mask butt cap. The weapon, however, appears to be all American in construction. A stippled border outlines the cock as well as the lock plate, which extends to a raised center point at the tail (popular among the Colonists). The flat triangular side plate, in turn, incorporates vertical lines at the rear and the engraved name "GEORGE SMITH," probably an owner. Note, too, that the burled walnut stock provides a pleasing curved grip but omits all raised carving except for a decorative splay design below the pointed barrel tang (top screw). A single cast brass thimble is inset at the entry hole for a wooden rammer.

| | | | |
|---|---|---|---|
| Length: 12-1/4" | Lock: 3-3/4" X 3/4" | Side Plate: 3-5/8" | Furniture: Brass |
| Barrel: 6-3/4", .47 cal. | Trigger Guard: 6" | Weight: 1.5 lbs. | |

**Richard Ulbrich Collection**

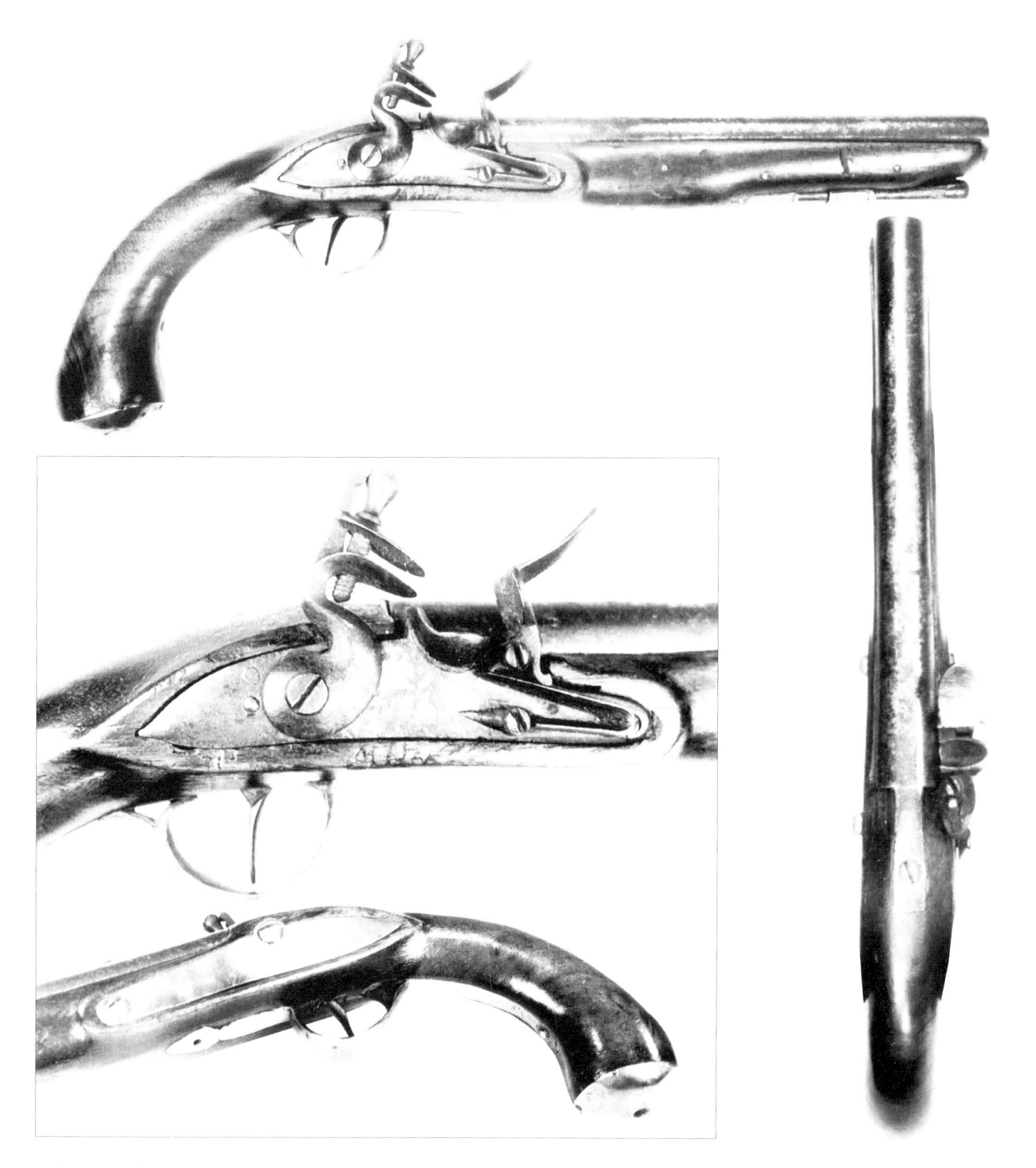

**35.PP  AMERICAN HOLSTER PISTOL**                                                                                                  Circa 1780–1800

A reused English nine-inch (.65 caliber) barrel with Tower double scepter private proofs and a two-screw trade pattern lock provided the primary elements for this American pistol. Its functional walnut stock adds only flat borders around the lock and side plate; however it extends and expands the butt apparently in recognition of the period's evolving hook handle. The elementary thin brass furniture, in turn, contributes a straight-edged butt cap with a short rear spur (held by a screw and four tacks), a flat triangular side plate, a crude locally cast trigger guard ending in an arrowhead terminal (pinned and nailed), and two sheet-formed thimbles for a wooden ramrod. Its rounded lock includes the usual commercial features of this period, that is, the cock's squared upper post with a forward notch, a top jaw slotted at the back, a round pan possessing a high rear extension yet omitting an exterior bridle, an oval frizzen top and a sharp-pointed frizzen spring finial. Note also that the long handle is more easily grasped by a gloved hand.

| | | | |
|---|---|---|---|
| Length: 15-3/8" | Lock: 4-3/8" X 7/8" | Side Plate: 4-3/4" | Furniture: Brass |
| Barrel: 9", .65 cal. | Trigger Guard: 6-1/2" | Weight: 1.7 lbs. | |

**Author's Collection**

*Chapter 5: Pistols*

**36.PP AMERICAN HORSEMAN PISTOL**                                                                                                                           Circa 1780

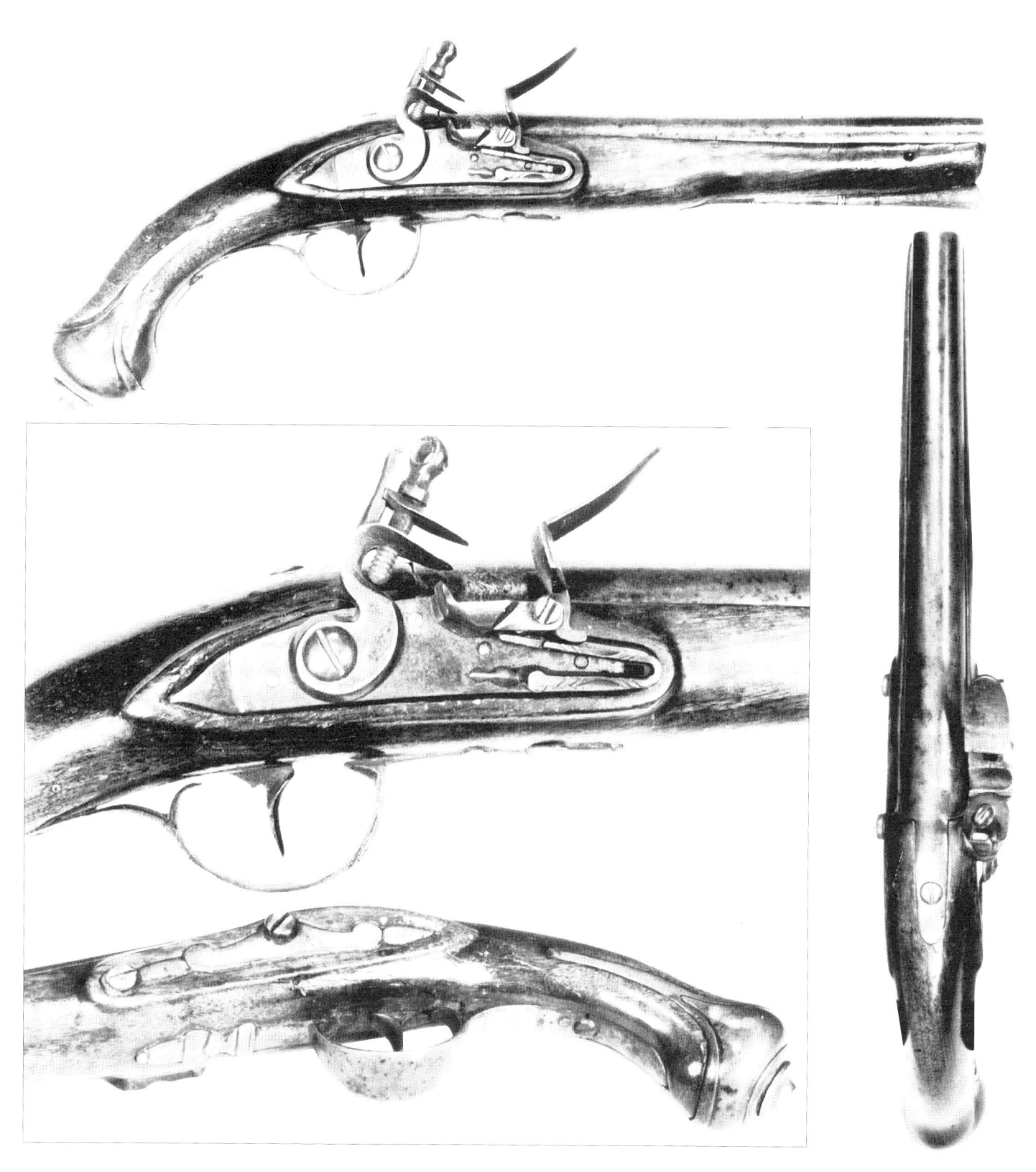

Several of this pattern are known. They were apparently produced in the Lancaster, Pennsylvania, and northern Maryland area for American mounted troops during the Revolution. Minor differences are found among their locks and barrels, yet the furniture and basic pattern are consistent—with European influences apparent. The interesting paneled side plate, for example, resembles some French forms, while the trigger guard reflects English design in its simplified acorn front terminal and split rear post on the bow. Notice also that the ridged butt cap, which includes side straps, is narrower than normal. The flat lock has a recessed tail seen on some French models, as well as a Germanic-type frizzen spring showing edge decorations plus an inside screw. Plain raised carving on the walnut stock borders both lock and side plate. In addition two sheet-brass pipes hold a trumpet-shaped wooden ramrod. The weapon's configuration with its original nine-inch pinned barrel is one of a number of American approximations of the contemporary British Light Dragoon Pistol Pattern 1759 (5.PP).

| | | | |
|---|---|---|---|
| Length: 15-1/2" | Lock: 4-1/2" X 7/8" | Side Plate 4-3/8" | Furniture: Brass |
| Barrel: 8-3/4", .65 cal. | Trigger Guard: 7-1/2" | Weight: 2.0 lbs. | |

**Robert Nittolo Collection**

*Chapter 5: Pistols*   **267**

**37.PP  AMERICAN HORSEMAN PISTOL**  Circa 1775–1780

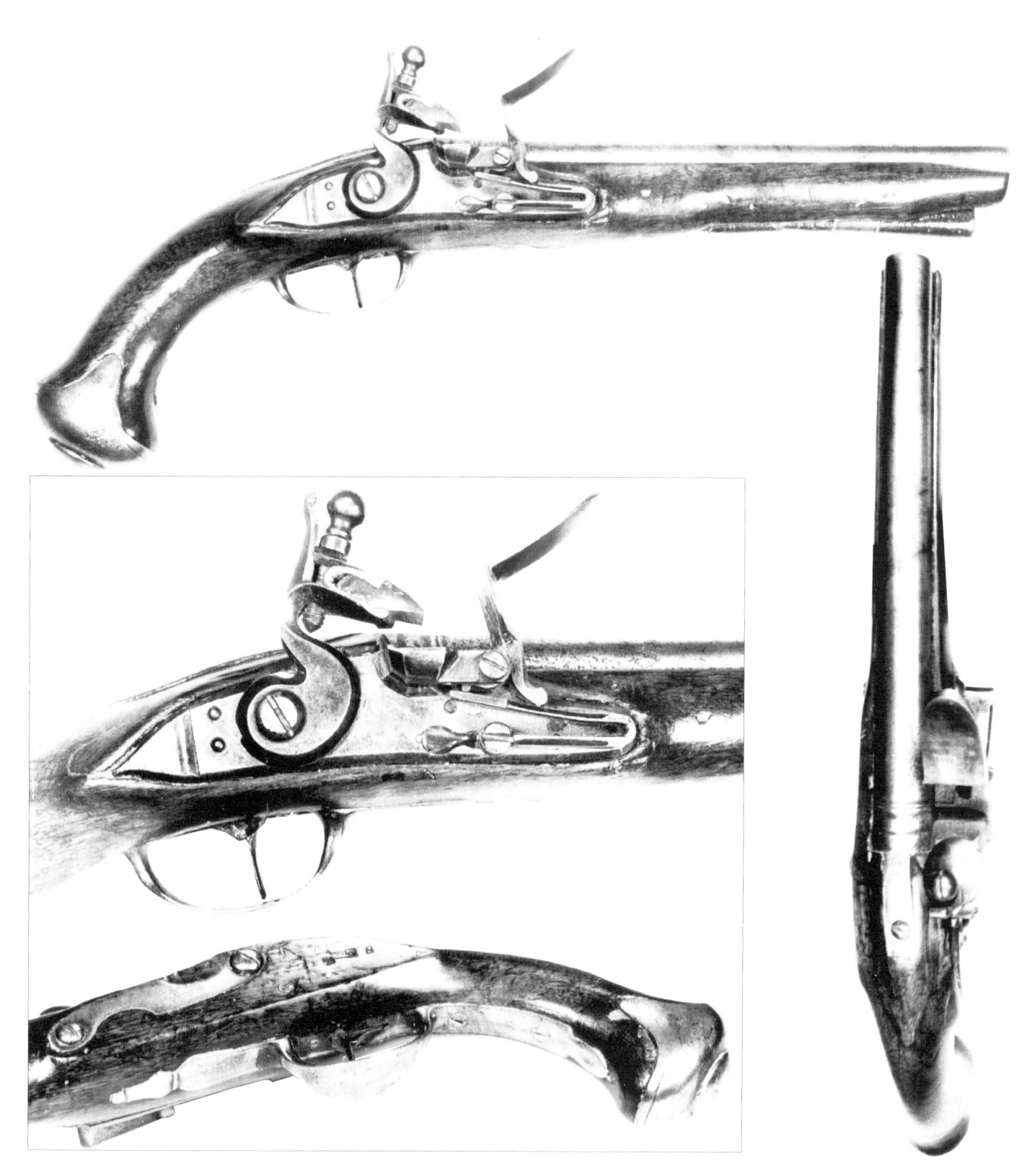

The above handgun is another American copy of the British Pattern 1759 in use by their light dragoons during the War for Independence (5.PP). The left side of its breech bears a small V-type stamp that is believed to be the Maryland proof mark as struck by Thomas Ewing, an inspector. English influence is obvious in the gun's profile, as well as the S-shaped flat side plate, round nine-inch barrel (.65 caliber; baluster breech) and abbreviated side lobes on the butt cap. However a number of variances were also introduced: a central European form of flat/beveled lock that includes a slashed tail, faceted pan with bridle and bulbous frizzen spring finial; iron furniture instead of brass; undulating carving in the walnut stock around the barrel tang to replace the usual beaver tail; as well as a trigger guard having a Germanic-type front terminal and lacking a split rear post on the bow. Two thimbles support a trumpet-shaped iron rammer. An escutcheon plate is omitted. Other marks are "GM / E" under the breech and "225" in the stock near the side plate.

| | | | |
|---|---|---|---|
| Length: 16-1/4" | Lock: 5-1/4" X 1-1/8" | Side Plate: 3-1/4" | Furniture: Iron |
| Barrel: 9-1/8", .65 cal. | Trigger Guard: 7-3/4" | Weight: 2.4 lbs. | |

**James D. Forman Collection**

Chapter 5: Pistols

**38.PP  AMERICAN HORSEMAN PISTOL**  Circa 1775–1780

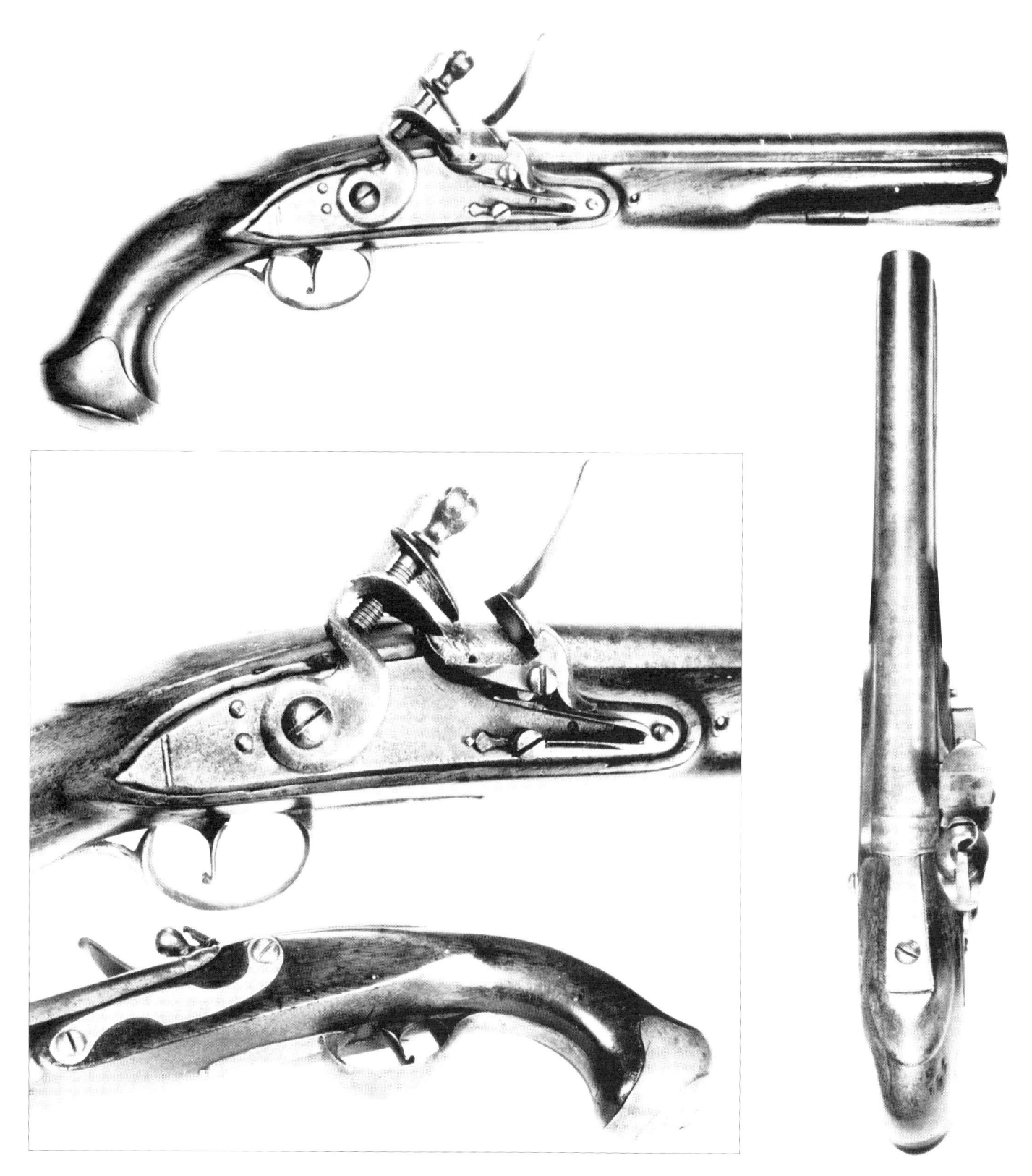

Virginia authorized James Hunter, with his key foreman, John Strode, to produce weapons for the Continental Army in 1775 at his iron forge on the Rappahannock River near Falmouth. Hunter's arms included muskets, rampart guns, pistols and swords (see 147.MM). Firearms manufacture was curtailed in 1780 because of British raiding parties. This rare example of his work is inscribed "RAPA FORGE" on the lock's tail and "I HUNTER" along the barrel. It is a near copy of the contemporary British Light Dragoon Pattern 1759 (5.PP) per the nine-inch barrel (.67 caliber; baluster breech ring), S-type side plate, tapered trigger guard, butt cap with abbreviated lobes and a walnut stock providing raised beaver-tail carving around the barrel tang. The flat/beveled American lock adds two vertical lines at the tail, as well as a slim squared upper post on the cock, a round pan with bridle and a unique frizzen spring finial. Its single rammer thimble for the wooden rod is probably a replacement. (Re: Swayze, bib. 145).

| | | | |
|---|---|---|---|
| Length: 15-1/8" | Lock: 5-1/4" X 1" | Side Plate: 3-3/8" | Furniture: Brass |
| Barrel: 9", .67 cal. | Trigger Guard: 6" | Weight: 2.2 lbs. | |

**Richard Ulbrich Collection**

Chapter 5: Pistols   269

**39.PP  AMERICAN HOLSTER PISTOL**  Circa 1740–1760

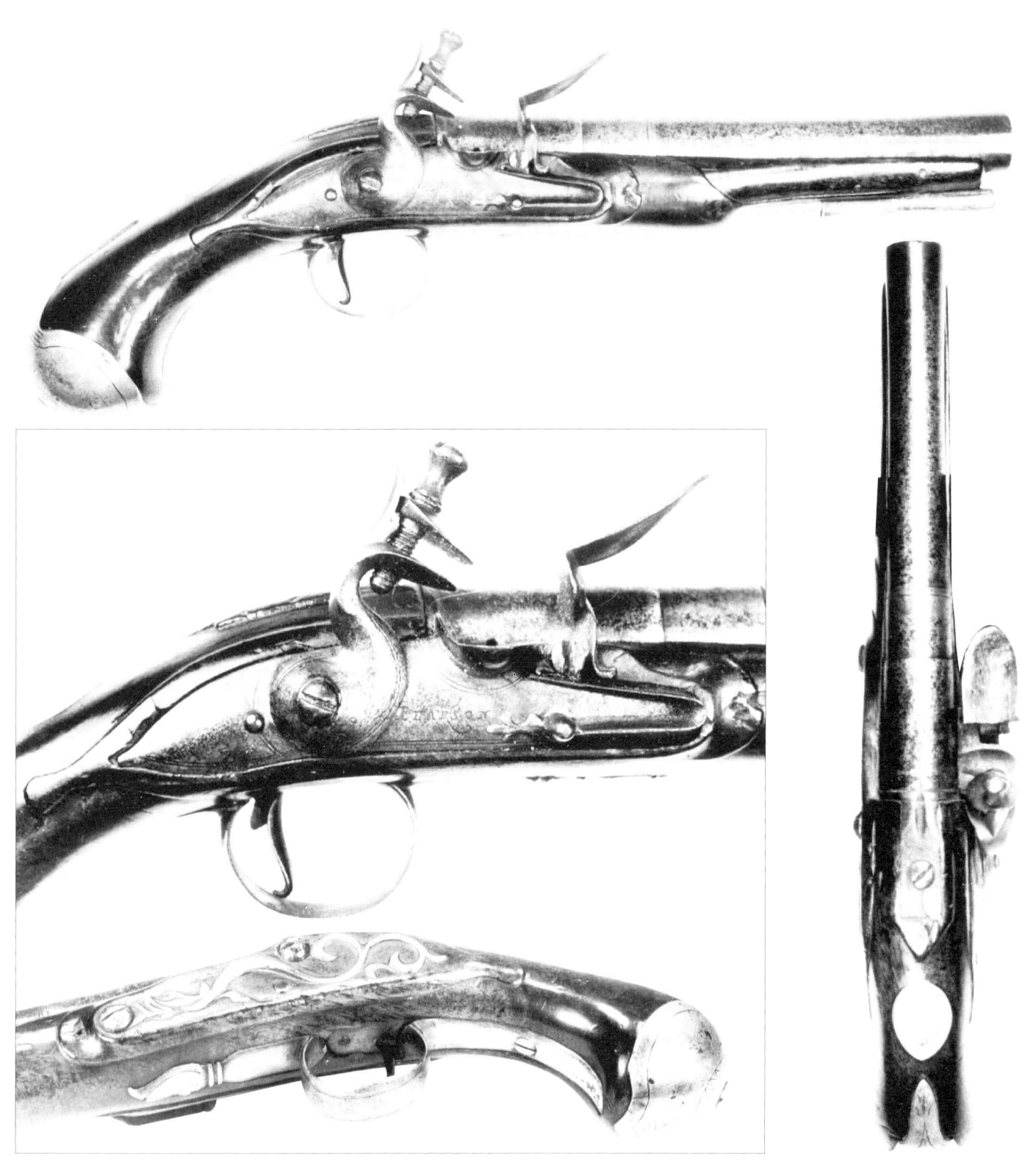

This interesting civilian/officer pistol combines diverse American and European features. Its delicately curved dragon side plate, for example, is a late 17th century Continental form, while the flame-shaped forward terminal on the trigger guard is found on early Queen Anne-period English patterns. The round seven-inch, .63 caliber, double-stepped flared barrel, in turn, retains faint London Gunmakers Company proofs. The walnut stock and remaining components have American Colonial characteristics, that is: a wide bulky grip ending in a substantial butt cap (similar to the screw barrel pistols, circa 1720); raised carving providing a stubby point below the barrel tang and stretched teardrop terminals behind the lock and side plate, as well as a forend ridge that rises at the rammer's entry hole; a single plain sheet-brass rammer pipe (wooden rod); and simple Colonial incised decorative lines on the butt cap and trigger bow. A plain ovoid escutcheon is held by two brass pins. Also note that the well-made rounded lock (no exterior bridle) is marked "I PEARSON," possibly an English maker but attributed to Joseph Pearson, an American Chester County, Pennsylvania, gunsmith.

| | | | |
|---|---|---|---|
| Length: 12-1/2" | Lock: 4-1/4" X 3/4" | Side Plate: 4" | Furniture: Brass |
| Barrel: 7", .62 cal. | Trigger Guard: 6" | Weight: 1.3 lbs. | |

**Author's Collection**

**40.PP AMERICAN HOLSTER PISTOL**                                                                                                          Circa 1770–1780

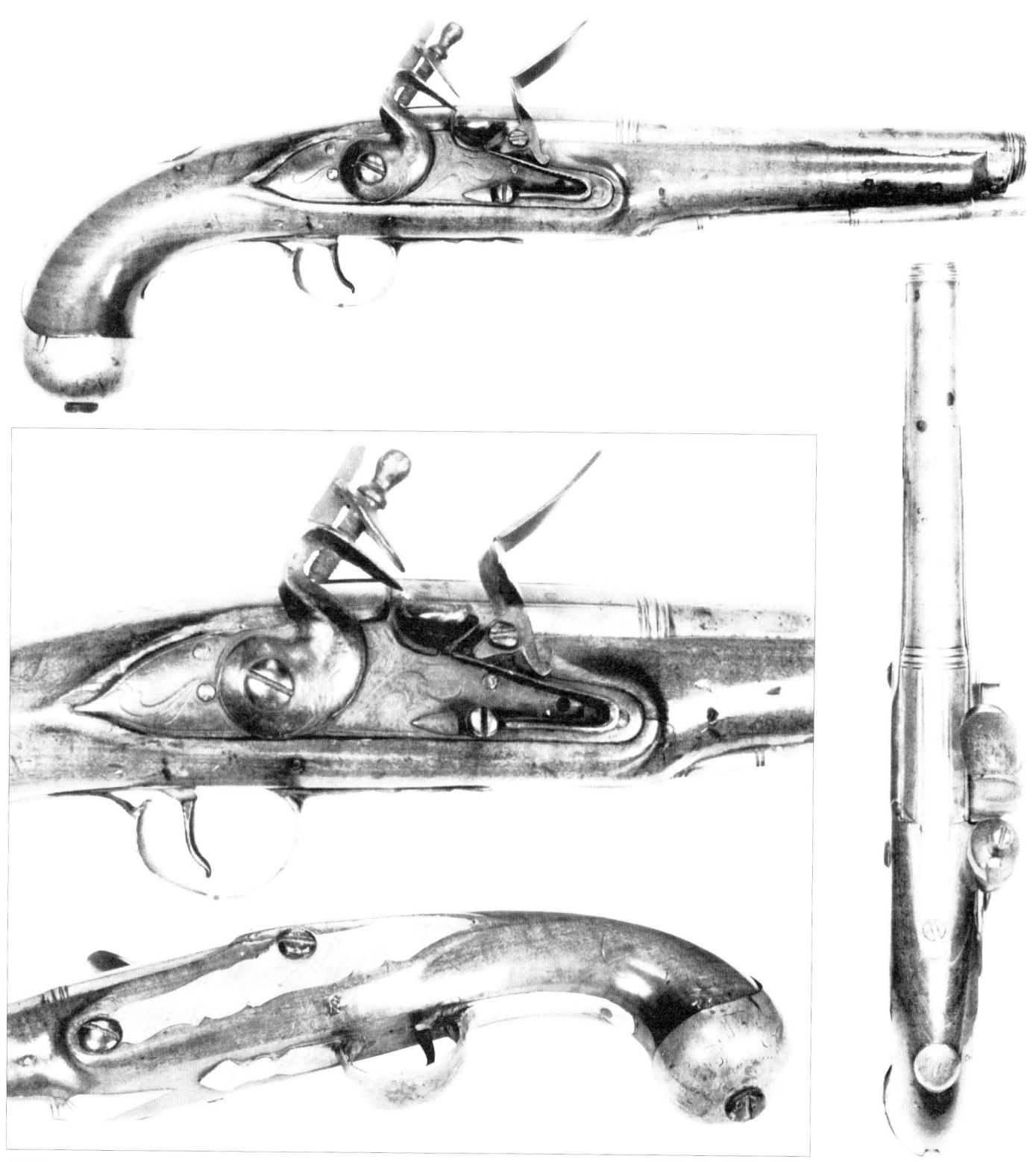

Such low-profile handguns were popular among American gunsmiths of this period, including Medad Hills of Goshen, Connecticut (re: Stickels, bib. 240). This distinctive striped maple stock omits all but the barest of raised carving yet cradles an impressive pinned brass barrel with a defined octagonal-paneled breech reaching 2-1/2 inches to a triple band and then a round surface to the ringed muzzle—to complete a semi-cannon form. The trade-type round lock shows typical 1760-period strawberry vine surface designs, plus a plain squared cock post, omitted outside bridle and spear-shaped frizzen spring finial. Its brass furniture, that is, the side plate, trigger guard, butt cap and two rammer thimbles (wooden rod) are all contemporary Colonial innovations. An oval silver escutcheon is engraved with the entwined initials "TC"—added after manufacture by an owner. No other markings are visible.

| | | | |
|---|---|---|---|
| Length: 13-7/8" | Lock: 4-3/4" X 1" | Side Plate: 4-3/4" | Furniture: Brass |
| Barrel: 7-3/4", .56 cal. | Trigger Guard: 5-1/2" | Weight: 1.8 lbs. | |

**Robert Nittolo Collection**

*Chapter 5: Pistols*

**41.PP  AMERICAN HORSEMAN PISTOL**  Circa 1760–1780

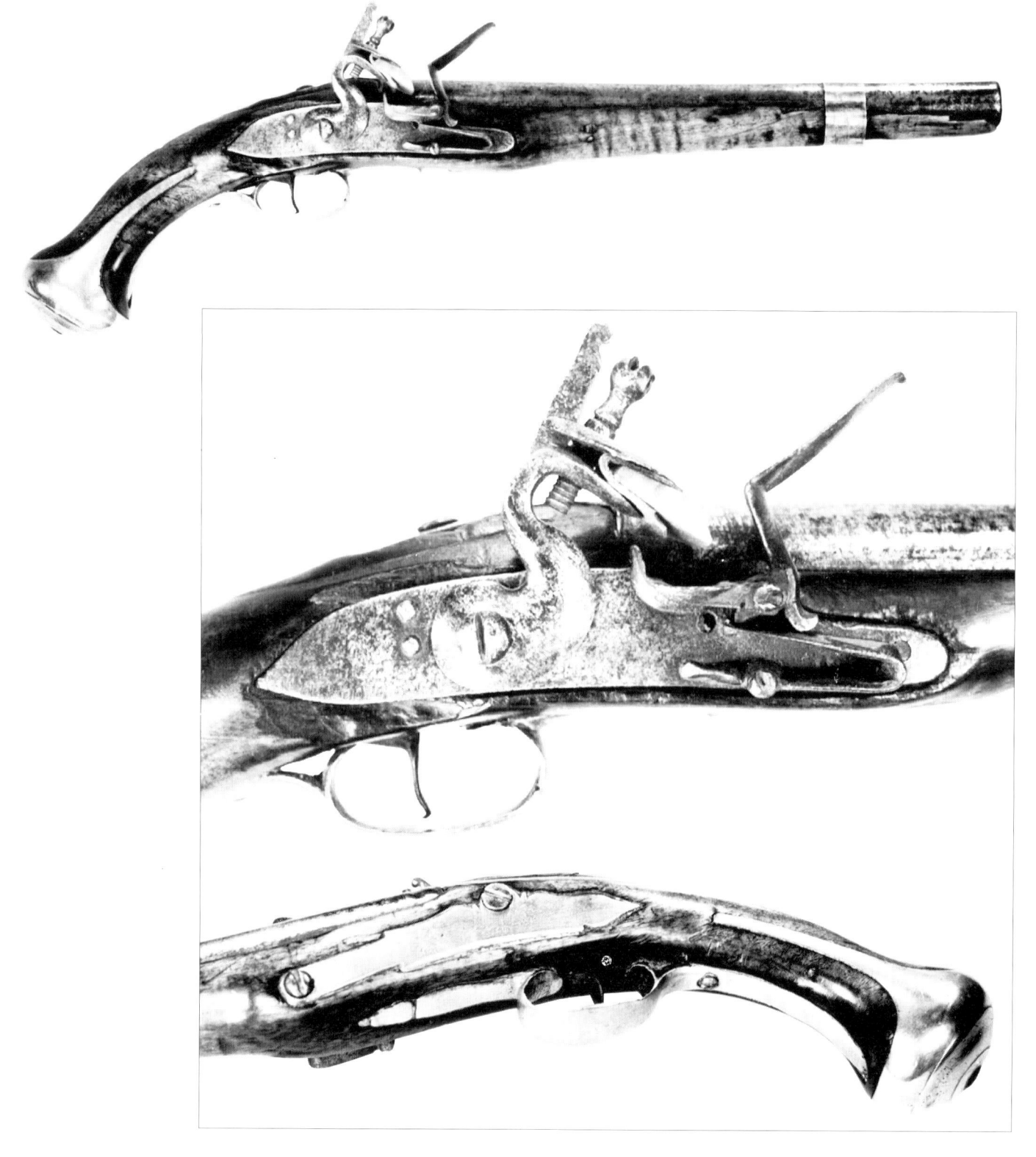

The long barrel of this handgun appears to have originated on a British dragoon pistol (like 3.PP) and bears faint Tower proofs at the breech. Its Brown Bess-style trigger guard and butt cap, as well as the French-type side plate, are apparently of Colonial manufacture. Also note the provincial, crude, narrow flat lock set into a striped-maple stock that is void of all carving. Even a ramrod channel is omitted—relying on an elementary sheet-brass band as the only furniture for the forend. (Note: some central European and Scandinavian pistols at that time also neglected the channel—carrying the ramrod on a neck lanyard.) Two additional pins help to secure the barrel. The weapon as a whole lacks any identifying markings and even excludes an escutcheon plate. As with most of these long military pistols, a smoothbore barrel and undersized ball were seldom effective beyond close range but served well for clubbing and even throwing after firing.

| | | |
|---|---|---|
| Length: 18-3/4" | Lock: 5-1/2" X 1" | Furniture: Brass |
| Barrel: 11-3/4", .68 cal. | Trigger Guard: 7-1/4" | Weight: 2.5 lbs. |

**42.PP  AMERICAN HORSEMAN PISTOL**  Circa 1740

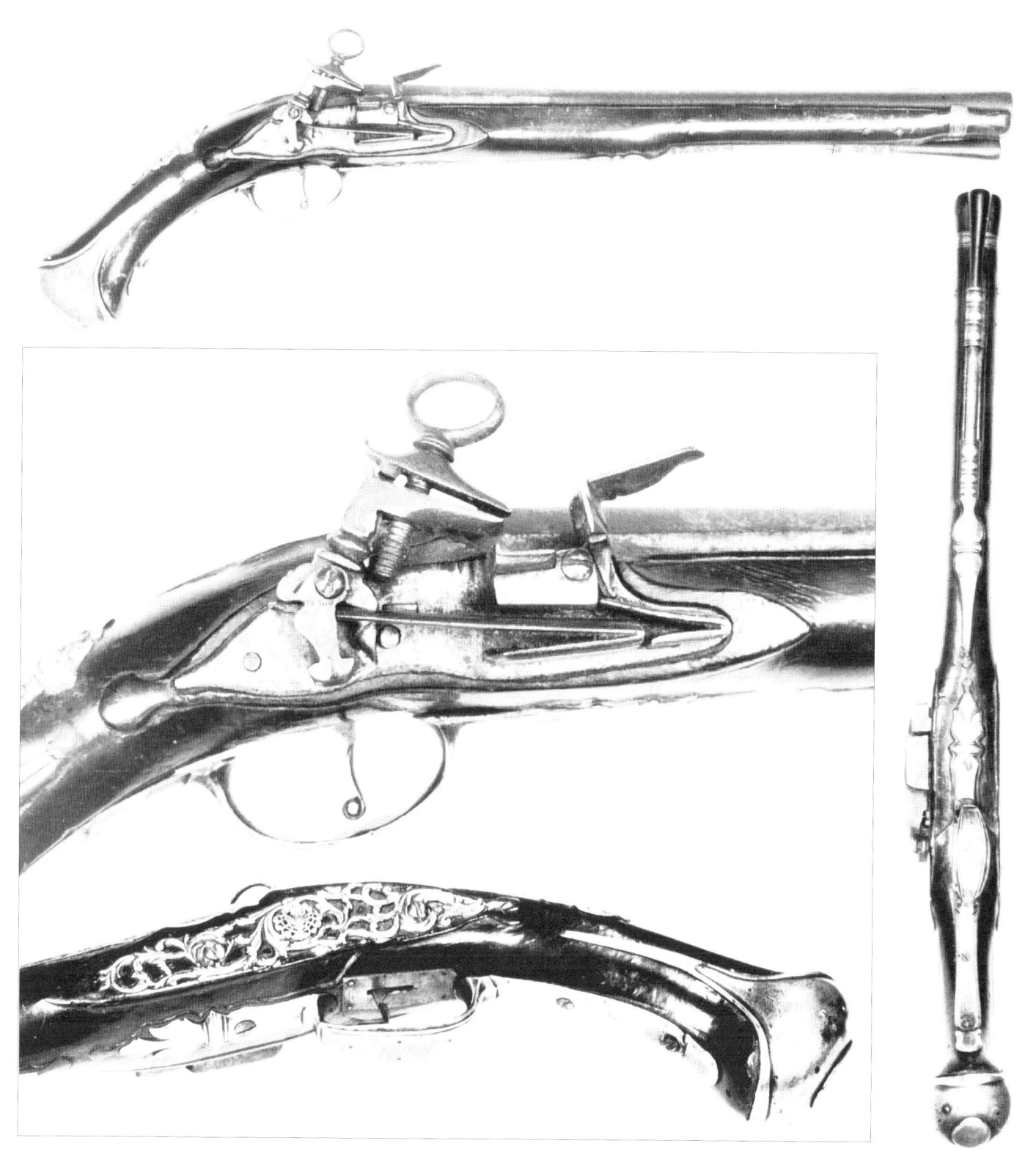

Much of the grace and majesty of America's Hudson Valley (New York) fowlers (see 110.MM–112.MM) are apparent in this pistol from that area. Note the typical Dutch-style furniture in the acanthus leaf terminal on the trigger guard, the bulbous butt cap with long side straps, an open foliage side plate and two baluster rammer thimbles (wooden trumpet-shaped rod). Its 14-1/2" (.70 caliber) pinned barrel is octagonal for 4-3/8 inches and continues a flat top panel to within 5/8 inch of the swamped muzzle. Moreover, a Spanish miquelet lock was reused by the gunsmith. It includes the usual mainspring on the outside, a ring-type cock screw and a lateral safety sear that projects out just forward of the hammer. An innovative squared supporting bridle was also added below the rectangular flash pan. Teardrop-type carving surrounds the lock, side plate and barrel tang. A raised brass escutcheon, plus a decorative silver badge in the side plate's center, are both later additions. The early practice of using a bottom screw to hold the barrel tang is also surprisingly incorporated in the gun.

Length: 21-3/4"  Lock: 4-5/8" X 1"  Furniture: Brass
Barrel: 14-1/2", .70 cal.  Trigger Guard: 8-1/4"  Weight: 2.6 lbs.

**Mike D'Ambra Collection**

*Chapter 5: Pistols*

**43.PP  AMERICAN HOLSTER PISTOLS**                                                       **Circa 1750–1770**

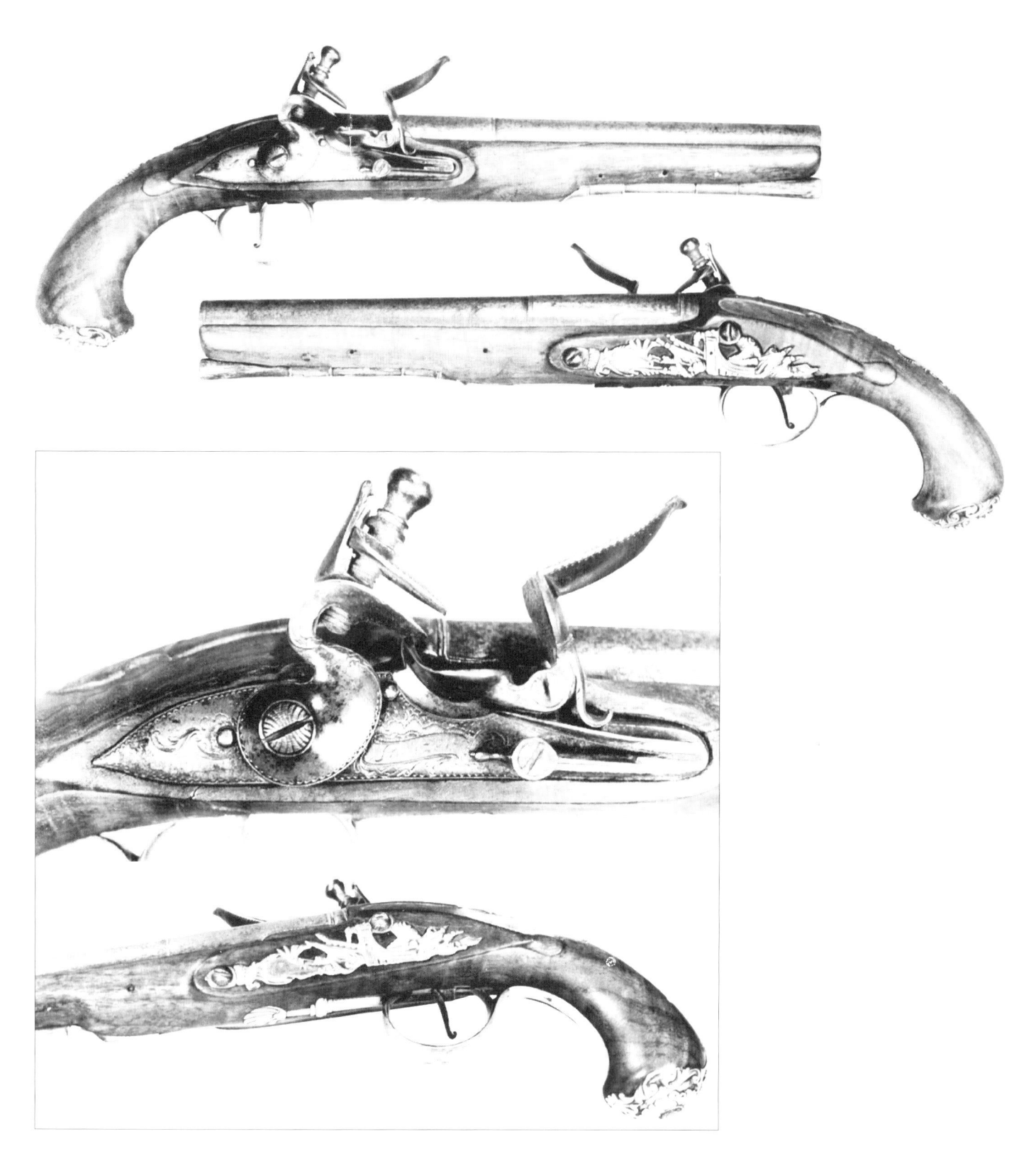

Although the pressures of war led Americans to create many utilitarian grade pistols for field service, their gunsmiths showed impressive capabilities when time and resources permitted. This pair of silver-mounted holster pistols is attributed to Pennsylvania and bears the name "SWITZER" on the lock plate under the pan. The English-style silver side plate with a rococo panoply display, the narrow trigger guard ending in a shell finial, and a foliage-decorated butt cap were popular in the mother country circa 1740 to 1760 and may have been imported as components. The locks, in turn, exhibit stippled outlines on the plate and cock—supplemented by incised lines covering the screw heads and frizzen spring edges. Of special interest is an elaborate escutcheon that features a shield inscribed with an arm holding a scimitar emerging from a cloud. The round barrels have a ring 2-5/8 inches above the breech, while two plain pipes hold the wooden rammers. Attractive walnut stocks provide raised borders (with unique end lobes) surrounding the lock and side plate, plus a splay below the barrel tang.

| | | |
|---|---|---|
| Length: 13-1/8" | Lock: 4-1/4" X 3/4" | Furniture: Silver |
| Barrel: 8-1/4", .56 cal. | Trigger Guard: 6-1/8" | Weight: 1.6 lbs. |

Chapter 5: Pistols

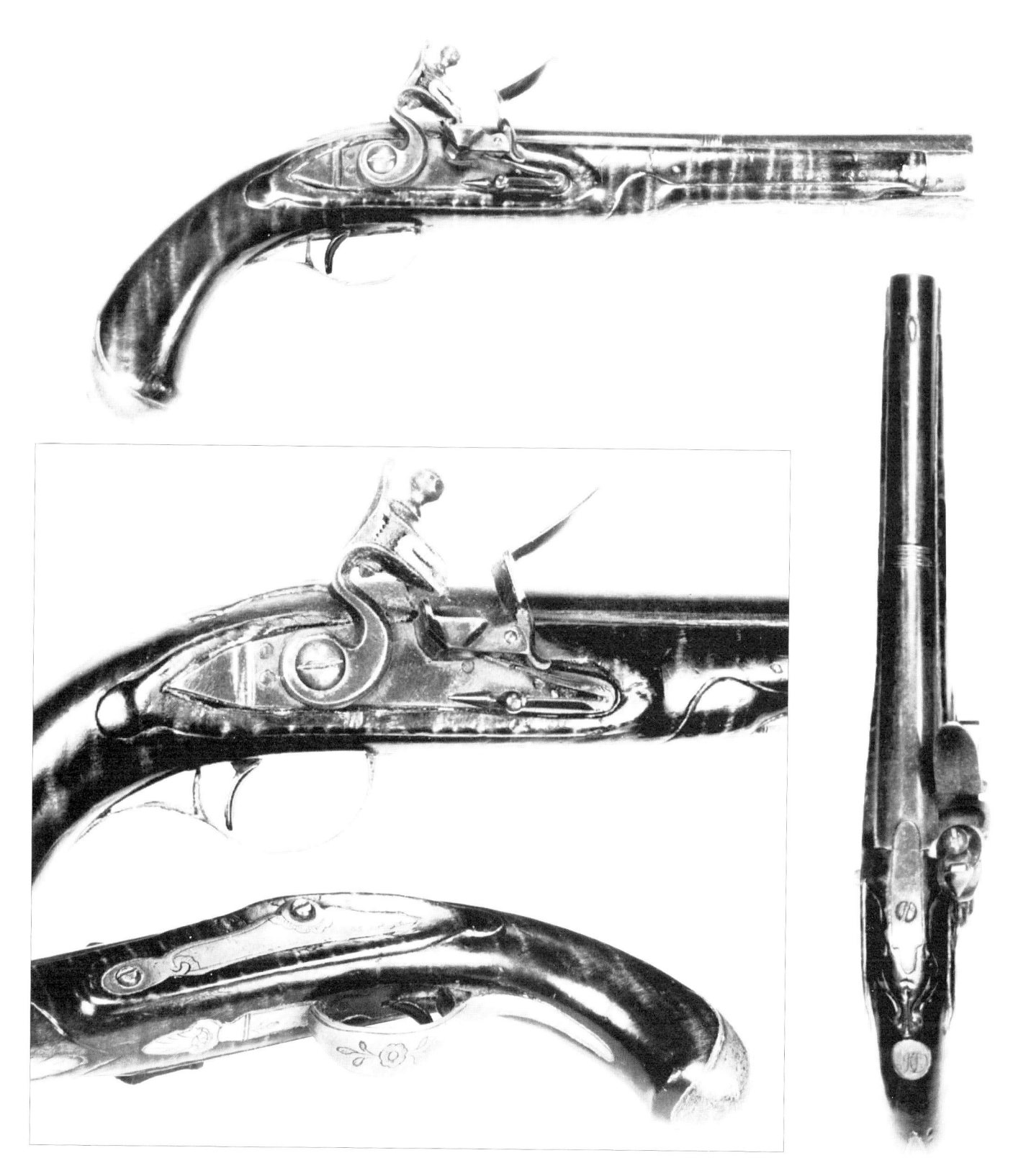

**44.PP AMERICAN "RIFLED" PISTOL**  Circa 1770–1785

Many of the makers of American long rifles also produced pistol counterparts. Few survived the Revolutionary War era, but this example from that period illustrates many of their features: a striped maple stock ending in a forend cap; a flat/beveled lock including a slashed tail, faceted pan and pointed frizzen spring finial; a pinned barrel usually octagonal and rifled (the one here is octagonal for 4-1/8 inches to a five-ring band, then round to the muzzle, which has a blade sight); stock carving such as the raised borders shown surrounding the lock, side plate and barrel tang, as well as an incised line on each side tracing the ramrod channel and outlining its tail pipe area; and functional but stylized furniture. This weapon's butt cap and side plate decoration suggest French influence, while its trigger guard displays a flower engraved on the bow. Its forward terminal is not unlike the acorn form—reflecting English exposure. The two sheet-brass thimbles, in turn, hold a wooden rammer. "JD" on the oval silver escutcheon is probably an owner's identification.

Length: 14-1/2"
Barrel: 8-1/2", .58 cal.
Lock: 4-1/2" X 3/4"
Trigger Guard: 6-1/4"
Side Plate: 4-1/8"
Weight: 1.8 lbs.
Furniture: Brass

**James D. Forman Collection**

Chapter 5: Pistols

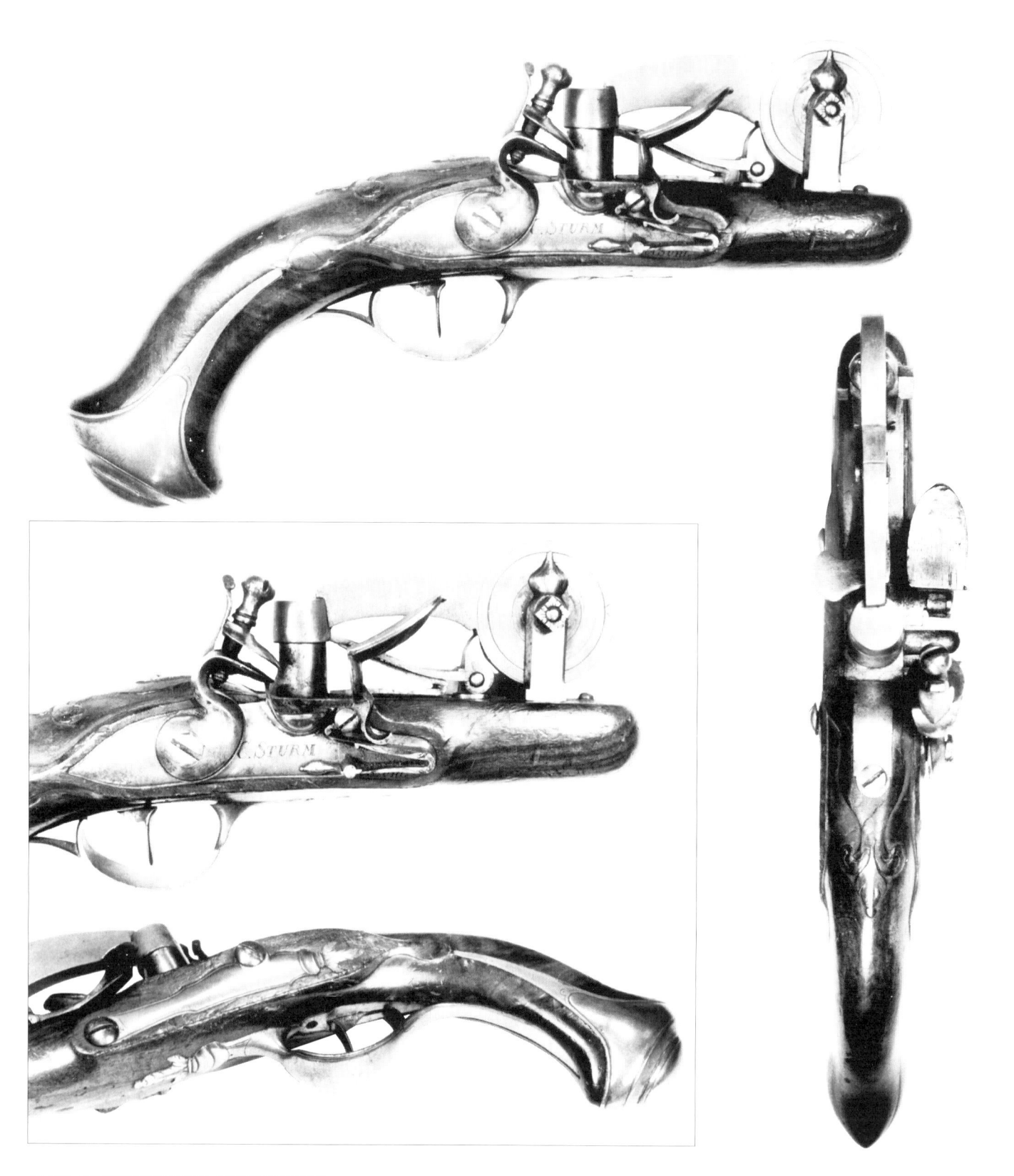

**45.PP POWDER TESTER *(EPROUVETTE)*** Circa 1740

The quality of black gunpowder varied because of the impurities of its ingredients, which were further altered by hygroscopic properties that changed its shooting performance depending on the amount of humidity in the air as well as the common practice of adding adulterating materials such as dirt, soot and coal dust. Thus it became necessary in most cases to test the strength of each lot. This was usually accomplished by an *eprouvette* as shown here on a pistol stock. Notice that the lock, side plate, trigger guard and butt cap are of normal handgun configuration. The barrel however has become a short vertical tube above the flashpan. Its upper end (muzzle) is covered with a cap attached to an arm reaching forward to a calibrated wheel. When the barrel is loaded with a measured amount of gunpowder and ignited by the normal flint action, the force of the powder's firing pushes up the cap to register its strength by the degree of rotation on the wheel. This German powder tester is marked "C STRUM, A Suhl." (Re: Howard, bib. 214).

| | | | |
|---|---|---|---|
| Length: 10" | Lock: 3-7/8" X 3/4" | Side Plate: 3-5/8" | Furniture: Brass |
| Barrel: 5/8" | Trigger Guard: 6-1/8" | Weight: 1.2 lbs. | |

**George C. Neumann Collection, Valley Forge National Historical Park**

276  *Chapter 5: Pistols*

# Chapter 6

# Bayonets... The Moment of Truth

The cries of men consumed in combat rise above the slamming cannon, chattering snare drums and screams of the wounded. Your hands and face are filthy with smears of black powder fouling from repeated firings of the musket—the barrel of which has long since become too hot to touch. The cartridge box flapping against your right hip offers only empty holes in its wooden block as your fingers dig clumsily to find a remaining round. The straight ranks of your battle lines, which began with controlled volleys, are now dangerously torn into forlorn groups separated by shredded gaps of the fallen. The

**THIRD NEW JERSEY REGIMENT AT CONNECTICUT FARMS (New Jersey), 1780**
By 1778 the Continental Line had mastered the discipline and élan of linear tactics. The result was a near-stalemate in the North, with Clinton in New York City and Washington ready to counter any attempted breakout, as shown in their hand-to-hand confrontation to stop this Hessian invasion into New Jersey.

*Chapter 6: Bayonets* 277

artificial surge of battlefield exhilaration that has sustained you is fading before the draining fatigue of overpowering exhaustion. Then they come—materializing through the clouds of smoke—one, two, perhaps even three long lines of the enemy advancing methodically—*tramp, tramp, tramp*—with muskets leveled, pointing deadly bayonet blades directly at you and your remaining comrades in relentless momentum. Somehow you must stop them. The moment of truth has arrived . . . and then they are upon you.

This was the climax of the typical 18th century battle. It did not offer the comfort and security of legend—that the Americans won because they wisely chose to fight from the cover of trees and walls. It was the harsh realities of the bayonet that usually decided victory or defeat. It was that combat of cold steel, hand-to-hand and face-to-face against the finest bayonet regiments in the world that Washington and his army had to confront and master before any hope of winning was even possible. Thus as we review the various bayonets presented here, it is important to remain aware that each is more than a pattern or transitional form needed to fill a gap in a collection or museum display. The bayonet, more than any other period weapon, testifies to the incredible personal courage, commitment and sacrifice required to overcome the impossible and achieve America's freedom.

At the time of the first American colonies, massed troops creating moving "hedgehogs" of spear points on long pikes were Europe's traditional battlefield formations. As the 1600s progressed, musket men with the new evolving firearm were steadily added to both flanks. By 1700 the two weapons had been combined by attaching a bayonet on an improved flintlock longarm to establish the basic tactics of 18th century battles, including the American War for Independence.

## PLUG BAYONETS

The practice of joining a blade with a long firearm reportedly began in the Basque area of Spain about 1580 as a dagger attached to a gun for hunting. The French then adopted this concept for military use about 1642 by inserting a long dagger having a tapered handle into the muzzle. Their term, *bayonet*, was apparently acquired from the cutlery center of Bayonne, which was well-known for knives and daggers. England purchased several hundred from France in 1662, and by the 1690s the plug bayonet had become a standard arm in Britain and most of continental Europe. Its shortcomings, however, were obvious: when pushed into the bore, the gun could not be fired; if jammed too tightly, reloading was not possible; and it was easily lost in combat. The tactics were established, but an improved pattern was needed (1.BB–6.BB).

## SOCKET BAYONETS

Again it was the French who by the 1670s pioneered a new version—the socket bayonet. This concept was quickly adopted in various forms and by 1700 had become a standard weapon. A cylindrical socket slid over a section of the barrel. It provided a short neck opposite the muzzle which offset the attached blade so that the firearm could be loaded and fired with the bayonet in place. Most designs had two or three slots cut (at right angles) in the socket. A rectangular stud was brazed above or below the muzzle, which slid through these slots as the bayonet was rotated during attachment. In final position the neck and blade projected out to the right side in the same horizontal plane as the musket barrel. Each socket was fitted individually to its assigned gun.

American Colonials had little need in their forested terrain for Europe's long pikes or even for the new bayonet at first. They specified the traditional secondary weapons (one was always carried in addition to the firearm) as either a short sword ("cutlass," "hanger") or a belt ax ("hatchet"). As the land was cleared and formations became more important, plug bayonets made their appearance in North America, probably beginning with professional English or French troops plus private purchases for local governments and individuals. Further large shipments from the mother country arrived beginning about 1700 in her effort to dispose of obsolete inventories.

Plug bayonets were listed in American arsenals by the 1680s and continued in use during the Revolutionary War as makeshift bayonets and daggers to fill the void of weapons. It is interesting to note that plug bayonets remained as civilian hunting arms well into the mid-1800s in parts of Spain, France and Germany.

By the 1740s the new socket bayonet was being listed with the sword and hatchet as an acceptable secondary arm for most provincial militias. While many were made locally in varying degrees of reliability, the majority followed England's pattern, shifting to the French form as their wartime shipments arrived.

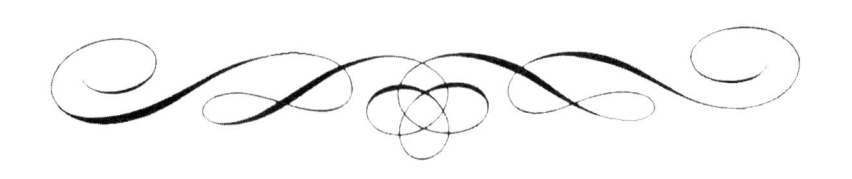

**1.BB  EUROPEAN PLUG BAYONET**  Circa 1680–1700

This long symmetrical blade and tapering wooden handle with an enlarged base (1-1/2" diameter) are typical of the large infantry patterns popular in central Europe during the late 17th century. The heavy blade includes a full length cutting edge, plus a 4-3/4" false edge and 3/8" ricasso. Notice also the crossguard that provides field tools and a means to dress a flint—having one quillon formed as a hammer, the other as a screwdriver. A 3/4" iron ferrule joins in a crude lapped seam.
Length: 21-1/4"      Handle: 7-7/8"      Blade: 13-3/8" X 1-3/8"
**George C. Neumann Collection, Valley Forge National Historical Park**

**2.BB  ENGLISH PLUG BAYONET**  Circa 1685–1700

There was little uniformity in plug bayonet patterns among British regiments prior to 1700, and they varied from plain utilitarian materials for enlisted men to impressive officer versions with ivory and silver. This was a popular design that adopted an earlier French practice of shaping pommel and quillon tips as human figures—in this case helmeted faces. Blades also differed greatly. The one shown is a true dagger form (symmetrical plus both edges sharpened). The tapering round hilt is mahogany with two ivory rings, while its crossguard and pommel are cast brass.
Length: 17-1/2"      Hilt: 6-3/8"      Blade: 11-1/8" X 1-1/8"
**Author's Collection**

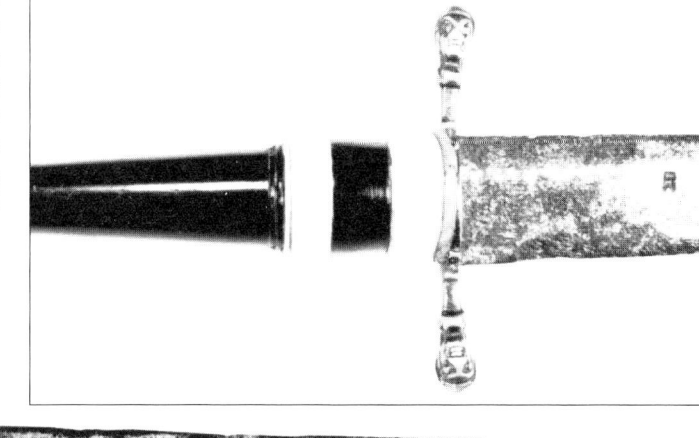

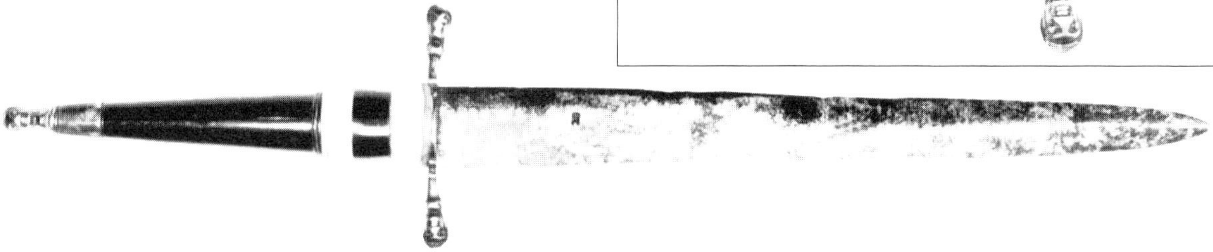

**3.BB  ENGLISH PLUG BAYONET**  Circa 1688–1700

Britain's Board of Ordnance showed little interest in standard models for plug bayonets before 1700. It did, however, issue suggested dimensions in 1686, and this form is one of the "official" patterns of that period—examples of which vary in size. Most 17th century English plugs were made by the London Cutlers Company that, like much of Europe, was not above forging the "king's head" ("konigskopf") of Solingen on its blades (visible here). The oak grip mounts a rounded brass pommel as well as a bulbous crossguard (3-1/2"). Its 11" single-edged blade includes a five-inch false edge.
Length: 17-1/2"      Hilt: 6-1/2"      Blade: 11" X 1-1/2"
**Author's Collection**

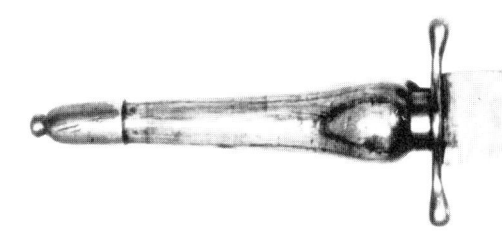

*Chapter 6: Bayonets*   279

**4.BB FRENCH "MARINE" PLUG BAYONET     Circa 1670–1700**
This plug bayonet with its impressive sword-type blade fits the French pattern described in 1695 for Marine troops that defended French Canada. Note the blade's dimensions: 15" X 1-1/2" (single edge sharpened), 5-1/4" false edge, and 3/16" fuller along the back. A scimitar mark is stamped into its face. The hilt has a reddish-brown fruitwood grip (ending in a 1-1/8" ball), a crude disk pommel, a 3/8" ferrule and a flint knapping/field tool crossguard providing hammer and screwdriver quillons (2-5/8 inches across).
Length: 20-3/8"          Hilt: 5-3/8"          Blade: 15" X 1-1/2"
**Author's Collection**

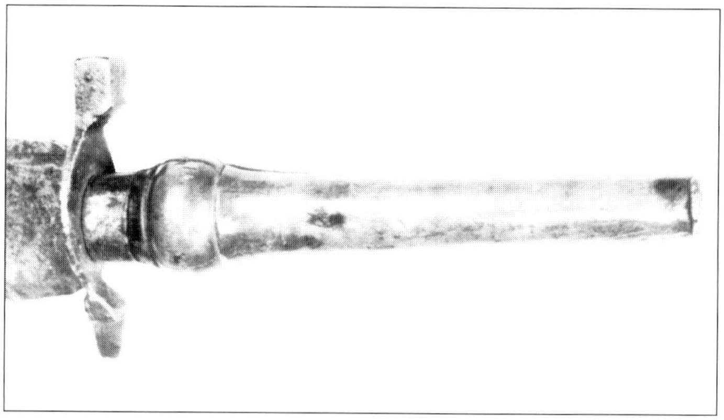

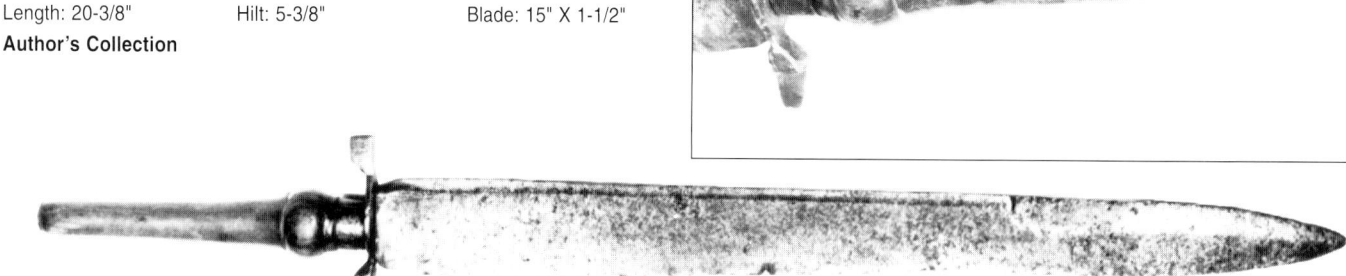

**5.BB AMERICAN PLUG BAYONET     Circa 1700–1740**
Although the English colonists received surplus plug bayonets from Britain, others were produced locally, as they required only a tapered handle to be shoved into a gun barrel, plus a basic straight blade. This rudimentary pattern was found in the muzzle of an early Colonial musket and is believed to be American made. The plain walnut grip tapers to form a 1-3/8" diameter ball above the simple flat iron crossguard, while the blade's thin tang passes up through the hilt and is flattened over a flat disk pommel at the upper end. The symmetrical blade measures 10-1/2 inches.
Length: 14-1/2"          Hilt: 4"          Blade: 10-1/2" X 1-5/16"
**George C. Neumann Collection, Valley Forge National Historical Park**

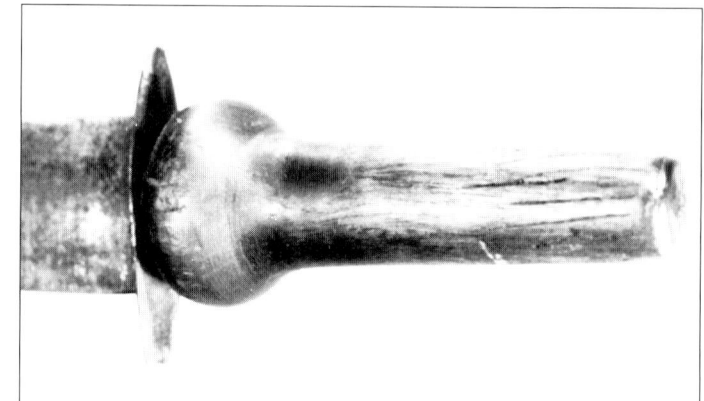

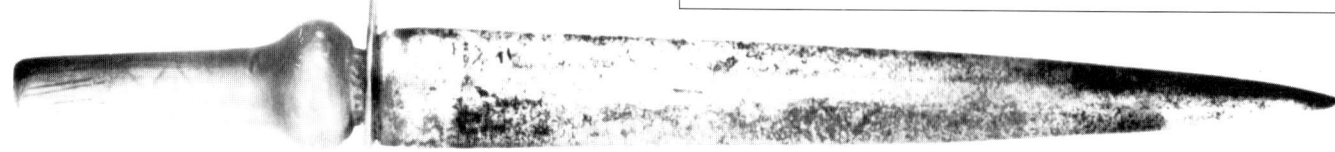

**6.BB AMERICAN PLUG BAYONET     Circa 1775–1780**
Facing a severe shortage of weaponry early in the Revolutionary War, the Colonials filled the gap temporarily with locally made spear-like pikes to defend fortified positions or to meet a charge of bayonets. This improvised plug bayonet appears to have converted a typical pike head by adding a squared base ring and a slightly tapered handle, which snugly fits into the muzzle of a Brown Bess. A cross-rivet through the spearhead's base secures the wood.
Length: 14"          Grip: 3-1/4"          Blade: 10-3/4"
**The Benninghoff Collection**

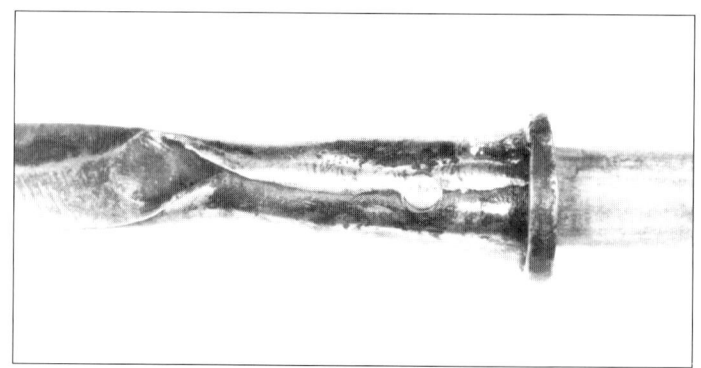

**7.BB  ENGLISH SPLIT SOCKET BAYONET      Circa 1700–1720**
Development of the new socket bayonet quickly established that a snug fit on the barrel required individual sizing for each of the wide variety of longarms in service. An early form to help ease the problem was this type of pattern, which combined a split socket that could easily adjust its diameter with a blade having a shell guard at the base to help trap an enemy's bayonet. The single-edged 10-7/8" blade includes a 3-1/2" false edge. Two right-angled mounting slots are present in the socket. A similar style appeared in France circa 1670 and was adopted by England before 1700.
Length: 16"           Socket: 3-7/8"           Blade: 10-7/8"
**George C. Neumann Collection, Valley Forge National Historical Park**

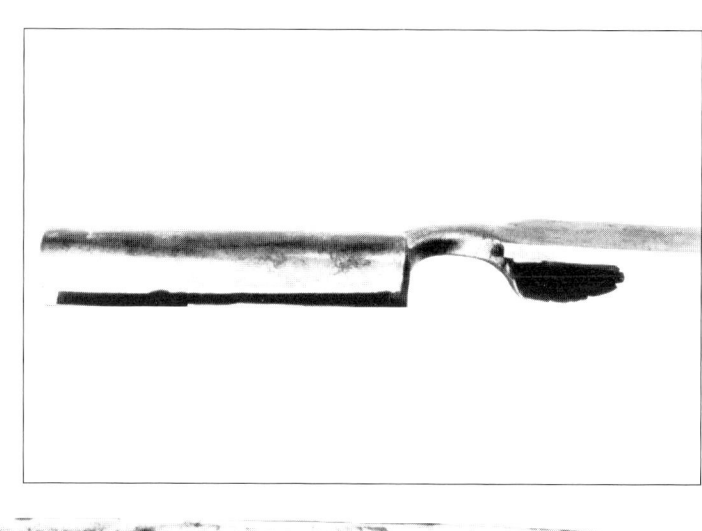

**8.BB  ENGLISH SHELL GUARD BAYONET      Circa 1710–1730**
During this period the eventual Brown Bess bayonet form was evolving. Its ultimate four-inch socket having an end ring and three mounting slots (for a top stud) is already apparent in this rare example. However an earlier broad vertical blade and shell guard continue. The reverse of its shell (2-1/8" X 2-1/8") is marked "L SORBY" (the maker); a neck stamp, in turn, reads "14 / 2." The impressive 19" blade has a flat back plus a cutting edge along the bottom, while its black leather scabbard (19-5/8" X 1-3/4") mounts brass fittings that include "3 / 71" on the stud.
Length: 24"           Socket: 4"              Blade: 19" X 1-1/2"
**Robert Nittolo Collection**

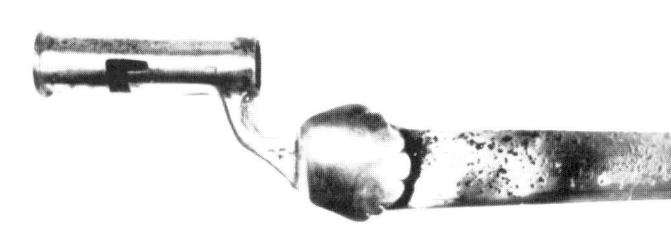

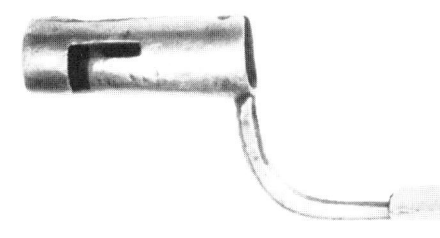

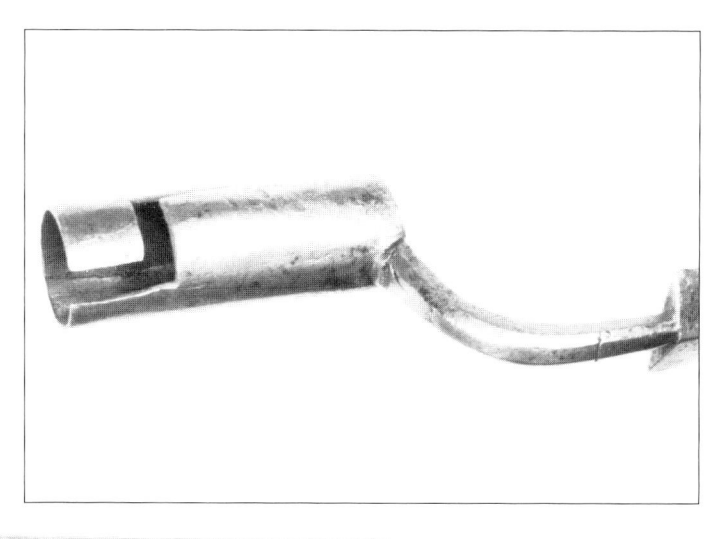

**9.BB  ENGLISH SOCKET BAYONET      Circa 1700–1715**
During the War of the Spanish Succession (1702–1713, Queen Anne's War), a vast array of weapons armed the British regiments. Many came from various sources on the Continent. The bayonet in this case was found on an early English musket and is crudely finished, showing a transitional mix of basic unrefined elements, for example: a 14" triangular blade still lacking fullers or a baseguard, a flawed octagonal neck ending in a narrowed socket joint, and a plain 3-1/8" socket (no ring) with a rough brazed seam along the top. The three mounting slots appear original.
Length: 19-1/2"       Socket: 3-1/8"          Blade: 14" X 1-1/8"
**Author's Collection**

*Chapter 6: Bayonets*   281

**10.BB  ENGLISH SOCKET BAYONET            Circa 1710–1720**
This design was apparently among the great variety of bayonets used by the British army in the formative period before the Board of Ordnance was able to enforce official patterns. Notice the wide straight rectangular neck (1/2" across) and 18-1/4" blade with its tapered shoulders, symmetrical double edges (unsharpened) and median ridge on both faces. It is unlike the developing English form, suggesting possible purchase from foreign suppliers. The 3-7/8" socket has three slots for a top barrel stud. (A mounted blade always ended up at the right of the muzzle.)
Length: 22-1/2"          Socket: 3-7/8"          Blade: 18-1/2"
**George C. Neumann Collection, Valley Forge National Historical Park**

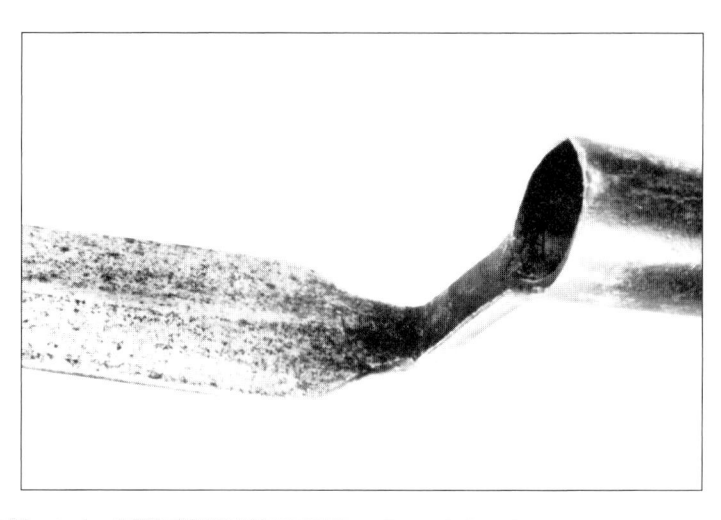

**11.BB  ENGLISH SOCKET BAYONET            Circa 1700–1720**
Here is another variation during this undisciplined era of the British socket bayonet. Like the preceding example, it omits a baseguard and mounts a blade with sloping shoulders and a median ridge on both faces (each slightly concave). The most unique feature, however, is the "cannon" socket design with baluster-type end rings. Also notice the growing acceptance of three mounting slots and the neck's raised collar joint at the socket.
Length: 18-7/8"          Socket: 3-9/16"          Blade: 14-1/8" X 1-1/8"
**Erik Goldstein Collection**

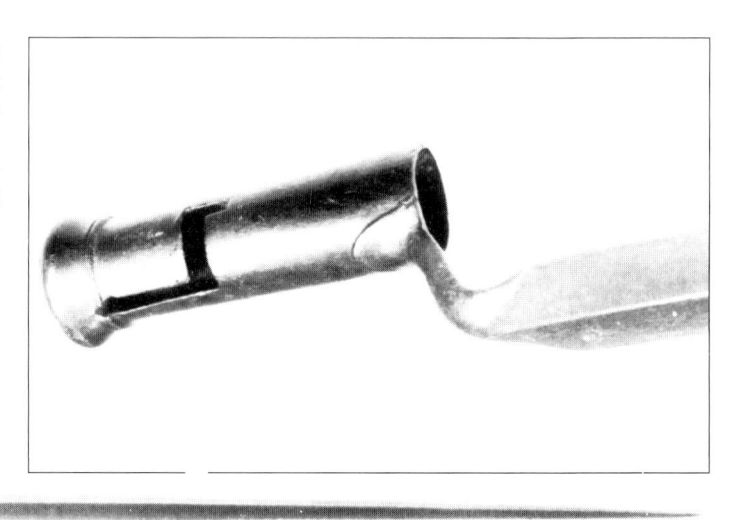

**12.BB  ENGLISH SOCKET BAYONET            Circa 1710–1720**
In this transitional stage of the new British socket bayonet, its eventual triangular blade is beginning to emerge. All three faces are concave and end at a pronounced half-circle baseguard. An extended oval neck, in turn, attaches to the plain socket (no end ring) with a rounded raised collar joint. The original two mounting slots apparently had a short third opening added during use to accomodate a larger barrel stud or to tighten its fit. The only marking is "20" on the socket's back end.
Length: 17-7/8"          Socket: 3-3/8"          Blade: 13" X 1-1/8"
**Author's Collection**

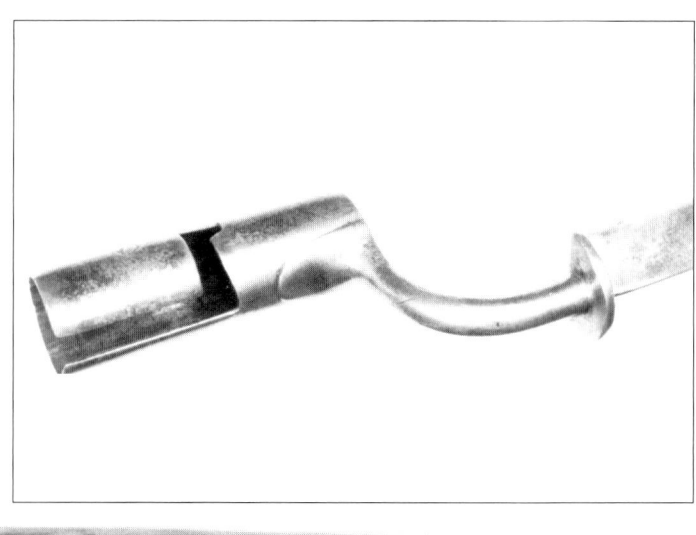

282      *Chapter 6: Bayonets*

**13.BB  ENGLISH SOCKET BAYONET         Circa 1710–1720**
Despite continued variances, further progress in Britain's pattern development is now evident by the addition of an end ring to the 3-5/8" cylindrical socket. Its three mounting slots (for a top stud) are becoming established, as well as the raised collar joint for its extended ovoid neck. This unusual blade (13-3/4") has a rare crescent cross-section with a rounded bottom and a concave upper face. The base guard is an expansive half circle. A rough top seam completes the socket; it is engraved "16."
Length: 19"          Socket: 3-1/2"          Blade: 13-3/4" X 1"
**Author's Collection**

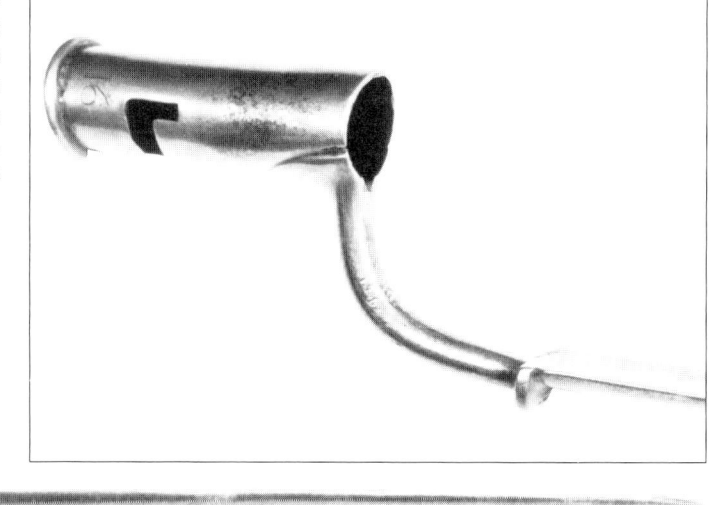

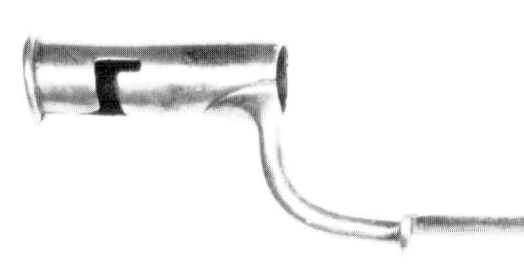

**14.BB  ENGLISH SOCKET BAYONET         Circa 1725–1740**
As the official Long Land musket pattern was finally specified during the 1720s, this new bayonet was also designated, and its basic configuration would continue into the next century. Notice the now-standard four-inch socket having a pronounced end ring and three-step slotting (always for a top barrel stud), the 17" triangular blade attached to a projecting baseguard, and a thick neck presenting a flattened front face. The raised collar joint is part of this pattern's early form. Its blade is wide (1-5/16 inches) with a slightly concave top and two bottom fullers.
Length: 21-1/2"          Socket: 4"          Blade: 16-5/8" X 1-5/16"
**Author's Collection**

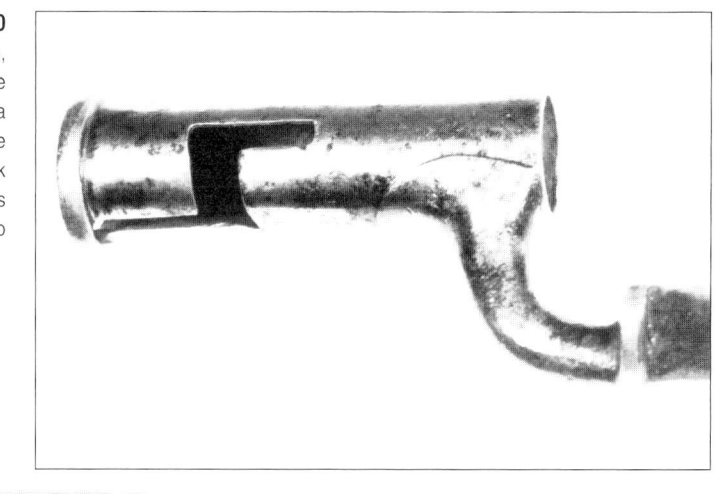

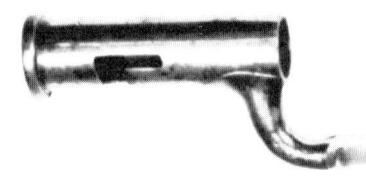

**15.BB  ENGLISH SOCKET BAYONET         Circa 1740–1760**
Notice these initial refinements of Britain's Long Land bayonet. The raised collar joint of the earlier version (14.BB) has been replaced by a smooth junction. Moreover the neck retains a flattened front surface but curves back slightly from the socket's end line. In addition, improved metallurgy now permitted the English to join a lower blade of iron with an upper blade section of steel—to combine flexibility at the base with rigid strength nearer the point (a faint line is visible two thirds distance from tip). This form was also adopted by the Sea Service in 1752.
Length: 21-3/4"          Socket: 4-1/8"          Blade: 16-7/8" X 1-3/8"
**Author's Collection**

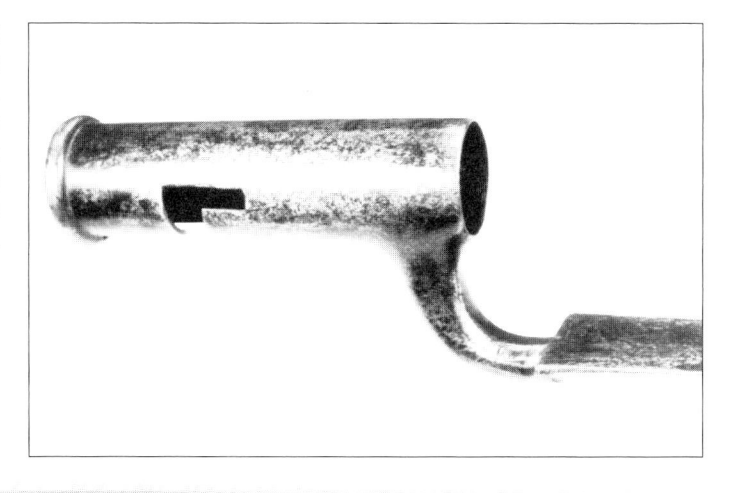

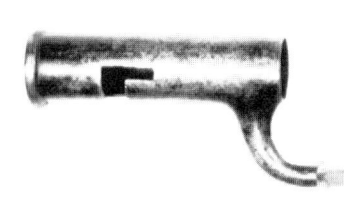

*Chapter 6: Bayonets*

**16.BB  ENGLISH SOCKET BAYONET  Circa 1760–1776**
There are two interesting observations here. First, the socket is marked at its forward end "F / 34 / 17RT" for the 17th Regiment of Foot, one of the most active of His Majesty's units—including the Battle of Princeton (the area where this arm was found). Second, it illustrates the manufacturing variances produced under wartime demands and cost cutting pressures. Notice, for example, this typical socket form is 3-3/4 inches instead of four inches, the blade's base has already narrowed to 1-3/16 inches with a flat upper face and its specified 17" length measures 16-3/4 inches.

Length: 21-3/8"          Socket: 3-3/4"          Blade: 16-3/4" X 1-3/16"
**Author's Collection**

**17.BB  ENGLISH (LIEGE) SOCKET BAYONET  Circa 1778–1785**
When France actively entered the war in 1778, England expanded its weapons procurement with contracts in Europe, especially Liege. They ordered the Short Land Pattern 1777 musket (16.MM) with bayonets that included minor changes (already being made) that would continue through the early 1800s, that is: a slight bend in the blade below the socket's axis, a down-curving beak-like point, a narrower base with less of a lip on the guard, and a flat upper surface. Note, too, the higher density, better quality Low Country steel that gives this example a smoother surface and greater weight.

Length: 21-5/8"          Socket: 4"          Blade: 16-7/8" X 1-3/16"
**Author's Collection**

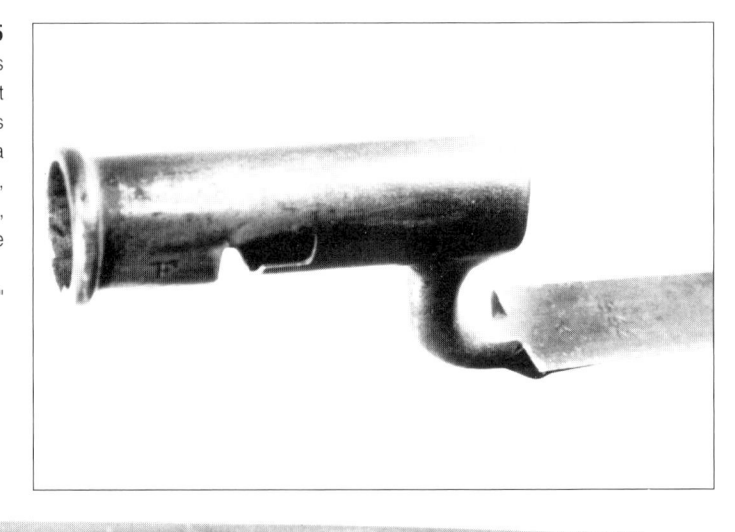

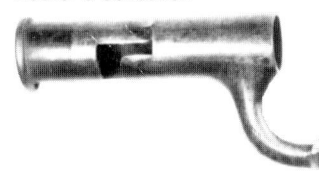

**18.BB  ENGLISH LIGHT INFANTRY CARBINE BAYONET PATTERN 1760          Circa 1760**
Once the basic Brown Bess bayonet pattern was established, the Board of Ordnance adjusted its configuration to fit other longarms. This variation was used with the Light Infantry Carbine Pattern 1760 (123.MM). The standard four-inch socket was retained, but its internal diameter was reduced to match the barrel's smaller bore (.65 caliber versus the musket's .75). The blade, in turn, copies the traditional triangular form yet measures 16-1/2 inches instead of the usual 17 inches and is narrowed to 1-1/8 inches. Both bottom fullers end 1-1/8 inch above the baseguard.

Length: 19-7/8"          Socket: 4"          Blade: 16-1/2" X 1-1/8"
**Author's Collection**

284     *Chapter 6: Bayonets*

**19.BB  ENGLISH ELIOTT CARBINE BAYONET PATTERN 1773   Circa 1773**
Britain's expanding light dragoons also adopted the basic infantry bayonet pattern to their carbines. This was the one sized to fit Eliott's Pattern 1773 (125.MM). The normal socket design with an end ring and three mounting slots (for a top stud) is shortened to 3-1/4 inches and has a smaller interior diameter for the .65 caliber carbine bore. Its down-sized triangular blade (13-3/8 inches) maintains the flat upper face, while both bottom fullers end 2-1/4 inches above the base. The name "OUGHTON" (a Birmingham maker) is stamped on the blade.
Length: 17-5/8"   Socket: 3-1/4"   Blade: 13-3/8" X 1"
**Author's Collection**

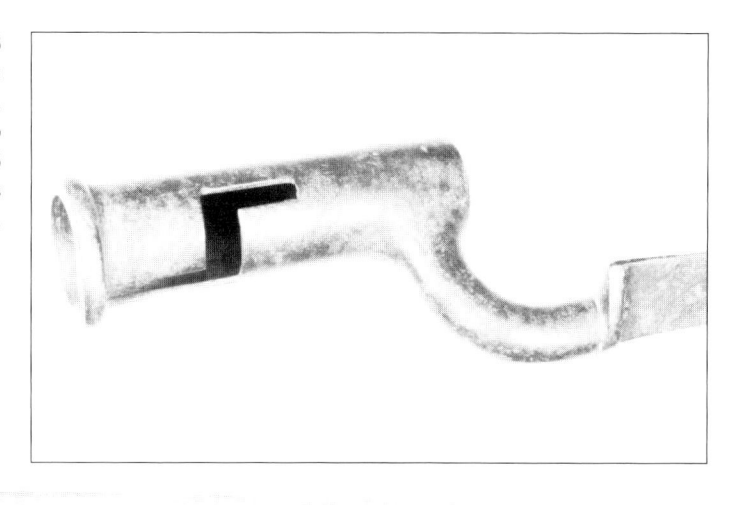

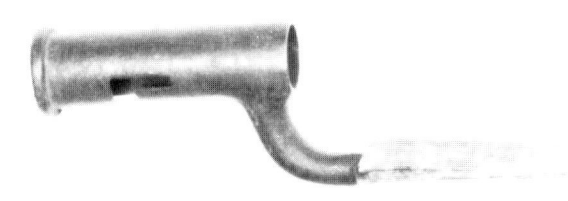

**20.BB  ENGLISH FERGUSON RIFLE BAYONET   Circa 1775–1780**
The traditional British musket had a top bayonet stud and no formal sights. The Ferguson military rifle (16.RR, 17.RR), however, added two sights and moved the stud under the muzzle—reflecting its aimed sighting and breechloading capabilities. Thus these special Ferguson bayonets were longer than usual (to offset a shorter barrel length) and slotted to fix the flat blade directly below the barrel instead of at the right side. This example accompanied a private contract rifle given to Loyalist Capt. A. de Peyster by Ferguson. (Re: Benninghoff, bib. 172)
Length: 29-5/8"   Socket: 4-1/4"   Blade: 24-5/8"
**Smithsonian Institution, James Watts de Peyster Collection**

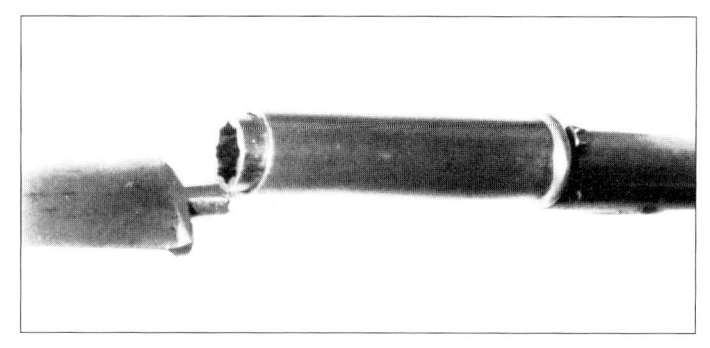

**21.BB  ENGLISH OFFICER'S FUSIL BAYONET   Circa 1750–1810**
Fusils were light muskets carried by officers. Since such longarms and their bayonets were purchased privately, they conformed to specifics of the owner's choice that varied in size and embellishments. Nevertheless most kept a semblance of the Long Land design, as seen in this fusil bayonet. The standard infantry pattern is followed but with scaled-down proportions: a three-inch socket that kept the established end ring and three slots; a reduced oval neck; plus the familiar triangular blade which was shortened to 12 inches yet copied the normal baseguard, flat face and two bottom fullers.
Length: 15-5/8"   Socket: 3"   Blade: 12" X 1"
**Author's Collection**

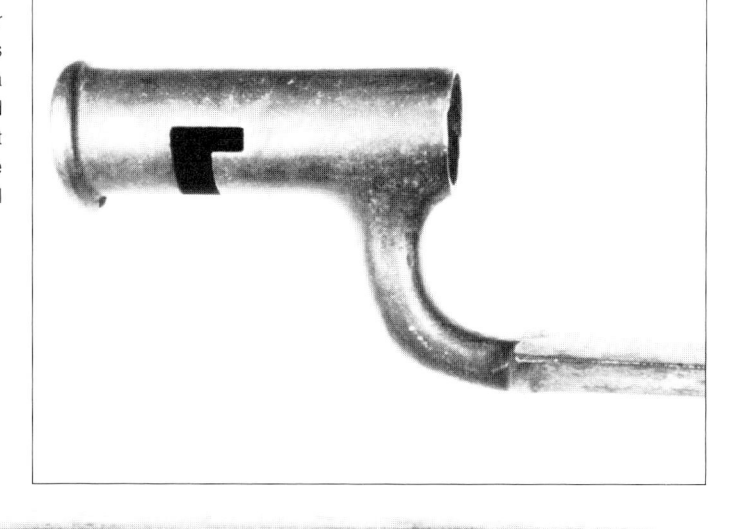

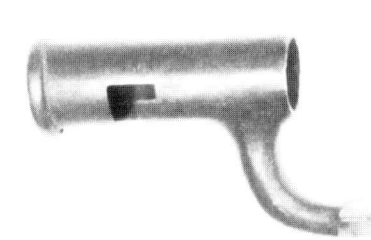

*Chapter 6: Bayonets*

**22.BB  ENGLISH EXPERIMENTAL BAYONET           Circa 1750–1775**

Experience in the field demonstrated that the right-angled open mounting slots were not reliable enough to secure a bayonet to the barrel. As a result various attachments and alterations were tested during this period. The example here adds a round spring held by a top screw. It follows the socket's curve to extend over the second slot in order to trap the barrel's stud in position. The third slot's extended length was probably a later alteration. This is a carbine/fusil size bayonet, but a similar clasp arrangement has been found on larger examples.

Length:14-1/4"            Socket: 3-1/4"            Blade: 10-1/8" X 1-1/8"

**Author's Collection**

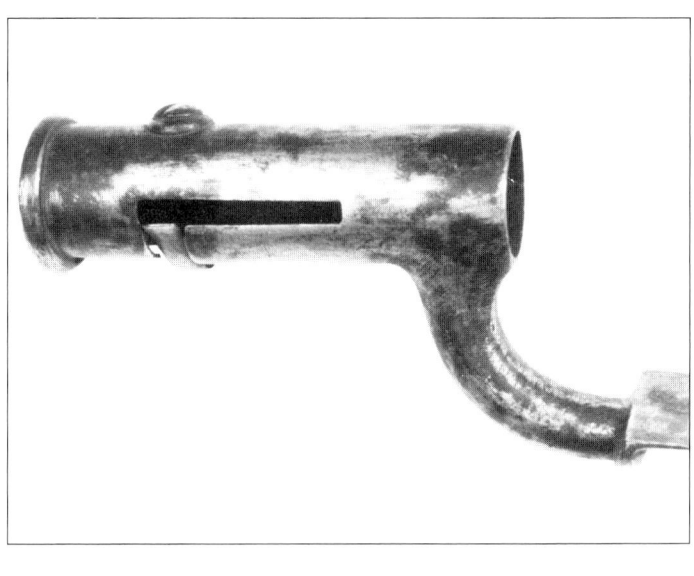

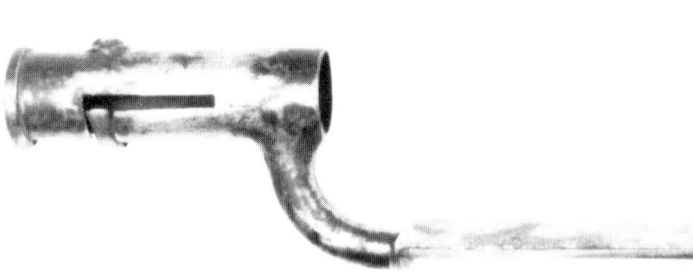

**23.BB  BRITISH EAST INDIA COMPANY BAYONET     Circa 1779**

This is *not* a Revolutionary War bayonet. It is included only for the reader's reference. At this time England's powerful East India Company was supplying their own army in India with private weapons (see 19.MM). They introduced this horizontal spring in the late 1770s. It is held by a rear screw and a small dovetail into the socket's ring to prevent rotation. The projection across the second slot locked the barrel stud in fixed position (third slot omitted). This is a fusil/carbine-size example. Marks include "E.I.C. heart symbol / MEMORY / 1779" along the socket.

Length: 16-1/2"           Socket: 3-1/4"            Blade: 12-1/2" X 1"

**Jim and Jay Kaplan Collection**

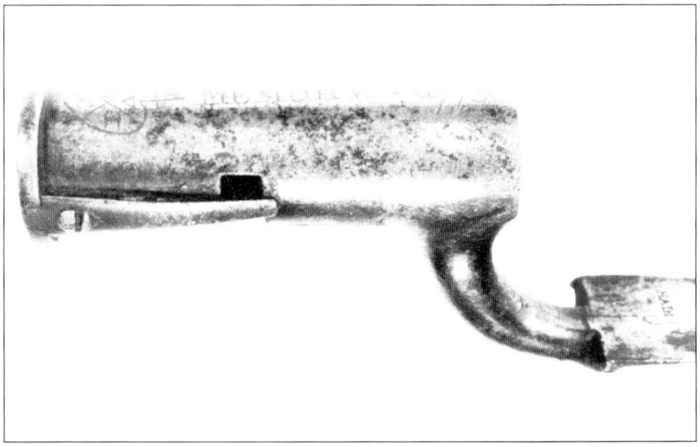

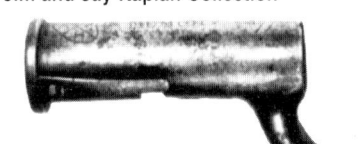

**24.BB  FRENCH "MARINE" SOCKET BAYONET        Circa 1690–1710**

Prior to 1755, when regular army regiments were first sent to North America, New France was garrisoned by *Les Compagnies Franches de la Marine*—special troops of the Ministry of Marine (Navy), which was responsible for offshore colonies. A distinctive bayonet issued to them until as late as 1740 (mostly from Tulle) had a long neck that expanded into a spearpoint. This example joins a plain 3-1/8" socket (two mounting slots) with a neck extending eight inches to a 7-3/4" triangular spearhead (all sides flat). The socket's top seam is sealed by copper, not brass (an early practice). An oval fleur-de-lis stamp appears in the upper blade face.

Length: 19"               Socket: 3-1/8"            Blade: 7-7/8" X 5/8"

**Author's Collection**

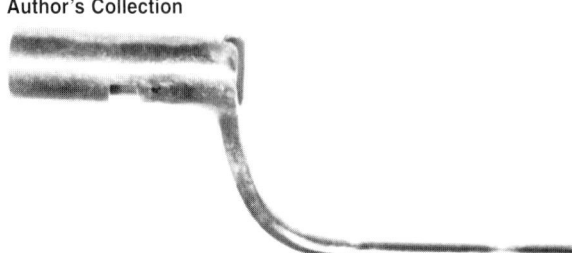

Chapter 6: Bayonets

### 25.BB  FRENCH "MARINE" SOCKET BAYONET     Circa 1700–1720

There was little adherence to firm specifications in these early years of France's spear-type bayonets. This version (versus 24.BB), for example, has a socket that retains the double mounting slots but adds a raised collar where the neck attaches to its front end (held by two rivets). Moreover the spearhead is still triangular in section with three flat sides yet is longer (8-7/8") and narrow (3/8"). The extended neck is thus reduced to 4-7/8 inches. No markings are visible.

Length: 17-1/8"            Socket: 3-1/8"            Blade: 8-7/8" X 3/8"

**George C. Neumann Collection, Valley Forge National Historical Park**

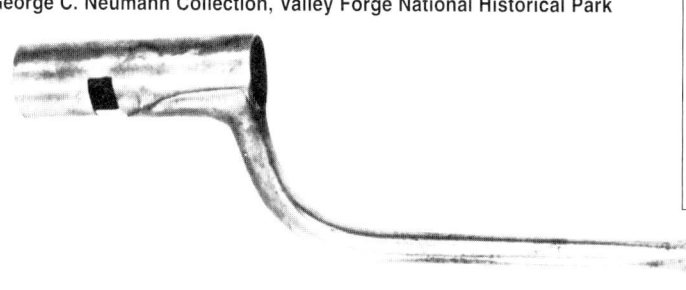

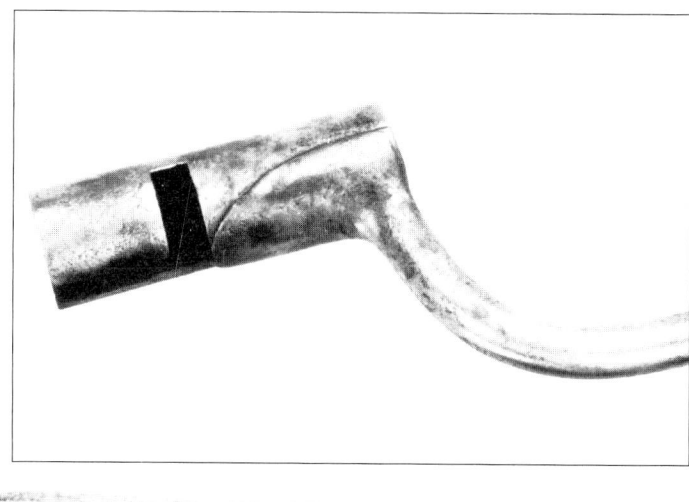

### 26.BB  FRENCH "MARINE" SOCKET BAYONET     Circa 1725–1740

The Tulle spear-type bayonet pattern specified in 1729 and 1734 contracts for Marine muskets in New France continued the cylindrical socket (2-7/8 inches, three slots here instead of the usual two) and added a single incised line bordering each end. The long slender neck projects forward 4-5/8 inches to a triangular 10" spearhead bearing a deep fuller in its upper face and two concave surfaces underneath. The neck's rear end, in turn, expands into a raised collar joint on the bottom side of the socket. There are no visible marks.

Length: 17-1/2"            Socket: 2-7/8"            Blade: 10"

**Don Troiani Collection**

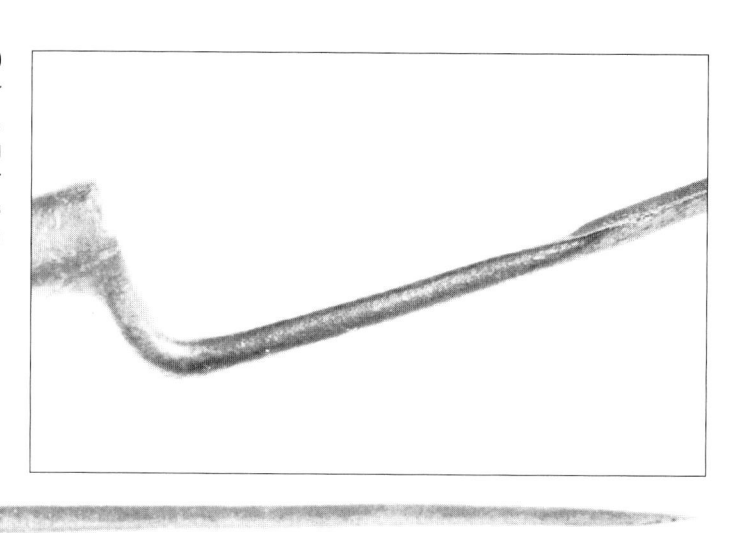

### 27.BB  SPEARHEAD SOCKET BAYONET     Circa 1710–1730

This variant of the French spear bayonet form was excavated near Fort Ticonderoga. Its neck reaches forward for 6-1/8 inches to a 9-5/8" triangular head that includes a deep V-shape fuller the length of its upper face, and both bottom sides are slightly concave. Of special interest is the three-inch socket that has added an unusual rear ring (1/8" high), retains a copper brazed top seam and omits a raised neck collar. Note also the three mounting slots cut to fit a bottom stud. It was found on a site only occupied by Americans (1776–1777) and might be their copy of an earlier French pattern.

Length: 18-1/2"            Socket: 3"            Blade: 9-5/8" X 11/16"

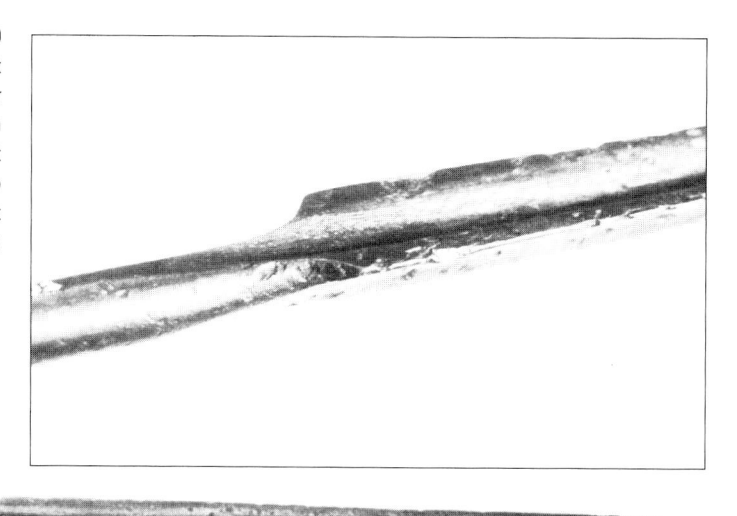

**Erik Goldstein Collection**

*Chapter 6: Bayonets*

**28.BB  FRENCH SOCKET BAYONET MODEL 1717     Circa 1715–1735**
To standardize its infantry weapons, the French army introduced a first official musket pattern in 1717 (38.MM). Its already existing bayonet form used a simple cylindrical socket (3" to 3-1/8") having two mounting slots (top barrel stud) and a triangular blade, of which each face was flat without fullers, plus either a sloping or squared rear end (blade lengths found: 14.9 inches to 12.8 inches). The neck, in turn, spread into a raised collar joint on the socket (some omitted the collar). This form continued until the early 1730s.

Length: 17"          Socket: 3"          Blade: 12-7/8" X 1"

**Jim and Jay Kaplan Collection**

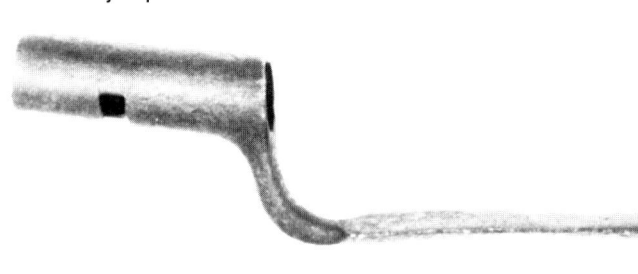

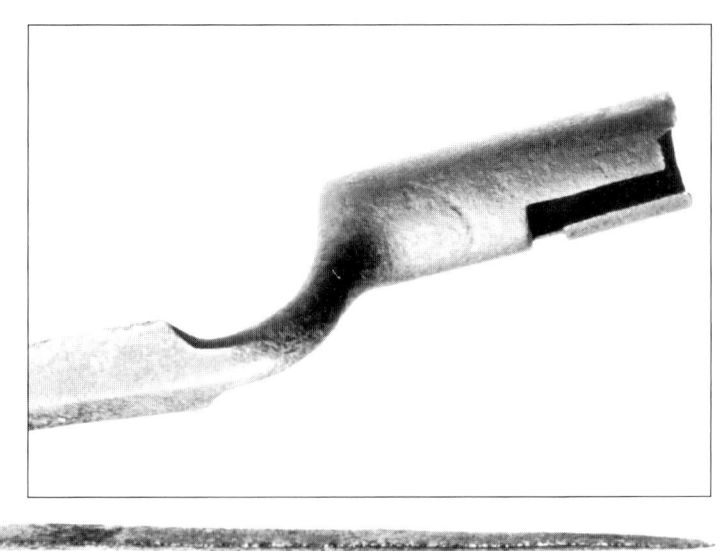

**29.BB  FRENCH SOCKET BAYONET MODEL 1728     Circa 1716–1745**
In 1728 France revised its musket pattern (39.MM), but bayonet date changes did not always coincide. A new design with deep concave bottom blade faces was authorized about 1716 and saw use through the mid-1740s (overlapping the Model 1717, 28.BB). Surviving examples vary, but this bayonet demonstrates its basic features. The 13" blade adopts two bottom hollow faces with a high median ridge, plus a slightly dished top surface having a 1/2" wide shallow fuller reaching back 6-1/2 inches from the tip. The oval neck ends in a raised socket joint (omitted in some). Its third slot was probably a later addition.

Length: 17-1/2"      Socket: 3-3/8"      Blade: 13" X 1"

**Author's Collection**

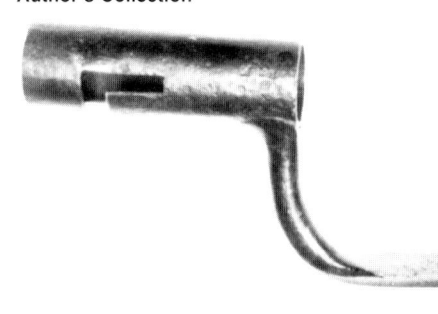

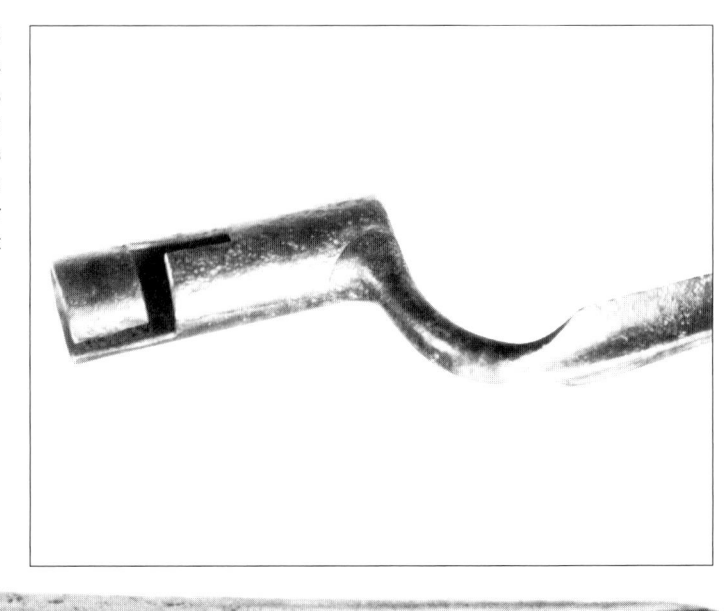

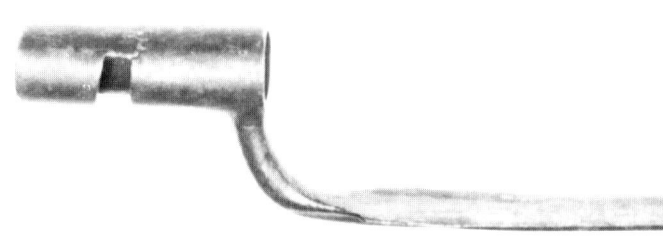

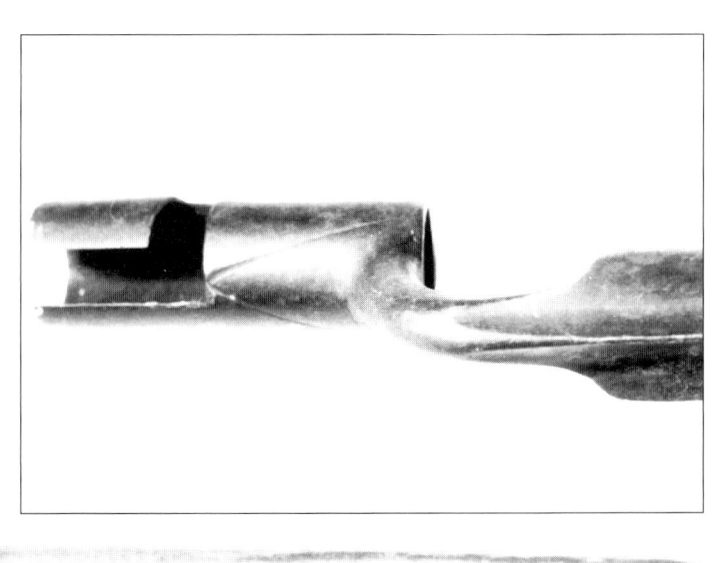

**30.BB  FRENCH SOCKET BAYONET MODEL 1750     Circa 1740–1754**
A few adjustments to the army's musket in 1746 created the model of that year (40.MM). The existing bayonet was also modified slightly during the 1740 to 1750 period and is usually designated the 1750 pattern. Its established configuration continued—with a simple socket (two mounting slots); a triangular blade (sloping shoulders) having a high bottom ridge between two deeply concave sides; and a slightly dished upper face including a shallow 1/2" wide fuller extending 6-1/2 inches from the tip. The previous raised neck/collar junction is disappearing, yet lingers with two token V-shaped incised lines.

Length: 18"          Socket: 3-3/16"     Blade: 13-3/8" X 1-1/16"

**Author's Collection**

**31.BB FRENCH SOCKET BAYONET MODEL 1754   Circa 1754–1763** 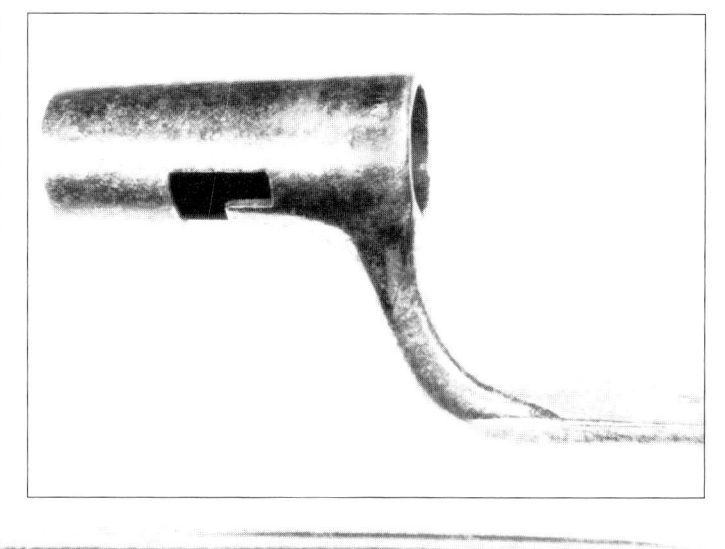
On the eve of the French and Indian War, France again modified its army musket as the Model 1754 (41.MM). The bayonet, in turn, was also altered. This 2-5/8" socket is shorter than the official 3-3/16" length, but most surviving examples found here are of this size. The new model added a third mounting slot (top barrel stud) and erased all evidence of the earlier raised joint at the socket/neck junction. Its triangular blade continues the two hollow bottom faces, but a slightly dished top surface adopts a narrower fuller (1/4 inch) reaching back 6-3/4 inches from the point.
Length: 17-1/2"      Socket: 2-5/8"      Blade: 13-5/8" X 1"
**Author's Collection**

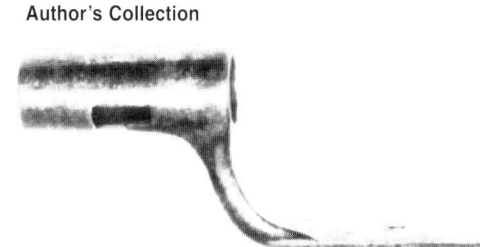

**32.BB FRENCH SOCKET BAYONET MODEL 1763   Circa 1763–1769** 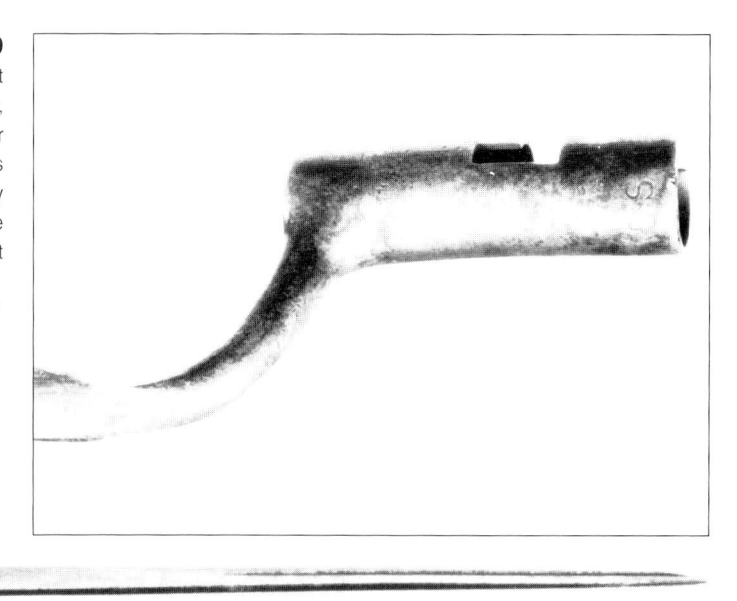
When the French army was reorganized after the French and Indian War, it developed new musket patterns in 1763 and 1766 (42.MM, 43.MM). The bayonet, however, received only minor adjustments, that is the socket became longer (3-3/8 inches) and retained three slots (now cut for a bottom barrel stud). Its triangular blade, in turn, kept the two bottom concave sides, as well as a slightly dished upper face (plus a 1/4" X 6-3/4" fuller at the tip). An early "US" surcharge is engraved at this socket's rear end. The same pattern was reused in 1773, cut for a top barrel stud.
Length: 18-1/4"      Socket: 3-3/8"      Blade: 13-1/4" X 1-1/8"
**Author's Collection**

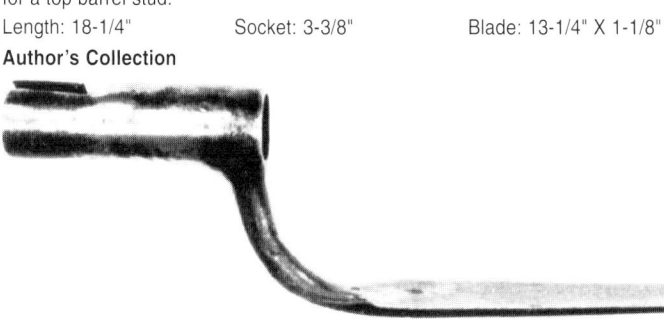

**33.BB FRENCH SOCKET BAYONET MODEL 1771   Circa 1771–1773** 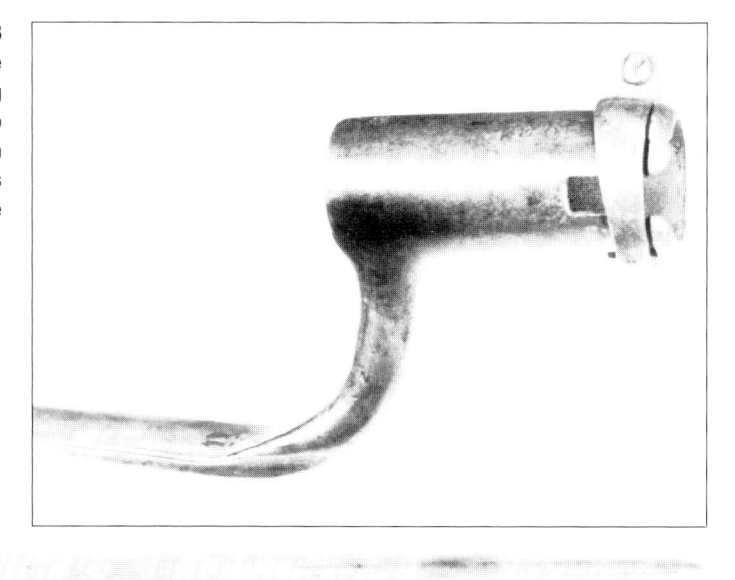
The search continued for an economical method to hold a bayonet firmly on the barrel. This arrangement with a short socket, single mounting slot and rotating rear locking band was introduced for the musket Model 1769/1770—to fit a top barrel stud. In 1771 the same pattern moved its slot for a bottom stud (as shown here). Notice the rear base ring and the rotating band that secures the stud. Its blade continues with two bottom hollow faces and a 1/4" X 5-3/4" top surface fuller at the point. Marks: "No 64" on the socket; two orb stamps in the blade.
Length: 17-1/2"      Socket: 2-5/8"      Blade: 13-3/4" X 1-1/8"
**Author's Collection**

*Chapter 6: Bayonets*

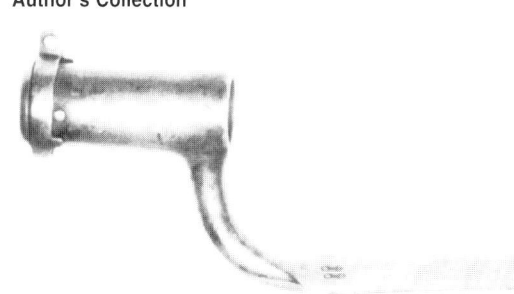

**34.BB FRENCH SOCKET BAYONET MODEL 1774   Circa 1774–1777**
The ongoing quest for a more reliable attachment led to this design in 1774. The infantry musket of that date (46.MM) had a clip project from the stock's forend. The new bayonet added a ring at the rear of the socket. When in place, the clip snapped over the ring to secure it. Note the short socket (2-3/4 inches) cut with three slots for a top barrel stud, a blade with two concave bottom faces, plus a flat top surface (including a 1/4" X 6-1/2" fuller at the point). Its neck is stamped "crown / A" (a Klingenthal mark; all official bayonets were made there after 1750).
Length: 17-5/8"        Socket: 2-3/4"        Blade: 13-1/2" X 1"
**Author's Collection**

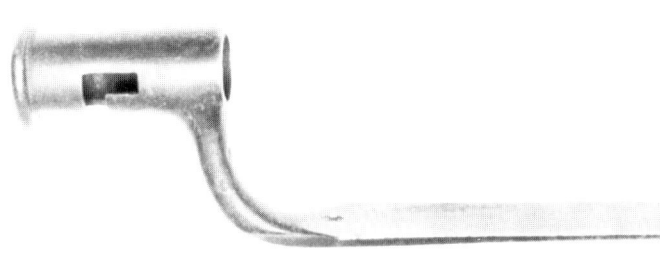

**35.BB FRENCH SOCKET BAYONET MODEL 1777        Circa 1777**
France's major weapon redesign in 1777 (47.MM) included the infantry's bayonet. Being the latest pattern, it was not included in their aid to America, but General Rochambeau's forces and other French troops carried them in their service here. Note the short socket (2-5/8 inches) with a permanent bridge over the first of three mounting slots. A center band, in turn, rises to allow the barrel's stud to enter and then rotates to secure it. A narrower blade retains the two concave bottom sides but now extends a dished top surface back to a raised 1-1/8" flat base panel.
Length: 18-1/8"        Socket: 2-5/8"        Blade: 14-1/2" X 7/8"
**Author's Collection**

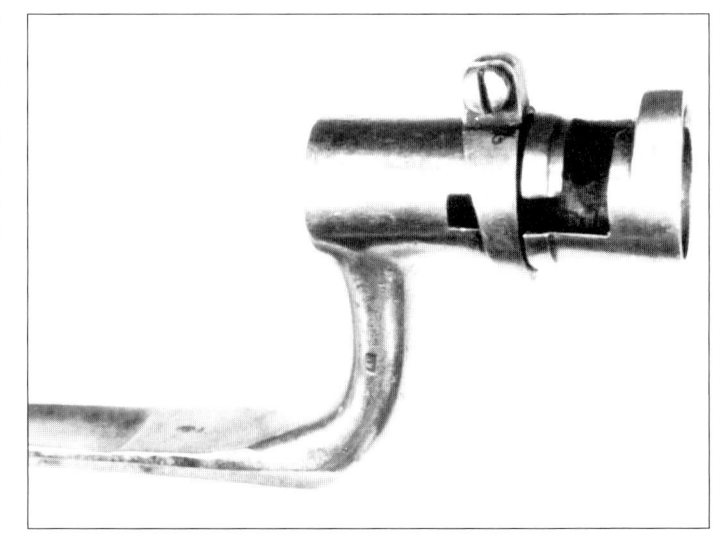

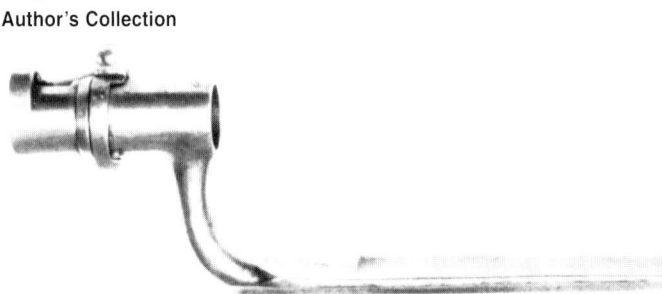

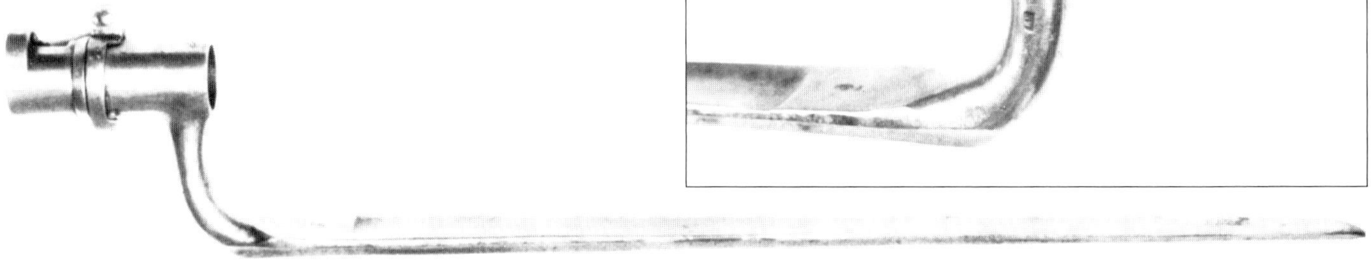

**36.BB FRENCH OFFICER'S CARBINE BAYONET MODEL 1752   Circa 1752**
It should be remembered that basic bayonet forms were adopted in varied dimensions for other service weapons. This short 11-1/2" example was scaled down and altered probably for a dragoon officer's 1752 carbine. A faceted neck ends in a raised collar where it joins the socket—which includes three slots for a top barrel stud. A diminutive blade, in turn, retains the French bottom ridge between two concave faces and a short top surface fuller (1/4" X 3-3/4") reaching back from the point. The familiar marking "E / maltese cross / C" is stamped at the base.
Length: 11-1/2"        Socket: 2-3/8"        Blade: 8-1/2" X 3/4"
**Author's Collection**

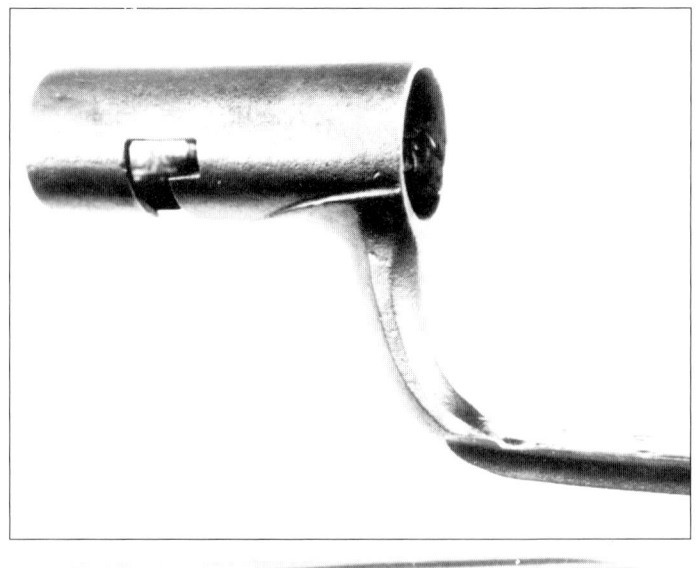

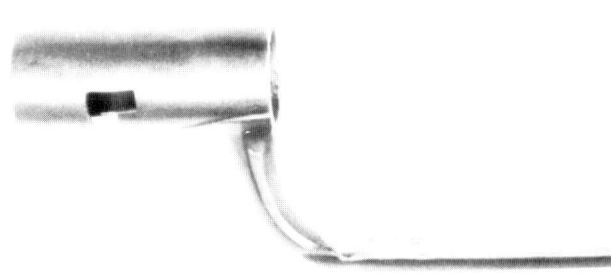

*290   Chapter 6: Bayonets*

**37.BB  SPANISH SOCKET BAYONET MODEL 1753      Circa 1753**
Spain joined America's Revolution in 1779. Their weaponry accompanied Spanish troops along the Gulf of Mexico (the Gen. Galvaz campaign) and as aid to both the Western frontier and Eastern rebels (musket 51.MM). Spain's earlier Model 1728 bayonet specified a 12-1/2" blade, but in 1753 a 14" length was authorized (most are slightly longer). Strong French influence is evident in its cylindrical socket (three slots, cut for either a top or bottom stud) and a triangular blade (two lower concave faces; flat top without a fuller). All elements appear thicker and heavier than the French.
Length: 18-1/2"        Socket: 2-7/8"        Blade: 14-7/8" X 1"
**Author's Collection**

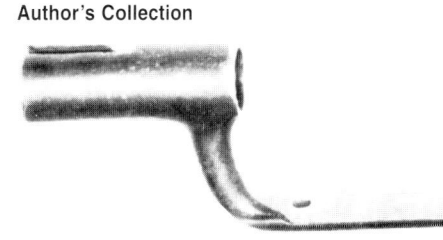

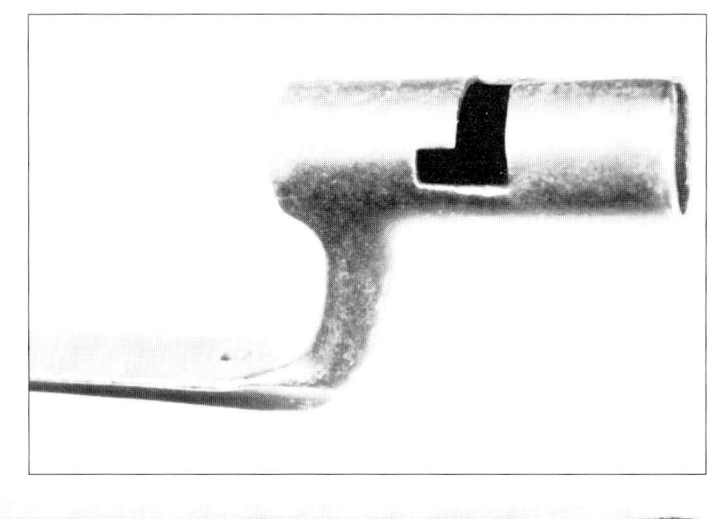

**38.BB  GERMAN SOCKET BAYONET   Prussian Model 1740**
The strongest German state at this time was Prussia, and its arms influenced many Germanic patterns, especially this Model 1740 (see 65.MM). Produced initially at Potsdam–Spandau, later contracts included Suhl, Liege, Zella and Essen. It usually had double lines at each socket end, a squared neck and three slots for a bottom barrel stud. The thick baseguard supports a triangular blade with two concave bottom fullers and a flat upper surface. One of this pattern was recovered from the Bennington, Vermont, battlefield (1777, Brunswick troops). (Re: Serbaroli, bib. 238)
Length: 18"        Socket: 3-1/4"        Blade: 13-1/2" X 1-1/4"
**Author's Collection**

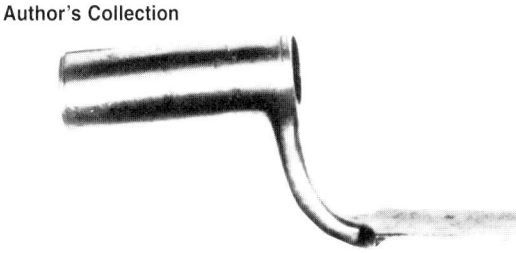

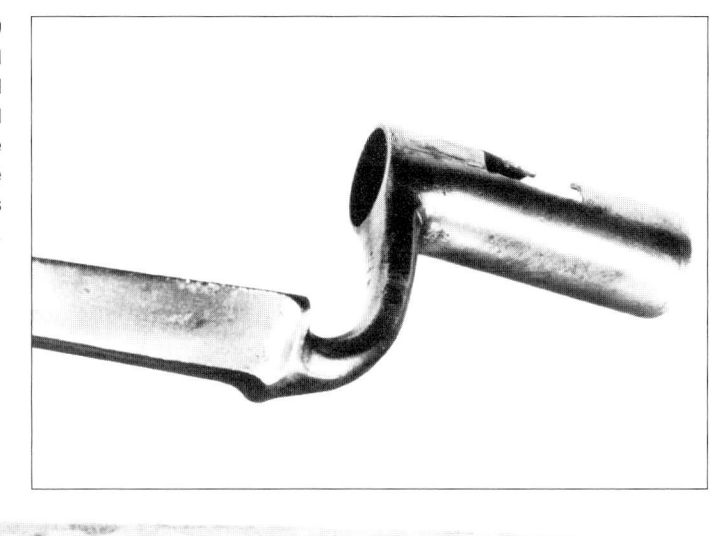

**39.BB  GERMAN SOCKET BAYONET            Circa 1740–1780**
Many of the Low Country–Germanic bayonets in the American Revolution accompanied the mercenaries serving the British, but others arrived as captured and surplus arms of prior wars through our allies or mixed shiploads from weapons dealers. This bayonet pattern showing socket end rings and a unique four-slot arrangement is associated with Saxony (a major contractor). Notice also the typical German squared neck with a raised collar junction, projecting baseguard and triangular blade (flat top, two concave bottom faces). Marks: "P" in neck; "No=7J" on the socket.
Length: 15-7/8"        Socket: 3-1/4"        Blade: 11-5/8" X 1-1/8"
**Author's Collection**

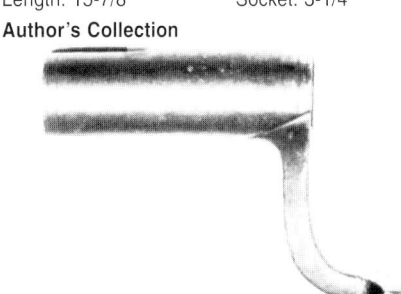

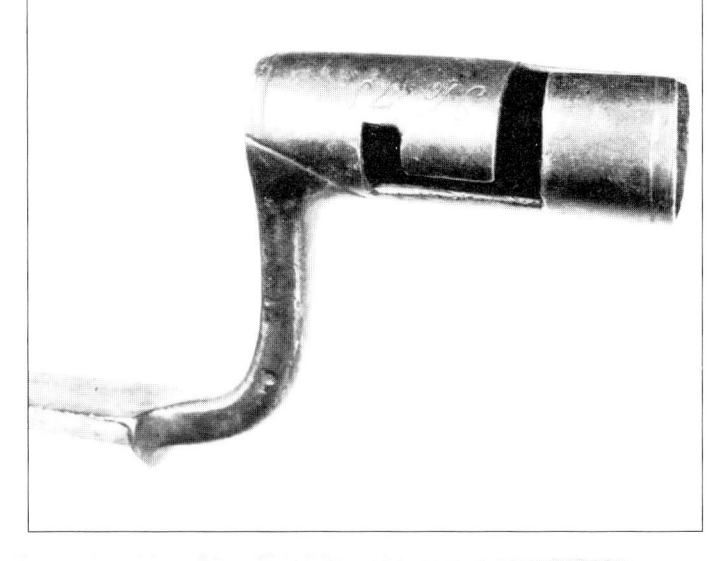

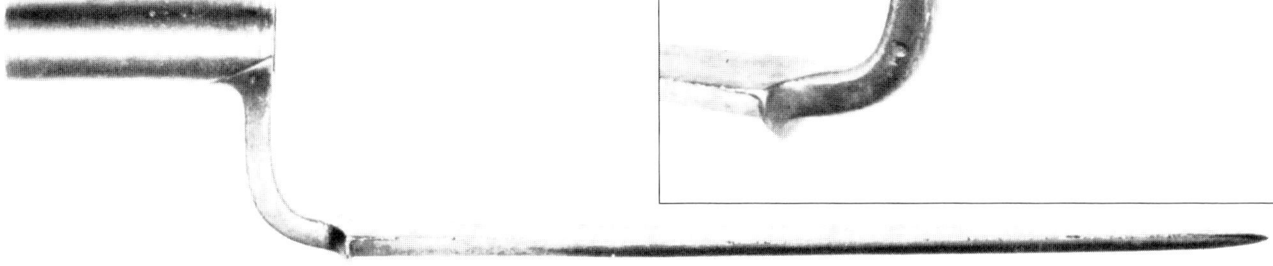

*Chapter 6: Bayonets*

### 40.BB  DUTCH/GERMAN SOCKET BAYONET    Circa 1730–1750

A mixture of central European influences is visible in this example. A thick-walled Germanic cylindrical socket includes three slots for a bottom barrel stud, and a sturdy triangular blade has both bottom faces fluted to within 2-1/4 inches of a raised baseguard. Yet the round-sectioned neck (set back 1/8 inch from the socket's front end), as well as the shallow dished upper face, suggest French styling. Engraved in the socket is "C 3 N.66" (3rd company, arm number 66) and "L" appears at the base of the blade.

Length: 18-1/4"    Socket: 3"    Blade: 14-3/8" X 1-1/8"

**Author's Collection**

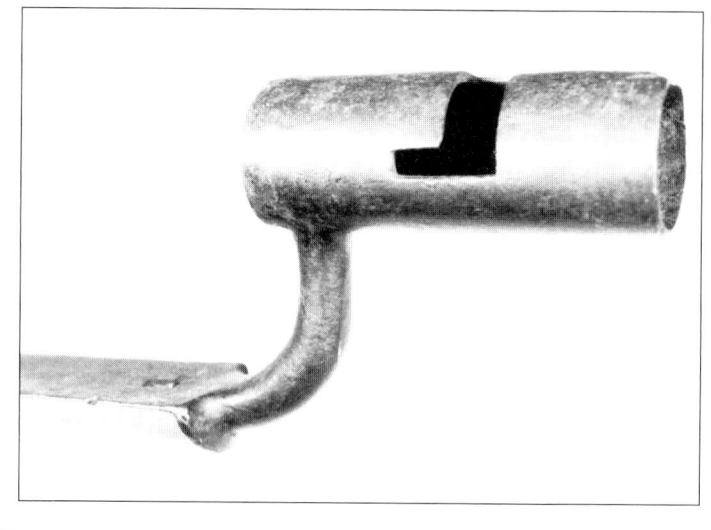

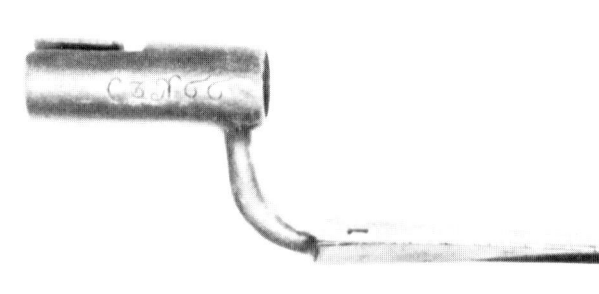

### 41.BB  DUTCH/GERMAN SOCKET BAYONET    Circa 1750–1780

A rear socket ring has been added to this bayonet (rare for Germanic patterns), and a thin rounded neck (versus the popular squared form) begins flush with the socket's front, then leads to a typical triangular blade (raised guard, two bottom fullered surfaces, flat top face). It also includes an unusual sloping point. A three-step slotting is cut for a bottom barrel stud. Note, too, the lingering resemblance to early century English patterns (for example, 13.BB). No marks are visible.

Length: 17-1/2"    Socket: 3"    Blade: 12-7/8" X 1"

**Author's Collection**

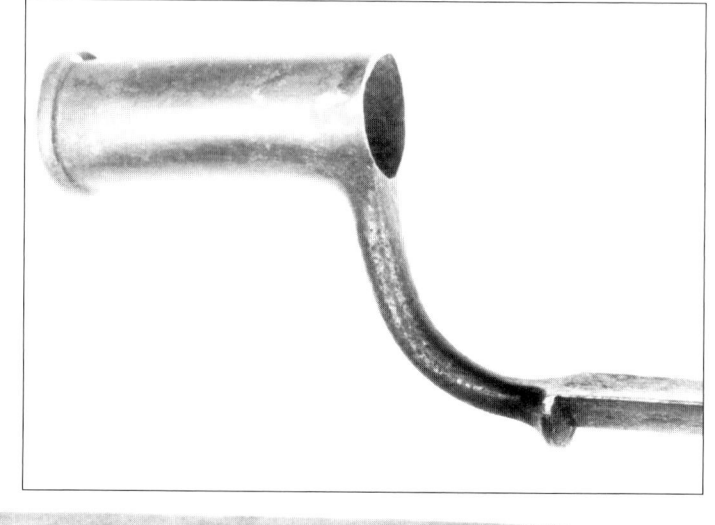

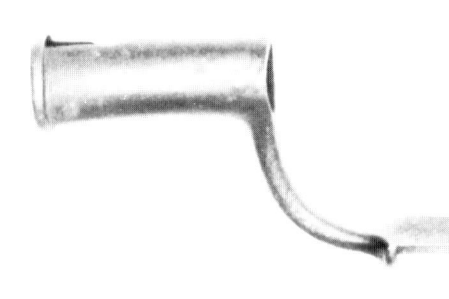

### 42.BB  AUSTRIAN SOCKET BAYONET MODEL 1767    Circa 1767

This heavy pattern was developed by Austria in 1748 and added its distinctive small rear socket hole by 1767. Like the French Model 1774 (46.MM) and some Dutch longarms (63.MM), an arched spring projecting from the musket's forend snapped into this opening to help anchor the bayonet. Moreover, the three mounting slots are now cut for a top stud. Its thick triangular blade, in turn, follows French styling by omitting a baseguard but adding a short three-inch top fuller at the tip, which has an abrupt angled point. The blade base is deeply stamped "P."

Length: 17-5/8"    Socket: 3-1/4"    Blade: 13-1/2" X 1-1/4"

**Author's Collection**

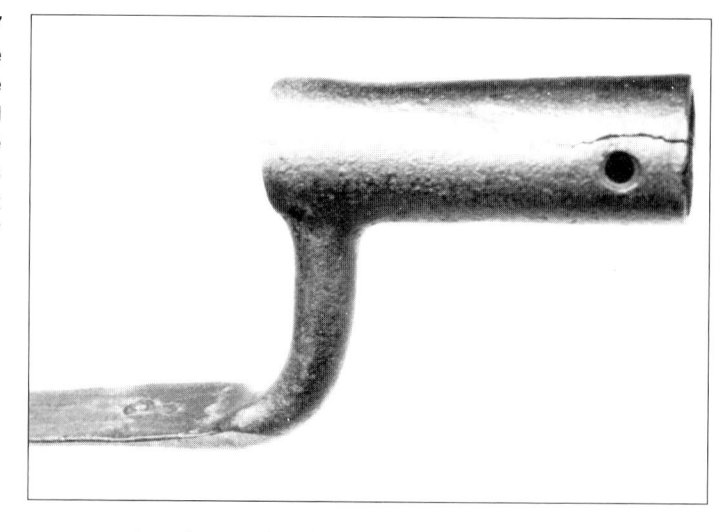

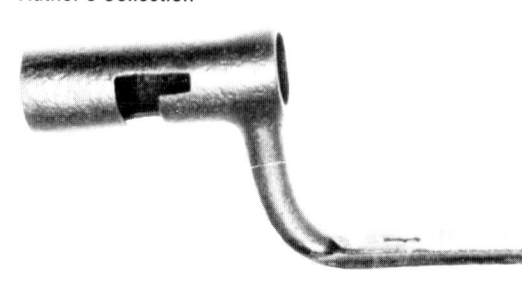

292    *Chapter 6: Bayonets*

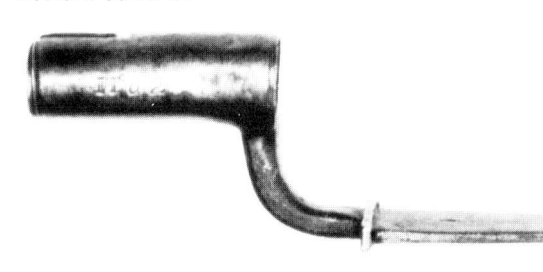

**43.BB DUTCH/GERMAN SOCKET BAYONET**  Circa 1730–1750

The long neck here is a reminder of early French spearpoint Marine bayonets (24.BB–27.BB), but it flows into a flattened blade (no guard) with both edges sharpened and three flats on the upper and lower faces—usually a Dutch form. In addition it retains the early practice of only two mounting slots which are cut for a top barrel stud (most German patterns at bottom). The higher steel density is also superior to most bayonets, another characteristic of the Low Countries at this time. Its large diameter thick-walled socket (one-inch inside diameter) is engraved "O / No=629."

Length: 16-3/4"     Socket: 3"     Blade: 11-1/2" X 1-1/8"
**Author's Collection**

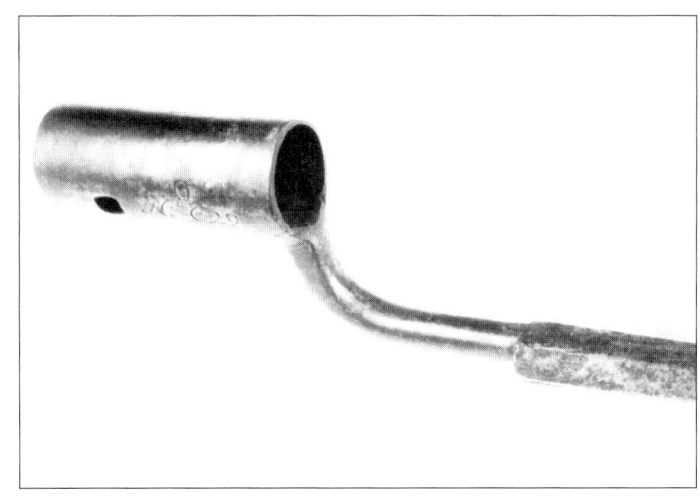

**44.BB DUTCH BAYONET**  Circa 1740–1760

This popular flat-bladed pattern with an oval baseguard is presumed to be Dutch or Liege, although it is also found on Germanic muskets. Having been discovered on French and Indian and Revolutionary War sites in America, it is believed to be part of the Low Country longarm shipments supplied by England to her colonists by the 1750s. The typical horizontal blade with its edges sharpened and three flat panels on both faces is found in various lengths. Its neck ends flush with a large bore socket (.92" inside diameter), which has the early double slots (bottom stud). Socket markings: "PN=117."

Length: 17"     Socket: 2-7/8"     Blade: 12-3/8" X 1-1/8"
**Author's Collection**

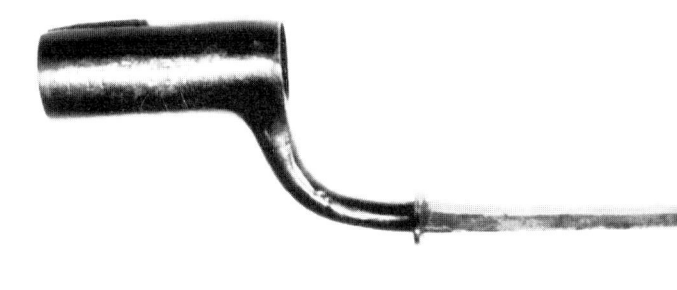

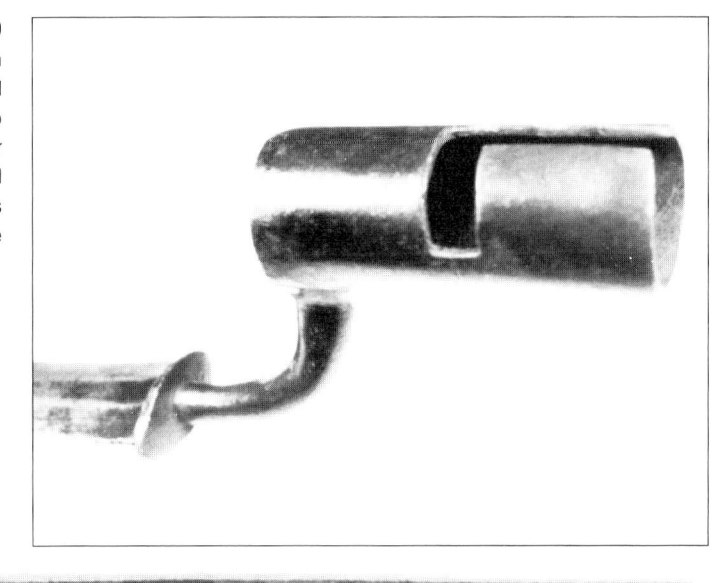

**45.BB DUTCH/GERMANIC SOCKET BAYONET**  Circa 1740–1760

The concept of a flattened horizontal blade illustrated in the previous Dutch bayonet (44.BB) is employed here but with Germanic features, that is: lines tracing each end of the large socket (.99" inside diameter; two slots for a bottom stud), a squared neck (chamfered corners), and a blade with flat faces and squared edges that become sharpened 2-1/8 inches from an abrupt point. The projecting baseguard is rectangular. Remains of this pattern have been found on French and Indian and Revolutionary War sites. This socket is engraved "No 62."

Length: 17-3/8"     Socket: 3-1/8"     Blade: 13" X 1-1/8"
**Author's Collection**

*Chapter 6: Bayonets*

**46.BB  GERMAN SOCKET BAYONET**          Circa 1730–1750

This is a further variation of the Germanic flat-bladed design. (The French dragoons used a similar form prior to 1750.) Note the substantial squared neck solidly attached to the end of its plain socket (three slots; bottom barrel stud) and a wide, thick horizontal blade that remains flat on each face. One edge is squared up to a 4-1/2" false edge; the other remains sharpened for its entire length. The crowned symbol marking on the blade face identifies a German state in that period as the Holy Roman Empire dissolved.

Length: 17-7/8"          Socket: 4-1/8"          Blade: 12-3/4" X 1-3/8"
**Fort Ticonderoga Collection**

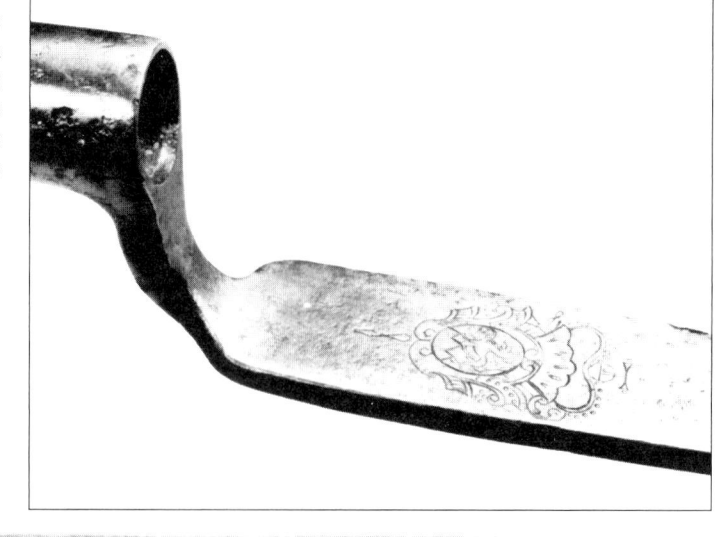

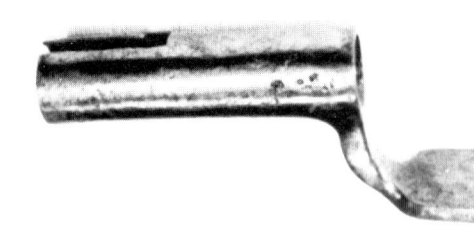

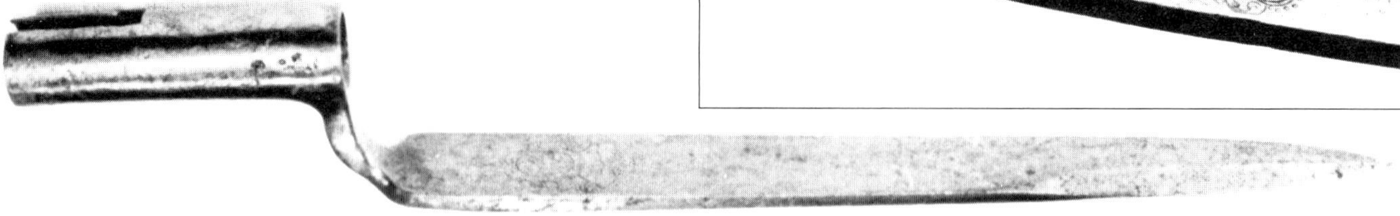

**47.BB  AMERICAN SOCKET BAYONET**          Circa 1775–1780

The American rebels employed European bayonets whenever available and followed their features in most locally made examples. Early in the war the familiar British patterns prevailed, but the French became more popular after 1777. This one is a remarkable copy of the current English Brown Bess form (15.BB). Yet its socket is 3-5/8 inches long (versus the British four inches), and the triangular blade ends at 16-1/4 inches (versus 17 inches). The prominent "US" and "E" markings at the blade's base are a typical Continental property surcharge plus a probable maker's sign.

Length: 20-1/2"          Socket: 3-5/8"          Blade: 16-1/4" X 1-1/8"
**Author's Collection**

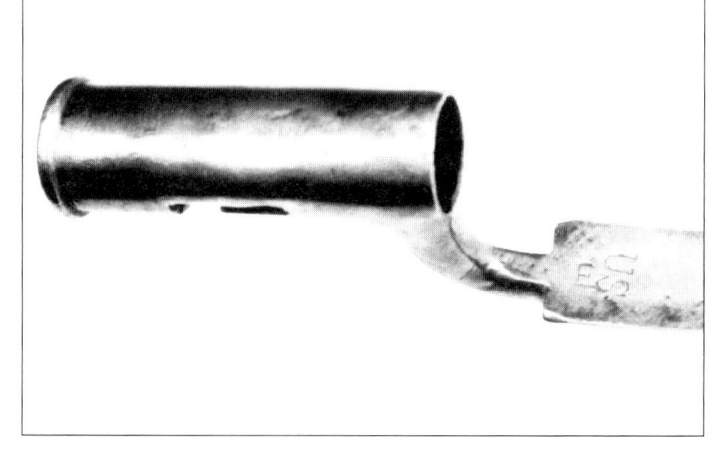

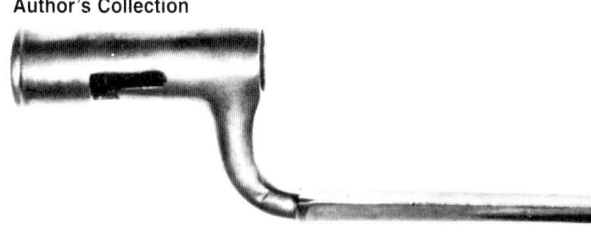

**48.BB  AMERICAN SOCKET BAYONET**          Circa 1775–1783

Most American bayonet makers were reluctant to identify their work. In this case, however, Lewis Prahl, a Pennsylvania Committee-of-Safety contractor has stamped "PRAHL" across the blade's base. A 3-3/4" socket with a thin end ring plus three-slots (top stud) approximates the English design and adds a 17" blade of British length. Yet it is a different shape that includes a rounded lower end (popular among Americans) plus a bottom median ridge with concave faces in the French fashion. The official Pennsylvania blade length of 16 inches was seldom followed.

Length: 21-1/4"          Socket: 3-3/4"          Blade: 17" X 1-1/8"
**Author's Collection**

294     *Chapter 6: Bayonets*

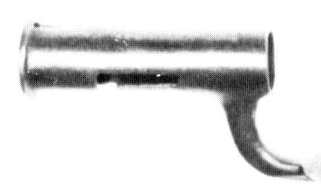

**49.BB  AMERICAN SOCKET BAYONET                    Circa 1775**

Elisha Buell, a gunsmith of Hebron, Connecticut, stamped "E BUEL" on the wide blade base of this American bayonet, which retains the basic English form. Its socket shows wear, but a straight seam remains along the top and a crude raised shoulder joint secured the neck. Buell's dimensions vary from Connecticut's specifications, but it was commonly done to meet wartime demands. For example, Buell's blade was 14-7/8 inches and the socket was 3-3/4" versus the state's 14 inches and four inches. Note: his postwar contracts specified French-style bayonets.

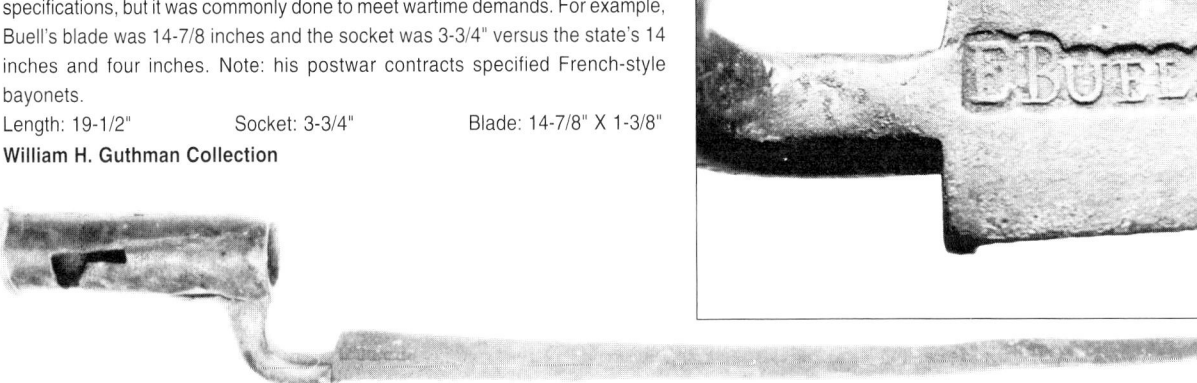

Length: 19-1/2"          Socket: 3-3/4"          Blade: 14-7/8" X 1-3/8"

**William H. Guthman Collection**


**50.BB  AMERICAN SOCKET BAYONET          Circa 1776–1780**

Like so many locally made bayonets, this example blends a shortened British-style socket including the rear ring with an innovative American flat-faced neck (note the sharp edges). A long 19" triangular blade (no top fuller) includes two French-type concave bottom faces and sloping shoulders. As shown, the blade's base is stamped by the Continental Army surcharge, "U.S," and the maker's name, "THOS WYLIE." Its lapped seam is still visible along the top of the socket.

Length: 22-5/16"          Socket: 3-1/8"          Blade: 19-3/16" X 1-7/16"

**J. Craig Nannos Collection**

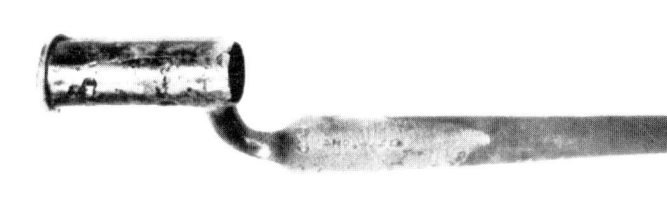

**51.BB AMERICAN SOCKET BAYONET          Circa 1777–1783**

As the Revolutionary War progressed, the great influx of French arms beginning in 1777 impacted the configuration of American-made weapons. The bayonet shown here is a close copy of France's Model 1774 (34.BB), although it omits the narrow front fuller on the blade's upper surface and adds a crude "US" surcharge at the base. The short three-slot socket with an end ring, the ovoid neck and the blade's bottom ridge between concave faces, however, reflect the contemporary French form.

Length: 17-1/8"          Socket: 2-5/8"          Blade: 13-1/2" X 1-1/8"

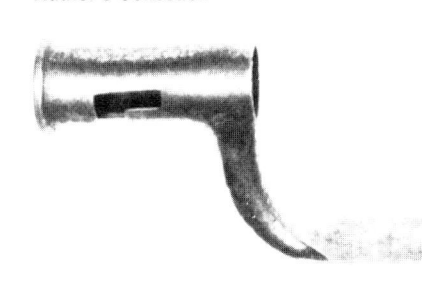

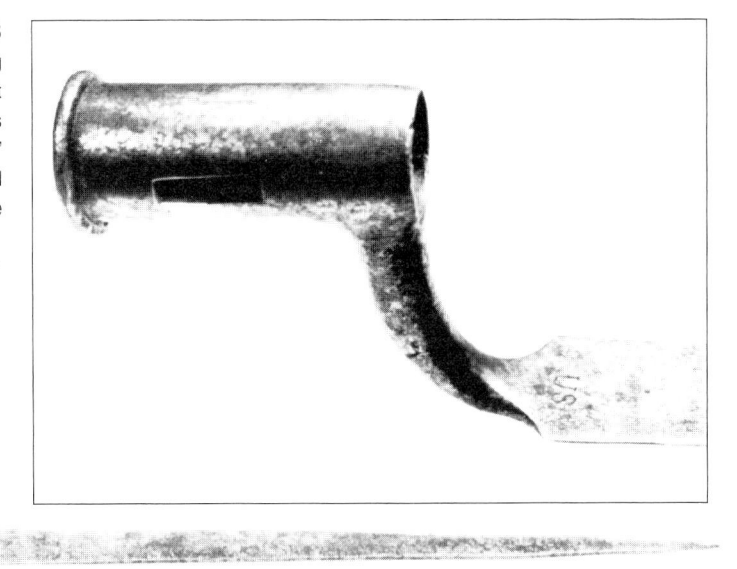

**Author's Collection**

*Chapter 6: Bayonets*   295

**52.BB  AMERICAN SOCKET BAYONET**         Circa 1740–1760

Forging wrought iron was as much an art as a science in the 18th century, and the smiths welcomed every opportunity to display their prowess. This unusual bayonet combines a simple socket (three slots for a top barrel stud) with a long slender neck curving down to an impressive horizontal blade, apparently styled after an officer's spontoon (see 34.PAA). Notice the expanded base plus tapering symmetrical blade bearing a low median ridge on both faces. It may not have been as sturdy as most, but the artistry is superb.

Length: 18"          Socket: 2-1/4"          Blade: 14-1/2" X 1-3/4"

**Fort Ticonderoga Collection**

**53.BB  AMERICAN SOCKET BAYONET**         Circa 1775–1790

Although the primitive construction of many American bayonets is understandable because of their expanded forging sites, the ability to create quality weapons was still present. One example is illustrated here. Note its high collar and oval neck that gracefully flows into the blade's raised bottom ridge. The triangular blade, in turn, has three flat faces and rear shoulders that were sculpted to form a scalloped base. The three mounting slots required a bottom barrel stud. No marks are visible.

Length: 14-3/4"          Socket: 2-1/2"          Blade: 11-1/2" X 7/8"

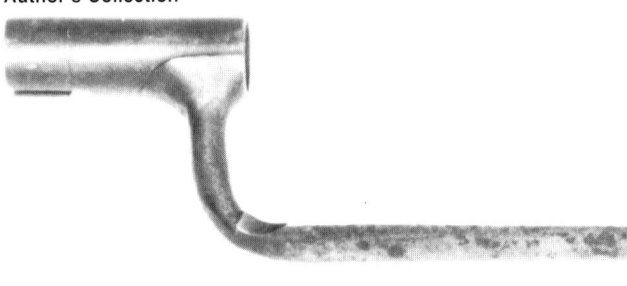

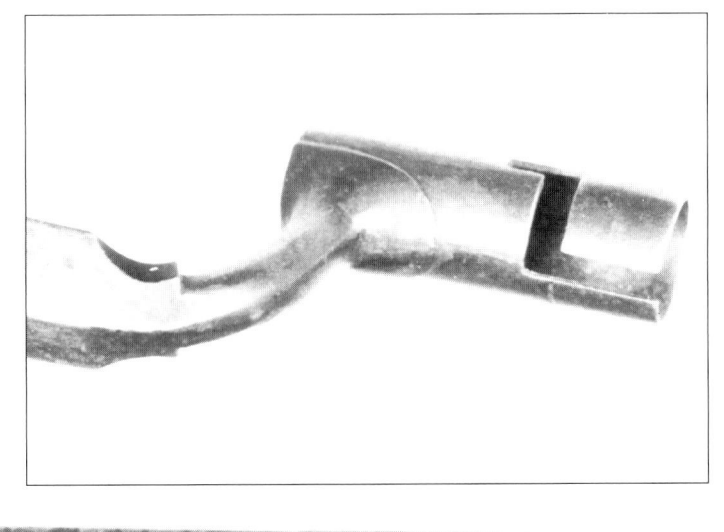

**Author's Collection**

**54.BB  AMERICAN SOCKET BAYONET**         Circa 1777–1785

An early French bayonet probably inspired this American example. Its cylindrical socket, raised collar at the neck junction and two concave lower blade faces follow features from France. Yet local variances are also apparent, for example, triple slotting for a bottom stud and a decorative line tracing the raised socket joint. Its flat upper blade omits a forward fuller and substitutes rounded instead of sharp-angled shoulders. Although lacking European craftsmanship, the piece is strong and reliable.

Length: 18-1/2"          Socket: 3-1/2"          Blade: 14-1/8" X 1-1/8"

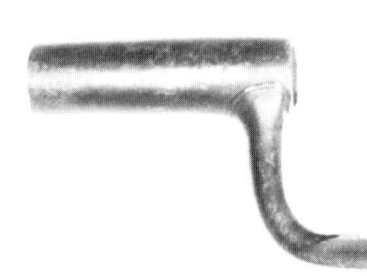

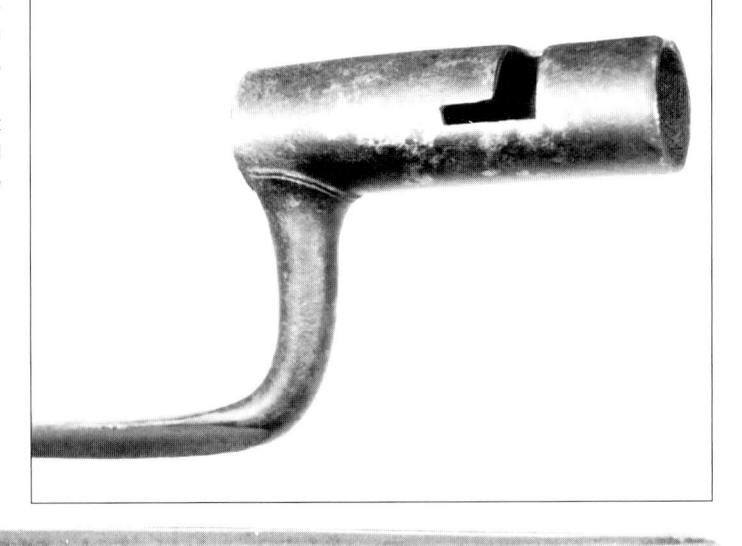

**Author's Collection**

**55.BB AMERICAN SOCKET BAYONET**            Circa 1740–1775

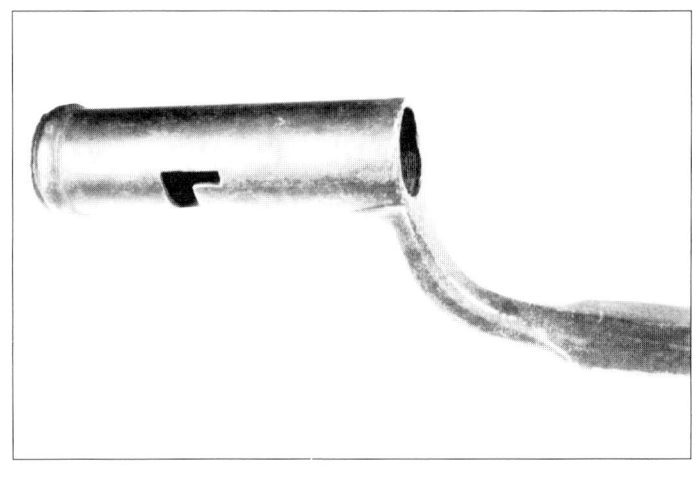

A similar Germanic pattern with a long projecting neck and flat blade may have inspired this Colonial bayonet. Notice that the proportions are not balanced, but its socket includes an indented raised ring at one end and a small collar joint at the other. The bulging neck presents a flat forward face flush with the socket; it then extends 1-1/4 inches into a 12-3/4" flat blade having a low median ridge on each face, flat side panels and sharpened edges. A forged seam is visible along the socket's top.

Length: 17-1/2"      Socket: 3-3/8"      Blade: 12-3/4" X 1-1/8"
**Author's Collection**

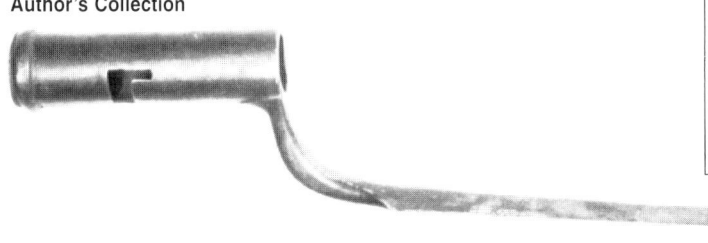

**56.BB AMERICAN THUMB SCREW BAYONET**      Circa 1775–1780

The search for a reliable method of holding the bayonet securely to the barrel continued during most of the 1700s. Several patterns in central Europe and Scandinavia added screws that penetrated the socket to enter indented spaces cut into the barrel. This version is believed to be a wartime American creation because of the marginal workmanship. Notice that its three slots accomodate a bottom stud, thus offering the wide flat thumb screw head as a high front sight. Observe also the blade's rounded shoulders, flat upper surface and bottom center ridge.

Length: 15-5/8"      Socket: 2-3/8"      Blade: 12-1/8" X 1"
**Erik Goldstein Collection**

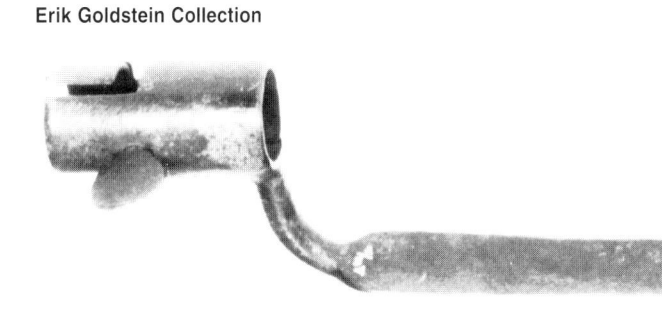

**57.BB AMERICAN SOCKET BAYONET**            Circa 1740–1760

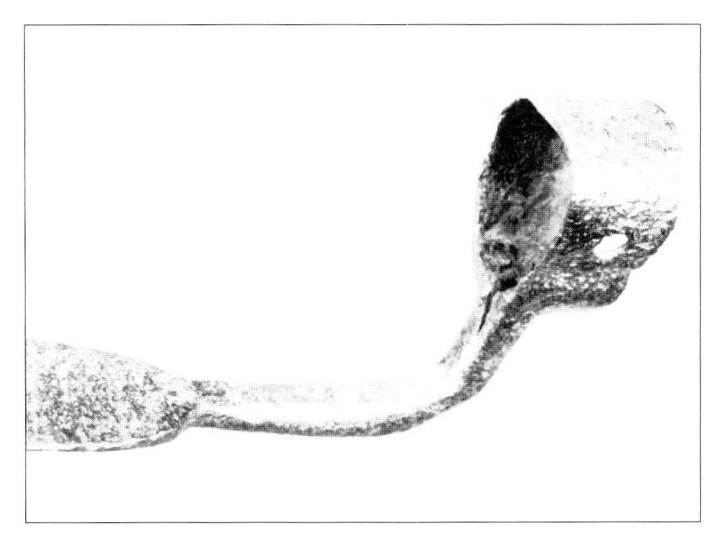

Dispersed production without common specifications leads to unusual innovations, as illustrated here. The crude forging created a one-inch long socket shaped to cover the gun's muzzle and wooden forend, thus positioning the blade under the muzzle instead of at the normal right side. A side socket hole, in turn, probably allowed for a locking screw or a spring catch device. The uneven neck projects forward two inches to a 12" thin horizontal blade that has rounded shoulders and two flat faces. No markings are present.

Length: 15"      Socket: 1"      Blade: 12" X 1-1/8"
**Tom Wnuck Collection**

*Chapter 6: Bayonets*

**58.BB  AMERICAN SOCKET BAYONET          Circa 1755–1780**

Despite the lack of balanced proportions found on European patterns, this local Colonial bayonet is a sturdy reliable weapon. Its socket has an English-type end ring and is solidly attached to the neck by an expanded raised collar weld. The neck displays a flattened front face and curves into a French-style triangular blade with two concave lower faces, plus a flat upper surface adding a short two-inch fuller at the point. Both edges were sharpened. The leather scabbard includes a simple frog and vertical belt loop (no metal).

Length: 16-3/8"          Socket: 3-1/4"          Blade: 12-1/2" X 1"

**Author's Collection**

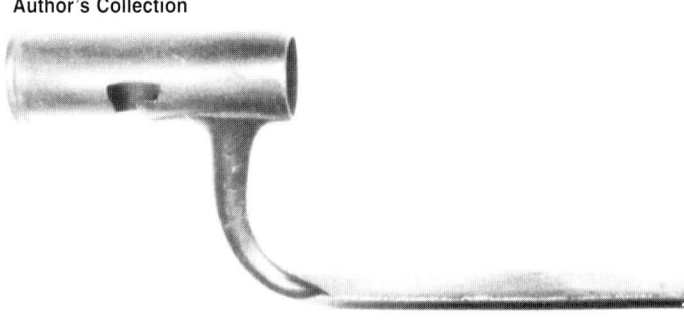

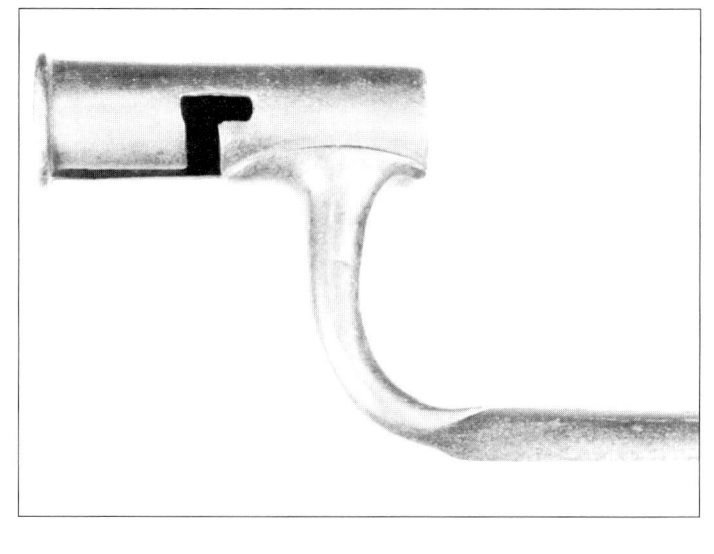

**59.BB  AMERICAN SOCKET BAYONET          Circa 1750–1780**

The essentials of a serviceable arm were provided for this American piece, despite the distorted features. It also suggests reference to the early British Brown Bess bayonet configuration (14.BB), that is, the end ring on its socket, a raised collar junction with the neck and a triangular blade including the projecting baseguard. Improvised design liberties, however, are apparent in the shortened (2-3/4") socket, slotting for a lower stud, and the absence of fullers alongside the blade's bottom center ridge.

Length: 17-1/4"          Socket: 2-3/4"          Blade: 13-1/4" X 1-1/4"

**Author's Collection**

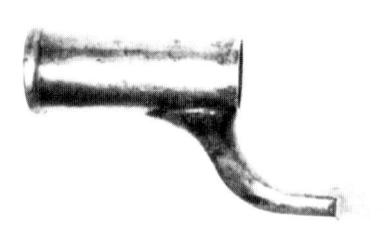

**60.BB  AMERICAN SOCKET BAYONET          Circa 1755–1780**

Rural blacksmithing created this bayonet. Yet the rugged strength it provided for combat is also apparent. The elementary thick-walled socket holds three mounting slots for a top barrel stud; its triangular blade, in turn, with flat faces and rounded rear shoulders, was forged in conjunction with a squared neck (faceted corners) leading to the crude shield-like raised socket joint.

Length: 16-1/4"          Socket: 3"          Blade: 12" X 1"

**Author's Collection**

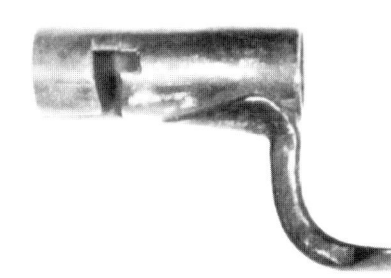

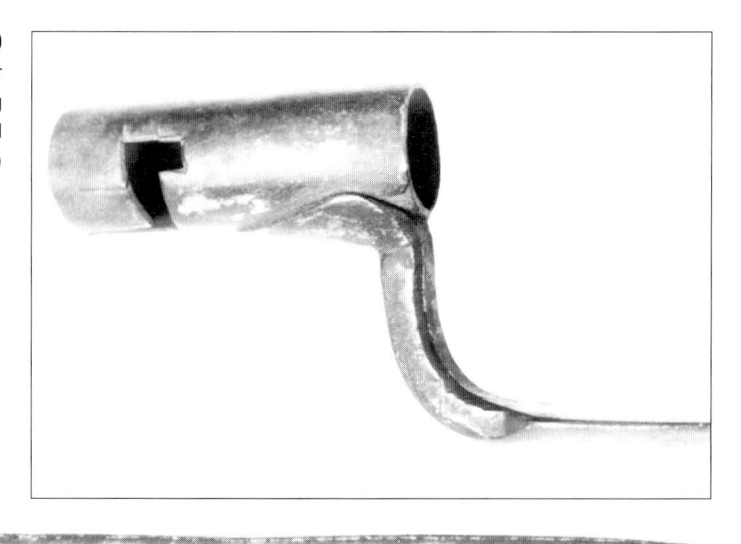

*Chapter 6: Bayonets*

**61.BB  AMERICAN SOCKET BAYONET        Circa 1755–1780**
Notice the emphasis on little more than basics to create the short but adequate bayonet shown here. Its bottom welded seam completed the socket (shaped from a plain rectangle of iron). The 9-3/4" French-type blade incorporates a high bottom ridge between two concave sides, a flat upper face and squared shoulders. It then continues into an indented oval neck that ends in a raised diamond-shaped joint at the socket. As with most American bayonets, there are no markings.
Length: 12-1/2"         Socket: 2-1/2"         Blade: 9-3/4" X 1"
**Author's Collection**

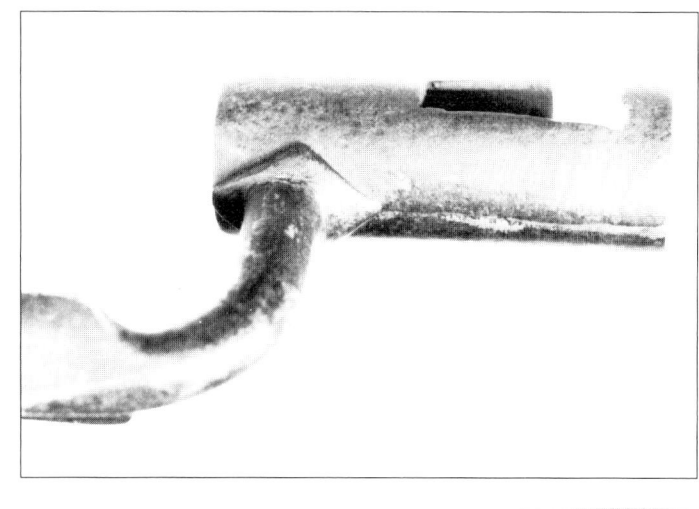

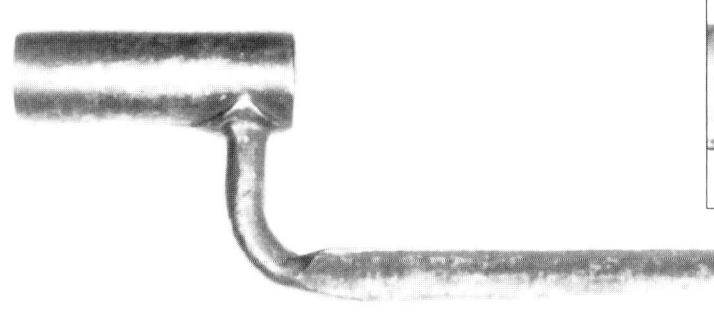

**62.BB  AMERICAN SOCKET BAYONET        Circa 1740–1760**
The awkwardness of this unbalanced pattern has surprisingly been repeated in other known examples, apparently by the same maker. Its rugged construction, large diameter socket (.99" inside diameter) and thickened six-sided point (like 17th century armor piercing pikes) suggests the American Colonies. The stocky triangular blade incorporates English-type side fullers underneath, as well as a flattened baseguard; the top surface is flat. Crude provincial forging characterizes the socket and oval neck, which are joined well back from the muzzle end.
Length: 17-3/8"         Socket: 3-1/2"         Blade: 13-1/2" X 1-1/8"
**Author's Collection**

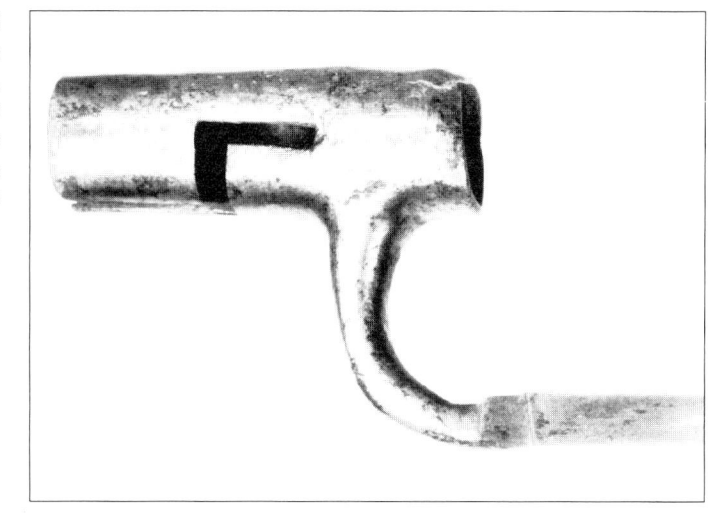

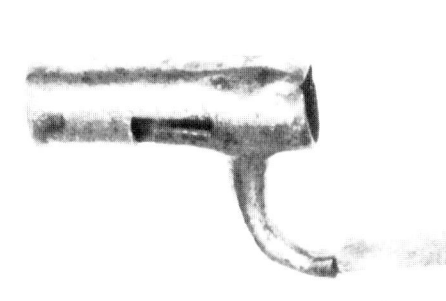

**63.BB  AMERICAN SOCKET BAYONET        Circa 1755–1780**
A cylindrical socket with only two mounting slots and a slender neck are similar to French styling, but this American bladesmith added his own variations. The socket has thick walls and is cut for a bottom barrel stud. Moreover its unique long thin blade (16-7/8" X 7/8") includes a half-round projecting baseguard and a top face concave for its entire length. Two bottom side fullers end three inches above the base. Although the blade's reach approximates Britain's standard bayonet's 17 inches, it lacks the sturdiness to counter it on the field.
Length: 21-1/4"         Socket: 2-7/8"         Blade: 16-7/8" X 7/8"
**Author's Collection**

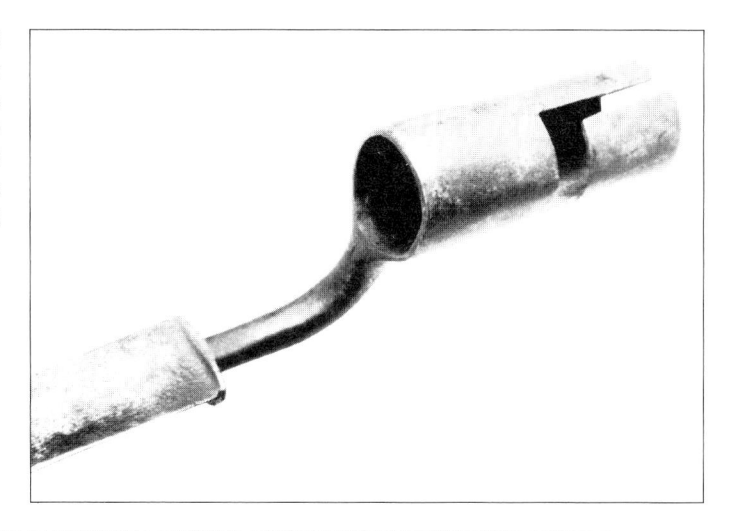

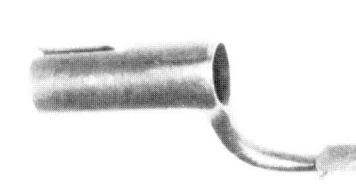

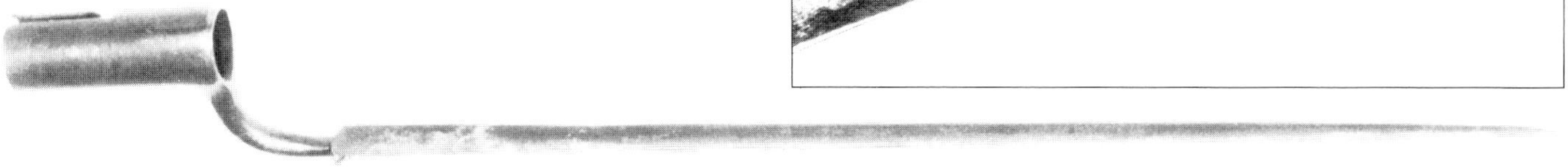

*Chapter 6: Bayonets*

**64.BB  AMERICAN SOCKET BAYONET**         Circa 1777–1785

The maker of this weapon created the illusion of an octagonal neck by adding three front panels to an otherwise oval cross section. Its upper connection to the short cylindrical socket is an abrupt crude weld; the other end extends into a French-type blade that rounds off the usual sharp shoulders but includes the raised bottom ridge flanked by concave faces. An upper flat surface adds a 3/8" by 2-1/2" shallow fuller leading back from the point. No marks are visible.

Length: 17-3/8"          Socket: 2-7/8"          Blade: 14" X 1"

**Author's Collection**

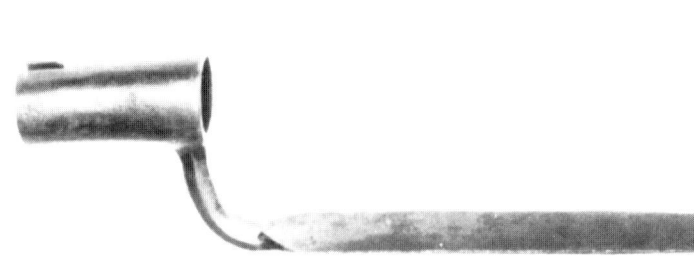

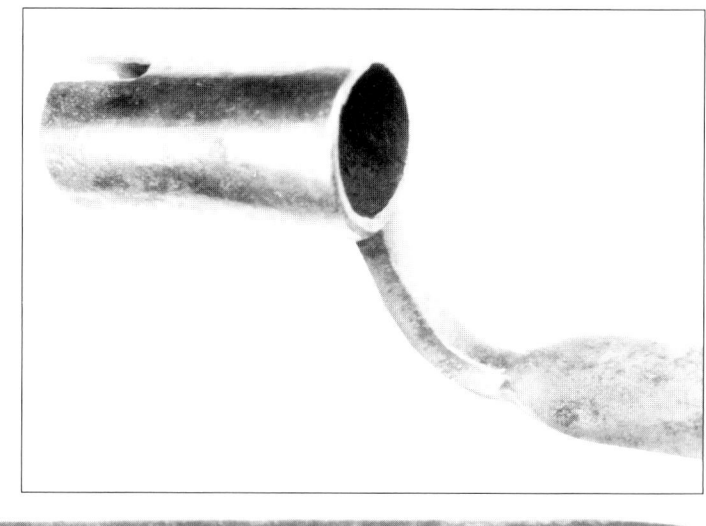

**65.BB  AMERICAN SOCKET BAYONET**         Circa 1740–1780

Here is another in this series of rough American bayonets that lack the finesse and balance of European patterns but were crafted as solid reliable fighting arms. The utilitarian socket, for example, displays an irregular lapped seam and a brief three-slot entry that indicates a barrel with its bottom stud set back 2-3/8 inches from the muzzle. A low, thick no-nonsense neck curves into the triangular blade—made with rounded shoulders and three flat faces.

Length: 16-3/4"          Socket: 3-1/4"          Blade: 12" X 1-1/8"

**Author's Collection**

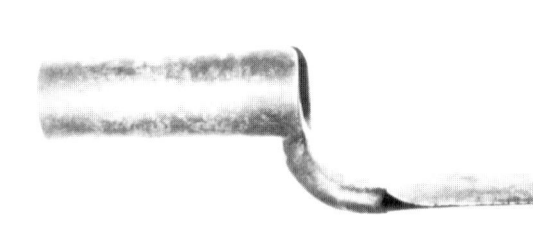

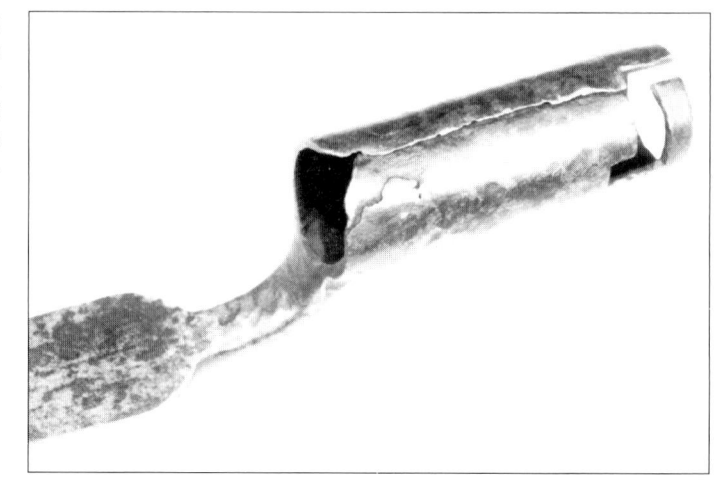

**66.BB  AMERICAN SOCKET BAYONET**         Circa 1755–1780

This design is suggestive of the popular Dutch pattern that also employed a plain socket and flat faceted blade (44.BB). Yet the roughly shaped neck is dangerously narrow at the socket junction. It also leads to a flattened irregular blade form beginning with a raised baseguard plus rounded shoulders and a low median ridge on both faces to create a diamond cross section. The socket is fitted for a bottom barrel stud (three slots) and sealed by a lapped seam along the top.

Length: 16-3/8"          Socket: 2-5/8"          Blade: 12-1/8" X 1-1/8"

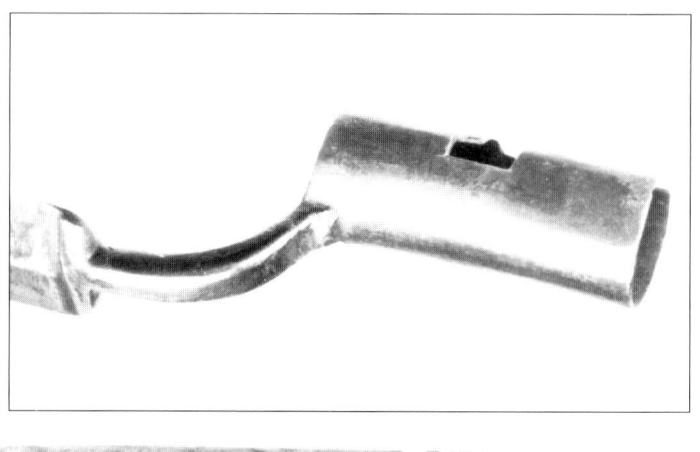

**Author's Collection**

### 67.BB  AMERICAN SPLIT-SOCKET BAYONET  Circa 1755–1777

Since each 18th century socket had to be sized individually to its assigned longarm, some bayonets have survived with the socket cut open for refitting to a later musket or, as in this case, originally made with an open slot for a simplified muzzle adjustment. Although the socket is thin-walled, its square-section neck anchors a rugged triangular blade shaped with three flat faces and rounded shoulders. Most American-made blades were shorter than their European counterparts.

Length: 16-1/2"         Socket: 3"          Blade: 11-5/8" X 1"
**Author's Collection**

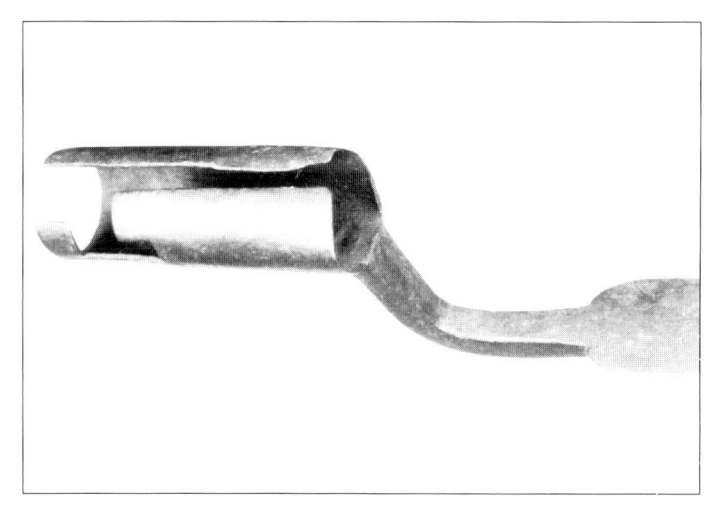

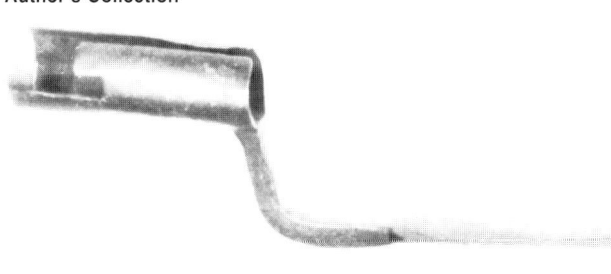

### 68.BB  AMERICAN SOCKET BAYONET  Circa 1755–1780

Although this four-inch socket with an end ring and triple slotting for a top stud copies the standard British Long Land bayonet, all else is purely provincial. A chunky neck projects horizontally forward from just below the muzzle for 1-1/2 inches to a flat double-edged rudely worked 8-1/2" blade. This appears to be its original size, which would stand little chance against the English 17" length but could have been effective in heavily forested terrain.

Length: 13-5/8"         Socket: 4"          Blade: 8-1/2" X 1-1/2"
**Tom Wnuck Collection**

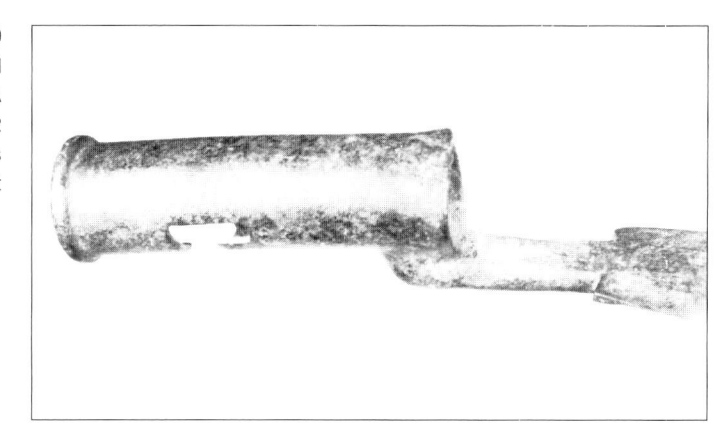

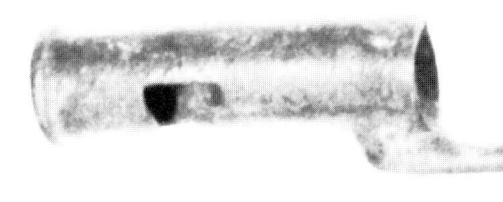

### 69.BB  AMERICAN SOCKET BAYONET  Circa 1775–1800

Colonial ingenuity was mustered to create this arrangement. To achieve a reliable attachment between socket and neck, the latter added a substantial ring at its upper end that encircled the socket's forward opening. A thinner band at the rear helped, in part, to restore balance. An unevenly forged blade flanks its bottom center ridge with concave faces—combined with a flat upper surface. No marks are present. Three mounting slots are positioned for a bottom barrel stud.

Length: 16-3/4"         Socket: 2-3/4"          Blade: 12-1/8" X 1"
**Author's Collection**

*Chapter 6: Bayonets*

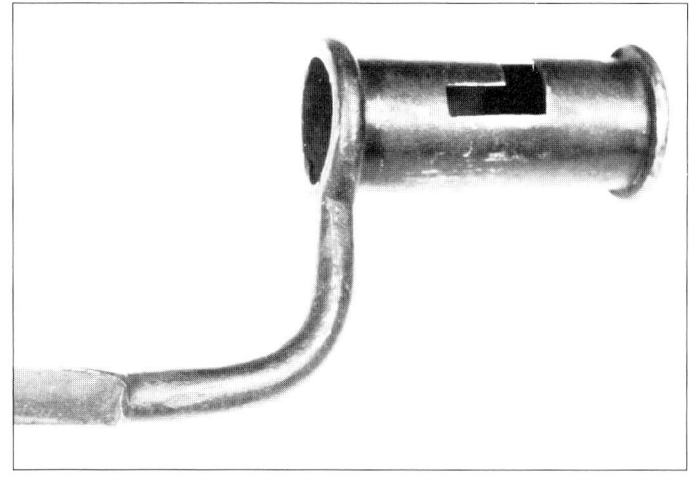

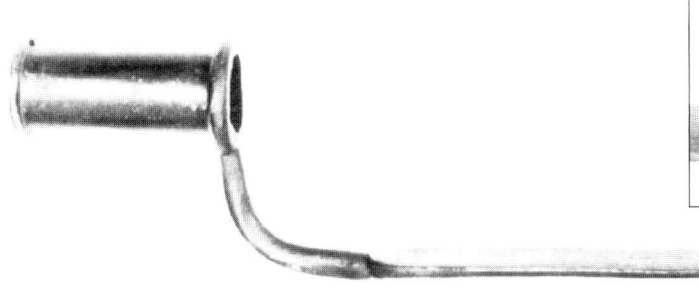

# Chapter 7

# Swords... Of Honor and Daring

By the time of the American Revolution, the sword had come to represent the importance of a civilian in a rigidly stratified society, the rank and resources of an officer, and the means to defend his honor in a duel. To the military horseman, soldier and seaman, it was a combat arm for close action survival. Moreover, many swords had earned a revered status in family tradition as they were passed down through generations. Although beginning to lose some importance by the later 1700s as the bayonet became the principal secondary field weapon and the need for civilian side arms waned, the sword in many forms and dimensions remained a dominant factor in our country's struggle for freedom.

Automatic forging of sword blades in Europe by heavy, water-powered equipment was already developed by the time the first English settlers arrived in North America. Solingen, Germany, was the chief blade supplier, supplemented by other centers such as Passau, Munich, Toledo in Spain and Italy's Milan. Most countries, including the American Colonies, imported these blades and added their own hilts. England attempted to create a domestic producer using former Solingen workmen at Hounslow from 1620–1634, but the venture failed. A second location at Shotley Bridge beginning in 1691 continued through the next century but at a marginal level. Meanwhile Birmingham became a major supplier for Britain. France, in turn, finally succeeded with a center at Klingenthal (Alsace) about 1729. None of these efforts, however, ended the world's dependency on imported blades in huge amounts from the established sources.

Lacking their own industry, the Colonists relied mostly on European swords and blades. Once the Revolution began, imports continued and were supplemented by available arms already in Colonial arsenals, plus complete

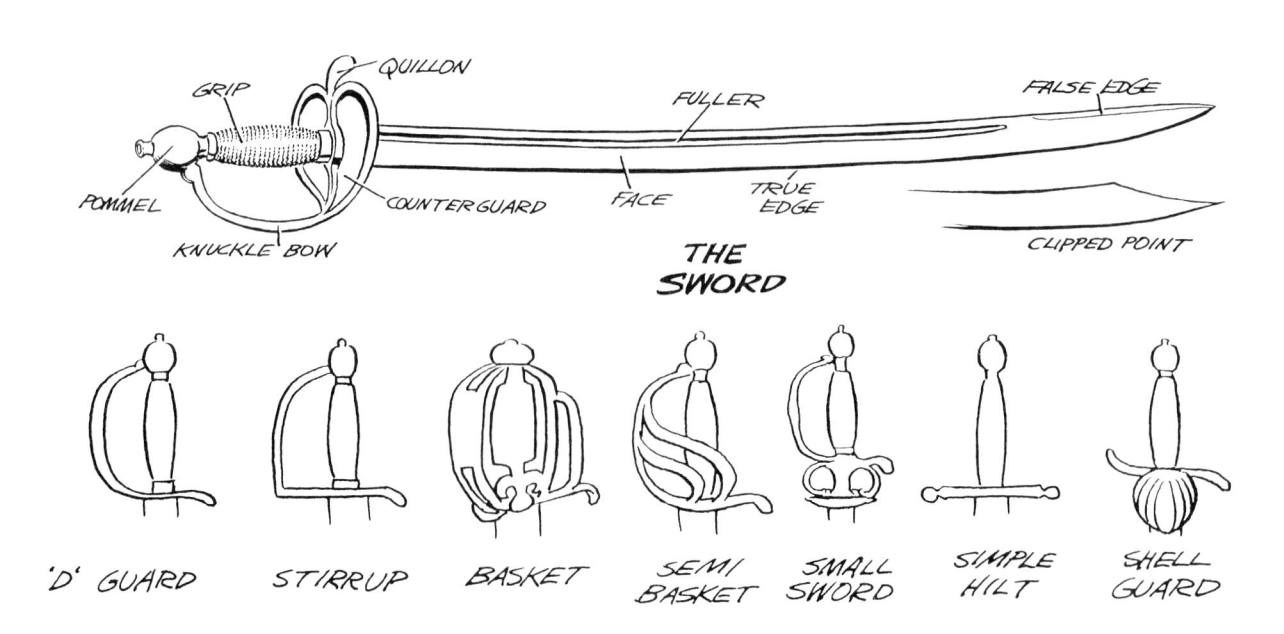

**LEE'S AMERICAN LEGION IN THE SOUTHERN CAMPAIGN, 1781**
Light dragoons usually fought from the saddle and carried carbines plus pistols, although their primary weapon was the saber. In later years of the war, they were often combined with light infantry to create small fast-moving attack forces ("legions"), especially in the South.

weapons produced by available craftsmen. This limited group varied from blacksmiths to trained cutlers, including some capable of excellent workmanship.

## BASIC SWORD CATEGORIES

The types of swords that participated in the American Revolution are grouped as follows:

*The Infantry Hanger* — A short fighting sword originally designated as the foot soldier's supplementary weapon for close combat (2.SS–52.SS). Its blade was usually slightly curved and 25 inches to 28 inches long with one cutting edge. As the bayonet gained acceptance, hangers gradually declined. Following the French and Indian War, a British 1768 warrant established that the only infantry to retain swords would be the sergeants of regiments, grenadier companies, fifers and drummers, plus the Highlanders (basket hilts). At the end of hostilities in 1783, they were retained mostly by sergeants.

France abolished such swords in 1764, except for grenadiers and sergeants. Many of the German mercenaries in America, however, continued to carry their hangers. Most American troops in 1775 were required to supply either a hanger, belt ax or bayonet as a second weapon, but by the later years, the majority of swords were in the hands of sergeants.

*The Short Saber* — This was the fighting weapon for many officers. It mounted a curved or straight, single-edged, cut-and-thrust blade averaging 28 inches to 32 inches (53.SS–83.SS).

*The Hunting Sword* — Developed as a supplementary arm for hunters, it later acquired embellishments to serve as a symbol of rank for officers in non-combat situations (84.SS–103.SS). The straight or curved blade was generally under 28 inches. American officers, lacking heavier swords, often carried them in the field.

*The Small Sword* — As the civilian sword associated with a gentleman, this was the favorite of most officers (104.SS–120.SS). Light and narrow, with a thin rapier-like blade, it required skill for a quick thrusting stroke. Blade forms varied from triangular to elliptical, hexagonal or diamond. The usual hilt included a simple knuckle bow, pas d'ane and a bilobate counterguard.

*The Horseman's Sword* — Typically a heavy saber, it had a straight or curved blade (usually single-edged) that measured 32 inches to 37 inches (126.SS–174.SS). Hilts ranged from a simple stirrup pattern to a full basket.

*The Naval Cutlass* — Resembling a hanger or short saber, it was the seaman's primary edged weapon in battle (175.SS–186.SS). Blades were curved or straight—usually sharpened along one side. The hilt's expanded guard was designed for maximum hand protection.

*Chapter 7: Swords*

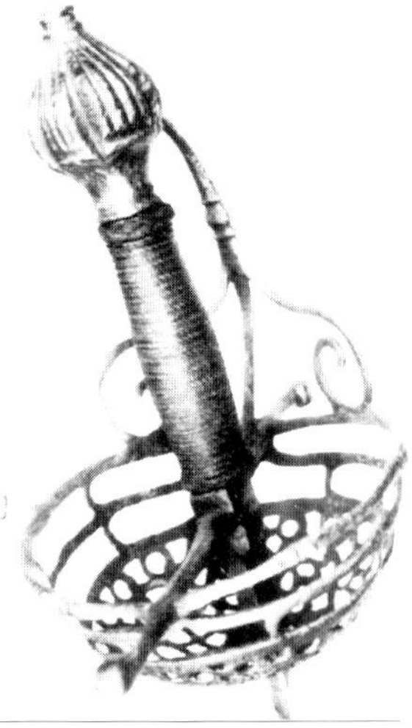

**1.SS  ENGLISH CUP-HILT RAPIER**                         Circa 1610–1630

Although dated long before the Revolutionary War, the cup-hilted rapier was the popular English sword form among America's early Jamestown and Plymouth colonists. One is included here for reference and in the belief that some were probably still in private hands during the 1700s for local use. Notice the long, slender thrusting blade, the typical pierced cup-guard, double quillons, wire-wrapped grip, side scrolled branches and bulbous pommel.

Length: 45-1/2"          Blade: 37-3/4" x 3/4"          Hilt: Iron

**Author's Collection's**

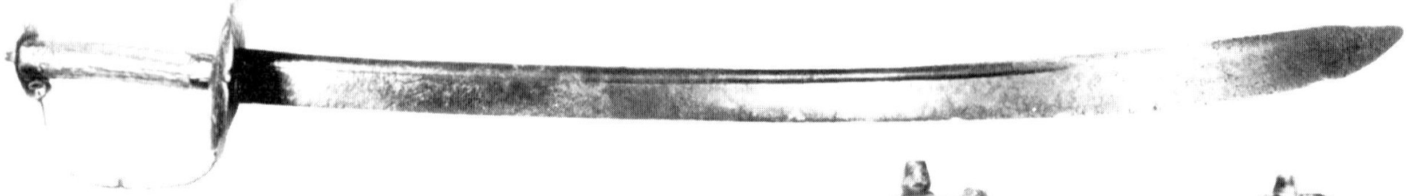

**2.SS  ENGLISH HANGER**                         Circa 1642–1660

This unique London pattern became popular at the time of Britain's Civil War (1642–1648). Most blades came from their Hounslow site or Germany's Solingen (whose running wolf marks are on this blade). Note the typical disk-like pommel, which is scrolled at the back to receive a flat knuckle bow with a mid-point simulated joint. The broad outboard counterguard contains three raised heads (usually political figures), while the iron hilt has an antler grip. Its curved blade ends in a clipped point.

Length: 32-3/4"          Blade: 27-3/8" X 1-1/4"          Hilt: Iron

**Author's Collection**

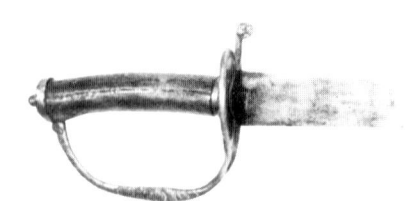

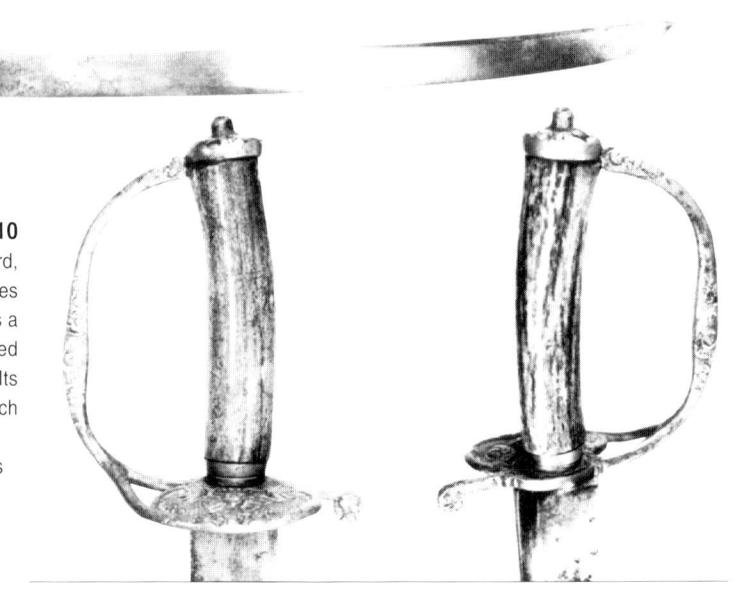

**3.SS  ENGLISH HANGER**                         Circa 1690–1710

One of Britain's infantry hangers in this period is described with a brass guard, antler grip and plain cutting edge. Note also that the tenuous knuckle bow divides to support the oval outer guard (none inboard). The staghorn handle secures a plain bottom ferrule and a disk-like pommel with a simple capstan. Raised designs are cast into the brass surfaces, including a cherub on the guard. Its curved, inexpensive blade contains flat faces, a 3/16" ricasso and a seven-inch false edge.

Length: 28-3/4"          Blade: 23-7/8" X 1-1/4"          Hilt: Brass

**Author's Collection**

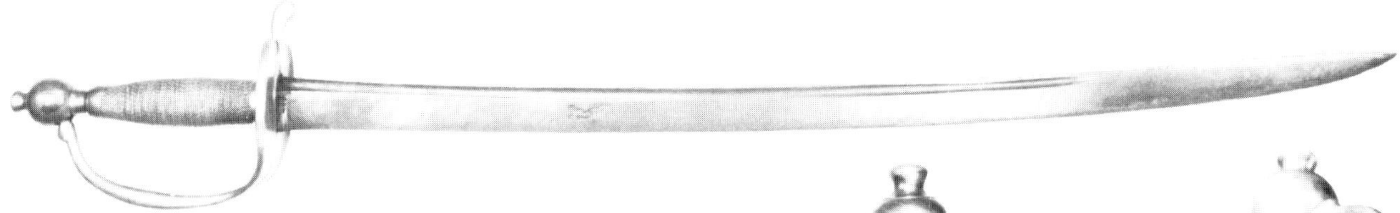

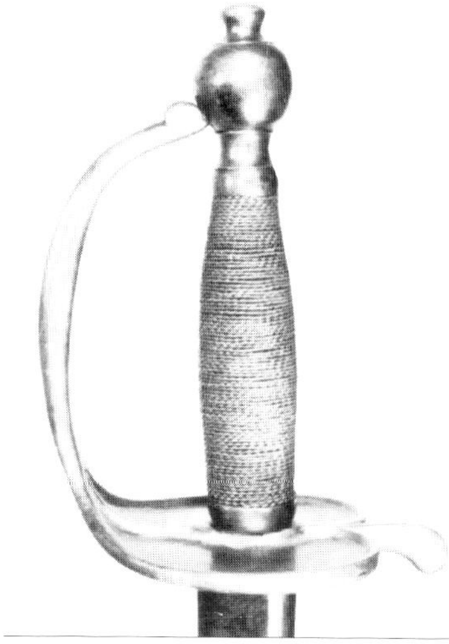

**4.SS ENGLISH HANGER**  Circa 1725–1750

The 18th century English colonel usually selected the swords for his regiment. This brass hilt mounting an oval pommel plus capstan, a simple knuckle bow and a recessed heart-shaped guard with ovoid quillon is typical of the period's battalion soldier's hanger. The form is often mistakenly called the Model 1742 because it appears in the Duke of Cumberland's clothing book of that date. Its wooden grip is wound with twisted brass wire, while the curved blade is stamped "SH" in a running fox figure (Samuel Harvey, Birmingham).

Length: 33-3/4"   Blade: 27-3/4" X 1-1/4"   Hilt: Brass
**Author's Collection**

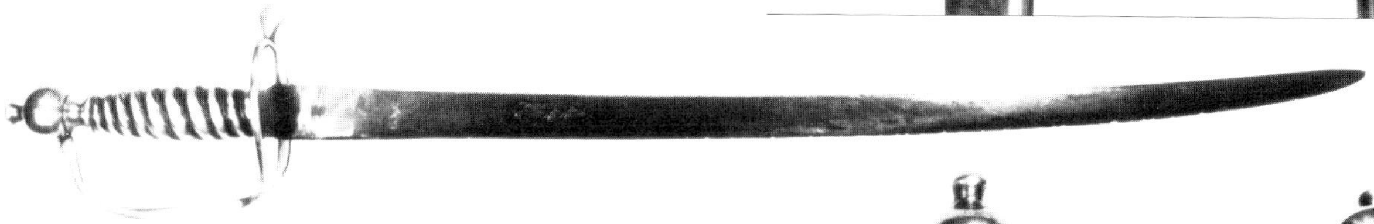

**5.SS ENGLISH HANGER**  Circa 1725–1740

Another of the popular British infantry hangers of this dating used a brass grip with accelerating spirals, a rounded pommel and raised capstan. A second casting created the combined knuckle bow, paneled heart-shaped guard, and lobed quillon. Many such patterns were contracted from Germany, as was probable in this case. A simple curved single-edged blade retains flat faces and the Germanic mark "C***." The guard's underside is crudely engraved "9" and "No 79."

Length: 29-1/2"   Blade: 24" X 1-1/8"   Hilt: Brass
**Author's Collection**

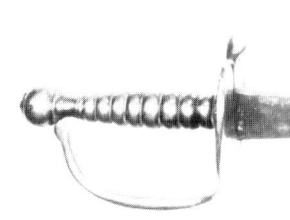

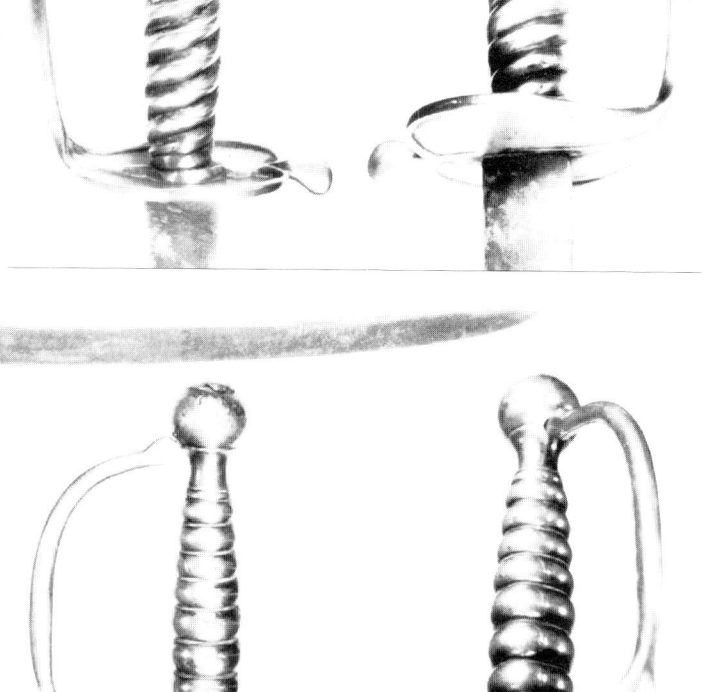

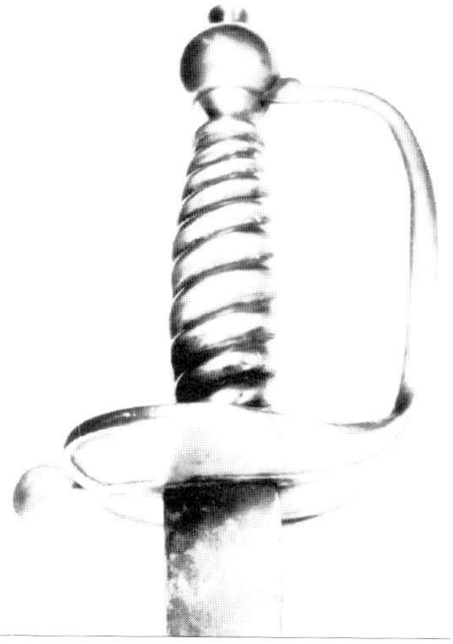

**6.SS ENGLISH HANGER**  Circa 1725–1750

Despite the preference by most British colonels toward inexpensive brass sword hilts for their battalion companies, pattern variations were common. The example shown here continues the two-piece cast hilt (see 5.SS) based on a heart-like counterguard and ovoid pommel but alters the grip with horizontal instead of spiraled ridges. The capstan has been lost in service. A common flat-faced single-edged Germanic blade bears their "C***" stamping.

Length: 28-1/2"   Blade: 23-3/4" X 1-3/16"   Hilt: Brass
**Author's Collection**

*Chapter 7: Swords*

**7.SS ENGLISH GRENADIER HANGER    Circa 1735–1755**

The single grenadier company in each English regiment, being an elite unit, was usually issued a different sword pattern than the regular battalion troops. Most of them used a basket or semi-basket hilt. In this case the common spiraled grip/paneled heart-like guard form (5.SS) has added a protective branch on each side. One is seen in Morier's paintings (1751). The hilt's underside is engraved "9 / 56" (the British "fraction," that is, unit nine, weapon 56).

Length: 32-1/8"    Blade: 26-1/4" X 1-1/4"    Hilt: Brass

**George C. Neumann Collection, Valley Forge National Historical Park**

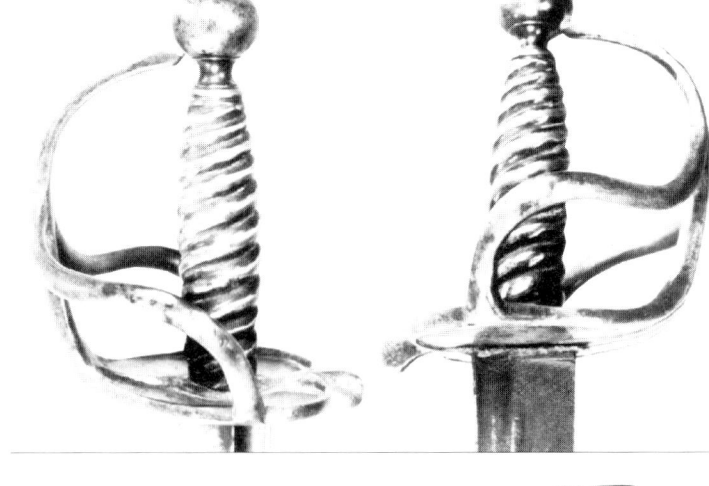

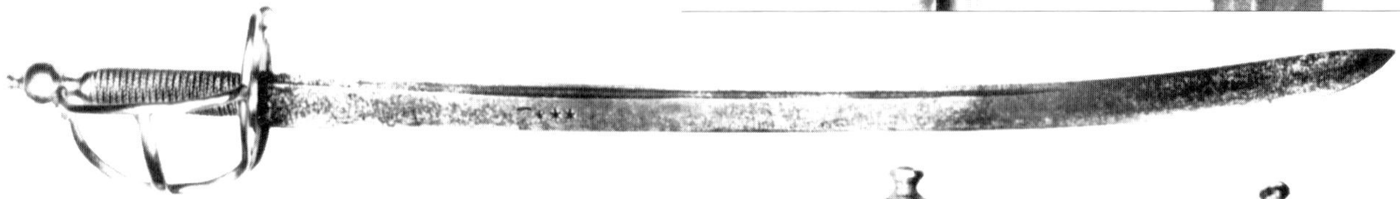

**8.SS ENGLISH GRENADIER HANGER    Circa 1740–1765**

Most British infantry hangers at this time used cast grips, but others, as shown here, chose to cover a wooden core with two side-by-side brass ropes (each of double strands), which were twisted in opposite directions to create a herringbone pattern. Note, too, the flat open heart-like guard, supplemented with a knuckle bow and outboard branch—joined by a horizontal strut to achieve a grenadier's semi-basket hilt. The common Germanic curved blade is stamped "C***."

Length: 32-3/4"    Blade: 26-5/8" X 1-1/4"    Hilt: Brass

**George C. Neumann Collection, Valley Forge National Historical Park**

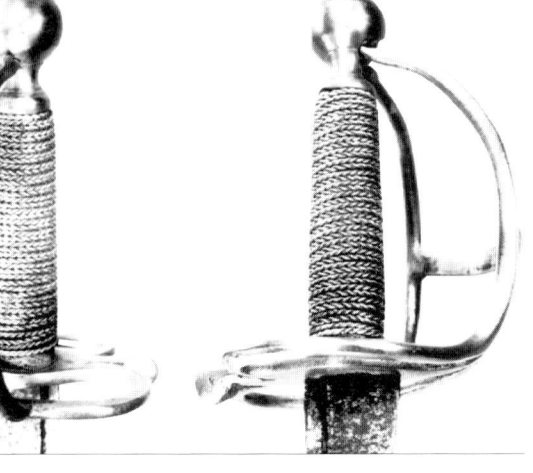

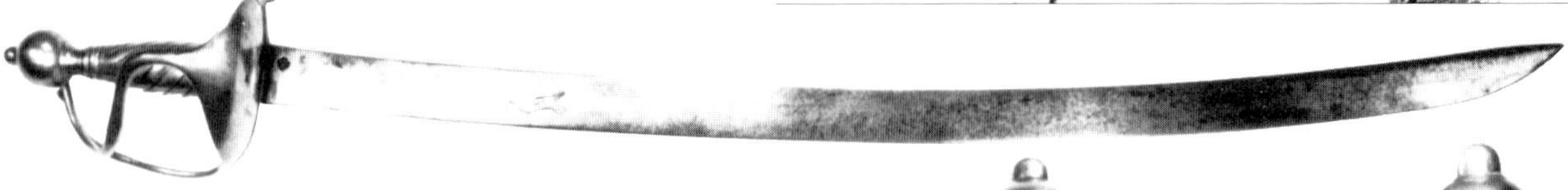

**9.SS ENGLISH GRENADIER HANGER    Circa 1735–1755**

The side branch and long blade here suggest a grenadier hanger. Note its unusual cast grip design, which simulates the popular raised spiral by incised lines, and the guard's evolution away from the recessed panel heart form to a smoothly dished contour. Moreover the original inboard half of the counterguard has been cut off—a favorite means of the soldier to ease leg chaffing. The English flat-faced blade is marked by Samuel Harvey ("SH" inside a running fox figure).

Length: 34-1/8"    Blade: 28-1/2" X 1-1/4"    Hilt: Brass

**Author's Collection**

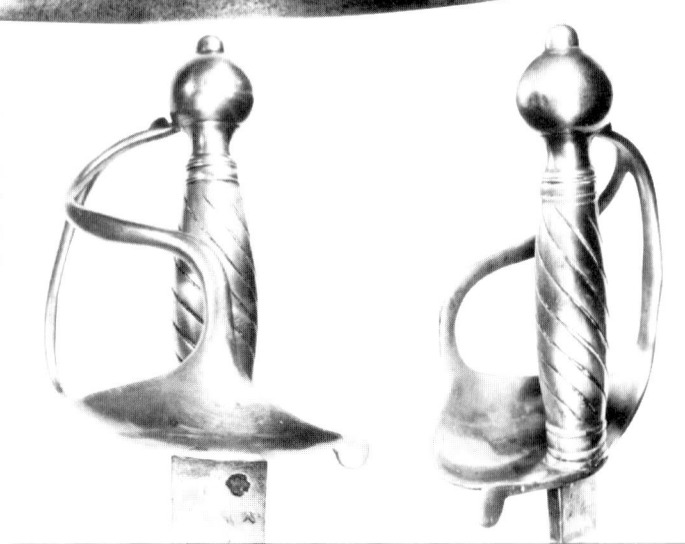

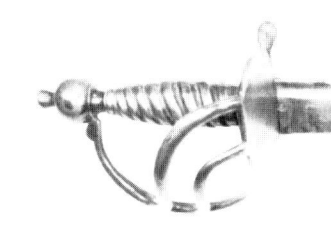

**10.SS  ENGLISH GRENADIER HANGER      Circa 1750–1768**
Two outboard branches connect the knuckle bow with a concave counterguard to create this semi-basket pattern. Today it is mistakenly called the Model 1751, referring to Morier's paintings of grenadiers in that year. Most of this style have English or Welsh county names engraved under the guard ("Denbigh-M" and "5 / 17" here), indicating initial use in Britain under their Militia Act of 1757. Its leather scabbard is stamped "crown / GR."
Length: 30-1/2"      Blade: 24-7/8" X 1-1/4"      Hilt: Brass
**Author's Collection**

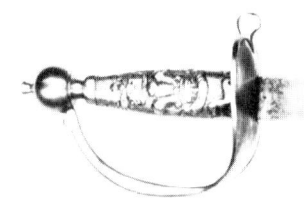

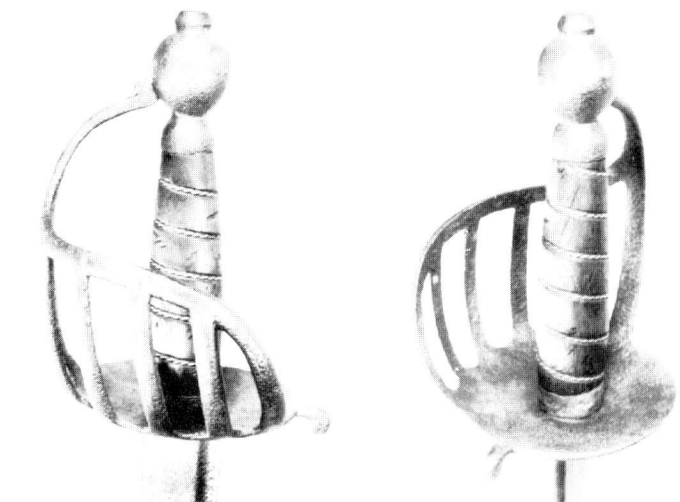

**11.SS  ENGLISH HANGER      Circa 1745–1760**
Because the regimental colonel purchased the swords privately for his troops, his regimental device was at times included. This impressive brass grip has the insignia of the famous 23rd Regiment of Foot, the Royal Welsh Fusiliers, cast into both sides (also see 21.SS). In addition, the hilt incorporates the evolved dished heart-shaped counterguard but retains raised borders underneath. A short 24-7/8" single-edged blade has flat faces and a 1/4" ricasso.
Length: 31"      Blade: 24-7/8" X 1-1/8"      Hilt: Brass
**George C. Neumann Collection, Valley Forge National Historical Park**

**12.SS  ENGLISH GRENADIER HANGER      Circa 1740–1755**
Some of the semi-basket hangers issued to grenadiers were iron-hilted. This interesting example provides a curving outboard branch supported by four vertical bars; they join a dished counterguard that is now oval instead of heart-shaped. The ovoid pommel, capstan and upper ferrule were forged as one piece. Its wooden grip, in turn, has lost the original leather wrapping and substituted a single channeled wire rope. "H" inside a fox figure marks the British blade.
Length: 33-1/2"      Blade: 27-3/4" X 1-3/8"      Hilt: Iron

Chapter 7: Swords

**13.SS  ENGLISH HANGER**  Circa 1650
A completely unique sword form used by the British featured a grotesque gargoyle (monster, lion, dog, etc.) pommel, which was apparently taken from the Kastane, the national sword of Ceylon. This early version is better defined than most and adds necklace-like designs plus finger ridges on the flat-sided grip. A double-lobed counterguard shows raised figures, while the knuckle bow bears a mid-point junction design. Its wide blade markings include "THE TOWER . . ." cut into a 1/4-inch back fuller.
Length: 27"         Blade: 23-3/8" X 1-3/8"         Hilt: Brass

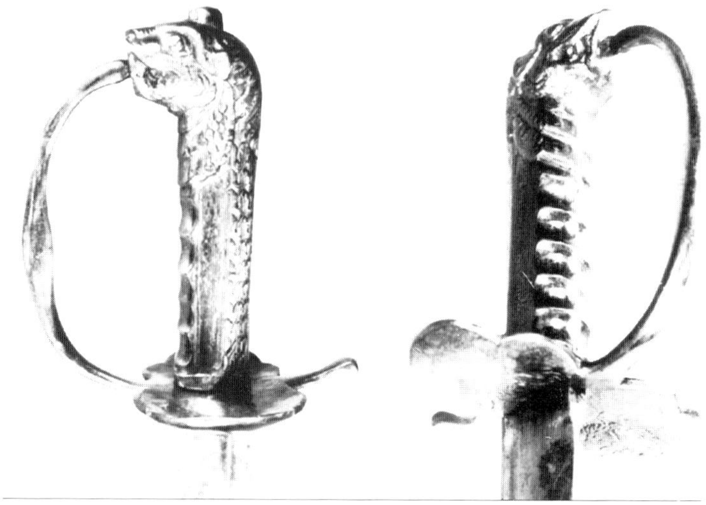

**14.SS  ENGLISH HANGER**  Circa 1690–1710
This evolving gargoyle-pommel sword (see 13.SS) retains a cast grip with finger ridges and flat sides but has softened the grotesque face and necklace decorations. It is cast in the same three pieces (two vertical grip halves and knuckle bow/guard). However the counterguard is now dished upward and the knuckle bow mid-point embellishment is gone. A later blade is stamped "T HOLLIER," an English cutler who rebladed them in the early 1700s. The sea service also used this form.
Length: 33"         Blade: 27-1/2" X 1-1/4"         Hilt: Brass
**George C. Neumann Collection, Valley Forge National Historical Park**

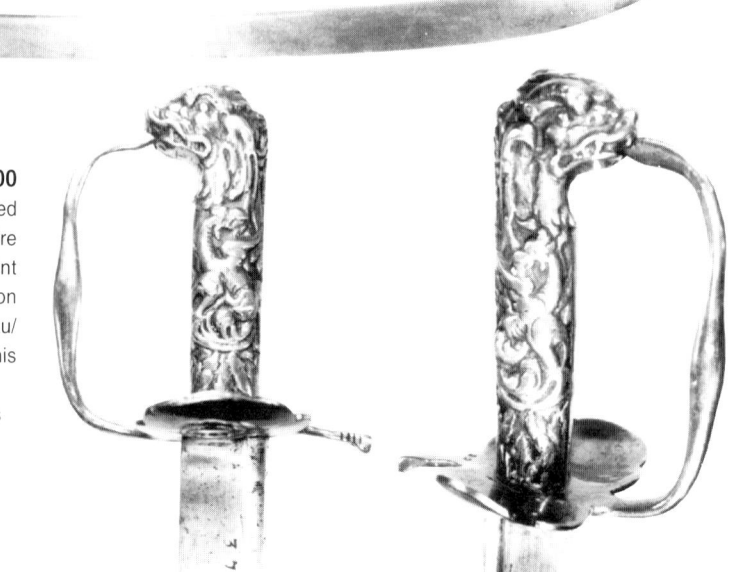

**15.SS  ENGLISH HANGER**  Circa 1680–1700
This alternate version of the early gargoyle sword pattern combines a less defined pommel head with interacting dragons and floral abstracts covering the entire grip. A single brass casting, in turn, joins the knuckle bow (no mid-point decoration), two lobed counterguards that curve upward (raised face designs on bottom) and a flattened quillon. The heavy blade is marked by crude Passau/Solingen running wolf marks (often faked), two anchor stamps and "370." This pattern also saw naval use.
Length: 33-1/2"         Blade: 28-1/8" X 1-1/4"         Hilt: Brass
**Author's Collection**

308    Chapter 7: Swords

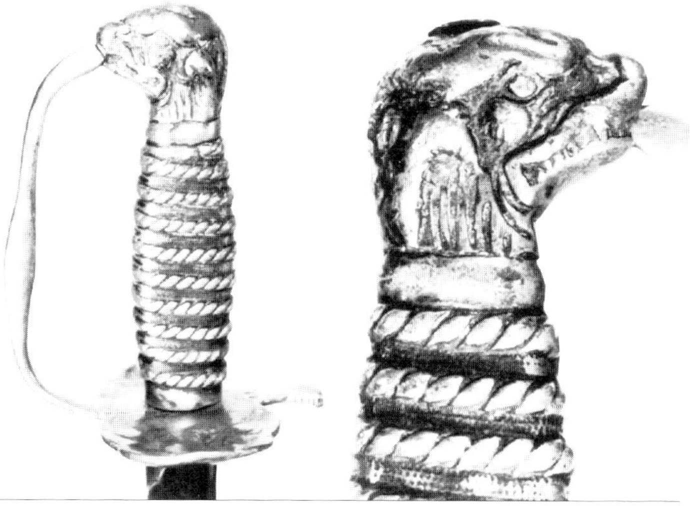

**16.SS  ENGLISH HANGER**                               Circa 1730–1750

As the 1700s progressed, the gargoyle head pommel became more inscrutable and added a cast rope spiral to the grip. Yet in this sword it is combined with the lingering late-17th century form of knuckle bow, upward dished counterguards and flat quillon. Raised designs appear on the underside. This type of pommel/grip (one piece) has been excavated at American sites of the Revolutionary War.

Length: 29-1/8"          Blade: 24" X 1"          Hilt: Brass

**Author's Collection**

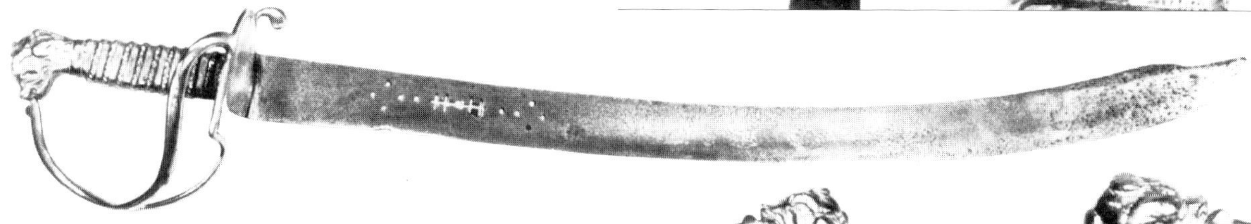

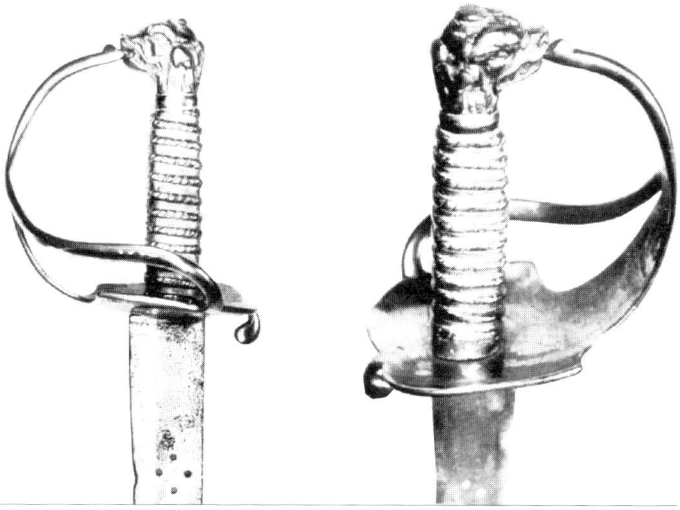

**17.SS  ENGLISH MUSICIAN'S HANGER**                    Circa 1745–1765

The maturing gargoyle pommel with its cast rope grip was, in this case, mounted with a broadened concave guard having abrupt rear shoulders, raised lower borders, an outboard side branch and a lobed quillon. Of further interest is the rare scimitar blade described as issued to British musicians under the 1768 warrant. Note the curved point and decorative dot/line designs punched through the blade, which are typical (see similar blade 50.SS). Both faces have a wide shallow concave fuller.

Length: 28-1/2"          Blade: 23-1/8" X 1-3/8"          Hilt: Brass

**Don Troiani Collection**

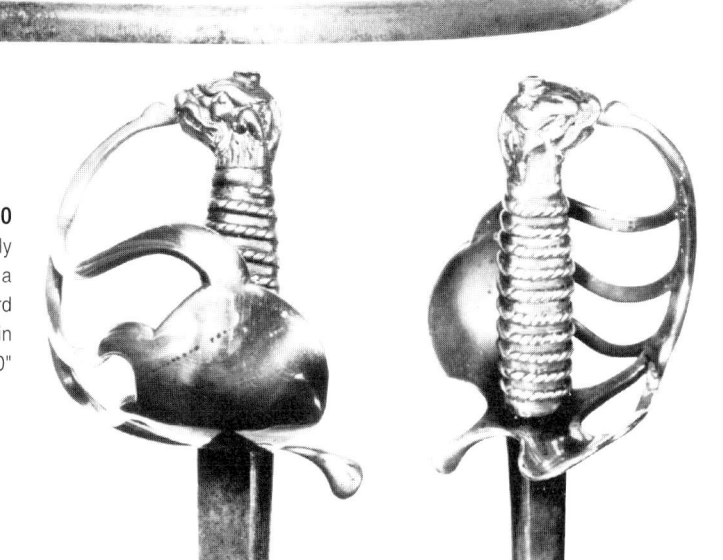

**18.SS  ENGLISH GRENADIER HANGER**                    Circa 1750–1780

This integral gargoyle pommel and raised rope grip was joined to an elaborately cast triple-branched hilt with a high oval outboard guard. It is identified as a grenadier sergeant's arm from the 16th Regiment of Foot (bottom of guard markings "XVI RT/GR No 39"). The sword was found in Georgia, an area in which that regiment served. A slightly curved single-edged blade (1/4" X 20" back fuller) is marked by the British running fox figure enclosing a faint "H."

Length: 31-5/8"          Blade: 26-1/2" X 1-1/4"          Hilt: Brass

**Don Troiani Collection**

Chapter 7: Swords   309

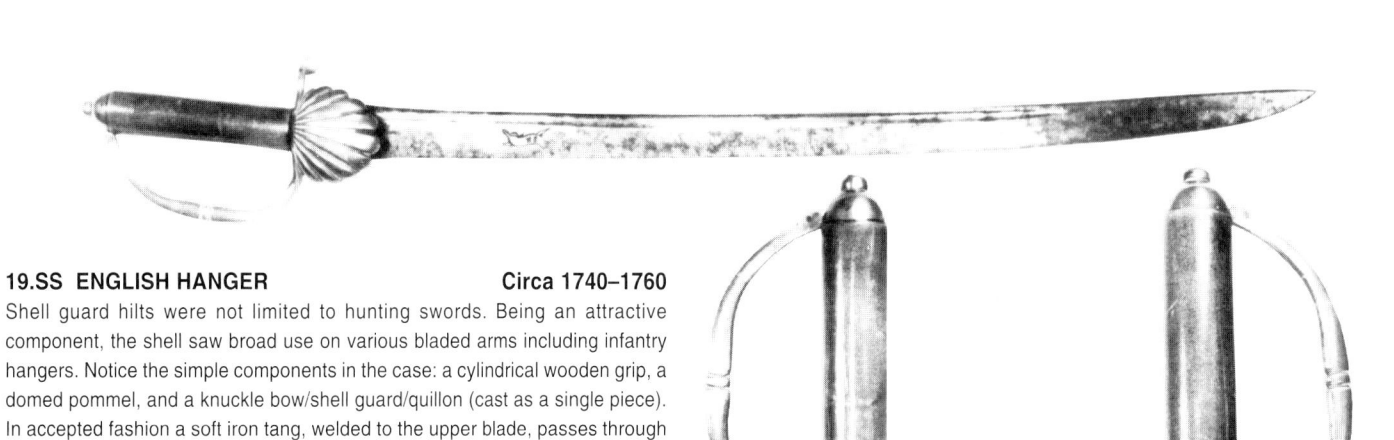

**19.SS ENGLISH HANGER**                        **Circa 1740–1760**

Shell guard hilts were not limited to hunting swords. Being an attractive component, the shell saw broad use on various bladed arms including infantry hangers. Notice the simple components in the case: a cylindrical wooden grip, a domed pommel, and a knuckle bow/shell guard/quillon (cast as a single piece). In accepted fashion a soft iron tang, welded to the upper blade, passes through holes in these units of the hilt to be hammered flat at the top.

Length: 29-5/8"        Blade: 24-5/8" X 1-1/4"        Hilt: Brass

**Author's Collection**

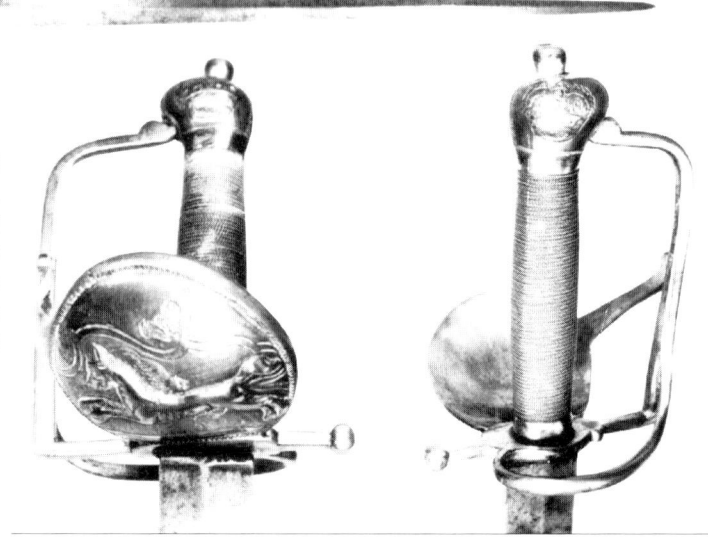

**20.SS ENGLISH HANGER**                        **Circa 1730–1755**

This unusual pattern is still reproduced for the warders in the Tower of London. Note that a raised crown has been cast into both sides of the unbalanced pommel and the Hanovarian horse (that is, King George) appears on the dished outer counterguard. The stirrup-shaped knuckle bow, in turn, spreads to form both an open inner guard and an outboard panel. The long straight blade has median ridges. A dug relic of this form is marked "Sr. W. P. No33," (probably Willliam Pepperrell's 51st Regiment).

Length: 35-3/8"        Blade: 29-1/2" X 1-1/4"        Hilt: Gilded Brass

**Author's Collection**

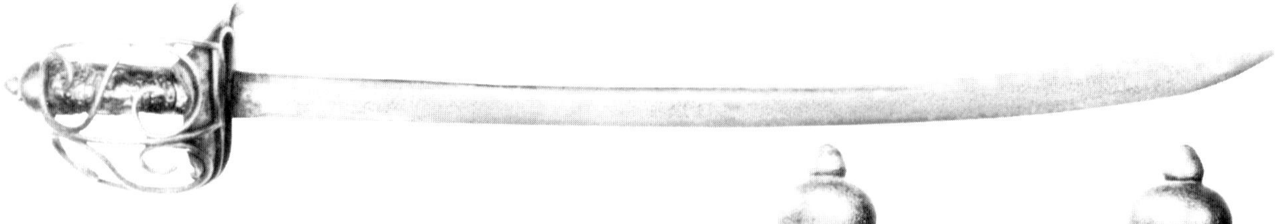

**21.SS ENGLISH GRENADIER HANGER**            **Circa 1740–1760**

One company of the ten in a British regiment was the elite grenadiers, with their tall caps. Unlike the eight battalion companies (regular soldiers) or the light infantry unit, grenadiers were usually issued basket-hilted swords. This "double S" iron pattern includes a thin sheet-metal grip (originally gilded) embossed with the insignia of the 23rd Regiment of Foot (Royal Welsh Fusiliers). The surviving leather base pad covers an open heart-shaped counterguard. (Also see 11.SS.)

Length: 30-1/8"        Blade: 24-1/2" X 1-1/8"        Hilt: Iron

**George C. Neumann Collection, Valley Forge National Historical Park**

**22.SS ENGLISH GRENADIER HANGER**  Circa 1750–1765

Most period grenadier swords were apparently hilted in iron (40 of the 46 shown in Morier's 1751 paintings, and 30 of them were basket-hilted). Notice the various shapes here in this semi-basket, as well as the broad ovoid pommel and raised capstan. A ring joins the elements under the pommel—at the top of a wooden grip covered by shagreen (fish- or sharkskin). The slightly curved blade is marked "S. HARVEY," (Samuel Harvey, Birmingham, circa 1748–1778).

Length: 37"  Blade: 30-3/4" X 1-1/4"  Hilt: Iron
**Erik Goldstein Collection**

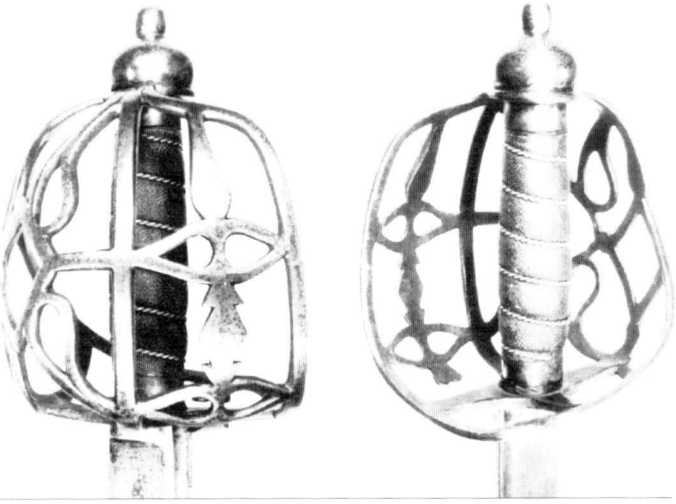

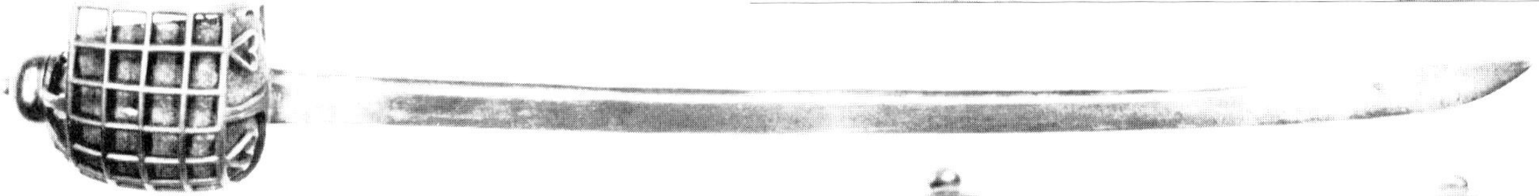

**23.SS ENGLISH GRENADIER HANGER**  Circa 1750–1765

This grenadier hanger continues the familiar British mid-century practice of a prominent capstan on a wide oval pommel just above a ring that secures all of the upper hilt components. In addition, the sturdy grid pattern semi-basket adds open heart forms that project into three lower openings. Note also the antler grip plus red wool liner with a thin buckskin backing. The common curved blade includes the usual 1/4" back fuller.

Length: 34-3/8"  Blade: 28-3/8" X 1-1/4"  Hilt: Iron
**George C. Neumann Collection, Valley Forge National Historical Park**

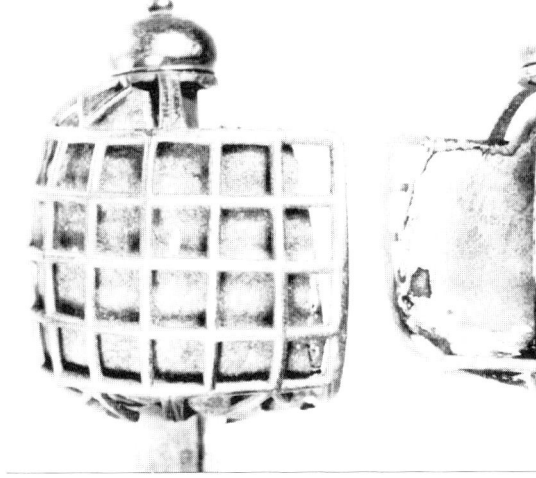

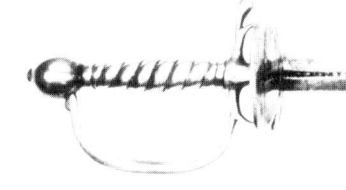

**24.SS FRENCH HANGER**  Circa 1695–1740

French preference for the rapier and its thrusting stroke is evident in both their grenadier and battalion company hangers prior to 1750. Most have a straight double-edged blade as seen here. This early pattern, usually associated with fusiliers, adopted the small sword format having an ovoid pommel, cast brass spiraled grip, pas-d'ane and a bilobate counterguard (dished, raised borders). The narrow blade is diamond in cross-section with a four-inch fuller below the hilt.

Length: 32-1/4"  Blade: 25-3/4" X 7/8"  Hilt: Brass
**Author's Collection**

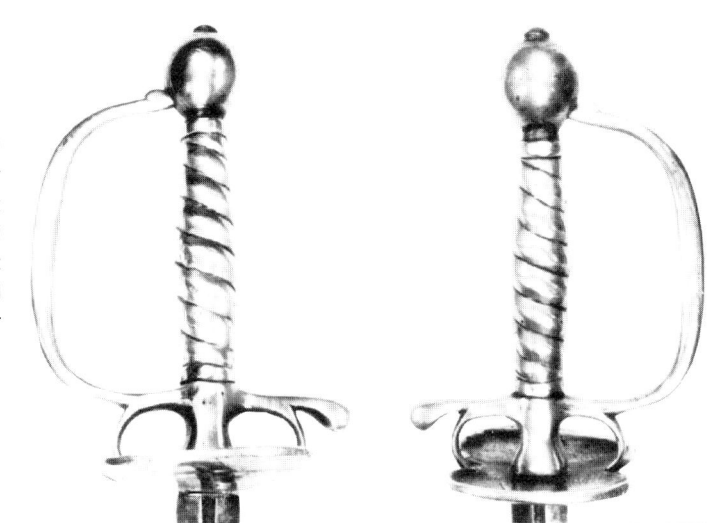

*Chapter 7: Swords*

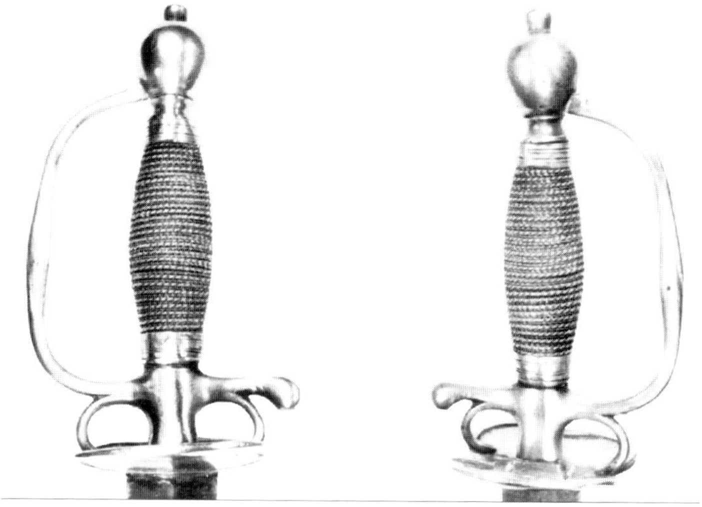

### 25.SS  FRENCH HANGER  Circa 1700–1750

France's affection for the small sword is evident in this popular hanger. The wooden grip is covered with two adjacent wire ropes (double strands) twisted in opposite directions to create a herringbone pattern. Unlike the English and Germans, who preferred equal size wire, the French usually had one rope larger than the other (as seen here). An ovoid pommel/capstan, D-guard, pas d'ane, 3/8" ferrules and a bilobate guard complete the hilt. Its straight blade has a typical abrupt point.

Length: 34-7/8"     Blade: 28-1/4" X 1-1/4"     Hilt: Brass

**Author's Collection**

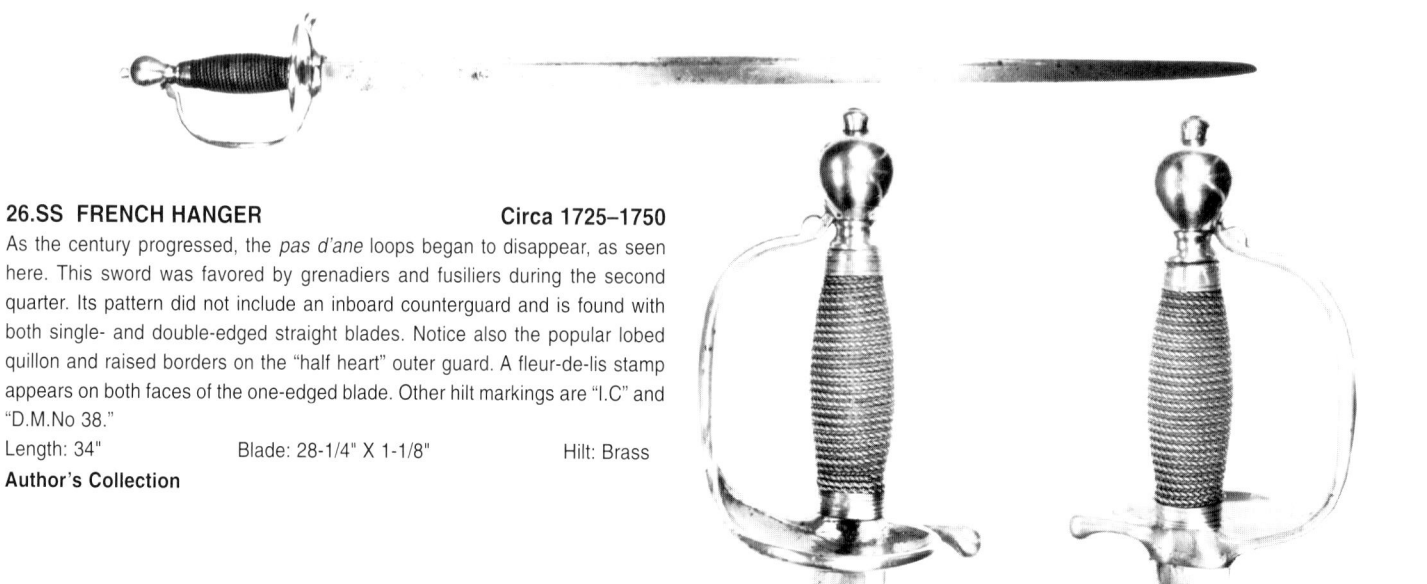

### 26.SS  FRENCH HANGER  Circa 1725–1750

As the century progressed, the *pas d'ane* loops began to disappear, as seen here. This sword was favored by grenadiers and fusiliers during the second quarter. Its pattern did not include an inboard counterguard and is found with both single- and double-edged straight blades. Notice also the popular lobed quillon and raised borders on the "half heart" outer guard. A fleur-de-lis stamp appears on both faces of the one-edged blade. Other hilt markings are "I.C" and "D.M.No 38."

Length: 34"     Blade: 28-1/4" X 1-1/8"     Hilt: Brass

**Author's Collection**

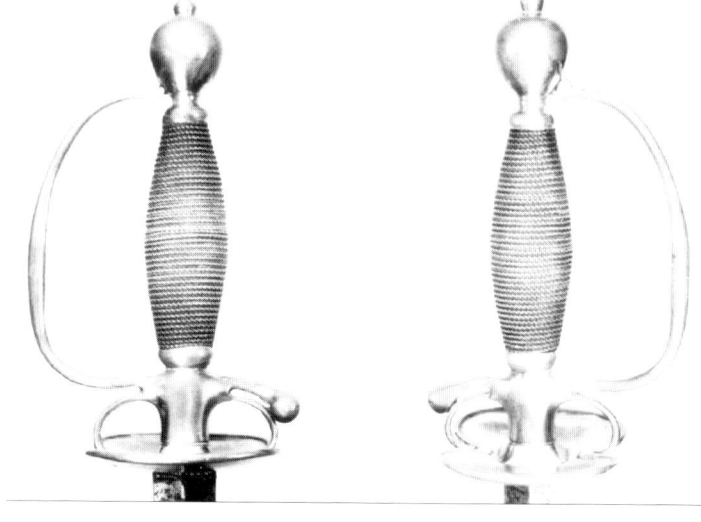

### 27.SS  FRENCH NON-COM HANGER  Circa 1710–1750

The basic elements of this non-commissioned or junior officer pattern are closer to the smaller and more delicate small sword, which also had widespread civilian acceptance. Note that the wooden grip is still wrapped by two different size wire ropes, but the ferrules are now cast as part of the pommel and knuckle bow. Both faces of the bilobate guard show raised borders. Its thin double-edged rapier-type blade has a diamond cross-section. The hilt was originally gilded.

Length: 34-1/4"     Blade: 28-1/4" x 7/8"     Hilt: Gilded Brass

**Author's Collection**

### 28.SS  FRENCH NON-COM HANGER  Circa 1710–1740
There was little control of sword designs among French regiments in the early 1700s, yet this use of facets on the pommel, knuckle bow and quillon was a favored pattern. The example shown is a form and quality frequently carried by non-coms and junior officers. Double brass wire ropes cover the grip between two-inch ferrules. Note also that the knuckle bow and *pas d'ane* are cast as one piece while incised decorations remain on the three-paneled sides of the double-edged blade.

Length: 36"  Blade: 29-1/4" X 3/4"  Hilt: Brass
**Author's Collection**

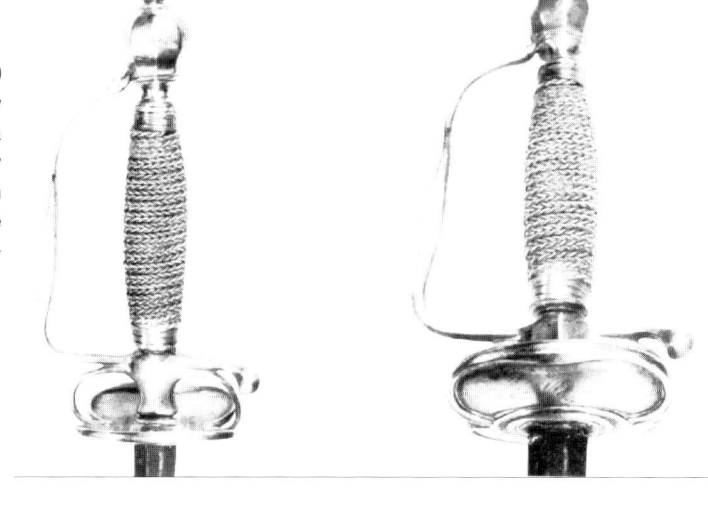

### 29.SS  FRENCH GRENADIER HANGER  Circa 1747–1764
In 1736 the official French infantry sword blade length was set at 27 inches. Previously it could vary but could not exceed 32 inches. A grenadier blade was then specified in 1747 to be single-edged, slightly curved and no longer than 32 inches. Yet the rulings were largely ignored by the colonels. This hilt with its vase-like pommel, dished heart-shaped guard, and smooth brass grip mounts a curved one-edged 26-1/2" blade marked "Vive Le Roy" and "Grenadier d'infantrie." It was found in Newport, Rhode Island.

Length: 32-3/4"  Blade: 26-1/4" X 1-1/16"  Hilt: Brass
**Don Troiani Collection**

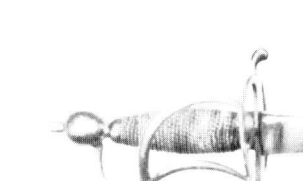

### 30.SS  FRENCH GRENADIER HANGER  Circa 1747–1764
France also used iron hilts as illustrated here. The double branch outboard guard is also found on some horseman sabers. In this design it attaches to an open heart-like counterguard having a cross-strut in each side. French tradition continues in the wire-wrapped grip and ovoid pommel with a sizable capstan. The slightly curving blade, in turn, retains a fleur-de-lis stamped on each side. A single fuller at the back measures 1/8" X 20".

Length: 34-1/2"  Blade: 28-1/2" X 1-1/4"  Hilt: Iron
**George C. Neumann Collection, Valley Forge National Historical Park**

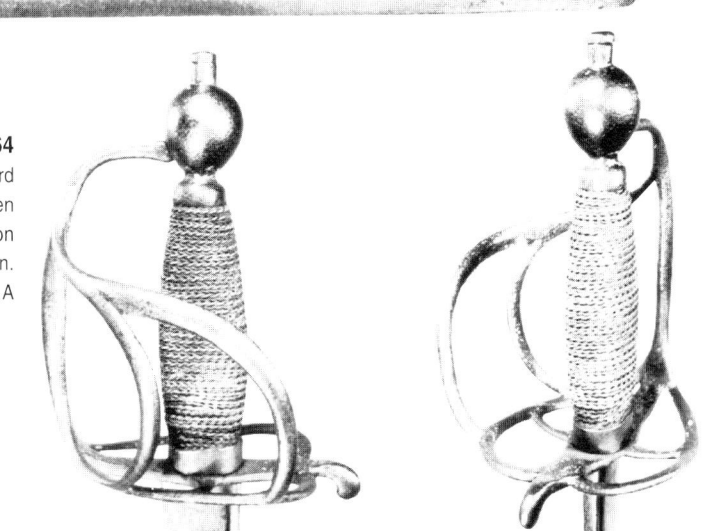

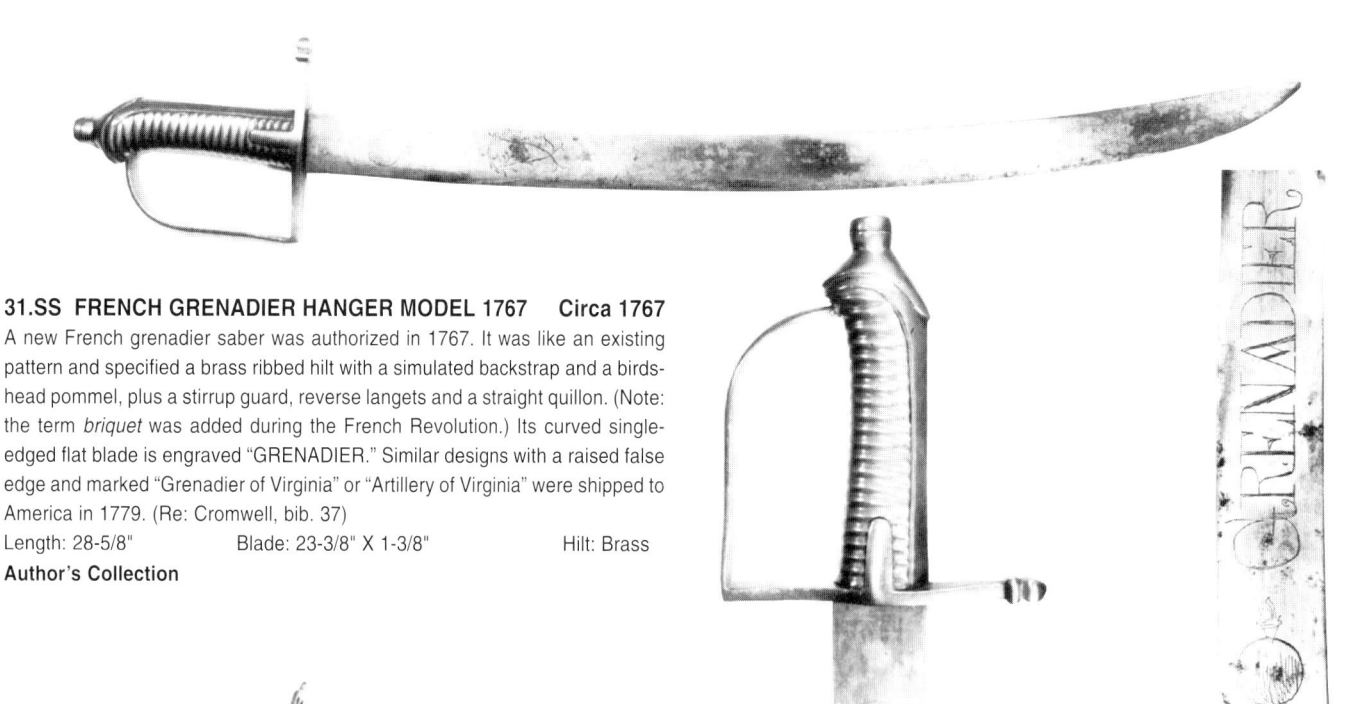

### 31.SS  FRENCH GRENADIER HANGER MODEL 1767    Circa 1767
A new French grenadier saber was authorized in 1767. It was like an existing pattern and specified a brass ribbed hilt with a simulated backstrap and a birds-head pommel, plus a stirrup guard, reverse langets and a straight quillon. (Note: the term *briquet* was added during the French Revolution.) Its curved single-edged flat blade is engraved "GRENADIER." Similar designs with a raised false edge and marked "Grenadier of Virginia" or "Artillery of Virginia" were shipped to America in 1779. (Re: Cromwell, bib. 37)
Length: 28-5/8"          Blade: 23-3/8" X 1-3/8"          Hilt: Brass
**Author's Collection**

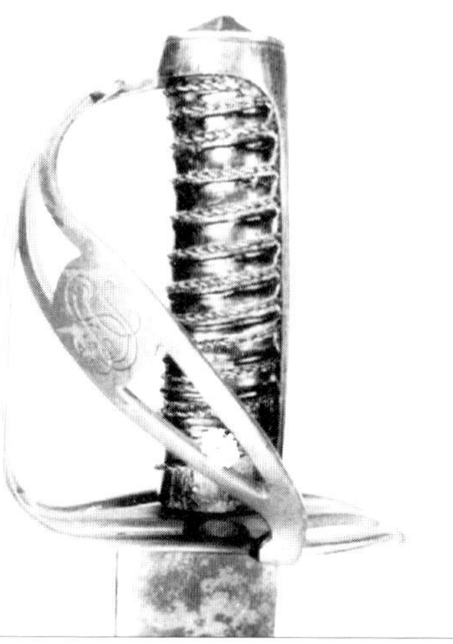

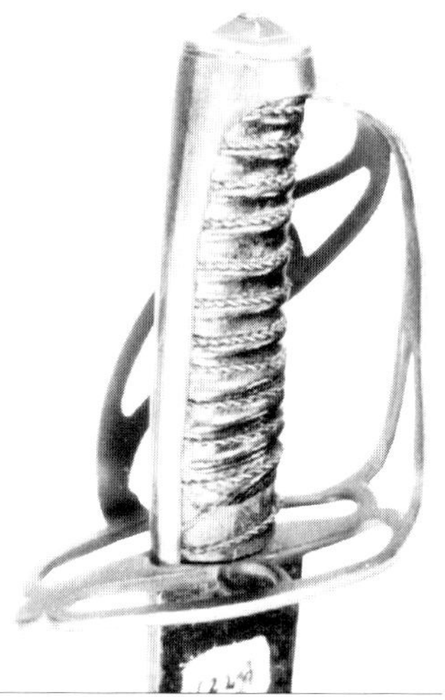

### 32.SS  FRENCH HANGER          Circa 1780–1783
The flattened pommel and diamond-shaped capstan of this hilt are forms usually associated with the end of the century. Yet excavation of this pattern in American Army camps circa 1780–1783 establishes that the design was developed earlier. Moreover the entwined "USA" inscribed on the panel of the outboard guard was also discovered on other accoutrements at these locations—suggesting that this was the short sword obtained for the Corps of Light Infantry by Lafayette. Note also the leather-covered grip.
Length: 30-7/8"          Blade: 25-1/2" X 7/8"          Hilt: Brass
**George Juno Collection**

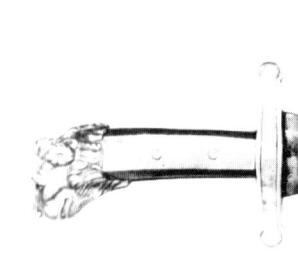

### 33.SS  FRENCH ARTILLERY SWORD          Circa 1771–1790
The famed Roman short sword *("gladius")* was the basis for this form adopted by the French land and naval artillery, which probably served in America with their forces. The design added articulate animal and birds-head pommels to a hilt with a crossguard showing indented panels. The typical double-edged blade includes two adjoining short fullers above a long center one on each face. The blade's mounting tang is the full width of the grip (edges visible). Marks: "SC No 29" on the hilt.
Length: 24-1/4"          Blade: 18-1/4" X 1-7/8"          Hilt: Brass
**George C. Neumann Collection, Valley Forge National Historical Park**

314    *Chapter 7: Swords*

**34.SS FRENCH ARTILLERY SWORD        Circa 1771–1790**
The well-defined eagle hilt pictured here was the most popular form of this French artillery sword pattern. Traces of gilding over the cast brass base and the insertion of plugs, in this example, to cover the usual three cross rivet heads visible along the grip, suggest use by an officer. Its blade also differs from the norm, with a low median ridge on each face (see 33.SS). Both edges have been sharpened. No markings are visible.
Length: 24-1/4"        Blade: 18-7/8" X 1-5/8"        Hilt: Brass
**Author's Collection**

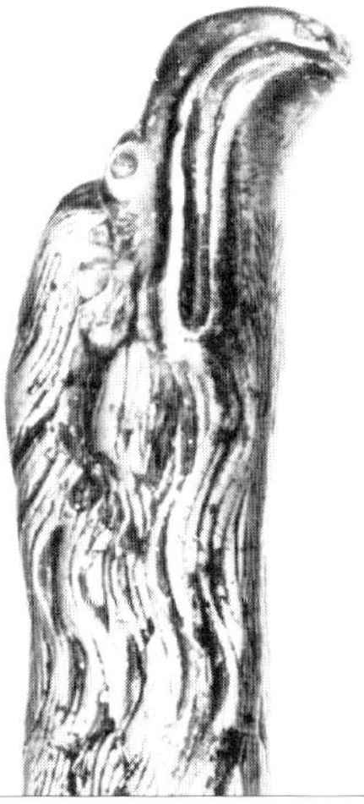

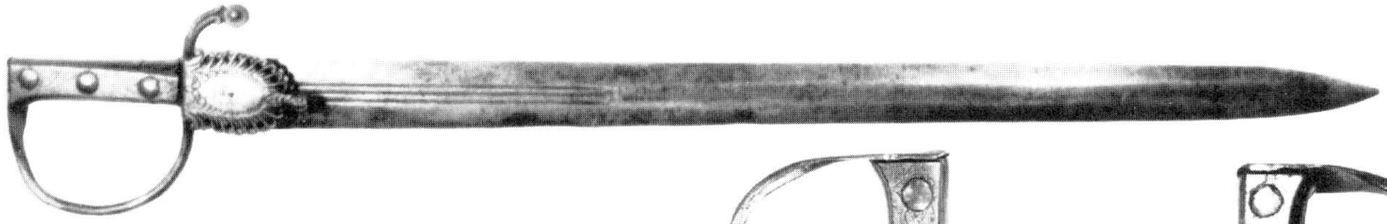

**35.SS SPANISH HANGER *("ESPADA ANCHA")*        Circa 1720–1790**
The *"espada ancha"* was the common sword of New Spain—developed in their North American colonies from a 17th century hunting broadsword. This officer's example includes a hilt with a wooden slab on each side of the wide blade tang—under another layer of outside iron panels (three cross rivets). Also note the plain D-guard, which is flat at the top and ends in an articulate quillon beyond an ornamented shell guard having a human head bottom finial. Its double-edged straight blade is typical.
Length: 31-1/4"        Blade: 27-1/8" X 1-5/8"        Hilt: Iron
**The Benninghoff Collection**

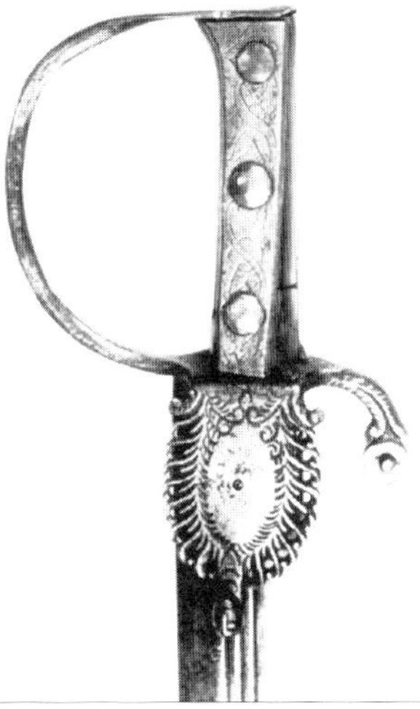

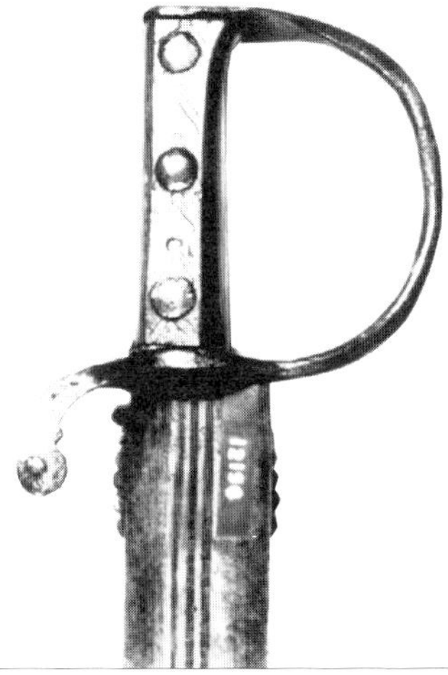

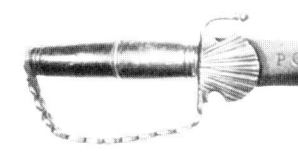

**36.SS SPANISH HANGER *("ESPADA ANCHA")*        Circa 1778**
Such popular Spanish colonial short swords undoubtedly saw service with the Bernardo de Galvaz expedition along the Gulf of Mexico from 1779–1781 and as part of their considerable aid to frontier Americans. This oval-section hilt has two pieces of horn meeting at a center disk. A rigid chain-like knuckle bow, in turn, leads to a typical down-curving quillon and outer shell guard. Its paneled straight blade is inscribed "POR EL REY CARLOS III" and "YNFANTA TO 1778."
Length: 29-1/2"        Blade: 25-1/4" X 1-1/4"        Hilt: Iron
**Tom Wnuck Collection**

*Chapter 7: Swords*

**37.SS GERMANIC HANGER**  Circa 1660–1680
Note several characteristics here of central European infantry swords from the mid-17th century: large bulbous ovals interrupting elements of the hilt; an inboard thumb ring (seldom, if ever, used by the English); a bulging pommel with raised capstan; and a long quillon ending in an expanded finial. This pattern adds a spiraled wooden grip, incised decoration (including a birds-head) in the guard panel's underside and a curved single-edged blade (two fullers).
Length: 35-1/4"   Blade: 29-1/2" X 1-1/8"   Hilt: Iron
**Author's Collection**

**38.SS GERMANIC HANGER**  Circa 1680–1710
Compared with the previous sword, evolution can be seen in the reduced size of the lobes on the hilt components, a narrower pommel and a bilobate counterguard having pierced panels inserted into each half. The traditional inboard thumb ring continues. Its wooden grip is covered by two wire ropes twisted in opposite directions—between two turks-head ferrules. A median ridge runs along both faces of the sturdy two-edged straight blade.
Length: 37-1/2"   Blade: 32 X 1-1/4"   Hilt: Iron
**George C. Neumann Collection, Valley Forge National Historical Park**

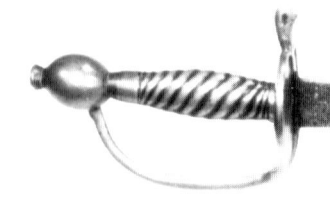

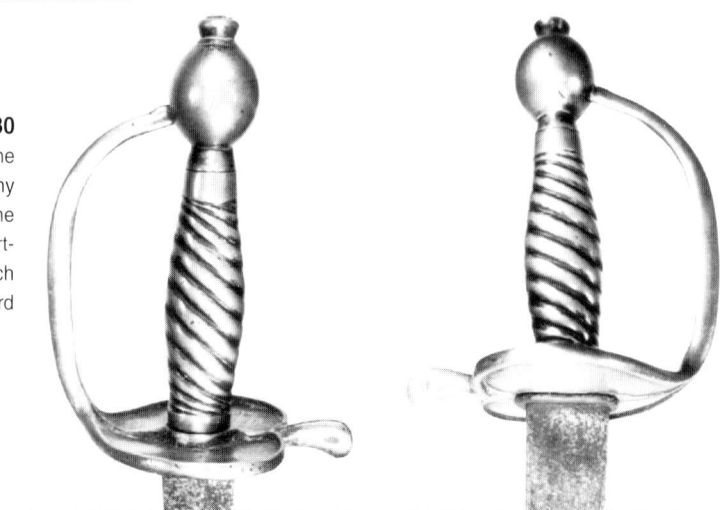

**39.SS GERMAN HANGER**  Circa 1740–1780
Such all-brass hilts were developed by Prussia about 1715. By mid-century the form had become popular across most of Europe and then accompanied many German mercenaries serving here during the American Revolution. Notice the large oval pommel and capstan, the cast brass spiraled grip, and the heart-shaped counterguard with recessed panels. Its large quillon was meant to catch an enemy's sword. This blade is curved with flat faces; some of these had inboard thumb rings.
Length: 29-1/2"   Blade: 23" X 1-1/8"   Hilt: Brass
**Author's Collection**

316   *Chapter 7: Swords*

**40.SS GERMAN HANGER**  Circa 1740–1780

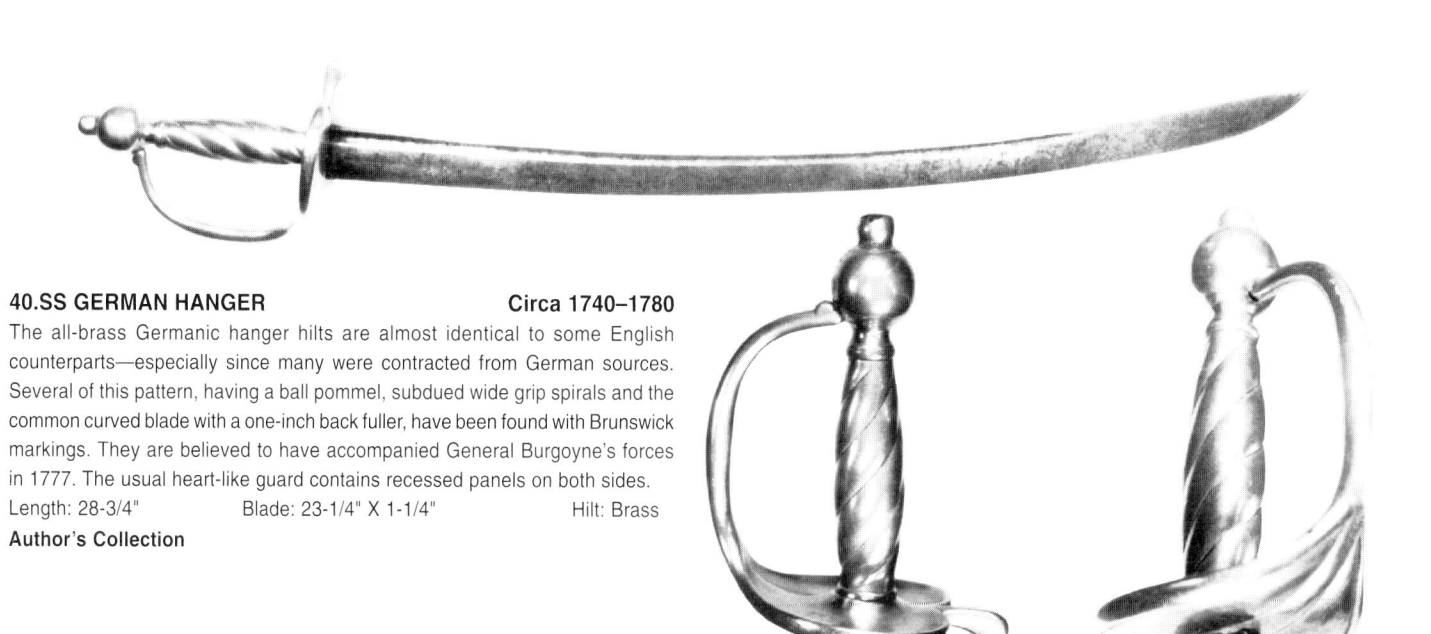

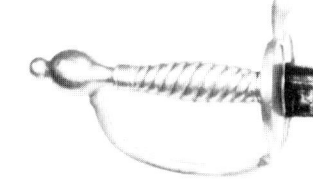

The all-brass Germanic hanger hilts are almost identical to some English counterparts—especially since many were contracted from German sources. Several of this pattern, having a ball pommel, subdued wide grip spirals and the common curved blade with a one-inch back fuller, have been found with Brunswick markings. They are believed to have accompanied General Burgoyne's forces in 1777. The usual heart-like guard contains recessed panels on both sides.
Length: 28-3/4"        Blade: 23-1/4" X 1-1/4"        Hilt: Brass
**Author's Collection**

**41.SS  GERMAN HANGER**  Circa 1760–1790

These all-brass hanger patterns show variations reflecting the various armies and regiments. This pommel, for example, is elongated into an inverted vase form, and the grip is narrower with a faster twist. Its cast knuckle bow, paneled heart-shaped guard and blunt quillon, in turn, follow accepted styling. The regiments often adorned their hilts with a sword knot (as shown, originally slipped over a man's wrist in combat); it usually adopted the color of the uniform lace or buttons.
Length: 30-3/8"        Blade: 24-1/4" X 1-1/4"        Hilt: Brass
**Author's Collection**

**42.SS  GERMANIC HANGER**  Circa 1750–1760

This pattern with its outer branch and upturned shell guard probably served in a grenadier company. Note the current accepted practice of wrapping thick cord around the wooden grip with intervals so that the leather covering would create channels for a spiraling wire rope. The birds-head pommel and quillon also reflect some French influence (31.SS). This sword knot's tassel is flat (versus the prior round example, 41.SS). An inboard thumb ring is also present.
Length: 35-1/4"        Blade: 30" X 1-1/4"        Hilt: Brass
**George C. Neumann Collection, Valley Forge National Historical Park**

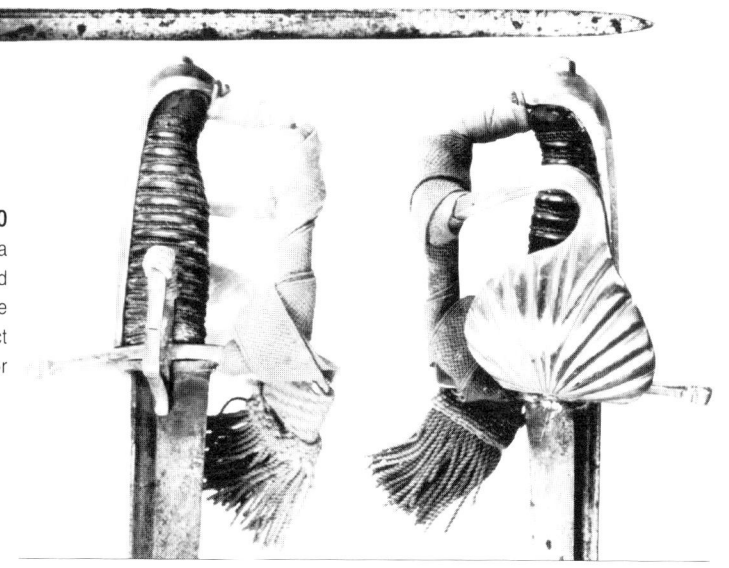

*Chapter 7: Swords*  317

**43.SS  GERMAN HANGER**  Circa 1767–1777
By these dates the backstrap hilt design with its birds-head pommel was in favor, usually accompanied by a leather-covered wooden grip (spiraled rope underneath). This Germanic pattern adds an engraved animal head at the top, plus a diamond-shaped double langet with a border design. The guard, in turn, is the evolving stirrup form. Such a pattern is associated with senior non-coms. Panoplies of arms appear on both faces of the single-edged blade (single fuller 5/16" X 22-1/2").
Length: 34-5/8"  Blade: 29-1/2" X 1-3/8"  Hilt: Brass
**George C. Neumann Collection, Valley Forge National Historical Park**

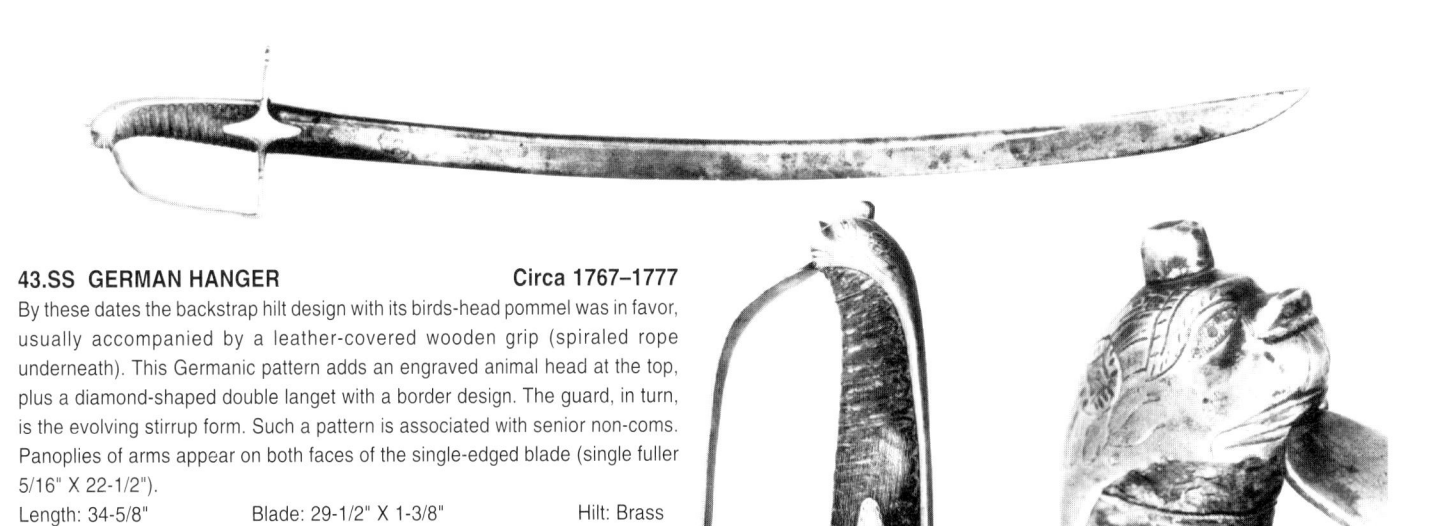

**44.SS  DUTCH HANGER**  Circa 1770–1785
Holland used various English and Germanic sword patterns in the 1700s, but this distinctive design was also employed. A quantity have been found in American Colonial sources. The brass backstrap with birds-head pommel ends abruptly to attach the upper end of its knuckle bow with a screw. In addition a pair of outer branches forms a semi-basket hilt above a common curved blade with a narrow back fuller. A similar later Danish hilt varied some elements, especially the quillon.
Length: 32"  Blade: 27" X 1-1/4"  Hilt: Brass
**Author's Collection**

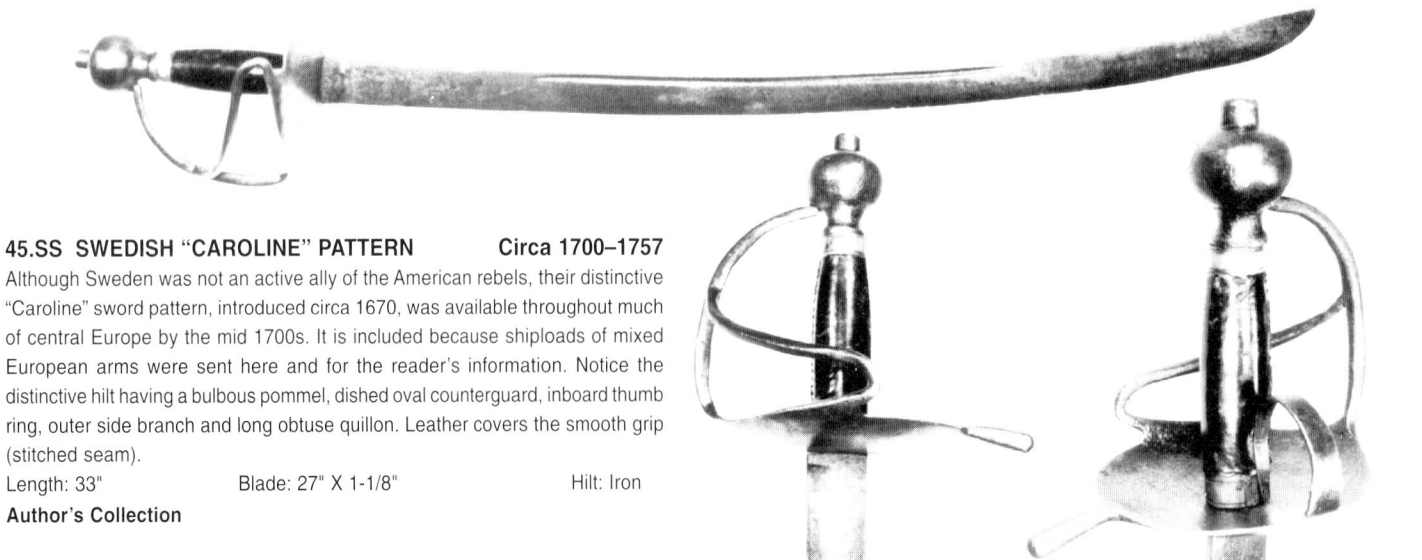

**45.SS  SWEDISH "CAROLINE" PATTERN**  Circa 1700–1757
Although Sweden was not an active ally of the American rebels, their distinctive "Caroline" sword pattern, introduced circa 1670, was available throughout much of central Europe by the mid 1700s. It is included because shiploads of mixed European arms were sent here and for the reader's information. Notice the distinctive hilt having a bulbous pommel, dished oval counterguard, inboard thumb ring, outer side branch and long obtuse quillon. Leather covers the smooth grip (stitched seam).
Length: 33"  Blade: 27" X 1-1/8"  Hilt: Iron
**Author's Collection**

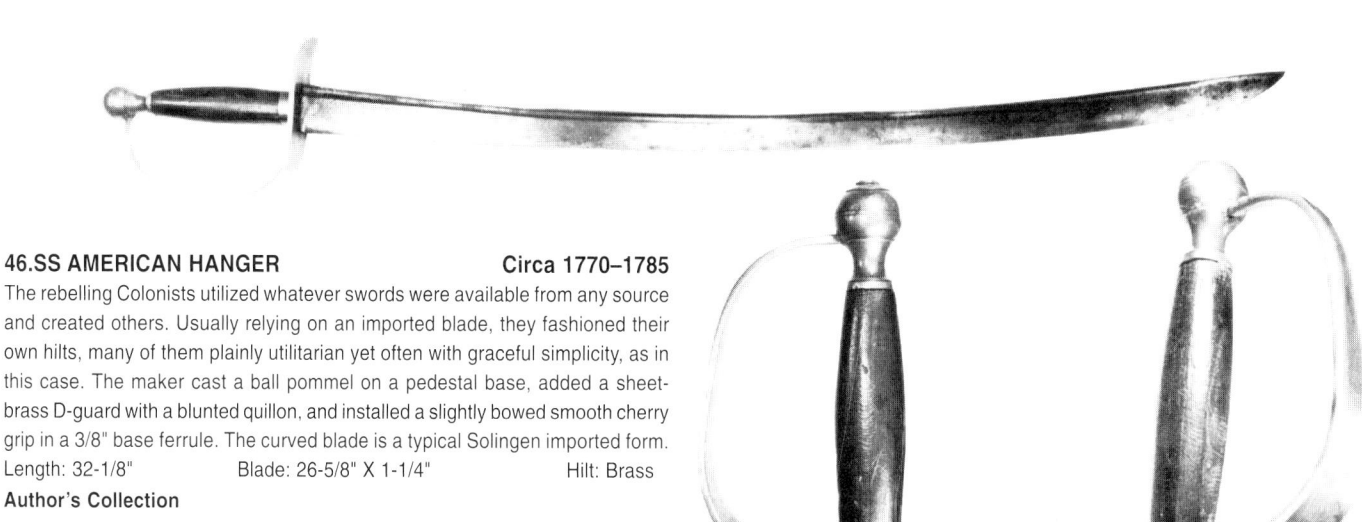

**46.SS AMERICAN HANGER**  Circa 1770–1785

The rebelling Colonists utilized whatever swords were available from any source and created others. Usually relying on an imported blade, they fashioned their own hilts, many of them plainly utilitarian yet often with graceful simplicity, as in this case. The maker cast a ball pommel on a pedestal base, added a sheet-brass D-guard with a blunted quillon, and installed a slightly bowed smooth cherry grip in a 3/8" base ferrule. The curved blade is a typical Solingen imported form.
Length: 32-1/8"   Blade: 26-5/8" X 1-1/4"   Hilt: Brass
**Author's Collection**

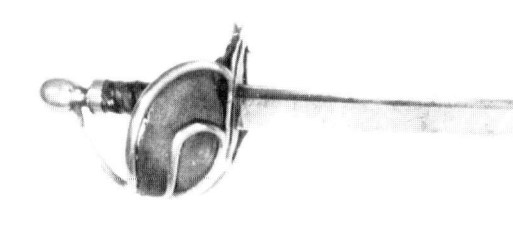

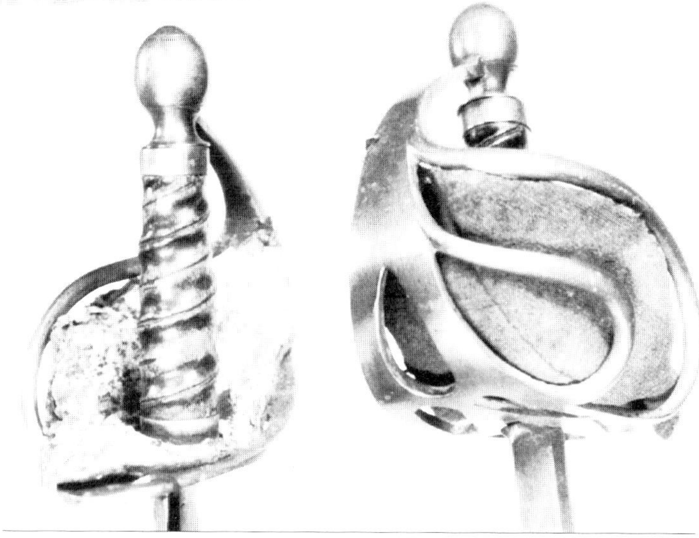

**47.SS AMERICAN HANGER**  Circa 1770–1790

This American-made semi-basket hilt may resemble British grenadier patterns, but the Continental Line did not include grenadiers. It probably was carried by a non-com or junior officer. The red wool liner with thin buckskin backing has survived. Notice the solidness of the brass hilt, which displays two outboard branches, and the olive-shaped pommel on a narrow neck. A wooden grip raises channeled ridges spiraling between two ferrules. Its German blade marks are "1745" and a "running wolf."
Length: 33-1/2"   Blade: 27-3/4" X 1-1/4"   Hilt: Brass
**Author's Collection**

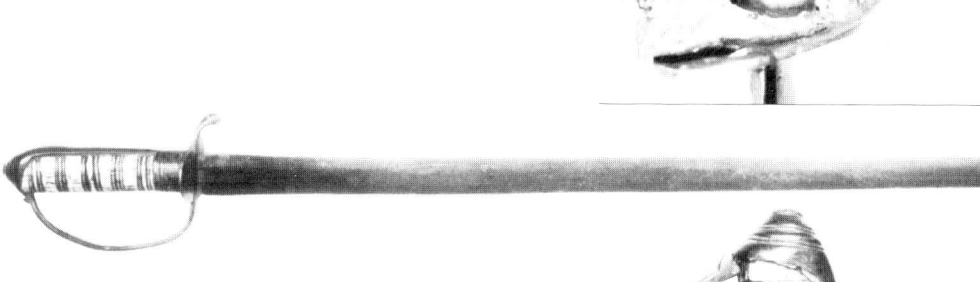

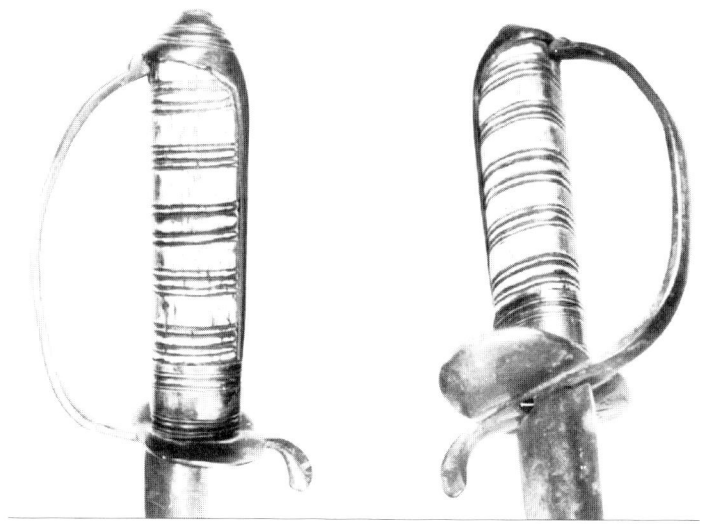

**48.SS AMERICAN HANGER**  Circa 1775–1785

The backstrap and birds-head form currently popular in Europe was copied for this American hilt. Note the uneven line decoration on the pommel, which is repeated on the 7/8" high ferrule and in various spacings along the polished bone grip. Its tenuous knuckle bow culminates in an unbalanced oval counterguard and quillon. "D2N" is engraved under the outboard guard. The straight double-edged blade has slightly convex faces.
Length: 33-7/8"   Blade: 28-1/4" X 1-1/4"   Hilt: Brass
**Author's Collection**

*Chapter 7: Swords*

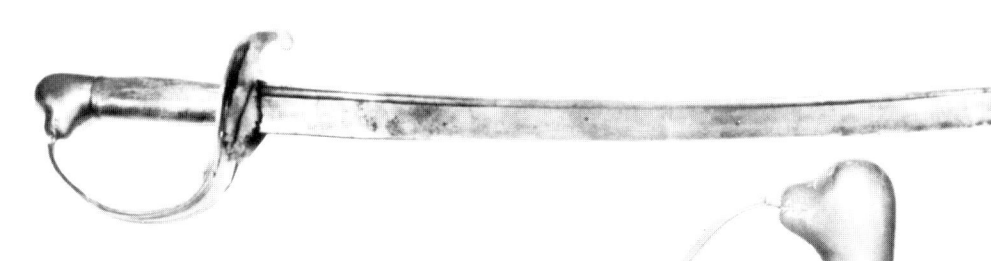

**49.SS  AMERICAN HANGER**                              Circa 1760–1780

The lack of subtle craftsmanship has not obscured the balance and poise of this primitive lion-head pommel. The limited features of its basic form, in fact, were created by use of a punch and chisel. A more professional broad D-guard has a decorative line along each edge and a crescent-like slot opposite both sides of the grip. The latter is a rude cylinder of apple wood. Three pieces of homespun sandwiched between the hilt and blade created a junction pad and scabbard cushion.

Length: 32"                Blade: 26-3/4" X 1-1/4"               Hilt: Brass

**William H. Guthman Collection**

**50.SS  AMERICAN HANGER**                              Circa 1760–1785

Occasionally an animal pommel appears as an integral part of a sword's handle, as shown here. A horse head in rural artistry with bared teeth is the upper section of this ivory grip, which adds lower spiraled grooves. Its broad iron hilt incorporates a series of double panels in the outboard guard. Of special interest is the reuse of a British musician's scimitar blade (see 17.SS). Note the two-inch curved tip, wide shallow fullers and typical pierced-dot design.

Length: 28-3/4"            Blade: 23-1/8" X 1-3/8"               Hilt: Iron

**Richard Ulbrich Collection**

**51.SS  AMERICAN HANGER**                              Circa 1777–1790

At the time of our War for Independence, flat pommels were beginning to appear in Europe, and the Colonists' desire for simplicity took ample advantage of it. The blade here, with its curved single-edged profile and single back fuller, is a common imported Germanic pattern. The provincial hilt was created with a stirrup knuckle bow and diamond-shaped guard (joined at the angle), plus an oval-sectioned cherry grip secured by a flat pommel (with capstan) and a lower 1/4" ferrule.

Length: 31-7/8"            Blade: 26-3/4" X 1-3/8"               Hilt: Brass

**Author's Collection**

*Chapter 7: Swords*

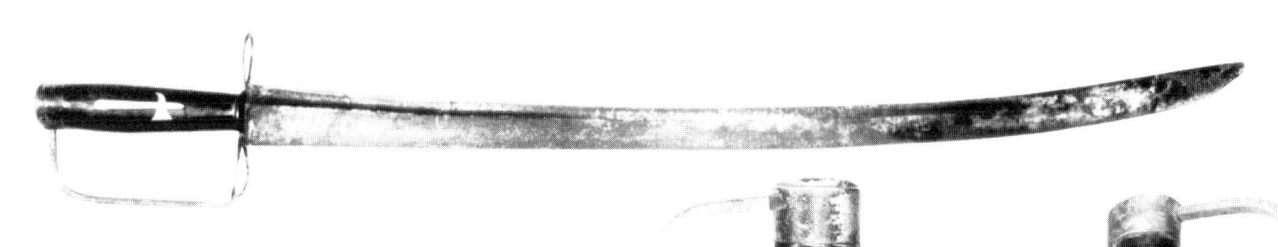

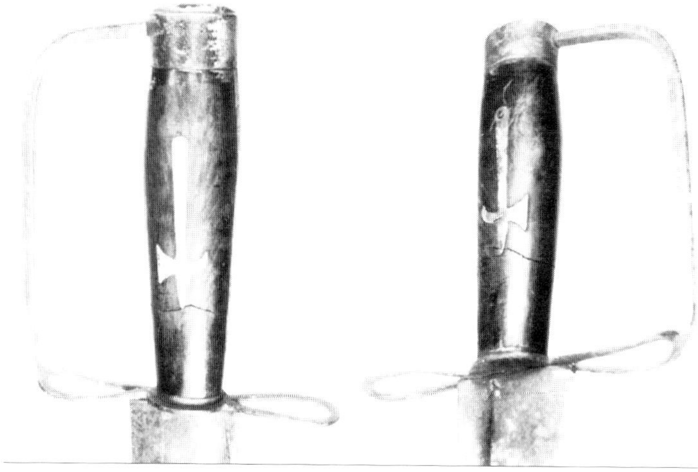

### 52.SS  AMERICAN HANGER  Circa 1778–1790
Although lacking the hilt strength for serious combat, this locally fashioned American pattern is intriguing. The would-be cutler joined a narrow squared knuckle bow with two open loops for a tenuous counterguard. The oval grip, in turn, was given a flat cap pommel and some individuality with a silver halberd tomahawk form inlaid in each side (possibly added later). Some of the hilt was once covered with a silver foil (a common practice of deception). The single-fuller blade is American.

Length: 30"  Blade: 25" X 1-1/2"  Hilt: Iron/Silver

**Tom Wnuck Collection**

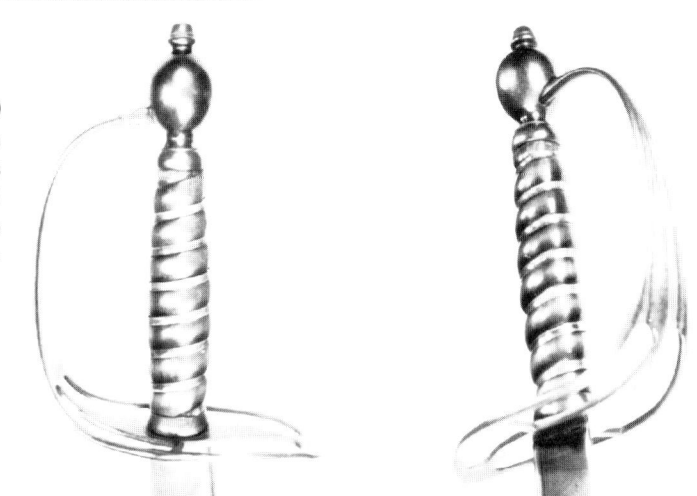

### 53.SS  ENGLISH SHORT SABER  Circa 1770–1780
This basic but pleasing British "four-slot" style was popular among both English and American officers. An olive-shaped pommel with a baluster capstan rises above the horn grip, which has spiraled channels holding a silver band. Its typical wide D-guard includes vertical fluting decoration on the back and expands to create four open panels—two on each side of the lower ferrule. A narrow single-edged blade joins a 1/4" X 16-1/4" fuller at the back with a 9-7/8" false edge.

Length: 32-1/4"  Blade: 26-1/8" X 1-1/8"  Hilt: Steel

**Author's Collection**

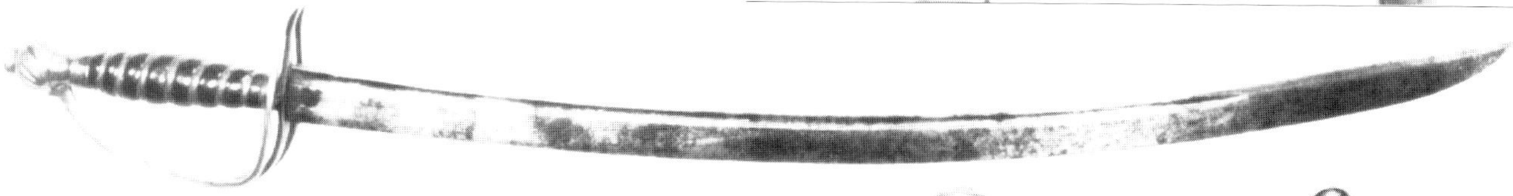

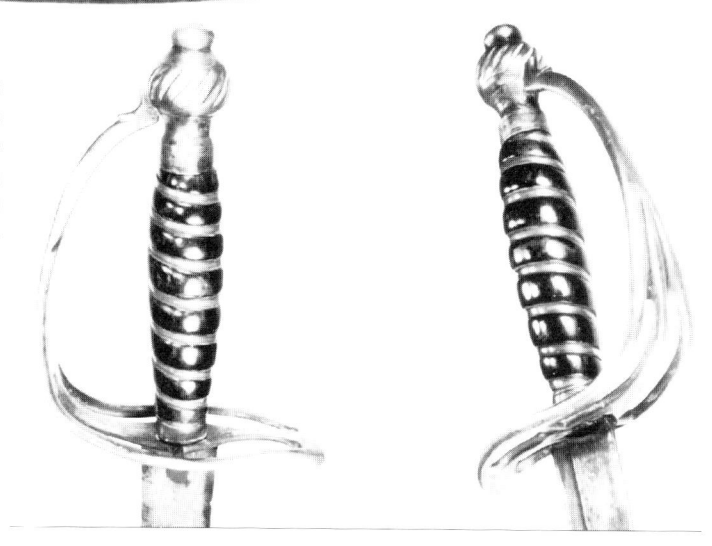

### 54.SS  ENGLISH SHORT SABER  Circa 1770–1783
The saber is a curved single-edged cutting sword. Those with shorter blades about 28 to 32 inches long are classified as short sabers and were the primary field weapons for commissioned officers in both armies. This variation of the common four-slot pattern has similar styling but a more rugged hilt and blade than the prior example (53.SS). Note its wider horn grip (silver band), the thicker D-guard, which omits back side fluting, and an innovative ball pommel with diagonal slotting.

Length: 32-3/4"  Blade: 26-3/4" X 1-1/4"  Hilt: Brass

**Author's Collection**

Chapter 7: Swords

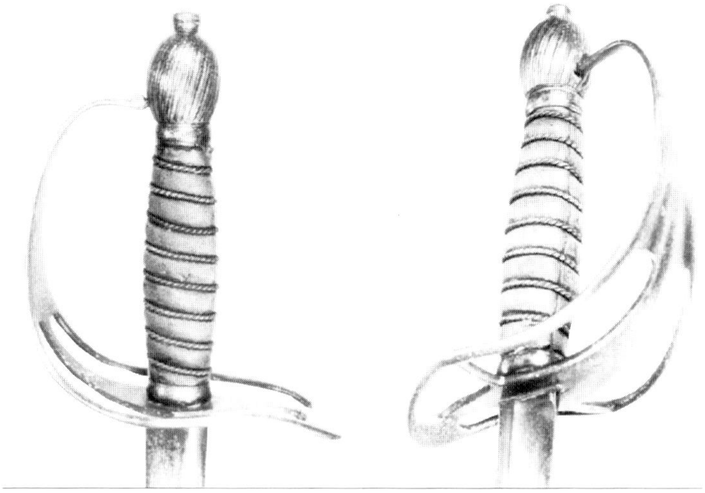

**55.SS  ENGLISH SHORT SABER**  Circa 1775–1790

This heavier variation of the four-slot format adds a tall domed steel pommel that provided better balance, a decorative enhancement and an effective back-handed jabbing opportunity in a melee. Its surface bears incised gadrooning. The wooden grip, in turn, is covered by shagreen (fishskin) with a twisted iron rope in the channels. The typical single-edged curving blade shows a 1/4" back fuller plus the English running fox figure on both faces.

Length: 34-3/8"  Blade: 28" X 1"  Hilt: Steel

**Author's Collection**

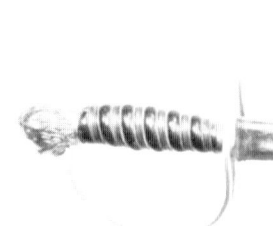

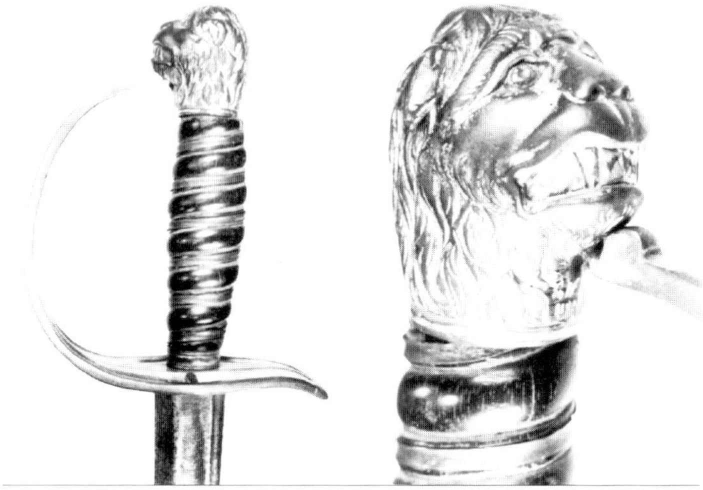

**56.SS  ENGLISH SHORT SABER**  Circa 1770–1785

The British lion head provided another version of the four-slot short saber. This well-crafted pommel is one of numerous lion interpretations observed (for example, 57.SS). A horn grip fills its spiraling grooves with a copper band. The D-shaped knuckle bow displays a decorative fluted back surface, as well as adding a simple incised quillon design. Originally the brass surface was gilded (usually to match the regimental uniform's buttons). Its typical light blade has two uneven fullers on each side.

Length: 31-1/8"  Blade: 25-1/2" X 1-1/8"  Hilt: Brass/Gilding

**Author's Collection**

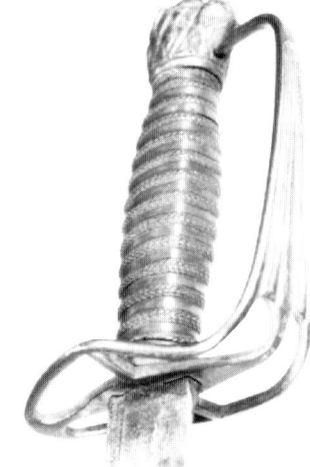

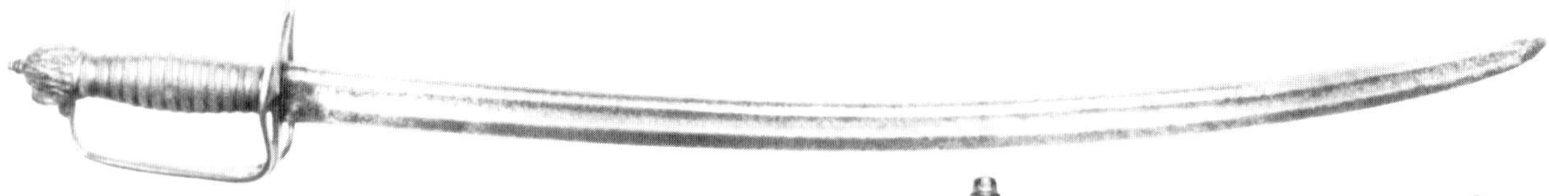

**57.SS  ENGLISH SHORT SABER**  Circa 1770–1785

It is instructive to compare this lion head four-slot pattern with the previous saber. They both follow the same design but, being officer swords, were purchased privately from different cutlers. Notice, for example, the varied lion form and the addition of a raised capstan. Moreover the guard still contains the four openings and fluting on the back, yet it has been given a right-angled profile. The wooden grip, too, is reshaped into four convex faces and wrapped in copper bands.

Length: 32-1/8"  Blade: 26-5/8" X 1-1/4"  Hilt: Brass/Gilding

**Author's Collection**

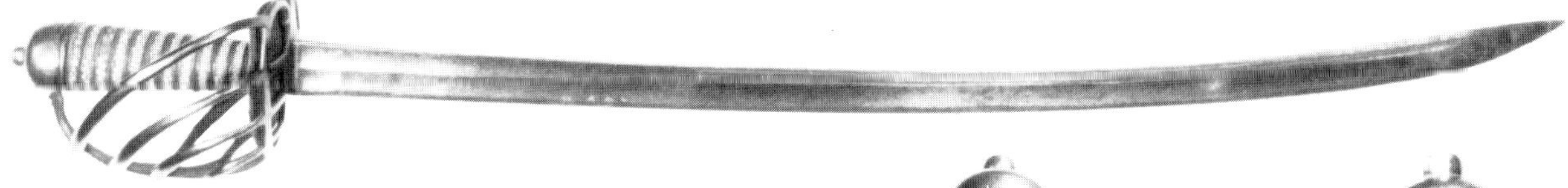

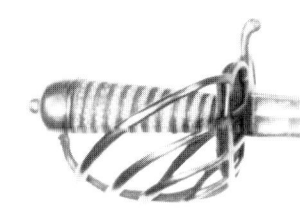

**58.SS  ENGLISH SHORT SABER         Circa 1750–1765**
Some of these short sabers had substantial hilts, such as this semi-basket form. Four curved branches protect the outer side, plus two more inboard. The earlier ovoid pommel shape is now reduced to a squat cap. Its grip, in turn, is wrapped in shagreen (fishskin) with three spiraled copper wire ropes and a 3/8" bottom ferrule. The counterguard, under the original red wool/buckskin pad, is a series of squared holes. Two 7/16" fullers dominate the curved light blade.
Length: 33-3/8"         Blade: 28-1/8" X 1-3/16"         Hilt: Iron
**Author's Collection**

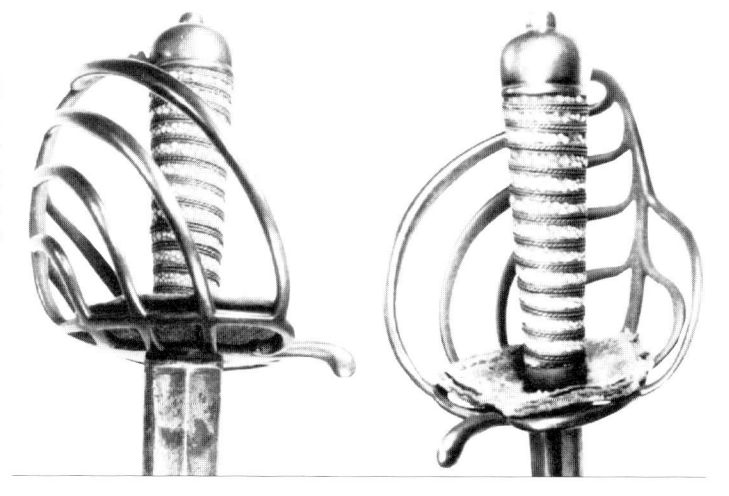

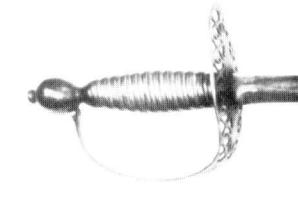

**59.SS  ENGLISH SHORT SABER (SPADROON)    Circa 1775–1790**
Cut steel hilt patterns, as seen here, were popular in Britain from circa 1750 to 1790. Note this ovoid pommel with a narrow neck and capstan; it secures (through a rear hole) the hooked end of a broad D-guard that includes pierced geometric designs and a rounded quillon. The four-sided grip is covered by spiraling steel and copper ropes plus a wide band. Its straight single-edged blade, in turn, is a "spadroon" form that had gained favor at this time. Note the 3/8" back fuller.
Length: 36-3/4"         Blade: 31" X 3/4"         Hilt: Steel
**Author's Collection**

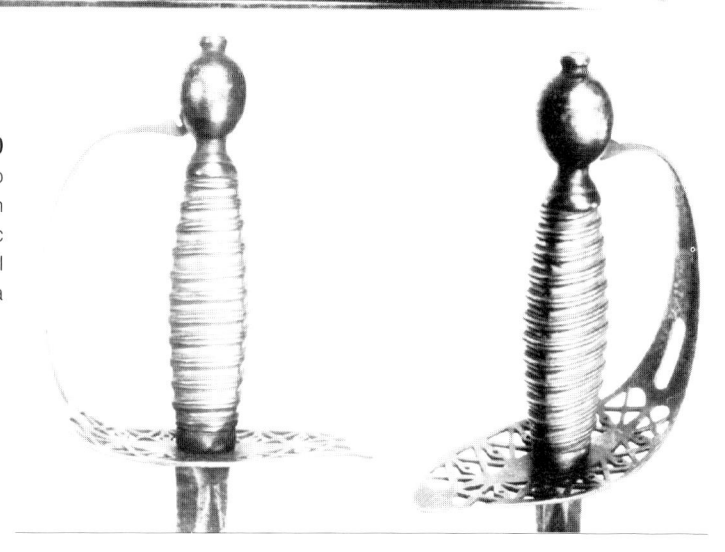

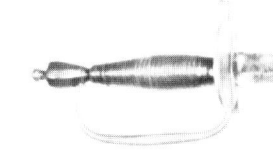

**60.SS  ENGLISH SHORT SABER (SPADROON)    Circa 1775–1796**
This basic hilt was adopted in 1796 as the first official sword pattern for English infantry officers. The design itself had been used by Prussian troops since the 1740s (see 119.SS). It was probably carried by some British and German officers (possibly even sergeants) in the American Revolution. When England abolished the spontoon in 1786, this official spadroon blade was mandated (32" X 1"), followed by the hilt in 1796. These earlier versions lacked the raised decorations of later examples.
Length: 37-3/4"         Blade: 32" X 1"         Hilt: Brass/Gilding
**Author's Collection**

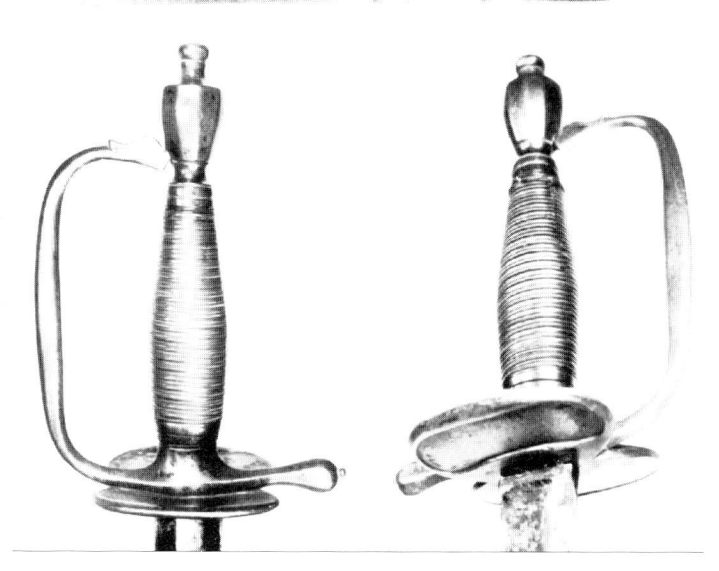

*Chapter 7: Swords*   323

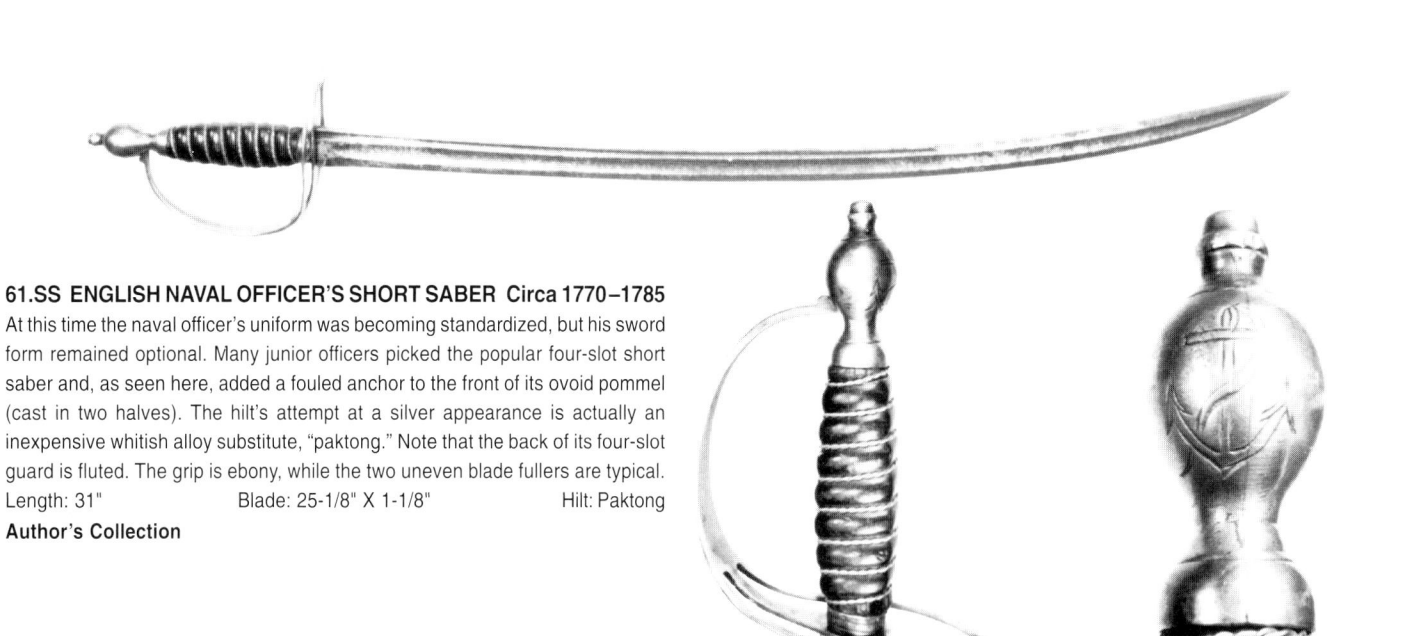

**61.SS  ENGLISH NAVAL OFFICER'S SHORT SABER  Circa 1770–1785**
At this time the naval officer's uniform was becoming standardized, but his sword form remained optional. Many junior officers picked the popular four-slot short saber and, as seen here, added a fouled anchor to the front of its ovoid pommel (cast in two halves). The hilt's attempt at a silver appearance is actually an inexpensive whitish alloy substitute, "paktong." Note that the back of its four-slot guard is fluted. The grip is ebony, while the two uneven blade fullers are typical.
Length: 31"  Blade: 25-1/8" X 1-1/8"  Hilt: Paktong
**Author's Collection**

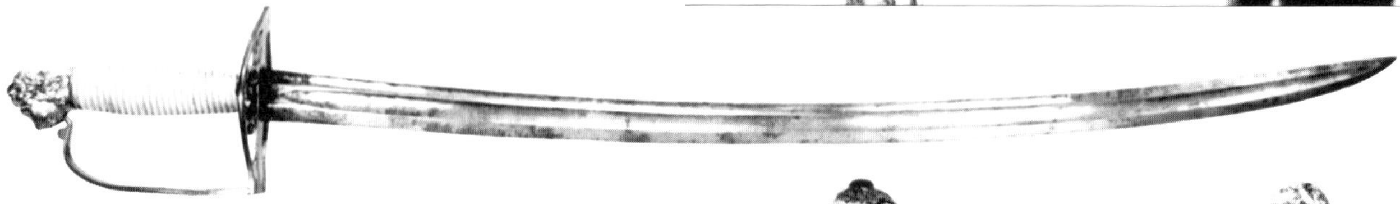

**62.SS  ENGLISH NAVAL OFFICER'S SHORT SABER  Circa 1780–1800**
A lion head pommel was mounted on a narrow-ribbed ivory grip in this naval officer's saber. The wide stirrup-hilt, in turn, is pierced by two fouled anchor designs—one through the lower knuckle bow and the other in the outboard guard. Its surface was gilded. Decorative lines also appear on the back side. The single-edged curved blade is usually associated with this pattern; it includes two fullers (1/4" X 19" and 3/8" X 26-1/8") plus an eight-inch false edge.
Length: 33"  Blade: 27" X 1-1/8"  Hilt: Brass/Gilding
**E. Norman Flayderman Collection**

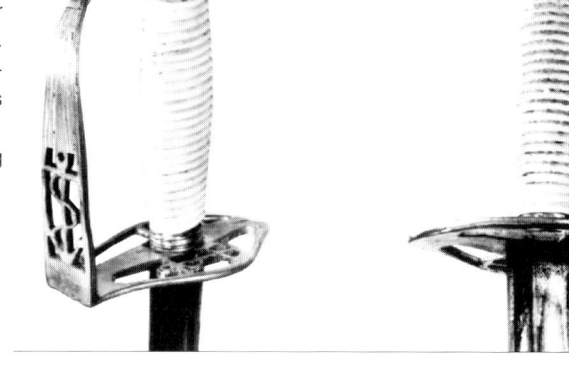

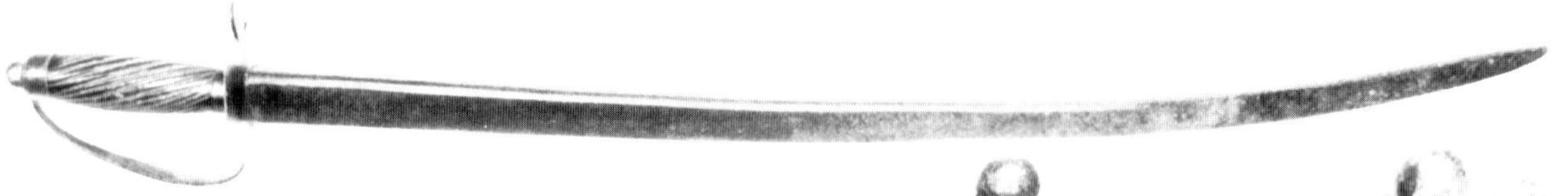

**63.SS  AMERICAN SHORT SABER  Circa 1770–1783**
Most American-made swords in the Revolutionary War employed a European imported or reused blade, but this short saber was totally a product of the New World. An undersized round pommel anchors a sheet-iron knuckle bow, which spreads into a flat heart-shaped guard and disk quillon. Also note the rudely grooved wooden grip bounded by two 1/2" ferrules. Its sturdy single-edged blade includes a long 7-1/2" false edge plus an irregular fuller at the back.
Length: 34"  Blade: 29" X 1-3/8"  Hilt: Iron
**Tom Wnuck Collection**

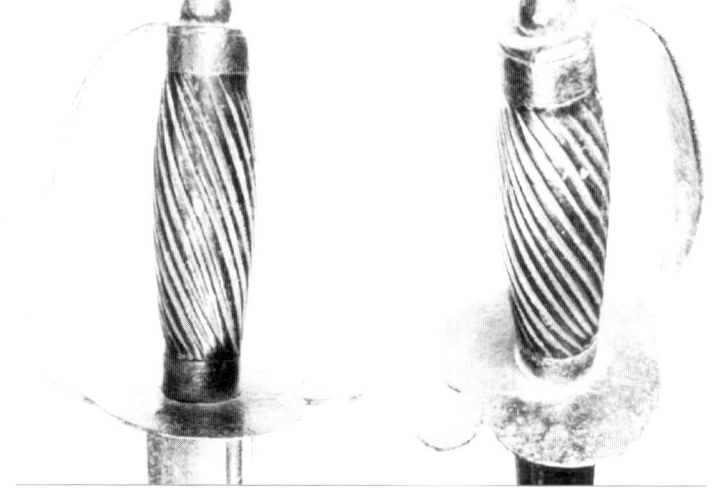

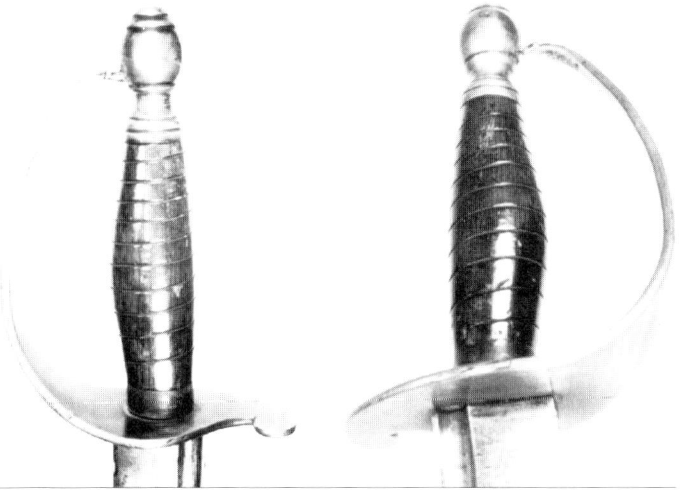

**64.SS AMERICAN SHORT SABER**          Circa 1770–1783

This American cutler disregarded popular European styling to create an unusual grace and balance with simple components. Notice, for example, the tiered rings on the oval pommel, the shaping of its sheet-brass knuckle bow into an expanded counterguard with a horizontal circular quillon, as well as a bulging rear profile of the wooden grip to achieve a final balance. The single-edged curving blade with a 1/4" back fuller and a seven-inch false edge is a typical imported pattern.

Length: 31-7/8"        Blade: 26-1/2" X l-1/4"        Hilt: Brass

**Author's Collection**

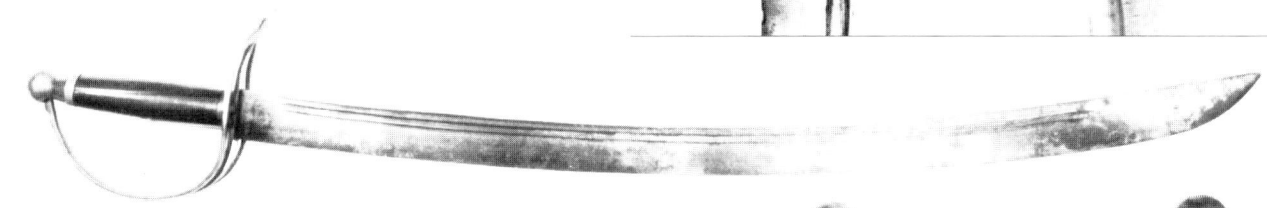

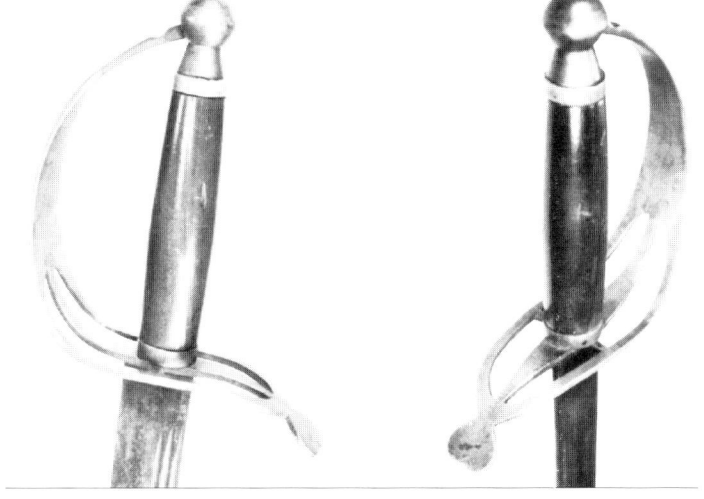

**65.SS AMERICAN SHORT SABER**          Circa 1775–1785

Strict utility probably determined this American hilt. An equatorial pommel sits on a truncated cone base, while the round-sectioned cherry grip rests in plain 1/4" ferrules without decorative carving. The escaping breach of discipline, however, appears in the extended heart finial at the end of the sheet-brass four-slot guard. A reduced version of the popular three-fuller Spanish saber blade is present. Its fullers each measure 1/8" X 20-1/2".

Length: 31-7/8"        Blade: 26-1/2" X 1-1/4"        Hilt: Brass

**Author's Collection**

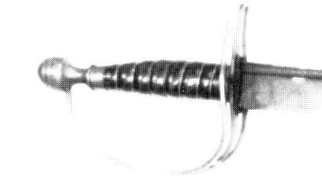

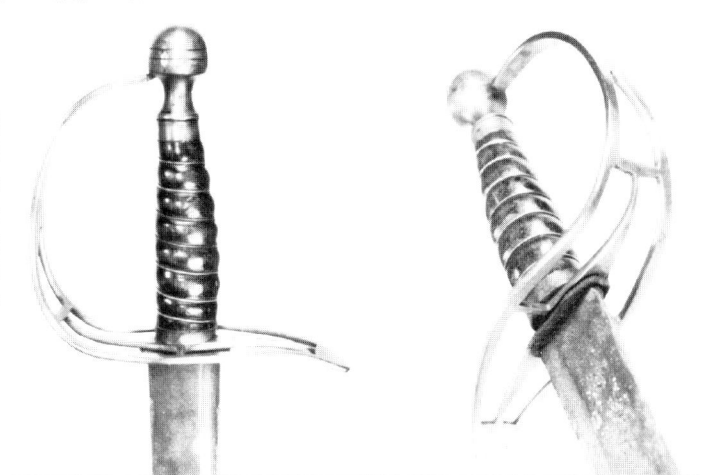

**66.SS AMERICAN SHORT SABER**          Circa 1770–1785

The unusual variants in this locally made American hilt are the high-domed mushroom pommel and the pregnant profile of the spiraled wooden grip. Its sheet-brass guard, in turn, adds a triangular opening behind the popular four side slots. It is intriguing to view how these rural Colonial cutlers, many of whom could neither read nor write, achieved such sensual artistry with the barest of elements. The popular Germanic imported blade includes the usual single back fuller.

Length: 31-5/8"        Blade: 26-1/2" X 1-1/4"        Hilt: Brass

**Author's Collection**

### 67.SS  AMERICAN SHORT SABER                Circa 1755–1780

A small truncated conical pommel completes this hilt, which in normal fashion passes a thin tang from the blade up through the components—to be hammered flat at the top. Its wooden grip is covered by a spiraled overlapping strip of leather and omits both ferrules. An elementary iron forged knuckle bow and blunt-ended counterguard harbor a three-inch leather oval that cushions the joint with its blade (a common practice). The heavy blade (3/8" fuller) bears a running dog mark.

Length: 34"            Blade: 27-7/8" X 1-3/8"            Hilt: Iron

**Tom Wnuck Collection**

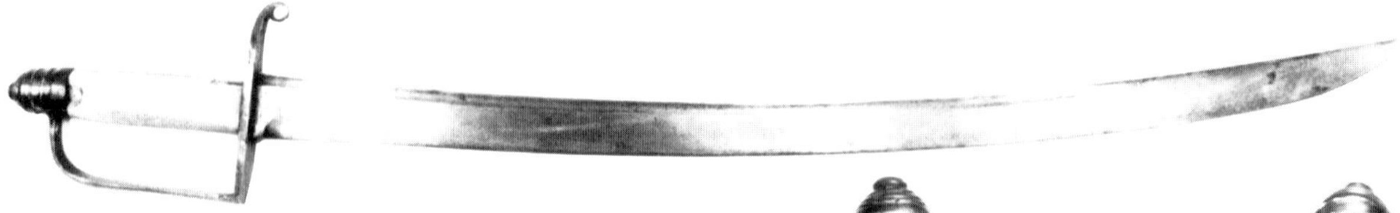

### 68.SS  AMERICAN SHORT SABER                Circa 1775–1790

An unusual turret-like pommel with thin ridges secures the upper end of this very solid brass stirrup hilt. The quillon is also a variant—having its center drilled through to create a ring form. Notice, too, the octagonal grip, which is fashioned from polished bone. (Regarding the grip's identification, bone contains small dark flecks versus ivory's wood-like warm flowing grain.) The typical slightly curved imported blade includes a normal 1/4" X 17-1/2" back fuller and a six-inch false edge.

Length: 29"            Blade: 23-3/4" X 1-1/4"            Hilt: Brass

**Author's Collection**

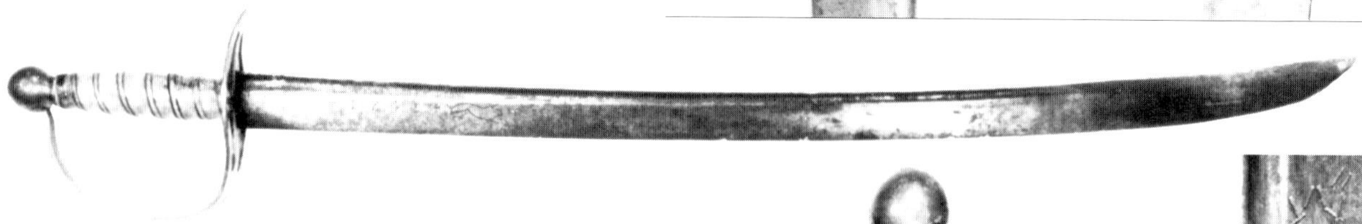

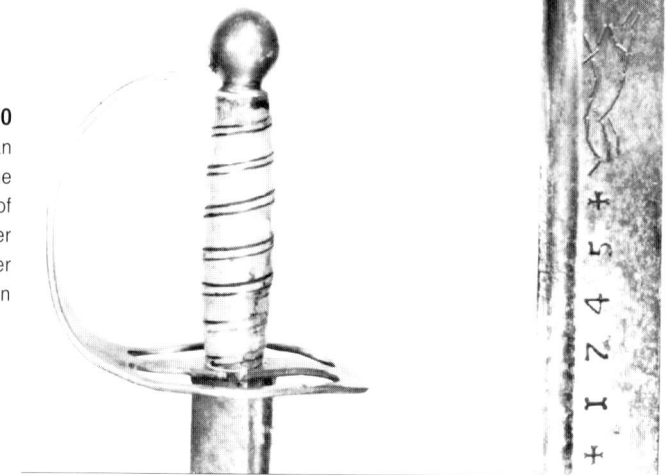

### 69.SS  AMERICAN SHORT SABER                Circa 1770–1780

A local hilt was added to an earlier Germanic blade to create this American weapon. The D-shaped guard is cut from sheet brass and expands to form the familiar four openings in its counterguard plus a blunted quillon point. A piece of polished bone, in turn, with channels and incised ridges defines the grip under a plain oval pommel. The usual curved blade having a single 1/4" back fuller and a 7-1/2" false edge is marked with the running wolf of Passau/Solingen and "1745."

Length: 33"            Blade: 27-1/2" X 1-1/4"            Hilt: Brass

**Author's Collection**

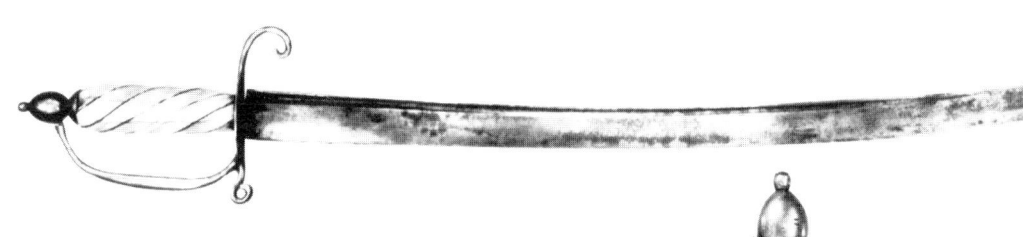

**70.SS  AMERICAN SHORT SABER**  Circa 1770–1785
A unique single brass casting transforms this hilt into a memorable pattern. Notice the plain D-type knuckle bow and expanded counterguard that suddenly come to life with double scrolled quillions of different sizes facing opposing directions. In addition, an olive-shaped pommel on a dome pedestal fits above the thick spiraled grip of polished bone. Its single-edged curving blade is a popular imported form.
Length: 32-1/2"          Blade: 26-1/2" X 1-1/4"          Hilt: Brass
**George C. Neumann Collection, Valley Forge National Historical Park**

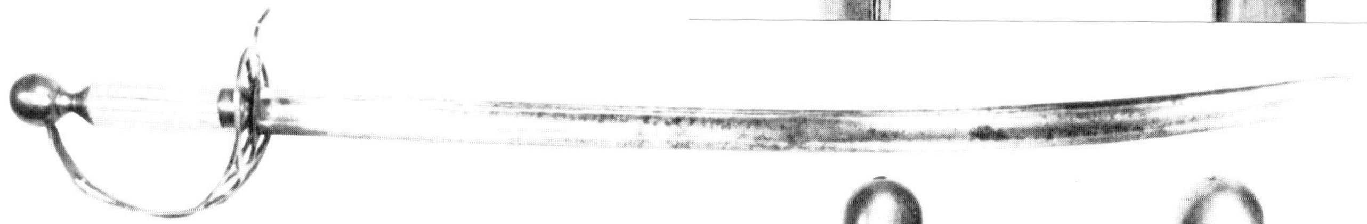

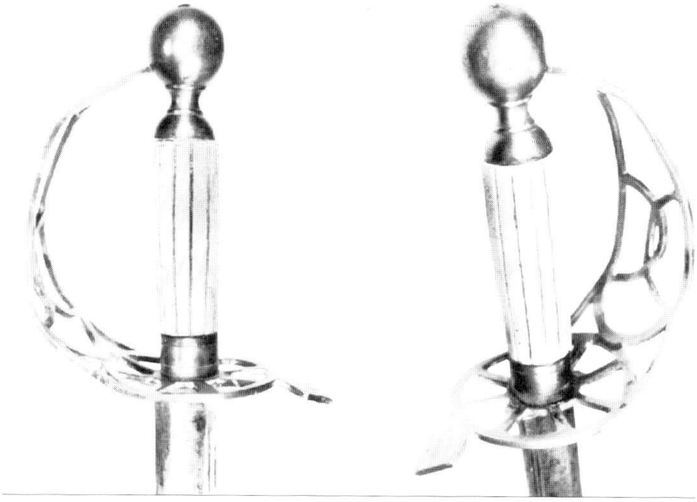

**71.SS  AMERICAN SHORT SABER**  Circa 1775–1785
One of the most pleasing and distinctive forms of these Colonial American hilts is the wagon hilt pattern. This saber, for example, takes a flat brass sheet and extracts various portions to create a wheel-like guard with a diamond quillon and tenuous open designs in the knuckle bow. It is balanced by a large ball pommel on a constricted neck above a vertically reeded hilt of bone. The equally impressive European blade displays two 1/16" back fullers above a 1/2" concave center one.
Length: 33-3/4"          Blade: 27-5/8" X 1-1/8"          Hilt: Brass
**Author's Collection**

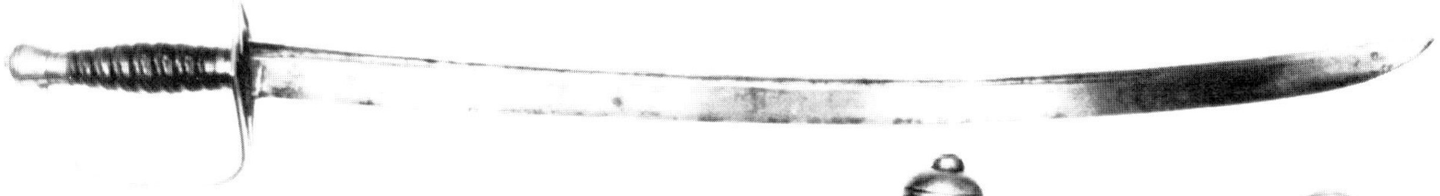

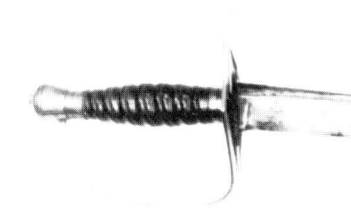

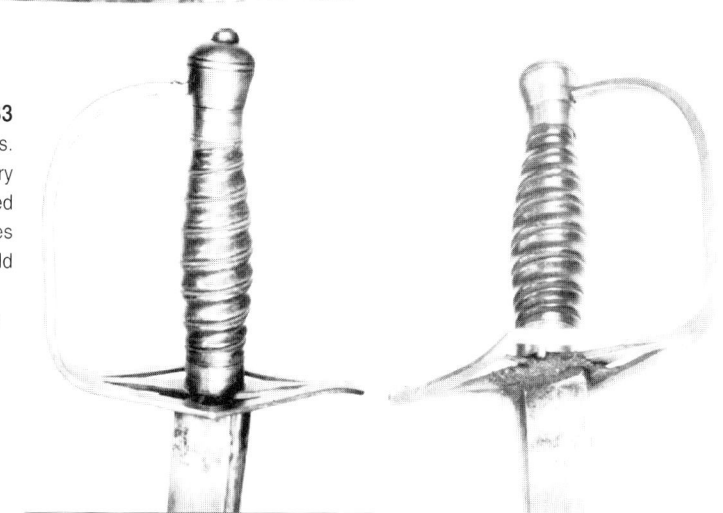

**72.SS  AMERICAN SHORT SABER**  Circa 1775–1783
A flat-domed pommel was a favorite component to many American swordsmiths. Note how this one seals off the top of the hilt and contains the bulbous cherry grip with its incised ridges. Of equal importance to the pattern is the pierced diamond-like guard that ends in a side curving quillon. Pairs of thin incised lines on the ferrules and pommel add further home-spun elegance. A swatch of old red wool cushions the junction with a typical imported single fuller blade.
Length: 32-1/8"          Blade: 26-3/4" X 1-1/4"          Hilt: Brass
**Author's Collection**

*Chapter 7: Swords*

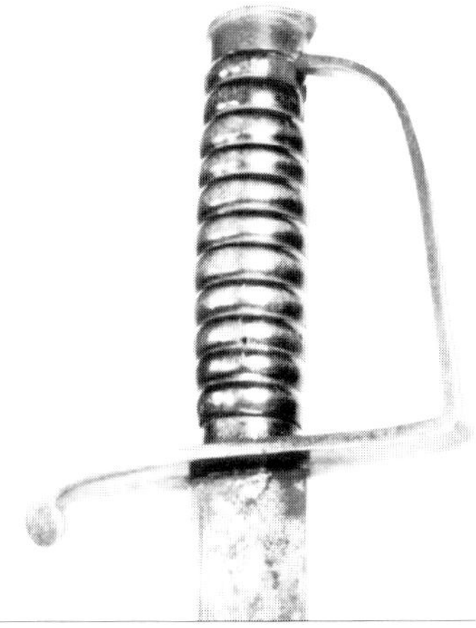

**73.SS  AMERICAN SHORT SABER**  Circa 1780–1800
Sword pattern elements that would gain greater acceptance following the Revolutionary War are emerging here, that is, the squared two-piece pommel with the flat top's projecting tail and a straight wooden grip carved in parallel ribbing. Its more contemporary forged iron stirrup knuckle bow and simple counterguard terminate in a downturned disk quillon. An irregular thin 1/8" back fuller, in turn, is part of the straight single-edged American-made blade.
Length: 34-7/8"          Blade: 29-3/4" X 1-1/4"          Hilt: Iron
**Author's Collection**

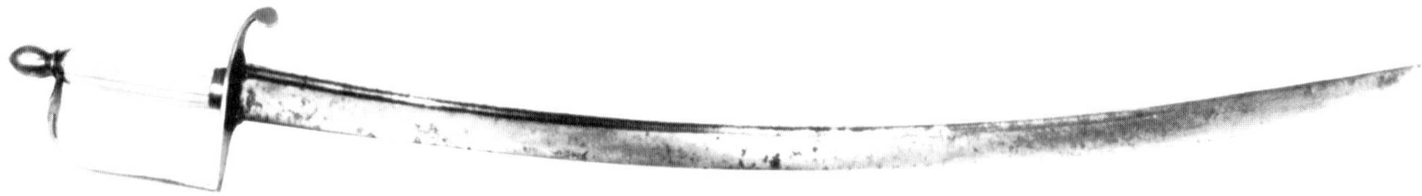

**74.SS  AMERICAN SHORT SABER**  Circa 1780–1800
This late-war officer's saber illustrates changes that would gain further acceptance in the Federal Period. Notice that the brass pommel is becoming longer and smaller; a bone grip shows vertical reeding with rounded ridges; and the stirrup hilt now includes a slot in its upper shoulder that would secure the sword knot (see 41.SS). Prior to this, the knot was looped around the knuckle bow, but by the 1790s a slot or small ring was common (also retrofitted to earlier arms, as in this case).
Length: 33-1/8"          Blade: 27-5/8" X 1-1/4"          Hilt: Brass
**Author's Collection**

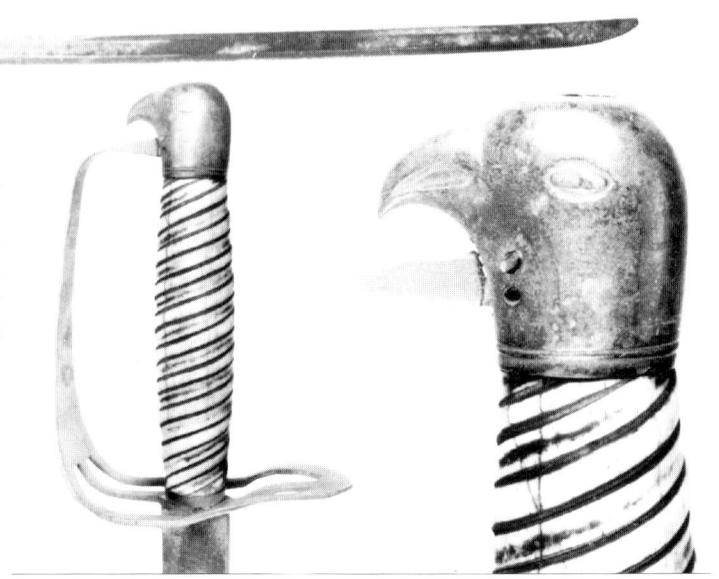

**75.SS  AMERICAN SHORT SABER**  Circa 1778–1795
Although the bald eagle was not accepted as America's emblem until its inclusion in the Great Seal of 1782, a wide range of animals, birds and vague creatures served on sword pommels for many prior years here and abroad. This primitive domed eagle form creates its eyes with incised lines and adds a short vaguely defined beak. A high bone grip bears spiraled channels, while the gaunt counterguard, in turn, contains a four-slot pattern. Its blade (two uneven fullers) has French markings.
Length: 36-1/2"          Blade: 30-1/4" X 1"          Hilt: Brass
**William H. Guthman Collection**

328    *Chapter 7: Swords*

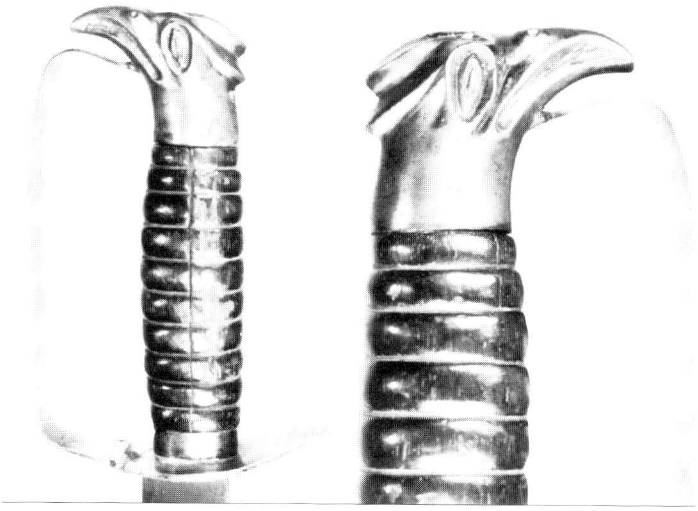

**76.SS  AMERICAN SHORT SABER**  Circa 1780–1800
Early swords included lions, dogs, eagles, hawks, doves and even dragons on their pommels. Others went further in their imaginations. This primitive American example suggests a rustic eagle or rooster. It speaks for the efforts by many isolated Colonists who often tried to reproduce high level craftsmanship remembered from prior urban or military exposure. The wooden hilt has parallel channels. Its provincial-made blade is crude but sturdy, with an uneven 1/8" fuller on one side.
Length: 31-1/2"      Blade: 25-1/4" X 1-1/4"      Hilt: Brass
**Tom Wnuck Collection**

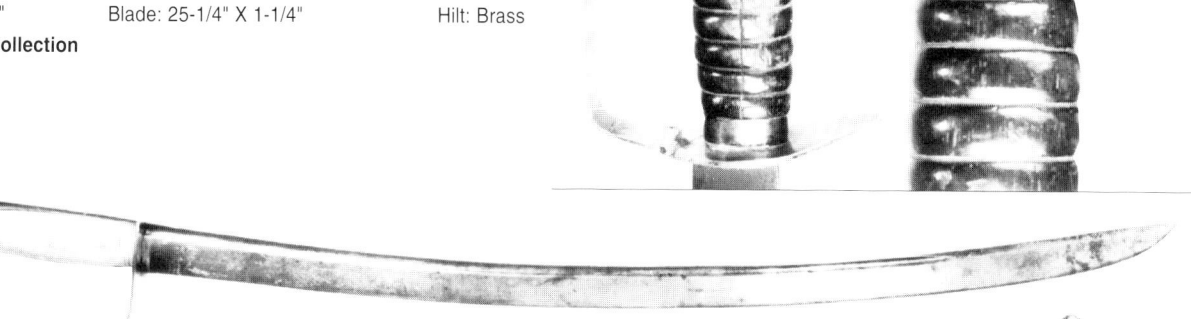

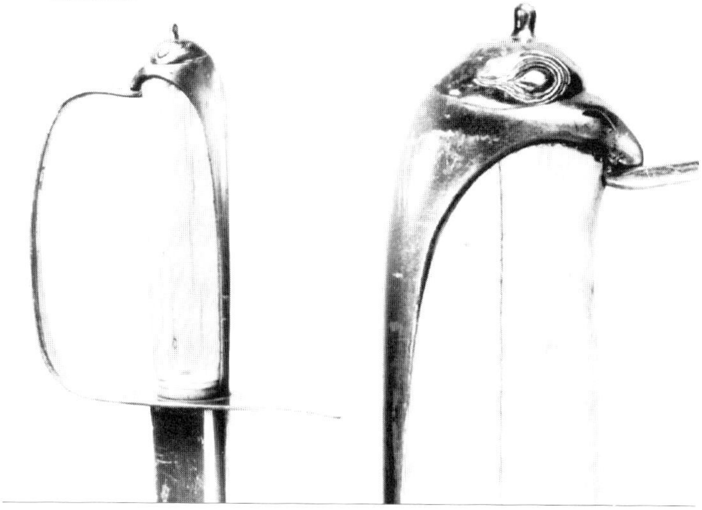

**77.SS  AMERICAN SHORT SABER**  Circa 1778–1795
Patterns with articulated bird's features on a backstrap/birds-head hilt were appearing in London by the 1770s. This more primitive American version has the crude incised details found on early Colonial interpretations. The backstrap supports a grip of polished bone with a simulated bottom ferrule cut into it, as well as a simple flat brass guard devoid of decoration. Its popular imported blade form displays panoplies of arms and floral displays on both faces.
Length: 33-1/4"      Blade: 27-1/2" X 1-1/4"      Hilt: Brass
**Fort Ticonderoga Collection**

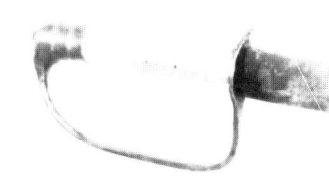

**78.SS  AMERICAN SHORT SABER**  Circa 1780–1800
Pewter was normally considered too soft and vulnerable for sword components, but someone employed it to cast this vague eagle pommel and guard. A raised ridge helps define the eye and beak, which join a continuing uneven rectangular knuckle bow, expanded guard and stubby 5/8" quillon. An octagonal piece of polished bone creates the grip. Its flat-sided blade also presents an increasing curve profile, which would progress further by 1800.
Length: 30-1/4"      Blade: 25" X 1-1/4"      Hilt: Pewter
**Author's Collection**

Chapter 7: Swords   329

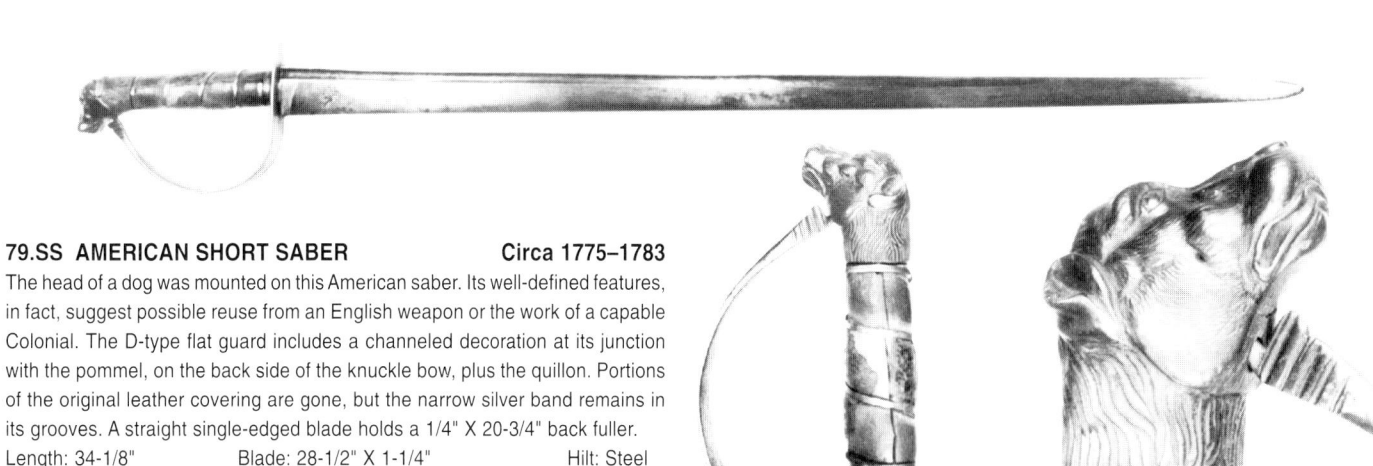

**79.SS  AMERICAN SHORT SABER**                Circa 1775–1783
The head of a dog was mounted on this American saber. Its well-defined features, in fact, suggest possible reuse from an English weapon or the work of a capable Colonial. The D-type flat guard includes a channeled decoration at its junction with the pommel, on the back side of the knuckle bow, plus the quillon. Portions of the original leather covering are gone, but the narrow silver band remains in its grooves. A straight single-edged blade holds a 1/4" X 20-3/4" back fuller.
Length: 34-1/8"          Blade: 28-1/2" X 1-1/4"           Hilt: Steel
**Author's Collection**

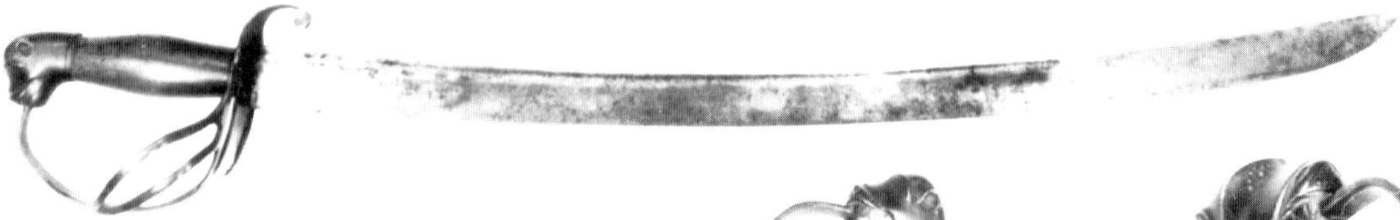

**80.SS  AMERICAN SHORT SABER**                Circa 1775–1783
The essential features of this American lion pommel were cast into the head. Note its triangular teeth, nostrils, raised brows and ears—supplemented by punched dots for the eyes. A double branch semi-basket guard is a well-made casting that includes raised ridges on the knuckle bow's back side and two open panels opposite the blade. The smooth surfaced bulbous grip, in turn, is cherry. Its common military-type Germanic imported blade bears a typical single back fuller.
Length: 32-1/4"          Blade: 26-1/2" X 1-3/8"           Hilt: Brass
**Robert Nittolo Collection**

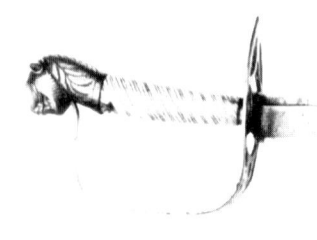

**81.SS  AMERICAN SHORT SABER**                Circa 1755–1785
Several swords with this unique happy lion are known. In usual fashion the figure is cast in two vertical sections split between the eyes. Many of the intriguing punched dot features were apparently added after the casting. Note also that the decorative parallel channels cut into the ivory grip meet in a V-pattern opposite the knuckle bow. Its flat brass counterguard, in turn, forms a pointed forward end and adds pierced geometric forms around the lower ferrule.
Length: 33"              Blade: 26-3/4" X 1-1/8"           Hilt: Brass
**George C. Neumann Collection, Valley Forge National Historical Park**

*330     Chapter 7: Swords*

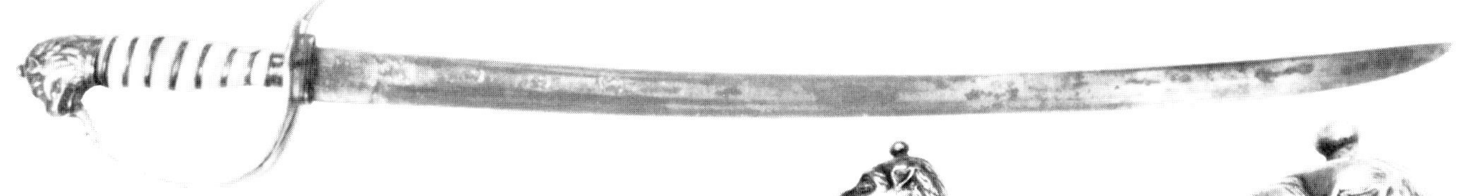

**82.SS AMERICAN SHORT SABER**  Circa 1776–1778
This attractive silver-mounted saber has its scabbard throat engraved "J BAILEY / FREDERICKSBURG." John Bailey was a prolific cutler in Fredericksburg, New York (1776–1778) and Fishkill, New York (1778–1784). Notice the well-sculptured lion head pommel (typically cast in two halves), the ivory grip (silver band) and the four-slot counterguard. Many of his blades came from the Weyersburg family in Solingen, Germany—marked "ANDREA FARRARA"—as in this case.
Length: 32-7/8"   Blade: 26-3/8" X 1-1/4"   Hilt: Silver
**James D. Forman Collection**

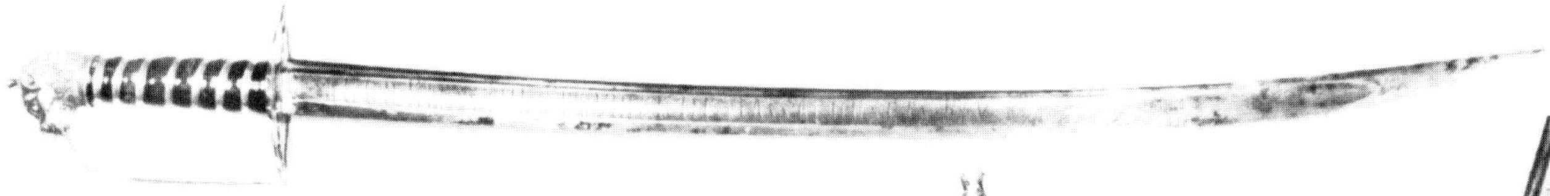

**83.SS AMERICAN SHORT SABER**  Circa 1760–1775
The silver-mounted saber pictured here is attributed to the maker John Bailey. Its attractive lion head pommel is slightly different from the preceding example. Moreover this stirrup-type knuckle bow joins a decorative open guard having a scalloped outer edge and a smooth inner border (to reduce chaffing). The wooden grip channels a silver band. Its two-fullered blade is engraved "GOD BLESS THE PROVINCE OF MASSACHUSETTS BAY." It is associated with a Capt. G. H. Collister.
Length: 32-7/8"   Blade: 27" X 1-1/8"   Hilt: Silver
**Fort Ticonderoga Collection**

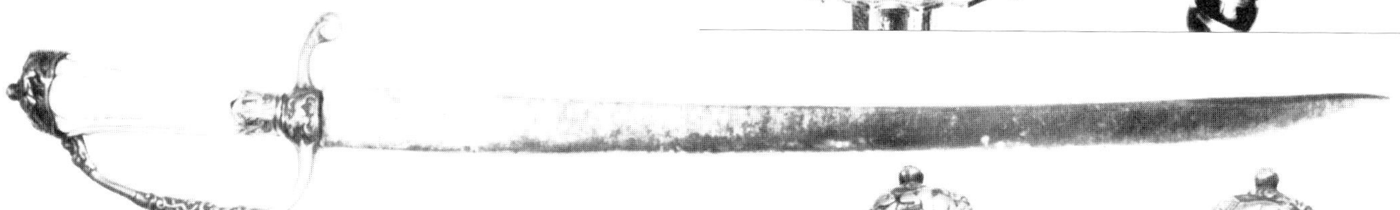

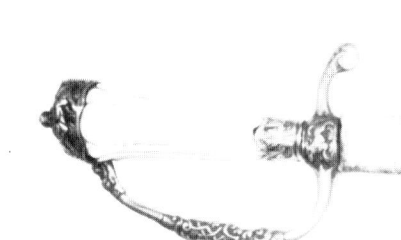

**84.SS EUROPEAN HUNTING SWORD**  Circa 1700–1720
During the 17th century, a short civilian sword became popular with hunters as a supplementary weapon and a means to dispatch wounded game. It usually mounted a straight or slightly curved cut-and-thrust blade that seldom exceeded 28 inches in length. This early heavy-hilted example has interwoven designs plus dogs and forest animals cast into the brass components. Raised panels outline a tapered bone grip. The flat gently curved blade retains engraved designs and a false edge.
Length: 24-5/8"   Blade: 19" X 1"   Hilt: Brass
**Author's Collection**

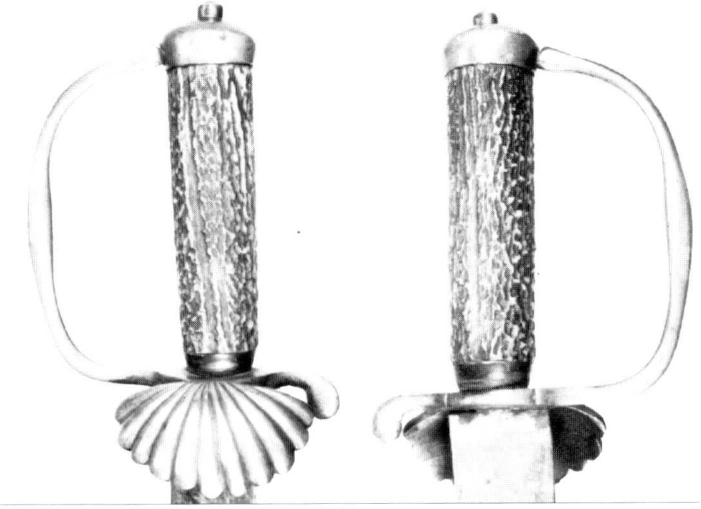

### 85.SS  EUROPEAN HUNTING SWORD        Circa 1710–1730

Originally designed for hunting, many of these swords assumed more general use and acquired basic characteristics. Although not suited for combat, they were often carried by American officers who lacked military patterns. This example (probably French) displays the popular cap-like pommel, slender knuckle bow, staghorn grip and lobed quillon. The evolving shell guard, in turn, retains the almost horizontal projection found in its early form. The Germanic blade is marked "C***."

Length: 27-3/4"        Blade: 22-3/4" X 1-1/4"        Hilt: Brass

**Douglas Neumann Collection**

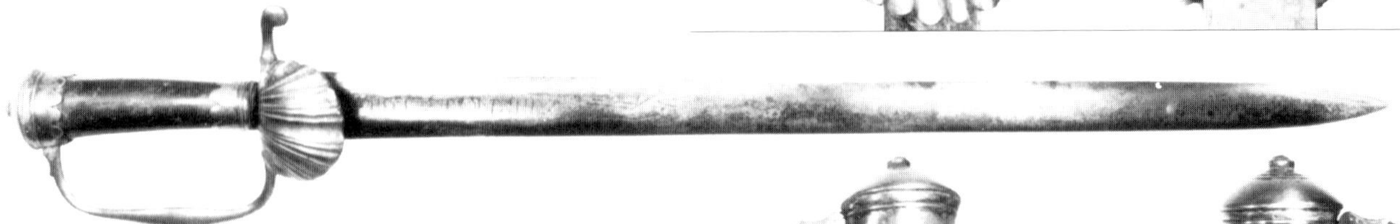

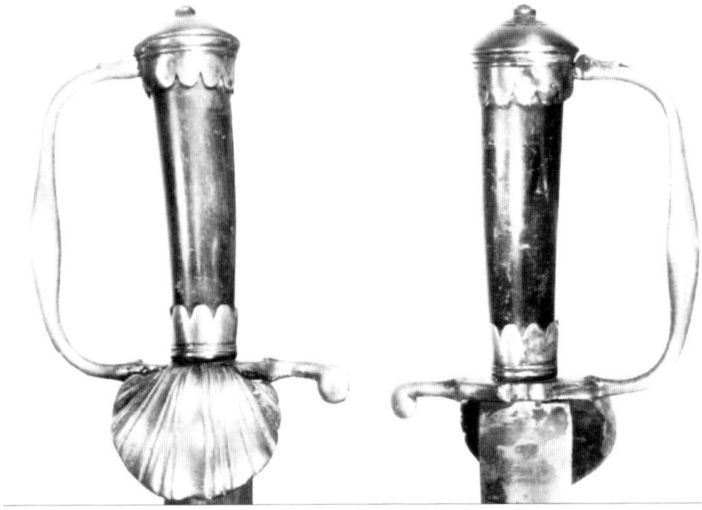

### 86.SS  EUROPEAN HUNTING SWORD        Circa 1740–1760

A number of the jaegers serving Britain during the Revolutionary War reportedly carried their personal rifles. This is the type of secondary weapon that probably accompanied them. Notice both the strength and simple artistry of its Germanic styling, that is, a sloped pommel with notches in its lower edge and bottom ferrule, a tapering horn grip, the D-type knuckle bow, a bulbous quillon and a ridged shell guard now in a more vertical position. The two-edged blade has the running wolf figure.

Length: 27-1/8"        Blade: 21-3/4" X 1-1/4"        Hilt: Brass

**Author's Collection**

### 87.SS  EUROPEAN HUNTING SWORD        Circa 1740–1760

Being privately owned, these weapons often acquired elaborate decorative features. Notice the pierced designs in this stylized shell guard, a pixy face on the cap-like pommel, raised foliage along the stubby counterguard and incised grooves across the bone grip. Its short curved blade includes a 5/8" X 16" fuller and a 4-3/4" false edge—as well as engraved panels filled with period geometric designs.

Length: 22-3/8"        Blade: 16-3/4" X 1"        Hilt: Brass

**Author's Collection**

### 88.SS EUROPEAN HUNTING SWORD
Circa                                                      1750–1770

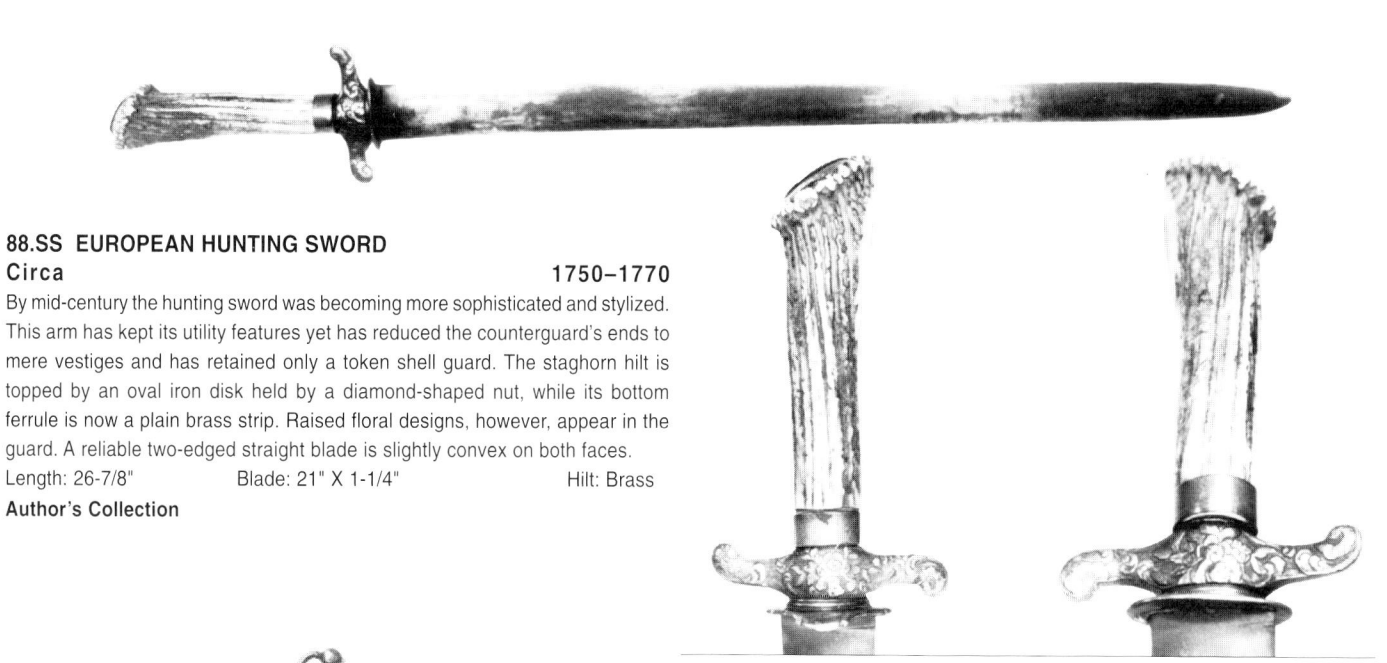

By mid-century the hunting sword was becoming more sophisticated and stylized. This arm has kept its utility features yet has reduced the counterguard's ends to mere vestiges and has retained only a token shell guard. The staghorn hilt is topped by an oval iron disk held by a diamond-shaped nut, while its bottom ferrule is now a plain brass strip. Raised floral designs, however, appear in the guard. A reliable two-edged straight blade is slightly convex on both faces.
Length: 26-7/8"       Blade: 21" X 1-1/4"                Hilt: Brass
**Author's Collection**

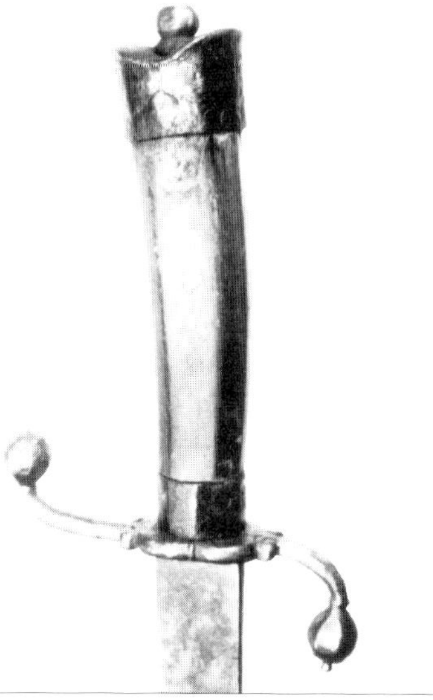

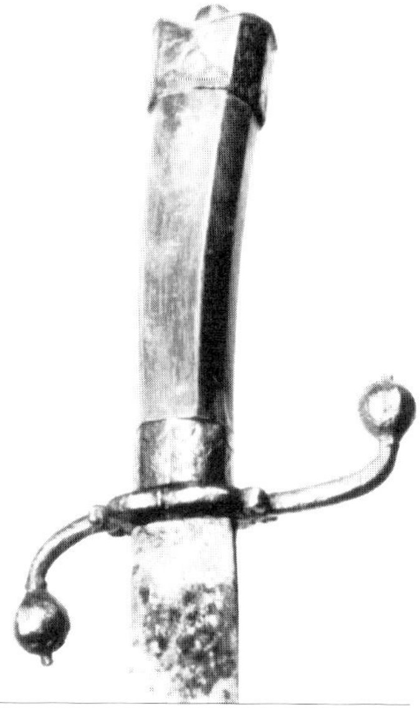

### 89.SS EUROPEAN HUNTING SWORD (CUTTOE) Circa 1650–1670
A longer variation of the hunting sword evolved in central Europe as a light "town" pattern ("cuttoe") which also became a symbol of rank for military officers. Observe this 17th century example found in Massachusetts. It has a slender single-edged flat blade and a gently curving faceted horn grip mounting both an octagonal bottom ferrule and a cleft upper pommel with capstan. The iron "S" guard includes a bulging quillon and stud finial at each end.
Length: 29-1/2"       Blade: 24-1/4" X 1"                Hilt: Iron
**Author's Collection**

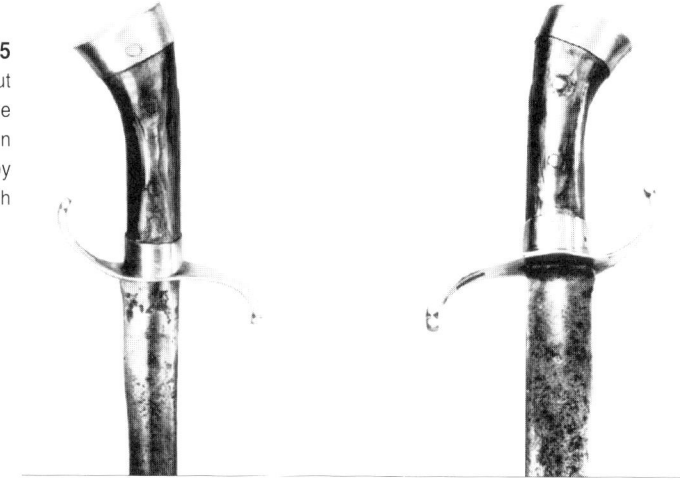

### 90.SS AMERICAN HUNTING SWORD (CUTTOE) Circa 1750–1775
American craftsmen also produced these short swords. This elementary but pleasing silver-hilted pattern is marked "C CHOUSO" in a rectangular cartouche on both faces of its quillon. He was a swordmaker associated with the Hudson Valley circa 1750 to 1780. The grip is a pair of horn panels pinned to the tang by two cross rivets. Its flat curving counterguard, in turn, adds a small finial at each end and is soldered to the 3/4" ferrule. The blade is also locally made.
Length: 32-1/4"       Blade: 27-1/4" X 1-1/8"              Hilt: Silver
**Former Harold L. Peterson Collection**

*Chapter 7: Swords*

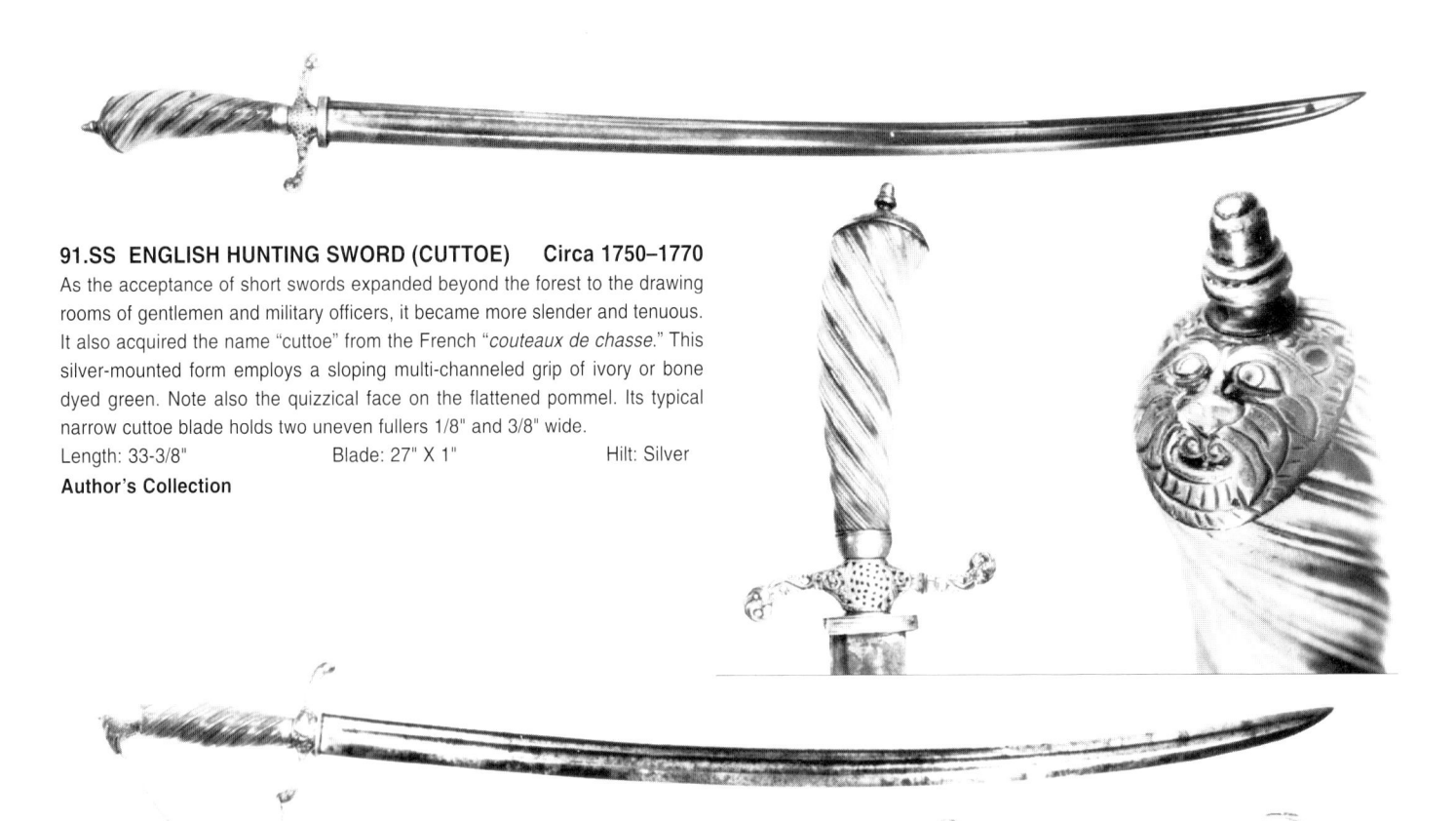

**91.SS  ENGLISH HUNTING SWORD (CUTTOE)    Circa 1750–1770**

As the acceptance of short swords expanded beyond the forest to the drawing rooms of gentlemen and military officers, it became more slender and tenuous. It also acquired the name "cuttoe" from the French "*couteaux de chasse*." This silver-mounted form employs a sloping multi-channeled grip of ivory or bone dyed green. Note also the quizzical face on the flattened pommel. Its typical narrow cuttoe blade holds two uneven fullers 1/8" and 3/8" wide.

Length: 33-3/8"            Blade: 27" X 1"            Hilt: Silver

**Author's Collection**

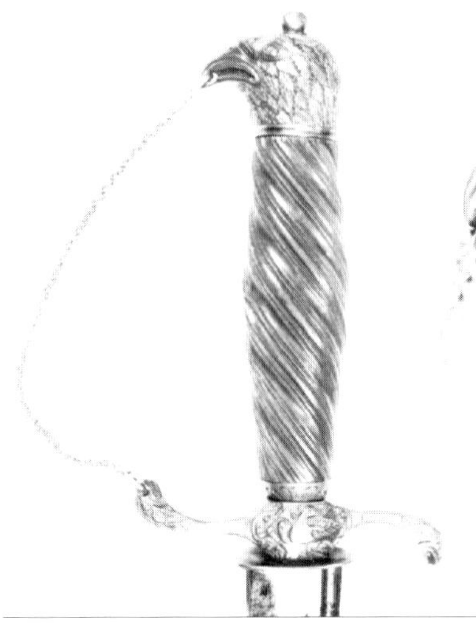

**92.SS  ENGLISH HUNTING SWORD (CUTTOE)    Circa 1769**

The established appeal of bird and animal heads is apparent in this English cuttoe's silver eagle pommel. It even adds eagle-like figures on both crossguard finials and the center panel. Also reflecting prevailing fashion, the finely grooved ivory hilt is dyed green, while a chain connects its guard and pommel. The silver scabbard throat is engraved "CAPT WM BROWN / N YORK 1769." Brown served in America with the 14th Regiment in 1768, the 35th in 1769 and the 52nd from 1772.

Length: 31-3/4"            Blade: 26" X 1"            Hilt: Silver

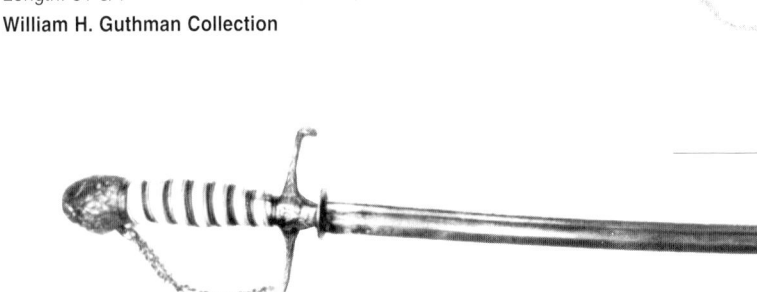

**William H. Guthman Collection**

**93.SS  ENGLISH HUNTING SWORD (CUTTOE)    Circa 1759–1770**

The large lion pommel of this steel-mounted cuttoe assumes a wincing expression to match a flattened nose. It anchors a double chain composed of figure-8 links (at right angles), plus a channeled ivory grip bearing four twisted wire ropes—two each of iron and brass. Notice also the mythological phoenix "rising from the ashes" at the center of the crossguard, which terminates in two multiple "claw" finials. The typical curved blade includes both a 1/8" and a 3/8" fuller.

Length: 34"            Blade: 26-3/4" X 1"            Hilt: Steel

**Author's Collection**

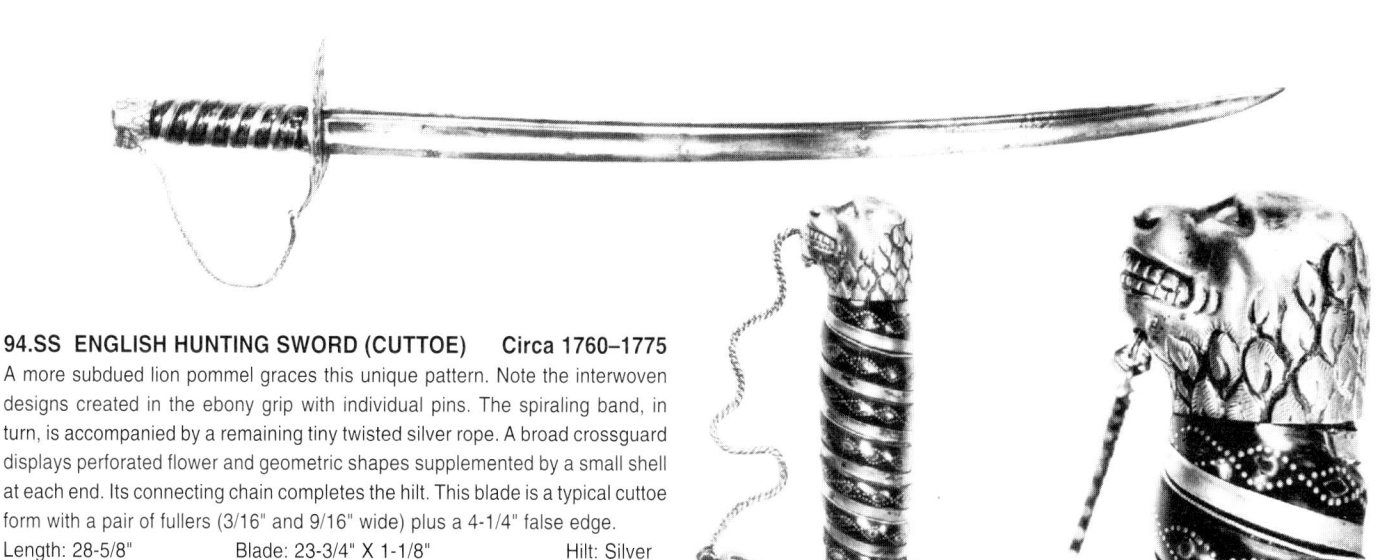

**94.SS ENGLISH HUNTING SWORD (CUTTOE)    Circa 1760–1775**
A more subdued lion pommel graces this unique pattern. Note the interwoven designs created in the ebony grip with individual pins. The spiraling band, in turn, is accompanied by a remaining tiny twisted silver rope. A broad crossguard displays perforated flower and geometric shapes supplemented by a small shell at each end. Its connecting chain completes the hilt. This blade is a typical cuttoe form with a pair of fullers (3/16" and 9/16" wide) plus a 4-1/4" false edge.
Length: 28-5/8"          Blade: 23-3/4" X 1-1/8"          Hilt: Silver
**Author's Collection**

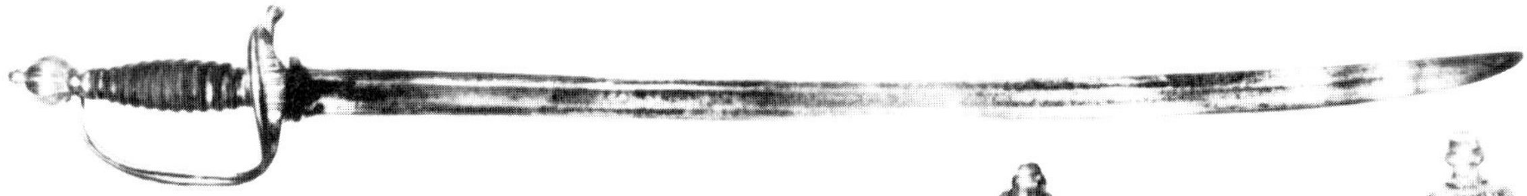

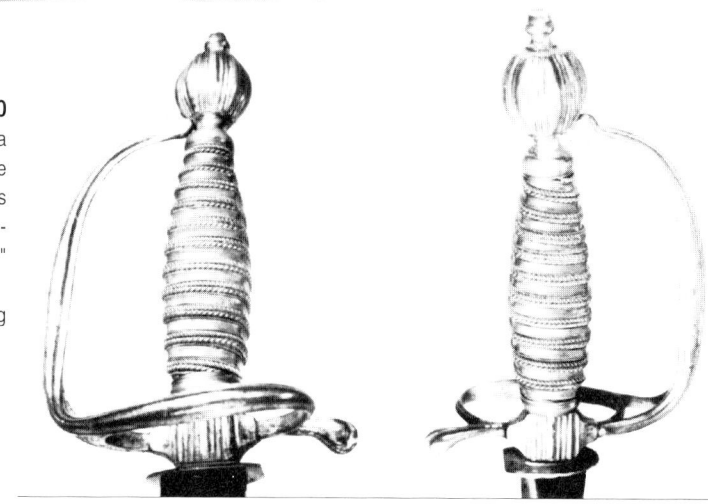

**95.SS ENGLISH HUNTING SWORD (CUTTOE)    Circa 1760–1770**
A more conventional D-guard hilt was chosen for this sword. It is gilded over a brass base and includes a ringed capstan, an incised oval pommel, a simple guard with an outboard loop and a lobed quillon. Double brass twisted ropes and a flat band cover the bulbous wooden grip. Its typical light cuttoe single-edged blade (below a small elliptical junction plate) has two uneven fullers (1/4" X 18-1/2"; 3/8" X 25-1/4") along with an eight-inch false edge.
Length: 32-3/4"          Blade: 26-3/8" X 1"          Hilt: Brass/Gilding
**Author's Collection**

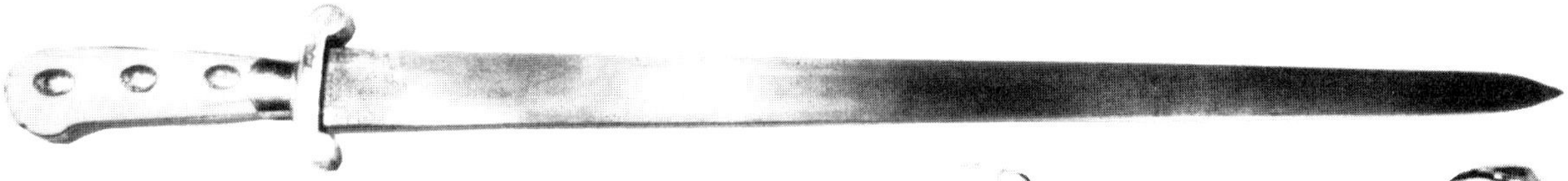

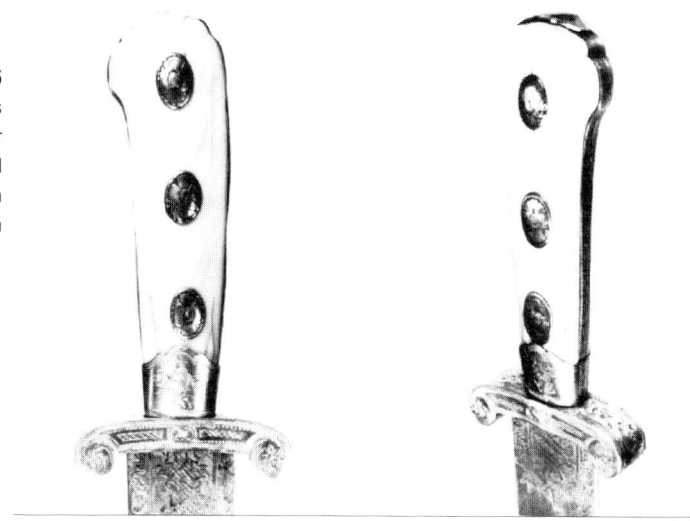

**96.SS AMERICAN HUNTING SWORD (CUTTOE)    Circa 1770–1776**
The distinctive hilt of this silver-mounted cuttoe is dominated by three oval disks with floral designs along the grip's two convex ivory faces. A 1/4" wide silver band, in turn, covers the side junction. Its slightly arched crossguard adds scrolled ends and bears extensive foliate and geometric decoration—which continue on the upper blade. The straight blade is sharpened along one side. This American arm has an association with the Revolutionary War 1776–1777 campaigns.
Length: 27-3/4"          Blade: 22-1/2" X 1-3/8"          Hilt: Silver
**George and Roseanne Juno Collection**

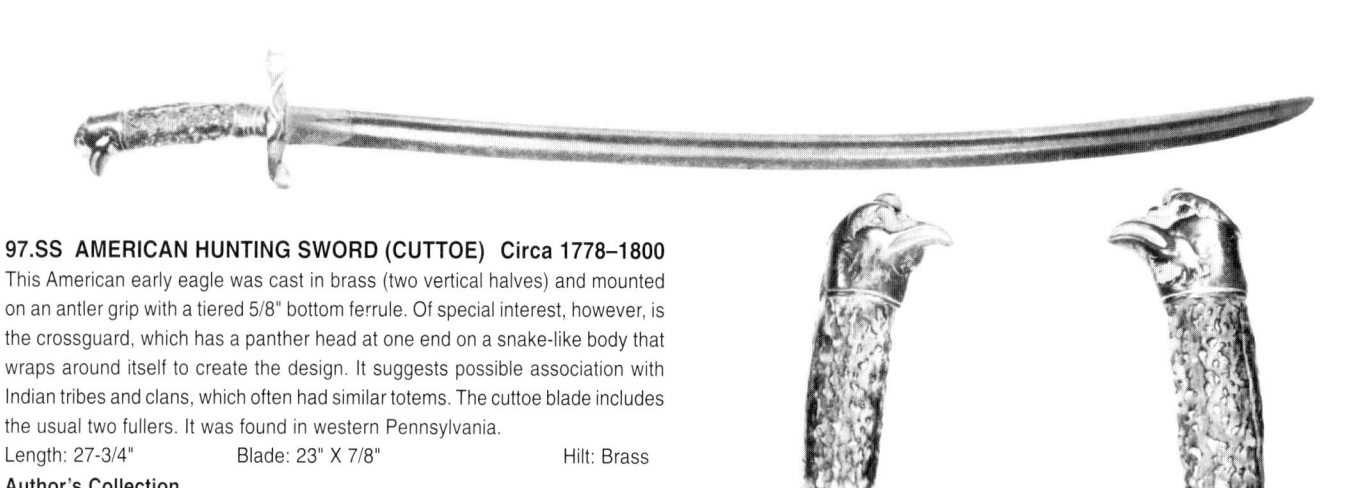

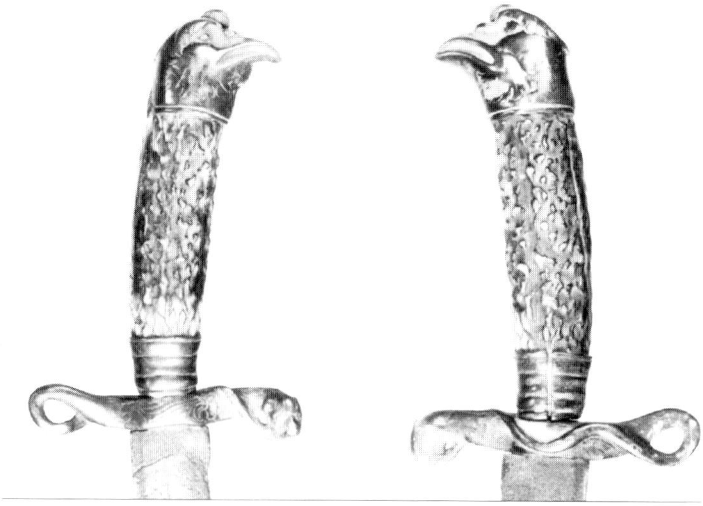

**97.SS AMERICAN HUNTING SWORD (CUTTOE)  Circa 1778–1800**
This American early eagle was cast in brass (two vertical halves) and mounted on an antler grip with a tiered 5/8" bottom ferrule. Of special interest, however, is the crossguard, which has a panther head at one end on a snake-like body that wraps around itself to create the design. It suggests possible association with Indian tribes and clans, which often had similar totems. The cuttoe blade includes the usual two fullers. It was found in western Pennsylvania.
Length: 27-3/4"   Blade: 23" X 7/8"   Hilt: Brass
**Author's Collection**

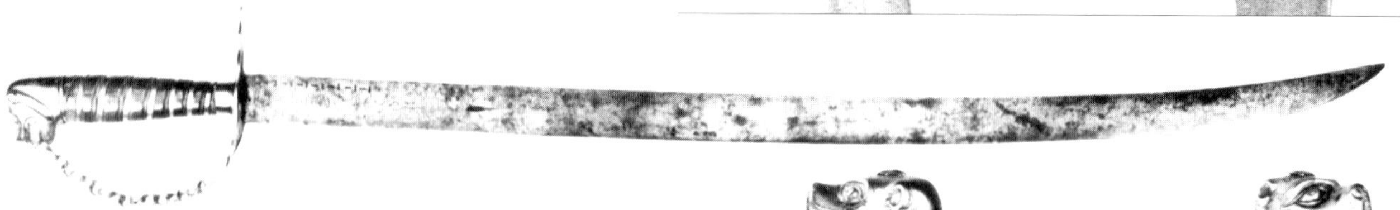

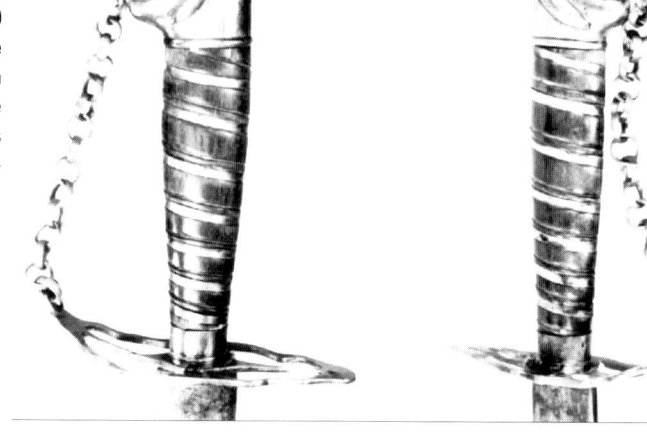

**98.SS AMERICAN HUNTING SWORD (CUTTOE)  Circa 1770–1780**
All of this sword's components are considered of American origin. The primitive lion/dog pommel was made from a single piece of brass. Its tapering wooden grip has a band in its spiraled groove and terminates at a 1/2" ferrule. Note the original chain, which was hand-formed into round links from flat brass strips having their outer surface reeded. A flat counterguard is pierced in typical four-slot fashion, while the flat blade bears staid provincial incised designs.
Length: 33-1/8"   Blade: 27-1/2" X 1-5/16"   Hilt: Brass
**George C. Neumann Collection, Valley Forge National Historical Park**

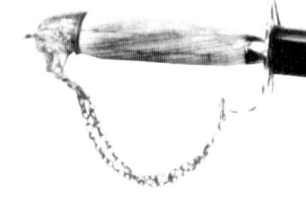

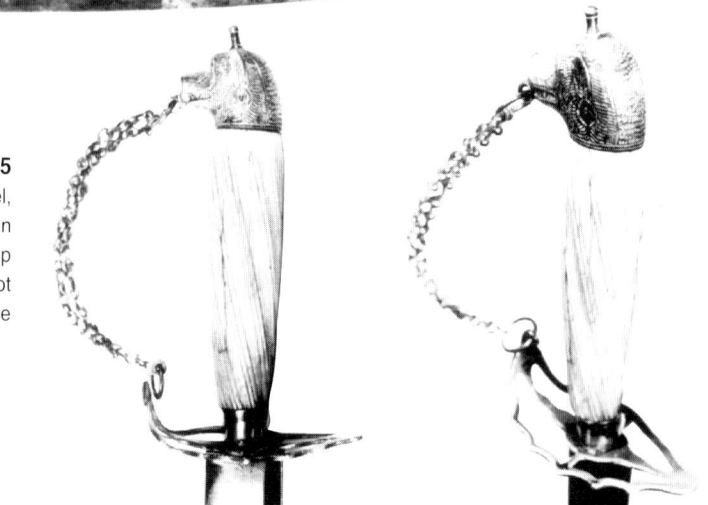

**99.SS AMERICAN HUNTING SWORD (CUTTOE)  Circa 1770–1785**
The dog-like features and shallow incised detail work on this silver animal pommel, as well as the high capstan and the absence of hallmarks, suggest an American origin. Also notice the tapered ivory grip and double chain that attaches to the tip of a two-ended counterguard. The guard's familiar pattern includes a four-slot design combined with a scalloped outer edge and a smooth inner one (to reduce clothing wear). Its imported blade is blued only on the upper half (common).
Length: 33-1/8"   Blade: 26-3/4" X 1-1/4"   Hilt: Silver
**Richard Ulbrich Collection**

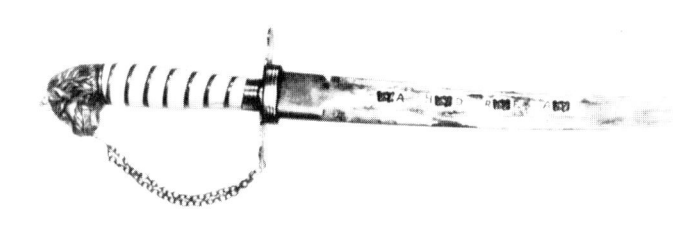

### 100.SS AMERICAN HUNTING SWORD (CUTTOE) Circa 1776–1778

John Bailey, America's prodigious swordmaker, produced this impressive cuttoe. He employed a well-defined lion pommel above a polished ivory grip and silver band. A double chain, in turn, connects both ends of the hilt. The flat scalloped guard adds a rear animal head terminal; it also attaches to an oval sheath cap. King's head stamps and "ANDREA FARARA" appear on the Solingen blade, while "J BAILEY Fecit (made by) Fredericksburgh" (New York) is on the silver scabbard throat.

Length: 33-3/8"   Blade: 27-1/4" X 1-1/4"   Hilt: Silver

**Richard Ulbrich Collection**

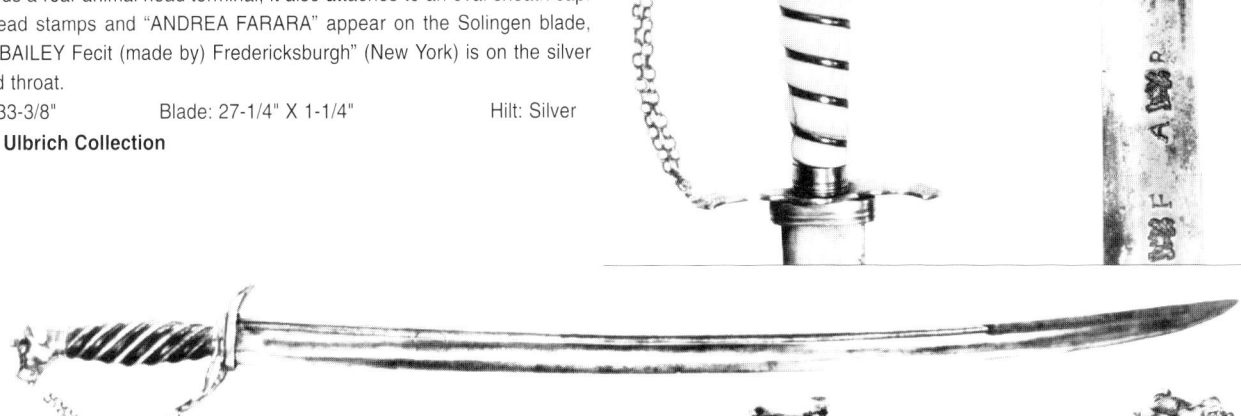

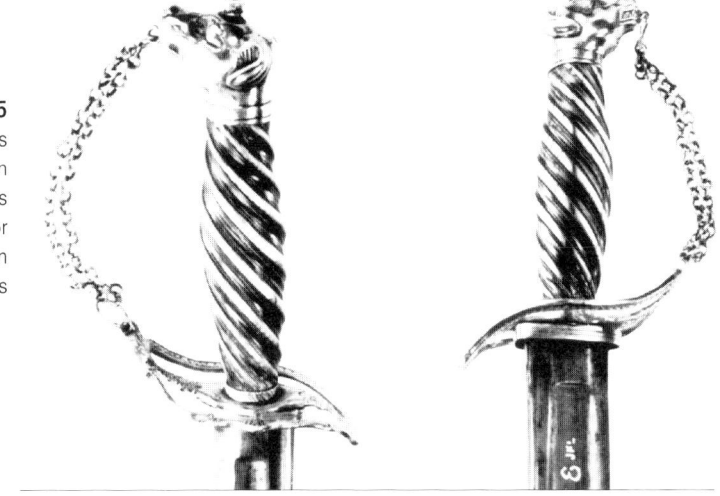

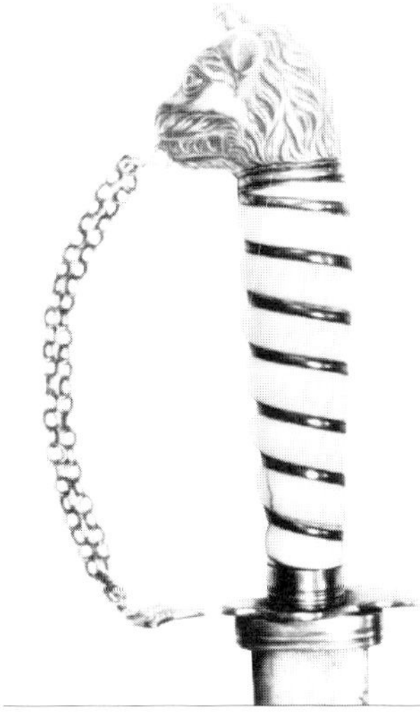

### 101.SS AMERICAN HUNTING SWORD (CUTTOE) Circa 1765–1775

This dog pommel silver cuttoe is believed to have been Ethan Allen's dress sword. The maker was Ephraim Brasher of New York (1744–1810). A thin gold wash covers the dog head and small jewels are inserted in the eyes. Its channeled grip is ivory. The double-ended counterguard contributes four interior openings plus a scalloped outside edge and smooth inner one—which adds an inlaid iron strip to reduce wear and tarnish stains. A British "crown / GR" remains on the blade.

Length: 32-7/8"   Blade: 27" X 1-1/4"   Hilt: Silver/Gold Wash

**Dr. John K. Lattimer Collection**

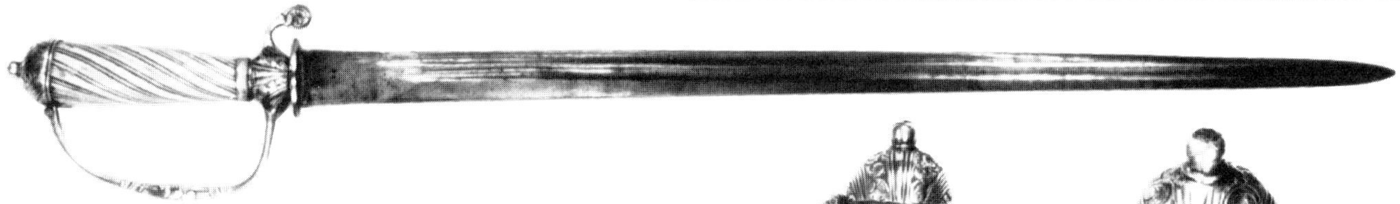

### 102.SS ENGLISH HUNTING SWORD (CUTTOE) Circa 1759–1782

D-guard patterns were also used on these slender cuttoe forms. The silver-hilted example in this case, by Britain's William Kinman, mounted a domed pommel and capstan on a gracefully spiraled ivory grip. Rococo-type decoration appears on all metal components of the hilt, including the center section of its tenuous knuckle bow. An oval disk completes the junction with a straight single-edged blade displaying two 1/4" fullers.

Length: 26"   Blade: 20-5/8" X 1"   Hilt: Silver

**Author's Collection**

*Chapter 7: Swords*

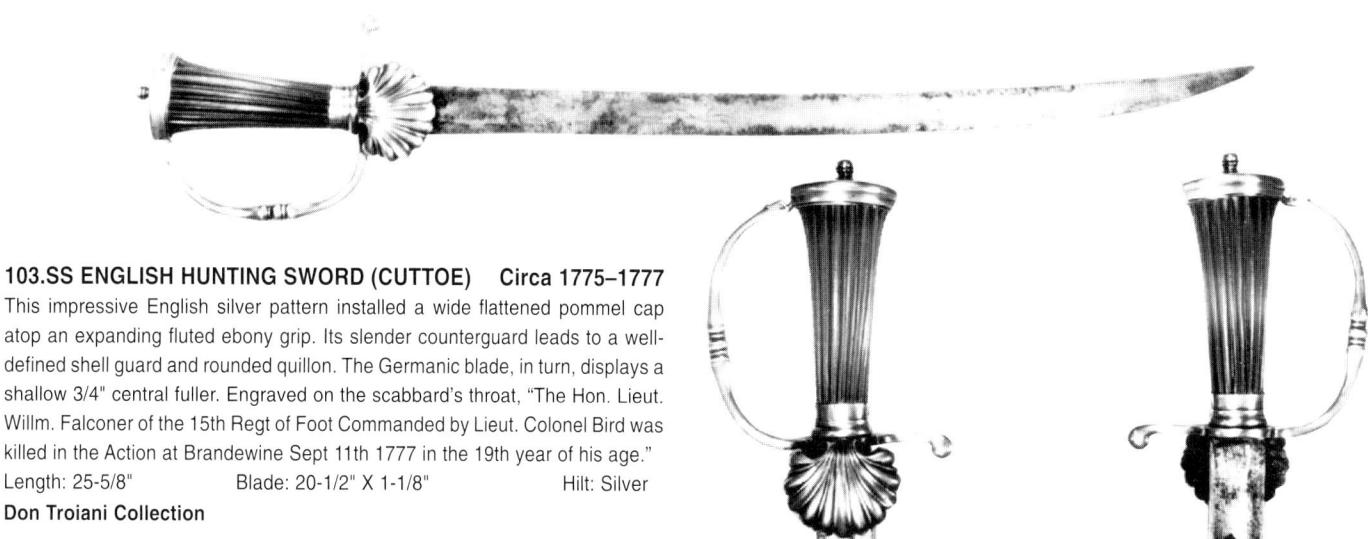

**103.SS ENGLISH HUNTING SWORD (CUTTOE)    Circa 1775–1777**
This impressive English silver pattern installed a wide flattened pommel cap atop an expanding fluted ebony grip. Its slender counterguard leads to a well-defined shell guard and rounded quillon. The Germanic blade, in turn, displays a shallow 3/4" central fuller. Engraved on the scabbard's throat, "The Hon. Lieut. Willm. Falconer of the 15th Regt of Foot Commanded by Lieut. Colonel Bird was killed in the Action at Brandewine Sept 11th 1777 in the 19th year of his age."
Length: 25-5/8"        Blade: 20-1/2" X 1-1/8"        Hilt: Silver
**Don Troiani Collection**

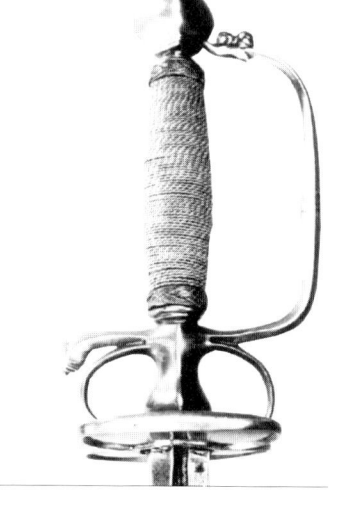

**104.SS  ENGLISH SMALL SWORD           Circa 1690–1700**
These long slender straight-bladed swords were civilian weapons and served most officers on both sides during the Revolutionary War. The pattern apparently evolved from Holland in the early 1600s to France and central Europe by mid century and into England with Charles II in 1660. By 1700 it had achieved this profile: a rounded pommel, squared knuckle bow, large *pas d'ane*, a bilobate counterguard with raised borders, a single wire-wrapped grip, and a thin triangular blade.
Length: 40-1/4"        Blade: 33-3/8" X 7/8"        Hilt: Brass/Silver Wash
**George C. Neumann Collection, Valley Forge National Historical Park**

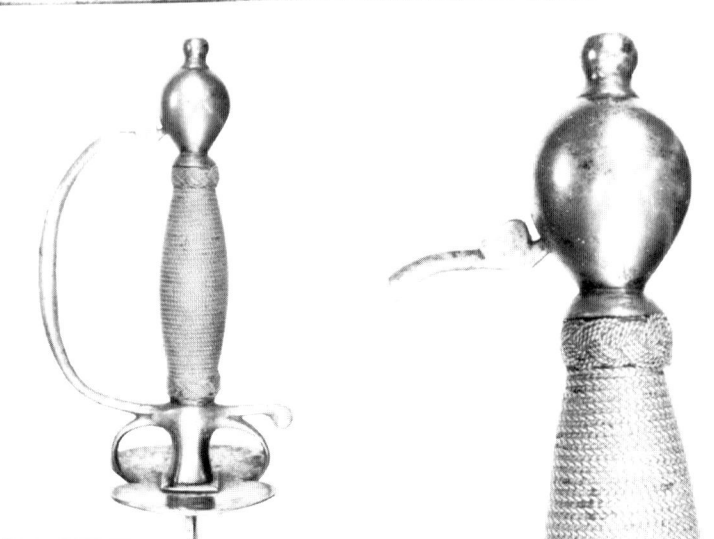

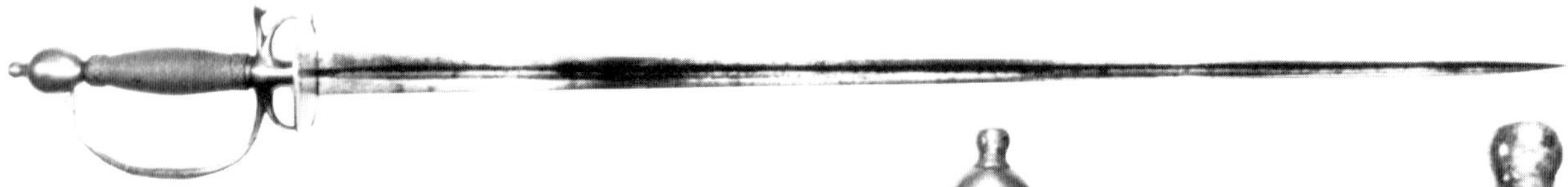

**105.SS  ENGLISH SMALL SWORD                  Circa 1720–1740**
By the 1720s the English small sword had achieved a simplicity and balance that was adopted and continued by many American swordsmiths through the Revolutionary War (see 113.SS). Notice this egg-like pommel, the D-shaped knuckle bow, rounded *pas d'ane*, and lobed quillon. Most had raised borders on the bilobate counterguard (only bottom here). The disciplined grip is a wooden core tightly wrapped by two adjacent wire ropes of different size, plus turks-head ferrules.
Length: 33-1/4"        Blade: 27" X 7/8"        Hilt: Steel
**Author's Collection**

338    *Chapter 7: Swords*

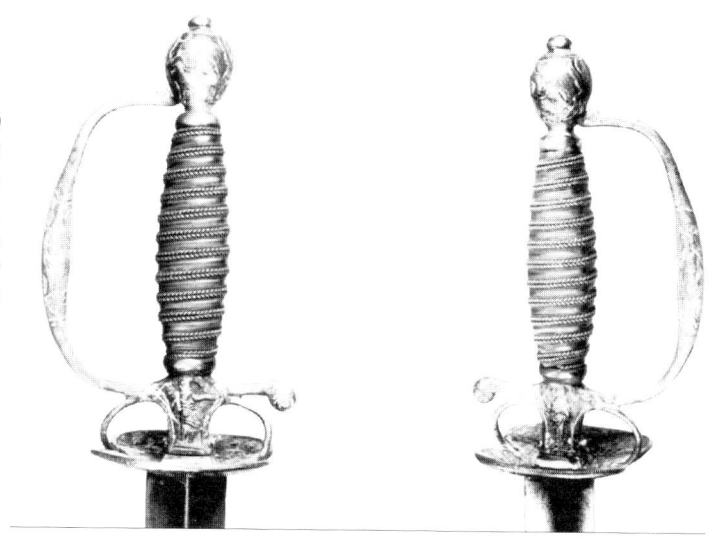

### 106.SS  ENGLISH SMALL SWORD     Circa 1720–1740

Being civilian "gentlemen's" weapons, many small swords acquired embellishments such as the raised classical figures seen here. Its brass base was coated with a gold wash—since hilt quality reflected the owner's social status. Of further interest is the colichemard blade form developed by the French; the wider section adjacent to the hilt could receive an opponent's blow, yet the slender forward end retained offensive dexterity. Its grip is wrapped by double ropes and a 1/8" band.

Length: 38-1/4"     Blade: 32" X 1-1/8"     Hilt: Brass/Gold Wash

**Author's Collection**

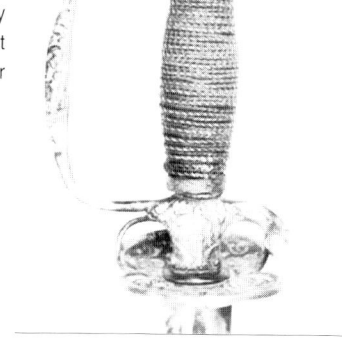

### 107.SS  FRENCH SMALL SWORD     Circa 1720–1750

The French were especially attracted to the small sword form and even carried it over into the patterns of their early infantry hangers (25.SS). The example here—covered with cast figures and foliage designs—is of the type favored by many of their junior officers. Also of interest, this double-edged cut-and-thrust blade includes a linear design cut through its center. The French preference for wire-wrapped grips and turks-head ferrules should also be noted.

Length: 35-1/2"     Blade: 29-3/8" X 1"     Hilt: Brass

**Author's Collection**

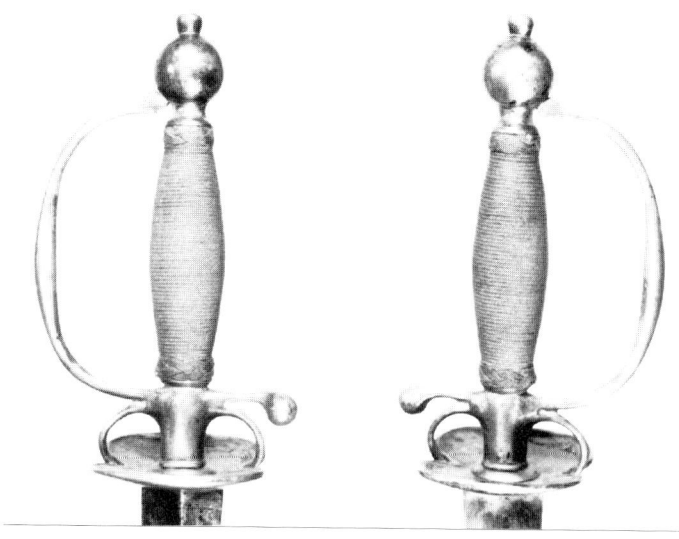

### 108.SS  SMALL SWORD     Circa 1750

By mid-century, evolution was apparent among most small swords: the pommel was now rounder, the squared knuckle bow profile had softened into a D-shape, the quillon was bending outward, and the *pas d'anes* were beginning to flatten. This brass hilt originally had a gold wash coating. In its simplicity the sword is typical of the form favored by many junior officers of both the American and King's armies. Its triangular blade is concave on two sides and has a 1/4" fuller in the other.

Length: 35-1/2"     Blade: 29-1/2" X 1-1/8"     Hilt: Brass/Gold Wash

**Author's Collection**

*Chapter 7: Swords*

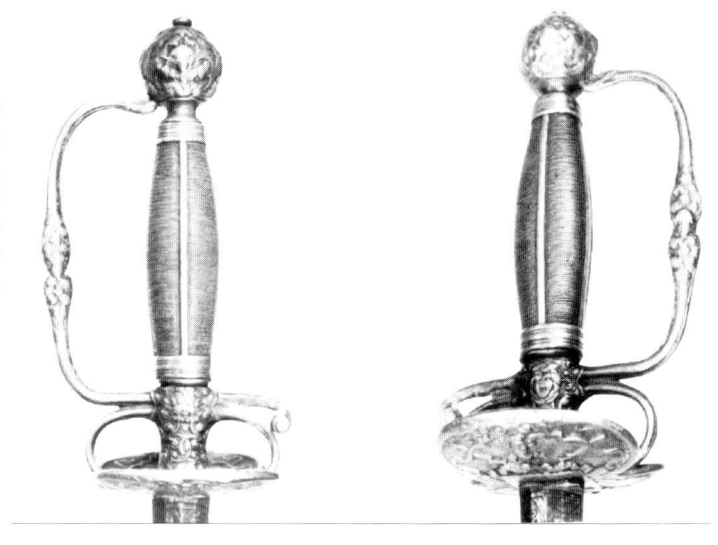

**109.SS FRENCH SMALL SWORD — Circa 1750–1760**

The French penchant to innovate is constantly seen on their swords. This wooden grip is typically wrapped by two adjacent wire ropes twisted in opposite directions. Yet four vertical struts appear for diversity. The blade, in turn, is hexagonal and bears the figures plus names of the disciples—as well as the phrases "Ne Me Tire Pas Sans Raison . . . Ne Me Remette Point Sans Honneur," ("Draw me not without reason . . . sheathe me not without honor"), which are found on many blades.

Length: 37-1/2"   Blade: 31-1/4" X 3/4"   Hilt: Brass

**Author's Collection**

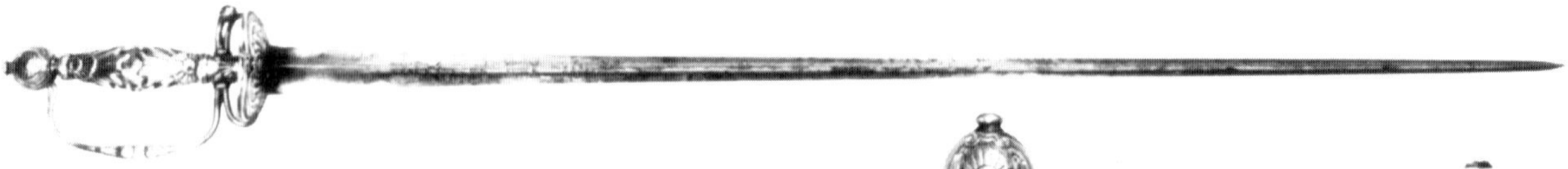

**110.SS FRENCH SMALL SWORD — Circa 1750–1770**

It appears that small sword decoration had no limitations. This silver-hilted example from the third quarter is embellished with French–Low Country-type rococo patterns—including stamps of the former. Notice that the round pommel is still dominant and a panel has been added between the *pas d'ane*, which, in turn, continue slowly to flatten and lose their earlier round shape. A typical long blade has engraved panels on its three concave faces.

Length: 36-1/4"   Blade: 30-1/4" X 1"   Hilt: Silver

**Author's Collection**

**111.SS AMERICAN SMALL SWORD — Circa 1740–1760**

As with many American-made weapons, the proper elements are present but the proportions are distorted. Moreover, these *pas d'ane* are of different sizes, and a cast ridge on the quillon's back side was never dressed (possibly to strengthen the narrow neck). In typical fashion the knuckle bow and *pas d'ane* were cast as a single piece. The shagreen (fishskin) grip covering is usually found on sabers. Its blade assumes a diamond cross-section below a 2-1/8" ricasso.

Length: 36"   Blade: 29-3/8" X 1/2"   Hilt: Brass

**George C. Neumann Collection, Valley Forge National Historical Park**

Chapter 7: Swords

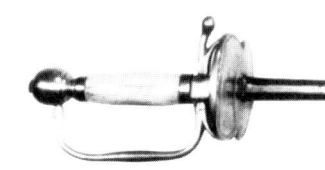

**112.SS  AMERICAN SMALL SWORD**  Circa 1760–1780

An American cutler added a touch of elegance here with an ivory grip, yet the cast brass components are overly large and distorted—including a heavy post under the lower ferrule. Military officers usually owned two or more swords—to cope with ceremonial and social occasions (for example, a small sword or cuttoe), as well as field combat (short saber or horseman's saber). These rapier-like patterns would also fight duels and required considerable training in thrust and parry techniques.

Length: 36-1/4"   Blade: 30" X 5/8"   Hilt: Brass

**Author's Collection**

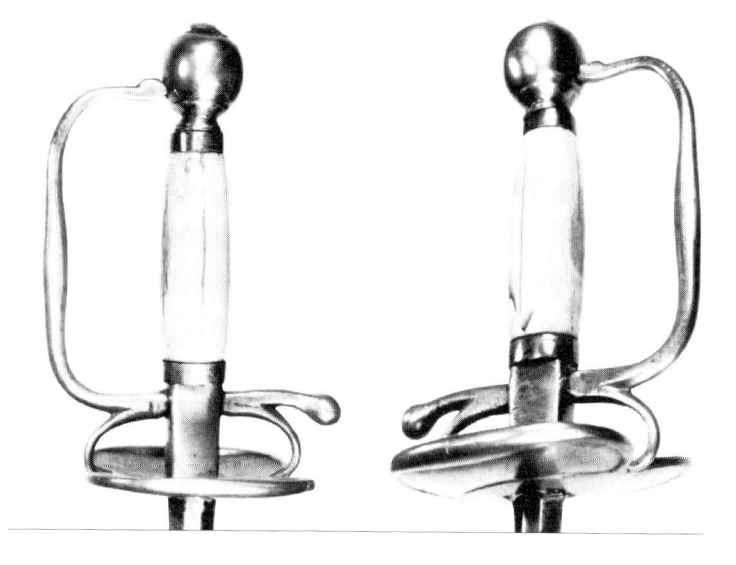

**113.SS  AMERICAN SMALL SWORD**  Circa 1750–1770

The basic unfettered small sword pattern prevalent in England circa 1720–1730 was still being made by many New World cutlers at the time of the Revolutionary War. Such provincials did not have hallmark regulations and this unmarked silver example is thought to be American. It adds two raised tiers to the pommel, as well as a single silver wire wrapped with the two usual ropes on the grip. The colichemard triangular blade (wide upper section) is probably an import.

Length: 34-3/4"   Blade: 29-1/8" X 1-1/4"   Hilt: Silver

**Author's Collection**

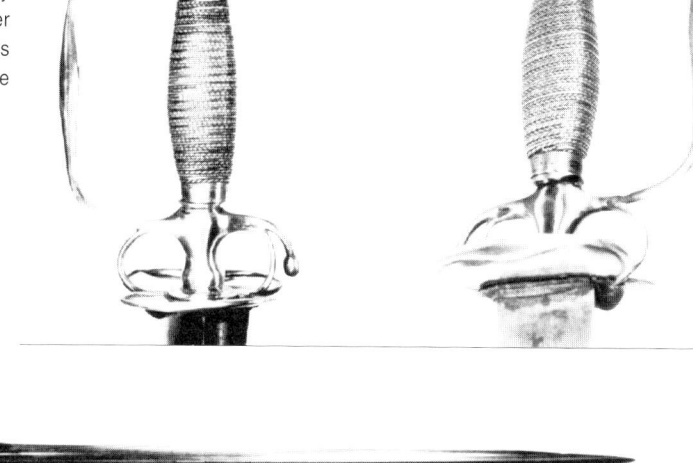

**114.SS  AMERICAN SMALL SWORD**  Circa 1765–1770

The boat guard illustrated in this American silver-hilted pattern was a popular small sword variation (see 115.SS). Notice that it required a second quillon at the rear. The maker's name appears on the outboard knuckle bow near its ball pommel, *"J OTIS"* (Jonathan Otis, Newport, Rhode Island, and Middletown, Connecticut, 1723–1791). The impressive capabilities of many American cutlers is again evidenced here. Its colichemard blade with the widened upper section had a silver-mounted leather scabbard.

Length: 32-3/4"   Blade: 25-1/2" X 1-3/8"   Hilt: Silver

**Hermann W. Williams, Jr. Collection**

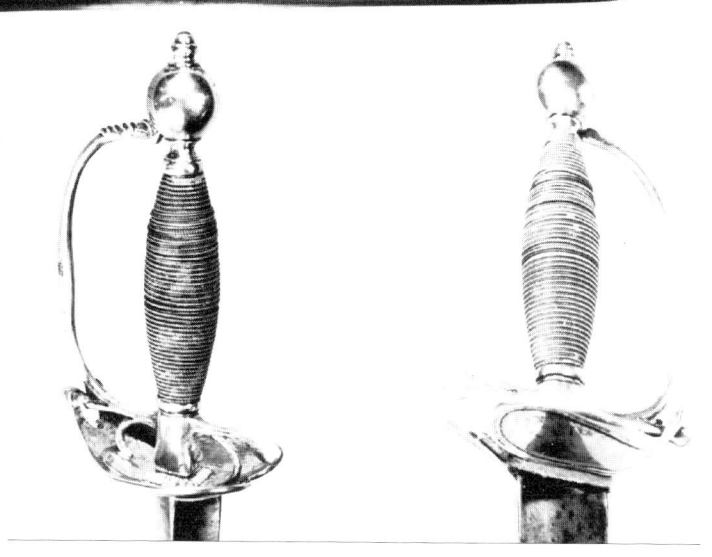

### 115.SS  EUROPEAN SMALL SWORD  Circa 1755–1770

Just past mid-century small swords began to acquire oval counterguards. One variation was the boat guard, which was stretched to harbor a second rear quillon. This one also protects the further lowered *pas d'ane* yet retains the traditional thick raised borders. The all-brass hilt has a copper hue and is decorated by the now-popular gadrooning (diagonal lines). Its blade, in turn, presents three concave sides plus two deep 1/8" fullers in the wide face.

Length: 35-1/2"    Blade: 29-5/8" X 1"    Hilt: Brass

**George C. Neumann Collection, Valley Forge National Historical Park**

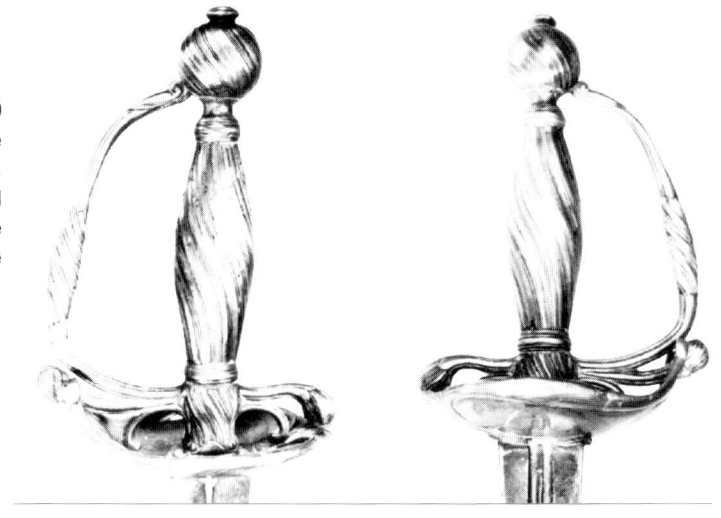

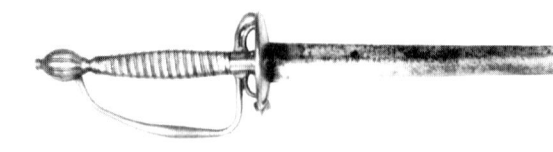

### 116.SS  FRENCH SMALL SWORD  Circa 1750–1787

This French military pattern is similar to a form carried by their king's household troops. Its long straight double-edged blade is wider than normal with a median ridge on each face. Of primary importance is the evolving small sword features that it illustrates. Notice that the pommel is now elongated, the grip (cast here) is stretched and thinner, and the *pas d'anes* have become flattened in profile. The bilobate guard continues, but the new oval form was gaining recognition.

Length: 35-3/4"    Blade: 29-1/8" X 1-1/8"    Hilt: Brass

**Author's Collection**

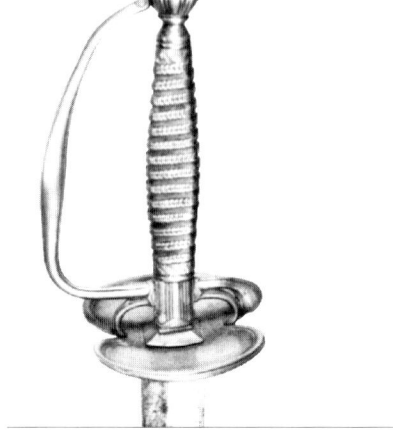

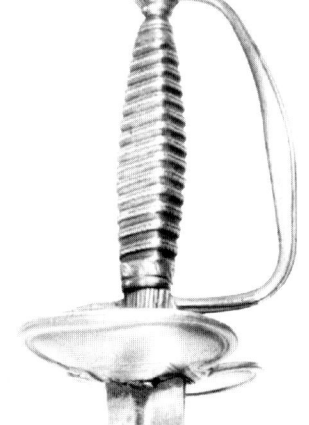

### 117.SS  FRENCH SMALL SWORD  Circa 1775–1790

By 1780 the small sword was entering its decline as the pattern rapidly deteriorated into a tenuous decorative form. The French example here illustrates this new phase: the previous bilobate guard is now a dished oval, the formerly rounded *pas d'anes* have become arches, the ball pommel has lengthened, and its grip is thinner and longer. The new reed-like gadrooning design is also present, as well as a rococo grip decoration. Moreover its silver surface is pressed over a copper base ("Sheffield plate").

Length: 38"    Blade: 31-1/8" X 3/4"    Hilt: Sheffield Plate

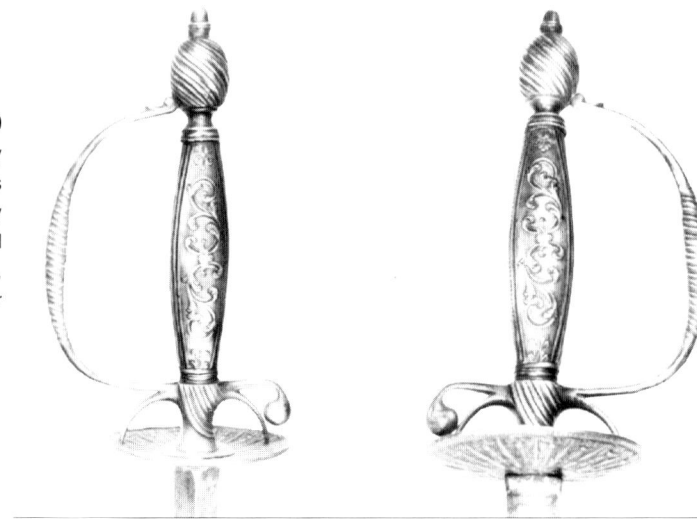

**Author's Collection**

Chapter 7: Swords

**118.SS  GERMANIC SMALL SWORD (RAPIER)    Circa 1750–1770**
The gentleman's slender small sword was also adopted to a heavy cast hilt and substantial double-edged blade—mostly for Germanic troops. Notice the faceted pommel, thick cast *pas d'ane* that curls upward and six-sided bulbous quillon with the early tip finial. Twisted wire ropes cover the wooden grip. Its equal-size bilobate guard panels, in turn, are of military field strength with raised borders on each face.
Length: 35-1/2"        Blade: 28-3/4" X 1-1/4"        Hilt: Brass
**Author's Collection**

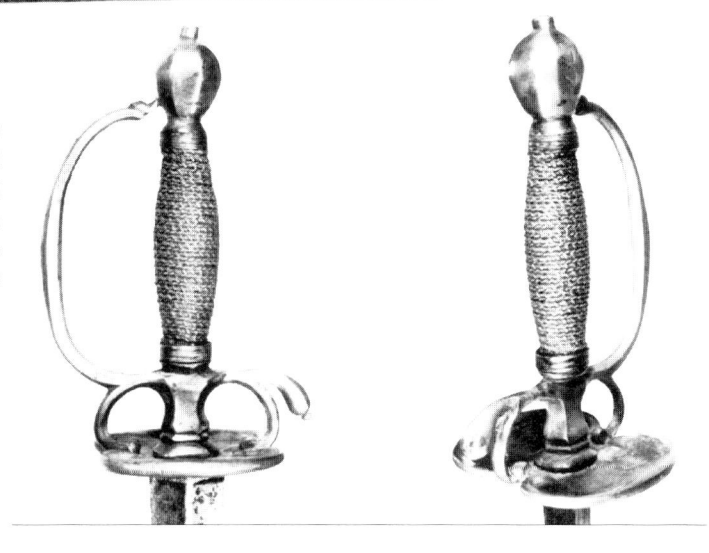

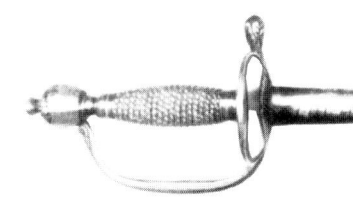

**119.SS  GERMAN SMALL SWORD (RAPIER)    Circa 1750–1785**
This basic design with its faceted pommel, dished bilobate counterguard and straight bulbous quillon (with minimal foliage decoration) was a Prussian infantry pattern beginning during the 1740s and continuing into the 1790s. Note the heavy twisted wire grip wrapping plus the absence of *pas d'anes*. Its straight two-edged, convex-faced blade is engraved "Pro Gloria Et Patria." Similar hilts were adopted by English officers (60.SS)—leading to their first official pattern in 1796.
Length: 35-3/8"        Blade: 28-5/8" X 1"        Hilt: Brass
**Author's Collection**

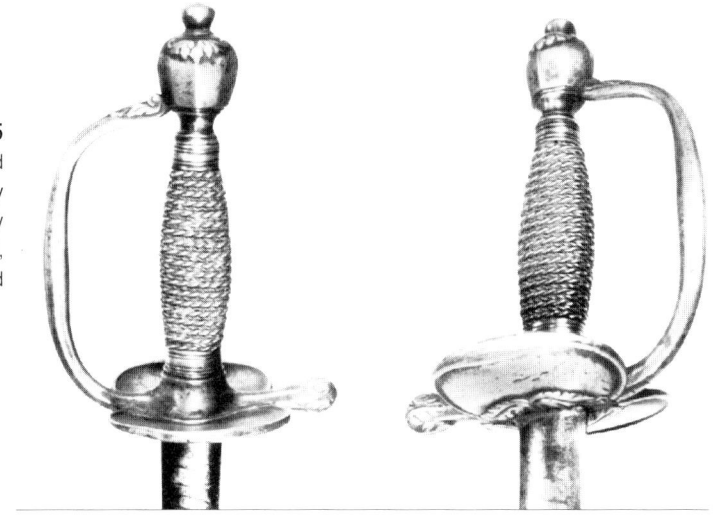

**120.SS  AMERICAN SMALL SWORD    Circa 1740–1760**
Adoption of the basic small sword features (that is, a light hilt and long thin blade) to heavier patterns (often omitting the *pas d'ane*) for field and combat capabilities was also practiced by American provincials. This almost primitive but serviceable weapon found in Pennsylvania has a plain whittled wooden grip and a squared pommel with decorative corner notches. Its simple knuckle bow creates a rectangular base for the grip above a double-ended boat-shaped flat guard.
Length: 35-1/8"        Blade: 29-3/4" X 1"        Hilt: Iron
**George C. Neumann Collection, Valley Forge National Historical Park**

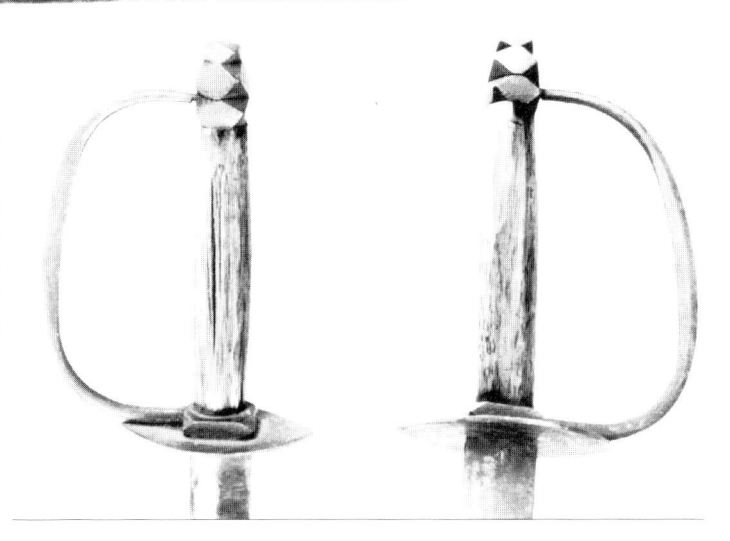

*Chapter 7: Swords*   343

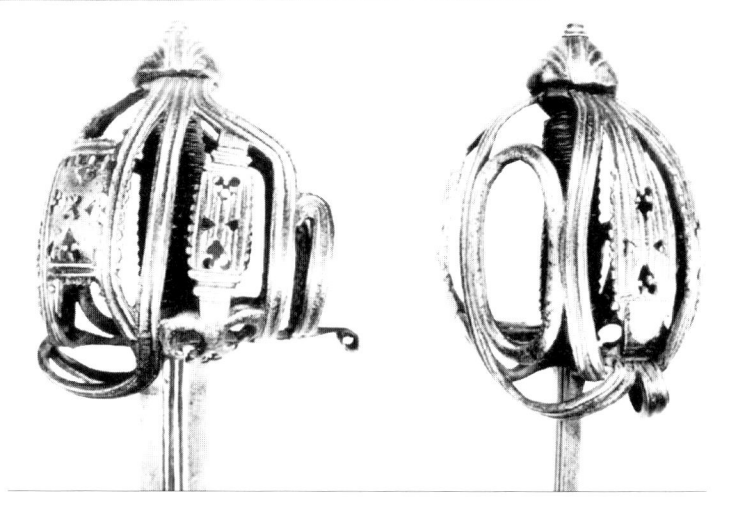

**121.SS  SCOTCH BROADSWORD**     Circa 1690–1717

Most Scottish hilts are classified into two "schools" of design—the traditional wide bar form from Glasgow and the round bar patterns of Stirling. The bottom of this basket is stamped "IS / G" for John Simpson (probably "The Elder"), a leading Glasgow swordsmith. Notice the typical Glasgow flat chiseled bars, scalloped and pierced rectangular junction plates plus side plates, as well as the fluted pommel. Its knuckle bow bears the arms of Colin Lindsay (1654–1722), the 3rd Earl of Balcarres (a Jacobite).

Length: 41-1/4"      Blade: 35-1/2" X 1-1/4"      Hilt: Iron

**James D. Forman Collection**

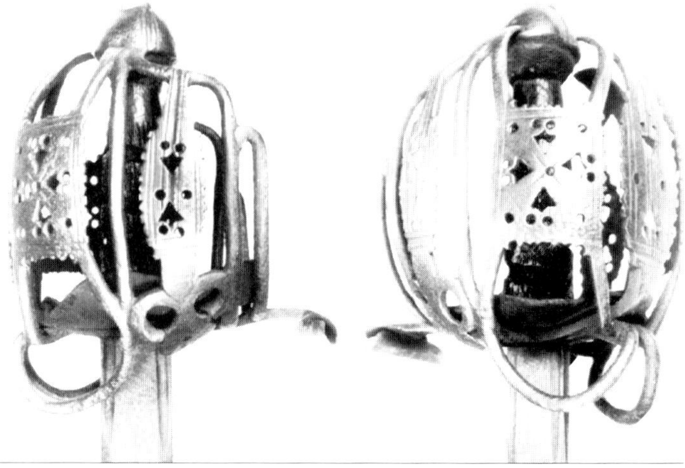

**122.SS  SCOTTISH BROADSWORD**     Circa 1714–1740

The "Stirling" basket hilts emphasized thin rounded bars instead of the wide straps of Glasgow (see 121.SS). John Allan developed the Stirling pattern, and his older son, Walter Allan, increased its popularity. Notice the typical Allan-style round section bars plus scalloped plates pierced by grouped holes and arrowheads. The guard's upper arms tuck into a shallow groove under the domed pommel. Its wide   quillon measures 2-1/8 inches across, while the double-edged straight blade has three fullers.

Length: 39-1/8"      Blade: 33" X 1-1/4"      Hilt: Iron

**Author's Collection**

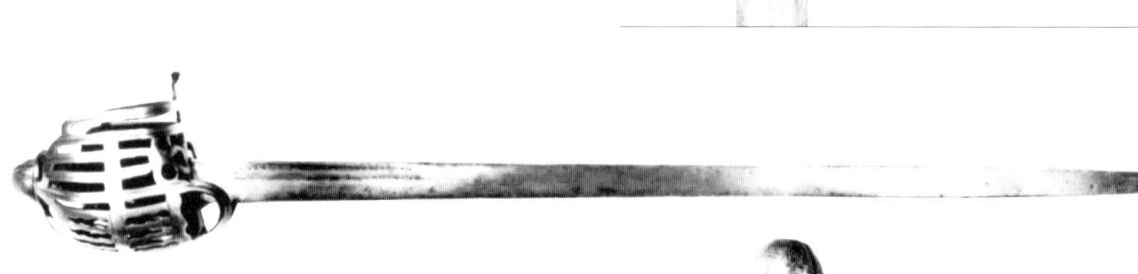

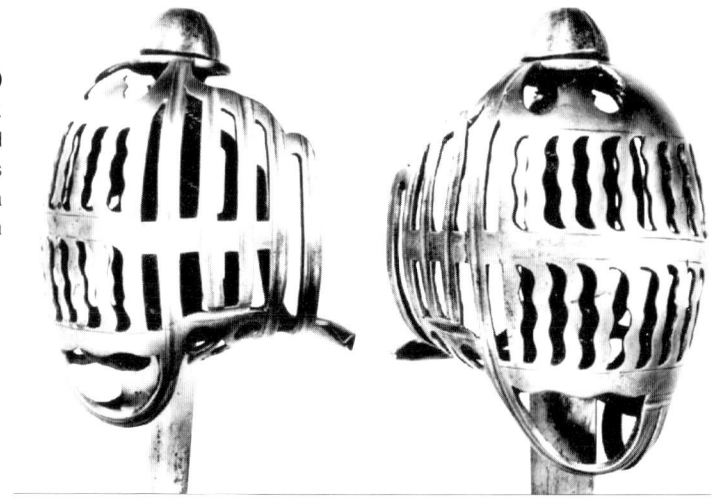

**123.SS  SCOTCH BACKSWORD**     Circa 1732–1759

Walter Allan of Stirling is considered by many the greatest Scottish hilt maker. His work contained impressive innovations, and this inexpensive officer's sword appears to be a copy of one of his forms. Note the use of parallel pierced openings to create a distinctive pattern. The three segment tips, in turn, are joined to a ring just below the domed pommel. Its imported Germanic blade is marked "Andria Farara" and has one edge ground flat to create a later backsword.

Length: 39-1/8"      Blade: 33-1/2" X 1-1/4"      Hilt: Iron

**George C. Neumann Collection, Valley Forge National Historical Park**

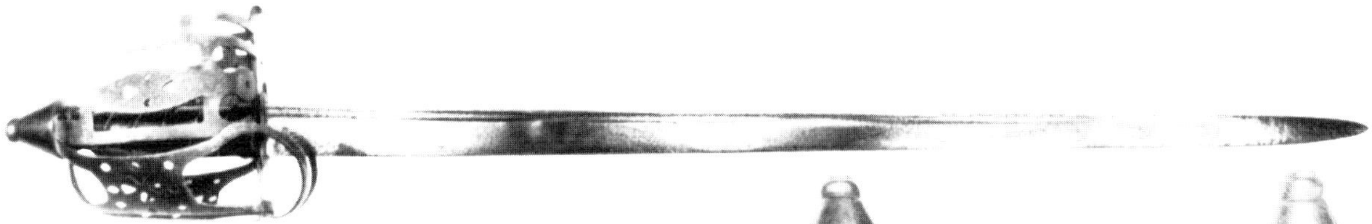

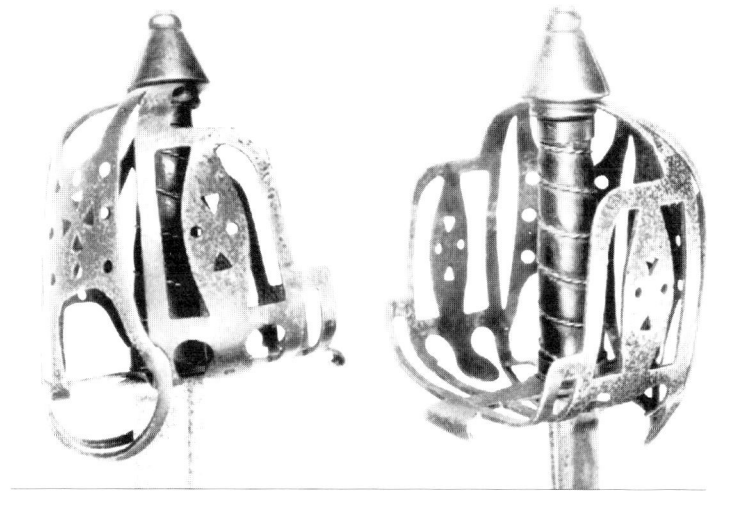

### 124.SS  SCOTTISH INFANTRY BACKSWORD    Circa 1757
In the middle 1700s, the English began issuing this inexpensive basket-hilted backsword to their Highland enlisted men, who carried them here in the French and Indian War. Although based on the traditional Scottish pattern, the hilts and blades were cheaply made in Birmingham by the two contractors Drury and Jefferies. Observe the familiar features in thin sheet iron, plus the distinctive conical pommel with its lower groove for the segment tips. The usual maker's blade stamp has been removed here.

Length: 35"   Blade: 28-5/8" X 1-1/4"   Hilt: Iron
**Author's Collection**

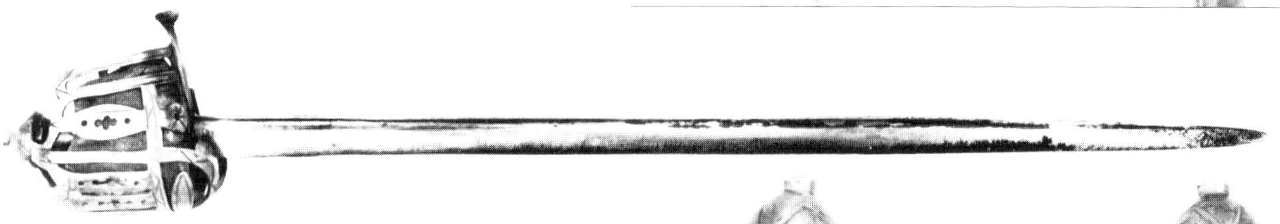

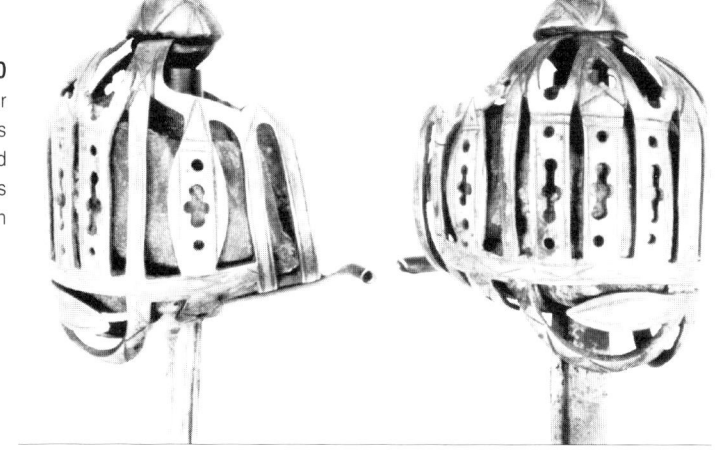

### 125.SS  SCOTTISH INFANTRY BACKSWORD    Circa 1760–1790
This military hilt style was popular with officers of the Highland regiments. Similar to designs by John Allan, Jr. during the 1740s, it includes a series of side plates that repeat pierced dot and slotted designs. The segment tips, in turn, extend into a slot circling the pommel's base. Of further interest are its special panels inside the arms of the hilt, plus a typical wide rolled quillon. Note also the British emphasis on a single-edged straight backsword blade.

Length: 36-3/4"   Blade: 31" X 1-1/8"   Hilt: Iron
**George C. Neumann Collection, Valley Forge National Historical Park**

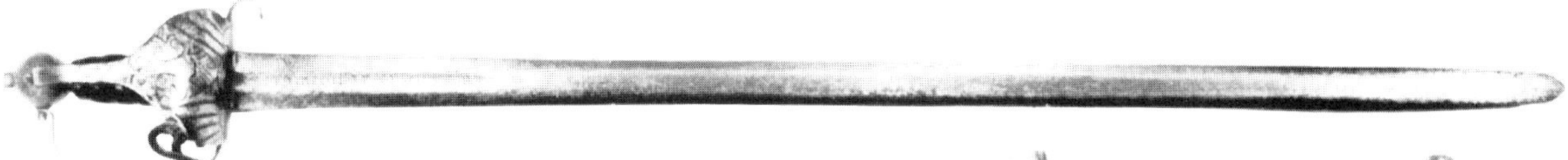

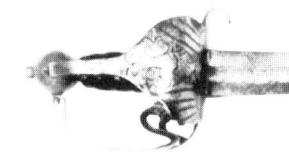

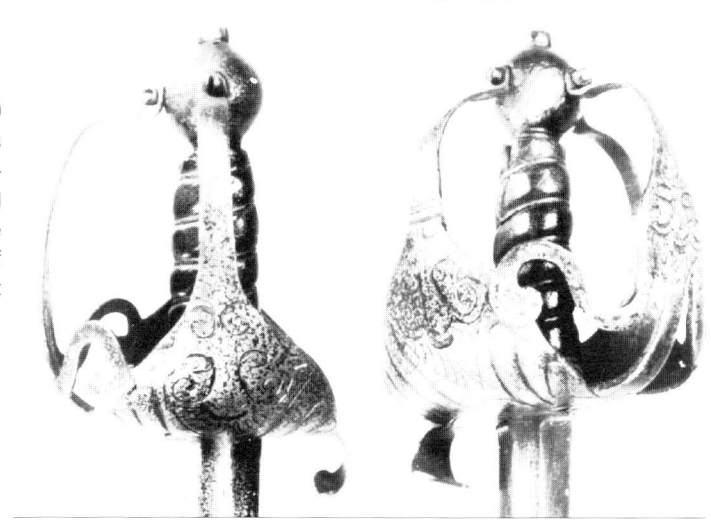

### 126.SS  ENGLISH HORSEMAN BROADSWORD    Circa 1630–1650
As the basket hilt gained favor with British horsemen during the 1600s, this "mortuary" form emerged and was used by both sides in their Civil War (1642–1648). A large ovoid pommel secures the guard segments by screws. Scrolled side branches, in turn, join the guard sections to create a semi-basket, while incised lines trace vague face figures (claimed to be the death mask of Charles I). Its early double-edged straight German blade is marked "Me Fecit Solingen." The hilt is rewrapped.

Length: 40"   Blade: 34" X 1-1/2"   Hilt: Iron
**George C. Neumann Collection, Valley Forge National Historical Park**

*Chapter 7: Swords*

**127.SS  ENGLISH HORSEMAN SABER            Circa 1750**
The British officially adopted the Scottish-type basket hilt for their dragoons circa 1707. By 1750 they had modified most of these arms with a flattened ovoid pommel above a ring joining the segment tips, plus an inboard oval opening that allowed both the sword and horse's reins to be controlled by one hand—freeing the other for a pistol or salute. The straight blade is now long and single-edged to deliver a primary thrusting rather than a cutting stroke (two fullers at the back).
Length: 38-1/2"      Blade: 32-3/4" X 1-1/2"      Hilt: Iron
**Author's Collection**

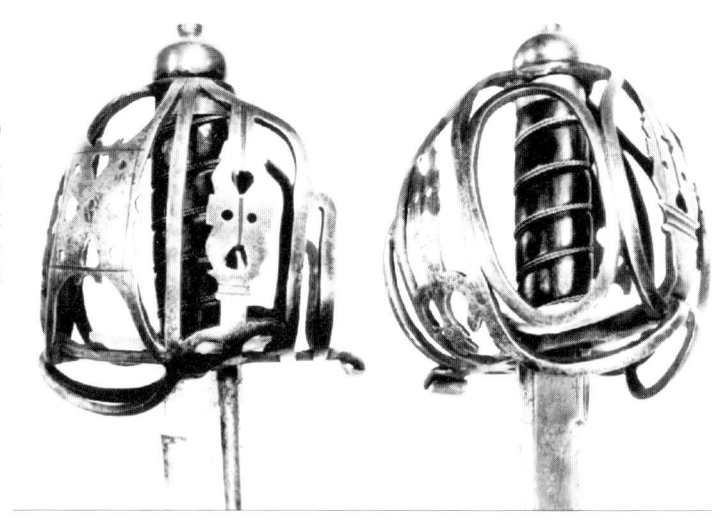

**128.SS  ENGLISH HORSEMAN SABER            Circa 1750–1770**
Although the basic British dragoon swords with long straight blades prevailed at this time, individual units varied their hilt designs. Note the innovative form here, for example; it has injected curving fish and serpents, as well as a series of shell patterns. However the established ovoid pommel, segment tip ring and inboard oval "reins" opening remain. Shagreen covers the grip. An early double-edged blade (probably reused) is marked "ANDRIA FERARA" (three center fullers).
Length: 39-1/2"      Blade: 33-1/4" X 1-1/4"      Hilt: Iron
**George C. Neumann Collection, Valley Forge National Historical Park**

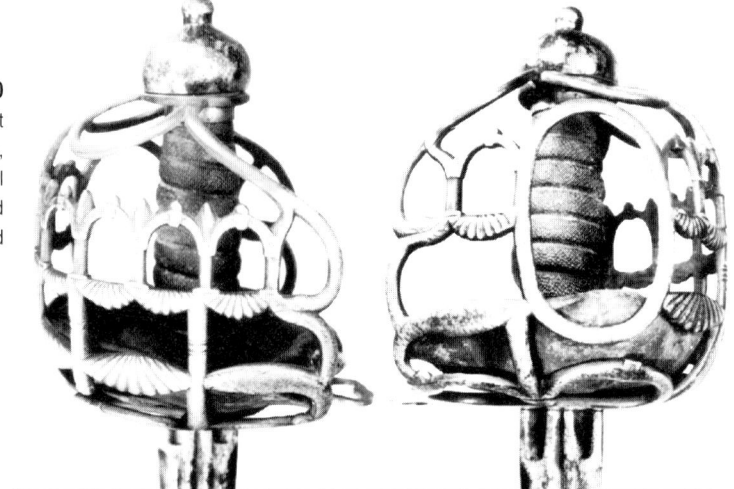

**129.SS  ENGLISH HORSEMAN SABER            Circa 1750**
A few British dragoon swords were mounted in brass. Although double panel S-hilts in iron were employed on grenadier hangers (21.SS), a third S-section was added here to create this three quarter basket. Observe the typical ovoid pommel, shagreen-covered grip and straight single-edged blade. A quillon is omitted, but the open guard expands at its front corners to protect the hand. Marks: "K/3=N=27" (King's Own Dragoons) on pommel; Solingen's "anchor" in the blade.
Length: 40"      Blade: 33-3/4" X 1-3/8"      Hilt: Brass
**Richard Ulbrich Collection**

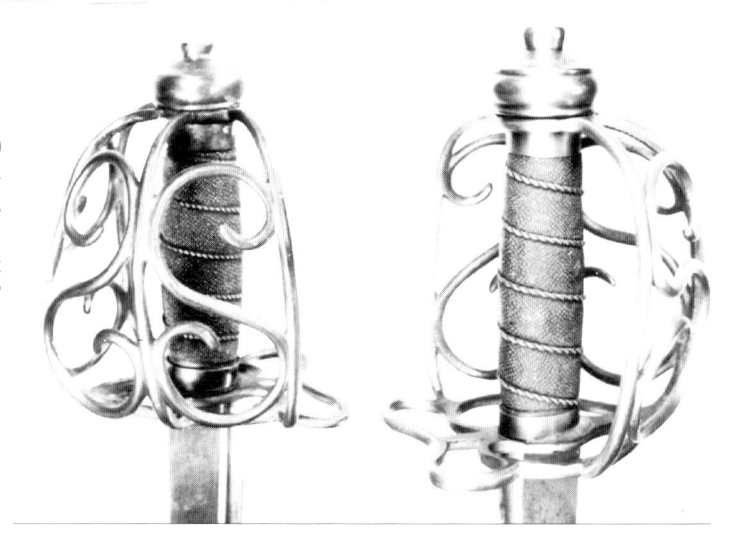

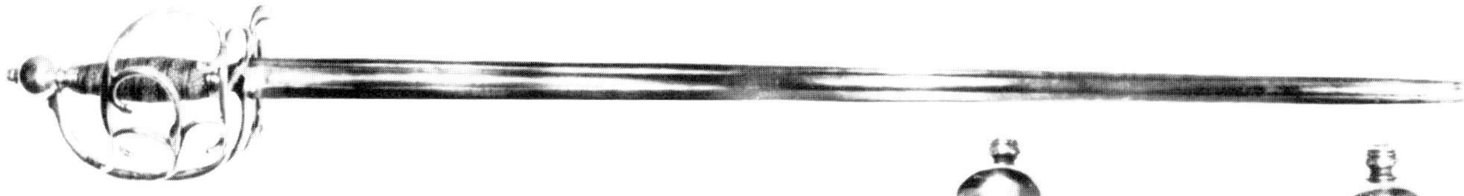

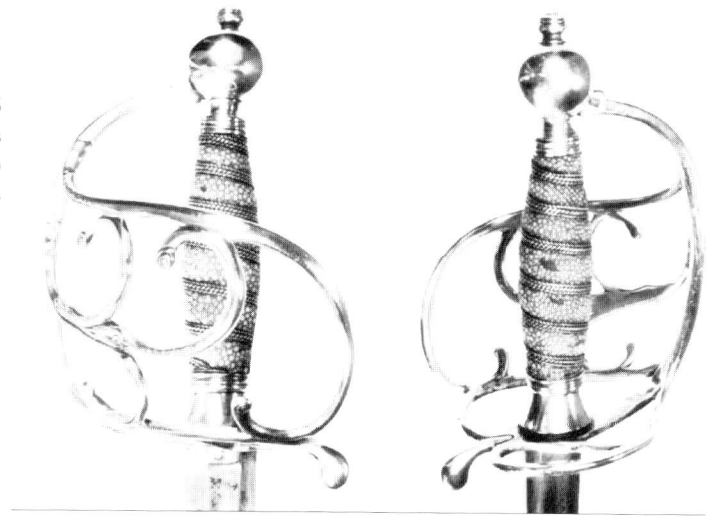

### 130.SS  ENGLISH HORSEMAN SWORD  Circa 1755
With the resources and freedom to select their own weapons, many officers indulged in innovative patterns. This impressive silver semi-basket includes two graceful side branches that expand into four scrolled terminals. Although its hallmarks are 1755 (see stamps on upper knuckle bow), the open heart guard, lobed quillon and ball pommel are more typical of the second quarter. Shagreen (fishskin) and three silver wire ropes cover the grip, above a straight single-edged blade.

Length: 38-1/2"        Blade: 32-3/8" X 1"        Hilt: Silver

**Erik Goldstein Collection**

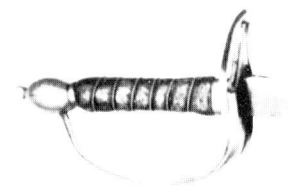

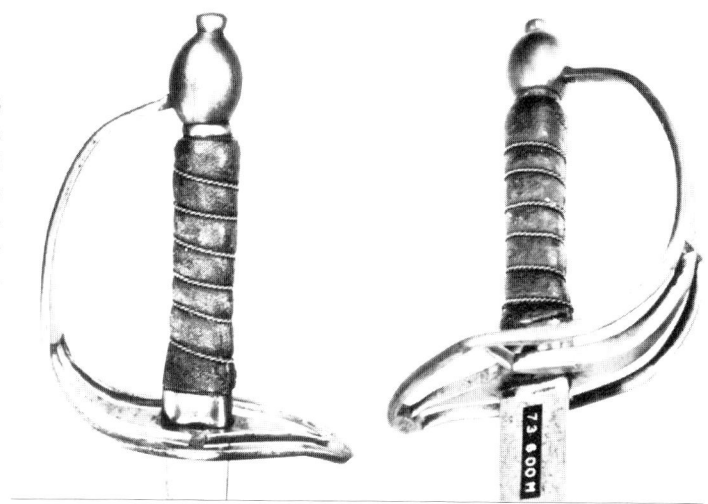

### 131.SS  ENGLISH LIGHT HORSEMAN SABER  Circa 1760–1788
In 1756 new light horse troops were added to the "heavy" dragoon regiments as a test. When it was successful, full light dragoon regiments were authorized during 1759. Their sword specifications lengthened the blade (not always followed) to 37 inches ("crooked or straight"). Note this example's high olive pommel and capstan, plus a sturdy D-type iron guard having the popular four slots and blunted end. "Crown / GR / IEFRIS" (Jefferys, London) is on the single-edged blade.

Length: 45-1/8"        Blade: 37-1/8" X 1-5/16"        Hilt: Iron

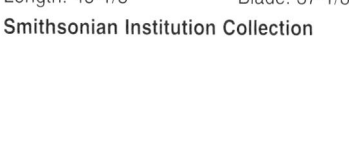

**Smithsonian Institution Collection**

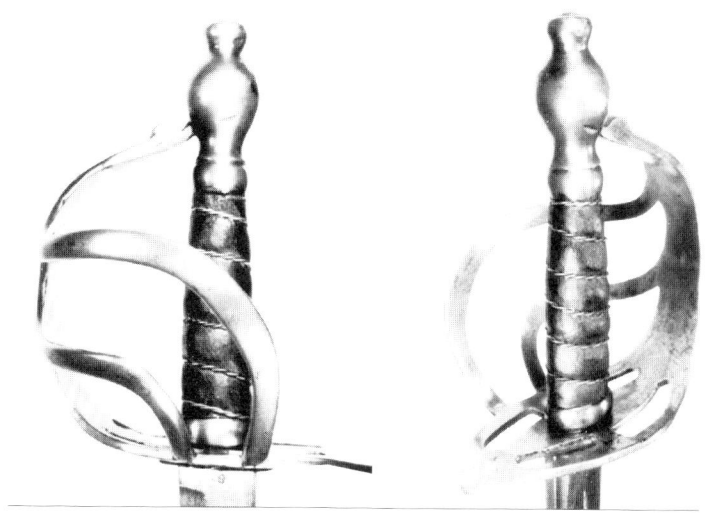

### 132.SS  ENGLISH LIGHT HORSEMAN SABER  Circa 1760–1788
Despite growing similarity in weapons between regiments, differences still existed, as seen here (versus 131.SS). The leather-wrapped grip and four-slot guard continue, but two side branches have been added and the pommel form is less defined. Its typical long straight single-edged blade, in turn, has two fullers–1/4" X 25-1/2" at the back, plus 1/2" X 34-3/4" in the center. Its ricasso is stamped "crown / 9" (a viewer's or inspector's mark with his identifying number).

Length: 42-3/4"        Blade: 36-1/8" X 1-1/4"        Hilt: Iron

**Author's Collection**

*Chapter 7: Swords*  347

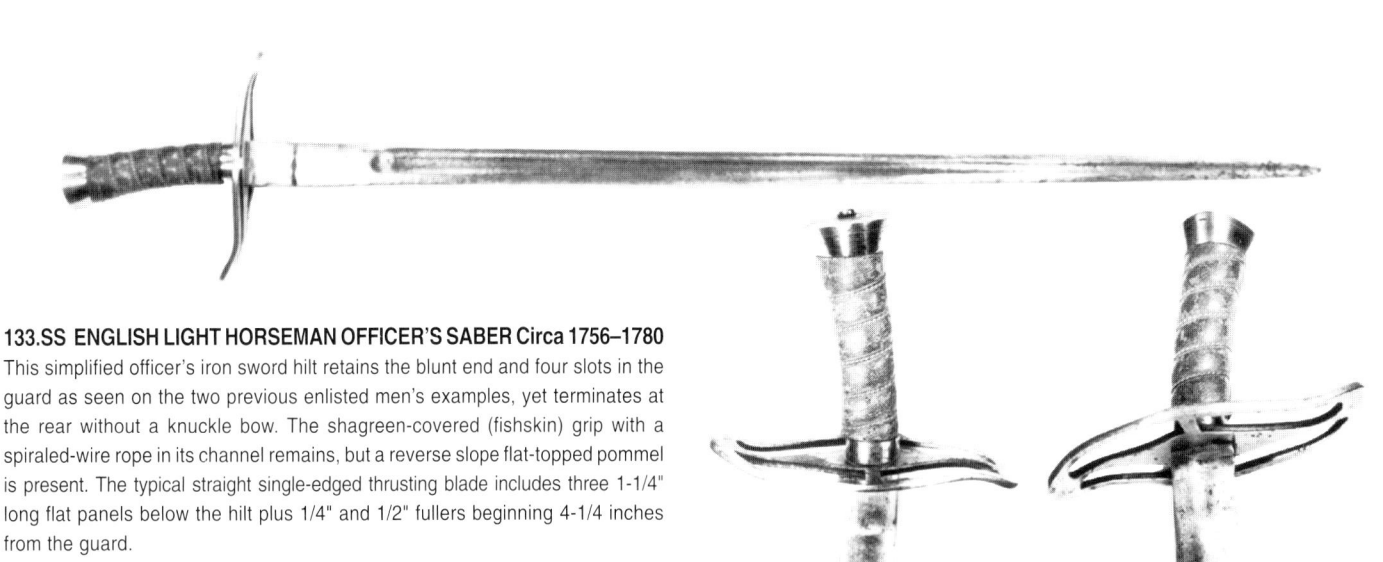

**133.SS ENGLISH LIGHT HORSEMAN OFFICER'S SABER Circa 1756–1780**
This simplified officer's iron sword hilt retains the blunt end and four slots in the guard as seen on the two previous enlisted men's examples, yet terminates at the rear without a knuckle bow. The shagreen-covered (fishskin) grip with a spiraled-wire rope in its channel remains, but a reverse slope flat-topped pommel is present. The typical straight single-edged thrusting blade includes three 1-1/4" long flat panels below the hilt plus 1/4" and 1/2" fullers beginning 4-1/4 inches from the guard.
Length: 41-1/2"    Blade: 35-3/4" X 1-3/8"    Hilt: Iron
**Don Troiani Collection**

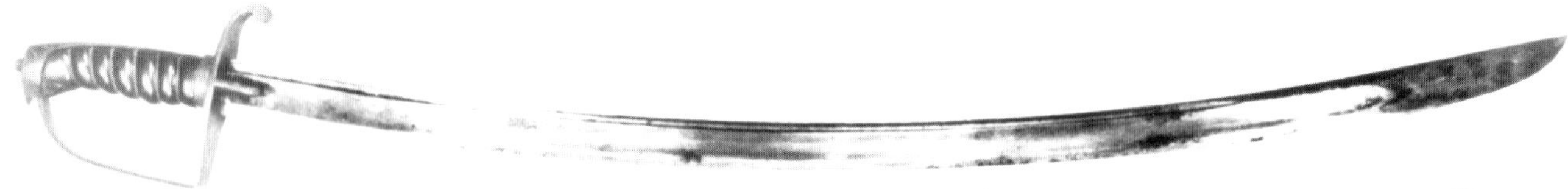

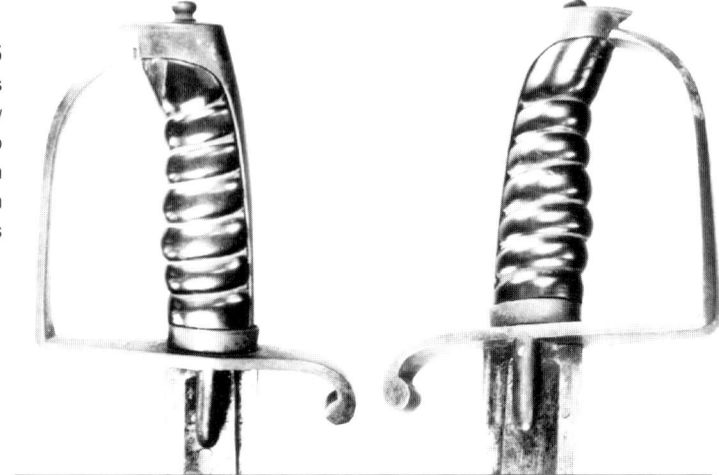

**134.SS FRENCH HUSSAR SABER    Circa 1765–1785**
Beginning in the 1750s, much of Europe adopted the lavish uniforms and weapons of the Hungarian Hussars. These spectacular light cavalrymen employed a new saber with a simple iron stirrup hilt having a backstrap, flat pommel, ribbed grip and curved single-edged blade (two fullers here). A langet (as shown) was often included. Among such new French units was Lauzon's Legion, which served in America's Revolution under Rochambeau—wearing the new hussar uniforms and probably using these saber patterns.
Length: 41-1/2"    Blade: 36" X 1-1/2"    Hilt: Iron
**George C. Neumann Collection, Valley Forge National Historical Park**

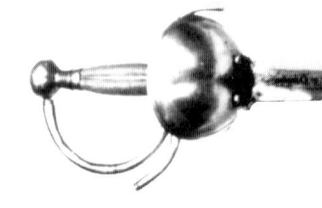

**135.SS SPANISH BROADSWORD    Circa 1750**
A distinctive broadsword pattern was developed in Spain during the late 1600s. Known as the "bilbo" today, it persisted until the mid-1800s. Observe this circa-1750 version's sturdy round knuckle bow (not attached to the pommel) that leads to double curving quillons and large rounded arms inside two deeply cupped guards (held by four screws). Twisted ropes of fine copper wire cover the grip. Its long two-edged straight blade has a center panel marked "AYZIVILLA" and "L."
Length: 41-3/4"    Blade: 34-3/4" X 1-1/2"    Hilt: Iron
**George C. Neumann Collection, Valley Forge National Historical Park**

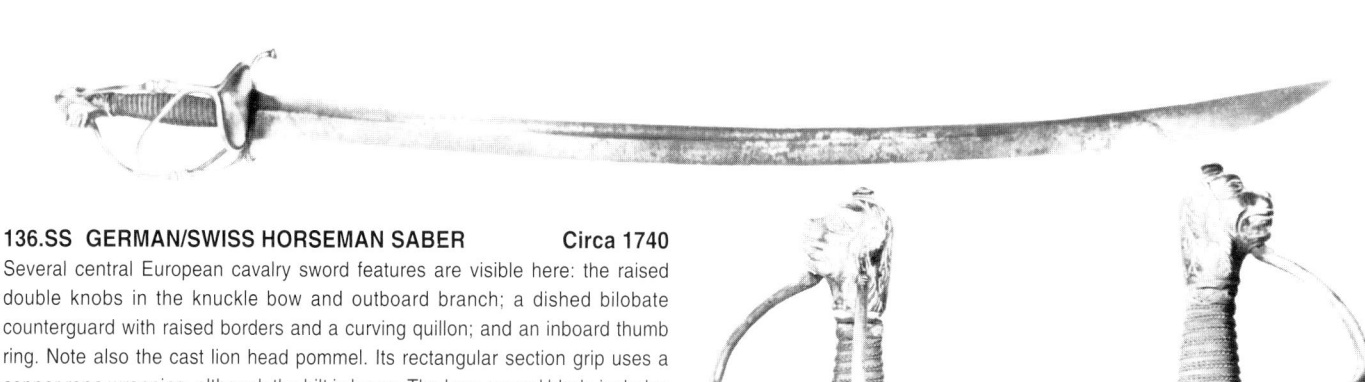

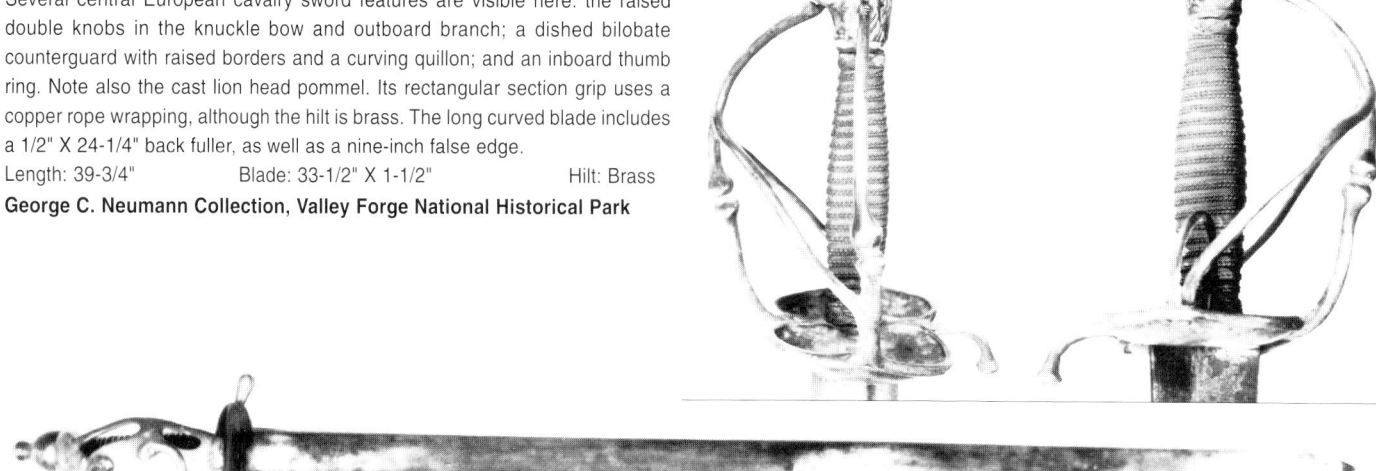

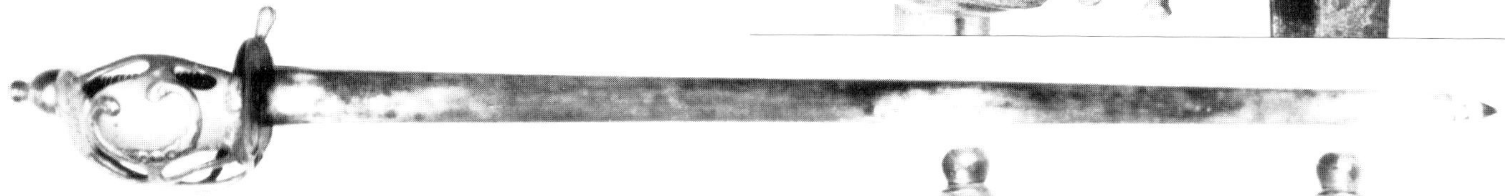

### 136.SS  GERMAN/SWISS HORSEMAN SABER    Circa 1740
Several central European cavalry sword features are visible here: the raised double knobs in the knuckle bow and outboard branch; a dished bilobate counterguard with raised borders and a curving quillon; and an inboard thumb ring. Note also the cast lion head pommel. Its rectangular section grip uses a copper rope wrapping, although the hilt is brass. The long curved blade includes a 1/2" X 24-1/4" back fuller, as well as a nine-inch false edge.

Length: 39-3/4"    Blade: 33-1/2" X 1-1/2"    Hilt: Brass

**George C. Neumann Collection, Valley Forge National Historical Park**

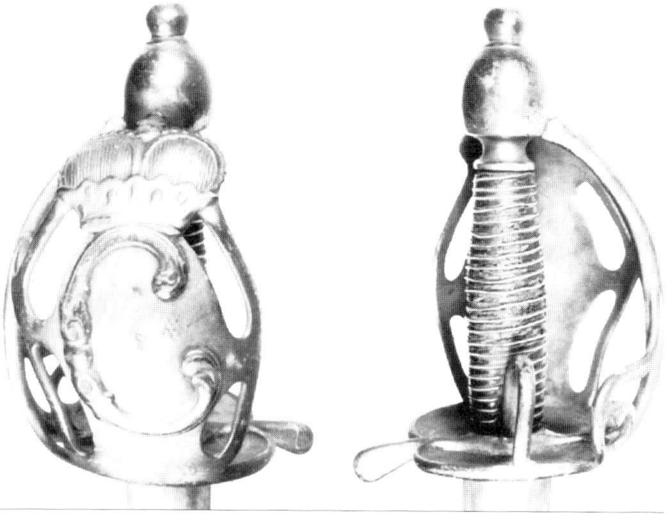

### 137.SS  BRUNSWICK DRAGOON SWORD    Circa 1750–1777
Prussian weapons served as patterns for many German states. Their Model 1732 Cuirassier broadsword, for example, was adopted for the Brunswick mercenaries by replacing the outer cast brass Prussian eagle panel with one showing a crown above "C" for Duke Charles I of Brunswick. This sword was recovered from the Bennington (Vermont) Battlefield (1777). Note the bilobate guard, thumb ring, single brass wire on the leather grip and double-edged convex blade (single edge in 1797).

Length: 43-1/4"    Blade: 36-1/4" X 1-1/2"    Hilt: Brass

**Commonwealth of Massachusetts Archives**

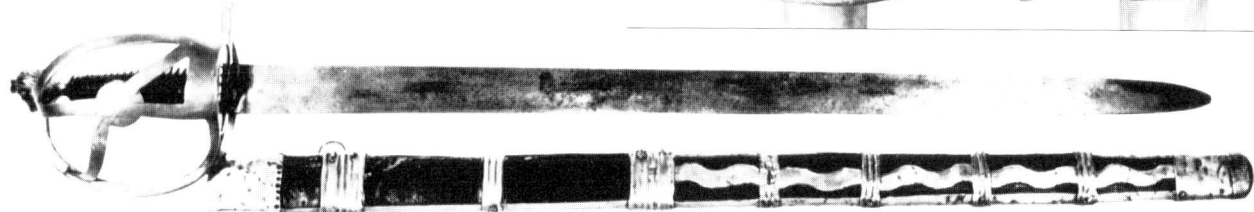

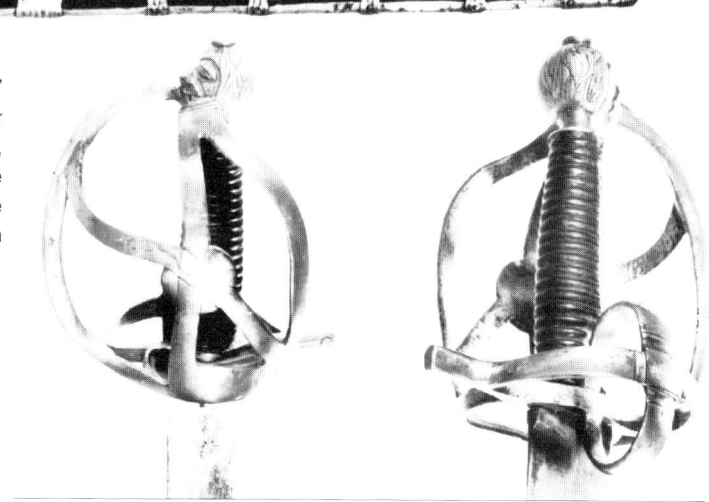

### 138.SS  GERMAN HORSEMAN BROADSWORD    Circa 1737–1797
Prussia's Model 1735 dragoon sword also served as a basic design for other German states. Notice its distinctive two branches crossing at a rounded junction, the solid paneled outboard guard, an open inboard bar and thumb ring, plus the lion pommel (usually a Prussian eagle). A single brass wire originally filled the leather grip's channels. This typical double-edged convex-faced blade has been shortened from about 37 inches.

Length: 43"    Blade: 33-3/4" X 1-5/8"    Hilt: Brass

**West Point Museum Collection**

*Chapter 7: Swords*

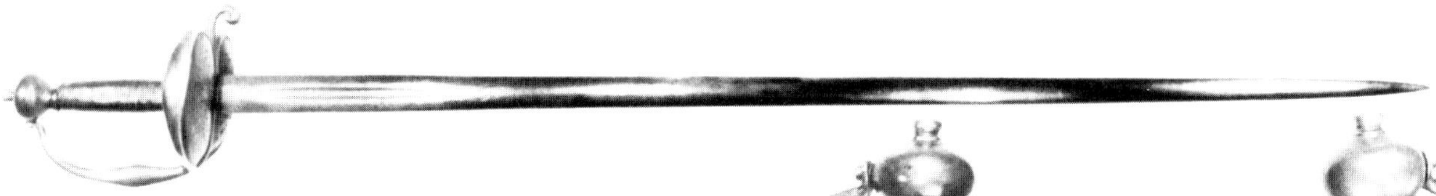

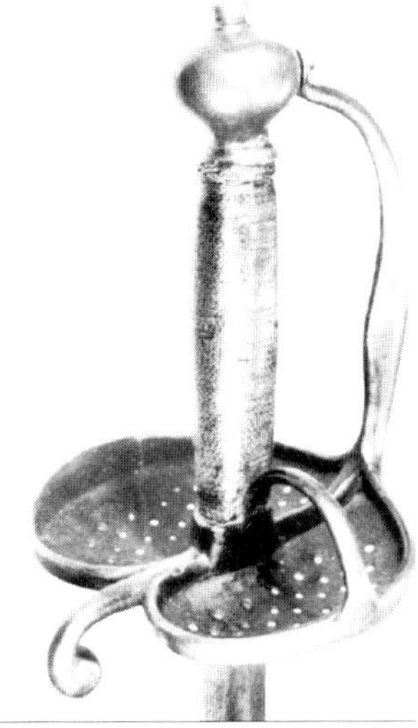

**139.SS EUROPEAN HORSEMAN BROADSWORD  Circa 1650–1690**
This famous "Walloon" pattern emerged from the 30 Years War (1616–1648) and saw service across northern Europe. Note the distinctive wide ovoid pommel, deep sunken pierced panels in a heart-shaped counterguard, curled quillon, inboard thumb ring and screw attaching the upper knuckle bow. Its wooden grip is covered by dual iron wire ropes and two turks-head ferrules. The straight double-edged blade, in turn, bears the running wolf mark plus "1414" (a mystical "cabalistic" number).

Length: 40-1/8"        Blade: 34-1/4" X 1"        Hilt: Iron
**Author's Collection**

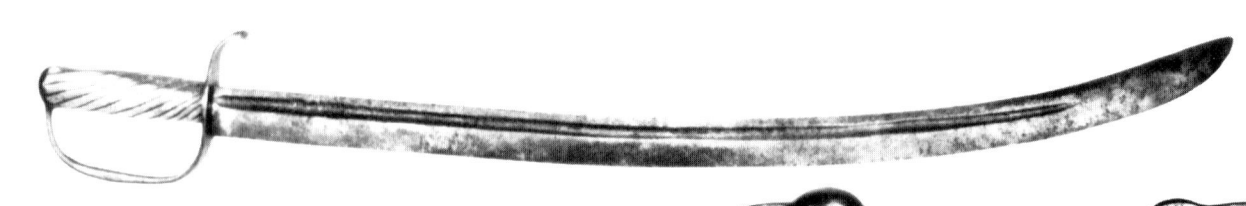

**140.SS  AMERICAN HORSEMAN SABER        Circa 1750–1780**
American mounted troops carried an array of European, local and mixed component swords. Horse units were attached to many provincial militia regiments but participated in the Revolution usually as limited groups or "legions" (combined with light infantry). This weapon is entirely of American manufacture. Observe its spiraled bone grip (old red paint remaining), D-shaped knuckle bow/guard, and common American blade form that accelerates its curve one third of the distance from its tip.

Length: 35-5/8"        Blade: 30-5/8" X 1-3/8"        Hilt: Iron
**Author's Collection**

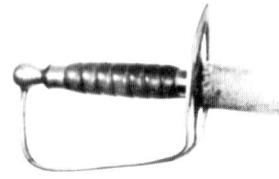

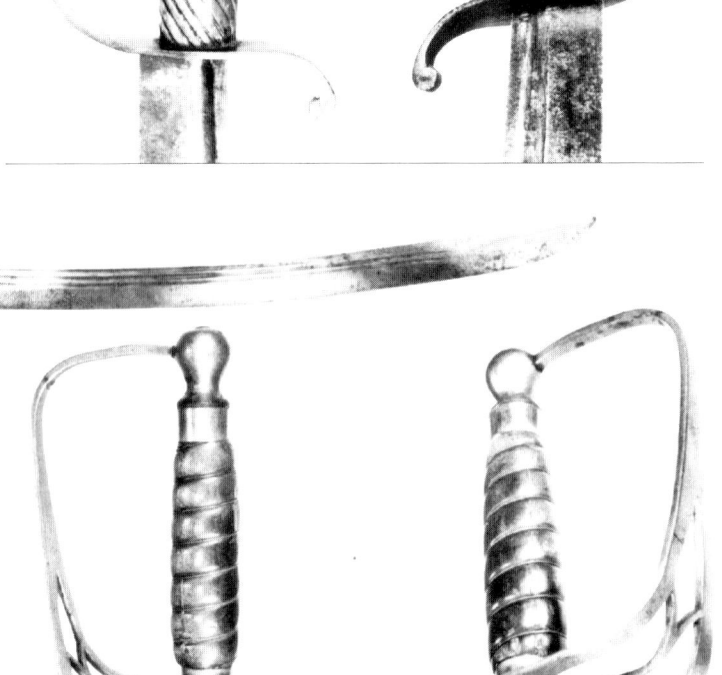

**141.SS  AMERICAN HORSEMAN SABER        Circa 1770–1785**
New England militia regiments frequently included horse troops. Their sabers varied but usually mounted European blades (mostly the Spanish three-fuller form seen here) plus a bare wooden grip, sheet-brass guard and a simple cast pommel—combined with a touch of local artistry. This example hooks the upper end of a flat brass knuckle bow into the top half of an ovoid pommel and adds geometric openings in the guard, as well as a spiraled cherry hilt in plain 1/2" ferrules.

Length: 37"        Blade: 31-1/2" X 1-3/8"        Hilt: Brass
**Author's Collection**

350    *Chapter 7: Swords*

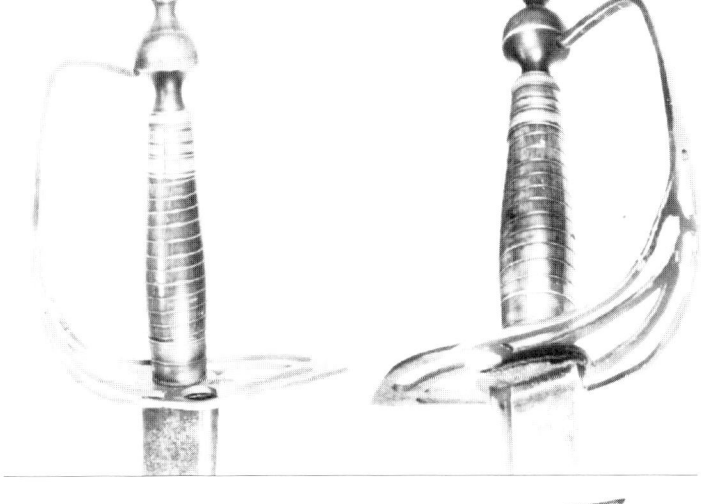

**142.SS  AMERICAN HORSEMAN SABER**     Circa 1770–1785
An input of homespun creativeness is evident here. Its flat sheet-brass guard spreads at the bottom to permit open geometric panels and ends at a center point—in familiar fashion. But a unique cast mushroom pommel with a tall shouldered capstan is combined with a channeled cherry grip (never covered); it is secured between two high ferrules that include decorative rings. The curved single-edged blade has a single back fuller and is blued for 14-1/4 inches below the hilt (common).
Length: 32-3/4"        Blade: 26-3/8" X 1-1/4"        Hilt: Brass
**Richard Ulbrich Collection**

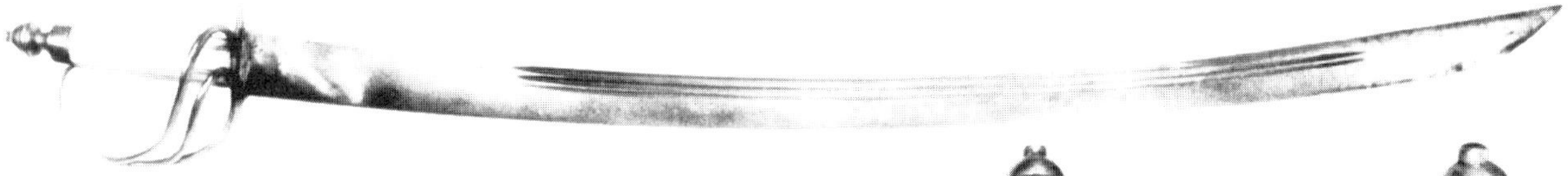

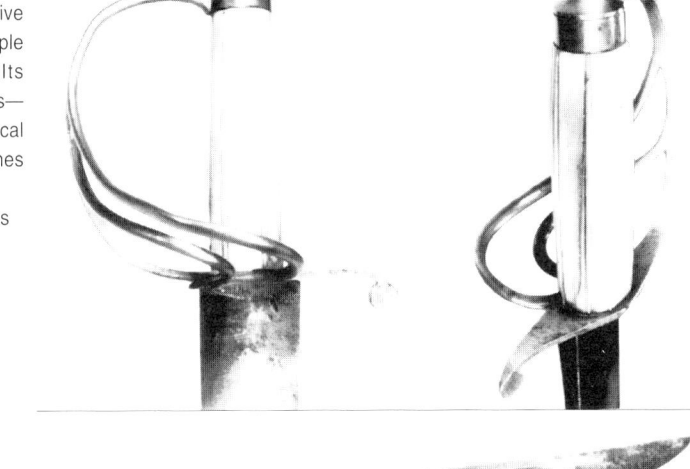

**143.SS  AMERICAN HORSEMAN SABER**     Circa 1778–1785
This further variation of the mushroom cap pommel displays a raised decorative ring and rises above a wide band that anchors the knuckle bow. The simple counterguard adds two curving side branches and a disk quillon. Its impressive polished bone grip is formed by vertical flat and rounded panels—which began to gain acceptance during the Revolution's second half. The typical Spanish blade, in turn, has three 1/4" parallel fullers beginning 6-1/2 inches below the hilt.
Length: 38-3/8"        Blade: 33" X 1-1/2"        Hilt: Brass
**Author's Collection**

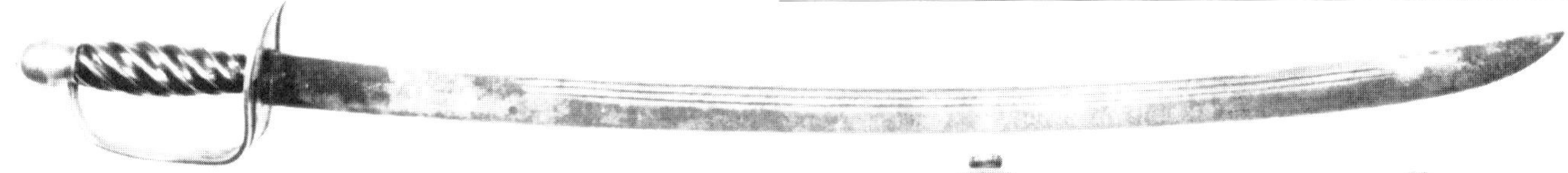

**144.SS  AMERICAN HORSEMAN SABER  Circa 1770–1785**
A subdued mushroom pommel and shaped wooden grip with 1/16" inlaid brass strips tracing its raised ridges contribute a special dignity to this saber. Incised lines also ring the upper cap and neck. Moreover the sheet-brass guard continues the contemporary American preference for pierced geometric designs. These curved single-edged imported Spanish blades with their three 1/4" fullers are believed to have been obtained mostly through the West Indies.
Length: 40-3/8"        Blade: 34-1/8" X 1-3/8"        Hilt: Brass
**Author's Collection**

*Chapter 7: Swords*

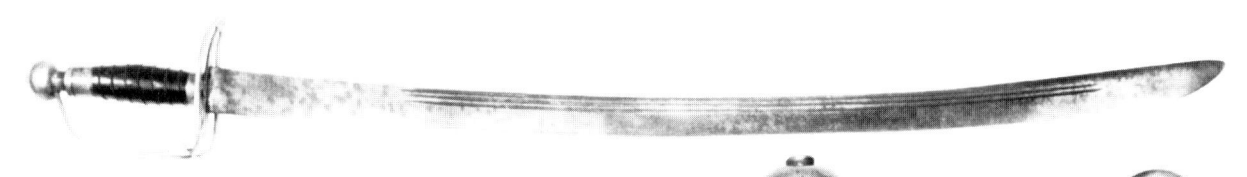

### 145.SS  AMERICAN HORSEMAN SABER    Circa 1770–1785
This hilt combines the typical New England flat sheet-brass guard, bared wooden grip and three-fullered blade. Yet it is more sturdy than most. Note the flattened ovoid cast pommel with disk-like capstan, the substantial whittled cherry grip that includes a single twisted wire in its narrow groove, and two plain but high ferrules (5/8", 1/2"). The guard's open panels above the three-fuller blade also add a spear-like window in the knuckle bow.

Length: 40"   Blade: 34-1/4" X 1-3/8"   Hilt: Brass

**Author's Collection**

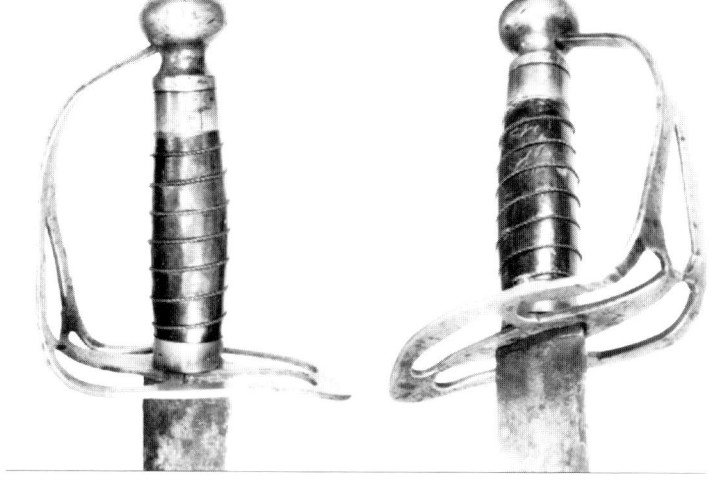

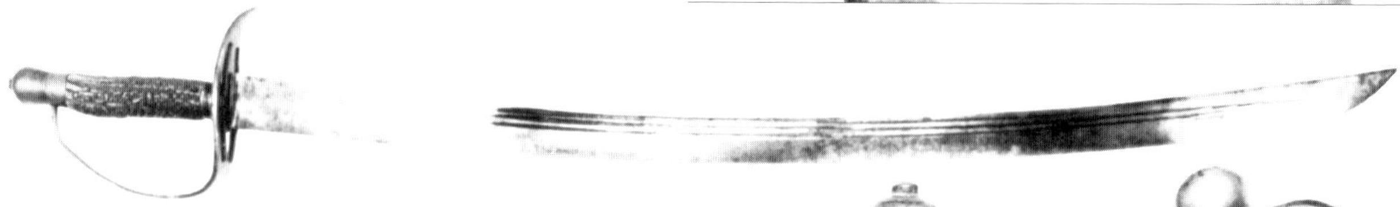

### 146.SS  AMERICAN HORSEMAN SABER    Circa 1775–1785
One of the popular sword grip variations was antler or staghorn—especially on hunting swords, cutlasses and even American horseman sabers as in this case. It was readily available, hard wearing and did not deteriorate in exposed conditions. The example here adds a domed pommel, wide ferrules and a conservative sheet-brass guard including only four openings. The ubiquitous Spanish three-fuller blade is again present—-with bluing on its upper 11-3/8 inches (common).

Length: 39"   Blade: 33" X 1-3/8"   Hilt: Brass

**Author's Collection**

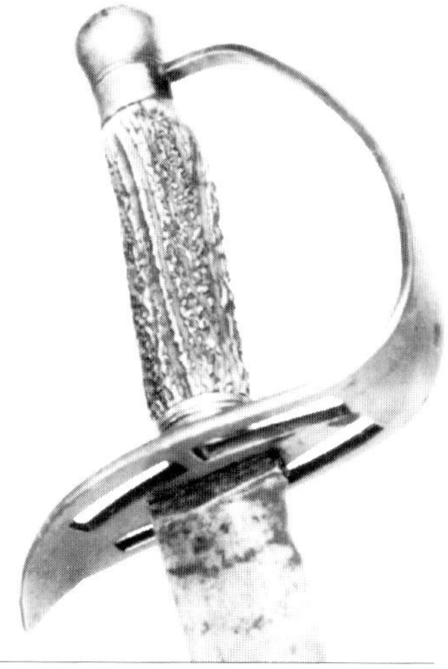

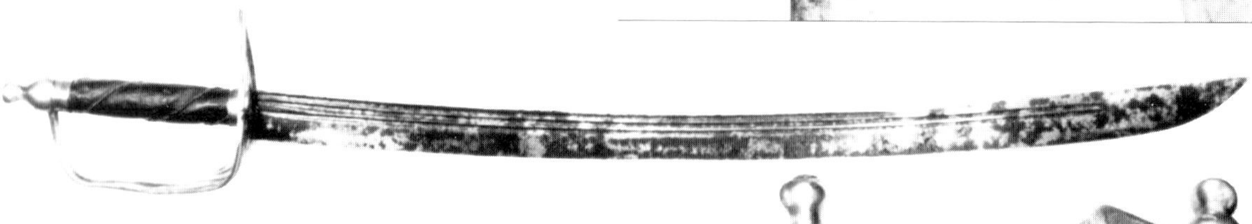

### 147.SS  AMERICAN HORSEMAN SABER    Circa 1760–1780
An American provincial chose to cast this rather intricate brass guard, which is obviously not of European styling. A subdued pommel with an exaggerated capstan rests above the leather-wrapped and spiraled wooden grip. Its multi-segmented guard ends in the popular center-pointed quillon; also note that the three-fuller blade was shortened at one time. The surviving leather scabbard retains brass mountings plus multiple X-incised decorative patterns.

Length: 34-1/2"   Blade: 28" X 1-3/8"   Hilt: Brass

**Author's Collection**

*Chapter 7: Swords*

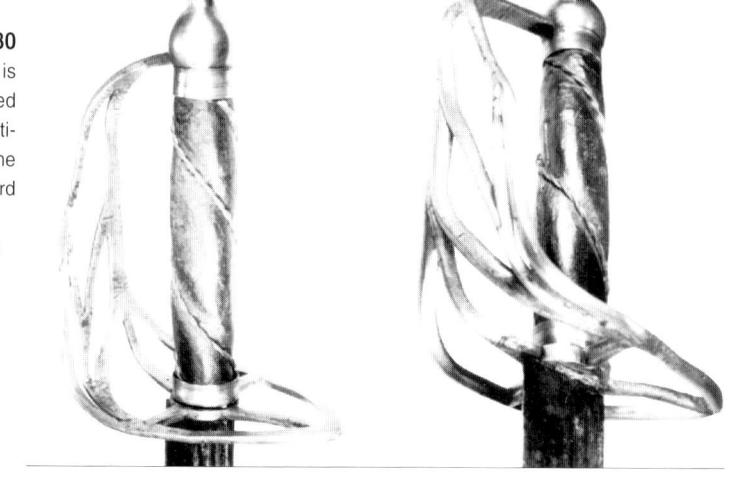

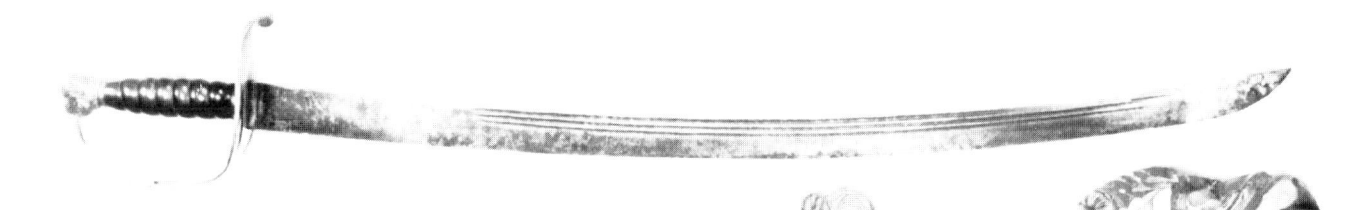

**148.SS  AMERICAN HORSEMAN SABER          Circa 1770–1785**
Following Europe's practice some Colonists added animal and bird heads as sword pommels. This crude American brass lion was cast in two vertical side halves. The ribbed wooden grip (never covered) sits in a 3/8" plain ferrule, while a guard of sheet brass hooks into the lion's mouth and terminates in a disk quillon at the other end. Its counterguard has only two side openings plus one in the knuckle bow. The usual three-fullered blade includes a 1/8" ricasso under the hilt.
Length: 38-1/2"          Blade: 33-1/4" X 1-1/2"          Hilt: Brass
**Author's Collection**

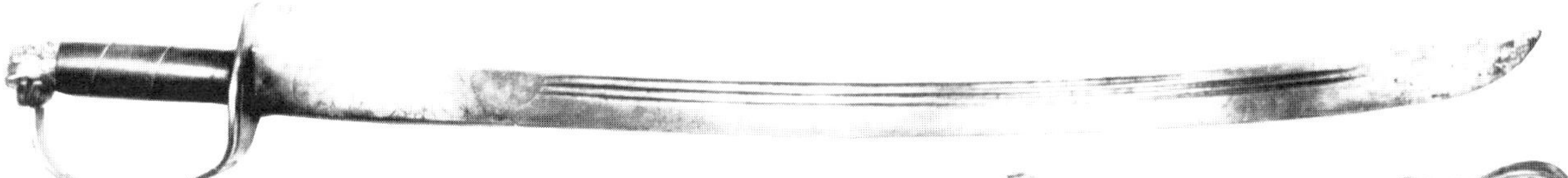

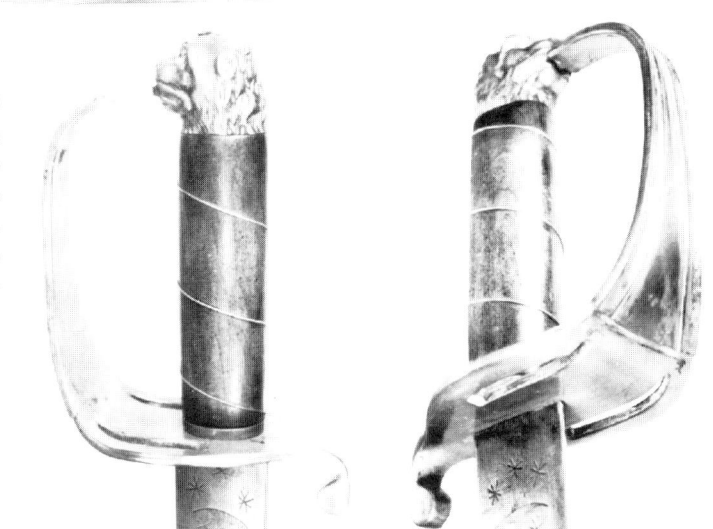

**149.SS  AMERICAN HORSEMAN SABER          Circa 1770–1785**
A more articulate brass lion pommel was mounted here—in conjunction with a substantial cast guard that raises channeled borders in a panel on the wide knuckle bow and two narrow open side slots cut through the counterguard. A smooth near-cylindrical cherry grip holds a single spiraled wire in a narrow groove. The common three-fuller blade bears engraved European "moon / stars, sun, and cloud / arm figures"—originally mystical in meaning but now purely decorative.
Length: 36-3/4"          Blade: 31-1/8" X 1-3/8"          Hilt: Brass
**Author's Collection**

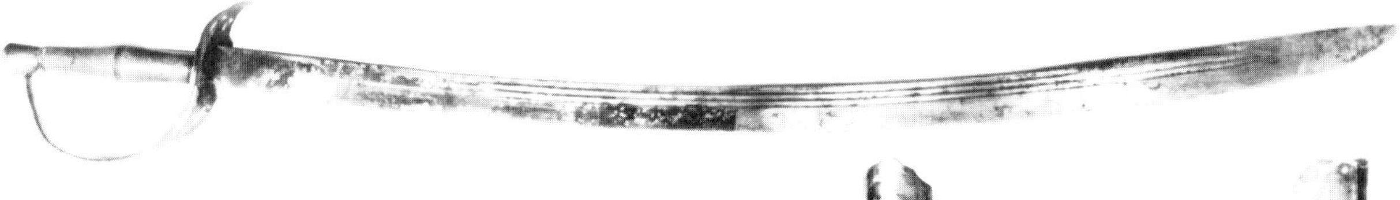

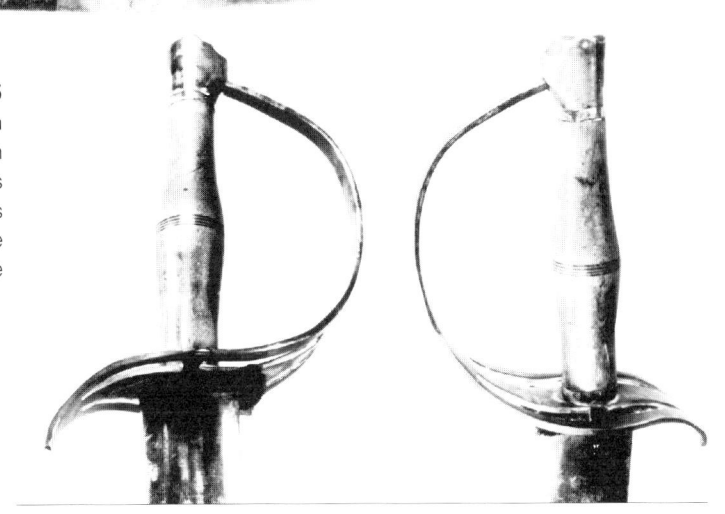

**150.SS  AMERICAN HORSEMAN SABER          Circa 1770–1785**
Another variation of the New England trooper's saber (often associated with New Hampshire) has this primitive pommel form with a rudimentary suggestion of an animal head. Also notice the well-proportioned maple grip including its raised center and effective four-line decoration. The broad brass guard displays the normal four side openings above the blade. A triple fullered Spanish blade retains an 8-1/2" false edge plus the original cloth cushion between it and the hilt.
Length: 38-1/2"          Blade: 33" X 1-1/2"          Hilt: Brass

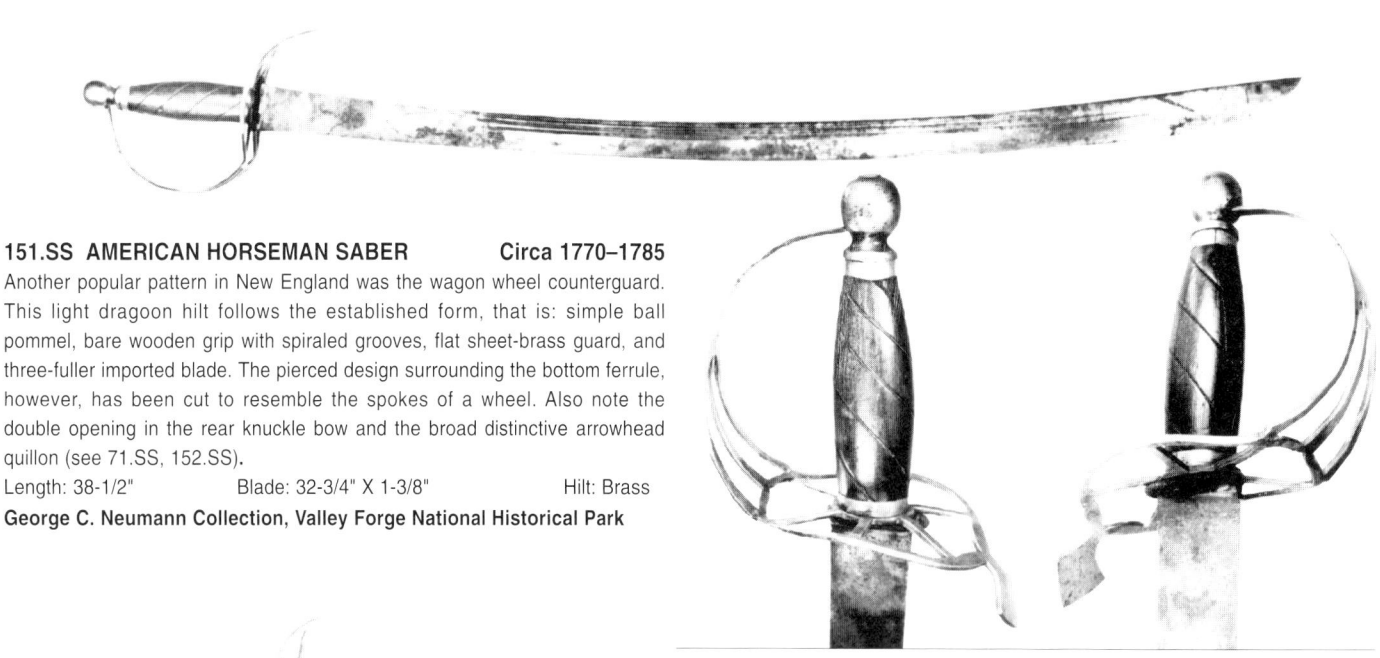

**151.SS AMERICAN HORSEMAN SABER    Circa 1770–1785**
Another popular pattern in New England was the wagon wheel counterguard. This light dragoon hilt follows the established form, that is: simple ball pommel, bare wooden grip with spiraled grooves, flat sheet-brass guard, and three-fuller imported blade. The pierced design surrounding the bottom ferrule, however, has been cut to resemble the spokes of a wheel. Also note the double opening in the rear knuckle bow and the broad distinctive arrowhead quillon (see 71.SS, 152.SS).
Length: 38-1/2"        Blade: 32-3/4" X 1-3/8"        Hilt: Brass
**George C. Neumann Collection, Valley Forge National Historical Park**

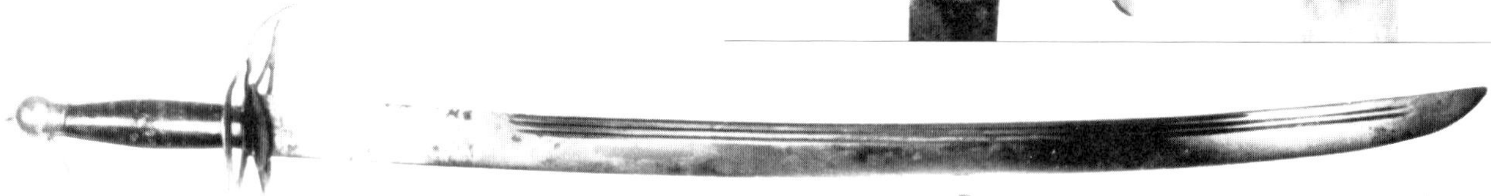

**152.SS AMERICAN HORSEMAN SABER    Circa 1775–1783**
The graceful proportions of the traditional American wagon wheel pattern seen in the previous illustration were often imitated, as pictured here on an iron-hilted saber. Note that the basic features are included—wheel-like guard openings, an arrowhead quillon, and paired knuckle bow piercings—but in more exaggerated and flamboyant proportions. Its ball pommel and capstan are a single piece; the smooth-faced wooden grip ends in two 1/4" brass ferrules.
Length: 36-1/2"        Blade: 30-3/4" X 1-1/2"        Hilt: Iron
**Tom Wnuck Collection**

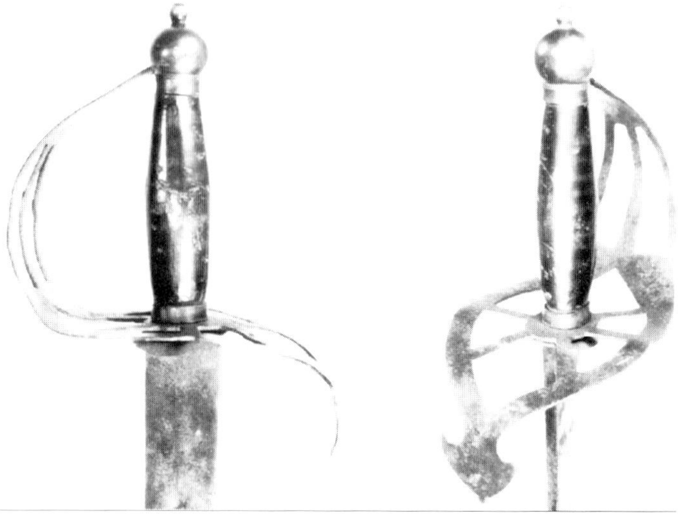

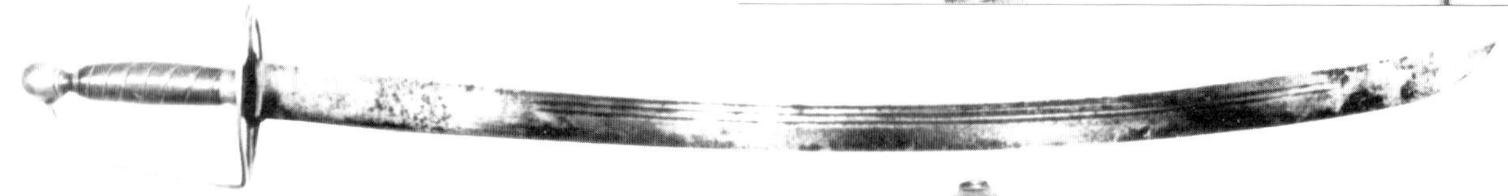

**153.SS AMERICAN HORSEMAN SABER    Circa 1770–1785**
Influence of the wagon wheel form is also found in other contemporary hilts. The one illustrated here has compressed the round guard into an oval, reduced its spokes to four and eliminated the arrowhead quillon. Yet vestiges of the basic configuration remain as part of a stirrup hilt profile. Note also the well-proportioned pommel with its top ridge and pedestal neck. As usual the blade is the three-fuller pattern having bluing covering 10-3/4 inches below the hilt.
Length: 38-7/8"        Blade: 32-7/8" X 1-3/8"        Hilt: Brass
**Author's Collection**

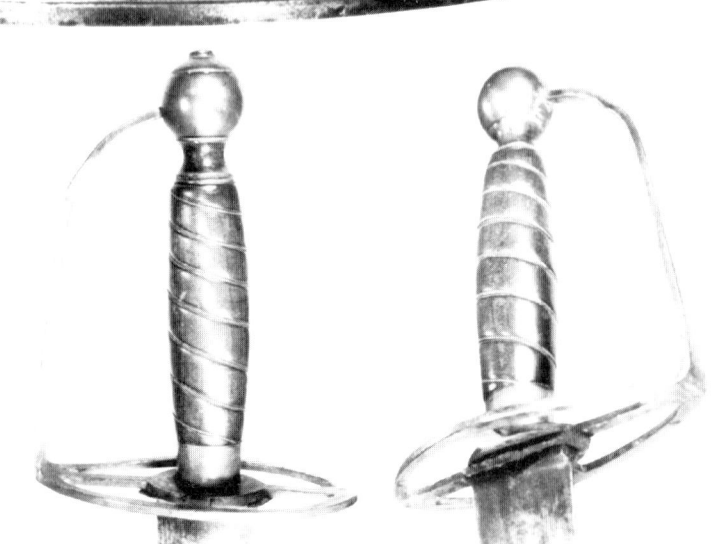

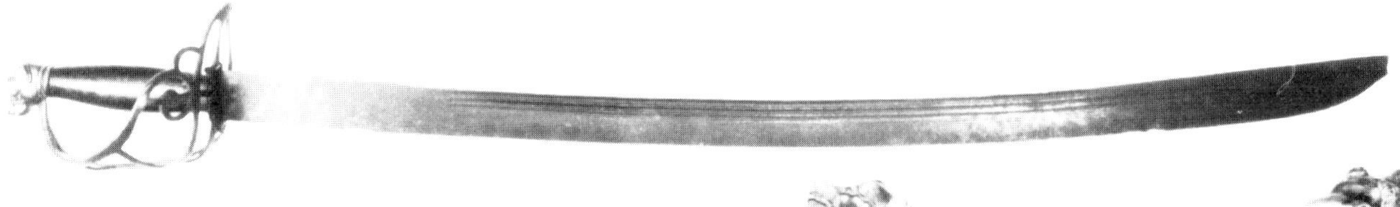

**154.SS  AMERICAN HORSEMAN SABER        Circa 1770–1785**
The popular D-guard with four side openings and a blunt quillon comprise the core of this impressive hilt, which added a side branch having an ornamental scroll opposite the blade (plus two lateral support bars). A realistic dog head cast in brass (one piece) presides over a smooth oval cherry grip in a 3/8" ferrule. It mounts the usual three-fuller Spanish blade. The saber was found in New Hampshire but is attributed to Col. James Scammon of Massachusetts.
Length: 40-1/2"         Blade: 34" X 1-3/8"         Hilt: Brass
**George C. Neumann Collection, Valley Forge National Historical Park**

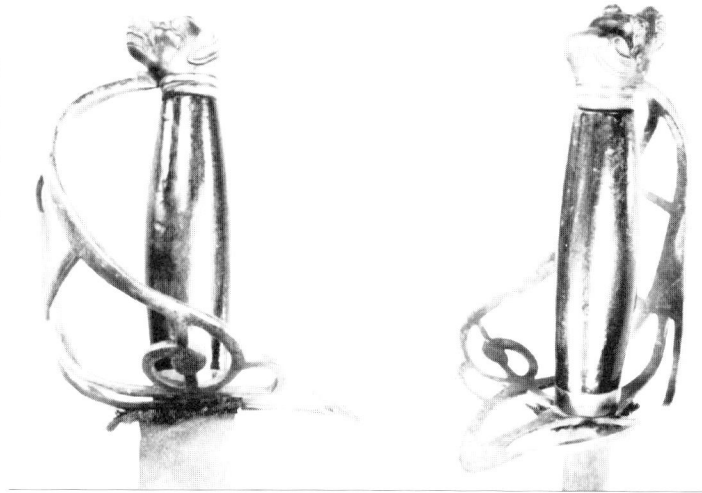

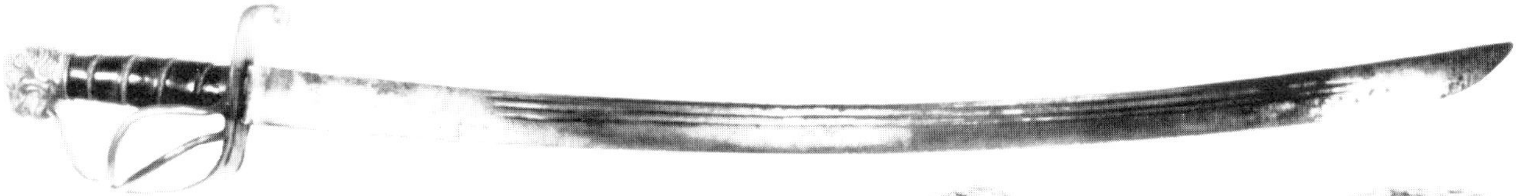

**155.SS  AMERICAN HORSEMAN SABER        Circa 1770–1785**
Several of this pattern are known and one is attributed to General Israel Putnam of Connecticut. The hilt is dominated by a grotesque lion head pommel above a channeled wooden grip retaining a decorative brass wire rope. Its bronze-colored flat counterguard is pierced once above each side of the blade and attaches two outboard branches (cast as a separate unit) to create a semi-basket hilt. "HR / NH" is cut into the back edge of its popular three-fuller single-edged cutting blade.
Length: 38-7/8"         Blade: 32-7/8" X 1-3/8"         Hilt: Brass
**Author's Collection**

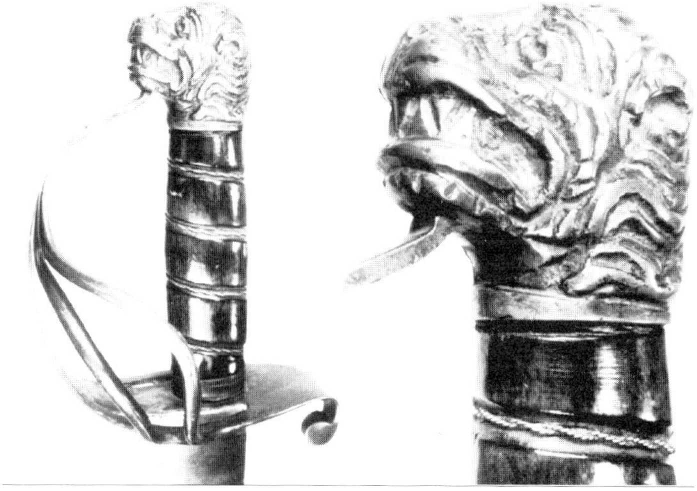

**156.SS  AMERICAN HORSEMAN SABER        Circa 1780–1790**
Toward the later years of the American War for Independence, counterguard patterns often took on an oval form and added an outer border of pierced loops as seen here. This American light dragoon saber also includes an eagle head pommel. Because its United States symbolism did not officially begin until the Great Seal of 1782, it was probably chosen from among the many creature forms offered by cutlers. The bulbous bare wooden grip is typical of the period.
Length: 39-1/8"         Blade: 33" X 1-3/8"         Hilt: Brass
**George C. Neumann Collection, Valley Forge National Historical Park**

Chapter 7: Swords   355

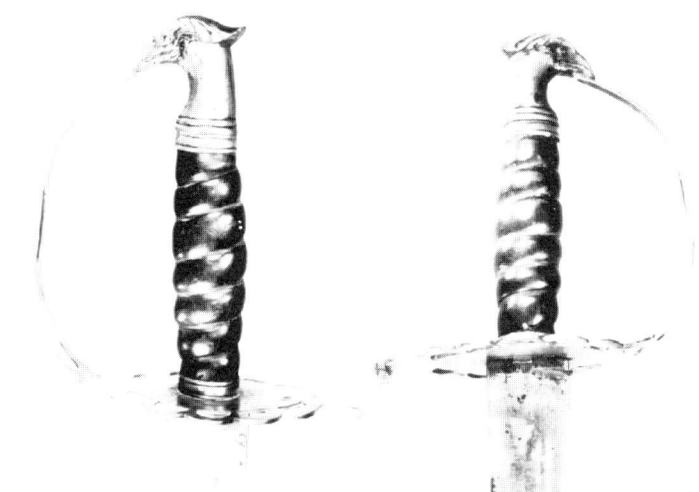

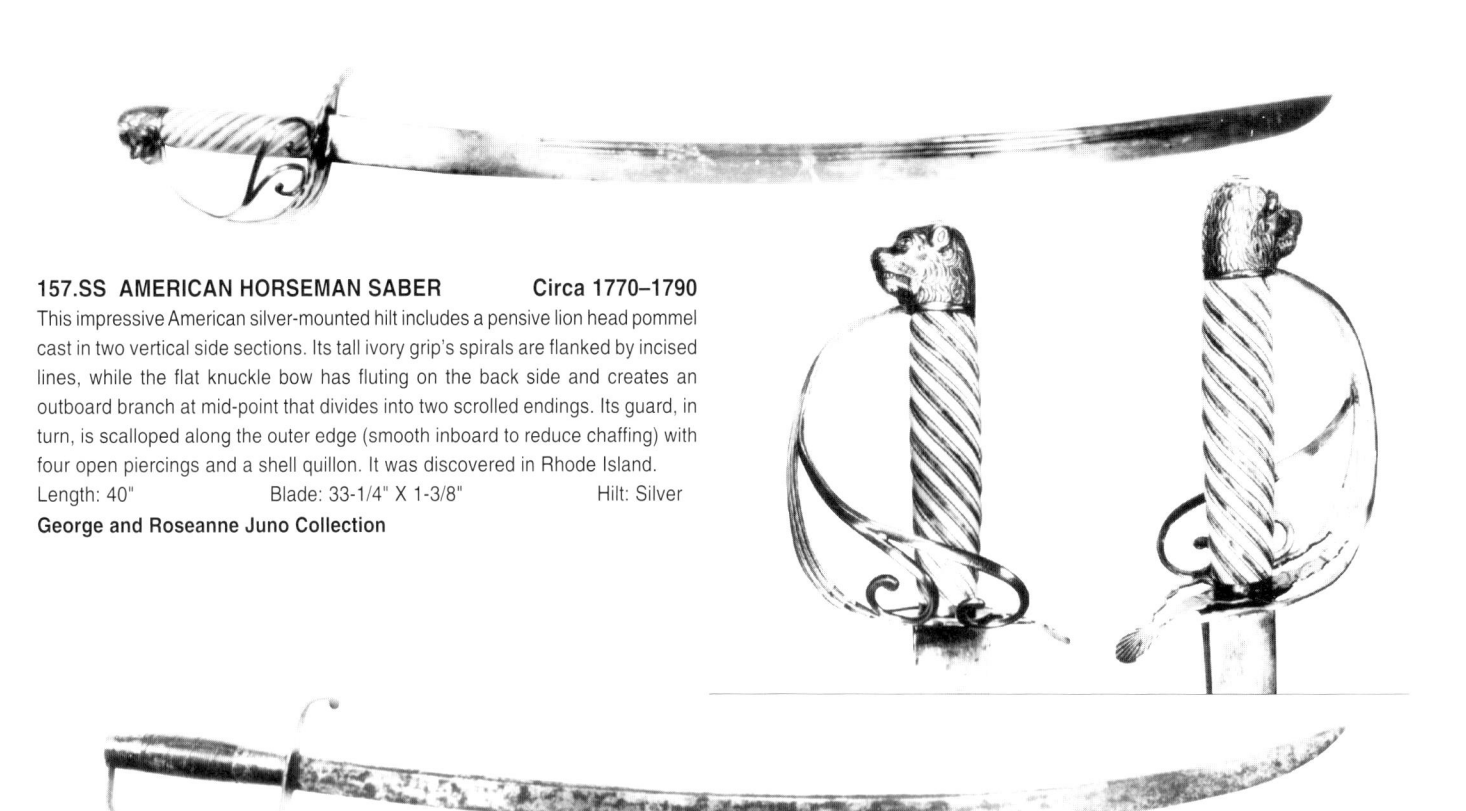

**157.SS  AMERICAN HORSEMAN SABER          Circa 1770–1790**
This impressive American silver-mounted hilt includes a pensive lion head pommel cast in two vertical side sections. Its tall ivory grip's spirals are flanked by incised lines, while the flat knuckle bow has fluting on the back side and creates an outboard branch at mid-point that divides into two scrolled endings. Its guard, in turn, is scalloped along the outer edge (smooth inboard to reduce chaffing) with four open piercings and a shell quillon. It was discovered in Rhode Island.
Length: 40"           Blade: 33-1/4" X 1-3/8"           Hilt: Silver
**George and Roseanne Juno Collection**

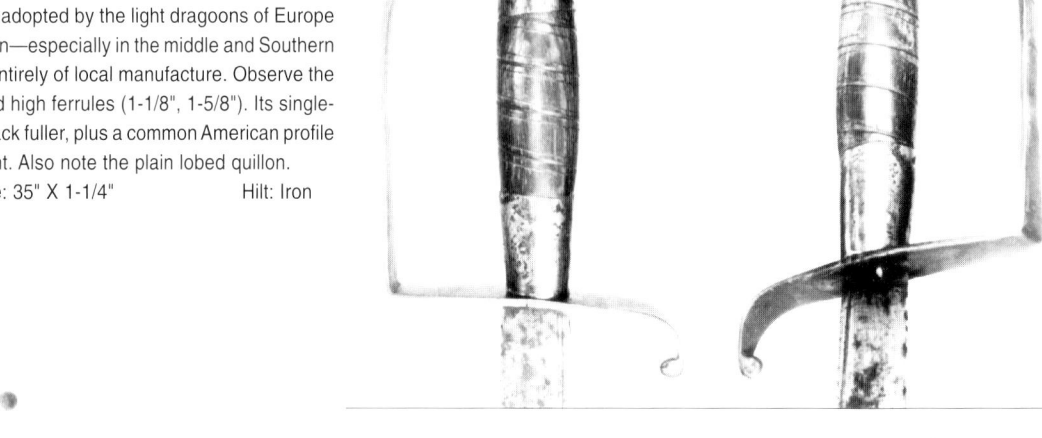

**158.SS  AMERICAN HORSEMAN SABER          Circa 1775–1783**
The right-angled stirrup hilt form newly adopted by the light dragoons of Europe was also favored by American horsemen—especially in the middle and Southern states. This iron-mounted example is entirely of local manufacture. Observe the grooved horn grip, flat cap pommel and high ferrules (1-1/8", 1-5/8"). Its single-edged blade displays an uneven 1/8" back fuller, plus a common American profile that accelerates its curve near the point. Also note the plain lobed quillon.
Length: 40-7/8"           Blade: 35" X 1-1/4"           Hilt: Iron
**Author's Collection**

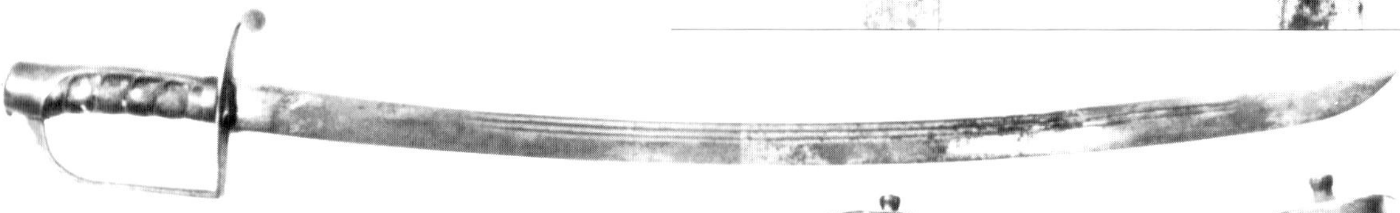

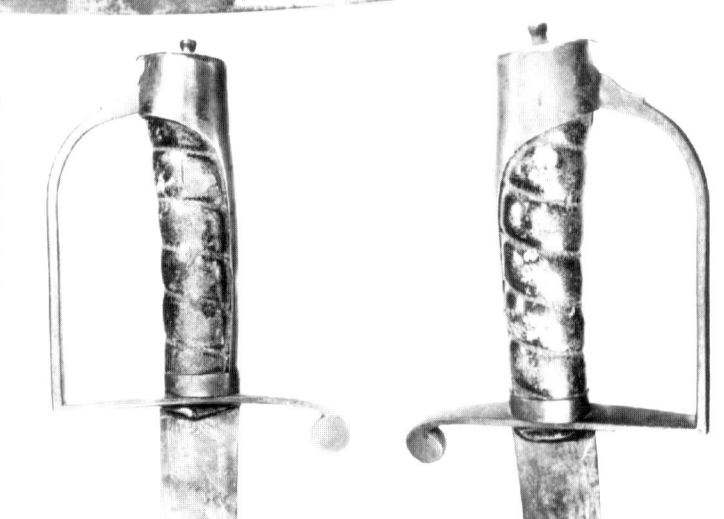

**159.SS  AMERICAN HORSEMAN SABER          Circa 1777–1790**
The rebels in New England also adopted the stirrup hilt, often with the French-style backstrap and squared pommel (134.SS). Note these wartime characteristics: a tall brass hilt with a high-shouldered knuckle bow, a backstrap and squared profile pommel plus capstan, a leather-covered grip, and a thin flat cap (rear point). Its three-fuller blade has two leather junction pads. The form varies from U.S. contracts circa 1798–1800, which had a tapered pommel, no capstan and a thicker cap). It was found in Newport, Rhode Island.
Length: 39-3/8"           Blade: 33" X 1-3/8"           Hilt: Brass
**Author's Collection**

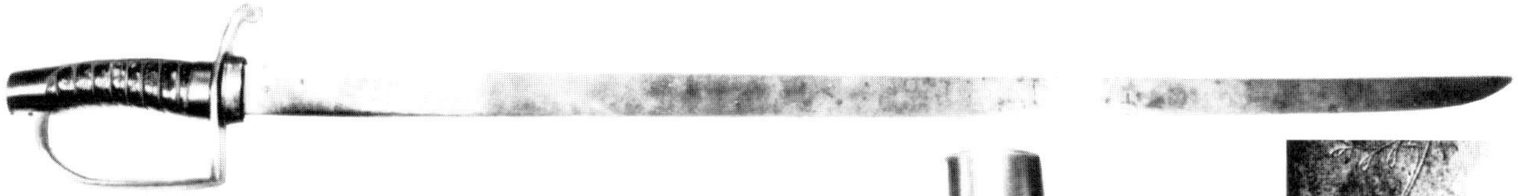

**160.SS  AMERICAN HORSEMAN SABER          Circa 1779**
In 1779 the Virginia agent Jacques LeMaire ordered 1500 to 2000 sword patterns of three forms from France's Klingenthal manufactory. Two resembled the French Model 1767 hanger (31.SS), but the third group was horseman blades marked "Dragoon of Virginia" between a visored cap and a flaming bomb, as well as "Victory or Death" with an arms panoply on the reverse. These blades were apparently given a variety of hilts in America. Note the typical iron stirrup hilt in this case with a sheath cap. (Re: Cromwell, bib. 37)

Length: 42"          Blade: 36-1/8" X 1-1/4"          Hilt: Iron

**William H. Guthman Collection**

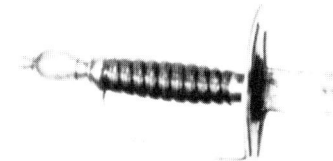

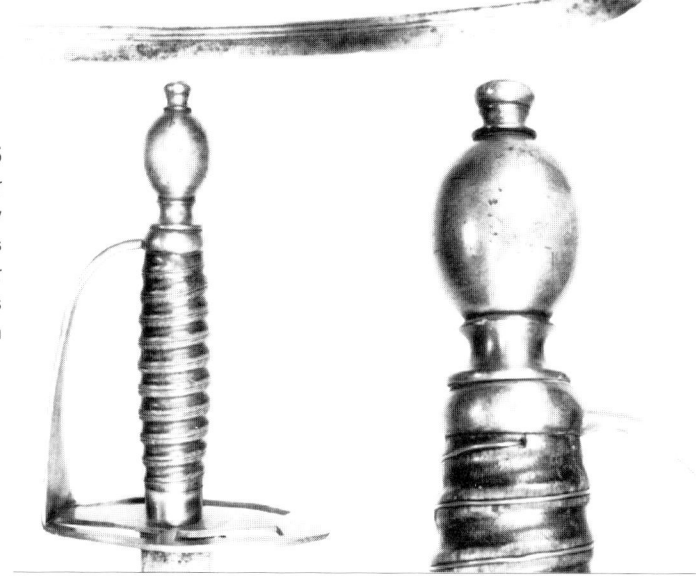

**161.SS  AMERICAN HORSEMAN SABER          Circa 1770–1785**
Estimates suggest that thirty percent of American Colonists could not read or write, yet many of their swordsmiths continually created an impressive dignity and balance in their work using only limited components. This classic hilt is tall (for a gloved hand) and combines a high ovoid pommel having a baluster capstan and pedestal neck above an uncovered grip with spiraled ridges highlighted by a brass wire. The flat four-slot stirrup guard, in turn, springs from an upper ferrule band.

Length: 41-1/4"          Blade: 33-5/8" X 1-3/8"          Hilt: Brass

**Author's Collection**

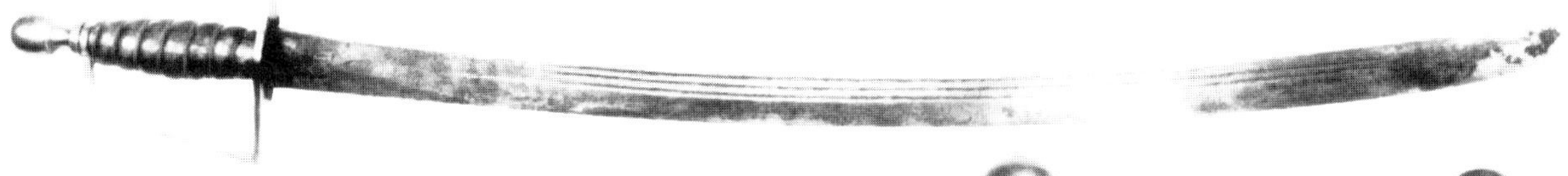

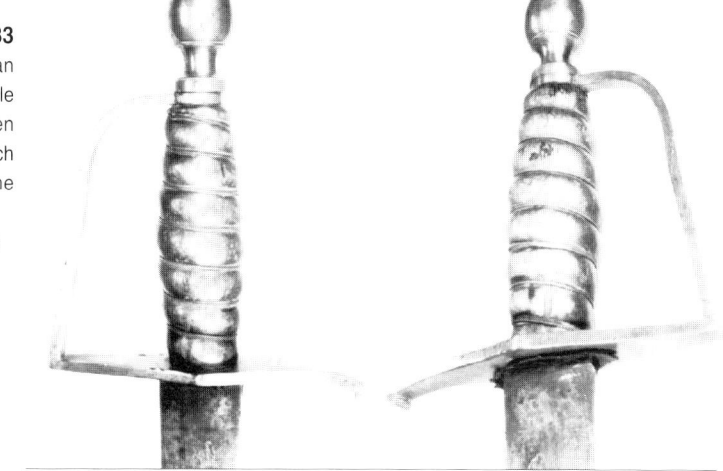

**162.SS  AMERICAN HORSEMAN SABER          Circa 1775–1783**
This American maker cast a thicker-than-normal brass stirrup guard with an integral mounting ring at the upper end of a squared knuckle bow. Meanwhile a cast ovoid pommel (narrow neck) rises above a channeled bare wooden grip that omitted ferrules. The counterguard spreads to an angled point on each side opposite the three-fuller blade. Note also the leather cushion at the guard/blade junction.

Length: 39-1/2"          Blade: 33-1/8" X 1-1/2"          Hilt: Brass

**Author's Collection**

Chapter 7: Swords   357

### 163. SS AMERICAN HORSEMAN SABER     Circa 1776–1783

As the Revolution progressed, many American horsemen adopted the stirrup-hilted saber. It was easier to manufacture and followed the new light dragoon patterns of Europe. This example found in Maine is completely local—combining only essential components, that is, an olive pommel above an iron ring that anchors a forged stirrup guard with four pierced openings. Its carved wooden grip was never covered, while the blade shows the abrupt "American curve" just before the point.

Length: 41-7/8"     Blade: 35-3/4" X 1-3/8"     Hilt: Iron

**Author's Collection**

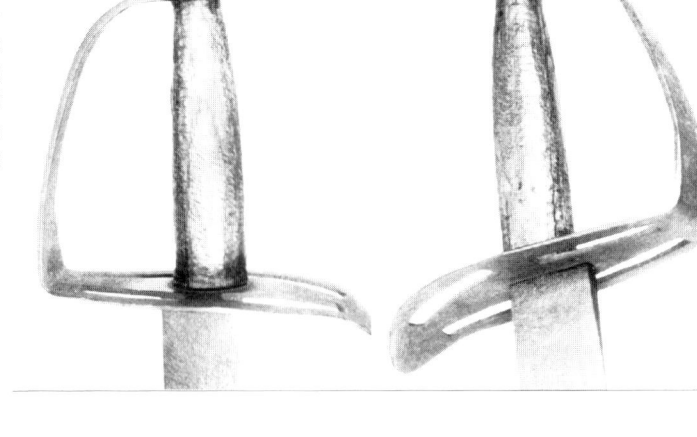

### 164. SS AMERICAN HORSEMAN SABER     Circa 1775–1783

On most of these American stirrup hilts the knuckle bow/guard was cast as a single piece. In some cases, however, as with this sword, the four-slot guard and tapered knuckle bow were cut separately and joined at the right angle. A low domed pommel with upper tiers is mounted on a bare (never covered) wooden grip that includes a spiraled single wire and pregnant bulge at the back. Its familiar imported Spanish blade displays three 1/4" fullers that begin 6-1/2 inches below the hilt.

Length: 40-1/2"     Blade: 34-3/4" X 1-3/8"     Hilt: Brass

**Author's Collection**

### 165. SS AMERICAN HORSEMAN SABER     Circa 1775–1783

This forged iron stirrup pattern includes a lengthened four-slot guard and, at the upper knuckle bow, extends an integral cap pommel—used on many American swords. The channeled wooden grip (1/4" base ferrule) has a later leather covering. Its slightly curved blade, in turn, shows an unusually wide 3/4" X 32" fuller. Marks: "PRAHL" (the Philadelphia maker) in the flat-sided blade and "H" on the knuckle bow's back face (sometimes attributed to James Hunter, Rappahannock Forge).

Length: 39-3/8"     Blade: 34-3/8" X 1-3/8"     Hilt: Iron

**William H. Guthman Collection**

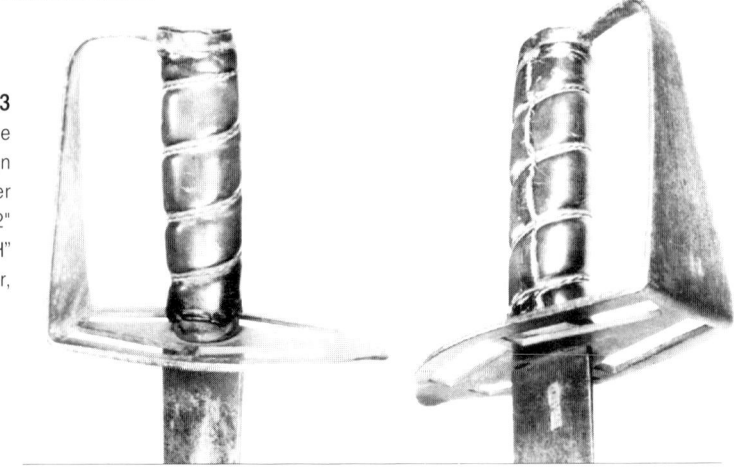

*Chapter 7: Swords*

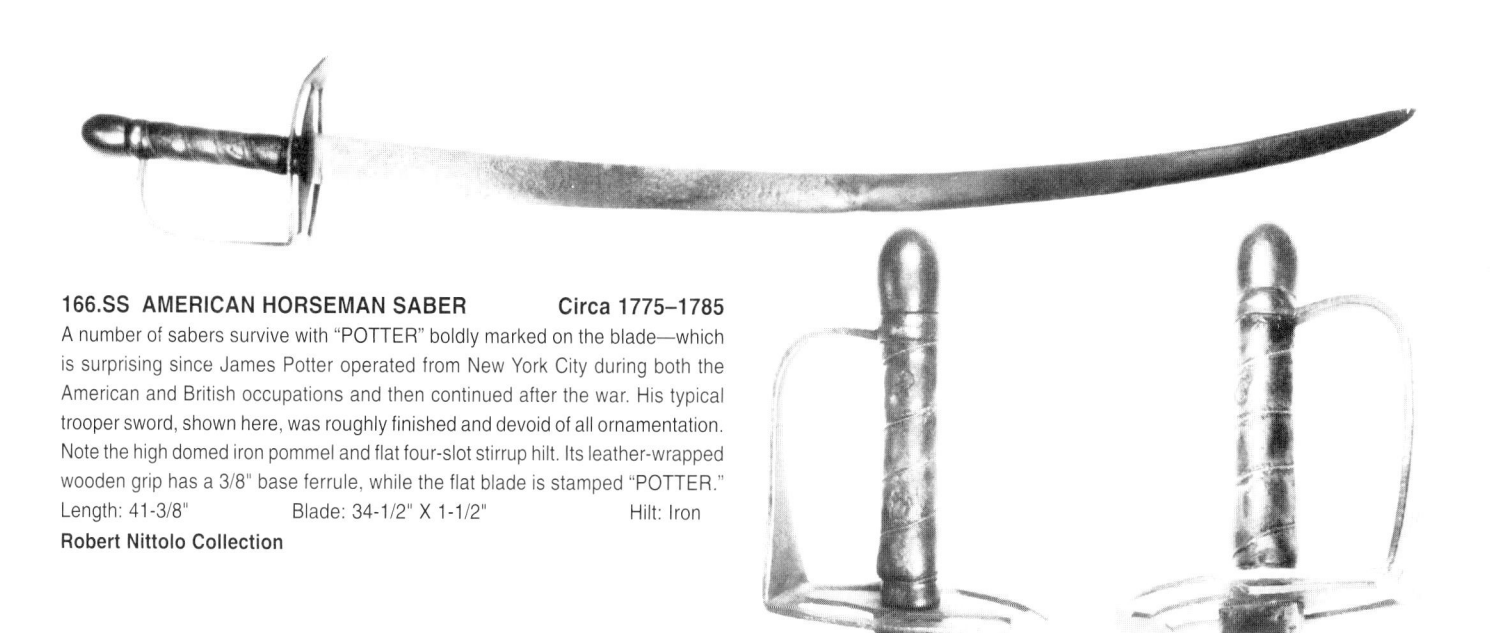

### 166.SS  AMERICAN HORSEMAN SABER  Circa 1775–1785
A number of sabers survive with "POTTER" boldly marked on the blade—which is surprising since James Potter operated from New York City during both the American and British occupations and then continued after the war. His typical trooper sword, shown here, was roughly finished and devoid of all ornamentation. Note the high domed iron pommel and flat four-slot stirrup hilt. Its leather-wrapped wooden grip has a 3/8" base ferrule, while the flat blade is stamped "POTTER."
Length: 41-3/8"            Blade: 34-1/2" X 1-1/2"            Hilt: Iron
**Robert Nittolo Collection**

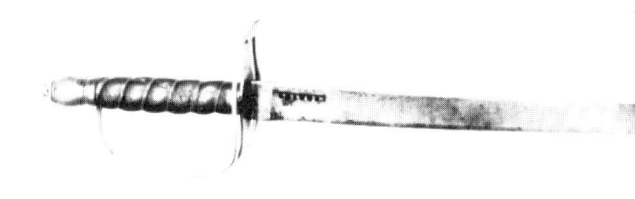

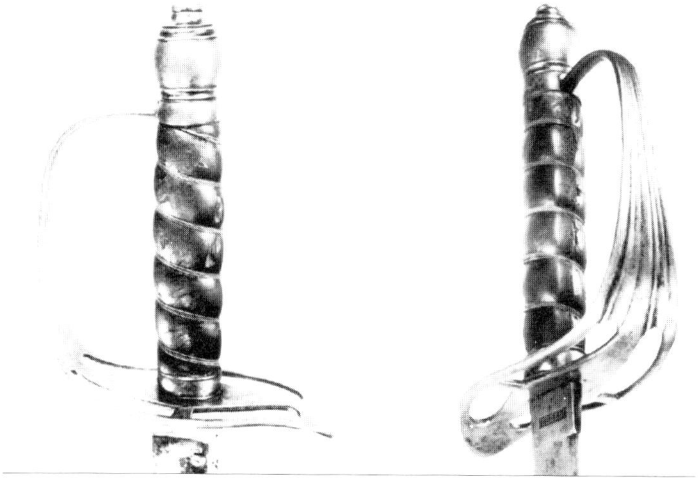

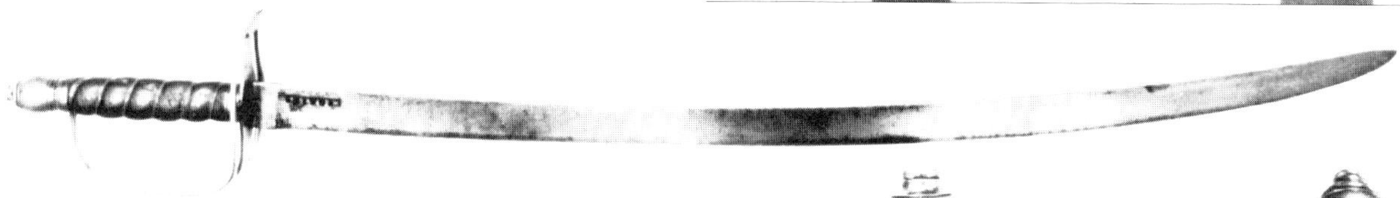

### 167.SS  AMERICAN HORSEMAN SABER  Circa 1775–1790
Also made by James Potter of New York City, this officer's saber is vastly better finished. It was used by Maj. Benjamin Talmadge of the 2nd Continental Dragoons. Notice that fluting has been added to the knuckle bow's back side, the tall pommel has acquired turned end rings and a capstan, while the blade includes a shallow broad fuller (normally a later feature). Its ricasso is stamped "POTTER" in a scalloped cartouche. Leather covers the wooden grip.
Length: 43-3/8"            Blade: 36" X 1-3/8"            Hilt: Iron
**E. H. Wilkins Collection, Smithsonian Institution**

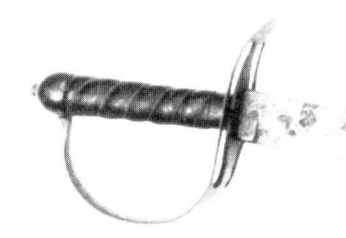

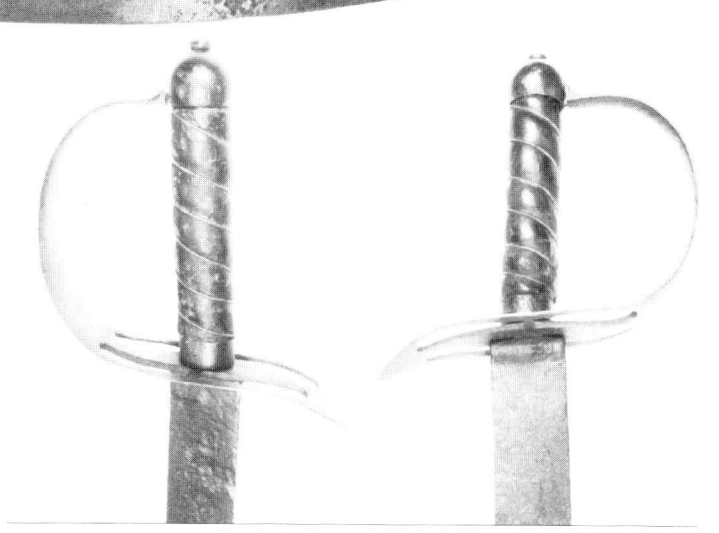

### 168.SS  AMERICAN SABER  Circa 1775–1790
Federal period advertisements list "Potter" marked blades being sold without hilts, which probably accounts for many unusual patterns attributed to him. This form, plus 166.SS and 167.SS, appear to be most representative of his designs. The leather-wrapped grip is now topped by a semi-domed cap pommel that receives the knuckle bow's upper end (versus an integral round ring on the others) and adopts a pronounced D-shaped profile that continues the four-slot guard. "POTTER" is stamped on the inboard ricasso of the short flat blade (possibly used for infantry).
Length: 35-5/8"            Blade: 26-1/4" X 1-1/2"            Hilt: Iron
**Robert Nittolo Collection**

*Chapter 7: Swords*

**169.SS AMERICAN HORSEMAN SABER**  Circa 1770–1790

Some provincial cutlers took the extra time to add bits of local elegance. This stirrup guard expands opposite the grip and again at the quillon to create an unusual form—filled with geometric openings and decorated along the edges with multiple strikes of a punch (typical Colonial practice). A tall ovoid pommel and capstan rise above a spiraled wooden grip (never wrapped). Its flat blade illustrates the American habit of a sudden curve just below the point.

Length: 40-1/8"     Blade: 33" X 1-1/2"     Hilt: Brass

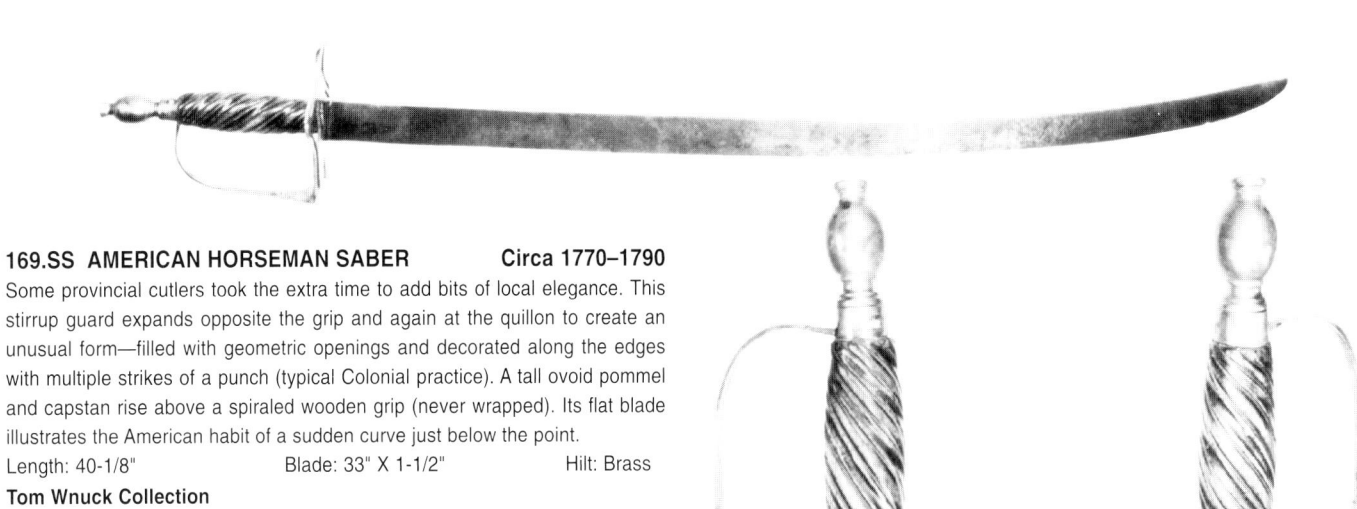

**Tom Wnuck Collection**

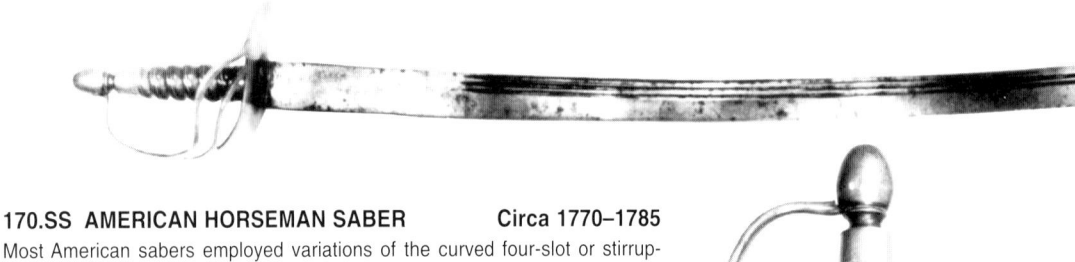

**170.SS AMERICAN HORSEMAN SABER**  Circa 1770–1785

Most American sabers employed variations of the curved four-slot or stirrup-shaped hilts. Yet the more demanding semi-basket was also popular. This wide solid counterguard includes two outboard side branches and hooks into an egg-shaped quillon over a broad channeled wooden grip (singled wire in ridge slot). A 1/2" ferrule exists at each end, while red wool swatches were added to cushion the grip (above the guard) and again with the three-fuller blade (below). "PS" is engraved under the hilt.

Length: 39-3/8"     Blade: 33-1/2" X 1-3/8"     Hilt: Brass

**Author's Collection**

**171.SS AMERICAN HORSEMAN SABER**  Circa 1775–1783

Although this counterguard is similar to the preceding sword the variances among American makers and localities are apparent: both outboard side branches curve differently at their lower connections, its spiraled cherry grip is narrower (never wrapped), and the inverted-vase pommel/capstan is less defined. Note also that the slightly curved single-edged Colonial blade bears only one irregular back fuller versus the more common three-fuller imported pattern.

Length: 39"     Blade: 33" X 1-3/8"     Hilt: Brass

**William Rose Collection**

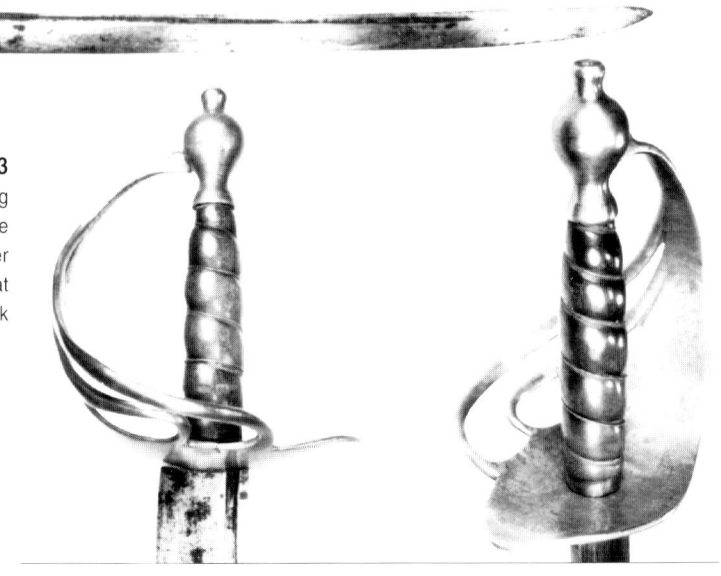

360   Chapter 7: Swords

### 172.SS  AMERICAN HORSEMAN SABER       Circa 1770–1785
All of these components are of American origin. The distinctive hilt form has also been seen on Colonial cutlasses, hangers and dragoon sabers. Notice its dominant pommel/capstan, the plain 1/4" ferrules and the sturdy leather-covered wooden grip with a 1/8" spiraled copper band. The broad dished iron counterguard includes two outboard branches, of which the higher one divides at the front (crude joints at each end). The local blade shows a single 1/4" back fuller.
Length: 39-5/8"          Blade: 33-3/4" X 1-1/4"          Hilt: Iron
**Author's Collection**

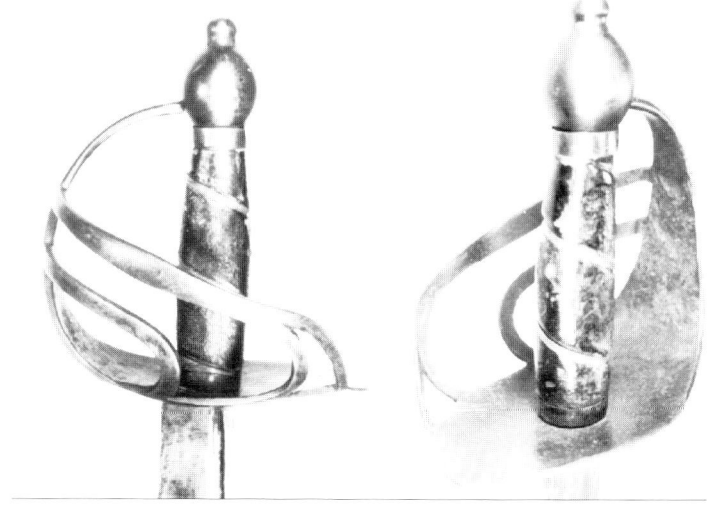

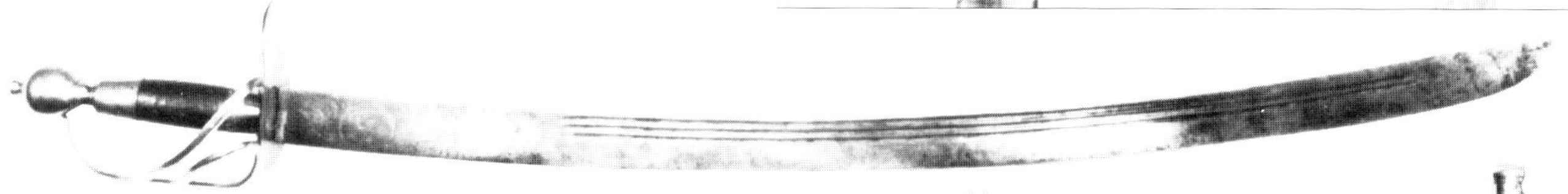

### 173.SS  AMERICAN HORSEMAN SABER       Circa 1770–1785
Simplicity and proportion have given this semi-basket hilt an impressive Colonial pattern. Notice how the overly large egg-shaped pommel and capstan are balanced by two deep one-inch ferrules plus a smooth oval wooden grip. Meanwhile a wide flattened counterguard projects two curved outer branches—without raised borders, pierced openings or decorations to interrupt its clean lines. The Spanish blade so popular in the Northeast begins its three fullers seven inches below the hilt.
Length: 40-1/4"          Blade: 33-3/8" X 1-3/8"          Hilt: Brass
**Richard Ulbrich Collection**

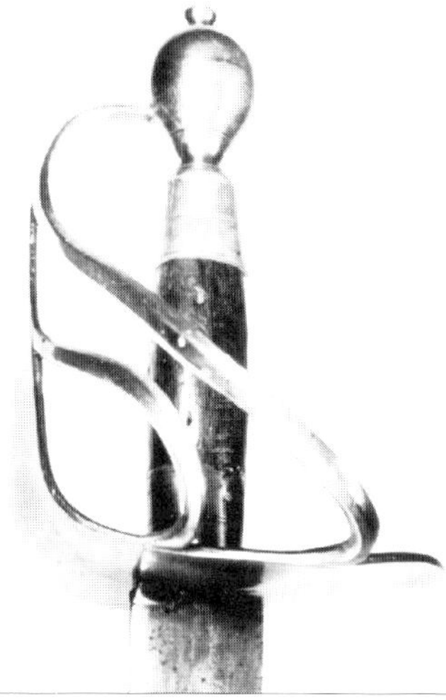

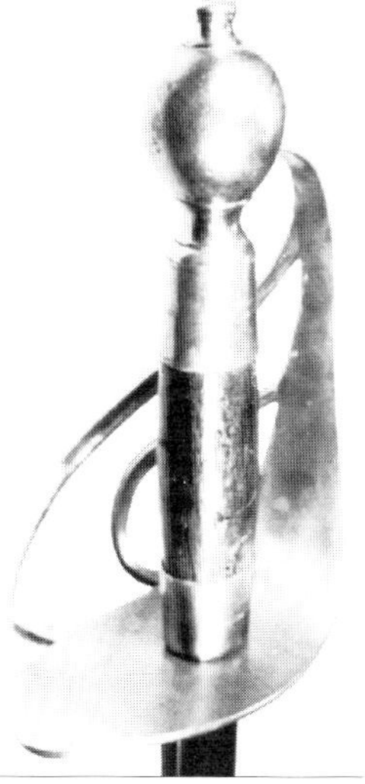

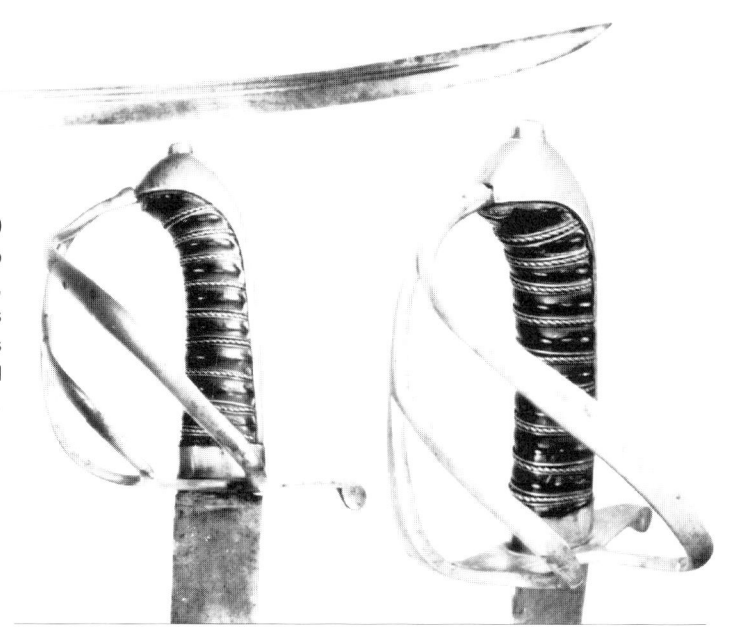

### 174.SS  AMERICAN HORSEMAN SABER       Circa 1777–1790
This saber reflects French influence with a backstrap rising from a 1/2" ferrule to form a birds-head pommel with a cylindrical capstan. Its curving knuckle bow, counterguard, two side branches and quillon were all molded as a single brass casting. The oval wooden grip created its channels by spiraling cord around its smooth surface before covering both with leather. A twisted brass rope flanked by two wires fills the grooves. It mounts the familiar three-fuller Spanish blade.
Length: 38-3/4"          Blade: 33-1/4" X 1-3/8"          Hilt: Brass
**Author's Collection**

*Chapter 7: Swords*

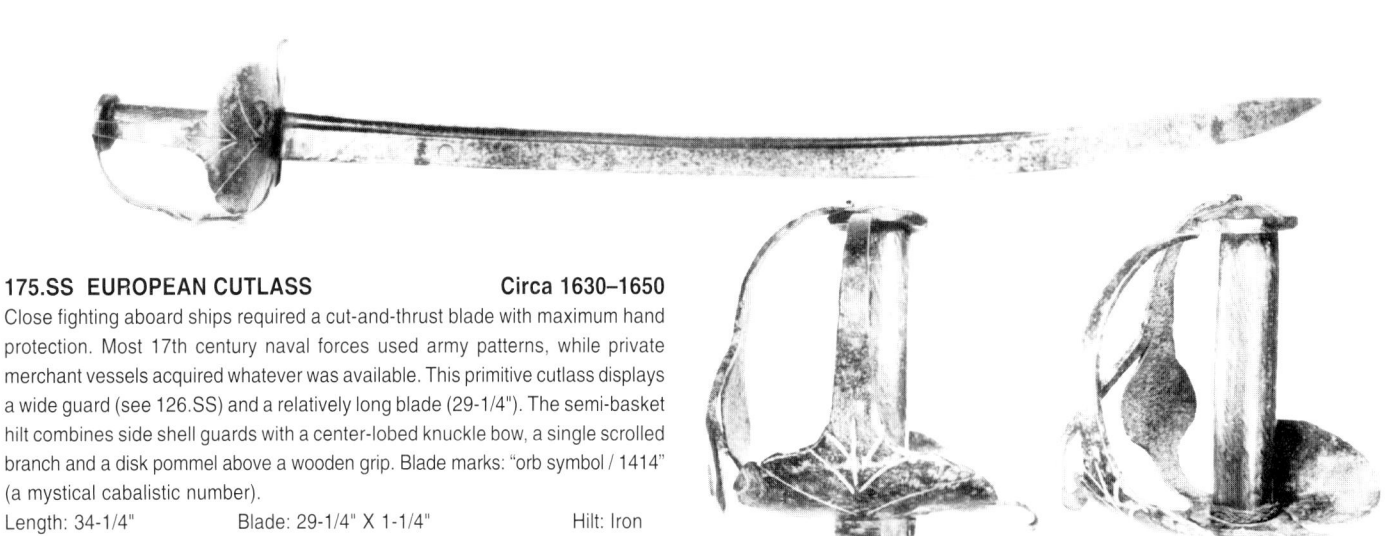

### 175.SS  EUROPEAN CUTLASS                Circa 1630–1650

Close fighting aboard ships required a cut-and-thrust blade with maximum hand protection. Most 17th century naval forces used army patterns, while private merchant vessels acquired whatever was available. This primitive cutlass displays a wide guard (see 126.SS) and a relatively long blade (29-1/4"). The semi-basket hilt combines side shell guards with a center-lobed knuckle bow, a single scrolled branch and a disk pommel above a wooden grip. Blade marks: "orb symbol / 1414" (a mystical cabalistic number).

Length: 34-1/4"         Blade: 29-1/4" X 1-1/4"         Hilt: Iron
**William H. Guthman Collection**

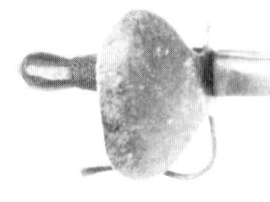

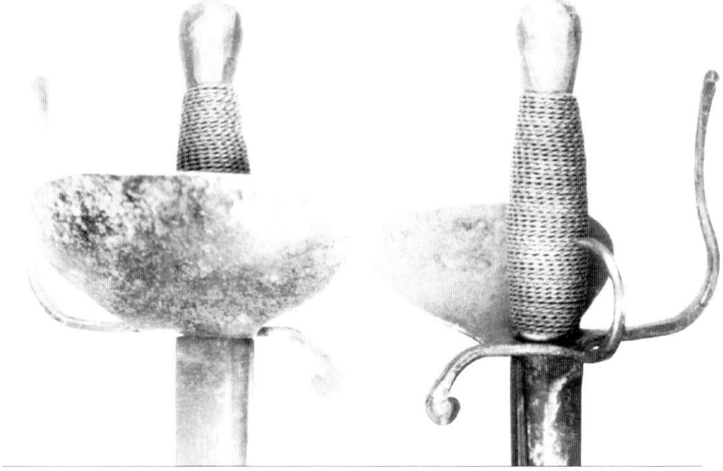

### 176.SS  EUROPEAN CUTLASS                Circa 1745

This mid-17th century Germanic cutlass pattern continued to be manufactured into the 1800s. The curved single fuller cutting blade with a raised 10" false edge is typically found bearing a crude Solingen (Passau) running wolf mark and a date—in this case "1745." Note its barely adequate hilt, limited to a crude pommel, an upturned shell guard, inboard thumb ring and pseudo knuckle bow. It was originally painted black for protection from the salt air, a common naval practice.

Length: 31-1/2"         Blade: 26-5/8" X 1-1/8"         Hilt: Iron
**Author's Collection**

### 177.SS  EUROPEAN CUTLASS                Circa 1700–1725

During the 1600s the term *cutlass* referred to any short cutting sword. By the mid-18th century, it usually identified use at sea. In the early 1700s, the short heavy blade was popular, while the inboard thumb ring was losing favor. Observe this typical shipboard pattern with a wide outboard shell guard and a simple bone grip, plus a tenuous knuckle bow/quillon having an integral flat disk pommel. Its hefty cutting blade contains a 1/4" X 16-1/2" back fuller and a seven-inch false edge.

Length: 28-1/8"         Blade: 23-3/4" X 1-1/2"         Hilt: Iron
**Author's Collection**

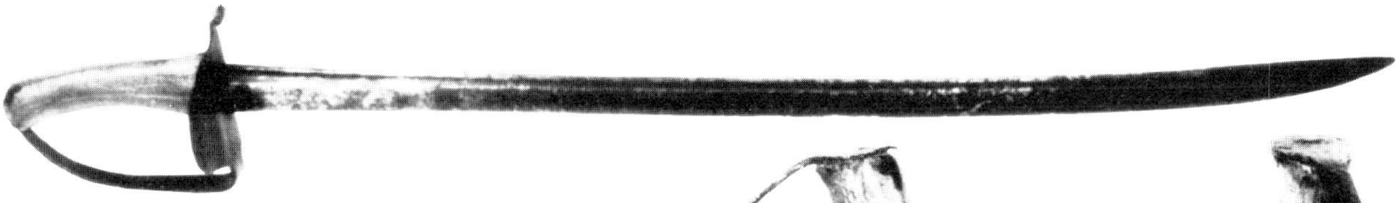

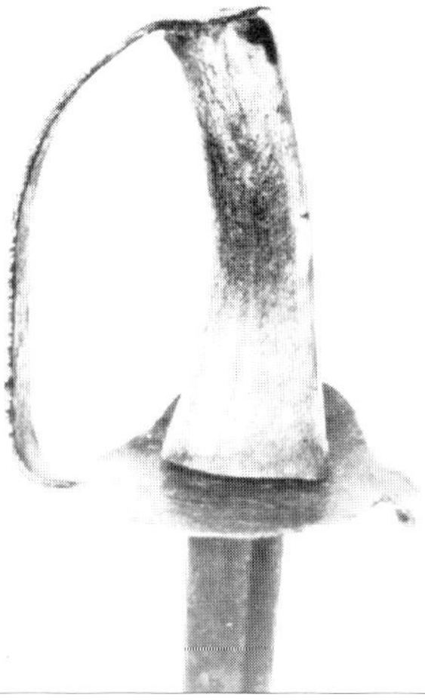

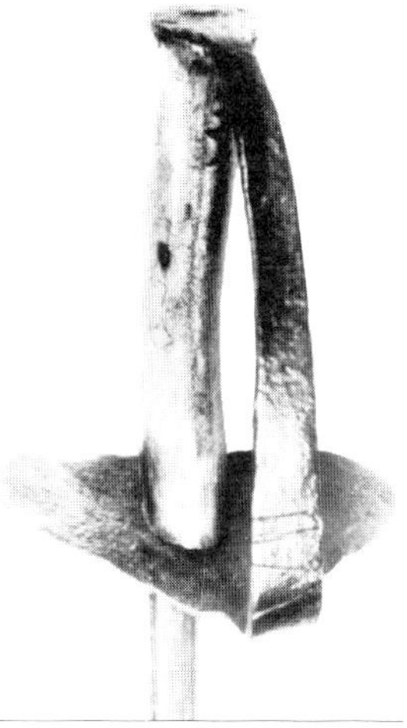

**178.SS  AMERICAN CUTLASS**  Circa 1750–1785

By the mid-1700s, the common naval arm had replaced its earlier shell form by a round flat guard, sheet-iron knuckle bow with an integral disk pommel and a wide rolled quillon to catch an opponent's stroke. This example uses a plain bone grip plus a single-edged blade. The "VII" crudely filed into its knuckle bow and cut into the grip identified it as cutlass number seven. In contemporary nautical practice, it was painted black.

Length: 31-5/8"   Blade: 27" X 1"   Hilt: Iron
**Author's Collection**

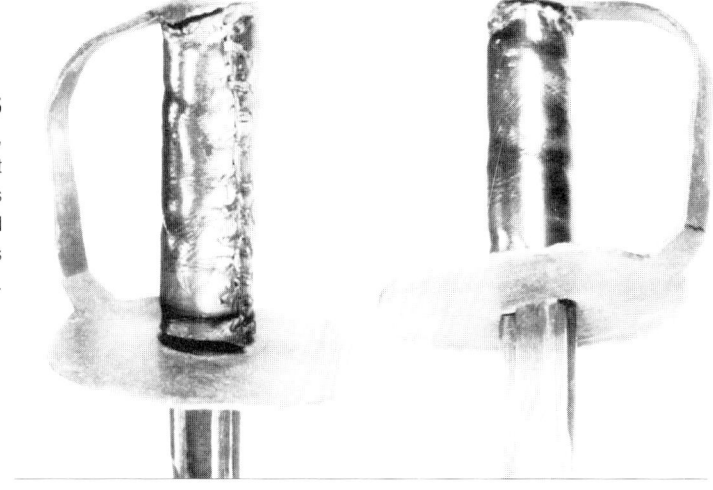

**179.SS  AMERICAN CUTLASS**  Circa 1750–1785

All seagoing vessels at that time carried small arms to counter wartime enemies, pirates or mutiny. Since most ships were privately owned, the thrifty merchant usually bypassed the cutler to have a blacksmith prepare crude but sturdy hilts for imported blades. This typical American example mounts a rough hand-forged round guard welded to a strap knuckle bow with an attached flat pommel. Its cylindrical wooden grip is covered by leather joined at a vertical stitched seam. The straight blade is two-edged.

Length: 30-1/4"   Blade: 26-1/2" X 1"   Hilt: Iron
**Author's Collection**

**180.SS  AMERICAN CUTLASS**  Circa 1750–1785

These hand-forged hilts with a flat rounded guard, elementary knuckle bow/quillon (notice the crude weld here) and a simple wood, bone or antler grip were the prevalent merchant/privateer cutlass form during our War for Independence. This American guard's edges have been bent in opposite directions and the quillon omitted. Its locally made blade presents flat faces and a seven-inch false edge. (Note: a typical soft iron tang on the blade passes through the hilt to secure all components.)

Length: 29-1/4"   Blade: 24-7/8" X 1-1/8"   Hilt: Iron
**Author's Collection**

Chapter 7: Swords

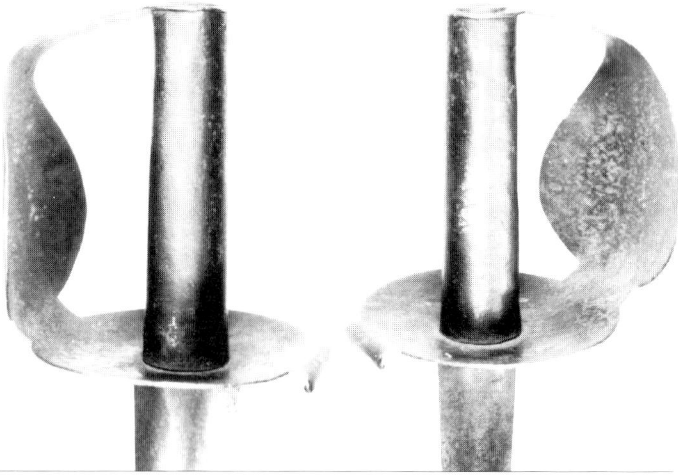

**181.SS  ENGLISH/AMERICAN CUTLASS**  Circa 1770–1790

By the middle 1700s, European navies finally began to specify cutlass patterns. The British preferred this new "double disk" or "figure 8" hilt which gave the round iron guard a slightly dished profile and added a second oval at the middle of the flat knuckle bow. Most examples covered the wooden grip by lapped sheet iron, kept the wide rolled quillon, and mounted a straight blade. Late century versions adopted grid-like cast iron grips. Most American versions are roughly finished.

Length: 32-1/2"         Blade: 27-1/2" X 1-1/2"         Hilt: Iron
**Author's Collection**

**182.SS  ENGLISH CUTLASS**  Circa 1750–1775

The evolving British "figure 8" naval pattern was supplemented in this case to create a more protective basket hilt. It is of heavy iron construction and originally painted black in the prevailing seagoing fashion. The flat knuckle bow adds a central disk form and is flanked by a strong branch on each side. An antler grip rests on a broad dished guard having a curled quillon. Its curved single-edged blade is marked "HARVEY" (Samuel Harvey, a Birmingham maker).

Length: 32-1/2"         Blade: 27-1/2" X 1-3/8"         Hilt: Iron
**Erik Goldstein Collection**

**183.SS  FRENCH CUTLASS**  Circa 1750–1760

France's effort toward a standard naval cutlass chose this "pontet simple" brass form about 1750. It includes a flat cast pommel with raised designs, a narrow knuckle bow, a sunken panel outboard guard and a lobed quillon. An inboard thumb ring rests on a small shell-like base next to its horn grip. Variations with raised ribbing in the guard and a faceted bone grip have been found at Crown Point and the Frigate *Machault* (sunk in Canada, 1760). Marking: "crown / R."

Length: 31"         Blade: 26-1/4" X 1-1/16"         Hilt: Brass
**Erik Goldstein Collection**

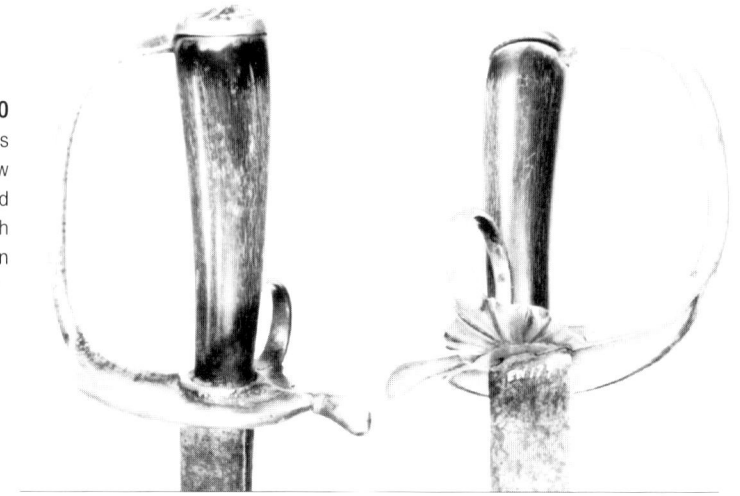

### 184.SS  FRENCH CUTLASS            Circa 1760–1790
Another frequent pattern in Europe and America was this broad dished sheet-iron guard that slowly narrowed to fit over the top of the wooden (ash) grip. Several have been found mounted on earlier French military blades. The straight single-edged blade in this case is from a circa 1725–1750 hanger and stamped with a fleur-de-lis on both faces (26.SS). Its single back fuller measures 1/4" X 19-1/2", while a leather oval cushions the hilt/blade junction.
Length: 30-3/4"        Blade: 26" X 1-1/4"       Hilt: Iron
**Author's Collection**

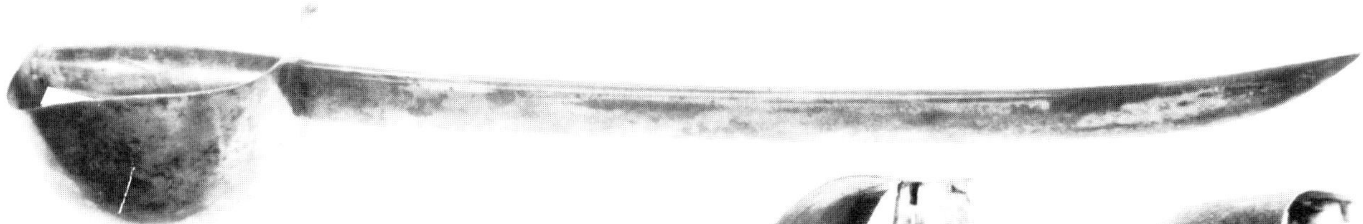

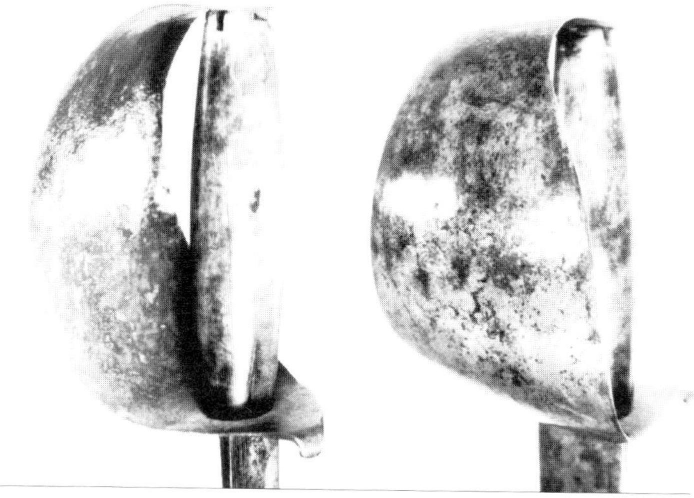

### 185.SS  EUROPEAN CUTLASS           Circa 1760–1790
This interesting naval variation took the basic broad sheet-iron guard of the previous example and rotated it 90 degrees to protect better the outside of the seaman's hand. The plain wooden grip has acquired a convex profile. Its short combat-weight cutting blade (uneven 3/16" back fuller) would have been ideal in close deck fighting. Such a massive outboard guard may have been an early version of France's later famous Model 1801.
Length: 26-7/8"       Blade: 21-1/2" X 1-5/8"       Hilt: Iron
**Author's Collection**

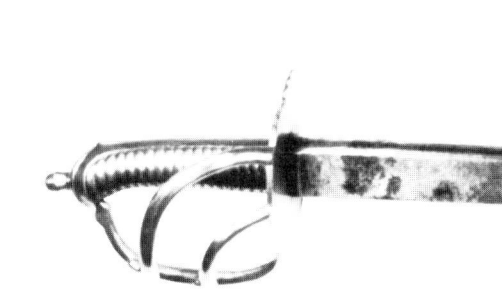

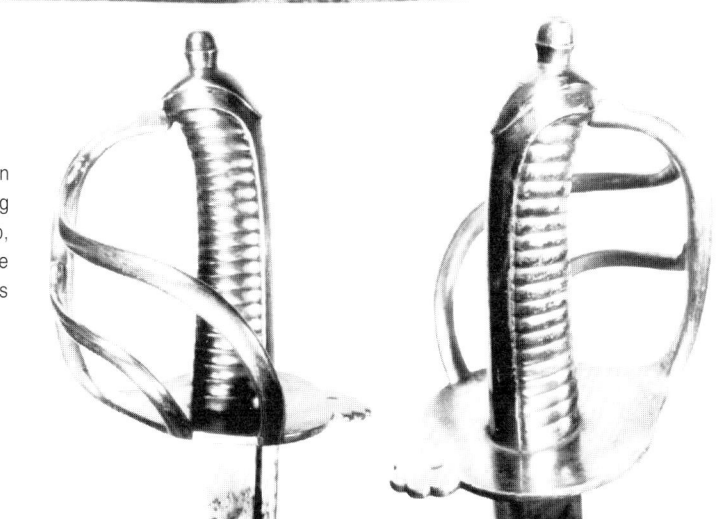

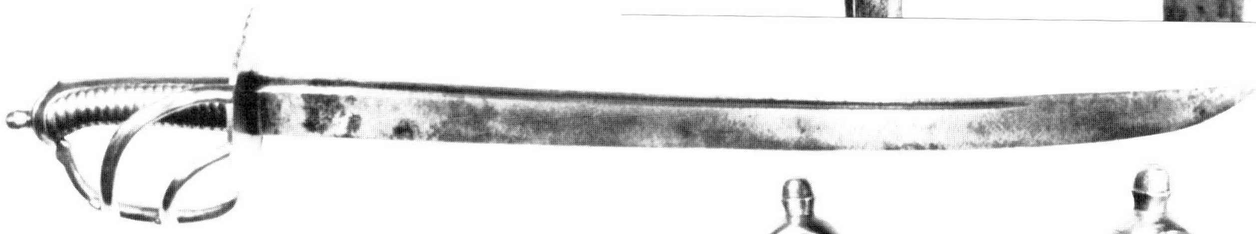

### 186.SS  FRENCH CUTLASS MODEL 1782
In 1782 France certified this brass model. It was apparently a form already in use and probably furnished to America, as well as to our privateers operating from French ports under Franklin's auspices. Notice that the cast backstrap, helmeted birds-head pommel and ribbed grip combination is a direct copy of the Model 1767 grenadier sword (31.SS). The flat guard with a five-lobe quillon plus two side branches was cast as a single piece. It is stamped "crown / R."
Length: 30"       Blade: 24-1/2" X 1-3/8"       Hilt: Brass
**George C. Neumann Collection, Valley Forge National Historical Park**

*Chapter 7: Swords*

# Chapter 8

# Polearms... Traditions of Rank and Combat

From about 1450 through the 17th century, long infantry pikes often exceeding eighteen feet in length created a wall of bristling spear points from closely packed formations of disciplined troops to dominate the European battlefield. The improving firearm however was gaining acceptance during the 1600s and by 1700 with the addition of a bayonet, which permitted its use in both capacities, the musket replaced the pike as the standard infantry weapon.

The long polearms did not die immediately, however. Having been established over centuries, they remained in limited use by both forces during the American Revolution.

## THE HALBERD

The halberd (or halpert) was the symbol of rank for sergeants of foot regiments. The British form resembled a battle-ax with a flaring cross-blade under a vertical spear point. It was mounted on a sturdy staff ("haft") usually of ash, walnut or hickory that included a conical iron point on the bottom ("butt cone," "ground iron"). The form was copied by the American militia and in turn carried over into the Continental Army in a wide variety of domestic designs. It served primarily as a means of identification on a busy battlefield and, per the sharpened edges of surviving examples, as a close-action weapon.

The halberd's importance was waning, however, especially in the woods of North America. General Braddock replaced it with a fusil (light musket) in 1755, followed by General Amherst in 1759. An official British warrant then sanctioned the change for all grenadier sergeants in 1768–1769. During the Revolutionary War, those polearms still in the King's service were largely limited to garrison duty. A sergeant's pike officially replaced the remaining British halberds in 1792 (1.PAA–10.PAA).

The Americans required halberds for sergeants and some corporals early in the war but, like the English,

**AMERICAN CORPS OF LIGHT INFANTRY AT YORKTOWN, 1781**
This commissioned officer carries a spontoon copied from the British pattern. It served as a symbol of rank and a means of signaling, as well as a close contact weapon. Note also the hunting horn (bugle horn) in the background, which was often used to transmit orders in these elite flank companies.

366   *Chapter 8: Polearms*

gradually retired them in preference to the fusil and bayonet. They varied in localized design but generally followed the British battle-ax form (18PAA–28PAA).

France's halberd copied the 17th century partizan with its broad blade and short base projections (32.PAA). The official length was set at six feet nine inches in 1703 (no official design), at which time grenadier sergeants switched to firearms. Line company sergeants were also changed to fusils in 1758 (although halberds were briefly reinstated from 1764 to 1766). They were present here during the French and Indian War (12.PAA–15.PAA).

The German halberds saw service throughout the Revolution. They resembled the French pattern but usually had a wider blade, shorter base projections and a regimental or landgrave device on the face (16.PAA–17.PAA).

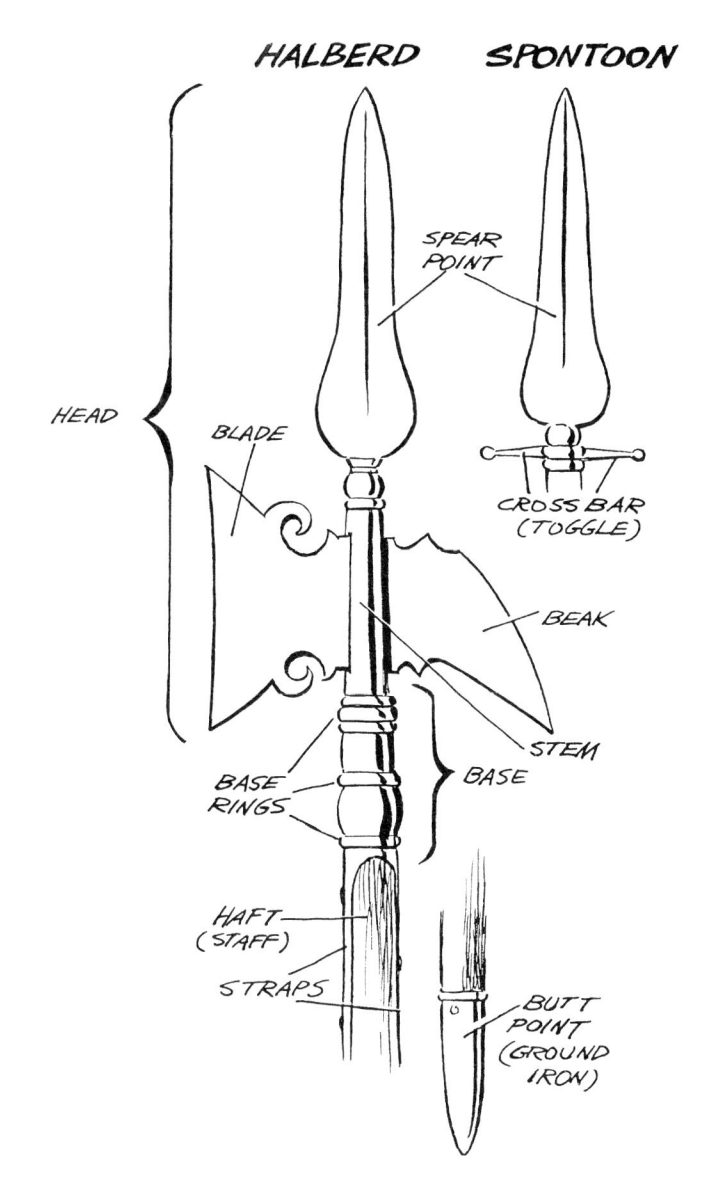

## THE SPONTOON

Shaped like a spear point on a six- to eight-foot pole, the spontoon (espontoon or half pike) was a fighting arm, signaling device and symbol of rank for the commissioned officer. The English army limited the spontoon's length to seven feet in 1768, when they also abolished it for grenadier officers. By 1786 the arm was officially withdrawn from service (33.PAA–34.PAA).

Washington favored the spontoon for his officers. In Valley Forge (1778) it was specified as a staff "six feet and a half, one and one quarter inches thick at largest part" plus "an iron point one foot long." Widespread compliance is doubted, but it officially remained throughout the war (35.PAA–57.PAA).

France ordered officers to discard spontoons in 1758 (although they were recalled from 1764 to 1766). They were with their North American forces in the French and Indian War (41.PAA–42.PAA).

German spontoons remained in active use in America during the Revolution. Their form usually included a broad symmetrical blade above a base with pierced patterns (43.PAA–46.PAA).

## THE PIKE

Especially during the early years of the War for Independence when the Americans lacked firearms for many of their troops, they resorted to the 17th century pike (also spear, trench spear or boarding pike). Local blacksmiths easily produced the heads, which were mounted on hafts often reaching to over twelve feet in length. They were primarily intended to defend entrenched positions or to meet a bayonet charge. Similar heads on shorter shafts (five to seven feet—"half pikes") were also used, especially on naval vessels as boarding pikes (58.PAA–69.PAA).

## THE LINSTOCK

This polearm for the artillery was developed with a center vertical spear point flanked by two side arms that secured the ends of a smoldering "match rope" used to ignite the cannon. By the time of the Revolution, most had been reduced to the two arms without a blade on a haft, often as short as two to four feet (29.PAA–31.PAA).

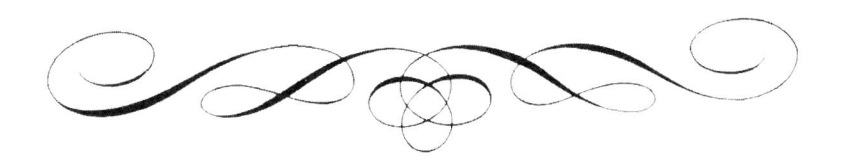

Chapter 8: Polearms

1.PAA  2.PAA  3.PAA

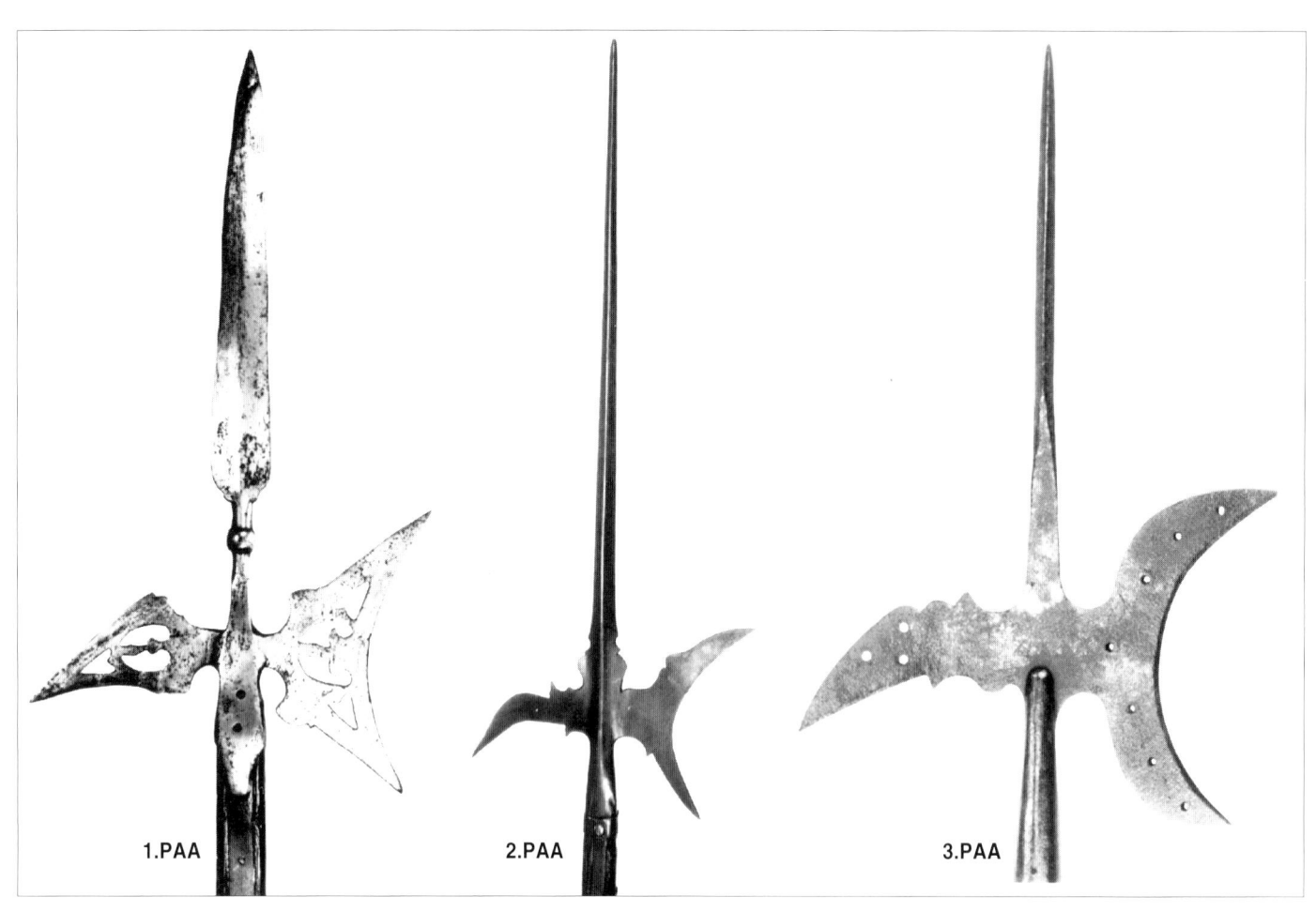

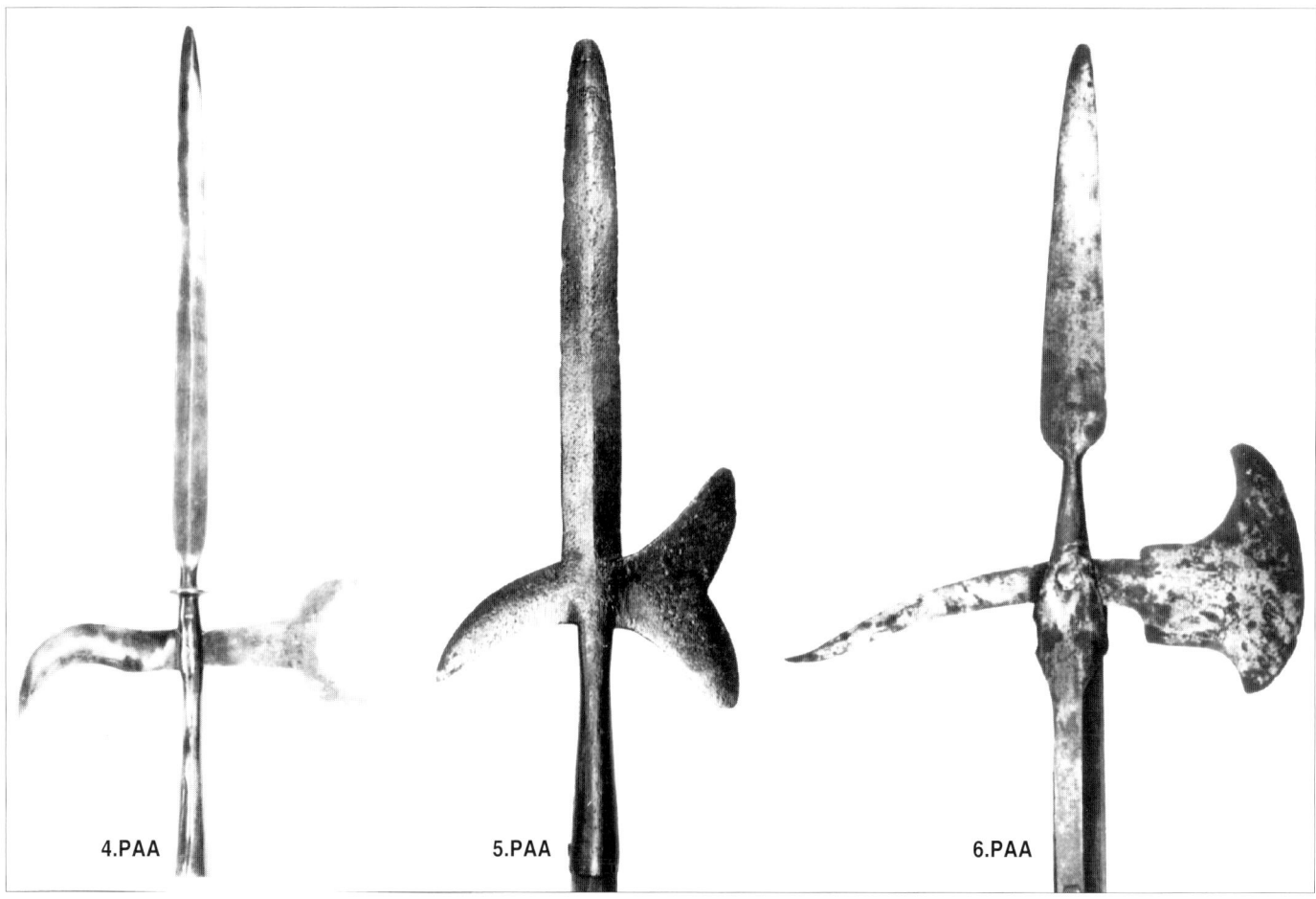

4.PAA  5.PAA  6.PAA

368  *Chapter 8: Polearms*

7.PAA      8.PAA      9.PAA

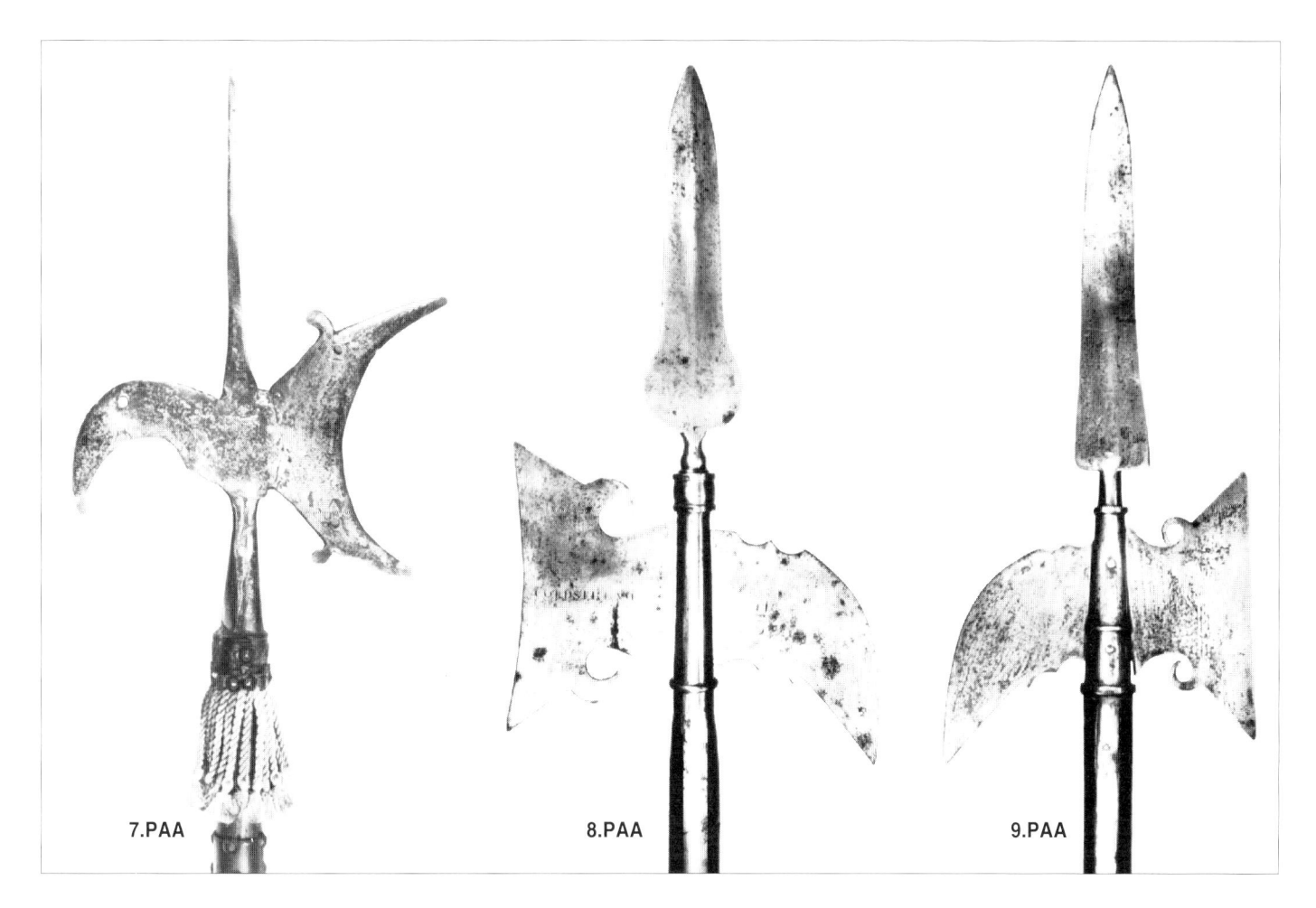

**1.PAA ENGLISH HALBERD**      Circa 1600–1680

This Pilgrim-period pattern has a typical long spear point (11-7/8") and pierced designs in the crosspiece. Its early base splits to fit onto the wedge-shaped top of an octagonal pole. The head was forged as a single unit; the side straps have been replaced.
George C. Neumann Collection, Valley Forge National Historical Park

**2.PAA AMERICAN HALBERD**      Circa 1680–1700

The long diamond-sectioned spear point is typical of many early American Colonial polearms. It is mounted on a squared haft with beaded corners and held by a separate strap nailed to each face. Note the deadly points it projects in each direction. The head is 29-1/4 inches high.
Author's Collection

**3.PAA AMERICAN HALBERD**      Circa 1690–1700

The narrow diamond-section point was paired with a locally forged crescent blade and beak by means of a visible dovetail joint. Note the unbalanced Colonial workmanship, pierced hole decorations and conical mounting socket. The height shown is 20-1/2 inches.
Author's Collection

**4.PAA AMERICAN HALBERD**      Circa 1700–1720

Notice this long thrusting spear point with a median ridge—as such arms were still considered active weapons in these early years. The crescent crosspiece, in turn, has now assumed a more symbolic role. Its finish and lapped seams are crudely done. Length shown: 23-5/8".
Author's Collection

**5.PAA AMERICAN HALBERD**      Circa 1720

This Colonial "fish tail" pattern was discovered in Cape Cod, Massachusetts. The long median ridge blade indicates continued emphasis as a fighting weapon at this date. It was forged as one integral piece. A single side nail attaches the round socket to the pole. Head: 19-3/4" high.
Author's Collection

**6.PAA AMERICAN HALBERD**      Circa 1680–1720

This almost-primitive but effective fighting head splits at the base to fit (wedge-shaped) on a squared haft with two 8-3/4" side straps (two nails each). A median ridge appears on only one spear face; both edges of the elongated blade/beak are sharpened. Head height is 15-1/4 inches.
Author's Collection

**7.PAA AMERICAN HALBERD**      Circa 1730–1740

The shortened 9-1/2" spike reflects an evolving ceremonial or symbolic role—often in local courts or meetings. Observe the crude forging, yet note also the attempts to improvise decoration with pierced holes, a rounded beak and projecting spurs. The restored tassels are typical. Head height: 16 inches.
Douglas Neumann Collection

**8.PAA ENGLISH HALBERD**      Circa 1740–1780

This is the period's classic British sergeant's halberd. Its removeable crossblade slides through a slot in the neck—held by the spear screwed down into an upper notch in the blade. Marks: "COLDSTREAM 11/3." Also compare the spear's bulbous form with the spontoon (34.PAA). Height: 81-1/4 inches total, 14-1/4 inches, head. This was found in New York City after the British evacuation.
Richard Ulbrich Collection

**9.PAA ENGLISH HALBERD**      Circa 1730–1760

Early variations in the basic English sergeant's halberd (8.PAA) are apparent in this squared spear point base and the double rivets securing the crosspiece. Its components are not removable. The head length is 15-7/8 inches; both side straps measure 11 inches (four cross rivets).
Author's Collection

*Chapter 8: Polearms*

| 10.PAA | 11.PAA | 12.PAA |

| 13.PAA | 14.PAA | 15.PAA |

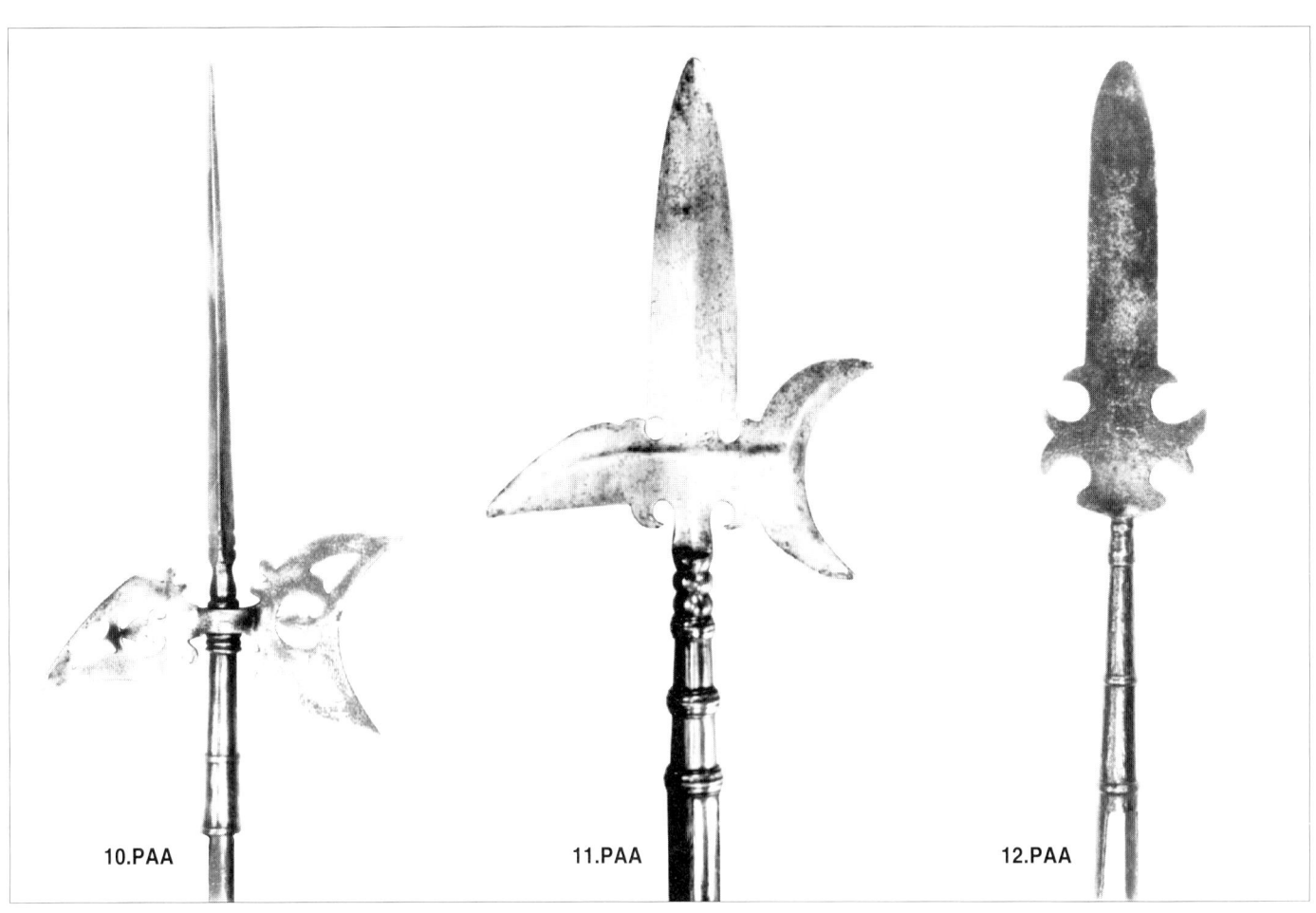

370   Chapter 8: Polearms

**16.PAA**  **17.PAA**  **18.PAA**

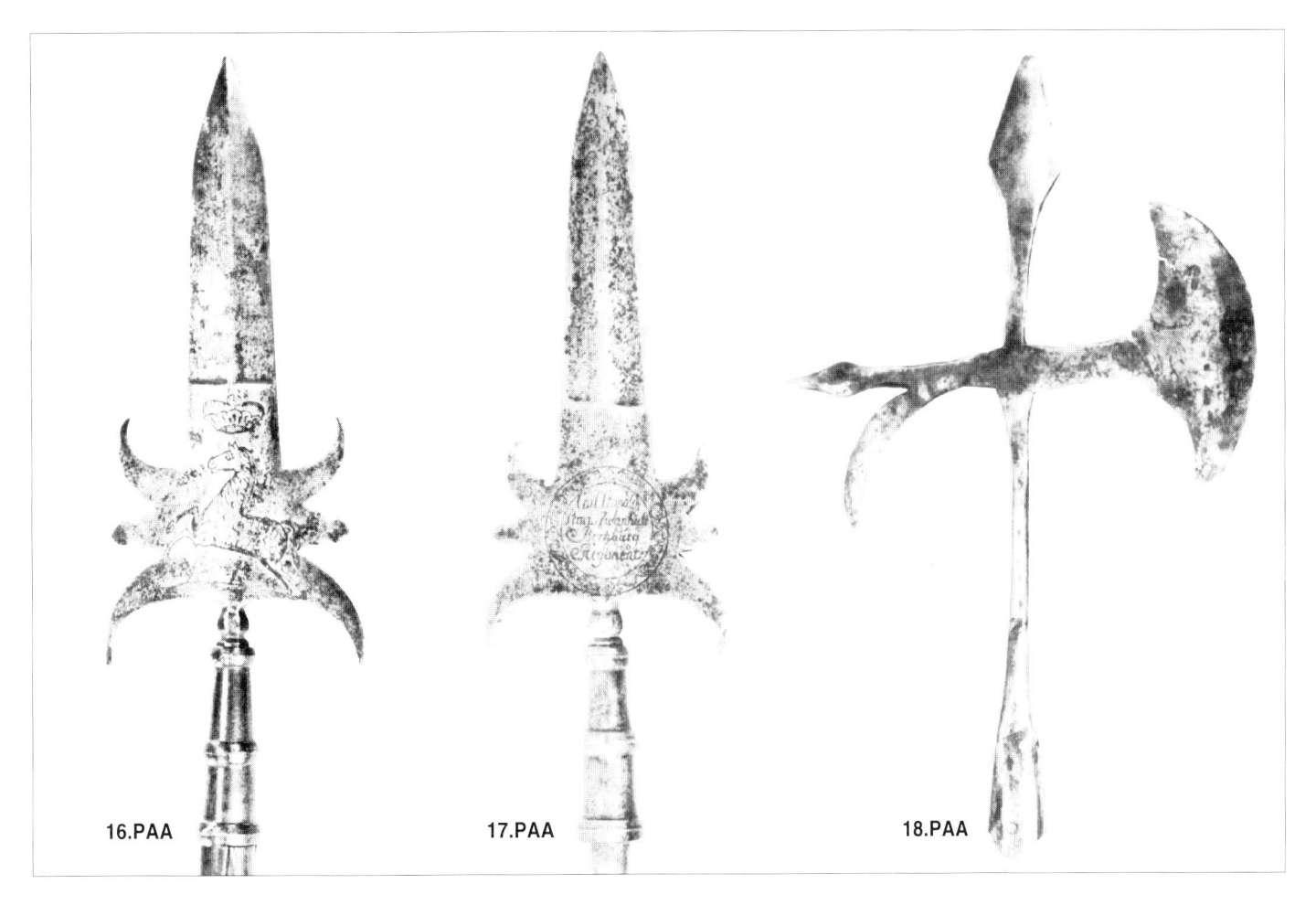

**10.PAA ENGLISH ARTILLERY HALBERD**  Circa 1740–1760
Notice the strength and quality of this British artillery halberd. The 13-1/2" square-sectioned spike is for combat, but the pierced blade and beak are becoming more ceremonial. They are joined by a collar through which the central shaft passes. Height: head 18-7/8 inches; two straps 12-1/4 inches (four cross rivets).
**Robert Nittolo Collection**

**11.PAA EUROPEAN HALBERD**  Circa 1740–1760
Here is a typical mid-century northern European pattern often copied by Americans. Forged as a single unit, the shorter and straighter elements are now more symbols than weapons. Also observe the Germanic rings on its socket. Marks: "R II.M.B. No 1" in the base. The head measures 15-1/2 inches; the straps, 20-3/4 inches.
**George C. Neumann Collection, Valley Forge National Historical Park**

**12.PAA FRENCH HALBERD**  Circa 1695–1740
Note this broad blade and the unique multi-spur design at the base that resembles a fleur-de-lis form. Its long socket bears raised rings, while the side straps have been cut off. The head was found in western Pennsylvania. It measures 15-3/4 inches in height (minus the side straps).
**Author's Collection**

**13.PAA FRENCH HALBERD**  Circa 1690–1730
French halberds were discontinued in 1766 but arrived in North America up through the French and Indian War and as part of Revolutionary War aid. This early long high ridged blade and the partizan-style base projections were favored by France versus Britain's battle-ax pattern (8.PAA). The head height is 16-1/4 inches.
**Author's Collection**

**14.PAA FRENCH HALBERD**  Circa 1700–1715
The elaborate head has extended arms, a faceted neck, an early high ridged blade and decoration including a sun figure (Louis XIV, the Sun King). Also see the French-style crossbar (toggle) set at right angles to the spear's face (like 42.PAA). This head is 14-1/8 inches high; its straps add 10-1/2 inches.
**Fort Ticonderoga Collection**

**15.PAA FRENCH HALBERD**  Circa 1720–1758
This classic French form has clearly evolved: the spear point's high center ridge is almost gone, the flamboyant base projections are shorter and less stylized, while its socket is simplified. The head is typical of those carried in the French and Indian War. It is 12-1/2 inches high.
**Author's Collection**

**16.PAA GERMAN HALBERD**  Circa 1760–1780
Germanic halberds usually resembled the French style but with a shorter spear, only a partial-length middle ridge, reduced base projections, raised rings on the socket and a blade that unscrewed. This engraved crown above a leaping horse identified Brunswick troops with Gen. Burgoyne. Head length: 8-3/8 inches.
**William H. Guthman Collection**

**17.PAA GERMAN HALBERD**  Circa 1776
The base engravings here read "CARL LEOPOLD / PRINZ Zu Anhalt / Berenberg Regiment" and "Compagnie / No 1" on the reverse. This grenadier company of the von Mirbach regiment was with Col. von Donop's corps at Bordentown, New Jersey, at the time of Washington's attack on Trenton. It was found in that area.
**Old Barracks Museum, Trenton, New Jersey**

**18.PAA AMERICAN HALBERD**  Circa 1720–1760
This innovative roughly forged provincial head added a diamond spear point above a crossblade ending in a split beak (note one end repeats the diamond form). Its long neck spreads into a brief mounting socket secured by one cross rivet. The total height shown is 17-3/4 inches.
**Author's Collection**

*Chapter 8: Polearms*  371

**19.PAA**      **20.PAA**      **21.PAA**

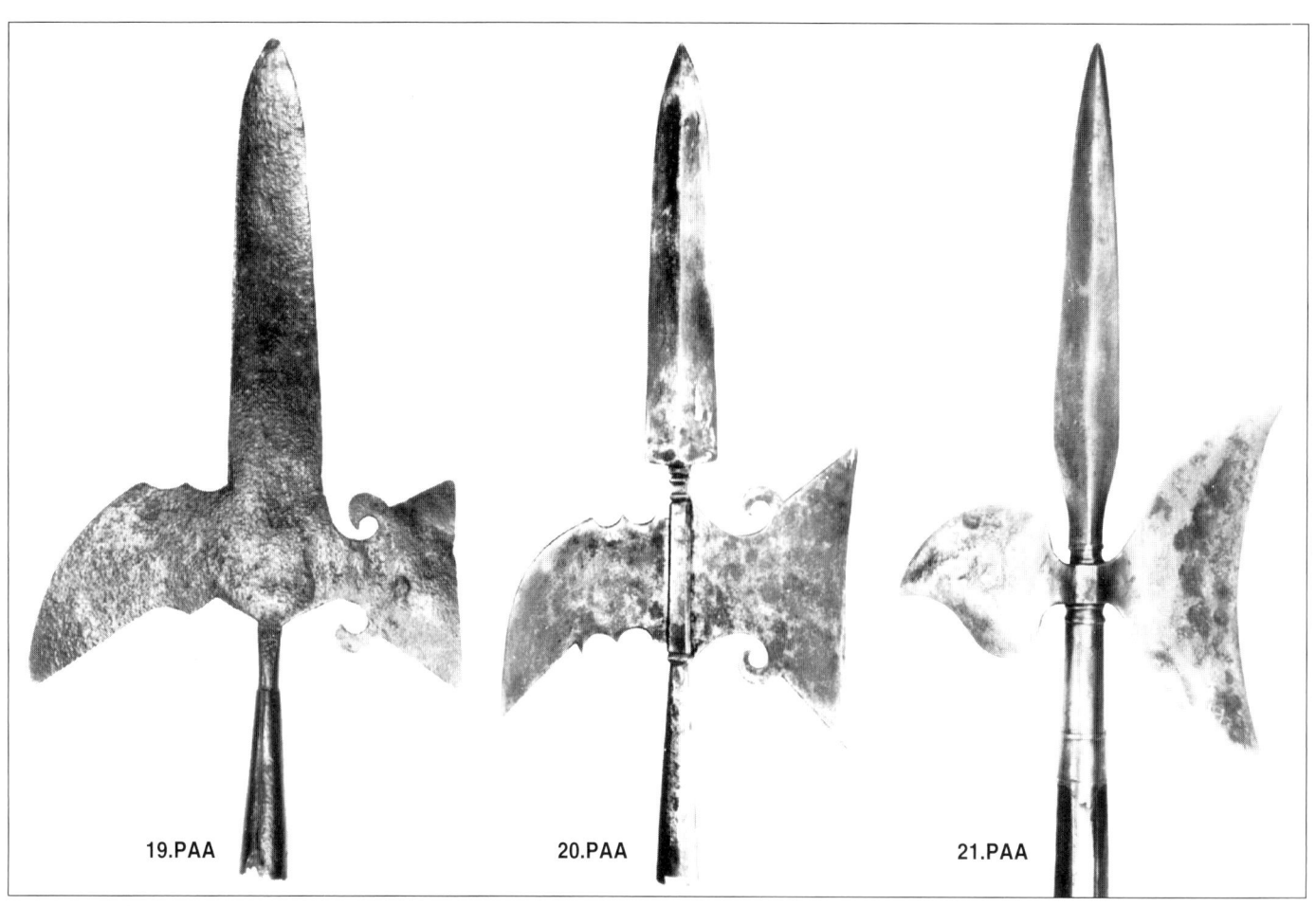

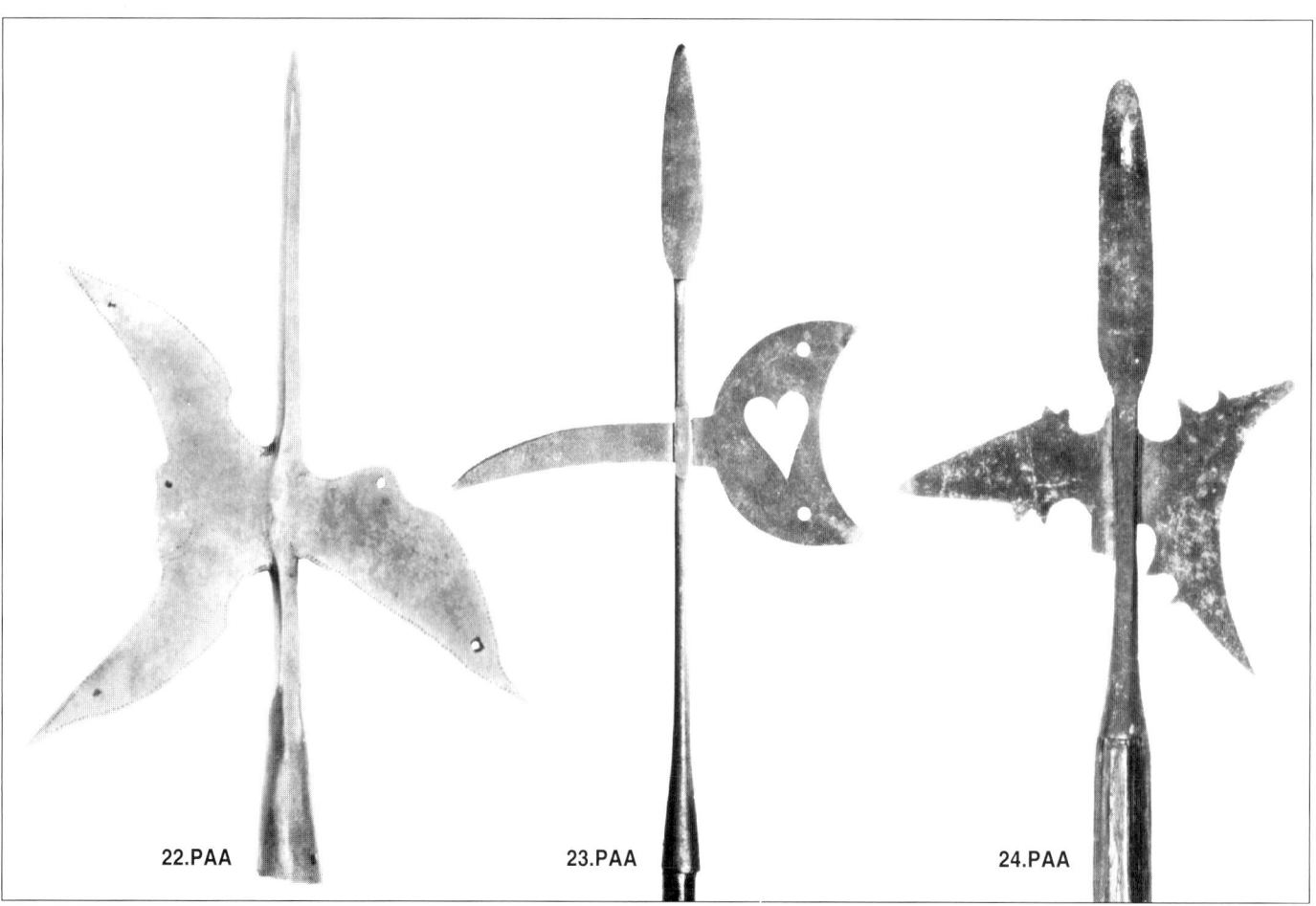

**22.PAA**      **23.PAA**      **24.PAA**

372     *Chapter 8: Polearms*

**19.PAA AMERICAN HALBERD**  Circa 1755–1780
Many American arms were crafted in rural areas based upon the maker's memory of patterns seen in the past. This attempt to replicate the standard British halberd (8.PAA) lost its proportions with a reduced blade size. It was found in central Pennsylvania and measures 15-3/4" high.
**Author's Collection**

**20.PAA AMERICAN HALBERD**  Circa 1760–1780
Several of this pattern from Pennsylvania are known. It was copied as a variant of the standard British sergeant's halberd (9.PAA). The spear does not unscrew, and the crosspiece is fixed in the slot of a squared stem. Both side straps are gone. Height shown: 20-3/4 inches.
**George C. Neumann Collection, Valley Forge National Historical Park**

**21.PAA AMERICAN HALBERD**  Circa 1740–1760
The spear point with its uneven median ridge is of fighting strength, while the cross-blade adds points for lateral strokes—including a widened beak (probably intended to balance the crescent blade). Its two nine-inch straps have a pair of cross rivets; the head height is 14-3/8 inches.
**Author's Collection**

**22.PAA AMERICAN HALBERD**  Circa 1740–1750
Although roughly forged, this provincial folk art halberd supplemented its long spike-like spear point and mounting socket by a flamboyant blade/beak with a crescent man-in-the-moon profile that is outlined in punched dots. The head height totals 17-1/2 inches.
**George C. Neumann Collection, Valley Forge National Historical Park**

**23.PAA AMERICAN HALBERD**  Circa 1754
Lacking the dictates of entrenched craft guilds, individual American smiths were often able to create real beauty from the simplist of forms. Note the balance here from a plain "leaf" spear, thin round/squared center stem, plus an extended beak and crescent blade with its pierced heart and dots. Dated 1754.
**George C. Neumann Collection, Valley Forge National Historical Park**

**24.PAA AMERICAN HALBERD**  Circa 1750–1770
By the time of the French and Indian War, halberds were becoming more symbols of rank than fighting weapons. This spear point is now shorter, and the sheet iron crosspiece adds raised decorative spurs (it passes through a slot in the squared shaft). Height: head 12-1/2 inches; straps 7-1/4 inches.
**Robert Nittolo Collection**

**25.PAA AMERICAN HALBERD**  Circa 1720–1740
The 17th century English halberd with pierced blade (1.PAA) was often copied by later Colonists. Note this 12" straight-sided spear, plus partizan shapes in the open designs of the blade and beak. Its spear unscrews; the crosspiece's collar surrounds the stem. Height: head 18"; straps 5-1/2".
**Fort Ticonderoga Collection**

**26.PAA AMERICAN HALBERD**  Circa 1750–1760
This is typical of the classic American halberd form of the mid-1700s. Notice the early armor-piercing point retained on the spear, the narrow squared shaft with raised rings and baluster turnings, plus the variety of dagger and geometric shapes piercing the scalloped blades. Head height: 17-7/8 inches.
**Author's Collection**

**27.PAA AMERICAN HALBERD**  Circa 1750–1760
This version of the classic Colonial head joins the blade and beak by a collar above a conical base. Its spear point unscrews. Of special interest is the impressive heart, dagger, cross, S-shapes and dot designs penetrating the blades. Total height with haft: 88 inches; head, 14-3/4 inches.
**William H. Guthman Collection**

*Chapter 8: Polearms*

28.PAA  29.PAA  30.PAA

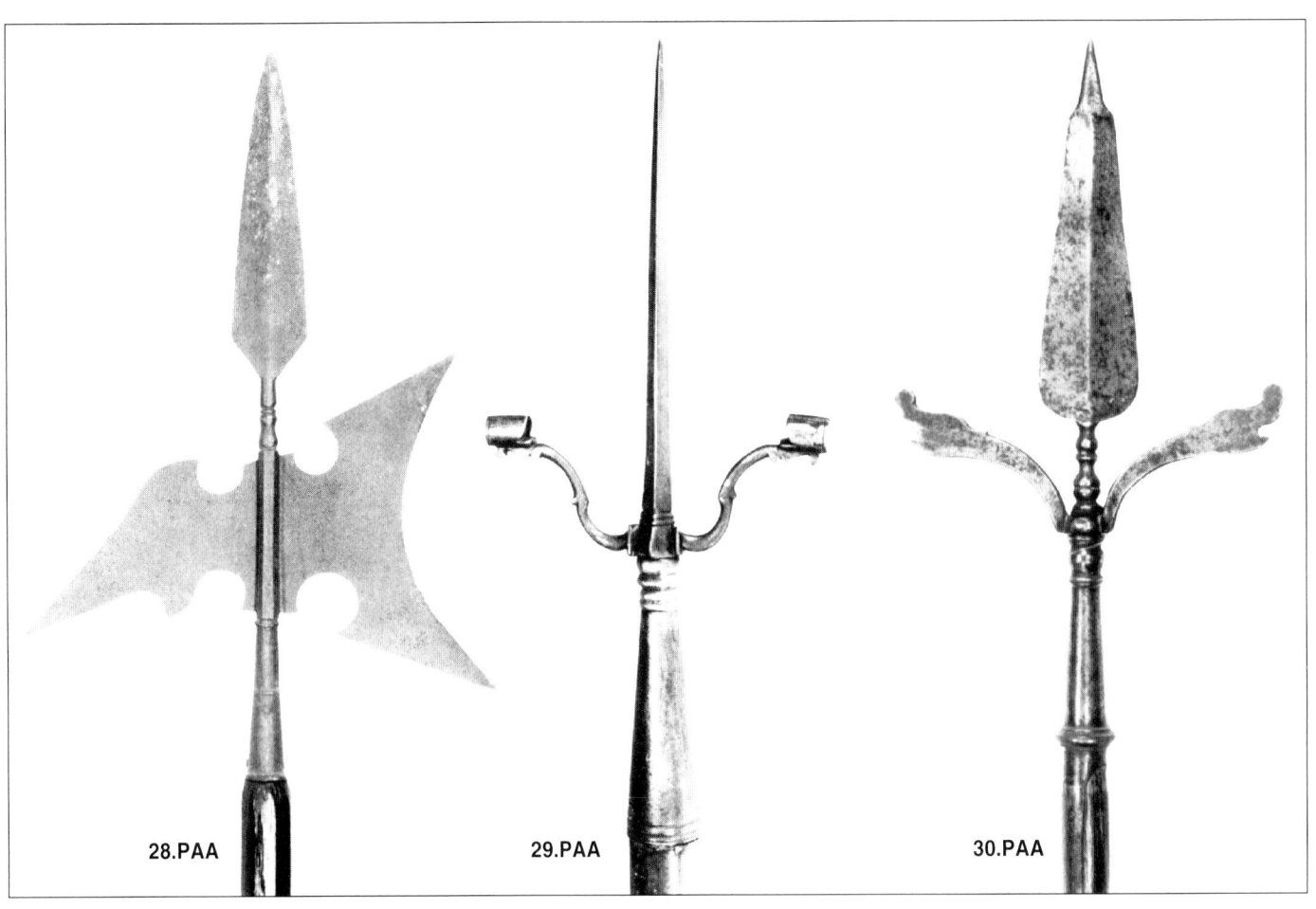

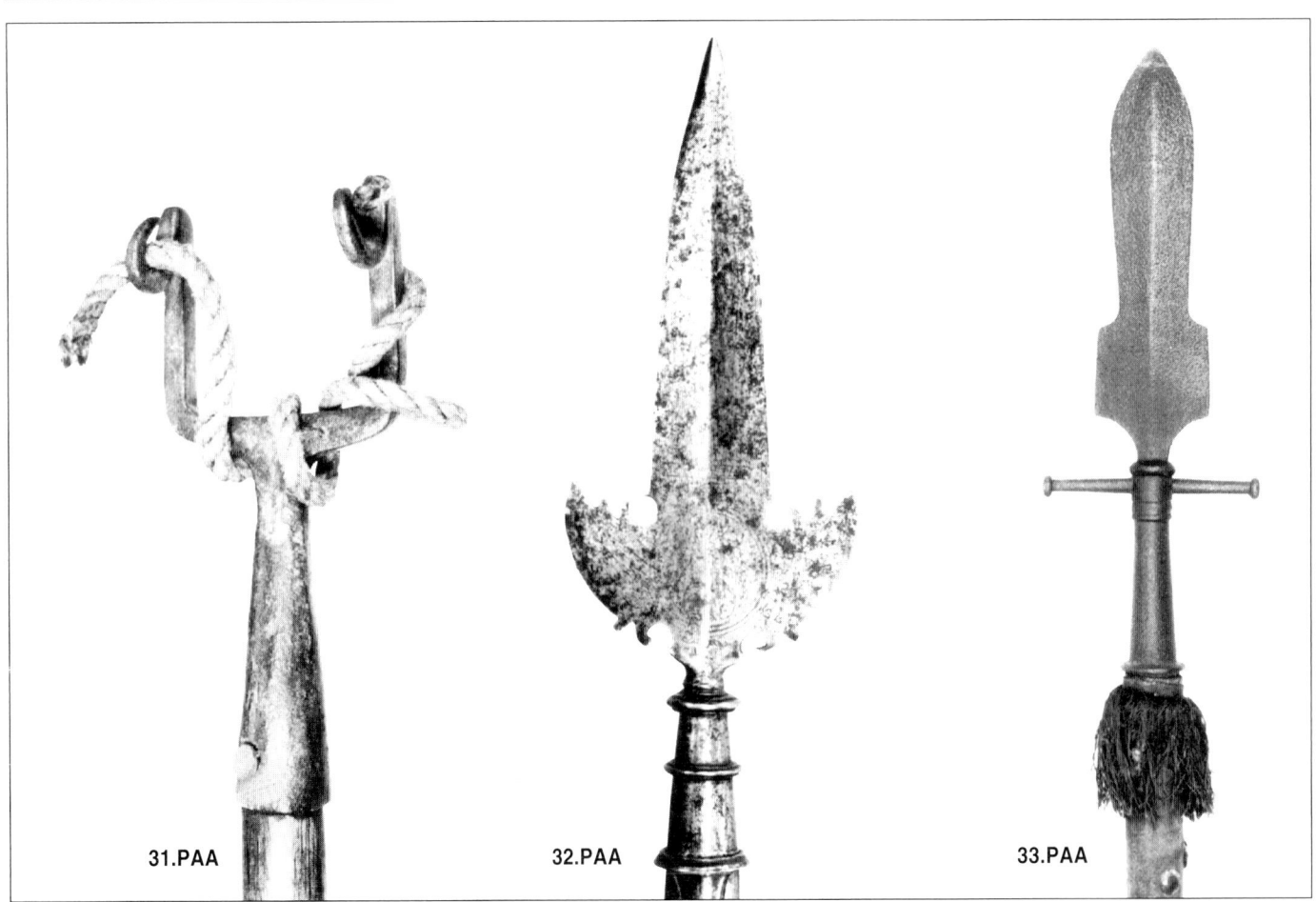

31.PAA  32.PAA  33.PAA

374   *Chapter 8: Polearms*

34.PAA  35.PAA  36.PAA

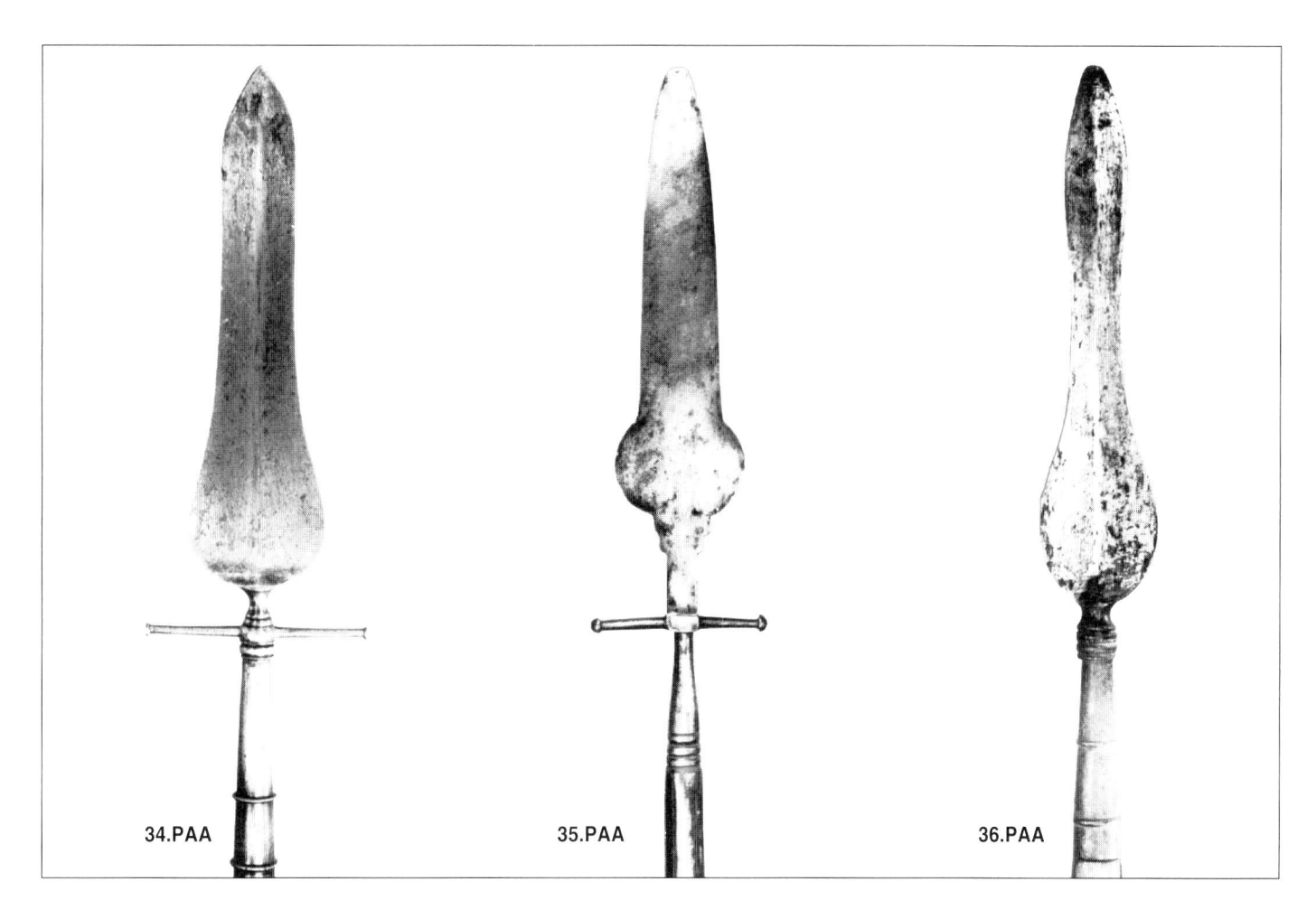

**28.PAA AMERICAN HALBERD**            Circa 1770–1785
Found in Newport News, Virginia, this well-balanced but light head illustrates its evolved emphasis as a symbol of rank as well as civil authority by the time of the Revolution. Observe the baluster stem below its spear and the scalloped cross blade profile. The head measures 14" high.
Author's Collection

**29.PAA EUROPEAN ARTILLERY LINSTOCK**      Circa 1670–1720
Such artillerymen's pole arms combined a spear point with two lower side branches that held the ends of a smoldering match rope used to ignite cannon. The tips of these arms are shaped as open slotted cylinders. Its rectangular sectioned spike, in turn, unscrews. Height: 12-3/8 inches.
George C. Neumann Collection, Valley Forge National Historical Park

**30.PAA EUROPEAN ARTILLERY LINSTOCK**         Dated 1753
This well-made European linstock includes a traditional armor-piercing tip on a spear point, which also unscrews. The two side branches split apart to hold the burning match rope ends. Note the animal heads on the arms and baluster turnings in the neck. It is marked "NH / 1753"; the head measures 14-1/2 inches.
Don Troiani Collection

**31.PAA AMERICAN ARTILLERY LINSTOCK**      Circa 1775–1783
By the time of the American Revolution, most linstocks had eliminated the center blade and retained only the two arms supporting the match rope as illustrated here. The typical haft was also shortened to two to four feet. This locally forged iron head is 6-1/2" high.
George C. Neumann Collection, Valley Forge National Historical Park

**32.PAA EUROPEAN PARTIZAN**              Circa 1650–1700
This partizan form with its tall blade, base projections and symmetrical profile was the polearm of most officers and dignitaries during the 17th century and influenced many spontoons, as well as halberds, during the 1700s. The height shown is 11-3/8 inches.
George C. Neumann Collection, Valley Forge National Historical Park

**33.PAA ENGLISH SPONTOON**              Circa 1760–1786
The expanded blade base, tapered socket and tassel-like "wig" at the bottom show 17th century partizan influence (32.PAA) on this English officer's spontoon. The crossbar ("toggle") is now common. The total length with haft is 80 inches; head height, 13-1/2 inches.
Author's Collection

**34.PAA ENGLISH SPONTOON**              Circa 1750–1780
This is the period's typical British spontoon pattern. The spearpoint is bulbous at the base, and its thin crossbar has a center collar through which the blade unscrews. All edges are sharpened. Head height: 13-3/4 inches; straps, 10-3/8 inches.
George C. Neumann Collection, Valley Forge National Historical Park

**35.PAA AMERICAN SPONTOON**           Circa 1755–1783
Compare this American spontoon copy with Britain's basic form (34.PAA). Note the round spear base, squared shank and the incised rings in the socket. It does not disassemble. Full length on the one-inch diameter haft is 75-3/8 inches. Separate heights: head 12-1/2 inches; straps 13-1/8 inches; ground iron 5-7/8 inches.
Author's Collection

**36.PAA AMERICAN SPONTOON**           Circa 1755–1783
Notice the pleasing symmetry of this slender blade, which reflects British influence. It unscrews at the base and has well-sharpened edges. The original wooden pole never mounted a ground iron. The total length is 77-5/8 inches; its two side straps measure six inches.
George C. Neumann Collection, Valley Forge National Historical Park

*Chapter 8: Polearms*     375

37.PAA  38.PAA  39.PAA  40.PAA

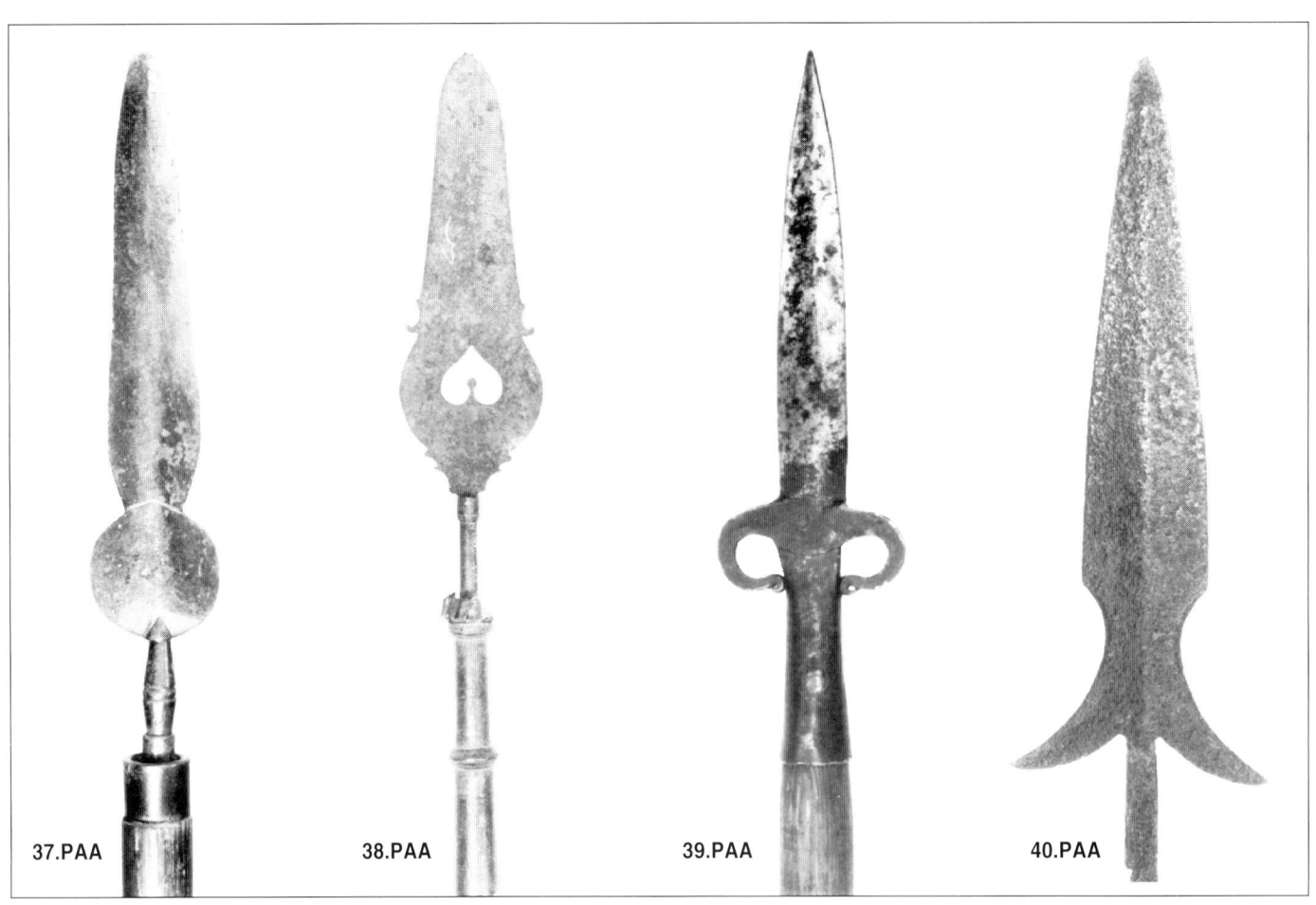

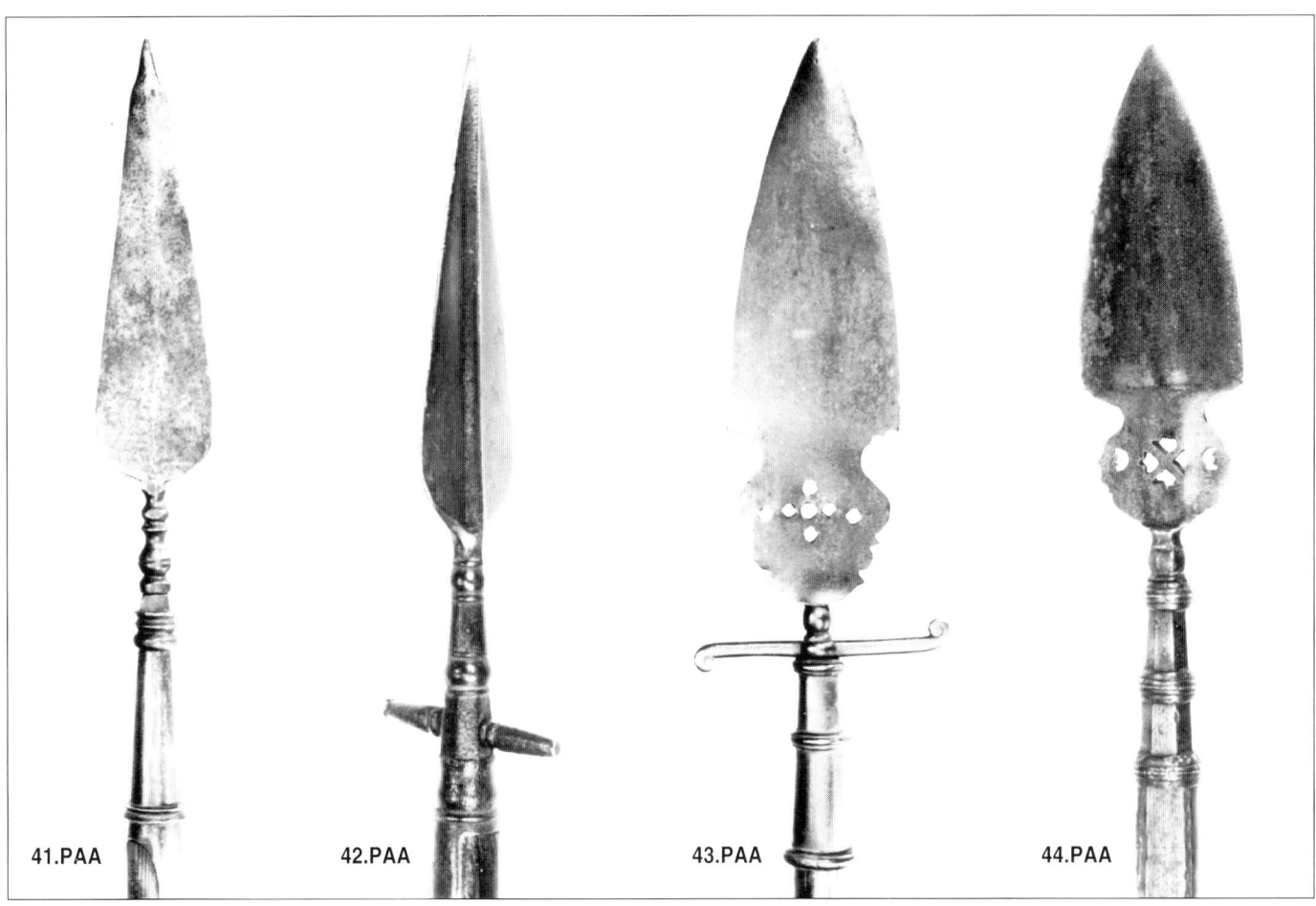

41.PAA  42.PAA  43.PAA  44.PAA

376  Chapter 8: Polearms

45.PAA     46.PAA     47.PAA     48.PAA

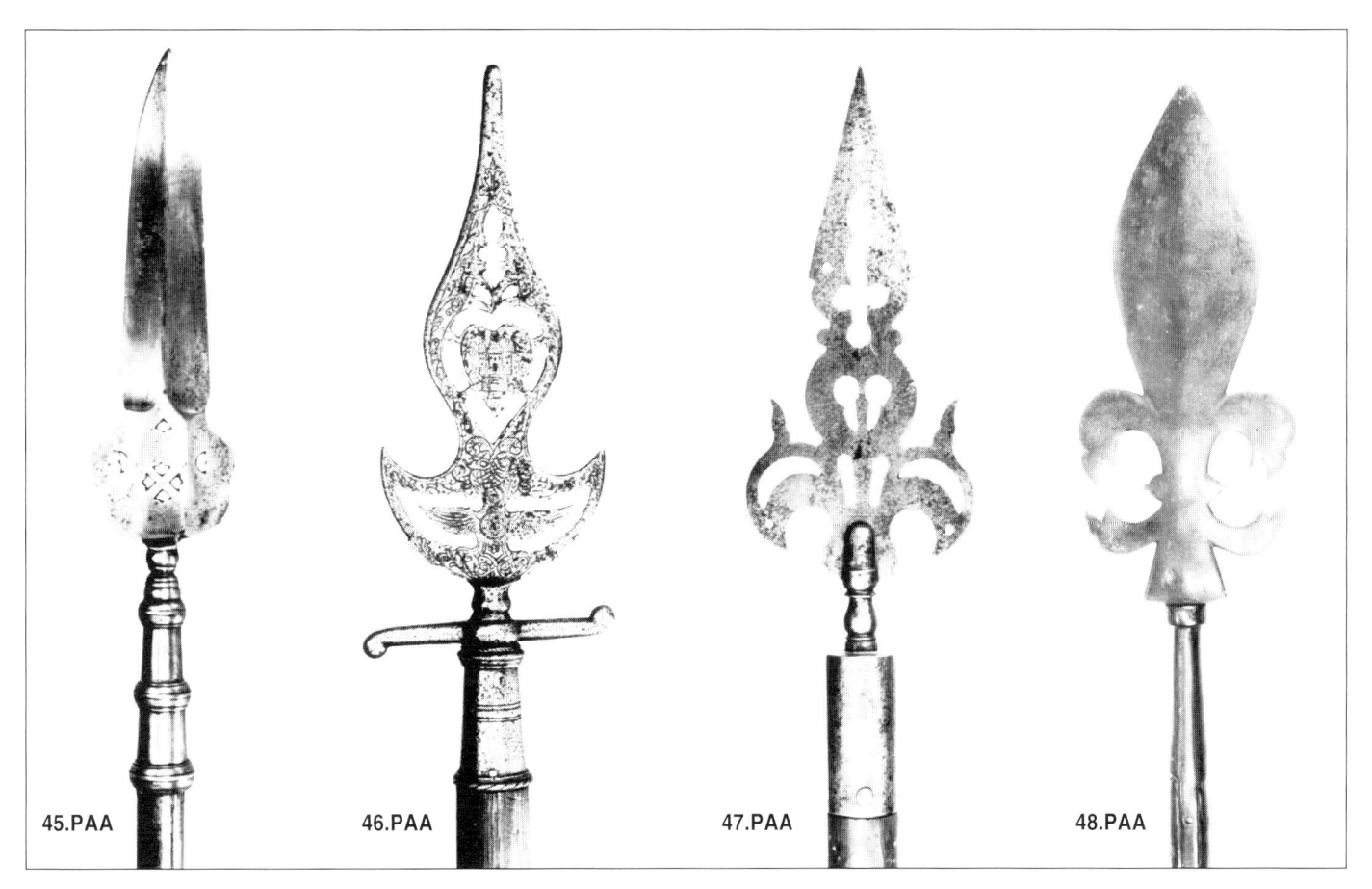

**37.PAA AMERICAN SPONTOON**     Circa 1755–1783
This crude but innovative spearpoint combines rounded shoulders with a disk-like base. It rests on a turned shank that penetrates the staff, which is bound by a 3/4" iron ferrule (band). Length on the one-inch diameter ash haft is 78-1/4 inches; the head is nine inches.
**Fort Ticonderoga Collection**

**38.PAA AMERICAN SPONTOON**     Circa 1740–1770
Found in central Pennsylvania, this simple pattern adds forge artistry with a bulbous blade base bearing a heart cutout and spurs along the edges. Tassel-like iron strips at mid-socket are further enhancements. Head shown: 14-1/2" high.
**Richard Ulbrich Collection**

**39.PAA AMERICAN SPONTOON**     Circa 1775–1780
This sturdy sharpened blade has a crosspiece welded across its base to achieve a "hands-on-hips" profile. Notice, too, the small curled finials. The tapered socket is wrapped iron—open on the reverse side. Head height: 11-3/4 inches.
**Author's Collection**

**40.PAA AMERICAN SPONTOON**     Circa 1755–1780
Excavated near Fort Ticonderoga, this simple head is a known form. All outer edges on the symmetrical blade and base projections are sharpened. Its flat tang was driven into the top of its haft. Height shown: 13 inches.
**Author's Collection**

**41.PAA FRENCH SPONTOON**     Circa 1740–1758
Note the earlier thickened armor-piercing tip on this popular French leaf blade. The pattern lacks a crossbar but adds baluster turnings to the neck. Head length to the base ring is 13-1/2 inches; the two straps measure 13-1/4 inches (four rivets).
**George C. Neumann Collection, Valley Forge National Historical Park**

**42.PAA FRENCH SPONTOON**     Circa 1710–1758
This was apparently the most popular French pattern of the period. Its leaf-shaped spearpoint has a high median ridge and the crossbar (toggle) pierces the faceted socket at right angles to the blade face. Head height, 8-3/4 inches; straps, eight inches.
**Author's Collection**

**43.PAA GERMAN SPONTOON**     Circa 1740–1780
The usual Germanic spontoon had a broad blade reduced at the base to a decorative silhouette with pierced designs. The crossbar curled in opposite directions, while a round or faceted socket mounted raised rings. This 16" blade unscrews.
**George C. Neumann Collection, Valley Forge National Historical Park**

**44.PAA GERMAN SPONTOON**     Circa 1750–1780
This Germanic variation (versus 43.PAA) omits the crossbar and adds a faceted socket with bulbous raised rings. Its straps have been cut. The crescent/arrow pierced base design is typical. Head height: 11 inches.
**Author's Collection**

**45.PAA GERMAN SPONTOON**     Circa 1760–1780
A further form found in German military prints shows this narrower blade with a median ridge above an enlarged circular base pierced with moon/arrow designs (no crossbar). The popular three large rings appear on its round socket. Head: 15" high.
**George C. Neumann Collection, Valley Forge National Historical Park**

**46.PAA GERMAN SPONTOON**     Circa 1710–1750
An earlier Germanic pattern believed still in use during America's Revolution had this scalloped outline similar to the partizan (32.PAA) with symbolic cutout designs, plus a crossbar as shown. The head is 10 inches in height.
**George C. Neumann Collection, Valley Forge National Historical Park**

**47.PAA AMERICAN SPONTOON**     Circa 1760–1770
Originating in northern Pennsylvania, this impressive scalloped and pierced flat iron blade is held in a slot of the turned shank that, in turn, is anchored to a deep cap on the staff. Its total length is 80-7/8 inches; the head height is 10-7/8 inches.
**Richard Ulbrich Collection**

**48.PAA AMERICAN SPONTOON**     Circa 1755–1780
Reflecting the broad Germanic patterns, this head attributed to Pennsylvania includes dual base projections with bird-like terminals under a wide leaf-shaped blade on a narrow shank. Head height: 15-5/8 inches.
**Author's Collection**

49.PAA  50.PAA  51.PAA  52.PAA

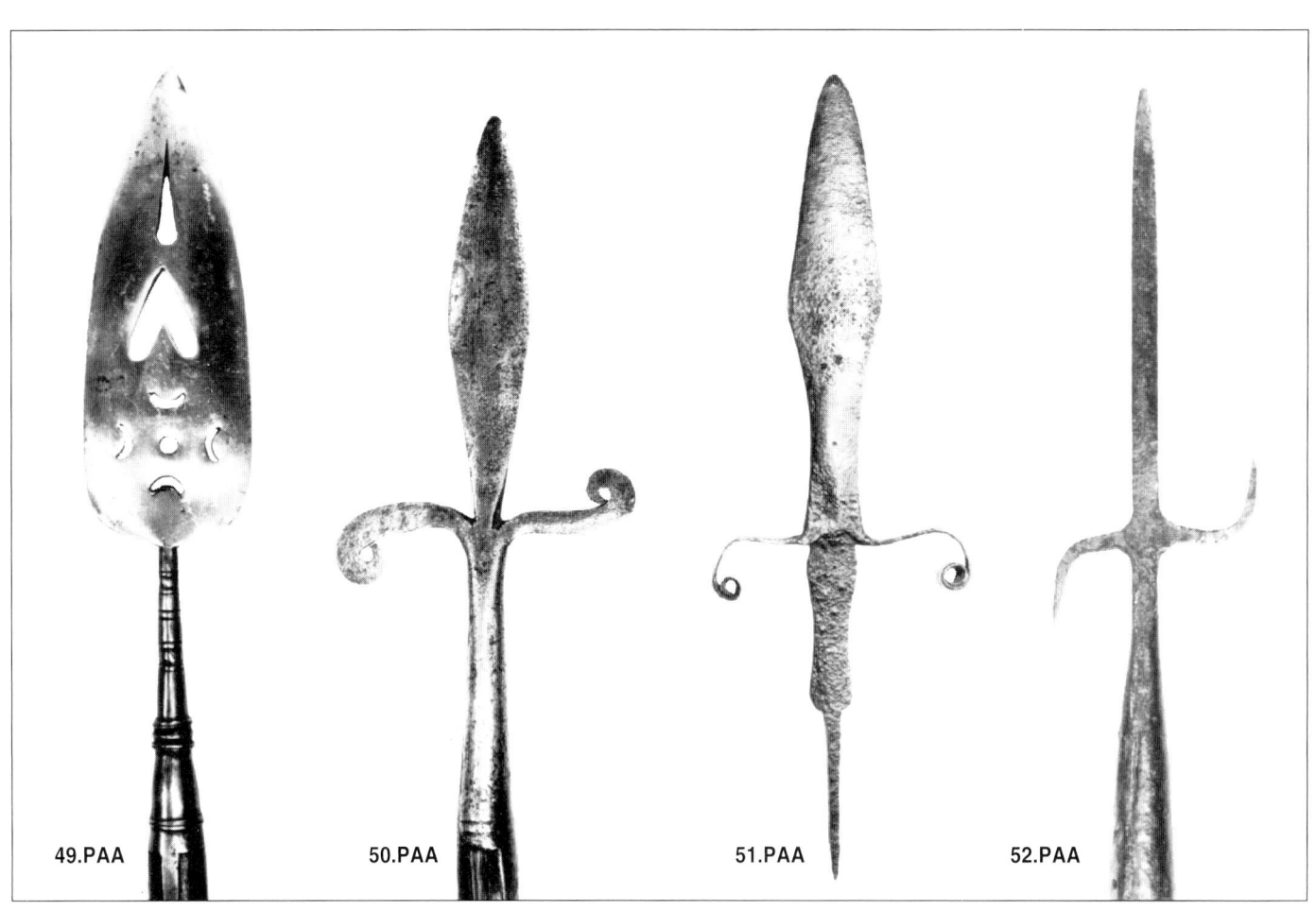

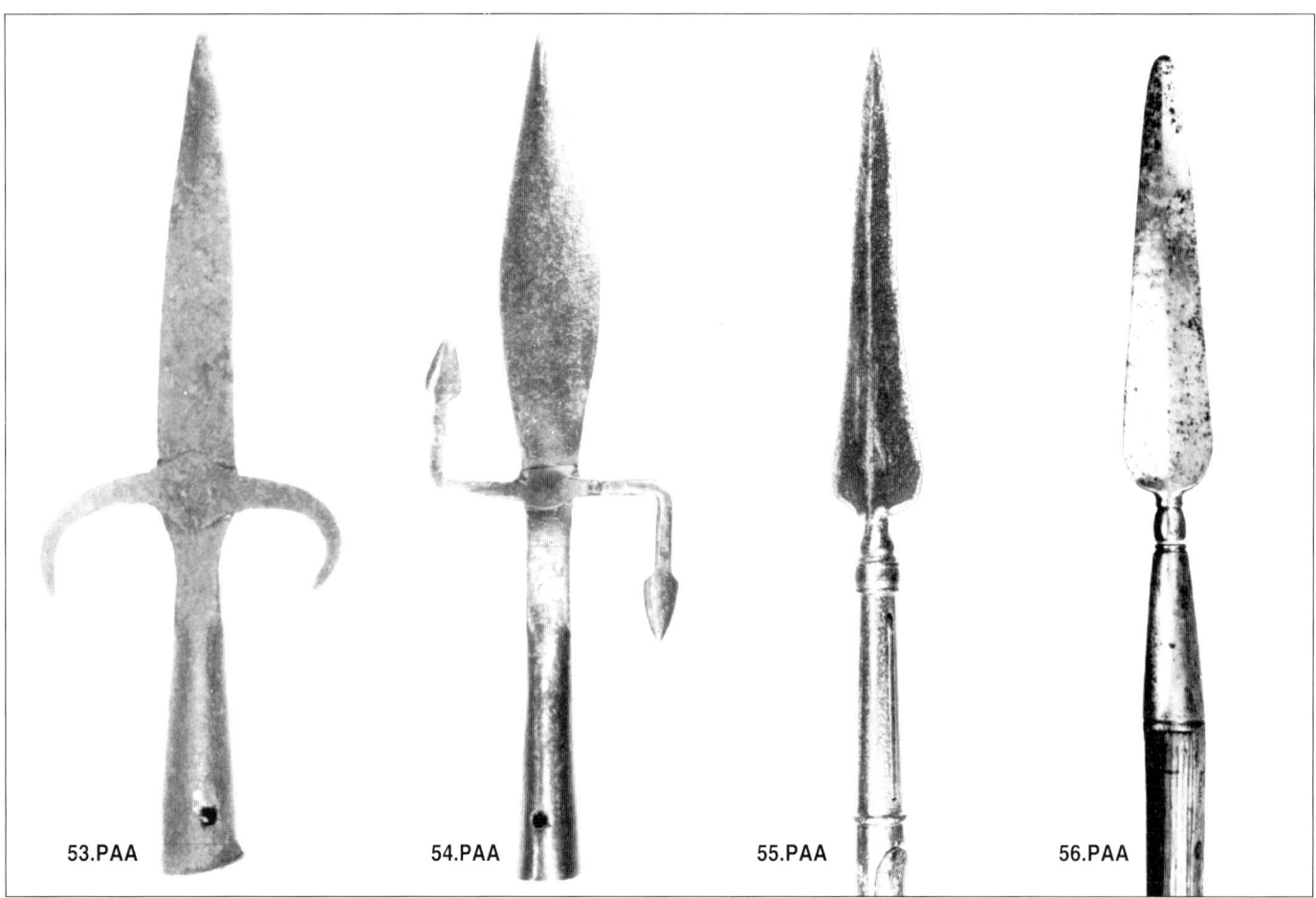

53.PAA  54.PAA  55.PAA  56.PAA

Chapter 8: Polearms

57.PAA  58.PAA  59.PAA  60.PAA

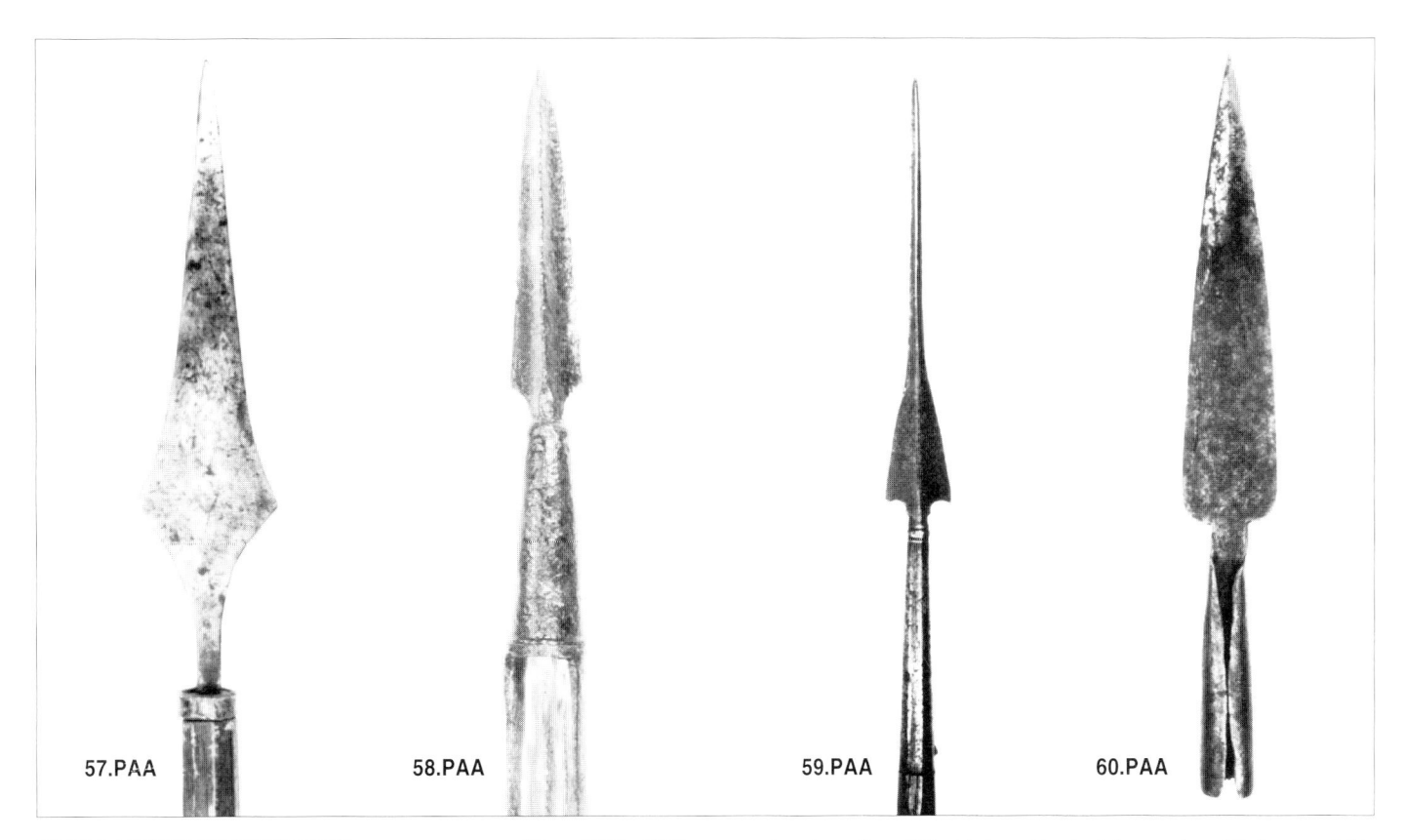

**49.PAA AMERICAN SPONTOON**  Circa 1755–1780
Additional German influence is apparent in this simple leaf blade pierced by a bleeding heart and a traditional crescent design. Observe, too, the multi-turnings in the narrow stem. Lengths: total, 82-1/4 inches; head, 12-3/8 inches; straps, 7-1/2 inches (haft, 1-1/8" diameter).
Author's Collection

**50.PAA AMERICAN SPONTOON**  Circa 1755–1783
Forged as one piece, this Colonial poleam mounts a convex leaf blade above a conical socket, while two flattened side branches curl in opposite directions. It was found in northern New York State. Height of head: 12-1/4 inches.
Author's Collection

**51.PAA AMERICAN SPONTOON**  Circa 1740–1780
Excavated in New York's Mohawk Valley, this roughly forged blade projects uneven scrolled branches from its base and continues to a nail-like shank that was driven into the top of its haft. Height shown: 18-1/8 inches.
Author's Collection

**52.PAA AMERICAN SPONTOON**  Circa 1720–1780
This obvious fighting head joins a long rectangular-sectioned thrusting blade to a simple lapped conical socket, with a rough S-crossbar welded across their junction. It is 15-1/2" high.
Author's Collection

**53.PAA AMERICAN SPONTOON**  Circa 1755–1780
Wartime pressures are indicated in this roughly forged head. The uneven convex blade shows a downturned crossbar welded across its base above a wrapped socket having an open seam on the reverse side. Height: 11-3/4 inches.
Author's Collection

**54.PAA AMERICAN SPONTOON**  Circa 1775–1780
A New England smith improved on the popular S-crossbar by adding right angles and arrowheads; they are flat on one side and rounded on the other. Its leaf blade continues down to a simple wrapped socket. Height shown: 13-1/4 inches.
Author's Collection

**55.PAA AMERICAN SPONTOON**  Circa 1775–1783
This head began as a standard British halberd (8.PAA) and was altered to a spontoon by cutting off the blade and beak at the opening of their cross slot in the shaft. Head to base ring, 14-1/8 inches; two straps, 15-5/8 inches.
Author's Collection

**56.PAA AMERICAN SPONTOON**  Circa 1775–1776
"PRAHL" appears on a strap of this weapon for Lewis Prahl of Philadelphia, who had American pike and sword contracts. This simple blade and socket could be a pike or spontoon; the latter was chosen because of its finished surface. Head: 11 inches; straps, 9-3/4 inches.
Hermann W. Williams, Jr. Collection

**57.PAA AMERICAN SPONTOON**  Circa 1775–1783
The diamond-like profile gained acceptance during the Revolution. This rural example drove the 10-3/4" blade's bottom spike into an octagonal haft (painted green; 1-1/8" diameter). The pole's ferrule band is lead.
Author's Collection

**58.PAA EUROPEAN PIKE**  Circa 1600–1700
Long infantry pikes (often 16 to 18 feet) brought to early America were impractical here and were often shortened to six- to eight-foot "half pikes." The triangular concave-faced point shown here springs from a tapered base (two straps cut off). Head height: 9-1/8 inches.
Author's Collection

**59.PAA EUROPEAN PIKE**  Circa 1600–1700
This 17th century pike head with its long armor-piercing nose and faceted socket was found with an old label, which read, "After the Revolution, used as a court-officer's staff at the Courthouse, Newburgh, N.Y." Total length: 86 inches; head, 16-3/4 inches.
Author's Collection

**60.PAA AMERICAN PIKE**  Circa 1775–1780
To fill the early weapons shortage during the Revolutionary War, local American blacksmiths produced large numbers of these crude but effective pike heads for the rebel army and naval vessels. This head is 11-3/4 inches long.
Author's Collection

*Chapter 8: Polearms*

61.PAA  62.PAA  63.PAA  64.PAA  65.PAA

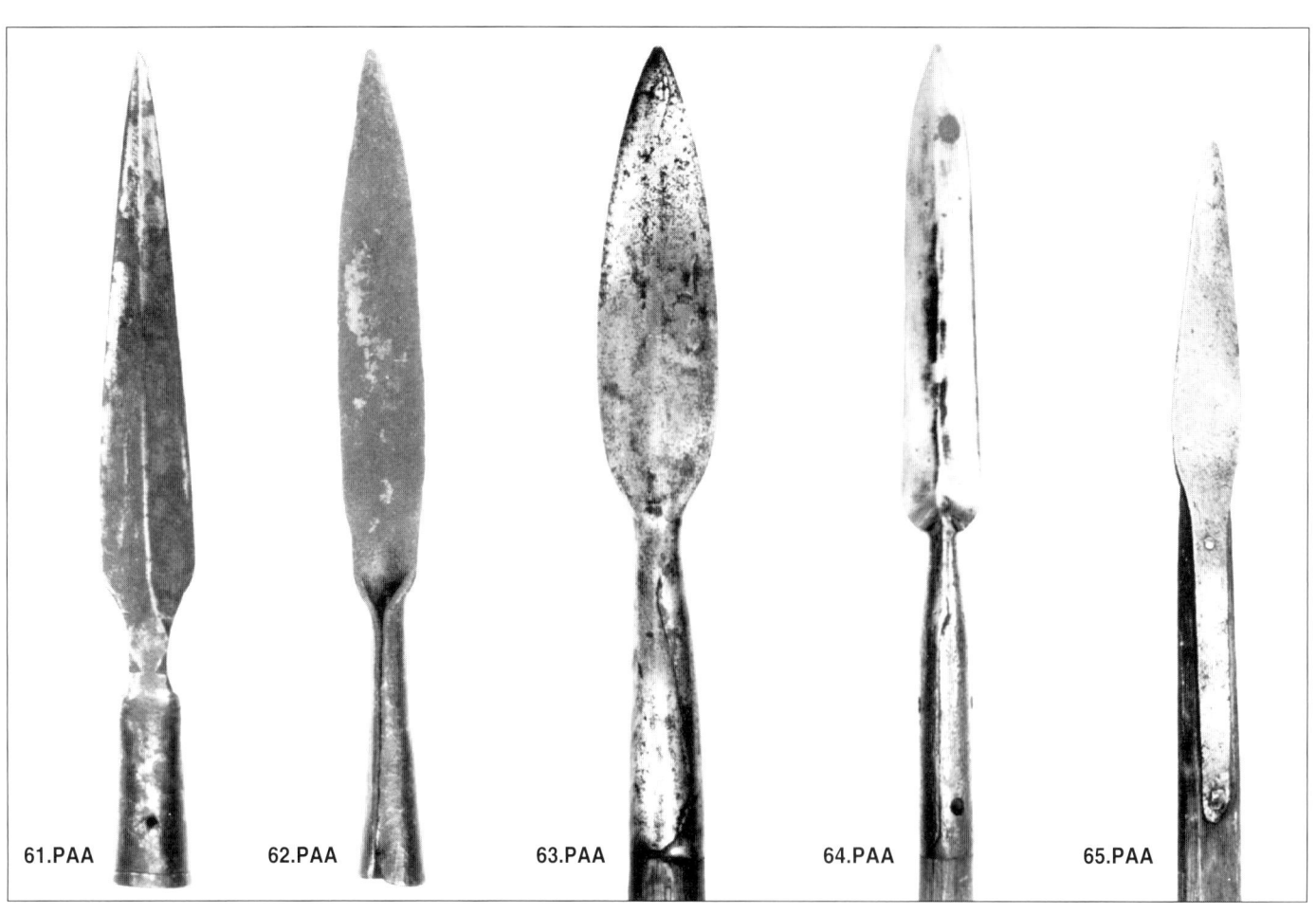

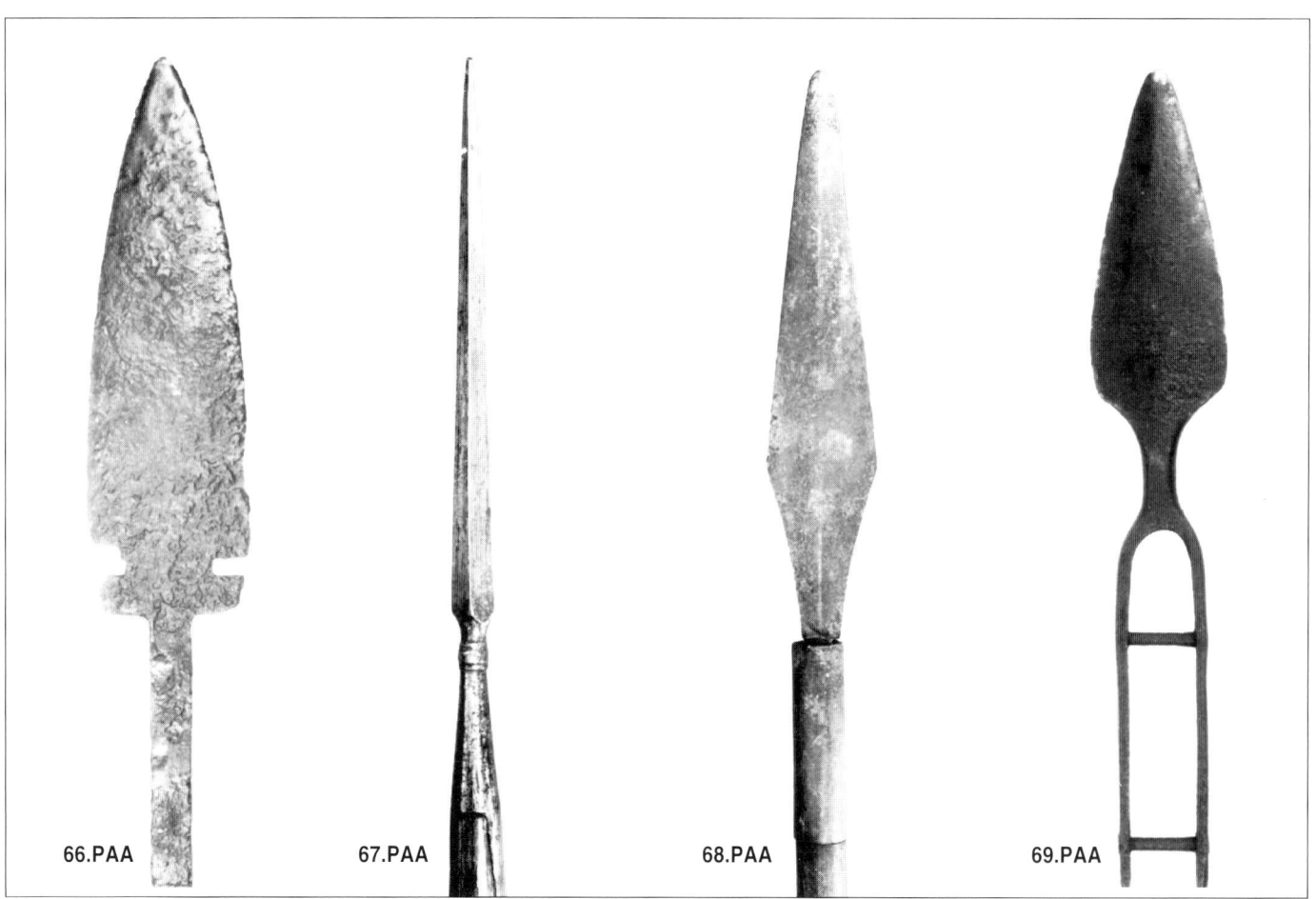

66.PAA  67.PAA  68.PAA  69.PAA

380  *Chapter 8: Polearms*

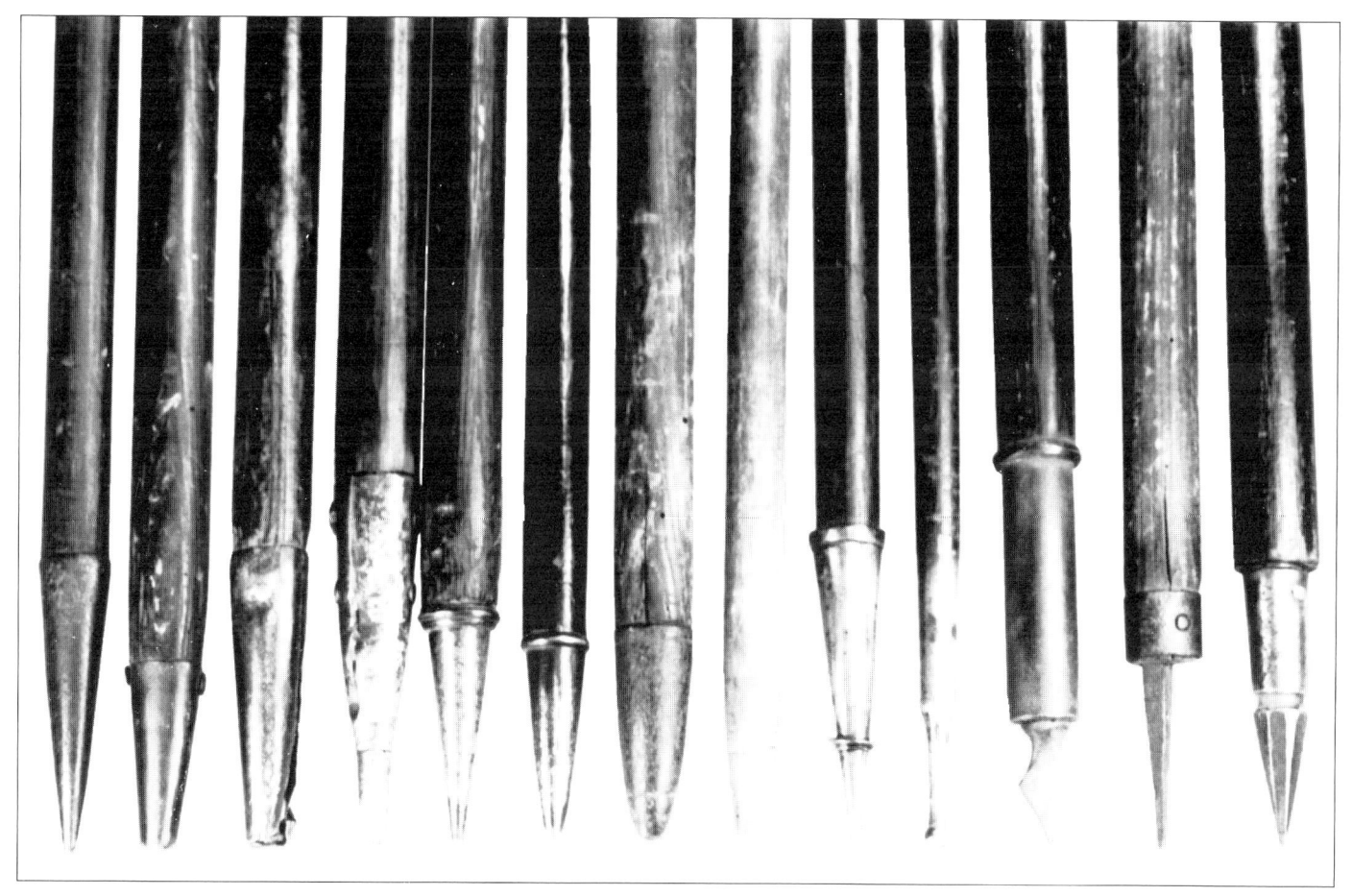

**AMERICAN POLEARMS, BUTT POINT VARIATIONS**
Equally as different as the polearm heads were the varieties of butt points at the other end of the haft to protect the wood from wear. Notice this range from a plain tapered uncovered tip to sheet and cast iron or brass in myriad forms.

**61. PAA AMERICAN PIKE**  Circa 1775–1780
This variant pike form has a sturdy center-ridged blade leading down to a mounting socket having an open seam on the reverse side. Note the bottom raised ring and the prideful notches struck into the neck. Head: 12-1/4" high.
Author's Collection

**62. PAA AMERICAN PIKE**  Circa 1775–1780
This rudely crafted spearhead includes a long narrow flattened blade with both edges sharpened. Its simple conical socket leaves an unlapped seam. The head length is 12-1/2 inches.
Author's Collection

**63. PAA AMERICAN PIKE**  Circa 1775–1780
Typical of American pikes, this leaf-shaped blade flows into a simple lapped mounting socket on a 1-1/8" diameter ash haft, which ends in a 6-1/8" conical ground iron. Lengths: total, 81-5/8 inches; head, 10-1/8 inches.
Author's Collection

**64. PAA AMERICAN PIKE**  Circa 1775–1780
Substantial heads of this shape have been found in the Fort Ticonderoga area. Note the thick center-ridged blade with honed edges and the socket having a center seam plus two cross-rivets. Head height: 18-3/8 inches.
Author's Collection

**65. PAA AMERICAN PIKE**  Circa 1775–1778
Several of this form have been discovered in Champlain Valley (New York) Revolutionary War sites. The thin flat blade splits into two mounting straps (two nails) on a wedge-shaped pole end. Head plus straps measure 14 inches.
Author's Collection

**66. PAA AMERICAN PIKE**  Circa 1775–1780
This rather fragile head is another shape found on Champlain Valley wartime sites. Cut from a flat sheet of iron with a bottom stud to insert into a slotted pole, its side notches create a simple crossbar. The head shown is 11-1/2 inches.
George C. Neumann Collection, Valley Forge National Historical Park

**67. PAA AMERICAN NAVAL PIKE**  Circa 1775–1800
Most American Revolutionary War pikes were interchangeable for land or sea. This slender design, however, is associated with naval use. The 8-1/4" square-sectioned spike tops a 2-3/8" socket. Two 4-5/8" straps hold three rivets.
George C. Neumann Collection, Valley Forge National Historical Park

**68. PAA AMERICAN NAVAL PIKE**  Circa 1775–1800
This Revolutionary War-period diamond-like blade has its bottom tang driven into the top of a 58-7/8" haft having a broad upper iron collar, plus a bottom band that permits the pole to project below it (not to scar the decks). Height: 69 inches.
George C. Neumann Collection, Valley Forge National Historical Park

**69. PAA AMERICAN PIKE**  Circa 1775–1780
Discovered in upper New York State, this sturdy convex-faced spearhead narrows to a thick neck and substantial side branches holding two cross rivets. It could be for land or sea use or even as a spontoon. Length shown: 12-1/2 inches.
Author's Collection

*Chapter 8: Polearms*

# Glossary of Terms

**Backstrap:** A metal strip along the back of a sword grip or pistol handle.
**Backsword:** A long sword with a single cutting edge.
**Barrel:** The metal tube of a firearm through which a bullet passes.
**Blunderbuss:** A short, large-caliber shoulder firearm with an expanded muzzle.
**Bore:** The interior diameter of a firearm barrel.
**Breech:** The rear end of a barrel (opposite the muzzle).
**Beavertail:** The traditional raised carving around the butt tang of British arms.
**Bridle:** A supporting strap on a lock, usually (inside) to brace the tumbler and (outside) to strengthen the frizzen screw.
**Broadsword:** A long sword with a double-edged blade.
**Butt Plate Tang:** The upper extension of the butt plate—reaching along the stock comb.
**Carbine:** A military light shoulder firearm with a reduced bore size.
**Cock:** A pivoting arm on a lock that holds the flint in its upper jaws.
**Comb:** The thin upper ridge along the top of the stock butt.
**Counterguard:** Part of the sword hilt—between the grip and blade.
**Cutlass:** A naval short saber, usually with a wide guard.
**Doglock:** An early gunlock having a rear latch to engage the cock for safety.
**Escutcheon:** A shaped metal piece on the "small" or "wrist" of the stock.
**Ferrule:** A supporting or binding base at either end of a sword grip.
**Finial:** An ornamental end, usually on sword quillons or trigger guards.
**Flash Pan:** A pan outside the barrel's touch-hole holding the priming powder.
**Flintlock:** A method of firearm ignition by striking flint against steel.
**Frizzen (Battery):** The pivoting steel piece struck by the flint to produce sparks.
**Fuller:** A groove cut into the face of a sword to improve balance, strengthen and reduce weight.
**Furniture:** Metal fittings on a firearm (not the barrel, lock or rammer).
**Fusil (Fusee):** A light smaller-bore musket carried by officers. Also the French word for a musket.
**Grip:** The part of a sword hilt normally held by the hand.
**Haft:** The shaft or handle of a polearm, tomahawk, etc., when longer than the blade.
**Halberd:** A polearm used by infantry sergeants.
**Hanger:** A short cutting sword carried mostly by foot soldiers.
**Head:** The upper part of a polearm mounted above the base.

**Hilt:** The grip, pommel, mountings and guard of a sword.
**Holster Pistol:** A military-style pistol normally used by an officer.
**Hunting Sword:** A short civilian sword originally carried while hunting.
**Inboard:** The side of a sword against the body when worn on the left side.
**Knuckle Bow:** The part of a sword guard designed to protect the knuckles.
**Lock plate:** The external iron plate upon which most of the lock parts are mounted.
**Matchlock:** An early ignition system using a match cord to ignite the powder.
**Miquelet Lock:** A Spanish flintlock form.
**Musket:** A military smoothbore, large caliber shoulder firearm.
**Musketoon:** A short, large caliber smoothbore musket or blunderbuss form.
**Muzzle:** The mouth or open end of a barrel.
**Outboard:** The side of a sword away from the body.
***Pas D'ane***: The two rings on a small sword hilt (one on each side of the *ricasso*).
**Pike:** A long military spear.
**Pommel:** The upper end of a sword hilt.
**Proof Marks:** Devices stamped on weapons to indicate completion of proofing tests.
**Quillon:** The end of a sword guard—after it passes the grip.
**Rammer:** A wooden or metal rod for ramming a charge down the barrel.
**Ricasso:** A squared blade area under the sword hilt or between the small sword *pas d'ane*.
**Rifle:** A shoulder arm with grooves cut inside the barrel.
**Short Saber:** A light cut-and-thrust sword worn by many officers.
**Side Plate:** A metal piece supporting the lock screws on the side of the stock opposite the lock.
**Small Sword:** A civilian sword with a thin straight thrusting blade.
**Snaphaunce:** An early form of flintlock ignition having a separate battery and pan cover.
**Spontoon:** An officer's spear-like polearm.
**Stock:** The wooden part of a firearm.
**Tang:** A narrow extension, e.g. the projecting rear of a barrel breech plug.
**Wall Gun (Rampart Gun):** A large smoothbore or rifled shoulder arm.
**Wheel-Lock:** An early ignition system using sparks from a wheel revolving against an iron pyrites or flint.

# Measurement Definitions

**Barrel: (1st Figure)** the length from the muzzle to the end of the breech (not including the tang); **(2nd Figure)** the actual measured bore caliber.
**Blade: (1st Figure)** the straight distance between the point and its contact with the hilt; **(2nd Figure)** the width of the blade at the hilt.
**Butt Tang:** A horizontal measurement from the tang's tip to the point opposite the upper plate's rearmost extension.
**Lock: (1st Figure)** the length of the lock plate; **(2nd Figure)** height of the plate between the cock and flashpan.
**Side Plate:** The front-to-back measurement.
**Total Length:** A straight line distance between the two outermost points.
**Trigger Guard:** The distance along the stock between the guard's two ends.

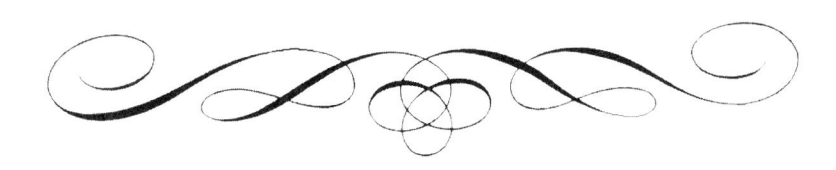

## NOMENCLATURE OF THE WEAPONS

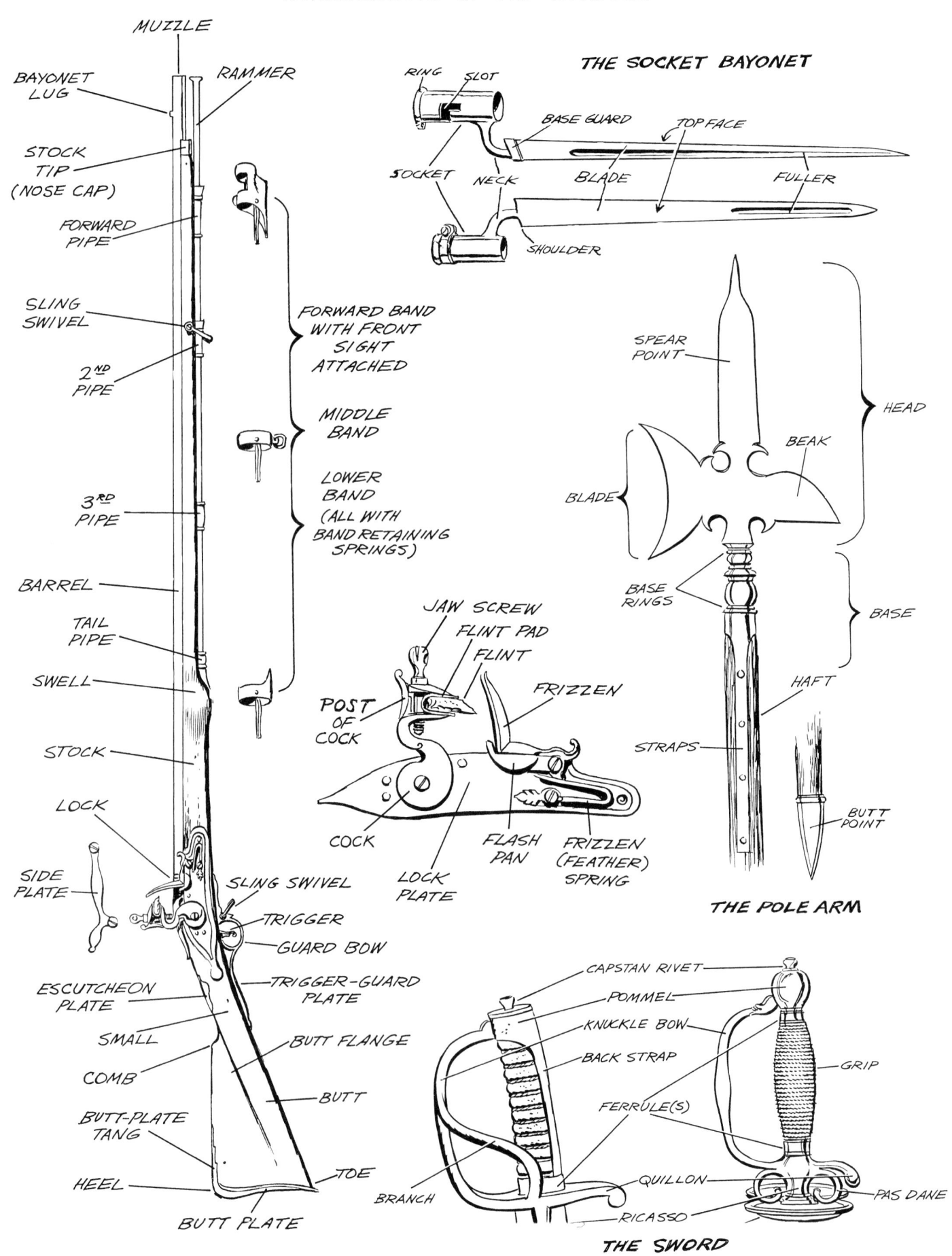

### THE SOCKET BAYONET

Labels: RING, SLOT, BASE GUARD, TOP FACE, SOCKET, NECK, BLADE, FULLER, SHOULDER

### The Musket

Labels: MUZZLE, RAMMER, BAYONET LUG, STOCK TIP (NOSE CAP), FORWARD PIPE, SLING SWIVEL, 2ND PIPE, FORWARD BAND WITH FRONT SIGHT ATTACHED, MIDDLE BAND, LOWER BAND (ALL WITH BAND RETAINING SPRINGS), 3RD PIPE, BARREL, TAIL PIPE, SWELL, STOCK, LOCK, SIDE PLATE, SLING SWIVEL, TRIGGER, GUARD BOW, ESCUTCHEON PLATE, TRIGGER-GUARD PLATE, SMALL, BUTT FLANGE, COMB, BUTT, BUTT-PLATE TANG, HEEL, TOE, BUTT PLATE

### The Lock

Labels: JAW SCREW, FLINT PAD, FLINT, FRIZZEN, POST OF COCK, COCK, FLASH PAN, FRIZZEN (FEATHER) SPRING, LOCK PLATE

### THE POLE ARM

Labels: SPEAR POINT, HEAD, BEAK, BLADE, BASE RINGS, BASE, HAFT, STRAPS, BUTT POINT

### THE SWORD

Labels: CAPSTAN RIVET, POMMEL, KNUCKLE BOW, BACK STRAP, GRIP, FERRULE(S), BRANCH, QUILLON, RICASSO, PAS DANE

384   Nomenclature

# Bibliography

This list does not include all of the sources used in preparing this book. It is intended only as a presentation of the major references and an indication of the range of material studied.

## I. TEXTS

1. Aarum, Finn, and Stein G. Saegrov. *Dolle-Bajonetten I Norsk Bruk.* Norway: Forsvarsmuseet, 1983.
2. Akershus. *Haermuseet.* Oslo: Saetrykk Av Arbok, 1956.
3. Annis, P. G. W. *Naval Swords.* Harrisburg, PA: Stackpole, 1970.
4. Aylward, J. D. *The Small Sword in England.* London: Hutchinson, 1960.
5. Bailey, D. W. *British Military Longarms, 1715-1815.* Harrisburg, PA: Stackpole, 1971.
6. Baxter, D. R. *Blunderbusses.* Harrisburg, PA: Stackpole, 1970.
7. Berg, Fred Anderson. *Encyclopedia of Continental Army Units.* Harrisburg, PA: Stackpole, 1972.
8. Bezek, Richard H. *American Swords and Sword Makers.* Boulder, CO: Paladin Press, 1994.
9. Blackmore, Howard L. *British Military Firearms.* New York: Arco, 1962.
10. Blackmore, Howard L. *Gunmakers of London, 1350-1850.* York, PA: George Shumway, 1986.
11. Blair, Claude. *European and American Arms.* New York: Crown, 1962
12. Blair, Claude, and Robert Woosnam-Savage. *Scottish Firearms.* Bloomfield, Ont.: Museum Restoration Service, 1995.
13. Bland, Humphrey. *A Treatise of Military Discipline.* London, 1746.
14. Boatner, Mark M. III. *Encyclopedia of the American Revolution.* New York: David McKay, 1966.
15. Bodle, Wayne K., and Jacqueline Thibaut. *Valley Forge Historical Research Report* Vols. 1–3. Valley Forge, PA: Valley Forge National Historical Park, 1980.
16. Boeheim, Wendelin. *Handbuch Der Waffenkunde.* Graz, Austria: Akademische Druck, 1966.
17. Boehret, Paul C. *The Committee-of-Safety Musket.* Philadelphia, PA: privately published, 1956.
18. Bottet, Maurice. *L'Arme Blanche De Guerre Francaise Au XVIII Siecle.* Paris: Leroy, 1910.
19. —. "L'Arme A Feu Portative Des Armees Francaises". Paris: F. De Nobele, 1968.
20. Bouchard, Russel. *Les Fusils de Traite en Nouvelle-France 1690-1760.* Chicoutimi, Que.: Musée du Saguenay #4, 1976.
21. —. *Leo Fusils de Tulle en Nouvelle-France: 1691-1741.* Journal des Armes enr. Chicoutimi, Que.: 1980.
22. —. *Les Fusils du poste de traite Pontchartrain 1690-1760.* University of Quebec, Chicoutimi, Que.: 1976.
23. Boudriot, Jean. *Armes a Feu Francaises.* Paris, 1961.
24. Bowling, A. H. *British Infantry Regiments 1660-1914.* London: Almark Publishing, 1970.
25. Brinckerhoff, Sidney B., and Pierce A. Chamberlain. *Spanish Military Weapons in Colonial America 1700-1821.* Harrisburg, PA: Stackpole, 1972.
26. Brooker, Robert E. Jr. *British Military Pistols 1603 to 1888.* American Society of Arms Collectors, 1978.
27. Brown, M. L. *Firearms in Colonial America.* Washington: Smithsonian Institution Press, 1980.
28. Brown, Rodney Hilton. *American Polearms 1526-1865.* New Milford, CT: N. Flayderman, 1967.
29. Burke, Joseph, and Colin Caldwell. *Hogarth.* New York: Harry N. Abrahams.
30. Butler, David F. *United States Firearms: The First Century, 1776-1875.* New York: Winchester Press, 1971.
31. Calver, William Louis, and Reginald Pelham Bolton. *History Written with a Pick and Shovel.* New York: New-York Historical Society, 1950.
32. United States Cartridge Company. Firearms Collection Catalog. Lowell, MA: U. S. Cartridge, 1947.
33. Chartrand, René. *Canadian Military Heritage 1000-1754.* Vol. 1. Montreal: Art Global, 1993.
34. —. *The French Soldier in Colonial America.* Ottawa, Ont.: Museum Restoration Service, 1984.
35. Chartrand, René, and Francis Back. *The French Army in the American War of Independence.* London: Osprey, 1991.

36. Clinton, Henry. *The American Rebellion.* Campaign narrative. Ed. William B. Willcox. New Haven, CT: Yale University Press, 1954.
37. Cromwell, Giles. *French Swords for Virginia 1779.* Ellicott City, MD: Courtney B. Wilson, 1995.
38. Curtis, Edward E. *The Organization of the British Army in the American Revolution.* New Haven, CT: Yale University Press, 1926.
39. Darling, Anthony D. *Red Coat and Brown Bess.* Bloomfield, Ont.: Museum Restoration Service, 1970.
40. —. *Weapons of the Highland Regiments 1740-1780.* Bloomfield, Ont.: Museum Restoration Service, 1995.
41. De Watteville, H. *The British Soldier.* New York: Putnam, 1954.
42. Diderot, Denis. *L'Encyclopedie, ou Dictionnaire Raisonne des Sciences, des Arts et des Metier.* Paris, 1763.
43. Dillon, John G. W. *The Kentucky Rifle.* New York: Ludlum & Beebe, 1946.
44. Eckert, Allan W. *The Wilderness War.* Boston: Little, Brown, 1978.
45. Elting, John. *American Army Life.* New York: Scribner, 1982.
46. Ffoulkes, Charles. *Arms and Armament.* London: George G. Harrrap, 1945.
47. Flayderman, Norm. *Flayderman's Guide to Antique American Firearms.* 6th Edition. Northbrook, IL: DBI Books, 1994.
48. Ford, Worthington Chauncey. *British Officers Serving in the American Revolution.* Brooklyn, NY: Historical Printing Club, 1897.
49. Forman, James D. *The Blunderbuss 1500-1900.* Bloomfield, Ont.: Museum Restoration Service, 1994.
50. Gallup, Andrew, and Donald F Shaffer. *La Marine: The French Colonial Soldier in Canada 1745-1761.* Bowie, MD: Heritage Books, 1992.
51. Gardner, Robert E. *Small Arms Makers.* New York: Crown, 1963.
52. George, John Nigel. *English Guns and Rifles.* Harrisburg, PA: Stackpole, 1947.
53. Gilkerson, William. *Boarders Away.* Vols. 1, 2. Lincoln, RI: Andrew Mowbray, 1991-93.
54. Glendenning, Ian. *British Pistols and Guns 1640-1840.* London: Cassell, 1951.
55. Gluckman, Arcadi. *United States Muskets, Rifles, and Carbines.* Harrisburg, PA: Stackpole, 1959.
56. Gluckman, Arcadi, and L. D Satterlee. *American Gun Makers.* Harrisburg, PA: Stackpole, 1953.
57. Goldstein, Erik. *The Bayonet in New France 1665–1760.* City? Ont.: Museum Restoration Service, 1997.
58. Grant, Madison. *The Kentucky Rifle Hunting Pouch.* York, PA: Maple Press, 1977.
59. Grimm, Jacob L. *Archaeological Investigation of Fort Ligonier 1960-1965.* Pittsburgh, PA: Carnegie Museum, 1970.
60. Grose, Francis. *Military Antiquities, A History of the English Army.* Vols. 1, 2. London, 1801.
61. Guthman, William H. *U. S. Army Weapons 1784-1791.* American Society of Arms Collectors, 1975.
62. Gyngell, Dudley S. Hawtrey. *Armourers' Marks.* London: Thorsons, 1959.
63. Hamilton, Edward P. *The French Army in America.* Bloomfield, Ont.: Museum Restoration Service, 1967.
64. Hamilton, T. M. *Colonial Frontier Guns.* Chadron, NE: Fur Press, 1980.
65. —. *Early Indian Trade Guns 1625-1775.* Lawton, OK: Museum of the Great Plains, 1968.
66. —. *Firearms on the Frontier: Guns at Fort Michilimackinac 1715-1781.* Mackinac Island, MI: Mackinac Island State Park Commission, 1976.
67. —. *Indian Trade Guns.* Union City, TN: Pioneer Press, 1982.
68. Hanson, Charles E. Jr. *The Northwest Gun.* Lincoln, NE: Nebraska State Historical Society, 1955.
69. Hanson, Lee, and Dick Ping Hsu. *Casemates and Cannonballs, Archaeological Investigations of Fort Stanwix.* Washington, D.C.: U. S. Dept. of Interior, 1975.
70. Hardin, Albert H. Jr. *The American Bayonet 1776-1964.* Philadelphia: Riling and Lentz, 1964.
71. Held, Robert. *The Age of Firearms.* New York: Harper, 1957.
72. Hicks, James E. *French Military Weapons 1717-1938.* New Milford, CT: N. Flayderman, 1964.
73. Hinde, Capt. *The Discipline of the Light Horse.* London, 1778.
74. Houlding, J. A. *French Arms Drill of the 18th Century 1703-1760.* Bloomfield, Ont.: Museum Restoration Service, 1988.
75. Johnson, Henry P. *Connecticut Military Record 1775-1848.* Hartford, CT: Adjutant-General of Connecticut, 1889.
76. Katcher, Philip R. N. *Armies of the American Wars 1753-1815.* New York: Hastings House, 1975.
77. —. *Encyclopedia of British, Provincial, and German Army Units 1775-1783.* Harrisburg, PA: Stackpole, 1973.
78. Kauffman, Henry A. *Early American Gunsmiths.* Harrisburg, PA: Stackpole, 1952
79. Kehoe, Vincent. *A Military Guide: The 10th Regiment of Foot of 1775.* 2nd ed. Somis, CA: privately published, 1993.
80. Kemp, Alan. *American Soldiers of the Revolution.* London: Almark 1970.
81. —. *The British Army in the American Revolution.* London: Almark, 1973.
82. Kindig, Joe Jr. *Thoughts on the Kentucky Rifle in Its Golden Age.* York, PA: Trimmer Printing, 1960.
83. Klay, Frank. *The Samuel E. Dyke Collection of Kentucky Pistols.* Leyden Press, 1964.
84. Krafft, John Charles Philip von. *Personal Journal.* New York: New-York Historical Society, 1884.
85. Laking, Guy Francis. *A Record of European Armour and Arms Through Seven Centuries.* London: G. Bell, 1922.
86. Latham, R. J. Wilkinson. *British Military Bayonets from 1700 to 1945.* London: Hutchinson, 1967.
87. Lavin, James D. *A History of Spanish Firearms.* New York: Arco, 1965.
88. Lawson, Cecil C. P. *A History of the Uniforms of the British Army.* Vols. 1–4. London: Norman Military Publications, 1940-1961.
89. Lenk, Torsten. *The Flintlock: Its Origin and Development.* Bramhall House, NY: 1965.
90. Lhoste, Jean, and Jean-Jacques Buigne. *Armes Blanches Francaises.* Paris: Editions du Portail, 1994.
91. Lichtenberg. *The World of Hogarth.* Boston: Houghton Mifflin, 1966.
92. Lindsay, Merrill. *The New England Gun, the First Two Hundred Years.* New York: New Haven Historical Society; David McKay, 1975.
93. Manarey, R. Barrie. *The Canadian Bayonet.* Edmonton, Alb.: Century Press, 1971.

94. Mann, James. *Wallace Collection Catalogues Vols. I, II.* London: William Clowes, 1962.
95. Martin, Joseph Plumb. *Private Yankee Doodle.* New York: Popular Library, 1963.
96. Massachusetts State. *Soldiers and Sailors of the Revolutionary War.* Vols. 1–17. Boston: Wright & Potter, 1896.
97. May, Robin, and G. A. Embleton. *The British Army in North America 1775-1783.* London: Osprey, 1974.
98. —. *Wolfe's Army.* London: Osprey, 1974.
99. May, W. E., and P. G. W. Annis. *Swords for Sea Service.* Vols. 1, 2. London: Her Majesty's Stationery Office, 1970.
100. Metropolitan Museum of Art. *Early Firearms of Great Britain and Ireland from the Collection of Clay P. Bedford.* New York: 1971.
101. Miller, A. E. Haswell, and N. P. Dawnay. *Military Drawings and Paintings in the Collection of Her Majesty the Queen.* London: Phaidon Press, 1966.
102. Moller, George D. *American Military Shoulder Arms.* Vols. 1, 2. Niwot: University Press of Colorado, 1993.
103. Montross, Lynn. *Rag, Tag, and Bobtail.* Scranton, PA: Haddon Craftsmen, 1952.
104. Moore, Warren. *Weapons of the American Revolution.* New York: Funk & Wagnalls, 1967.
105. Mowbray, E. Andrew. *The American Eagle-Pommel Sword.* Lincoln, RI: *Man at Arms*, 1988.
106. Müller, Heinrich. *Die Bewaffnung, Das Heerwesen in Brandenburg und PreuBen von 1640 bis 1806.* Berlin: Brandenburgisches Verlagshaus, 1991.
107. Neal, W. Keith. *Spanish Guns and Pistols.* London: G. Bell, 1955.
108. Neumann, George C. *The History of Weapons of the American Revolution.* New York: Harper & Row, 1967.
109. —. *Swords and Blades of the American Revolution.* Harrisburg PA: Stackpole, 1973.
110. Neumann, George C., and Frank J. Kravic. *Collector's Illustrated Encyclopedia of the American Revolution.* Harrisburg, PA: Stackpole, 1975.
111. *New York in the Revolution.* Vols. 1, 2. Albany, NY: J. B. Lyons, 1904.
112. Norman, A. V. B. *Small Swords and Military Swords.* London: Arms and Armour Press, 1967.
113. Peterkin, Ernest W. *The Exercise of Arms in the Continental Infantry.* Bloomfield, Ont.: Museum Restoration Service, 1989.
114. Peterson, Harold L. *Arms and Armor in Colonial America.* Harrisburg, PA: Stackpole, 1956.
115. —. *Encyclopedia of Firearms.* New York: Dutton, 1964.
116. —. *The American Sword 1775-1945.* New Hope, PA: River House, 1954.
117. —. *The Book of the Continental Soldier.* Harrisburg, PA: Stackpole, 1968.
118. Priest, Graham. *The Brown Bess Bayonet 1720-1860.* Norwich, Eng.: Tharston Press, 1986.
119. Rankin, Robert H. *Small Arms of the Sea Services.* New Milford, CT: N. Flayderman, 1972.
120. Ravenshear, Kit. *English Commercial Guns 1685-1730.* New Berlin, PA: privately published, 1995.
121. —. *The King's Musket.* New Berlin, PA: privately published, 1992.
122. —. *The Guns of Louis XV.* New Berlin, PA: privately published, 1993.
123. Reilly, Robert M. *American Socket Bayonets and Scabbards.* Lincoln, RI: Andrew Mowbray, 1990.
124. Riling, Joseph R. *Baron Von Steuben and His Regulations.* Philadelphia: Ray Riling Arms, 1966.
125. Rogers, H. C. B. *Weapons of the British Soldier.* London: Seeley Service, 1960.
126. Rogers Island Historical Association. *Exploring Rogers Island.* Fort Edward, NY: 1969.
127. Russel, Carl P. *Firearms, Traps and Tools of the Mountain Men.* New York: Knopf, 1967.
128. —. *Guns on the Early Frontiers.* Los Angeles: University of California Press, 1957.
129. Saxe, Field Marshal Count. *Reveries on Memories upon the Art of War.* Trans. London, 1757.
130. Scheer, George F., and Hugh E. Rankin. *Rebels and Redcoats.* New York: World Publishing, 1957.
131. Sellers, Frank M. *American Gunsmiths.* Highland Park, NJ: Gun Room Press, 1983.
132. Shumway, George. *Jaeger Rifles, Collected Articles Published in Muzzle Blasts.* York, PA: Shumway, 1994.
133. —. *Rifles of Colonial America.* 2 vols. Longrifle Series. York, PA: Shumway, 1980.
134. Simes, Thomas. *The Military Medley.* London, 1768.
135. —. *The Regulator to Form the Officer.* London, 1780.
136. Skennerton, Ian D., and Robert Richardson. *British and Commonwealth Bayonets.* Margate, Australia: Ian D. Skennerton, 1986.
137. Smid, Jan, and Petr Moudry. *Bayonetten Der Habsburger Monarchie 1683-1918.*
138. Smith, George. *An Universal Military Dictionary.* London: J. Millan, 1779.
139. Sprouse, Deborah A. *A Guide to Excavated Colonial and Revolutionary War Artifacts.* Turbotville, PA: Heritage Trails, 1988.
140. Stephens, Frederick. *A Collector's Pictorial Book of Bayonets.* Harrisburg, PA: Stackpole, 1971.
141. Stockel, Johan F. *Haandskydevaabens Bedommelse.* Copenhagen, 1947.
142. Stone, George Camerone. *A Glossary of the Construction, Decoration, and Use of Arms and Armor.* New York: Jack Brussel, 1961.
143. Stone, Lyle M. *Fort Michilimackinac 1715-1781, An Archaeological Perspective.* East Lansing, MI: Michigan State University Museum, 1974.
144. Sullivan, Catherine. *Legacy of the Machault.* Hull, Quebec: Parks Canada, 1986.
145. Swayze, Nathan L. *The Rappahannock Forge.* American Society of Arms Collectors, 1976.
146. Trevelyan, George Otto. *The American Revolution.* New York: David McKay, 1964.
147. Tuchman, Barbara W. *The First Salute.* New York: Ballantine, 1988.
148. Upper Canada Historical Arms Society. *The Military Arms of Canada.* Bloomfield, Ont.: Museum Restoration Service, 1963.
149. Van Rensselaer, Stephen. *American Firearms.* Watkins Glen, NY: Century House, 1947.

150. Vial, Jean-Pierre. *Atlas de la Baionnette de Collection, Tome I, Le Nouveau Kiesling.* France: Editions du Portail, 1995.
151. Von Krafft, John C. D. *Journal 1776-1784.* New York: New-York Historical Society, 1882.
152. Wagner, Edward. *Cut and Thrust Weapons.* London: Spring Books, 1967.
153. Wallace, John. *Scottish Swords and Dirks.* Harrisburg, PA: Stackpole, 1970.
154. Ward, Christopher. *The War of the Revolution.* Vols. 1, 2. New York: Macmillan, 1952.
155. Webster, Donald B. Jr. *American Socket Bayonets 1717-1873.* Bloomfield, Ont.: Museum Restoration Service, 1964.
156. Wilber, C. Keith. *Picture Book of the Continental Soldier.* Harrisburg, PA: Stackpole, 1969.
157. —. *Picture Book of the Revolution's Privateers.* Harrisburg, PA: Stackpole, 1973.
158. Wilkinson, Frederick. *Edged Weapons.* Garden City, NY: Doubleday, 1970.
159. —. *Small Arms.* London: Ward Lock, 1965.
160. Windham, William. *A Plan of Discipline for the Use of the Norfolk Militia.* London, 1759.
161. Wright, John Womack. *Some Notes on the Continental Army.* Vails Gate, NY: National Temple Hill, 1963.
162. Wyler, Seymour B. *The Book of Old Silver.* New York: Crown, 1937.

## II. PERIODICALS

163. "American Pole Arms or Shafted Weapons." *Bulletin of the Fort Ticonderoga Museum.* 5 (July 1939).
164. Ahearn, Bill. "Colonial Firearms Displayed at the Princton Battlefield." *The Gun Report* May 1994.
165. —. "First Model British Brown Bess Long Land Pattern Musket Marked 53rd Regiment." *The Gun Report* Nov. 1990.
166. —. "Guns of the 53rd British Regiment—Revisited." *The Gun Report* June 1993.
167. —. "Identifying American Revolutionary War Firearms." *The Gun Report* Aug. 1992.
168. Bailey, DeWitt. "British Military Small Arms in North America 1755-1783." *Bulletin of the American Society of Arms Collectors* 1994.
169. —. "The Ordance System, British Government Small Arms Manufacture 1714-1783." *Black Powder* 1989.
170. Baird, Donald. "An 18th Century Fusil by Richard Wilson—London." *Arms Collecting* 6.1 (Feb. 1968).
171. Bazelon, Bruce S., and John B. Trussell. "Arming the Associators: The Documentation of a Pennsylvania Committee of Safety Musket." *Man at Arms* Sept./Oct. 1983.
172. Benninghoff, Herman II. "Art and Archaeology and the Study of the American War for Independence." *Bulletin of the American Society of Arms Collectors* #73 (Oct. 1995).
173. —. "The Evolved Longarm in North America 1750-1850." *Bulletin of the American Society of Arms Collectors* #64 (May 1991).
174. Blackmore, Howard L. "British Military Firearms in Colonial America." *Bulletin of the American Society of Arms Collectors* #25, 1972.
175. —. "Dutch Muskets for Ireland 1706-1715." *Arms Collecting* (Aug. 1994).
176. Bouchard, Russel. "The Trade Gun in New France, 1690-1760." *Canadian Journal of Arms Collecting* 15:1 (1977).
177. Burgoyne, John W. "A Classic Queen Anne Pistol by William Turvey of London." *Arms Collecting* 31.1 (Feb. 1993).
178. —. "Queen Anne Style Boxlock Pistols c.1750-1780." *Arms Collecting* 32.2 (May 1994).
179. Carroll, Don. "The Brown Bess Musket Regimentally Marked." *The Gun Report* Jan. 1990.
180. Chapman, Frederick T., and John R. Elting. "Brunswick Regiment of Dragoons 1776-1783." *Journal of the Company of Military Historians* 12.1 (1960).
181. Colton, Richard T. "The Snaphaunce." *Man at Arms* Nov./Dec. 1992.
182. Copeland, Peter. "Weapons of the Pyrates and Buccaneers 1665-1725." *Man at Arms* Jan./Feb. 1982.
183. Corry, Noel. "The Spanish Miquelet Lock." *The Gun Report* June 1962.
184. Darling, Anthony D. "An 18th English Military Rifle." *Canadian Journal of Arms Collecting* 10.2.
185. —. "History Engraved on a Barrel." *The Gun Report* Jan. 1971.
186. —. "The British Infantry Hangers." *Canadian Journal of Arms Collecting* 8.4 (Nov. 1970).
187. —. "Weapons of the British Dragoon (Circa 1750)." *The Gun Report* Oct. 1972.
188. Darling, Anthony D., and Jane Brooks. "A Regimentally-Marked Mid 18th Century British Infantry Sword in the Concord Antiquarian Museum." *Arms Collecting* 24.2 (May 1986).
189. Dean, Bashford. "On American Polearms." *Metropolitan Museum Studies* 1 (1928).
190. Dorlodot, Albert de. "Memorandum on Military and Naval Supplies Manufactured in Belgium and Other Forms of Aid for the Continental Forces 1775-1782." Unpublished manuscript, 1948.
191. duMont, John S. "J Bailey, America's Famous Revolutionary War Sword Maker." *Man at Arms* Mar./Apr. 1987.
192. Englehardt, A. "The Story of European Proof Marks." *The Gun Digest* 1953.
193. Evans, Roger D. C. "The Plug Bayonet in Colonial America." Parts 1–3. *Journal of the Society of American Bayonet Collectors* 14; 15; 16.
194. Forman, James D. "Committee of Safety Muskets." *Canadian Journal of Arms Collecting* 10.4 (Nov. 1972).
195. —. "Guns of the American Indians." *Man at Arms* Nov./Dec. 1979.
196. —. "The Blunderbuss Pistol." *Man at Arms* Nov./Dec. 1985.
197. —. "The Evolution of the Kentucky Pistol." *Man at Arms* July/Aug. 1981.
198. —. "The Hessian and His Musket." *Arms Collecting* 15.4 (1977).
199. Fox, Christopher D. "New British Musket Discovered." *The Haversack* 5.1 (Autumn 1995).
200. Godwin, Brian. "The English Snaphance, Some Newly Discovered Examples." *Arms Collecting* 32.4 (Nov. 1994).
201. Gooding, S. James. "Gunmakers to The Hudson's Bay Co." *Arms Collecting* 13.1 (1975).
202. —. "Trade Guns of The Hudson's Bay Company 1670-1700." *Arms Collecting* 13.3 (1975).

203. Gordon, Lewis H. Jr. "The British Cavalry and Dragoon Pistol." Parts 1, 2. *Canadian Journal of Arms Collecting* 5.4–6.1 (Nov. 1967–Feb. 1968).
204. —. "The British Military Blunderbuss and Musketoon." *Canadian Journal of Arms Collecting* 5.3 (Aug. 1967).
205. Gousse, André. "Grenadier Muskets in New France." *Company of Military Historians Journal* Spring 1989.
206. Gusler, Wallace B. "18th Century Virginia Rifles." *Man at Arms* Sept./Oct. 1982.
207. Gutchess, Alan D. "Weapons of the 18th Century American Frontier: A Restocked Hybrid Trade Fusil Examined." *The Gun Report* Feb. 1996.
208. Guthman, William H. "Colonial Swords of New England." Parts 1–3. *Man at Arms* Sept./Oct. 1982–Sept./Oct. 1989.
209. —. "Committee of Safety Musket? Prove It!" *Man at Arms* July/Aug. 1979.
210. Haarman, Albert W. "The Hessian Army and the Corps in North America 1776-1783." *The Company of Military Historians Journal* 14.3 (1962).
211. Haarman, Albert W., and Donald Holst. "The Friedrich Von Germann Drawings of Troops in the American Revolution." *The Company of Military Historians Journal* 16.1 (1964).
212. Hanson, Charles E. Jr. "Fur Traders' Pistols." *The American Society of Arms Collectors Journal* 62 (May 1990).
213. Howard, Gordon T. "Trade Guns of the North West Co." *Arms Collecting* 2.3 (Aug. 1964).
214. Howard, Robert A. "Powder Testers at the Hagley Museum and Library." *Man at Arms* July/Aug. 1989.
215. Hunter, Tony. "The Frontal Assault of Infantry in the 18th and 19th Centuries." *Muzzleloader* Mar./Apr. 1996.
216. Katsianos, Charles. "Firearms of the French Galley Navy." *Arms Gazette* 11/77.
217. —. "The English Sea Service Pistols of the 18th Century." *The American Rifleman* Oct. 1977.
218. Lattimer, John K. "An Exhibition of Silver Hilted Swords by American Silversmiths of the Colonial, Revolutionary, and Federal Periods." *Bulletin of the Fort Ticonderoga Museum* 11.6 (1965).
219. "Sword Hilts by Early American Silversmiths." *Antiques Magazine* Feb. 1965.
220. Manders, Eric, and George A. Snook. "New England Independent Companies 1675-1676." *The Company of Military Historians Journal* 2 (1964).
221. Marsden, Joseph R. "The Bayonets at Fort Ligonier, Pennsylvania 1758-1766." *The Company of Military Historians Journal* 46.4 Winter 1994).
222. Mayer, J. R. "Medad Hills, Connecticut Gunsmith." *Magazine Antiques* July 1943.
223. McKenzie, Lynton. "British Holster Pistols." *Muzzle Blasts* Jan. 1993.
224. Mowbray, E. Andrew. "Small Swords—Overlooked Collectibles." *Man at Arms* Jan./Feb. 1979.
225. Mulligan, Robert E. Jr. "The City of New York Muskets of 1755-1775." *Man at Arms* Mar./Apr. 1991.
226. Neal, W. Keith. "The Ferguson Rifle and Its Origins." *The American Society of Arms Collectors Journal*.
227. Neumann, George C. "Firearms of the Revolution." Series. *The American Rifleman* July-Oct. 1967.
228. —. "Revolutionary War Rifles: Accurate but of Limited Use." *The American Rifleman* Oct. 1973.
229. —. "The Pennsylvania Prahl Bayonet." *The Company of Military Historians Journal* 47.1 (Spring 1995).
230. Ray, Fred Jr., and Frederick P. Todd. "British 42nd (Royal Highland) Regiment of Foot, 1759-1760." *The Company of Military Historians Journal* 8.2 (1956).
231. Reid, William. "Walter Allan, Armourer in Stirling." *The Scottish Art Review* 9.1 (1963).
232. Reilly, Robert M. "The Evolution of the Socket Bayonet in America." *Man at Arms* July/Aug. 1985.
233. Renoux, Pierre. "French Bayonets 1717-1780." *Society of American Bayonet Collectors Journal* 14 (Winter 1995).
234. Ravenshear, Kit. "Ketland and Co." *Man at Arms* Sept./Oct. 1988.
235. —. "The 1734 Tulle Contract Marine Musket." Report to Fortress Louisbourg National Historic Park Workshop, 1978.
236. Schmidt, Peter. "Evolution of the India Pattern Brown Bess." *The Gun Report* May 1973.
237. Scott, J. G. "Basket-Hilted Swords of Glasgow Make." *The Scottish Art Review* 9.1 (1963).
238. Serbaroli, Joseph A. Jr. "The Prussian Model 1740 (Bayonet)." *The American Society of Bayonet Collectors Journal* 12 (Summer 1995).
239. Serven, James E. "The Long Rifle of Pennsylvania." *The American Rifleman* June 1969.
240. Stickels, George A. "The William Smith Pistols Made by Medad Hills." *The Gun Report* Sept. 1979.
241. Switlik, Matthew C. "Shooting the Famous Ferguson Rifle." *The American Rifleman* Aug. 1971.
242. Vuillemin, Henri. "Modele 1728 Le Fusil de Fontenoy." *Gazette des Armes* 167 (July 1987).
243. Weaver, Phil. "Flintlock Era Linear Warfare." Brigade of the American Revolution.
244. Webster, Donald B. Jr. "American Wall Guns." *The American Rifleman* Aug. 1963.
245. Wheeler, Robert F. "The Infantry Hanger During the Revolution." *The American Arms Collector* Apr. 1957.
246. Whisker, James B. "Some Early New York Gunsmiths." *The Gun Report* Dec. 1995.
247. Wolf, Paul J. "Powder Testers." *The American Arms Collector* Oct. 1958.
248. Wood, Stephen. "Blades of Glory: Swords of the Scottish Infantry 1756-1900." *The American Society of Arms Collectors Bulletin* 72 (1995).

# Index

Allen, E. 195
Allen, Ethan 337
Allen, John 344, 345
Allen, Walter 344
Amherst, Jeffrey 76, 366
Ammunition 11, 12, 16, 20, 21
Amsterdam 15, 19, 107, 112, 177
Amusette (see "Wall Guns")
Anhalt-Zerbst 226
Anne, Queen 14, 17, 34, 37, 38, 42, 53, 77, 121, 127, 150, 159, 163, 183, 186, 200, 201, 270
Annely, Edward and Thomas 145, 153, 119, 170, 317, 371
Antes, William 265
Arnold, Benedict 162
Artillery 13, 171, 172, 193, 314, 315, 374

Bailey, John 331, 337
Barker, M. 227, 229
Bayonets 5, 13, 15, 17, 20, 44, 123, 278, 366; *American* 280, 294–301; *Dutch* 292, 293; *English* 17, 20, 279, 281–286; *French* 17, 19, 20, 44, 280, 286–290; *Germanic* 279, 291–294; *Spanish* 291
Bayonne (France) 278
Behr, I. I. 120
Bennington (Vt.) 23, 45, 119, 291, 349
Birmingham 14, 16, 17, 52, 162, 175, 227, 285, 302, 305, 311, 345, 364
Bissell, Issac 244
Blachon, Jerome 259
Black Powder 5, 6–13, 277
Blunderbusses 20; *American* 186; *English* 44, 183, 184, 187–191, 247; *French* 185
Board of Ordnance 14, 16, 68, 82, 170, 227, 238, 282
Bond, Edward 14
Boscowen 76
Boston (Mass.) 15, 150, 152, 163
Braddock, Edward 366
Brandywine (Penn.) 228, 338
Brasher, Ephraim 337
Brown Bess Patterns: *Long Land* 17, 58–61, 72–76, 129, 154; *Short Land* 17, 64–68; *Marine or Militia* 17, 62, 63
Brown, John 61
Brown, William 334
Brunswick 15, 23, 45, 119, 291, 317, 349, 371
Buccaneer Muskets 102, 103, 141, 199
Buell, E. 295
Bullet Molds 21
Bumford, John 232
Bunker Hill 11, 13, 15, 22, 166
Burgoyne, John 61, 119, 170, 317, 371
Buttall, I. 72

Canada 18, 84–89, 146, 164, 206, 250, 280, 364
Canteen 32, 33
Cape Cod (Mass.) 369
Carbines 20; *American* 20; *Dutch* 177; *English* 20, 34, 39, 44, 46, 167–176; *French* 20, 46, 49, 179–182
Cargill, Benjamin 128
Carrier 196
Carteron, Nicholas 89, 209
Cartridge Boxes 21–29
Champlain Valley 381
Chandler, Stephen 37, 131
Chapin, Joseph 165
Charleville 14, 17, 19, 91, 94, 96, 103, 125, 180, 181, 254
Childs, Elisha 128
Chouso, C. 333
Churchel, Jannah 142
Clarkson, Joseph 233
Collumbell 70
Committees of Safety 126, 131, 135, 137, 139, 144, 147, 294
Compagnies Franches de la Marine 18, 27, 84, 85–87, 89, 286
Conant, L. A. 124
Concord (Mass.) 13, 15, 31, 123, 139
Connecticut 15, 125, 126, 128, 131, 142, 144, 165, 210, 264, 295, 341, 355
Connecticut Farms 277

Continental Congress 19
Continental Line 13, 15, 28
Cookson, John 163
Corbau, Godefroi 109
Crown Point 132
Culemborg Manufactory 112, 113
Cumberland, Duke of 305

**D** Grasse 105
Dickert, Jacob 221
Domino (French Musket) 86
Doud, John 128
Doud & Norton 142
Drury 345
Dublin Castle 17, 18, 61, 140, 176, 237
Duke of Choiseul 18
Dunmore, Earl of 55
Durham (Conn.) 126
Dutch 16, 19, 68, 107, 108–113, 152, 160-162, 177, 260, 363, 273, 318, 338

**E**ast India Co. 14, 17, 65, 68, 69, 191, 286
Easton (Mass.) 137
Edge 62, 77, 143, 236
Egg, Durs 229
Eliott, George 20, 169, 174–176, 236, 285
England (see categories)
Eprouvette 276
Essen 19, 291
Ewing, Thomas 268

**F**alconer, William 338
Farmer 59, 234
Ferguson, Patrick 228, 229, 285
Fishkill (N.Y.) 331
Flintlocks 7–10, 16–19, 34–50, 51–210; *Blunderbusses* 20, 183–191; *Carbines* 20, 34, 44, 167–182; *Fowlers* 15, 19, 20, 42–45, 50, 150 166; *Fusils* 19–20, 46, 70, 71, 98–100, 144–147; *Muskets* 16–19, 34–50, 51 143, 148, 149; *Pistols* 230–275; *Rifles* 12, 13, 19, 32, 45, 48, 150, 211–229; *Shoulder Mortar* 198; *Trade Guns* 20, 38, 43, 48, 199–210; *Volley Gun* 82;

*Wall Guns* 20, 192–197
Flints 18, 143
Fournier 102, 125
Fowlers 15, 19, 20, 42–45, 50, 103, 128, 141, 142, 144, 150–166, 263
France 5, 10, 13, 17–19, 278
Frederick the Great 15, 115, 262
Fredericksburg (Va.) 15, 37, 133
Fredericksburgh (N.Y.) 331, 337
French & Indian War 17, 62, 74, 75, 87, 90, 92, 101 109, 110, 122, 124, 173, 196, 205, 209, 253, 289, 293, 303, 345, 367, 371, 372
Fusils 19–20; *American* 142, 144–147; *English* 70, 71; *French* 19, 98–100, 146

**G**alton 168, 227
Galvaz, Bernardo de 101, 291, 315
Generaliteit 113
George (Kings I–III) 14, 55, 86, 310
Georgia 224, 309
German Manufactories 16, 17, 50, 112, 114, 118, 226
German Troops (see "Hessians")
Gerrish, John 150
Girard 252
Glasgow 344
Goshen (Conn.) 126, 128, 142, 271
Grady, William 133
Grenade Launcher 81
Grice, William 63, 170, 171, 175, 227
Griffin & Tow 239
Gunpowder (see "Black Powder")

**H**adley 127
Halberd (see "Pole Arms")
Hall, J. 72, 183
Hartford, Colonel 233
Hartford (Conn.) 131, 264
Harvard (Mass.) 148, 164
Harvey, Samuel 15, 305, 311, 364
Hawkins 240
Hawley 56
Heckstall 202
Hesse Cassel 226
Hessians 5, 15, 17, 23, 155, 226, 277, 332, 370
Heylin, Joseph 247
Hills, Benoni 126, 142

Hills, John 126
Hills, Medad 126, 128, 271
Holland (see "Dutch")
Hollier, Thomas 59, 308
Holy Roman Empire 19, 118, 294
Horns, Powder 30, 31
Hudson Valley (N.Y.) 50, 153, 160 162, 263 273
Hudson's Bay Co. 14, 205
Huguenot, French 211
Hunter, James 197, 269, 358
Hunting Bags 212

**I**ndia Pattern 65, 68, 69, 76
Indians 205, 208, 336
Italy 8, 302

**J**aeger 211, 213, 214, 226, 332
Jamestown (Va.) 211, 304
Jefferies 345, 347
Jordan 76, 81, 126, 234
Jover, W. 243

**K**astane 308
Ketland 14, 71, 223
Kinman, William 337
Klingenthal 290, 302, 357

**L**afayette 314
Lake George 166
Lancaster (Mass.) 164
Lancaster (Penn.) 215, 216, 220, 221, 223, 267
Lane, T. 242
Lauzon's Legion 348
Lee, Harry 303
Leonard, Eliphalet 137
Lexington (Mass.) 13, 15, 31, 123, 139, 164
Liege 15, 16, 17, 19, 41, 43, 66, 107, 114, 120, 185, 201, 284, 291, 293
Lilien 15, 89
Linear Warfare 5, 11–13
Linstock (see "Pole Arms")
Lock Actions 6–10, 34–38; *Doglock* 16, 19, 34, 38, 51; *English* 9, 34; *Flintlock* 7–10; *French Lock* 10, 17, 35; *Matchlock* 6, 7; *Miquelet* 8, 9, 273; *Snaphaunce* 8; *Wheellock* 7

Index  **391**

London Cutlers Company 279
London Gunmakers Company 14, 16, 71, 72, 74, 75, 80, 161, 187, 191, 199, 204, 232, 233 238–240, 242, 246, 248, 270
Lord, F. 61
Louisbourg 87, 124, 166
Lovis 196
Low Countries 19, 39, 112, 114, 115, 117, 119, 120, 131, 136, 152, 185, 194, 201, 217, 251, 284, 291, 293
Loyalists 15, 16, 17, 19, 168, 227, 285
Ludlam, I. 70

Maastricht 19, 107, 109
Machault 105, 364
Maine 358
Man, Jacob 123
Mannheim 214
Marine Ministry (France) 17–19, 84–88, 146, 206, 208, 250
Marines 17, 39, 49, 62–64
Marseille 105
Maryland 15, 138, 211, 224, 267, 268
Masonic 135
Massachusetts 15, 30, 119, 123, 124, 137, 139, 148, 152, 154, 164, 166, 331, 333, 355, 369
Matchlock 6, 7
Maubeuge 14, 17, 19, 91, 93, 253, 254
May, B. 214
Memory 286
Middletown (Conn.) 341
Militia 13, 15, 17, 39, 49, 62, 63, 64, 126, 135, 136, 142, 144, 151, 153, 157, 158, 161, 224, 263
Minories 16, 203
Miquelet Lock 8, 273
Mohawk Valley (N.Y.) 3, 379
Monlieu 208
Monmain 251
Morier 307, 311
Mortar, Shoulder 198
Munich 302
Murdoch T. 245
Murray, Lord John 244
Musician 309, 320
Musketoon (see "Carbines")
Muskets 16–20, 34–50, 51–143; *American* 19, 37, 38, 42, 45, 47, 121–143; *Dutch* 19, 36, 39, 41, 45–47, 50, 107–114, 123, 125, 177; *English* 16, 17, 38, 39, 43, 44, 46, 48, 49, 51–81, 108, 128; *French* 17–20, 35, 38, 40, 43–48, 83–97, 102–106, 123–125,178 179; *Germanic* 19, 36, 41, 43, 45–47, 109, 112, 114–120, 132, 155; *Spanish* 24, 36, 40, 45, 49, 101, 125

Naval (see "Sea Service")
Netherlands (see "Dutch")
New France 206, 209, 250, 280
New Hampshire 15, 93, 119, 136, 353, 355
New Jersey 15, 74, 75, 145, 153
New Orleans 101
New Windsor (N.Y.) 158
New York 12, 33, 73, 123, 145, 160–162, 265, 273, 331, 337, 359, 369, 379, 381
Newburgh (N.Y.) 379
Newport (R.I.) 97, 100, 313, 341, 356
Newport News (Va.) 375
Nicholson, Edward 54
Nicholson, John 147
Nock, Henry 82
North Carolina 212, 215
Northampton (Mass.) 166
Northwest Gun 205, 209
Norton, Ebenezer 128

Oerton, Christian 219
Otis, Jonathan 341
Oughton 285

Page, John 38, 144
Passau 15, 302, 308
Pearson, Joseph 270
Pennsylvania 15, 135, 145, 147, 157, 211, 213, 215, 216, 219, 220–225, 267, 270, 274, 294, 336, 343, 371, 372, 377
Pepperrell, William 310
Perkins, Joseph 95
Peyster, Frederic de 229, 285
Philadelphia 130, 145, 147, 265, 358, 379

Pike (see "Pole Arms")
Pistols 230–275; *American* 230, 231, 263–275; *Dutch* 260; *English* 230–249; *French* 20, 230, 231, 250–259; *Germanic* 261, 262
Pistor, T. W. 226
Pitcairn, John 244
Plymouth (Mass.) 211, 304
Pocock 57
Pole Arms 15, 70, 98, 366, 367; *Butt Points* 381; *Halberds* 368–374; *Linstocks* 374; *Pikes* 379–381; *Spontoons* 374–379
Pomeroy, Seth 166
Portsmouth (N.H.) 93
Potsdam-Spandau 19, 36, 41, 47, 50, 115, 118, 261, 262, 291
Potter, James 359
Powder Tester (see "Eprouvette")
Powell 61
Prahl, Lewis 294, 358, 379
Pratt, John 17, 65, 68
Predden, William 34, 55
Preston (Conn.) 144
Princeton (N.J.) 123, 284
Proofs 14–17 (see individual arms)
Prussia 36, 41, 45, 47, 50, 115–119, 261, 291, 316, 323, 349
Puffer, Jonathan 164
Putnam, Israel 355

Quebec 73

Rampart Gun (see "Wall Guns")
Rappahannock Forge 37, 197, 269, 358
Rea, John 187
Redding (Penn.) 215, 220
Recruiting 15
Reenactors 5
Regiments: *American*, 3rd NJ 277, 1st NY 73, 3rd NY 73, 13th Continentals 123, 2nd Cont. Dragoons 359; *English*, Coldsteam Guards 369, No. British Fusiliers 170, King's Own Dragoons 346, Queen's Rangers 65, 3rd Rgt. Foot Guards 55, 4th Rgt. (King's Own) 154, 8th (King's Rgt.) 57,

14th Rgt. 334, 15th Rgt. 154, 338, 16th Rgt. 309, 17th Rgt. 284, 23rd Rgt. (Royal Welch) 12, 58, 307, 310, 33rd Rgt. 56, 35th Rgt. 334, 42nd (RHR) 244, 52nd Rgt. 334, 53rd Rgt. 61, 71st Rgt. 64, 15th Lt. Drag. 174, 16th Lt. Drag. 176, 235, 236, 17th Lt. Drag. 175, 236; *German*, Von Mirbach 371

Rhode Island 15, 123, 341, 356
Richards 124
Rifles 12, 13, 19, 150, 211–229; *American* 42, 45, 48, 150, 215–225; *English* 227–229; *German* 213, 214, 226
Rochambeau 97, 290, 348
Rotterdam 107
Royal Foresters 20, 176, 235
Royal Welch Fusiliers 12, 58, 307, 310

**S**add, Matthew 264
St. Etienne 14, 17–19, 85, 88, 89, 91, 92, 97, 105, 106, 114, 156, 179, 181, 182, 196, 206, 207, 209, 252, 254, 257, 259
Saratoga (N.Y.) 28, 170, 211
Savannah (Ga.) 100
Sawyer, Phineas 148, 164
Saxony 291
Scammon, James 355
Schmalkalden 226
Schroyer, George 215
Schuyler, Philip 162
Screw-Barrel Pistols 241–243
Sea Service: *Muskets* 17, 19, 34, 35, 39, 40, 44, 46, 48, 49, 76–82, 99, 102–106, 149, 308, 362–365; *Pikes* 367, 379, 381; *Pistols* 231, 232, 248, 249, 253, 254, 258, 259; *Swords* 324, 362–365
Sheppard 248
Shot Bags 30
Shotley Bridge 302
Simcoe, John 65
Simpson, John 344
Snaphaunce 8
Solingen 15, 19, 67, 107, 279, 302, 304, 308

Sorby, L. 281
South Carolina 109, 122, 212, 215
Spain 5, 8, 15, 68, 278, 291, 302, 315, 348
Spanish Succession, War of 16, 17, 52
Spontoon (see "Pole Arms")
Stamps 167
Stark, John 119
Stirling 344
Strode, John 269
Strum, C. 276
Suhl 15, 19, 41, 107, 114, 276, 291
Surcharge Marking (U.S.) 13, 95, 114, 289, 294
Sweden 318
Swiss 211, 349
Switzer 274
Sword Knot 317, 328
Swords: 15, 302, 303; *Cutlasses* 362–365; *Hangers* 304–321; *Hunting/Cuttoes* 331–338; *Horseman* 345–361; *Rapiers* 304, 343; *Short Sabers* 321–331; *Small Swords* 338–343

**T**actics 5, 11–13, 15, 18, 277, 278
Take-Down Fowler 158
Talmadge, Benjamin 359
Thomas, Louis 257
Thompson, Abijah 139
Thuringen 19
Ticonderoga, Fort 61, 73, 76, 287, 377, 381
Tittensor, John 192
Toledo 302
Tories (see "Loyalists")
Toussaint 102
Tower Armory 14, 17, 34, 39, 58, 127
Trade Guns 20, 38, 43, 48, 199–210
Trenton (N.J.) 123, 145, 153, 371
Trulock, I. 61
Tulle 14, 17, 18, 19, 35, 38, 43, 48, 84, 85–87, 89, 121, 124, 146, 182, 206, 207, 210, 250, 258, 286

**V**alley Forge 367
Varick, Richard 162
Vermont 23, 45, 119, 291, 349

Vernon 173
Vinial 105
Virginia 15, 37, 133, 140, 197, 211, 222, 224, 240, 269, 314, 357, 374
Voight, Henry 130
Volley Gun 82
Von Steuben 13

**W**aite, Lt. Col. 58
Walker 200
Wall Guns 20, 192–197
Walloon 350
Washington, George 5, 12, 240, 278, 367
Waters, John 246
Watkeys, Henry 158
Watkin, R. 188
Whateley 190
Whatley 229
Wheel-Lock 7
Willets 170, 174, 227
Wilson, James 82
Wilson, Richard 14, 38, 56, 57, 69, 73–75, 160, 191, 203–205, 240, 241
Windsor (Conn.) 165
Woburn (Mass.) 139
Wooldridge, Richard 53
Wylie, Thomas 295

**Y**ork (Penn.) 215
Yorktown (Va.) 100, 105, 366

**Z**ella 107, 291

*Index* 393

# Other books from Mowbray Publishers...

## MUSKETS OF THE REVOLUTION

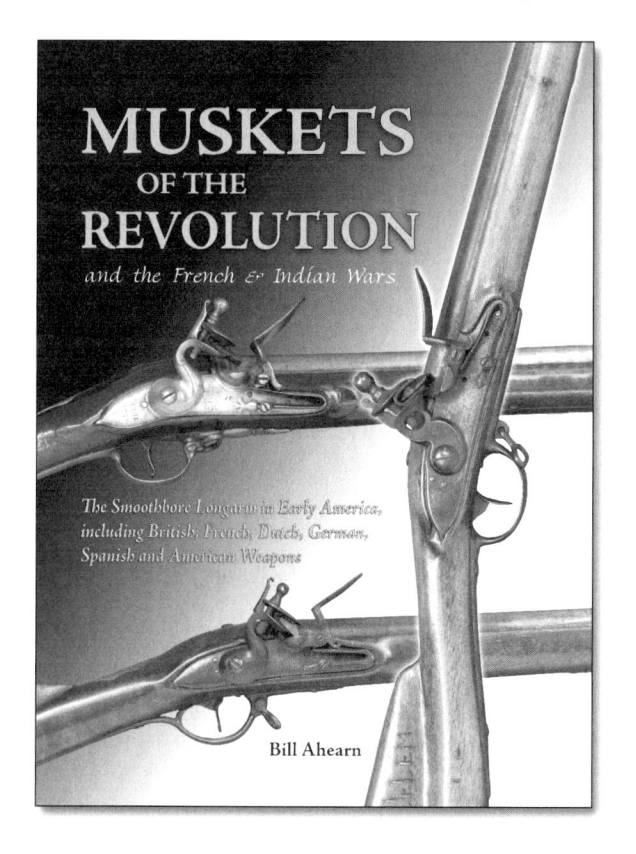

### and the French & Indian Wars

The exciting, true story of the guns that fought the American Revolution by **Bill Ahearn**, including intimate details of the men who carried them and the desperate battles in which they served. Not just a technical study of old firearms, this is a tribute to the bravery of the men who fought on both sides of that epic conflict and a celebration of the tools of freedom that have become so much a part of our national character. Includes many never-before-published photos! 248 pages • 8.5" x 11" Nearly 500 photos and illustrations.
**Hardcover. $49.99 + $4.50 p/h**

## THE BROWN BESS

An all-new, pattern-by-pattern, full-color collector's guide by Erik Goldstein and Stuart Mowbray. This book covers them all, including the India Patterns! ALMOST 1,000 COLOR PHOTOS! 160 pages • 11" x 8.5"
**Softcover • $39.99 + $4.50 p/h**

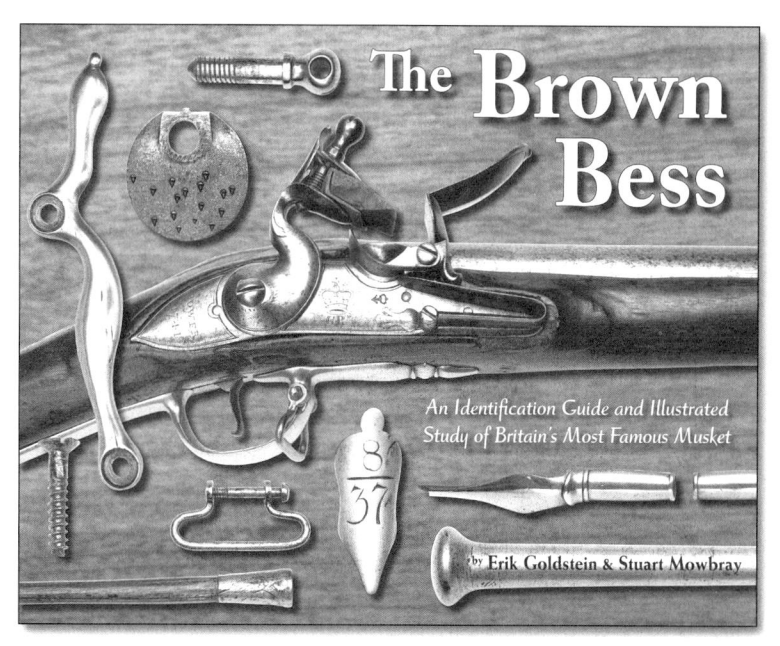

---

To order a book or a subscription to *Man at Arms*, contact:

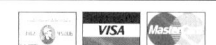

**Mowbray Publishers, Inc. • 54 East School Street • Woonsocket, RI 02895**

**Call 1-800-999-4697** • Outside the U.S., call (401) 597-5055

Visit us at www.gunandswordcollector.com   EMAIL ORDERS TO: ORDERS@MANATARMSBOOKS.COM

*ASK FOR A FREE CATALOG • Personal Checks, Money Orders, VISA, MasterCard and Amer. Express acepted*

# Subscribe Today!

## Man at ARMS for the GUN AND SWORD COLLECTOR

*Get all the news and information you need from the world's leading source on antique gun collecting.*

Six times a year, *Man at Arms for the Gun and Sword Collector* brings the whole world of gun collecting right into your home, with entertaining and authoritative articles and lots of large color pictures of your favorite antique firearms. And, as the NRA's official "Journal for the American Arms Collector, we can give you special, exlusive features like NRA Collector News and the NRA's Gun Show Calendar.

A one-year subscription (six issues) to *Man at Arms for the Gun and Sword Collector* is $32.00; $62.00 for two years. Call 1-800-999-4697 or visit our website to order your subscription. VISA, MasterCard, American Express, PayPal, money orders and personal checks accepted. Foreign subscribers please add $10 for surface postage. Make checks or money orders payable to *Man at Arms*.

TO ORDER, VISIT OUR WEBSITE: **www.gunandswordcollector.com**

or call toll free **(800) 999-4697**  Outside of the U.S., call **(401) 597-5055**

YOU CAN ALSO SEND A CHECK OR MONEY ORDER TO:

**ANDREW MOWBRAY, INC./PUBLISHERS**
**54 East School Street, Woonsocket, RI 02895**